Pearson New International Edition

Effective Small Business Management

Norman Scarborough
Tenth Edition

PEARSON

Pearson Education Limited
Edinburgh Gate
Harlow
Essex CM20 2JE
England and Associated Companies throughout the world

Visit us on the World Wide Web at: www.pearsoned.co.uk

ISBN 10: 1-292-02064-4
ISBN 13: 978-1-292-02064-8

British Library Cataloguing-in-Publication Data
A catalogue record for this book is available from the British Library

Printed in the United States of America

Table of Contents

Entrepreneurs: The Driving Force Behind Small Business

The future belongs to those who believe in their dreams.

—Eleanor Roosevelt

It doesn't matter how many times you fail. No one is going to care about your failures, and neither should you. All you have to do is learn from them because all that matters in business is that you get it right once. Then everyone can tell you how lucky you are.

—Mark Cuban

Learning Objectives

Upon completion of this chapter, you will be able to:

1 Define the role of the entrepreneur in the U.S. economy.
2 Describe the entrepreneurial profile.
3 Explain how entrepreneurs spot business opportunities.
4 Describe the benefits of owning a small business.
5 Describe the potential drawbacks of owning a small business.
6 Explain the forces that are driving the growth in entrepreneurship.
7 Discuss the role of diversity in small business and entrepreneurship.
8 Describe the contributions small businesses make to the U.S. economy.
9 Put business failure into the proper perspective.
10 Explain how entrepreneurs can avoid the major pitfalls of running a business.

From Chapter 1 of *Effective Small Business Management: An Entrepreneurial Approach*, 10/e. Norman M. Scarborough.

1. Define the role of the entrepreneur in the U.S. economy.

Welcome to the world of the entrepreneur! Every year, entrepreneurs in the United States launch nearly 6 million businesses.[1] These people, who come from diverse backgrounds, are striving to realize that Great American Dream of owning and operating their own business. Some of them have chosen to leave the security of the corporate hierarchy in search of independence, others have been forced out of large corporations as a result of downsizing, and still others have from the start chosen the autonomy that owning a business offers. The impact of these entrepreneurs on the nation's economy goes far beyond their numbers, however. The resurgence of the entrepreneurial spirit they are spearheading is the most significant economic development in recent business history. These heroes of the new economy are introducing innovative products and services, pushing back technological frontiers, creating new jobs, opening foreign markets, and, in the process, sparking the U.S. economy.

Entrepreneurs, once shunned as people who could not handle a "real" job in the corporate world, now are the heroes of the economy. They create companies, jobs, wealth, and innovative solutions to some of the world's most vexing problems, from relief for sore feet to renewable energy sources. "The story of entrepreneurship entails a never ending search for new and imaginative ways to combine the factors of production into new methods, processes, technologies, products, or services," says one government economist who has conducted extensive research on entrepreneurship's impact.[2] In short, small business is "cool," and entrepreneurs are the rock stars of the business world.

The last several decades have seen record numbers of entrepreneurs launching businesses. One important indicator of the popularity of entrepreneurship is the keen interest expressed by students in creating their own businesses. Increasing numbers of young people are choosing entrepreneurship as a career (some of them while they are still in school) rather than joining the ranks of the pinstriped masses in major corporations. When many young people hear the phrase "corporate America," they do not think of career opportunities; instead, images of the television show *The Office* come to mind. In short, the probability that you will become an entrepreneur at some point in your life has never been higher!

Research suggest that entrepreneurial activity remains vibrant not only in the United States but around the world as well. According to the Global Entrepreneurship Monitor (GEM), a study of entrepreneurial activity across the globe, 8 percent of the U.S. population aged 18 to 64, nearly one in 12 adults, is engaged in entrepreneurial activity. The study also found that 10.9 percent of people in the 49 GEM countries analyzed are involved in starting a new business (see Figure 1).[3]

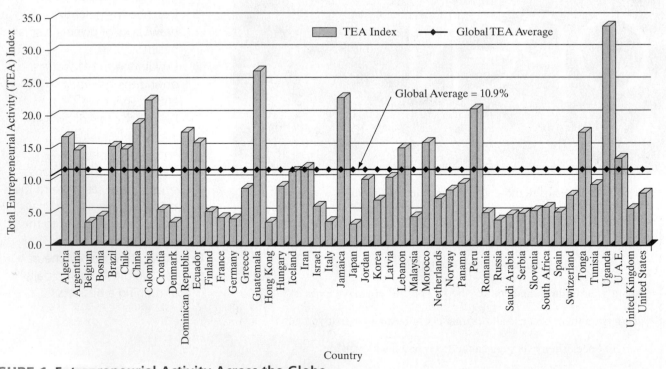

FIGURE 1 Entrepreneurial Activity Across the Globe
Persons per 100 Adults, 18–64 Years Old Engaged in Entrepreneurial Activity
Source: Global Entrepreneurship Monitor, 2008.

Entrepreneurs in every corner of the world are launching businesses thanks to technology that provides easy access to both local and global markets at start-up. Even countries that traditionally are not known as hotbeds of entrepreneurial activity are home to promising start-up companies. Despite discouraging entrepreneurial activity for generations, China is now home to an estimated 36 million small businesses.

ENTREPRENEURIAL
Profile

Jack Ma: Alibaba

Jack Ma – founder of Alibaba.com.

Source: Imaginechina/AP Images

Perhaps China's most famous entrepreneur is Jack Ma, founder of Alibaba, an Internet-based company that connects Chinese companies with business partners around the world. At age 12, Ma taught himself English by serving as a guide to tourists before going on to study English at Hangzhou Teachers University. When he graduated, Ma was assigned to teach in a university, earning the equivalent of about $15 per month. He discovered the Internet while serving as an interpreter for a trade delegation in Seattle, Washington, and when he returned to China, borrowed $2,000 to launch China Pages, China's first Internet company. Ma's next goal was to launch an e-commerce business with global reach. "In 1999," he says, "I gathered 18 people in my apartment and spoke to them for 2 hours about my vision. Everyone put their money on the table, and that got us $60,000 to start Alibaba," a name Ma took from *One Thousand and One Nights*, a collection of tales commonly known as Arabian Nights. Ma took Alibaba public in 2008, and the company, now valued at $26 billion, has expanded into online search. "I want to create one million jobs, change China's social and economic environment, and make it the largest Internet market in the world," says the visionary entrepreneur who also has launched Taobao, an online auction site.[4]

In recent years, large companies in the United States and around the world have engaged in massive downsizing campaigns, dramatically cutting the number of managers and workers on their payrolls. This flurry of "pink slips" has spawned a new population of entrepreneurs—"castoffs" from large corporations (many of whom thought they would be lifetime ladder-climbers in their companies) with solid management experience and many productive years left before retirement.

One casualty of this downsizing has been the long-standing notion of job security in large corporations, which all but destroyed the concept of loyalty and has made workers much more mobile. In the 1960s, the typical employee had worked for an average of four employers by the time he or she reached age 65; today, the average employee has had eight employers by the time he or she is 30.[5] Members of Generation X (those born between 1965 and 1980) and Generation Y (those born between 1981 and 1995), in particular, no longer see launching a business as being a risky career path. Having witnessed large companies lay off their parents after many years of service, these young people see entrepreneurship as the ideal way to create their own job security and career success! They are eager to control their own destinies.

This downsizing trend among large companies also has created a more significant philosophical change. It has ushered in an age in which "small is beautiful." Twenty-five years ago, competitive conditions favored large companies with their hierarchies and layers of management; today, with the pace of change constantly accelerating, fleet-footed, agile, small companies have the competitive advantage. These nimble competitors dart into and out of niche markets as they emerge and recede; they move faster to exploit opportunities the market presents; and they use modern technology to create within a matter of weeks or months products and services that once took years and all of the resources a giant corporation could muster. The balance has tipped in favor of small entrepreneurial companies.

Entrepreneurship also has become mainstream. Although launching a business is never easy, the resources available today make the job much simpler today than ever before. Thousands of colleges and universities offer courses in entrepreneurship, the Internet hosts a sea of information on launching a business, sources of capital that did not exist just a few years ago are now available, and business incubators hatch companies at impressive rates. Once looked down on as a choice for people unable to hold a corporate job, entrepreneurship is now an accepted and respected part of our culture.

Another significant shift in the bedrock of our nation's economic structure is influencing this swing in favor of small companies. The nation is rapidly moving away from an industrial economy to a knowledge-based one. What matters now is not so much the factors of production but *knowledge* and *information*. The final impact of this shift will be as dramatic as the move from an agricultural economy to an industrial one that occurred 200 years ago in the United States. A knowledge-based economy favors small businesses because the cost of managing and transmitting knowledge and information is very low, and computer and information technologies are driving these costs lower still.

No matter why they start their businesses, entrepreneurs continue to embark on one of the most exhilarating—and one of the most frightening—adventures ever known: launching a business. It's never easy, but it can be incredibly rewarding, both financially and emotionally. One successful business owner claims that an entrepreneur is "anyone who wants to experience the deep, dark canyons of uncertainty and ambiguity and wants to walk the breathtaking highlands of success. But I caution: Do not plan to walk the latter until you have experienced the former."[6] True entrepreneurs see owning a business as the real measure of success. Indeed, entrepreneurship often provides the only avenue for success to those who otherwise might have been denied the opportunity.

Who are these entrepreneurs, and what drives them to work so hard with no guarantee of success? What forces lead them to risk so much and to make so many sacrifices in an attempt to achieve an ideal? Why are they willing to give up the security of a steady paycheck working for someone else to become the last person to be paid in their own companies? This chapter will examine the entrepreneur, the driving force behind the American economy.

Source: www.CartoonStock.com

What Is an Entrepreneur?

2. Describe the entrepreneurial profile.

At any given time, an estimated 10.1 million adults in the United States are engaged in launching a business, traveling down the path of entrepreneurship.[7] An **entrepreneur** is one who creates a new business in the face of risk and uncertainty for the purpose of achieving profit and growth by identifying opportunities and assembling the necessary resources to capitalize on those opportunities. Entrepreneurs usually start with nothing more than an idea—often a simple one—and then organize the resources necessary to transform that idea into a sustainable business. In essence, entrepreneurs are *disrupters*, upsetting the traditional way of doing things by creating new ways to do them. One business writer says that an entrepreneur is "someone who takes nothing for granted, assumes change is possible, and follows through; someone incapable of confronting reality without thinking about ways to improve it; and for whom action is a natural consequence of thought."[8]

What entrepreneurs have in common is the ability to spot opportunities and the willingness to capitalize on them.

ENTREPRENEURIAL
Profile

Zac Workman: ZW Enterprises

Zac Workman – founder of ZW Enterprises.
Source: Chris Meyer

As a high school All-American swimmer, Zac Workman made a habit of drinking an energy drink after each 5-hour swim practice. The drink "tasted awful, but it gave me energy, so I kept drinking it," he says. After his freshman year at Indiana University, Workman began studying the energy drink market and recognized the opportunity for an energy drink that actually tasted good, was made from natural ingredients, and avoided the postdrink crash that comes with high-sugar and high-caffeine drinks. The 21-year-old took a 75-year-old family recipe for fruit punch and added the necessary ingredients to formulate an energy drink. After several drink manufacturers rejected his idea, Workman partnered with Power Brands, a California-based beverage development company, to perfect his drink. Workman designed the black and red can himself but collaborated with chemists to develop an energy drink that could be mass produced; after 10 attempts, they were successful. Workman tapped his family for $200,000 in start-up capital and launched ZW Enterprises, the company that markets his energy drink, Punch. Sales are on track to reach $1 million, and the finance and entrepreneurship major says that running his company is making him a better student. "I'm sitting in class learning business strategies meant to be applied in the professional world," he says, "but I actually get to do that when I go home."[9]

A recent Gallup survey reported that 61 percent of adults in the United States would like to start a business so that they can be their own boss.[10] The reality, however, is although many people dream of owning a business, most of them never actually launch a company. Those who do take the entrepreneurial plunge, however, will experience the thrill of creating something grand from nothing; they will also discover the challenges and the difficulties of building a business "from scratch." Whatever their reasons for choosing entrepreneurship, many recognize that true satisfaction comes only from running their own businesses the way they choose.

Researchers have invested a great deal of time and effort over the last decade studying these entrepreneurs and trying to paint a clear picture of the entrepreneurial personality. Although these studies have produced several characteristics entrepreneurs tend to exhibit, none of them has isolated a set of traits required for success. We now turn to a brief summary of the entrepreneurial profile.[11]

1. *Desire and willingness to take initiative.* Entrepreneurs feel a personal responsibility for the outcome of ventures they start. They prefer to be in control of their resources and to use those resources to achieve self-determined goals. They are willing to step forward and build businesses based on their creative ideas.

2. *Preference for moderate risk.* Entrepreneurs are not wild risk-takers but are instead *calculating* risk-takers. Unlike "high-rolling, riverboat gamblers," they rarely gamble. Entrepreneurs often have a different perception of the risk involve in a business situation. The goal may appear to be high—even impossible—from others' perspective, but entrepreneurs typically have thought through the situation and believe that their goals are reasonable and attainable. Entrepreneurs launched many now-famous businesses, including Burger King, Microsoft, FedEx, Disney, CNN, MTV, HP, and others, during economic recessions when many people believed their ideas and their timing to be foolhardy.

This attitude explains why so many successful entrepreneurs failed many times before finally achieving their dreams. For instance, Milton Hershey, founder of one of the world's largest and most successful chocolate makers, started four candy businesses, all of which failed, before he launched the business that would make him famous. The director of an entrepreneurship center says that entrepreneurs "are not crazy, wild-eyed risk takers. Successful entrepreneurs understand the risks [of starting a business] and figure out how to manage them."[12] Good entrepreneurs become risk *reducers*, and one of the best ways to minimize the risk in any entrepreneurial venture is to create a sound business plan.

3. *Confidence in their ability to succeed.* Entrepreneurs typically have an abundance of confidence in their ability to succeed, and they tend to be optimistic about their chances for business success. Entrepreneurs face many barriers when starting and running their companies, and a healthy dose of optimism can be an important component in their ultimate success. "Entrepreneurs believe they can do anything," says one researcher.[13]

4. *Self-reliance.* Entrepreneurs do not shy away from the responsibility for making their businesses succeed. Perhaps that is why many entrepreneurs persist in building businesses even when others ridicule their ideas as follies. Their views reflect those of Ralph Waldo Emerson in his essay "Self Reliance":

> You will always find those who think they know what is your duty better than you know it. It is easy in the world to live after the world's opinion; it is easy in solitude to live after our own; but the great man is he who in the midst of the crowd keeps with perfect sweetness the independence of solitude.[14]

5. *Perseverance.* Even when things don't work out as they planned, entrepreneurs don't give up. They simply keep trying. Real entrepreneurs follow the advice contained in the Japanese proverb, "Fall seven times; stand up eight."

ENTREPRENEURIAL
Profile

Gail Borden:
Borden Inc.

Entrepreneur Gail Borden (1801–1874) was a prolific inventor, but most of his inventions, including the terraqueous wagon (a type of prairie schooner that could travel on land or water) and a meat biscuit (a mixture of dehydrated meat and flour that would last for months), never achieved commercial success. After witnessing a small child die from contaminated milk, Borden set out to devise a method for condensing milk to make it safer for human consumption in the days before refrigeration. For 2 years he tried a variety of methods, but every one of them failed. Finally, Borden developed a successful vacuum condensation process, won a patent for it, and built a company around the product. It failed, but Borden persevered. He launched another condensed milk business, this time with a stronger capital base, and it succeeded, eventually becoming Borden Inc., a multibillion-dollar conglomerate that still makes condensed milk using the process Borden developed 150 years ago. When he died, Borden was buried beneath a tombstone that reads, "I tried and failed. I tried again and succeeded."[15]

6. *Desire for immediate feedback.* Entrepreneurs like to know how they are doing and are constantly looking for reinforcement. Tricia Fox, founder of Fox Day Schools, Inc., claims, "I like being independent and successful. Nothing gives you feedback like your own business."[16]

7. *High level of energy.* Entrepreneurs are more energetic than the average person. That energy may be a critical factor given the incredible effort required to launch a start-up company. Long hours—often 60 to 80 hours a week—and hard work are the rule rather than the exception. Building a successful business requires a great deal of stamina.

8. *Competitiveness.* Entrepreneurs tend to exhibit competitive behavior, often early in life. They enjoy competitive games and sports and always want to keep score!

9. *Future orientation.* Entrepreneurs tend to dream big and then formulate plans to transform those dreams into reality. They have a well-defined sense of searching for opportunities. They look ahead and are less concerned with what they accomplished yesterday than what they can do tomorrow. Ever vigilant for new business opportunities, entrepreneurs *observe* the same events other people do, but they *see* something different.

Taking this trait to the extreme are **serial entrepreneurs,** those who create multiple companies, often running more than one business simultaneously. These entrepreneurs take multitasking to the extreme. Serial entrepreneurs get a charge from taking an idea, transforming it into a business, and repeating the process.

ENTREPRENEURIAL
Profile

Stuart Skorman:
Clerkdogs.com

At age 60, Stuart Skorman launched his sixth company, Clerkdogs.com, a Web site that recommends movies based on an analysis of 36 attributes of users' favorite films and the insights of dozens of former video-store employees. Skorman, a former corporate executive, decided to become an entrepreneur at age 36, when he launched Empire Video, a chain of video rental stores. He went on to start Reel.com, a Web site that serves as a hub for information about films and the film industry, which he sold to Hollywood Video for $100 million. Skorman also launched Elephant Pharmacy, a company that he sold to CVS Pharmacies in 2006. Not all of his ventures have succeeded, however. He lost $20 million on a doomed dot-com start-up, Hungryminds.com, but, like a genuine entrepreneur, Skorman continued to create businesses.[17] "I'm the creative guy you want to start with, but I'm not the management guy you want to run [a business]," says Skorman, explaining his serial entrepreneur tendencies.[18]

10. *Skill at organizing.* Building a company "from scratch" is much like piecing together a giant jigsaw puzzle. Entrepreneurs know how to put the right people and resources together to accomplish a task. Effectively combining people and jobs enables entrepreneurs to bring their visions to reality.

11. *Value of achievement over money.* One of the most common misconceptions about entrepreneurs is that they are driven wholly by the desire to make money. To the contrary, *achievement* seems to be the primary motivating force behind entrepreneurs; money is simply a way of "keeping score" of accomplishments—a *symbol* of achievement. "Money is not the driving motive of most entrepreneurs," says Nick Grouf, founder of a high-tech company. "It's just a very nice by-product of the process."[19]

Other characteristics exhibited by entrepreneurs include:

■ *High degree of commitment.* Launching a company successfully requires total commitment from the entrepreneur. Business founders often immerse themselves completely in their businesses. "The commitment you have to make is tremendous; entrepreneurs usually put everything on the line," says one expert.[20] That commitment helps overcome business-threatening mistakes, obstacles, and pessimism from naysayers, however. Entrepreneurs' commitment to their ideas and the businesses those ideas spawn determine how successful their companies ultimately become.

■ *Tolerance for ambiguity.* Entrepreneurs tend to have a high tolerance for ambiguous, ever-changing situations—the environment in which they most often operate. This ability to handle uncertainty is critical, because these business builders constantly make decisions using new, sometimes conflicting, information gleaned from a variety of unfamiliar sources.

■ *Flexibility.* One hallmark of true entrepreneurs is their ability to adapt to the changing demands of their customers and their businesses. In this rapidly changing world economy, rigidity often leads to failure. As society, its people, and their tastes change, entrepreneurs also must be willing to adapt their businesses to meet those changes. Successful entrepreneurs are willing to allow their business models to evolve as market conditions warrant.

■ *Tenacity.* Obstacles, obstructions, and defeat typically do not dissuade entrepreneurs from doggedly pursuing their visions. Successful entrepreneurs have the willpower to conquer the barriers that stand in the way of their success.

What conclusion can we draw from the volumes of research conducted on the entrepreneurial personality? Entrepreneurs are not of one mold; no one set of characteristics can predict who will become entrepreneurs and whether they will succeed. Indeed, *diversity* seems to be a central characteristic of entrepreneurs. As you can see from the examples in this chapter, *anyone*—regardless of age, race, gender, color, national origin, or any other characteristic—can become an entrepreneur. There are no limitations on this form of economic expression, and Hans Becker is living proof.

ENTREPRENEURIAL
Profile

Hans Becker: Armadillo Tree & Shrub

While serving a 5-year prison term in Cleveland, Texas, Hans Becker, 46, enrolled in the Prison Entrepreneurship Program (PEP), a nonprofit organization founded by former Wall Street executive Catherine Rohr that teaches the tools of entrepreneurship to inmates. Participants take classes in both business and life skills and work with mentors from colleges, churches, and the business community. When Becker was released, he used the $500 that family members gave him to buy yard tools and launched Armadillo Tree & Shrub, a landscape business, in Dallas. Armadillo generates as much as $10,000 per month in sales during the busy season and employs eight workers. "PEP taught me that people in business would accept me for who I am as long as I build a business that is solid and ethical," says Becker. "That gave me hope." Becker is one of 58 PEP graduates who have started their own businesses, which range from T-shirt printing to software development. Fewer than 10 percent of PEP graduates land back in jail, compared to a recidivism rate of more than 50 percent for released prisoners nationwide.[21]

Entrepreneurship is not a genetic trait; it is a skill that is learned. The editors of *Inc.* magazine claim, "Entrepreneurship is more mundane than it's sometimes portrayed . . . .You don't need to be a person of mythical proportions to be very, very successful in building a company."[22] As you read this text, we hope that you will pay attention to the numerous small business examples and will notice not only the creativity and dedication of the entrepreneurs behind them but also the diversity of those entrepreneurs.

▶ ENTREPRENEURSHIP IN ACTION ▶

Can a Pair of Helium Heads Build a Successful Business?

Entrepreneur-turned-venture-capitalist Guy Kawasaki says that entrepreneurs are willing to ask the fundamental question, "Wouldn't it be neat if . . . ?" Steve Jobs wondered, "Wouldn't it be neat if people could take their favorite music with them wherever they go?" and the result was the best-selling iPod. Copreneurs Brian and Alexandra (Alex) Hall asked, "Wouldn't it be neat if people could ride in a zeppelin?" and launched Airship Adventures Zeppelin NT (New Technology) in Mountain View, California.

Alex, an astrophysicist, and Brian, a successful software entrepreneur, came up with their zeppelin business idea after Brian took a ride on a zeppelin while he was in Germany in 2006 shortly before the couple married. The Halls approached Deutsche Zeppelin-Reederei, a German company that made zeppelins during their heyday in the 1930s and restarted production in 2001, about buying one of the company's $15 million airships. (Zeppelins and blimps are not the same. Blimps are short-range balloons with navigational fins; a zeppelin is designed for long-distance flights and has a metal infrastructure that contains multiple bags filled with inert helium rather than with explosive hydrogen, which doomed the *Hindenburg* in 1937.) With the help of a business plan, the Halls raised $8.5 million from private investors, including technology

entrepreneur and investor Esther Dyson, to start the only passenger zeppelin business in the United States. (Before they started flying, Alex says that they actually called the Federal Aviation Administration and said, "You probably need to regulate us, but you don't have any zeppelin regulations on the books.")

The Hall's airship, the *Eureka*, is 246 feet long, and its spacious cabin accommodates one pilot, one flight attendant, and 12 passengers. The cabin has oversized panoramic windows (the views are phenomenal) and a 180-degree rear observation window and love seat that wraps around the entire aft cabin. Its vectored thrust engines can propel the Eureka at speeds of up to 78 miles per hour. The *Eureka* is one of only three functioning zeppelins in the world.

Based at Moffett Field in Mountain View, California, the *Eureka* takes passengers on leisurely, peaceful flights around San Francisco, Silicon Valley, and Napa Valley. The Halls recently took the airship to Los Angeles and Hollywood and sold out every flight within 48 hours of arriving. Flights cost $500 per hour per person, and a typical flight lasts between 1 and 2 hours. When traveling for a special event in another city—for example, from their home base in Mountain View to Los Angeles—the Halls sell tickets for $1,500 each for these "flightseeing" excursions.

Because it is a rigid airship filled with helium, the *Eureka* cannot fly in heavy rain or fog or in winds that exceed 20 knots. Cancelled flights due to poor weather, particularly in California's rainy season from November to March, present a significant problem for the young company. In their first year of operation, the Halls had to cancel one-third of their flights during the rainy season, which significantly lowered the company's sales and strained its cash flow. Discussions with experienced pilots about the Bay Area fog revealed to the Halls that afternoons are the best time to fly. The Halls also have lifted off from airfields in Oakland and Monterey to avoid cancelling flights. To maximize flight time and the company's revenue, they also are considering moving their operation to Los Angeles during the Bay Area's rainy season.

California law requires Airship Adventures to hold customers' payments in escrow until the customers actually fly, which further restricts the company's working capital. In addition, the Federal Aviation Administration requires the Eureka to be grounded for 1 month each year for an annual inspection. Taking the airship out of service that long costs an estimated $1.3 million in lost revenue. Operating costs include payments on the zeppelin, rent for the hangar space, insurance, helium, salaries for their full-time staff (which includes Kate Board, the only female zeppelin pilot in the world) and part-time ground crews, and other expenses. The Halls anticipate sales of $9 million, which will allow them to break even, assuming that they can sell advertising space on the 57-foot-tall craft to a company that is looking for a highly-visible, unique way to advertise.

Despite the challenges they face, the Halls, who admit that they are "helium heads," are zealous about their business. They are exploring how best to capitalize on the strengths that their location offers and are testing the market for a winery tour weekend and a ski weekend that would take passengers to Lake Tahoe. The Halls would like to expand their business into two other markets, including one on the East coast. "We'd like more ships," says Brian. "Three is the sweet spot." The Halls see their business as more than one that simply takes passengers on flights in a unique airship with a storied past. "Every day we create memories and smiles," says Brian. "You can't look at our ship and be grumpy."

1. If you were one of the potential investors whom the Halls approached for start-up capital, how would you have responded? What questions would you have asked them?
2. What do you predict for the future of this business?
3. Identify some of the most significant challenges facing the Halls and Airship Ventures. What strategies can you suggest they use to deal with them?

Sources: Based on Ian Mount, "It's Not a Blimp. It's a Zeppelin," *FSB,* November 2008, p. 20; Chris Taylor, "Helium Heads," *FSB,* April 2009, pp. 80–83; "The Ship," Airship Adventures, *www.airshipventures.com/factsandfigures.php;* "Airship Ventures' Eureka Returns Home After Receiving Star Treatment in Los Angeles," *Reuters,* May 27, 2009, *www.reuters.com/article/pressRelease/idUS209827+27-May-2009+MW20090527.*

How to Spot Entrepreneurial Opportunities

3. Explain how entrepreneurs spot business opportunities.

One of the tenets of entrepreneurship is the ability to create new and useful ideas that solve the problems and challenges people face every day. "Entrepreneurs innovate," said management legend Peter Drucker. "Innovation is the special instrument of entrepreneurship."[23] Entrepreneurs achieve success by creating value in the marketplace when they combine resources in new and different ways to gain a competitive edge over rivals. Entrepreneurs can create value in a number of ways— inventing new products and services, developing new technology, discovering new knowledge, improving existing products or services, finding different ways of providing more goods and services with fewer resources, and many others. Indeed, finding new ways of satisfying customers' needs, inventing new products and services, putting together existing ideas in new and different ways, and creating new twists on existing products and services are hallmarks of the entrepreneur.

What is the entrepreneurial "secret" for creating value in the marketplace? In reality, the "secret" is no secret at all: it is applying creativity and innovation to solve problems and to capitalize on opportunities that people face every day. **Creativity** is the ability to develop new ideas and to discover new ways of looking at problems and opportunities. **Innovation** is the ability to *apply* creative solutions to those problems and opportunities to enhance or to enrich people's lives. Harvard's Ted Levitt says that creativity is *thinking* new things, and innovation is *doing* new things. In short, entrepreneurs succeed by *thinking and doing* new things or old things in new ways. Simply having a great new idea is not enough; turning the idea into a tangible product, service, or business venture is the essential next step.

Entrepreneurs' ability to build viable businesses around their ideas has transformed the world. From King Gillette's invention of the safety razor (Gillette) and Mary Kay Ash's use of a motivated team of consultants to sell her cosmetics (Mary Kay Cosmetics) to Steve Jobs and Steve Wozniak building the first personal computer in a California garage (Apple) and Fred

Smith's concept for delivering packages overnight (FedEx), entrepreneurs have made the world a better place to live. How do entrepreneurs spot opportunities? Although there is no single process, the following techniques will help you learn to spot business opportunities in the same way these successful entrepreneurs did.

Monitor Trends and Exploit Them Early On

Astute entrepreneurs watch both national and local trends that are emerging and then build businesses that align with those trends. Detecting a trend early on and launching a business to capitalize on it enables an entrepreneur to gain a competitive advantage over rivals. The Pew Foundation predicts that mobile devices such as smart phones will surpass computers as the primary tool for Internet connectivity by 2020, and entrepreneurs are working to capitalize on the growing popularity of mobile devices. Since Apple launched the App Store, an online store that sells a multitude of clever applications for its popular iPhone, iPod Touch, and iPad products, entrepreneurs have been racing to create the next "killer app," introducing applications that do everything from providing clever games and recipes for mixed drinks to checking prices on products and creating personal radio stations. In the App Store's first 8 months, customers downloaded an average of 1 million applications per month!

ENTREPRENEURIAL
Profile
Ge Wang: Sonic Mule

Ge Wang, cofounder of Sonic Mule, a company that creates applications for the iPhone, developed Ocarina, an app that transforms the iPhone into a flute that allows users to create music by blowing into the microphone and changing cords by touching circles that appear on the screen. Tilting the phone changes the vibrato rate. Customers downloaded 700,000 copies of Ocarina, which costs 99 cents, in just 4 months, making it one of the most successful applications in the App Store.[24]

Take a Different Approach to an Existing Market

Another way to spot opportunities is to ask if there is another way to reach an existing market with a unique product, service, or marketing strategy. Entrepreneurs are famous for finding new, creative approaches to existing markets and turning them into business opportunities.

ENTREPRENEURIAL
Profile
Michael and Tun Flancman: Poo Poo Paper Company

Many business sell paper made the traditional way from wood pulp, but copreneurs Michael and Tun Flancman take a completely different approach, making a thick, textured paper out of dung from elephants, panda bears, and other animals! (It is disinfected and odorless.) Their company, the Poo Poo Paper Company, collects the dung from domesticated Asian elephant herds and other animals that work on farms and tourist attractions in Thailand. The company's 65 employees boil the dung for several hours to sanitize it and then add fiber from various seasonal fruits that serve as a binding element. They add bleach or color and spread the resulting cakes onto mesh screens that dry in the sun. Once the sheets are dry, workers transform them into sheets of paper, envelopes, and other products that the Flancmans sell to more than 620 retail outlets around the world. The Poo Poo Paper Company generates annual sales of $500,000, and the Flancmans donate a portion of every sale to elephant welfare and conservation programs.[25]

Put a New Twist on an Old Idea

Sometimes entrepreneurs find opportunities by taking an old idea and giving it a unique twist. The result can lead to a profitable business venture.

ENTREPRENEURIAL
Profile
Jason Gaxiola: Green Grass at Last

Jason Gaxiola, owner of Green Grass at Last, saw a business opportunity in the housing "bust" in Las Vegas, Nevada. Thousands of homes were in foreclosure, and their neglected lawns were brown and unappealing. Gaxiola thought that the same trick that groundskeepers of baseball fields and golf courses have used for years to make their grass look so luxuriant—a mixture of ammonia, fertilizer, and green dye—would rejuvenate the lawns of the abandoned houses and make them easier to sell. Taking an old idea and giving it a new twist worked; Green Grass treats an average of two foreclosed properties a day and charges $250 for a 500-square-foot lawn.[26]

Look for Creative Ways to Use Existing Resources

Another way entrepreneurs uncover business opportunities is to find creative ways to use existing resources. This requires them to cast aside logic and traditional thinking.

ENTREPRENEURIAL
Profile

Rory Cutaia:
Greenfields Coal

Rory Cutaia, founder of Greenfields Coal, looked at spent coal mines and saw opportunity. His company has developed a way to extract bits of coal from the sludge left behind after a mine closes and that most people see as waste and an environmental hazard. Greenfields Coal also has developed a substance that binds the tiny pieces of recovered coal into briquettes that have the same properties as deep-mined coal and are easy to ship. Cutaia recently purchased the rights to an abandoned coal mine in West Virginia and has set up a processing plant on site that will reclaim 10 million tons of coal from the sludge that once was considered waste.[27]

Realize That Others Have the Same Problem You Do

Another way to spot business opportunities is to recognize that other people face the same problems that you do. Providing a product or service that solves those problems offers the potential for a promising business.

ENTREPRENEURIAL
Profile

Nicole DeBoom:
SkirtSports

Nicole DeBoom – founder of SkirtSports, Boulder, Colorado.
Source: AP Wide World Photos

For years, Nicole DeBoom, a world-class triathlete, wore high-performance running shorts that were designed for men—until she caught a glimpse of her reflection in a store window while running in a pair of them. The look, she decided, was less than flattering, even for someone as fit as she was. Back at home, DeBoom scribbled "Pretty!" on a sheet of paper and decided to create a line of exercise clothing that was designed specifically for active women and would marry high performance with attractive design. The result was SkirtSports, a Boulder, Colorado-based company that designs and markets a line of running skirts, dresses, tank tops, sports bras, and hoodies that are sold in more than 300 stores across the United States. To promote her company, DeBoom created a series of "Skirt Chaser" races in which women runners in a "Catch Me" wave get a 3-minute head start over men runners. A block party and fashion show featuring SkirtSports products (of course) follow the fun-filled race. "I made a product because I wanted to perform better myself," says DeBoom. "Other women were looking for the same thing. We were besieged by women who said, 'What took you so long?'"[28]

Notice What Is Missing

Sometimes entrepreneurs spot viable business opportunities by noticing what is *missing*. The first step is to determine whether a market for the missing product or service actually exists (perhaps the reason it does not exist is that there is no potential market), which is one of the objectives of building a business plan.

ENTREPRENEURIAL
Profile

Chris Vicino: Dogs
on Wheels

Chris Vicino, a native of New York City, grew tired of his career in finance on Wall Street and moved to Greenville, South Carolina, a small, fast-growing city of 60,000 people. While strolling the downtown district with his wife one day, Vicino noticed that there were no hot dog vendors like the ones he was so accustomed to seeing on most street corners in New York City. After purchasing all the necessary licenses and a cart, Vicino opened Dogs on Wheels and began selling classic New York style hot dogs to hungry Southerners.[29]

No matter which methods they use to detect business opportunities, true entrepreneurs follow up their ideas with action, building companies to capitalize on their ideas.

The Benefits of Owning a Small Business

4. Describe the benefits of owning a small bussiness.

Surveys show that owners of small businesses believe they work harder, earn more money, and are happier than if they worked for a large company. Entrepreneurs enjoy many benefits of owning a small business, including the following:

Opportunity to Gain Control over Your Own Destiny

Entrepreneurs cite controlling their own destinies as one of the benefits of owning their own businesses. Owning a business provides entrepreneurs the independence and the opportunity to achieve what is important to them. Entrepreneurs want to "call the shots" in their lives, and they use their businesses to bring this desire to life. Numerous studies of entrepreneurs in several countries report that the primary incentive for starting their businesses is "being my own boss." Entrepreneurs reap the intrinsic rewards of knowing they are the driving forces behind their businesses. Wendy Wade, who at age 57 accepted a buyout package from Best Buy, where she had worked as a human resource executive for 9 years, to start her own consulting business, says, "Part of the attraction is taking control of my destiny, including my financial destiny. I'm not risk averse."[30]

Opportunity to Make a Difference

Increasingly, entrepreneurs are starting businesses because they see an opportunity to make a difference in a cause that is important to them. Known as **social entrepreneurs**, these business builders seek to find innovative solutions to some of society's most pressing and most challenging problems. Whether it is providing low-cost, sturdy housing for families in developing countries, promoting the arts in small communities, or creating a company that educates young people about preserving the earth's limited resources, entrepreneurs are finding ways to combine their concerns for social issues and their desire to earn good livings. Although they see the importance of building viable, sustainable businesses, social entrepreneurs' primary goal is to use their companies to make a positive impact on the world.

ENTREPRENEURIAL
Profile

Michael Reynolds: Earthship Biotecture

In the early 1970s, before recycling and sustainability became popular, Michael Reynolds, then a recent graduate in architecture, began experimenting with building houses out of waste material and trash. Today, Reynolds is the CEO of Earthship Biotecture, a company in Taos, New Mexico, that builds self-sufficient homes called "earthships" because they are made from natural and recycled materials (including aluminum cans, plastic bottles, and car tires), use solar and wind power, and generate their own electricity and water. "We're building homes today that have a $100 a year total utility bill," he says. Reynolds is an innovator in the field of biotecture (a term he coined to describe the marriage of biology and architecture), the science of designing buildings and environments in a sustainable way. In addition to their environmental friendliness and sustainability, the houses also feature the latest in creature comforts, including high-speed wireless Internet service, fireplaces, flat-screen TVs, and more. "We have just scratched the surface of what is possible in terms of using the materials that are discarded by modern society," says Reynolds, whose company has built earthship homes all around the world.[31]

Opportunity to Reach Your Full Potential

Too many people find their work boring, unchallenging, and unexciting. But to most entrepreneurs, there is little difference between work and play; the two are synonymous. Roger Levin, founder of Levin Group, the largest dental practice management consulting firm in the world, says, "When I come to work every day, it's not a job for me. I'm having fun!"[32]

Entrepreneurs' businesses become the instrument for self-expression and self-actualization. Owning a business challenges all of an entrepreneur's skills, abilities, creativity, and determination. The only barriers to success are self-imposed. "It's more exciting to get a company from zero to $100 million than to get a billion-dollar company to its next $100 million," says Dick

Harrington, former CEO of Thomson Reuters and now a principal at Cue Ball, a venture capital firm that invests in promising small companies.[33] Entrepreneurs' creativity, determination, and enthusiasm—not limits artificially created by an organization (e.g., the "glass ceiling")—determine how high they can rise.

Opportunity to Reap Impressive Profits

Although money is *not* the primary force driving most entrepreneurs, the profits their businesses can earn are an important motivating factor in their decisions to launch companies. If accumulating wealth is high on your list of priorities, owning a business is usually the best way to achieve it. Indeed, nearly 75 percent of those on the *Forbes* list of the 400 richest Americans are first-generation entrepreneurs![34] Self-employed people are four times more likely to become millionaires than those who work for someone else. According to researchers Thomas Stanley and William Danko, the typical American millionaire is first-generation wealthy; owns a small business in a less-than-glamorous industry, such as welding, junk yards, or auctioneering; and works between 45 and 55 hours per week.[35]

ENTREPRENEURIAL
Profile
*Marco Giannini:
Dogswell*

As a child growing up with Emily, his beloved white German shepherd, Marco Giannini knew that he wanted to work with animals. At age 27, Giannini's dream came true when he came up with the idea of making premium dog treats that are infused with nutrients to keep dogs healthy. He scrounged up $30,000 in capital to produce the first batch of all-natural chicken jerky treats. He packaged the jerky treats into 5-ounce bags and visited more than 200 independent pet stores in California, many of whom agreed to carry the product, which Giannini called Dogswell. Giannini has expanded the Dogswell line to include dry and canned dog food and has launched similar products for cats under the Catswell brand. Dogswell has grown rapidly, from $500,000 in sales in its first full year to $21 million today, and has made Giannini a millionaire while still in his 30s.[36]

Opportunity to Contribute to Society and Be Recognized for Your Efforts

Often, small business owners are among the most respected—and most trusted—members of their communities. In fact, a recent survey by Zogby International and WeMedia reports that 63 percent of U.S. citizens say that entrepreneurs and small business owners (whom survey participants ranked first) will lead the nation to a better future.[37] Entrepreneurs enjoy the trust and the recognition they receive from the customers they have served faithfully over the years. Playing a vital role in their local business systems and knowing that the work they do has a significant impact on how smoothly our nation's economy functions is yet another reward for entrepreneurs.

Opportunity to Do What You Enjoy Doing

A common sentiment among small business owners is that their work *really* isn't work. In fact, a recent survey by Wells Fargo/Gallup Small Business Index reports that 89 percent of business owners say they do not plan to fully retire from their businesses![38] Most successful entrepreneurs choose to enter their particular business fields because they have an interest in them and enjoy those lines of work. Many of them have made their avocations (hobbies) their vocations (work) and are glad they did! These entrepreneurs are living the advice Harvey McKay offers: "Find a job doing what you love, and you'll never have to work a day in your life."

The Potential Drawbacks of Entrepreneurship

5. Describe the potential drawbacks of owning a small business.

Although owning a business has many benefits and provides many opportunities, anyone planning to enter the world of entrepreneurship should be aware of its potential drawbacks. "If you aren't 100 percent sure you want to own a business," says one business consultant, "there are plenty of demands and mishaps along the way to dissuade you."[39]

Uncertainty of Income

Opening and running a business provides no guarantees that an entrepreneur will earn enough money to survive. Even though business owners tend to earn more than wage-and-salary workers, some small businesses barely generate enough revenue to provide the owner-manager with an adequate income. The median income of small business owners ($59,708) is 56 percent higher than the median income of full-time wage and salary workers ($38,376), but business owners' income tends to be much more variable.[40] In the early days of a start-up, a business often cannot provide an attractive salary for its founder and meet all of its financial obligations, which means that the entrepreneur may have to live on savings for a time. The regularity of income that comes with working for someone else is absent because the owner is always the last one to be paid. The founder of a flavor and fragrances manufacturing operation recalls the time his bank unexpectedly called the company's loans just before Thanksgiving, squeezing both the company's and the family's cash flow. "We had planned a huge Christmas party, but we canceled that," recalls his wife. "And Christmas. And our usual New Year's trip."[41]

Risk of Losing Your Entire Invested Capital

The small business failure rate is relatively high. According to a study by the National Federation of Independent Businesses (NFIB), 34 percent of new businesses fail within 2 years, and 56 percent shut down within 4 years. Within 6 years, 60 percent of new businesses will have folded.[42]

A failed business can be financially and emotionally devastating. Before launching their businesses, entrepreneurs should ask themselves whether they can cope financially and psychologically with the consequences of failure. They should consider the risk-reward trade-off before putting their financial and mental well-being at risk:

- What is the worst that could happen if I open my business and it fails?
- How likely is the worst to happen?
- What can I do to lower the risk of my business failing? (See Table 1)
- If my business were to fail, what is my contingency plan for coping?

Long Hours and Hard Work

The average small business owner works 54 hours per week, compared to the 39.5 hours per week the typical U.S. production employee works.[43] A Small Business Watch survey reports that 61 percent of small business owners work 6 or 7 days a week.[44] In many start-ups, 10- to 12-hour days and 6- or 7-day workweeks with no paid vacations are the *norm*. Thirty percent of business owners say that they have not taken a vacation of at least 1 week in 4 years or more.[45] Sleep researcher James Maas of Cornell University estimates that entrepreneurs lose 700 hours of sleep the year in which they launch their companies, which is equivalent to the amount of sleep that a

TABLE 1 Top Five Reasons Start-up Businesses Fail

Research by the U.S. Small Business Administration shows the following top five reasons that start-up companies fail. Make sure that your business does not fall victim to them!

1. **Insufficient start-up capital.** Starting a business with too little capital is a sure recipe for failure. Experts suggest that entrepreneurs have the cash equivalent of 6 months of expenses available.

2. **Lack of managerial experience.** Passion for starting a company is important, but entrepreneurs also should have skills and experience in key business areas such as cash flow management, marketing, financing, inventory control, and others.

3. **Bad location.** Selecting the proper location is a key to success for many businesses. Your location should be convenient for your company's target customers.

4. **Poor inventory control.** Entrepreneurs in businesses that carry inventory must manage it closely. Carrying too much inventory ties up valuable cash, which can sink a new business.

5. **Lack of initial planning.** There is a reason that the mantra of many small business counselors is "business plan." Creating a comprehensive plan allows entrepreneurs to determine whether a business idea is likely to succeed and to identify the steps they must take to create a successful company.

Source: Greg Lopez, "Five Creative Ways to Start a New Small Business in a Turbulent Economy," Small Business Administration, Office of Advocacy, November 2008, p. 1.

parent loses in the first year of a baby's life.[46] Dan Croft left a top management job at a large mobile communications company to start Mission Critical Wireless, a small business that helps other businesses select and implement wireless communication systems. Croft's 25 years of experience in the industry allowed him to make a smooth transition to entrepreneurship, but there were a few surprises. "The highs are much higher, the lows are much lower, and the lack of sleep is much greater," jokes Croft, referring to the long hours his new role requires.[47]

Because they often must do everything themselves, owners experience intense, draining workdays. "I'm the owner, manager, secretary, and janitor," says Cynthia Malcolm, who owns a salon called the Hand Candy Mind and Body Escape in Cheviot, Ohio.[48] Many business owners start down the path of entrepreneurship thinking that they will own a business only to discover later that the business owns them!

Lower Quality of Life Until the Business Gets Established

The long hours and hard work needed to launch a company can take their toll on the remainder of an entrepreneur's life. Business owners often find their roles as husbands and wives or fathers and mothers take a back seat to their roles as company founders. Marriages and friendships are too often casualties of small business ownership. Part of the problem is that entrepreneurs are most likely to launch their businesses between the ages of 25 and 34, just when they start their families.

ENTREPRENEURIAL
Profile

Peyton Anderson:
Affinergy Inc.

Peyton Anderson, owner of Affinergy Inc., a 12-person biotech firm located in Research Triangle Park, North Carolina, struggles to balance the demands of his young company and his family, which includes three children under the age of 4. "I do a lot of work from 9 P.M. to midnight," says Anderson, "and I try to keep Saturday open to do things with the kids." He also uses flextime during the week to spend more time with his family, but maintaining balance is an ongoing battle, especially when managing a young company. "Even while I'm singing to them in the bathtub, in the back of my mind, I'm grinding on stuff at work," admits Anderson.[49]

High Levels of Stress

Launching and running a business can be an extremely rewarding experience, but it also can be a highly stressful one. Most entrepreneurs have made significant investments in their companies, have left behind the safety and security of a steady paycheck, and have mortgaged everything they own to get into business. Failure often means total financial ruin, as well as a serious psychological blow, and that creates high levels of stress and anxiety. "Being an entrepreneur takes sheer guts and demands far more than an 'employee' mentality," says Jamie Kreitman, founder of Kreitman Knitworks Ltd., a company specializing in whimsical apparel and footwear.[50]

Complete Responsibility

Owning a business is highly rewarding, but many entrepreneurs find that they must make decisions on issues about which they are not really knowledgeable. When there is no one to ask, pressure can build quickly. The realization that the decisions they make are the cause of success or failure of the business has a devastating effect on some people. Small business owners realize quickly that *they* are the business.

Discouragement

Launching a business requires much dedication, discipline, and tenacity. Along the way to building a successful business, entrepreneurs will run headlong into many obstacles, some of which may appear to be insurmountable. Discouragement and disillusionment can set in, but successful entrepreneurs know that every business encounters rough spots and that perseverance is required to get through them.

Why the Boom: The Fuel Feeding the Entrepreneurial Fire

6. Explain the forces that are driving the growth in entrepreneurship.

What forces are driving this entrepreneurial trend in our economy? Which factors have led to this age of entrepreneurship? Some of the most significant ones follow.

Entrepreneurs as Heroes

An intangible but very important factor is the attitude that Americans have toward entrepreneurs. Around the world, the most successful entrepreneurs have hero status and serve as role models for aspiring entrepreneurs. Business founders such as Michael Dell (Dell), Oprah Winfrey (Harpo Studios and Oxygen Media), Richard Branson (Virgin), Robert Johnson (Black Entertainment Television), and Phil Knight (Nike) are to entrepreneurship what Tiger Woods and Peyton Manning are to sports. The media reinforces entrepreneurs' hero status with television shows such as *The Apprentice* with Donald Trump, *Shark Tank,* and *Dragons' Den*, which is broadcast in 12 nations and features entrepreneurs who pitch their ideas to a panel of tough business experts who have the capital and the connections to make a budding business successful. Even China's state-owned Central Television has its own version of *Dragons' Den*.[51] More than 75 countries on 6 continents now participate in Global Entrepreneurship Week, a celebration of entrepreneurship that involves more than 3 million people and is sponsored by the Kauffman Foundation.[52]

Entrepreneurial Education

People with more education are more likely to start businesses than those with less education, and entrepreneurship, in particular, is an extremely popular course of study among students at all levels. A rapidly growing number of college students see owning a business as an attractive career option, and in addition to signing up for entrepreneurship courses, many of them are launching companies while in school. Today, more than 2,300 colleges and universities offer at least 1 course in entrepreneurship or small business management, up from just 16 in 1970![53] More than 500 colleges and universities now offer entrepreneurship majors at both undergraduate and graduate levels, up from just 175 in 1990.[54] More than 200,000 students are enrolled in entrepreneurship classes across the United States, and many colleges and universities are having trouble meeting the demand for courses in entrepreneurship and small business management.

Economic and Demographic Factors

Most entrepreneurs start their businesses between the ages of 25 and 44, and the number of U.S. citizens in that age range stands at more than 83.6 million! The economic growth over the last 20 years has created many business opportunities and a significant pool of capital for launching companies to exploit them.

Shift to a Service Economy

The service sector accounts for 80 percent of the jobs (up from 70 percent in the 1950s) and 48 percent of the gross domestic product (GDP) in the United States.[55] Because of their relatively low start-up costs, service businesses have been very popular with entrepreneurs. The booming service sector has provided entrepreneurs with many business opportunities, from hotels and health care to computer maintenance and Web-based services.

ENTREPRENEURIAL
Profile

Rob Kalin: Etsy

At age 25, Rob Kalin, created Etsy, a Web site that serves as an online marketplace for handmade items of all sorts, from jewelry and paintings to handbags and furniture, in 2005 with two classmates at New York University. The Brooklyn, New York–based online handmade marketplace has attracted 200,000 vendors and 1.8 million members in 150 countries. Etsy charges vendors a listing fee and a small commission on each sale. With an average of 30,000 items sold on Etsy each day, Kalin's company generates annual revenue of $100 million, up from $166,000 in its first year. Etsy, which has attracted more than $27 million in investments from venture capital firms Accel Partners and Union Square Ventures, has become a gathering place for artisans and buyers who are passionate about handmade goods.[56]

Technology Advancements

With the help of modern business tools—the Internet, personal computers, tablet computers, personal digital assistants, smart phones, copiers, color printers, instant messaging, and voice mail—even one person working at home can look like a big business. At one time, the high cost of such technological wizardry made it impossible for small businesses to compete with larger companies that could afford the hardware. Now the cost of sophisticated technology is low enough that even the smallest companies can use technology to gain a competitive edge. A survey conducted by the Canadian Federation of Independent Businesses reports that 77 percent of business owners say that technology allows them to differentiate their companies from the competition.[57] Although entrepreneurs may not be able to manufacture heavy equipment in their spare bedrooms, they can run a service- or information-based company from their homes very effectively and look like any *Fortune* 500 company to customers and clients.

Outsourcing

Entrepreneurs have discovered that they do not have to do everything themselves. Because of advances in technology, entrepreneurs can outsource many of the operations of their companies and retain only those in which they have a competitive advantage. Doing so enhances their flexibility and adaptability to ever-changing market and competitive conditions.

ENTREPRENEURIAL
Profile
Paul Carpenter: Sinol USA

Paul Carpenter operates Sinol USA, a small company in Newtown, Connecticut, that markets a line of natural nasal sprays that relieve sinus headaches and infections, with just two full-time employees, a bookkeeper and a receptionist. Since launching Sinol, which generates sales of more than $2 million, in 2005, Carpenter has outsourced most of the company's operations. The spray is packaged by a company in Oxford, Connecticut, in bottles from a Canadian manufacturer. Sinol uses independent sales representatives in New Jersey and California, a San Diego company fills corporate orders, and a New Haven, Connecticut, company fills individuals' orders. Carpenter recently established a relationship with a marketing firm in Washington, D.C.[58]

Independent Lifestyle

Entrepreneurship fits the way Americans want to live—independent and self-sustaining. Increasingly, entrepreneurs are starting businesses for lifestyle reasons. They want the freedom to choose where they live, the hours they work, and what they do. Although financial security remains an important goal for most entrepreneurs, lifestyle issues such as more time with family and friends, more leisure time, and more control over work-related stress also are important. To these "lifestyle entrepreneurs," launching businesses that give them the flexibility to work the hours they prefer and live where they want to are far more important than money.

E-commerce and the World Wide Web

The proliferation of the **World Wide Web,** the vast network that links computers around the globe via the Internet and opens up endless oceans of information to its users, has spawned thousands of entrepreneurial ventures since its beginning in 1993. As online shopping becomes easier, more engaging, and more secure for shoppers, e-commerce will continue to grow. Forrester Research predicts that online retail sales in the United States will increase from $141.3 billion in 2008 to $249 billion in 2014.[59] Many entrepreneurs see the power of the Web and are putting it to use, but others have been slow to establish a presence on the Web. A recent study by Elance and Microsoft reports that just 48 percent of small businesses have Web sites, and many of the owners of those businesses do not know enough about their sites to capitalize on the opportunities that the Web offers.[60] For many small companies, however, the Web is an essential tool.

ENTREPRENEURIAL
Profile
Jonathan Forgacs: Pillow Décor

At Pillow Décor, a Vancouver, Canada-based retailer and wholesaler of decorative pillows, Internet sales account for more than 90 percent of sales. Jonathan Forgacs opened a retail showroom and spent the next 6 months working with e-commerce companies to create an efficient, easy-to-use Web site that allows visitors to browse the company's extensive product line of more than 1,000 types of unique pillows that range in price from $10 to $300. Forgacs credits much of Pillow Décor's $1.8 million in annual sales to the company's search engine optimization strategy and its use of pay-per-click ads.[61]

International Opportunities

No longer are small businesses limited to pursuing customers within their own borders. The dramatic shift to a global economy has opened the door to tremendous business opportunities for those entrepreneurs willing to reach across the globe. Although the United States is an attractive market for entrepreneurs, approximately 95 percent of the world's population lives outside its borders. With so many opportunities in international markets, even the smallest businesses can sell globally, particularly with the help of the Internet. Jonathan Forgacs, cofounder of Pillow Décor, the Canadian company that sells decorative pillows, says that more than 98 percent of sales originate outside of Canada.[62]

Small companies with fewer than 100 employees account for 91 percent of the 266,500 U.S. businesses that export goods and services; however, they generate only 21 percent of the nation's export sales.[63] The most common barriers to international trade cited by small business owners are difficulty locating potential customers and problems finding reliable foreign sales representatives to handle their products.[64] Although "going global" can be fraught with many dangers and problems, many entrepreneurs are discovering that selling their products and services in foreign markets is not really as difficult as they originally thought. Patience, diligence, and a management commitment to exporting are essential elements. As business becomes increasingly global in nature, international opportunities for small businesses will continue to grow rapidly in the twenty-first century.

IN THE ENTREPRENEURIAL
SPOTLIGHT   Collegiate Entrepreneurs

For growing numbers of students, college is not just a time of learning, partying, and growing into young adulthood; it is fast becoming a place for building a business. Today, more than 2,300 colleges and universities offer courses in entrepreneurship and small business management, and many of them have trouble meeting the demand for these classes. "There's been a change in higher education," says William Green, dean of the entrepreneurship program at the University of Miami. "Entrepreneurship has become a mainstream activity." In addition to regular classroom courses, colleges increasingly are adding an extra dimension to their entrepreneurship programs, including interactions with the local business community, mentoring relationships with other entrepreneurs, networking opportunities with potential investors, and participation in business plan competitions. "Entrepreneurial education is a contact sport," says Allan R. Cohen, dean of the graduate program at Babson College.

Many college students expect to apply the entrepreneurial skills they are learning in their classes by starting businesses while they are still in college. When Jessyca Blood enrolled in the Wolff Center for Entrepreneurship at the University of Houston, her goal was to capitalize on her love of fashion and launch her own clothing line. While Jessyca was in school, her sister, Jaymi, asked her to create some outfits for her teacup Yorkshire terrier, Paris. The doggie couture was such a hit with pet owners that Jessyca decided to change her plans. "It was an opportunity," she says. "I made a total switch from fashion apparel to pet clothes." Using a 60-page business plan that she created for one of her classes, Jessyca raised $15,000 in capital and started Jess & Co., a company that makes a variety of clothing for dogs, ranging from T-shirts and hoodies to coats and dresses, which she sells in small specialty pet boutiques in Houston and on her company's Web site (*www.jessandco.com*). Jessyca credits the Wolff Center for Entrepreneurship for helping her launch her business successfully. Since graduating, Jessyca has focused on running Jess & Co. full time. The company generates more than $100,000 in annual sales, and Jessyca already is developing plans to enter international markets with her line of canine fashions.

Sean Belnick launched his company, Bizchairs.com, at age 14, well before he enrolled in college. Belnick had been selling items on eBay and learned enough about the office furniture business from his stepfather, Gary Glazer, to spot an opportunity to build a successful niche business selling office chairs online. Belnick observed that when furniture retailers called to place an order with his stepfather, who was a manufacturer's representative for several furniture companies, Glazer would call the manufacturer and have the item shipped either to the store or directly to the customer. Belnick, a product of the Internet Age, realized that moving the process online would lower costs and improve customer service and convenience. He approached Glazer about listing some office chairs online. "I saw an industry that had virtually no presence online and realized there was an opportunity to build a more efficient way to get furniture to people," he says. Just a freshman in high school, Belnick launched his online company from his bedroom with just $600 and began selling a product line that consisted of fewer than 100 office chairs.

By the time Belnick enrolled in the Goizueta Business School at Emory University in Atlanta, his company's sales had reached $24 million! (His stepfather handles the daily operations of the company while Belnick is in school, where he is majoring in business.) Belnick has expanded the company's product line to include more than 25,000 items in categories that range from office and home furniture to medical equipment and school furnishings. Bizchair.com's annual sales are approaching $50 million. "Pick any one element and do it better than any of your competitors," says Belnick. "Once you have successfully established your initial position, you can grow from there." Now, with more than 100 employees, Bizchair.com sells furniture to colleges and universities, other small businesses, large corporations, and government agencies. When asked about the advice for other young entrepreneurs, Belnick says, "Don't be afraid to take risks. Just make sure they are calculated and not careless risks. You have your whole life to succeed."

1. Some critics contend that entrepreneurship cannot be taught. What do you think?
2. In addition to the normal obstacles of starting a business, what other barriers do collegiate entrepreneurs face?
3. What advantages do collegiate entrepreneurs have when launching a business?
4. What advice would you offer a fellow college student about to start a business?
5. Work with a team of your classmates to develop ideas about what your college or university could do to create a culture that supports entrepreneurship on your campus or in your community.

Sources: Based on David Port, "Get Smarter," *Entrepreneur*, April 2009, pp. 51–56; Nichole L. Torres, "Launch Pad to Success," *Entrepreneur*, October 2008, pp. 61–81; Sandra Bretting, "Aiming to Be Top Dog in Canine Fashion," *Houston Chronicle*, October 25, 2008, *www.chron.com/disp/story.mpl/headline/biz/6077543.html*; Joel Holland, "Breaking Business Models," *Entrepreneur*, March 2009, p. 102; "5 Questions with Sean Belnick, *Catalyst*, October 15, 2008, *http://archives.catalystmag.com/Multimedia/Sean_Belnick_Interview.html*; Lori Johnston, "Young Entrepreneur Distinguished Self in Office Furniture Business," *Atlanta Business Chronicle*, December 7, 2007, *www.bizjournals.com/atlanta/stories/2007/12/10/smallb1.html*; "Interview with Sean Belnick," Retire@21, *www.retireat21.com/interview/interview-with-sean-belnick-making-millions-selling-business-chairs*; Patricia B. Gray, "Can Entrepreneurship Be Taught?" *FSB*, March 2006, pp. 34–51.

The Cultural Diversity of Entrepreneurship

7. Discuss the role of diversity in small business and entrepreneurship.

As we have seen, virtually anyone has the potential to become an entrepreneur. The entrepreneurial sector of the United States consists of a rich blend of people of all races, ages, backgrounds, and cultures. It is this cultural diversity that is one of entrepreneurship's greatest strengths. We turn our attention to those who make up this diverse fabric we call entrepreneurship.

Young Entrepreneurs

Young people are setting the pace in entrepreneurship. Disenchanted with their prospects in corporate America and willing to take a chance to control their own destinies, scores of young people are choosing entrepreneurship as their primary career path. Generation X, made up of those people born between 1965 and 1980, is the most entrepreneurial generation in history. There is no slowdown in sight as Generation Y, the Millennials, begins to flex its entrepreneurial muscles. The Kauffman Foundation reports that entrepreneurial activity in the United States is highest for the leading edge of the Baby Boomer generation, people between the ages of 55 and 64, and those between 35 and 44, but those in the 20 to 24 age group also exhibit strong entrepreneurial tendencies (see Figure 2).[65] However, there is no age requirement to be a successful entrepreneur.

ENTREPRENEURIAL
Profile

Laura Osmond: Wear to Win

When Laura Osmond began playing golf at age 11, she noticed that the popularity of the sport was growing among adolescents and that the supply of attractive golf attire for young girls was extremely limited. During Laura's freshman year at Wake Forest University, where she plays on the women's golf team, she and her mother had several conversations about the idea of launching a business that would provide stylish, comfortable clothing for young female golfers. As Laura and her mother were moving Laura out of her dorm at the end of her freshman year, they decided to

FIGURE 2
Entrepreneurial Activity by Age Group

Source: Kauffman Index of Entrepreneurial Activity, 1996–2009.

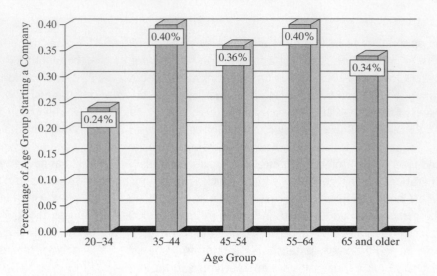

stop by the university's Office of Entrepreneurship and Liberal Arts, where they gathered information on how to write a business plan. By the end of the summer, Laura and her mother, Cindy, had assembled a top-notch plan that incorporated market research (including the results of focus group sessions with golfers at tournaments and from surveys conducted on Survey Monkey), sales, earnings, and cash-flow estimates, an analysis of potential suppliers, and other important topics. During her sophomore year, Laura and her mother launched Wear to Win, a company that designs and markets golf apparel for women between the ages of 12 and 22. Using the slogan, "Inspiring golfwear for aspiring young women," the company sells golf stylish skorts, tops, and belts and plans to add shorts, vests, pants, raingear, and travel accessories in the future. Now a senior at Wake Forest, Laura is juggling academic work, golf, and Wear to Win. She recently was one of three winners of the university's highest award for excellence in entrepreneurship.[66]

Women Entrepreneurs

Despite years of legislative effort, women still face discrimination in the workforce. However, small business has been a leader in offering women opportunities for economic expression through employment and entrepreneurship. Increasing numbers of women are discovering that the best way to break the "glass ceiling" that prevents them from rising to the top of many organizations is to start their own companies (see Figure 3). The freedom that owning their own companies gives them is one reason that entrepreneurship is a popular career choice for women. In fact, women now own 40 percent of all privately-held businesses in the United States, and many of them are in fields that traditionally have been male dominated.

FIGURE 3
Entrepreneurial Activity by Gender

Source: 2008 Kauffman Index of Entrepreneurial Activity, p. 5.

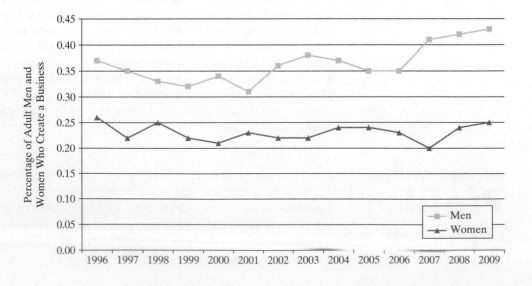

ENTREPRENEURIAL
Profile

Maria de Lourdes Sobrino: Lulu's Dessert

Maria de Lourdes ("Lulu") Sobrino – founder of Lulu's Dessert Company.

Source: AP Wide World Photos

Already an experienced entrepreneur, Maria de Lourdes ("Lulu") Sobrino decided in 1982 to introduce to the United States market a ready-to-eat gelatin dessert that was a dietary staple in her native Mexico. Using an old family recipe, Sobrino launched Lulu's Dessert and began making by hand batches of gelatin, rice pudding, and flan (custard) desserts in a tiny storefront in Torrance, California, where she turned out 300 cups of desserts a day. Soon, local grocery stores were carrying her desserts, and as profits increased Sobrino reinvested them in her company. Today, after nearly 30 years of hard work, Lulu's Dessert sells more than 50 million dessert cups a year through Walmart, Costco, and other supermarkets across the United States. Sobrino's company, which now sells sugar-free and all-natural versions of its desserts, employs 78 workers and generates $8 million in annual sales.[67]

Although the businesses women start tend to be smaller than those men start, their impact is anything but small. Women-owned companies in the United States employ 13 million workers and generate approximately $1.9 trillion in revenue.[68] Women entrepreneurs have even broken through the comic-strip barrier. Blondie Bumstead, long a typical suburban housewife married to Dagwood, owns her own catering business with her best friend and neighbor, Tootsie Woodly!

Minority Enterprises

Like women, minorities also are choosing entrepreneurship more often than ever before. Hispanics, Asians, and African-Americans, respectively, are most likely to become entrepreneurs. Hispanics represent the fastest-growing segment of the U.S. population and exhibit the greatest level of entrepreneurial activity among minorities in the United States (See Figure 4). More than 1.6 million Hispanic-owned companies employ more than 1.5 million people and generate more than $220 billion in annual sales.[69]

Minority entrepreneurs see owning their own businesses as an ideal way to battle discrimination, and minority-owned companies have come a long way in the last decade. The most recent *Index of Entrepreneurial Activity* by the Ewing Marion Kauffman Foundation shows that Hispanics are 55 percent more likely to start a business than whites, and Asians are 13 percent more likely.[70] Minority entrepreneurs in the United States own more than 18 percent of all businesses in the United States, generate $668 billion in annual revenue, employ 4.7 million workers, and start their businesses for the same reason that most entrepreneurs do: to control their own

FIGURE 4
Minority Business Ownership in the United States

Source: Based on *Minorities in Business: A Demographic Review of Minority Business Ownership*, Small Business Administration, Office of Advocacy, April 2007, p. 5.

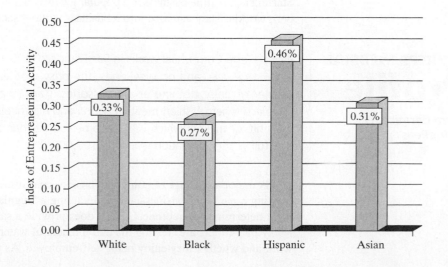

destinies.[71] The future is promising for this new generation of minority entrepreneurs who are better educated, have more business experience, have more entrepreneurial role models, and are better prepared for business ownership than their predecessors.

Chris Gardner: Gardner Rich and Company

After serving in the Navy, Chris Gardner took a job as a medical supply salesman in San Francisco but soon became interested in becoming a stockbroker. Gardner worked his way into a training program at Dean Witter Reynolds, but the meager salary he earned required him to spend many nights in a homeless shelter or in a subway station bathroom. Gardner's tremendous work ethic distinguished him from the other members in the program, and he joined the brokerage house after passing his licensing exam on the first attempt. In 1987, Gardner started Gardner Rich and Company, a specialized brokerage firm in New York City that serves some of the largest businesses and institutions in the world. Now a highly successful entrepreneur, Gardner, whose life story was the inspiration for the 2006 film, *The Pursuit of Happyness,* is a well-known philanthropist, giving back to his community with donations of time and money.[72]

Immigrant Entrepreneurs

The U.S. has always been a "melting pot" of diverse cultures, and many immigrants have been lured to this nation by its economic freedom. Unlike the unskilled "huddled masses" of the past, today's immigrants arrive with far more education and experience and a strong desire to succeed. They play an especially important role in technology industries. A study by Duke University's Vivek Wadhwa reports that immigrant entrepreneurs founded 25.3 percent of all technology firms in the United States over a recent 10-year period.[73]

Immigrant entrepreneurs own 12.5 percent of businesses in the United States and are 30 percent more likely to start businesses than are non-immigrants.[74] Although many immigrants come to the United States with few assets, their dedication and desire to succeed enable them to achieve their entrepreneurial dreams.

ENTREPRENEURIAL Profile

Al Guerra: Kelvin International

At age 10, Al Guerra emigrated to the United States from Cuba in 1961 when Fidel Castro came into power. Guerra's father, who had been a car dealer in Havana, left Cuba first and settled in Boston, where Guerra and, eventually, the rest of his family joined him. Guerra worked hard, went to college, became an engineer, and started a part-time business while working at Jefferson Labs. His company, Kelvin International, a business that makes cryogenic (ultralow-temperature) equipment, grew, and Guerra left Jefferson Labs to run his company full time. Kelvin International now sells to customers around the globe and recently expanded its operations to accommodate its fast growth. "Don't forget," says Guerra, "Most immigrants have the risk gene already built in."[75]

Part-Time Entrepreneurs

Starting a part-time business is a popular gateway to entrepreneurship. Part-timers have the best of both worlds. They can ease into a business without sacrificing the security of a steady paycheck.

ENTREPRENEURIAL Profile

Terra Carmichael: FlyingPeas

By day, Terra Carmichael works in San Francisco at Yahoo! the search engine company, but from 9 P.M. to 2 A.M. and on weekends, the busy mother of two manages FlyingPeas, an online retailer of baby clothing and accessories. Carmichael plans to transition into her business ("a place where fashion meets function and hip meets high quality") full time when its annual sales hit $2 million, which is likely to be sooner than later given that her company's sales in its first full year of operation reached $100,000.[76]

A major advantage of going into business part-time is the lower risk in case the venture flops. Starting a part-time business and maintaining a "regular" job can challenge the endurance of the most determined entrepreneur, but it does provide a safety net in case the business venture fails. Many part-timers are "testing the entrepreneurial waters" to see whether their business ideas will work and whether they enjoy being self-employed. As part-time ventures grow, they absorb more of the entrepreneur's time until they become full-time businesses. "There comes a point when you cannot get up and go to work because the only thing you want to do is your company," says Divya Gugnani, who left her job with a venture capital firm to start BehindtheBurner.com, a Web site that features cooking tips and techniques. "The passion is so infectious."[77]

Home-Based Business Owners

More than 12 percent of the households in the United States operate home-based businesses, generating $427 billion a year in sales.[78] Fifty-three percent of all small businesses are home-based, but most of them are very small with no employees.[79] In the past, home-based businesses tended to be rather unexciting cottage industries, such as making crafts or sewing. Today's home-based businesses are more diverse; modern home-based entrepreneurs are more likely to be running high-tech or service companies with millions of dollars in sales. Because of their low-cost locations, home-based businesses generate higher gross profit margins than companies that have locations outside the home. Less costly and more powerful technology and the Internet, which are transforming many ordinary homes into "electronic cottages," will continue to drive the growth of home-based businesses. The average home-based business generates revenues of $62,523 and earns a net income of $22,569.[80]

On average, someone starts a home-based business every 11 seconds.[81] The biggest advantage home-based businesses offer entrepreneurs is the cost savings of not having to lease or buy an external location. Home-based entrepreneurs also enjoy the benefits of flexible work and lifestyles. (One survey of home-based workers reports that 39 percent work in sweat pants and shirts, and 10 percent work naked![82])

ENTREPRENEURIAL
Profile

Valerie Johnson: Big Feet Pajamas

The idea for Valerie Johnson's home-based business came to her at a party when the host's young son wandered in wearing his footed pajamas. Every adult at the party talked about how comfortable they looked and how the pajamas brought back pleasant childhood memories. "It's too bad they don't make those for grown-ups," said one. "I'd love a pair." It was then that Johnson realized that she had discovered not only a business opportunity, but also a product that evoked warm childhood memories for many people. She kept her job in investor relations but worked evenings from the basement of her Las Vegas home to start her company, which she named Big Feet Pajamas. She found a local costume designer to create prototype pajamas, began researching the apparel industry, and used Alibaba.com to locate potential factories in China to manufacture the pajamas. Wanting to explain the details of her prototypes and to check out the factories firsthand, Johnson flew to China and put down $50,000 of her own money to secure an order of 5,000 pairs of footed pajamas. Then she rented a 10-foot-square booth at the Magic Apparel Show, a huge trade show that attracts buyers for large and small stores from around the world, to display the prototypes and to take orders. At the show, she made many valuable contacts, collected dozens of e-mail addresses, and accepted orders. When the 5,000 pairs of pajamas arrived at her home (completely filling her garage), Johnson activated the e-commerce section of her Web site, and "within 60 seconds, we had our first order," she says. Within a week, demand was so strong that she ordered more pajamas from her Chinese manufacturer. When Big Feet pajamas, which sell from $40 to $120, were selected as celebrity gifts for the Oscars the next year, the publicity caused the company's sales to take off. Big Feet Pajamas' annual sales are $2.5 million, and Johnson, who continues to run the company from her home, is reinvesting the profits to fuel its growth.[83]

Table 2 offers 18 guidelines home-based entrepreneurs should follow to be successful.

Family Business Owners

A **family-owned business** is one that includes two or more members of a family with financial control of the company. They are an integral part of our economy. Nearly 90 percent of the 29.3 million businesses in the United States are family-owned and managed. These companies account for 62 percent of total employment in the United States, 78 percent of all new jobs, and

TABLE 2 Rules for a Successful Home-based Business

Rule 1. Do your homework. Much of a home-based business's potential for success depends on how much preparation an entrepreneur makes *before* ever opening for business. Your local library and the Internet are excellent sources of information on customers, industries, competitors, and other important topics.

Rule 2. Find out what your zoning restrictions are. In some areas, local zoning laws make running a business from home illegal. Avoid headaches by checking these laws first. You can always request a variance.

Rule 3. Create distinct zones for your family and business dealings. Your home-based business should have its own dedicated space. About half of all home-based entrepreneurs operate out of spare bedrooms. The best way to determine the ideal office location is to examine the nature of your business and your clients. Avoid locating your business in your bedroom or your family room.

Rule 4. Focus your home-based business idea. Avoid the tendency to be "all things to all people." Most successful home-based businesses focus on a niche, whether it is a particular customer group, a specific product line, or in some other specialty.

Rule 5. Discuss your business rules with your family. Running a business from your home means you can spend more time with your family . . . and that your family can spend more time with you. Establish the rules for interruptions up front.

Rule 6. Select an appropriate business name. Your first marketing decision is your company's name, so make it a good one! Using your own name is convenient, but it's not likely to help you sell your product or service.

Rule 7. Buy the right equipment. Modern technology allows a home-based entrepreneur to give the appearance of any *Fortune* 500 company, but only if you buy the right equipment. A well-equipped home office should have a separate telephone line, a fast computer, a sturdy printer, a high-speed Internet connection, a copier/scanner, and an answering machine (or voice mail).

Rule 8. Dress appropriately. Being an "open-collar worker" is one of the joys of working at home. However, when you need to dress up (to meet a client, make a sale, meet your banker, close a deal), do it! Avoid the tendency to lounge around in your bathrobe all day.

Rule 9. Learn to deal with distractions. The best way to fend off the distractions of working at home is to create a business that truly interests you. Budget your time wisely. Remember: Your productivity determines your company's success.

Rule 10. Realize that your phone can be your best friend . . . or your worst enemy. As a home-based entrepreneur, you'll spend lots of time on the phone. Be sure you use it productively.

Rule 11. Be firm with friends and neighbors. Sometimes friends and neighbors get the mistaken impression that because you're at home, you're not working. If someone drops by to chat while you're working, tactfully ask him or her to come back "after work."

Rule 12. Maximize your productivity. One advantage of working from home is flexibility. Learn the times during which you tend to work at peak productivity, whether that occurs at 2 P.M. or 2 A.M., and build your schedule around them.

Rule 13. Create no-work time zones. Because their businesses are always nearby, the tendency for some home-based entrepreneurs is to work all the time, which is not healthy. Set boundaries that separate work and no work times and stick to them.

Rule 14. Take advantage of tax breaks. Although a 1993 Supreme Court decision tightened considerably the standards for business deductions for an office at home, many home-based entrepreneurs still qualify for special tax deductions on everything from computers to cars. Check with your accountant.

Rule 15. Make sure you have adequate insurance coverage. Some homeowner's policies provide adequate coverage for business-related equipment, but many home-based entrepreneurs have inadequate coverage on their business assets. Ask your agent about a business owner's policy (BOP), which may cost as little as $300 to $500 per year.

Rule 16. Understand the special circumstances under which you can hire outside employees. Sometimes zoning laws allow in-home businesses, but they prohibit hiring employees. Check local zoning laws carefully.

Rule 17. Be prepared if your business requires clients to come to your home. Dress appropriately. (No pajamas!) Make sure your office presents a professional image.

Rule 18. Get a post office box. With burglaries and robberies on the rise, you are better off using a PO Box address rather than your specific home address. Otherwise you may be inviting crime.

Rule 19. Network. Isolation can be a problem for home-based entrepreneurs, and one of the best ways to combat it is to network. It's also an effective way to market your business.

Rule 20. Be proud of your home-based business. Merely a decade ago there was a stigma attached to working from home. Today, home-based entrepreneurs and their businesses command respect. Be proud of your company!

Sources: Pamela Slim, "5 Keys to Making Your Home Office Work," *Open Forum*, June 24, 2009, *www.openforum.com/idea-hub/topics/the-world/article/5-keys-to-making-your-home-office-work-pamela-slim*; Lynn Beresford, Janean Chun, Cynthia E. Griffin, Heather Page, and Debra Phillips, "Homeward Bound," *Entrepreneur*, September 1995, pp. 116–118; Jenean Huber, "House Rules," *Entrepreneur*, March 1993, pp. 89–95; Hal Morris, "Home-Based Businesses Need Extra Insurance," *AARP Bulletin*, November 1994, p. 16; Stephanie N. Mehta, "What You Need," *Wall Street Journal*, October 14, 1994, p. R10; Jeffery Zbar, "Home Free," *Business Start-Ups*, June 1999, pp. 31–37.

generate 64 percent of the U.S. Gross Domestic Product (GDP). Not all of them are small; 33 percent of the *Fortune* 500 companies are family businesses.[84]

"When it works right," says one writer, "nothing succeeds like a family firm. The roots run deep, embedded in family values. The flash of the fast buck is replaced with long-term plans. Tradition counts."[85]

Fireworks by Grucci, a company now in its fifth generation of family leadership, is one family business that has managed to beat the odds. Donna Grucci Butler, the great-great-great-granddaughter of company founder Angelo Lanzetta, grew up working in the family business and is now its president. Fireworks by Grucci puts on more than 250 fireworks shows each year and generates more than $10 million in annual revenue. The company's list of credits includes seven presidential inaugurations, four Olympic games, and three World's Fairs.[86]

Despite their magnitude, family businesses face a major threat—a threat from within: management succession. Only 33 percent of family businesses survive to the second generation; just 12 percent make it to the third generation; and only 3 percent survive to the fourth generation and beyond.[87] Business periodicals are full of stories describing bitter disputes among family members that have crippled or destroyed once-thriving businesses, usually because the founder failed to create a succession plan. To avoid the senseless destruction of valuable assets, founders of family businesses should develop plans for management succession long before retirement looms before them.

Copreneurs

"**Copreneurs**" are entrepreneurial couples who work together as co-owners of their businesses. More than 1.2 million husband-and-wife teams operate businesses in the United States.[88] Unlike the traditional "Mom & Pop" (Pop as "boss" and Mom as "subordinate"), copreneurs divide their business responsibilities on the basis of their skills, experience, and abilities rather than on gender. Studies suggest that companies co-owned by spouses represent one of the fastest growing business sectors.

Managing a small business with a spouse may appear to be a recipe for divorce, but most copreneurs say not. "There are days when you want to kill each other," says Mary Duty, who has operated Poppa Rollo's Pizza with her husband for 20 years. "But there's nothing better than working side-by-side with the [person] you love."[89] Successful copreneurs learn to build the foundation for a successful working relationship *before* they ever launch their companies. Some of the characteristics they rely on include:

- An assessment of how well their personalities will mesh in a business setting
- Mutual respect for each other and one another's talents
- Compatible business and life goals—a common "vision"
- A view that they are full and equal partners, not a superior and a subordinate
- Complementary business skills that each acknowledges in the other and that lead to a unique business identity for each spouse
- A clear division of roles and authority—ideally based on each partner's skills and abilities—to minimize conflict and power struggles
- The ability to keep lines of communication open, talking and listening to each other about personal as well as business issues
- The ability to encourage each other and to lift up a disillusioned partner
- Separate work spaces that allow them to escape when the need arises
- Boundaries between their business life and their personal life so that one doesn't consume the other
- A sense of humor
- An understanding that not every couple can work together

Although copreneuring isn't for everyone, it works extremely well for many couples and often leads to successful businesses.

ENTREPRENEURIAL

Profile

*Kathy Van Zeeland
and Bruce Makowsky:
Kathy Van Zeeland*

While working for shoe company Nine West, where they created a handbag division, Kathy Van Zeeland and her husband Bruce Makowsky started a part-time handbag business of their own. Their bags, which they marketed under the Kathy Van Zeeland brand, proved to be popular because they couple utilitarian designs with stylish patterns and fabrics and are priced at less than $100. The rapid growth of their company convinced the copreneurs to leave their jobs to operate their company full time. Five years after Zeeland and Makowsky launched their company, more than 1,300 stores across the United States were selling Kathy Van Zeeland bags. The company also sells bags through the QVC shopping network and operates 40 retail outlets in Italy and across Asia. Zeeland and Makowksy recently sold their company to LF USA, a global consumer goods company, for $330 million but agreed to remain as co-presidents of the business.[90]

Corporate Castoffs

Concentrating on trying to operate more efficiently, corporations have been downsizing, shedding their excess bulk, and slashing employment at all levels in the organization. These downsizing victims or "corporate castoffs" have become an important source of entrepreneurial activity. Skittish about downsizing at other large companies they might join, many of these castoffs are choosing instead to create their own job security by launching their own businesses or buying franchises. They have decided that the best defense against future job insecurity is an entrepreneurial offense. Armed with years of experience, tidy severance packages, a working knowledge of their industries, and a network of connections, these former managers are setting out to start companies of their own. Some 20 percent of these discharged corporate managers become entrepreneurs, and many of those left behind in corporate America would like to join them. A study by Robert Half Management Resources reports that 32 percent of executives at large companies would leave to start their own companies if they could afford to do so.[91]

ENTREPRENEURIAL

Profile

*Dawn Newsome and
Karen Ponischil:
Moonlight Creative
Group*

When a large bank eliminated the marketing department where Dawn Newsome and Karen Ponischil worked, the pair decided to make Moonlight Creative Group, the part-time marketing and advertising agency they had launched just a few months before, a full-time business. They used their own money and credit cards to finance the expansion, moving the company from a spare bedroom in Ponischil's home to a professional office building. Moonlight's sales have grown steadily, and the entrepreneurs now employ five workers. Newsome says that freedom is the best part of owning a business. "The freedom to set your own schedule, to determine the types of clients you want to work with, and to control your own destiny."[92]

Corporate "Dropouts"

The dramatic downsizing in corporate America has created another effect among the employees left after restructuring: a trust gap. The result of this trust gap is a growing number of "dropouts" from the corporate structure who then become entrepreneurs. Although their workdays may grow longer and their incomes may shrink, those who strike out on their own often find their work more rewarding and more satisfying because they are doing what they enjoy and they are in control.

Because they often have college degrees, a working knowledge of business, and years of management experience, both corporate castoffs and dropouts may ultimately increase the small business survival rate. Better-trained, more experienced entrepreneurs are less likely to fail in business. Many corporate castoffs and dropouts choose franchising as the vehicle to business ownership because it offers the structure and support with which these former corporate executives are most comfortable.

Retired Baby Boomers

Members of the Baby Boom Generation (1946–1964) are retiring, but many of them are not idle; instead, they are launching businesses of their own. A recent survey by the American

Colonel Harland Sanders, founder of Kentucky Fried Chicken (now KFC).

Source: AP Wide World Photos

Association of Retired Persons reports that 15 percent of baby boomers expect to own a business in retirement.[93] A study by the Kauffman Foundation shows that the level of entrepreneurial activity among people age 55 to 64 actually is higher than that among people age 20 to 34 (refer to Figure 2), a pattern that has held for the last decade. Many entrepreneurs start their entrepreneurial ventures late in life. At age 65, Colonel Harland Sanders, for example, began franchising the fried chicken business that he had started 3 years earlier, a company that became Kentucky Fried Chicken (now known as KFC).

To finance their businesses, retirees often use some of their invested "nest eggs," or they rely on the same sources of funds as younger entrepreneurs, such as banks, private investors, and others.

ENTREPRENEURIAL
Profile

Judith Moore: Charleston Cookie Company

At age 61, after retiring from a career as a marriage and family therapist, Judith Moore transformed her baking hobby into a profitable business. Moore's Charleston Cookie Company, based in a 5,000-square-foot warehouse in Charleston, South Carolina, makes a variety of delectable cookies that it sells online, by mail, and through upscale retail outlets such as New York's Dean & Deluca and The Sanctuary at Kiawah Island. Moore's inspiration to start her business came around Christmas in 2001. "I went on a quest for the perfect chocolate chip cookie, but I couldn't find one," she recalls. Like a true entrepreneur, Moore created her own recipe, developed a business plan, and launched the Charleston Cookie Company, which now generates more than $1 million in annual sales. When it comes to pursuing an entrepreneurial venture, "you'd better be doing something you love," advises Moore. "If you're not risk tolerant, you should not be running a business regardless of how old you are."[94]

The Contributions of Small Businesses

8. Describe the contributions small businesses make to the U.S. economy.

Of the 29.3 million businesses in the United States today, approximately 29.2 million, or 99.7 percent, can be considered "small." Although there is no universal definition of a small business, a common delineation of a **small business** is one that employs fewer than 100 people. They thrive in virtually every industry, although the majority of small companies are concentrated in the service, construction, and retail industries (see Figure 5). Their

**FIGURE 5
Small Business
by Industry**

Source: SBA, 2009

Pie chart segments:
- Services 51.1%
- Other 4.4%
- Construction 13.4%
- Manufacturing 4.4%
- Wholesale 5.4%
- Retail 11.8%
- Finance, Insurance, & Real Estate 9.5%

contributions to the economy are as numerous as the businesses themselves. For example, small companies employ 50.2 percent of the nation's private sector workforce, even though they possess less than one-fourth of total business assets.[95] Small companies also pay 45 percent of the total private payroll in the United States. Because they are primarily labor intensive, small businesses actually create more jobs than do big businesses. The Small Business Administration (SBA) estimates that small companies create 79 percent of the net new jobs each year in the United States.[96]

David Birch, president of the research firm Arc Analytics, says that the ability to create jobs is not distributed evenly across the small business sector, however. His research shows that just 6 percent of these small companies create 70 percent of the net new jobs, and they do so across all industry sectors—not just in "hot" industries. Birch calls these job-creating small companies "gazelles," those growing at 20 percent or more per year with at least $100,000 in annual sales. His research also identified "mice," small companies that never grow much and don't create many jobs. The majority of small companies are "mice." Birch tabbed the country's largest businesses "elephants," which have continued to shed jobs for several years.[97] In an updated study, researchers found that small companies with fewer than 20 employees accounted for 93.8 percent of all "high-impact firms," those that have both fast revenue and employment growth. These high-impact companies make up less than 3 percent of all businesses but account for almost all of the employment and revenue growth in the U.S. economy.[98]

Not only do small companies lead the way in creating jobs, but they also bear the brunt of training workers for them. Small businesses provide 67 percent of workers with their first jobs and basic job training. Small companies offer more general skills instruction and training than large ones, and their employees receive more benefits from the training than do those in larger firms. Although their training programs tend to be informal, in-house, and on-the-job, small companies teach employees valuable skills—from written communication to computer literacy.[99]

Small businesses also produce 51 percent of the country's private GDP and account for 47 percent of business sales.[100] In fact, the U.S small business sector is the world's third largest "economy," trailing only the economies of the United States and China. Small businesses also play an integral role in creating new products, services, and processes. Small companies produce 13 times more patents per employee than do large firms, and many of those patents are among the most significant inventions in their fields. A study by the SBA reports that the smallest businesses, those with fewer than 25 employees, produce the greatest number of patents per employee.[101] Many important inventions trace their roots to an entrepreneur; for example, the zipper, the personal computer, FM radio, air conditioning, the escalator, the light bulb, the helicopter, and the automatic transmission all originated in small businesses. Entrepreneurs continue to create innovations designed to improve people's lives in areas that range from energy and communications to clothing and toys.

LESSONS FROM THE STREET-SMART → entrepreneur

Bulletproofing Your Start-up

It happens thousands of times every day: Someone comes up with a great idea for a new business, certain that the idea is going to be "the next big thing." Technology advances, the Internet, increased global interconnectivity, and computer-aided-design tools that allow inventors to go from the idea stage to creating a prototype faster than ever have made transforming a great idea into reality much easier than at any point in the past. In addition, entrepreneurial training, improved access to information, and greater awareness of entrepreneurship as a career choice have made it easier than ever to launch a business. However, *succeeding* in business today is as challenging as it ever was.

What steps can a potential entrepreneur with a great idea take to build a "bulletproof" start-up? Take these tips from the Street-Smart Entrepreneur:

Step 1. Test to see whether your idea really is a good one

The reality is that transforming an idea into a successful business concept is much like the television show *American Idol*. For every person who really is a great singer, there are 99 people who can't stay on key but who *think* they are great singers. This step involves getting a reality check from other people—and not just friends and relatives who may not tell you what they really think about your idea because they don't want to hurt your feelings. The goal is to determine whether your business idea really has market potential. One key is to involve potential customers and people who are knowledgeable about the particular industry into which your idea fits in evaluating your idea.

This step requires potential entrepreneurs to maintain a delicate balance between getting valuable feedback on their idea and protecting it from those who might steal it. Before they reveal their ideas to other people, some would-be entrepreneurs rely on nondisclosure agreements, contracts in which the other party promises not to use the idea for their own gain or to reveal it to others. Typically, the feedback, input, and advice entrepreneurs get at this phase far outweigh the risks of disclosing their ideas to others.

Sometimes entrepreneurs discover that Step 1 is as far as they should go; otherwise, they would be wasting time, talent, and resources. Other entrepreneurs receive confirmation that they really are on to something at this step. Jesse Vendley grew up in Calexico, California, a town in southern California near the Mexican border. When he moved to New York to work as an advertising copywriter, Vendley enjoyed cooking meals for his friends using family recipes such as carne asada, a richly flavored steak dish. Vendley began to think seriously about opening a Mexican-themed restaurant but wanted to test the market for it first. His solution: Start with a food cart. With his two brothers, Brian and Dave, Vendley launched Calexico Carne Asada and began selling meals from a food cart in New York's SoHo district. The stellar food that the aspiring restaurateurs served generated lots of "buzz" across the city, and soon the brothers had a second cart in operation. Calexico's reputation was sealed when it won the Vendy Competition, the equivalent of the Oscars for food cart vendors in New York City. Their market test proved to be so successful that Calexico has opened a permanent Calexico restaurant in Brooklyn, and the feedback that Vendley and his entrepreneurial team received while running the cart has given them confidence that their permanent restaurant will be a hit.

Step 2. Start building your entrepreneurial team

Nearly half of all new business ventures are started by teams of people. As one business writer observes, "Launching a company isn't just a full-time job; in many cases, it's three full-time jobs." Perhaps that is why a study of 2,000 businesses by researchers at Marquette University found that companies started by teams of entrepreneurs are nearly 16 times more likely to become high-growth ventures than those started by solo entrepreneurs. Indeed, launching a company is a demanding task that requires a diverse blend of skills, abilities, and experience that not every individual possesses. If that is the case, the best alternative is to launch your company with others whose skills, abilities, and experience *complement* rather than *mirror* yours. Picking the right entrepreneurial players is as essential to business success as picking the best kids to be on your kickball team was in grammar school! However many people it may require, ideally a start-up team includes a "big picture" strategic thinker, a top-notch networker with marketing and sales know-how, and a hands-on technical person who understands the business opportunity at the "nuts-and-bolts" level.

Step 3. Focus on one thing, something about which you are passionate

"Do what you do better than anyone else, but don't try to do it all," advises one business writer. A common mistake that destroys many new businesses is trying to do too much from the outset. For small businesses especially, focusing on a niche increases the probability of success, especially if it is something that ignites the passion in an entrepreneur's heart. The best strategy is to determine what you do well and what you love to do (they often are the same) and figure out a way to build a business around it. When Christine Marchuska was laid off from her investment banking job during the recent financial crisis, she decided to pursue her passion for fashion and, with her brother Justin, launched Marchuska, an eco-friendly collection of T-shirts, and CMarchuska, which sells an eco-friendly line of fashionable dresses. Christine says that she and Justin are creating "something that we both believe in and are passionate about. We have never been afraid of failure, but we are afraid of not living out our dreams."

Step 4. Do your research and create a business plan

Smart entrepreneurs know that creating a business plan is an important step in building a successful company even if they are not seeking capital from external sources. Starting a company without a business plan is like trying to build a house without a set of blueprints. Even though a business plan is a valuable document that entrepreneurs use in many ways, the real value in creating a plan lies in the *process*. Developing a plan requires entrepreneurs to address an array of important issues, ranging from which form of ownership is best and how much capital is required to researching their target customers and preparing financial and cash flow forecasts.

While Andrew Smith was a student at Dartmouth's Tuck School of Business, he partnered with an inventor of aerodynamic panels that can be added to transport trucks to dramatically improve their fuel efficiency. Together they created a business plan, which they entered in the 2006 Rice Business Plan Competition. Their plan for ATDynamics won first place, which provided $20,000 in prize money, a $100,000 investment from the GOOSE Society (a group of entrepreneurs who help other entrepreneurs launch promising businesses), and access to consultants and mentors. Refining the panels to fit almost all of more than 2 million tractor-trailers in the United States took another 2 years. ATDynamics began shipping its first kits in late 2008, and sales have been climbing steadily. The Society of Automotive Engineers says that the ATDynamics aerodynamic kit improves the fuel economy of tractor-trailers by 12 percent. California recently passed a law that requires every truck entering the state to be equipped with aerodynamic panels, and Smith expects other states to follow suit. Returning to speak to the competitors in the 2008 Rice Business Plan Competition, Smith reflected on the value of the business plan to the success of ATDynamics. "I have given the same elevator pitch more than a thousand times to prospective investors and others," he says.

Sources: Based on Sara Wilson, "Laid Off in 2008? Start a Business in 2009," *Entrepreneur*, February 2009, pp. 73–77; Gregory T. Huang, "Three Things Every Start-up Should Do, as Inspired by the UW Business Competition," *Xconomy*, April 30, 2009, *www.xconomy.com/seattle/2009/04/30/three-things-every-startup-should-do-as-inspired-by-uw-business-competition*; Katy McLaughlin, "Food Truck Nation," *Wall Street Journal*, June 5, 2009, *http://online.wsj.com/article/SB10001424052970204456604574201934018170554.html*; Patrick Huguenin, "3 Brothers Behind Calexico Are Improving the a la Cart Menu," *New York Daily News*, October 26, 2008, *www.nydailynews.com/lifestyle/food/2008/10/26/2008-10-26_3_brothers_behind_calexico_are_improving.html*; Michael V. Copeland and Om Malik, "How to Build a Bulletproof Startup," *Business 2.0*, June 2006, pp. 76–92; Michael V. Copeland and Andrew Tilin, "The New Instant Companies," *Business 2.0*, June 2005, pp. 82–94; Daniel Roth, "The Amazing Rise of the Do-It-Yourself Economy," *Fortune*, May 30, 2005, pp. 45–46; "Visionaries," Marchuska, *www.marchuska.com/visionaries.html*; David Kaplan, "60 Seconds to Sell It," *Houston Chronicle*, April 5, 2008, *www.chron.com/CDA/archives/archive.mpl?id=2008_4544150*; "7 Business Plan Superstars: ATDynamics," *FSB*, April 15, 2009, *http://money.cnn.com/galleries/2009/smallbusiness/0904/gallery.bizplan_superstars.smb/2.html*.

Putting Failure into Perspective

9. Put business failure into the proper perspective.

Because of their limited resources, inexperienced management, and lack of financial stability, small businesses suffer a relatively high mortality rate (see Figure 6). Studies by the SBA suggest that 54 percent of new businesses will have failed within 4 years. Put another way, a new business has an almost identical chance of surviving as a Japanese kamikaze pilot had of surviving World War II.[102] Why are entrepreneurs willing to endure these odds?

Because they are building businesses in an environment filled with uncertainty and shaped by rapid change, entrepreneurs recognize that failure is likely to be a part of their lives; yet, they are not paralyzed by that fear. "The excitement of building a new business from scratch is far greater than the fear of failure," says one entrepreneur who failed in business several times before finally succeeding.[103] Instead, they use their failures as a rallying point and as a means of defining their companies' reason for being more clearly. They see failure for what it really is: an opportunity to learn what doesn't work! Successful entrepreneurs have the attitude that failures

FIGURE 6
Small Business
Survival Rate

Source: NFIB Business Policy Guide 2003, p. 16.

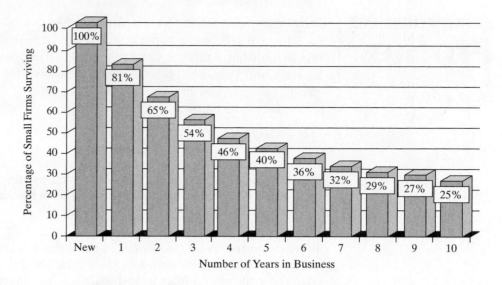

are simply stepping stones along the path to success. Walt Disney was fired from a newspaper job because, according to his boss, he "lacked ideas." Disney also went bankrupt several times before he created Disneyland.

Failure is a natural part of the creative process. The only people who never fail are those who never do anything or never attempt anything new. Baseball fans know that Babe Ruth held the record for career home runs (714) for many years, but how many know that he also held the record for strikeouts (1,330)? Successful entrepreneurs realize that hitting an entrepreneurial home run requires a few strikeouts along the way, and they are willing to accept that. Lillian Vernon, who started her mail-order company with $2,000 in wedding gift money, says, "Everybody stumbles . . . The true test is how well you pick yourself up and move on, and whether you're willing to learn from that."[104]

One hallmark of successful entrepreneurs is the ability to fail *intelligently*, learning why they failed so that they can avoid making the same mistake again. They know that business success does not depend on their ability to avoid making mistakes but to be open to the lessons each mistake brings. They learn from their failures and use them as fuel to push themselves closer to their ultimate target. Entrepreneurs are less worried about what they might lose if they try something and fail than about what they miss if they fail to try.

Entrepreneurial success requires both persistence and resilience, the ability to bounce back from failures. Thomas Edison discovered about 1,800 ways *not* to build a light bulb before hitting upon a design that worked—and would revolutionize the world. R. H. Macy failed in business seven times before his department store in New York City became a success. Entrepreneur Bryn Kaufman explains this "don't quit" attitude, "If you are truly an entrepreneur, giving up is not an option."[105]

How to Avoid the Pitfalls

10. Explain how entrepreneurs can avoid the major pitfalls of running a business.

As valuable as failure can be to the entrepreneurial process, no one sets out to fail. We now examine the ways to avoid becoming another failure statistic and gain insight into what makes a start-up successful. Entrepreneurial success requires much more than just a good idea for a product or service. It also takes a solid plan of execution, adequate resources (including capital and people), the ability to assemble and manage those resources, and perseverance. The following suggestions for success follow naturally from the causes of business failures.

Know Your Business in Depth

We have already emphasized the need for the right type of experience in the business. Get the best education in your business area you possibly can *before* you set out on your own. Read everything you can—trade journals, business periodicals, books, Web pages—relating to your industry. Personal contact with suppliers, customers, trade associations, and others in the same industry is another excellent way to get important knowledge.

Before copreneurs Jim and Melissa Voss launched Chloe & Grace, a shop in Greenville, South Carolina, that sells upscale home accessories and gifts, they had lengthy career stints at major retailers in cities across the United States. Jim had opened and managed retail stores for 22 years, and Melissa had been an account executive for a coffee franchise. The couple was able to parlay all that they had learned about retailing "on someone else's dime" into the opportunity to have their own business.[106]

Like Jim and Melissa Voss, successful entrepreneurs are like sponges, soaking up as much knowledge as they can from a variety of sources, and they continue to learn about their businesses, markets, and customers as long as they are in business.

Prepare a Business Plan

To wise entrepreneurs, a well-written business plan is a crucial ingredient in business success. Without a sound business plan, a company merely drifts along without any real direction and often stalls out when it faces its first challenge. Yet, entrepreneurs, who tend to be people of action, often jump right into a business venture without taking time to prepare a written plan outlining the essence of the business. "Most entrepreneurs don't have a solid business plan," says one business owner. "But a thorough business plan and timely financial information are critical. They help you make the important decisions about your business; you constantly have to monitor what you're doing against your plan."[107]

Manage Financial Resources

The best defense against financial problems is developing a practical financial information system and then using this information to make business decisions. No entrepreneur can maintain control over a business unless he or she is able to judge its financial health.

The first step in managing financial resources effectively is to have adequate start-up capital. Too many entrepreneurs begin their businesses with too little capital. One experienced business owner advises, "Estimate how much capital you need to get the business going and then double that figure." In other words, launching a business almost always costs more than *any* entrepreneur expects. Establishing a relationship early on with at least one reliable lender who understands your business is a good way to gain access to financing when a company needs capital for growth or expansion.

The most valuable financial resource to any small business is *cash*; successful entrepreneurs learn early on to manage it carefully. Although earning a profit is essential to its long-term survival, a business must have an adequate supply of cash to pay its bills. Some entrepreneurs count on growing sales to supply their company's cash needs, but it almost never happens. Growing companies usually consume more cash than they generate; and the faster they grow, the more cash they gobble up!

Understand Financial Statements

Every business owner must depend on records and financial statements to know the condition of his or her business. All too often, these records are used only for tax purposes rather than as vital control devices. To truly understand what is going on in the business, an owner must have at least a basic understanding of accounting and finance.

When analyzed and interpreted properly, a company's financial statements are reliable indicators of its health. They can be quite helpful in signaling potential problems. For example, declining sales or profits, rising debt, and deteriorating working capital are all symptoms of potentially lethal problems that require immediate attention.

Learn to Manage People Effectively

No matter what kind of business you launch, you must learn to manage people. Every business depends on a foundation of well-trained, motivated employees. No entrepreneur can do everything alone. The people an entrepreneur hires ultimately determine the heights to which the company can climb—or the depths to which it can plunge. Attracting and retaining a corps of quality employees is no easy task, however; it remains a challenge for every small business owner. One entrepreneur alienated employees with a memo chastising them for skipping lines on interoffice envelopes (the cost of a skipped line was two-thirds of a penny) while he continued to use a chauffeur-driven luxury car and to stay at exclusive luxury hotels while traveling on business.[108] Entrepreneurs quickly learn that treating their employees with respect, dignity, and compassion usually translates into their employees treating customers in the same fashion. Successful entrepreneurs value their employees and constantly find ways to show it.

Set Your Business Apart from the Competition

The formula for almost certain business failure involves becoming a "me-too business"—merely copying whatever the competition is doing. Successful entrepreneurs find a way to convince their customers that their companies are superior to their competitors even if they sell similar products or services.

Maintain a Positive Attitude

Achieving business success requires an entrepreneur to maintain a positive mental attitude toward business and the discipline to stick with it. Successful entrepreneurs recognize that their most valuable resource is their time, and they learn to manage it effectively to make themselves and their companies more productive. None of this, of course, is possible without passion—passion for their businesses, their products or services, their customers, their communities. Passion is what enables a failed business owner to get back up, try again, and make it to the top! One business writer says that growing a successful business requires entrepreneurs to have great faith in themselves and their ideas, great doubt concerning the challenges and inevitable obstacles they will face as they build their businesses, and great effort—lots of hard work—to make their dreams become reality.[109]

Conclusion

As you can see, entrepreneurship lies at the heart of this nation's free enterprise system; small companies truly are the backbone of our economy. Their contributions are as many and as diverse as the businesses themselves. Indeed, diversity is one of the strengths of the U.S. small business sector. Although there are no secrets to becoming a successful entrepreneur, there are steps that entrepreneurs can take to enhance the probability of their success.

As you can see, the journey down the road of entrepreneurship will be an interesting and exciting one. Let's get started!

Chapter Review

1. Define the role of the entrepreneur in business.
   - Record numbers of people have launched companies over the past decade. The boom in entrepreneurship is not limited solely to the United States; many nations across the globe are seeing similar growth in the small business sector. A variety of competitive, economic, and demographic shifts have created a world in which "small is beautiful."
   - Society depends on entrepreneurs to provide the drive and risk-taking necessary for the business system to supply people with the goods and services they need.

2. Describe the entrepreneurial profile.
   - Entrepreneurs have some common characteristics, including a desire for responsibility, a preference for moderate risk, confidence in their ability to succeed, desire for immediate feedback, a high energy level, a future orientation, skill at organizing, and a value of achievement over money. In a phrase, they are high achievers.

3. Explain how entrepreneurs spot business opportunities.
   - Entrepreneurs rely on creativity and innovation to build successful businesses. They spot business opportunities using the following techniques: Monitor trends and exploit them early on, take a different approach to an existing market, put a new twist on an old idea, look for creative ways to use existing resources, realize that others have the same problem you do, and notice what is missing.

4. Describe the benefits of owning a small business.
   - Entrepreneurs establish and manage small businesses to gain control over their lives, make a difference, become self-fulfilled, reap impressive profits, contribute to society, and do what they enjoy doing.

5. Describe the potential drawbacks of owning a small business.
   - Small business ownership has some potential drawbacks. There are no guarantees that the business will make a profit or even survive. The time and energy required to manage a new business may have dire effects on the owner and family members.

6. Explain the forces that are driving the growth in entrepreneurship.
   - Several factors are driving the boom in entrepreneurship, including entrepreneurs portrayed as heroes, better entrepreneurial education, economic and demographic factors, a shift to a service economy, technology advancements, more independent lifestyles, e-commerce, and increased international opportunities.

7. Discuss the role of diversity in small business and entrepreneurship.
   - Several groups are leading the nation's drive toward entrepreneurship—young people, women, minorities, immigrants, "part-timers," home-based business owners, family business owners, copreneurs, corporate castoffs, corporate dropouts, and retired baby boomers.

8. Describe the contributions small businesses make to the U.S. economy.
   - The small business sector's contributions are many. They make up 99.7 percent of all businesses, employ 50.2 percent of the private sector workforce, create 79 percent of the new jobs in the economy, produce 51 percent of the country's private gross domestic product (GDP), and account for 47 percent of business sales. Small companies also create 13 times more innovations per employee than large companies.

9. Put business failure into the proper perspective.
   - The failure rate for small businesses is higher than for big businesses, and profits fluctuate with general economic conditions. SBA statistics show that 54 percent of new businesses will have failed within 4 years.
   - Because they are building businesses in an environment filled with uncertainty and shaped by rapid change, entrepreneurs recognize that failure is likely to be a part of their lives; yet, they are not paralyzed by that fear. Successful entrepreneurs have the attitude that failures are simply stepping stones along the path to success.
10. Explain how small business owners can avoid the major pitfalls of running a business.
   - Small business owners can employ several general tactics to avoid failure. The entrepreneur should know the business in depth, develop a solid business plan, manage financial resources effectively, understand financial statements, learn to manage people effectively, set the business apart from the competition, and maintain a positive attitude.

Discussion Questions

1. What forces have led to the boom in entrepreneurship in the United States?
2. What is an entrepreneur? Give a brief description of the entrepreneurial profile.
3. *Inc.* magazine claims, "Entrepreneurship is more mundane than it's sometimes portrayed . . . you don't need to be a person of mythical proportions to be very, very successful in building a company." Do you agree? Explain.
4. What are the major benefits of business ownership?
5. Which of the potential drawbacks to business ownership are most critical?
6. Briefly describe the role of the following groups in entrepreneurship: women, minorities, immigrants, "part-timers," home-based business owners, family business owners, copreneurs, corporate castoffs, and corporate dropouts.
7. What contributions do small businesses make to our economy?
8. Describe the small business failure rate.
9. How can the small business owner avoid the common pitfalls that often lead to business failures?
10. Why is it important to study the small business failure rate?
11. Explain the typical entrepreneur's attitude toward failure.
12. One entrepreneur says that too many people "don't see that by spending their lives afraid of failure, they *become* failures. But when you go out there and risk as I have, you'll have failures along the way, but eventually the result is great success if you are willing to keep risking . . . For every big 'yes' in life, there will be 199 'nos.'" Do you agree? Explain.
13. What advice would you offer an entrepreneurial friend who has just suffered a business failure?
14. Noting the growing trend among collegiate entrepreneurs launching businesses while still in school, one educator says, "A student whose main activity on campus is running a business is missing the basic reason for being here, which is to get an education." Do you agree? Explain.

 This text is accompanied by the best-selling business planning software, Business Plan Pro™ by Palo Alto Software, Inc. This end-of-chapter feature along with the software can assist you in four ways as you accomplish the goal of creating a business plan:

1. *Structure.* Business Plan Pro provides a structure to the process of creating a business plan. There are general business plan standards and expectations, and Business Plan Pro has a recognized and well-received format that lends credibility to your plan. A comprehensive plan that follows a generally recognized outline adds credibility and, if it is a part of the plan's purpose, increases its chances of being funded.
2. *Efficiency.* Business Plan Pro will save you time. Once you become familiar with the interface, Business Plan Pro creates all of the essential financial statements for you using the information the software prompts you to enter. The income statement, balance sheet, and profit and loss statement are formatted once the data is there.

3. *Examples.* Business Plan Pro includes dozens of example business plans. Seeing examples of other plans can be a helpful learning tool to create a plan that is unique to your product or service and your market.
4. *Appearance.* Business Plan Pro automatically incorporates relevant tables and graphs into the text. The result is a cohesive business plan that combines text, tables, and charts and enhances the impact of your document.

Writing a business plan is more than just creating a document. The process can be the most valuable benefit of all. A business plan "tells a story" about your business. It addresses why the business concept is viable, who your target market is, what you offer that market, why the business offers a unique value, how you are going to reach your market, how your business is going to be funded, and—based on your projections—how it will be financially successful.

Creating a business plan is a learning process. For a start-up business, completing a business plan allows you to better understand what to do before you start writing checks and seek funding. Owners of existing businesses can benefit from writing a business plan to better address the challenges they face and optimize the opportunities before them. Business Plan Pro is a tool to assist you with this process. The software guides you through the process by asking a series of questions with software "wizards" to help build your business plan as you put the vision of your business on paper.

At the end of chapter, a Business Plan Pro activity applies the concepts discussed in that chapter. These activities will enable you to build your plan one step at a time in manageable components. You will be able to assemble your plan in a way that captures the information you know about your business and raise key questions that will push you to learn more in areas you may not have considered. Business Plan Pro will guide you through each step to complete your plan as you progress through this text. This combination of learning concepts and then applying them in your business plan can be powerful. It represents a critical step toward launching a business or establishing a better understanding of the business you now own.

The following exercises will lead you through the process of creating your own business plan. If you or your team does not have a business concept in mind, select a business idea and work through these steps.

The EasyPlan Wizard™ within Business Plan Pro is another optional resource that will guide you through the process of creating your business plan and, just as you follow the guidance chapter offers, this will not proceed chronologically through the business plan outline that appears in Business Plan Pro. Instead, it skips from section to section as you build concepts about your business, the products and services you offer, the markets you will serve, and your financial information. You can use the wizard or follow the sections of the business plan outline based on the guidance. Both options will lead you through the entire process and help you create a comprehensive business plan.

On the Web

First, visit the Companion Web site designed for this text at *www.pearsonhighered.com/scarborough*. Locate the "Business Plan Resource" tab at the top along with the chapter and review the information in that section. The information and links here will be a resource for you as you work through this chapter and develop your business plan.

In the Software

Follow the instructions included on the CD to install Business Plan Pro. After you first open Business Plan Pro—preferably on a PC with an Internet connection—open the "Sample Plan

Browser." The Sample Plan Browser allows you to preview a library of sample business plans. You will find numerous business plan examples ranging from restaurants to accounting firms to nonprofit organizations. A tool will help sort through these plans based on a specific industry or key words. Don't be concerned about finding a plan that is identical to your business concept. Instead, look for plans that contain parallel characteristics, such as a product or service plan, or one that is targeted to consumers rather than business customers. Review several of these plans to get a better idea of the outline and content. This may give you a clearer vision of what your business plan will look like.

Click the "Sample Plan Browser" within the software and review these two plans: "The Daily Perc" and "Corporate Fitness."

1. Compare the table of contents of each plan. What differences do you notice?
2. Review the executive summary of each plan. What is the key difference in these two business concepts?
3. What similarities do the plans share regarding the reason the plans were written?
4. As you look through the plans, what are some common tables and charts you find embedded in the text? What value do these tables and charts offer the reader?

Building Your Business Plan

Open Business Plan Pro and select the choice that allows you to start a new plan. You may want to view the movie that will give you an animated and audio overview of the software. Then allow the EasyPlan Wizard to "ask" you about your start date, the title of your plan, and other basic information including:

1. Do you sell products or services?
2. Is your business a profit of a nonprofit organization?
3. Is your business a start-up operation or an ongoing business?
4. What kind of business plan do you want to create? (Choose "complete business plan.")
5. Do you want to include the SWOT analysis? (Check this box.)
6. Will you have a Web site?
7. A series of financial questions to structure the financial aspects of your plan with assistance throughout.
8. Do you want to prepare a plan for three years (a standard plan) or a longer term plan of five years, both with a one-year monthly breakdown?

Save these decisions by using the drop-down menu under "File" and clicking "Save" or by clicking the "Save" icon at the top right of the menu bar. You can change your response to these decisions at any time as you build your plan.

Review the outline of your plan by clicking on the "Preview" icon on the top of your screen, or by clicking "File," "Print," and then "Preview" within the Print window. Based on your responses to the wizard questions, you will now see the outline of your business plan. The software will enable you to change and modify the plan outline in any way you choose at any time. Business Plan Pro will help you build your plan one step at a time.

Endnotes

1. Robert W. Farlie, *Kauffman Index of Entrepreneurial Activity*, 1996–2007, April 2008, Ewing Marion Kauffman Foundation, p. 1.

2. Akbar Sadeghi, "The Births and Deaths of Business Establishments in the United States," *Monthly Labor Review*, December 2008, p. 3.

3. Niels Bosma, Zoltan J. Acs, Erkko Autio, Alicia Coduras, and Jonathan Levie, *Global Entrepreneurship Monitor: 2008 Executive Report*, Babson College, Universidad del Desarrollo, and London Business School (Boston, MA: 2009), p. 20.

4. Jack Ma and Rebecca Fannin, "How I Did It: Jack Ma, Alibaba.com," *Inc.*, January 2008, *www.inc.com/magazine/20080101/how-i-did-it-jack-ma-alibaba.html*; "Corporate Overview," Alibaba.com, *www.alibaba.com/aboutalibaba/aligroup/jack.html*.

5. Adrian Woolridge, "Global Heroes," *The Economist*, March 14, 2009, p. 8.

6. Jeffry A. Timmons, "An Obsession with Opportunity," *Nation's Business*, March 1985, p. 68.

7. "Panel Study on Entrepreneurial Dynamics," Kauffman Foundation Entrepreneurship Research Portal, *http://research.kauffman.org/cwp/appmanager/research/researchDesktop?_nfpb=true&_pageLabel=research_dataDetail&awebcurl=Research/DataSet_01.htm*.

8. Jerry Useem, "The Risk-Taker Returns," *FSB*, May 2001, p. 70.

9. Allie Townsend, "A Jolt of Energy, Minus the Crash," *Inc.*, March 2009, pp. 83–84; "*Inc.* Recognizes Kelley School Student's Company as One of 'America's Coolest College Start-Ups,'" Indiana University News Room, February 23, 2009, *http://newsinfo.iu.edu/news/page/normal/10018.html*.

10. Frank Ross, "Most Americans Want to Be Their Own Boss," *All Business*, April 20, 2009, *www.allbusiness.com/reports-reviews-sections/polls-surveys/12278487-1.html*.

11. David McClellan, *The Achieving Society* (Princeton, NJ: Van Nostrand, 1961), p. 16; Nancy Michaels, "Entrepreneurship: An Alternative Career Choice," *U.S. News & World Report*, March 24, 2003, p. 45; Susan Ward, "So You Want to Start a Small Business? Part 2: The Personality of the Entrepreneur," *Small Business Canada*, *http://sbinfocanada.about.com/library/weekly/aa082900b.htm*.

12. Charles Gerena, "Nature vs. Nurture," *Region Focus*, Fall 2005, p. 19.

13. Max Chafkin, Donna Fenn, April Joyner, Ryan McCarthy, Kate Pastorek, and Nitasha Tiku, "Cool, Determined, and Under 30," *Inc.*, October 2008, p. 101.

14. Ralph Waldo Emerson, "Essays: First Series," Emerson.com, *www.emersoncentral.com/selfreliance.htm*.

15. Jeffrey Shuman and David Rottenberg, "Famous Failures," *Small Business Start-Ups*, February 1999, pp. 32–33; Francis Huffman, "A Dairy Tale," *Entrepreneur*, February 1999, p. 182; "Gail Borden," Famous Texans, *www.famoustexans.com/GailBorden.htm*.

16. Sabin Russell, "Being Your Own Boss in America," *Venture*, May 1984, p. 40.

17. Anne Field, "Bouncing From Start-Up to Start-Up and Loving It," Gathering of Angels, *http://gatheringofangels.com/News/bouncing.html*; Howard Yellen, "The Making of a Serial Entrepreneur," Larta Institute, January 10, 2005, *www.larta.org/LAVox/articlelinks/2005/050110_making.asp*.

18. Jennifer Wang, "Confessions of Serial Entrepreneurs," *Entrepreneur*, January 2009 *www.entrepreneur.com/startingabusiness/successstories/article199436.html*.

19. Stephanie N. Mehta, "Young Entrepreneurs Are Starting Business After Business," *Wall Street Journal*, March 19, 1997, p. B2.

20. Roger Rickleffs and Udayan Gupta, "Traumas of a New Entrepreneur," *Wall Street Journal*, May 10, 1989, p. B1.

21. Mike Hofman, "Some Good Earners," *Inc.*, February 2009, pp. 21–22; Annalyn Censky, "Starting a Business from Behind Bars," *FSB*, July 30, 2008, *http://askfsb.blogs.fsb.cnn.com/2008/07/30/starting-a-business-behind-bars/*; Zoe Sandvig, "Program Turns Felons into Businessmen," *Washington Times*, March 26, 2009, *www.washingtontimes.com/news/2009/mar/26/felons-get-the-business/#*.

22. John Case, "The Origins of Entrepreneurship," *Inc.*, June 1989, p. 52.

23. Adrian Woolridge, "Global Heroes," *The Economist*, March 14, 2009, p. 4.

24. Farhad Manjoo, "App Mania," *Fast Company*, May 2009, pp. 73–79; Jeffrey M. O'Brien, "The Wizards of Apps," *Fortune*, May 25, 2009, pp. 29–30; Yukari Iwatani Kane, "Apple Apps Ahead," *Wall Street Journal*, April 29, 2009, *http://online.wsj.com/article/SB123980962988921409.html*.

25. Emily Lambert, "Waste? Not!" *Forbes*, June 16, 2008, p. 122.

26. Jia Lynn Yang, "Gang Green," *Fortune*, April 27, 2009, pp. 12–13.

27. Jess McCuan, "Turning Slurry Back into Coal," *Inc.*, April 2009, pp. 46–47.

28. Nichole L. Torres, "First Flip to Hip," *Entrepreneur*, September 2008, pp. 84–86; "SkirtSports History," SkirtSports, *http://skirtsports.com/about-skirtsports/*.

29. John Boyanoski, "Hot Idea Comes to Downtown," *GSA Business*, June 30, 2006, p. 22.

30. Richard C. Morais, "Investing in Yourself," *Forbes*, April 27, 2009, p. 46.

31. Dennis Nishi, "A Builder of Castles Made of Trash," *Wall Street Journal*, June 16, 2009. P. D14 "Q&A: Michael Reynolds, Earthship Architect," *CNN*, September 4, 2007, *www.cnn.com/2007/BUSINESS/08/29/skewed.michaelreynolds/*; "About Earthship Biotecture," *Earthship Biotecture, www.earthship.net/index.php?option=com_content&view=article&id=4&Itemid=58*.

32. Roger P. Levin, "You've Got to Love It or Leave It," *Success*, December 2000/January 2001, p. 22.

33. "The Knowledge," *FSB*, May 2009, p. 90.

34. Matthew Miller and Duncan Greenberg, "The Forbes 400," *Forbes*, September 17, 2008, *www.forbes.com/2008/09/16/forbes-400-billionaires-lists-400list08_cx_mn_0917richamericans_land.html*.

35. Mary Diebel, "4.6 Million Americans Are Millionaires," *The Sacramento Bee*, July 16, 2001, *http://24hour.sacbee.com/24hour/business/story/632161p-678117c.html*; Sheryl Nance, "You Can Be a Millionaire," *Your Company*, June/July 1997, pp. 26–33.

36. Nichole L. Torres, "Young Millionaires: Marco Giannini," *Entrepreneur*, September 2008, p. 63; Alexa Nyland, "He's Making Pet Food the Natural Way," *Los Angeles Business Journal*, November 17, 2008, p. B1.

37. Anita Campbell, "Small Businesses Will Lead Us to a Better Future," *Small Biz Trends*, February 26, 2009, *http://smallbiztrends.com/2009/02/small-businesses-lead-future.html*.

38. Dennis Jacobs, "Most Small Business Owners Don't Plan to 'Fully' Retire," *Gallup*, March 10, 2008, *www.gallup.com/poll/104866/four-smallbusiness-owners-dont-plan-retire.aspx*.

39. Gayle Sato-Stodder, "Never Say Die," *Entrepreneur*, December 1990, p. 95.

40. "Salary Survey Report for Job: Owner/Operator, Small Business," Payscale, July 5, 2009, *www.payscale.com/research/US/Job=Owner_%2F_Operator,_Small_Business/Salary*; "Usual Weekly Earnings of Wage and Salary Workers: First Quarter 2009," Bureau of Labor Statistics, April 16, 2009, p. 1.

41. Anne Fisher, "Is Your Business Ruining Your Marriage?" *FSB*, March 2003, pp. 63–71.

42. Scott Shane, "Start-up Failure Rates: The REAL Numbers," *Small Business Trends*, April 28, 2008, *http://smallbiztrends.com/2008/04/startup-failure-rates.html*; "Frequently Asked Questions," Small Business Administration, Office of Advocacy, October 2005, p. 2.

43. Matt Phillips, "Average Workweek," *Wall Street Journal Blogs*, July 2, 2009, *http://blogs.wsj.com/marketbeat/2009/07/02/average-workweek-nobody-is-going-to-be-hiring-anytime-soon/*; Denise O'Berry, "How Small Business Owners Feel About Doing Business," *All Business*, December 20, 2006, *www.allbusiness.com/operations/3872887-1.html*.

44. "Small Business Owners Working Longer Hours," *Rent to Own Industry News*, May 26, 2009, *http://rtoonline.com/Content/Article/may09/smal-business-owners-work-hours-survey-052609.asp*.

45. "Small Business Owners Working Longer Hours," *Rent to Own Industry News*, May 26, 2009, *http://rtoonline.com/Content/Article/may09/smal-business-owners-work-hours-survey-052609.asp*.

46. Anne Fisher, "Make Sleep Work for You," *FSB*, September 2008, pp. 85–90.

47. Jennifer Wang, "Not Ready to Retire?" *Entrepreneur*, March 2009, pp. 73–79.

48. Geoff Williams, "Guiding Light," *Entrepreneur B.Y.O.B.*, August 2003, p. 84.

49. Mark Henricks, "Parent Trap?" *Entrepreneur*, September 2005, pp. 17–18.

50. Pattie Simone, "You Can Do It!" *Entrepreneur*, July 2006, pp. 94–101.

51. Adrian Woolridge, "Global Heroes," *The Economist*, March 14, 2009, pp. 8–9.

52. "Global Entrepreneurship Week: 2008 in Review," *Unleashing Ideas*, www.unleashingideas.org/review08.

53. Nichole L. Torres, "Launch Pad to Success," *Entrepreneur*, October 2008, pp. 62–81; Raymund Flandez, "An Education in Itself," *Wall Street Journal*, September 25, 2006, p. R10.

54. Jim Hopkins, "Venture Capital 101: Entrepreneur Courses Increase," *USA Today*, January 5, 2004, p. 1B.

55. "USTR Focus on Services," Office of the United States Trade Representative, *www.ustr.gov/Trade_Sectors/Services/Section_Index.html*.

56. Max Chafkin, Donna Fenn, April Joyner, Ryan McCarthy, Kate Pastorek, and Nitasha Tiku, "Cool, Determined, and Under 30," *Inc.*, October 2008, p. 99; Linda Tischler, "The Fast Company 50: #44: Etsy," *Fast Company*, February 2009, *www.fastcompany.com/fast50_09/profile/list/etsy*. "Small Business Success: Etsy," CNN, March 20, 2009, *www.cnn.com/video/#/video/living/2009/03/20/sbs.selling.online.cnn*.

57. "Survey: Entrepreneur's Hard Work Earns Respect," HP Newsroom, October 15, 2007, *http://h41131.www4.hp.com/ca/en/pr/10152007a.html*.

58. Mina Kimes, "Small Company, Big Profit," *FSB*, October 2008, *http://money.cnn.com/2008/10/08/smallbusiness/when_less_means_more.fsb/index.htm*.

59. Erick Schonfeld, "Forrester Forecast: Online Retail Sales Will Grow to $250 Billion by 2014," *Tech Crunch*, March 8, 2010, *http://techcrunch.com/2010/03/08/forrester-forecast-online-retail-sales-will-grow-to-250-billion-by-2014*.

60. Stuart J. Johnston, "Survey Finds Small Business Optimistic on 2009," *Internet News*, January 16, 2009, *www.internetnews.com/bus-news/article.php/3796716/Survey+Finds+Small+Business+Optimistic+on+2009.htm*.

61. Vangie Beal, "E-Commerce Profile: PillowDecor.com," *E-Commerce*, March 4, 2009, *www.ecommerce-guide.com/news/trends/article.php/3808511*; "About Pillow Décor," Pillow Décor, *www.pillowdecor.com/aboutus.asp*.

62. Vangie Beal, "E-Commerce Profile: PillowDecor.com," *E-Commerce*, March 4, 2009, *www.ecommerce-guide.com/news/trends/article.php/3808511*.

63. *A Profile of U.S. Exporting Companies, 2006–2007*, U.S. Census Bureau, U.S. Department of Commerce, Washington, DC: April 9, 2009, p. 6.

64. Lara Chamberlain, *NFIB National Small Business Poll: International Trade*, Volume 4, Issue 1, 2004, National Federation of Independent Businesses, pp. 1, 4.

65. Maria Minniti, William Bygrave, and Erkko Autio, Global Entrepreneurship Monitor: Executive Summary, Babson College and the London Business School, January 2006, p. 33.

66. Aimee Mepham, "Wear to Win," *Entrepreneurship and Liberal Arts Newsletter*, Wake Forest University, November 2008, *http://entrepreneurship.wfu.edu/newsletter/wear-to-win.html*; "About Us," Wear to Win, *www.weartowin.com/about.php*; "Laura Ormson Named a Wake Forest Hobbs Award Winner," *Entrepreneurship and Liberal Arts Newsletter*, April 2009, *http://entrepreneurship.wfu.edu/newsletter/hobbs-winners.html*.

67. Angus Loten, "The Sweet Taste of Success," *MSNBC*, July 13, 2008, *www.msnbc.msn.com/id/25561551/*; "Maria de Lourdes Sobrino Biography," Lulu's Dessert, *www.lulusdessert.com/bio.html*.

68. "Key Facts About Women-Owned Businesses: The Overall Picture, 2008–2009," Center for Women's Business Research, *www.womensbusinessresearchcenter.org/research/keyfacts/*.

69. David J. Hall, "Hispanic Businesses Recognized at National Small Business Week," U.S. Small Business Administration, May 21, 2009, pp. 1–2.

70. Robert W. Fairlie, *2008 Kauffman Index of Entrepreneurial Activity*, Kauffman Foundation, April 2009, p. 10.

71. Ying Lowrey, *Minorities in Business: A Demographic Review of Minority Business Ownership*, U.S. Small Business Administration, Office of Advocacy, April 2007, pp. 13–14; *Minority Biz Fast Facts*, U.S. Department of Commerce, Minority Business Development Agency, *www.mbda.gov/minoritybizfacts/*; *2007 SRP Arizona Business Study: Focus on Minority Owned Businesses*, SRP and Arizona State University Hispanic Research Center, 2007, p. 1.

72. "Famous Black Entrepreneurs and Executives: Christopher Gardner," *Black Enterprise*, *www.blackentrepreneurprofile.com/profile-full/archive/2007/january/article/christopher-gardner/*.

73. Vivek Wadhwa, "Foreign-Born Entrepreneurs: An Underestimated American Resource," *Kauffman Thoughtbook*, Kauffman Foundation (Kansas City, Missouri: 2009), p. 178.

74. John McDowell, "Immigrant Owned Business's Contribution to the Economy Detailed in New Report," U.S. Small Business Administration, November 12, 2008, p.1.

75. Betty Joyce Nash, "Immigrant Entrepreneurs: Talent, Technology, and Jobs," *Region Focus*, Fall 2008, pp. 20–22.

76. Helen Coster, "Don't Quit Your Day Job," *Forbes*, July 21, 2008, pp. 60-62; "About Us," FlyingPeas, *www.flyingpeas.com/info.html*.

77. Sarah E. Needleman, "A Toe in the Water," *Wall Street Journal*, February 23, 2009, p. R7.

78. "Home-Based Business Facts," National Black Business Trade Association, *www.inc.com/articles/2007/12/home.html*.

79. Tamara Schweitzer, "Escape from Cubicle Hell," *Inc.*, December 2007, *www.inc.com/articles/2007/12/home.html*.

80. Joanne H. Pratt, "The Impact of Location on Net Income: A Comparison of Homebased and Non-Homebased Sole Proprietors," *Small Business Research Summary*, Small Business Administration, Office of Advocacy, May 2006, p. 1.

81. Laurence Baxter, "Home-based Business Facts," *eZine Articles*, June 12, 2009, *http://ezinearticles.com/?Home-Based-Business-Facts-and-Statistics&id=2469758*.

82. "The Ticker," *Information Week*, March 8, 2006, p. 18.

83. Patricia B. Gray, "Sleeper Sell," *FSB*, April 2009, p. 15; Wes Moss, "Starting from Scratch: Valerie Johnson of Big Feet Pajama Co. Went from Stockbroker to Pajama Mogul," *New York Daily News*, June 20, 2009, *www.nydailynews.com/money/small_biz/2009/06/20/2009-06-20_from_stockbroker_to_pajama_magnate_the_inspiring_story_of_valerie_johnson.html*.

84. "Facts and Figures on Family Business in the U.S.," The Family Firm Institute, *www.ffi.org/looking/fbfacts_us.cgi*.

85. Erick Calonius, "Blood and Money," *Newsweek*, Special Issue, p. 82.

86. Liz Welch, "Things I Can't Live Without: Donna Grucci Butler," *Inc.*, July 2006, p. 70; "About Us," Fireworks by Grucci, *www.grucci.com/aboutus.html*.

87. "Facts and Perspectives on Family Business in the U.S.," The Family Firm Institute, *www.ffi.org/looking/fbfacts_us.pdf*.

88. "Facts About Family Business," S. Dale High Center for Family Business at Elizabethtown College, *www.centerforfamilybusiness.org/facts.asp*.

89. "Love and the Bottom Line: Couples in Business Find High Rewards and Risks," *Nando Times News*, *http://archive.nandotimes.com/newsroom/nt/0212bizcpl.html*.

90. "LF USA to Acquire Van Zeeland, Inc.," Berns Communication Group, August 13, 2008, *www.bernscommunications.com/pr_081308.php*; Sara Wilson, "In Good Hands," *Entrepreneur*, June 2008, p. 140.

91. Stephen Taub, "For Most, It's Just a Dream: Being Your Own Boss," *CFO*, September 18, 2007, *www.cfo.com/article.cfm/9826799?f=related*.

92. Kirsten Valle, "Can't Land a Job? Create Your Own," *Charlotte Observer*, May 24, 2009, *www.charlotteobserver.com/business/story/740918.html*.

93. "Boomers Becoming Their Own Boss in Retirement," *Marketing Charts*, October 23, 2007, *www.marketingcharts.com/direct/boomers-becoming-their-own-boss-in-retirement-2104/*.

94. Jennifer Wang, "Not Ready to Retire?" *Entrepreneur*, March 2009, pp. 75–79; Lindsay Danzell, "Local Company Reaches Profitability," *Charleston Regional Business Journal*, February, 7, 2007, p. 16.

95. "Small Business Profile: United States," U.S. Small Business Administration, Office of Advocacy, January 2009, p. 1.

96. Steve Green, "Small Businesses Key to Economic Recovery, Report Says," *Las Vegas Sun*, January 26, 2009, *www.lasvegassun.com/news/2009/jan/26/small-businesses-key-economic-recovery-report-says/*.

97. *NFIB Small Business Policy Guide* (Washington, DC: NFIB Education Foundation, 2000), p. 30; "Help Wanted," *Inc, Special Report: The State of Small Business 1997*, pp. 35–41; "The Job Factory," *Inc, Special Report: The State of Small Business 2001*, pp. 40–43; "The Gazelle Theory," *Inc, Special Report: The State of Small Business 2001*, pp. 28–29.

98. Zoltan Acs, William Parsons, and Spencer Tracy, "High Impact Firms: Gazelles Revisited," Small Business Administration, Office of Advocacy, June 2008, pp. 1–2.

99. Jules Lichtenstein, "Small Businesses Provide Flexible Training to Job Market Entrants," *Small Business Advocate*, April 2009, p. 4; Preston McLaurin, "Small Businesses Are Winners," *S.C. Business Journal*, May 2000, p. 10.

100. *"FAQs,"* U.S. Small Business Administration (Washington, DC, 2007), *http://app1.sba.gov/faqs/faqIndexAll.cfm?areaid=24*; Kathryn Kobe, "The Small Business Share of GDP," Small Business Research Summary, Small Business Administration, Office of Advocacy, April 2007, *www.sba.gov/advo/research/rs299tot.pdf*.

101. Anthony Breitzman and Diana Hicks, *An Analysis of Small Business Patents by Industry and Firm Size*, U.S. Small Business Administration, November 2008, pp. 1–2.
102. "World War II Diary," *History Detectives*, Season 6, Episode 1, *www.pbs.org/opb/historydetectives/pdf/601_wardiary.pdf*, p. 3.
103. Michael Warshaw, "Great Comebacks," *Success*, July/August 1995, p. 43.
104. Michael Barrier, "Entrepreneurs Who Excel," *Nation's Business*, August 1996, p. 28.
105. Clint Willis, "Try, Try Again," *Forbes ASAP*, June 2, 1997, p. 63.
106. Jeanne Brooks, "Uncertain Future Stares Greenville Store Owner in Face," *Greenville News*, June 21, 2009, pp. 1A, 3A.
107. Stephanie Barlow, "Hang On!" *Entrepreneur*, September 1992, p. 156.
108. Jared Sandberg, "Counting Pizza Slices, Cutting Water Cups—You Call This a Budget?" *Wall Street Journal*, January 21, 2004, p. B1.
109. Rhonda Abrams, "Building Blocks of Business: Great Faith, Great Doubt, Great Effort," *Business*, March 4, 2001, p. 2.

Appendix

My Friends' Bookstore Plan

Dana Waters

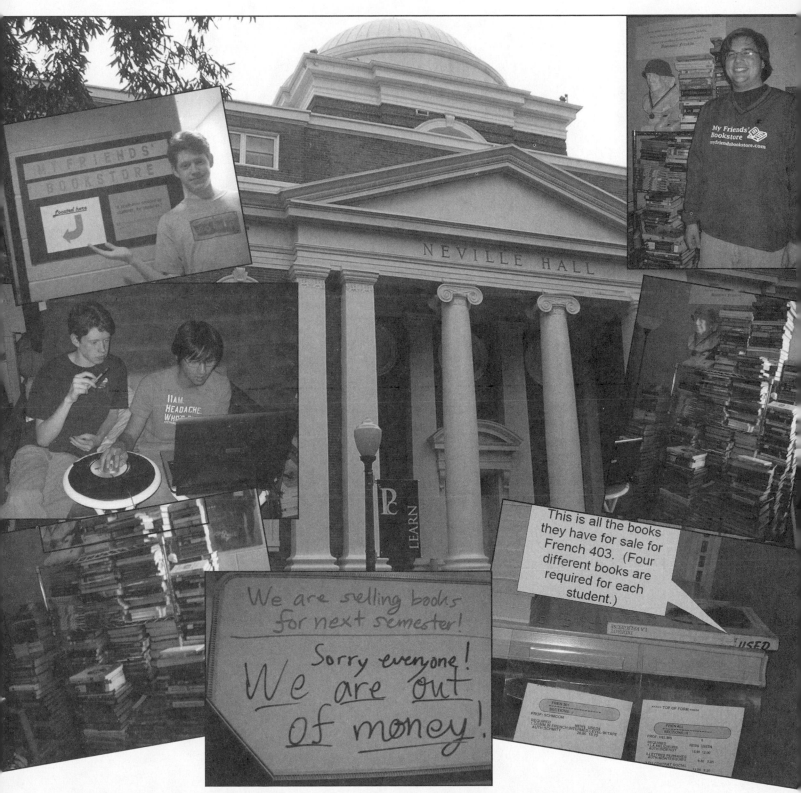

Contents

1. Executive Summary

My Friends' Bookstore is a college store that operates out of Presbyterian College (PC). It buys books from students and sells them to other students on campus as well as to millions of students online. It is run by college students in a dorm room, thereby avoiding many of the costs incurred by traditional college stores. By focusing on used textbooks, we are able to capitalize on the 35.1 percent gross margin and under-price our competitors.

By providing dorm room delivery and pick-up of textbooks, lower prices, and a fully functional Web site, My Friends' Bookstore will vault past its competition.

After conducting a very successful trial run during the Fall 2006/Spring 2007 semesters, partners Dana Waters, Scott Mumbauer, and Jonathan Choi were able to learn valuable lessons about running a used textbook store, all while making a profit from an investment of $15,000. Many businesses take up to three years to make profit, but My Friends' Bookstore was able to earn a profit after only two months!

This business plan ultimately serves to show the incredible opportunity of investing in a revolutionary new college store that allows the personal touch of a small business to reach a global market.

1.1. Objectives

1. To create an online bookstore that serves the needs of Presbyterian College students.
2. To earn 30 percent market share and achieve name recognition as the "on campus" book-store by 2008.
3. To achieve a net income of $5,000 by year two and $10,000 by year three (see Figure 1).
4. To provide better prices, convenience, and customer satisfaction than competitors.

1.2. Mission

My Friends' Bookstore is dedicated to buying and selling books to students at fair, competitive prices while providing the highest possible level of customer service and satisfaction. We strive to provide convenience and timeliness to all of our customers while maintaining a positive relationship with the faculty and administrative staff at Presbyterian College.

1.3. Keys to Success

The keys to success for My Friends' Bookstore are:

1. *Cost Leadership.* Selling textbooks and other course materials at competitive prices across a majority of academic departments. My Friends' Bookstore must provide all relevant materials for all classes that are covered.

FIGURE 1
Financial Highlights

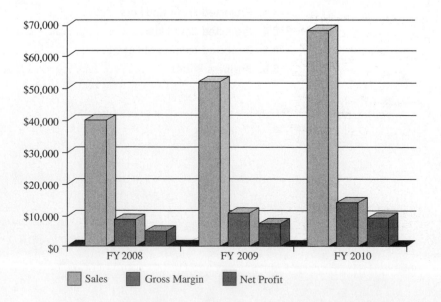

44

2. *Location*. Offering convenience through reliable and timely deliveries and pick-ups. There is no physical location, which makes fast response time to customers essential to providing more convenience than a traditional bookstore.

3. *Customer Loyalty*. Buying textbooks from students at competitive and fair prices so that they will recognize the benefits of using My Friends' Bookstore. That loyalty will generate a solid customer base and increase total sales.

4. *Customer Satisfaction*. Provide satisfaction for 100 percent of our customers. My Friends' Bookstore strives to keep a close and positive relationship with every customer through the use of personal greeting strategies, newsletters, customer feedback, and quick response times to customers' questions or complaints.

2. Company Summary

Store Location Although My Friends' Bookstore is run entirely online, its storage facility currently is located in a dorm room at Presbyterian College (PC). This allows for storage, deliveries, and pick-ups to be made from a convenient and central location.

Store Operation My Friends' Bookstore uses a Web site that allows for all sales and purchases to be conducted online; therefore, it is technically open 24/7. It also has a phone line in the dorm room for students to call with questions or to make sales and purchases. Book deliveries and purchases are usually conducted between the hours of 12 P.M. and 11 P.M. My Friends' Bookstore is staffed by three full-time partners as well as up to five part-time employees who serve as telephone support representatives, e-mail and Web site technicians, and book delivery persons.

Store Policies My Friends' Bookstore accepts cash on delivery (CODs), all major credit cards, and PayPal. Books sold to My Friends' Bookstore cannot be refunded at any time. Books bought from My Friends' Bookstore can be returned for any reason within 14 days with receipt up until the final day of book sales.

2.1. Company Ownership

My Friends' Bookstore is organized as a partnership among the three general partners of G. Dana Waters, Scott B. Mumbauer, and Jonathan H. Choi. Each owns 33.33 percent of the company. Dana Waters handles the accounting and legal duties; Scott Mumbauer works with financing and loan duties; and Jonathan Choi works with pricing, marketing strategies, and the company's Web site design. All partners share daily business duties evenly.

2.2. Company History

My Friends' Bookstore was created by two Presbyterian College students on September 5, 2006, to provide students with an alternative to the "typical" campus bookstore that generally overcharged students for textbooks and underpaid them for their used textbooks at the end of the semester. After getting permission from college administrators to set up on campus, My Friends' Bookstore surprised everyone in its almost "overnight" success.

My Friends' Bookstore is privately financed by family members and private investors (or angels). More than $15,000 was invested into the company for its first trial run in December 2006. This money covered start-up costs, including launching a grassroots advertising campaign with T-shirts and hoodies and buying more than 700 books from students and online sources. At the beginning of the next semester, they sold these books to students at competitive prices, most of which were lower than those the campus bookstore offered. They have sold the remaining inventory online through Amazon.com. The company's first major struggles soon began. Several books were reported stolen and campus police confiscated nearly $200 worth of books from My Friends' Bookstore. Tensions rose as My Friends' Bookstore tried to follow the rules established by residence life and campus police, while running a full-time bookstore and going to class full time. Sales were also less than expected, and a large portion of inventory had to be listed on Amazon.com, which charges a 15 percent commission on every book sold. This greatly reduced the store's profit margin, which was already very low to compete with competitors' prices. The founders of My Friends' Bookstore have learned a great deal from this trial run and implemented changes to increase sales and profits. The owners have changed their strategy to increase their

Past Performance

	FY 2007
Sales	$ 16,743
Gross margin	$ 1,257
Gross margin %	7.51%
Operating expenses	$ 1,646
Inventory turnover	6.23

	FY 2007
Balance sheet	
Current assets	
Cash	$ 8,290
Inventory	$ 4,974
Other current assets	$ 100
Total current assets	$ 13,364
Long-term assets	
Long-term assets	$ 0
Accumulated depreciation	$ 0
Total long-term assets	$ 0
Total assets	$ 13,364
Current liabilities	
Accounts payable	$ 0
Current borrowing	$ 0
Other current liabilities (interest free)	$ 5,500
Total current liabilities	$ 5,500
Long-term liabilities	$ 0
Total liabilities	$ 5,500
Paid-in capital	$ 15,500
Retained earnings	($24,109)
Earnings	$ 16,473
Total capital	$ 7,864
Total capital and liabilities	$ 3,364
Other inputs	
Payment days	1

profit margin based on Amazon.com's commission and to increase sales with better and larger advertising campaigns to encourage more PC students to buy. The founders believe that the convenience they offer will increase their customer base when their largest competitor, the campus bookstore, moves to its downtown, off-campus location.

My Friends' Bookstore has gained a competitive advantage in the market by providing students with fair and competitive prices, emphasizing the convenience of buying and selling their books on the company's Web site as well as delivering books to students' dorm rooms free of charge, and above all, providing a level of customer satisfaction and knowledge that only students can provide to other students.

3. Products

My Friends' Bookstore sells predominantly used textbooks bought from Presbyterian College students and online. Therefore, there is no set supplier. The suppliers are students and online sellers whose prices and products vary greatly from semester to semester, even day-to-day.

The textbook market is very competitive and unstable. As new editions come out, the value of previous editions of textbooks greatly depreciates almost immediately. Therefore, knowledge of when new editions are coming out is essential for maintaining a competitive advantage in buying and selling textbooks.

Books from virtually every academic department offered at Presbyterian College are bought and sold. All books are purchased based on the Amazon.com retail price, and on the expected demand of the book and the current quantity in stock. To maintain a strong customer base, the owners must begin to provide all books and materials for PC classes on its Web site instead of offering only some of the materials required for them. This, of course, is not essential when selling books to non-PC customers.

Books are sold first to PC students, and the rest of the inventory is listed online. A new Web site is in the works that will allow customers to buy books directly from the Web site with credit cards and PayPal, whereas the original system involved sending PayPal invoices to individual customers, which was a very tedious and time-consuming process. This Web site will also allow all inventory to be cross-listed on eBay, thus allowing My Friends' Bookstore to reach a broader market.

4. Market Analysis Summary

College Store Industry Information The college textbook market totaled $6.5 billion in 2004–2005. The total sales for college stores totaled nearly $11.2 billion in 2004–2005.[1]

Breakdown of College Store Sales*

Course materials	58.40%	$6.524 billion
Computer products	14.10%	$1.577 billion
Insignia merchandise	11.40%	$1.278 billion
Other merchandise	6.40%	$0.718 billion
Student supplies	5.50%	$0.614 billion
General/trade books	4.20%	$0.465 billion
Total	100.00%	$11.172 billion

*Based on 2004–2005 estimates.

CAMPUS STORE OWNERSHIP. According to the National Association of College Stores' approximately 4,450 college stores serve 4,236 institutions in the United States."[2] This is equivalent to 1.05 stores per institution. More than 3,000 of these stores are NACS members. Their members are an accurate representation of the average college store. They are divided by ownership as follows:

**FIGURE 2
Campus Store
Ownership/Operations**

Source: National Association of College Stores, 2007.

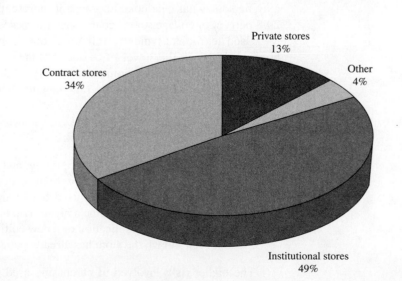

Private stores
13%

Other
4%

Contract stores
34%

Institutional stores
49%

FIGURE 3
NACS Membership by Estimated Sales

Source: National Association of College Stores, 2007.

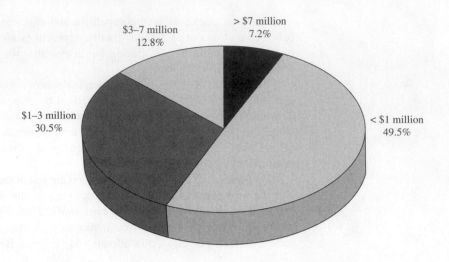

For example, Presbyterian College's current bookstore is a contract store, and My Friends' Bookstore is a private store. Many college stores are owned by student associations and also fall under the Private Stores category.[3]

COLLEGE STORE ANNUAL SALES. According to the NACS, college stores' sales vary greatly based on the size of the institution. Average annual sales are approximately $6 million, but most college stores generate sales of less than $3 million (see Figure 3).[4]

USED TEXTBOOK MARKET. Textbooks and other course materials make up nearly 59 percent of all college stores' sales.

New texts	40.80%	$4.284 billion
Used texts	17.10%	$1.796 billion
Course packs	1.10%	$0.116 billion
Total course material	**59.0%**	**$6.195 billion**
Total store sales	**100.00%**	**$10.5 billion**

Source: NACS 2007 College Store Industry Financial Report, National Association of Bookstores, 2007.

New textbooks generate the greatest percentage of the typical college store's sales. My Friends' Bookstore caters mainly to the used book niche of the textbook market. This market may be somewhat overlooked because it represents a small portion of the total market. Only 29.8 percent of college stores' course materials sales come from used textbooks.

Used textbooks typically sell for about 75 percent of the original price of new textbooks.[5] However, this lower price does not mean a lower profit margin. The margin on used textbooks is 35.1 percent, compared to only 22.3 percent on new textbooks.[6] For Fall 2006 (the latest data available), the average new textbook price is $53, compared to $44 for used textbooks.

Unfortunately, there are additional costs attached with the used textbook market. According to the NACS's analysis of used textbooks:

The process of acquiring, cleaning, pricing, and re-shelving used books involves significantly more time than that of new textbooks and increases college stores operating expenses.[7] In addition, because used books are non-returnable to publishers (as new books are), college stores assume a higher risk on their used book inventory. There is also the possibility that the publication of a new edition will make inventoried used textbooks obsolete, even though the store has already purchased them.[8]

The higher risks involved in purchasing used textbooks may explain why new textbooks make up a larger portion of most college stores sales. They may be less willing to invest a large portion of their resources into inventory that carries a higher risk of obsolescence. By studying used textbook trends, My Friends' Bookstore can reduce the high risks associated with used textbooks and turn this normally higher-risk market into a higher-profit market.

WHERE THE NEW TEXTBOOK DOLLAR GOES. As Figure 4 shows, college stores retain only 22.2 cents per dollar on new textbooks. Therefore, by focusing on the used textbook market, My Friends' Bookstore can avoid the 77.8 cents per dollar publisher/freight fees *and* earn a higher level of profit, all while paying less per book.

THE ONLINE COLLEGE STORE ADVANTAGE. According to the National Association of College Stores (NACS), only 2.8 percent of college sales are from online purchases.[10] This means that only 1.6 percent of college stores' total textbook sales are conducted online. There are many advantages to adding online capabilities to a college store, such as My Friends' Bookstore, including the following:

- Ease of returns
- Ability to pick up items immediately
- One-stop shopping
- Accurate information on which textbooks students need for courses
- The trust and security of buying from a well-known source with an on-campus location
- The primary target audience, college students, is accustomed to making purchases online.

MY FRIENDS' BOOKSTORE'S ONLINE ADVANTAGE. This "click and mortar" strategy can be highly successful if implemented properly. My Friends' Bookstore can capitalize on all of these advantages. All books are sold through a Web site with a secure checkout system. These books

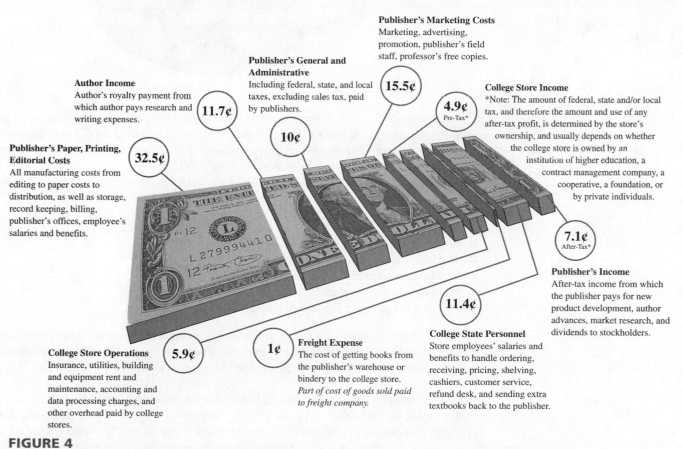

Publisher's Marketing Costs
Marketing, advertising, promotion, publisher's field staff, professor's free copies.

Publisher's General and Administrative
Including federal, state, and local taxes, excluding sales tax, paid by publishers.

Author Income
Author's royalty payment from which author pays research and writing expenses.

College Store Income
*Note: The amount of federal, state and/or local tax, and therefore the amount and use of any after-tax profit, is determined by the store's ownership, and usually depends on whether the college store is owned by an institution of higher education, a contract management company, a cooperative, a foundation, or by private individuals.

Publisher's Paper, Printing, Editorial Costs
All manufacturing costs from editing to paper costs to distribution, as well as storage, record keeping, billing, publisher's offices, employee's salaries and benefits.

11.7¢

15.5¢

4.9¢ Pre-Tax*

10¢

32.5¢

7.1¢ After-Tax*

Publisher's Income
After-tax income from which the publisher pays for new product development, author advances, market research, and dividends to stockholders.

11.4¢

College Store Operations
Insurance, utilities, building and equipment rent and maintenance, accounting and data processing charges, and other overhead paid by college stores.

5.9¢

1¢

Freight Expense
The cost of getting books from the publisher's warehouse or bindery to the college store. *Part of cost of goods sold paid to freight company.*

College State Personnel
Store employees' salaries and benefits to handle ordering, receiving, pricing, shelving, cashiers, customer service, refund desk, and sending extra textbooks back to the publisher.

FIGURE 4
Where the New Textbook Dollar Goes*

*College store numbers are averages and reflect the most current 2004–2005 data gathered by the National Association of College Stores. Publisher numbers are estimates based on data provided by the Association of American Publishers.

(© 2006 by the National Association of College Stores.)

are then delivered to the students' dorms free-of-charge at the time they request. Refunds are as easy as a phone call or an e-mail. The owners know which textbooks to stock by talking to individual professors to determine which books they require for their classes. Because My Friends' Bookstore has been on campus since Fall 2006, it has made a name for itself as being fast, convenient, and fair to all students. My Friends' Bookstore's online advantage is accomplished by combining the benefits of a traditional college store with the ease and convenience of online purchasing.

HIGHER EDUCATION STATISTICS. There are 4,236 institutions of higher education in the United States. Most colleges have fewer than 10,000 students (see Figure 5), which is ideal for My Friends' Bookstore's current capacity. This size allows a relatively small number of students (2 to 3) to have the ability to keep in contact with professors, apply effective marketing strategies for a small campus, and handle the volume of books sold with relative ease. This smaller size also requires less financing than trying to compete with a college store at a large campus.

FIGURE 5
College Enrollment Statistics

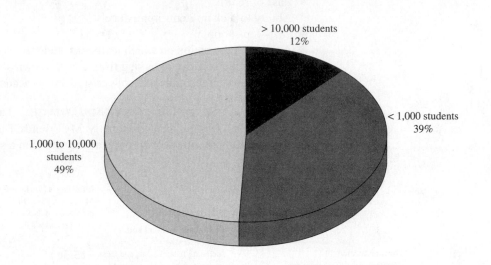

> 10,000 students
12%

< 1,000 students
39%

1,000 to 10,000 students
49%

There were 17.3 million college students in 2004, which represents an increase of 21 percent in enrollment since 1994. The number of female students increased faster (25 percent) than male students (16 percent). The number of young students is also increasing; the number of enrolled students under 25 increased nearly 31 percent since 1990.[11]

An *Almanac 2007–2008* survey of college students published by the *Chronicle of Higher Education* found the following:

- 86 percent were undergraduates
- 61 percent of students attended four-year institutions
- 43 percent were between the ages of 15 and 21
- 32.9 percent were between the ages of 22 and 30
- 56.6 percent were women
- 59.9 percent of the total attended college or university full time[12]

Although the majority of students at higher education institutions are white, nearly 30 percent of students are minorities (see Figure 6). The number of Asian/Pacific Islanders and Hispanics has increased the most (6 percent and 10 percent since 1974, respectively).[13]

COLLEGE STUDENTS' SPENDING IN COLLEGE STORES. Students spent an average of $763 at a college store in 2005–2006, up from $720 in the previous academic year. Spending does not differ greatly between public and private or between two-year and four-year higher education institutions. The College Board reports that students, on average, spent between $850 and $942 on textbooks and supplies in 2005–2006, up from $801 to $904 in 2004–2005.[14] Based on these statistics, Presbyterian College's student population of 1,200 yields $864,000 in potential college store sales per academic year.

FIGURE 6
Ethnic Background of Enrolled Students

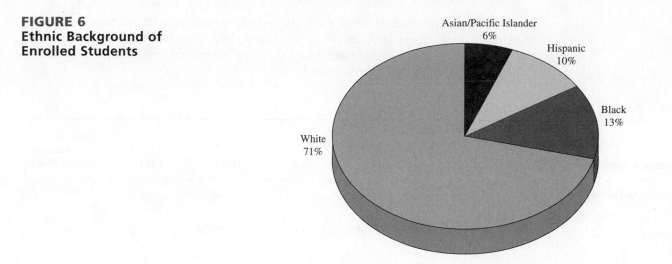

COLLEGE STUDENTS' SPENDING AND THE INTERNET. More than 93 percent of college students, an estimated 16.4 million users, access the Internet in a given month.[15] Nearly 90 percent of college students own a computer, and more than 67 percent have a high-speed Internet connection.[16] College students spend more than $210 billion a year.[17] Approximately 75 percent of students have a job, in which they earn $645 per month on average. Meanwhile, parents contribute an extra $154 a month to their income. This means a typical college student spends $13,000 each year.[18]

College students are price sensitive when they shop. More than 93 percent of college students say that low-price is a determining factor when they make purchases.[19] College students frequently use the Internet to make purchases. One recent survey found that:

- 98 percent of college students have bought something online.
- 54 percent of students have purchased a product because of online advertising.
- 34 percent find online advertising to be the most influential means to get them to learn more about a product.[20]

Another survey found that Facebook, a social-networking site, is the most popular Web site among people ages 17 to 24. Half of females and more than one-third of males list it as their favorite Web site.[21] My Friends' Bookstore began using the marketing power of Facebook during its first semester of operation by creating a My Friends' Bookstore group that Facebook members can join. Within one week, the page had nearly 200 members at a college of 1,200 students. By using Facebook, My Friends' Bookstore sent messages to members about buying and selling textbooks. It also allowed customers to comment on their experiences and list how much money they received for the books they sold to My Friends' Bookstore. Only a few days after the creation of the Facebook group, the number of views of My Friends' Bookstore's Web site (*www.myfriendsbookstore.com*) increased more than 285 percent.

College students spend a significant amount of time researching products and companies before making a purchase, and usually that purchase is online.[22] College students also have "considerable swaying power" over their peers.[23] It is essential to market to students effectively so that they visit the Web site and tell their friends about their experience.

4.1. Market Segmentation

MY FRIENDS' BOOKSTORE'S MARKET ANALYSIS. My Friends' Bookstore has found that it is more profitable to provide books for general education classes rather than for upper-level courses. This is due to the high number of students, on average, that are enrolled in a general education course. The books are also more readily available to buy and sell at Presbyterian College and online because of the high volume of students taking these classes across colleges and universities in the United States. Most Presbyterian College customers, when asked about why they purchased a general education book from My Friends' Bookstore, said that they thought that My Friends' Bookstore would be carrying a high number of general education textbooks, but very few upper-level textbooks. Therefore, focusing on the general education textbook market is essential to provide for the customer's needs.

Market Analysis

Potential Customers	Growth	2007	2008	2009	2010	2011	Compound Annual Growth Rate
Presbyterian College Students	5%	1,200	1,260	1,323	1,389	1,458	4.99%
College Students in United States	2%	16,400,000	16,744,400	17,096,032	17,455,049	17,821,605	2.10%
Total	2.10%	16,401,200	16,745,660	17,097,355	17,456,438	17,823,063	2.10%

4.2. Target Market Segment Strategy

TARGET CUSTOMERS. The primary customer target is Presbyterian College students. Due to PC's small size, marketing campaigns can reach almost everyone on campus with relative ease.

- These customers are predominantly ages 18 to 24.[24]
- There are approximately 1,200 students—48 percent male and 52 percent female.[25]
- 95 percent of students live on campus.[26]
- The average cost for textbooks for each student per semester: $555.00.[27]

As previously mentioned, the typical college student spends $13,000 each year. Therefore, Presbyterian College students spend more than $15,600,000 every year!

The secondary customer target is college students at other universities who purchase textbooks online through Amazon.com or eBay. My Friends' Bookstore's new, proposed Web site will include a cross-listing of all inventory on eBay, thereby reaching a large portion of the online textbook market beyond Presbyterian College.

PRESBYTERIAN COLLEGE MARKETING STRATEGIES. Because of the relatively small size of the campus, My Friends' Bookstore has found that word-of-mouth can be the most effective marketing tool. In addition, the following marketing tools were used during the Fall 2006/Spring 2007 period.

- Flyers
- T-shirts and hoodies
- Direct mail advertisements
- Facebook messaging
- E-mailing customers about updates and special offers

Despite the variety of advertising techniques that the founders used, many students still were unaware of My Friends' Bookstore after the first semester of operation. This was because the founders had made only a small investment in marketing because the first semester of operation was meant to be a trial run for the business. In essence, the founders were engaging in business prototyping to determine whether their idea was viable. The owners will implement new marketing strategies on a larger scale for the next buying and selling period, including more personal advertising and efforts to reach people who have not yet purchased from My Friends' Bookstore. The owners are working to retain the company's existing customer base with special offers for returning customers. To date, 228* students have sold books to My Friends' Bookstore, and 131 students have purchased books from the company.

---

*228 includes some repeat customers; it should also be noted that the $14,000 used to buy back books was used over 3 days rather than the planned 7-day buyback period due to the enormous success of offering better prices for books and the fact that word of the excellent buy-back prices we offer students spread like wildfire across campus.

4.3. Industry Analysis

THE COLLEGE TEXTBOOK INDUSTRY.   The college bookstore industry is unique because sellers for the most part do not get to choose the products they sell. They sell the books that professors choose for their classes. Therefore, the demand of textbooks is governed by professors and students, and the supply of textbooks is provided by publishers and wholesalers. It is the college store's responsibility as a retailer to resell textbooks to college students.[28]

The *NACS 2006 College Store Industry Financial Report* shows that the average gross margin on new textbooks is 22.3 percent, a figure that has not greatly changed since 1989. The average gross margin for used textbooks is considerably higher, reaching 35.1 percent. This is normal compared to other retail industries where annual gross margins range from 19.2 to 50.4 percent. However, there are also higher risks associated with used textbooks, including the fact that stores cannot return them to publishers and that new editions are constantly coming out.[29]

After publisher and store costs, the average college store retains only about 4 cents per dollar on every textbook it sells.[30] My Friends' Bookstore is run out of a college dorm room, and it is able to set lower prices than a typical college bookstore because it has few of these costs (no rent, no utilities, etc.).

Many students try to find the lowest-cost textbooks. Textbook prices have steadily been increasing an average of 6 percent annually, almost twice the rate of inflation.[31] Textbooks sold on the Internet often are much cheaper than at a college store because publishers who sell to international markets must compete locally by setting competitive prices in the areas in which they are selling books. In addition, foreign-based textbook suppliers often set their online prices much lower than their U.S.-based competitors.[32]

College students spend a great deal of their income on online purchases. However, according to a 2005 Student Watch™ survey, only 23 percent of students buy their textbooks online. Moreover, one-third of these online sales are made on college stores' Web sites.[33] Online retailers such as Amazon.com and eBay account for slightly more than 15 percent of college textbook sales. This is a great advantage for a click-and-mortar strategy such as that of My Friends' Bookstore. By providing the on-campus availability and reliability of a traditional college store and the convenience and lower prices of an online store, My Friends' Bookstore has a strong advantage over both of its major competitors.

Major Competitors

1. Traditional college stores (85 percent of the market)
2. Online retailers, such as Amazon.com and eBay (15 percent of the market)

Traditional College Stores. Traditional college stores typically have higher prices than online stores, operate from established physical locations (off-campus in the case of Presbyterian College), and sell a variety of college-related items in addition to textbooks. They make the most profit from used textbooks, student supplies, and "insignia items" such as apparel displaying the name of the institution. The gross profit margins of each category of items are shown below:

	Average	25th Percentile	Median (Mid-Point)	75th Percentile
New texts	22.3%	19.7	22.4	24.5
Custom published materials	23.8%	15.8	23.0	31.7
Used texts	35.1%	33.1	35.8	38.3
Total course books	25.9%	23.3	25.8	28.6
Trade books	26.0%	22.1	28.2	33.7
Medical reference books	22.2%	—	20.5	—
Total trade books	25.5%	20.4	26.7	33.7

(Continued)

	Average	25th Percentile	Median (Mid-Point)	75th Percentile
Total book sales	25.8%	23.4	26.0	28.5
Computer hardware	7.5%	3.3	7.8	12.7
Computer software	16.6%	12.2	17.0	22.2
Computer supplies	26.2%	16.8	26.1	34.5
Total computer products	16.1%	10.7	14.5	22.1
Student supplies	37.9%	33.1	39.0	43.6
Medical instruments	28.1%	—	—	—
Total supplies	36.2%	31.7	38.7	43.5
Insignia items	37.7%	32.4	40.3	44.7
Other merchandise	31.5%	24.9	32.5	40.1
Total non-book sales	31.5%	25.1	31.3	38.6
Total sales	**27.2%**	**23.9**	**27.2**	**30.2**

Source: "2007 College Store Margins," National Association of College Stores, 2007, *www.nacs.org/public/research/margins.asp.* © NACS 2006 College Store Industry Financial Report.

Online Retailers. Amazon.com has seen an increase of 18 percent from 2004 to 2005 in its book, music, and DVD sectors. Nearly one-third of the books sold on Amazon.com are through third-party sellers, such as individuals and businesses. Third-party sellers accounted for more than 28 percent of Amazon.com's total sales in 2005.[34] Although these third-party sellers are direct competitors, My Friends' Bookstore has used Amazon.com to its advantage by selling its remaining inventory through the Web site with great success (and often underpricing its competitors).

eBay has seen an increase in textbook sales of 180 percent per year.[35] An eBay textbook marketing forum has the following to say about the booming textbook industry:

> Each year during the months of August–September and January–February, textbook sales soar on eBay. Textbook sellers have found that they can sell very profitably on eBay because of the high average selling price of a textbook (often $70 to $120 per book!) and the significant turnover of textbooks each college semester. Imagine, every few months there is a new source of supply (the end of a semester when students sell their textbooks) and a new source of demand (the beginning of each semester when students need to buy their textbooks). Because of the large volume of quickly turning inventory, profits can be substantial for sellers in this category.[36]

My Friends' Bookstore also takes advantage of eBay by cross-listing all of its inventory with eBay and competing with that market. Therefore, My Friends' Bookstore's uses its two largest online competitors as marketing channels to reach new customers in new markets.

ANNUAL TEXTBOOK SALES. Students spend more than $6.5 billion on textbooks annually,[37] an amount that makes up nearly 40 percent of total annual book sales of $16.6 billion.[38] Textbook sales are very seasonal, revolving around the beginning and end of academic semesters. As Figure 7 shows, January, August, September, and December produce the highest monthly textbook sales at college bookstores.

4.3.1. COMPETITION AND BUYING PATTERNS. Competition in the online textbook industry is based mainly on three factors:

1. Delivery time
2. Price
3. Ability to verify that the book is the right one for a class[39]

Most textbook buyers want to have their books delivered as fast as possible.[40] During its first selling period, My Friends' Bookstore noticed that more than half of all buyers on Amazon.com opted to pay for expedited shipping ($5.99 versus $3.49). This need for speedy delivery occurs

FIGURE 7
2005 Bookstore Sales in Billions of $

Source: National Association of College Stores, 2007.

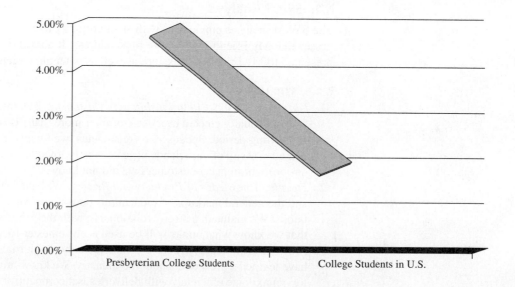

because most students do not shop for their textbooks until after they have attended a class and learned about the materials that are required for the course. My Friends' Bookstore can capitalize on all of these factors. Textbooks for classes are determined by talking to professors, the price is set to be competitive with both college stores and online markets, and books are delivered in person, thus cutting out shipping time and costs.

Reputation is also an important factor. My Friends' Bookstore is located on campus; it is currently building a strong reputation with Presbyterian College students. Likewise, on Amazon.com, My Friends' Bookstore has 96 percent positive ratings, which lets buyers know that the seller is reliable.

The actual product, textbooks, is bought based on condition. Demand for a textbook is based solely on whether a professor requires it for a class. Therefore, students do not shop around for different textbooks but instead search for the best price and condition. Therefore, My Friends' Bookstore emphasizes buying textbooks in good condition because poor condition books sell for much less than a "like new" book.

Because of the high turnover of inventory, it is essential to keep customers coming back so that they will buy and sell books. The textbook industry is unique because it also buys from the same customers to whom it sells; therefore, college stores must focus on keeping customers satisfied or they will lose twice the amount of business a normal store would lose.

FIGURE 8
Market Analysis (C.A.G.R.)

5. Web Plan Summary

My Friends' Bookstore's Web site is the source for all of the business's sales. Its e-commerce strategy is based on instilling trust in potential customers and providing easy access, simple payment options, and detailed information about the books that are required for each class. The Web site is PayPal verified, provides the ability to pay with a credit card, and lists all the books required for every class in every department on campus. In addition, prices for every book are clearly listed and, when available, the price of the campus bookstore is also listed. We also show the percentage difference in our prices and those of our competitors to illustrate our low prices.

My Friends' Bookstore contacts customers mainly through e-mail, but a phone line is available for customers who prefer to place orders over the phone. A professional company runs the Web site and provides a shopping cart, credit card payment, and inventory uploading. The inventory listed on our Web site is also cross-listed with eBay so that the company reaches the online textbook market without any extra effort.

5.1. Web Site Marketing Strategy

Our online marketing strategy involves listing all of the benefits and conveniences of our business to encourage students to buy from us. We clearly list all of our prices and will soon include pictures next to the books that we list for sale to help students verify they are buying the right book. Talking to each professor to determine required textbooks for each course is essential, and this information is listed online so that students can see the books they need to buy before they ever attend class. Prices and price differences are listed to show customers the benefit of buying from a cheaper, online bookstore.

Our online business allows us to process a virtually unlimited number of orders with relative ease. We simply deliver the books, implement the proper marketing strategy, and address customer concerns.

5.2. Development Requirements

Ongoing Costs:

- Web site fee, monthly: $24.95
- Yearly domain registration fee: $15.00
- Credit card and PayPal commissions: variable (example: $1.39 + 3 percent of price)
- Site design: Free (done by ourselves)
- Site updates: Free (done by ourselves)
- Traffic reports: Included in Web site fee
- Shopping cart, inventory, and eBay access: Included in Web site fee

6. Strategy and Implementation Summary

6.1. SWOT Analysis

The SWOT analysis provides us with an opportunity to examine the internal strengths and weaknesses that My Friends' Bookstore must address. It also allows us to examine the opportunities presented to My Friends' Bookstore as well as potential threats.

6.1.1. STRENGTHS

1. *Close and Personal Relationship with Customers.* The owners of My Friends' Bookstore have personally greeted every one of their more than 300 customers during the first buying and selling period. Because we are students, we know our fellow students better than anyone else. Many of our friends have been very loyal to us, and their positive word-of-mouth has brought in many customers we did not know.
2. *Detailed Knowledge of Products and Pricing.* We have learned how prices fluctuate online and the general markups of the campus bookstore. We also buy and sell our own textbooks. We maintain a strong relationship with the professors at Presbyterian College so that we know what books will be used each semester for each course.
3. *Previous Experience.* We have conducted a thorough trial run of the bookstore business and have learned a great deal about the industry. We know how to manage cash flow and inventory, maximize efficiency with deliveries, set competitive prices for books, and market to

students. All partners have gained a great deal of knowledge about running a bookstore efficiently.

4. *Strong Reputation at Presbyterian College and Online.* We are known on campus as having fair prices and looking out for students' best interests. Many students strongly and actively support our endeavor and favor us over the campus bookstore based on principle alone. On Amazon.com, we have a positive feedback rating of nearly 100 percent, a rating that ensures potential customers who may not be familiar with us that we are reliable and honest sellers.

5. *Complementary Skills of Founding Partners.* Dana Waters is a business management major, and is currently enrolled in a small business management course to help improve My Friends' Bookstore. He has a vast knowledge of computers, accounting, pricing, and customer service. Scott Mumbauer is a music major with a minor in Business Administration. He helped to secure the financial backing, which allowed the business to conduct a successful trial run. Jonathan Choi handles the company's pricing and specializes in managing and updating the My Friends' Bookstore Web site.

6. *Sound Financial Backing.* The founders launched My Friends' Bookstore with capital from family members. When the company's rapid growth quickly outstripped the capacity of family financing, the owners presented their business plan to the Palmetto Bank, which granted the business a $15,000 unsecured line of credit. The company used the entire line of credit, repaid it, and now has increased its line of credit to $25,000.

7. *Cost Leadership Strategy.* Because prices are so important to students, pursuing a cost leadership strategy is key to the company's success. This strategy allows us to maintain a price advantage over competitors. Our low costs allow us to underprice competitors and still generate a reasonable profit.

8. *A Reputation for Providing Convenience for Customers.* My Friends' Bookstore combines the best of both worlds. It provides the convenience of shopping online 24/7 and paying instantly with a credit card, while providing fast dorm room delivery. This gives the company a competitive advantage over traditional college stores with limited hours and online stores that require shipping times and fees.

9. *Recognition That My Friends' Bookstore is not an Official College Store.* Because we are not affiliated with Presbyterian College, we do not have to pay commissions to the college like the campus bookstore does. We also have the freedom to operate however we see fit, and we are not under the influence of the college.

10. *Potential to Expand Market Share.* Many potential customers have not discovered us yet. As we increase our marketing efforts, we will be able to increase our share of the market.

6.1.2. WEAKNESSES

1. *Limited Time of Partners.* In addition to being entrepreneurs, we are also full-time students. The buyback period is in the middle of exam week, and we must hire friends to help us run the bookstore and limit the strain it puts on our schedules.

2. *Not an Official College Store.* This is both a strength and a weakness. As a weakness, Presbyterian College cannot provide us with funding, aid, or guidance. We must talk to professors about textbooks and gather information ourselves.

3. *Limited Storage Capacity.* We are limited by the size of our dorm room. We have converted one entire dorm room into temporary storage for textbooks until they are sold. We are exploring the possibility of renting a larger storage space not far from campus.

4. *Operating Under the Authority of the College's Residence Life Office, Administration, and Campus Police.* We are allowed to operate on college grounds only as long as we abide by the rules set by the college. Because of the college's contractual relationship with the company that operates the "official" bookstore, we may have to move our operations off campus.

6.1.3. OPPORTUNITIES.

The most important opportunity in the Presbyterian College market is that the campus bookstore is moving off campus. Its new location requires students to drive downtown to buy and sell textbooks. Therefore, My Friends' Bookstore's convenience will be much more beneficial to Presbyterian College students who do not want to drive downtown.

Another opportunity is the potential to expand our sales to both Presbyterian College and online purchases. As college enrollment increases along with textbook prices, the opportunity for profit increases as well.

6.1.4. THREATS. Threats to My Friends' Bookstore include:

1. *Used Textbooks Becoming Outdated when a New Edition Comes Out.* This is especially dangerous over the summer because we must wait four months until our inventory will begin selling again (with the exception of summer school).
2. *Competition from the Campus Bookstore.* The campus bookstore attempts to compete with our convenience and/or low prices.
3. *Lower Prices from Online Sellers That We Cannot Match.* Occasionally we must list some books at prices that are lower than the purchase price of the book. This usually happens when new editions come out, and the market is "flooded" with older editions at very low prices.
4. *Theft.* My Friends' Bookstore stores its books in a dorm room, making security essential. Also, large amounts of cash are necessary to buy back books, and this may attract thieves.

6.2. Competitive Edge

My Friends' Bookstore has a competitive edge because it combines the best benefits of traditional college stores and online retailers: convenience, ease of use, 24/7 operation with a Web Site, fast and free delivery, and personal knowledge of the books required for each class are a few of the many examples.

My Friends' Bookstore prides itself on customer service and satisfaction. Our goal is to provide not only a monetary benefit of saving students money, but also the intangible benefit of dealing with students who know and understand them. We strive to provide for their best interests while still making profits.

Our reputation as a high quality company will continue to spread across Presbyterian College and the online market. Our superior customer service is unmatched by any of our competitors. Therefore, our market share should steadily increase for many years to come.

6.3. Marketing Strategy

Our marketing strategy focuses on the following:

- Offering low prices
- Providing all of the right books for each class
- Building a solid reputation as a good company with total customer satisfaction
- Continuing to increase marketing to reach new customers in both the Presbyterian College and online textbook markets

6.4. Sales Strategy

Our sales strategy focuses on the following:

- We will offer specials to encourage people to buy and sell books from us.
- There is very little "convincing" customers to buy books. Because our business is conducted entirely online, the best way to close sales is to be up front about the benefits our Web site and bookstore offer customers.
- Order processing involves sending confirmation e-mails to customers, fixing any problems that occur along the way, delivering books in a timely fashion, and above all making sure the customer is satisfied.
- Inventory rosters must be as accurate as possible to ensure that we do not accept orders for books that we do not have in inventory.
- We will offer a 14-day return/exchange policy to build trust with our customers and maintain retention and loyalty.

6.4.1. SALES FORECAST. The sales forecast is based on an actual net profit margin of 20 to 25 percent, although our goal is to reach 30 percent profit. By investing all of the profits back into the business, we hope to attain a steady 30 percent growth in sales. Sales are based on the

typical sales period for textbooks, mainly August and September, and January and February. For each season, we forecast 75 percent of sales occurring in the first month, and the remaining 25 percent occurring in the second month. Virtually all of our expenses are variable costs; therefore, the company's cost of goods sold increases at about 30 percent, the same percentage as the increase in sales.

Sales Forecast

	FY 2008	FY 2009	FY 2010
Sales			
Textbooks	$77,460	$147,140	$204,210
Total sales	$77,460	$147,140	$204,210

	FY 2008	FY 2009	FY 2010
Direct cost of sales			
Textbook purchases	$52,000	$94,000	$134,000
Subtotal direct cost of sales	$52,000	$94,000	$134,000

FIGURE 9
Sales Monthly

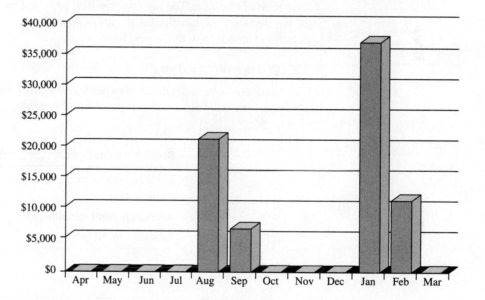

FIGURE 10
Sales by Year

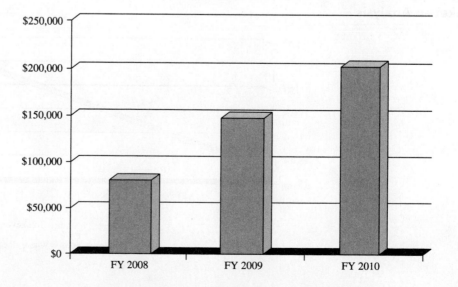

7. Management Summary

My Friends' Bookstore is comprised of:

- 3 full-time partners
- Up to 5 part-time employees who work during peak volume periods

Additional partners may be added as the business grows in size.

7.1. Personnel Plan

Personnel are needed only during peak volume sales and buyback periods and when the owners are otherwise unable to operate the business themselves. These costs are based on hourly wages, which are $6.50 per hour.

8. Financial Plan

We expect our business to grow at a very rapid rate of 30 percent, which is limited by the amount of financing that we can attain for the business through investments and loans. We also plan to reinvest all profit back into the business to further expand our company's growth.

8.1. Important Assumptions

Sales occur entirely through our online storefront; therefore, we incur no sales tax. All loans are for a term of one-year. The interest-free loan provided by a private lender can be paid back over the course of several months, but the financial forecasts assume that the amount will be paid back in full one month prior to the next loan.

8.2. Breakeven Analysis

Our business has virtually no fixed expenses other than Web site fees and advertising. Therefore, our breakeven point is very low, at just $100 per month.

Breakeven Analysis	
Monthly revenue breakeven	$100
Assumptions	
Average percent variable cost	67%
Estimated monthly fixed cost	$ 33

FIGURE 11
Breakeven Analysis

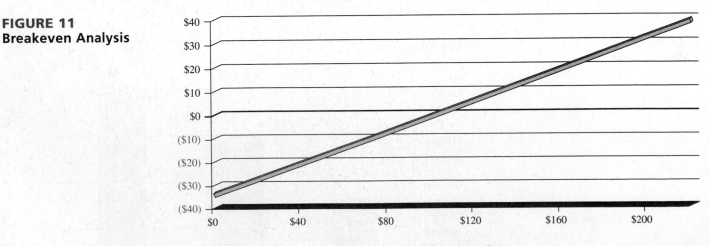

Monthly Breakeven Point

Breakeven point = where line intersects with 0

8.3. Projected Profit and Loss

We expect to see rapid growth in our sales as we continue to finance our company through loans and retained earnings, which will allow us to sell more textbooks. A 20 to 25 percent net profit margin also allows a significant amount of profit to be reinvested into the company, which further increases the cash available to buy textbooks. Because of the highly seasonal nature of our business, the company experiences huge swings in profit on a monthly basis (see Figure 12), but its annual profit increases at a steady rate (see Figure 13).

Pro Forma Profit and Loss

	FY 2008	FY 2009	FY 2010
Sales	$77,460	$147,140	$204,210
Direct costs of goods	$52,000	$ 94,000	$134,000
Other costs of goods	$ 0	$ 0	$ 0
Cost of goods sold	$52,000	$ 94,000	$134,000
Gross margin	$25,460	$ 53,140	$ 70,210
Gross margin %	32.87%	36.12%	34.38%
Expenses			
Payroll	$ 0	$ 0	$ 0
Marketing/promotion	$ 80	$ 90	$ 100
Depreciation	$ 0	$ 0	$ 0
Web site fee	$ 300	$ 300	$ 300
Domain registration fee	$ 15	$ 15	$ 15
Total operating expenses	$ 395	$ 405	$ 415
Profit before interest and taxes	$25,065	$ 52,735	$ 69,795
Earnings before interest, taxes and depreciation	$25,065	$ 52,735	$ 69,795
Interest expense	$ 1,039	$ 2,133	$ 3,467
Taxes incurred	$ 7,208	$ 15,181	$ 19,899
Net profit	$16,818	$ 35,421	$ 46,430
Net profit/sales	21.71%	24.07%	22.74%

FIGURE 12
Profit Monthly

FIGURE 13
Profit Yearly

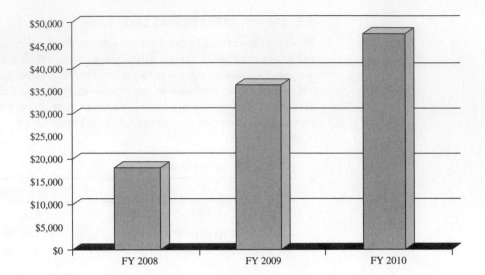

FIGURE 14
Gross Margin Monthly

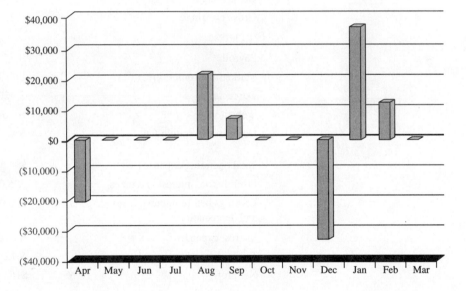

FIGURE 15
Gross Margin Yearly

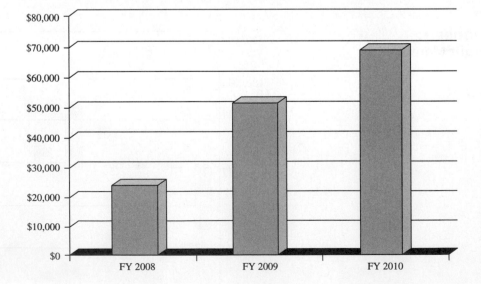

8.4. Projected Cash Flow

Cash flow is also very important due to the high seasonality of the business. As the business grows, its yearly cash balance greatly increases. Some months show a negative cash flow during periods of low sales, but the monthly cash balance stays relatively high (see Figure 16).

Pro Forma Cash Flow

	FY 2008	FY 2009	FY 2010
Cash received			
Cash from operations			
Cash sales	$ 77,460	$147,140	$204,210
Subtotal cash from operations	$ 77,460	$147,140	$204,210
Additional cash received			
Sales tax, VAT, HST/GST received	$ 0	$ 0	$ 0
New current borrowing	$ 0	$ 0	$ 0
New other liabilities (interest-free)	$ 20,000	$ 20,000	$ 20,000
New long-term liabilities	$ 32,000	$ 74,000	$114,000
Sales of other current assets	$ 0	$ 0	$ 0
Sales of long-term assets	$ 0	$ 0	$ 0
New investment received	$ 0	$ 0	$ 0
Subtotal cash received	$129,460	$241,140	$338,210
Expenditures	FY 2008	FY 2009	FY 2010
Expenditures from operations			
Cash spending	$ 0	$ 0	$ 0
Bill payments	$ 87,568	$126,358	$178,711
Subtotal spent on operations	$ 87,568	$126,358	$178,711
Additional cash spent			
Sales tax, VAT, HST/GST paid out	$ 0	$ 0	$ 0
Principal repayment of current borrowing	$ 0	$ 0	$ 0
Other liabilities principal repayment	$ 20,000	$ 20,000	$ 20,000
Long-term liabilities principal repayment	$ 17,335	$ 60,667	$100,667
Purchase other current assets	$ 0	$ 0	$ 0
Purchase long-term assets	$ 0	$ 0	$ 0
Dividends	$ 0	$ 0	$ 0
Subtotal cash spent	$124,903	$207,024	$299,377
Net cash flow	$ 4,557	$ 34,116	$ 38,833
Cash balance	$ 12,847	$ 46,963	$ 85,795

FIGURE 16
Cash Flow

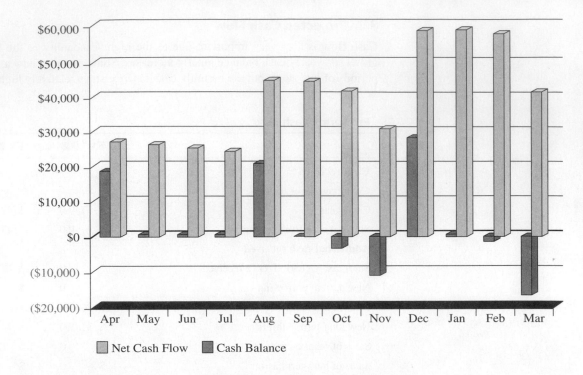

8.5. Projected Balance Sheet

Our balance sheet shows that our business will experience rapid growth, leading to a significant increase in inventory, sales, and long-term liabilities in the form of loans. Although liabilities are projected to increase throughout the next several years, capital and retained earnings are also projected to increase. Our net worth is expected to increase substantially as our business becomes more profitable, thus allowing more retained earnings to be reinvested into the business and further expanding the financial capacity of the business.

Pro Forma Balance Sheet

	FY 2008	FY 2009	FY 2010
Assets			
Current assets			
Cash	$12,847	$ 46,963	$ 85,795
Inventory	$32,000	$ 57,846	$ 82,462
Other current assets	$ 100	$ 100	$ 100
Total current assets	$44,947	$104,909	$168,357
Long-term assets			
Long-term assets	$ 0	$ 0	$ 0
Accumulated depreciation	$ 0	$ 0	$ 0
Total long-term assets	$ 0	$ 0	$ 0
Total assets	$44,947	$104,909	$168,357

(Continued)

	FY 2008	FY 2009	FY 2010
Liabilities and capital			
Current liabilities			
Accounts payable	$ 100	$ 11,307	$ 14,991
Current borrowing	$ 0	$ 0	$ 0
Other current liabilities	$ 5,500	$ 5,500	$ 5,500
Subtotal current liabilities	$ 5,600	$ 16,807	$ 20,491
Long-term liabilities	$14,665	$ 27,999	$ 41,332
Total liabilities	$20,265	$ 44,805	$ 61,823
Paid-in capital	$15,500	$ 15,500	$ 15,500
Retained earnings	($7,636)	$ 9,182	$ 44,604
Earnings	$16,818	$ 35,421	$ 46,430
Total capital	$24,682	$ 60,104	$106,533
Total liabilities and capital	$44,947	$104,909	$168,357
Net Worth	$24,682	$ 60,104	$106,533

8.6. Business Ratios

Our business ratios are included and compared to a retail bookstore.

Ratio Analysis

	FY 2008	FY 2009	FY 2010	Industry Profile
Sales growth	362.64%	89.96%	38.79%	6.22%
Percentage of total assets				
Inventory	71.19%	55.14%	48.98%	28.92%
Other current assets	0.22%	0.10%	0.06%	28.31%
Total current assets	100.00%	100.00%	100.00%	84.87%
Long-term assets	0.00%	0.00%	0.00%	15.13%
Total assets	100.00%	100.00%	100.00%	100.00%
Current liabilities	12.46%	16.02%	12.17%	45.48%
Long-term liabilities	32.63%	26.69%	24.55%	15.42%
Total liabilities	45.09%	42.71%	36.72%	60.90%
Net worth	54.91%	57.29%	63.28%	39.10%
Percentage of sales				
Sales	100.00%	100.00%	100.00%	100.00%
Gross margin	32.87%	36.12%	34.38%	12.95%
Selling, general, & administrative expenses	11.16%	12.04%	11.64%	6.26%
Advertising expenses	0.10%	0.06%	0.05%	0.54%
Profit before interest and taxes	32.36%	35.84%	34.18%	0.94%

(*Continued*)

Ratio Analysis   (*Continued*)

	FY 2008	FY 2009	FY 2010	Industry Profile
Main ratios				
Current	8.03	6.24	8.22	1.62
Quick	2.31	2.80	4.19	0.85
Total debt to total assets	45.09%	42.71%	36.72%	65.08%
Pre-tax return on net worth	97.34%	84.19%	62.26%	2.82%
Pre-tax return on assets	53.45%	48.23%	39.40%	8.08%

	FY 2008	FY 2009	FY 2010	
Additional ratios				
Net profit margin	21.71%	24.07%	22.74%	n/a
Return on equity	68.14%	58.93%	43.58%	n/a
Activity ratios				
Inventory turnover	2.17	2.09	1.91	n/a
Accounts payable turnover	880.08	12.17	12.17	n/a
Payment days	27	15	26	n/a
Total asset turnover	1.72	1.40	1.21	n/a
Debt ratios				
Debt to net worth	0.82	0.75	0.58	n/a
Current liab. to liab.	0.28	0.38	0.33	n/a
Liquidity ratios				
Net working capital	$39,348	$88,102	$147,865	n/a
Interest coverage	24.13	24.72	20.13	n/a
Additional ratios				
Assets to sales	0.58	0.71	0.82	n/a
Current debt/total assets	12%	16%	12%	n/a
Acid test	2.31	2.80	4.19	n/a
Sales/net worth	3.14	2.45	1.92	n/a
Dividend payout	0.00	0.00	0.00	n/a

Sales Forecast

		Apr-07	May-07	Jun-07	Jul-07	Aug-07	Sep-07	Oct-07	Nov-07	Dec-07	Jan-08	Feb-08	Mar-08
Sales													
Textbooks	0%	$ 0	$ 0	$ 0	$ 0	$21,450	$7,150	$ 0	$ 0	$ 0	$36,660	$12,200	$ 0
Other	0%	$ 0	$ 0	$ 0	$ 0	$ 0	$ 0	$ 0	$ 0	$ 0	$ 0	$ 0	$ 0
Total sales		$ 0	$ 0	$ 0	$ 0	$21,450	$7,150	$ 0	$ 0	$ 0	$36,660	$12,200	$ 0
Direct cost of sales													
Textbook purchases		$20,000	$ 0	$ 0	$ 0	$ 0	$ 0	$ 0	$ 0	$32,000	$ 0	$ 0	$ 0
Other		$ 0	$ 0	$ 0	$ 0	$ 0	$ 0	$ 0	$ 0	$ 0	$ 0	$ 0	$ 0
Subtotal direct cost of sales		$20,000	$ 0	$ 0	$ 0	$ 0	$ 0	$ 0	$ 0	$32,000	$ 0	$ 0	$ 0

Pro Forma Cash Flow

		Apr-07	May-07	Jun-07	Jul-07	Aug-07	Sep-07	Oct-07	Nov-07	Dec-07	Jan-08	Feb-08	Mar-08
Cash received													
Cash from operations													
Cash sales		$0	$0	$0	$0	$21,450	$7,150	$0	$0	$0	$36,660	$12,200	$0
Subtotal cash from operations		$0	$0	$0	$0	$21,450	$7,150	$0	$0	$0	$36,660	$12,200	$0
Additional cash received													
Sales Tax, VAT, HST/GST received	0.00%	$0	$0	$0	$0	$0	$0	$0	$0	$0	$0	$0	$0
New current borrowing		$0	$0	$0	$0	$0	$0	$0	$0	$0	$0	$0	$0
New other liabilities (interest-free)		$10,000	$0	$0	$0	$0	$0	$0	$0	$10,000	$0	$0	$0
New long-term liabilities		$10,000	$0	$0	$0	$0	$0	$0	$0	$22,000	$0	$0	$0
Sales of other current assets		$0	$0	$0	$0	$0	$0	$0	$0	$0	$0	$0	$0
Sales of long-term assets		$0	$0	$0	$0	$0	$0	$0	$0	$0	$0	$0	$0
New investment received		$0	$0	$0	$0	$0	$0	$0	$0	$0	$0	$0	$0
Subtotal cash received		$20,000	$0	$0	$0	$21,450	$7,150	$0	$0	$32,000	$36,660	$12,200	$0

	Apr-07	May-07	Jun-07	Jul-07	Aug-07	Sep-07	Oct-07	Nov-07	Dec-07	Jan-08	Feb-08	Mar-08
Expenditures												
Expenditures from operations												
Cash spending	$ 0	$ 0	$ 0	$ 0	$ 0	$ 0	$ 0	$ 0	$ 0	$ 0	$ 0	$ 0
Bill payments	$ 970	$ 71	$ 66	$ 61	$ 271	$ 6,357	$ 2,120	$ 42	$ 1,198	$33,783	$ 10,901	$ 3,656
Subtotal spent on operations	$ 970	$ 71	$ 66	$ 61	$ 271	$ 6,357	$ 2,120	$ 42	$ 1,198	$33,783	$ 10,901	$ 3,656
Additional cash spent												
Sales Tax, VAT, HST/GST paid out	$ 0	$ 0	$ 0	$ 0	$ 0	$ 0	$ 0	$ 0	$ 0	$ 0	$ 0	$ 0
Principal repayment of current borrowing	$ 0	$ 0	$ 0	$ 0	$ 0	$ 0	$ 0	$ 0	$ 0	$ 0	$ 0	$ 0
Other liabilities principal repayment	$ 0	$ 0	$ 0	$ 0	$ 0	$ 0	$ 0	$ 10,000	$ 0	$ 0	$ 0	$ 10,000
Long-term liabilities principal repayment	$ 833	$ 833	$ 833	$ 833	$ 833	$ 833	$ 833	$ 833	$ 2,667	$ 2,667	$ 2,667	$ 2,667
Purchase other current assets	$ 0	$ 0	$ 0	$ 0	$ 0	$ 0	$ 0	$ 0	$ 0	$ 0	$ 0	$ 0
Purchase long-term assets	$ 0	$ 0	$ 0	$ 0	$ 0	$ 0	$ 0	$ 0	$ 0	$ 0	$ 0	$ 0
Dividends	$ 0	$ 0	$ 0	$ 0	$ 0	$ 0	$ 0	$ 0	$ 0	$ 0	$ 0	$ 0
Subtotal cash spent	$ 1,804	$28,976	$ 899	$ 894	$ 1,105	$ 7,190	$ 2,953	$ 10,875	$ 3,865	$36,450	$ 13,568	$ 16,323
Net cash flow	$18,196	($ 904)	($ 899)	($ 894)	$20,345	($ 40)	($ 2,953)	($10,875)	$28,135	$ 210	($ 1,368)	($ 16,323)
Cash balance	$26,486	$25,582	$24,683	$23,789	$44,134	$44,094	$ 41,141	$ 30,266	$58,401	$58,611	$ 57,243	$ 40,920

Endnotes

1. "Higher Education Retail Market Facts and Figures 2007," National Association of College Stores, *www.nacs.org/public/research/higher_ed_retail.asp*.
2. Ibid.
3. Ibid.
4. Ibid.
5. "FAQ on Used Textbooks." National Association of College Stores, June 2007, *www.nacs.org/common/research/faq_usedbooks.pdf*.
6. "Higher Education Retail Market Facts and Figures 2007," National Association of College Stores, *www.nacs.org/public/research/higher_ed_retail.asp*.
7. Ibid.
8. Ibid.
9. "Fast Facts," National Center for Education Statistics, *www.nces.ed.gov/fastfacts/display.asp?id=98*.
10. "Higher Education Retail Market Facts and Figures 2007," National Association of College Stores, *www.nacs.org/public/research/higher_ed_retail.asp*.
11. "Fast Facts," National Center for Education Statistics, *www.nces.ed.gov/fastfacts/display.asp?id=98*.
12. "Higher Education Retail Market Facts and Figures 2007," National Association of College Stores, *www.nacs.org/public/research/higher_ed_retail.asp*.
13. Robyn Greenspan, "College Students Surf, Spend," ClickZ, February 13, 2003, *www.clickz.com/showPage.html?page=1583871*.
14. "College Students Tote $122 Billion in Spending Power Back to Campus This Year," Harris Interactive, August 14, 2004, *www.harrisinteractive.com/news/allnewsbydate.asp?NewsID=835*.
15. Robyn Greenspan, "College Students Surf, Spend," ClickZ, February 13, 2003, *www.clickz.com/showPage.html?page=1583871*.
16. "College Students Tote $122 Billion in Spending Power Back to Campus This Year," Harris Interactive, August 14, 2004, *www.harrisinteractive.com/news/allnewsbydate.asp?NewsID=835*.
17. "Higher Education Retail Market Facts and Figures 2007," National Association of College Stores, *www.nacs.org/public/research/higher_ed_retail.asp*.
18. "Online Advertising Motivates College Students to Buy," *MarketingVox*, February 8, 2006, *www.marketingvox.com/archives/2006/02/08/online_advertising_motivates_college_students_to_buy/*.
19. "College Students Pick Facebook as Favorite Site," *MarketingVox*, December 4, 2006, *www.marketingvox.com/archives/2006/12/04/college-students-pick-facebook-as-favorite-site/*.
20. "Online Advertising Motivates College Students to Buy," *MarketingVox*, February 8, 2006, *www.marketingvox.com/archives/2006/02/08/online_advertising_motivates_college_students_to_buy/*.
21. "College Students Tote $122 Billion in Spending Power Back to Campus This Year," Harris Interactive, August 14, 2004, *www.harrisinteractive.com/news/allnewsbydate.asp?NewsID=835*.
22. "FAQ on College Textbooks," National Association of College Stores, June 2007, *www.nacs.org/common/research/faq_textbooks.pdf*.
23. Ibid.
24. Ibid.
25. Ibid.
26. Ibid.
27. Morris Rosenthal, "North American Book Market," Foner Books, *www.fonerbooks.com/booksale.htm*.
28. "EBay Workshop: Selling Textbooks on eBay," eBay.com, *forums.ebay.com/db2/thread.jspa?threadID=410167803*.
29. Ibid.
30. "Higher Education Retail Market Facts and Figures 2007," National Association of College Stores, *www.nacs.org/public/research/higher_ed_retail.asp*.
31. "EBay Workshop: Selling Textbooks on eBay," eBay.com, *forums.ebay.com/db2/thread.jspa?threadID=410167803*.
32. Ibid.

Strategic Management and the Entrepreneur

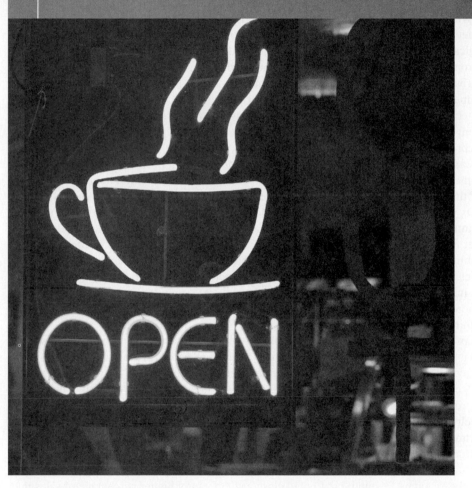

Learning Objectives

Upon completion of this chapter, you will be able to:

1 Understand the importance of strategic management to a small business.

2 Explain why and how a small business must create a competitive advantage in the market.

3 Develop a strategic plan for a business using the nine steps in the strategic planning process.

4 Discuss the characteristics of three basic strategies: low-cost, differentiation, and focus.

5 Understand the importance of controls such as the balanced scorecard in the planning process.

To accomplish great things, we must not only act but also dream;

not only plan but also believe.

—Anatole France

Strategy without tactics is the slowest route to victory. Tactics

without strategy is the noise before defeat.

—Sun Tzu

From Chapter 2 of *Effective Small Business Management: An Entrepreneurial Approach*, 10/e. Norman M. Scarborough.

Few activities in the life of a small business are as vital—or as overlooked—as that of developing a strategy for success. Too often, entrepreneurs brimming with optimism and enthusiasm launch businesses destined for failure because their founders never stop to define a workable strategy that sets them apart from their competition. Because entrepreneurs tend to be people of action, they often find the process of developing a strategy dull and unnecessary. Their tendency is to start a business, try several approaches, and see what works. Without a cohesive plan of action, however, these entrepreneurs have as much chance of building a successful business as a defense contractor attempting to build a jet fighter without blueprints. Companies that lack clear strategies may achieve success in the short-run, but as soon as competitive conditions stiffen or an unanticipated threat arises, they usually "hit the wall" and fold. Without a basis for differentiating itself from a pack of similar competitors, the best a company can hope for is mediocrity in the marketplace.

In today's global competitive environment, any business, large or small, that is not thinking and acting strategically is extremely vulnerable. Every business is exposed to the forces of a rapidly changing competitive environment, and in the future small business executives can expect even greater change and uncertainty. From sweeping political changes around the planet and rapid technological advances to more intense competition and newly emerging global markets, the business environment has become more turbulent and challenging for entrepreneurs. Although this market turbulence creates many challenges for small businesses, it also creates opportunities for those companies that have in place strategies to capitalize on them. Small companies now have access to technology, tools, and techniques that once were available only to large companies, enabling them to achieve significant, sometimes momentous, results.

Entrepreneurs' willingness to create change, to experiment with new business models, and to break traditional rules have become more important than ever. Rather than merely respond to the chaos in the environment, small companies that are prepared actually can *create* the disruptions that revolutionize their industries and gain a competitive edge. Just as sales of music CDs were at their peak, Steve Jobs' Apple Computer revolutionized the music industry with the introduction of the iPod. Apple now has a commanding 70 percent market share in the market for MP3 players, and its iTunes Music Store became the world's leading music retailer within 5 years of its launch, selling more than 8 *billion* song downloads. In addition, Apple does not wait on rivals to render its iPod products obsolete with better, more powerful versions; instead, the company disrupts its own products! Apple introduced the iPod Touch just 24 months after it released the highly successful iPod Nano and continues that pattern today with both the iPod and the iPhone.[1]

Perhaps the biggest change entrepreneurs face is unfolding now: the shift in the world's economy from a base of *financial* to *intellectual* capital. Intellectual capital is the knowledge and information a company acquires and uses to create a competitive edge in its market segment. "Knowledge is no longer just a factor of production," says futurist Alvin Toffler. "It is the *critical* factor of production."[2] Most small companies have significant stockpiles of valuable knowledge that can help them gain an edge in the marketplace—from customers' purchasing patterns to how one department uses Excel to forecast product demand. The key is putting it to good use. Norm Brodsky, a serial entrepreneur who founded eight successful businesses, discovered the importance of intellectual capital early on in his business career, and it is a competitive advantage that he continues to rely on today. "I found that I could close a significantly higher percentage of sales than my competitors simply by knowing more than they did about the customer, its representatives, and every other aspect of the deal," he says. "That's still true today." Brodsky explains what happens at his records storage business before a potential customer comes on site.

We prepare thoroughly. Before the customer's people arrive, I go online and find out as much as I can about the organization's structure, mission, and history. My salespeople give me a full briefing on the visitors I'm about to meet—what they're like as individuals, whom else they're considering, how the decision will be made, and so on. I tailor my presentation accordingly.

The result of Brodsky's use of the knowledge in his company is a closing rate that exceeds 95 percent for all prospective customers who visit his company's facility.[3]

Unfortunately, much of the knowledge that resides in many small companies sits idle or is shared only by happenstance on an informal basis. This scenario is the equivalent of having a bank account without a checkbook or an ATM card to access it! The key is learning how to utilize the knowledge a company accumulates over time as a strategic resource and as a competitive weapon. **Knowledge management** is the practice of gathering, organizing, and disseminating the collective wisdom and experience of a company's employees for the purpose of strengthening its competitive position. "Organizations that harness knowledge and put it to good use are able to gain a clear competitive advantage," says Eric Lesser, a consultant at IBM's Institute for Knowledge Management.[4] Knowledge management enables companies to get more innovative products to market faster, respond to customers' needs more quickly, and solve (or avoid altogether) problems more efficiently. Because of their size and simplicity, small businesses have an advantage over large companies when it comes to managing knowledge. Knowledge management requires a small company to identify what its workers know, incorporate that knowledge into the business and distribute it where it is needed, and leverage it into more useful knowledge.

Increasingly, a company's intellectual capital is likely to be the source of its competitive advantage in the marketplace. **Intellectual capital** has three components:[5]

1. *Human capital*—the talents, skills, and abilities of a company's workforce.
2. *Structural capital*—the accumulated knowledge and experience in its industry and in business in general that a company possesses. It can take many forms, including processes, software, patents, copyrights, and, perhaps most important, the knowledge and experience of the people in a company.
3. *Customer capital*—the established customer base, positive reputation, ongoing relationships, and goodwill a company builds up over time with its customers.

Increasingly, entrepreneurs are recognizing that the capital stored in these three areas forms the foundation of their ability to compete effectively and that they must manage this intangible capital base carefully. Every business uses all three components in its strategy, but the emphasis they place on each component varies.

The rules of the competitive game of business are undergoing dramatic change. Entrepreneurs must recognize that the business forecast calls for continued chaos and disruption with the certainty of new opportunities and a slight chance of disaster. To be successful in this environment, entrepreneurs can no longer do things in the way they've always done them. They must learn to be initiators and agents of change. The late management guru Peter Drucker said that the key challenge for managers in the twenty-first century is leading change and that doing so successfully requires leaders "to abandon yesterday," leaving behind the products, services, management styles, marketing techniques, and other ideas that no longer work.[6] Unfortunately, for most managers, abandoning yesterday is no easy task because it is what they know and are most comfortable with.

Fortunately, successful entrepreneurs have at their disposal a powerful weapon to cope with a chaotic environment filled with disarray and constant disruptions: the process of strategic management. **Strategic management** is a process that involves developing a game plan to guide the company as it strives to accomplish its vision, mission, goals, and objectives and to keep it from straying off its desired course. The idea is to give the entrepreneur a blueprint for matching the company's strengths and weaknesses to the opportunities and threats in the environment.

Building a Competitive Advantage

2. Explain why and how a small business must create a competitive advantage in the market.

The goal of developing a strategic plan is to create for the small company a **competitive advantage**—the aggregation of factors that differentiates a small business from its competitors and gives it a unique and superior position in the market. From a strategic perspective, the key to business success is to develop a unique competitive advantage, one that creates value for customers, is sustainable, and is difficult for competitors to duplicate. No business can be everything to everyone. In fact, one of the biggest pitfalls many entrepreneurs stumble into is failing to differentiate their companies from the crowd of competitors. Entrepreneurs often face the challenge of setting their companies apart from their larger, more powerful competitors (who can easily outspend them) by using the creativity, speed, flexibility, and special abilities their businesses offer customers.

After conducting a strategic assessment of Garner's Natural Life's competitive advantage, owner Candace Garner made a bold decision to pare down her company and refocus on what it does best: vitamins, health supplements, and herbal remedies. Founded in Greenville, South Carolina, in 1979, the company was among the first to capitalize on the rapid growth in organic foods and eventually moved into a 20,000-square-foot store that included a selection of organic grocery items and an all-natural café. As larger chains such as Whole Foods, Fresh Market, and others aggressively caught on to the trend toward "natural" foods and expanded their organic food offerings, Garner's faced intense competition from rivals whose size and sales volume gave them a distinct cost and marketing edge. Garner's strategic assessment revealed that the company's core business—vitamins, health supplements, and herbal remedies—accounted for 50 percent of sales, even though only 15 percent of floor space was dedicated to it. "It time to reinvent ourselves and evolve back to our roots," says Garner. "We grew from the vitamins and herbs. That's always been the core of our business." Garner's relocated to a new 3,500-square-foot store in a shopping center anchored by a Fresh Market grocery store, which has generated increased customer traffic at Garner's. With its refocused strategy, the new Garner's profits are back on track thanks to another of its core strengths, an experienced staff of knowledgeable, well-trained, and enthusiastic employees who are passionate about the products they sell.[7]

Over the long run, a company gains a sustainable competitive advantage through its ability to develop a set of core competencies that enable it to serve its target customers better or to operate more efficiently than its rivals. **Core competencies** are a unique set of skills, knowledge, or abilities that a company develops in key areas, such as superior quality, customer service, innovation, engineering, team-building, flexibility, speed, responsiveness, and others that allow it to perform vital processes to world-class standards and to vault past competitors. They are the things that a company does best and does far better than its competitors.

Since its founding in 1833 by Christian Frederick Martin, the C.F. Martin Company, the oldest guitar maker in the world, has developed a core competency in manufacturing quality acoustic guitars using handcrafting techniques that the company has perfected over time. Currently led by Christian Martin IV, the sixth-generation CEO of the family business, Martin has used its nearly 180 years of experience in the art of guitar building to introduce many innovative features and designs that have made the company the industry leader. C.F. Martin relies on the skills of experienced craftspeople, many of whom have been with the company for decades, to produce its sole product: stellar acoustic guitars that sell for as much as $109,000. The company counts many famous artists, including Sting, Jimmy Buffett, and Eric Clapton, among its customers.[8]

Typically, a company is likely to build core competencies in no more than three to five (sometimes fewer) areas. These core competencies are the source of a company's competitive advantage and are usually quite enduring over time. Markets, customers, and competitors may change, but a company's core competencies are more durable, forming the building blocks for *everything* a company does. In fact, to be effective, these competencies must be sustainable over time. They also should be difficult for competitors to duplicate and must provide customers with a valuable perceived benefit. Small companies' core competencies often have to do with the advantages of their size—agility, speed, closeness to their customers, superior service, or ability to innovate. In short, they use their "smallness" to their advantage, doing things that their larger rivals cannot. The key to success is to build core competencies (or to identify the ones a company already has) and concentrate them on providing superior service and value for a company's target customers.

Developing core competencies does *not* necessarily require a company to spend a great deal of money. It does, however, require an entrepreneur to use creativity, imagination, experience, and vision to identify or develop those things that the business does best and that are most important to its target customers. Building a company's strategy on the foundation of its core competencies allows a business to gain a sustainable competitive edge over its rivals.

Another guitar maker, PRS Guitars, founded in 1985 by Paul Reed Smith, has built a competitive edge similar to the one that C.F. Martin enjoys, but in a different area: electric guitars. Paul Smith built his first electric guitar for a college music class and has been building high-end guitars of stellar quality ever since. Smith, a musician, field tested his early designs while playing at his band's gigs and incorporated design changes using those tests and customer feedback. "Over 10 years, we went through three headstocks, several renditions of body shapes, many tremolo designs, and many experiments with woods and construction methods to get the right mix," says Smith. To build its high-quality electric guitars, PRS uses a blend of high-tech automation and hand craftsmanship. "If the best guitar results from using a robot for one procedure and a lot of hand-sanding or hand-inlaying for another, that's the way we do it," he says. Another core competency is the company's workforce, 80 percent of whom are musicians, "who treat each guitar as if it is their own," says Smith.[9]

When it comes to developing a strategy for establishing a competitive advantage, small companies have a variety of natural advantages over their larger competitors. The typical small business has fewer product lines, a more clearly defined customer base, and a limited geographic market area. Entrepreneurs usually are in close contact with their markets, giving them valuable knowledge on how to best serve their customers' needs and wants. Because of the simplicity of their organization structures, small business owners are in touch with employees daily, often working side-by-side with them, allowing them to communicate strategic moves firsthand. Consequently, small businesses find that strategic management comes more naturally to them than to larger companies with their layers of bureaucracy and far-flung operations.

Strategic management can increase a small company's effectiveness, but entrepreneurs first must have a process designed to meet their needs and their business's special characteristics. It is a mistake to attempt to force a big company's strategic management process onto a small business, because a small business is not merely a little big business. Because of their size and their particular characteristics—limited resources, a flexible managerial style, an informal organizational structure, and adaptability to change—small businesses need a different approach to the strategic management process. The strategic management procedure for a small business should include the following features:

- Use a relatively short planning horizon—2 years or less for most small companies.
- Be informal and not overly structured; a "shirt-sleeve" approach is ideal.
- Encourage the participation of employees and outside parties to improve the reliability and creativity of the resulting plan.
- Do not begin with setting objectives because extensive objective-setting early on may interfere with the creative process of strategic management.
- Maintain flexibility; competitive conditions change too rapidly for any plan to be considered permanent.
- Focus on strategic *thinking*, not just planning, by linking long-range goals to day-to-day operations.

The Strategic Management Process

3. Develop a strategic plan for a business using the nine steps in the strategic planning process.

One of the most important tasks a business owner must perform is to look ahead—to peer into the future—and then devise a strategy for meeting the challenges and opportunities it presents. Strategic management, the best way to accomplish this vital task, is a continuous process that consists of nine steps:

Step 1   Develop a clear vision and translate it into a meaningful mission statement.

Step 2   Assess the company's strengths and weaknesses.

Step 3	Scan the environment for significant opportunities and threats facing the business.
Step 4	Identify the key factors for success in the business.
Step 5	Analyze the competition.
Step 6	Create company goals and objectives.
Step 7	Formulate strategic options and select the appropriate strategies.
Step 8	Translate strategic plans into action plans.
Step 9	Establish accurate controls.

Step 1. Develop a Clear Vision and Translate It into a Meaningful Mission Statement

VISION. Throughout history, the greatest political and business leaders have been visionaries. Whether the vision is as grand as Martin Luther King, Jr.'s "I Have a Dream" speech or as simple as Ray Kroc's devotion to quality, service, cleanliness, and value at McDonald's, the purpose is the same: to focus everyone's attention and efforts on the same target. The vision touches everyone associated with the company—employees, investors, lenders, customers, and the community. It is an expression of what entrepreneurs believe in and the values on which they build their businesses. Highly successful entrepreneurs are able to communicate their vision and their enthusiasm about that vision to those around them. "Strategic planning is worthless unless there is first a strategic vision," says entrepreneur and author John Naisbitt.[10]

A vision statement addresses the question "What kind of company do we want to become?" In his book, *Daring Visionaries: How Entrepreneurs Build Companies, Inspire Allegiance, and Create Wealth*, Ray Smilor describes the importance of vision:[11]

> Vision is the organizational sixth sense that tells us why we make a difference in the world. It is the real but unseen fabric of connections that nurture and sustain values. It is the pulse of the organizational body that reaffirms relationships and directs behavior.

A vision is the result of an entrepreneur's dream of something that does not exist yet and the ability to paint a compelling picture of that dream for everyone to see. A clearly defined vision helps a company in four ways:

1. *Vision provides direction.* Entrepreneurs who spell out the vision for their company focus everyone's attention on the future and determine the path the business will take to get there.
2. *Vision determines decisions.* The vision influences the decisions, no matter how big or how small, that owners, managers, and employees make every day in a business. This influence can be positive or negative, depending on how well defined the vision is. One writer explains, "Almost all workers are making decisions, not just filling out weekly sales reports or tightening screws. They will do what they think [is] best. If you want them to do as the company thinks best too, then you must [see to it that] they have an inner gyroscope aligned with the corporate compass."[12] That gyroscope's alignment depends on an entrepreneur's vision and how well he or she transmits it throughout the company.
3. *Vision motivates people.* A clear vision excites and ignites people to action. People want to work for a company that sets its sights high and establishes targets that are worth pursuing.
4. *Vision allows a company to persevere in the face of adversity.* Small companies, their founders, and their employees face a multitude of challenges as they grow. Having a vision that serves as a "guiding star" inspires everyone in the company to work through challenging times.

Vision is based on an entrepreneur's values. Successful entrepreneurs build their businesses around a set of three to six core values, which might range from respect for the individual and encouraging innovation to creating satisfied customers and making the world a better place to live. These values become the foundation on which the entire company and its strategy are built. Even though the environment in which a company operates may undergo turbulent disruptions and changes, the core values on which it is built remain constant. Truly visionary entrepreneurs see their companies' primary purpose as much more than just "making money." When Henry C. Turner started Turner Construction Company in 1902 in New York City, he identified three core values to guide his business: teamwork (people-focused), integrity (highest ethical standards), and commitment (client-driven). The company has grown into one of the largest construction and building services company in the United States, handling more than 1,600 construction projects around the world in a typical year, and the same principles on which Turner founded the company continue to guide it. Some of Turner Construction's most famous projects include Bloomingdales' Department Store, LaGuardia Airport, the Rock and Roll Hall of Fame and Museum, and Ericcson Stadium.[13]

Danny Meyer, an author and the owner of New York City's Union Square Café, compares a company's core values to the banks of a river. "[Core values] are the riverbanks that guide us as we refine and improve our performance," he says. "A lack of riverbanks creates estuaries and cloudy waters that are confusing to navigate. I want a crystal-clear, swiftly flowing stream."[14] The best way to create that crystal-clear, swiftly flowing stream of core values and to translate them into action is to create a written mission statement that communicates the company's values to everyone it touches.

MISSION STATEMENT.   A mission statement addresses the first question of any business venture: "What business am I in?" Establishing the purpose of the business in writing must come first to give the company a sense of direction. The mission is the mechanism for making it clear to everyone the company touches "why we are here" and "where we are going." Because a mission statement reflects the company's core values, it helps create an emotional bond between a company and its stakeholders, especially its employees and its customers. Without a concise, meaningful mission statement, a small business risks wandering aimlessly in the marketplace, with no idea of where to go or how to get there.

ENTREPRENEURIAL
Profile

Shawn Foster: Foster's Grille

Shawn Foster, former corporate chef at Atlanta's famous Palm Restaurant, opened his first casual restaurant, Foster's Grille, in Manassas, Virginia, in 1999. Foster's Grille, which is known for its "2-big-for-2-hands" Charburger and hand-cut fries, is guided by its mission statement: "Foster's Grille is committed to providing our guests with the highest quality food and energetic service in a clean, relaxed, and upbeat family-friendly, neighborhood-style grill." Everything at Foster's Grille, now with 22 franchised outlets, is made with fresh ingredients, and heat lamps and microwave ovens are forbidden. Restaurant staff hand-cut potatoes twice a day for fresh fries, squeeze lemons to make lemonade, and bake homemade cakes for dessert. "My mission was to create the ultimate burger of the finest quality meats and serve it to people with other great menu offerings in an atmosphere that they could look forward to coming to with their friends, family, and colleagues," says Foster.[15]

Elements of a Mission Statement.   A sound mission statement need not be lengthy to be effective. Three key issues entrepreneurs and their employees should address as they develop a mission statement for their businesses include:

- The *purpose* of the company: What are we in business to accomplish?
- The *business* we are in: How are we going to accomplish that purpose?
- The *values* of the company: What principles and beliefs form the foundation of the way we do business?

A company's mission statement may be the most essential and basic communication that it puts forward. If the people on the plant, shop, retail, or warehouse floor don't know what a company's mission is, then, for all practical purposes, it does not have one! The mission statement expresses the company's character, identity, and scope of operations, but writing it is only half the battle, at best. The most difficult part is living that mission every day. *That's* how employees decide what really matters. To be effective, a mission statement must become a natural part of the organization, embodied in the minds, habits, attitudes, and decisions of everyone in the company every day. Consider the mission statement of Fetzer Vineyards, a California vineyard whose acreage is 100 percent organic with no chemical pesticides, herbicides, fungicides, or fertilizers, and the message it sends to company stakeholders:

We are an environmentally and socially conscious grower, producer, and marketer of wines of the highest quality and value.

Working in harmony with respect for the human spirit, we are committed to sharing information about the enjoyment of food and wine in a lifestyle of moderation and responsibility. We are dedicated to the continuous growth and development of our people and our business.[16]

A company may have a powerful competitive advantage, but it is wasted unless (1) the owner has communicated that advantage to workers, who, in turn, are working hard to communicate it to customers and potential customers, and (2) customers are recommending the company to their friends because they understand the benefits they are getting from it that they cannot get elsewhere. *That's* the real power of a mission statement.

LESSONS FROM THE STREET-SMART entrepreneur

Reinventing Your Business

Having faced the worst economic recession since the 1930s, many entrepreneurs recognize that their customers' buying behavior and, perhaps more important, attitudes have changed, perhaps permanently. These changes mean that entrepreneurs must reinvent their businesses to maintain their success. A recent survey by *Forbes* and research company Innosight reports that 79 percent of 500 business owners say that the environment has increased the need for transforming businesses. What are the keys to reinventing your business successfully? Consider these tips from the Street-Smart Entrepreneur:

Tip 1. Get comfortable with chaos

The globalization of business, technology advancement, and rapidly changing economic conditions mean that entrepreneurs can no longer expect long periods of stabilized economic prosperity. Instead, they must be prepared to face constant turbulence punctuated by opportunities for growth. Successful entrepreneurs make this important mental shift and are willing to reinvent their companies to capitalize on the opportunities that chaos creates. Chaos requires reinvention, and small companies are much more flexible and fleet-footed at reinventing themselves than their larger rivals.

Tip 2. Stay in contact with your customers

Businesses that constantly realign their product and service offerings to meet their customers' changing needs have a competitive edge. Small companies maintain closer contact with their customers than large businesses, which gives them the advantage. Entrepreneurs who listen to their customers; who conduct surveys, polls, and focus groups; and who simply just spend time with customers find it easy to stay in tune with their customers' needs, expectations, and demands. Ashton and Elaine Barrington started Elaine's as a gift shop in Clinton, South Carolina, a small town with a population of 10,000. After a few years, customer feedback prompted them to add a coffee shop inside their store. Before the Barringtons decided to expand the coffee shop to include a lunch menu, they tested the idea first on a small scale. Customers gave their overwhelming approval, and the Barringtons remodeled their store, making Jitters, their coffee shop and café, a larger part of their store. When a severe recession caused sales of gift items to plummet, the Barrington's decision to reinvent their business proved to be a wise one. "Jitters has been the salvation of our business," says Ashton.

Tip 3. Focus on providing value to your customers

In a severe recession, customers, even upscale ones, change their buying behavior and carefully evaluate every potential purchase, looking always for *value*. Companies that find creative ways to add value to their products and services and help their customers solve problems will be the ones that succeed. A study by the research firm Nielsen reports that customers' willingness to purchase innovative products and services in good and bad economic environments has remained constant over the last 30 years. Adding value does not have to be complex or expensive. One furniture retailer increased the average sale at his company by adding a monitored play area for children, which allowed parents to spend more time browsing and shopping.

Tip 4. Look for new markets

In a chaotic environment, game-changing companies look for more than ways to cut costs; they look for new markets to enter. How can you change your existing business model to reach another market, perhaps one that exists with your current customers? When sales of low-end vinyl-lined pools declined during the recession, the family owners of Sparkle

Pool, a small company in Weston, West Virginia, decided to exit that market even though the company had been in the business for three generations. General manager Bob Pirner says that the family decided to shift its pool business toward upscale customers who want custom-designed pools and "aquascapes," an area in which the youngest generation of family members had been developing expertise. Sparkle Pools' unique installations now range from $50,000 to $300,000, a significant increase over the typical $12,000 to $16,000 installation for a vinyl pool. In spite of the recession, entering the new market has allowed the company to increase its sales by 30 percent to more than $1.2 million.

Tip 5. Hitch a ride on a wave

Like a surfer catching the perfect wave, successful entrepreneurs constantly watch for meaningful trends (not fads) and find ways to capitalize on them. Dave Chewey, owner of Garden Associates Landscape Architecture for 19 years, tapped into the trend toward environmental preservation and began marketing more effectively his company's experience and expertise in creating sustainable landscapes. Emphasizing landscapes with native, drought-tolerant plants and offering new services such as installing solar energy panels, conducting home energy audits, and installing efficient geothermal energy systems, helped offset a 60 percent decline in sales among the company's target customers, owners of upscale homes. Chewey says that existing customers have accounted for 80 percent of the new sales.

Sources: Based on Chris Pentilla, "Evolve," *Entrepreneur*, May 2009, pp. 43–45; Suzanne Barlyn, "New and Improved," *Wall Street Journal*, April 23, 2009, p. R4.

Step 2. Assess the Company's Strengths and Weaknesses

Having defined the vision and the mission of the business, entrepreneurs can turn their attention to assessing company strengths and weaknesses. Competing successfully demands that a business create a competitive strategy that is built on and exploits its strengths and overcomes or compensates for its weaknesses. **Strengths** are positive internal factors that contribute a company's ability to achieve its mission, goals, and objectives. **Weaknesses** are negative internal factors that inhibit the accomplishment of its mission, goals, and objectives.

Identifying strengths and weaknesses helps an entrepreneur understand her business as it exists (or will exist). An organization's strengths should originate in its core competencies because they are essential to its ability to remain competitive in each of the market segments in which it competes. The key is to build a successful strategy using the company's underlying strengths as its foundation and matching those strengths against competitors' weaknesses. Honest Tea, a company started by Seth Goldman and Barry Nalebuff that sells a line of teas made from organic ingredients, has built its strategy on its strengths—the quality, freshness, and health aspects of its all-natural, organic products and an understanding of its core customers' preferences—to compete successfully against much larger and more financially capable rivals in the intensely competitive beverage industry.

One effective technique for taking a strategic inventory is to prepare a balance sheet of the company's strengths and weaknesses (see Table 1). The positive side should reflect important skills, knowledge, or resources that contribute to the company's success. The negative side should record honestly any limitations that detract from the company's ability to compete. This balance sheet should analyze all key performance areas of the business—human resources, finance, production, marketing, product development, organization, and others. This analysis should give entrepreneurs a more realistic perspective of their business, pointing out foundations on which they can build future strengths and obstacles that they must remove for business progress.

TABLE 1 Identifying Company Strengths and Weaknesses

Strengths (Positive Internal Factors)	Weaknesses (Negative Internal Factors)

Step 3. Scan the Environment for Significant Opportunities and Threats Facing the Business

OPPORTUNITIES.   Once entrepreneurs have taken an internal inventory of company strengths and weaknesses, they must turn to the external environment to identify any opportunities and threats that might have a significant impact on the business. **Opportunities** are positive external options that the firm can exploit to accomplish its mission, goals, and objectives. The number of potential opportunities is limitless, but an entrepreneur should focus only on a small number (probably two or three at most) of those that are consistent with the company's vision, core values, and mission. Otherwise, they may jeopardize their core business by losing focus and trying to do too much at once.

ENTREPRENEURIAL
Profile

Napoleon Barragan:
Dial-a-Mattress

Napoleon Barragan launched Dial-a-Mattress in 1976 with a simple idea: to sell mattresses directly to customers (in those days with a toll-free telephone number). For three decades, the company grew steadily, eventually giving customers the option of buying online through the company's Web site. Annual sales reached $150 million, but in 2001 the company strayed from its core competency of direct sales and began opening retail stores. Unfortunately, Dial-a-Mattress managers lacked the skill and experience required to select the right retail locations. Although online and telephone sales continued to climb, the ill-fated foray into retail stores had plunged the company into debt, and Barragan was forced to sell his bankrupt company to rival Sleepy's.[17]

When identifying opportunities, entrepreneurs must pay close attention to new potential markets. Are competitors overlooking a niche in the market? Is there a better way to reach customers? Are customers requesting new products or product variations? Are trends in the industry creating new opportunities to serve customers? Have environmental changes created new markets? Entrepreneurs are discovering business opportunities that help customers deal with escalating energy costs.

ENTREPRENEURIAL
Profile

Gary Grossman, Peter
Santangeli, Matthew
Smith, Jonathan Gay,
and Robert Tatsumi:
Greenbox Technology

Greenbox Technology, a company founded in 2007 by five former employees of Macromedia, provides a Web-based application that provides customers historic and real-time feedback on energy consumption by their home or business, giving them the power to understand and reduce their energy use and their environmental footprint. By allowing people to see how much energy they use, Greenbox technology will "set a new standard for energy intelligence in the home," says cofounder Jonathan Gay.[18]

THREATS.   Sixty-five million years ago, a giant asteroid or comet smashed into the earth, causing catastrophic damage to the environment that lasted for years and wiped out the dinosaurs. Today, astronomers monitor the heavens with their telescopes, watching for "near-earth objects" that pose the same threat to our planet today. In the same way, small businesses must be on the lookout for threats that could destroy their companies. **Threats** are negative external forces that hamper a company's ability to achieve its mission, goals, and objectives. Threats to the business can take a variety of forms, such as new competitors entering the local market, a government mandate regulating a business activity, an economic recession, rising interest rates, technology advances that make a company's product obsolete, and many others. The struggling U.S. auto industry poses a threat for many small businesses, ranging from automotive suppliers to bars. Kelly's Bar, located near an auto assembly plant and an axle supplier in Detroit, Michigan, has catered to automotive workers for years but saw sales decline 75 percent in just 8 months as nearby factories scaled back production or closed. "Autoworkers just don't go out like they used to," says bartender Cyndi Crooks. "This is the worst we've seen."[19]

Source: Cartoon Features Syndicate

"I suggest we all roll up in a tight little ball until the danger is past."

Movie theater owners face serious threats to their business from a variety of sources, including increasingly sophisticated home-theater systems that contain DVD players and high-definition big-screen televisions, pay-per-view movies available on demand, crooks who distribute black-market copies of films (sometimes before the original is released), and other forms of entertainment, ranging from iPods and YouTube to video games such as *Guitar Hero* and the Internet. The result has been an overall decline in movie ticket sales. In 1946, movie theaters sold 4 billion tickets (an average of 28 movies per year for each American); in a typical year, movie theaters sell nearly 1.4 billion tickets, which means that the average American goes to the movies fewer than five times per year.[20] Although theater owners cannot directly control the threats their businesses face, they must prepare a strategic plan to shield their businesses from these threats.

Opportunities and threats are products of the interactions of forces, trends, and events outside the direct control of the business. By monitoring demographic trends as well as trends in their particular industries, entrepreneurs can sharpen their ability to spot most opportunities and threats well in advance, giving themselves time to prepare for them.

ENTREPRENEURIAL Profile

*Shari Redstone:
Cinema De Lux*

To deal with the threats facing their businesses, theater owners are changing the way they do business in an effort to lure customers from their in-home theaters and back to the (really) big screen. "We are trying our hardest to get people out of the house to see a movie," says Shari Redstone, president of family-owned National Amusements, a chain of 1,500 movie theaters located around the world. "We simply must give people an experience they can't get elsewhere." To do that, Redstone has converted several theaters in the chain into Cinema De Lux (CDL) theaters that offer moviegoers amenities such as martini bars, upscale concessions (even a mini Ben & Jerry's outlet), a concierge desk to help patrons with tickets or cabs, a lobby that boasts a baby grand piano and a virtual soccer game for kids, "directors' halls" (reserved seating in premier locations with cushy leather rocking recliners), digital projection and high-tech sound systems capable of broadcasting crisp images in 3D, and "love seats" on the last two rows of the theater. CDL theaters also include two private-function rooms that can be rented for birthday parties, social gatherings, or corporate events. The company also recently began adding live entertainment venues in some of its theater complexes.[21]

TABLE 2 Identifying Opportunities and Threats

Opportunities (Positive External Factors)	Threats (Negative External Factors)

Table 2 provides a form that allows entrepreneurs to take a strategic inventory of the opportunities and threats facing their companies.

Table 3 provides an analytical tool that is designed to help entrepreneurs to identify the threats that pose the greatest danger to their companies.

Step 4. Identify the Key Factors for Success in the Business

KEY SUCCESS FACTORS. Every business is characterized by a set of controllable factors that determine the relative success of market participants. Identifying, understanding, and manipulating these factors allow a small business to gain a competitive advantage in its market segment. By focusing efforts to maximize their companies' performance on these key success

TABLE 3 Identifying and Managing Major Threats

Every business faces threats, but entrepreneurs cannot afford to be paranoid or paralyzed by fear when it comes to dealing with them. At the same time, they cannot afford to ignore threats that have the potential to destroy their businesses. The most productive approach to dealing with threats is to identify those that would have the most severe impact on a small company and those that have the highest probability of occurrence.

Research by Greg Hackett, president of management think tank MergerShop, has identified 12 major sources of risk that can wreak havoc on a company's future. The following table helps entrepreneurs to determine the threats on which they should focus their attention.

Source	Specific Threat	Severity (1 = Low, 10 = High)	Probability of Occurrence (0 to 1)	Threat Score (Severity × Probability, Max = 10)
Channels of distribution				
Competition				
Demographic changes				
Globalization				
Innovation				
Waning customer or supplier loyalty				
Offshoring or outsourcing				
Stage in product life cycle				
Government regulation				
Influence of special interest groups				
Influence of stakeholders				
Changes in technology				

Once entrepreneurs have identified specific threats facing their companies in the 12 areas (not necessarily all 12), they rate the severity of the impact of each on their company on a 1 to 10 scale. Then, they assign probabilities (between 0 and 1) to each threat. To calculate the threat score, entrepreneurs simply multiply the severity of each threat by its probability. (The maximum threat score is 10.) The higher a threat's score, the more attention it demands. Typically, one or two threats stand out above all of the others, and those are the ones on which entrepreneurs should focus.

Source: Adapted with permission from Edward Teach, "Apocalypse Soon," *CFO*, September 2005, pp. 31–32.

factors, entrepreneurs can achieve dramatic strategic advantages over their competitors. Companies that understand these key success factors tend to be leaders of the pack, whereas those who fail to recognize them become also-rans.

Key success factors come in a variety of different patterns depending on the industry. Simply stated, they are the factors that determine a company's ability to compete successfully in an industry. Bruce Milletto, owner of Bellissimo Coffee Info-Group, a coffee-business consulting firm, says that to be successful coffee shops must focus on three key success factors: high-quality coffee products, stellar customer service, and a warm, inviting ambience that transforms a coffeehouse into a destination where people want to gather with their friends.

ENTREPRENEURIAL Profile

Martin and Kerry Mayorga: Mayorga Coffee

Martin Mayorga started a coffee-roasting business with his wife Kerry in 1998 and then opened a retail coffee store in Silver Springs, Maryland, that focuses on specialty imported coffee beans. With these key success factors in mind, Mayorga created a shop that looks more like a lounge than a retail store, with its plush leather family-style seating. The Mayorgas also have added an entertainment factor by including musical entertainment and allowing customers to view the entire roasting process on its custom-made bean roaster, attractive extras for customers looking for a way to relax after a busy day at work.[22]

Simply stated, key success factors determine a company's ability to compete in the marketplace. Sometimes these sources of competitive advantages are based on cost factors, such as manufacturing cost per unit, distribution cost per unit, or development cost per unit. More often, these key success factors are less tangible but are just as important, such as product quality, customer service, convenient store locations, availability of customer credit, relationships with distributors, name recognition, and others. For example, one restaurant owner identified the following key success factors for his business:

- Tight cost control (labor, 15–18 percent of sales and food costs, 35–40 percent of sales)
- Trained, dependable, and honest in-store managers
- Close monitoring of waste
- Convenient location
- High food quality
- Consistent food
- Clean restaurants
- Friendly and attentive service from a well-trained waitstaff

These controllable variables determine the ability of any restaurant in his market segment to compete. Restaurants that lack these key success factors are not likely to survive, whereas those that build these factors into their strategies will prosper. However, before entrepreneurs can build a strategy on the foundation of the industry's key success factors, they must identify them. Table 4 presents a form to help entrepreneurs identify the most important success factors and their implications for the company.

TABLE 4 Identifying Key Success Factors

List the key success factors that your business must possess if it is to be successful in its market segment.

Key Success Factor	How your company rates . . .
1	Low 1 2 3 4 5 6 7 8 9 10 High
2	Low 1 2 3 4 5 6 7 8 9 10 High
3	Low 1 2 3 4 5 6 7 8 9 10 High
4	Low 1 2 3 4 5 6 7 8 9 10 High
5	Low 1 2 3 4 5 6 7 8 9 10 High
Conclusions:	

Step 5. Analyze the Competition

Ask small business owners to identify the greatest challenge they face, and one of the most common responses is *competition*. A recent study of top executives by consulting firm McKinsey and Company reports that 85 percent say that their industries are becoming more competitive. What factors are driving the increased levels of competition? Smarter rivals, more companies competing on low price, and rising customer awareness top the list.[23] Small companies increasingly are under fire from larger, more powerful rivals, including general retailers such as Walmart and specialty big-box stores such as Home Depot, PetSmart, and Office Depot. Keeping tabs on rivals' strategic movements through competitive intelligence programs is a vital strategic activity. According to one small business consultant, "Business is like any battlefield. If you want to win the war, you have to know who you're up against."[24] The primary goals of a competitive intelligence program include the following:

- Avoiding surprises from existing competitors' new strategies and tactics
- Identifying potential new competitors
- Improving reaction time to competitors' actions
- Anticipating rivals' next strategic moves
- Improving your ability to differentiate your company's products and services from those of your competitors
- Defining your company's competitive edge

Unfortunately, most small companies fail to gather competitive intelligence because their owners mistakenly assume that it is too costly or simply unnecessary. The Global Market Intelligence Survey reports that only 35 percent of businesses use competitive intelligence in most or all of the company's key decisions.[25] In reality, the cost of collecting information about competitors typically is minimal, but it does require discipline.

COMPETITOR ANALYSIS. Sizing up the competition gives entrepreneurs a more realistic view of the market and their companies' position in it. Yet not every competitor warrants the same level of attention in a strategic plan. *Direct competitors* offer the same products and services, and customers often compare prices, features, and deals from these competitors as they shop. *Significant competitors* offer some of the same products and services. Although their product or service lines may be somewhat different, there is competition with them in several key areas. *Indirect competitors* offer the same or similar products or services only in a small number of

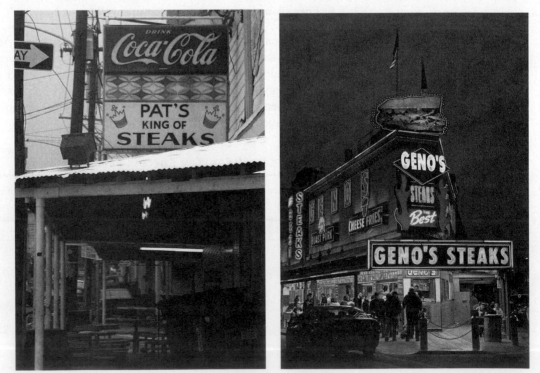

Pat's King of Steaks and Geno's, which are located across the street from one another in Philadelphia, are direct competitors in the market for Philly cheesesteaks.

Sources: (left photo) AP Photo/Dan Loh and (right photo) Mira/Alamy Images areas, and their target customers seldom overlap yours. Entrepreneurs should monitor closely the actions of their direct competitors, maintain a solid grasp of where their significant competitors are heading, and spend only minimal resources tracking their indirect competitors. For instance, two of Philadelphia's landmark businesses, Pat's King of Steaks and Geno's Steaks, are direct competitors in the market for Philly cheesesteaks. Their locations—across the street from one another—make it easy for each to keep track of the other. Pat's and Geno's charge the same prices for their sandwiches, and both claim to be the home of the original Philly cheesesteak sandwich.[26]

A competitive intelligence exercise enables entrepreneurs to update their knowledge of competitors by answering the following questions:

- Who are your major competitors and where are they located? Bob Dickinson, president of Carnival Cruise Lines, considers his company's main competition to be land-based theme parks and casinos rather than other cruise lines. Why? Because 89 percent of American adults have never been on a cruise![27]
- What distinctive competencies have they developed?
- How do their cost structures compare to yours? Their financial resources?
- How do they market their products and services?
- What do customers say about them? How do customers describe their products or services; their way of doing business; the additional services they might supply?
- What are their key strategies?
- What are their strengths? How can your company surpass them?
- What are their primary weaknesses? How can your company capitalize on them?
- What messages are they communicating to their customers?
- Are new competitors entering the market?

A small business owner can collect a great deal of information about competitors through low-cost competitive intelligence (CI) methods, including the following:

- Read industry trade publications for announcements from competitors.
- Ask questions of customers and suppliers on what they hear competitors may be doing. In many cases, this information is easy to gather because some people love to gossip.
- Talk to employees, especially sales representatives and purchasing agents. Experts estimate that 70 to 90 percent of the competitive information a company needs already resides with employees who collect it in their routine dealings with suppliers, customers, and other industry contacts.[28]
- Attend trade shows and collect competitors' sales literature.
- Watch for employment ads from competitors; knowing what types of workers they are hiring can tell you a great deal about their future plans.
- Conduct patent searches for patents that competitors have filed. This gives important clues about new products they are developing.
- Environmental Protection Agency reports can provide important information about the factories of manufacturing companies, including the amounts and the kinds of emissions released. A private group, Environmental Protection, also reports emissions for specific plants.[29]
- Learn about the kinds and amounts of equipment and raw materials competitors are importing by studying the *Journal of Commerce Port Import Export Reporting Service (PIERS)* database. These clues can alert an entrepreneur to new products a competitor is about to launch.
- If appropriate, buy the competitors' products and assess their quality and features. Benchmark their products against yours. The owner of an online gift basket company periodically places orders with his primary competitors and compares their packaging, pricing, service, and quality to his own.[30]
- Obtain credit reports on each of your major competitors to evaluate their financial condition. Dun & Bradstreet and other research firms also enable entrepreneurs to look up profiles of competitors that can be helpful in a strategic analysis.
- Publicly held companies must file periodic reports with the Securities and Exchange Commission (SEC), including quarterly 10-Q and annual 10-K reports. These are available at the SEC's Web site.

- Check out the resources of your local library, including articles, computerized databases, and online searches. Press releases, which often announce important company news, can be an important source of competitive intelligence. Many companies supply press releases through *PR Newswire*. For local competitors, review back issues of the area newspaper for articles on and advertisements by competitors.

- Use the vast resources of the Internet to learn more about your competitors. The Internet enables entrepreneurs to gather valuable competitive information at little or no cost. "Businesses need to make sure that they have the right people spending enough time looking for the right kind of information and that there is a mechanism for getting this intelligence into decision making loops," says one expert on business intelligence.[31] (Refer to the text's Web site at *www.pearsonhighered.com/scarborough* for an extensive listing of useful small business Web sites.)

- Visit competing businesses periodically to observe their operations. Sam Walton, founder of Walmart, was famous for visiting competitors' operations to see what he could learn from them.

Using the information gathered, a business owner can set up teams of managers and employees to evaluate key competitors and make recommendations on strategic actions that will improve the company's competitive position against each one.

Entrepreneurs can use the results of the competitor intelligence analysis to construct a competitive profile matrix for each market segment in which the firm operates. A **competitive profile matrix** allows entrepreneurs to evaluate their firms against the major competitor on the key success factors for their market segments (refer to Table 4). The first step is to list the key success factors identified in Step 4 of the strategic planning process and to attach weights to them reflecting their relative importance. Table 5 shows a sample competitive profile matrix for a small company. (For simplicity, the weights in this matrix sum to 1.00.) In this example, notice that product quality is the most important key success factor, which is why its weight (.35) is the highest.

The next step is to identify the company's major competitors and to rate each one (and your company) on each of the key success factors:

If factor is a:	Rating is:
Major weakness	1
Minor weakness	2
Minor strength	3
Major strength	4

Once the rating is completed, the owner simply multiplies the weight by the rating for each factor to get a weighted score, and then adds up each competitor's weighted scores to get a total weighted score. The results will show which company is strongest, which is the weakest, and which of the key success factors each one is best and worst at meeting. The matrix shows entrepreneurs how their companies "measure up" against competitors on the industry's key success

TABLE 5 Sample Competitive Profile Matrix

Key Success Factors (from Step 5)

	Weight	Your Business Rating	Your Business Score	Competitor 1 Rating	Competitor 1 Score	Competitor 2 Rating	Competitor 2 Score
Ability to innovate	0.20	2	0.40	1	0.20	1	0.20
Customer service	0.25	4	1.00	1	0.25	2	0.50
Convenience	0.10	3	0.30	3	0.30	4	0.40
Product quality	0.35	4	1.40	2	0.70	2	0.70
Product selection	0.10	2	0.20	4	0.40	3	0.30
Total	**1.00**		**3.30**		**1.85**		**2.10**

factors and gives them an idea of which strategies they should employ to gain a competitive advantage over their rivals. For instance, the company in Table 5 should compete by emphasizing its product quality and its customer service (both are major strengths for the company but are weaknesses for its rivals) and not its product selection (which is a minor weakness for the company but is a strength for its rivals).

Step 6. Create Company Goals and Objectives

Before entrepreneurs can build a comprehensive set of strategies, they must first establish business goals and objectives, which give them targets to aim for and provide a basis for measuring their companies' performance. Without them, entrepreneurs cannot know where their businesses are going or how well they are performing.

GOALS. **Goals** are the broad, long-range attributes that a business seeks to accomplish; they tend to be general and sometimes even abstract. Goals are not intended to be specific enough for a manager to act on but simply state the general level of accomplishment sought. What level of sales would you like for your company to achieve in 5 years? Do you want to boost your market share? Does your cash balance need strengthening? Would you like to enter a new market or increase sales in a current one? Do you want your company to be the leader in its market segment? Do you want to improve your company's customer retention level? What return on your investment do you seek? Researchers Jim Collins and Jerry Porras studied a large group of businesses and determined that one of the factors that set apart successful companies from unsuccessful ones was the formulation of very ambitious, clear, and inspiring long-term goals. Collins and Porras called them BHAGs ("Big Hairy Audacious Goals," pronounced "bee-hags") and say that their main benefit is to inspire and focus a company on important actions that are consistent with its overall mission. BHAGs are bold, daring, and exciting, and they operate on a long time frame, 10 to 30 years.[32] In their classic book, *Built to Last: Successful Habits of Visionary Companies*, Collins and Porras explain the role of BHAGs to a company:

> A true BHAG is clear and compelling and serves as a unifying focal point of effort and acts as a catalyst for team spirit. It has a clear finish line, so the organization can know when it has achieved the goal; people like to shoot for finish lines. A BHAG engages people—it reaches out and grabs them in the gut. It is tangible, energizing, highly focused.[33]

ENTREPRENEURIAL
Profile

Keith Lavitt: Super Enterprises

Every fall, Keith Lavitt, co-owner of Super Enterprises, a wholesale distributor of upscale windows and doors with locations in New York, New Jersey, and Georgia, gathers input from his employees for the purpose of formulating goals for the upcoming year. Lavitt and his employees develop an initial draft of the company's goals by October, revise them, and publish them by year-end. "Once the goals are set, we have monthly updates on where we are compared to our goals," says Lavitt.[34]

Defining broad-based goals helps entrepreneurs to focus on the next phase—developing specific, realistic objectives.

OBJECTIVES. **Objectives** are more specific targets of performance. They define the things that entrepreneurs must accomplish if they are to achieve their goals and overall mission. Common objectives address profitability, productivity, growth, efficiency, markets, financial resources, physical facilities, organizational structure, employee well-being, and social responsibility. The objectives a company sets determine the level of success it achieves. Establishing profitability targets is *not* enough. Instead, entrepreneurs must set objectives and measure performance in those critical areas that determine their companies' ability to be profitable—a concept that Collins calls a company's true economic denominators. These economic denominators might be the cost of acquiring a customer, sales per labor hour, the customer retention rate, the rate of inventory turnover, or some other factor. Unfortunately, Collins claims that fewer than 10 percent of all companies understand what their true economic denominators are.

Well-written objectives have the following characteristics:

They are specific. Objectives should be quantifiable and precise. For example, "to achieve a healthy growth in sales" is not a meaningful objective; but "to increase retail sales by 12 percent and wholesale sales by 10 percent in the next fiscal year" is precise and spells out exactly what management wants to accomplish.

They are measurable. Entrepreneurs should be able to plot their companies' progress toward its objectives; this requires a well-defined reference point from which to start and a scale for measuring progress.

They are assignable. Unless an entrepreneur assigns responsibility for an objective to an individual, it is unlikely that the company will ever achieve it. Creating objectives without giving someone responsibility for accomplishing them is futile.

They are realistic, yet challenging. Objectives must be within the reach of the organization or motivation evaporates. However, entrepreneurs and their employees must set challenging objectives. (Remember the importance of BHAGs.) In other words, the more challenging an objective is (within realistic limits), the higher the performance will be. Set objectives that will test you, your business, and its employees; that's how companies become market leaders.

They are timely. Objectives must specify not only what is to be accomplished but also when it is to be accomplished. A time frame for achievement is important.

They are written down. This writing process does not have to be complex; in fact, the manager should make the number of objectives relatively small, from 5 to 15.

The strategic planning process works best when managers and employees are actively involved jointly in setting objectives. Developing a plan is top management's responsibility, but executing it falls to managers and employees; therefore, encouraging them to participate in the process broadens the plan's perspective and increases the motivation to make the plan work. In addition, managers and employees know a great deal about the organization and usually are willing to share this knowledge.

▶ ENTREPRENEURSHIP IN ACTION ▶

A Company That Loves to Turn the World Upside Down

In 1994, Peter Schnabel left his post at Intamin AG, a Swiss company that specializes in making roller coasters, to start a competing company, Premier Rides. Schnabel convinced Jim Seay, the executive in charge of developing new rides for amusement park operator Six Flags, to join the fledgling company. Seay, now the sole owner and president of Premier Rides, manages the busiest designer of steel roller coasters in the United States, a Millersville, Maryland-based company that has installed more than 30 major theme park attractions, including Mr. Freeze at Six Flags Over Texas, Speed at the NASCAR Café in Las Vegas, and Revenge of the Mummy at Universal Studios in Orlando, Florida. A constant challenge is developing new, ever-edgier rides that push the limits of engineering while maintaining safety as a top priority. "Guests are very sophisticated these days," says Seay. "Their level of expectations is very high."

Given his background in the amusement industry, Seay understood from the earliest days of the company one of the most important key success factors in the roller coaster design business: offering a unique product. Because theme parks are locked in a battle for market share, they demand attractions that are one-of-a-kind. Virtually every roller coaster that the company designs is unique, and each one pushes the envelope a bit further, which requires a culture of creativity. To achieve that culture, Seay has organized Premier around its design and engineering functions and outsources all other activities, including construction of its coasters. "Premier is very innovative," says Bill Linkenheimer, an officer in the American Coaster Enthusiasts, a fan club for amusement park aficionados. "It's the go-to company for parks that want to build something customized. Its people are willing to do anything."

Designing and building a new roller coaster takes several years and costs anywhere from $5 million to $20 million. Premier Rides works closely with amusement park managers in a process that closely resembles scripting a movie. "They come up with the idea," says Seay. "We come up with the technology to meet the vision." To create the

Jim Seay, owner of Premier Rides, stands in front of a roller coaster that uses linear induction motor technology. Seay's company created the award-winning technology that revolutionized roller coasters and has rocketed Premier Rides to the top of the industry.

Source: AP Wide World Photos

popular Revenge of the Mummy ride for Universal Studios, Premier took a seven-act storyboard that the theme park's creative team developed and turned its engineers loose to generate ideas for bringing the ride to life. For instance, the storyboard called for the coaster to back up abruptly and spin 180 degrees.

A proprietary propulsion system that Premier Rides developed called the linear induction motor (LIM) allows the company to make its roller coasters among the most innovative on the market. Unlike a traditional roller coaster, which relies on gravity for energy, LIM uses a series of computer-controlled electromagnets that power up in rapid sequence to accelerate cars at any point along a ride. The LIM system can create incredible bursts of speed, propelling riders from zero to 60 miles per hour in just 3 seconds! LIM produces enough energy to pull roller coaster cars through 30 vertical curves, 25 horizontal curves, and 4 upside down loops. In addition to its ability to produce energy and speed anywhere along a roller coaster's track, LIM is an amazingly simple and reliable system that produces few breakdowns. "Other than the wheels of the coaster, there are no moving parts," says Ben Lovelace, one of Premier's engineers.

Premier has survived a shakeout in the roller coaster industry. Two of Premier's competitors, Arrow Dynamics and Giovanola, recently declared bankruptcy after their projects went over budget. Learning from his competitors' mistakes, Seay is particularly vigilant about Premier Rides' finances and cost estimates. To avoid taking the company on a financial roller coaster ride, he manages the company very conservatively. "A company needs financial discipline to be successful," he says. "We pride ourselves on having no debt, cash on hand, and a significant line of credit."

1. Search online for information about the amusement industry. Identify three key success factors in the industry.
2. Visit Premier Rides' Web site. Describe the company's strengths and weaknesses. What opportunities and threats does the company face?
3. Which of the three strategies described in this chapter is Premier Rides pursuing? What advice can you offer Jim Seay about the company's strategy?

Sources: Based on Jeff Wise, "Masters of Disaster," *FSB*, March 2009, pp. 76–79; "Rides," Premier Rides, *www.premier-rides.com/rides.htm*.

Step 7. Formulate Strategic Options and Select the Appropriate Strategies

4. Discuss the characteristics of three basic strategies: low-cost, differentiation, and focus.

By this point in the strategic management process, entrepreneurs should have a clear picture of what their businesses do best and what their competitive advantages are. Similarly, they should know their companies' weaknesses and limitations as well as those of their competitors. The next step is to evaluate strategic options and then prepare a game plan designed to achieve the company's mission, goals, and objectives.

STRATEGY. A **strategy** is a road map an entrepreneur draws up of the actions necessary to fulfill a company's mission, goals, and objectives. In other words, the mission, goals, and objectives spell out the *ends*, and the strategy defines the *means* for reaching them. A strategy is the master plan that covers all of the major parts of the organization and ties them together into a unified whole. The plan must be action-oriented—that is, it should breathe life into the entire planning process. Entrepreneurs must build a sound strategy based on the preceding steps that uses their company's core competences as the springboard to success. Joseph Picken and Gregory Dess, authors of *Mission Critical: The 7 Strategic Traps that Derail Even the Smartest Companies,* write, "A flawed strategy—no matter how brilliant the leadership, no matter how effective the implementation—is doomed to fail. A sound strategy, implemented without error, wins every time."[35] A successful strategy is comprehensive and well-integrated, focusing on establishing the key success factors that the entrepreneur identified in Step 4.

ENTREPRENEURIAL
Profile

Scott and Melissa Coleman: La Puerta Originals

Scott and Melissa Coleman of La Puerta Originals.

Source: La Puerta Originals

Architect and custom home builder Scott Coleman identified early on that sustainable and environmentally friendly construction practices were emerging as key success factor in the home-building industry. Scott and his wife Melissa launched La Puerta Originals, a business in Santa Fe, New Mexico, that scours the world for antique and reclaimed wood and metal products that can be incorporated into the design of their clients' upscale homes. "We are proud that our work not only adds warmth and beauty to your home, but helps to preserve our world's natural resources," says Scott. La Puerta Originals, now with annual sales of $4.4 million, boasts a large collection of antique architectural wood materials in the United States, including more than 6,000 doors; yet each piece comes with its own provenance. "I take them to the wood and tell them the story behind it," he says.[36]

THREE STRATEGIC OPTIONS. The number of strategies from which entrepreneurs can choose is infinite. When all of the glitter is stripped away, however, three basic strategies remain. In his classic book, *Competitive Strategy,* Michael Porter defines three strategies: (1) cost leadership, (2) differentiation, and (3) focus (see Figure 1).

Cost Leadership. A company pursuing a **cost leadership strategy** strives to be the lowest-cost producer relative to its competitors in the industry. Many small companies attempt to compete by offering low prices, but low costs are a prerequisite for success. "You can't compete on price if you can't compete on cost," explains small business researcher Scott Shane.[37] Cost control on all fronts is paramount in companies that pursue this strategy. Economies of scale that are associated with large-scale operations are a common source of a company's cost advantage (high volume = low per unit costs), which makes executing a successful cost leadership strategy difficult for small businesses. However, small companies can build low-cost strategies in a number of ways. The most successful cost leaders know the areas in which they have cost advantages over their competitors and use them as the foundation for their strategies.

FIGURE 1
Three Strategic Options

Source: Michael Porter, *Competitive Strategy,* Free Press, New York: 1980. pp. 35–41.

	Source of Competitive Advantage	
	Uniqueness Perceived by Customer	**Low-Cost Position**
Entire Industry	Differentiation	Cost Leadership
Niche	Focus	

(Target Market)

Low-cost leaders have a competitive advantage in reaching buyers whose primary purchase criterion is price, and they have the power to set the industry's price floor. This strategy works well when buyers are sensitive to price changes, when competing firms sell the same commodity products, and when companies can benefit from economies of scale. Not only is a low-cost leader in the best position to defend itself in a price war, but it also can use its power to attack competitors with the lowest price in the industry. "You have to be the lowest-cost producer in your patch," says the president of a small company that sells the classic commodity product—cement.[38]

ENTREPRENEURIAL
Profile

*William Wang:
Vizio Inc.*

Before he turned 30, William Wang was a successful entrepreneur whose company, MAG Innovision, specialized in computer display screens. In 2002, Wang used $600,000 from the sale of MAG Innovision to launch Vizio Inc., which has surged past industry icons such as Sony, Sharp, and Samsung to become the fastest-growing maker of flat-panel televisions in North America. Wang's well-executed cost leadership strategy, much of which he developed from the mistakes he made at MAG Innovision, is the key to the company's success. When he started Vizio ("Where vision meets value"), high-definition televisions sold for $8,000, but Wang's vision was to offer quality products and to keep costs low, enabling his company to sell TVs at half the going price. "When I started this business, I believed we could do all of the things we're doing today," he says. A lean operating strategy has been a hallmark of the Irvine, California-based company since its first day of operation. Outsourcing most functions, including tech support, warehousing, shipping, and research and development, and keeping its employee ranks lean hold operating costs well below the industry average. Vizio's overhead costs are less than 1 percent of its sales, far below the 10 percent of sales that those costs represent at its competition. "Every single dime counts," says Wang. Because concept development, marketing, and customer service are keys to success, Wang intentionally keeps them in-house. Vizio's distribution network is consistent with its low-cost strategy, relying on discount chains such as Sam's Club, Costco, and others to reach mass market purchasers who tend to be price sensitive.[39]

Dangers exist in following a cost leadership strategy. Some companies attempt to compete on price even though their cost structure is not the lowest in the market. Other companies focus exclusively on lower manufacturing costs, without considering the impact of purchasing, distribution, or overhead costs. Another danger is misunderstanding the company's true cost drivers. For instance, one furniture manufacturer drastically underestimated its overhead costs and, as a result, was selling its products at a loss. Finally, a company may pursue a low-cost leadership strategy so zealously that it essentially locks itself out of other strategic choices.

Under the right conditions, a cost leadership strategy executed properly can be an incredibly powerful strategic weapon. Small discount retailers that live in the shadows of Walmart and thrive even when the economy slows succeed by relentlessly pursuing low-cost strategies. Small retail chains such as Fred's, Dollar General, Family Dollar, and 99 Cents Only cater to low- and middle-income customers who live in inner cities or rural areas. These small-box discounters incur rental costs that are one-tenth of those incurred by traditional retail stores by carefully choosing inexpensive locations in areas that are close to their target customers. Because their typical customer has an income of about $35,000, they offer inexpensive products such as food, health and beauty products, cleaning supplies, clothing, and seasonal merchandise, and many of the items they stock are closeout buys (purchases made as low as 10 cents on the dollar) on brand name merchandise. They also are committed to squeezing unnecessary costs out of their operations. Every decision the founders of these companies make—from the low-cost locations of their headquarters with their spartan facilities to their efficient distribution centers—emphasizes cost containment and is designed to appeal to the bargain-hunting nature of their target audiences. For instance, 99 Cents Only, whose name describes its merchandising strategy, is housed in a no-frills warehouse in an older section of City of Commerce, California. Dollar General has reduced its cost with its EZStore system, a labor-saving strategy that streamlines inventory restocking by using prestocked carts that employees literally roll off of delivery trucks straight onto the retail floor.[40]

Differentiation. A company following a **differentiation strategy** seeks to build customer loyalty by positioning its goods or services in a unique or different fashion. In other words, a company strives to be better than its competitors at something that its customers value. The primary benefit of successful differentiation is the ability to generate higher profit margins because of customers' heightened brand loyalty and reduced price sensitivity. There are many ways to create a differentiation strategy, but the key is to be special at something that is important to customers and offers them unique value such as quality, convenience, flexibility, performance, or style. "You'd better be on top of what it is your customers value and continually improve your offerings to better deliver that value," advises Jill Griffin, a strategic marketing consultant.[41] Any small company that can offer products or services that larger competitors do not, improve a product's or service's performance, reduce the customer's risk of purchasing it, or enhance the customer's status or self-esteem has the potential to differentiate.

ENTREPRENEURIAL
Profile

Ed McBride:
Steel Is Alive

Ed McBride has taken the ordinary charcoal grill and turned it into a work of art while creating a unique image for his business, Steel Is Alive. Rather than buy a standard charcoal grill, McBride, a sculptor, decided to make his own. In keeping with his artistic flair, McBride built a 5-foot-tall charcoal grill in the shape of a dragon, which he later sold for $65,000. Buoyed by his success, McBride officially added custom-built grills to his line of artistic creations, the latest of which incorporates another dragon, this one 9 feet tall with a wingspan of 10 feet. The design also includes a small dragon that heats a Dutch oven with his "dragon breath." Sales price: $90,000.[52]

Even in industries in which giant companies dominate, small companies that differentiate themselves can thrive even when they cannot compete effectively on the basis of price. The grocery industry is dominated by several large chains, but many small grocers are achieving success with differentiation strategies that are designed to appeal to their target customers. The average grocery store carries 46,852 items, and most of the large chains carry very similar, often identical, products and compete primarily on price. Many small, independent grocers stock unique products, often from small, local producers and growers, that customers cannot find in large, generic chain stores. Small grocers are installing high-tech scanners that speed checkout time, and some are using "smart" shopping carts that tally products as customers add them and, by accepting debit or credit cards, allow customers to avoid checkout lines altogether. Others offer extra services such as in-store babysitting, gourmet ready-to-cook and ready-to-eat meals, upscale in-store cafés, delivery services, and well-trained employees who take the time to help customers select the right ingredients for that special meal. Although these small grocers may not be able to compete with large chains on price, they are using their size to their advantage and are attracting customers who are looking for more than the lowest food prices.[43]

The key to a successful differentiation strategy is to build it on a *distinctive competence* (discussed earlier in this chapter)—something the small company is uniquely good at doing in comparison to its competitors. Common bases for differentiation include superior customer service, special product features, complete product lines, a custom-tailored product or service, instantaneous parts availability, absolute product reliability, supreme product quality, extensive product knowledge, and the ability to build long-term, mutually beneficial relationships with customers. To be successful, a differentiation strategy must create the perception of value to the customer. No customer will purchase a good or service that fails to produce a *perceived* value, no matter how *real* that value may be. One business consultant advises, "Make sure you tell your customers and prospects what it is about your business that makes you different. Make sure that difference is in the form of a true benefit to the customer."[44] Travel agents have been under siege by a host of strategic threats for more than a decade. The number of travel agents has declined from 124,000 in 2000 to fewer than 85,000 today. Those who are most successful are finding ways to differentiate themselves and to offer extra value for their customers.

Margaret and Pierre Faber, two adventurers with PhDs from Oxford University (his in business, hers in anthropology), founded Classic Africa in 1999 as an ecotourism company with the intent of sharing their passion for southern Africa's wilderness, wildlife, and people with discerning travelers from around the world. Pierre, a native of South Africa, grew up tracking animals in the bush outside Johannesburg. Classic Africa offers its guests the option of a standard tour or a customized itinerary, which is the more popular option. The Fabers arrange small group trips, which range in price from about $5,000 to $25,000, for about 500 clients each year at camps in South Africa, Namibia, Botswana, Zambia, and Zimbabwe. Guests enjoy the rugged comfort of the camps, which range from luxurious accommodations to more rustic and basic settings. Their offerings include photographic safaris (some of them on elephant) for Africa's exotic wildlife and gorgeous scenery and side trips to unique venues, such as Africat, a veterinary hospital for Africa's wild cats, such as the leopard, the cheetah, and the lion.[45]

Pursuing a differentiation strategy includes certain risks. One danger is trying to differentiate a product or service on the basis of something that does not boost its performance or lower its cost to the buyer. Another pitfall is trying to differentiate on the basis of something that customers do not perceive as important. Business owners also must consider how long they can sustain a product's or service's differentiation; changing customer tastes make the basis for differentiation temporary at best. Imitations and "knock-offs" from competitors also pose a threat to a successful differentiation strategy. For instance, designers of high-priced original clothing see much cheaper knock-off products on the market shortly after their designs hit the market. Another danger of this strategy is over-differentiating and charging so much that a company prices its products out of its target customers' reach. Another risk is focusing only on the physical characteristics of a product or service as a basis for differentiating it and ignoring important psychological factors—status, prestige, image, and style. For many successful companies, psychological factors are key elements in differentiating their products and services from those of competitors.

Focus. A **focus strategy** recognizes that not all markets are homogeneous. In fact, in any given market, there are many different customer segments, each having different needs, wants, and characteristics. The principal idea of this strategy is to select one (or more) segment(s); identify customers' special needs, wants, and interests; and then approach them with a good or service designed to excel in meeting these needs, wants, and interests. Focus strategies build on *differences* among market segments. Using a focus strategy, entrepreneurs concentrate on serving a niche in the market that larger companies are overlooking or underestimating rather than trying to reach the entire market.

A focus strategy is ideally suited to many small businesses, which often lack the resources to reach a national market. Their goal is to serve their narrow target markets more effectively and efficiently than do competitors that pound away at the broad market. Common bases for building a focus strategy include zeroing in on a small geographic area, targeting a group of customers with similar needs or interests (e.g., left-handed people), or specializing in a specific product or service (e.g., petite clothing).

Jane Tattersall, owner of Tattersall Sound & Pictures in Toronto, Canada, specializes in providing postproduction sound design for films and television shows. A subtle yet important part of any film, sound design involves incorporating the ideal sounds, which range from birds singing and horns honking to horses walking on cobblestones and cars exploding, at the right point in a scene once it has been filmed. Tattersall, her 9 full-time employees, and 15 freelancers located around the world have built a constantly growing library of more than 80,000 sound effects from which they can draw. Taking a recording device with her wherever she goes, Tattersall once stopped for 20 minutes on a deserted German back road at 4 A.M. to record the sounds of nightingales. "I'm trying to create reality," she says. Selecting and editing the sounds for a film typically takes 6 weeks, and mixing and refining it requires another 3 weeks. Toronto is the heart of Canada's thriving film industry, and Tattersall's company has built a strong reputation in its niche, having won more than 75 awards in its 20-plus years of business. "I just love filling in the canvas of sound on a film," says Tattersall.[46]

Like Tattersall, the most successful focusers build a competitive edge by concentrating on specific market niches and serving them better than any other competitor can. Essentially, this strategy depends on creating value for the customer either by being the lowest-cost producer or by differentiating the product or service in a unique fashion, but doing so in a narrow target segment. Speedy service, a unique product or service, specialized knowledge, superior customer service, value pricing, and convenience are just some of the ways that companies using focus strategies meet their target customers' unique needs. To be worth targeting, a niche must be large enough to be profitable, reachable through marketing, and capable of sustaining a business over time (in other words, not a passing fad). Examples of small companies competing successfully in small, yet profitable, niches include the following:

- Lena Blackburne Baseball Rubbing Mud, has supplied mud, which removes the gloss from new baseballs and makes them easier to grip, to every Major League Baseball team since 1959. Jim Bintliff, the third-generation president of the family business, which is located in Delran, New Jersey, still collects the special mud from the same secret location along the Delaware River that company founder Lena Blackburne discovered in 1938. Bintliff, who ages the mud for 6 months before selling it in 3-pound containers, recently began selling to a few NFL teams that have discovered that the mud makes footballs easier to grip.[47]
- Eric Shannon and Andrew Strauss started Oh My Dog Supplies, a San Francisco–based online company, to target dog owners who appreciate quality and craftsmanship and want more for their dogs than the run-of-the-mill goods found in the average pet store. In fact, the company's Web site promotes the top reason to buy from Oh My Dog Supplies: "Because your dog is unique. You want him or her to have cooler stuff than the dog next door that is stuck with gear from the big boring corporate Pet Super-Franchise."

Jim Bintliff collects mud that his company, Lena Blackburne Baseball Rubbing Mud, will process and sell to Major League Baseball teams to get slick new baseballs ready for play.

Source: Coke Whitworth\AP Wide World Photos

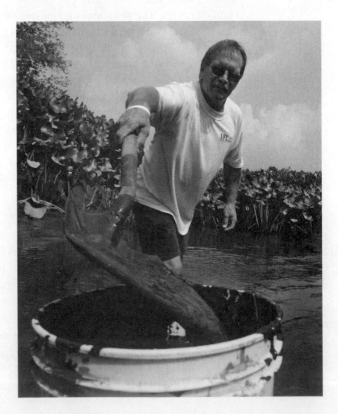

The company's product line includes elevated feeders (easier on digestion), all-natural gourmet food, luxurious couches and chaise lounges, and seat belts and car booster seats for dogs on the go.[48]

- Cretors, based in Chicago, Illinois, specializes in manufacturing popcorn poppers and other concession equipment for movie theaters and amusement parks. In the 1890s, Charles Cretors built a steam-powered nut roaster for his confectionary business and soon began using it to make popcorn. Nearly 120 years later, Charles D. Cretors, the founder's great-grandson, his son, Andrew, and 75 employees continue to make popcorn poppers that range from a basic popper priced at $700 to $500,000 industrial poppers used by snack food companies. The family-owned business generates annual sales of more than $15 million by focusing on its niche.[49]

The rewards of dominating a niche can be huge, but pursuing a focus strategy does carry risks. Companies sometimes must struggle to capture a large enough share of a small market to be profitable. A niche must be big enough for a company to generate a profit. A successful focus strategy also brings with it a threat: invasion by competitors. If a small company is successful in its niche, there is the danger of larger competitors entering the market and eroding or controlling it. Sometimes a company with a successful niche strategy gets distracted by its success and tries to branch out into other areas. As it drifts farther away from its core strategy, it loses its competitive edge and runs the risk of confusing or alienating its customers. Muddying its image with customers puts a company in danger of losing its identity.

A successful strategic plan identifies a complete set of success factors—financial, operating, and marketing—that, taken together, produce a competitive advantage for a small business. The resulting action plan distinguishes the firm from its competitors by exploiting its competitive advantages. The focal point of this entire strategic plan is the customer. The customer is the nucleus of any business, and a competitive strategy will succeed only if it is aimed at serving customers better than the competitor does. An effective strategy draws out the competitive advantage in a small company by building on its strengths and by making the customer its focus. It also defines methods for overcoming a company's weaknesses, and it identifies opportunities and threats that demand action.

IN THE ENTREPRENEURIAL

SPOTLIGHT Strategies for Success

Most entrepreneurs who launch businesses face established rivals with greater name recognition, more resources, bigger budgets, and existing customer bases. How can a small start-up company compete effectively against that? It all boils down to creating a winning strategy and then executing it. The entrepreneurs profiled here developed strategies for their companies that set them apart from their rivals and gave them a competitive edge in their respective markets.

Book Soup

Book Soup, a small, independent bookstore that has served its loyal customers from its location on Hollywood's legendary Sunset Boulevard for 31 years, sets itself apart by stocking more than 60,000 titles and specializing in hard-to-find books from small, international, and university publishers. Rather than attempting to compete on price with bookstore chains and online rivals, Book Soup emphasizes extensive collections of books on subjects that appeal to its target customers, such as film, art, photography, music, celebrity biographies, controversial nonfiction, and literary fiction. The quirky little store also features a regular schedule of appearances by authors for readings, which are followed by book signings. Authors who have appeared at Book Soup include Malcolm Gladwell (*Outliers*), Ralph Nader, (*The Seventeen Traditions*), and Barbara Benjamin Marcus (*Inside Out*, a book about drag queens). Signed first editions are a big draw to the store's target customers. Inside the store and on the company's Web site, shoppers can find reading recommendations from employees (all of whom are book fanatics) that point out books customers might otherwise overlook. The Book Soup Web site also includes links to a company blog and to its MySpace page as well as podcasts of author readings and interviews.

Bogdan Reels

Stanley Bogdan began making reels for fly fishermen in 1940 while working for the Rollins Engine Company, a manufacturer of steam engines. In 1955, he quit his job and began making reels full time. Today, Stanley's son, Steve, and his wife, Sandy, own Bogdan Reels, which hand-builds reels in 15 sizes, from those designed to catch the smallest trout to those made to handle a hard-charging Atlantic salmon. In a high-tech world, Bogdan's process is extremely low-tech. Except for a few springs, every part of a Bogdan reel is machined and fitted in a small garage-sized workshop in New Ipswich, New Hampshire, on a 50-year-old milling machine and a 130-year-old lathe. The company doesn't even own a computer.

The most unique feature of a Bogdan reel is the drag, a mechanical device that allows a fisherman to slow and then fight a hooked fish. Smoothness is the secret to a good drag, and Stanley invented a double-brake system that uses two spring-supported brake shoes that gently, but firmly, clamp down on the spinning disc, minimizing the chances of a fish breaking off. The unique drag makes a distinct whirring sound that one happy customer who owns six Bogdan reels describes as "the muted joy of exultation." Even though the price of a reel ranges from $1,300 to $2,200, Bogdan, which turns out only 100 or so reels a year, has a 3-year waiting list. Bogdan reels are so hard to come by that used ones often sell for more than new ones, fetching as much as $3,000 on eBay!

1. Which of the three strategies described in this chapter are these companies using? Explain.
2. What advantages does successful execution of their strategies produce for Book Soup and Bogdan Reels?
3. What are the risks associated with the strategies of these companies?

Sources: Based on "Book Soup for the Soul," *Get to the Point Marketing Inspiration*, July 27, 2009, pp. 1–2; "About Book Soup," Book Soup, *www.booksoup.com/about.html*; Monte Burke, "The Reel Deal," *Forbes*, April 13, 2009, p. 80.

Step 8. Translate Strategic Plans into Action Plans

When it comes to strategic planning, entrepreneurs typically do not lack vision. Success, however, requires matching vision with execution. No strategic plan is complete until it is put into action. Entrepreneurs must convert strategic plans into operating plans that guide their companies on a daily basis and become a visible, active part of their businesses. A small business cannot benefit from a strategic plan sitting on a shelf collecting dust.

IMPLEMENT THE STRATEGY. To make the plan workable, business owners should divide the plan into projects, carefully defining each one by the following:

Purpose. What is the project designed to accomplish?

Scope. Which areas of the company will be involved in the project?

Contribution. How does the project relate to other projects and to the overall strategic plan?

Resource requirements. What human and financial resources are needed to complete the project successfully?

Timing. Which schedules and deadlines will ensure project completion?

Once entrepreneurs assign priorities to these projects, they can begin to implement the strategic plan. Involving employees and delegating adequate authority to them is essential because these projects affect them most directly.

If an organization's people have been involved in the strategic management process to this point, they will have a better grasp of the steps they must take to achieve the organization's goals as well as their own professional goals. Early involvement of the workforce in the strategic management process is a luxury that larger businesses cannot achieve. Commitment to achieve the company's objectives is a powerful force for success, but involvement is a prerequisite for achieving total employee commitment. Without a committed, dedicated team of employees working together to implement strategy, a company's strategy, no matter how well planned, usually fails.

When putting their strategic plans into action, small companies must exploit all of the competitive advantages of their size by:

- Responding quickly to customers' needs
- Remaining flexible and willing to change
- Continually searching for new emerging market segments
- Building and defending market niches
- Erecting "switching costs" through personal service and special attention
- Remaining entrepreneurial and willing to take risks
- Acting with lightning speed to move into and out of markets as they ebb and flow
- Constantly innovating

Although it is possible for competitors to replicate a small company's strategy, it is much more difficult for them to mimic the way in which it implements and executes its strategy.

Step 9. Establish Accurate Controls

5. Understand the importance of controls such as the balanced scorecard in the planning process.

So far, the planning process has created company objectives and has developed a strategy for reaching them, but rarely, if ever, will the company's actual performance match stated objectives. Entrepreneurs quickly realize the need to control actual results that deviate from plans.

CONTROLLING THE STRATEGY. Planning without control has little operational value, and a sound planning program requires a practical control process. The plans created in this process become the standards against which actual performance is measured. It is important for everyone in the organization to understand—and to be involved in—the planning and controlling process.

Controlling projects and keeping them on schedule means that the owner must identify and track key performance indicators. The source of these indicators is the operating data from the company's normal business activity; they are the guideposts for detecting deviations from established standards. Accounting, production, sales, inventory, and other operating records are primary sources of data an entrepreneur can use for controlling activities. For example, on a customer service project, performance indicators might include the number of customer complaints, orders returned, on-time shipments, and a measure of order accuracy.

To evaluate the effectiveness of their strategies and to link them to everyday performance, many companies are developing **balanced scorecards**, a set of measurements unique to a company that includes both financial and operational measures and gives managers a quick yet comprehensive picture of the company's total performance against its strategic plan. The key to linking strategy and day-to-day organizational performance is identifying the right factors and measurements to be included on the scorecard. (Recall the discussion of the true economic denominators or critical numbers in Step 6 of the strategic management process, creating goals and objectives.) One writer says that a balanced scorecard:

> is a sophisticated business model that helps a company understand what's really driving its success. It acts a bit like the control panel on a spaceship—the business equivalent of a flight speedometer, odometer, and temperature gauge all rolled into one. It keeps track of many things, including financial progress and softer measurements—everything from customer satisfaction to return on investment—that need to be managed to reach the final destination: profitable growth.[50]

Rather than sticking solely to the traditional financial measures of a company's performance, the balanced scorecard gives managers a comprehensive view from *both a financial and an operational perspective*. The premise behind such a scorecard is that relying on any single measure of company performance is dangerous. Just as a pilot in command of a jet cannot fly safely by focusing on a single instrument, an entrepreneur cannot manage a company by concentrating on a single measurement. The complexity of managing a business demands that an entrepreneur be able to see performance measures in several areas simultaneously. Those measures might include traditional standards such as financial ratios or cash flow performance and gauges of product innovation, customer satisfaction, retention, and profitability as well as measures of vendor performance and inventory management.

Properly used, an entrepreneur can trace the elements on the company's balanced scorecard back to its overall strategy and its mission, goals, and objectives. The goal is to develop a reporting system that does not funnel meaningful information only to a few decision makers but to make it available in a timely manner throughout the entire company, enabling employees at *all* levels to make decisions based on strategic priorities. A balanced scorecard reporting system should collect, organize, and display meaningful information that managers and employees need to make daily decisions that are congruent with the company's overall strategy, and it must do so in a concise, easy-to-read, timely manner. When creating a balanced scorecard for a company, the key is to establish goals for each critical indicator of company performance and then create meaningful measures for each one. Although some elements will apply to many businesses, a company's scorecard should be unique. The balanced scorecard looks at a business from five important perspectives (see Figure 2):[51]

1. *Customer Perspective.* How do customers see us? Customers judge companies by at least four standards: time (how long it takes the company to deliver a good or service), quality (how well a company's product or service performs in terms of reliability, durability, and accuracy), performance (the extent to which a good or service performs as expected), and service (how well a company meets or exceeds customers' expectations of value). Because customer-related goals are external, managers must translate them into measures of what the company must do to meet customers' expectations.

2. *Internal Business Perspective.* On what factors must we excel? The internal factors that managers should focus on are those that have the greatest impact on customer satisfaction and retention and on company effectiveness and efficiency. Developing goals and measures for factors such as quality, cycle time, productivity, costs, and others that employees directly influence is essential.

3. *Innovation and Learning Perspective.* Can we continue to improve and create value? This view of a company recognizes that the targets required for success are never static; they are constantly changing. If a company wants to continue its pattern of success, it cannot stand still; it must continuously improve. A company's ability to innovate, learn, and improve determines its future. These goals and measures emphasize the importance of continuous improvement in customer satisfaction and internal business operations.

4. *Financial Perspective.* How do we look to investors? The most traditional performance measures, financial standards tell how much the company's overall strategy and its execution are contributing to

FIGURE 2
The Balanced Scorecard

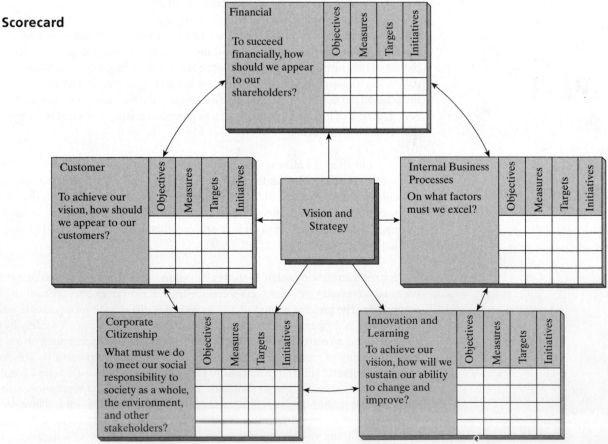

its bottom line. These measures focus on factors such as profitability, growth, and investor value. On balanced scorecards, companies often break their financial goals into three categories: survival, success, and growth. Companies use these measures to make sure that their strategies drive their budgets rather than allowing their budgets to determine their strategies.

5. *Corporate citizenship.* How well are we meeting our social responsibility to society as a whole, the environment, the community, and other external stakeholders? Even the smallest companies must recognize that they have a responsibility to be good business citizens. This part of the scorecard focuses on measuring a small company's social and environmental performance.

Although the balanced scorecard is a vital tool that helps managers keep their companies on track, it is also an important tool for changing behavior in an organization and for keeping everyone focused on what really matters. As conditions change, managers must make corrections in performances, policies, strategies, and objectives to get performance back on track. Increasingly, companies are linking performance on the metrics included in their balanced scorecards to employees' compensation. A practical control system is also economical to operate. Most small businesses have no need for a sophisticated, expensive control system. The system should be so practical that it becomes a natural part of the management process.

Conclusion

The strategic planning process does *not* end with the nine steps outlined here; it is an ongoing procedure that a small business owner must repeat. With each round, the entrepreneur gains experience, and the steps become much easier. The planning process outlined here is designed to be as simple as possible. No small business should be burdened with an elaborate, detailed formal planning process that it cannot easily use.

This strategic planning process teaches entrepreneurs a degree of discipline that is important to their businesses' survival. It helps them to learn about their businesses, their competitors, and, most important, their customers. It forces them to recognize and evaluate their companies' strengths and weaknesses as well as the opportunities and threats facing them. It also encourages entrepreneurs to define how they will set their businesses apart from the competition. Although strategic planning cannot guarantee success, it does dramatically increase a small company's chances of survival in a hostile business environment.

Chapter Review

1. Understand the importance of strategic management to a small business.
   - Strategic planning, which often is ignored by small companies, is a crucial ingredient in business success. The planning process forces potential entrepreneurs to subject their ideas to an objective evaluation in the competitive market.
2. Explain why and how a small business must create a competitive advantage in the market.
   - The goal of developing a strategic plan is for the small company to create a competitive advantage—the aggregation of factors that sets the small business apart from its competitors and gives it a unique position in the market. Every small firm must establish a plan for creating a unique image in the minds of its potential customers.
3. Develop a strategic plan for a business using the nine steps in the strategic planning process.
   - Small businesses need a strategic planning process designed to suit their particular needs. It should be relatively short, be informal and not structured, encourage the participation of employees, and not begin with extensive objective setting. Linking the purposeful action of strategic planning to an entrepreneur's little ideas can produce results that shape the future.

   Step 1. *Develop a clear vision and translate it into a meaningful mission statement.* Highly successful entrepreneurs are able to communicate their vision to those around them. The firm's mission statement answers the first question of any venture: What business am I in? The mission statement sets the tone for the entire company.

Step 2. *Assess the company's strengths and weaknesses.* Strengths are positive internal factors; weaknesses are negative internal factors.

Step 3. *Scan the environment for significant opportunities and threats facing the business.* Opportunities are positive external options; threats are negative external forces.

Step 4. *Identify the key factors for success in the business.* In every industry, key factors determine a firm's success, and so they must be an integral part of a company's strategy. Key success factors are relationships between a controllable variable (e.g., plant size, size of sales force, advertising expenditures, product packaging) and a critical factor that influences the firm's ability to compete in the market.

Step 5. *Analyze the competition.* Business owners should know their competitors almost as well as they know their own companies. A competitive profile matrix is a helpful tool for analyzing competitors' strengths and weaknesses.

Step 6. *Create company goals and objectives.* Goals are the broad, long-range attributes that the firm seeks to accomplish. Objectives are quantifiable and more precise; they should be specific, measurable, assignable, realistic, timely, and written down. The process works best when subordinate managers and employees are actively involved.

Step 7. *Formulate strategic options and select the appropriate strategies.* A strategy is the game plan the firm plans to use to achieve its objectives and mission. It must center on establishing for the firm the key success factors identified earlier. Three strategic options include cost leadership, differentiation, and focus strategies.

Step 8. *Translate strategic plans into action plans.* No strategic plan is complete until the owner puts it into action.

Step 9. *Establish accurate controls.* Actual performance rarely, if ever, matches plans exactly. Operating data from the business serve as guideposts for detecting deviations from plans. Such information is helpful when plotting future strategies.

The strategic planning process does not end with these nine steps; rather, it is an ongoing process that the owner will repeat.

4. Discuss the characteristics of three basic strategies: low-cost, differentiation, and focus.
   • Three basic strategic options are cost leadership, differentiation, and focus. A company pursuing a cost leadership strategy strives to be the lowest-cost producer relative to its competitors in the industry.
   • A company following a differentiation strategy seeks to build customer loyalty by positioning its goods or services in a unique or different fashion. In other words, the firm strives to be better than its competitors at something that customers value.
   • A focus strategy recognizes that not all markets are homogeneous. The principal idea of this strategy is to select one (or more) segment(s), identify customers' special needs, wants, and interests, and approach them with a good or service designed to excel in meeting these needs, wants, and interests. Focus strategies build on differences among market segments.

5. Understand the importance of controls such as the balanced scorecard in the planning process.
   • Just as a pilot in command of a jet cannot fly safely by focusing on a single instrument, an entrepreneur cannot manage a company by concentrating on a single measurement. The balanced scorecard is a set of measurements unique to a company that includes both financial and operational measures and gives managers a quick yet comprehensive picture of the company's total performance.

Discussion Questions

1. Why is strategic planning important to a small company?
2. What is a competitive advantage? Why is it important for a small business to establish one?
3. What are the steps in the strategic management process?
4. What are strengths, weaknesses, opportunities, and threats? Give an example of each.
5. What is competitive intelligence? What benefits does it offer a small company?
6. Explain the characteristics of effective objectives. Why is setting objectives important?

7. What are business strategies? Explain the three basic strategies from which entrepreneurs can choose. Give an example of each one.
8. Describe the three basic strategies available to small companies. Under what conditions is each most successful?
9. How is the controlling process related to the planning process?
10. What is a balanced scorecard? What value does it offer entrepreneurs who are evaluating the success of their current strategies?

This chapter is designed to help you think about your business from a strategic perspective. This involves describing your business objectives, drafting your mission statement, identifying "keys to success," conducting a SWOT analysis, and making initial comments about your strategy and your competitive advantage.

On the Web

Visit the Companion Web site at *www.pearsonhighered.com/scarborough* and click the "Business Plan Resources" tab. Scroll down and find the information with the heading "Standard Industry Classification Codes" (SIC codes). Step through the process to find the SIC code associated with your industry. Then, review the information associated with the "Competitor Analysis" section. This information may provide insight into learning more about your industry competitors on a global, national, or even on a local basis.

In the Software

Open your plan in Business Plan Pro. Add text to the strategic areas mentioned in this chapter. Don't worry about perfecting this information. Instead, capture your main thoughts and ideas so you can revisit these topics, add detail, and make certain the sections are congruent with your entire plan. Reviewing some examples of each of these sections in one or more of the sample plans that you had selected earlier may be helpful.

Review the following sections, as they appear, in one or more of the sample plans that you identified earlier:

- Mission Statement
- Objectives
- SWOT Analysis
- Keys to Success
- Competition, Buying Patterns, and Main Competitors

- Value Proposition
- Competitive Edge
- Strategy & Implementation Summary

Note the information captured in these sections of the plans. The text in some areas may be quite elaborate, whereas in other areas it might be brief and contain only bullet points. As you look at each plan, determine whether it provides the needed information under each topic and think about the type of information to include in your plan.

Building Your Business Plan

Here are some tips you may want to consider as you tackle each of these sections:

- *Mission statement.* Use your mission statement to establish your fundamental goals for the quality of your business offering. The mission statement represents the opportunity to answer the questions: What business are you in and why does your business exist? This may include the value you offer and the role customers, employees, and owners play in providing and benefiting from that value. A good mission statement can be a critical element in defining your business and communicating this definition to key stakeholders including investors, partners, employees, and customers.
- *Objectives.* Objectives should be specific goals that are quantifiable and measurable. Setting measurable objectives will enable you to track your progress and measure your results.
- *SWOT analysis.* What are the internal strengths and weaknesses of your business? As you look outside the organization, what are the external opportunities and threats? List the threats and opportunities and then assess what this tells you about your business. How can you leverage your strengths to take advantage of the opportunities ahead? How can you improve or minimize the areas of weaknesses?

■ *Keys to success.* Virtually every business has critical aspects that make the difference between success and failure. These may be brief bullet point comments that capture key elements that will make a difference in accomplishing your stated objectives and realizing your mission.

■ *Competition, buying patterns, and main competitors.* Discuss your ideal position in the market. Think about specific kinds of features and benefits your business offers and how they are unique compared to what is available to your market today. Why do people buy your services instead of the services your competitors offer? Discuss your primary competitors' strengths and weaknesses. Consider their service offerings, pricing, reputation, management, financial position, brand awareness, business development, technology, and any other factors that may be important. What market segments do they occupy? What strategy do they appear to pursue? How much of a competitive threat do they present?

■ *Value proposition.* A value proposition is a clear and concise statement that describes the tangible value-based result a customer receives from using your product or service. The more specific and meaningful this statement is from a customer's perspective, the better. Once you have your value proposition, look at your organization—and your business plan—in terms of how well you communicate it and fulfill your promise to your customers or clients.

■ *Your competitive edge.* A competitive edge builds on your value proposition and seeks to capture the unique value—in whatever terms the customer defines that value—that your business offers. Your competitive edge may be through your product, customer service, method of distribution, pricing, or promotional methods. It describes how your business is uniquely different from all others in a way that is meaningful to customers and sustainable over time.

■ *Strategy and implementation.* This is a section that you will build upon and, for now, make comments that capture your plans for the business. This describes the game plan and provides focus to realize your venture's objectives and mission. Based on your initial strategic analysis, which of the three business strategies—low cost, differentiation, or focus—will you use to give your company a competitive advantage? How will this strategy capitalize on your company's strengths and appeal to your customer's need? Later you will build upon this information as you formulate action plans to bring this strategic plan to life.

Capture your ideas in each of these sections and continually ask yourself about the relevance of this information. If it does not add value to your business plan, there is no need to include this information.

Endnotes

1. L. Gordon Crovitz, "How the Music Industry Can Get Digital Satisfaction," *Wall Street Journal*, January 12, 2009, p. A11; Fred Vogelstein, "Mastering the Art of Disruption," *Fortune*, February 6, 2006, pp. 23–24; Prince McLean, "Apple: 50% of Our Traditional MP3 Buyers New to iPod," *AppleInsider*, July 21, 2009, *www.appleinsider.com/articles/09/07/21/apple_retains_70_of_mp3_player_share_50_of_ipod_buyers_new.html*.

2. Alvin Toffler, "Shocking Truths About the Future," *Journal of Business Strategy*, July/August 1996, p. 6; Russ Juskalian, "Knowledge Drives Future, Creates Wealth, Authors Say," *USA Today*, May 15, 2006, p. 5B.

3. Norm Brodsky, "Be Prepared," *Inc.*, January 2006, pp. 53–54.

4. Samuel Greenguard, "Knowledge Management Can Turbocharge Your Company," *Beyond Computing*, November/December 2000, p. 28.

5. Thomas A. Stewart, "You Think Your Company's So Smart? Prove It," *Fortune*, April 30, 2001, p. 188.

6. Geoffrey Colvin, "Managing in Chaos," *Fortune*, October 2, 2006, pp. 76–82.

7. David Dykes, "Relocation, Revamping a Natural for Garner's," *Greenville News*, September 7, 2008, p. 1E.

8. "About Martin," C.F. Martin and Company, *www.martinguitar.com/news/aboutmartin.html*; Susan Koomar, "Strummin' Fun: Free Factory Tours at Martin Guitar," *Pike County Press and Port Jervis News*, July 20, 2009, *http://pikecountypress.com/wordpress/2009/07/30/strummin%E2%80%99-fun-free-factory-tours-at-martin-guitar/*.

9. "Paul Reed Smith: Entrepreneur of the Year," Ultimate Guitar, July 11, 2007, *www.ultimate-guitar.com/news/press_releases/paul_reed_smith_entrepreneur_of_the_year.html*; Paul Reed Smith, "The Journey Begins," PRS Guitars, *www.prsguitars.com/inside/history.html*; Tom Wheeler, "The Journey Continues," PRS Guitars, *www.prsguitars.com/inside/history.html*.

10. "John Naisbitt Quotes," ThinkExist, *http://thinkexist.com/quotation/strategic-planning-is-worthless-unless-there-is/363708.html*.

11. Ray Smilor, *Daring Visionaries: How Entrepreneurs Build Companies, Inspire Allegiance, and Create Wealth* (Avon, MA: Adams Media Corporation, 2001), pp. 12–13.

12. Thomas A. Stewart, "Why Values Statements Don't Work," *Fortune*, June 10, 1996, p. 137.

13. "Core Values," Turner Construction Company, *www.turnerconstruction.com/corporate/content.asp?d=5736*; "Turner News: Special Centennial Issue," Turner Constrction Company, March 2002, pp. 1, 19.

14. Danny Meyer, "The Saltshaker Theory," *Inc.*, October 2006, p. 70.

15. Carol Lewis, "For a True Charburger, Race to Foster's Grille," *Urbana Gazette*, January 24, 2008, *www.fostersgrille.com/PDF_Files/Urbana-Gazette-net.pdf*; Chelsea Mann, "Under the Toque: Foster's Grille Fosters Neighborhood Feel," *Nation's Restaurant News*, July 14, 2008, *www.nrn.com/article.aspx?keyword=%20Shawn%20Kearney%20Tang&menu_id=1388&id=356548*; "Foster's Grill Fills Fast-Casual Burger Void: Projects 100 Franchises in Next Four Years," *FranchiseGator*, April 14, 2008, *www.franchisegator.com/articles/foster%27s-grille-fills-fast-casual-burger-void-projects-100-franchises-in-next-four-years/*.

16. "About Our Winery: Mission Statement," Fetzer Vineyards, *www.fetzer.com/fetzer/wineries/philosophy.aspx*.

17. Sarah E. Needleman, "Dial-a-Mattress Retailer Blames Troubles on Stores, Executive Team," *Wall Street Journal*, July 14, 2009, *http://online.wsj.com/article/SB124752875953235607.html*.

18. Kim Orr, "Power Rangers," *Entrepreneur*, February 2009, pp. 22–25; Katie Fehrenbacher, "Greenbox, Silver Springs Score Oklahoma Utility Deal," Earth2Tech, August 20, 2008, *http://earth2tech.com/2008/08/20/greenbox-silver-springs-score-oklahoma-utility-deal/*.

19. Alex Taylor III and Lawrence Delevigne, "Motor City Blues," *Fortune*, February 2, 2009, p. 13.

20. "U.S. Movie Market Summary 1995–2009," *The Numbers*, July 31, 2009, *www.the-numbers.com/market/*; Andy Serwer, "Extreme Makeover," *Fortune*, May 29, 2006, pp. 108–116.

21. "National Amusements Launches 'Center Stage,'" National Amusements, January 5, 2009, *www.nationalamusements.com/*

about/press.asp; "National Theater Unveils Luxury Theater in Brazil," National Amusements, March 27, 2007, *www.nationalamusements.com/about/press.asp*; Kate Kelly, "The Multiplex Under Siege," *Wall Street Journal*, December 24–25, 2005, pp. P1, P5; Andy Serwer, "Extreme Makeover," *Fortune*, May 29, 2006, pp. 108–116.

22. Nicole L. Torres, "Roast of the Town," *Entrepreneur B.Y.O.B.*, March 2003, p. 118; "Company History," Mayorga Coffee Roasters, *www.mayorgacoffee.com/about_01_2.html*.

23. "Executive Outlook," *Sales and Marketing Management's Performance Newletter*, May 29, 2006, p. 1.

24. Carolyn Z. Lawrence, "Know Your Competition," *Business Startups*, April 1997, p. 51.

25. *Global Market Intelligence Survey*, Global Intelligence Alliance, February 2008, p. 5.

26. David Whitford, "Sandwich Superheroes," *FSB*, June 2003, p. 20; "Our History," Geno's Steaks, *www.genosteaks.com*; "History," Pat's King of Steaks, *www.patskingofsteaks.com/history.htm*.

27. Julia Boorstin, "Cruising for a Bruising?" *Fortune*, June 9, 2003, pp. 143–150; Martha Brannigan, "Cruise Lines Look to the Land to Get Boomers on Board," *Wall Street Journal*, December 6, 1999, p. B4.

28. Shari Caudron, "I Spy, You Spy," *Industry Week*, October 3, 1994, p. 36.

29. Stephen D. Solomon, "Spies Like You," *FSB*, June 2001, pp. 76–82.

30. Dan Brekke, "What You Don't Know Can Hurt You," *Smart Business*, March 2001, pp. 64–76.

31. David H. Freedman, "Somebody's Watching You," *Inc.*, September 2005, pp. 75–76.

32. Mark Henricks, "In the BHAG," *Entrepreneur*, August 1999, pp. 65–67.

33. Jim Collins and Jerry Poras, *Built to Last: Successful Habits of Visionary Companies* (New York: HarperBusiness, 1994), p. 232.

34. Jamie Herzlich, "Small Business: Setting Goals to Meet the Economy's Challenges," *Newsday*, June 1, 2009, *www.newsday.com/columnists/jamie-herzlich/small-business-setting-goals-to-meet-economy-s-challenges-1.748411*.

35. Joseph C. Picken and Gregory Dess, "The Seven Traps of Strategic Planning," *Inc.*, November 1996, p. 99.

36. Malika Zouhali-Worrall, "Domestic Bliss," *FSB*, November 2008, p. 100; "Our Story," La Puerta Originals, *www.lapuertaoriginals.com/story/*.

37. Ian Mount, "Myth Busters," *FSB*, November 2008, p. 30.

38. Kambiz Foroohar, "Step Ahead—and Avoid Fads," *Forbes*, November 4, 1996, pp. 172–176.

39. Sara Wilson, "Picture It," *Entrepreneur*, July 2008, p. 43; Matt McClellan, "The Big Picture," *Smart Business Orange County*, June 2008,

www.sbnonline.com/Local/Article/14706/77/0/The_big_picture.aspx; "Vizio Announces Grand Opening of a New Customer Service Based Sales and Support Center," *Reuters*, May 14, 2009, *www.reuters.com/article/pressRelease/idUS137503+14-May-2009+PRN20090514*.

40. Suzanne Kapner, "The Mighty Dollar," *Fortune*, April 27, 2009, pp. 64–66; Matthew Boyle, "The King of Cheap Stuff," *Fortune*, November 14, 2005, p. 220; Ann Zimmerman, "Behind the Dollar-Store Boom: A Nation of Bargain Hunters," *Wall Street Journal*, December 13, 2004, pp. A1, A10; Brendan Coffey, "Every Penny Counts," *Forbes*, September 30, 2002, pp. 68–70; Amber McDowell, "Discount Retailers Prosper Amid Economic Instability," *Greenville News Business*, December 23, 2002, pp. 6, 13; Tony Taylor, "S.C. a Growth Center for Discount Retailer," *GSA Business*, November 25, 2005, pp. 3, 9; Debbie Howell, "Dollar General Market to Grow 70 in 2006," *DSN Retailing Today*, December 19, 2005, *www.findarticles.com/p/articles/mi_m0FNP/is_23_44/ai_n15969632*.

41. Debra Phillips, "Leaders of the Pack," *Entrepreneur*, September 1996, p. 127.

42. Brandi Stewart, "Grilled Dragon," *FSB*, September 2008, p. 27; "Barbeque Sculptures," Steel Is Alive, *www.steelisalive.com/bbqsculptures.htm*.

43. Damian Joseph, "Supermarket Strategies: What's New at the Grocer," *BusinessWeek*, June 8, 2009, *www.businessweek.com/innovate/content/jun2009/id2009068_540314.htm*; Ted Mininni, "How Can Supermarkets Truly Differentiate?" *Marketing Profs Daily Fix*, June 30, 2009, pp. 1–2.

44. Phillips, "Leaders of the Pack," p. 127.

45. Maggie Overfelt, "Breakfast with Cheetahs," *FSB*, June 2008, pp. 88–92; "About Us," Classic Africa, *http://classicafrica.com/aboutus/about.htm*.

46. Caitlin Kelly, "She Hunts and Gathers Sounds," *Wall Street Journal*, July 29, 2009, *http://online.wsj.com/article/SB10001424052970204261704574274364012713436.html*.

47. Jim Bintliff, "Joy in Mudville," *FSB*, September 2008, pp. 34–35; Kasey Wehrum, "Behind the Scenes," *Inc.*, April 2009, pp. 16–17.

48. KC Ifeanyi, "The Lap of Luxury," *FSB*, March 2009, pp. 90–91.

49. Patrick J. Sauer, "Behind the Scenes," *Inc.*, October 2008, pp. 22–23; "History," Cretors, *www.cretors.com/History-set.htm*.

50. Joel Kurtzman, "Is Your Company Off Course? Now You Can Find Out Why," *Fortune*, February 17, 1997, p. 128.

51. Robert S. Kaplan and David P. Norton, "The Balanced Scorecard—Measures That Drive Performance," *Harvard Business Review*, January–February 1992, pp. 71–79.

Choosing a Form of Ownership

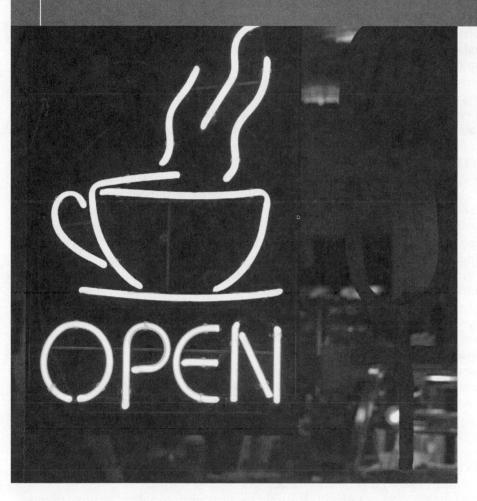

Learning Objectives

Upon completion of this chapter, you will be able to:

1 Discuss the issues that entrepreneurs should consider when evaluating different forms of ownership.

2 Describe the advantages and disadvantages of the sole proprietorship.

3 Describe the advantages and disadvantages of the partnership.

4 Describe the advantages and disadvantages of the corporation.

5 Describe the features of the alternative forms of ownership, such as the S corporation, the limited liability company, and the joint venture.

Whenever you see a successful business, someone once made a

courageous decision.

—Peter F. Drucker

To survive, men and business and corporations must serve.

—John H. Patterson

From Chapter 3 of *Effective Small Business Management: An Entrepreneurial Approach*, 10/e. Norman M. Scarborough.
Copyright © 2012 by Pearson Education. Published by Prentice Hall. All rights reserved.

1. Discuss the issues that entrepreneurs should consider when evaluating different forms of ownership.

One of the first decisions an entrepreneur faces when starting a business is selecting the form of ownership for the new venture. Too often, entrepreneurs give little thought to the decision, which can lead to problems because it has far-reaching implications for the business and its owners—from the taxes the company pays and how it raises money to the owner's liability for the company's debts and his or her ability to transfer the business to the next generation. Although the decision is not irreversible, changing from one form of ownership to another can be expensive, time consuming, and complicated.

There is no single "best" form of business ownership. Each form has its own unique set of advantages and disadvantages. The key to choosing the right form of ownership is to understand the characteristics of each business entity and to know how they affect an entrepreneur's business and personal circumstances.

The following are some of the most important issues an entrepreneur should consider in choosing a form of ownership:

- *Tax considerations.* Graduated tax rates, the government's constant modification of the tax code, and the year-to-year fluctuations in a company's income require an entrepreneur to calculate the firm's tax responsibility under each ownership option every year. Changes in federal or state tax codes may have a significant impact on the firm's "bottom line" and the entrepreneur's personal tax exposure.
- *Liability exposure.* Certain forms of ownership offer business owners greater protection from personal liability from financial problems, faulty products, and lawsuits. Entrepreneurs must evaluate the potential for legal and financial liabilities and decide the extent to which they are willing to assume personal responsibility for their companies' obligations. Individuals with significant personal wealth or a low tolerance for the risk of loss may benefit from forms of ownership that provide greater protection of their personal assets.
- *Start-up and future capital requirements.* The form of ownership can affect an entrepreneur's ability to raise start-up capital. Some forms of ownership are better than others when obtaining start-up capital, depending on how much capital is needed and the source from which it is to be obtained. As a business grows, capital requirements increase, and some forms of ownership make it easier to attract outside financing.
- *Control.* Certain forms of ownership require an entrepreneur to relinquish some control over the company. Before selecting a business entity, entrepreneurs must decide how much control they are willing to sacrifice in exchange for resources from others.
- *Managerial ability.* Entrepreneurs must assess their own ability to successfully manage their companies. If they lack skill or experience in certain areas, they should consider a form of ownership that allows them to involve individuals who possess those needed skills or experience into the company.
- *Business goals.* The projected size and profitability of the business influence the form of ownership an entrepreneur chooses. Businesses often evolve into different forms of ownership as they grow, but moving from some formats can be complex and expensive. Legislation may change and make current ownership options no longer attractive.
- *Management succession plans.* When choosing a form of ownership, business owners must look ahead to the day when they will pass their companies on to the next generation or to a buyer. Some forms of ownership better facilitate this transition than others. In other cases, when the owner dies, so does the business.
- *Cost of formation.* Some forms of ownership are much more costly and involved to create. Entrepreneurs must weigh the benefits and the costs of the form they choose.

Traditionally, business owners have been able to choose from three major forms of ownership: the sole proprietorship, the partnership, and the corporation. Other hybrid forms of ownership include the S corporation, the limited liability company, and the joint venture. This chapter describes the characteristics, advantages, and disadvantages of these forms of business ownership. Figure 1 provides an overview of the various forms of ownership.

The Sole Proprietorship

2. Describe the advantages and disadvantages of the sole proprietorship.

The **sole proprietorship** is the simplest and most popular form of ownership. This form of business ownership is designed for a business owned and managed by one individual. The sole proprietor is the only owner and ultimate decision maker for the business. Its simplicity and ease

FIGURE 1
Forms of Business Ownership

Source: Based on data from *Sources of Income*, Internal Revenue Service.

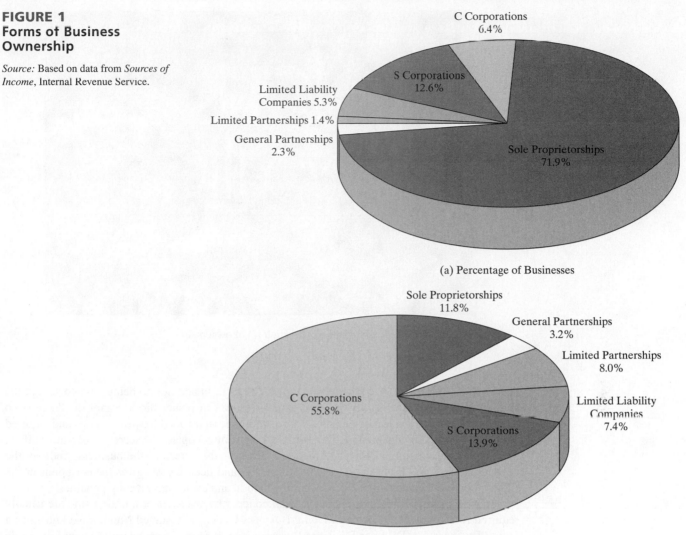

(a) Percentage of Businesses

(b) Percentage of Net Income

of formation make the sole proprietorship the most popular form of ownership, comprising nearly 72 percent of all businesses in the United States.

Advantages of a Sole Proprietorship

Sole proprietorships offer the following advantages:

SIMPLE TO CREATE. One attractive feature of the sole proprietorship is the ease and speed of its formation. For example, if entrepreneurs want to form a business under their own names (J. Jolly Financial Consulting), they simply obtain the necessary business licenses from state, county, and/or local governments and begin operation. In most cases, an entrepreneur can complete all of the necessary steps in a single day because few barriers exist to creating a sole proprietorship.

ENTREPRENEURIAL
Profile

David Polatseck: Business Licenses

Entrepreneurs can download more than 50,000 federal, state, and local license and permit applications from the Airmont, New York–based Business Licenses Web site (*www.businesslicenses.com*). For as little as $20 per form, entrepreneurs can learn which forms they must file, access the necessary forms, get supporting documents, and file and archive them online without having to make trips to multiple government offices. The company also offers a comprehensive Business License Compliance Package that provides entrepreneurs with a complete, customized list of all of the licenses, permits, and tax registration documents they must file to open and operate their businesses. According to cofounder David Polatseck, the 60-employee company has helped more than 10,000 small business customers across the United States.[1]

107

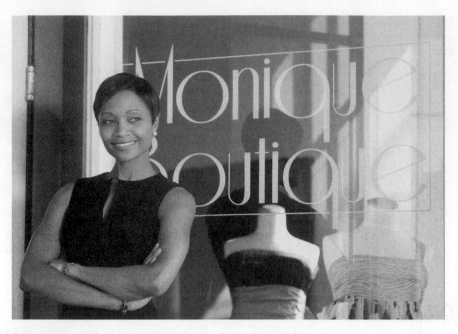

Sole proprietorships are the most common form of ownership.

Source: Blend Images\SuperStock, Inc.

LEAST COSTLY FORM OF OWNERSHIP TO ESTABLISH. In addition to being easy to set up, the sole proprietorship is generally the least expensive form of ownership to establish. There is no need to create and file legal documents, such as those recommended for partnerships and required for corporations. An entrepreneur, for example, may simply contact the secretary of state's office, select a business name, identify the location, describe the nature of the business, and pay the appropriate fees and license costs. Paying these fees and license costs gives the entrepreneur the right to conduct business in that particular jurisdiction and avoids aggravating penalties.

In many jurisdictions, entrepreneurs who conduct business under a trade name are usually required to acquire a Certificate of Doing Business Under an Assumed Name (also known as a Doing Business As (DBA) or Fictitious Business Name) from the secretary of state. Some sole proprietors use their own names as their company names, such as Bob Smith Towing Service. Others prefer to come up with creative company names as a way of distinguishing themselves in the market and creating the right impression with their target customers.

The fee for the Certificate of Doing Business Under an Assumed Name is usually nominal. Acquiring this certificate involves conducting a search to verify that the name chosen for the business is not already registered as a trademark or service mark with the secretary of state. Filing this certificate also notifies the state of the owners of the business. Additionally, most states now require notice of the trade name to be published in a newspaper serving the trade area of the business.

PROFIT INCENTIVE. One major advantage of operating as a sole proprietorship is that once the entrepreneur has paid all of the company's expenses, he or she can keep the remaining after-tax

LESSONS FROM THE STREET-SMART → entrepreneur

Get That Name Right!

The owners of Rise and Dine Restaurants, a chain of 15 breakfast and lunch restaurants based in Columbus, Ohio, decided to change the name of the business to Sunny Street Café. Market research showed that customers associated the name "Rise and Dine" with breakfast only and that many of them were unaware that the chain also was open for lunch. "We want our customers to know that we offer an extensive lunch menu with plenty of variety," says Chief Operating Officer Joe Deavenport. "Our tagline, 'A Bright Spot for Breakfast and Lunch' will resonate well with our target audience and capture the essence of our brand."

As Sunny Street Café's experience shows, choosing a memorable business name can be one of the most enjoyable—and most challenging—aspects of starting a business. Some entrepreneurs invest as much in the creation of their business names as they do in developing their business ideas. Ideally, a business name should convey the expertise, value, and uniqueness of the company and its products or services. Darrin Piotrowski saw a need for fast, affordable, and reliable computer service in his native New Orleans, Louisiana, and borrowed $300 from his mother to start Rent-a-Nerd as a part-time business from his apartment. The clever name caught people's attention, and Piotrowski's customer service kept them coming back. The business grew quickly, and Piotrowski soon quit his job to run Rent-a-Nerd full time.

Gerald Lewis, owner of CDI Designs, a brand consulting company that specializes in helping retail food businesses, says that the right name is essential. "In retailing, the market is so segmented that [a name must] convey very quickly what the customer is going after," he says. "For example, if it is a warehouse store, it has to convey that impression. If it's an upscale store selling high-quality food, it has to convey that impression. The name combined with the logo is very important in doing that."

Whatever the image you want to communicate to your customers, try the following process from the Street-Smart Entrepreneur:

1. Decide the most appropriate single quality of the business that you want to convey. Avoid sending a mixed or inappropriate message. Remember that a name is the first and single most visible attribute of a company. Your business's name will appear on all advertising and printed materials and, if done effectively, will portray its personality, make it stand out in a crowd, and help it to stick in the minds of consumers. Remember: The more your name communicates about your business to your customers, the less effort you have to expend to educate them about what your company does.

2. Select a name that is short, attention-getting, and memorable. Avoid names that are hard to spell, pronounce, or remember.

3. Be creative and have fun with a name but follow the guidelines of good taste. When Paul and Barbara Rasmussen started a store in Vancouver, British Columbia, that sells manufactured and custom-made sofas, they decided to name it Sofa So Good.

4. Make sure the name has longevity and does not limit your business. Although many small businesses operate locally, choosing a "local" name restricts a company that wants to expand its area of operation. For example, the name "Richmond Bakery" may not be suitable if the company wants to expand beyond the borders of Richmond.

5. Select a name that creates a positive image for your business. Is Rent-a-Wreck attractive because you think you will save money on a car rental, or does the name put you off because you question the reliability of its cars? Lord of the Fries is a Melbourne, Australia-based business that specializes in selling fresh, hand-cut fries topped with a variety of international sauces.

6. Once you have selected a name, try it out on friends and family. Does the name resonate, or does it create looks of bewilderment?

7. Once you are comfortable with your choice, conduct a name search to make sure that no one else in your jurisdiction has already claimed the name. This is an especially important task for companies whose Web site addresses use the company name. Registering a name with the proper office provides immediate protection.

8. Another tactic in coming up with a great name is to visualize your customers. What are your customers like? What are their ages, genders, lifestyles, and locations? What characteristics of your company are most important to your customers? Classic examples of companies that have used this approach include ServiceMaster, In-N-Out Burgers, and Value-Rite. According to Dave Batt, president of the marketing consulting firm Everest Communications Inc. in Geneva, Illinois, "The more targeted your product or service is to a specific demographic, the more specific your name should be to appeal to that target."

The number of potential names for a company is almost limitless. Coming up with the right one can help you create a lasting brand image for your business. Choosing a name that is distinctive, memorable, and positive can go a long way toward helping you achieve success in your business venture. What's in a name? Everything!

Sources: Based on Andrew Raskin, "The Name of the Game," *Inc.*, February 2000, pp. 31–32; Rhonda Adams, "Sometimes Business Success Is All in the Name," *Business*, July 23, 2000, p. 3; Thomima Edmark, "What's in a Name?" *Entrepreneur*, October 1999, pp. 163–165; Steve Nubie, "Naming Names—Why a Good Business Plan Can Help You Name Your Company," *Entrepreneur*, May 2000, *www.entrepreneur.com/ magazine/businessstartupsmagazine/2000/may/26080.html;* "How to Name Your Business" *Entrepreneur*, April 23, 2005, *www.entrepreneur.com/ startingabusiness/startupbasics/namingyourbusiness/article21774.html;* "Rent-a-Nerd Life Story," Rent-a-Nerd, *www.rent-a-nerd.net/about_us/ about_us.shtml.*

profits. The profit incentive is a powerful one, and among entrepreneurs profits represent an excellent way of "keeping score" in the game of the business.

TOTAL DECISION-MAKING AUTHORITY. Because sole proprietors are in total control of operations, they can respond quickly to changes. The ability to respond quickly is an asset in a rapidly shifting market, and the freedom to set the company's course of action is both a major motivational and strategic force. For people who thrive on seeking new opportunities, the freedom of fast, flexible decision making is vital. The entrepreneur solely directs the operations of the business.

NO SPECIAL LEGAL RESTRICTIONS. The proprietorship is the least regulated form of business ownership. In a time when government demands for information seem never-ending, this feature has merit.

EASY TO DISCONTINUE. If an entrepreneur decides to discontinue operations, he or she can terminate the business quickly, even though he or she will still be liable for all of the business's outstanding debts and obligations.

Disadvantages of the Sole Proprietorship

Although the advantages of a proprietorship are extremely attractive to most people who are contemplating starting a new business, it is important to recognize that this form of ownership has some significant disadvantages.

UNLIMITED PERSONAL LIABILITY. The greatest disadvantage of a sole proprietorship is the unlimited personal liability of the owner; the sole proprietor is *personally* liable for all business debts. In the eyes of the law, the entrepreneur and the business are one in the same. The proprietor owns all of the business's assets, and if the business fails, creditors can force the sale of those assets to cover its debts. The company's debts are the owner's debts. If unpaid business debts remain, creditors also can force the sale of the proprietor's *personal* assets to cover repayment. State laws vary, but most states require creditors to leave the failed business owner a minimum amount of equity in a home, a car, and some personal items. The reality: *Failure of the business can ruin a sole proprietor financially.*

LIMITED ACCESS TO CAPITAL. If the business is to grow and expand, a sole proprietor often needs additional financial resources. However, many proprietors already have invested their available resources into their business and may have used their personal assets as collateral on existing loans. Therefore, it may be difficult for sole proprietors to borrow additional funds. A sole proprietorship is limited to whatever capital the owner can contribute and whatever money the owner can borrow. Unless proprietors have substantial personal wealth, they may find it difficult to raise additional money while maintaining sole ownership. Most banks and other lending institutions have well-defined formulas for determining a borrower's eligibility.

LIMITED SKILLS AND ABILITIES. A sole proprietor may not possess the full range of skills that running a successful business requires. An entrepreneur's education, training, and work experiences may have taught him or her a great deal, yet there are areas in which their decision-making ability will benefit from the insight of others. Many business failures occur because owners lack skill, knowledge, and experience in areas that are vital to business success. Owners may tend to push aside problems they do not understand or do not feel comfortable with in favor of those they can solve more easily. Unfortunately, the problems they set aside seldom solve themselves.

FEELINGS OF ISOLATION. Running a business alone allows an entrepreneur maximum flexibility, but it also creates feelings of isolation; there is no one to turn to for help in solving problems or getting feedback on a new idea. Most entrepreneurs report that they sometimes feel alone and frightened when they must make decisions knowing that they have nowhere to turn for advice or guidance. The weight of each critical decision rests solely on the proprietor's shoulders.

LACK OF CONTINUITY OF THE BUSINESS. If the proprietor dies, retires, or becomes incapacitated, the business automatically terminates. Lack of continuity is inherent in a sole proprietorship. Unless a family member or employee can take over, the future of the business could be in jeopardy. Because people look for secure employment and the opportunity for advancement, proprietorships often have trouble recruiting and retaining good employees. If no one is trained to run the business, creditors can petition the court to liquidate the assets of the dissolved business to pay outstanding debts.

A sole proprietorship is ideal for entrepreneurs who want to keep their businesses relatively small and simple. Some entrepreneurs, however, find that forming partnerships is one way to overcome the disadvantages of the sole proprietorship. For instance, a person who lacks specific managerial skills or has insufficient access to needed capital can compensate for those weaknesses by forming a partnership with someone who has complementary management skills or money to invest.

The Partnership

3. Describe the advantages and disadvantages of the partnership.

A **partnership** is an association of two or more people who co-own a business for the purpose of making a profit. In a partnership, the co-owners (partners) legally share a business's assets, liabilities, and profits according to the terms of an established partnership agreement. The law does not require a written partnership agreement, also known as the articles of partnership, but it is wise to work with an attorney to develop an agreement that documents the exact status and responsibility of each partner. Partners may think they know what they are agreeing to, only to find that there was not a clear understanding about the role and obligation of each partner. The **partnership agreement** is a document that states all of the terms of operating the partnership for the protection of each partner involved. Every partnership should be based on a comprehensive written agreement. When problems arise between partners, the written document becomes invaluable.

When no partnership agreement exists, the Uniform Partnership Act, which will be discussed later in this chapter, governs the partnership, but its provisions may not be as favorable as a specific agreement drafted by the partners. Creating a partnership agreement is not necessarily costly. In most cases, the partners can review sample agreements and discuss each of the provisions in advance. Once they have reached an understanding, an attorney can draft the final document.

Banks often want to review the partnership agreement before lending the business money. Perhaps the most important benefit of a partnership agreement is that it addresses, in advance, sources of potential conflict that could result in partnership battles and the dissolution of a business that could have been successful. Documenting these details before they occur—especially for challenging issues such as profit splits, contributions, workloads, decision-making authority, dispute resolution, and others—help avoid tension in a partnership that could lead to business failure or dissolution of the partnership.

Partners!

Source: Masterfile Royalty Free Division

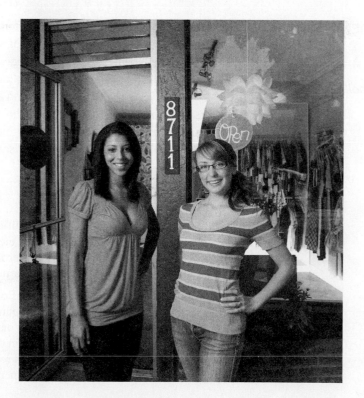

A partnership agreement can include any terms the partners want (unless they are illegal). A standard partnership agreement includes the following information:

1. *Name of the partnership.*
2. *Purpose of the business.* What is the reason the partners created the business?
3. *Domicile of the business.* Where will the business be located?
4. *Duration of the partnership.* How long will the partnership last?
5. *Names of the partners and their legal addresses.*
6. *Contributions of each partner to the business, at the creation of the partnership and later.* This includes each partner's investment in the business. In some situations, a partner may contribute assets that do not appear on the balance sheet. Experience, sales contacts, or a good reputation in the community may be some reasons for asking a person to join a partnership.
7. *Agreement on how the profits or losses will be distributed.*
8. *Agreement on salaries or drawing rights against profits for each partner.*
9. *Procedure for expansion through the addition of new partners.*
10. *Distribution of the partnership's assets if the partners voluntarily dissolve the partnership.*
11. *Sale of the partnership interest.* How can partners sell their interests in the business?
12. *Absence or disability of one of the partners.* If a partner is absent or disabled for an extended period of time, should the partnership continue? Will the absent or disabled partner receive the same share of profits as she did before her absence or disability? Should the absent or disabled partner be held responsible for debts incurred while unable to participate?
13. *Voting rights.* In many partnerships, partners have unequal voting power. The partners may base their voting rights on their financial or managerial contributions to the business.
14. *Decision-making authority.* When can partners make decisions on their own, and when must other partners be involved?
15. *Financial authority.* Which partners are authorized to sign checks, and how many signatures are required to authorize bank transactions?
16. *Handling tax matters.* The Internal Revenue Service requires partnerships to designate one person to be responsible for handling the partnership's tax matters.
17. *Alterations or modifications of the partnership agreement.* No document is written to last forever. Partnership agreements should contain provisions for alterations or modifications. As a business grows and changes, partners often find it necessary to update their original agreement. If no written partnership agreement exists and a dispute arises, the courts apply the Uniform Partnership Act.

ENTREPRENEURIAL
Profile
Cot Campbell: Dogwood Stable

Dogwood Stable in Aiken, South Carolina, offers investors the chance to participate in horseracing by creating four- and eight-share general partnerships that own its racehorses. According to Dogwood Stable president Cot Campbell, Dogwood retains a 5 percent interest in the partnership, and investors purchase either a 23.75 percent or 11.84 percent stake at prices that typically range from $30,000 to $75,000. The odds of earning an attractive return are rather low (only 17 percent of racehorses win at least $25,000 per year, the average annual cost of boarding and training one), but it happens on occasion. The payoff for most investors is the thrill of being an owner and having the opportunity to participate in the "sport of kings" for a relatively small investment.[2]

The Uniform Partnership Act

The **Uniform Partnership Act,** or **UPA,** codifies the body of law dealing with partnerships in the United States. Under the UPA, the three key elements of any partnership are common ownership interest in a business, sharing the business's profits and losses, and the right to participate in managing the partnership. Under the act, each partner has the right to:

1. Share in the management and operations of the business.
2. Share in any profits the business might earn from operations.
3. Receive interest on additional advances made to the business.
4. Be compensated for expenses incurred in the name of the partnership.
5. Have access to the business's books and records.
6. Receive a formal accounting of the partnership's business affairs.

"I'd like to congratulate Jenkins for making pard'ner."

The UPA also describes the partners' obligations. Each partner is obligated to:

1. Share in any losses sustained by the business.
2. Work for the partnership without salary.
3. Submit differences that may arise in the conduct of the business to majority vote or arbitration.
4. Give the other partners complete information about all business affairs.
5. Give a formal accounting of the partnership's business affairs.

To meet these obligations, partners must abide by the following duties:

- *Duty of loyalty.* Each partner has a fiduciary responsibility to the partnership and, as such, must always place the interest of the partnership above his or her personal interest.
- *Duty of obedience.* This duty requires each partner to adhere to the provision of the partnership agreement and the decisions made by the partnership.
- *Duty of care.* As the name implies, each partner is expected to behave in ways that demonstrate the same level of care and skill that a reasonable manager in the same position would use under the same circumstances. Failure to live up to this duty is considered negligence.
- *Duty to inform.* All information relevant to the management of the business must be made available to all partners.

Beyond what the law prescribes, a partnership is based on mutual trust and respect. Any partnership missing those elements is destined to fail. Like sole proprietorships, partnerships also have advantages and disadvantages.

Advantages of the Partnership

EASY TO ESTABLISH. Like the proprietorship, the partnership is relatively easy and inexpensive to establish. The owners must obtain the necessary business license and submit a minimal number of forms. In most states, partners must file a Certificate for Conducting Business as Partners if the business operates under a trade name.

COMPLEMENTARY SKILLS. In successful partnerships, the parties' skills and abilities complement one another, strengthening the company's managerial foundation. The synergistic effect created when partners of equal skill and creativity collaborate effectively results in outcomes that reflect the contributions of all involved. In his book *The Illusions of Entrepreneurship*, Scott Shane says that businesses that are founded by teams of entrepreneurs (not necessarily partners) are more likely to succeed than those that are founded by a single entrepreneur.[3]

ENTREPRENEURIAL
Profile

Norm Brodsky and Sam Kaplan: CitiStorage

For years, Norm Brodsky, founder of CitiStorage, a document storage company in New York City, resisted taking on a partner because he knew that many partnerships fall apart. Finally, Brodsky brought his trusted friend Sam Kaplan in as a partner because he saw that Kaplan's values and philosophies were similar to his own and that Kaplan's strengths were skills that he lacked. With his strong background in finance, Kaplan had an immediate impact on the company. He took over the management of CitiStorage's finances and introduced systems and practices that were rare in a small company. "While I still think it's a bad idea to start a business with one, I've come to realize that ending with a partner is another matter—especially if the other person is someone like Sam," says Brodsky.[4]

DIVISION OF PROFITS. There are no restrictions on how partners may distribute the company's profits as long as they are consistent with the partnership agreement and do not violate the rights of any partner. The partnership agreement should articulate the nature of each partner's contribution and proportional share of profits. If the partners fail to create an agreement, the UPA states that the partners share equally in the partnership's profits, regardless of the proportional amount of their original capital contributions.

LARGER POOL OF CAPITAL. A partnership can significantly broaden the pool of capital available to a business. Each partner's asset base supports a larger borrowing capacity than either partner would have had alone. This may become a critical factor because undercapitalization is a common cause of business failures.

ABILITY TO ATTRACT LIMITED PARTNERS. Not every partner must take an active role in the operation of a business. Partners who take an active role in managing a company and who share in its rewards, liabilities, and responsibilities are **general partners**. Every partnership must have at least one general partner (although there is no limit on the number of general partners a business can have). General partners have unlimited personal liability for the company's debts and obligations and are expected to take an active role in managing the business.

Limited partners are financial investors who do not participate in the day-to-day affairs of the partnership and seek to limit their risk. Limited partners cannot take an active role in the operation of the company and have limited personal liability for the company's debts and obligations. If the business fails, limited partners lose only what they have invested in the partnership itself and no more. If limited partners are "materially and actively" involved in a business— defined as spending more than 500 hours a year in the company—they will be treated as general partners and will lose their limited liability protection. Silent partners and dormant partners are special types of limited partners. **Silent partners** are not active in a business but generally are known to be members of the partnership. **Dormant partners** are neither active nor generally known to be associated with the business.

A limited partnership can attract investors by offering them limited liability and the potential to realize a substantial return on their investments if the business is successful. Many individuals find it profitable to invest in high-potential small businesses but *only* if they avoid the disadvantages of unlimited liability. Limited partnerships will be discussed in greater detail later in this chapter.

LITTLE GOVERNMENTAL REGULATION. Like the proprietorship, the partnership form of ownership is not burdened with reporting requirements.

FLEXIBILITY. Although not as flexible as sole proprietorships, partnerships can react quickly to changing market conditions. In large partnerships, however, getting all partners' approval on key decisions can slow a company's ability to react. Unless the partnership agreement states otherwise, each partner has a single vote in the management of the company no matter how large his or her contribution to the partnership is.

TAXATION. The partnership itself is not subject to federal taxation. It serves as a conduit for the profit or losses it earns or incurs; its net income or loss is passed through the individual partners as personal income, and the partners, not the business, pay income tax on their distributive shares. The partnership, like the proprietorship, avoids the "double taxation" disadvantage associated with the corporate form of ownership.

Disadvantages of the Partnership

Business partnerships can be complicated and frustrating. Before taking on a partner, every entrepreneur should double-check the decision to be sure that the prospective business partner is adding value to the business. "I would never, ever, ever advise someone to go into a partnership unless it's necessary," says Clay Nelson, a Santa Barbara business advisor who works with partners.[5] For some entrepreneurs, taking on a partner *is* necessary; for others, it is a mistake. Before entering into a partnership, entrepreneurs must consider their disadvantages.

UNLIMITED LIABILITY OF AT LEAST ONE PARTNER. At least one member of every partnership must be a general partner. The general partner has unlimited personal liability for the partnership's debts. In most states, certain property belonging to a proprietor or a general partner is exempt from attachment by creditors of a failed business. The most common is the homestead exemption, which allows the debtor's home to be sold to satisfy debt but stipulates that a certain dollar amount be reserved to allow the debtor to find other shelter. State laws commonly exempt certain personal property items from attachments by creditors. For example, household furniture (up to a specified amount), clothing and personal possessions, government or military pensions, and bonuses are protected and cannot be seized to satisfy an outstanding business debt.

CAPITAL ACCUMULATION. Although the partnership form of ownership is superior to the sole proprietorship when it comes to attracting capital, it also presents limitations. The partnership is generally not as effective in raising funds as the corporate form of ownership, which can acquire capital by selling shares of ownership to outside investors.

DIFFICULTY IN DISPOSING OF PARTNERSHIP INTEREST. Most partnership agreements restrict how partners can dispose of their shares of the business. Usually, a partner is required to sell his interest to the remaining partners. Even if the original agreement contains such a requirement and clearly delineates how the value of each partner's ownership will be determined, there is no guarantee that other partners will have the financial resources to buy the seller's interest. When the money is not available to purchase a partner's interest, the other partners may be forced to either accept a new partner or to dissolve the partnership and distribute the remaining assets. Under previous versions of the UPA, when a partner withdrew from a partnership (an act called dissociation), the partnership automatically dissolved, which required the remaining partners to form a new partnership. Current provisions of the UPA, however, do not require dissolution and allow the remaining partners to continue to operate the business without the withdrawing partner. The withdrawing partner no longer has the authority to represent the business or to take part in managing it.

POTENTIAL FOR PERSONALITY AND AUTHORITY CONFLICTS. In some ways, a partnership is similar to a marriage. The compatibility of partners' work habits, goals, ethics, and general business philosophies are an important ingredient in a successful relationship. Friction among partners is inevitable and can be difficult to control. The key is to have in place a comprehensive partnership agreement and open lines of communication. The demise of many partnerships can be traced to interpersonal conflicts and the lack of a partnership agreement to resolve them. Knowing potential partners well and having a conflict resolution plan in place result in better outcomes when dealing with the inevitable conflicts that occur when there is a fundamental difference of opinion on one or more critical business decisions.

PARTNERS ARE BOUND BY THE LAW OF AGENCY. Each partner acts as an agent for the business and can legally bind the other partners to a business agreement. This agency power requires all partners to exercise good faith and reasonable care in performing their responsibilities. For example, if a partner signs a 3-year lease for new office space, dramatically increasing the operation costs of the business beyond what the business can afford, the partnership is legally bound to that agreement.

Some partnerships survive a lifetime; others experience difficulties and ultimately are dissolved. In a partnership, the continued exposure to personal liability for partners' actions may wear down the general partners. Knowing that they could lose their personal assets because of a partner's bad business decision is a fact of life in partnerships. Conflicts between or among partners can force a business to close. Unfortunately, few partnerships have a mutually agreed upon means for conflict resolution, such as mediation or arbitration, which can help partners resolve underlying conflicts and keep the business operating. Without such a mechanism, disagreements can escalate to the point where the partnership is dissolved and the business ceases to operate.

ENTREPRENEURIAL
Profile
John and Jim Martin

Brothers John and Jim Martin started a retail clothing shop as equal partners. The business proved successful, and over the years the brothers opened two additional shops. Five of their children are now active in the business, three from John's family and two from Jim's. Plans to open another store had been vetoed by Jim's family, which brought to the surface a range of underlying issues involving work practices and compensation that had gone unresolved for years. The brothers attempted to resolve the dispute through direct negotiation over several months but were unsuccessful. Their accountant realized the impact the dispute was having on the business and suggested mediation. Both families agreed, and with the mediator's help the families began communicating for the first time in years. In addition to saving the family business, a key outcome of the mediation process was the restoration of the relationships among family members, who finally realized that unresolved problems do not disappear and that it is better to address problems when they occur.[6]

Limited Partnerships

A **limited partnership** is a modification of a general partnership. Limited partnerships are composed of at least one general partner and at least one limited partner. The general partner is treated, under law, in the same manner as in a general partnership, which means that he or she has unlimited personal liability for the partnership's debts. Limited partners are treated as *investors* in the business venture with limited liability and therefore can lose only the amount they have invested in the business. There is no limit on the number of limited partners in a limited partnership.

Most states recognize the ratified Revised Uniform Limited Partnership Act. To form a limited partnership, the partners must file a certificate of limited partnership in the state in which the partnership plans to conduct business. The certificate of limited partnership should include the following information:

1. The name of the limited partnership.
2. The general character of its business.
3. The address of the office of the firm's agent authorized to receive summonses or other legal notices.
4. The name and business address of each partner, specifying which ones are general partners and which are limited partners.
5. The amount of cash contributions actually made, and agreed to be made in the future, by each partner.
6. A description of the value of noncash contributions made or to be made by each partner.
7. The times at which additional contributions are to be made by any of the partners.

LESSONS FROM THE STREET-SMART ➤ entrepreneur

How to Avoid a Business Divorce

Starting a business with another person or team of people offers many advantages, including a greater chance for success than starting a business solo. Ben Cohen and Jerry Greenfield (Ben & Jerry's Homemade), Bill Hewlett and Dave Packard (Hewlett-Packard), and Sam, Jack, Harry, and Albert Warner (Warner Brothers) were as successful in business as Fred Astaire and Ginger Rogers were in dancing and Laurel and Hardy were in comedy. However, operating a business with others also presents challenges in the form of personality conflicts, differing business philosophies, workload expectations, and a variety of other important issues. Like marriage partners, business co-owners together experience happiness and heartbreak, good times and bad times, and success and failure. In addition, some business partnerships, like some marriages, fall apart. Before going into business with someone else, consider the following advice from the Street-Smart Entrepreneur on how to avoid a business divorce.

Tip #1. Know your co-owners and make sure the "fit" is good

One of the biggest mistakes entrepreneurs make is jumping into a business with other people before they get to know them. Ideally, business co-owners' business goals are compatible and their skill sets are complementary. One of the best ways to get to know potential co-owners is to work on small projects together *before* launching a business together. Alicia Rockmore and Sarah Welch, cofounders of Buttoned Up, Inc., an online company that sells organizational products aimed specifically at women, worked together on and off for 8 years in their respective corporate jobs before they decided to take the entrepreneurial plunge together. Each woman brings to the business a different skill set, but what ties them together is "respect for each other's business judgment," says Welch.

Tip #2. Divide responsibilities based on ability, experience, and interest

One of the greatest advantages of creating a company with others is the ability to create a whole that is greater than the sum of its parts. To do so, however, requires each cofounder to do what he or she does best. In one successful landscape design company, one partner's expertise lies in creating unique landscape designs that are suited to the local climate, and the other partner handles the business affairs, including marketing and finance.

Tip #3. Put it in writing

Before launching a business with someone else, take the time to put together an operating agreement in writing—whatever form of ownership you choose. The document should spell out the division of responsibilities and duties, the decision-making process and final authority, the division of profits, compensation, exit strategies, and other important matters. Avoid the tendency to go into business with someone else, no matter how close you may be, with nothing more than a handshake and high hopes. Doing so is like playing Russian roulette with your business.

Tip #4. Realize that conflicts will occur

Conflict is a natural part of any relationship. Co-owners will never agree on every aspect of operating a company. However, tempers tend to flare and disagreements arise when co-owners find themselves in a crucible, under pressure to make decisions or deal with a business crisis. The key is to have a mechanism such as an operating agreement in place for dealing with conflict when it does occur. The *worst* approach co-owners can take is to ignore or cover up the conflict. Unaddressed conflicts seldom resolve themselves.

Tip #5. Keep the lines of communication open

The best way to deal with conflict is to talk and work through it. That requires co-owners to maintain open lines of communication with one another. When Dr. Shaparak Kemarei and Dr. Marjaneh Hedayat decided to become partners in a laser hair-removal practice, they often called each other after business hours to discuss issues, a procedure that imposed on their family time. Soon they established a better way of maintaining daily communication: Twice a day they set aside a designated time to devote to discussing business issues and regularly select management books to read and discuss together. "Even if we don't agree, we talk about everything, come to an understanding, and move on," says Dr. Hedayat. "That's how a business grows."

Sources: Based on Shelly Banjo, "Before You Tie the Knot," *Wall Street Journal*, November 26, 2007, p. R4; Alexander Stein, "Make Your Partnership Work," *FSB*, May 2009, p. 19.

8. Whether and under what conditions a limited partner has the right to grant limited partner status to an assignee of his or her interest in the partnership.
9. If agreed upon, the time or the circumstances when a partner may withdraw from the firm.
10. If agreed upon, the amount of, or the method of determining, the funds to be received by a withdrawing partner.
11. Any right of a partner to receive distributions of cash or other property from the firm, and the circumstances for such distributions.
12. The time or circumstances when the limited partnership is to be dissolved.
13. The rights of the remaining general partners to continue the business after the withdrawal of a general partner.
14. Any other matters the partners want to include.

Although limited partners do not have the right to take an active role in managing the business, they can make management suggestions to general partners, inspect the business, and access and make copies of business records. A limited partner is, of course, entitled to a share of the business's profit (or loss) as agreed upon and specified in the certificate of limited partnership.

Limited Liability Partnerships

Many states now recognize **limited liability partnerships, or LLPs**, in which all partners in the business are limited partners, having only limited liability for the debts and obligations of the partnership. Most states restrict LLPs to certain types of professionals, such as attorneys, physicians, dentists, accountants, and others. Just as with any limited partnership, the partners must file a certificate of limited partnership in the state in which the partnership plans to conduct business. As with other partnership forms, an LLP does not pay taxes; its income is passed through to the limited partners, who pay personal taxes on their shares of the company's net income.

The Corporation

4. Describe the advantages and disadvantages of the corporation.

The corporation is the most complex of the three major forms of business ownership. A **corporation** is an artificial legal entity created by the state that can sue or be sued in its own name, enter into and enforce contracts, hold title to and transfer property, and be found civilly and criminally liable for violations of the law.[7] The life of the corporation is independent of its owners, and shareholders can transfer their ownership in the business to others.

Corporations, also known as **C corporations**, are creations of the state. When a corporation is founded, it accepts the regulations and restrictions of the state in which it is incorporated and any other state in which it chooses to conduct business. A corporation that conducts business in the state in which it is incorporated is a **domestic corporation**. When a corporation conducts business in another state, that state considers it to be a **foreign corporation**. Corporations that are formed in other countries and conduct business in the United States are referred to as **alien corporations**.

Corporations have the power to raise capital by selling shares of ownership to outside investors. Some corporations have thousands of shareholders, and others have only a handful of owners. **Publicly held corporations** have a large number of shareholders, and their stock is usually traded on one of the organized stock exchanges. **Closely held corporations** have shares that are controlled by a relatively small number of people, often family members, relatives, or friends. Their stock is not traded on any stock exchange but instead, is passed from one generation to the next. Many small corporations are closely held.

In general, a corporation must report annually its financial operations to its home state's secretary of state. These financial reports become public record. If the corporation's stock is sold in more than one state, the corporation must comply with federal regulations governing the sale of corporate securities and stringent reporting requirements. There are substantially more reporting requirements for a corporation than for the other forms of ownership.

Requirements for Incorporation

Most states allow entrepreneurs to incorporate without the assistance of an attorney. Some states even provide incorporation kits to help in the incorporation process. Although it is less expensive for entrepreneurs to complete the process themselves, doing so may not be ideal, because overlooking some provisions of the incorporation process can create legal and tax problems. In some states, the application process is complex and the required forms are confusing. Entrepreneurs usually can find an attorney or an online service to help them incorporate their businesses for a reasonable fee.

Once the owners decide to form a corporation, they must choose the state in which to incorporate. If the business will operate in a single state, it usually makes sense to incorporate in that state. States differ—sometimes dramatically—in the requirements they place on the corporations they charter and in how they treat corporations chartered in other states. States also differ in the tax rates imposed on corporations, the restrictions placed on their activities, the capital required to incorporate, and the fees or organization tax charged to incorporate.

Every state requires a certificate of incorporation or charter to be filed with the secretary of state. The following information is generally required to be in the certificate of incorporation:

1. *The corporation's name.* The corporations must choose a name that is not so similar to that of another firm in that state that it causes confusion or lends itself to deception. It must also include a term such as *corporation, incorporated, company,* or *limited* to notify the public that they are dealing with a corporation.

2. *The corporation's statement of purpose.* The incorporators must state in general terms the intended nature of the business. The purpose must, of course, be lawful. For example, a retailer of office furniture might describe its purpose as "engaging in the sale of office furniture and fixtures." The purpose should be broad enough to allow for some expansion in the activities of the business as it develops.

3. *The company's time horizon.* Most corporations are formed with no specific termination date and will continue "in perpetuity." However, it is possible to incorporate for a specific duration of time, for example, a period of 50 years.

4. *Names and addresses of the incorporators.* The incorporators must be identified in the articles of incorporation and are liable under the law to attest that all information in this document is correct. In some states, one or more of the incorporators must reside in the state the corporation is being created.

5. *Place of business.* The post office address of the corporation's principal office must be listed. This address, for a domestic corporation, must be in the state in which incorporation takes place.

6. *Capital stock authorization.* The articles of incorporation must include the amount and class (or type) of capital stock the corporation wants to be authorized to issue. This is not the number of shares it must issue; a corporation also must define the different classification of stock and any special rights, preferences, or limits each class has.

7. *Capital required at the time of incorporation.* Some states require a newly formed corporation to deposit in a bank a specific percentage of the stock's par value before incorporating.

8. *Provisions for preemptive rights, if any, that are granted to stockholders.* If arranged, **preemptive rights** state that stockholders have the right to purchase new shares of stock before they are offered to the public.

9. *Restrictions on transferring share.* Many closely held corporations—those owned by a few shareholders, often family members—require shareholders who are interested in selling their stocks to offer it first to the corporation. Shares the corporation itself owns are called **treasury stock**. To maintain control over their ownership, many closely held corporations exercise this right, known as the **right of first refusal**.

10. *Names and addresses of the officers and directors of the corporation.*

11. *Rules under which the corporation will operate.* **Bylaws** are the rules and regulations the officers and directors establish for the corporation's internal management and operation.

Once the secretary of state of the incorporating state approves a request for incorporation and the corporation pays its fees, the approved articles of incorporation become its **corporate charter**. With the corporate charter as proof that the corporation legally exists, the next order of business is to hold an organizational meeting for the stockholders to formally elect directors, who, in turn, will appoint the corporate officers.

Corporations account for the greatest proportion of sales and profits than other forms of ownership, but like the preceding forms of ownership, they have advantages and disadvantages.

Advantages of the Corporation

LIMITED LIABILITY OF STOCKHOLDERS. The primary reason most entrepreneurs choose to incorporate is to gain the benefit of limited liability, which allows investors to limit their liability to the total amount of their investment. This legal protection of personal assets outside the business is of critical concern to many investors. The shield of limited liability often is not impenetrable, however. Because start-up companies generally present higher levels of risk, lenders and other creditors require the owners to *personally* guarantee loans made to the corporation. Experts estimate that 95 percent of small business owners have to sign personal guarantees to get the financing they need. By making these guarantees, owners place their personal assets at risk (just as in a proprietorship) despite choosing the corporate form of ownership.

Court decisions have extended the personal liability of small corporation owners beyond the financial guarantees that banks and other lenders require, "piercing the corporate veil" more than ever before. Courts are increasingly holding corporate owners personally liable for environmental, pension, and legal claims against their corporations. Courts will pierce the corporate veil and hold owners liable for the company's debts and obligations if the owners deliberately commit criminal or negligent acts when handling corporate business. Corporate shareholders most commonly lose their liability protection, however, because owners and officers have commingled corporate funds with their own personal funds. Failing to keep corporate and personal funds separate is often a problem, particularly in closely held corporations.

Steps to avoid legal difficulties include the following:

- *File all of the reports and pay all of the necessary fees required by the state in a timely manner.* Most states require corporations to file reports with the secretary of state annually. Failing to do so jeopardizes the validity of a corporation and opens the door for personal liability problems for its shareholders.
- *Hold annual meetings to elect officers and directors.* In a closely held corporation, the officers elected may *be* the shareholders, but that does not matter. Corporations formed by an individual are not required to hold meetings, but the sole shareholder must file a written consent form.
- *Keep minutes of every meeting of the officers and directors, even if it takes place in the living room of the founders.* It is a good idea to elect a secretary who is responsible for recording the minutes.
- *Make sure that the corporation's board of directors makes all major decisions.* Problems arise in closely held corporations when one owner makes key decisions alone without consulting the elected board.
- *Make it clear that the business is a corporation by having all officers sign contracts, loan agreements, purchase orders, and other legal documents in the corporation's name rather than their own names.* Failing to designate their status as agents of the corporation can result in the officer's being held personally liable for agreements they think they are signing on the corporation's behalf.
- *Keep corporate assets and the personal assets of the owners separate.* Few things make courts more willing to hold shareholders personally liable for a corporation's debts than commingling corporate and personal assets. In some closely held corporations, owners have been known to use corporate assets to pay their personal expenses (or vice versa) or to mix their personal funds with corporate funds into a single bank account. Protecting the corporation's identity by keeping it completely separate from the owner's personal identities is critical.

ENTREPRENEURIAL
Profile

Dennis Kozlowski: Tyco International Ltd.

In one of the most famous cases of corporate abuse, former Tyco International Ltd. CEO Dennis Kozlowski and former finance chief Mark Swartz were sentenced to up to 25 years in prison after shareholders learned about the executives' extravagant personal lifestyles, which they paid for with company funds. For example, the corporation paid for a $2 million toga birthday party for Kozlowski's wife on a Mediterranean island and an $18 million Manhattan apartment with a $6,000 shower curtain. Kozlowski and Swartz were also accused of giving themselves more than $150 million in illegal bonuses, forgiving loans to themselves, and manipulating the company's stock price. After a 4-month trial, the jury deliberated 11 days before returning 22 guilty verdicts on counts of grand larceny, falsifying business records, securities fraud, and conspiracy.[8]

ABILITY TO ATTRACT CAPITAL. Corporations have proved to be the most effective form of ownership for accumulating large amounts of capital, largely due to the protection of limited liability. Restricted only by the number of shares authorized in its charter (which can be amended), the corporation can raise money to begin business and to finance expansion by selling shares of its stock to investors. A corporation can sell its stock to a limited number of private investors, called a **private placement**, or to the public, which is referred to as a **public offering**. In fact, the ability to facilitate financing is one of the most significant advantages of a corporation, especially those in need of major capital infusions. "If you're thinking about going public, there's no question that C corps are the best vehicle," says Hillel Bennett, an attorney who specializes in corporate law.[9]

ABILITY TO CONTINUE INDEFINITELY. As a separate legal entity, a corporation can continue indefinitely or in perpetuity unless limited by its charter. Unlike a proprietorship or partnership in which the death of a founder ends the business, the corporation lives beyond the lives of those who created it. This perpetual life gives rise to the next major advantage of the corporation, transferable ownership.

TRANSFERABLE OWNERSHIP. If stockholders in a corporation are displeased with the business's progress, they can sell their shares to someone else. Millions of shares of stock representing ownership in companies are traded daily on the world's stock exchanges. Shareholders also can transfer their stock through inheritance to a new generation of owners. Throughout these transfers of ownership, the corporation seamlessly continues to conduct business as usual. Because only a small number of people, often company founders, family members, or employees, own the stock of closely held corporations, the resale market for shares is limited and the transfer of ownership may be difficult.

Disadvantages of the Corporation

COST AND TIME INVOLVED IN THE INCORPORATION PROCESS. Corporations can be costly and time consuming to establish. As the owners give birth to this artificial legal entity, the gestation period can be prolonged. In some states, an attorney must handle the incorporation, but in most states entrepreneurs can complete all of the required forms themselves. However, an entrepreneur must exercise great caution when incorporating without the help of an attorney. In addition to potential legal expenses, incorporating a business requires fees that do not apply to proprietorships or partnerships. Creating a corporation can cost between $500 and $3,000, with the average cost around $1,500.

DOUBLE TAXATION. As a separate legal entity, a corporation must pay taxes on its net income to the federal, most state, and many local governments. Before stockholders receive any net income as dividends, a corporation must pay these taxes at the corporate tax rate. Then stockholders must pay taxes on the dividends they receive from these same profits at the individual tax rate. Thus, a corporation's profits are taxed twice—once at the corporate level and again at the individual level. This **double taxation** is a distinct disadvantage of the corporate form of ownership. Figure 2 shows a comparison of a small company's tax bill organized as a C corporation and as an S corporation or limited liability company.

POTENTIAL FOR DIMINISHED MANAGERIAL INCENTIVES. As corporations grow, they often require additional managerial expertise beyond that which the founder can provide. Because they created their companies and often have most of their personal wealth tied up in the business, entrepreneurs have an intense interest in ensuring their success and are willing to make sacrifices for their businesses. Professional managers an entrepreneur brings in to help run the business as it grows do not always have the same degree of dedication or loyalty to the company. As a result, the business may suffer without the founder's energy, care, and devotion. One way to minimize this potential problem is to link managers' (and even employees') compensation to the company's financial performance through profit-sharing or bonus plans. Corporations also can stimulate managers' and employees' incentive on the job by creating an **employee stock ownership plan, or ESOP**, in which managers and employees become part owners in the company.

FIGURE 2
Tax Rate Comparison:
C Corporation and
S Corporation or Limited
Liability Company

The form of ownership that an entrepreneur chooses has many important business implications, not the least of which is the amount of taxes the business or entrepreneur must pay. A recent study by the Small Business Administration's Office of Advocacy reports that, on average, taxes consume 19.8 percent of the typical small company's net income. The study also shows the average effective tax rate (the actual amount of taxes paid by a company as a percentage of its net income) for small businesses under each form of ownership:

Form of Ownership	Average Effective Federal Tax Rate
Sole proprietorship	13.3%
Partnership	23.6%
S corporation	26.9%
C corporation	17.5%
All small businesses	19.8%

Although these averages are revealing, entrepreneurs must consider the tax bills their particular companies incur under the various forms of ownership. For example, S corporations do not pay taxes on their net income. Instead, that income passes through to the owners, who pay taxes on it at their individual tax rates. C corporations, in contrast, pay a corporate tax on their net income. If the C corporation pays out some or all of that net income as dividends to shareholders, the dividends are taxed a second time at the shareholders' individual tax rates. Therefore, the tax obligations for an owner of an S corporation may be considerably lower than that of a C corporation.

The following example illustrates the effect of these tax rate differentials. This somewhat simplified example assumes that a small company generates a net income of $500,000 and that all after-tax income is distributed to the owners.

	C Corporation	S Corporation or LLC
Corporate or LLC net income	$500,000	$500,000
Maximum corporate tax	39%	0%
Corporate tax	**$170,000**	**0**
After-tax income	$330,000	$500,000
Maximum shareholder tax rate	33%	35%
Shareholder tax	**$49,500***	**$175,000****
Total tax paid	**$219,500**	**$175,000**
(Corporate tax plus Shareholder tax)		
Total tax savings by choosing S corporation or limited liability company		**$44,500**

* Using the marginal 15% tax rate on dividends: $330,000 × 15% = $49,500

** Using the marginal 35% tax rate on ordinary income: $500,000 × 35% = $175,000

LEGAL REQUIREMENTS AND REGULATORY RED TAPE. Corporations are subject to more legal and financial requirements than other forms of ownership. Entrepreneurs must meet stringent requirements to accurately record and report business transactions in a timely manner. They must hold annual meetings and consult the board of directors about major decisions that are beyond day-to-day operations. Managers may be required to submit major decisions to the stockholders for approval. Corporations that are publicly held must also file quarterly and annual reports with the Securities and Exchange Commission (SEC). Failure to follow state and federal regulations has led to problems for many corporations.

POTENTIAL LOSS OF CONTROL BY THE FOUNDERS. When entrepreneurs sell shares of ownership in their companies, they relinquish some degree of control. In corporations that require large capital infusions, entrepreneurs may have to give up a significant amount of control, so much, in fact, that they become minority shareholders. Losing majority ownership—and therefore control—of their companies leaves founders in a precarious position. They no longer have the power to determine the company's direction; "outsiders" do. The founders' shares may become so diluted that majority shareholders may vote them out of their jobs.

Professional Corporations

A **professional corporation** offers professionals such as lawyers, doctors, dentists, accountants, and others the advantages of the corporate form of ownership. Corporate ownership is ideally suited for licensed professionals, who must always be concerned about malpractice lawsuits, because it offers limited liability. For example, if three doctors form a professional corporation, none of them would be liable for the malpractice of the other. (Of course, each would be liable for his or her own actions.) Professional corporations are created in the same way as regular corporations. They often are identified by the abbreviation P.C. (professional corporation), P.A. (professional association), or S.C. (service corporation).

Alternative Forms of Ownership

5. Describe the features of the alternative forms of ownership, such as the S corporation, the limited liability company, and the joint venture.

In addition to the sole proprietorship, the partnership, and the corporation, entrepreneurs can choose other forms of ownership, including the S corporation, the limited liability company, and the joint venture.

The S Corporation

The Internal Revenue Service Code created the Subchapter S corporation in 1954. More commonly known as an S corporation, this form of ownership has undergone modifications in its legal requirements. An **S corporation** is a distinction that is made only for federal income tax purposes and is, in terms of its legal characteristics, no different from any other corporation. Small businesses seeking S corporation status must meet the following criteria:

1. It must be a domestic (U.S.) corporation.
2. It cannot have a nonresident alien as a shareholder.
3. It can issue only one class of common stock, which means that all shares must carry the same distribution or liquidation rights. Voting rights, however, may differ. In other words, an S corporation can issue voting and nonvoting common stock.
4. It must limit its shareholders to individuals, estates, and certain trusts, although tax-exempt entities such as ESOPs and pension plans can be shareholders.
5. It cannot have more than 100 shareholders (increased from 75).
6. No more than 25 percent of the corporation's gross revenues during three successive tax years can be from passive investment income.

By increasing the number of shareholders allowed in S corporations to 100, the new law makes succession planning easier for business owners. Founders now can pass their stock on to their children and grandchildren without worrying about exceeding the maximum allowable number of owners. The larger number of shareholders also gives S corporations greater ability to raise capital by attracting more investors.

The new law also allows S corporations to own subsidiary companies. Previously, the owners of S corporations had to establish separate businesses if they wanted to launch new ventures, even those closely related to the S corporation. This change is especially beneficial to entrepreneurs with several businesses in related fields. They can establish an S corporation as the "parent" company and then set up multiple subsidiaries as either S or C corporations as "offspring" under it. Because they are separate corporations, the liabilities of one business cannot spill over and destroy the assets of another.

Violating any of the requirements for an S corporation automatically terminates a company's S status. If a corporation meets the criteria for an S corporation, its shareholders must elect to be treated as one. (The corporation must have been eligible for S status for the entire year.) To make the election of S status effective for the current tax year, an entrepreneur must file IRS Form 2553 within the first 75 days of the tax year. *All* shareholders must consent to have the corporation treated as an S corporation.

ADVANTAGES OF AN S CORPORATION. S corporations retain all of the advantages of a regular corporation, including continuity of existence, transferability of ownership, and limited personal liability for its owners. The most notable provision of the S corporation is that it passes all of its profits or losses through to the *individual* shareholders and its income is taxed only *once* at the individual tax rate. Thus, electing S corporation status avoids the double-taxation disadvantage of a C corporation. In essence, the tax treatment of an S corporation is exactly like that of a partnership; its owners report their shares of the company's profits on their individual income tax returns and pay taxes on those profits at the individual rate, even if they never take the money out of the business.

Another advantage of the S corporation is that it avoids the tax C corporations pay on the assets that have appreciated in value and are sold. S corporations owners also enjoy the ability to make year-end payouts to themselves when net income is high. To minimize their tax bills, some S corporation owners pay themselves minimal salaries, which are subject to Social Security and Medicare taxes, and instead make large dividend distributions, which are not subject to those taxes, to themselves. In a C corporation, owners have no such luxury because the IRS watches for excessive compensation to owners and managers. However, the IRS is trying to eliminate this loophole, arguing that it costs the U.S. Treasury billions of lost revenue annually.

DISADVANTAGES OF AN S CORPORATION. Although tax implications should not be the sole criterion when choosing a form of ownership, they are important to business owners. Congress's constant tinkering with the tax code means that the tax advantages that the S corporation offers may not be permanent. S corporations lose their attractiveness if either personal

IN THE ENTREPRENEURIAL
SPOTLIGHT Wild Thymes on the Farm

In 1970, Enid Stettner and her husband, Fred, left their corporate careers (fashion designer and film producer, respectively) in New York City, moved to the quaint, nineteenth-century farmhouse in the Hudson Valley that they had purchased a decade earlier, and started farming. Ten years later, Enid, a self-taught cook, created a business plan for an idea that she had dreamed about for many years: making and selling a line of flavored vinegars made from homegrown herbs and fruits in unusual flavors, such as opal basil, hot pepper, and blueberry. She named her company Wild Thymes and began selling the hand-bottled, gourmet products at local farmers markets and craft fairs. Using her own creativity and suggestions from customers, Enid began developing new recipes, and within a few years Wild Thymes' reputation and notoriety had grown to the point that retailers such as Whole Foods, Crate and Barrel, Williams-Sonoma, and others contacted Enid about carrying her company's products in their stores. Enid says that her experience as a fashion designer allowed her to create packaging that helped sell Wild Thymes' quality products.

Enid recognized that her company had the potential to grow, and she took some time off to travel with her eldest daughter, Ann, to find inspiration for new product ideas. Their time traveling together made Enid and Ann realize that they would make a great business team. Both were creative cooks, have similar business philosophies, and possess complementary business skills. Enid had experience in food production, and Ann, who had spent more than a decade as a marketing executive in television and sports in New York City, brought the sales and marketing experience that Wild Thymes needed to reach its potential.

Wild Thymes truly is a family-owned business. Enid handles new product development, manufacturing, distribution, and accounting. Ann is in charge of recipe development, in-house sales, marketing, and public relations, and Fred still manages daily operations. Each member of the family management team contributes to the company based on his or her strengths; as a result, Wild Thymes has prospered. They have expanded the company's product line to include dipping sauces, marinades, chutneys, and salad dressings. "It was like starting over [in business]," says Enid. Wild Thymes has won many culinary awards and is perfectly positioned to capitalize on several significant trends in the food industry, including a preference for all-natural, organic, and healthy products. "Our products are sold at the premier specialty and natural food stores nationwide, through our mail order catalog, and through our Web site," says Enid. "Although we've grown we still make every single product on our farm."

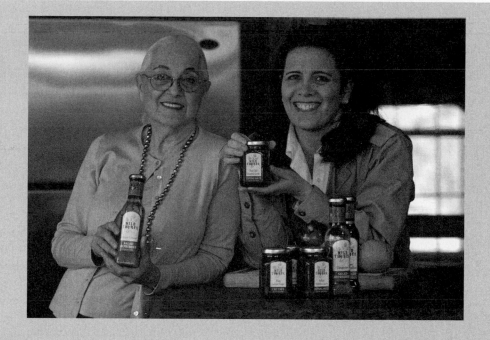

Enid and Ann Stettner, owners of Wild Thymes.

Source: Mike Groll\AP Wide World Photos

1. When Wild Thymes was faced with the opportunity for growth, Enid decided to bring her daughter into the business to help her capitalize on that opportunity. What are the benefits of adding a co owner at such a critical point in a company's life? What are the risks of doing so?

2. Suppose that Enid Stettner had approached you when she was starting Wild Thymes for advice on the form of ownership she should choose. What questions would you ask her?

3. Refer to question 2. Which forms of ownership would you have recommended that Enid avoid? Which form of ownership would you have recommended that she use? Explain.

Sources: Based on Erin Madison, "Moms and Daughters Running Businesses Together," *Great Falls Tribune*, August 10, 2009, *www.greatfallstribune.com/article/20090810/BUSINESS/908100320/Moms+and+daughters+running+businesses+together;* "About Us," Wild Thymes Farm, *www.wildthymes.com/aboutus.asp.*

income tax rates rise above those of C corporation rates, or C corporation rates fall below personal income tax rates.

In addition to the tax implications of choosing an S corporation, owners should consider the following factors in their decision:

- The size of the company's net profits
- The tax rates of its shareholders
- Strategic plans and their timing to sell the company or transition ownership
- The impact of the C corporation's double-taxation penalty on income distributed as dividends

WHEN IS AN S CORPORATION A WISE CHOICE? Choosing S corporation status is usually beneficial to start-up companies that anticipate net losses and to highly profitable firms with substantial dividends to pay out to shareholders. In these cases, owners can use the losses to offset other income, thus reducing their tax bills. Companies that plan to reinvest most of their earnings to finance growth also find S corporation status favorable. Small business owners who intend to sell their companies in the future prefer S status over C status because the capital gains tax on the sale of the assets of an S corporation is lower than those on the sale of a C corporation.

Small companies with the following characteristics are *not* likely to benefit from S corporation status:

- Highly profitable companies with large numbers of shareholders in which most of the profits are passed on to shareholders as compensation or retirement benefits

- Shareholders who pay marginal tax rates that are higher than the marginal tax rates that C corporations pay
- Fast-growing companies that must retain most of their earnings to finance growth and capital spending
- Corporations in which the cost of employee benefits to shareholders exceeds the tax savings that S status produces

The Limited Liability Company

Like an S corporation, the limited liability company (LLC) is a hybrid structure that features elements of a partnership and a corporation. Because of the advantages it offers and its flexibility, the LLC is the fastest growing form of business ownership. LLCs provide owners with many of the benefits of S corporations but are not subject to the restrictions imposed on S corporations. For instance, an LLC offers its owners limited liability without imposing any requirements on their characteristics or any ceiling on their numbers. LLCs do not restrict members' ability to become involved in managing the company, unlike a limited partnership, which prohibits limited partners from participating in day-to-day management of the business.

Although an LLC can have just one owner, most have multiple owners (called *members*). LLCs offer their members the advantages of limited liability and avoiding the double taxation imposed on C corporations. Like an S corporation, an LLC does not pay income taxes; its income flows through to the members, who are responsible for paying income taxes on their shares of the LLC's net income. LLCs permit its members to divide income, and thus tax liability, as they see fit, just as in a partnership.

These advantages make the LLC an ideal form of ownership for companies in many diverse industries. Peter Helmetag and John Fernsell created Ibex Outdoor Clothing, a small company based in Woodstock, Maine, that designs high-performance merino and organic wool outdoor clothing, as an LLC. After emerging bankruptcy filing in 2009, automaker Chrysler was reformed as an LLC.

Creating an LLC is much like creating a corporation. Forming an LLC requires an entrepreneur to file the articles of organization with the secretary of state. The LLC's **articles of organization**, similar to the corporation's articles of incorporation, establish the company's name, its method of management (board-managed or member-managed), its duration, and the names and addresses of each organizer. In most states, the company's name must contain the words *limited liability company*, *limited company*, or the letters LLC or LC. An LLC can have a defined duration, or it can elect to be an "at-will" LLC that has no specific term of duration Although an operating agreement is not required by law, it is essential for entrepreneurs who form LLCs to create one. The LLC **operating agreement** is similar to a corporation's bylaws and outlines the provisions governing the way the LLC will conduct business by defining members' voting rights and power, their percentages of ownership, how profits and losses are distributed, and other important matters. To ensure that an LLC is classified as a partnership for tax purposes, an entrepreneur must carefully draft the operating agreement. The operating agreement must create an LLC that has more characteristics of a partnership than of a corporation to maintain this favorable tax treatment. Specifically, an LLC cannot have any more than two of the following four corporate characteristics:

1. *Limited liability.* Limited liability exists if no member of the LLC is personally liable for the debts or claims against the company. Because entrepreneurs who choose this form of ownership usually get limited liability protection, the operating agreement almost always contains this characteristic.
2. *Continuity of life.* Continuity of life exists if the company continues to exist despite changes in stock ownership. To avoid continuity of life, any LLC member must have the power to dissolve the company. Most entrepreneurs choose to omit this characteristic from their LLC's operating agreements. Thus, if one member of an LLC resigns, dies, or declares bankruptcy, the LLC automatically dissolves and all remaining members must vote to keep the company going.
3. *Free transferability of interest.* Free transferability of interest exists if each LLC member has the power to transfer his ownership to another person without the consent from other members. To avoid this characteristic, the operating agreement must state that the recipient of a member's LLC stock cannot become a substitute member without the consent of the remaining members.

4. *Centralized management.* Centralized management exists if a group that does not include all LLC members has the authority to make management decisions and to conduct company business. To avoid this characteristic, the operating agreement must state the company elects to be "member-managed."

Despite their universal appeal to entrepreneurs, LLCs present some disadvantages. For example, they can be expensive to create. Although LLCs may be ideally suited for an entrepreneur launching a new company, it may pose problems for business owners who are considering converting an existing business to an LLC. Switching to an LLC from a general partnership, a limited partnership, or a sole proprietorship reorganizing to bring in new owners is usually not a problem. However, owners of corporations and S corporations can incur large tax obligations if they convert their companies to LLCs.

Joint Venture

A **joint venture** is very much like a partnership, except that it is formed for a specific purpose. For instance, suppose that you have a 500-acre tract of land 60 miles from Chicago. This land has been cleared and is normally used for farming. One of your friends has solid contacts among major musical groups and would like to put on a concert. You expect prices for your agricultural products to be low this summer, so you and your friend form a joint venture for the specific purpose of staging a 3-day concert. Your contribution will be the exclusive use of the land for 1 month, and your friend will provide all of the performers, as well as the technicians, facilities, and equipment. All costs will be paid out of receipts, the net profits will be split, and you will receive 20 percent for the use of your land. When the concert is over, the facilities removed, and the accounting for all costs completed, you and your friend split the profits 20-80, and the joint venture will terminate. The "partners" form a new joint venture for each new project they undertake. The income derived from a joint venture is taxed as if it had been generated from a partnership.

Table 1 summarizes the key features of the sole proprietorship, the partnership, the C corporation, the S corporation, and the limited liability company.

TABLE 1 Characteristics of the Major Forms of Ownership

Characteristic	Sole Proprietorship	General Partnership	Limited Partnership	C Corporation	S Corporation	Limited Liability Company
Definition	A for-profit business owned and operated by one person	A for-profit business jointly owned and operated by two or more people	One general partner and one or more partners with limited liability and no rights of management	An artificial legal entity separate from its owners and formed under state and federal laws	An artificial legal entity that is structured like a C corporation but taxed by the federal government like a partnership	A business entity that provides limited liability like a corporation but is taxed like a partnership. Owners are referred to as members
Ease of formation	Easiest form of business to set up. If necessary, acquire licenses and permits, register fictitious name, and obtain taxpayer identification	Easy to set up and operate. A written partnership agreement is highly recommended. Must acquire an Employer ID number. If necessary, register fictitious name.	File a certificate of limited partnership with the secretary of state. Name must show that business is a limited partnership. Must have written agreement, and must keep certain records.	File articles of incorporation and other required reports with the secretary of state. prepare bylaws and follow corporate formalities	Must meet all criteria to file as an S corporation. Must file timely election with the IRS (within $2\frac{1}{2}$ months of first taxable year).	File articles of organization with the secretary of state. Adopt operating agreement, and file necessary reports with the secretary of state. The name must show it is a limited liability company.
Owner's personal liability	Unlimited	Unlimited for general partners, limited for limited partners	Limited	Limited	Limited	Limited

(continued)

TABLE 1 Continued

Characteristic	Sole Proprietorship	General Partnership	Limited Partnership	C Corporation	S Corporation	Limited Liability Company
Number of owners	One	Two or more	At least one general partner and any number of limited partners	Any number	Maximum of 100 with restrictions as to who they are	One (A few states require two or more)
Tax liability	Single tax: personal tax rate	Single tax: partners pay on their proportional shares at their individual rate	Same as general partnership	Double tax: corporation pays tax and shareholders pay tax on dividends distributed	Single tax: owners pay on their proportional shares at individual rate	Single tax: members pay on their proportional shares at individual rate
Current maximum tax rate	35%	35%	35%	39% corporate plus 35% individual	35%	35%
Transferability of ownership	Fully transferable through sale or transfer of company assets	May require consent of all partners	Same as general partnership	Fully transferable	Transferable (but transfer may affect S status)	Usually requires consent of all members
Continuity of the business	Ends on death or insanity of proprietor or upon termination by proprietor	Dissolves upon death, insanity, or retirement of a general partner (business may continue)	Same as general partnership	Perpetual life	Perpetual life	Perpetual Life
Cost of formation	Low	Moderate	Moderate	High	High	High
Liquidity of the owner's investment in the business	Poor to average	Poor to average	Poor to average	High	High	High
Ability to raise capital	Low	Moderate	Moderate to high	Very high	High	High
Formation procedure	No special steps required other than buying necessary licenses	No written partnership agreement required (but highly advisable)	Must comply with state laws regarding limited partnership	Must meet formal requirements specified by state law	Must follow same procedures as C corporation, then elect S status with IRS	Must meet formal requirements specified by state law

Chapter Review

1. Discuss the issues that entrepreneurs should consider when evaluating different forms of ownership.
   - The key to choosing the "right" form of ownership is to understand the characteristics of each and know how they affect an entrepreneur's personal and business circumstances.
   - Factors to consider include tax implications, liability expense, start-up and future capital requirements, control, managerial ability, business goals, management succession plans, and cost of formation.
2. Describe the advantages and disadvantages of the sole proprietorship.
   - A sole proprietorship is a business owned and managed by one individual and is the most popular form of ownership.
   - Sole proprietorships offer these advantages:
     - Simple to create
     - Least costly to form

- Owner has total decision-making authority
- No special reporting requirements or legal restrictions
- Easy to discontinue
- Sole proprietorships suffer from these disadvantages:
  - Unlimited personal liability of owner
  - Limited managerial skills and capabilities
  - Limited access to capital
  - Lack of continuity
3. Describe the advantages and disadvantages of the partnership.
- A partnership is an association of two or more people who co-own a business for the purpose of making a profit.
- Partnerships offer these advantages:
  - Easy to establish
  - Complementary skills of partners
  - Division of profits
  - Large pool of capital available
  - Ability to attract limited partners
  - Little government regulation
  - Flexibility
  - Tax advantages
- Partnerships suffer from these disadvantages:
  - Unlimited liability of at least one partner
  - Difficulty in disposing of partnership interest
  - Lack of continuity
  - Potential for personal and authority conflicts
  - Partners are bound by the law of agency
4. Describe the advantages and disadvantages of the corporation.
- A limited partnership operates like any other partnership except that it allows limited partners—primarily investors who cannot take an active role in managing the business—to become owners without subjecting themselves to unlimited personal liability of the company's debts.
- A corporation is a separate legal entity and the most complex of the three basic forms of ownership.
- To form a corporation, an entrepreneur must file the articles of incorporation with the state in which the company will incorporate.
- Corporations offer these advantages:
  - Limited liability of stockholder
  - Ability to attract capital
  - Ability to continue indefinitely
  - Transferable ownership
- Corporations suffer from these disadvantages:
  - Cost and time in incorporation
  - Double taxation
  - Potential for diminished managerial incentives
  - Legal requirement and regulatory red tape
  - Potential loss of control by the founders
5. Describe the features of the alternative forms of ownership, such as the S corporation, the limited liability company, and the joint venture.
- An S corporation offers its owners limited liability protection but avoids the double taxation of C corporations.
- A limited liability company, like the S corporation, is a cross between a partnership and a corporation and offers the advantages of each. However, it operates without the restrictions imposed on an S corporation. To create a limited liability company, an entrepreneur must file the articles of organization and the operating agreement with the secretary of state.
- A joint venture is like a partnership, except that is it formed for a specific purpose.

Discussion Questions

1. What factors should an entrepreneur consider before choosing a form of ownership?
2. Why are sole proprietorships the most popular form of ownership?
3. How does personal conflict affect partnerships? What steps might partners take to minimize personal conflict?
4. Why are the articles important to a successful partnership? What issues should the articles of partnership address?
5. Can one partner commit another to a business deal without the other's consent? Why and what are the potential ramifications?
6. Explain the differences between a domestic corporation, a foreign corporation, and an alien corporation.
7. What issues should the certificate of incorporation cover?
8. How does an S corporation differ from a regular corporation?
9. What role do limited partners play in a partnership? What will happen if a limited partner takes an active role in managing the business?
10. What advantages does a limited liability company offer over an S corporation? Over a sole proprietorship?
11. How is an LLC created? How does this differ from creating an S corporation?
12. What criteria must an LLC meet to avoid double taxation?
13. How does a joint venture differ from a partnership?
14. In what circumstances might a joint venture be applicable?

Selecting the form of your business is an important decision. As the chapter describes, this decision will affect the number of business owners, tax obligations, the time and cost to form the entity, the ability to raise capital, and options to transfer ownership.

On the Web

Review the business entity links associated with the Companion Web site at *www.pearsonhighered.com/scarborough*. This may provide additional information and resources to assist with your form of business. Enter the search term "business entity" in your favorite search engine and note the resources and information that this term generates.

Go to the Sample Plan Browser in Business Plan Pro and look at these three business plans: Calico Computer Consulting, a sole proprietorship; Lansing Aviation, a limited liability company; and Southeast Health Plans Inc., a corporation. After reviewing the executive summaries of each of these plans, why do you think the owners selected this form of ownership? Consider their respective industries: What are the advantages and disadvantages that each of these business entities offer the owners? Why are these choices a good match for the business entities relating to ease of starting, liability, control, ability to raise capital, and transfer of ownership?

In the Software

Go to the section of Business Plan Pro called "Company Ownership." As you look at the comparison matrix of "Characteristics of the

Major Forms of Ownership," Table 1, consider the ramifications of your choice.

- If the business is a sole proprietorship or a partnership and the business is sued, you may be personally liable. Is the nature of your business one that may present this type of risk? Is this an appropriate business entity based on that potential outcome?
- Once your business becomes profitable, what are the potential tax ramifications compared to your current situation?
- If your goal is to retain control of the company over the long term, will the form of ownership you have chosen enable you to do so?
- How much should you budget for legal fees and other expenditures to form the business?
- How much time do you estimate you will need to invest to establish this business entity?
- Will you need to raise capital? How much capital will the venture require? Is this form of ownership optimal for accomplishing that objective?

As you review the instructions provided within Business Plan Pro, refer to the "Characteristics of the Major Forms of Ownership" in Table 1 to help you select the form of ownership that is best for you and your venture.

Building Your Business Plan

Review the work that you have completed on your business plan to date. Does the form of ownership you have chosen "fit" your vision and the scope of the business? Will this choice of business entity offer the type of protection flexibility you desire for your business? You may also want to include comments in your plan regarding changing factors that may require you to reexamine your form of ownership in the future.

Endnotes

1. Ian Mount, "Business Licenses to Go," *FSB*, March 2007, p. 14; "FAQs," Business Licenses, *www.businesslicenses.com/faqs.php#q2*.
2. Denis Blake, "Howdy Partner," *Horseman's Journal*, Spring 2009, *www.nationalhbpa.com/HorsemensJournalDisplay.asp?section=3&key1=11461*; Katy Marquadt, "The Ups and Downs of Owning a Racehorse," *Kiplinger's*, May 2006, pp. 56–59.
3. Matthew Bandyk, "Five Things Entrepreneurs Should Know About Business Partners," *U.S. News and World Report*, May 6, 2008, *www.usnews.com/articles/business/small-business-entrepreneurs/2008/ 05/06/5-things-entrepreneurs-should-know-about-business-partners.html*.
4. Norm Brodsky, "Sam and Me," *Inc.*, June 2006, p. 65.
5. Stephanie Clifford, "Until Death, or Some Other Sticky Problem, Do Us Part," *Inc.*, November 2006, pp. 104–110.
6. "Dispute Resolution: Partnerships," Australian Government, Department of Innovation, Industry, Science and Research, February 14, 2008, *www.innovation.gov.au/General/OSB-MarketsSection/Pages/DisputeResolutionPartnerships.aspx*.
7. Henry R. Chesseman, *Business Law*, 5th ed. (Upper Saddle River, NJ: Pearson Prentice Hall, 2004), p. 675.
8. Grace Wong, "Kozlowski Gets up to 25 Years," *CNN/Money*, September 19, 2005, *http://money.cnn.com/2005/09/19/news/newsmakers/kozlowski_sentence/*.
9. Jill Andresky Fraser, "Perfect Form," *Inc.*, *www.inc.com/magazine/19971201/1368.html*, page 3.

Franchising and the Entrepreneur

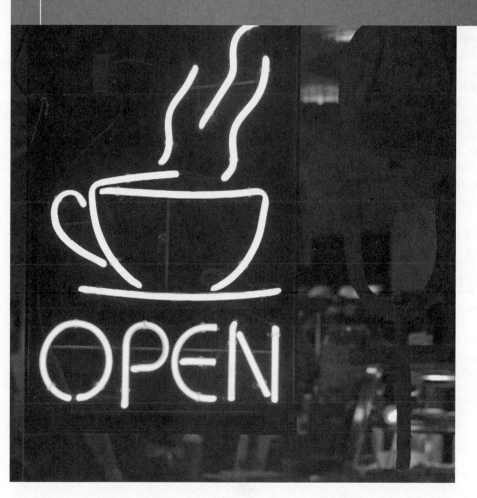

Mistakes are the portals of discovery.

—James Joyce

Good judgment comes from experience. Experience comes from

bad judgment.

—Bob Packwood

Learning Objectives

Upon completion of this chapter, you will be able to:

1 Explain the importance of franchising in the U.S. and global economy.
2 Define the concept of franchising.
3 Describe the different types of franchises.
4 Describe the benefits and limitations of buying a franchise.
5 Describe the legal aspects of franchising, including the protection offered by the FTC's Trade Regulation Rule.
6 Explain the right way to buy a franchise.
7 Describe a typical franchise contract and its primary provisions.
8 Explain current trends shaping franchising.
9 Describe the potential of franchising a business as a growth strategy.

1. Explain the importance of franchising in the U.S. and global economy.

One day while Staci Deal was shopping in Indiana, the 22-year-old University of Arkansas apparel studies major discovered Plato's Closet, a 240-outlet franchise aimed at teens and young adults that buys and resells gently used clothing at discount prices. "This would go over great in Fayetteville (Arkansas, her hometown)," she thought. When she returned to Fayetteville, which Deal describes as "a hip college town," she convinced her father-in-law to lend her the money to purchase a Plato's Closet franchise, making her the youngest franchise owner in the chain. Deal's fashion and business instincts were on the mark: In its first full year of operation, her store generated $1 million in sales. Deal, now with 20 employees, is investing $400,000 to open a second store near a large community college in nearby Rogers, Arkansas.[1]

Franchises like Staci Deal's are an important part of the American business system. Much of franchising's popularity arises from its ability to offer those who lack business experience the chance to own and operate a business with a high probability of success. Franchising's reach now extends far beyond the traditional fast-food outlets and auto dealerships. Shoppers can buy nearly every kind of good or service imaginable through franchises—from waste-eating microbes and health care to hardware and pet sitting. More than 854,000 franchise outlets operate in the United States, employing nearly 9.6 million people and generating $835 billion in annual output, an amount that represents 5.8 percent of the nation's gross domestic product.[2]

Franchising also has a significant impact on the global economy as well. The International Franchise Association reports that over the last decade almost half of all business units established by U.S. franchisors were outside the country.[3] One study reports that 52 percent of the U.S.-based franchise companies support international operations and that an average of 30 percent of their total franchise units are located overseas. Preferred areas for international expansion are Europe and the Pacific Rim countries, and many have high expectations for China in the future. Nearly 80 percent of these companies plan to open new units outside the United States within the next 3 years.[4]

What Is a Franchise?

2. Define the concept of franchising.

In **franchising**, semi-independent business owners (franchisees) pay fees and royalties to a parent company (franchisor) in return for the right to become identified with its trademark, to sell its products or services, and often to use its business format and system. Franchisees do not establish their own autonomous businesses; instead, they buy a "success package" from the franchisor, who shows them how to use it. Franchisees, unlike independent business owners, don't have the freedom to change the way they run their businesses—for example, shifting advertising strategies or adding new products—but they do have access to a formula for success that the franchisor has worked out. Fundamentally, when they buy their franchises, franchisees are purchasing a successful business

FRANCHISES AVAILABLE

Brown.

model. The franchisor provides a business system and the expertise to make it work; the entrepreneur brings the investment, spirit, and drive necessary to implement the system successfully.

Many franchisees say that buying a franchise is like going into business *for* yourself but not *by* yourself. Although franchisees own their own outlets, they must operate them according to the system that the franchisor has developed. One writer explains:

> The science of franchising is an exacting one; products and services are delivered according to tightly-wrapped operating formulas. There is no variance. A product is developed and honed under the watchful eye of the franchisor, then offered by franchisees under strict quality standards. The result: a democratization of products and services. Hamburgers that taste as good in Boston as in Beijing. Quick lubes available to everyone, whether they drive a Toyota or a Treblinka.[5]

Entrepreneurs who insist on doing things their own way usually do not make good franchisees. Successful franchisors claim that failing to follow the formula that they have developed is one of the main reasons that franchisees fail. "First and foremost, franchising demands that you 'follow the system,'" says Nicholas Bibby, a franchise consultant. "Whether the business is a major food brand or a home-based franchise, you must be a team player who is willing to follow the rules. If changing the order of things is among your favorite pastimes, think seriously about another form of self-employment. The best franchises simply have the best systems."[6] In other words, successful franchisees tend to follow the franchisor's business recipe. This standardized, formulaic approach lies at the core of franchising success.

Types of Franchising

3. Describe the different types of franchises.

Franchising includes three basic types of systems: tradename franchising, product distribution franchising, and pure franchising. Each of these forms of franchising allows franchisees to benefit from the parent company's identity.

Tradename franchising involves being associated with a brand name, such as True Value Hardware or Western Auto. In tradename franchising, a franchisee purchases the right to become identified with the franchisor's trade name without distributing particular products exclusively under the manufacturer's name.

Product distribution franchising involves licensing the franchisee to sell specific products under the manufacturer's brand name and trademark through a selective, limited distribution network. This system is commonly used to market automobiles (General Motors and Toyota), gasoline products (Exxon and Chevron), soft drinks (Pepsi Cola and Coca-Cola), bicycles, appliances, cosmetics, and other products.

Pure franchising (or **comprehensive** or **business format franchising**) involves providing the franchisee with a complete business format. This highly structured relationship includes a license for a trade name, the products or services to be sold, the physical plant, the methods of operation, a marketing strategy plan, a quality control process, a two-way communications system, and the necessary business services. The franchisee purchases the right to use all of the elements of a fully integrated business operation. Business format franchising is the most common and the fastest growing of the three types of franchising, accounting for 85.1 percent of all franchise outlets in the United States.[7] It is common among fast-food restaurants, hotels, business service firms, car rental agencies, educational institutions, and many other types of businesses.

The Benefits of Buying a Franchise

4-A. Describe the benefits of buying a franchise.

The primary reason for franchising's success is the mutual benefits it offers both franchisors and franchisees. The ideal franchising relationship is a partnership based on trust and a willingness to work together for mutual success (see Figure 1). The most successful franchisors are the ones that see their franchisees as business partners. They recognize that *their* success depends on their *franchisees'* success.

Franchisees get the opportunity to own a small business relatively quickly, and, because of the identification with an established product and brand, a franchise often reaches the breakeven

FIGURE 1
The Franchising Relationship

Source: Adapted from *Economic Impact of Franchised Businesses: A Study for the International Franchise Association*, National Economic Consulting Practice of PriceWaterhouseCoopers (IFA Educational Foundation, New York: 2004), pp. 3, 5. Reprint courtesy of IFA Educational Foundation.

Element	The Franchisor	The Franchisee
Site selection	Oversees and approves; may choose site	Chooses site with franchisor's approval
Design	Provides prototype design	Pays for and implements design
Employees	Makes general recommendations and training suggestions	Hires, manages, and fires employees
Products and services	Determines product or service line	Modifies only with franchisor's approval
Prices	Can only recommend prices	Sets final prices
Purchasing	Establishes quality standards; provides list of approved suppliers; may require franchisees to purchase from the franchisor	Must meet quality standards; must purchase only from approved suppliers; must purchase from supplier if required.
Advertising	Develops and coordinates national ad campaign; may require minimum level of spending on local advertising	Pays for national ad campaign; complies with local advertising requirements; gets franchisor approval on local ads
Quality control	Sets quality standards and enforces them with inspections; trains franchisees	Maintains quality standards; trains employees to implement quality systems
Support	Provides support through an established business system	Operates business on a day-to-day basis with franchisor's support

point faster than an independent business would. Still, most new franchise outlets don't break even for at least 6 to 18 months.

Franchisees also benefit from the franchisor's business experience. In fact, experience is, in essence, what a franchisee buys from a franchisor. The franchisor's knowledge, expertise, and experience in the industry provide a competitive advantage for franchisees. Given the thin margin for error in a start-up business, entrepreneurs cannot afford to make too many mistakes. In a franchising arrangement, the franchisor already has worked out the kinks in the system, often by trial and error, and franchisees benefit from that experience. Franchisors already have climbed up the learning curve and share with their franchisees the secrets to success that they have learned. This ability to draw on the franchisor's experience and benefit from their support acts as a safety net for entrepreneurs as they build their businesses.

Before jumping into a franchise opportunity, an entrepreneur should ask, "What can a franchise do for me that I cannot do for myself?" The answer depends on one's particular situation and is just as important as a systematic evaluation of any franchise opportunity. After careful deliberation, an entrepreneur may conclude that a franchise offers nothing that he or she cannot do on his or her own or it may turn out that a franchise is the key to success for an entrepreneur.

ENTREPRENEURIAL
Profile

David Ambinder:
Mr. Handyman

David Ambinder worked as an executive on Wall Street for 25 years before being laid off from Lehman Brothers just before the financial services company went bankrupt. Rather than take a chance on another corporate layoff, Ambinder decided to create his own job security by owning his own business. For Ambinder, the structure, support, and safety net of a franchise were ideal. "For me, it's the right move," he says. After investigating several franchise options, Ambinder opened a Mr. Handyman franchise, a company that provides skilled repairmen for a variety of home repair jobs, in Union, New Jersey. Ambinder is one of many corporate castoffs and dropouts who have discovered that franchising offers them the ideal blend of corporate support to which they are accustomed and the freedom of entrepreneurship.

Let's explore the advantages of buying a franchise.

A Business System

One major benefit of joining a franchise is gaining access to a business system with a proven track record. In many cases, franchisors provide their franchisees with turnkey operations, allowing entrepreneurs to get their businesses up and running much faster, more efficiently, and more effectively than if they launched their own companies. Using the franchisor's business system as a guide, franchisees can be successful even though they may have little or no experience in the industry.

Management Training and Support

Franchisors want to give their franchisees a greater chance for success than independent businesses and offer management training programs to franchisees prior to opening a new outlet. Many franchisors, especially the well-established ones, also provide follow-up training and consulting services. This service is vital because most franchisors do not require a franchisee to have experience in the business. These programs teach franchisees the details they need to know for day-to-day operations as well as the nuances of running their businesses successfully. "Just putting a person in business, giving him a trademark, patting him on the [back], and saying, 'Good luck,' is not sufficient," says one franchise consultant.[8]

Training programs often involve both classroom and on-site instruction to teach franchisees the basic operations of the business—from producing and selling the goods or services to purchasing raw materials and completing paperwork. Franchisees at Zaxby's, a fast-casual chain of chicken restaurants, receive 6 weeks of training in a variety of venues before opening their stores. The first component of the program involves classroom training at Zaxby's headquarters, where they learn about the company's culture and expectations. Then franchisees go into Zaxby's restaurants, where they learn the details of daily operations from existing franchisees. For the final part of their training, franchisees return to headquarters to learn about Zaxby's franchise support system and to take a final written and hands-on test.[9] Franchisees at Plato's Closet, the chain of resale shops that focuses on clothing for teens and young adults, spend 2 weeks learning how to develop a business plan, secure financing, hire and manage employees, buy and sell inventory,

Zaxby's, a fast-casual chain of chicken restaurants, offers franchisees 6 weeks of training before franchisees open their stores and ongoing support once they are in business.

Source: Alamy Images

and use the company's proprietary computer software system to manage their stores. The strength of that training program is one factor that gave Charlotte Knowles, a former schoolteacher with no experience in retail clothing, the confidence to open a Plato's Closet franchise in Greenville, South Carolina.[10] Although these training programs are beneficial to running a successful franchise, franchisees should not expect a 2- to 6-week program to make them management experts. The necessary management skills for any business are too complex to learn in any single course.

Many franchisors supplement their start-up training programs with ongoing instruction and support to ensure franchisees' continued success. Franchisors often provide field support to franchisees in customer service, quality control, inventory management, and general management. Franchisors may assign field consultants to guide new franchisees through the first week or two of operation after the grand opening. Zaxby's offers its franchisees a Web-based Learning Center, where they can take refresher courses, view videos, listen to podcasts, participate in discussion boards, and access an online library.[11]

ENTREPRENEURIAL
Profile

Wendy Steele and Stuart and Marian German: Einstein Bros. Bagels

When Wendy Steele and two partners, Stuart and Marian German, decided to open a restaurant in Augusta, Georgia, they chose an Einstein Bros. Bagels franchise. The Lakewood, Colorado-based chain of restaurants, which serves bagels, soups, sandwiches, and wraps, appealed to the cofounders because none of them had significant experience in the restaurant business. They saw the franchisor's training and support system as one key to their success. "Einstein's has been wonderful in their training and complete support," says Steele. The co-owners plan to open 3 more locations within 4 years.[12]

Brand Name Appeal

Franchisees purchase the right to use a known and advertised brand name for a product or service, giving them the advantage of identifying their businesses with a widely recognized name. Customers recognize the identifying trademark, the standard symbols, the store design, and the products of an established franchise. In fact, a basic tenet of franchising is cloning the franchisor's success. Customers can be confident that the quality and content of a meal at McDonald's in Fort Lauderdale will be consistent with a meal at a San Francisco McDonald's. Because of a franchise's name recognition, franchisees who have just opened their outlets often discover a ready supply of customers eager to purchase their products or services. Entrepreneurs who launch independent businesses may have to work for years and spend many thousands of dollars in advertising to build a customer base of equivalent size. One franchising expert explains, "The day you open a McDonald's franchise, you have instant customers. If you choose to open [an independent] hamburger restaurant, you'd have to spend a fortune on advertising and promotion before you'd attract [that many] customers."[13]

Standardized Quality of Goods and Services

The quality of the goods or service franchisees sell determines the franchisor's reputation. Building a sound reputation in business can be a slow process, although destroying a good reputation takes no time at all. If some franchisees are allowed to operate at substandard levels, the image of the entire chain suffers irreparable damage; therefore, franchisors demand strict compliance with uniform standards of quality and service throughout the chain. Many franchisors conduct periodic inspections of local facilities to assist in maintaining acceptable levels of performance. Maintaining quality is so important that most franchisors retain the right to terminate the franchise contract and to repurchase the outlet if the franchisee fails to comply with established standards.

National Advertising Programs

An effective advertising program is essential to the success of virtually all franchise operations. Marketing a brand name product or service over a wide geographic area requires a far-reaching advertising campaign. A regional or national advertising program benefits all franchisees, and most franchisors have one. Typically, these advertising campaigns are organized and controlled by the franchisor, but franchisees actually pay for the campaigns. In fact, a recent study reported that 79 percent of franchisors require franchisees to contribute to a national advertising fund (the average amount is

2 percent of sales).[14] For example, Subway franchisees pay 3.5 percent of gross revenues to the Subway national advertising program. The franchisor pools these funds to create a cooperative advertising program, which has more impact than if the franchisees spent the same amount of money separately. The result is that franchisees associated with a well-developed system do not have to struggle for recognition in the local marketplace as much as an independent owner might.

Many franchisors also require franchisees to spend a minimum amount on local advertising. In fact, 41 percent of franchisors require their franchisees to invest in local advertising (once again, the average amount is 2 percent of sales).[15] To supplement their national advertising efforts, both Wendy's and Burger King require franchisees to spend at least 3 percent of gross sales on local advertising. Some franchisors assist franchisees in designing and producing local advertising. Many companies help franchisees create promotional plans and provide press releases, advertisements, and special materials such as signs and banners for grand openings and special promotions.

Financial Assistance

Purchasing a franchise can be just as expensive (if not more so) than launching an independent business. Although franchisees typically invest a significant amount of their own money in their businesses, most of them need additional financing. Some franchisors are willing to provide at least a portion of that additional financing through their own internal financing programs. A basic principle of franchising is to use franchisees' money to grow the franchisor's business, but some franchisors realize that because start-up costs have reached breathtakingly high levels they must provide financial help for franchisees. A study by FRANdata, a franchising research company, reports that 20 percent of franchisors offer direct financing to their franchisees (see Figure 2).[16] Small franchise systems are more likely to provide direct financial assistance to franchisees than are larger, established franchisors. Once a franchisor locates a suitable prospective franchisee, it may offer the qualified candidate direct financial assistance in specific areas, such as purchasing equipment, inventory, or even the franchise fee. For instance, Snap-On Tools, a 90-year-old franchise company with 4,800 franchises worldwide that sell tools to mechanics and other technicians from mobile stores on wheels, has an internal financing program that will finance all but $25,000 of the initial franchise investment, which ranges from $150,000 to $280,000.[17]

Traditionally, financial assistance from franchisors takes a form other than direct loans or short-term credit. Franchisors usually assist qualified franchisees with establishing relationships with banks, nonbank lenders, and other sources of funds. The support and connections from the franchisor enhance a franchisee's credit standing because lenders recognize the lower failure rate among established franchises. Tight credit standards in the last several years have made this benefit all the more important to prospective franchisees. "A few years ago we handed new franchisees off to a list of lenders," says John Dring of Cartridge World North America, a franchise in Emeryville, California. "Today we have 25 managers in the field working hand-in-hand with four or five national lenders to make sure they're comfortable with our concept."[18]

FIGURE 2
Franchisor Financial Assistance

Source: The Profile of Franchising 2006, International Franchise Association (Washington, DC: 2007), p. 70.

The Small Business Administration (SBA) has created a program called the Franchise Registry that is designed to provide financing for franchisees through its loan guarantee programs. The Franchise Registry streamlines and expedites the loan application process for franchisees who pass the screening tests at franchises that are members of the Registry. More than 1,000 franchises, ranging from AAMCO Transmissions (automotive repair) to Zaxby's (fast-food chicken restaurants), participate in the Franchise Registry program. Approximately 6.3 percent of all SBA loan guarantees go to franchisees, and the amount typically ranges from $250,000 to $500,000.[19] Franchisees interested in the Franchise Registry program should visit its Web site at www.franchiseregistry.com.

Proven Products and Business Formats

A franchisee is purchasing the franchisor's experience, expertise, products, and support. A franchise owner does not have to build the business from scratch. Rather than relying solely on personal ability to establish a business and attract a clientele, the franchisee can depend on the methods and techniques of an established business. These standardized procedures and operations greatly enhance the franchisee's chances of success and avoid the most inefficient type of learning—trial and error. "When we say 'Do things our way,' it's not just an ego thing on the part of the franchisor," says an executive at Subway Sandwiches and Salads. "We've proven it works."[20]

Reputable franchisors also invest resources in researching and developing new products and services, improving on existing ones, and tracking market trends that influence the success of its product line. Many franchisees cite this as another key benefit of the franchising arrangement.

Centralized Buying Power

A franchisee has a significant advantage over the independent small business through the franchisor's centralized and large-volume buying power. If franchisors sell goods and materials to franchisees—and not all do—they may pass on to franchisees any cost savings through volume discounts. For example, it is unlikely that a small, independent ice cream parlor could match the buying power of Baskin-Robbins with its 6,000 stores. In many instances, economies of scale simply preclude independent owners from successfully competing head-to-head on price with franchise operations.

Site Selection and Territorial Protection

A proper location is critical to the success of any small business, and franchises are no exception. In fact, franchise experts consider the three most important factors in franchising to be *location*, *location*, and *location*. Becoming affiliated with a franchise may be the best way to get into prime locations. McDonald's, for example, is well known for its ability to obtain prime locations in high-traffic areas for its restaurants. Although choosing a location is the franchisee's responsibility, the franchisor reserves the right to approve the final site. Many franchisors will conduct an extensive location analysis for new outlets (usually for a fee). A thorough demographic and statistical analysis of potential locations is essential to selecting the site that offers the best potential for success.

Some franchisors offer territorial protection, which gives the franchisee the right to exclusive distribution of brand name goods or services within a particular geographic area. Under such an agreement, a franchisor agrees not to sell another franchised outlet or to open a company-owned unit within the franchisee's defined territory. The size and description of a franchisee's territory varies from one franchise to another. For example, one restaurant franchise agrees not to license another franchisee within a 3-mile radius of existing locations. The purpose of this protection is to prevent an invasion of existing franchisees' territories and the accompanying dilution of sales. The owner of a fast-food franchise saw his store's sales decline from $15,000 per week to $8,000 per week when another franchisee opened a second outlet in the same small Connecticut town. Because the franchisor offered no territorial protection, however, the owner of the original franchise could do nothing about his nearby competitor from the same chain.[21]

Unfortunately for franchisees, fewer franchisors now offer their franchisees territorial protection, and franchise owners may find they are in close proximity to each other. As competition for top locations escalates, disputes over the placement of new franchise outlets have become a source of friction between franchisors and franchisees. Existing franchisees charge that franchisors are encroaching on their territories by granting new franchises in such close proximity that their sales are diluted. Franchise experts consistently cite territorial encroachment as the number one threat to franchisees.

Increased Chance for Success

Investing in a franchise is not risk-free. Between 200 and 300 new franchise companies enter the market each year, and many do not survive. For instance, nine franchisees of Cork and Bottle, a retail wine store franchise, face an uncertain future after their Florida-based franchisor declared bankruptcy. Although they no longer have the support of a franchisor, the franchisees meet periodically to discuss ways to keep the brand alive without the support of the parent company.[22] Scott Shane, who has conducted extensive research on both entrepreneurs and franchises, says that the failure rate for young franchise systems is higher than that of older, more established ones. "Twenty years from their start, less than 20 percent of the franchisors will still be around," he says.[23] In an attempt to accelerate their growth, some franchisors are minimizing the risk that franchisees take by offering guaranteed buy-backs of outlets that fail to meet certain performance targets. Maaco, an automotive repair franchisee, will buy back (with limitations) any new franchise that does not reach $750,000 in sales in its first 15 months of operation.[24]

Despite the fact that franchising offers no guarantees of success, experts contend that franchising is less risky than building a business from the ground up. The tradition of success for franchises is attributed to the broad range of services, assistance, guidelines, and the comprehensive business system the franchisor provides. Statistics regarding the success of a given franchise must be interpreted carefully, however. For example, sometimes when a franchise is in danger of failing, the franchisor often repurchases or relocates the outlet and does not report it as a failure.* As a result, some franchisors boast of never experiencing a failure.

A recent study of franchises reports that the success rate of franchisees is higher when a franchise system:

- Requires franchisees to have prior industry experience.
- Requires franchisees to actively manage their stores (no "absentee" owners).
- Has built a strong brand name.
- Offers training programs designed to improve franchisees' knowledge and skills.[25]

The risk involved in purchasing a franchise is two-pronged: success—or failure—depends on the franchisee's managerial skills and motivation and on the franchisor's business experience, system, and support. Many franchisees are convinced that franchising has been the key to their success in business.

Drawbacks of Buying a Franchise

4-B. Describe the limitations of buying a franchise.

The benefits of franchising can mean the difference between success and failure for some entrepreneurs. Prospective franchisees must understand the disadvantages of franchising before choosing this method of doing business. Perhaps the biggest drawback of franchising is that a franchisee must sacrifice some freedom to the franchisor. Other disadvantages include the following.

Franchise Fees and Ongoing Royalties

Virtually every franchisor imposes fees and demands a share of franchisees' sales revenue in return for the use of the franchisor's name, products or services, and business system. The fees and the initial capital requirements vary among the different franchisors. The total investment required for a franchise varies from around $1,000 for some home-based service franchises to $6.5 million or more for hotel and motel franchises. For example, Jan-Pro, a commercial cleaning franchise, requires a capital investment that ranges from just $3,300 to $54,300, and Snap Fitness, a 24-hour fitness center, estimates that the total cost of opening a franchise ranges from $77,400 to $272,800. Sonic Drive-In Restaurants, a chain that sells a variety of fast-food items that range from breakfast dishes and hot dogs to hamburgers and slushes in the retro atmosphere of a 1950s curbside diner, requires an investment of $1.2 million to $3.2 million, depending on land acquisition and building construction costs.

---

*As long as an outlet's doors never close, most franchisors do not count it as a failure even if the outlet has struggled for survival and has been through a series of owners who have tried unsuccessfully to turn around its performance.

Start-up costs for franchises often include a variety of fees. Most franchises impose a franchise fee up front for the right to use the company name. The average up-front fee that franchisors charge is $25,147.[26] Sonic Drive-In charges a franchise fee of $45,000. Other franchise start-up costs might include a location analysis, site purchase and preparation, construction, signs, fixtures, equipment, management assistance, and training. Some franchise fees include these costs, but others do not. For example, Closets by Design, a company that designs and installs closet and garage organizers, entertainment centers, and home office systems, charges a franchise fee ranging from $24,500 to $39,900, which includes both a license for an exclusive territory and management training and support. Before signing any contract, a prospective franchisee should determine the total cost of a franchise, something every franchisor is required to disclose in item 10 of its Franchise Disclosure Document (see the "Franchising and the Law" section later in this chapter).

Franchisors also impose continuing royalty fees as revenue-sharing devices. The royalty usually involves a percentage of gross sales with a required minimum or a flat fee levied on the franchise. (In fact, 82 percent of franchisors charge a royalty based on a percentage of franchisees' sales.[27]) Royalty fees range from 1 to 11 percent, and the average royalty rate is 6.7 percent.[28] The Atlanta Bread Company charges franchisees a royalty of 5 percent of gross sales, which is payable weekly, and Cold Stone Creamery charges a royalty of 6 percent of gross sales. These ongoing royalties increase a franchisee's overhead expenses significantly. Because the franchisor's royalties and fees (the total fees the average franchisor collects amount to 8.4 percent of a franchisee's sales) are calculated as a percentage of a franchisee's sales, the franchisor gets paid, even if the franchisee fails to earn a profit.[29] Sometimes unprepared franchisees discover (too late) that a franchisor's royalties and fees are the equivalent of the normal profit margin for a franchise. To avoid this problem, prospective franchisees should determine exactly how much fees will be and then weigh the benefits of the services and benefits the fees cover. One of the best ways to do this is to itemize what you are getting for your money and then determine whether the cost is reasonable. Getting details on all expenses—the amount, the time of payment, and the financing arrangements—is important. It is critical that entrepreneurs find out which items, if any, are included in the initial franchise fee and which fees represent additional expenditures.

Strict Adherence to Standardized Operations

Although franchisees own their businesses, they do not have the autonomy of independent owners. The terms of the franchise agreement govern the franchisor–franchisee relationship. That agreement requires franchisees to operate their outlets according to the principles spelled out in the franchisor's operations manual. Typical topics covered in the manual include operating hours, dress codes, operating policies and procedures, product or service specifications, and confidentiality requirements.

To protect its public image, franchisors require franchisees to maintain certain operating standards. If a franchise constantly fails to meet the minimum standards established for the business, the franchisor may terminate its license. Many franchisors determine compliance with standards with periodic inspections and mystery shoppers. Mystery shoppers work for a survey company and, although they look like any other customer, are trained to observe and then later record on a checklist a franchise's performance on key standards such as cleanliness, speed of service, employees' appearances and attitudes, and others. At times, strict adherence to franchise standards may become a burden to some franchisees. A franchisee may believe that the written reports the franchisor demands require an excessive amount of time or that enforcing specific rules that he or she thinks are unfair is not in the best interest of his or her business.

Restrictions on Purchasing

To maintain quality standards, franchisors sometimes require franchisees to purchase products, supplies, or special equipment from the franchisor or from approved suppliers. For example, KFC requires that franchisees use only seasonings blended by a particular company because a poor image for the entire franchise could result from some franchisees using inferior products to cut costs. The franchise contract spells out the penalty for using unapproved suppliers, which usually is termination of the franchise agreement. MaggieMoos International, an ice cream franchise, sued two franchisees for failure to use the company's proprietary ice cream mix because the company was concerned about the impact of inferior products on the integrity of its brand.[30]

Before signing with a franchisor, prospective franchisees should investigate the prices that the franchisor and approved suppliers charge for supplies.

Profile
Marty Tate: Quiznos

Several franchisees in the Quiznos sandwich chain filed a class-action lawsuit against the franchisor alleging that the company requires franchisees to buy practically all of their supplies—including the meat and the cheese for sandwiches, bathroom soap, payroll and accounting systems, and even the piped-in music—from the franchisor or its approved suppliers at inflated prices, which caused their stores to be unprofitable. "We can't make money," says Marty Tate, a franchisee who owns a Quiznos outlet in Pennsylvania. He claims that 40 percent of his sales go to cover food costs, the ongoing royalty, and the franchise advertising fee.[31]

A franchisor may legally set the prices it charges for the products it sells to franchisees, but it cannot control the retail prices franchisees charge for the products they sell. A franchisor can *suggest* retail prices for a franchisee's products and services, but it cannot force the franchisee to abide by them. To do so would be a violation of the Robinson-Patman Act. For instance, even though most fast-food franchisors promote their "dollar menus," many franchisees charge more than $1 for those items. One long-time franchisee, who charges $1.29 for a double cheeseburger, says that if he had to price them at $1, he "couldn't stay in business."[32] Franchisors do influence the prices that their franchisees charge in other ways, however. A common technique is to offer discount coupons that franchisees must honor. One sandwich company's franchisees complained that the franchisor's discount coupons were cutting into their profit margins so severely that they could not make a profit on sales of the discounted items. "This company never saw a discount it didn't like," says one franchisee. "Those great discounts are financed solely by franchisees."[33]

Limited Product Line

In most cases, the franchise agreement stipulates that franchisees can sell only those products approved by the franchisor. Franchisees must avoid selling any unapproved products through their outlets unless they are willing to risk cancellation of their franchise license. Franchisors strive for standardization in their product lines so that customers, wherever they may be, know what to expect. Some companies allow franchisees to modify their product or service offerings to suit regional or local tastes, but only with the franchisor's approval. When Heavenly Hams franchisee Felix Mirando spotted an opportunity to sell ready-made box lunches to employees at corporate offices near his franchise, he asked for and received approval from the franchisor to add the item to his menu.[34]

A franchise may be required to carry an unpopular product or be prevented from introducing a desirable one by the franchise agreement. Some franchises discourage franchisees from deviating from the standard "formula" in any way, including experimenting with new products and services. However, other franchisors encourage and even solicit new ideas and innovations from their franchisees.

Profile
Herb Peterson: McDonald's

Herb Peterson, a McDonald's franchisee in Santa Barbara, California, created the highly successful Egg McMuffin while experimenting with a Teflon-coated egg ring that gave fried eggs rounded corners and a poached appearance. Peterson put his round eggs on English muffins, adorned them with Canadian bacon and melted cheese, and showed his creation to McDonald's CEO Ray Kroc. Even though Kroc had just eaten lunch, he devoured two of them and was sold on the idea. The catchy name came about later when the Krocs were having dinner with another McDonald's executive, Fred Turner, and his wife, Patty, who suggested the Egg McMuffin name. In 1975, McDonald's became the first fast-food franchise to open its doors for breakfast, and the Egg McMuffin became a staple on the breakfast menu, which accounts for 15 percent of McDonald's sales. McDonald's franchisees also came up with the ideas for the Big Mac and the Happy Meal.[35]

Market Saturation

Franchisees in fast-growing systems reap the benefits of the franchisor's expanding reach, but they also may encounter the downside of a franchisor's aggressive growth strategy: market saturation. As the owners of many fast-food, sandwich, and yogurt and ice cream franchises have discovered, market saturation is a very real danger. Fast-growing franchises run the risk of having outlets so close together that they cannibalize sales from one another. Franchisees of one fast-growing ice cream chain claim that the franchisor's rapid expansion has resulted in oversaturation in some markets, causing them to struggle to reach their breakeven points. Some franchisees saw their sales drop precipitously and were forced to close their outlets.

Although some franchisors offer franchisees territorial protection, others do not. Territorial encroachment has become a hotly contested issue in franchising as growth-seeking franchisors have exhausted most of the prime locations and are now setting up new franchises in close proximity to existing ones. In some areas of the country, franchisees are upset, claiming that their markets are oversaturated and their sales are suffering.

Limited Freedom

When franchisees purchase their franchises and sign the contract, they agree to sell the franchisor's product or service by following its prescribed formula. When McDonald's rolls out a new national product, for instance, all franchisees put it on their menus. Franchisors want to ensure success, and most monitor their franchisees' performances closely. Strict uniformity is the rule rather than the exception. This feature of franchising is the source of the system's success, but it also gives many franchisees the feeling that they are reporting to a "boss." Entrepreneurs who want to be their own bosses and to avoid being subject to the control of others most likely will be frustrated as franchisees. Highly independent, "go-my-own-way" individuals probably should not choose the franchise route to business ownership. Table 1 offers a Franchise Evaluation Quiz designed to help potential franchisees decide whether a franchise is right for them.

Franchising and the Law

5. Describe the legal aspects of franchising, including the protection offered by the FTC's Trade Regulation Rule.

The franchising boom of the late 1950s brought with it many prime investment opportunities. However, the explosion of legitimate franchises also ushered in with it numerous fly-by-night franchisors who defrauded their franchisees. By the 1970s, franchising was rife with fraudulent practitioners. Thousands of people lost millions of dollars to criminals and unscrupulous operators

TABLE 1 A Franchise Evaluation Quiz

Taking the emotion out of buying a franchise is the goal of this self-test developed by Franchise Solutions, Inc., a franchise consulting company in Portsmouth, New Hampshire. Circle the number that reflects your degree of certainty or positive feelings for each of the following 12 statements: 1 is low; 5 is high.

	Low				High
1. I would really enjoy being in this kind of business.	1	2	3	4	5
2. This franchise will meet or exceed my income goals.	1	2	3	4	5
3. My people-handling skills are sufficient for this franchise.	1	2	3	4	5
4. I understand fully my greatest challenge in this franchise, and I feel comfortable with my abilities.	1	2	3	4	5
5. I have met with the company management and feel compatible.	1	2	3	4	5
6. I understand the risks with this business and am prepared to accept them.	1	2	3	4	5
7. I have researched the competition in my area and feel comfortable with the potential market.	1	2	3	4	5
8. My family and friends think this is a great opportunity for me.	1	2	3	4	5
9. I have had an adviser review the disclosure documents and the franchise agreement.	1	2	3	4	5
10. I have contacted a representative number of the existing franchisees; they were overwhelmingly positive.	1	2	3	4	5
11. I have researched this industry and feel comfortable about the long-term growth potential.	1	2	3	4	5
12. My background and experience make this franchise an ideal choice.	1	2	3	4	5

The maximum score on the quiz is 60. A score of 45 or below means that either the franchise opportunity is unsuitable or that you need to do more research on the franchise you are considering.

Source: Roberta Maynard, "Choosing a Franchise," *Nation's Business*, October 1996, p. 57.

IN THE ENTREPRENEURIAL
SPOTLIGHT   The Appeal of Franchising

Neil Erlich knew that he wanted to be an entrepreneur when he helped start a contracting business when he was just 14 years old. During his junior year at Sonoma State University, Erlich, with help from his father, a corporate executive, began investigating franchise options that would suit his interests and skills. They honed in on the automotive service industry and reviewed the FDDs of several franchises, including Meineke, Jiffy Lube, and Midas, before settling on Express Oil Change. Erlich was particularly impressed with the support that Express Oil Change offered its franchisees. When Erlich graduated with a business degree, his father put up $375,000 to help him purchase and set up the $1.5 million franchise operation. Erlich, who is the youngest franchisee in the Express Oil Change system, sees the franchisor's support as one of the greatest benefits of choosing to open a franchise rather than an independent business of his own. "[The franchisor] is there for you," he says. "It's very comforting."

Like Erlich, a growing number of college graduates and twenty-something adults who are disenchanted with the prospects of a dull job in the corporate grind are looking to franchising as a promising career choice. Indeed, franchising is attracting people of all ages and backgrounds, from corporate dropouts and military veterans to retired baby boomers and corporate castoffs. "People say, 'I put 20 years into a company, and because they ran into some tough times, they let me go,'" explains Ray Titus, head of the United Franchise Group. "They think, 'Do I want to put myself into a position where I may get laid off again?' Instead, they take control of their future by running their own businesses." For many of them, franchising is the perfect fit. Luis Ricardo Galindo had been with Lenovo Corporation for years when the company decided to close the Boca Raton, Florida, office, where he worked. Not willing to risk another corporate layoff, Galindo began working with a franchise broker to identify franchises that would be right for him. Eventually, Galindo settled on Molly Maids, a franchise that specializes in residential house cleaning and is resistant to economic downturns. Because credit was so tight, Galindo tapped his retirement account to finance his franchise, which opened recently.

Retirees who are looking for second careers also are turning to franchising as well. "They've got school-of-hard-knocks experience and business skills that they can apply on day one at a franchise," says Michael Shay of the International Franchise Association. Six months after Kathy McAvoy-Rogalski retired at age 56 from a large pharmaceutical company, she and her husband, James purchased a Fetch Pet Care franchise in Yonkers, New York. With annual sales exceeding $43 billion, the pet products and services industry is the seventh largest retail sector in the United States. Fetch Pet Care allows franchisees to operate their pet-sitting and dog-walking businesses from their homes, which keeps start-up and operating costs low. In its first year of operation, revenues for their business were $55,000, more than their financial forecasts had indicated. Their major costs were paying their staff of seven dog walkers and sitters and paying the franchise royalty fee, which is 5 percent of gross sales, and the cooperative advertising fee, which is 1.5 percent of gross sales. "It's the perfect way to earn extra money," says McAvoy-Rogalski of her franchise.

Franchising can be the ideal path to owning a business for people in almost any phase of professional life, whether they are retirees looking for a new direction and extra income or recent college graduates who are ready to embark on exciting careers. "Boosted by a brand name, training, advertising, and an established business plan, a franchise can ease the struggle and the risk of opening a business and still let you call some shots."

1. These examples show people at different stages of their professional lives choosing to become business owners with the help of a franchise. What conclusions can you draw from their stories about the benefits and appeal of franchising?
2. What are the disadvantages of investing in a franchise?
3. Suppose that one of your friends who is about to graduate is considering purchasing a franchise. What advice would you offer him or her before signing the franchise contract?

Sources: Based on Deborah L. Cohen, "Young Entrepreneurs Bypass Corporate Rat Race," Reuters, August 20, 2009, *www.reuters.com/article/deborahCohen/idUSTRE57J2XS20090820*; Allison Ross, "Unemployed Pinning Hopes on Franchise Ventures," *Palm Beach Post*, May 11, 2009, pp. 1F, 6F; Dave Carpenter, "Older Workers Turn to Franchises in Recession," MSNBC, February 5, 2009, *www.msnbc.msn.com/id/29039605*.

who sold flawed business concepts and phantom franchises to unsuspecting investors. In an effort to control the rampant fraud in the industry and the potential for deception inherent in a franchise relationship, California in 1971 enacted the first Franchise Investment Law. This law and those of 14 other states[†] that have since passed similar laws requires franchisors to register a Uniform Franchise Offering Circular (UFOC) and deliver a copy to prospective franchisees before any offer or sale of a franchise. The UFOC establishes full disclosure guidelines for the franchising company and gives potential franchisees the ability to protect themselves from unscrupulous franchisors. In October 1979, the Federal Trade Commission (FTC) adopted similar legislation at the national level that established full disclosure guidelines for any company selling franchises and was designed to give potential franchisees the information they needed to protect themselves from unscrupulous franchisors.

In 2008, the FTC replaced the UFOC with a similar document, the **Franchise Disclosure Document (FDD)**, which requires all franchisors to disclose detailed information on their operations at least 14 days before a franchisee signs a contract or pays any money. The FDD applies to all franchisors, even those in the 35 states that lack franchise disclosure laws. The purpose of the regulation is to assist potential franchisees' investigations of a franchise deal and to introduce consistency into the franchisor's disclosure statements. The FTC also established a "plain English" requirement for the FDD that prohibits legal and technical jargon and makes a document easy to read and understand. The FTC's philosophy is not so much to prosecute abusers as to provide information to prospective franchisees and help them to make intelligent decisions. Although the FTC requires each franchisor to provide a potential franchisee with this information, it does not verify its accuracy. Prospective franchisees should use this document only as a starting point for their investigations.

In its FDD, a franchisor must include a sample franchise contract, 3 years of audited financial statements, and information on the following 23 items:

1. Information identifying the franchisor and its affiliates and describing the franchisor's business experience and the franchises being sold.
2. Information identifying and describing the business experience of each of the franchisor's officers, directors, and managers responsible for the franchise program.
3. A description of the lawsuits in which the franchisor and its officers, directors, and managers have been involved. Although most franchisors will have been involved in some type of litigation, an excessive number of lawsuits, particularly if they relate to the same problem, is alarming. Another red flag is an excessive number of lawsuits brought against the franchisor by franchisees. "The history of the litigation will tell you the future of your relationship [with the franchisor]," says the founder of a maid-service franchise.[36]
4. Information about any bankruptcies in which the franchisor and its officers, directors, and managers have been involved.
5. Information about the initial franchise fee and other payments required to obtain the franchise, the intended use of the fees, and the conditions under which the fees are refundable.
6. A table that describes all of the other fees that franchisees are required to make after startup, including royalties, service fees, training fees, lease payments, advertising or marketing charges, and others. The table also must include the due dates for the fees.
7. A table that shows the components of a franchisee's total initial investment. The categories covered are pre-opening expenses, the initial franchise fee, training expenses, equipment, opening inventory, initial advertising fee, signs, real estate (purchased or leased), equipment, opening inventory, security deposits, business licenses, initial advertising fees, and other expenses, such as working capital, legal and accounting fees. These estimates, usually stated as a range, give prospective franchisees an idea of how much their total start-up costs will be.
8. Information about quality requirements of goods, services, equipment, supplies, inventory, and other items used in the franchise and where franchisees may purchase them, including required purchases from the franchisor.
9. A cross-reference table that shows the location in the FDD and in the franchise contract of the description of the franchisee's obligations under the franchise contract.

[†]The 15 states requiring franchise registration are: California, Hawaii, Illinois, Indiana, Maryland, Michigan, Minnesota, New York, North Dakota, Oregon, Rhode Island, South Dakota, Virginia, Washington, and Wisconsin.

10. A description of any financial assistance available from the franchisor in the purchase of the franchise. Although many franchisors do not offer direct financial assistance to franchisees, they may have special arrangements with lenders who help franchisees find financing.

11. A description of all obligations the franchisor must fulfill in helping a franchisee prepare to open and operate a unit, including site selection, advertising, computer systems, pricing, training, (a table describing the length and type of training is required) and other forms of assistance provided to franchisees. This usually is the longest section of the FDD.

12. A description of any territorial protection that the franchise receives and a statement as to whether the franchisor may locate a company-owned store or other franchised outlet in that territory. The franchisor must specify whether it offers exclusive or nonexclusive territories. Given the controversy in many franchises over market saturation, franchisees should pay close attention to this section.

13. All relevant information about the franchisor's trademarks, service marks, trade names, logos, and commercial symbols, including where they are registered. Prospective franchisees should look for a strong trade or service mark that is registered with the U.S. Patent and Trademark Office.

14. Similar information on any patents, copyrights, and proprietary processes the franchisor owns and the rights franchisees have to use them.

15. A description of the extent to which franchisees must participate personally in the operation of the franchise. Many franchisors look for "hands-on" franchisees and discourage or even prohibit "absentee owners."

16. A description of any restrictions on the goods or services that franchises are permitted to sell and with whom franchisees may deal. The agreement usually restricts franchisees to selling only those items that the franchisor has approved.

17. A table that describes the conditions under which the franchise may be repurchased or refused renewal by the franchisor, transferred to a third party by the franchisee, and terminated or modified by either party. This section also addresses the methods established for resolving disputes, usually either mediation or arbitration, between franchisees and the franchisor.

18. A description of the involvement of celebrities and public figures in the franchise.

19. A complete statement of the basis for any earnings claims made to the franchisee, including the percentage of existing franchises that have actually achieved the results that are claimed. Franchisors that make earnings claims must include them in the FDD, and the claims must "have a reasonable basis" at the time they are made. However, franchisors are *not* required to make any earnings claims at all; in fact, 81.7 percent of franchisors do not, primarily because of liability concerns about committing such numbers to writing.[37]

20. A table that displays system-wide statistical information about the expansion or the contraction of the franchise over the last 3 years. This section also includes the current number of franchises, the number of franchises projected for the future and the states in which they are to be sold, the number of franchises terminated, the number of agreements the franchisor has not renewed, the number of franchises that have been sold to new owners, the number of outlets the franchisor has repurchased, and a list of the names and addresses (organized by state) of other franchisees in the system and of those who have left the system within the last year. Contacting some of the franchisees who have left the system can alert would-be franchisees to potential problems with the franchise.

21. The franchisor's audited financial statements.

22. A copy of all franchise and other contracts (leases, purchase agreements, and others) that the franchisee will be required to sign.

23. A standardized, detachable "receipt" to prove that the prospective franchisee received a copy of the FDD. The FTC now allows franchisors to provide the FDD to prospective franchisees electronically.

The typical FDD is from 100 to 200 pages long, but every potential franchisee should read and understand it. Unfortunately, many do not, which often results in unpleasant surprises for franchisees. The information contained in the FDD neither fully protects a potential franchise from deception nor does it guarantee success. The FDD does, however, provide enough information to begin a thorough investigation of the franchisor and the franchise deal, and prospective franchisees should use it to their advantage.

The Right Way to Buy a Franchise

6. Explain the right way to buy a franchise.

The FDD can help potential franchisees to identify and avoid dishonest franchisors. The best defenses a prospective entrepreneur has against making a bad investment decision or against unscrupulous franchisors are preparation, common sense, and patience. A thorough investigation before investing in a franchise reduces the risk of being hoodwinked into a nonexistent franchise or a system that is destined to fail. Asking the right questions and resisting the urge to rush into an investment decision helps potential franchisees avoid unscrupulous franchisors.

Despite existing disclosure requirements, dishonest franchisors are still in operation, often moving from one state to another just ahead of authorities. Potential franchisees must beware. Franchise fraud has destroyed the dreams of many hopeful franchisees and has robbed them of their life savings. Because dishonest franchisors tend to follow certain patterns, well-prepared franchisees can avoid getting burned. The following clues should arouse the suspicion of an entrepreneur about to invest in a franchise:

- Claims that the franchise contract is "the standard one" and that "you don't need to read it." There is no standard franchise contract.
- A franchisor who fails to give you a copy of the required disclosure document, the FDD, at your first face-to-face meeting.
- A marginally successful prototype store or no prototype at all.
- A poorly prepared operations manual outlining the franchise system or no manual (or system) at all.
- An unsolicited testimonial from "a highly successful franchisee." Scam artists will hire someone to pose as a successful franchisee, complete with a rented luxury car and expensive-looking jewelry and clothing, to "prove" how successful franchisees can be and to help close the sale. Use the list of franchisees in item 20 of the FDD to find real franchisees and ask them plenty of questions.
- An unusual amount of litigation brought against the franchisor. In this litigious society, companies facing lawsuits is a common situation. However, too many lawsuits are a sign that something is amiss. This information is found in item 3 of the FDD.
- Verbal promises of large future earnings without written documentation. Remember: If franchisors make earnings claims, they *must* document them in item 19 of the FDD.
- A high franchisee turnover rate or a high termination rate. This information is described in item 20 of the FDD.
- Attempts to discourage you from allowing an attorney to evaluate the franchise contract before you sign it.
- No written documentation to support claims and promises.
- A high pressure sale—sign the contract now or lose the opportunity. This tactic usually sounds like this: "Franchise territories are going fast. If you hesitate, you are likely to miss out on the prime spots."
- Claiming to be exempt from federal laws requiring complete disclosure of franchise details in an FDD. If a franchisor does not have an FDD, run—don't walk—away from the deal.
- "Get-rich-quick schemes," promises of huge profits with only minimum effort.
- Reluctance to provide a list of present franchisees for you to interview.
- Evasive, vague answers to your questions about the franchise and its operation.

Not every franchise "horror story" is the result of dishonest franchisors. In fact, most franchising problems are due to franchisees buying legitimate franchises without proper research and analysis. They end up in businesses they do not enjoy and that they are not well suited to operate. The following steps will help any potential franchisee make the right franchise choice.

Evaluate Yourself

Henry David Thoreau's advice to "know thyself" is excellent advice for prospective franchisees. Before looking at any franchise, entrepreneurs should study their own traits, goals, experience, likes, dislikes, risk-orientation, income requirements, time and family commitments, and other characteristics. Knowing how much you can invest in a franchise is important, but it is not the only factor to consider. The following are valuable questions for the entrepreneur to ask:

- Will you be comfortable working in a structured environment?
- What kinds of franchises fit your desired lifestyle?
- Do you want to sell a product or a service?

- Do you enjoy working with the public?
- Do you like selling?
- What hours do you expect to work?
- Do you want to work with people, or do you prefer to work alone?
- Which franchise concepts mesh best with your past work experience?
- What activities and hobbies do you enjoy?
- What income do you expect a franchise to generate?
- How much can you afford to invest in a franchise?
- Will you be happy with the daily routine of operating the franchise?

Most franchise contracts run for 10 years or more, making it imperative that prospective franchisees conduct a complete inventory of their interests, likes, dislikes, and abilities before buying a franchise.

Research the Market

Entrepreneurs should research the market in the areas they plan to serve before shopping for a franchise:

- How fast is the surrounding area growing?
- In which areas is that growth occurring fastest?
- Is the market for the franchise's product or service growing or declining?
- How strong is the competition?
- Who are your potential customers?
- What are their characteristics?
- What are their income and education levels?
- What kinds of products and services do they buy?
- What gaps exist in the market?

Investing time in the local library or on the Internet to determine whether an area has a sufficient number of the franchise's target customers is essential to judging an outlet's potential for success.

Solid market research should tell a prospective franchisee whether a particular franchise is merely a passing fad. Steering clear of fads and into long-term trends is a key to sustained success in franchising. The secret to distinguishing between a fad that will soon fizzle and a meaningful trend that offers genuine opportunity is finding products or services that are consistent with fundamental demographic and lifestyle patterns of the population. That requires sound market research that focuses not only on local market opportunities but also on the "big picture." For instance, a growing number of aging baby boomers is creating an opportunity for franchises that provide cleaning, home care, and home improvement services.

Consider Your Franchise Options

Tracking down information on prospective franchise systems is easier now than ever before. Franchisors publish information about their systems on the Internet. These listings can help potential franchisees find a suitable franchise within their price ranges. Many cities host franchise trade shows throughout the year, where hundreds of franchisors gather to sell their franchises. Many business magazines such as *Entrepreneur, Inc.*, and others devote at least one issue and a section of their Web sites to franchising, where they often list hundreds of franchise opportunities.

Get a Copy of the FDD and Study It

Once you narrow down your franchise choices, contact each franchise and get a copy of the franchise FDD. Then read it! The FDD is an important tool in your search for the right franchise. When evaluating a franchise opportunity, what should a potential franchisee look for? Although there is no guarantee of success, the following characteristics make a franchisor stand out:

- *A unique concept or marketing approach.* "Me-too" franchises are no more successful than "me-too" independent businesses. Pizza franchisor Papa John's has achieved an impressive growth rate by emphasizing the quality of its ingredients, whereas Domino's is known for its fast delivery.
- *Profitability.* A franchisor should have a track record of profitability and so should its franchisees. If a franchisor is not profitable, its franchisees are not likely to be either. Franchisees who follow the business format should expect to earn a reasonable rate of return.
- *A registered trademark.* Name recognition is difficult to achieve without a well-known and protected trademark.

Just like the famous detective, Sherlock Holmes, a prospective franchisee should investigate thoroughly to determine which franchise is right for him or her.

Source: Picture Desk, Inc./Kobal Collection

- *A business system that works.* A franchisor should have in place a system that is efficient and is well documented in its manuals. After all, a proven business system lies at the heart of what a franchisee purchases from a franchisor.
- *A solid training program.* One of the most valuable components of a franchise system is the training it offers franchisees. The system should be relatively easy to learn.
- *Affordability.* A franchisee should not have to take on an excessive amount of debt to purchase a franchise. Being forced to borrow too much money to open a franchise outlet can doom a business from the outset. Respectable franchisors verify prospective franchisees' financial qualifications as part of the screening process.
- *A positive relationship with franchisees.* The most successful franchises are those that see their franchisees as partners—and treat them accordingly. "You want companies that award franchises, not sell them," says one franchise consultant.[38]

The FDD covers the 23 items discussed earlier and includes a copy of the company's franchise agreement and any contracts accompanying it. Although the law requires an FDD to be written in plain English rather than "legalese," it is best to have an attorney with franchise experience review the FDD and discuss its provisions with you. The franchise contract summarizes the details that will govern the franchisor–franchisee relationship over its life. The contract outlines exactly the rights and the obligations of each party and sets the guidelines that govern the franchise relationship. Franchise contracts typically are long term; 50 percent run for 15 years or more, making it extremely important for prospective franchisees to understand their terms before they sign a contract.

Particular items in the FDD that entrepreneurs should focus on include the franchisor's experience (items 1 and 2), current and past litigation against the franchisor (item 3), the fees and total investment (items 5, 6, and 7), and the franchisee turnover rate for the past 3 years (item 20). The **franchisee turnover rate**, the rate at which franchisees leave the system, is one of the most revealing items in the FDD. If the turnover rate is less than 5 percent, the franchise probably is sound; however, a rate approaching 20 percent is a sign of serious, underlying problems in a franchise. Although virtually every franchisor has been involved in lawsuits, an excessive amount of litigation against a franchisor over a particular matter should alert a prospective franchisee to potential problems down the road. Determining what the cases were about and whether they have been resolved is important.

Talk to Existing Franchisees

Although the FDD contains valuable information, it is only the starting point for researching a franchise opportunity thoroughly. Perhaps the best way to evaluate the reputation of a franchisor is to interview (in person) several franchise owners who have been in business at least 1 year about the positive and the negative aspects of the agreement and whether the franchisor delivered what it promised. Knowing what they know now, would they buy the franchise again? Another useful technique is to monitor franchisees' blogs, where prospective franchisees can learn the "real story" of running a franchise.

Another revealing exercise is to spend an entire day with at least one (preferably more) franchisee to observe firsthand what it is like to operate a franchise unit. Some prospective franchisees work in an existing outlet, sometimes without pay, to get a sense of what the daily routine is like. Item 20 of the FDD lists all of a company's current franchisees and former franchisees who have left the system within the last year and their contact information, which makes it easy for potential franchisees to contact them. It is wise to interview former franchisees to get their perspectives on the franchisor–franchisee relationship. Why did they leave?

Before brother and sister Whitney and Ryan Berger purchased a Cold Stone Creamery franchise in Baltimore, Maryland, they used the information in the FDD to contact every existing and former franchisee listed in it. Their due diligence paid off; they now own three Cold Stone Creamery stores in Maryland that generate annual sales of $1.5 million.[39]

Table 2 provides some important questions to ask current franchisees.

Ask the Franchisor Some Tough Questions

Take the time to visit the franchisor's headquarters and ask plenty of questions about the company and its relationship with its franchisees. You will be in this relationship a long time, and you need to know as much about it as possible beforehand. Important questions to ask include:

1. What skills does a successful franchisee need? (Then consider how you measure up.)
2. What is the franchisor's philosophy concerning the franchisor–franchisee relationship? How do franchisees and the franchisor resolve conflicts? (Ask for specific examples.)
3. What are the most common causes of the problems that franchisees encounter?
4. How would you describe the company's culture?
5. How much input do franchisees have into the system?
6. What are the franchisor's future expansion plans? How will they affect your franchise?
7. Are you entitled to an exclusive territory?
8. What kind of profits can you expect? (If the franchisor made no earnings claims in item 19 of the FDD, why not?)
9. Has the franchisor terminated any franchisee's contracts? If so, why?
10. Have any franchisees failed? If so, why?
11. Does the franchisor have a well-formulated strategic plan?

Make Your Choice

The first lesson in franchising is "Do your homework before you get out your checkbook." Only after conducting a thorough analysis of a franchise opportunity can you make an informed choice about which franchise is right for you. Then it is time to put together a solid business plan to serve as your road map to success with the franchise you have selected. The plan also is a valuable tool for attracting financing to purchase your franchise.

ENTREPRENEURIAL
Profile

Rocco Valluzo:
Microtel Inn and Suites

Rocco Valluzo, a second-generation McDonald's franchisee, decided to make the leap from the restaurant business to the hotel business after his wife stayed at a Microtel Inns and Suites and marveled at the smoothly operating business system. Before signing on with Microtel, Valluzo did his homework. In addition to evaluating the local market and conducting a location analysis, Valluzo says that he "toured properties and looked at the franchise cost and what the service fees would be." His preparation has paid off. His hotel reached the point of profitability within 6 months of opening, and he is already making plans to open three more locations. "The key to success is having the support of the franchisor," he says.[40]

TABLE 2 Questions to Ask Existing Franchisees

A key ingredient in any prospective franchisee's evaluation of a franchise opportunity is to visit existing franchisees and ask them questions about their relationship with the franchisor. "What you need to know from franchisees is what the franchisor does that makes it worth the fees," says one franchise consultant. The following questions will reveal how well the franchisor supports its franchisees and the nature of the franchisor–franchisee relationship:

1. How much did it cost to start your franchise?

2. How much training did you receive at the outset? How helpful was it?

3. How prepared were you when you opened your franchise?

4. Does the franchisor provide you with adequate ongoing support? How much? Are you pleased with the level of support you receive? What is the nature of this support?

5. Is the company available to answer your questions? How often do you contact the company? What is the typical response?

6. How much marketing assistance does the franchisor provide? Is it effective? How can you tell?

7. Do franchisees have input into the development of new products or services?

8. Which of your expectations has the franchisor met? Failed to meet?

9. How often does someone from the franchise check on your operation? What is the purpose of those visits?

10. What is a "typical day" like for you? How do you spend most of your time?

11. Which day-to-day tasks do you enjoy performing most? Least?

12. How much did your franchise gross last year? How much do you expect to gross this year? What has been the pattern of your outlet's sales since you started?

13. Is your franchise making a profit? If so, how much? What is your net profit margin?

14. How long did you operate before your outlet began to earn a profit? Is your outlet consistently profitable?

15. What is your franchise's breakeven point? How long did it take for your franchise to reach the breakeven point?

16. Has your franchise met your expectations for return on investment (ROI)?

17. Is there a franchisee association? Do you belong to it? What is its primary function?

18. Does the franchisor sponsor system-wide meetings? Do you attend? Why?

19. Does the franchisor listen to franchisees?

20. What changes would you recommend the franchisor make in its business system?

21. Where do you purchase supplies, equipment, and products for your franchise? Are the prices you pay reasonable?

22. How much freedom do you have to run your business?

23. Does the franchisor encourage franchisees to apply their creativity to running their businesses or does it frown upon innovation in the system?

24. Has the franchisor given you the tools you need to compete effectively?

25. How much are your royalty payments and franchise fees? What do you get in exchange for your royalty payments? Do you consider it to be a good value?

26. Are you planning to purchase additional territories or franchises? Why?

27. Has the franchisor lived up to its promises?

28. Looking back, what portions of the franchise contract would you change?

29. What are communications with the franchisor like?

30. How would you describe franchisees' relationship with the franchisor? How would you describe your relationship with the franchisor?

31. Are most franchisees happy with the franchise system? With the franchisor?

32. What advice would you give to someone considering purchasing a franchise from this franchisor?

33. Knowing what you know now, would you buy this franchise again?

Sources: Based on Carol Tice, "How to Research a Franchise," *Entrepreneur*, January 2009, pp. 112–119; Andrew A. Caffey, "Analyze This," *Entrepreneur*, January 2000, pp. 163–167; Roger Brown, "Ask More Questions of More People Before Deciding, Then Plan to Work Very Hard," *Small Business Forum*, Winter 1996/1997, pp. 91–93; Roberta Maynard, "Choosing a Franchise," *Nation's Business*, October 1996, pp. 56–63; Andrew A. Caffey, "The Buying Game," *Entrepreneur*, January 1997, pp. 174–177; Julie Bawden Davis, "A Perfect Match," *Business Start-Ups*, July 1997, pp. 44–49.

Make Sure You Select the Right Franchise

Finding the right franchise is no easy task, but the results are well worth the effort—*if* you make the right choice. The Street-Smart Entrepreneur identifies the most common mistakes that first-time franchisees make.

Mistake 1. Not knowing what they want in a franchise

Start by evaluating your personal and business interests. What type of work and activities do you enjoy? Which ones do you dislike? What are your financial expectations? Failing to define your goals increases the chance you will make the wrong choice.

Mistake 2. Buying a franchise they cannot afford

Franchises can be expensive, and you must know how much you can afford to spend before you go shopping for a franchise. A sure-fire recipe for failure is buying a franchise that breaks the budget. Franchises are available in a myriad of price ranges, from just a few thousand dollars to several million dollars. Determine the price range that best fits your budget before you begin reviewing franchise packages.

Mistake 3. Failing to ask existing and former franchisees about the franchise

One of the best ways to determine what your franchise experience will be is to talk with current and former franchisees. Item 20 of the FDD provides the necessary information for you to contact these people. Visit their operations and ask them *lots* of questions about the franchise system and how well it works, the franchisor, and the franchisor–franchisee relationship.

Mistake 4. Failing to read the fine print

The FDD is a valuable document for potential franchisees, but only for those who actually read it and use it to make a franchising decision. After you narrow down your potential franchise choices, get their FDDs and review them. Many potential franchisees find it helpful to go through the FDD and the franchise contract with an experienced franchise attorney, who can point out potential problem areas.

Mistake 5. Failing to get professional help

Inexperienced franchise shoppers believe that paying attorneys and accountants to help them understand the FDD and the franchise contract is a waste of money. Wrong! The franchise contract governs the franchisor–franchisee relationship, and most contracts run for at least 10 years. Make sure you understand its terms clearly before you sign a franchise contract.

Mistake 6. Buying in too early

Buying into a new franchise concept offers advantages (refer to Figure 3). However, doing so involves some risk because some new franchise operations have not worked the "bugs" out of their business systems or are not prepared to teach their systems effectively to franchisees. Established franchises have proven track records of success and typically involve less risk, but that security comes at a higher price. If you are considering buying into a new franchise, be extra diligent in your investigation of the opportunity.

Mistake 7. Falling for exaggerated earnings claims

One question of paramount interest to potential franchisees is "How much money can I expect to earn from a franchise?" Item 19 of the FDD includes a statement of the basis for any earnings claims that franchisors make. Any financial representations that a franchisor makes must represent the earnings that an average franchisee can expect, not the results of the top-performing franchise. However, the FDD does not require franchisors to make earnings claims. In fact, fewer than 20 percent of franchisors make any earnings claims in their FDDs. "An earnings claim is an opportunity to showcase your company," says Charlie Simpson, a top manager at Great Clips, a hairstyling franchise with more than 2,700 salons. "[Doing so] provides instant credibility with a candidate." Remember: Any earnings claims franchisors make must be backed by *facts*. If a franchise does not provide any information on franchisees' expected earnings, what is the reason? Potential franchisees need access to statistics on expected earnings so that they can assemble reasonable financial forecasts for their business plans.

Mistake 8. Neglecting to check the escape clause

Most franchise contracts include options for getting out of the franchise relationship for both the franchisor and the franchisee. Under what circumstances can the franchisor end the relationship? Under what circumstances can you end the relationship? What is the cost associated with terminating the franchise agreement?

Sources: Based on Eddy Goldberg and Kerry Pipes, "How Much Can I Earn?" Franchising.com, August 18, 2008, *www.franchising.com/articles/385/;*

Andrew A. Caffey, "Watch Your Step," *Entrepreneur B.Y.O.B.*, August 2002, p. 82; Todd D. Maddocks, "Write the Wrong," *Entrepreneur B.Y.O.B.*, January 2001, pp. 152–155; Kerry Pipes, "Franchisee Lifestyles, Franchise Update, *www.franchise-update.com/fuadmin/articles/article_FranchiseeLifestyles5.htm*; "Franchise How-To Guides: The Paper Trail," *Entrepreneur, www.entrepreneur.com/franchises/buyingafranchise/howtoguides/article36392-4.html.*

Franchise Contracts

7. Describe a typical franchise contract and its primary provisions.

The amount of franchisor–franchisee litigation has risen steadily in recent years. Franchising's popularity as a business system has created growing pains that have resulted in an increase in the number of franchise-related lawsuits. A common source of much of this litigation is the interpretation of the franchise contract's terms. Most often, difficulties arise after the agreement is in operation. Because a franchisor's attorney prepares franchise contracts, the provisions favor the franchisor, giving minimal protection to franchisees. A franchise contract summarizes the details that will govern the franchisor–franchisee relationship over its life. It outlines exactly the rights and the obligations of each party and sets the guidelines that govern the franchise relationship. To protect potential franchisees from having to rush into a contract without clearly understanding it, the FTC requires that franchisees receive a completed contract with all revisions at least 5 business days before it is signed.

Every potential franchisee should have an attorney evaluate the franchise contract and review it with the investor before signing anything. Too many franchisees don't discover unfavorable terms in their contracts until *after* they have invested in a franchise. By then, however, it's too late to negotiate changes. Although most large, established franchisors are not willing to negotiate the franchise contract's terms ("The contract is what it is"), many smaller franchises will negotiate some terms, especially for highly qualified candidates. Figure 3 describes the advantages and the disadvantages of buying a new versus an established franchise.

Although franchise contracts cover everything from initial fees and continuing payments to training programs and territorial protection, three terms are responsible for most franchisor-franchisee disputes: termination of the contract, contract renewal, and transfer and buyback provisions.

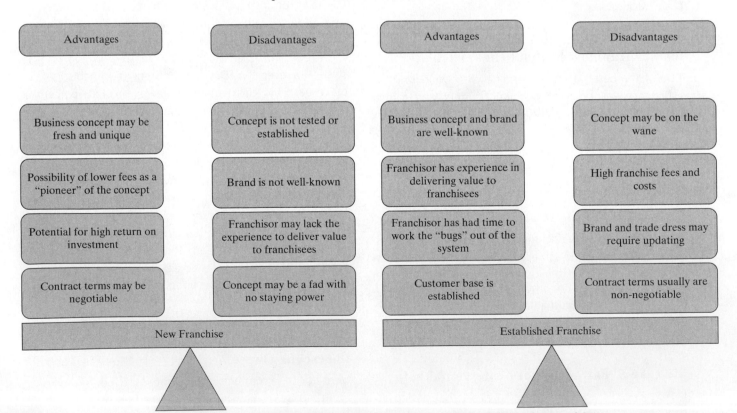

FIGURE 3 Advantages and Disadvantages of Buying a New vs. an Established Franchise

Termination

One of the most litigated subjects of a franchise agreement is the termination of the contract by either party. Most contracts prohibit termination "without just cause." However, prospective franchisees must be sure they know exactly when and under what conditions they—and the franchisor—can terminate the contract. Generally, the franchisor has the right to cancel a contract if a franchisee declares bankruptcy, fails to make required payments on time, or fails to maintain quality standards.

Renewal

Franchisors usually retain the right to renew or refuse to renew franchisees' contracts. If a franchisee fails to make payments on schedule or does not maintain quality standards, the franchisor has the right to refuse renewal. In some cases, the franchisor has no obligation to offer contract renewal to the franchisee when the contract expires.

When a franchisor grants renewal, the two parties must draw up a new contract. Frequently, the franchisee must pay a renewal fee and may be required to fix any deficiencies of the outlet or to modernize and upgrade it. The FTC's Trade Regulation Rule requires the franchisor to disclose these terms before any contracts are signed.

Transfer and Buybacks

Unlike owners of independent businesses, franchisees typically are not free to sell their businesses to just anyone. Under most franchise contracts, franchisees cannot sell their franchises to a third party or transfer them to others without the franchisor's approval. In most instances, franchisors do approve a franchisee's request to sell an outlet to another person.

Most franchisors retain the right of first refusal in franchise transfers, which means the franchisee must offer to sell the outlet to the franchisor first. For example, McDonald's Corporation recently repurchased 13 restaurants under its first refusal clause from a franchisee who was ready to retire. If the franchisor refuses to buy the outlet, the franchisee may sell it to a third party who meets the franchisor's approval, applying the same standards that buyers of new franchises must meet.

Trends in Franchising

8. Explain current trends shaping franchising.

Franchising has experienced three major growth waves since its beginning. The first wave occurred in the early 1970s when fast-food restaurants used the concept to grow rapidly. The fast-food industry was one of the first to discover the power of franchising, but other businesses soon took notice and adapted the franchising concept to their industries. The second wave took place in the mid-1980s as the U.S. economy shifted heavily toward the service sector. Franchises followed suit, springing up in every service business imaginable—from maid services and copy centers to mailing services and real estate. The third wave began in the early 1990s and continues today. It is characterized by new, low-cost franchises that focus on specific market niches. In the wake of major corporate downsizing and the burgeoning costs of traditional franchises, these new franchises allow would-be entrepreneurs to get into proven businesses faster and at lower costs. These companies feature start-up costs from $2,000 to $250,000 and span a variety of industries—from leak detection in homes and auto detailing to day care and cost-reduction consulting. Here we detail other significant trends in franchising.

Changing Face of Franchisees

Franchisees today are a more diverse group than in the past. A study by the International Franchise Association reports that minorities own 19.3 percent of all franchises and women own 25 percent of them.[41] Modern franchisees also are better educated, are more sophisticated, have more business acumen, and are more financially secure than those of just 20 years ago. People of all ages and backgrounds are choosing franchising as a way to get into business for themselves. A survey by Franchise Business Review reports that 13 percent of franchisees are between the ages of 18 and 34.[42] Franchising also is attracting skilled, experienced businesspeople who are opening franchises in their second careers and whose goal is to own multiple outlets that cover entire states or regions. Many of them are former corporate managers—either corporate castoffs or corporate dropouts—looking for a new start on a more meaningful and rewarding career. They have the financial resources, management skills and experience, and motivation to operate their franchises successfully. Experts estimate that 35 to 40 percent of new franchisees are people who have experienced a layoff or some type of job displacement.[43]

After experiencing a layoff from her job in the human resources department of a large bank, Debbie Michaels decided to purchase a franchise from Expense Reduction Analysts, a company with more than 1,150 locations around the world that specializes in helping businesses lower their expenses. "I thought I would live and die in corporate America," she says, "but I've never been happier." As part of her severance package, Michaels worked with franchise-consulting firm FranNet to match her experience, strengths, and career goals with the right franchise opportunity.[44]

International Opportunities

One of the major trends in franchising is the internationalization of American franchise systems. Increasingly, franchising is becoming a major export industry for the United States; in fact, since 1997, nearly half of all franchises sold by U.S.-based franchisors have been located in other countries.[45] Increasingly, U.S. franchises are moving into international markets to boost sales and profits as the domestic market becomes saturated. A survey by the International Franchise Association reports that 52 percent of U.S.-based franchisors have an international presence, which reprensents a 20 percent increase in international franchising since 1996. According to the study, 79 percent of U.S.-based franchisors plan to open franchised units outside the United States within the next 3 years.[46] For example, Yum! Brands, the parent company of Taco Bell, Pizza Hut, KFC, A&W All-American Food, and Long John Silver's, has more than 36,000 franchised restaurants in 100 countries. The company, which derives more than half of its profits from international locations, already has a significant presence in China and plans to expand its operations there and in India.[47] In 1980, franchise legend McDonald's had restaurants in 28 countries; today, the company

International markets represent a significant growth market for franchisors. This McDonald's outlet in Shanghai is one of more than 1,000 that the company has opened in China.

Source: Alamy Images

operates outlets in 118 nations.[48] Europe is the primary market for U.S. franchisors, with Pacific Rim countries, Canada, and South America following, but China and India are becoming franchising "hot spots."[49] These markets are most attractive to franchisors because they are similar to the U.S. market—rising personal incomes, strong demand for consumer goods, growing service economies, and spreading urbanization.

As they venture into foreign markets, franchisors have learned that adaptation is one key to success. Although they keep their basic systems intact, franchises that are successful in foreign markets quickly learn how to change their concepts to adjust to local cultures and to appeal to local tastes. For instance, fast-food chains in other countries often must make adjustments to their menus to please locals' palates. In India, a nation that is predominantly Hindu and reveres cows, beef-based sandwiches do not appear on menus. Instead, fast-food franchises sell sandwiches made from chicken, lamb, and vegetable patties. Venezuelan diners prefer mayonnaise with their french fries, and in Chile customers want avocado on their hamburgers. In Japan, McDonald's (known as "Makudonarudo") franchises sell shrimp burgers, rice burgers, seaweed soup, vegetable croquette burgers, and katsu burgers (cheese wrapped in a roast pork cutlet topped with katsu sauce and shredded cabbage) in addition to their traditional American fare. In the Philippines, the McDonald's menu includes a spicy Filipino-style burger, spaghetti, and chicken with rice. In some countries in Europe, McDonald's franchises sell beer. In China, Burger King offers localized menu items such as pumpkin porridge, deep-fried twisted dough sticks called *you tiao*, and *shaobing*, a toasted sesame seed cake that is a traditional Chinese snack.

IN THE ENTREPRENEURIAL
SPOTLIGHT   India: A Hot Spot for Franchising

As franchisors have found wringing impressive growth rates from the domestic market increasingly difficult, they have begun to export their franchises to international markets, including those with developing economies. Indeed, franchising is ideally suited for developing economies because it allows people with limited business experience and financial resources to become part of an established business. India, with a population of more than1 billion people, is attracting the attention of franchisors across the globe. More than 750 franchisors now operate in India, where the franchising industry is growing at an annual rate of 30 percent. India's middle class, which currently stands at 50 million, is expected to grow to 583 million by 2025, a growth rate that appeals to franchisors. India also has 35 cities with populations that exceed 1 million people compared to just 9 in the United States. The Global Retail Development Index published by management consulting firm A.T. Kearney ranks India as the most attractive market globally for retail investment.

Although franchises in a multitude of industries operate in India, fast-food franchises such as McDonald's, Pizza Hut, and others, were among the first to enter the Indian market. Their vision is paying off; the pizza market in India has been growing at an annual rate of 40 percent. Pizza Hut, which recently was named the "most trusted food service brand" in India for the fifth consecutive year, operates 156 restaurants in 35 Indian cities. In India, per capita incomes are growing but remain relatively low by Western standards, which requires franchisees to be conscious of the prices they charge. At Pizza Hut locations, Indian customers can purchase a four-course meal for two that includes a chicken tikka pan pizza, a garlic bread called *naan*, tomato soup, and mango ice cream for just $6.25. Because 80 percent of Indians are vegetarians, pizza chains such as Pizza Hut and Domino's include many vegetarian items on their menus and are fanatical about keeping the vegetarian and nonvegetarian sections of their kitchens separate. One of Domino's Pizza's most popular items in India is a $3 Veggie Lovers personal pan pizza.

McDonald's operates 157 restaurants in India and recently announced plans to open nearly 200 more by 2015. To appeal to Indian customers, McDonald's has modified its traditional U.S. menu significantly; the company's restaurants serve no beef or pork in any of their dishes. Instead, the Indian McDonald's menu offers burger "lookalikes" that are made of vegetables and spices and are seasoned to local tastes. For instance, restaurants serve the McVeggie sandwich (a vegetarian patty made from peas, carrots, green beans, red bell pepper, potatoes, onions, rice, and seasonings), Curry Pans (a vegetable medley baked on a spiced bread with a cheese topping), and the Pizza McPuff (a mixture of vegetables and spices inside a pastry). The only nonvegetarian items on the McDonald's

Indian menu are served with either chicken or fish. Outlets offer a chicken version of the Curry Pan, a Filet-O-Fish sandwich (one of the few items on the Indian menu that is the same as in U.S. McDonald's restaurants), and sandwiches made with grilled or fried chicken patties. "Today 70 percent of our menu is 'Indianized,'" says Vikram Bakshi, managing director of McDonald's India North.

U.S. franchisors operating in India know that it will take time for their investments to come to fruition, but they believe the payoffs will be worth the wait. Success requires patience and commitment. "We are planting the seeds for a bigger future," says Sam Su, president of Yum! Restaurants China.

1. What steps should U.S.-based franchisors take when establishing outlets in foreign countries?
2. Describe the opportunities and the challenges franchisors face when entering emerging markets such as India.

3. Use the Web as a resource to develop a list of at least five suggestions that will help new franchisors looking to establish outlets in India.

Sources: Based on "Pizza Hut Named Most Trusted in India," *Reuters*, June 25, 2009, *www.reuters.com/article/pressRelease/idUS153010+ 25-Jun-2009+BW20090625*; "The Future Is Bright for Franchising in India," *Franchise Direct*, *www.franchisedirect.com/information/trendsfacts/ thefutureisbrightforfranchisinginindia/8/345*; "What You Can and Can't Get at McDonald's in India," *Indiamarks*, February 26, 2009, *www. indiamarks.com/guide/What-You-Can-and-Can%27t-Get-at-McDonalds- India . . ./1739*; Sheridan Prasso, "India's Pizza Wars," *Fortune*, October 1, 2007, pp. 61–64; Dhawal Shah, "India: Market for the Masses," *Franchising World*, June 2008, *www.franchise.org/Franchise-News-Detail. aspx?id=40638*; "McDonald's India to Open 180–190 More Restaurants by 2015," *Financial Express*, May 26, 2009, *www.financialexpress.com/ news/mcdonalds-india-to-open-180190-more-restaurants-by-2015/466279/*; "Global Leading Pizza and Pasta Restaurant Chain[6] 'The Pizza Company' Expanding to Indian Market Through Franchise India Internationa," *India PR Wire*, June 3, 2009, *www.indiaprwire.com/pressrelease/restaurants/ 2009060326721.htm*.

Smaller, Nontraditional Locations

As the high cost of building full-scale locations continues to climb, franchisors are searching out nontraditional locations in which to build smaller, less expensive outlets. Based on the principle of **intercept marketing**, the idea is to put a franchise's products or services directly in the paths of potential customers, wherever that may be. Franchises are putting scaled-down outlets on college campuses, in sports arenas, in hospitals, in airports, and in zoos. Customers are likely to find a mini-Wendy's or Subway sandwich shop inside a convenience store or a Walmart Super Center, a Dunkin' Donuts outlet in an airport, or a Maui Wowi kiosk at a sports stadium or arena. The 7,000-member Brentwood Baptist Church in Houston has a McDonald's franchise in its lifelong learning center. The church co-owns the franchise with one of its members, who owns six McDonald's franchises.[50]

Baskin-Robbins, a Canton, Massachusetts-based franchise with 5,800 outlets in 36 countries, recently introduced a scaled-down version of its stores called BR Express that occupies just 200 square feet and sells only soft-serve ice cream in special flavors with a variety of available toppings. These express outlets are opening in high-traffic locations such as college campuses, airports, museums, and inside the company's Dunkin' Donuts franchises.[51] Many franchisees have discovered that smaller outlets in nontraditional locations generate nearly the same sales volume as full-sized outlets at just a fraction of the cost. Establishing outlets in innovative locations will be a key to continued franchise growth in the domestic market.

Conversion Franchising

The trend toward **conversion franchising**, in which owners of independent businesses become franchisees to gain the advantage of name recognition, will continue. One study found that 72 percent of North American franchise companies use conversion franchising in their domestic markets and 26 percent use the strategy in foreign markets.[52] In a franchise conversion, the franchisor gets immediate entry into new markets and experienced operators; franchisees get increased visibility and often experience a significant sales boost.

Multiple-Unit Franchising

Twenty-five years ago, the typical franchisee operated a single outlet. Today, however, modern franchisees strive to operate multiple franchise units. In **multiple-unit franchising (MUF)**, a franchisee opens more than one unit in a broad territory within a specific time period. According to the International Franchise Association, 19.8 percent of franchisees are multiple-unit owners, a number that is expected to increase over the next several years. These multiple-unit franchisees own 52.6 percent of all franchise units. Although the typical multiple-unit franchise owns 4.5 outlets, it is no longer unusual for a single franchisee to own 25, 75, or even 100 units.[53]

ENTREPRENEURIAL

Profile

Darrell Lamb and Adam Fuller: Oil Express

Business partners Darrell Lamb and Adam Fuller own 24 Oil Express franchises in the Southeast and have plans to purchase more of the quick-lube outlets, which they describe as a "Steady Eddy" business that generates consistent revenues and profits, no matter what overall economic conditions are. "We're in the right industry at the right time with the right franchise concept," says Lamb.[54]

Franchisors are finding that multiple-unit franchising is an efficient way to do business. For a franchisor, the time and cost of managing 10 franchisees each owning 12 outlets are much less than managing 120 franchisees each owning one outlet. A multiple-unit strategy also accelerates a franchise's growth rate. For instance, to reach its goal of adding 5,000 new outlets within 5 years, Allied Domecq Quick Service Restaurants, the company that sells Baskin-Robbins, Dunkin' Donuts, and Togo's franchises, began recruiting multiple-unit franchisees in 17 major markets in the United States. Many of the franchisees the company selected were existing franchisees looking to expand their businesses, but others were newcomers to the chain.[55]

Not only is multiple-unit franchising an efficient way to expand quickly, but it also is effective for franchisors who are targeting foreign markets, where having a local representative who knows the territory is essential.

The popularity of multiple-unit franchising has paralleled the trend toward increasingly experienced, sophisticated franchisees, who set high performance goals that a single outlet cannot meet. For franchisees, multiple-unit franchising offers the opportunity for rapid growth without leaving the safety net of the franchise. In addition, franchisees may be able to get fast-growing companies for a bargain when franchisors offer discounts off of their standard fees for buyers who purchase multiple units.

Although operating multiple units offers advantages for both franchisors and franchisees, there are dangers. Operating multiple units requires franchisors to focus more carefully on selecting the right franchisees—those who are capable of handling the additional demands of multiple units. The impact of selecting the wrong franchise owners is magnified when they operate multiple units and can create huge headaches for the entire chain. Franchisees must be aware of the dangers of losing their focus and becoming distracted if they take on too many units. In addition, operating multiple units means more complexity, because the number of business problems franchisees face also is multiplied.

Master Franchising

A **master franchise** (or **subfranchise** or **area developer**) gives a franchisee the right to create a semi-independent organization in a particular territory to recruit, sell, and support other franchisees. A master franchisee buys the right to develop subfranchises within a territory or, sometimes, an entire country. Like multiple-unit franchising, subfranchising "turbocharges" a franchisor's growth.

Many franchisors use master franchising to open outlets in international markets because the master franchisees understand local laws and the nuances of selling in local markets. NexCen Brands, the parent company of MaggieMoo's Ice Cream & Treatery and Marble Slab Creamery, recently signed a master franchise agreement for Singapore with Thirtythree Private Limited. The contract calls for the master franchisee to open at least 8 franchises over 10 years, a move that will introduce the company's first franchised ice cream stores to Asia.[56]

Cobranding

Some franchisors also are discovering new ways to reach customers by teaming up with other franchisors selling complementary products or services. A growing number of companies are **cobranding** (or **piggybacking**) outlets—combining two or more distinct franchises under one roof. This "buddy system" approach works best when the two franchise ideas are compatible and appeal to similar customers. At one location, a Texaco gasoline station, a Pizza Hut restaurant, and a Dunkin' Donuts, all owned by the same franchisee, work together in a piggyback arrangement to draw customers. Cold Stone Creamery, an ice cream franchise, and the Rocky Mountain Chocolate Factory, a franchise that sells freshly made chocolate candy and other sweets, recently began a co-branding arrangement. Both companies have seen sales increase appreciably. "Demand for ice cream peaks in the summer, and demand for gourmet chocolates peaks during the winter holiday season," says Dan Beem, president of Cold Stone Creamery.[57] Properly planned, cobranded franchises can magnify many times over the sales and profits of separate, self-standing outlets.

Serving Dual-Career Couples and Aging Baby Boomers

Now that dual-career couples have become the norm, the market for franchises offering convenience and time-saving devices is booming. Customers are willing to pay for products and services that will save them time or trouble, and franchises are ready to provide them. For instance, Maid Brigade, a residential cleaning franchise with nearly 500 locations across the United States and Canada that has been franchising since 1979, aims its cleaning service at busy professionals who prefer to "spend their time pursuing careers, hobbies and enjoying family and friends" rather than cleaning their homes.[58]

Other areas in which franchising is experiencing rapid growth include home delivery of meals, continuing education and training (especially computer and business training), leisure activities (such as hobbies, health spas, and travel-related activities), products and services aimed at home-based businesses, and health care.

A number of franchises are aiming at one of the nation's largest population segments: aging baby boomers. About 37.3 million people, 12.5 percent of the U.S. population, are 65 or older, and by 2030 that number is expected to double to 72 million. An AARP survey shows that 90 percent of senior citizens want to remain in their homes as they age, which is creating a great business opportunity for franchises such as Home Instead Senior Care, a company that provides in-home non-health-care services to senior citizens.[59]

▶ E N T R E P R E N E U R S H I P   IN ACTION ▶

Franchising the Taste of Yumm!

"Mary Anne has an amazing memory for taste," says Mark Beauchamp, her husband and business partner. "She can recall the moment when she experiences a new flavor—a fresh herb in Italy or a spice in the Far East." Mary Anne's culinary ability provided the momentum for her to open a restaurant, the Wild Rose Café & Deli. Her continuous culinary experimentation led to the creation of a type of "sauce," for lack of a better term. The sauce combines flavors and healthy ingredients from around the world—brown rice with red and black beans mixed with salsa and spices and topped with picante sauce—and offers an inviting texture and an incredible flavor.

Mary Anne made the sauce for her own lunch, but soon employees discovered it and began asking Mary Anne for it. Before long, customers found out about it as well and began ordering it. "Almost without exception, my customers would take a bite, roll their eyes heavenward, do a little knee-dip and say, "'Yumm . . . what is this?'" recalls Mary Anne. That reaction resulted in naming the creation Yumm! Sauce. Yumm! Sauce's reputation continued to spread and ultimately changed the future of their restaurant in ways Mary Anne and Mark, then a commercial realtor, could not have imagined.

The Beauchamps moved their restaurant to a location that would generate more customer traffic, changed the name to Café Yumm!, and updated the menu to feature Mary Anne's Original Yumm! Sauce, along with the traditional soups and deli sandwiches. Variations on the theme include a beanless version with jasmine rice and fresh avocado, brown rice with chipotle chili, and zucchini-and-tomato stew with rice, beans, and sauce. Customers can top any of these off with cheese, tomato, avocado, sour cream, black olives, and cilantro for a satisfying, well-balanced meatless meal. Other menu options include chili or Chilean zucchini stew straight up, flour tortilla wraps, and salads. The café also sells Original Yumm! Sauce by the jar.

The new restaurant was an immediate hit with customers. The residents of Eugene, Oregon—a college town best known for its love for the sport of track and its organic culture—responded quickly. Within 5 years, the couple had opened a second restaurant. The customer response was encouraging and surprised the Beauchamps. "We never expected to come up with a product and business that would resonate with so many people," says Mary Anne.

By this time, Mark had left his real estate career to join Mary Anne, who would much rather cook than manage a business. Their skills are complementary in every respect. Mary Anne is creative and has an in-depth restaurant background, and Mark is a linear thinker with a business mind.

The anticipated growth pains came, and the logistics of making the sauce presented problems. "With increases in demand and kitchens with only so much space, Mary Anne was physically not able to make enough sauce to meet the needs of our customers," says Mark. He formed a relationship with a food manufacturer to produce the Original Yumm! Sauce in large quantities, which would enable the copreneurs to meet the needs of their growing restaurants and to sell Yumm! Sauce through specialty food stores and grocery stores, including Whole Foods. It was a natural fit.

With the success of their restaurants and the popularity of their Yumm! Sauce, the Beauchamps began receiving requests to purchase franchises. The idea of franchising Café Yumm! was "organic," according to Mark. "We didn't intend to create a franchise; it just evolved as the business changed." Analyzing their business, the copreneurs decided that they would be able to meet the basic needs of a franchise arrangement—to showcase profitable operations and to systematize, formulate, and teach the business model and its operation to other people. Mark also realized that franchising Café Yumm! would require them to create an entirely new kind of business: one that sold and supported franchises. They hired a franchise consultant and began making changes to the business system that would benefit franchisees by creating a more manageable, systematic business. They also had to raise the capital—$1 million—from private investors to create the franchise system, meet all regulatory requirements, and market the system to franchisees.

Today, Mark is focusing on opening another company-owned restaurant that will serve as the state-of-the-art model for the franchise system. Mary Anne and Mark have sold several franchises, which cost between $300,000 and $500,000 to start. In return for an extensive training program and a business system, Café Yumm! franchisees pay a $35,000 franchise fee, an ongoing royalty of 6 percent of gross sales, and an advertising fee of up to 3 percent of gross sales. "We are just at the beginning stages of selling franchises and we are excited about what is ahead," says Mark. "As long as our customers continue to say 'yumm!' we know we are on the right track."

1. How did the Beauchamps' duties change when they began franchising their business?
2. What challenges might Café Yumm! face in the next phase of the franchise evolution as more franchisees buy into the system and expect to optimize the profitability of their individual restaurants?
3. Identify the benefits and the risks for franchisees who are considering investing in a relatively new franchise such as Café Yumm!.

Sources: "Franchise Opportunities," Café Yumm!, *www.cafeyumm.com/franchise.html*; personal contact with Mark Beauchamp, July 17, 2007.

Franchising as a Growth Strategy

9. Describe the potential of franchising a business as a growth strategy.

Entrepreneurs with established and tested business models can use franchising as a growth strategy by becoming franchisors. Franchising enables business owners to use other people's money to grow their businesses with minimal capital investment on the part of the franchisor. Franchisees put up the funds to start their businesses, infuse capital into the franchising operation through the franchise fee, and generate ongoing cash flow for the franchisor from ongoing royalty fees and other charges. In short, franchising turbocharges a small company's growth.

To create a successful franchise operation, an entrepreneur must meet the following criteria:

UNIQUE CONCEPT. To make a successful franchise operation, a business must have a unique concept that gives it a competitive edge in the marketplace. For instance, an entrepreneur may develop a new twist on fast food, a better way to exercise, or a new process for removing dents from cars.

ENTREPRENEURIAL
Profile

Mary Obana and Michael Lannon: Koko FitClub LLC

Mary Obana and her husband Michael Lannon discovered that only 16 percent of U.S. adults belong to a fitness club. In light of this fact, they developed a business, Koko FitClub, that offers clients the benefits of a personal trainer without the high cost. When members visit a Koko FitClub, they insert a key (actually a flash drive) into a computer-controlled system that monitors their exercise patterns. On each subsequent trip, the computer devises a 30-minute workout that is customized to the member's current level of fitness and his or her fitness goals. In their first year of franchising, Obana and Lannon sold 40 franchises. "Being different is essential," says Obana. "Imagine the ability to introduce something that's game-changing to the market."[60]

REPLICABLE. To make a successful franchise operation, an entrepreneur's business model must be replicable. Can potential franchisees reproduce the success of the original unit regardless of location? Is there a business system in place that an entrepreneur can teach to franchisees? In addition, is the owner willing to relinquish some control to these new owners? Franchising requires an entrepreneur to leave the business's daily operations (and its reputation) largely in the hands of franchisees.

EXPANSION PLAN. When entrepreneurs make the decision to franchise, they must develop a sound expansion plan. New franchisors must consider issues such as the speed of growth, territorial development, support services, staffing, and fee structure. The entire plan demands a well-conceived strategy for supporting franchisees and a rigorous financial analysis.

DUE DILIGENCE. Launching a successful franchise requires undertaking an extensive due diligence process, researching legal issues, acquiring necessary trademarks, creating a Web site, and writing training manuals for franchisees. Regardless of how a franchise generates revenue, an entrepreneur has two new business roles: selling franchises and servicing franchisees. "Franchising is like starting an entirely new business venture within the existing business structure," says Jim Thomas, a former top manager of the Taco Time International franchise. "The business now becomes a legally responsible support system with an entirely new set of responsibilities."[61]

LEGAL GUIDANCE. Enlisting professional assistance from a franchise attorney is essential. One of the most important roles of the franchise attorney is to prepare the franchise disclosure document (FDD). Every franchisor must provide to prospective franchisees an FDD that covers the 23 items discussed earlier in this chapter. Recall that 15 states require approval of the FDD before the franchisor can sell franchises. Obtaining legal approval, producing audited financial statements, and marketing the franchise concept is not cheap. Entrepreneurs can expect to invest a minimum of $100,000 to $750,000 to launch a franchise business.[62]

SUPPORT FOR FRANCHISEES. Once a franchise operation is running, the franchisor must have the resources available to train franchisees in the operation of the business system, assist them through the start-up phase, and provide ongoing product support for them.

Conclusion

Franchising has proved its viability in the U.S. economy and has become a key part of the small business sector because it offers many would-be entrepreneurs the opportunity to own and operate a business with a greater chance for success. Despite its impressive growth rate to date, the franchising industry still has a great deal of room left to grow, especially globally. Current trends combined with international opportunities—China as just one example—indicate that franchising will continue to play a vibrant role in the global business economy.

Chapter Review

1. Explain the importance of franchising in the U.S. and global economy.
   - Through franchised businesses, consumers can buy nearly every good or service imaginable—from singing telegrams and computer training to tax services and waste-eating microbes.
   - A new franchise opens somewhere in the world every 6.5 minutes! Franchises generate $835 billion in annual output in the United States, and they employ nearly 9.6 million people in more than 100 major industries.
2. Define the concept of franchising.
   - Franchising is a method of doing business involving a continuous relationship between a franchisor and a franchisee. The franchisor retains control of the distribution system, whereas the franchisee assumes all of the normal daily operating functions of the business.

3. Describe the different types of franchises.
   - The three types of franchising are trade name franchising, where the franchisee purchases only the right to use a brand name; product distribution franchising, which involves a license to sell specific products under a brand name; and pure franchising, which provides a franchisee with a complete business system.

4. Describe the benefits and limitations of buying a franchise.
   - The franchisor has the benefits of expanding his business on limited capital and growing without developing key managers internally. The franchisee also receives many key benefits: management training and counseling, customer appeal of a brand name, standardized quality of goods and services, national advertising programs, financial assistance, proven products and business formats, centralized buying power, territorial protection, and greater chances for success.
   - Potential franchisees should be aware of the disadvantages involved in buying a franchise: franchise fees and profit sharing, strict adherence to standardized operations, restrictions on purchasing, limited product lines, possible ineffective training programs, and less freedom.

5. Describe the legal aspects of franchising, including the protection offered by the FTC's Trade Regulation Rule.
   - The FTC's Trade Regulation Rule is designed to help the franchisee evaluate a franchising package. It requires each franchisor to disclose information covering 23 topics at least 10 days before accepting payment from a potential franchisee. This document, the Franchise Disclosure Document (FDD) is a valuable source of information for anyone considering investing in a franchise.

6. Explain the right way to buy a franchise.
   - To buy a franchise the right way requires that you: evaluate yourself, research your market, consider your franchise options, get a copy of the franchisor's FDD and study it, talk to existing franchisees, ask the franchisor some tough questions; and make your choice.

7. Describe a typical franchise contract and its provisions.
   - The amount of franchisor–franchisee litigation has risen steadily over the past decade. Three terms are responsible for most franchisor–franchisee disputes: termination of the contract, contract renewal, and transfer and buyback provisions.

8. Explain current trends shaping franchising.
   - Trends influencing franchising include: international opportunities; the emergence of smaller, nontraditional locations; conversion franchising; multiple-unit franchising; master franchising; piggyback franchising (or cobranding); and products and services targeting aging baby boomers.

9. Describe the potential of franchising a business as a growth strategy.
   - Franchising a business can be an effective method to grow a business using the investments of the franchisees. It does involve a highly litigious and regulated process that demands specialized legal professions and imposes an entirely new set of administrative demands on the business to establish and administer this complex system.

Discussion Questions

1. What is franchising?
2. Describe the three types of franchising and provide an example of each.
3. How does franchising benefit the franchisor?
4. Discuss the advantages and the disadvantages of franchising for the franchisee.
5. How beneficial to franchisees is a quality training program? What types of entrepreneurs may benefit most from this training?

6. Compare the failure rates for franchises with those of independent businesses. What are some of the reasons for this difference?
7. Why might an independent entrepreneur be dissatisfied with a franchising arrangement?
8. What clues might indicate an unreliable franchisor?
9. Should a prospective franchisee investigate before investing in a franchise? If so, how and in what areas?

10. What is the function of the FTC's Trade Regulation Rule? What function does the FDD perform?
11. Outline the rights the Trade Regulation Rule gives all prospective franchisees.
12. What is the source of most franchisor–franchisee litigation? Which party does the standard franchise contract favor?
13. Describe the current trends affecting franchising within the United States and internationally.
14. One franchisee says, "Franchising is helpful because it gives you somebody (the franchisor) to get you going, nurture you, and shove you along a little. However, the franchisor won't make you successful. That depends on what you bring to the business, how hard you are prepared to work, and how committed you are to finding the right franchise for you." Do you agree? Explain your response.
15. Why might an entrepreneur consider franchising to be an attractive growth strategy?
16. What should an entrepreneur be prepared for in considering franchising as a viable alternative?

Most franchisors require a business plan as a part of the application process. In many cases, the franchisor will specify the elements that the business plan should include and may provide a business plan outline unique to the franchise. Determine the expectations regarding the content and structure of the business plan. Does the franchisor have a business plan outline or a sample plan available for review?

On the Web

Go to the Companion Web site *www.pearsonhighered.com/scarborough* and click the tab. Review the online franchise resources that are available. One of those links is to "The World Franchise Directory." Click that link and enter the first letter of a familiar franchise, the letter "S" for example. The number of franchise systems, many of them with an international presence, is staggering. Now, click the sample plan tab and review the sample franchise plan in this section of Business Plan Pro. What unique characteristic do you notice about this business plan compared to others you have seen?

Select a franchise. Visit its corporate Web site and begin the process to request franchise information. Note specific questions regarding sources of capital. Access to capital will be a major qualification in determining whether an applicant is "franchise worthy."

In the Software

To meet the needs of a specific franchise business plan, modify the outline in Business Plan Pro to match the franchisor's recommendation. First, view the outline in the left-hand navigation window and click the "Plan Outline" icon or go to the "View" menu and click "Outline." Then, right-click on each of those topics that you need to change, move, or delete to meet the franchisor's requirements. Move topics up or down the outline with the corresponding arrows to place them in the correct sequence. To change topics from headings to subheadings, "Demote" the topic. The "Promote" option moves a subheading left to a more dominant position.

Building Your Business Plan

Continue developing the franchise business plan based on that outline. Use information and verbiage that is familiar to the franchise system whenever possible. This plan may be one of dozens received that week, and demonstrating knowledge, competence, and credibility is important. The franchise business plan can be a sales tool to position the applicant as an informed and attractive prospective franchise owner.

Endnotes

1. Jason Daley, "Fashion Forward—Frugally," *Entrepreneur*, July 2009, p. 98; Karen Spencer, "Young and In Charge," *Pink*, June 2008, *www.pinkmagazine.com/franchise/women/2008/young_franchisees.html*; Eve Tahmincioglu, "Franchising Frenzy," *Business on Main*, *http://businessonmain.msn.com/knowledgeexchange/articles/expert.aspx?cp-documentid=20741785*; Lana F. Flowers, "UA Student Plans Opening of Second Plato's Closet," *Morning News*, February 7, 2009, *www.nwaonline.net/articles/2009/02/07/business/020809bizplatoscloset.txt*.
2. "Franchised Business Outlook," *International Franchise Association*, January 7, 2009, p. 1.
3. David J. Kaufmann, "What a Ride!" *Entrepreneur*, May 2007, pp. 108, 109.
4. Hachemi Aliouche, "Rosenberg Center Study Confirms Global Franchise Growth," *Franchising World*, August 1, 2006, *www.allbusiness.com/retail-trade/1189645-1.html*.
5. Gregory Matusky, "The Franchise Hall of Fame," *Inc.*, April 1994, pp. 86–89.
6. Personal contact with Nicholas A. Bibby, The Bibby Group, *www.bibbygroup.com*, May 2, 2007.
7. *Economic Impact of Franchised Businesses, Volume 2: Executive Summary and Highlights*, International Franchise Association and Price Waterhouse Coopers (Washington, DC: 2007), pp. 10, 15.
8. Janean Huber, "Franchise Forecast," *Entrepreneur*, January 1993, p. 73.
9. Maya Norris, "Franchisees Benefit from Learning 2.0 at Zaxby's," *Chain Leader*, January 15, 2009, *www.chainleader.com/article/CA6629891.html*.
10. Louise Witt, "Franchising: The Great Entrepreneurial Gambit," *FSB* Special Advertising Section, December 2002/January 2003, pp. 51–52; Mark Jones, "Getting Hip with Plato's Closet," *USA Business*, September 22, 2003, pp. 3, 7.

11. Norris, "Franchisees Benefit from Learning 2.0 at Zaxby's."

12. LaTina Emerson, "Chain Operations Offer Some Sense of Security in Hard Times," *Augusta Chronicle*, July 26, 2009, *http://chronicle. augusta.com/stories/2009/07/26/bus_542019.shtml;* LaTina Emerson, "Einstein Bros. Bagels Opens," *Augusta Chronicle*, March 31, 2009, *http://chronicle.augusta.com/stories/2009/03/31/ bus_516589.shtml.*

13. Janean Huber, "Franchise Forecast," *Entrepreneur*, January 1993, p. 73.

14. *The Profile of Franchising 2006*, International Franchise Association (Washington, DC: 2007), p. 67.

15. Ibid., p. 67.

16. Ibid., p. 70.

17. Jonathan Maze, "Tight Credit Is Turning Franchisors into Lenders," *Franchise Times*, April 2009, *www.franchisetimes.com/content/ story_result.php?article=01307.*

18. Julie Bennett, "Good Shepherds," *Franchise Times*, June–July 2008, *www.franchisetimes.com/content/story_result.php?article=00930.*

19. Darrell Johnson and John Reynolds, "A Study of Franchise Loan Performance in the SBA Guaranty Programs," *Franchising World*, September 2007, pp. 53–56; Richard Gibson, "How to Finance a Franchise," *Wall Street Journal*, March 17, 2008, p. R8.

20. Stephanie Barlow, "Sub-Stantial Success," *Entrepreneur*, January 1993, p. 126.

21. Julie Bennet and Cheryl Babcock, *Franchise Times Guide to Selecting, Buying, and Owning a Franchise*, *Franchise Times* and Sterling Publishing, p. 255.

22. Jonathan Maze, "Cork and Bottle," August 2008, *Franchise Times*, *www.franchisetimes.com/content/story.php?article=00954;* "7 Franchises That Went Bankrupt," *CNNMoney*, July 21, 2009, *http://money.cnn.com/galleries/2009/smallbusiness/0907/gallery.8_fran chises_that_went_bankrupt.smb/2.html.*

23. Richard Gibson, "Why Franchisees Fail," *Wall Street Journal*, April 30, 2007, p. R9.

24. Jonathan Maze, "Guaranteed," *Franchise Times*, September 2008, *www.franchisetimes.com/content/story_result.php?article=01011.*

25. Steven C. Michael and James G. Combs, "Entrepreneurial Failure: The Case of Franchisees," *Journal of Small Business Management*, January 2008, Volume 46, Number 1, pp. 75–90.

26. *The Profile of Franchising 2006*, 62.

27. *The Profile of Franchising* (Washington, DC: FRANDATA Corp and the IFA Educational Foundation, 2000), p. 123.

28. *The Profile of Franchising 2006*, p. 66.

29. Ibid., p. 68.

30. Rachel Sams, "Good Partnerships Gone Bad," *Baltimore Business Journal*, September 16–22, 2005, pp. 1–2.

31. Jim Coen, "Quiznos Franchisees Walloped by Recession," *Let's Talk Franchising*, October 21, 2008, *www.franchiseperfection.com/ blog/?p=327;* Julie Creswell, "When Disillusion Sets In," *New York Times*, February 24, 2007, *www.nytimes.com/2007/02/24/ business/24quiznos.html.*

32. Richard Gibson, "McDonald's Franchisees Grumble over Dollar Menu," *Wall Street Journal*, May 21, 2008, p. B3.

33. Richard Gibson, "The Inside Scoop," *Wall Street Journal*, June 16, 2008, *http://wsj.com/article/SB121321718319265569.html?mod= Financing_1.*

34. Steve Cooper, "Creative Endeavors," *Entrepreneur*, January 2003, pp. 126–128.

35. Janet Adamy, "For McDonald's, It's a Wrap," *Wall Street Journal*, January 30, 2007, pp. B1–B2; "The Birth of the Egg McMuffin," McDonald's, March 15, 2009, *www.aboutmcdonalds.com/mcd/ students/amazing_stories/the_birth_of_the_egg_mcmuffin.html.*

36. Elaine Pofeldt, "Success Franchisee Satisfaction Survey," *Success*, April 1999, p. 59.

37. *The Profile of Franchising 2006*, International Franchise Association (Washington, DC: 2007), p. 77.

38. Carol Tice, "How to Research a Franchise," *Entrepreneur*, January 2009, p. 117.

39. Tracy Stapp, "The Right Ingredients," *Entrepreneur*, October 2008, p. 98; Karen Spencer, "Young and In Charge," *Pink*, June 2008, *www.pinkmagazine.com/franchise/women/2008/young_franchisees.html.*

40. Amy Covington, "Microtel Inns & Suites; The Rocco Valluzo Story," *Franchise Prospector*, April 2007, *www.franchiseprospector.com/ success/microtel-rocco-valluzo.php.*

41. John Reynolds, "Minorities, Women Have Big Stake in Franchised Businesses," International Franchise Association, October 22, 2007, *www.franchise.org/Franchise-Industry-News-Detail.aspx?id=35934.*

42. Jacy Cochran, "Generation Y: Make Way for the Fresh Faces of Franchising," *AllBusiness*, January 1, 2007, *www.allbusiness. com/retail-trade/3969190-1.html.*

43. Christian Conte, "Former SunTrust Executive Finds Happiness in Franchising," *Jacksonville Business Journal*, June 19, 2009, *http://jacksonville.bizjournals.com/jacksonville/stories/2009/06/22/ story3.html.*

44. Ibid.

45. David J. Kaufman, "What a Ride!" *Entrepreneur*, May 2007, pp. 108–113.

46. Udo Schlentrich and Hachemi Aliouche, "Rosenberg Center Study Confirms Global Franchise Growth," International Franchise Association, August 1, 2006, *www.edwardsglobal.com/pdf/ Rosenberg_Center.pdf.*

47. Andrew Leckey, "Overseas Markets Key to Yum Brands' Growth," *Richmond Times-Dispatch*, June 1, 2009, *www2.timesdispatch.com/rtd/ business/local_other/article/LECK01_20090529-224507/270842/.*

48. *McDonald's Corporation 2009 Annual Report*, p. 24.

49. Udo Schlentrich and Hachemi Aliouche, "Rosenberg Center Confirms Global Franchise Growth," *Franchising World*, August 2006, *www.franchise.org/Franchise-News-Detail.aspx?id=31120.*

50. Zaheera Wahid, "Twist and Shout," *Business Start-Ups*, February 2000, p. 85; Elizabeth Bernstein, "Holy Frappuccino," *Wall Street Journal*, August 31, 2001, pp. W1, W8; "Holy Fries," ABC13.com, *http://abclocal.go.com/ktrk/news/020601_sn_holyfries.html.*

51. Steve Adams, "The Latest Scoop on Baskin-Robbins," *Patriot Ledger*, June 27, 2009, *www.patriotledger.com/business/x942416304/The- latest-scoop-on-Baskin-Robbins*; Elissa Elan, "Baskin-Robbins Targets On-Site Venues with Express Unit," *Nation's Restaurant News*, February 10, 2009, *www.nrn.com/breakingNews.aspx?id=363024.*

52. Richard C. Hoffman and John F. Preble, "Convert to Compete: Competitive Advantage through Conversion Franchising," *Journal of Small Business Management*, Volume 41, No. 2, July 2003, pp. 187–204.

53. Carol Tice, "Running the Numbers," *Entrepreneur*, July 2009, pp. 87–95.

54. Julie Bennett, "Multi-Unit Franchisees See Upside to Downturn," *Wall Street Journal*, April 16, 2009, p. D6.

55. Joseph Wheeler, "The Multi-Unit Franchise Revolution," *Area Developer*, October 10, 2004, *www.areadeveloper.us/archive.shtml.*

56. "Marble Slab and MaggieMoo's Head to Singapore," *QSR*, February 20, 2009, *www.qsrmagazine.com/articles/news/story.phtml?id=8101.*

57. "Cold Stone Creamery, Chocolatier to Co-Brand Stores," *Nation's Restaurant News*, November 13, 2008, *www.nrn.com/%28X%281% 29F%2852lTE0nwL5sdRZgNXHL36xVHkYtica8Vi5gT7x4n3HuT5JTbX MWKxxMKpG7JketVM4UUXK4Qjb5PtyUZ87wyKGb3TMQKCLGvfBe LDuXLHN01%29%29/breakingNews.aspx?menu_id= 1368&id=360128.*

58. "Do You Need Maid Brigade?" Maid Brigade, *www.maidbrigade. com/whoneedsmaidbrigade.php.*

59. Raymund Flandez, "A Look at High-Performing Franchises," *Wall Street Journal*, February 12, 2008, p. B5; Lindsay Holloway, James Park, Nichole L. Torres, and Sara Wilson, "This Just In . . ." *Entrepreneur*, January 2008, pp. 100–110.

60. Tracy Stapp, "Breaking the Mold," *Entrepreneur*, September 2009, pp. 87–90.

61. Personal contact with Jim Thomas, May 16, 2007.

62. Amy Joyce, "The Art of the Successful Franchise," *Washington Post*, Monday, April 30, 2007, p. D1.

Buying an Existing Business

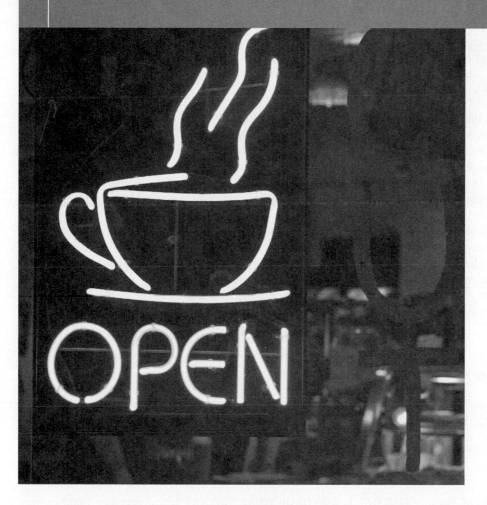

Learning Objectives

Upon completion of this chapter, you will be able to:

1 Understand the advantages and disadvantages of buying an existing business.
2 List the steps involved in the *right* way to buy a business.
3 Describe the various methods used in valuing a business.
4 Discuss the process of negotiating the deal.

Although our intellect always longs for clarity and certainty, our

nature often finds uncertainty fascinating.

—Karl von Clausewitz

A pessimist sees the difficulty in every opportunity: an optimist

sees the opportunity in every difficulty.

—Winston Churchill

From Chapter 5 of *Effective Small Business Management: An Entrepreneurial Approach*, 10/e. Norman M. Scarborough.
Copyright © 2012 by Pearson Education. Published by Prentice Hall. All rights reserved.

The entrepreneurial experience always involves risk. One way to minimize the risk of entrepreneurship is to purchase an existing business rather than to create a new venture. Buying an existing business requires a great deal of analysis and evaluation to ensure that what the entrepreneur is purchasing meets his or her needs and expectations. Exercising patience and taking the necessary time to research a business before buying it are essential to getting a good deal. Research conducted by Stanford's Center for Entrepreneurial Studies reports that the average business purchase takes 19 months from the start of the search to the closing of the deal.[1] In too many cases, the excitement of being able to implement a "fast entry" into the market causes an entrepreneur to rush into a deal and make unnecessary mistakes in judgment.

Before buying any business, an entrepreneur must conduct a thorough analysis of the business and the opportunity that it presents. According to Russell Brown, author of *Strategies for Successfully Buying or Selling a Business*, "You have access to the company's earnings history, which gives you a good idea of what the business will make and an existing business has a proven track record; most established organizations tend to stay in business and keep making money."[2] If vital information such as audited financial statements and legal clearances are not available, an entrepreneur must be especially diligent.

Smart entrepreneurs conduct thorough research before negotiating a purchase price for a business. The following questions provide a good starting point:

- Is this the type of business you would like to operate?
- Will this business offer a lifestyle that you find attractive?
- What are negative aspects of owning this type of business?
- Are there any skeletons in the company closet that might come back to haunt you?
- Is this the best market and the best location for this business?
- Do you know the critical factors that must exist for this business to be successful?
- Do you have the experience required to operate this type of business? If not, will the current owner be willing to stay on for a time to teach you the "ropes"?
- If the business is profitable, why does the current owner(s) want to sell? Can you verify the current owner's reason for selling?
- If the business is currently in decline, do you have a plan to return the business to profitability? How confident are you that your turnaround plan will work?
- Have you examined other similar businesses that are currently for sale or that have sold recently to determine what a fair market price for the company is?

The time and energy invested in evaluating an existing business pays significant dividends by allowing an entrepreneur to acquire a business that will continue to be successful or to avoid purchasing a business that is heading for failure.

Buying an Existing Business

Advantages of Buying an Existing Business

1-A. Understand the advantages of buying an existing business.

The following are some of the most common advantages of purchasing an existing business.

SUCCESSFUL BUSINESSES OFTEN CONTINUE TO BE SUCCESSFUL. A business that has been profitable for some time often reflects an owner who has established a solid customer base, has developed successful relationships with critical suppliers, and has mastered the day-to-day operation of the business. When things have gone well, it is important for a new owner to make changes slowly and retain the relationships with customers, suppliers, and staff that have made the business a success. This advantage often accompanies the second advantage, using the experience of the previous owner.

LEVERAGING THE EXPERIENCE OF THE PREVIOUS OWNER. In cases in which the business has a history of success, a new owner may negotiate with the current owner to stay on as a consultant for a time. This allows a smooth transition during which the seller introduces the new owner to customers and suppliers and shows the new owner the secrets of making the company work. The previous owner can also be very helpful in unmasking the unwritten rules of business—whom to trust, expected business behavior, and many other critical intangibles. Hiring the previous owner as a consultant for the first few months can be a valuable investment. Learning from the previous owner's experience increases a buyer's chance for continued success.

THE TURN-KEY BUSINESS. Starting a company can be a daunting, time-consuming task, and buying an existing business is one of the fastest pathways to entrepreneurship. When things go well, purchasing an existing business saves the time and energy required to plan and launch a new business. The buyer gets a business that is already generating cash and perhaps profits as well. The day the entrepreneur takes over the ongoing business is the day revenues begin. Tom Gillis, an entrepreneur and management consultant in Houston, Texas, says, "Acquiring an established company becomes attractive in three situations: when you haven't found 'the idea' that really turns you on and you find it in an existing business; when you have more money than you have time to start a business from scratch; and when you want to grow but lack a compatible product, service, location or particular advantage that is available from an owner who wants out." According to Gillis, the critical question is: "What do I gain by acquiring this business that I would not be able to achieve on my own?"[3]

SUPERIOR LOCATION. When the location of the business is critical to its success, purchasing a business that is already in the right location may be the best choice. In fact, an existing business's greatest asset may be its location. A location that provides a significant competitive advantage may be reason enough for an entrepreneur to decide to buy instead of build. Opening a second-class location and hoping to draw customers often proves fruitless.

EMPLOYEES AND SUPPLIERS ARE IN PLACE. Experienced employees who choose to continue to work for the company are a significant resource because they can help the new owner learn the business. In addition, an existing business has an established set of suppliers with a history of business transactions. Vendors can continue to supply the business while the new owner assesses the products and services of other vendors. Thus, the new owner can take the time needed to evaluate alternative suppliers.

INSTALLED EQUIPMENT WITH KNOWN PRODUCTION CAPACITY. Acquiring and installing new equipment imposes a tremendous strain and uncertainty on a fledgling company's financial resources. The buyer of an existing business can determine the condition of the plant and equipment, its capacity, its remaining life, and its value before buying the business. In many cases, the entrepreneur can purchase the existing physical facilities and equipment at prices that are significantly below their replacement costs. In some businesses, purchasing these assets may be the best part of the deal.

INVENTORY IN PLACE. The proper mix and amount of inventory is essential to both cost control and sales volume. A business with too little inventory cannot satisfy customer demand, and too much inventory ties up excessive amounts of capital, increases costs, reduces profitability, and increases the likelihood of cash flow problems. Many successful established business owners have learned a proper balance of inventory. Knowing the "right" amount of inventory to keep on hand can be extremely valuable, especially for buyers of businesses that experience seasonal fluctuations or those that must meet the needs of high-volume customers.

ESTABLISHED TRADE CREDIT. Previous owners also have established trade credit relationships of which the new owner can take advantage. The business's proven track record gives the new owner leverage in negotiating favorable trade credit terms. No supplier wants to lose a good customer.

EASIER ACCESS TO FINANCING. Investors and bankers often perceive the risk associated with buying an existing business with a solid history of performance to be lower than that of an unknown start-up. This may make it easier for the new owner to secure financing. A buyer can point to the existing company's track record and to the plans for improving it to convince potential lenders to finance the purchase. Many lenders will finance 50 to 75 percent of the purchase price of a business, depending on a number of factors, such as the industry in which it operates, its track record of success, and its profits, cash flow, assets, and collateral.[4] In addition, in many business purchases, buyers use a built-in source of financing, the seller.

HIGH VALUE. Some existing businesses are real bargains. If the current owner must sell quickly, he or she may have to set a bargain price for the company that is below its actual worth. Any special skills or training required to operate the business limit the number of potential buyers; therefore, the more specialized the business is, the greater the likelihood is that a buyer will find a bargain. If the owner wants a substantial down payment or the entire selling price in cash, there may be few qualified buyers, but those who do qualify may be able to negotiate a good deal.

Disadvantages of Buying an Existing Business

1-B. Understand the disadvantages of buying an existing business.

Buying an existing business does have disadvantages that a prospective buyer must consider.

CASH REQUIREMENTS. One of the most significant challenges to buying a business is acquiring the necessary funds for the initial purchase price. "[Because] the business concept, customer base, brands, and other fundamental work have already been done, the financial costs of acquiring an existing business is usually greater then starting one from nothing," observes the Small Business Administration.[5]

THE BUSINESS IS LOSING MONEY. A business may be for sale because it is no longer—or never has been—profitable. Owners can use various creative accounting techniques that make a company's financial picture appear to be much more positive than it actually is. The maxim "let the buyer beware" is sound advice in the purchase of a business. Any buyer who is unwilling to conduct a thorough analysis of the business usually ends up paying a much higher price down the road when the business turns out to be struggling.

Although buying a money-losing business is risky, it is not necessarily taboo. If a business analysis indicates that the company is poorly managed, suffering from neglect, or overlooking a prime opportunity, a new owner may be able to turn it around. However, buying a struggling business without a well-defined plan for solving the problems it faces is an invitation to disaster.

ENTREPRENEURIAL
Profile

*Philip Schram and
Buffalo Wings
and Rings*

While working for an auto parts maker in Cincinnati, Ohio, Philip Schram learned that a coworker's father was selling an underperforming restaurant franchise, Buffalo Wings and Rings, that he had started in 1988. After analyzing the six-store chain and developing a plan for turning it around, Schram purchased the chicken wings and onion rings franchise. "Since I was a boy, I dreamed of owning a business," he says. Schram worked with franchisees to increase the company's marketing, promotion, and branding efforts; refurbished the chain's stores to give them

Philip Schram (right), CEO of Buffalo Wings and Rings, talks with vice-president Nader Masadeh outside one of the company's restaurants.

Source: Tom Uhlman\AP Wide World Photos

a fresher, consistent look; and expanded the menu. The changes worked. Within 2 years, the number of outlets had grown to 43 and sales had increased from $6 million to $20 million. Schram continues to expand the chain across the Midwest and recently opened a new franchisee training headquarters in Cincinnati.[6]

Unprofitable businesses often result from at least one of the following problems:

- High inventory levels
- Excessively high wage and salary expenses due to excess pay or inefficient use of personnel
- Excessively high compensation for the owner
- Inadequate accounts receivable collection efforts
- Excessively high rental or lease rates
- High-priced maintenance costs or service contracts
- Poor location or too many locations for the business to support
- Inefficient equipment
- Intense competition from rivals
- Prices that are too low
- Low profit margins
- Losses due to employee theft, shoplifting, and fraud

Like Philip Schram, a potential buyer usually can trace the causes of a company's lack of profitability by analyzing a company and its financial statements. The question is: Can the new owner take steps to resolve the problems and return the company to profitability?

PAYING FOR ILL WILL. Just as proper business dealings can create goodwill, improper business behavior or unethical practices can create ill will. A business may look great on the surface, but customers, suppliers, creditors, or employees may have negative feelings about their dealings with it. Too many business buyers discover—after the sale—that they have inherited undisclosed credit problems, poor supplier relationships, soon-to-expire leases, lawsuits, building code violations, and other problems created by the previous owner. Vital business relationships may have begun to deteriorate, but their long-term effects may not yet be reflected in the company's financial statements. Ill will can permeate a business for years. The only way to avoid these problems is to investigate a prospective purchase target thoroughly *before* moving forward in the negotiation process.

CURRENT EMPLOYEES ARE UNSUITABLE. If a new owner plans to make changes in a business, current employees may not suit the company's needs. Some workers may have a difficult time adapting to the new owner's management style and the new vision for the company. Previous managers may have kept marginal employees because they were close friends or had been with the company for a long time. The new owner, therefore, may have to make some very unpopular termination decisions. For this reason, employees may feel threatened by new ownership. In some cases, employees who may have wanted to buy the business themselves but could not afford it are resentful. They may see the new owner as the person who "stole" their opportunity. Bitter employees are not likely to be productive workers and may have difficulty fitting in to the new management structure.

LOCATION HAS BECOME UNSATISFACTORY. What was once an ideal location may no longer be because of changing demographic patterns. Recently opened malls and shopping centers, new competitors, or traffic pattern changes can spell disaster, especially for a small retail shop. Prospective buyers must evaluate the current market in the area surrounding the business as well as its potential for future growth and expansion. Researching all zoning, traffic, and land development plans with appropriate jurisdictions, such as the city, county, or state, is important as well.

OBSOLETE OR INEFFICIENT EQUIPMENT AND FACILITIES. Potential buyers sometimes neglect to have an expert evaluate a company's building and equipment before they purchase it. They may discover all too late that the equipment is obsolete and inefficient, which increases operating expenses to excessively high levels. Modernizing equipment and facilities is seldom inexpensive.

THE CHALLENGE OF IMPLEMENTING CHANGE. Planning for change is much easier than implementing it. Methods and procedures the previous owner used created precedents that can be difficult or awkward for a new owner to change. For example, if the previous owner granted volume-based discounts to customers, it may be difficult to eliminate that discount without losing some of those customers. The previous owner's policies—even those that are unwise—can influence the changes the new owner can make. Implementing changes to reverse a downward sales trend in a turnaround situation can be just as difficult as eliminating unprofitable procedures. Convincing alienated customers to return can be an expensive and laborious process that may take years.

OBSOLETE INVENTORY. Inventory has value only when it is salable. Too many potential owners make the mistake of trusting a company's balance sheet to provide them with the value of its inventory. The inventory value reported on a company's balance sheet is seldom an accurate reflection of its real market value. A company's inventory may reflect the value at the time of purchase but inventory, especially technology-related inventory, can depreciate quickly. The value reported on the balance sheet reflects the original cost of the inventory, *not* its actual market value. In fact, inventory and other assets reported as having value may be completely worthless because they are outdated and obsolete. It is the buyer's responsibility to discover the *real* value of the assets before negotiating a purchase price for the business.

VALUING ACCOUNTS RECEIVABLE. Like inventory, accounts receivable rarely are worth their face value. The prospective buyer should age the accounts receivable to determine their collectibility. The older the receivables are, the less likely they are to be collected, and, consequently, the lower their actual value. Table 1 shows a simple but effective method of evaluating accounts receivable once the buyer ages them.

THE BUSINESS MAY BE OVERPRICED. Most business sales involve the purchase of the company's assets rather than its stock. A buyer must be sure which assets are included in the deal and what their real value is. Many people purchase businesses at prices far in excess of their true value. If a buyer accurately values a business's accounts receivable, inventories, and other assets, he or she will be in a better position to negotiate a price that will allow the business to be profitable. Making payments on a business that was overpriced is a millstone around the new owner's neck, making it difficult to keep the business afloat.

TABLE 1 Valuing Accounts Receivable

A prospective buyer asked the current owner of a business about the value of her accounts receivable.

The owner's business records showed $101,000 in accounts receivable. However, when the prospective buyer aged them and then multiplied the resulting totals by his estimated probabilities of collection, he discovered their *real* value.

Age of Accounts (Days)	Amount	Probability of Collection	Value (Amount × Probability of Collection)
0–30	$40,000	95%	$38,000
31–60	$25,000	88%	$22,000
61–90	$14,000	70%	$9,800
91–120	$10,000	40%	$4,000
121–150	$7,000	25%	$1,750
151+	$5,000	10%	$500
Total	**$101,000**		**$76,050**

Had he blindly accepted the "book value" of these accounts receivable, this prospective buyer would have overpaid by nearly $25,000 for them!

IN THE ENTREPRENEURIAL
SPOTLIGHT Buying the Li'l Guy

Christina and David Sloan, third-generation co-owners of Li'l Guy Foods, a family business founded in 1965 in Kansas City, Missouri, that manufactures Mexican foods, recently decided that it was time to sell because the 30-employee company was facing financial pressure from rising food, energy, and packaging costs. The cost of corn, a major ingredient in the company's product line, had increased by 150 percent in just a few months, eradicating the savings the Sloans had experienced by cutting out one production shift. "We were under an assault on [profit] margins," says David, which made prospective buyers nervous because they were buying the company's future earning potential. "We had cut over 35 percent of our expenses and were still having trouble," he says. "We started noticing that across the country tortilla companies just like ours were going out of business."

The Sloans decided that selling the family business was the best way to ensure its survival. They put out the word that the company was for sale but were disappointed in the lack of prospective buyers. They realized that "there weren't a lot of people wanting to jump into this industry," says David. However, one of Li'l Guy Foods' greatest assets was a base of loyal small restaurant customers who recognized the high quality of its products and were willing to pay for them. The Li'l Guy Foods brand had strong customer awareness in the local area, and the company was generating $3.3 million in annual sales.

Tortilla King, another small food maker based in Moundridge, Kansas, with 120 employees, saw an opportunity to expand its product line and its market share. The larger company, which was founded in 1992, had more sophisticated systems in place than did Li'l Guy Foods, including a commodities-hedging system that shielded the company from sudden shocks in the prices of raw materials such as corn. In addition, Tortilla King understood the food manufacturing business, and the two companies had done business with one another in the past.

After analyzing Li'l Guy Foods, the president of Tortilla King, Juan Guardiola, decided to buy the company. "It made a lot of sense to merge," he says. Over the course of several weeks, the two companies negotiated a deal for an undisclosed purchase price that included shifting production to Tortilla King's brand new manufacturing plant in Wichita, Kansas, but maintaining Lil'Guy Foods' brand name and distribution center in Missouri. Tortilla King absorbed all of Li'l Guy Foods' employees, even paying to relocate 20 manufacturing employees to Moundridge, Kansas. David and his sister Christina agreed to stay on with the company and have seats on Tortilla King's six-member board.

Just before the deal was about to close, the bank that had agreed to provide the financing for the purchase pulled out as a result of the upheaval in the financial industry. Not wanting to see the deal collapse, the Sloans decided to finance the purchase of their company themselves. Tortilla King made a down payment, and the Sloans agreed to finance the balance of the purchase price over 5 years at 8 percent interest. "It wasn't the ideal transaction for us," admits David. "I would rather have had it a lot cleaner." However, when the bank withdrew its financial support, the Sloans knew that the only way to close the deal was to provide seller financing.

"Li'l Guy Foods has a very good market share and complement well what we're trying to do with our company," says Tortilla King president Guardiola. "Food manufacturing has gotten to be such an expensive endeavor, small businesses have to join forces to take on the big guys."

1. What was the motivation behind the Sloans' decision to sell Li'l Guy Foods? Are you surprised that so few potential buyers expressed interest in the company? Explain.
2. How common is seller financing in the sale of small companies such as Li'l Guy Foods? How are these deals typically structured?
3. What benefits can Tortilla King expect as a result of buying Li'l Guy Foods?

Sources: Arden Dale and Simona Covel, "Sellers Offer a Financial Hand to Their Buyers," *Wall Street Journal*, November 13, 2008, p. B6; Suzanna Sategemeyer, "Li'l Guy Sells to Tortilla King, Moves Manufacturing to Wichita," *Kansas City Business Journal*, September 12, 2008, *http://kansascity.bizjournals.com/kansascity/stories/2008/09/15/story2.html.*

How to Buy a Business

2. List the steps involved in the *right* way to buy a business.

Buying an existing business can be risky if approached haphazardly. Kevin Mulvaney, a professor of entrepreneurship at Babson College and a consultant to business sellers, says that 50 to 75 percent of all business sales that are initiated fall through.[7] To avoid blowing a deal or making costly mistakes, an entrepreneur-to-be should follow these steps:

1. Conduct a self-inventory, objectively analyzing your skills, abilities, and personal interests to determine the type(s) of business that offers the best fit.

2. Develop a list of the criteria that define the "ideal business" for you.
3. Prepare a list of potential candidates that meet your criteria.
4. Thoroughly investigate the potential acquisition targets that meet your criteria. This *due diligence process* involves practical steps, such as analyzing financial statements and making certain that the facilities are structurally sound. The goal is to minimize the pitfalls and problems that can arise when buying any business.
5. Explore various financing options for buying the business.
6. Negotiate a reasonable deal with the existing owner.
7. Ensure a smooth transition of ownership.

We now address each of these important steps.

Self-Analysis of Skills, Abilities, and Interests

The first step in buying a business is conducting a "self-audit" to determine the ideal business. Consider, for example, how the following questions could produce valuable insights into the best type of business for an entrepreneur. These answers will provide an important personal guide that might help you avoid a costly mistake:

- What business activities do you enjoy most? What activities do you enjoy the least?
- Which industries interest you most? Which interest you the least?
- What kind of business do you want to buy?
- What kinds of businesses do you want to *avoid?*
- In what geographic area do you want to live and work?
- What do you expect to get out of the business?
- How much can you put into the business—in both time and money?
- What business skills and experience do you have? Which ones do you lack?
- How easily can you transfer your existing skills and experience to other types of businesses? In what kinds of businesses would that transfer be easiest?
- How much risk are you willing to take?
- What size company do you want to buy?

Answering those and other questions *beforehand* will allow you to develop a list of criteria that a company must meet before it should be a purchase candidate.

Develop a List of Criteria

Based on the answers to the self-inventory questions, the next step is to develop a list of criteria that a potential business acquisition must meet. Investigating every business that you find for sale is a waste of time. The goal is to identify the characteristics of the "ideal business" for you so that you can focus on the most viable candidates as you wade through a multitude of business opportunities. These criteria will provide specific parameters against which you can evaluate potential acquisition candidates.

Prepare a List of Potential Candidates

Once you know the criteria and parameters for the ideal candidate, you can begin your search. One technique is to start at the macro level and work down. Drawing on the resources of the Internet and the library, government publications, and industry trade associations and reports, buyers can discover which industries are growing fastest and offer the greatest potential for future growth. For entrepreneurs with a well-defined idea of what they are looking for, another effective approach is to begin searching in an industry in which they have experience or knowledge.

Typical sources for identifying potential acquisition candidates include the following:

- The Internet—several sites, such as BizBuySell.com, BizQuest.com, and others, have listings of business brokers and companies for sale
- Business brokers
- Bankers
- Accountants
- Investment bankers
- Trade associations
- Industry contacts, such as suppliers, distributors, customers, and others

- Contacting owners of businesses you would like to buy (even if they're not advertised "for sale")
- Newspaper and trade journal listings of businesses for sale (e.g., the Business Opportunities section of the *Wall Street Journal*)
- "Networking" through social and business contact with friends and relatives

Buyers should consider all businesses that meet their criteria—even those that may not be listed for sale. Just because a business does not have a "for sale" sign in the window does not mean it is not for sale. In fact, the hidden market of companies that might be for sale but are not advertised as such is one of the richest sources of top-quality businesses. Getting the word out that a buyer has an interest in buying a particular type of business often leads to the discovery of many rich business opportunities.

ENTREPRENEURIAL
Profile
Randy Hoyle and and Niche Equipment

"For a long time I had thought about owning my own business where I could make my own decisions," Randy Hoyle says. When the company he worked for transferred him again, Hoyle "saw this as my chance." Rather than starting a business, Hoyle decided that buying one was best for him. "I wanted to have income faster than a startup would entail, so I focused on finding an ongoing business that also had a good upside." To find the best companies, Hoyle expanded his search beyond companies that were officially listed for sale. "None of the companies I contacted was 'for sale,'" says Hoyle, who worked with a consultant to find potential candidates. "We got a listing of businesses for which my background could be a good fit, and we sent letters to those businesses to find out what interest they had in selling. We mailed 600 letters, narrowed it down to 20 to 25 that we actually visited and then to three that were final candidates for which we did serious due diligence." The search, which took about 9 months of full-time effort, ultimately led to Hoyle's purchase of Niche Equipment, a wholesale distributor of office equipment with six employees and more than $1 million in annual revenues.[8]

The Due Diligence Process: Investigating and Evaluating Potential Acquisition Candidates

Due diligence involves studying, reviewing, and verifying all of the relevant information concerning the top acquisition candidates. This step involves investigating the most attractive business candidates in greater detail. The goal of the due diligence process is to discover exactly what the buyer is purchasing and avoid any unpleasant surprises *after* the deal is closed. Exploring a company's character and condition through the Better Business Bureau, credit-reporting agencies, the company's bank, its vendors and suppliers, your accountant, your attorney, and through other resources increases the odds that an entrepreneur gets a good deal on a business with the

Source: ©Thaves. Reprinted by permission.

capacity to succeed. It is important to invest in the due diligence process; you may choose to pay now or pay—usually far more—later.[9]

A thorough analysis of a potential acquisition candidate usually requires an entrepreneur to assemble a team of advisors. Finding a suitable business, structuring a deal, and negotiating the final bargain involves many complex legal, financial, tax, and business issues, and good advice can be a valuable tool. Many entrepreneurs involve an accountant, an attorney, an insurance agent, a banker, and a business broker to serve as consultants during the due diligence process.

The due diligence process involves investigating five critical areas of the business and the potential deal:

1. *Motivation:* Why does the owner want to sell?
2. *Asset valuation:* What is the real value of the firm's assets?
3. *Market potential:* What is the market potential for the company's products or services?
4. *Legal issues:* What legal aspects of the business represent known or hidden risks?
5. *Financial condition:* Is the business financially sound?

MOTIVATION. Why does the owner want to sell? Every prospective business owner should investigate the *real* reason the business owner wants to sell. In addition to a planned retirement, the most common reasons businesses are for sale usually fall into three categories:[10]

1. The seller is not making enough money in the business.
2. The seller has a personal reason for selling, such as health, boredom, or burnout.
3. The seller is aware of pending changes in the business or the business environment that will adversely affect its future.

These changes may include a major competitor entering the market, a degraded location, leasing problems, cash-flow issues, or a declining customer base. In other cases, owners decide to cash in their business investments and diversify into other types of assets. Every prospective buyer should investigate *thoroughly* the reason a seller gives for selling a business. Remember: Let the buyer beware!

Businesses do not last forever, and most owners know when the time has come to sell. Some owners do not feel obliged to disclose to potential buyers the whole story of their motivation for selling. In every business sale, the buyer bears the responsibility of determining whether the business is a good value. Visiting local business owners may reveal general patterns about the area and its overall vitality. The local Chamber of Commerce also may have useful information. Suppliers and competitors may be able to shed light on why a business is for sale. Combining this collection of information with an analysis of the company's financial records, a potential buyer should be able to develop a clear picture of the business and its real value.

ASSET VALUATION. A prospective buyer should examine the business's assets to determine their value. Questions to ask about assets include:

- Are the assets really useful or are they obsolete?
- Will the assets require replacement soon?
- Do the assets operate efficiently?
- Are the assets reasonably priced?

A potential buyer should check the condition of the equipment and the building. It may be necessary to hire a professional to evaluate the major components of the building, such as its structure and its plumbing, electrical, and heating and cooling systems. Renovations are seldom inexpensive or simple, and unexpected renovations can punch a gaping hole in a buyer's budget.

What is the status of the firm's existing inventory? Is it able to be sold at full price? How much of it would the buyer have to sell at a loss? Is it consistent with the image the new owner wants to project? Determining the value of inventory and other assets may require an independent appraisal because sellers often price them above their actual value. These items typically constitute the largest portion of a business's value, and a potential buyer should not accept the seller's asking price blindly. Remember: *Book value is not the same as market value.* Value is determined in the market, not on a balance sheet. Well-prepared buyers usually can purchase equipment and fixtures at prices that are substantially lower than book value.

Other important factors that the potential buyer should investigate include the following:

1. *Accounts receivable.* If the sale includes accounts receivable, the buyer must check their quality before purchasing them. How creditworthy are the accounts? What portion of them is past due? By aging the accounts receivable, the buyer can judge their quality and determine their *real* value. (Refer to Table 1.)

2. *Lease arrangements.* Is the lease included in the sale? When does it expire? What restrictions does it have on renovation or expansion? What is the status of the relationship with the property owner? The buyer should determine beforehand any restrictions the landlord has placed on the lease. Does the lease agreement allow the seller to assign the lease to a buyer? The buyer must negotiate all necessary changes with the landlord and get them in writing prior to buying the business.

3. *Business records.* Accurate business records can be a valuable source of information and can tell the story of the company's pattern of success—or lack of it! Unfortunately, many business owners are sloppy record keepers. Consequently, a potential buyer and his or her team may have to reconstruct critical records. It is important to verify as much information about the business as possible. For instance, does the owner have current customer mailing lists? These can be valuable marketing tools for a new business owner.

4. *Intangible assets.* Determining the value of intangible assets is much more difficult than computing the value of the tangible assets, yet intangible assets can be one of the most valuable parts of a business acquisition. Does the sale include intangible assets such as trademarks, patents, copyrights, or goodwill? Edward Karstetter, Director of Valuation Services at USBX says, "The value placed on intangible assets such as people, knowledge, relationships, and intellectual property is now a greater proportion of the total value of most businesses than is the value of tangible assets such as machinery and equipment."[11]

5. *Location and appearance.* The location and appearance of the building are important to most businesses because they send clear messages to potential customers. Every buyer should consider the location's suitability for today and for the near future. Potential buyers also should check local zoning laws to ensure that the changes they want to make are permissible. In some areas, zoning laws are very difficult to change and can restrict the business's growth.

MARKET POTENTIAL. What is the market potential for the company's products or services? No one wants to buy a business with a dying market. A thorough market analysis leads to an accurate and realistic sales forecast for the buyer. This research should tell a buyer whether he or she should consider a particular business and help define the trend in the business's sales and customer base. Two important aspects of a market analysis include learning about customers and competitors.

Customer Characteristics and Composition. A business owner should analyze both the existing and potential customers before purchasing an existing business. Discovering why customers buy from the business and developing a profile of the existing customer base allows the buyer to identify a company's strengths and weaknesses. The entrepreneur should answer the following questions:

- Does the business have a well-defined customer base? Is it growing or shrinking?
- Who are my customers in terms of race, age, gender, and income level?
- What do customers expect the business to do for them?
- What needs are they satisfying when they buy from the company?
- How often do customers buy?
- Do they buy in seasonal patterns?
- How loyal are present customers?
- Why do some potential customers *not* buy from the business?
- How easily can the company attract new customers? Will the new customers be significantly different from existing customers?
- Is the customer base from a large geographic area, or do they all live near the business?

Analyzing the answers to these questions helps a potential buyer to develop a marketing plan. Ideally, the buyer will keep the business attractive to existing customers and change features of its marketing plan to attract new customers.

Competitor Analysis. A potential buyer must identify the company's direct competitors, the businesses that sell the same or similar products or services. The potential profitability and survival of the business may depend on the behavior of these competitors. In addition to analyzing direct competitors, buyers should evaluate the trend in the level of competition. Answering the following questions provides valuable insight:

- How many similar businesses have entered the market in the last 5 years?
- How many similar businesses have closed in the last 5 years?
- What caused them to fail?
- Has the market already reached the saturation point? Being a late comer in a saturated market is plagued with challenges.

When evaluating the competitive environment, the prospective buyer should answer additional questions:

- What are the characteristics that have led to the success of the company's most direct competitors?
- How do the competitors' sales volumes compare with those of the business the entrepreneur is considering?
- What unique services do competitors offer?
- How well organized and coordinated are the marketing efforts of competitors?
- How strong are competitors' reputations?
- What are their strengths and weaknesses?
- How can you gain market share in this competitive environment?

The intent of competitor analysis is to determine the company's current competitive situation and the competitive landscape in which the firm will be forced to compete.

LEGAL ISSUES. What legal aspects of the business represent known or hidden risks? Business buyers face myriad legal pitfalls. The most significant legal issues involve liens, bulk transfers, contract assignments, covenants not to compete, and ongoing legal liabilities.

Liens. The key legal issue in the sale of any asset is typically the proper transfer of good title from seller to buyer. However, because most business sales involve a collection of assorted assets, the transfer of a good title is complex. Some business assets may have **liens** (creditors' claims) against them, and unless those liens are satisfied before the sale, the buyer must assume them and become financially responsible for them. One way to reduce this potential problem is to include a clause in the sales contract that states that any liability not shown on the balance sheet at the time of sale remains the responsibility of the seller. A prospective buyer should have an attorney thoroughly investigate all of the assets for sale and their lien status before buying any business.

Bulk Transfers. A **bulk transfer** is a transaction in which a buyer purchases all or most of a business's inventory (as in a business sale). To protect against surprise claims from the seller's creditors after purchasing a business, the buyer should meet the requirements of a bulk transfer under Section 6 of the Uniform Commercial Code. Suppose that an owner owing many creditors sells his business to a buyer. The seller, however, does not use the proceeds of the sale to pay his or her debts to business creditors. Instead, he "skips town," leaving his creditors unpaid. Without the protection of a bulk transfer, those creditors could make claim (within 6 months) to the assets that the buyer purchased in order to satisfy the previous owner's debts. To be effective, a bulk transfer must meet the following criteria:

- The seller must give the buyer a sworn list of existing creditors.
- The buyer and the seller must prepare a list of the property included in the sale.
- The buyer must keep the list of creditors and the list of property for 6 months.
- The buyer must give notice of the sale to each creditor at least 10 days before he takes possession of the goods or pays for them (whichever is first).

By meeting these criteria, a buyer acquires free and clear title to the assets purchased, which are not subject to prior claims from the seller's creditors. Because Section 6 can create quite a burden on a business buyer, several states have repealed it, and more are likely follow. Many states have revised Section 6 to make it easier for buyers to notify creditors. Under the revised rule, if a business has more than 200 creditors, the buyer may notify them by public notice rather than by contacting them individually.

Contract Assignments. A buyer must investigate the rights and the obligations he or she would assume under existing contracts with suppliers, customers, employees, lessors, and others. To continue the smooth operation of the business, the buyer must assume the rights of the seller under existing contracts. For example, the current owner may have 4 years left on a 10-year lease that he or she will assign to the buyer (if the lease allows assignment). A seller can assign most contractual rights unless the contract specifically prohibits the assignment or the contract is personal in nature. For instance, loan contracts sometimes prohibit assignments with **due-on-sale clauses**. These clauses require the buyer to pay the full amount of the remaining loan balance or to finance the balance at prevailing interest rates. Thus, the buyer cannot assume the seller's loan at a lower interest rate. In addition, a seller usually cannot assign his or her credit arrangements with suppliers to the buyer because they are based on the seller's business reputation and are personal in nature. If contracts such as these are crucial to the business operation and cannot be assigned, the buyer must negotiate new contracts.

The prospective buyer also should evaluate the terms of other contracts the seller has, including the following:

- Patent, trademark, or copyright registrations
- Exclusive agent or distributor contracts
- Insurance contracts
- Financing and loan arrangements
- Union contracts

Covenants Not to Compete. One of the most important and most often overlooked legal considerations for a prospective buyer is negotiating a **covenant not to compete** (or a **restrictive covenant**) with the seller. Under a restrictive covenant, the seller agrees not to open a competing store within a specific time period and geographic area of the existing one. (The buyer must negotiate the covenant directly with the owners, not the corporation; if the corporation signs the agreement, the owner may not be bound by it.) However, the covenant must be a part of a business sale and must be reasonable in scope in order to be enforceable. Without this protection, a buyer may find his new business eroding beneath his or her feet.

Ongoing Legal Liabilities. Finally, a potential buyer must look for any potential legal liabilities the purchase might expose. These typically arise from three sources: physical premises, product liability claims, and labor relations.

Physical Premises. The buyer must first examine the physical premises for safety. Is the employees' health at risk because of asbestos or some other hazardous material? If a manufacturing environment is involved, does it meet Occupational Safety and Health Administration (OSHA) and other regulatory agency requirements?

Product Liability Claims. The buyer must consider whether the product contains defects that could result in **product liability lawsuits**, which claim that a company is liable for damages and injuries caused by the products or services it sells. Existing lawsuits might be an omen of more to follow. In addition, the buyer must explore products that the company has discontinued because he or she might be liable for them if they prove to be defective. The final bargain between the parties should require the seller to guarantee that the company is not involved in any product liability lawsuits.

Labor Relations. The relationship between management and employees is a key to a successful transition of ownership. Does a union represent employees in a collective bargaining agreement? The time to discover sour management–labor relations is before the purchase, not after.

The existence of liabilities such as these does not necessarily eliminate a business from consideration. Insurance coverage can shift risk from the potential buyer, but the buyer should check to see whether the insurance covers lawsuits resulting from actions taken before the purchase. Despite conducting a thorough search, a buyer may purchase a business only to discover later the presence of hidden liabilities such as unpaid back taxes or delinquent bills, unpaid pension fund contributions, undisclosed lawsuits, or others. Including a clause in the purchase agreement that imposes the responsibility for such hidden liabilities on the seller can protect a buyer from unpleasant surprises after the sale.

FINANCIAL CONDITION. Is the business financially sound? Any investment in a company should produce a reasonable salary for the owner and a healthy return on the money invested. Otherwise, it makes no sense to purchase the business. Therefore, every serious buyer must analyze the records of the business to determine its financial health. Accounting systems and methods can vary tremendously from one company to another, and buyers usually benefit from enlisting the assistance of an accountant. Some business sellers know all of the tricks to make profits appear to be higher than they actually are. For example, a seller might lower costs by gradually eliminating equipment maintenance or might boost sales by selling to marginal customers who will never pay for their purchases. Techniques such as these can artificially inflate a company's earnings, but a well-prepared buyer will be able to see through them. For a buyer, the most dependable financial records are audited statements, those prepared by a certified public accountant in accordance with generally accepted accounting principles (GAAP). Unfortunately, most small businesses that are for sale do not have audited financial statements.

A buyer also must remember that he or she is purchasing the future earning potential of an existing business. To evaluate a company's earning potential, a buyer should review past sales, operating expenses, and profits as well as the assets used to generate those profits. The buyer must compare current balance sheets and income statements with previous ones and then develop projected statements for the next 2 or 3 years. Sales tax records, income tax returns, and financial statements are valuable sources of information.

Earnings trends are another area to analyze. Are profits consistent over time, or have they been erratic? If there are fluctuations, what caused them? Is this earnings pattern typical in the industry, or is it a result of unique circumstances or poor management? If these fluctuations are caused by poor management, can a new manager make a difference? Some of the financial records that a potential buyer should examine include the income statement, balance sheet, tax returns, owner's compensation, and cash flow.

Income Statements and Balance Sheets for at Least 3 Years. It is important to review data from several years because creative accounting techniques can distort financial data in any single year. Even though buyers are purchasing the future earning power of a business, they must remember that many businesses intentionally show low profits to minimize the owners' tax bills. Low profits should prompt a buyer to investigate their causes.

Income Tax Returns for at Least 3 Years. Comparing basic financial statements with tax returns can reveal discrepancies of which the buyer should be aware. Some small business owners "skim" from their businesses; that is, they take money from sales without reporting it as income. Owners who skim often claim that their businesses are more profitable than their tax returns show. However, buyers should not pay for "phantom profits."

Owner's and Family Members' Compensation. Owner compensation is especially important in small companies, and the smaller the company, the more important it is. Although many companies do not pay their owners what they are worth, some compensate their owners lavishly. Buyers must consider the impact of benefits such as company cars, insurance contracts, country club memberships, and the like. It is important to adjust the company's income statements for the salary and benefits that the seller has paid himself or herself and family members.

Cash Flow. Most buyers understand the importance of evaluating a company's profit history, but few recognize the need to analyze its cash flow. They assume that if earnings are adequate, the company will have sufficient cash to pay all of its expenses and to provide an adequate salary for them. *That is not necessarily the case.* Before closing any deal, a buyer should convert the company's financial statements into a cash-flow forecast. This forecast must take into account not only existing debts and obligations but also any additional debts the buyer plans to take on. It should reflect any payments the buyer will make to the seller if the seller finances part of the purchase price. The critical question is: Can the company generate sufficient cash to be self-supporting under the new financial structure?

Don't Get Burned When You Buy a Business

Rather than experience the expense, sweat, and toil of starting a new business, many entrepreneurs buy an existing business from someone who has gone through the process of starting a venture and proving its worth. Buying a business, however, is rife with potential pitfalls, and an unprepared entrepreneur can easily get burned. The Street-Smart Entrepreneur offers the following tips for buying an existing business:

■ **Recognize that you are not just buying a company; you are buying a livelihood and a lifestyle.** Buyers of small businesses are not just buying assets and inventories and leases, they are also choosing a lifestyle. "You have to look at the fact that you're buying a job and, hopefully, a decent return on investment," says Glen J. Cooper, a certified business appraiser in Portland, Maine. "Part of what you'll want to do is look at how much you can realistically expect the business to be able to pay you for your work and how much of a return on your investment you can get in the form of additional profit beyond your own compensation." The business may be the single most significant determinant of your future lifestyle; therefore, choose it carefully.

■ **Explore seller financing.** Recent turbulence in the financial industry has made banks hesitant to make loans to business buyers. Fortunately, buyers have a built-in source of capital available: the seller. Seller financing "is almost a mandatory piece of the deal," says business broker Domenic Rinaldi. In a typical deal, the buyer makes a down payment to the seller that ranges from 20 to 70 percent of the purchase price. The seller takes a note for the balance, which the buyer repays over 3 to 10 years. When Alex Shlepakov, founder of Network One, a business based in Elk Grove Village, Illinois, that provides network support services to small businesses, decided to sell the company, he offered to finance a portion of the selling price. Shlepakov accepted a large down payment from the buyers and agreed to finance the balance over 2.5 years. Shlepakov says that providing financing is a tangible way for sellers to demonstrate confidence in the business that they are selling.

■ **Use professional advisors.** When it comes to conducting due diligence on a potential target company, smart entrepreneurs turn to professionals—accountants, attorneys, business brokers, and others—for valuable insight and advice. "I strongly, strongly advise hiring professionals such as attorneys and accountants to help buyers with the potential legal and financial issues or pitfalls of any purchase," says Nick Nicholson, business broker and owner of Atlanta-based Nicholson & Associates.

■ **Link the final price to customer retention.** In many small businesses, particularly service businesses, a significant part of what a buyer is receiving is the existing client or customer base. In sales of these businesses, the agreed-upon price often is based on the company's ability to retain a certain percentage of customers. If the company's customer base declines after the buyer takes over, the agreement calls for a reduction in the selling price.

■ **Get the seller to stick around.** Buyers usually benefit from having the previous owner stay on during the transition period following the sale. The complexity of the business and the new owner's familiarity with the industry determine whether the time frame is a few weeks or a few years. The previous owner may have years of experience and knowledge of the industry and the local community that would be highly valuable to the buyer. Negotiating a deal for the seller to stay on for a time takes a great deal of pressure off of an inexperienced buyer.

■ **Do your homework on valuation techniques.** As you can see from this chapter, valuing a business is partly an art and partly a science. Smart entrepreneurs educate themselves in advance about the various methods practitioners in the industry use to value businesses. Remember that a common technique for estimating the value of a business is to apply a multiple to its earnings before interest and taxes (EBIT). However, the multiples used vary significantly across industries.

In many ways, buying a business is easier than starting a business from scratch, but buying a business poses a unique set of challenges and potential pitfalls. Following these tips from the Street-Smart Entrepreneur lowers the probability that you will get burned when you buy a business.

Sources: Based on Arden Dale and Simona Covel, "Sellers Offer a Financial Hand to Their Buyers," *Wall Street Journal*, November 13, 2008, p. B6; Joseph Anthony, "Seven Tips for Buying a Business," Microsoft Small Business Center, *www.microsoft.com/smallbusiness/resources/startups/business_opportunities/7_tips_for_buying_a_business.aspx.*

Michael and Xochi Birch sold their social networking site Bebo to AOL for $850 million.

Source: UPPA/Photoshot/Newscom

Methods for Determining the Value of a Business

3. Describe the various methods used in valuing a business.

Business valuation is part art and part science. The sheer number of variables that influence the value of a privately owned business make establishing a price difficult. These factors include the nature of the business itself, its position in the market or industry, the outlook for the market or industry, the company's financial status and stability, its earning capacity, intangible assets (such as patents, trademarks, and copyrights), the value of similar companies that are publicly owned, and many others. The median selling price of a private company is $560,000, according to a database compiled by Business Valuation Resources, a company that tracks private company transactions (see Figure 1).[12] However, some businesses sell for much more. Xochi and Michael Birch recently sold Bebo, the social networking site they built, to industry giant AOL, which was looking to expand its social media presence, for $850 million. Even though Bebo was small compared to Facebook and MySpace, the Birch's 3-year-old company had built a huge following in Great Britain.[13]

Assessing the value of the company's tangible assets usually is straightforward, but assigning a price to the intangible assets, such as goodwill, almost always creates controversy. The seller expects the value of the goodwill to reflect the hard work and long hours invested in building the business. The buyer, however, is willing to pay only for those intangible assets that produce

FIGURE 1
Selling Prices of Private Companies

Source: Business Valuation Resources, 2009. *http://www.bvmarketdata.com/defaulttextonly.asp?f=Database%20Chart*

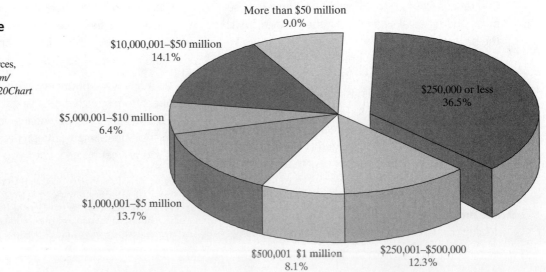

More than $50 million
9.0%

$10,000,001–$50 million
14.1%

$5,000,001–$10 million
6.4%

$1,000,001–$5 million
13.7%

$500,001 $1 million
8.1%

$250,001–$500,000
12.3%

$250,000 or less
36.5%

extra income. How can a buyer and a seller arrive at a fair price? There are few hard-and-fast rules in establishing the value of a business, but the following guidelines can help:

- There is no single best method for determining a business's worth because each business sale is unique. A practical approach is to estimate a company's value using several techniques, review those values, and then determine the range in which most of the values converge.
- The deal must be financially feasible for both parties to be viable. The seller must be satisfied with the price received for the business, and the buyer cannot pay an excessively high price that requires heavy borrowing that strains cash flow from the outset.
- The buyer should have access to all business records.
- Valuations should be based on facts, not feelings or fiction.
- The two parties should deal with one another openly, honestly, and in good faith.

The main reason that buyers purchase existing businesses is to get their future earning potential. The second most common reason is to obtain an established asset base; it is much easier to buy assets than to build them. Although some valuation methods take these goals into consideration, many business sellers and buyers simplify the process by relying on rules of thumb to estimate the value of a business. For instance, one rule for valuing sporting goods stores is 30 percent of its annual sales plus its inventory.[14] Other rules use multiples of a company's net earnings to value the business. Although the multipliers vary by industry, most small companies sell for 2 to 12 times their earnings before interest and taxes (EBIT), with an average selling price of between 6 and 7 times EBIT.[15] For instance, a study by Business Valuation Resources of 2,168 business sales over a recent 3-year period shows that the median selling price of a restaurant is 2.45 times EBIT, the median price of a car wash is 6.27 times EBIT, and the median price of a business consulting service is 11.56 times EBIT.[16] Factors that increase the value of the multiplier include proprietary products and patents; a strong, diversified customer base; an above-average growth rate; a strong, balanced management team; and a dominant market share. Factors that decrease the value of the multiplier include generic, "me-too" products; dependence on a single customer or a small group of customers for a significant portion of sales; reliance on the skills of a single manager (e.g., the founder); declining market share; and dependence on a single product for generating sales.[17]

This section describes three basic techniques—the balance sheet method, the earnings approach, and the market approach—and several variations on them for determining the value of a hypothetical business, Luxor Electronics.

Balance Sheet Technique

The balance sheet method computes the book value of a company's **net worth**, or **owner's equity** (net worth = assets − liabilities) and uses this figure as the value. A criticism of this technique is that it oversimplifies the valuation process. The problem with this technique is that it fails to recognize reality: Most small businesses have market values that exceed their reported book values.

The first step is to determine which assets are included in the sale. In most cases, the owner has some personal assets that he or she does not want to sell. Professional business brokers can help the buyer and the seller arrive at a reasonable value for the collection of assets included in the deal. Remember that net worth on a financial statement will likely differ significantly from actual net worth in the market. Figure 2 shows the balance sheet for Luxor Electronics. This balance sheet shows that the company's net worth is:

$$\$266,091 - \$114,325 = \$151,766$$

VARIATION: ADJUSTED BALANCE SHEET TECHNIQUE. A more realistic method for determining a company's value is to adjust the book value of net worth to reflect the actual market value. The values reported on a company's books may either overstate or understate the true value of assets and liabilities. Typical assets in a business sale include notes and accounts receivable, inventory, supplies, and fixtures. If a buyer purchases notes and accounts receivable, he or she should estimate the likelihood of their collection and adjust their value accordingly (refer to Table 1).

FIGURE 2
Balance Sheet for Luxor Electronics, June 30, 20XX

ASSETS		
Current Assets		
Cash		$11,655
Accounts receivable		15,876
Inventory		56,523
Supplies		8,574
Prepaid insurance		5,587
Total current assets		**$98,215**
Fixed Assets		
Land		$24,000
Buildings	$141,000	
less accumulated depreciation	51,500	89,500
Office equipment	$12,760	
less accumulated depreciation	7,159	5,601
Factory equipment	$59,085	
less accumulated depreciation	27,850	31,235
Trucks and autos	$28,730	
less accumulated depreciation	11,190	17,540
Total fixed assets		**$167,876**
Total Assets		**$266,091**
LIABILITIES		
Current Liabilities		
Accounts payable		$19,497
Mortgage payable		5,215
Salaries payable		3,671
Note payable		10,000
Total current liabilities		**$38,383**
Long-Term Liabilities		
Mortgage payable		$54,542
Note payable		21,400
Total long-term liabilities		**$75,942**
Total Liabilities		**$114,325**
OWNER'S EQUITY		
Owner's Equity (Net Worth)		$151,766
Total Liabilities + Owner's Equity		**$266,091**

In manufacturing, wholesale, and retail businesses, inventory is usually the largest single asset in the sale. Taking a physical inventory count is the best way to determine accurately the condition and quantity of goods to be transferred. The sale may include three types of inventory, each having its own method of valuation: raw materials, work-in-process, and finished goods. Before accepting any inventory value, a buyer should evaluate the condition of the goods to avoid being stuck with inventory that he or she cannot sell.

Fixed assets transferred in a sale might include land, buildings, equipment, and fixtures. Business owners frequently carry real estate and buildings on their books at their original purchase prices, which typically are well below their actual market value. Equipment and fixtures, depending on their condition and usefulness, may increase or decrease the value of the business. Appraisals of these assets on insurance policies are helpful guidelines for establishing market value. In addition, business brokers can be useful in determining the current value of fixed assets. Some brokers use an estimate of what it would cost to replace a company's physical assets (less a reasonable

FIGURE 3
Adjusted Balance Sheet for Luxor Electronics, June 30, 20XX

ASSETS			
Current Assets			
Cash		$11,655	
Accounts receivable		10,051	
Inventory		39,261	
Supplies		7,492	
Prepaid insurance		5,587	
Total current assets			$74,046
Fixed Assets			
Land		$52,000	
Buildings	$177,000		
less accumulated depreciation	51,500	115,500	
Office equipment	$11,645		
less accumulated depreciation	7,159	4,486	
Factory equipment	$50,196		
less accumulated depreciation	27,850	22,346	
Trucks and autos	$22,550		
less accumulated depreciation	11,190	11,360	
Total fixed assets			$205,692
Total Assets			**$279,738**
LIABILITIES			
Current Liabilities			
Accounts payable		$19,497	
Mortgage payable		5,215	
Salaries payable		3,671	
Not payable		10,000	
Total current liabilities			$38,383
Long-Term Liabilities			
Mortgage payable		$54,542	
Note payable		21,400	
Total long-term liabilities			$75,942
Total Liabilities			**$114,325**
OWNER'S EQUITY			
Owner's Equity (Net Worth)			$165,413
Total Liabilities + Owner's Equity			**$279,738**

allowance for depreciation) to determine their value. As indicated by the adjusted balance sheet in Figure 3, the adjusted net worth for Luxor Electronics is $279,738 − $114,325 = $165,413, which indicates that some of the entries on its books did not accurately reflect market value.

Business valuations based on any balance sheet methods suffer one major drawback: They do not consider the future earnings potential of the business. These techniques value assets at current prices and do not consider them as tools for creating future profits. The next method for computing the value of a business is based on its expected future earnings.

Earnings Approach

The buyer of an existing business is purchasing its future income potential. The **earnings approach** is more refined than the balance sheet method because it considers the future income potential of the business.

VARIATION 1: EXCESS EARNINGS METHOD. This method combines both the value of a company's existing assets (less its liabilities) and an estimate of its future earnings potential to determine the selling price for the business. One advantage of the **excess earnings method** is that it offers an estimate of goodwill. **Goodwill** is the difference between an established, successful business and one that has yet to prove itself. Goodwill is based on the company's reputation and its ability to attract customers. This intangible asset often creates problems in a business sale. A common method of valuing a business is to compute its tangible net worth and then to add an often arbitrary adjustment for goodwill. A buyer should not accept blindly the seller's arbitrary adjustment for goodwill because it is likely to be inflated.

The excess earnings method provides a reasonable approach for determining the value of goodwill. It measures goodwill by the amount of profit the business earns above that of the average firm in the same industry. It also assumes that the owner is entitled to a reasonable return on the company's adjusted tangible net worth.

Step 1   *Compute adjusted tangible net worth.* Using the previous method of valuation, the buyer should compute the company's adjusted tangible net worth. Total tangible assets (adjusted for market value) minus total liabilities yields adjusted tangible net worth. In the Luxor Electronics example, and as shown in Figure 2, the adjusted tangible net worth is $279,738 − $114,325 = $165,413.

Step 2   *Calculate the opportunity costs of investing in the business.* **Opportunity costs** represent the cost of forgoing a choice; that is, what income does the potential buyer give up by purchasing the business? If the buyer chooses to purchase the assets of a business, he or she cannot invest his or her money elsewhere. Therefore, the opportunity cost of the purchase is the amount that the buyer could have earned by investing the same amount *in a similar risk investment*.

Three components determine the rate of return used to value a business: (1) the basic, risk-free return, (2) an inflation premium, and (3) the risk allowance for investing in the particular business. The basic, risk-free return and the inflation premium are reflected in investments such as U.S. Treasury bonds. To determine the appropriate rate of return for investing in a business, the buyer must add to this base rate a factor reflecting the risk of purchasing the company. The greater the risk involved, the higher the rate of return. An average-risk business typically indicates a 20 to 25 percent rate of return. For Luxor Electronics, the opportunity cost of the investment is $165,413 × 25% = $41,353.

The second part of the buyer's opportunity cost is the salary that he or she could have earned working for someone else. For the Luxor Electronics example, if the buyer purchases the business, he or she must forgo a salary of, say, $35,000 that he or she could have earned working elsewhere. Adding these amounts yields a total opportunity cost of 41,353 + 35,000 = $76,353.

Step 3   *Project net earnings.* The buyer must estimate the company's net earnings for the upcoming year before subtracting the owner's salary. Averages can be misleading; therefore, the buyer must be sure to investigate the *trend* of net earnings. Have the earnings risen steadily over the past 5 years, dropped significantly, remained relatively constant, or fluctuated wildly? Past income statements provide useful guidelines for estimating earnings. In the Luxor Electronics example, the buyer and an accountant project net earnings to be $88,000.

Step 4   *Compute extra earning power.* A company's **extra earning power** is the difference between forecasted earnings (step 3) and total opportunity costs of investing (step 2). Many small businesses that are for sale do not have extra earning power (i.e., excess earnings), and they show marginal or no profits. The extra earning power of Luxor Electronics is: $88,000 − $76,353 = $11,647.

Step 5   *Estimate the value of intangibles.* The buyer can use the business's extra earning power to estimate the value of its intangible assets. Multiplying the extra earning power by a years-of-profit figure yields an estimate of the intangible assets' value. The years-of-profit figure for a normal-risk business typically ranges from three to four. A high-risk business may have a years-of-profit figure of one, whereas a well-established firm might use a figure of seven.

Rating the company on a scale of 1 (low) to 7 (high) on the following factors allows an entrepreneur to calculate a reasonable years-of-profit figure to use to estimate the value of the intangibles:[18]

Factor	Score						
	1	2	3	4	5	6	7
1. Risk	More risky				Less risky		
2. Degree of competition	Intense competition				Few competitors		
3. Industry attractiveness	Fading				Attractive		
4. Barriers to entry	Low				High		
5. Growth potential	Low				High		
6. Owner's reason for selling	Poor performance				Retiring		
7. Age of business	Young				10+ years old		
8. Current owner's tenure	Short				10+ years		
9. Profitability	Below average				Above average		
10. Location	Problematic				Desirable		
11. Customer base	Limited and shrinking				Diverse and growing		
12. Image and reputation	Poor				Stellar		

To calculate the years-of-profit figure, the entrepreneur adds the score for each factor and divides by the number of factors (in this example, 12). For Luxor Electronics, the scores are as follows:

Risk	3
Degree of competition	2
Industry attractiveness	4
Barriers to entry	2
Growth potential	4
Owner's reason for selling	6
Age of business	6
Owner's tenure	6
Profitability	4
Location	4
Customer base	3
Image and reputation	5
Total	49

Thus, for Luxor Electronics the years-of-profit figure is $49 \div 12 = 4.1$ and the value of intangibles is $11,647 \times 4.1 = \$47,752$.

Step 6   *Determine the value of the business.* To determine the value of the business, the buyer simply adds together the adjusted tangible net worth (step 1) and the value of the intangibles (step 5). Using this method, the value of Luxor Electronics is $165,413 + \$47,752 = \$213,165$.

Both the buyer and seller should consider the tax implications of transferring goodwill. Because the *buyer* can amortize both the cost of goodwill and a restrictive covenant over 15 years, the tax treatment of either would be the same. However, the *seller* would prefer to have the amount of the purchase price in excess of the value of the assets allocated to goodwill, which is a capital asset. The gain on the capital asset is taxed at the lower capital gains rates. If that same amount were allocated to a restrictive covenant (which is negotiated with the seller personally, not the business), the seller must treat it as ordinary income, which is taxed at regular rates that currently are higher than the capital gains rates.

VARIATION 2: CAPITALIZED EARNINGS APPROACH. Another earnings approach capitalizes expected net earnings to determine the value of a business. The buyer should prepare his own pro forma income statement and should ask the seller to prepare one also. Many appraisers use a 5-year weighted average of past sales (with the greatest weights assigned to the most recent years) to estimate sales for the upcoming year.

Once again, the buyer must evaluate the risk of purchasing the business to determine the appropriate rate of return on the investment. The greater the perceived risk, the higher the return the buyer will require. Risk determination is always somewhat subjective, but it is a necessary consideration for proper evaluation.

The **capitalized earnings approach** divides estimated net earnings (after subtracting the owner's reasonable salary) by the rate of return that reflects the risk level. For Luxor Electronics, the capitalized value (assuming a reasonable salary of $35,000) is:

$$\frac{\text{Net earnings (after deducting owner's salary)}}{\text{Rate of return}} = \frac{\$88,000 - \$35,000}{25\%} = \$212,000$$

Companies with lower risk factors offer greater certainty and, therefore, are more valuable. In this example, a lower rate of return of 10 percent yields a value of $530,000 compared to those with higher risk factors of 50 percent rate of return, which produces a value of $106,000. Most normal-risk businesses use a rate-of-return factor ranging from 20 to 25 percent. The lowest risk factor that most buyers would accept for any business ranges from 15 to 18 percent.

VARIATION 3: DISCOUNTED FUTURE EARNINGS APPROACH. This variation of the earnings approach assumes that a dollar earned in the future will be worth less than that same dollar today. Using the **discounted future earnings approach**, the buyer estimates the company's net income for several years into the future and then discounts these future earnings back to their present value. The resulting present value is an estimate of the company's worth. The present value represents the cost of the buyers' giving up the opportunity to earn a reasonable rate of return by receiving income in the future instead of today.

To visualize the importance of present value and the time value of money, consider two $1 million sweepstakes winners. Rob wins $1 million in a sweepstakes, and he receives it in $50,000 installments over 20 years. If Rob invests every installment at 8 percent interest, he will have accumulated $2,288,098 at the end of 20 years. Lisa wins $1 million in another sweepstakes, but she collects her winnings in one lump sum. If Lisa invests her $1 million today at 8 percent, she will have accumulated $4,660,957 at the end of 20 years. The dramatic difference in their wealth—Lisa is now worth nearly $2,373,000 more—is the result of the time value of money.

The discounted future earnings approach has five steps:

Step 1   *Project earnings for 5 years into the future.* One way is to assume that earnings will grow by a constant amount over the next 5 years. Perhaps a better method is to develop three forecasts—pessimistic, most likely, and optimistic—for each year and find a weighted average using the following formula:

$$\text{Forecasted earnings for year } i = \frac{\begin{array}{c}\text{Pessimistic} \\ \text{earnings} \\ \text{for year } i\end{array} + \begin{array}{c}4 \times \text{Most Likely} \\ \text{earnings for} \\ \text{year } i\end{array} + \begin{array}{c}\text{Optimistic} \\ \text{earnings} \\ \text{year } i\end{array}}{6}$$

The most likely forecast is weighted 4 times greater than the pessimistic and optimistic forecasts; therefore, the denominator is the sum of the weights (1 + 4 + 1 = 6). For Luxor Electronics, the buyer's earnings forecasts are:

Year	Pessimistic	Most Likely	Optimistic	Weighted Average
XXX1	$75,000	$88,000	$92,000	**$86,500**
XXX2	78,000	91,000	98,000	**90,000**
XXX3	82,000	95,000	105,000	**94,500**
XXX4	85,000	103,000	109,000	**101,000**
XXX5	88,000	110,000	115,000	**107,167**

The buyer must remember that the further into the future he forecasts, the less reliable the estimates will be.

Step 2   *Discount these future earnings using the appropriate present value factor.* The appropriate present value factor can be found by looking in published present value tables or by solving the equation

$$1/(1+k)^t$$

where k = rate of return

and t = time (year 1, 2, 3, ... n)

The rate that the buyer selects should reflect the rate that he or she could earn on an investment of similar risk. Because Luxor Electronics is a normal-risk business, the buyer chooses 25 percent.

Year	Income Forecast (Weighted Average)	Present Value Factor (at 25 percent)	Net Present Value
XXX1	$86,500	.8000	$69,200
XXX2	90,000	.6400	57,600
XXX3	94,500	.5120	48,384
XXX4	101,000	.4096	41,369
XXX5	107,167	.3277	35,116
Total			**$251,670**

Step 3   *Estimate the income stream beyond 5 years.* One technique suggests multiplying the 5th-year income by 1/(rate of return). For Luxor Electronics, the estimate is:

Income beyond year 5 = $111,667 × (1/25%) = $428,667

Step 4   *Discount the income estimate beyond 5 years using the present value factor for the 6th year.* For Luxor Electronics:

Present value of income beyond year 5: $428,667 × 0.2621 = $112,372

Step 5   *Compute the total value of the business.*

Total value: $251,670 + $117,372 = $364,042

The primary advantage of this technique is that it evaluates a business solely on the basis of its future earnings potential, but its reliability depends on making accurate forecasts of future earnings and on choosing a realistic present value factor. The discounted future earnings approach is especially well suited for valuing service businesses, whose asset bases are often small, and for companies experiencing high growth rates.

Market Approach

The **market** (or **price/earnings**) **approach** uses the price/earnings ratios of similar businesses to establish the value of a company. The buyer must use businesses whose stocks are publicly traded in order to get a meaningful comparison. A company's price/earnings ratio (or P/E ratio) is the price of one share of its common stock in the market divided by its earnings per share (after deducting preferred stock dividends). To get a representative P/E ratio, the buyer should average the P/Es of as many similar businesses as possible.

The buyer multiplies the average P/E ratio by the private company's estimated earnings to compute a company's value. For example, suppose that the buyer found four companies comparable to Luxor Electronics, but whose stock is publicly traded. Their P/E ratios are:

Company 1	3.3
Company 2	3.8
Company 3	4.3
Company 4	4.1
Average	3.875

This average P/E ratio produces a value of $341,000:

$$\text{Value} = \text{Average P/E ratio} \times \text{Estimated net earnings}$$
$$3.875 \times \$88,000 = \$341,000$$

The most significant advantage of the market approach is its simplicity. However, the market approach method does have several disadvantages, including:

1. **Necessary comparisons between publicly traded and privately owned companies.** The stock of privately owned companies is illiquid; therefore, the P/E ratio used is often subjective and lower than that of publicly held companies.
2. **Unrepresentative earnings estimates.** The private company's net earnings may not realistically reflect its true earnings potential. To minimize taxes, owners usually attempt to keep profits low and rely on benefits to make up the difference.
3. **Finding similar companies for comparison.** Often, it is extremely difficult for a buyer to find comparable publicly held companies when estimating the appropriate P/E ratio.
4. **Applying the after-tax earnings of a private company to determine its value.** If a prospective buyer is using an after-tax P/E ratio from a public company, he also must use the after-tax earnings from the private company.

Despite its drawbacks, the market approach is useful as a general guideline to establishing a company's value.

The Best Method

Which of these methods is best for determining the value of a small business? Simply stated, there is no single best method. These techniques yield a range of values, and buyers should look for values that cluster together and then use their best judgment to determine an offering price. The final price of the business depends on the value estimates that the buyer derives and the negotiating skills of both parties.

Negotiating the Deal

4. Discuss the process of negotiating the deal.

Once an entrepreneur has established a reasonable value for the business, the next step in making a successful purchase is negotiating a suitable deal. Most buyers do not realize that the price they pay for a company often is not as crucial to its continued success as the terms of the purchase. In other words, *the structure of the deal—the terms and conditions of payment—is more important than the actual price the seller agrees to pay.*

Wise business buyers attempt to negotiate the best price they can, but they pay more attention to negotiating favorable terms: how much cash they pay out and when, how much of the price the seller is willing to finance and for how long, the interest rate at which the deal is financed, and others. The buyer's primary concern is to ensure that the deal does not endanger the company's financial future and that it preserves the company's cash flow.

On the surface, the negotiation process may appear to be strictly adversarial. Although each party may be trying to accomplish objectives that are at odds with those of the opposing party, the negotiation process does not have to be conflict-oriented. The process goes more smoothly and faster if the two parties work to establish a cooperative relationship based on honesty and trust from the outset. A successful deal requires both parties to examine and articulate their respective positions while trying to understand the other party's position. Recognizing that neither of them will benefit without a deal, both parties must work to achieve their objectives while making certain concessions to keep the negotiations alive.

To avoid a stalled deal, both buyer and seller should go into the negotiation with a list of objectives ranked in order of priority. Prioritizing desired outcomes increases the likelihood that both parties will get most of what they want from the bargain. Knowing which terms are most (and least) important enables the parties to make concessions without regret and avoid getting bogged down in unnecessary details. If, for instance, the seller insists on a term that the buyer cannot agree to, the seller can explain why he cannot concede on that term and then offer to give up something in exchange. The following negotiating tips can help parties reach a mutually satisfying deal:

■ *Know what you want to have when you walk away from the table.* What will it take to reach your business objectives? What would the perfect deal be? Although it may not be possible to achieve it, defining the perfect deal may help to identify which issues are most important to you.

- *Develop a negotiation strategy.* Once you know where you want to finish, decide where you will start and remember to leave some room to give. Try not to be the first one to mention price. Let the other party do that; then negotiate from there.
- *Recognize the other party's needs.* For a bargain to occur, both parties must believe that they have met at least some of their goals. Asking open-ended questions can provide insight to the other side's position and enable you to understand why it is important.
- *Be an empathetic listener.* To truly understand what the other party's position is, you must listen attentively.
- *Focus on the issue, not on the person.* If the negotiation reaches an impasse, a natural tendency is to attack the other party. Instead, focus on developing a workable solution to accomplish your goals.
- *Avoid seeing the other side as "the enemy."* This type of an attitude reduces the negotiation to an "I win, you lose" mentality that only hinders the process.
- *Educate; don't intimidate.* Rather than trying to bully the other party into accepting your point of view, explain the reasoning and the logic behind your proposal.
- *Be patient.* Resist the tendency to become angry and insulted at the proposals the other party makes. Similarly, do not be in such a hurry to close the deal that you give in on crucial points.
- *Remember that "no deal" is an option.* What would happen if the negotiations failed to produce a deal? In most negotiations, walking away from the table *is* an option. In some cases, it may be the best option.
- *Be flexible and creative.* Always have a fallback position—an alternative that, although less-than-ideal, is acceptable to you and to the other party.

In general, the seller of the business is looking to:

- Get the highest price possible for the company.
- Sever all responsibility for the company's liabilities.
- Avoid unreasonable contract terms that might limit future opportunities.
- Maximize the cash from the deal.
- Minimize the tax burden from the sale.
- Make sure the buyer will make all future payments.

The buyer seeks to:

- Get the business at the lowest price possible.
- Negotiate favorable payment terms, preferably over time.
- Get assurances that he is buying the business he thinks it is.
- Avoid enabling the seller to open a competing business.
- Minimize the amount of cash paid up front.

Entrepreneurs who are most effective at acquiring a business know how important it is to understand the complex emotions that influence the seller's behavior and decisions. For many sellers, the businesses that they created have been a significant part of their lives and have defined their identities. They nurtured their companies through their infancy and helped them grow, and letting them go is not easy. Sellers may be asking themselves, "What will I do now? Where will I go each morning? Who will I be without my business?" The negotiation process may bring these questions to light as it requires sellers to, in effect, put a price tag on their life's work. For these reasons, the potential buyer must negotiate in a manner that displays sensitivity and respect.

The "Art of the Deal"

Both buyers and sellers must recognize that no one benefits without an agreement. Both parties must work to achieve their goals while making concessions to keep the negotiations alive.

Figure 4 is an illustration of two people prepared to negotiate for the purchase and sale of a business. The buyer and seller both have high and low bargaining points in this example:

- The buyer would like to purchase the business for $900,000 but would not pay more than $1,300,000.

FIGURE 4
Identifying the Bargaining Zone

The seller would like to get $1,500,000 for the business but would not take less than $1,000,000.

- The seller would like to get $1,500,000 for the business but would not take less than $1,000,000.
- If the seller insists on getting $1,500,000, there will be no deal.
- Likewise, if the buyer stands firm on an offer of $900,000, there will be no deal.

The bargaining process usually leads both parties into the *bargaining zone*, the area within which the buyer and the seller can reach an agreement. It extends from above the lowest price the seller is willing to take to below the maximum price the buyer is willing to pay. The dynamics of this negotiation process and the needs of each party ultimately determine whether the buyer and seller can reach an agreement and, if so, its terms.

Learning to negotiate successfully means mastering "the art of the deal." The following guidelines help the parties involved see the negotiation as a conference, which is likely to produce positive results, rather than as a competition, which will likely spiral downward into conflict.

ESTABLISH THE PROPER MIND-SET. Successful negotiations are built on a foundation of trust. The first step in any negotiation should be to establish a climate of trust and communication. Too often, buyers and sellers rush into putting their chips on the bargaining table without establishing a rapport with one another:

UNDERSTAND THE RULES. Recognize the "rules" of successful negotiations:

- Everything is negotiable.
- Take nothing for granted.
- Consider the other party's perspective.
- Be willing to explore a variety of options.
- Seek solutions that are mutually beneficial.

DEVELOP A NEGOTIATING STRATEGY. One of the biggest mistakes business buyers can make is entering negotiations with only a vague notion of the strategies they will employ. To be successful, a negotiator must be able to respond to a variety of situations that are likely to arise, and that requires a strategy. Every strategy has an upside and a downside, and effective negotiators know what they are.

BE CREATIVE. When negotiations stall or come to an impasse, negotiators must seek creative alternatives that benefit both parties or, at a minimum, get the negotiations started again.

KEEP EMOTIONS IN CHECK. A short temper and an important negotiation make ill-suited partners. The surest way to destroy trust and to sabotage a negotiation is to lose one's temper and lash out at the other party. Anger leads to poor decisions.

BE PATIENT. Sound negotiations often take a great deal of time, especially when one is buying a business from the entrepreneur who founded it. The seller's ego is woven into the negotiation process, and wise negotiators recognize this. Persistence and patience are the keys to success in any negotiation involving the sale of the business.

DON'T BECOME A VICTIM. Well-prepared negotiators are not afraid to walk away from deals that are not right for them.

▶ ENTREPRENEURSHIP IN ACTION ▶

What's the Deal?

Country Lanes North

Robert Carlson started Country Lanes North, a 24-lane bowling alley in Duluth, Minnesota, in 1976 with two partners. Carlson gradually bought out his partners and brought his two sons into the business as owners. Scott Carlson, who began working at the bowling alley in high school, took over the management of Country Lanes when his father semi-retired in the late 1990s. Scott has considered borrowing the money to buy out his father and his brother so that he can have sole ownership of the business, but tight financial markets are making it difficult to find the necessary capital. "I have always worked for my father," says Scott. "Now it's time to cash out and let him enjoy his retirement."

In addition to the bowling alley, Country Lanes North, which includes 2.5 acres of land, contains three outdoor volleyball courts, two bars, and a restaurant. Approximately 55 percent of the company's $750,000 in annual revenue comes from bowling, 34 percent comes from food and beverage sales, and the remainder comes from the pro shop and equipment rentals. Although the company's revenue peaked at $1 million in 2003, sales for the current year are running 30 percent above those of the previous year. Four other bowling alleys operate in the Duluth area, but Country Lanes North recently signed an agreement to host an upcoming United States Bowling Congress state championship. Online competitors have cut into sales at the pro shop, and the hardwood alleys will require resurfacing within the next 10 years at an estimated cost of $120,000. The Carlson's asking price is $2.4 million, which includes $20,000 in inventory and $500,000 in equipment. Scott wants to stay with the company and manage it for the new owner. "I've been living my dream here," he says, "and I would like to keep living it."

Classic Pizza Crust

In 1998, Dominick Fimiano, started Classic Pizza Crust, a maker of frozen pizza dough and crusts and complete, ready-to-bake pizzas in Pompano Beach, Florida. Customers include schools, hospitals, bowling alleys, amusement parks, and others that have small kitchens and require pizzas that are easy to heat and serve. In 2003, Fimiano borrowed $700,000, which he used to purchase equipment for a modern manufacturing plant. The move resulted in a sales growth spurt, and Fimiano sees more growth potential for the company in the future even though the company has spent very little on marketing in recent years. Capitalizing on that growth potential would require Fimiano to borrow more capital, but at age 70 Fimiano is ready to retire. Anthony Fimiano, Dominick's oldest son, has played a key role in the company's growth but does not have the capital necessary to fuel the company's growth. Dominick is looking for a buyer who will allow Anthony, 31, to continue to work at the company.

Dominick's asking price is $1.2 million, which includes the new equipment. Because Dominick plans to use the sale proceeds to pay off the company's debt, the buyer will not have to assume any significant liabilities. The buyer can assume Classic Pizza Crust's $9,300 monthly lease on the $10,000-square-foot building the company occupies. Annual sales are expected to increase to $1.5 million next year from $885,000 this year, but the company's profits have been uneven in recent years.

1. Assume the role of a prospective buyer for these two businesses. How would you conduct the due diligence necessary to determine whether they would be good investments?
2. Do you notice any red flags or potential sticking points in either of these deals? Explain.
3. Which techniques for estimating the value of a business described in this chapter would be most useful to a prospective buyer of these businesses? Are the owners' asking prices reasonable?

Sources: Based on Darren Dahl, "Business for Sale: A 24-Lane Bowling Center, for $2.4 Million," *Inc.*, July–August 2009, p. 28; Darren Dahl, "Business for Sale: For the Seasoned Buyer," *Inc.*, November 2008, p. 32.

Structuring the Deal

To make a negotiation work, the buyer and the seller must structure the deal in a way that is acceptable to both parties. Several options are available.

STRAIGHT BUSINESS SALE. A straight business sale may be best for a seller who wants to step down and turn over the reins of the company to someone else. A study of small business sales in 60 categories found that 94 percent were asset sales; the remaining 6 percent involved the sale of stock. About 22 percent were for cash, and 75 percent included a down payment with a note carried by the seller. The remaining 3 percent relied on a note from the seller with no down payment. When the deal included a down payment, it averaged 33 percent of the purchase price. Only 40 percent of the business sales studied included covenants not to compete. Although cash only deals are not viable for most business buyers, they typically produce a discount of 10 to 15 percent of the asking price.[19]

Although selling a business outright is often the safest exit path for an entrepreneur, it is usually the most expensive. Sellers who want cash and take the money up front may face a significant tax burden. They must pay a capital gains tax on the sale price less their investments in the company. Nor is a straight sale an attractive exit strategy for those who want to stay on with the company or for those who want to surrender control of the company gradually rather than all at once.

Ideally, a buyer has already begun to explore the options available for financing the purchase. (Recall that many entrepreneurs include bankers on their teams of advisors.) If traditional lenders shy away from financing the purchase of an existing business, buyers often find themselves searching for alternative sources of funds. Fortunately, most business buyers discover an important source of financing built into the deal: the seller. Typically, a deal is structured so that the buyer makes a down payment to the seller, who then finances a note for the balance. The buyer makes regular principal and interest payments over time—perhaps with a larger balloon payment at the end—until the note is paid off. A common arrangement involves a down payment with the seller financing the remaining 20 to 70 percent of the purchase price over time, usually 3 to 10 years.

Sellers must be willing to finance a portion of the purchase price, particularly when credit is tight.

ENTREPRENEURIAL
Profile

Rick Hunt and Risk Removal

During a recent recession, Rick Hunt knew that he and his partners would have to accept a note for at least part of the purchase price of their Fort Collins, Colorado-based environmental services company, Risk Removal. With annual sales of $3 million and a good reputation in a lucrative niche market (the company removes asbestos and lead paint from buildings), Risk Removal had attracted attention from several buyers, but none had been able to close a financing deal. Hunt hired a business broker, and within months he and his partners had accepted an offer from a buyer who had experience in the business and could pay 25 percent of the purchase price in cash. A bank financed 50 percent of the price, and Hunt and his partners accepted a 5-year promissory note at 7 percent interest for the remaining 25 percent.[20]

SALE OF CONTROLLING INTEREST. Sometimes business owners sell a majority interest in their companies to investors, competitors, suppliers, or large companies with an agreement that the seller will stay on after the sale. This gives potential buyers more confidence in the acquisition if they know the current owner is willing to commit to a management contract for a few years. For the seller who does not want to retire or start a new business, a management contract can be an excellent source of income. Sellers rarely stay with their former companies for long, however, particularly when the new owner begins making significant changes to its operation.

ENTREPRENEURIAL
Profile

Chris DeWolfe and Tom Anderson and MySpace

Chris DeWolfe and Tom Anderson, cofounders of the social networking site MySpace, sold their company to News Corp., a media conglomerate for $650 million and agreed to stay on to manage the business for 4 years. News Corp., however, ousted DeWolfe and Anderson 7 months before their contracts were to expire and replaced them with a former top manager at Facebook.[21]

A variation on this option is an **earn-out**, a deal in which the seller agrees to accept a percentage of the asking price and stays on to manage the business for a few more years under the new owner. The remaining payment to the seller is contingent on the company's performance; the more profit the company generates during the earn-out period, the greater the payout to the seller. One disadvantage of this method for the seller is the risk of receiving a lower price if the company fails to meet the financial performance targets. One entrepreneur who sold his Internet business to a large company with an earn-out provision that proved to be worthless when the business failed says that because earn outs are risky for the seller, they should make up no more than 50 percent of the total deal.[22]

ENTREPRENEURIAL
Profile

*James Essey and
TemPositions*

James Essey, CEO of TemPositions, a temporary staffing company based in New York City, recently purchased a competing staffing company in Queens, New York—Vintage Personnel—using an earn-out. The seller accepted a percentage of the selling price up front and agreed to stay on for 3 years, during which time he will receive 30 percent of Vintage Personnel's gross profits.[23]

RESTRUCTURE THE COMPANY. Another way for business owners to cash out gradually is to replace the existing corporation with a new one, formed with other investors. The owner essentially is performing a leveraged buyout of his own company. For example, assume that you own a company worth $15 million. You form a new corporation with $12 million borrowed from a bank and $3 million in equity: $1.5 million of your own equity and $1.5 million in equity from an investor who wants you to stay on with the business. The new company buys your company for $15 million. You net $13.5 in cash ($15 million minus your $1.5 million equity investment) and still own 50 percent of the new leveraged business (see Figure 5). For a medium-size business whose financial statement can justify a significant bank loan, this is an excellent alternative. This can be an option in cases where both parties agree that the seller should remain involved in the business.

Other Alternatives

FAMILY LIMITED PARTNERSHIP. Entrepreneurs who want to pass their businesses on to their children should consider forming a family limited partnership. Using this exit strategy, entrepreneurs can transfer their businesses to their children without sacrificing control over the business. The owner takes the role of general partner while the children become limited partners. The general partner keeps just 1 percent of the company, but the partnership agreement gives him or her total control over the business. The children own 99 percent of the company but have little or no say over how to run the business. Until the founder decides to step down and turn the reins of the company over to the next generation, he or she continues to run the business and sets up significant tax savings for the ultimate transfer of power.

EMPLOYEE STOCK OWNERSHIP PLAN (ESOP). Some owners cash out by selling to their employees through an **employee stock ownership plan (ESOP)**. An ESOP is a form of employee benefit plan in which a trust created for employees purchases their employers' stock. Here's how an ESOP works: The company transfers shares of its stock to the ESOP trust, and the trust uses the stock as collateral to borrow enough money to purchase the shares from the company. The company guarantees payment of the loan principal and interest and makes tax-deductible contributions to the trust to repay the loan. The company then distributes the stock to employees' accounts using a predetermined formula (see Figure 6). In addition to the tax benefits an ESOP offers, the plan permits the owner to transfer all or part of the company to employees as gradually or as suddenly as preferred.

**FIGURE 5
Restructuring a Business
for Sale**

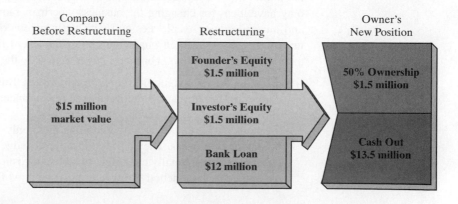

195

FIGURE 6
A Typical Employee Stock Ownership Plan (ESOP)

Source: Corey Rosen, "Sharing Ownership with Employees," *Small Business Reports*, December 1990, p. 63.

To use an ESOP successfully, a small business should be profitable (with pretax profits exceeding $100,000) and should have a payroll of at least $500,000 a year. In general, companies with fewer than 15 to 20 employees do not find ESOPs beneficial. For companies that prepare properly, however, ESOPs offer significant financial and managerial benefits. Owners get to sell off their stock at whatever annual pace appeals to them. There is no cost to the employees, who eventually get to take over the company, and for the company the cost of the buyout is fully deductible.

ENTREPRENEURIAL
Profile

Irene Firmat and James Emmerson and Full Sail Brewing

Source: Full Sail Brewing Company

In 1987, Irene Firmat and her husband, James Emmerson, launched a microbrewery, Full Sail Brewing, in a former fruit cannery in Hood River, Oregon. Production in their first year was just 287 barrels of beer, but customers enjoyed the company's hearty brews, and the business grew. In 1999, Firmat and Emmerson decided to establish an ESOP so that they could eventually turn ownership of the brewery over to their employees. Today, 55 of Full Sail Brewing's 90 employees are owners of the business. When Firmat and Emmerson decide to step down, they will be able to sell the brewery, which now produces 90,000 barrels of beer annually, to the people who have the greatest stake in it.[24]

SELL TO AN INTERNATIONAL BUYER. In an increasingly global marketplace, small U.S. businesses have become attractive buyout targets for foreign companies. In many instances, foreign companies buy U.S. businesses to gain access to a lucrative, growing market. They look for a team of capable managers, whom they typically retain for a given time period. They also want companies that are profitable, stable, and growing. Selling to foreign buyers can have disadvantages, however. Foreign buyers typically purchase 100 percent of a company, thereby making the previous owner merely an employee. Relationships with foreign owners also can be difficult to manage.

Ensure a Smooth Transition

Once the parties have negotiated a deal, the challenge of facilitating a smooth transition arises. No matter how well planned the sale is, there are always surprises. For instance, the new owner may have ideas for changing the business—perhaps radically—that cause a great deal of stress and anxiety among employees and with the previous owner. Charged with such emotion and uncertainty, the transition phase may be difficult and frustrating—and sometimes painful. To avoid a bumpy transition, a business buyer should do the following:

- Concentrate on communicating with employees. Business sales are fraught with uncertainty and anxiety, and employees need reassurance. Take the time to explain your plans for the company.
- Be honest with employees. Avoid telling them only what they want to hear.
- Listen to employees. They have intimate knowledge of the business and its strengths and weaknesses and usually can offer valuable suggestions. Keep your door and your ears open and come in as somebody who is going to be good for the company.

- Devote time to selling the vision for the company to its key stakeholders, including major customers, suppliers, bankers, and others.
- Consider asking the seller to serve as a consultant until the transition is complete. The previous owner can be a valuable resource.

Chapter Review

1. **Understand the advantages and disadvantages of buying an existing business.**
   - The *advantages* of buying an existing business include: a successful business may continue to be successful; the business may already have the best location; employees and suppliers are already established; equipment is installed and its productive capacity known; inventory is in place and trade credit established; the owner hits the ground running; the buyer can use the expertise of the previous owner; the business may be a bargain.
   - The *disadvantages* of buying an existing business include: an existing business may be for sale because it is deteriorating; the previous owner may have created ill will; employees inherited with the business may not be suitable; its location may have become unsuitable; equipment and facilities may be obsolete; change and innovation are hard to implement; inventory may be outdated; accounts receivable may be worth less than face value; the business may be overpriced.

2. **Conduct the detailed level of analysis necessary before buying a business.**
   - Buying a business can be a treacherous experience unless the buyer is well prepared. The right way to buy a business is: analyze your skills, abilities, and interests to determine the ideal business for you; prepare a list of potential candidates, including those that might be in the "hidden market"; investigate and evaluate candidate businesses and evaluate the best one; explore financing options before you actually need the money; and, finally, ensure a smooth transition.
   - Rushing into a deal can be the biggest mistake a business buyer can make. Before closing a deal, every business buyer should investigate five critical areas:
     1. Why does the owner wish to sell? Look for the real reason.
     2. Determine the physical condition of the business. Consider both the building and its location.
     3. Conduct a thorough analysis of the market for your products or services. Who are the present and potential customers? Conduct an equally thorough analysis of competitors, both direct and indirect. How do they operate and why do customers prefer them?
     4. Consider all of the legal aspects that might constrain the expansion and growth of the business. Did you comply with the provisions of a bulk transfer? Negotiate a restrictive covenant? Consider ongoing legal liabilities?
     5. Analyze the financial condition of the business, looking at financial statements, income tax returns, and especially cash flow.

3. **Describe the various methods used in the valuation of a business.**
   - Placing a value on a business is part art and part science. There is no single best method for determining the value of a business. The following techniques (with several variations) are useful: the balance sheet technique (adjusted balance sheet technique); the earnings approach (excess earnings method, capitalized earnings approach, and discounted future earnings approach); and the market approach.

4. **Discuss the process of negotiating the deal.**
   - Selling a business takes time, patience, and preparation to locate a suitable buyer, strike a deal, and make the transition. Sellers must always structure the deal with tax consequences in mind. Common exit strategies include a straight business sale, forming a family limited partnership, selling a controlling interest in the business, restructuring the company, selling to an international buyer, and establishing an employee stock ownership plan (ESOP).
   - The first rule of negotiating is never confuse price with value. The party who is the better negotiator usually comes out on top. Before beginning negotiations, a buyer should identify the factors that are affecting the negotiations and then develop a negotiating strategy. The best deals are the result of a cooperative relationship based on trust.

Discussion Questions

1. What advantages can an entrepreneur who buys a business gain over one who starts a business from scratch?
2. How would you go about determining the value of the assets of a business if you were unfamiliar with them?
3. Why do so many entrepreneurs run into trouble when they buy an existing business? Outline the steps involved in the *right* way to buy a business.
4. When evaluating an existing business that is for sale, what areas should an entrepreneur consider? Briefly summarize the key elements of each area.
5. How should a buyer evaluate a business's goodwill?
6. What is a restrictive covenant? Is it fair to ask the seller of a travel agency located in a small town to sign a restrictive covenant for 1 year covering a 20-square-mile area? Explain.

7. How much negative information can you expect the seller to give you about the business? How can a prospective buyer find out such information?
8. Why is it so difficult for buyers and sellers to agree on a price for a business?
9. Which method of valuing a business is best? Why?
10. Outline the different exit strategies available to a seller.
11. Explain the buyer's position in a typical negotiation for a business. Explain the seller's position. What tips would you offer a buyer about to begin negotiating the purchase of a business?
12. What benefits might you realize from using a business broker? What are the disadvantages?

This chapter addresses buying an existing business. If you are purchasing an existing business, determine whether the company has a business plan. If so, how recent is that plan? Is it representative of the current state of the organization? Is access available to other historical information including historical sales information and financial statements, such as the profit and loss, balance sheet, and cash flow statements? These documents are valuable resources to understand the business and develop a plan for its future.

On the Web

If the business has a Web site, review that site to assess the "online personality" of the business. Gather as much information as possible about the business from the Web site. Does it match the information from the owner and other documents? Conduct an online search for the business name and the owners' names. Note what you find and, again, determine whether this information correlates with information from other sources.

Review the executive summaries of these ongoing business plans through the Sample Plan Browser in Business Plan Pro:

- Machine Tooling
- Salvador's Sauces
- Sample Software Company
- Take Five Sports Bar
- Web Solutions, Inc.

Scan the table of contents and find the section of the plan with information on the company's past performance. What might this historical information indicate about the future potential of the venture? Which of these businesses present the greatest profit potential based on their past performance? Which business represents the greatest risk based on these same criteria? How might this risk influence the purchase price?

In the Software

If the company has sales, profits, and other information available, enter it into Business Plan Pro. First, select the "existing" business plan option in the opening window. If you have access to an electronic version of the company's plan you are considering purchasing, copy and paste text from a word processing document directly into Business Plan Pro by using the "Paste Special" option and then select the option "Without Formatting." This step will help to keep the formatting in order. Go to the "Company Summary" section and include the results of the due diligence process. The financial statements of the business, including the balance sheet, profit and loss, and cash flow statements from the past 3 years will be valuable. This will set a baseline for the future sales and expense scenarios. This process may help to better assess the business's future earning potential and its current value.

Building Your Business Plan

One of the advantages of using Business Plan Pro is the ease of creating multiple financial scenarios. This can be an excellent way to explore multiple "what if" options. Once the business is up and running, updating the plan during the fiscal year and on an annual basis can be a quick and easy process. This will be an efficient way to keep the plan current and, by saving each of these files based on the date for the example, offer an excellent historical account of the business.

Endnotes

1. David E. Gumpert, "Buying a Biz Instead of Starting One," *BusinessWeek,* August 21, 2006, *www.businessweek.com/smallbiz/content/aug2006/ sb20060821_514069.htm?chan=search.*

2. Julie Bawden Davis, "Buying an Existing Business? You'd Better Shop Around," *Entrepreneur,* August 1999, *www.entrepreneur.com/magazine/ entrepreneur/1999/august/18132.html.*

3. Lin Grensing-Pophal, "Decide Whether You'll Buy an Existing Business, a Business Opportunity, a Franchise, or Go It Alone," *Business Start-Ups,* December 2000.

4. Lil Sawyer, "Buying a Business: The Safer Alternative," *About.com, http://entrepreneurs.about.com/od/buyingabusiness/a/buyingabusiness .htm.*

5. "Buying a Business," Small Business Administration, *www. sba.gov/smallbusinessplanner/start/buyabusiness/SERV_SBP_S_ BUYB.html.*

6. Mina Kimes, "Sales Take Wing," *FSB,* December 2008/January 2009, p. 27; David Farkas, "Buffalo Wings and Rings Is Taking Flight," *Chain Leader,* September 1, 2009, *www.chainleader.com/article/ CA6686882.html.*

7. Justin Martin, "The Time to Sell Is Now!" *FSB,* September 2006, pp. 28–43.

8. B. G. Yovovich, "Why Start a Business When You Can Buy One?" *Satisfaction Magazine.com, www.satisfactionmag.com/index.php/2006/10/ why-start-a-business-when-you-can-buy-one/.*

9. Mark Blayney, *Buying a Business and Making It Work* (Oxford, England: How To Books Ltd., 2005), p. 420.

10. Robert F. Klueger, *Buying and Selling a Business: A Step by Step Guide* (New York: John Wiley & Sons, Inc., 2004), p. 12.

11. Edward Karstetter, "How Intangible Assets Affect Business Value," *Entrepreneur,* May 6, 2002, *http://Entrepreneur.com/article/ 0,4621,299514,00.html.*

12. "BV Market Data Database Summary," Business Valuation Resources, September 1, 2009, *www.bvmarketdata.com/defaulttextonly. asp?f=bvmdtable.*

13. Jason Del Rey, "This Couple Just Made $500 Million," *Inc.,* August 2008, pp. 19–20.

14. "Valuation Rule of Thumb," BizStats, *www.bizstats.com/reports/ valuation-rule-thumb.asp.*

15. Darren Dahl, "The Most Valuable Companies in America," *Inc.,* April 2008, pp. 97–105.

16. Ryan McCarthy, "A Buyer's Market," *Inc.,* June 2009, pp. 82–92.

17. James Laabs, "What Is Your Company Worth?" The Business Sale Center, *www.businesssalecenter.com/new_page_3.htm.*

18. "Business Planning Tools: Buying and Selling a Small Business," MasterCard Worldwide, *www.mastercard.com/us/business/en/smallbiz/ businessplanning/businessplanning.html,* p. 11.

19. Ryan McCarthy, "A Buyer's Market," *Inc.,* June 2009, p. 85.

20. Jeanne Lee, "Exit Strategies," *FSB,* April 2009, p. 49.

21. Emily Steel, "News Corp. May Sideline MySpace Founders," *Wall Street Journal,* April 23, 2009, p. B1; Julia Angwin and Emily Steel, "Founders Step Aside at MySpace," *Wall Street Journal,* April 23, 2009, *http://online.wsj.com/article/SB124043324710044929. html.*

22. Brandi Stewart and Scott Wainner, "Seller's Remorse," *FSB,* December 2008/January 2009, pp. 41–42.

23. Ryan McCarthy, "A Buyer's Market," *Inc.,* June 2009, p. 85.

24. Aaron Smith, "When Workers Take Charge: Full Sail Brewing Company," *CNNMoney,* September 23, 2009, *http://money.cnn.com/ galleries/2009/smallbusiness/0909/gallery.worker_owner_coop.smb/2. html;* Mark Graves, "Full Sail Brewing Woos New Audience with Dark Beer," *The Oregonian,* June 25, 2009, *www.oregonlive.com/business/ index.ssf/2009/06/full_sail_brewing_woos_new_aud.html.*

Conducting a Feasibility Analysis and Crafting a Winning Business Plan

Learning Objectives

Upon completion of this chapter, you will be able to:

1 Present the steps involved in conducting a feasibility analysis.
2 Explain the benefits of creating an effective business plan.
3 Explain the three tests every business plan must pass.
4 Describe the elements of a solid business plan.
5 Explain the "five Cs of credit" and why they are important to potential lenders and investors reviewing business plans.
6 Understand the keys to making an effective business plan presentation.

Before you build a better mouse trap, it helps to know if there are

any mice out there.

—Mortimer B. Zuckerman

Good fortune is what happens when opportunity meets with

planning.

—Thomas Alva Edison

For many entrepreneurs, the easiest part of launching a business is coming up with an idea for a new business concept or approach. Business success, however, requires much more than just a great new idea. Once entrepreneurs develop an idea for a business, the next step is to subject it to a feasibility analysis to determine whether they can transform the idea into a viable business. A **feasibility analysis** is the process of determining whether an entrepreneur's idea is a viable foundation for creating a successful business. Its purpose is to determine whether a business idea is worth pursuing. If the idea passes the feasibility analysis, the entrepreneur's next step is to build a solid business plan for capitalizing on the idea. If the idea fails to pass muster, the entrepreneur drops it and moves on to the next opportunity. He or she has not wasted valuable time, money, energy, and other resources creating a full-blown business plan, or worse, launching a business that is destined to fail because it is based on a flawed concept. Although it is impossible for a feasibility study to guarantee an idea's success, conducting a study reduces the likelihood that entrepreneurs will waste their time pursuing fruitless business ventures.

A feasibility study is *not* the same as a business plan; both play important, but separate, roles in the start-up process. A feasibility study answers the question, "Should we proceed with this business idea?" Its role is to serve as a filter, screening out ideas that lack the potential for building a successful business, *before* an entrepreneur commits the necessary resources to building a business plan. A feasibility study primarily is an *investigative* tool. It is designed to give an entrepreneur a picture of the market, sales, and profit potential of a particular business idea. Will a ski resort located here attract enough customers to be successful? Will customers in this community support a sandwich shop with a retro rock-n-roll theme? Can we build the product at a reasonable cost and sell it at a price customers are willing and able to pay? Does this entrepreneurial team have the ability to implement the idea successfully?

A business plan, in contrast, is a planning tool for transforming an idea into reality. It builds on the foundation of the feasibility study but provides a more comprehensive analysis than a feasibility study. It functions primarily as a planning tool, taking an idea that has passed the feasibility analysis and describing how to turn it into a successful business. Its primary goals are to guide entrepreneurs as they launch and operate their businesses and to help them acquire the financing needed to launch.

Feasibility studies are particularly useful when entrepreneurs have generated multiple ideas for business concepts and must winnow their options down to the "best choice." They enable entrepreneurs to explore quickly the practicality of each of several potential paths for transforming an idea into a successful business venture. Sometimes the result of a feasibility study is the realization that an idea simply won't produce a viable business—no matter how it is organized. In other cases, a study shows an entrepreneur that the business idea is a sound one but it must be organized in a different fashion to be profitable.

Research suggests that, whatever their size, companies that engage in business planning outperform those that do not. A business plan offers:

- A systematic, realistic evaluation of a venture's chances for success in the market
- A way to determine the principal risks facing the venture
- A "game plan" for managing the business successfully
- A tool for comparing actual results against targeted performance
- An important tool for attracting capital in the challenging hunt for money

The feasibility study and the business plan play important but separate roles in the start-up process. This chapter describes how to build and use these vital business documents, and it will help entrepreneurs create business plans that will guide them on their entrepreneurial journey and help them attract the capital they need to launch and grow their businesses.

Conducting a Feasibility Analysis

1. Present the steps involved in conducting a feasibility analysis.

A feasibility analysis consists of three interrelated components: an industry and market feasibility analysis, a product or service feasibility analysis, and a financial feasibility analysis (see Figure 1). "Making a critical evaluation of your business concept at an early stage will allow you to discover, address, and correct any fatal flaws before investing time in preparing your business plan," says Timothy Faley, managing director of the Samuel Zell & Robert H. Lurie Institute for Entrepreneurial Studies at the University of Michigan.[1]

FIGURE 1
Elements of a Feasibility Analysis

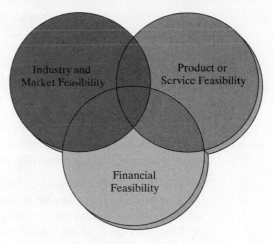

Industry and Market Feasibility Analysis

When evaluating the feasibility of a business idea, entrepreneurs find a basic analysis of the industry and targeted market segments a good starting point. The focus in this phase is twofold: (1) to determine how attractive an industry is overall as a "home" for a new business and (2) to identify possible niches a small business can occupy profitably.

The first step in assessing industry attractiveness is to paint a picture of the industry with broad strokes, assessing it from a "macro" level. Answering the following questions will help establish this perspective:

- How large is the industry?
- How fast is it growing?
- Is the industry as a whole profitable?
- Is the industry characterized by high profit margins or razor-thin margins?
- How essential are its products or services to customers?
- What trends are shaping the industry's future?
- What threats does the industry face?
- What opportunities does the industry face?
- How crowded is the industry?
- How intense is the level of competition in the industry?
- Is the industry young, mature, or somewhere in between?

Addressing these questions helps entrepreneurs determine whether the potential for sufficient demand for their products and services exists.

A useful tool for analyzing an industry's attractiveness is Porter's Five Forces model developed by Michael E. Porter of the Harvard Business School (see Figure 2). Five forces interact with one another to determine the setting in which companies compete and hence the attractiveness of the industry: (1) the rivalry among competing firms, (2) the bargaining power of suppliers,

FIGURE 2
Porter's Five Forces Model

Source: Adapted from Michael E. Porter, "How Competitive Forces Shape Strategy," *Harvard Business Review*, Volume 57, No. 2, March–April 1979, pp. 137–145. Reprinted by permission of Harvard Business School Publishing.

(3) the bargaining power of buyers, (4) the threat of new entrants, and (5) the threat of substitute products or services.

RIVALRY AMONG COMPANIES COMPETING IN THE INDUSTRY. The strongest of the five forces in most industries is the rivalry that exists among the businesses competing in a particular market. Much like the horses running in the Kentucky Derby, businesses in a market are jockeying for position in an attempt to gain a competitive advantage. When a company creates an innovation or develops a unique strategy that transforms the market, competing companies must adapt or run the risk of being forced out of business. This force makes markets a dynamic and highly competitive place. Generally, an industry is more attractive when:

- The number of competitors is large, or, at the other extreme, quite small (fewer than five).
- Competitors are not similar in size or capability.
- The industry is growing at a fast pace.
- The opportunity to sell a differentiated product or service is present.

BARGAINING POWER OF SUPPLIERS TO THE INDUSTRY. The greater the leverage that suppliers of key raw materials or components have, the less attractive is the industry. For instance, because they supply the chips that serve as the "brains" of PCs and because those chips make up a sizeable portion of the cost of a computer, chip makers such as Intel and Advanced Micro Devices (AMD) exert a great deal of power over computer manufacturers such as Dell, HP, and Gateway. Generally, an industry is more attractive when:

- Many suppliers sell a commodity product to the companies in it.
- Substitute products are available for the items suppliers provide.
- Companies in the industry find it easy to switch from one supplier to another or to substitute products (i.e., "switching costs" are low).
- When the items suppliers provide the industry account for a relatively small portion of the cost of the industry's finished products.

BARGAINING POWER OF BUYERS. Just as suppliers to an industry can be a source of pressure, buyers also have the potential to exert significant power over businesses, making it less attractive. When the number of customers is small and the cost of switching to competitors' products is low, buyers' influence on companies is high. Famous for offering its customers low prices, Walmart, the largest company in the world, is also well known for applying relentless pressure to its 21,000 suppliers for price concessions, which it almost always manages to get.[2] Generally, an industry is more attractive when:

- Industry customers' "switching costs" to competitors' products or to substitutes are relatively high.
- The number of buyers in the industry is large.
- Customers demand products that are differentiated rather than purchase commodity products that they can obtain from any supplier (and subsequently can pit one company against another to drive down price).
- Customers find it difficult to gather information on suppliers' costs, prices, and product features—something that is becoming much easier for customers in many industries to do by using the Internet.
- The items companies sell to the industry account for a relatively small portion of the cost of their customers' finished products.

THREAT OF NEW ENTRANTS TO THE INDUSTRY. The larger the pool of potential new entrants to an industry, the greater is the threat to existing companies in it. This is particularly true in industries where the barriers to entry, such as capital requirements, specialized knowledge, access to distribution channels, and others are low. Generally, an industry is more attractive to new entrants when:

- The advantages of economies of scale are absent. Economies of scale exist when companies in an industry achieve low average costs by producing huge volumes of items (e.g., computer chips).
- Capital requirements to enter the industry are low.

- Cost advantages are not related to company size.
- Buyers are not extremely brand-loyal, making it easier for new entrants to the industry to draw customers away from existing businesses.
- Governments, through their regulatory and international trade policies, do not restrict new companies from entering the industry.

THREAT OF SUBSTITUTE PRODUCTS OR SERVICES. Substitute products or services can turn an entire industry on its head. For instance, many makers of glass bottles have closed their doors in recent years as their customers—from soft drink bottlers to ketchup makers—have switched to plastic containers, which are lighter, less expensive to ship, and less subject to breakage. Printed newspapers have seen their readership rates decline as new generations of potential readers turn to online sources of news that are constantly updated. Generally, an industry is more attractive when:

- Quality substitute products are not readily available.
- The prices of substitute products are not significantly lower than those of the industry's products.
- Buyers' cost of switching to substitute products is high.

After surveying the power these five forces exert on an industry, entrepreneurs can evaluate the potential for their companies to generate reasonable sales and profits in a particular industry. In other words, they can answer the question, "Is this industry a good home for my business?" Table 1 provides a matrix that allows entrepreneurs to assign quantitative scores to the five forces influencing industry attractiveness. Note that the *lower* the score for an industry, the *more* attractive it is.

The next step in assessing an industry is to identify potentially attractive niches. Many small businesses prosper in a market by sticking to niches that are too small to attract the attention of large competitors. Occupying an industry niche enables a business to shield itself to some extent from the power of the five forces. The key question entrepreneurs must address is "Can we identify a niche that is large enough to produce a profit, or can we position our company uniquely in the market to differentiate it from the competition in a meaningful way?" Entrepreneurs who have designed successful focus or differentiation strategies for their companies can exploit these niches to their advantage.

TABLE 1 Five Forces Matrix

Assign a value to rate the importance of each of the five forces to the industry on a 1 (not important) to 5 (very important) scale. Then assign a value to reflect the extent to which each force poses a threat to the industry. Multiply the importance rating in column 2 by the threat rating in column 3 to produce a weighted score. Add the weighted scores in column 3 to get a total weighted score. This score measures the industry's attractiveness. The matrix is a useful tool for comparing the attractiveness of different industries.

Force	Importance (1 = Not Important, 5 = Very Important)	Threat to Industry (1 = Low, 3 = Medium, 5 = High)	Weighted Score Col 2 × Col 3
Rivalry among companies competing in the industry	5	2	10
Bargaining power of suppliers in the industry	2	2	4
Bargaining power of buyers	2	4	8
Threat of new entrants to the industry	3	4	12
Threat of substitute products or services	4	1	4
		Total	**38**

Minimum Score = 5 (Very attractive)
Maximum Score = 125 (Very unattractive)

Questions entrepreneurs should address in this portion of the feasibility analysis include:

- Which niche in the market will we occupy?
- How large is this market segment, and how fast is it growing?
- What is the basis for differentiating our product or service from competitors?
- Do we have a superior business model that will be difficult for competitors to reproduce?

Companies can shield themselves from some of the negative impact of these five forces by finding a niche and occupying it.

<table>
<tr><td>

ENTREPRENEURIAL
Profile

Patrick Gottsch and RFD-TV

</td><td>

Patrick Gottsch has found success in a niche in the competitive cable television business that is dominated by giant companies. His RFD-TV, a television network he founded in 1988 in Omaha, Nebraska, specializes in programming aimed at rural communities, broadcasting an unusual mix of shows in four categories: agriculture ("This Week in AgriBusiness"), equine, ("Training Mules and Donkeys"), entertainment (reruns of the 1970s variety show "Hee Haw" and new shows such as the "Big Joe Polka Show"), and rural lifestyle ("Ms. Lucy's Cajun Classroom"). Gottsch's RFD-TV has become one of the most successful networks you've never heard of, reaching 40 million homes in 20 countries and generating $25 million in annual revenues.[3]

</td></tr>
</table>

One technique for gauging the quality of a company's business model involves **business prototyping**, in which entrepreneurs test their business models on a small scale before committing serious resources to launch a business that might not work. Business prototyping recognizes that every business idea is a hypothesis that needs to be tested before an entrepreneur takes it to full scale. If the test supports the hypothesis and its accompanying assumptions, it is time to launch a company. If the prototype flops, the entrepreneur scraps the business idea with only minimal losses and turns to the next idea.

The Internet is a valuable business prototyping tool because it gives entrepreneurs easy and inexpensive access to real live potential customers. Entrepreneurs can test their ideas by selling their products on established sites such as eBay or by setting up their own Web sites to gauge customers' response.

<table>
<tr><td>

ENTREPRENEURIAL
Profile

Jennifer and Brad Fallon and My Wedding Favors

</td><td>

Jennifer and Brad Fallon were looking for a business that Jennifer could run from home. The idea for an online wedding favors business came to Jennifer, whose corporate job required extensive travel, while she was planning their wedding. She began to research the potential for her business idea and discovered that more than 100,000 people per month conduct online searches for the term "wedding favors." At that point, she says, "I knew the idea had potential." Her research also revealed more than 822,000 existing Web sites that sold wedding favors, which meant that a successful search engine marketing strategy would be a key success factor. Fortunately, her husband Brad was a leading expert in that field!

To test their business idea, the Fallons set up a simple online store for just $50 per month with Yahoo! In its first month of operation, My Wedding Favors generated $10,000 in sales. Within 3 months, sales had grown to $80,000, and the Fallons knew that their business idea had passed the feasibility test. The couple worked hard to refine their search engine optimization strategy, and as sales continued to climb, they expanded their product line and rented a warehouse in which to store their inventory.

Jennifer continues to work from home even though My Wedding Favors has become a leader in the market with a full-time staff of six employees and sales of $350,000 per month.[4]

</td></tr>
</table>

Product or Service Feasibility Analysis

Once entrepreneurs discover that sufficient market potential for their product or service idea actually exists, they sometimes rush in with their exuberant enthusiasm ready to launch a business without actually considering whether they can actually produce the product or provide the service at a reasonable cost. A product or service feasibility analysis determines the degree to which a product or service idea appeals to potential customers and identifies the resources necessary to produce the product or provide the service. This portion of the feasibility analysis addresses two questions:

- Are customers willing to purchase our goods and services?
- Can we provide the product or service to customers at a profit?

Entrepreneurs need feedback from potential customers to successfully answer these questions. Conducting **primary research** involves collecting data firsthand and analyzing it; **secondary research** involves gathering data that has already been compiled and is available, often at a very reasonable cost or sometimes even free. In both types of research, gathering both quantitative and qualitative information is important to drawing accurate conclusions about a product's or service's market potential. Primary research tools include customer surveys, focus groups, prototypes, and in-home trials.

CUSTOMER SURVEYS AND QUESTIONNAIRES. Keep them short. Word your questions carefully so that you do not bias the results and use a simple ranking system (e.g., a 1-to-5 scale, with 1 representing "definitely would not buy" and 5 representing "definitely would buy"). Test your survey for problems on a small number of people before putting it to use. Web surveys are inexpensive, easy to conduct, and provide feedback fast.

FOCUS GROUPS. A **focus group** involves enlisting a small number of potential customers (usually 8 to 12) to provide feedback on specific issues about your product or service (or the business idea itself). Listen carefully for what focus group members like and don't like about your product or service as they tell you what is on their minds. The founders of one small snack food company that produced apple chips conducted several focus groups to gauge customers' acceptance of the product and to guide many key business decisions, ranging from the product's name to its packaging. Once again, consider creating virtual focus groups on the Web; one small bicycle retailer conducts 10 online focus groups each year at virtually no cost and gains valuable marketing information from them. Feedback from online customers is fast, convenient, and real-time.

PROTOTYPES. An effective way to gauge the viability of a product is to build a prototype of it. A **prototype** is an original, functional model of a new product that entrepreneurs can put into the hands of potential customers so that they can see it, test it, and use it. Prototypes usually point out potential problems in a product's design, giving inventors the opportunity to fix them even before they put the prototype into customers' hands. The feedback customers give entrepreneurs based on prototypes often leads to design improvements and new features, some of which the entrepreneurs might never have discovered on their own. Makers of computer software frequently put prototypes of new products into customers' hands as they develop new products or improve existing ones. Known as *beta tests*, these trials result in an iterative design process in which software designers collect feedback from users and then incorporate their ideas into the product for the next round of tests.

IN-HOME TRIALS. One technique that reveals some of the most insightful information into how customers actually use a product or service is also the most challenging to coordinate: in-home trials. An **in-home trial** involves sending researchers into customers' homes to observe them as they use the company's product or service.

Secondary research, which is usually less expensive to collect than primary data, includes the following sources.

TRADE ASSOCIATIONS AND BUSINESS DIRECTORIES. To locate a trade association, use *Business Information Sources* (University of California Press) or the *Encyclopedia of Associations* (Gale Research). To find suppliers, use *The Thomas Register of American Manufacturers* (Thomas Publishing Company) or *Standard and Poor's Register of Corporations, Executives, and Industries* (Standard and Poor Corporation). *The American Wholesalers and Distributors Directory* includes details on more than 18,000 wholesalers and distributors.

DIRECT MAIL LISTS. You can buy mailing lists for practically any type of business. *The Standard Rates and Data Service (SRDS) Directory of Mailing Lists* (Standard Rates and Data) is a good place to start looking.

DEMOGRAPHIC DATA. To learn more about the demographic characteristics of customers in general, use *The Statistical Abstract of the United States* (Government Printing Office). Profiles of more specific regions are available in *The State and Metropolitan Data Book* (Government Printing Office). *The Sourcebook of Zip Code Demographics* (CACI, Inc.) provides detailed breakdowns of the population in every zip code in the country. *Sales and Marketing Management's Survey of Buying Power* (Bill Communications) has statistics on consumer, retail, and industrial buying.

CENSUS DATA. The Bureau of the Census publishes a wide variety of reports that summarize the wealth of data found in its census database, which is available at most libraries and at the Census Bureau's Web site at *www.census.gov*.

FORECASTS. The *U.S. Global Outlook* traces the growth of 200 industries and gives a 5-year forecast for each one. Many government agencies, including the Department of Commerce, offer forecasts on everything from interest rates to the number of housing starts. A government librarian can help you find what you need.

MARKET RESEARCH. Someone may already have compiled the market research you need. *The FINDex Worldwide Directory of Market Research Reports, Studies, and Surveys* (Cambridge Information Group) lists more than 10,600 studies available for purchase. Other directories of business research include *Simmons Study of Media and Markets* (Simmons Market Research Bureau Inc.) and the *A.C. Nielsen Retail Index* (A.C. Nielsen Company).

ARTICLES. Magazine and journal articles pertinent to your business are a great source of information. Use the *Reader's Guide to Periodical Literature*, the *Business Periodicals Index* (similar to the Reader's Guide but focuses on business periodicals), and *Ulrich's Guide to International Periodicals* to locate the ones you need.

LOCAL DATA. Your state Department of Commerce and your local Chamber of Commerce will very likely have useful data on the local market of interest to you. Call to find out what is available.

THE INTERNET. Entrepreneurs can benefit from the vast amount of market research information available on the Web. This is an efficient resource with up-to-date information, and much of it is free.

Financial Feasibility Analysis

The final component of a feasibility analysis involves assessing the financial feasibility of a proposed business venture. At this stage of the process, a broad financial analysis is sufficient. If the business concept passes the overall feasibility analysis, an entrepreneur should conduct a more thorough financial analysis when creating a full-blown business plan. The major elements to be included in a financial feasibility analysis include the initial capital requirement, estimated earnings, and the resulting return on investment.

CAPITAL REQUIREMENTS. Just as a Boy Scout needs fuel to start a fire, an entrepreneur needs capital to start a business. Some businesses require large amounts of capital, but others do not. Typically, service businesses require less capital to launch than manufacturing or retail businesses. Start-up companies often need capital to purchase equipment, buildings, technology, and other tangible assets as well as to hire and train employees, promote their products and services, and establish a presence in the market. A good feasibility analysis provides an estimate of the amount of start-up capital an entrepreneur will need to get the business up and running.

ENTREPRENEURIAL
Profile

*Shawn Donegan and
Mike Puczkowski and
Trac Tool Inc.*

Before launching Trac Tool Inc., a Cleveland, Ohio-based business that markets Speed Rollers, a paint application system aimed at professional paint contractors, entrepreneurs Shawn Donegan and Mike Puczkowski estimated that they needed $150,000 to launch the company and bring the Speed Rollers paint system to market. Their invention features an airless paint pump that feeds paint onto one of two rollers, eliminating the need to dip the rollers into a paint tray and making the system three times faster than using traditional rollers. They spent most of their start-up capital to develop and test the prototype and to introduce the product at the Painting and Decorating Contractors of America trade show.[5]

ESTIMATED EARNINGS. In addition to producing an estimate of the start-up company's capital requirements, an entrepreneur also should forecast the earning potential of the proposed business. Industry trade associations and publications such as the *RMA Annual Statement Studies* offer guidelines on preparing sales and earnings estimates. From these, entrepreneurs can estimate the financial results they and their investors can expect to see from the business venture.

RETURN ON INVESTMENT. The final aspect of the financial feasibility analysis combines the estimated earnings and the capital requirements to determine the rate of return the venture is expected to produce. One simple measure is the rate of return on the capital invested, which is calculated by dividing the estimated earnings the business yields by the amount of capital invested in the business. Although financial estimates at the feasibility analysis stage typically are rough, they are an important part of the entrepreneur's ultimate "go" or "no go" decision about the business ventures. A venture must produce an attractive rate of return relative to the level of risk it requires. This risk-return trade-off means that the higher the level of risk a prospective business involves, the higher the rate of return it must provide to the entrepreneur and investors. Why should an entrepreneur take on all of the risks of starting and running a business that produces a mere 3 or 4 percent rate of return when he or she could earn that much in a risk-free investment at a bank or other financial institution?

Wise entrepreneurs take the time to subject their ideas to a feasibility analysis like the one described here, whatever outcome it produces. If the analysis suggests that transforming the idea into a viable business is not feasible, the entrepreneur can move on to the next idea, confident that he or she has not wasted valuable resources launching a business destined to fail.

If the analysis shows that the idea has real potential as a profitable business, the entrepreneur can pursue it, using the information gathered during the feasibility analysis as the foundation for building a sound business plan. We now turn our attention to the process of developing a business plan.

IN THE ENTREPRENEURIAL
SPOTLIGHT A Business Plan: Don't Launch Without It

A recent study by the Small Business Administration reports that entrepreneurs who create business plans in the early stages of the start-up process are more likely to actually launch companies and complete typical start-up activities such as acquiring a patent, attracting capital, and assembling a start-up team more quickly than entrepreneurs who do not. "Early formal planners are doers," write the study's authors. "Challenging prospective entrepreneurs to accomplish a formal business plan early in the venture creation process enables them to engage in additional start-up behaviors that further the process of venture creation."

Geo-Logical

Daniel Stewart is one entrepreneur who believes in the value of building a business plan. Stewart was running a sink-hole remediation business, Geo-Logical, that he had created with a partner in Port Richey, Florida, when he realized that operating their business effectively required a unified software platform rather than the hodgepodge of software applications that they had been using to manage the projects on which the company was working. Stewart worked with a software developer to create a program that allowed his company to create proposals, track projects' status, send invoices promptly, and, most important, complete projects on time and within budget. The engineering companies and other businesses with which Geo-Logical worked took notice and began asking to purchase the software.

Stewart realized that to capitalize on this business opportunity he needed a business plan. Although Stewart and his partner were not seeking external financing, they decided that developing a business plan would be a crucial element in the company's success. "We're our own investors," says Stewart, "but to be a responsible entrepreneur, you have to see things as they are." Their first task was to conduct a feasibility analysis of their business idea, which involved analyzing the software package's market potential and preparing a fundamental financial forecast. Enthusiastic feedback from potential customers convinced them that a significant market existed for the product. Stewart and his partner also created three sets of financial projections: a most likely forecast, an optimistic one, and a disaster scenario. Creating the plan also brought them to the realization that they needed to add to their team someone who was experienced in starting and managing a software company. Stewart and his partner recruited to their board of directors Jim Eddy, who had started and managed to profitability three technology start-ups, before launching their software company, Envala. All of their planning paid off. Envala, which targets small companies with its productivity software, is growing rapidly and now has customers across North America, Europe, and the Caribbean.

Roaring Lion Energy Drink

When Sean Hackney began writing his business plan, his intent was not to start a company but to convince a soft-drink maker to hire him. When Hackney, who had worked for Red Bull North America, showed the plan to his father, a corporate attorney, and a family friend who had been a managing director for Red Bull, "they said, 'Don't send this

to Coke or Pepsi. Start the business, and we'll help you,'" he recalls. Hackney took their advice and launched Roaring Lion Energy Drink. Based on customer feedback, he chose to distribute the energy drink as a boxed syrup that distributors can serve with a soda-dispensing gun rather than in cans, which restaurants, bars, and nightclubs dislike because of the storage space they require and the wasted product they create. In its first year of operation, Roaring Lion generated $900,000 in sales. It reached its break-even point within 16 months. The company now boasts sales of $6.2 million and has customers across the United States and Europe. "We've grown the business from a $62,000 investment to the number two energy drink in bars and nightclubs," says Hackney. He credits the original business plan he wrote and has since updated several times with much of Roaring Lion's success. "I had a lot of stuff in my head that needed to be put on paper," he says. Hackney still relies on a regularly updated plan to guide the company, which now has 32 employees.

1. Some entrepreneurs claim that creating a business plan is not necessary for launching a successful business venture. Do you agree? Explain.
2. What benefits do entrepreneurs who create business plans before launching their companies reap?
3. Suppose that a friend who has never taken a course in entrepreneurship tells you about a business that he or she is planning to launch. When you ask about a business plan, the response is, "Business plan? I don't have time to write a business plan! I know this business will succeed." Write a one-page response to your friend's comment.

Sources: Based on Mark Henricks, "Do You Really Need a Business Plan?" *Entrepreneur,* December 2008, pp. 93–95; Ricardo Baca, "Red Bull vs. Lion in Bar Mixer Duel," *BevNet,* September 24, 2003, *www.bevnet.com/news/2003/09-24-2003-redbull.asp*; Kelly Spors, Advance Planning Pays Off for Start-Ups," *Wall Street Journal,* February 9, 2009, *http://blogs.wsj.com/independentstreet/2009/02/09/advance-planningpays-off-for-start-ups.*

The Benefits of Creating a Business Plan

2. Explain the benefits of an effective business plan.

Any entrepreneur who is in business or is about to launch a business needs a well-conceived and factually based business plan to increase the likelihood of success. For decades, research has proved that companies that engage in business planning outperform those that do not. A recent study by the Small Business Administration reports that entrepreneurs who write business plans early on are two-and-a-half times more likely to actually start their businesses than those who do not.[6] Unfortunately, many entrepreneurs never take the time to develop plans for their businesses, and the implications of the lack of planning are all too evident in the high failure rates that small companies experience.

A **business plan** is a written summary of an entrepreneur's proposed business venture, its operational and financial details, its marketing opportunities and strategy, and its managers' skills and abilities. There is no substitute for a well-prepared business plan, and there are no shortcuts to creating one. The plan serves as an entrepreneur's road map on the journey toward building a successful business. As a small company's guidebook, a business plan describes the direction the company is taking, what its goals are, where it wants to be, and how it's going to get there. The plan is written proof that an entrepreneur has performed the necessary research, has studied the business opportunity adequately, and is prepared to capitalize on it with a sound business model. A business plan is an entrepreneur's best insurance against launching a business destined to fail or mismanaging a potentially successful company.

A business plan serves two essential functions. First, it guides the company's operations by charting its future course and devising a strategy for following it. The plan provides a battery of tools—a mission statement, goals, objectives, budgets, financial forecasts, target markets, and strategies—to help the entrepreneur lead the company successfully. A solid business plan provides managers and employees a sense of direction when everyone is involved in creating and updating it. As more team members become committed to making the plan work, it takes on special meaning. It gives everyone targets to shoot for, and it provides a yardstick for measuring actual performance against those targets, especially in the crucial and chaotic start-up phase of the business. Creating a plan also forces entrepreneurs to subject their ideas to the test of reality. The greatest waste of a completed business plan is to let the plan go unused. When properly done, a plan becomes an integral and natural part of a company. In other words, successful entrepreneurs actually *use* their business plans to help them build strong companies.

<table>
<tr><td>

ENTREPRENEURIAL
Profile

Rhonda Abrams and The Planning Shop

</td><td>

Rhonda Abrams, founder of The Planning Shop, a small publisher of books and tools for entrepreneurs, says that the business plan that she and her employees craft every year has played an important role in her company's success. "Developing a business plan is a key to long-term business survival and success," she says. Abrams credits her company's strategic plan for helping her team identify a new market opportunity that later allowed the business to survive the bankruptcy of its former distributor.[7]

</td></tr>
</table>

The second function of the business plan is to attract lenders and investors. A business plan must prove to potential lenders and investors that a venture will be able to repay loans and produce an attractive rate of return. They want proof that an entrepreneur has evaluated the risk involved in the new venture realistically and has a strategy for addressing it. Unfortunately, many small business owners approach potential lenders and investors without having prepared to sell their business concepts. Kristie Price, founder of Noah's Arf, a pet day-care center in Portland, Oregon, credits the business plan she created with the help of Business Plan Pro for helping her land the financing she needed for her company. "That business plan is what sold me to the bank and got me my first $200,000," she says.[8] A collection of figures scribbled on a note pad to support a loan application or investment request is not enough. Applying for loans or attempting to attract investors without a solid business plan rarely attracts needed capital. The best way to secure the necessary capital is to prepare a sound business plan. The quality of an entrepreneur's business plan weighs heavily in the final decision to lend or invest funds. It is also potential lenders' and investors' first impression of the company and its managers. Therefore, the finished product should be highly polished and professional in both form and content.

Building a plan forces a potential entrepreneur to look at his or her business idea in the harsh light of reality. To get external financing, an entrepreneur's plan must pass three tests with potential lenders and investors: (1) the reality test, (2) the competitive test, and (3) the value test. The first two tests have both an external and internal component:

3. Explain the three tests that every business plan must pass.

REALITY TEST. The external component of the reality test revolves around proving that a market for the product or service really does exist. It focuses on industry attractiveness, market niches, potential customers, market size, degree of competition, and similar factors. Entrepreneurs who pass this part of the reality test prove in the marketing portion of their business plan that there is strong demand for their business idea.

The internal component of the reality test focuses on the product or service itself. Can the company *really* build it for the cost estimates in the business plan? Is it truly different from what competitors are already selling? Does it offer customers something of value?

COMPETITIVE TEST. The external part of the competitive test evaluates the company's relative position to its key competitors. How do the company's strengths and weaknesses match up with those of the competition? Do competitors' reactions threaten the new company's success and survival?

The internal competitive test focuses on management's ability to create a company that will gain an edge over existing rivals. To pass this part of the competitive test, a plan must prove the quality, skill, and experience of the venture's management team. What other resources does the company have that can give it a competitive edge in the market?

VALUE TEST. To convince lenders and investors to put their money into the venture, a business plan must prove to them that it offers a high probability of repayment or an attractive rate of return. Entrepreneurs usually see their businesses as good investments because they consider the intangibles of owning a business—gaining control over their own destinies, freedom to do what they enjoy, and others; lenders and investors, however, look at a venture in colder terms: dollar-for-dollar returns. A plan must convince lenders and investors that they will earn an attractive return on their money.

Even after completing a feasibility analysis, entrepreneurs sometimes do not come to the realization that "this business just won't work" until they build a business plan. Have they wasted valuable time? Not necessarily! The time to find out that a business idea will not succeed is in the planning stages *before* committing significant money, time, and effort to the venture. It is much less expensive to make mistakes on paper than in reality. In other cases, a business plan reveals important problems to overcome before launching a company. Exposing these flaws and then addressing them enhances the chances of a venture's success. Business plans can help nascent entrepreneurs nail down important aspects of their concept and sometimes prevent costly mistakes.

The real value in preparing a plan is not as much in the plan itself as it is in the *process* the entrepreneur goes through to create the plan. Although the finished product is extremely useful, the process of building the plan requires entrepreneurs to explore all areas of the business and subject their ideas to an objective, critical evaluation from many different angles. What entrepreneurs learn about their industry, target customers, financial requirements, competition, and other factors is essential to making their ventures successful. Building a business plan is one controllable factor that reduces the risk and uncertainty of launching a company.

IN THE ENTREPRENEURIAL
SPOTLIGHT The Battle of the Plans

The four members of In Context Solutions (ICS), a start-up market research company that has developed the technology to create customized virtual stores that allow retailers to understand their customers' behavior quickly and inexpensively, were feeling the pressure of the high-stakes competition. More than 300 teams had submitted business plans to the Rice Business Plan Competition, one of the largest and richest business plan competitions in the world, and just 42 of them had made the final cut. Over the course of the next 3 days, the ICS team would be competing against some of the most promising start-up companies in the world, and the stakes were high—$800,000 in cash and prizes and, more important, valuable exposure to well-connected judges with money of their own to invest and access to the financing they needed to enable their companies to grow. "There are no toy businesses here," says one judge, himself a successful technology entrepreneur. In fact, since the Rice Business Plan Competition began in 2001,

more than 228 teams have competed, and nearly 90 of them have launched their companies successfully, raising more than $150 million in early stage financing.

The ICS team stumbled in the practice round but came back strong when the scores counted, securing one of the 12 spots in the final competition. One of the team's toughest competitors was Dynamics, a company founded by Jeffrey Mullen, a patent attorney and electrical engineer. Mullen has developed a magnetic strip that can be placed on a credit card that supports a constantly changing number, a technology that the credit card companies have been trying to accomplish for years. Overcoming a major obstacle of previous attempts to improve credit card technology, Dynamics' system allows companies to use their existing credit card readers. Not only does Dynamics' technology provide enhanced security by making credit card theft more difficult, but it also allows users to combine multiple cards onto one piece of plastic, giving them the ability to

BiologicsMD, a company created by students at the University of Arkansas that is commercializing a new drug to treat osteoporosis, was the winner at a recent Rice Business Plan Competition.

Source: 2007 Rice Alliance\Rice University

charge purchases to different accounts using just one card. Mullen's Pittsburgh-based company already had seven employees, had been negotiating with several venture capital firms, and was working with several banks to bring his technology to market.

At the awards banquet at the end of the Rice Business Plan Competition, ICS came in 12th, but the team was not downcast. "We came in 12th out of 300-plus teams that submitted plans," said Kristine Wexler. The team was already talking about how to use the feedback from the judges to improve their business plan for the business plan competition at their own school, the University of Chicago's Booth School of Business, and in meetings with potential investors. Many judges were impressed with ICS's technology and business plan. "I think they're as likely to succeed as any startup I've seen," said Tim Berry, founder of Palo Alto Software.

In the end, Dynamics proved to be the competition's winner, taking first prize of $20,000 and $305,000 in investments and business services. Dynamics also received the prestigious $100,000 Technology Award from Opportunity Houston (which it can collect only if it moves from Pittsburgh to Houston) and a $125,000 investment from the GOOSE Society of Texas. The ICS team, which raised $200,000 from family and friends to start the company, went back to the

same source for $225,000 more in capital. However, one judge in the business plan competition is negotiating with ICS for a $100,000 investment. Another judge from software giant Oracle has promised to set up meetings with some of Oracle's clients as another possible source of capital for ICS

1. What benefits do entrepreneurs who compete in business plan competitions such as the one at Rice University gain?
2. Work with a team of your classmates to brainstorm ideas for establishing a business plan competition on your campus. How would you locate judges? What criteria would you use to judge the plans? What prizes would you offer winners?
3. Using the ideas you generated in question 2, create a two-page proposal for establishing a business plan competition at your school.

Sources: Based on Adriana Gardella, "Rice Business Plan Awards 2009," *FSB*, June 2009, pp. 80–85; Shara Rutberg, "Student Grudge Match: Wirelessly Zapping Pain," *CNNMoney*, May 22, 2008, *http://money.cnn.com/galleries/2008/fsb/0804/gallery.rice_b_plan_competition_08.fsb/4.html*; "Rice Business Plan Competition Announces $111 Million in Funding Raised by Past Competitors," *Rice Alliance Digest Newsletter*, March 5, 2009, p. 2.

The Elements of a Business Plan

4. Describe the elements of a solid business plan.

Wise entrepreneurs recognize that every business plan is unique and must be tailored to the specific needs of their business. They avoid the off-the-shelf, "cookie-cutter" approach that produces a look-alike business plan. The elements of a business plan may be standard, but the way entrepreneurs tell their stories should be unique and reflect their enthusiasm for the new venture. In fact, the best business plans usually are those that tell a compelling story in addition to the facts. For those making a first attempt at writing a business plan, seeking the advice of individuals with experience in this process often proves helpful. Accountants, business professors, attorneys, and consultants with Small Business Development Centers (SBDCs) are excellent sources of

Source: The *Wall Street Journal*/
Cartoon Features Syndicate

"I love the business plan. I can see a lot of scheming went into it."

advice when creating and refining a plan. (To locate an SBDC, visit the Small Business Administration's Web SBDC Web page at *www.sba.gov/aboutsba/sbaprograms/sbdc/sbdclocator/ SBDC_LOCATOR.html.*) Remember, though, that you should be the one to author your business plan, not someone else.

Initially, the prospect of writing a business plan may appear to be overwhelming. Many entrepreneurs would rather launch their companies and "see what happens" than invest the necessary time and energy defining and researching their target markets, outlining their strategies, and mapping out their finances. After all, building a plan is hard work—it requires time, effort, and thought. However, it is hard work that pays many dividends, and not all of them are immediately apparent. Entrepreneurs who invest their time and energy building plans are better prepared to face the hostile environment in which their companies will compete than those who do not.

Entrepreneurs can use business planning software available from several companies to create their plans. Some of the most popular programs include Business Plan Pro* (Palo Alto Software), PlanMaker (Power Solutions for Business), and Plan Write (Business Resources Software). Business Plan Pro, for example, encompasses every aspect of a business plan—from the executive summary to the cash flow forecasts. These packages help entrepreneurs organize the material they have researched and gathered, and they provide helpful tips on plan writing as well as templates for creating financial statements. Business planning software may help to produce professional-looking business plans, but there is a potential drawback: the plans they produce may look as if they came from the same mold. That can be a turn-off for professional investors who review hundreds of business plans each year. Entrepreneurs will benefit by making the content and appearance of their plan look professional and unique.

A business plan typically ranges from 20 to 40 pages in length. Shorter plans may be too brief to be of value, and those much longer than this run the risk of never getting used or read! This section explains the most common elements of a business plan. However, entrepreneurs must recognize that, like every business venture, every business plan is unique. An entrepreneur should use the following elements as the starting point for building a plan and should modify them, as needed, to better tell the story of his or her new venture.

*Business Plan Pro is available at nominal cost with this text.

Title Page and Table of Contents

A business plan should contain a title page with the company's name, logo, and address as well as the names and contact information of the company's founders. Many entrepreneurs also include the copy number of the plan and the date on which it was issued on the title page. Business plan readers appreciate a table of contents that includes page numbers so that they can locate the particular sections of the plan in which they are most interested.

The Executive Summary

To summarize the presentation for each potential financial institution or for investors, the entrepreneur should write an executive summary. It should be concise—a maximum of two pages—and should summarize all of the relevant points of the proposed business. After reading the executive summary, anyone should be able to understand the entire business concept and what differentiates the company from the competition. The executive summary is a synopsis of the entire plan, capturing its essence in a condensed form. It should explain the basic business model and the problem the business will solve for customers, briefly describing the owners and key employees, target market(s), financial highlights (e.g., sales and earnings projections, the loan or investment requested, how the funds will be used, and how and when any loans will be repaid or investments cashed out), and the company's competitive advantage. Much like Abraham Lincoln's Gettysburg Address, which at 256 words lasted just 2 minutes and is hailed as one of the greatest speeches in history, a good executive summary provides a meaningful framework for potential lenders and investors of the essence of a company.

The executive summary is a written version of what is known as "the elevator pitch." Imagine yourself on an elevator with a potential lender or investor. Only the two of you are on the elevator, and you have that person's undivided attention for the duration of the ride, but the building is not very tall! To convince the investor that your business idea is a great investment, you must condense your message down to its essential elements—key points that you can communicate in no more than 2 minutes. In the Babcock Elevator Competition at Wake Forest University, students actually ride an elevator 27 floors with a judge, where they have the opportunity to make their elevator pitches in just 2 minutes. "The competition was designed to simulate reality," says Stan Mandel, creator of the event and director of the Angell Center for Entrepreneurship. Winners receive the chance to make 20-minute presentations of their business plans to a panel of venture capitalists, who judge the competition using criteria that range from the attractiveness of the business idea and the value proposition it offers to the quality of the plan's marketing and financial elements.[9]

Like a good movie trailer, an executive summary is designed to capture readers' attention and draw them into the plan. If it misses, the chances of the remainder of the plan being read are minimal. A coherent, well-developed summary introducing the rest of the plan establishes a favorable first impression of the business and the entrepreneur behind it and can go a long way toward obtaining financing. A good executive summary should allow the reader to understand the business concept and how it will make money as well as answering the ultimate question from investors or lenders: "What's in it for me?" Although the executive summary is the first part of the business plan, it should be the last section you write.

Mission and Vision Statement

A mission statement expresses an entrepreneur's vision for what his or her company is and what it is to become. It is the broadest expression of a company's purpose and defines the direction in which it will move. It anchors a company in reality and serves as the thesis statement for the entire business plan by answering the question, "What business are we in?" Every good plan captures an entrepreneur's passion and vision for the business, and the mission statement is the ideal place to express them.

Company History

The owner of an existing small business should prepare a brief history of the operation, highlighting the significant financial and operational events in the company's life. This section should describe when and why the company was formed, how it has evolved over time, and what the owner envisions for the future. It should highlight the successful accomplishment of past objectives and should convey the company's image in the marketplace.

Business and Industry Profile

To acquaint lenders and investors with the industry in which a company competes, an entrepreneur should describe it in the business plan. This section should provide the reader with an overview of the industry or market segment in which the new venture will operate. Industry data such as market size, growth trends, and the relative economic and competitive strength of the major firms in the industry set the stage for a better understanding of the viability of a new business. Strategic issues such as ease of market entry and exit, the ability to achieve economies of scale or scope, and the existence of cyclical or seasonal economic trends further help readers to evaluate the new venture. This part of the plan also should describe significant industry trends and key success factors as well as an overall outlook for its future. Information about the evolution of the industry helps the reader comprehend its competitive dynamics. The *U.S. Industrial Outlook Handbook* is an excellent reference that profiles a variety of industries and offers projections for future trends in them. Another useful resource of industry and economic information is the *Summary of Commentary on Current Economic Conditions*, more commonly known as the *Beige Book*. Published eight times a year by the Federal Reserve, the *Beige Book* provides detailed statistics and trends in key business sectors and in the overall economy. It offers valuable information on topics ranging from tourism and housing starts to consumer spending and wage rates. Entrepreneurs can find this wealth of information on the Web at *www.minneapolisfed.org/bb/*.

This section should contain a statement of the company's general business goals and then work down to a narrower definition of its immediate objectives. Together they should spell out what the business plans to accomplish, how, and when. **Goals** are broad, long-range statements of what a company plans to achieve in the future that guide its overall direction. In other words, they address the question, "Where do I want my company to be in 3 to 5 years?"

Objectives are short-term, specific performance targets that are specific, measurable, and assignable. Every objective should reflect some general business goal and include a technique for measuring progress toward its accomplishment. To be meaningful, an objective must have a time frame for achievement. Both goals and objectives should relate to the company's basic mission. In other words, accomplishing each objective should move a business closer to achieving its goals, which, in turn, should move it closer to its mission.

Business Strategy

An even more important part of the business plan is the owner's view of the strategy needed to meet—and beat—the competition. In the previous section, an entrepreneur defined where he or she wants to take the business by establishing goals and objectives. This section addresses the question of how to get there—business strategy. Here an entrepreneur explains how he or she plans to gain a competitive edge in the market and what sets his or her business apart from the competition. A key component of this section is defining what makes the company unique in the eyes of its customers. One of the quickest routes to business failure is trying to sell "me-too" products or services that offer customers nothing newer, better, bigger, faster, or different.

This section of the business plan should outline the methods the company will use to meet the key success factors cited earlier. If, for example, making sales to repeat customers is critical to success, an entrepreneur must devise a plan of action for achieving a customer retention rate that exceeds that of existing companies in the market.

Description of Firm's Product or Service

An entrepreneur should describe the company's overall product line, giving an overview of how customers use its goods or services. Drawings, diagrams, and illustrations may be required if the product is highly technical. It is best to write product and service descriptions so that laypeople can understand them. A statement of a product's position in the product life cycle might also be helpful. An entrepreneur should include a summary of any patents, trademarks, or copyrights that protect the product or service from infringement by competitors. Finally, the plan should include an honest comparison of the company's product or service with those of competitors, citing specific advantages or improvements that make its goods or services unique and indicating plans for creating the next generation of goods and services that will evolve from the present product line. Ideally, a product or service offers high-value benefits to customers and is difficult for competitors to duplicate.

TABLE 2 Transforming Features into Meaningful Benefits

For many entrepreneurs, there's a big gap between what a business is selling and what its customers are buying. The following exercise is designed to eliminate that gap.

First, develop a list of the features your company's product or service offers. List as many as you can think of, which may be 25 or more. Consider features that relate to price, performance, convenience, location, customer service, delivery, reputation, reliability, quality, features, and other aspects.

The next step is to group features that have similar themes together by circling them in the same color ink. Then translate those groups of features into specific benefits to your customers by addressing the question "What's in it for me?" from the customer's perspective. (Note: It usually is a good idea to ask actual customers why they buy from you. They usually give reasons that you never thought of.) As many as six or eight product or service (or even company) features may translate into a single customer benefit, such as saving money or time or making life safer. Don't ignore intangible benefits, such as increased status; they can be more important than tangible benefits.

Finally, combine all of the benefits you identify into a single benefit statement. Use this statement as a key point in your business plan and to guide your company's marketing strategy.

Product or Service *Features*	Product or Service *Benefits*

Benefit Statement:

Source: Based on Kim T. Gordon, "Position for Profits," *Business Start-Ups*, February 1998, pp. 18–20.

One danger entrepreneurs must avoid in this part of the plan is the tendency to dwell on the features of their products or services. This problem is the result of the "fall-in-love-with-your-product" syndrome, which often afflicts inventors. Customers, lenders, and investors care less about how much work, genius, and creativity went into a product or service than about what it will do for them. The emphasis of this section should be on defining the benefits customers get by purchasing the company's products or services, rather than on just a "nuts and bolts" description of the features of those products or services. A **feature** is a descriptive fact about a product or service (e.g., "an ergonomically designed, more comfortable handle"). A **benefit** is what the customer gains from the product or service feature (e.g., "fewer problems with carpal tunnel syndrome and increased productivity"). Advertising legend Leo Burnett once said, "Don't tell the people how good you make the goods; tell them how good your goods make them."[10] This part of the plan must describe how a business will transform tangible product or service features into important but often intangible customer benefits—for example, lower energy bills, faster access to the Internet, less time writing checks to pay monthly bills, greater flexibility in building floating structures, shorter time required to learn a foreign language, or others. Remember: *Customers buy benefits, not product or service features.* Table 2 offers an easy exercise designed to help entrepreneurs translate their products' or services' features into meaningful customer benefits.

ENTREPRENEURIAL
Profile

Håkan and Annika Olsson and First Penthouse

While renovating their top-floor apartment in Stockholm, Sweden, civil engineers Håkan and Annika Olsson came up with a unique idea for creating high-quality modular penthouses that could be manufactured in factories and installed atop existing flat-roof buildings. When the couple moved to London, they purchased aerial photographs of the city and marked all of the flat-roof buildings in red ink. "We knew we had a good business idea when the whole picture was red," says Håkan. After conducting more research and building a business plan, the Olssons launched First Penthouse, a company that specializes in rooftop development. Their business model adds value both for tenants, who get penthouse living quarters where none existed before, and for landlords, whose property values are enhanced by the addition of the modular penthouses. The entire process, from design to open house, takes just 10 weeks, one-fourth the time required to complete a similar structure using conventional techniques. First Penthouse offers the benefit of a convenient 1-day installation and guarantees no disturbances to existing residents. To avoid disturbing current tenants, the Olssons use special "quiet" tools and place soundproof mats over the roofs as they work. As sales grow, the Olssons plan to take their concept into other large urban markets around the world.[11]

Marketing Strategy

One of the most important tasks a business plan must fulfill is proving that a viable market exists for a company's goods or services. A business plan must identify and describe a company's target customers and their characteristics and habits. Defining the target audience and its potential is one of the most important—and most challenging—parts of building a business plan. Narrowing its target market enables a small company to focus its limited resources on serving the needs of a specific group of customers rather than attempting to satisfy the desires of the mass market. Creating a successful business depends on an entrepreneur's ability to attract real customers who are willing and able to spend real money to buy its products or services. Perhaps the worst marketing error an entrepreneur can commit is failing to define his target market and trying to make the business "everything to everybody." Small companies usually are much more successful focusing on a specific market niche or niches where they can excel at meeting customers' special needs or wants.

Proving that a profitable market exists involves two steps: showing customer interest and documenting market claims.

SHOWING CUSTOMER INTEREST. An important element of any business plan is showing how a company's product or service provides a customer benefit or solves a customer problem. Entrepreneurs must be able to prove that their target customers actually need or want their goods or services and are willing to pay for them. Venture capitalist Kathryn Gould, who has reviewed thousands of business plans, says that she looks for plans that focus on "target customers with a compelling reason to buy. The product must be a 'must-have.'"[12]

Proving that a viable market exists for a product or service is relatively straightforward for a company already in business but can be quite difficult for an entrepreneur with only an idea. In this case, the key is to find a way to get primary customer data. For instance, an entrepreneur might build a prototype of the product and offer it to several potential customers to get written testimonials and evaluations to show to investors. The entrepreneur also could sell the product to several customers, perhaps at a discount, on the condition that they provide evaluations of it. Doing so proves that there are potential customers for the product and allows customers to experience the product in operation. Getting a product into customers' hands is also an excellent way to get valuable feedback that can lead to significant design improvements and increased sales down the road.

ENTREPRENEURIAL
Profile
Charley Moore and RocketLawyer

Charley Moore originally launched RocketLawyer, a Web site that targets entrepreneurs with a variety of legal documents ranging from basic contracts and corporate documents to noncompete agreements and Web site design contracts, using a fee-per-downloaded-document business model. After several months in business, the site's analytics showed Moore that even though the site was attracting large numbers of visitors, its abandonment rate was stifling the company's revenue. "We were charging [our customers] a couple of hundred dollars less than other sites or the cost of hiring a lawyer," says Moore, "but we were asking them to pay for every document they wanted to download. It was still a lot of money for most folks." Based on feedback from customers, Moore changed the business model that he had developed in his business plan. "We decided to go with a 'first one free' model to accommodate customers who wanted to try our service," he explains. RocketLawyer also added a $40 monthly membership that gives customers unlimited access to legal documents and to online document storage. The revamped business model produced results immediately. Sales increased from $1 million to $5 million in just 1 year, and the number of RocketLawyer customers climbed from 150,000 to 900,000.[13]

DOCUMENTING MARKET CLAIMS. Too many business plans rely on vague generalizations such as, "This market is so huge that if we get just 1 percent of it, we will break even in 8 months." Statements such as these usually reflect nothing more than an entrepreneur's unbridled optimism, and, in most cases, are quite unrealistic! In *The Art of the Start*, entrepreneur and venture capitalist Guy Kawasaki calls this the Chinese Soda Lie: "If just 1 percent of the people in China drink our soda, we will be more successful than any company in the history of mankind."[14] The problems with this reasoning are (1) few markets, especially the niche markets that small businesses often pursue, are as large as that, and (2) capturing 1 percent of a big market is extremely difficult to do, especially for a small company. Capturing a large share of a small, well-defined niche market is much more realistic for a small company than is winning a small share of a huge market.

Entrepreneurs must support claims of market size and growth rates with *facts*, and that requires market research. Results of market surveys, customer questionnaires, and demographic studies lend credibility to an entrepreneur's frequently optimistic sales projections. Quantitative market data are important because they form the basis for all of the company's financial projections in the business plan.

As you learned earlier in the section on conducting a feasibility analysis, one effective documentation technique involves business prototyping, in which entrepreneurs test their business models on a small scale before committing serious resources to a business that might not work. Business prototyping recognizes that every business idea is a hypothesis that should be tested before an entrepreneur takes it to full scale. If the test supports the hypothesis and its accompanying assumptions, it is time to launch a company. If the prototype flops, the entrepreneur scraps the business idea with only minimal losses and turns to the next idea.

One of the main purposes of the marketing section of the plan is to lay the foundation for financial forecasts that follow. Sales, profit, and cash forecasts must be founded on more than wishful thinking. An effective market analysis should address the following items:

Target Market. Who are the company's target customers? How many of them are in the company's trading area? What are their characteristics (age, gender, educational level, income, and others)? What do they buy? Why do they buy? When do they buy? What expectations do they have about the product or service? Will the business focus on a niche? How does the company seek to position itself in the market(s) it will pursue? Knowing customers' needs, wants, and habits, what should be the basis for differentiating the business in their minds?

Advertising and Promotion. Only after entrepreneurs understand their companies' target markets can they design a promotion and advertising campaign to reach those customers most effectively and efficiently. Which media are most effective in reaching the target market? How will they be used? How much will the promotional campaign cost? How will the promotional campaign position the company's products or services? How can the company benefit from publicity? How large is the company's promotional budget?

Market Size and Trends. Assessing the size of the market is a critical step. How large is the potential market? Is it growing or shrinking? Why? Are customers' needs changing? Are sales seasonal? Is demand tied to another product or service?

<table>
<tr><td>

ENTREPRENEURIAL
Profile

Neil Malhotra and NP Solutions

</td><td>

One of the largest potential markets in the world of biotechnology is patients who suffer from lower back pain. Many people experience some form of degenerative disc disease beginning in their late twenties, but the majority of sufferers are not disabled enough for highly invasive and risky treatments, such as spinal fusion. Neil Malhotra, a neurosurgeon and cofounder of NP Solutions, spotted a business opportunity and developed a much less invasive treatment called RejuvaDisc, which involves injecting a small amount of hydrogel (a biocompatible polymer) into the affected disc. "Lower back pain is responsible for 15 million physicians' visits a year," Malhotra told the judges in a recent business plan competition at the University of Pennsylvania's Wharton School of Business, in which the company placed first.[15]

</td></tr>
</table>

Location. For many businesses, choosing the right location is a key success factor. For retailers, wholesalers, and service companies, the best location usually is one that is most convenient to their target customers. Using census data and other market research, entrepreneurs can determine the sites with the greatest concentrations of their customers and locate there. Which sites put the company in the path of its target customers? Maps that show customer concentrations (available from census maps and other sources), traffic counts, the number of customers using a particular train station and when, and other similar types of information provide evidence that a solid and sizable customer base exists. Do zoning regulations restrict the use of a site? For manufacturers, the location issue often centers on finding a site near their key raw materials or near their primary customers. Using demographic reports and market research to screen potential sites takes the guesswork out of choosing the "right" location for a business.

Pricing. What does the product or service cost to produce or deliver? Before opening a restaurant, for example, an entrepreneur should know *exactly* what it will cost to produce each item on the menu. Failing to know the total cost (including the cost of the food as well as labor, rent, advertising, and other indirect costs) of putting a plate in front of a customer is a recipe for failure. Cost is just one part of the pricing equation. Another significant factor to consider is the image a company is trying to create in the market. "Price really is more of a marketing tool than it is a vehicle for cost recovery," says Peter Meyer, author of *Creating and Dominating New Markets*. "People will pay more for a high value product or solution, so be sure to research your [product's or service's] total value."[16]

Other pricing issues that a plan should address include: What is the company's overall pricing strategy? Will the planned price support the company's strategy and desired image? Given the company's cost structure, will the price produce a profit? How does the planned price compare to those of similar products or services? Are customers willing to pay it? What price tiers exist in the market? How sensitive are customers to price changes? Will the business sell to customers on credit? Will it accept credit cards? Will the company offer discounts?

Distribution. This portion of the plan should describe the channels of distribution that the business will use (the Internet, direct mail, in-house sales force, sales agents, retailers, or others) to distribute its products and services. Will distribution be extensive, selective, or exclusive? What is the average sale? How large will the sales staff be? How will the company compensate its sales force? What are the incentives for salespeople? How many sales calls does it take to close a sale? What can the company do to make it as easy as possible for customers to buy?

Competitor Analysis

An entrepreneur should describe the new venture's competition. Failing to assess competitors realistically makes entrepreneurs appear to be poorly prepared, naive, or dishonest, especially to potential lenders and investors. The plan should include an analysis of each significant competitor. Entrepreneurs who believe they have no competitors are only fooling themselves and are raising a huge red flag to potential lenders and investors. Gathering information on competitors' market shares, products, and strategies is usually not difficult. Trade associations, customers, industry journals, marketing representatives, and sales literature are valuable sources of data. This section of the plan should focus on demonstrating that the entrepreneur's company has an advantage over its competitors and address these questions:

- Who are the company's key competitors?
- What are their strengths and weaknesses?
- What are their strategies?
- What images do they have in the marketplace?
- How successful are they?
- What distinguishes the entrepreneur's product or service from others already on the market, and how will these differences produce a competitive edge?

Firsthand competitor research is particularly valuable.

Owners' and Managers' Résumés

The most important factor in the success of a business venture is its management, and financial officers and investors weight heavily the ability and experience of a company's managers in financing decisions. A plan should include the résumés of business officers, key directors, and any person with at least 20 percent ownership in the company. This is the section of the plan in which entrepreneurs have the chance to sell the qualifications and the experience of their management team. Remember: *Lenders and investors prefer experienced managers.* Ideally, they look for managers with at least 2 years of operating experience in the industry they are targeting.

A résumé should summarize each individual's education, work history (emphasizing managerial responsibilities and duties), and relevant business experience. Lenders and investors look for the experience, talent, and integrity of the people who will breathe life into the plan. This portion of the plan should show that the company has the right people organized in the right fashion for success. One experienced private investor advises entrepreneurs to remember the following:

- Ideas and products don't succeed; people do. Show the strength of your management team. A top-notch management team with a variety of proven skills is crucial. Arthur Rock, a legend in the venture capital industry, says, "I invest in people, not ideas."[17]
- Show the strength of key employees and how you will retain them. Most small companies cannot pay salaries that match those at large businesses, but stock options and other incentives can improve employee retention.
- Enhance the strength of the management team with a capable, qualified board of advisors. A board of directors or advisors consisting of industry experts lends credibility and can complement the skills of the management team.

Plan of Operation

To complete the description of the business, an entrepreneur should construct an organization chart identifying the business's key positions and the people who occupy them. Assembling a management team with the right stuff is difficult, but keeping it together until the company is established can be even harder. Thus, entrepreneurs should describe briefly the steps taken to encourage important officers to remain with the company. Employment contracts, shares of ownership, and perks are commonly used to keep and motivate key employees.

Finally, a description of the form of ownership (sole proprietorship, partnership, joint venture, C corporation, S corporation, or LLC, for example) and of any leases, contracts, and other relevant agreements pertaining to the operation is helpful.

Pro Forma (Projected) Financial Statements

One of the most important sections of the business plan is an outline of the proposed company's financial statements—the "dollars and cents" of the proposed venture. In fact, one survey found that 74 percent of bankers say that financial documentation is the most important aspect of a business plan for entrepreneurs who are seeking loans.[18] For an existing business, lenders and investors use past financial statements to judge the health of the company and its ability to repay loans or generate adequate returns; therefore, an owner should supply copies of the firm's financial statements from the past 3 years. Ideally, these statements should be audited by a certified public accountant because most financial institutions prefer that extra reliability although a financial review of the statements by an accountant sometimes may be acceptable.

Whether assembling a plan for an existing business or for a start-up, an entrepreneur should carefully prepare projected (pro forma) financial statements for the operation for the next year using past operating data, published statistics, and research to derive forecasts of the income statement, balance sheet, cash forecast (always!), and a schedule of planned capital expenditures. Although including only most likely forecasts in the business plan is acceptable, entrepreneurs also should develop forecasts for pessimistic and optimistic conditions that reflect the uncertainty of the future in case potential lenders and investors ask for them.

It is essential for financial forecasts to be realistic. Entrepreneurs must avoid the tendency to "fudge the numbers" just to make their businesses look good. Experienced lenders and investors can detect unrealistic forecasts easily. In fact, some venture capitalists automatically discount an entrepreneur's financial projections by as much as 50 percent. After completing these forecasts, an entrepreneur should perform a break-even analysis for the business.

It is also important to include a statement of the *assumptions* on which these financial projections are based. Potential lenders and investors want to know how an entrepreneur derived forecasts for sales, cost of goods sold, operating expenses, accounts receivable, collections, accounts payable, inventory, taxes, and other items. Spelling out realistic assumptions gives a plan more credibility and reduces the tendency to include overly optimistic estimates of sales growth and profit margins. Greg Martin, a partner in the venture capital company Redpoint Ventures, says, "I have problems with start-ups making unrealistic assumptions—how much money they need or how quickly they can ramp up revenue. Those can really kill a deal for me."[19]

The Loan or Investment Proposal

The loan or investment proposal section of the business plan should state the purpose of the financing, the amount requested, and the plans for repayment or, in the case of investors, an attractive exit strategy. When describing the purpose of the loan or investment, an entrepreneur must specify the planned use of the funds. Entrepreneurs should state the precise amount requested and include relevant backup data, such as vendor estimates of costs or past production levels.

Another important element of the loan or investment proposal is the repayment schedule or exit strategy. A lender's main consideration when granting a loan is the reassurance that the applicant will repay, whereas an investor's major concern is earning a satisfactory rate of return. Financial projections must reflect a company's ability to repay loans and produce adequate returns. Without this proof, a request for funding stands little chance of being approved. It is necessary for the entrepreneur to produce tangible evidence that shows the ability to repay loans or to generate attractive returns. Developing an exit strategy, such as the option to cash out through an acquisition or a public offering, is important.

Finally, an entrepreneur should include a realistic timetable for implementing the proposed plan. This should include a schedule showing the estimated start-up date for the project and noting all significant milestones along the way.

A business plan must present an honest assessment of the risks facing the new venture. Evaluating risk in a business plan requires an entrepreneur to walk a fine line, however. Dwelling too much on everything that can go wrong discourages potential lenders and investors from financing the venture. Ignoring the project's risks makes those who evaluate the plan see the entrepreneur as either naive, dishonest, or unprepared. The best strategy is to identify the most significant risks the venture faces and then to describe the plans the entrepreneur has developed to avoid them altogether or to overcome the negative outcome if the event does occur. The accompanying "Lessons from the Street-Smart Entrepreneur" feature explains how two simple diagrams communicate effectively to investors both the risks and the rewards of a business venture.

LESSONS FROM THE STREET-SMART entrepreneur

Visualizing a Venture's Risks and Rewards

When reviewing business plans, lenders and investors naturally focus on the risks and the rewards of a business venture. Rather than taking dozens of pages of text and charts to communicate these important concepts to investors, entrepreneurs can use the following simple graphs to convey accurately both the potential risk and the returns of their proposed businesses. The first diagram shows the amount of money an entrepreneur needs to launch the business, the time required to reach the point of positive cash flow, and the anticipated amount of the payoff.

In this diagram, the depth of the hole shows lenders and investors how much money it will take to start the business, and the length of the chasm shows how long it will take to reach positive cash flow.

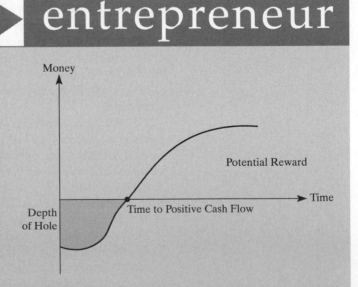

Experienced business owners know that cash flow is the lifeblood of any business. A company can operate (at least in the short run) without earning a profit, but it cannot survive without cash flow. Shallow cash holes and short times to positive cash flow are ideal, but businesses can tolerate deeper holes and longer cash chasms *as long as their founders have a plan in place to carry the company through until cash flow does become positive.*

The second diagram that follows complements the first. It shows investors the range of possible returns and the probability of achieving them. In the following example, investors can see that there is a 15 percent chance that their investments will be complete losses. The flat section shows that there is a very small chance that investors will lose only a small amount of money. The hump in the middle says that investors have a significant chance of earning between 15 and 45 percent on their money. (Note the probability of these returns is about the same as that of a total loss.) Finally, there is a small chance that their initial investments will yield a 200 percent rate of return.

This diagram portrays what investors intuitively understand: Most companies either fail big or achieve solid success.

Source: Adapted from William A. Sahlman, "How to Write a Great Business Plan," *Harvard Business Review*, July/August 1997, pp. 98–108. Reprinted by permission of Harvard Business School Publishing.

There is a difference between a *working* business plan—the one the entrepreneur is using to guide her business—and the *presentation* business plan—the one he or she is using to attract capital. Although coffee rings and penciled-in changes in a working plan don't matter (in fact, they're a *good* sign that the entrepreneur is actually using the plan), they have no place on a plan going to someone outside the company. A plan is usually the tool that an entrepreneur uses to make a first impression on potential lenders and investors. To make sure that impression is a favorable one, an entrepreneur should follow these tips:

- Realize that first impressions are crucial. Make sure the plan has an attractive (but not an expensive) cover.
- Make sure the plan is free of spelling and grammatical errors and "typos." It is a professional document and should look like one.
- Make it visually appealing. Use color charts, figures, and diagrams to illustrate key points. Don't get carried away, however, and end up with a "comic book" plan.
- Include a table of contents with page numbers to allow readers to navigate the plan easily. Reviewers should be able to look through a plan and quickly locate the sections they want to see.
- Make it interesting. Boring plans seldom get read; a good plan tells an interesting story.
- A plan must prove that the business will make money. In one survey of lenders, investors, and financial advisors, 81 percent said that, first and foremost, a plan should prove that a venture will earn a profit.[20] Start-ups do not necessarily have to be profitable immediately, but sooner or later (preferably sooner), they must make money.
- Use computer spreadsheets to generate a set of realistic financial forecasts. They allow entrepreneurs to perform valuable "what if" (sensitivity) analysis in just seconds.
- *Always* include cash flow projections. Entrepreneurs sometimes focus excessively on their proposed venture's profit forecasts and ignore cash flow projections. Although profitability is important, lenders and investors are much more interested in cash flow because they know that's where the money to pay them back or to cash them out comes from.
- The ideal plan is "crisp," long enough to say what it should but not so long that it is a chore to read. Entrepreneur and venture capitalist Guy Kawasaki says that for him the ideal business plan is just 20 pages long, including 2 pages of financial projections.[21]
- Tell the truth. Absolute honesty is always critical when preparing a business plan.

Business plans are forecasts about the future that an entrepreneur plans to create, something that one expert compares to "taking a picture of the unknown," which is a challenging feat!

As uncertain and difficult to predict as the future may be, an entrepreneur who launches a business without a plan arguing that "trying to forecast the future is pointless" is misguided. In the *Harvard Business Review*, William Sahlman says that "the best business plans . . . are like movies of the future. They show the people, the opportunity, and the context from multiple angles. They offer a plausible, coherent story of what lies ahead. They unfold the possibilities of action and reaction."[22] That's the kind of "movie" an entrepreneur should strive to create in a plan.

▶ ENTREPRENEURSHIP IN ACTION ▶

A Plan for BabyCakes

Erin McKenna left her parents and 11 brothers and sisters in San Diego, California, striking out for New York City to pursue her dream of becoming a fashion designer. Several months later, she was working as a fashion assistant at a magazine, a job that not only paid very little but was so far from her dream that it also "was demoralizing," says McKenna. She had to take on a second job as a waitress just to pay her bills. One day, she quit the fashion assistant's job and prayed, "Let me find a job that feeds my soul."

Back in her small apartment, McKenna wanted to make a batch of her favorite comfort food, chocolate chip cookies. Unfortunately, several months before, McKenna had discovered that, like 12 million other Americans, she suffered from food allergies, particularly wheat gluten, sugar, flour, and dairy products. That weekend, she attended a children's birthday party where the hostess offered McKenna some "baby cake" and explained that it might taste different because her son had food allergies, in fact, the same ones that McKenna suffered from.

"What a cute name," McKenna thought. "Perfect for a bakery for kids with food allergies." Back at home, she called her brother, who is a chef in California, and suggested that he start a bakery for people with allergies. "Why don't you do it?" he asked.

"Me? You're in the food business."

"It's your idea," her brother insisted. "You have food allergies. You know how to bake. You can make this work."

"I tried to talk myself out of it," admits McKenna, "but I felt my heart quicken, the way it used to when I sketched designs for dresses. Was this the job that would feed my soul?" After talking with her mother about the idea, McKenna decided to pursue a new dream: to start a bakery for people who suffer from food allergies. She downloaded a business plan format from the Internet and began researching the industry. McKenna discovered that millions of people who suffered from food allergies were switching to vegetarian and vegan products, sales of which were $1.2 billion annually.

Launching a bakery that used no flour, soy, sugar, or other "traditional" baking ingredients meant that McKenna had to develop new recipes. "There was no cookbook available that was doing what I set out to do, so recipe development was an insanely rocky road," she recalls. "I never went to culinary school and had to teach myself not only how to make my way around the kitchen but also how to play in this crazy culinary obstacle course I had put myself in." Working at a nearby restaurant, she began experimenting to develop recipes for her bakery. Health food stores near her apartment stocked all of the ingredients she needed, such as coconut oil (which provides a butter flavor), agave nectar (a natural sweetener with no aftertaste), xanthan gum (a substitute for wheat gluten), and gluten-free baking mix. Many experiments failed. "There were plenty of cookies that went into the trash after one bite," she recalls.

After a year of experimenting, McKenna had developed recipes for a line of delicious all-natural products, including cupcakes, cookies, brownies, and pastries, that people who suffered from food allergies could enjoy. Late in 2005 with just $85,000 in capital, she opened the first BabyCakes bakery in New York City's Lower East Side in a building equipped with hardwood floors and a tin ceiling, ideal for the image she wanted to create for her business. McKenna painted the walls pink and decorated them with 1960's memorabilia. A friend, Wendy Mullin, owner of the popular clothing label Built by Wendy, designed BabyCakes' uniforms.

The store was an instant hit with customers, reaching its break-even point in just 7 months, despite BabyCakes' modest gross profit margin. Cupcakes, which cost $2 each to make, sell for $3. Sales recently hit $1.2 million, which generated $497,000 in gross profit and $100,000 in net income. McKenna projects sales for the upcoming year to be $1.8 million, and by the end of the year she plans to open a second store in Los Angeles. A second New York

Erin McKenna, founder of BabyCakes.

Source: BabyCakes Bakery

City location is slated for the following year. "I want to focus on growing my business into a brand," she says. Many customers have approached McKenna about buying BabyCakes franchises, an idea that she finds intriguing. She continues to create cookbooks and is considering introducing BabyCakes-branded packaged foods that would sell in upscale health food stores.

The company also faces challenges. Because BabyCakes uses highly specialized ingredients, the number of suppliers, although growing, currently is limited, which makes its ingredient costs high. Other companies have noticed the rapid growth in the allergy-friendly food market and are opening competing stores. At least eight other similar bakeries operate in the United States, including one near Los Angeles that sells vegan products, and many of them have names that are very similar to BabyCakes.

All of McKenna's plans for BabyCakes require capital, however—more capital than the company can generate internally at this point.

1. What steps should Erin McKenna take to secure the capital she needs to expand BabyCakes and realize her dream of building a brand?
2. Create a business plan outline for Erin McKenna that would help her sell her ideas for expanding BabyCakes to potential lenders and investors.
3. Develop a list of at least 10 suggestions for McKenna to use when she presents her business plan to potential lenders and investors.

Sources: Based on Erin McKenna, "Sweet Dreams," *Guideposts*, December 2009, pp. 80–81; "Erin McKenna: BabyCakes Bakery," *Goop*, http://goop.com/newsletter/49/en/; "The Ultimate Start-up Reality Check," *Inc.*, July 2008, pp. 89–91.

What Lenders and Investors Look for in a Business Plan

5. Explain the "five Cs of credit" and why they are important to potential lenders and investors reviewing business plans.

To increase their chances of success when using their business plans to attract capital, entrepreneurs must be aware of the criteria lenders and investors use to evaluate the creditworthiness of entrepreneurs seeking financing. Lenders and investors refer to these criteria as the five Cs of credit: capital, capacity, collateral, character, and conditions.

CAPITAL. A small business must have a stable capital base before any lender will grant a loan. Otherwise the lender would be making, in effect, a capital investment in the business. Most lenders refuse to make loans that are capital investments because the potential for return on the investment is limited strictly to the interest on the loan, and the potential loss would probably exceed the reward. In fact, the most common reasons that banks give for rejecting small business loan applications are undercapitalization and too much debt. Investors also want to make sure that entrepreneurs have invested enough of their own money into the business to survive the tenuous start-up period.

CAPACITY. A synonym for capacity is *cash flow.* Lenders and investors must be convinced of a company's ability to meet its regular financial obligations and to repay the bank loan, and that takes cash. More small businesses fail from lack of cash than from lack of profit. It is possible for a company to be showing a profit and still run out of cash. Lenders expect a business to pass the test of liquidity; they study closely a small company's cash flow position to decide whether it has the capacity required to succeed.

Entrepreneurs who score high on the 5 c's of credit are more likely to receive the financing they need to launch their businesses.

Source: David Young\PhotoEdit Inc.

COLLATERAL. Collateral includes any assets an entrepreneur pledges to a lender as security for repayment of the loan. If an entrepreneur defaults on the loan, the bank has the right to sell the collateral and use the proceeds to satisfy the loan. Typically, lenders make very few unsecured loans (those not backed by collateral) to business start-ups. Bankers view an entrepreneur's willingness to pledge collateral (personal or business assets) as an indication of dedication to making the venture a success.

CHARACTER. Before putting money into a small business, lenders and investors must be satisfied with the owner's character. An evaluation of character frequently is based on intangible factors such as honesty, competence, polish, determination, knowledge, experience, and ability. Although the qualities judged are abstract, this evaluation plays a critical role in a lender's or investor's decision.

Lenders and investors know that most small businesses fail because of poor management, and they try to avoid extending loans to high-risk entrepreneurs. Preparing a solid business plan and a polished presentation can go far in convincing potential lenders and investors of an entrepreneur's ability to manage a company successfully.

CONDITIONS. The conditions surrounding a loan request also affect the owner's chance of receiving funds. Banks consider factors relating to the business operation, such as potential growth in the market, competition, location, form of ownership, and loan purpose. Again, the owner should provide this relevant information in an organized format in the business plan. Another important condition influencing the banker's decision is the shape of the overall economy, including interest rate levels, the inflation rate, and demand for money. Although these factors are beyond an entrepreneur's control, they still are an important component in a lender's decision.

The higher a small business scores on these five Cs, the greater its chance will be of receiving a loan or an investment. Wise entrepreneurs keep this in mind when preparing their business plans and presentations.

The Pitch: Making the Business Plan Presentation

6. Understand the keys to making an effective business plan presentation.

Lenders and investors are impressed by entrepreneurs who are informed and prepared when requesting a loan or investment. When entrepreneurs try to secure funding from lenders or investors, the written business plan almost always precedes the opportunity to meet face-to-face. The written plan must first pass muster before an entrepreneur gets the opportunity to present the plan in

LESSONS FROM THE STREET-SMART → entrepreneur

The Right Way to Write a Business Plan

Would-be entrepreneurs quickly learn the importance of writing a business plan for their prospective ventures. However, many of them believe that the only reason to create a plan is to attract capital from lenders and investors. That is a fallacy. The Street-Smart Entrepreneur offers the following tips about writing a business plan:

1. **Write a plan for the right reason.** Although a business plan is an essential tool in the hunt for capital, the primary purpose of writing a plan is to help the entrepreneurial team to identify its goals, objectives, strategies, tactics, and basis for a competitive edge in the market—in short, to lay the foundation for a successful business.

2. **Make sure you include the right elements.** There is no "best way" to write a business plan. Like the businesses they reflect, each one is unique; however, every plan should contain certain elements to maximize its value to both the entrepreneurial team and to potential lenders and investors. This chapter explains these elements; make sure that your plan covers them.

3. **Demonstrate that you understand the industry's key success factors.** Every industry is characterized by key success factors—often just two or three of them—and your plan must prove that you understand them. You also must show how your strategy incorporates these key success factors into your company.

4. **Obsess over the executive summary.** OK, "obsess" may be a bit extreme, but it emphasizes the importance of the executive summary. Most lenders and investors do not read entire plans, but they do read their executive summaries. If the executive summary hooks them, they are more likely to read the rest of the plan—and provide the capital to get the business off the ground. Entrepreneur and venture capitalist Guy Kawasaki explains the importance of the executive summary this way: "If it isn't fantastic, eyeball-sucking, pulse-altering, people won't read beyond it to find out who's on your great team, what's your business model, and why your product is curve-jumping, paradigm-shifting, and revolutionary." Remember that the executive summary is a written version of your elevator pitch.

5. **Make your financial projections realistic and keep them under control.** Entrepreneurs tend to be very optimistic, a trait that often shows up in the exuberant (and often unrealistic) financial forecasts for their companies. Research your industry thoroughly to make sure that your forecasts are reasonable; few items turn off potential lenders and investors as excessively optimistic forecasts. In addition, avoid the tendency to use spreadsheet programs to churn out dozens of pages of financial projections. Kawasaki advises, "Reduce your Excel hallucinations and provide a forecast of the key metrics of your business—for example, the number of paying customers."

6. **Write deliberately, act emergently.** When you write your plan, write deliberately, as though you know exactly what you are going to do to make your company successful. ("You're probably wrong," says Kawasaki, "but you take your best shot.") Because the reality of start-ups rarely reflects even the best plans of the entrepreneurs who launch them, entrepreneurs must act emergently, changing their strategies quickly as they execute the plan and learn the realities of the market.

7. **Avoid the most common planning mistakes that entrepreneurs make.** The following are some of the most common mistakes that entrepreneurs make when presenting their plans to potential lenders and investors, and the result is almost always the same—rejection:

- *"Our financial projections are quite conservative."* Some business plans for start-up companies show sales growth rates in the thousands of percent and revenues hitting $100 million in year 3. Then the entrepreneur presenting the plan claims that the estimates are conservative.

- *"Key employees will be joining us as soon as we raise the capital to launch."* Remember that potential lenders and investors are putting their money into a capable management team and not merely a great idea for a product or service. Although it is common for start-up companies to have some gaps in their organization charts, entrepreneurs should have a team of committed managers already in place.

- *"All we must do to be successful is to capture 1 percent of the market."* As this chapter points out, this is known as the Chinese Soda Lie. The probability that a start-up company will be able to capture 1 percent of a huge market is miniscule, and experienced lenders and investors know this. Instead, focus on defining your company's strategy for capturing a large share of a niche market.

■ *"We are confident that customers will be clamoring to buy our product or service."* Market research is a valuable component of a business plan, but the best plans offer tangible evidence of customer interest in a product or service, even if it is just a product or business prototype. In other words, be sure to include both primary and secondary market research in your plan.

Sources: Based on John W. Mullins, "Why Business Plans Don't Deliver," *Wall Street Journal,* June 22, 2009, p. R3; Julie Fields, "Lies to Make a VC Groan," *BusinessWeek,* December 29, 2000, *www.businessweek.com/smallbiz/content/dec2000/sb20001229_421.htm;* Guy Kawasaki, "The Zen of Business Plans," *How to Change the World,* January 21, 2006, *http://blog.guykawasaki.com/2006/01/the_zen_of_busi.html.*

person. Usually, the time for presenting a business opportunity is short, often no more than just a few minutes. (When presenting a plan to a venture capital forum, the allotted time is usually less than 20 minutes and rarely more than 30.) When the opportunity arises, an entrepreneur must be well prepared. It is important to rehearse, rehearse, and then rehearse some more. It is a mistake to begin by leading the audience into a long-winded explanation about the technology on which the product or service is based. Within minutes most of the audience will be lost, and so is any chance the entrepreneur has of obtaining the necessary financing for the new venture. A business plan presentation should cover five basic areas:

1. Your company and its products and services. The presentation should answer in simple terms the first question that every potential lender and investor has: What does your company do?
2. The problem to be solved, preferably told in a personal way through a compelling story. Is it eliminating the time, expense, and anxiety of waiting for the results of medical tests with a device that instantly reads blood samples or making hearing aids more effective at filtering out background noise while enhancing the dominant sound for the user?
3. A description (again in simple terms) of your company's solution to the problem. Ideally, the solution your company has developed is unique and serves as the foundation of your company's competitive edge in the marketplace.
4. Your company's business model. This part of the presentation explains how your company makes money and includes figures such as revenue per sale, expected gross profit, net profit margins, and other relevant statistics. This is your opportunity to show lenders and investors how your company will produce an attractive payback or payoff.
5. Your company's competitive edge. Your presentation should identify clearly the factors that set your company apart from the competition.

ENTREPRENEURIAL
Profile

Levi and Tomicah Tilleman-Dick and Iris Inc.

Levi and Tomicah Tilleman-Dick, cofounders of Iris Inc., a company they formed to market the improved internal combustion engine that their father developed before he died, have learned the importance of these five elements to their business plan presentation. "Know your audience," says Levi. At a recent business plan competition, with the help of a prototype engine, the brothers demonstrated not only the 80 percent improvement in efficiency that their Internally Radiated Impulse Structure (IRIS) engine provides but also its ability to generate more power and to reduce harmful emissions. They also mention the company's four patents and its board of advisors, which includes a former top executive at a major automotive company and a former consultant to the automotive industry. The essence of their pitch: cheaper, cleaner transportation for people.[24]

No matter how good a written business plan is, entrepreneurs who stumble through the presentation will lose the deal. Entrepreneurs who are successful raising the capital their companies need to grow have solid business plans and make convincing presentations of them. Some helpful tips for making a business plan presentation to potential lenders and investors include:

■ Prepare. Good presenters invest in preparing their presentations and knowing the points they want to get across to their audiences.

- Practice your delivery and then practice some more.
- Demonstrate enthusiasm about the business, but don't be overemotional.
- Focus on communicating the dynamic opportunity your idea offers and how you plan to capitalize on it. Fight the temptation to launch immediately into a lengthy discourse about the details of your product or service or how much work it took to develop it. Otherwise, you'll never have the chance to describe the details to lenders and investors.
- Hook investors quickly with an up-front explanation of the new venture, its opportunities, and the anticipated benefits to them.
- Use visual aids. They make it easier for people to follow your presentation. Don't make the mistake of making the visuals the "star" of the presentation, however. Visual aids should punctuate your spoken message and focus the audience's attention on the key points.
- Explain how your company's products or services solve some problem, and emphasize the factors that make your company unique.
- Offer proof. Integrate relevant facts into your presentation to prove your plan's claims, customers' satisfaction with your company's products or services, and its profit potential.
- Hit the highlights. Specific questions will bring out the details later. Don't get caught up in too much detail in early meetings with lenders and investors.
- Keep the presentation "crisp," just like your business plan. Otherwise, says one experienced investor, "Information that might have caused an investor to bite gets lost in the endless drone."[25]
- Avoid the use of technical terms that will likely be above most of the audience. Do at least one rehearsal before someone who has no special technical training. Tell him or her to stop you anytime he or she does not understand what you are talking about. When this occurs (and it likely will), rewrite that portion of your presentation.
- Remember that every potential lender and investor you talk to is thinking "What's in it for me?" Be sure to answer that question in your presentation.
- Close by reinforcing the potential of the opportunity. Be sure you have sold the benefits the investors will realize when the business succeeds.
- Be prepared for questions. In many cases, there is seldom time for a long "Q&A" session, but interested investors may want to get you aside to discuss the details of the plan.
- Anticipate the questions the audience is most likely to ask and prepare for them in advance.
- Be sensitive to the issues that are most important to lenders and investors by reading the pattern of their questions. Focus your answers accordingly. For instance, some investors may be interested in the quality of the management team, whereas others are more interested in marketing strategies. Be prepared to offer details on either.
- Follow up with every investor to whom you make a presentation. Don't sit back and wait; be proactive. They have what you need—investment capital. Demonstrate that you have confidence in your plan and have the initiative necessary to run a business successfully.

Conclusion

Although there is no guarantee of success when launching a business, the best way to insure against failure is create a business plan. A good plan serves as a strategic compass that keeps a business on course as it travels into an uncertain future. In addition, a solid plan is essential to raising the capital needed to start a business; lenders and investors demand it. "There may be no easier way for an entrepreneur to sabotage his or her request for capital than by failing to produce a comprehensive, well-researched, and, above all, credible business plan," says one small business expert.[26] Of course, building a plan is just one step along the path to launching a business. Creating a successful business requires entrepreneurs to put the plan into action. The chapter in this text focus on putting your business plan to work.

Suggested Business Plan Elements

Although every company's business plan will be unique, reflecting its individual circumstances, certain elements are universal. The following outline summarizes these components.

   I. Executive Summary (not to exceed two pages)
      A. Company name, address, and phone number
      B. Name(s), addresses, and phone number(s) of all key people

    C. Brief description of the business, its products and services, the customer problems they solve, and the company's competitive advantage

    D. Brief overview of the market for your products and services

    E. Brief overview of the strategies that will make your company successful

    F. Brief description of the managerial and technical experience of key people

    G. Brief statement of the financial request and how the money will be used

    H. Charts or tables showing highlights of financial forecasts

II. Vision and Mission Statement

    A. Entrepreneur's vision for the company

    B. "What business are we in?"

    C. Values and principles on which the business stands

    D. What makes the business unique? What is the source of its competitive advantage?

III. Company History (for existing businesses only)

    A. Company founding

    B. Financial and operational highlights

    C. Significant achievements

IV. Industry Profile and Overview

    A. Industry analysis

        1. Industry background and overview

        2. Significant trends

        3. Growth rate

        4. Barriers to entry and exit

        5. Key success factors in the industry

        6. Outlook for the future

    B. Stage of growth (start-up, growth, maturity)

V. Business Strategy

    A. Desired image and position in market

    B. Company goals and objectives

        1. Operational

        2. Financial

        3. Other

    C. SWOT analysis

        1. Strengths

        2. Weaknesses

        3. Opportunities

        4. Threats

    D. Competitive strategy

        1. Cost leadership

        2. Differentiation

        3. Focus

VI. Company Products and Services

    A. Description

        1. Product or service features

        2. Customer benefits

        3. Warranties and guarantees

        4. Unique selling proposition (USP)

    B. Patent or trademark protection

    C. Description of production process (if applicable)

        1. Raw materials

        2. Costs

        3. Key suppliers

        4. Lead times

    D. Future product or service offerings

VII. Marketing Strategy

    A. Target market

        1. Problem to be solved or benefit to be offered

        2. Demographic profile

        3. Other significant customer characteristics

    B. Customers' motivation to buy

    C. Market size and trends

       1. How large is the market?

       2. Is it growing or shrinking? How fast?

    D. Personal selling efforts

       1. Sales force size, recruitment, and training

       2. Sales force compensation

       3. Number of calls per sale

       4. Amount of average sale

    E. Advertising and promotion

       1. Media used—reader, viewer, listener profiles

       2. Media costs

       3. Frequency of usage

       4. Plans for generating publicity

    F. Pricing

       1. Cost structure

         a. Fixed

         b. Variable

       2. Desired image in market

       3. Comparison against competitors' prices

       4. Discounts

       5. Gross profit margin

    G. Distribution strategy

       1. Channels of distribution used

       2. Sales techniques and incentives for intermediaries

    H. Test market results

       1. Surveys

       2. Customer feedback on prototypes

       3. Focus groups

VIII. Location and Layout

    A. Location

       1. Demographic analysis of location vs. target customer profile

       2. Traffic count

       3. Lease/Rental rates

       4. Labor needs and supply

       5. Wage rates

    B. Layout

       1. Size requirements

       2. Americans with Disabilities Act compliance

       3. Ergonomic issues

       4. Layout plan (suitable for an appendix)

IX. Competitor Analysis

    A. Existing competitors

       1. Who are they? Create a competitive profile matrix.

       2. Strengths

       3. Weaknesses

    B. Potential competitors: Companies that might enter the market

       1. Who are they?

       2. Impact on your business if they enter

X. Description of Management Team

    A. Key managers and employees

       1. Their backgrounds

       2. Experience, skills, and know-how they bring to the company

    B. Résumés of key managers and employees (suitable for an appendix)

    C. Future additions to management team

    D. Board of directors or advisors

XI. Plan of Operation
  A. Form of ownership chosen and reasoning
  B. Company structure (organization chart)
  C. Decision making authority
  D. Compensation and benefits packages

XII. Financial Forecasts (suitable for an appendix)
  A. Key assumptions
  B. Financial statements (year 1 by month, years 2 and 3 by quarter)
      1. Income statement
      2. Balance sheet
      3. Cash flow statement
  C. Break-even analysis
  D. Ratio analysis with comparison to industry standards (most applicable to existing businesses)

XIII. Loan or Investment Proposal
  A. Amount requested
  B. Purpose and uses of funds
  C. Repayment or "cash out" schedule (exit strategy)
  D. Timetable for implementing plan and launching the business

XIV. Appendices (supporting documentation, including market research, financial statements, organization charts, résumés, and other items)

Chapter Review

1. Present the steps involved in conducting a feasibility analysis.
  • A feasibility analysis consists of three interrelated components: an industry and market feasibility analysis, a product or service feasibility analysis, and a financial feasibility analysis. The goal of the feasibility analysis is to determine whether an entrepreneur's idea is a viable foundation for creating a successful business.

2. Explain the benefits of an effective business plan.
  • A business plan serves two essential functions. First and more important, it guides the company's operations by charting its future course and devising a strategy for following it. The second function of the business plan is to attract lenders and investors. Applying for loans or attempting to attract investors without a solid business plan rarely attracts needed capital. Rather, the best way to secure the necessary capital is to prepare a sound business plan.

3. Explain the three tests every business plan must pass.
  • Reality test. The external component of the reality test revolves around proving that a market for the product or service really does exist. The internal component of the reality test focuses on the product or service itself.
  • Competitive test. The external part of the competitive test evaluates the company's relative position to its key competitors. The internal competitive test focuses on the management team's ability to create a company that will gain an edge over existing rivals.
  • Value test. To convince lenders and investors to put their money into the venture, a business plan must prove to them that it offers a high probability of repayment or an attractive rate of return.

4. Describe the elements of a solid business plan.
  • Although a business plan should be unique and tailor-made to suit the particular needs of a small company, it should include the following basic elements: an executive summary, a mission statement, a company history, a business and industry profile, a description of the company's business strategy, a profile of its products or services, a statement explaining its marketing strategy, a competitor analysis, owners' and officers' résumés, a plan of operation, financial data, and the loan or investment proposal.

5. Explain the "five Cs of credit" and why they are important to potential lenders and investors reviewing business plans.

- Small business owners need to be aware of the criteria bankers use in evaluating the creditworthiness of loan applicants—the five Cs of credit, which are capital, capacity, collateral, character, and conditions.
  - Capital. Lenders expect small businesses to have an equity base of investment by the owner(s) that will help support the venture during times of financial strain.
  - Capacity. A synonym for capacity is cash flow. The bank must be convinced of the firm's ability to meet its regular financial obligations and to repay the bank loan, and that takes cash.
  - Collateral. Collateral includes any assets the owner pledges to the bank as security for repayment of the loan.
  - Character. Before approving a loan to a small business, the banker must be satisfied with the owner's character.
  - Conditions. The conditions—interest rates, the health of the nation's economy, industry growth rates, etc.—surrounding a loan request also affect the owner's chance of receiving funds.

6. Understand the keys to making an effective business plan presentation.

- Lenders and investors are favorably impressed by entrepreneurs who are informed and prepared when requesting a loan or investment.
- Tips include: demonstrate enthusiasm about the venture, but don't be overemotional; "hook" investors quickly with an up-front explanation of the new venture, its opportunities, and the anticipated benefits to them; use visual aids; hit the highlights of your venture; don't get caught up in too much detail in early meetings with lenders and investors; avoid the use of technological terms that will likely be above most of the audience; rehearse your presentation before giving it; close by reinforcing the nature of the opportunity; and be prepared for questions.

Discussion Questions

1. What is involved in a feasibility analysis, and what value might it provide?
2. Why should an entrepreneur develop a business plan?
3. Why do entrepreneurs who are not seeking external financing need to prepare business plans?
4. Describe the major components of a business plan.
5. How can an entrepreneur seeking funds to launch a business convince potential lenders and investors that a market for the product or service really does exist?
6. What are the 5 Cs of credit? How do lenders and investors use them when evaluating a request for financing?
7. How would you prepare to make a formal presentation of your business plan to a venture capital forum?

This chapter begins with a discussion of the feasibility analysis to test the viability of your business concept. The following exercises will assist you in validating your business idea. You will also begin to work through the situation analysis part of the plan to enable you to better understand the market. Be as objective as possible as you work through these exercises. Rely on your ability to gather information and make realistic assessments and projections as the exercises require.

On the Web

Go to the Companion Web site at *www.pearsonhighered.com/scarborough* and click the "Business Plan Resource" tab. If you have not yet done so, find the Standard Industry Classification Code associated with your industry. You will find a link in the SIC Code information that will connect you to a resource to help you. Explore the information and links that are available on that site to learn more about the size of the industry, its growth, trends, and issues. Apply Porter's five forces model based on the industry and its SIC code. Assess the power of the five forces—the bargaining power of buyers, the power of suppliers, threat of new entrants, the threat of substitute products, and the level of rivalry. Again, you will find additional information on Porter's five forces model in the "Strategy" section of this same site. Look for information on the Web that may assist you with this analysis. Based on this information, how attractive do you consider this industry? How would you assess the opportunity this industry presents? Does this information encourage you to become involved in this industry, or does it highlight significant challenges?

In the Software

Your text may have come with "Business Feasibility Plan Pro." This software walks you through the essential steps of assessing the feasibility of your business concept. This software will address the overall feasibility of the product or service, help conduct an industry assessment, review management skills, and guide you through a preliminary financial analysis. The software provides "feedback-based" input in four components of the feasibility analysis with a numerical assessment. You can then export this information directly into Business Plan Pro.

Business Plan Pro is another resource to help you assess the feasibility of your business concept in the areas of product, service, market organization, and financial feasibility. For example, you can enter the initial capital requirements for the business in the start-up and expenses section. The sales forecast will help forecast revenues and help to determine the anticipated return on investment. If you have these estimates available, enter that information into your plan. Now look at the profit and loss statement. At what point, if any, does that statement indicate that your venture will begin generating a profit? In what year does that occur? Do you find that amount of time acceptable? If you are seeking investors, will they find that schedule attractive? Is the return on investment promising, and does this venture merit taking on the associated level of risk? We will talk more about these sections of the plan.

Review the start-up sample plans called "IntelliChild.com" and "Fantastic Florals."

1. What was the total amount of the start-up investment for each of these plans?
2. At what point, in months or years, did the plan indicate that it would begin making a profit?

3. What was the total profit projected in the following year, after breakeven occurred?
4. Based on the break-even point, which of these ventures is most attractive?
5. Based on the projections by year 3, which plan appears to offer the greatest financial potential?
6. How does the scale and potential of these two opportunities compare to those in your plan?

Building Your Business Plan

Review the information in the "Market Analysis" section. Continue to add information in this section based on the outline. Go to the "Sales Strategy" section and find information to help project expenses. You may enter the numbers in the table yourself or use the wizard that will pop up to assist you with this process. You may click and drag the visual graph to build that forecast base or enter the actual data. If the business is a start-up venture, expenses will include those figures along with ongoing expense projections. At this point, do not worry about the accuracy of the projections. Enter the estimates you have even if they are just "rough" estimates; you can change them at any time. Look at the profit and loss statement. At what point in time will your business begin making a profit? Do you find this profit picture to be acceptable?

As you build your plan, check to see that the outline and structure of the plan tells your story. Although the outline in Business Plan Pro is not identical to the outline presented in the chapter, right-clicking the outline allows you to move, add, and delete any topic you choose to modify the plan outline.

Endnotes

1. Timothy Faley, "Is Your Business Idea Feasible?" *Inc.*, October 1, 2005, *www.inc.com/resources/startup/articles/20051001/analysis.html.*
2. Charles Fishman, "The Wal-Mart You Don't Know," *Fast Company*, December 2003, *www.fastcompany.com/magazine/77/walmart.html.*
3. Ryan Blitstein, "The Cable Cowboy," *Fast Company*, November 2009, pp. 70–72.
4. Michelle Anton and Jennifer Basye Sander, "Start a Wedding Favors Business," *Entrepreneur*, May 11, 2007, *www.entrepreneur.com/ebusiness/sellingonline/article178158.html*; "About Us," My Wedding Favors, *www.myweddingfavors.com/info.html*; Tom Spinks, Kimberly Spinks Burleson, and Lindsay Spinks Shepherd, "Prepare to Be a Millionaire," Prepare to Be a Millionaire, February 1, 2008, *www.preparetobeamillionaire.com/features.pdf.*
5. Don Debelak, "Join Hands," *Entrepreneur's Be Your Own Boss*, October 2000, pp. 138–140; "Speed Rollers: Features and Benefits," Speed Rollers, *www.speedrollers.com/cms/site/c2b92193a60be297/index.html.*
6. Mark Henricks, "Do You Really Need a Business Plan?" *Entrepreneur*, December 2008, pp. 93–95; Kelly Spors, "Advance Planning Pays Off for Start-Ups," *Wall Street Journal*, February 9, 2009, *http://blogs.wsj.com/independentstreet/2009/02/09/advance-planning-pays-off-for-start-ups/.*
7. Rhonda Abrams, "Get Going on a New Business Plan," *Greenville News*, January 25, 2009, pp. 1E, 3E.
8. Kristie Price, "Business Plan Software," *Entrepreneur*, August 2009, p. 30.
9. "The Business Plan Competition," Wake Forest Schools of Business, *http://business.wfu.edu/default.aspx?id=279*; Stan Mandel, "The Elevator Pitch (EP): Engage People, Move to Action . . . In Two Minutes," *Office of Entrepreneurship and Liberal Arts Newsletter*, January 2006, *http://entrepreneurship.wfu.edu/newsletter/the-elevator-pitch.html.*
10. "Advice from the Great Ones," *Communication Briefings*, January 1992, p. 5.
11. Mike Hanlon, "Bespoke Apartments Created in 24 Hours," *GizMag*, September 15, 2006, *www.gizmag.com/go/6324/*; Adam McCulloch, "Prefab with a View," *Business 2.0*, May 2005, p. 70; "The Company," First Penthouse, *www.firstpenthouse.com/new/company/.*
12. Edward Clendaniel, "The Professor and the Practitioner," *Forbes ASAP*, May 28, 2001, p. 57.
13. Karen E. Klein, "To Beat the Recession, Reinvent Your Business," *BusinessWeek*, October 23, 2009, *www.businessweek.com/smallbiz/content/oct2009/sb20091023_229168.htm.*
14. Guy Kawasaki, *The Art of the Start* (Penguin: New York, 2004), p. 130.
15. "Business Plan Competition 2007: The 'Eight Great' Make Their Pitch," *Knowledge@Wharton*, *http://knowledge.wharton.upenn.edu/article.cfm?articleid=1738&CFID=34214186&CFTOKEN=67394551&jsessionid=9a308e717020131243d5.*
16. Jeff Wuorio, "Get an 'A' in Researching a Business Idea," *Microsoft bCentral*, *www.bcentral.com/articles/wuorio/140.asp.*

17. William A. Sahlman, "How to Write a Great Business Plan," *Harvard Business Review*, July/August 1997, p. 100.
18. "Raising Money," *Entrepreneur*, July 2005, p. 58.
19. Michael V. Copeland, "How to Make Your Business Plan the Perfect Pitch," *Business 2.0*, September 2005, p. 88.
20. Karen Axelton, "Good Plan, Stan," *Business Start-Ups*, March 200, p. 17.
21. Kawasaki, *The Art of the Start,* p. 69.
22. Sahlman, "How to Write a Great Business Plan," p. 105.
23. "Prepping Yourself for Credit," *Your Company*, April/May 1997, p. 9.
24. "Startup Showdown: The Winners," *CNN Money*, April 22, 2009, *http://money.cnn.com/galleries/2009/smallbusiness/0904/gallery.Rice_business_plan_competition_winners.smb/3.html*; "About Us," IRIS, Inc., *www.irisengine.com/599.html*.
25. David R. Evanson, "Capital Pitches That Succeed," *Nation's Business*, May 1997, p. 41.
26. Jill Andresky Fraser, "Who Can Help Out with a Business Plan?" *Inc.*, June 1999, p. 115.

Creating a Solid Financial Plan

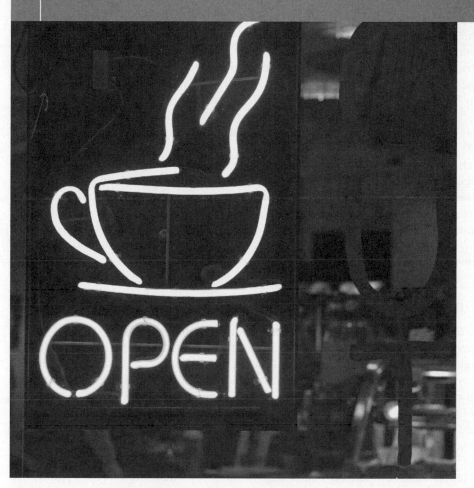

Learning Objectives

Upon completion of this chapter, you will be able to:

1. Understand the importance of preparing a financial plan.
2. Describe how to prepare financial statements and use them to manage a small business.
3. Create projected financial statements.
4. Understand basic financial statements through ratio analysis.
5. Explain how to interpret financial ratios.
6. Conduct a break-even analysis for a small company.

You can't tell who's swimming naked until after the tide goes out.

—David Darst

In the wake of numerous corporate financial scandals in which managers misrepresented their companies' financial positions, one pundit offers this definition of EBIT (in reality, earnings before interest and taxes): "earnings before irregularities and tampering."

—Mortimer B. Zuckerman

From Chapter 7 of *Effective Small Business Management: An Entrepreneurial Approach*, 10/e. Norman M. Scarborough.

1. Understand the importance of preparing a financial plan.

One of the most important steps in launching a new business venture is fashioning a well-designed, practical, realistic financial plan. Potential lenders and investors expect to see a financial plan before putting their money into a start-up company. More important, however, a financial plan is a vital tool to help entrepreneurs manage their businesses more effectively, steering their way around the pitfalls that cause failures. Entrepreneurs who ignore the financial aspects of their businesses run the risk of watching their companies become another failure statistic. Many empirical studies have verified the positive correlation between the degree of planning (including financial planning) that entrepreneurs engage in and the success of their new ventures. These studies also show a significant positive relationship between formal planning by small companies and their financial performance.[1] One financial expert says of small companies, "Those that don't establish sound controls at the start are setting themselves up to fail."[2]

However, both research and anecdotal evidence suggests that a significant percentage of entrepreneurs run their companies without any kind of financial plan and never analyze their companies' financial statements as part of the decision-making process. Why is the level of financial planning and analysis so low among entrepreneurs? The primary reason is the lack of financial know-how. One survey of small business owners by Greenfield Online found that accounting was the most intimidating part of managing their businesses and that more than half had no formal financial training at all.[3] To reach profit objectives, entrepreneurs cannot afford to be intimidated by financial management and must be aware of their companies' overall financial position and the changes in financial status that occur over time. Norm Brodsky, a veteran entrepreneur and author, says, "When you learn the basics of accounting, you realize that the numbers aren't as complicated as you feared and that you're developing the knowledge you need to be in control of your company."[4]

This chapter focuses on some very practical tools that help entrepreneurs to develop workable financial plans, keep them focused on their company's financial plans, and enable them to create a plan for earning a profit. They can use these tools to anticipate changes and plot an appropriate profit strategy to meet them head on. These profit planning techniques are not difficult to master, nor are they overly time consuming. We will discuss the techniques involved in preparing projected (pro forma) financial statements, conducting ratio analysis, and performing break-even analysis.

Basic Financial Reports

2. Describe how to prepare financial statements and use them to manage a small business.

Before we begin building projected financial statements, it would be helpful to review the basic financial reports that measure a company's overall financial position: the balance sheet, the income statement, and the statement of cash flows. Every business, no matter how small, will benefit from preparing these basic financial statements. Building them is the first step toward securing a small company's financial future. Most accounting experts advise entrepreneurs to use one of the popular computerized small business accounting programs, such as Intuit's market-leading QuickBooks, Sage's Peachtree Accounting, or Microsoft's Small Business Accounting, to manage routine record-keeping tasks that form the underlying framework of these financial statements. These programs make analyzing a company's financial statements, preparing reports, and summarizing data a snap. A survey by Microsoft, however, reports that less than half of small companies use dedicated accounting software; most use a combination of homemade spreadsheets and paper records to handle their accounting needs.[5] Working with an accountant to set up a smoothly functioning accounting system at the outset and then having an employee or a part-time bookkeeping service enter the transactions is most efficient for the businesses that use these packages.

The Balance Sheet

Like a digital camera, the balance sheet takes a "snapshot" of a business, providing owners with an estimate of the company's worth on a given date. Its two major sections show the assets a business owns and the claims creditors and owners have against those assets. The balance sheet is usually prepared on the last day of the month. Figure 1 shows the balance sheet for a small business, Sam's Appliance Shop, for the year ended December 31, 201X.

The balance sheet is built on the fundamental accounting equation: Assets = Liabilities + Owner's equity. Any increase or decrease on one side of the equation must be

FIGURE 1
Balance Sheet, Sam's
Appliance Shop
For Year Ending December 31, 201X

Assets		
Current assets		
Cash		$49,855
Accounts receivable	$179,225	
Less allowance for doubtful accounts	$6,000	$173,225
Inventory		$455,455
Prepaid expenses		$8,450
Total current assets		$686,985
Fixed assets		
Land		$59,150
Buildings	$74,650	
Less accumulated depreciation	$7,050	$67,600
Equipment	$22,375	
Less accumulated depreciation	$1,250	$21,125
Furniture and fixtures	$10,295	
Less accumulated depreciation	$1,000	$9,295
Total fixed assets		$157,170
Intangibles (goodwill)		$3,500
Total assets		$847,655
Liabilities		
Current liabilities		
Accounts payable		$152,580
Notes payable		$83,920
Accrued wages/salaries payable		$38,150
Accrued interest payable		$42,380
Accrued taxes payable		$50,820
Total current liabilities		$367,850
Long-term liabilities		
Mortgage		$127,150
Note payable		$85,000
Total long-term liabilities		$212,150
Owner's Equity		
Sam Lloyd, capital		$267,655
Total liabilities and owner's equity		$847,655

offset by an equal increase or decrease on the other side, hence the name *balance sheet*. It provides a baseline from which to measure future changes in assets, liabilities, and owner's equity (or net worth). The first section of the balance sheet lists the company's **assets** (valued at cost, not actual market value) and shows the total value of everything the business owns. **Current assets** consist of cash and items to be converted into cash within 1 year or within the normal operating cycle of the company, whichever is longer, such as accounts receivable and inventory, and **fixed assets** are those acquired for long-term use in the business. **Intangible assets** include items that, although valuable, do not have tangible value, such as goodwill, copyrights, and patents.

The second section shows the company's **liabilities**—the creditors' claims against the company's assets. **Current liabilities** are those debts that must be paid within 1 year or within the normal operating cycle of the company, whichever is longer, and **long-term liabilities** are those that come due after 1 year. This section of the balance sheet also shows the **owner's equity**, the value of the owner's investment in the business. It is the balancing factor on the balance sheet, representing all of the owner's capital contributions to the business plus all accumulated earnings not distributed to the owner(s).

The Income Statement

The **income statement** (or profit and loss statement, or "P&L") compares expenses against revenue over a certain period of time to show the firm's net income or loss. Like a digital video recorder, the income statement provides a "moving picture" of a company's profitability over time. The annual P&L statement reports the bottom line of the business over the fiscal or calendar year. Figure 2 shows the income statement for Sam's Appliance Shop for the year ended December 31, 201X.

To calculate net income or loss, owners record sales revenue for the year, which includes all income that flows into the business from the sale of goods and services. Income from other sources (rent, investments, interest) also must be included in the revenue section of the income statement. To determine net revenue, owners subtract the value of returned items and refunds from gross revenue. **Cost of goods sold** represents the total cost of purchasing (including shipping) the merchandise that the company sells during the year. Wholesalers and retailers calculate cost of goods sold by adding purchases to beginning inventory and subtracting ending inventory. Service companies typically have no cost of goods sold.

Subtracting the cost of goods sold from net sales revenue results in a company's **gross profit**. Allowing the cost of goods sold to get out of control whittles away a company's gross profit, virtually guaranteeing a net loss at the bottom of the income statement. Dividing gross profit by net sales revenue produces the **gross profit margin**, a percentage that every entrepreneur should watch closely. If a company's gross profit margin slips too low, it is likely that it will operate at a

FIGURE 2
Income Statement, Sam's Appliance Shop
For Year Ending December 31, 201X

Net sales revenue		$1,870,841
Cash sales	$561,252	
Credit sales	$1,309,589	
Cost of goods sold		
Beginning inventory, 1/1/xx	$805,745	
+ Purchases	$939,827	
Goods available for sale	$1,745,572	
− Ending inventory, 12/31/xx	$455,455	
Cost of goods sold		$1,290,117
Gross profit		$580,724
Operating expenses		
Advertising	$139,670	
Insurance	$46,125	
Depreciation		
Building	$18,700	
Equipment	$9,000	
Salaries	$224,500	
Travel	$4,000	
Entertainment	$2,500	
Total operating expenses		$444,495
General expenses		
Utilities	$5,300	
Telephone	$2,500	
Postage	$1,200	
Payroll taxes	$25,000	
Total general expenses		$34,000
Other expenses		
Interest expense	$39,850	
Bad check expense	$1,750	
Total other expenses		$41,600
Total expenses		$520,095
Net income		$60,629

loss (negative net income). A declining gross profit margin also restricts a company's ability to invest in revenue-generating activities, such as marketing, advertising, and business development.

Many business owners whose companies are losing money mistakenly believe that the problem is inadequate sales volume; therefore, they focus on pumping up sales at any cost. In many cases, however, the losses are due to an inadequate gross profit margin, and pumping up sales only deepens their losses! Repairing a poor gross profit margin requires a company to raise prices, cut manufacturing or purchasing costs, refuse orders with low profit margins, or add new products with more attractive profit margins. *Increasing sales will not resolve the problem.* One business owner admits that he fell victim to this myth of profitability. His company was losing money, and in an attempt to correct the problem he focused his efforts on boosting sales. His efforts were successful, but the results were not. The costs he incurred to add sales produced withering gross profit margins, and by the time he deducted operating costs the business had incurred an even greater net loss! Cash flow suffered, the business could not pay its bills on time, and the owner ended up filing bankruptcy. Now a successful business owner, this entrepreneur says, "Ever since, I've tracked my gross [profit] margins like a hawk."[6] Monitoring the gross profit margin over time and comparing it to those of other companies in the same industry are important steps to maintaining a company's long-term profitability.

Operating expenses include those costs that contribute directly to the manufacture and distribution of goods. General expenses are indirect costs incurred in operating the business. "Other expenses" is a catch-all category covering all other expenses that don't fit into the other two categories. Total revenue minus total expenses gives the company's **net income (or loss)**. Reducing expenses increases a company's net income, and even small reductions in expenses can add up to big savings.

ENTREPRENEURIAL
Profile

Jay Goltz and Chicago Art Source

Jay Goltz, owner of a picture-framing and home furnishings business in Chicago, recently purchased a machine that shreds cardboard, making it suitable as a packing material. Not only did the move eliminate the cardboard the company was putting into landfills, but it also allowed Goltz to save $10,000 per year on purchases of packing material.[7]

Business owners must be careful when embarking on cost-cutting missions, however. Although minimizing costs can improve profitability, entrepreneurs must be judicious in their cost-cutting, taking a strategic approach rather than imposing across-the-board cuts. Brad Smith, CEO of Intuit, a company that develops software and provides business services for small businesses, knows that research and development and product innovation are keys to the company's success. "We're not going to cut innovation," he vows. "For 25 years, this company has been fueled by new product innovation. We're protecting the innovation pipeline so that [our future] is strong."[8] Cutting costs in areas that are vital to a company's success—such as a retail jeweler cutting its marketing budget during a recession—can inhibit its ability to compete and do more harm than good. In fact, a study by McGraw-Hill Research reports that companies that advertise consistently even during recessions perform better in the long run; companies that advertised aggressively during a recent recession generated sales that were 256 percent higher than those that did not advertise consistently.[9]

In other cases, entrepreneurs on cost-cutting vendettas alienate employees and sap worker morale by eliminating nitpicking costs that affect employees but retaining expensive perks for themselves. One business owner enraged employees by cutting the budget for the company Christmas party to $5 (for the whole event) and encouraging employees not to skip lines on interoffice envelopes (which, one worker calculated, cost the company $0.0064 per skipped line). Although his reasons for cutting costs were valid, this CEO lost all credibility because employees knew that he had a chauffeur drive him to work every day and when he traveled he stayed only at upscale, butler-serviced hotels![10]

The Statement of Cash Flows

The **statement of cash flows** shows the changes in a company's working capital from the beginning of the accounting period by listing the sources of funds and the uses of these funds. Many small businesses never need such a statement; instead, they rely on a cash budget, a less formal managerial tool that tracks the flow of cash into and out of a company over time. Sometimes, however, creditors, lenders, investors, or business buyers may require this information.

To prepare the statement of cash flows, owners must assemble the balance sheets and the income statements summarizing the present year's operations. They begin with the company's net income for the accounting period (from the income statement). Then they add the sources of funds—borrowed funds, owner contributions, decreases in accounts payable, decreases in inventory, depreciation, and any others. Depreciation is listed as a source of funds because it is a non-cash expense that is deducted as a cost of doing business. Because the owners have already paid for the item being depreciated, its depreciation is a source of funds. Next the owners subtract the uses of these funds—plant and equipment purchases, dividends to owners, repayment of debt, increases in accounts receivable, decreases in accounts payable, increases in inventory, and so on. The difference between the total sources and the total uses of funds is the increase or decrease in working capital. By investigating the changes in their companies' working capital and the reasons for them, owners can create a more practical financial plan of action for the future.

These statements are more than just complex documents used only by accountants and financial officers. When used in conjunction with the analytical tools described in the following sections, they can help entrepreneurs map their companies' financial future and actively plan for profit. Merely preparing these statements is not enough, however; entrepreneurs and their employees must *understand and use* the information contained in them to make the business more effective and efficient.

IN THE ENTREPRENEURIAL
SPOTLIGHT Open Book Management

In 1982, Jack Stack led a management buyout of a failing division of International Harvester that refurbished engines. In one of the most highly leveraged buyouts in corporate history, the managers invested $100,000 of their own money and borrowed $9 million to purchase the business, leaving the company, Springfield Remanufacturing Company (SRC), with an incredible debt to equity ratio of 90 to 1! Facing a huge debt load and a short time horizon to turn SRC around, Stack and his team of managers knew that one key to success was to ignite a passion for the company among its employees. Stack's idea was to give everyone in the factory—from cam rod grinders to purchasing agents—access to SRC's financial statements and teach them how to read, analyze, and understand the company's critical numbers.

Managers met with teams of employees in weekly meetings to discuss the numbers, answer questions, and solicit ideas about how to improve them in a process he called "open book management," a revolutionary concept at the time. The idea behind open book management, says Stack, "is to get employees to start approaching their jobs as if they owned the place, which, in fact, they might." Some companies that practice open book management, including SRC, share ownership of the business with their employees through employee stock ownership plans (ESOPs). "Our goal was to teach our employees to think and act like owners," says Stack. "We started by trying to improve their financial literacy by turning topics like accounting into a game. We played this game with real money, however, and the game's pieces were each and every employee's quality of life. We called it The Great Game of Business."

Using The Great Game of Business, managers transformed employees into owners of every line of the company's balance sheet, income statement, and cash flows statement, which enabled workers at every level of operation to understand how they could move the numbers in the right direction. "Rather than having some engineer with a stopwatch trying to get people to work faster for less money, open book management gives everyone the chance to see what they need to do to succeed," says Stack. In its first full year of operation, SRC lost $60,500 on sales of $16 million. Within 10 years, the company was earning a profit of $1.3 million on sales of $66 million. Today, SRC is the leading success story of open book management, having evolved into a collection of 37 employee-owned businesses that employ more than 1,200 workers and make everything from race car engines to home furnishings.

Stack's daughter, who owns a small upscale clothing store in Missouri, learned the lessons of open book management from her father. She operates her small business using open book management with her seven employees. "She now has seven people who think like she does," observes Stack. "They now understand inventory turns and profit margins and the relationship between the two."

Growing numbers of entrepreneurs are realizing that, done properly, open book management has the potential to light a fire in employees' eyes, make businesses more profitable, and transform the way in which they operate. When Dorian Drake International, a business that provides sales, marketing, and logistics services to companies overseas, began using open book management, employees realized that some departments were receiving discounts from vendors, but others were not. The employees took the initiative to negotiate the same discounts for all departments, a move that helped the company go from a loss of $500,000 on sales of $32 million to a profit of $200,000 with no increase in sales in the company's first year of open book management. "I saw open book as an opportunity to send a message to our staff that said, 'We trust you,'" says CEO Ed Dorian, Jr. "We not only trust your intentions, but we also trust your ability to help us."

1. Use online resources to identify the management principles upon which open book management is based and prepare a two-page summary of your findings.
2. What benefits does open book management offer a company and its employees?
3. Conduct an online search for a company that uses open book management and write a one-page summary of its experience with this technique. Identify at least two keys to the successful use of open book management.
4. Why do many entrepreneurs resist opening their companies' books to employees? Would you be willing to do so? Explain.

Sources: Based on Jack Stack, "Introducing 'Open the Books': Why Would Anyone Do This?" *New York Times*, December 15, 2009, *http://boss.blogs. nytimes.com/2009/12/15/introducing-open-the-books-why-would-anyone-do-this/*; Jack Stack, "The Great Game of Business," *Institute for Entrepreneurial Excellence*, April 10, 2010, *www.entrepreneur.pitt.edu/eventfiles/1010.pdf*; Darren Dahl, "Open Book Management Lessons for Detroit," *New York Times*, May 21, 2009, *www.nytimes.com/2009/05/21/business/smallbusiness/21open.html*; Laura Lorber, "An Open Book," *Wall Street Journal*, February 23, 2009, p. R8; Jack Stack, "Open Wide," *Inc.*, January–February 2009, p. 76.

Creating Projected Financial Statements

3. Create projected financial statements.

Creating projected financial statements helps entrepreneurs transform their business goals into reality. These projected financial statements answer such questions as: What profit can the business expect to earn? If the founder's profit objective is x dollars, what sales level must the business achieve? What fixed and variable expenses can the owner expect at that level of sales? The answers to these and other questions are critical in formulating a successful financial plan for the small business.

This section focuses on creating projected income statements and balance sheets for the small business. These projected (pro forma) statements estimate the profitability and the overall financial condition of the business in the immediate future. They are an integral part of convincing potential lenders and investors to provide the financing needed to get the company off the ground. In addition, because these statements forecast a company's financial position, they help entrepreneurs plan the route to improved financial strength and healthy business growth. In other words, they lay the foundation for a pathway to profitability.

Because an established business has a history of operating data from which to construct pro forma financial statements, the task is not nearly as difficult as it is for the beginning business. When creating projected financial statements for a business start-up, entrepreneurs typically rely on published statistics that summarize the operation of similar-size companies in the same industry. These statistics are available from a number of sources (described later), but this section draws on information found in *RMA Annual Statement Studies*, a compilation of financial data on thousands of companies across hundreds of industries [organized by North American Industry Classification (NAICS) and Standard Industrial Classification (SIC) Codes]. Because conditions and markets change so rapidly, entrepreneurs who develop financial forecasts for start-ups should focus on creating projections for 2 years into the future. Investors mainly want to see that entrepreneurs have realistic expectations about their companies' income and expenses and when they expect to start earning a profit.

Projected Statements for the Small Business

One of the most important tasks confronting an entrepreneur is to determine the capital required to launch the business and to keep going until it begins to generate positive cash flow. The amount of money needed to begin a business depends on the type of operation, its location, inventory requirements, sales volume, credit terms, and other factors. Every new company must have enough capital to cover all start-up costs, including funds to rent or buy plant, equipment, and tools as well as to pay for employees' salaries and wages, advertising, licenses, insurance, utilities, travel, and other expenses. In addition, the owner must maintain a reserve of capital to carry the company until it begins to produce positive cash flow. Too often, entrepreneurs are overly optimistic in their financial plans and fail to recognize that expenses initially exceed income for most small firms, which creates a drain on its cash flow. This period of net losses and the resulting cash drain is normal and may last from just a few months to several years. During this time, entrepreneurs must be able to meet payroll, maintain adequate inventory, take advantage of cash discounts, pay all other business expenses, grant customer credit, and meet their personal obligations. Figure 3 provides a model that shows the connections among the various financial forecasts (income statement, balance sheet, and cash flow) entrepreneurs should include in their business plans.

THE PROJECTED INCOME STATEMENT. When creating a projected income statement, the first step is to create a sales forecast. An entrepreneur has two options: develop a sales forecast and work down or set a profit target and work up. Many entrepreneurs prefer to use the latter method—targeting a profit figure and then determine the sales level they must achieve to reach it. Of course, it is important to compare this sales target against the results of the marketing plan to determine whether it is realistic. Although financial forecasts are projections, they must be based in reality; otherwise, they are nothing more than hopeless dreams.

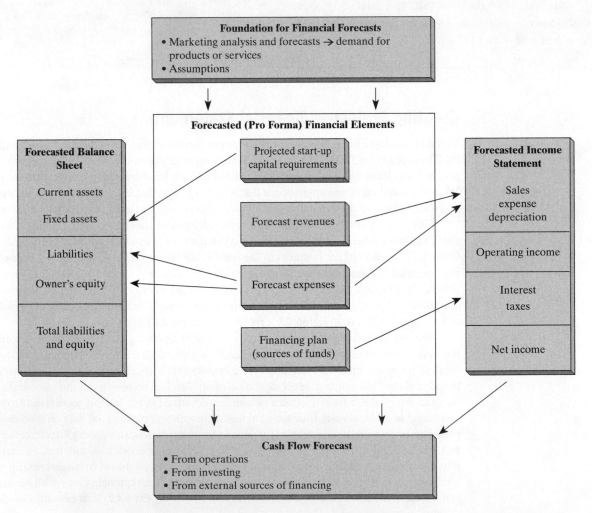

FIGURE 3
Financial Forecasting Model

Source: Adapted from Benjamin B. Gansel, "Financial Planning in Business Venturing," *International Journal of Entrepreneurship and Innovation Management, Special Issue: Strategic Approach for Successful Business Plan* 8(4), 2008, pp. 436–450. Reprinted by permission of Inderscience.

The next step is to estimate all of the expenses the business will incur to generate those sales. In any small business, the resulting profit must be large enough to produce a return for the time the owners spend operating the business and a return on their financial investment in the business. Ideally, a small company's net income after taxes should be at least as much as the owner could earn by working for someone else. An adequate profit must also include a reasonable return on the owner's total financial investment in the business. If a would-be owner has $200,000 and can invest it in securities that earn 8 percent, pouring the money into a small business that yields only 3 percent may not be the best course of action.

An entrepreneur's target income is the sum of a reasonable salary for the time spent running the business and a normal return on the amount invested in the firm. Determining this amount is the first step in creating the pro forma income statement.

The next step is to translate this target profit into a sales estimate for the forecasted period. To calculate net sales from a target profit, the owner needs published statistics for this type of business. Suppose an entrepreneur wants to launch a small retail flower shop and has determined that his target income is $30,000 for the upcoming year. Statistics gathered from *RMA Annual Statement Studies* show that the typical florist's net profit margin (net profit ÷ sales) is 7.2 percent. Using this information, he can compute the sales level required to produce a net profit of $30,000:

$$\text{Net profit margin} = \frac{\text{net profit}}{\text{sales (annual)}}$$

Solving for net sales produces the following result:

$$\text{Sales} = \frac{\$30,000}{0.072}$$
$$= \$416,667$$

Now the entrepreneur knows that to earn a net profit of $30,000 (before taxes), he must achieve annual sales of $416,667. To complete the projected income statement, the entrepreneur simply applies the appropriate statistics from *RMA Annual Statement Studies* to the annual sales figure. Because the statistics for each income statement item are expressed as percentages of sales, the entrepreneur merely multiplies the proper statistic by the annual sales figure to obtain the desired value. For example, cost of goods sold usually comprises 46.6 percent of sales for the typical small flower shop. The owner of this new flower shop expects the cost of goods sold to be the following:

$$\text{Cost of goods sold} = \$416,667 \times 46.6\% = \$194,167$$

The flower shop's complete projected income statement is shown as follows:

Net sales	(100%)	$416,667
− Cost of goods sold	(46.6%)	319,811
Gross profit margin	(53.4%)	$222,500
− Operating expenses	(46.2%)	192,500
Net income (before taxes)	(7.2%)	$30,000

At this point, the business appears to be a lucrative venture. But remember: This income statement represents a goal that the entrepreneur may not be able to attain. The next step is to determine whether this required sales volume is reasonable. One useful technique is to break down the required annual sales volume into daily sales figures. Assuming the shop will be open 6 days per week for 52 weeks (312 days), the owner must average $1,335 per day in sales:

$$\text{Average daily sales} = \frac{\$416,667}{312\,\text{days}}$$
$$= \$1,335/\text{day}$$

This calculation gives the owner a better perspective of the sales required to yield an annual profit of $30,000.

To determine whether the profit expected from the business will meet or exceed the entrepreneur's target income, the prospective owner should create an income statement based on a realistic sales estimate. The previous analysis showed this entrepreneur what sales level is needed to reach the desired profit. But what happens if sales are lower or higher? To answer that question, he must develop a reliable sales forecast using market research techniques.

Suppose that after gathering information from the industry trade association and conducting a marketing survey of local customers, the prospective florist projects that first year sales for the proposed business will be only $395,000. Using this expected sales figure to develop a pro forma income statement yields the following result:

Net Sales	(100%)	$395,000
− Cost of Goods Sold	(46.6%)	184,070
Gross Profit Margin	(53.4%)	210,930
− Operating Expenses	(46.2%)	182,490
Net Income (before taxes)	(7.2%)	$28,440

Based on sales of $395,000, this entrepreneur should expect a net income (before taxes) of $28,440. If this amount is acceptable as a return on the investment of time and money in the business, he should proceed with his planning.

At this stage in developing the financial plan, the owner should create a more detailed picture of the company's expected operating expenses. One method is to use the statistics found in publications such as *Dun & Bradstreet's Cost of Doing Business* or reports from industry trade associations. These publications document selected operating expenses (expressed as a percentage of net sales) for different lines of businesses. Although publications such as these offer valuable guidelines for preparing estimates of expenses, the most reliable estimates of a start-up company's expenses are those that entrepreneurs develop for their particular locations. Expenses such as rent, wages, salaries, benefits, utilities, and others vary dramatically from one part of the nation to another, and entrepreneurs must be sure that their forecasted expenses reflect the real cost of operating their particular businesses. Internet searches and a few telephone calls usually produce the necessary cost estimates.

To ensure that they have overlooked no business expenses in preparing their business plans, entrepreneurs should list all of the initial expenses they will incur and have an accountant review the list. Figures 4 and 5 show two useful forms designed to help assign dollar values to anticipated expenses. Totals derived from this list of expenses should approximate the total expense figures calculated from published statistics. Naturally, an entrepreneur should be more confident of the total from his own list of expenses because this reflects his particular set of circumstances.

Entrepreneurs who follow the top-down approach to building an income statement—developing a sales forecast and working down to net income—must be careful to avoid falling into the trap of excessive optimism. Many entrepreneurs using this method overestimate their anticipated revenues and underestimate their actual expenses, and the results can be disastrous. To avoid this problem, some experts advise entrepreneurs to use the rule that many venture capitalists apply when they evaluate business start-ups: Divide revenues by two, multiply expenses by two, and if the business can still make it, it's a winner!

THE PROJECTED BALANCE SHEET. In addition to projecting the small company's net profit or loss, the entrepreneur must develop a pro forma balance sheet outlining the fledgling company's assets and liabilities. Most entrepreneurs' primary focus is on the potential profitability of their businesses, but the assets their businesses use to generate profits are no less important. In many cases, small companies begin life on weak financial footing because their owners fail to determine their firms' total asset requirements. To prevent this major oversight, the owner should prepare a projected balance sheet listing every asset the business will need and all the claims against these assets.

ASSETS. Cash is one of the most useful assets the business owns; it is highly liquid and can quickly be converted into other tangible assets. But how much cash should a small business have at its inception? Obviously, there is no single dollar figure that fits the needs of every small firm. One practical rule of thumb, however, suggests that the company's cash balance should cover its operating expenses (less depreciation, a noncash expense) for one inventory turnover period. Using this rule, we can calculate the cash balance for the small flower shop as follows:

Estimated Monthly Expenses	Your estimate of monthly expenses based on sales of $_____ per year.	Your estimate of how much cash you need to start your business. (See column 3.)	What to put in column 2. (These figures are typical for one kind of business. You will have to decide how many months to allow for in your business.)
ITEM	**COLUMN 1**	**COLUMN 2**	**COLUMN 3**
Salary of owner-manager	$	$	2 times column 1
All other salaries and wages			3 times column 1
Rent			3 times column 1
Advertising			3 times column 1
Delivery expense			3 times column 1
Supplies			3 times column 1
Telephone and telegraph			3 times column 1
Other utilities			3 times column 1
Insurance			Payment required by insurance company
Taxes, including Social Security			4 times column 1
Interest			3 times column 1
Maintenance			3 times column 1
Legal and other professional fees			3 times column 1
Miscellaneous			3 times column 1
Starting costs you have to pay only once			Leave column 2 blank
Fixtures and equipment			Fill in worksheet 3 and put the total here
Decorating and remodeling			Talk it over with a contractor
Installation of fixtures and equipment			Talk to suppliers from whom you buy these
Starting inventory			Suppliers will probably help you estimate this
Deposits with public utilities			Find out from utilities companies
Legal and professional fees			Lawyer, accountant, and so on
Licenses and permits			Find out from city offices what you have to have
Advertising and promotion for opening			Estimate what you'll use
Accounts receivable			What you need to buy more stock until credit customers pay
Cash			For unexpected expenses or losses, special purchases, etc.
Other			Make a separate list and enter total
Total Estimated Cash You Need to Start		$	Add up all the numbers in column 2

FIGURE 4
Anticipated Expenses

Source: U.S. Small Business Administration, *Checklist for Going into Business,* Small Marketers Aid No. 71 (Washington, DC: GPO, 1982), pp. 6–7.

List of Furniture, Fixtures, and Equipment

Leave out or add items to suit your business. Use separate sheets to list exactly what you need for each of the items below.	If you plan to pay cash in full, enter the full amount below and in the last column.	If you are going to pay by installments, fill out the columns below. Enter in the last column your down payment plus at least one installment.			Estimate of the cash you need for furniture, fixtures, and equipment.
		Price	Down payment	Amount of each installment	
Counters	$	$	$	$	$
Storage shelves and cabinets					
Display stands, shelves, tables					
Cash register					
Safe					
Window display fixtures					
Special lighting					
Outside sign					
Delivery equipment if needed					
Total Furniture, Fixtures, and Equipment (enter this figure also in worksheet 2 under Starting Costs You Have to Pay Only Once)					$

FIGURE 5
Anticipated Expenditures for Fixtures and Equipment

Source: U.S. Small Business Administration, *Checklist for Going into Business,* Small Marketers Aid No. 71 (Washington, DC: GPO, 1982), pp. 6–7.

Operating expenses = $182,490 (from projected income statement)

Less depreciation (1.9% of annual sales) = $7,505 (a noncash expense)

Equals cash expenses (annual) = $174,985

$$\text{Cash requirement} = \frac{\text{cash expenses}}{\text{average inventory turnover ratio}}$$

$$= \frac{174,985}{13.6*}$$

$$= \$12,867$$

*from *RMA Annual Statement Studies.*

Notice the inverse relationship between a small company's average inventory turnover ratio and its cash requirements. The faster a business turns its inventory, the shorter the time its cash is tied up in inventory, and the smaller is the amount of cash at start-up the company requires. For instance, if this florist could turn its inventory 17 times per year, its cash requirement would be $182,655 ÷ 17, or $10,293.

INVENTORY. Another decision facing the entrepreneur is how much inventory the business should carry. An estimate of the amount of required inventory can be calculated from the information found on the projected income statement and from published statistics:

Cost of goods sold = $184,070 (from projected income statement)

$$\text{Average inventory turnover} = \frac{\text{Cost of goods sold}}{\text{Inventory level}}$$

$$= 13.6 \text{ times/year}$$

Rearranging the equation to solve for inventory level produces the following:

$$\text{Average inventory level} = \frac{\$184,070}{13.6 \text{ times/year}}$$

$$= \$13,535$$

The entrepreneur also includes $1,800 in miscellaneous current assets. Suppose the estimate of fixed assets is as follows:

Fixtures (including refrigeration units)	$54,500
Office equipment	5,250
Computers/Cash register	5,125
Signs	7,200
Miscellaneous	1,500
Total	**$73,575**

LIABILITIES. To complete the projected balance sheet, the owner must record all of the small company's liabilities, the claims against the assets. The florist was able to finance 50 percent of inventory and fixtures ($34,018) through suppliers and has a short-term note payable of $3,750. The only other major claim against the store's assets is a note payable to the entrepreneur's father-in-law for $25,000. The difference between the company's total assets ($101,776) and its total liabilities ($62,768) represents the owner's investment in the business (owner's equity) of $39,008.

The final step is to compile all of these items into a projected balance sheet, as shown in Figure 6.

Ratio Analysis

4. Understand basic financial statements through ratio analysis.

Would you be willing to drive a car on an extended trip without being able to see the dashboard displays showing fuel level, engine temperature, oil pressure, battery status, or the speed at which you were traveling? Not many people would! Yet many small business owners run their companies exactly that way. They never take the time to check the vital signs of their businesses using their "financial dashboards." The result: Their companies develop engine trouble, fail, and leave them stranded along the road to successful entrepreneurship.

Smart entrepreneurs know that once they have their businesses up and running with the help of a solid financial plan, the next step is to keep the company moving in the right direction with the help of proper financial controls. Establishing these controls—and using them consistently—is one of the keys to keeping a business vibrant and healthy. Business owners who don't often are shocked to learn that their companies are in serious financial trouble *and they never knew it.*

A smoothly functioning system of financial controls is essential to achieving business success. These systems serve as an early warning device for underlying problems that could destroy a young business. They allow an entrepreneur to step back and see the big picture

FIGURE 6
Projected Balance Sheet for a Small Flower Shop

Assets			Liabilities	
Current assets			**Current liabilities**	
Cash	$12,867		Accounts payable	$34,018
Inventory	13,535		Note payable	3,750
Miscellaneous	1,800			
Total current assets	$28,201		Total current liabilities	$37,768
Fixed Assets			**Long-term liabilities**	
Fixtures	$54,500		Note payable	$25,000
Office equipment	5,250			
Computers/cash register	5,125		Total liabilities	$62,768
Signs	7,200			
Miscellaneous	1,500			
Total fixed assets	$73,575		**Owner's equity**	$39,008
Total assets	$101,776		**Total liabilities and owner's equity**	$101,776

and to make adjustments in the company's strategic direction when necessary. According to one writer:

A company's financial accounting and reporting system will provide signals, through comparative analysis, of impending trouble, such as:

- Decreasing sales and falling profit margins.
- Increasing overhead.
- Growing inventories and accounts receivable.

These are all signals of declining cash flows from operations, the lifeblood of every business. As cash flows decrease, the squeeze begins:

- Payments to vendors become slower.
- Maintenance on production equipment lags.
- Raw material shortages appear.
- Equipment breakdowns occur.

All of these begin to have a negative impact on productivity. Now the downward spiral has begun in earnest. The key is hearing and focusing on the signals.[11]

What are these signals, and how does an entrepreneur go about hearing and focusing on them? One extremely helpful tool is ratio analysis. **Ratio analysis**, a method of expressing the relationships between any two accounting elements, provides a convenient technique for performing financial analysis. When analyzed properly, ratios serve as barometers of a company's financial health. Using ratios as benchmarks allows entrepreneurs to determine, for example, whether their companies are carrying excessive inventory, experiencing heavy operating expenses, collecting payments from their customers slowly, managing to pay its debts on time, and to answer other questions relating to the efficient operation of their businesses. Unfortunately, few business owners actually compute financial ratios and use them in managing their businesses!

Clever business owners use financial ratio analysis to identify problems in their businesses while they are still problems, not business-threatening crises. Tracking these ratios over time permits an owner to spot a variety of "red flags" that are indications of these problem areas. This is critical to business success because an entrepreneur cannot solve problems he or she does not know exist! Business owners also can use ratio analysis to increase the likelihood of obtaining bank loans. By analyzing their financial statements with ratios, entrepreneurs can anticipate potential problems and identify important strengths in advance. When evaluating a business plan or a loan request, lenders often rely on ratio analysis to determine how well managed a company is and how solid its financial footing is.

How many ratios should a small business manager monitor to maintain adequate financial control over the firm? The number of ratios an entrepreneur can calculate is limited only by the number of accounts recorded on the company's financial statements. However, tracking too many ratios only creates confusion and saps the meaning from an entrepreneur's financial analysis. The secret to successful ratio analysis is *simplicity*, focusing on just enough ratios to provide a clear picture of a company's financial standing.

12 Key Ratios

In keeping with the idea of simplicity, this section describes 12 key ratios that enable most business owners to monitor their companies' financial position without becoming bogged down in financial details. This chapter presents examples and explanations of these ratios based on the balance sheet and the income statement for Sam's Appliance Shop shown in Figures 1 and 2. We will group them into four categories: liquidity ratios, leverage ratios, operating ratios, and profitability ratios.

LIQUIDITY RATIOS. **Liquidity ratios** tell whether a small business will be able to meet its maturing obligations as they come due. These ratios can forewarn entrepreneurs of impending cash flow problems. A small company with solid liquidity not only is able to pay its bills on time but also is in a position to take advantage of attractive business opportunities as they arise. Liquidity ratios measure a company's ability to convert its assets into cash quickly and without a loss of value to pay its short-term liabilities. The two most common measures of liquidity are the current ratio and the quick ratio.

1. **Current Ratio.** The **current ratio** measures a small company's solvency by showing its ability to pay current liabilities from current assets. It is calculated in the following manner:

$$\text{Current ratio} = \frac{\text{Current assets}}{\text{Current liabilities}}$$

$$= \frac{\$686,985}{\$367,850}$$

$$= 1.87:1$$

Sam's Appliance Shop has $1.87 in current assets for every $1 it has in current liabilities.

Current assets are those that an entrepreneur expects to convert into cash in the ordinary business cycle, and normally include cash, notes or accounts receivable, inventory, and any other short-term marketable securities. Current liabilities are short-term obligations that come due within 1 year and include notes or accounts payable, taxes payable, and accruals.

The current ratio is sometimes called the working capital ratio and is the most commonly used measure of short-term solvency. Typically, financial analysts suggest that a small business maintain a current ratio of at least 2:1 (i.e., $2 of current assets for every $1 of current liabilities) to maintain a comfortable cushion of working capital. Generally, the higher a company's current ratio, the stronger its financial position, but a high current ratio does not guarantee that a company is using its assets in the most profitable manner. For example, a business maintaining excessive balances of idle cash or overinvesting in inventory would likely have a high current ratio.

With its current ratio of 1.87:1, Sam's Appliance Shop could liquidate its current assets at 53.5 percent (1 ÷ 1.87 = 53.5%) of book value and still manage to pay its current creditors in full.

2. **Quick Ratio.** The current ratio can sometimes be misleading because it does not show the quality of a company's current assets. For instance, a company with a large number of past-due receivables and stale inventory could boast an impressive current ratio and still be on the verge of financial collapse. The **quick ratio** (or the **acid test ratio**) is a more conservative measure of a firm's liquidity because it shows the extent to which its most liquid assets cover its current liabilities. This ratio includes only a company's "quick assets"—those assets that a company can convert into cash immediately if needed—and excludes the most illiquid asset of all, inventory. It is calculated as follows:

$$\text{Quick ratio} = \frac{\text{Quick assets}}{\text{Current liabilities}}$$

$$= \frac{\$686,985 - \$455,455}{\$367,850}$$

$$= 0.63:1$$

Sam's has 63 cents in quick assets for every $1 of current liabilities.

The quick ratio is a more rigorous test of a company's liquidity. It expresses capacity to repay current debts if all sales income ceased immediately. Generally, a quick ratio of 1:1 is considered satisfactory. A ratio of less than 1:1 indicates that the small company is overly dependent on inventory and on future sales to satisfy short-term debt. A quick ratio of more than 1:1 indicates a greater degree of financial security.

LEVERAGE RATIOS. **Leverage ratios** measure the financing supplied by a company's owners against that supplied by its creditors; they show the relationship between the contributions of investors and creditors to a company's capital base. Leverage ratios serve as gauges of the depth of a company's debt. These ratios show the extent to which an entrepreneur relies on debt capital (rather than equity capital) to finance the business. Leverage ratios provide one measure of the degree of financial risk in a company. Generally, small businesses with low leverage ratios are less affected by economic downturns, but the returns for these firms are lower during economic booms. Conversely, small firms with high leverage ratios are more vulnerable to economic slides because their debt loads demolish cash flow; however, they have greater potential for large profits. "Leverage is a double-edged sword," says one financial expert. If it works for you, you can really build something. If you borrow too much, it can drag a business down faster than anything."[12] Companies that end up declaring bankruptcy most often take on more debt than the business can handle.

Creditors of Dial-a-Mattress, a company launched in 1976 by Napoleon Barragan that for more than 30 years sold mattresses by telephone and later over the Internet, recently forced the company into bankruptcy after Dial-a-Mattress failed to make payments on the significant debt load it had acquired. In 2001, the company moved away from its core strategy and opened nearly 50 retail stores, most of which were located in low traffic areas that failed to produce sufficient sales. Revenue actually increased, but the poorly located stores and the additional costs of operating them destroyed Dial-a-Mattress's ability to generate a profit and hampered its cash flow. Just 2 years after its annual sales peaked at $150 million, the company fell behind in payments to its creditors, who filed an involuntary bankruptcy petition against it. Dial-a-Mattress's balance sheet showed $9.37 million in assets and $11.14 million in liabilities. Barragan agreed to pay creditors 84 cents of each dollar owed them and to sell the company's telephone and Internet division to Sleepy's, a competing chain of mattress stores with more than 700 locations and sales of $831 million.[13]

The following ratios help entrepreneurs keep their debt levels manageable.

3. Debt Ratio. A small company's **debt ratio** measures the percentage of total assets financed by its creditors. The debt ratio is calculated as follows:

$$\text{Debt ratio} = \frac{\text{Total debt (or liabilities)}}{\text{Total assets}}$$

$$= \frac{\$367,850 + \$212,150}{\$847,655}$$

$$= 0.68:1$$

Sam's creditors have claims of 68 cents against every $1 of assets that Sam's Appliance Shop owns, which means that creditors have contributed twice as much to the company's asset base as the company's owners have.

Total debt includes all current liabilities and any outstanding long-term notes and bonds. Total assets represent the sum of the firm's current assets, fixed assets, and intangible assets. A high debt ratio means that creditors provide a large percentage of the firm's total financing and, therefore, bear most of its financial risk. Owners generally prefer higher leverage ratios; otherwise, business funds must come either from the owners' personal assets or from taking on new owners, which requires them to surrender more control over the business. In addition, with a greater portion of the firm's assets financed by creditors, the owner is able to generate profits with a smaller personal investment. However, creditors typically prefer moderate debt ratios because a lower debt ratio indicates a smaller chance of creditor losses in case of liquidation. To lenders and creditors, high debt ratios mean a high risk of default.

4. Debt to Net Worth Ratio. A small company's **debt to net worth ratio** also expresses the relationship between the capital contributions from creditors and those from owners. This ratio compares what the business "owes" to "what it is worth." It is a measure of a company's ability to meet both its creditor and owner obligations in case of liquidation. The debt to net worth ratio is calculated as follows:

$$\text{Debt to net worth ratio} = \frac{\text{Total debt (or liabilities)}}{\text{Tangible net worth}}$$

$$= \frac{\$367,850 + \$212,150}{\$267,655 - \$3,500}$$

$$= 2.20:1$$

Sam's Appliance Shop owes creditors $2.20 for every $1 of equity that Sam owns.

Total debt is the sum of current liabilities and long-term liabilities, and tangible net worth represents the owners' investment in the business (capital + capital stock + earned surplus + retained earnings) less any intangible assets (e.g., goodwill) the company shows on its balance sheet.

The higher this ratio, the lower the degree of protection afforded creditors if the business fails. A high debt to net worth ratio means that the firm has less capacity to borrow; lenders and creditors see the firm as being "borrowed up." In addition, carrying high levels of debt limits a company's options and restricts managers' flexibility. Quite simply; there isn't much "wiggle room" with a debt-laden balance sheet. Metro-Goldwyn-Mayer (MGM), the venerable Hollywood movie studio that has produced many legendary movies since the 1920s, including *The Wizard of Oz* and *A Christmas Story*, has amassed so much debt and the resulting interest expense that it lacks the cash to produce significant numbers of films. In one recent year, MGM released only one film and had to count on DVD sales from its archive of 4,100 titles for revenue. As sales slipped, the company's earnings also fell, stretching its ability to make interest payments and its financial fortunes continued on a vicious downward spiral, forcing the studio to look for a buyer to save it from failure.[14]

A low debt to net worth ratio typically is associated with a higher level of financial security, giving the business greater borrowing potential. As a company's debt to net worth ratio approaches 1:1, its creditors' interest in the business approaches that of the owners. If the ratio is greater than 1:1, creditors' claims exceed those of the owners, and the business may be undercapitalized. In other words, the owners have not supplied an adequate amount of capital, forcing the business to take on too much debt.

5. Times Interest Earned Ratio. The **times interest earned ratio** earned is a measure of a small company's ability to make the interest payments on its debt. It tells how many times the company's earnings cover the interest payments on the debt it is carrying. This ratio measures the size of the cushion a company has in covering the interest on its debt load. The times interest earned ratio is calculated as follows:

$$\text{Times interest earned} = \frac{\text{Earnings before interest and taxes (or EBIT)}}{\text{Total interest expense}}$$

$$= \frac{\$60,629 + \$39,850}{\$39,850}$$

$$= 2.52:1$$

Sam's Appliance Shop's earnings are 2.5 times greater than its interest expense.

MGM, which released *The Wizard of Oz* in 1939, is saddled by so much debt that the company lacks the cash to produce a sufficient number of new films.

Source: apaphotos\Newscom

EBIT is the company's net income (earnings) *before* deducting interest expense and taxes; the denominator measures the amount the business paid in interest over the accounting period.

A high times interest earned ratio suggests that the company has little difficulty meeting the interest payments on its loans; creditors see this as a sign of safety for future loans. Conversely, a low ratio is an indication that the company is overextended in its debts. A company's earnings are not able to cover its debt service if this ratio is less than one. "I look for a [times interest earned] ratio of higher than three-to-one," says one financial analyst, "which indicates that management has considerable breathing room to make its debt payments. When the ratio drops below one-to-one, it clearly indicates management is under tremendous pressure to raise cash. The risk of default or bankruptcy is very high."[15] Many creditors look for a times interest earned ratio of at least 4:1 to 6:1 before pronouncing a company a good credit risk.

Debt is a powerful financial tool, but companies must handle it carefully—just as a demolitionist handles dynamite. Like dynamite, too much debt can be dangerous. Trouble looms on the horizon for companies whose debt loads are so heavy that they must starve critical operations such as research and development, customer service, and others just to pay interest on the debt. Because their interest payments are so large, highly leveraged companies find that they are restricted when it comes to spending cash, whether on normal operations, acquisitions, or capital expenditures. Unfortunately, some companies go on borrowing binges, push their debt loads beyond the safety barrier and end up struggling for survival.

ENTREPRENEURIAL
Profile
Goody's Family Clothing

Just 3 months after emerging from bankruptcy, Goody's Family Clothing, a Knoxville, Tennessee-based retailer founded in 1953, announced that it would close its remaining 287 stores and liquidate the company's assets. Driven into bankruptcy by a heavy debt burden, Goody's closed 74 underperforming stores in an attempt to streamline its operations and reorganize. However, faltering sales, a dismal holiday season (during which retailers typically generate 40 percent of their annual sales), and the resulting operating losses sealed the company's fate.[16]

Some entrepreneurs are so averse to debt that they run their companies with a minimum amount of borrowing, relying instead on their business's cash flow to finance growth. Jerry Edwards, president of Chef's Expressions, a small catering company, manages to generate annual sales of $2 million with just a $20,000 line of credit. "We've always funded our growth out of cash flow," says Edwards. "I had a credit line that I didn't dip into for 10 years!"[17] Growth may be slower for these companies, but their owners do not have to contend with the dangers of debt. Managed carefully, however, debt can boost a company's performance and improve its productivity. Its treatment in the tax code also makes debt a much cheaper means of financing growth than equity.

OPERATING RATIOS. **Operating ratios** help entrepreneurs evaluate their companies' performances and indicate how effectively their businesses are using their resources. The more effectively its resources are used, the less capital a small business will require. These five operating ratios are designed to help entrepreneurs spot those areas they must improve if their businesses are to remain competitive.

6. Average Inventory Turnover Ratio. A small company's **average inventory turnover ratio** measures the number of times its average inventory is sold out, or turned over, during the accounting period. This ratio tells owners how effectively and efficiently they are managing their companies' inventory. It indicates whether their inventory level is too low or too high and whether it is current or obsolete and priced correctly. The average inventory turnover ratio is calculated as follows:

$$\text{Average inventory turnover ratio} = \frac{\text{Cost of goods sold}}{\text{Average inventory}}$$

$$= \frac{\$1,290,117}{(\$805,745 + \$455,455) \div 2}$$

$$= 2.05 \text{ times/year}$$

Sam's Appliance Shop turns its inventory about two times a year, or once every 178 days.

Average inventory is found by adding a company's inventory at the beginning of the accounting period to the ending inventory and dividing the result by two.

This ratio tells an entrepreneur how fast the merchandise is moving through the business and helps to balance the company on the fine line between oversupply and undersupply. To determine the average number of days units remain in inventory, the owner can divide the average inventory turnover ratio into the number of days in the accounting period (e.g., 365 ÷ average inventory turnover ratio). The result is called **days' inventory** (or **average age of inventory**). Auto dealerships often use days of inventory on hand as a measure of performance and consider 50 to 60 days' worth of new cars to be an adequate inventory. Used car dealers' goal is to have 35 to 45 days' worth of used cars in inventory. Slow-turning inventory cannibalizes car dealers' profitability because of the interest expense they incur. The National Auto Dealers Association estimates that a used car that sells within 10 to 30 days generates an average gross profit of $2,000; however, if that same car sits on the lot for 90 days before it sells, the average gross profit falls to $875 (an occurrence known in the industry as "lot rot").[18] Companies with below-average inventory turnover ratios usually suffer from an illiquid inventory characterized by obsolescence, overstocking, stale merchandise, or poor purchasing procedures.

Businesses that turn their inventories more rapidly than average require a smaller inventory investment to produce a particular sales volume. That means that these companies tie up less cash in inventory that sits idly on shelves. For instance, if Sam's could turn its inventory four times each year instead of just two, the company would require an average inventory of just $322,529 instead of the current level of $630,600 to generate sales of $1,870,841. Increasing the number of inventory turns would free up more than $308,000 currently tied up in excess inventory! Sam's would benefit from improved cash flow and higher profits.

The inventory turnover ratio can be misleading, however. For example, an excessively high ratio could mean the firm has a shortage of inventory and is experiencing stockouts. Similarly, a low ratio could be the result of planned inventory stockpiling to meet seasonal peak demand. Another problem is that the ratio is based on an inventory balance calculated from 2 days out of the entire accounting period. Thus, inventory fluctuations due to seasonal demand patterns are ignored, which may bias the resulting ratio. There is no universal, ideal inventory turnover ratio.

Too much inventory creates financial and cash flow problems for a small company.

Source: eightfish\Alamy Images

Financial analysts suggest that a favorable turnover ratio depends on the type of business, its size, its profitability, its method of inventory valuation, and other relevant factors. The most meaningful basis for comparison is other companies of similar size in the same industry. For instance, the typical drugstore turns its inventory about 12 times per year, but a retail shoe store averages just 2 inventory turns a year.

7. **Average Collection Period Ratio.** A small company's **average collection period ratio** (or **days sales outstanding, DSO**) tells the average number of days it takes to collect accounts receivable. To compute the average collection period ratio, the entrepreneur must first calculate the firm's receivables turnover. Given that Sam's *credit* sales for the year were $1,309,589 (out of the total sales of $1,870,841), the company's receivables turnover ratio is as follows:

$$\text{Receivables turnover ratio} = \frac{\text{Credit sales (or net sales)}}{\text{Accounts receivable}}$$

$$= \frac{\$1,309,589}{\$179,225}$$

$$= 7.31 \text{ times/year}$$

Sam's Appliance Shop turns its receivables 7.31 times per year. This ratio measures the number of times a company's accounts receivable turn over during the accounting period. The higher a company's receivables turnover ratio, the shorter the time lag between making a sale and collecting the cash from it.

Entrepreneurs use the following formula to calculate a company's average collection period ratio:

$$\text{Average collection period ratio} = \frac{\text{Days in accounting period}}{\text{Receivables turnover ratio}}$$

$$= \frac{365 \text{ days}}{7.31}$$

$$= 50.0 \text{ days}$$

Sam's Appliance Shop's accounts receivable are outstanding for an average of 50 days. Typically, the higher a company's average collection period ratio, the greater is its chance of bad debt losses. Sales don't count unless a company collects the revenue from them!

One of the most useful applications of the collection period ratio is to compare it to the industry average and to the firm's credit terms. This comparison indicates the degree of the small company's control over its credit sales and collection techniques. One rule of thumb suggests that a company's collection period ratio should be no more than one-third greater than its credit terms. For example, if a small company's credit terms are "net 30," its average collection period ratio should be no more than 40 days (30 + 30 × 1/3). For this company, a ratio greater than 40 days would indicate poor collection procedures, such as sloppy record keeping or failure to send invoices promptly.

ENTREPRENEURIAL
Profile

Nick Ypsilantis and AccuFile

Nick Ypsilantis, CEO of AccuFile, a company that provides library staff and services to businesses, has learned the importance of sending invoices promptly. Before the company tightened its accounts receivable procedures, cash flow was a constant problem, forcing Ypsilantis to borrow money on a line of credit. By sending invoices sooner and following up promptly on past-due accounts, AccuFile has reduced its average collection period to 41 days and has not had to use its credit line.[19]

Just as Nick Ypsilantis has learned, slow payers represent great risk to small businesses. Many entrepreneurs proudly point to rapidly rising sales only to find that they must borrow money to keep their companies going because credit customers are paying their bills in 45, 60, or even 90 days instead of 30. Slow receivables often lead to a cash crisis that can cripple a business. Table 1 shows how lowering its average collection period ratio can save a company money.

8. **Average Payable Period Ratio.** The converse of the average collection period ratio, the **average payable period ratio** (or **days payables outstanding, DPO**), tells the average number of days it

TABLE 1 How Lowering Your Average Collection Period Can Save You Money

Too often, entrepreneurs fail to recognize the importance of collecting their accounts receivable on time. After all, collecting accounts is not as glamorous or as much fun as generating sales. Lowering a company's average collection period ratio, however, can produce tangible—and often significant—savings. The following formula shows how to convert an improvement in a company's average collection period ratio into dollar savings:

$$\text{Annual savings} = \frac{(\text{Credit sales} \times \text{Annual interest rate} \times \text{Number of days average collection period is lowered})}{365}$$

where

Credit sales = company's annual credit sales in $.

Annual interest rate = the interest rate at which the company borrows money.

Number of days average collection period is lowered = the difference between the previous year's average collection period ratio and the current one.

Example

Sam's Appliance Shop's average collection period ratio is 50 days. Suppose that the previous year's average collection period ratio was 58 days, an 8-day improvement. The company's credit sales for the most recent year were $1,309,589. If Sam borrows money at 8.75 percent, this 6-day improvement has generated savings for Sam's Appliance Shop of:

$$\text{Savings} = \frac{\$1,309,589 \times 8.75\% \times 8\,\text{days}}{365\,\text{days}} = \$2,512$$

By collecting his accounts receivable just 8 days faster, on average, Sam has saved his business more than $2,500! Of course, if a company's average collection period ratio increases, the same calculation will tell the owner how much that change costs.

Source: Based on "Days Saved, Thousands Earned," *Inc. Magazine,* November 1995, p. 98.

takes a company to pay its accounts payable. Like the average collection period, it is measured in days. To compute this ratio, first calculate the payables turnover ratio. Sam's payables turnover ratio is as follows:

$$\text{Payables turnover ratio} = \frac{\text{Purchases}}{\text{Accounts payable}}$$
$$= \frac{\$939,827}{\$152,580}$$
$$= 6.16\,\text{times/year}$$

To find the average payable period, we use the following computation:

$$\text{Average payable period ratio} = \frac{\text{Days in accounting period}}{\text{Payables turnover ratio}}$$
$$= \frac{365\,\text{days}}{6.16}$$
$$= 59.3\,\text{days}$$

Sam's Appliance Shop takes an average of about 59 days to pay its accounts with vendors and suppliers.

An excessively high average payable period ratio may indicate that a company is enjoying extended credit terms from its suppliers or it may be a sign of a significant amount of past-due accounts payable. Although sound cash management calls for business owners to keep their cash as long as possible, slowing payables too drastically can severely damage a company's credit rating.

Ideally, the average payable period matches (or exceeds) the time it takes to convert inventory into sales and ultimately into cash. In this case, the company's vendors are financing its inventory and its credit sales. Amazon.com reaps the benefits of this situation. On average, it does not pay its vendors until 31 days *after* it collects payment from its customers.[20]

To make this comparison, an entrepreneur subtracts the company's average collection period (days sales outstanding, DSO) from its average collection period ratio (days payables outstanding, DPO) to calculate the **company's float**, the net number of days of cash that flow into or out of a company. Sam's Appliance Shop's float is:

$$\text{Float} = \text{DPO} - \text{DSO} = 59.3 - 50.0\,\text{days} = 9.3\,\text{days}$$

A positive value for float is desirable because it means that cash will accumulate in a company over time. Multiplying float by a company's average daily sales tells Sam how much the company's cash balance will change over the course of the year as a result of its collection and payable processes. For Sam's Appliance Shop:

$$\text{Change in cash position} = \$1,870,841 \div 365 \text{ days} \times 9.3 \text{ days} = \$47,668$$

Another meaningful comparison for this ratio is against the credit terms offered by suppliers (or an average of the credit terms offered). If the average payable period ratio slips beyond vendors' credit terms, it is an indication that the company is suffering from cash shortages or a sloppy accounts payable procedure and its credit rating is in danger. If this ratio is significantly lower than vendors' credit terms, it may be a sign that a business is not using its cash most effectively.

9. **Net Sales to Total Assets.** A small company's **net sales to total assets ratio** (also called the **total assets turnover ratio**) is a general measure of its ability to generate sales in relation to its assets. It describes how productively a company employs its assets to produce sales revenue. The total assets turnover ratio is calculated as follows:

$$\text{Total assets turnover ratio} = \frac{\text{Net sales}}{\text{Net total assets}}$$

$$= \frac{\$1,870,841}{\$847,655}$$

$$= 2.21{:}1$$

Sam's Appliance Shop generates $2.21 in sales for every dollar of assets.

The denominator of this ratio, net total assets, is the sum of all of the firm's assets (cash, inventory, land, buildings, equipment, tools, everything it owns) less depreciation. This ratio is meaningful only when compared to that of similar firms in the same industry category. A total assets turnover ratio below the industry average suggests that a small company is not generating an adequate sales volume for its asset size.

In a recent National Federation of Independent Businesses (NFIB) survey, 32 percent of small businesses report poor sales as their number one problem. More than half of business owners report lower earnings from the previous year and point to poor sales as the primary

" NO, SIMMS, I SAID I WANT TO SEE A **PROFIT** AROUND HERE."

cause.[21] If a company's sales fall too far, it operates below its break-even point and cannot stay in business for long. Tweeter, a small chain of specialty electronics stores, recently closed its doors, citing poor sales and the "severe liquidity crisis" it caused.[22]

PROFITABILITY RATIOS. **Profitability ratios** indicate how efficiently a small company is being managed. They provide the owner with information about a company's ability to generate a profit. They focus on a company's "bottom line;" in other words, they describe how successfully the business is using its resources to generate a profit.

10. Net Profit on Sales Ratio. The **net profit on sales ratio** (also called the **profit margin on sales** or the **net profit margin**) measures a company's profit per dollar of sales. This ratio (which is expressed as a percentage) shows the number of cents of each sales dollar remaining after deducting all expenses and income taxes. The profit margin on sales is calculated as follows:

$$\text{Net profit on sales ratio} = \frac{\text{Net income}}{\text{Net sales}} \times 100\%$$

$$= \frac{\$60,629}{\$1,870,841} \times 100\%$$

$$= 3.24\%$$

Sam's Appliance Shop keeps 3.24 cents in profit out of every dollar of sales it generates.

A recent study by *Inc.* magazine and Sageworks shows that the average net profit margin for privately held companies normally falls between 5 and 6.5 percent, but this ratio varies from one industry to another. The retail industry typically produces a net profit on sales ratio that falls between 2 and 4 percent, but profit margins in the health care field range between 10 and 16 percent.[23] If a company's profit margin on sales is below the industry average, it is a sign that its prices are relatively low, that its costs are excessively high, or both.

ENTREPRENEURIAL
Profile

Shelly Fireman and Fireman Hospitality Group

Rising costs are putting pressure on many restaurants' profit margins. "[Profit] margin pressures are insane," says Shelly Fireman, who owns several upscale restaurants in New York City. Fireman points to rising costs for everything from food and rent to wages and insurance as the culprits that are draining his company's profit margins. Whatever industry they are in, businesses facing this dilemma can cover the increased costs of doing business with higher prices, settle for lower profit margins, or cut expenses elsewhere. Fireman, like most of his competitors, has raised prices but is concerned about the dampening effect that might have on sales. To counter higher food costs, the owner of one small chain of restaurants fine-tuned his recipes to control costs. Eliminating olive oil from his marinara sauce saved the business $17,000 in 1 year.[24]

If a company's net profit on sales ratio is excessively low, the owner should check the gross profit margin (net sales minus cost of goods sold expressed as a percentage of net sales). A reasonable gross profit margin varies from industry to industry, however. For instance, a service company may have a gross profit margin of 75 percent, whereas a manufacturer's may be 35 percent. If this margin slips too low, it puts the company's ability to generate a profit and stay in business in jeopardy.

11. Net Profit to Assets. The **net profit to assets** ratio (also known as the **return on assets, ROA**) ratio tells how much profit a company generates for each dollar of assets that it owns. This ratio describes how efficiently a business is putting to work all of the assets it owns to generate a profit. It tells how much net income an entrepreneur is squeezing from each dollar's worth of the company's assets. It is calculated as follows:

$$\text{Net profit on assets ratio} = \frac{\text{Net income}}{\text{Total assets}} \times 100\%$$

$$= \frac{\$60,629}{\$847,655} \times 100\%$$

$$= 7.15\%$$

Sam's Appliance shop earns a return of 7.15 percent on its asset base.

This ratio provides clues about the asset intensity of an industry. Return on assets ratios that are below 5 percent are indicative of asset-intense industries that require heavy investments in assets to stay in business (e.g., manufacturing companies). Return on assets ratios that exceed 20 percent tend to occur in asset-light industries such as business or personal services—for example, advertising agencies and computer services. A net profit to assets ratio that is below the industry average suggests that a company is not using its assets very efficiently to produce a profit.

Another common application of this ratio is to compare it to the company's cost of borrowed capital. Ideally, a company's return on assets ratio (ROA) should exceed the cost of borrowing money to purchase those assets. Companies that experience significant swings in the value of their assets over the course of a year often use an average value of the asset base over the accounting period to get a more realistic estimate of this ratio.

12. **Net Profit to Equity.** The **net profit to equity ratio** (or the **return on net worth ratio**) measures the owners' rate of return on investment (ROI). Because it reports the percentage of the owners' investment in the business that is being returned through profits annually, it is one of the most important indicators of a company's profitability or management's efficiency. The net profit to equity ratio is computed as follows:

$$\text{Net profit to equity ratio} = \frac{\text{Net income}}{\text{Owner's equity (or net worth)}} \times 100\%$$

$$= \frac{\$60,629}{\$267,655} \times 100\%$$

$$= 22.65\%$$

This ratio compares profits earned during the accounting period with the amount the owners have invested in the business during that time. If this interest rate on the owners' investment is excessively low, some of this capital might be better employed elsewhere. A business should produce a rate of return that exceeds its cost of capital.

LESSONS FROM THE [STREET-SMART] entrepreneur

Identify How Your Company Will Make Money

When they launch their businesses, entrepreneurs instinctively know that their companies must make a profit to survive. However, many entrepreneurs never take the time to examine the factors in their business models that drive their companies' profitability. The following model is a useful tool for visualizing these factors, analyzing their impact on a company's profits, and identifying strategies for improving them so that a business can improve its profitability. The Street-Smart Entrepreneur identifies four factors that determine a company's ability to produce an attractive profit: revenue drivers, margins, operating leverage, and volumes (see Figure 1).

Revenue drivers include all of the ways a company generates revenue. For instance, an automobile dealership's revenue drivers may be new cars sales, used cars sales, auto leases, service, parts, and short-term rentals. As another example, one small jewelry store identified its revenue generators as new jewelry, estate jewelry, watches, and gift items. Small companies with extensive inventories such as

Figure 1. Four Key Elements of a Firm's Economic Model

hardware stores can organize their revenue-generating product lines into a manageable number of major categories; for example, power tools, hand tools, lawn and garden, home repair, plumbing, electrical, and others. The next step is to assess the impact of each of the company's revenue drivers on total sales and their interaction with one another. For instance, an auto dealer may discover that the business generates more sales from used cars than from new cars.

Entrepreneurs must then consider how much control they have over pricing their revenue drivers. Pricing may be either fixed or flexible. A company relies on fixed pricing if it sells goods or services at standard prices without negotiation or variation. For example, item prices on a restaurant menu are fixed. Flexible pricing means that a company can offer different prices depending on when customers make a purchase, how many items they purchase, whether other items are bundled into the purchase, and other variables. Even though a restaurateur may be limited to fixed pricing on the menu, he or she would be able to use flexible pricing on catering jobs. Flexible pricing gives entrepreneurs greater ability to maximize total revenue (and profitability).

Margins reflect how much each revenue driver contributes to the company's profitability. Margins are the price that a customer pays minus the cost to the company of providing that good or service. A small company can increase its margins either by raising its prices or by improving its efficiency and providing goods and services at lower costs. The goal is to determine which revenue drivers are capable of generating the greatest profit. For instance, an auto dealership may find that its profit margin on used cars is much higher than new cars and that the margin on auto repairs is higher still.

Volumes are another important determinant of a company's profitability. A small company's volume depends on the number of sales transactions it generates over a given time period and the value of each transaction. For instance, a fast-food restaurant counts on selling a large number of relatively low-priced meals, but an upscale restaurant generates revenue from a smaller number of meals at much higher average prices. At the fast-food restaurant, the average check may be $5.80, but at the upscale restaurant the average check may be $45.80.

Operating leverage is the impact that a change in a company's sales volume has on its net income. If a small company achieves positive **operating leverage**, its expenses as a percentage of sales revenues flatten or even decline as sales increase. As a result, the company's net profit margin will increase as it grows. Operating leverage is a function of a business's cost structure. Companies that have high levels of fixed costs have high operating leverage; conversely, companies that have high levels of variable costs have low operating leverage. Profits are more volatile when a company has high operating leverage, because slight changes in revenue cause dramatic swings in profits as the company's sale fluctuate above and below its break-even point.

Once entrepreneurs have analyzed the four components of a company's profitability, they can formulate strategies to enhance them (see Figure 2). For instance, if a company's current business model is characterized by a single revenue driver, low margins, low volumes, and high operating leverage, it is not likely to be a highly profitable venture. The entrepreneur in this situation, however, might change the business model to make it more profitable by asking the following questions:

■ Can I add more revenue drivers to my business?
■ How can I increase the number of transactions and/or the average transaction size that make up our volume?

Figure 2. Keys to Profitability

- What can I do to reduce the level of fixed costs in my company?
- Can I change to a flexible pricing strategy and move away from a fixed pricing strategy?
- How can I improve the efficiency with which my company provides products and services to customers?
- In what other ways can I improve my company's profit margins?

Ron Towry, owner of Truck Gear SuperCenter, a small truck accessories business, was able to increase his company's sales by 25 percent and profits by 32 percent after making a strategic decision to begin selling his products at wholesale to truck and auto dealerships in addition to selling to his traditional retail customers. Although the company's wholesale prices and profit margins were lower, wholesale customers purchased in higher volumes, and Towry's company could sell to them at a lower cost per transaction, resulting in higher sales and profits.

Sources: Adapted from April Murdoch and Michael Morris, "Is Your Economic Model Working?" *Orange Entrepreneur*, Fall 2006, pp. 16–19; Ron Stodghill, "Bolt Down Those Costs," *FSB*, May 2006, pp. 85–87.

Interpreting Business Ratios

5. Explain how to interpret financial ratios.

Ratios are useful yardsticks when measuring a small company's performance and can point out potential problems before they develop into serious crises. However, calculating these ratios is not enough to ensure proper financial control. In addition to knowing how to calculate these ratios, the owner must understand how to interpret them and apply them to managing the business more effectively and efficiently.

Not every business measures its success with the same ratios. In fact, key performance ratios vary dramatically across industries and even within different segments of the same industry. Entrepreneurs must know and understand which ratios are most crucial to their companies' success and focus on monitoring and controlling those. Many successful entrepreneurs identify or develop ratios that are unique to their own operations to help them achieve success. Known as **critical numbers**, these barometers of business success measure financial and operational aspects of a company's performance. When these critical numbers are headed in the right direction, a business is on track to achieve its objectives.

ENTREPRENEURIAL
Profile

Pat Croce and Sports Physical Therapists

When Pat Croce founded Sports Physical Therapists, a business that grew into a chain of 40 sports medicine centers, he discovered that the number of new patient evaluations was the critical number he needed to track. This measure told Croce how much new business he could expect in the coming months. If the number climbed, he knew that he must begin adding staff immediately.[25]

Examples of critical numbers include:

- The load factor, the number of seats filled with passengers, on a luxury bus targeting business travelers with daily trips from downtown Boston to midtown Manhattan.[26]
- The number of cases shipped per employee at a food distributor.
- Food costs as a percentage of sales for a restaurant. To maintain profitability, many restaurateurs strive to keep their food costs between 22 and 30 percent of sales.[27] At Dos Caminos, a Mexican restaurant in New York City, chef Ivy Stark's goal is to keep the restaurant's food cost at or below 26 percent of sales. Stark relies on a five-page spreadsheet generated each morning to keep food costs under control.[28]
- Subscriber renewal rates at a magazine.
- Room occupancy rates at a hotel. Although a particular hotel's break-even occupancy rate depends on its cost structure, the average occupancy rate required for hotels to break even ranges from 62 to 65 percent. Other critical numbers in the hospitality industry include the average daily room rate and the revenue per available room (RevPAR).[29]
- The percentage of rework at a photo processor. Because the percentage of rework is an important determinant of profitability, this processor graphs this critical number and posts it weekly.

To maintain their profitability, many restaurateurs strive to keep their food costs between 22 and 30 percent of sales.

Source: Jim West\Alamy Images

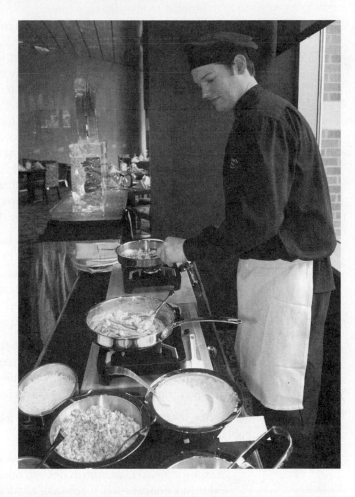

Critical numbers may be different for two companies in the same industry, depending on their strategies. The key is identifying *your* company's critical numbers, monitoring them, and then driving them in the right direction. That requires communicating the importance of critical numbers to employees and giving them feedback on how well the business is achieving them.

ENTREPRENEURIAL
Profile

Norm Brodsky and CitiStorage

Over time, Norm Brodsky, owner of CitiStorage, a highly successful records-storage business in New York City that targets law firms, accounting firms, and hospitals, discovered that his company's critical number was the number of new boxes put into storage each week, so he began tracking it closely. "Tell me how many new boxes came in during [a month]," he says, "and I can tell you our overall sales figure for [that month] within 1 or 2 percent of the actual figure." That particular critical number surprised Brodsky because new boxes account for only a small percentage of total sales; yet the new-box count was the key to allowing Brodsky to forecast his company's future. Once, during a period of rapid growth (about 55 percent a year), Brodsky saw on his Monday morning report that the new-box count had fallen by 70 percent in the previous week. Alarmed, Brodsky temporarily stopped expanding the company's workforce to see whether the drop was an aberration or the beginning of a business slowdown. A few weeks later, he knew that the market had changed and that sales growth had slowed to 15 percent. By using his company's critical number, Brodsky avoided excessive labor costs, a nasty cash crisis, and a morale-destroying layoff and was able to keep his company on track.[30]

One of the most valuable ways to utilize ratios is to compare them with those of similar businesses in the same industry. By comparing the company's financial statistics to industry averages, an entrepreneur can identify problem areas and develop a plan to improve them. "By themselves, these numbers are not that meaningful," says one financial expert of ratios, "but when you compare them to [those of] other businesses in your industry, they suddenly come alive because they put your operation in perspective."[31]

The principle behind calculating these ratios and critical numbers and then comparing them to industry norms is the same as that of basic medical tests in the health care profession. Just as a healthy person's blood pressure and cholesterol levels should fall within a range of normal values, so should a financially healthy company's ratios. A company cannot deviate too far from these normal values and remain successful for long. When deviations from "normal" do occur (and they will), an entrepreneur should focus on determining the cause of the deviations. In some cases, deviations are the result of sound business decisions, such as taking on inventory in preparation for the busy season, investing heavily in new technology, and others. In other instances, however, ratios that are out of the normal range for a particular type of business are indicators of what could become serious problems for a company. When comparing a company's ratios to industry standards, entrepreneurs should ask the following questions:

- Is there a significant difference in my company's ratio and the industry average?
- If so, is this a *meaningful* difference?
- Is the difference good or bad?
- What are the possible causes of this difference? What is the most likely cause?
- Does this cause require that I take action?
- What action should I take to correct the problem?

When used properly, ratio analysis can help owners identify potential problem areas in their businesses early on—*before* they become crises that threaten their very survival. Several organizations regularly compile and publish operating statistics, including key ratios, summarizing the financial performance of many businesses across a wide range of industries.

INDUSTRY GUIDES AND STUDIES. The local library should subscribe to most of these publications:

- *RMA Annual Statement Studies.* The Risk Management Association publishes its *Annual Statement Studies*, showing ratios and other financial data for more than 750 different industrial, construction, wholesale, retail, and service categories.
- *Dun & Bradstreet's Key Business Ratios.* Since 1932, Dun & Bradstreet has published *Key Business Ratios*, which encompasses more than 800 business categories.
- *Almanac of Business and Industrial Financial Ratios.* This handy guide provides key ratios and financial data in 50 areas organized by company size for nearly 200 industries.
- *Industry Spotlight.* Published by Schonfeld & Associates, this publication, which covers more than 250 industries, contains financial statement data and seventeen key ratios from more than 95,000 tax returns. *Industry Spotlight* also provides detailed financial information for both profitable companies and those with losses.
- *Standard and Poor's Industry Surveys.* In addition to providing information on financial ratios and comparative financial analysis, these surveys also contain useful details on how the industry operates, current industry trends, key terms in the industry, and others.

ONLINE RESOURCES. Many companies publish comparative financial resources online. Some require subscriptions, but others are free:

- BizStats publishes financial statements and ratios for 95 business categories for sole proprietorships, S corporations, and corporations.
- Reuters provides an overview of many industries that includes industry trends and news as well as financial ratios.
- A subscription to Lexis/Nexis allows users to view detailed company profiles, including financial reports and analysis, for publicly held companies.

INDUSTRY ASSOCIATIONS. Virtually every type of business is represented by a national trade association, which publishes detailed financial data compiled from its membership. For example, the owner of a small coffee shop could consult the National Coffee Association (and its newsletter, *The Coffee Reporter*), the Specialty Coffee Association of America, the International Coffee Organization, or a variety of state coffee associations for financial statistics relevant to his operation.

GOVERNMENT AGENCIES. Several government agencies, including the Federal Trade Commission, Interstate Commerce Commission, Department of Commerce, Department of Agriculture, and Securities and Exchange Commission, offer a great deal of financial operating data on a variety of industries, although the categories are more general. In addition, the IRS annually publishes *Statistics of Income,* which includes income statement and balance sheet statistics compiled from income tax returns. The IRS also publishes the *Census of Business* that gives a limited amount of ratio information.

What Do All of These Numbers Mean?

Learning to interpret financial ratios just takes a little practice! This section and Table 2 will show you how it's done by comparing the ratios from the operating data already computed for Sam's Appliance Shop to those taken from RMA's *Annual Statement Studies.* (The industry median is the ratio falling exactly in the middle when sample elements are arranged in ascending or descending order.) Calculating the variance from the industry median ((company ratio – industry median) ÷ industry median) helps entrepreneurs identify the areas in which the company is out of line with the typical company in the industry.

TABLE 2 Ratios: Sam's Appliance Shop Versus the Industry Average

Ratio	Sam's Appliance Shop	Industry Median	Variance (%)
Liquidity ratios tell whether a small business will be able to meet its maturing obligations as they come due.			
1. Current ratio	1.87:1	1.60:1	16.7%
Explanation: Sam's Appliance Shop falls short of the rule of thumb of 2:1, but its current ratio is above the industry median by a significant amount. Sam's should have no problem meeting its short-term debts as they come due. By this measure, the company's liquidity is solid.			
2. Quick ratio	0.63:1	0.50:1	25.9%
Explanation: Again, Sam's is below the rule of thumb of 1:1, but the company passes this test of liquidity when measured against industry standards. Sam's relies on selling inventory to satisfy short-term debt (as do most appliance shops). If sales slump, the result could be liquidity problems for Sam's.			
Leverage ratios measure the financing supplied by the company's owners against that supplied by its creditors and serve as a gauge of the depth of a company's debt.			
3. Debt ratio	0.68:1	0.62:1	10.4%
Explanation: Creditors provide 68 percent of Sam's total assets, very close to the industry median of 64 percent. Although Sam's does not appear to be overburdened with debt, the company might have difficulty borrowing additional money, especially from conservative lenders.			
4. Debt to net worth ratio	2.20:1	2.30:1	−4.5%
Explanation: Sam's Appliance Shop owes $2.20 to creditors for every $1.00 the owners have invested in the business (compared to $2.30 in debt to every $1.00 in equity for the typical business). Although this is not an exorbitant amount of debt by industry standards, many lenders and creditors see Sam's as "borrowed up." Borrowing capacity is somewhat limited because creditors' claims against the business are more than twice those of the owners.			
5. Times interest earned ratio	2.52:1	2.10:1	20.1%
Explanation: Sam's earnings are high enough to cover the interest payments on its debt by a factor of 2.52, better than the typical firm in the industry, whose earnings cover its interest payments just two times. Sam's Appliance Shop has a cushion when meeting its interest payments.			
Operating ratios evaluate a company's overall performance and show how effectively it is putting its resources to work.			
6. Average inventory turnover ratio	2.05 times/year	4.4 times/year	−53.5%
Explanation: Inventory is moving through Sam's at a very slow pace, *half* that of the industry median. The company has a problem with slow-moving items in its inventory and, perhaps, too much inventory. Which items are they, and why are they slow moving? Does Sam need to drop some product lines?			

(continued)

TABLE 2 Continued

Ratio	Sam's Appliance Shop	Industry Median	Variance (%)
7. Average collection period ratio	50.0 days	10.5 days	376.3%
Explanation: Sam's Appliance Shop collects the average accounts receivable after 50 days, compared with the industry median of about 11 days, nearly five times longer. A more meaningful comparison is against Sam's credit terms; if credit terms are net 30 (or anywhere close to that), Sam's has a dangerous collection problem, one that drains cash and profits and demands *immediate* attention!			
8. Average payable period ratio	59.3 days	23.0 days	158.1%
Explanation: Sam's payables are nearly significantly slower than those of the typical firm in the industry. Stretching payables too far could seriously damage the company's credit rating, causing suppliers to cut off future trade credit. This could be a sign of cash flow problems or a sloppy accounts payable procedure. This problem, which indicates that the company suffers cash flow problems, also demands *immediate* attention.			
9. Net sales to total assets ratio	2.21:1	3.4:1	−35.1%
Explanation: Sam's Appliance Shop is not generating enough sales, given the size of its asset base. This could be the result of a number of factors—improper inventory, inappropriate pricing, poor location, poorly trained sales personnel, and many others. The key is to find the cause . . . *fast*!			
Profitability ratios measure how efficiently a firm is operating and offer information about its bottom line.			
10. Net profit on sales ratio	3.24%	4.3%	−24.6%
Explanation: After deducting all expenses, 3.24 cents of each sales dollar remains as profit for Sam's—nearly 25 percent below the industry median. Sam should review his company's gross profit margin and investigate its operating expenses, checking them against industry standards and looking for those that are out of balance.			
11. Net profit to assets ratio	7.15%	4.0%	78.8%
Explanation: Sam's generates a return of 7.15 percent for every $1 in assets, which is nearly 79 percent *above* the industry median. Given his asset base, Sam is squeezing an above-average return from his company. This could be an indication that Sam's business is highly profitable; however, given the previous ratio, this is unlikely. It is more likely that Sam's asset base is thinner than the industry average.			
12. Net profit to equity ratio	22.65%	16.0%	41.6%
Explanation: Sam's Appliance Shop's owners are earning 22.65 percent on the money they have invested in the business. This yield is well above the industry median and, given the previous ratio, is more a result of the owner's relatively low investment in the business than an indication of its superior profitability. Sam is using O.P.M. (Other People's Money) to generate a profit.			

When comparing ratios for their individual businesses to published statistics, entrepreneurs must remember that the comparison is made against averages. Owners should strive to achieve ratios that are at least as good as these average figures. The goal should be to manage the business so that its financial performance is better than the industry average. As owners compare financial performance to those covered in the published statistics, they inevitably will discern differences between them. They should note those items that are substantially out of line from the industry average. However, a ratio that varies from the average does not necessarily mean that a small business is in financial jeopardy. Instead of making drastic changes in financial policy, entrepreneurs must explore why the figures are out of line. Steve Cowan, co-owner of Professional Salon Concepts, a wholesale beauty products distributor, routinely performs such an analysis on his company's financial statements. "I need to know whether the variances for expenses and revenues for a certain period are similar," he says. "If they're not, are the differences explainable? Is an expense category up just because of a decision to spend more, or were we just sloppy?"[32]

In addition to comparing ratios to industry averages, owners should analyze their firms' financial ratios over time. By themselves, these ratios are "snapshots" of the firm's finances at a single instant; but by examining these trends over time, the owner can detect gradual shifts that otherwise might go unnoticed until a financial crisis is looming (see Figure 7).

FIGURE 7
Sam's Appliance Shop
Current Ratio Trend

▶ E N T R E P R E N E U R S H I P **IN ACTION** ▶

In Search of a New Business Model

Abby and Daniel Larson started their small gift shop, Abby's Gift Emporium, in 2001 with financing from their own pockets and a bank loan of $40,000. At first, sales were slow as the company began to build name recognition and a base of loyal customers, but the Larsons managed to ring up sales of $250,000 in their first year of operation. Their business grew, and by 2005, they had repaid their original bank loan and had established a $75,000 line of credit at the local branch of a large national bank. They often relied on the line of credit to fill seasonal shortfalls in their cash flow and to extend credit to their customers, some of whom stretched their credit terms well beyond the "net 30" terms that the Larsons offered.

Abby's Gift Emporium had expanded its product line to include unique gifts that customers could not find at large discount stores. Some of the items the store sold came from local craftspeople who created unique gift items and jewelry. For instance, one local entrepreneur took pieces of antique jewelry that were broken and transformed them into unique pins, necklaces, and earrings. Another local supplier made beautiful jewelry in vibrant colors and striking patterns from glass.

Sales increased from year to year, and the Larsons decided to move into a larger space just a few doors down from their original location. The move required them to borrow $150,000 from their bank, and the Larsons spent two months remodeling and renovating their new space. Although they were somewhat reluctant to take on the debt, the Larsons discovered that customers responded to the larger store with its fresh new look and layout. "The

new store gave us more room to design the creative displays that we had envisioned since we opened," says Abby.

Despite their success, the Larsons wondered about their pricing policies and the profit margins they were generating. "Even though our sales have increased to more than $900,000, our profits haven't kept pace," says Daniel. "We're just not sure what we're doing wrong."

The Larsons decided to experiment with a coffee bar in their store. They came up with the idea while talking with some of their customers, who complained that the only place in their small town to get a cup of coffee was at one of the fast-food restaurants. "You two should open a coffee bar," said one customer. As other customers came into the store, the Larsons asked them whether they would buy coffee if they opened a coffee bar; 83 percent said that they would. Soon the Larsons were remodeling a corner of their store, transforming it into a coffee bar. The move paid off, and the coffee bar not only added $40,000 a year to the gift shop's sales, but it also increased its profitability. "The profit margins on coffee are much better than on the average gift," says Daniel. Some customers sat at the tables the Larsons set up at the coffee bar, and others walked around the store, perusing the selection of gifts. "We discovered that adding the coffee bar also increased sales in the gift shop," says Abby.

Together the Larsons draw a modest salary of $1,000 per week, but the business pays for their $350 per month car payment and their monthly health insurance premium of $800. Although neither Daniel nor Abby has taken courses in business, they have worked hard to learn the basics of financial management. "We're trying to be more disciplined in managing the financial aspects of the business," says Daniel. "Our next step is to begin building budgets and forecasting our cash flow." Abby's Gift Emporium pays rent of $4,000 per month, payroll is $8,000 per month, and taxes average $6,000 per month. Although their inventory purchases fluctuate depending on the season, the Larsons estimate that they spend an average of $18,000 per month purchasing inventory from their vendors and suppliers. "We estimate that we have to generate sales of about $29,000 per month to stay in business," says Daniel.

Unfortunately, Abby's Gift Emporium's sales declined 28 percent during a recent economic recession. Compounding the problem of declining sales, turmoil in the financial industry caused the Larson's bank to cancel the store's $75,000 line of credit. "We've always kept our debt under control and repaid every dime we've ever borrowed," says a frustrated Abby, "but that doesn't seem to matter to the bank. We are in the process of talking with a smaller community bank about transferring our accounts there. However, they can't promise us a $75,000 line of credit right away." The Larsons have resorted to using a business credit card to finance some of their business expenses. "It's not the way we want to finance our expenses, but right now, we don't have much choice," says Daniel.

The Larsons have responded by making some tough decisions. "Unfortunately, we had cut our staff to a minimum, reduced salaries, and minimized expenses every place we can find," says Abby. "Even though we no longer have a line of credit, we have managed to keep our shelves full by making credit card purchases and begging the vendors who sell to us on credit for 90-day payment terms." The Larsons are concerned about the risk of using high-interest credit cards to finance their company's purchases. The company's tight cash flow also has affected their ability to purchase inventory, and they suspect that their lack of a structured pricing policy has a negative impact on their company's profit margins.

1. Work with a team of your classmates to generate ideas to help Abby and Daniel Larson to establish a sound financial base for Abby's Gift Emporium.
2. Refer to the "Lessons from the Street-Smart Entrepreneur" feature in this chapter and review the model described there. Use the model to analyze Abby's Gift Emporium's business model. Work with a team of your classmates to use the questions posed in the "Street-Smart Entrepreneur" feature to make suggestions for changing their business model to a more successful one.

Break-Even Analysis

6. Conduct a break-even analysis for a small company.

Another key component of every sound financial plan is a break-even analysis (or cost–volume–profit analysis). A small company's **break-even point** is the level of operation (sales dollars or production quantity) at which it neither earns a profit nor incurs a loss. At this level of activity, sales revenue equals expenses; that is, the company "breaks even." A business that generates sales that are greater than its break-even point will generate a profit, but one that operates below its break-even point will incur a net loss. Red Roof Inn, a chain that owns 210 hotels and has an additional 130 franchisees, recently defaulted on its debt payments after the company's occupancy rate slipped to 50.7 percent, well below its break-even point of 62 percent.[33]

By analyzing expenses using break-even analysis, an entrepreneur can calculate the minimum level of activity required to keep a business in operation. These techniques can then be refined to project the sales needed to generate a desired level of profit. Most potential lenders and investors require entrepreneurs to prepare a break-even analysis so that they can judge the earning potential of a new business and the likelihood that it will be successful. In addition to its being a simple, useful screening device for financial institutions, break-even analysis also can serve as a planning device for entrepreneurs. It can show an entrepreneur who might have unreasonable expectations about a business idea just how unprofitable a proposed business venture is likely to be.

Calculating the Break-Even Point

A small business owner can calculate a firm's break-even point by using a simple mathematical formula. To begin the analysis, the owner must determine fixed expenses and variable expenses. **Fixed expenses** are those that do not vary with changes in the volume of sales or production (e.g., rent, depreciation expense, insurance, salaries, lease or loan payments, and others). **Variable expenses**, in contrast, vary directly with changes in the volume of sales or production (e.g., raw material costs, sales commissions, hourly wages, and others).

Some expenses cannot be neatly categorized as fixed or variable because they contain elements of both. These semivariable expenses change, although not proportionately, with changes in the level of sales or production (electricity would be one example). These costs remain constant up to a particular production or sales volume and then climb as that volume is exceeded. To calculate the break-even point, an entrepreneur must separate these expenses into their fixed and variable components. A number of techniques can be used (which are beyond the scope of this text), but a good cost accounting system can provide the desired results.

Here are the steps an entrepreneur must take to compute the break-even point using an example of a typical small business, the Magic Shop:

Step 1   *Determine the expenses the business can expect to incur.* With the help of a budget, an entrepreneur can develop estimates of sales revenue, cost of goods sold, and expenses for the upcoming accounting period. The Magic Shop expects net sales of $950,000 in the upcoming year, with a cost of goods sold of $646,000 and total expenses of $236,500.

Step 2   *Categorize the expenses estimated in step 1 into fixed expenses and variable expenses and separate semivariable expenses into their component parts.* From the budget, the owner anticipates variable expenses (including the cost of goods sold) of $705,125 and fixed expenses of $177,375.

Step 3   *Calculate the ratio of variable expenses to net sales.* For the Magic Shop, this percentage is $705,125 ÷ $950,000 = 74 percent. The Magic Shop uses 74 cents out of every sales dollar to cover variable expenses, leaving 26 cents ($1.00 − 0.74) as a contribution margin to cover fixed costs and make a profit.

Step 4   *Compute the break-even point by inserting this information into the following formula:*

$$\text{Break-even sales (\$)} = \frac{\text{Total fixed cost}}{\text{Contribution margin expressed as a percentage of sales}}$$

For the Magic Shop,

$$\text{Break-even sales} = \frac{\$177,375}{0.26}$$
$$= \$682,212$$

Thus, the Magic Shop will break even with sales of $682,212. At this point, sales revenue generated will just cover total fixed and variable expense. The Magic Shop will earn no profit and will incur no loss. To verify this, make the following calculations:

Sales at break-even point	$682,212
− Variable expenses (74% of sales)	−504,837
Contribution margin	177,375
− Fixed expenses	−177,375
Net income (or net loss)	$ 0

Some entrepreneurs find it more meaningful to break down their companies' annual break-even point into a daily sales figure. If the Magic Shop will be open 312 days per year, then the average daily sales it must generate just to break even is $682,212 ÷ 312 days, or $2,187 per day.

Adding a Profit

What if the Magic Shop's owner wants to do *better* than just break even? The analysis can be adjusted to consider such a possibility. Suppose the owner expects a reasonable profit (before taxes) of $80,000. What level of sales must the Magic Shop achieve to generate this? He can calculate this by treating the desired profit as if it were a fixed cost. In other words, he modifies the formula to include the desired net income:

$$\text{Sales (\$)} = \frac{\text{Total fixed expenses + Desired net income}}{\text{Contribution margin expressed as a percentage of sales}}$$
$$= \frac{\$177,375 + \$80\,000}{0.26}$$
$$= \$989,904$$

To achieve a net profit of $80,000 (before taxes), the Magic Shop must generate net sales of $989,904. Once again, if we transform this sales annual volume into a daily sales volume, we get: $989,904 ÷ 312 days = $3,173 per day.

Break-Even Point in Units

Some small businesses may prefer to express the break-even point in units produced or sold instead of in dollars. Manufacturers often find this approach particularly useful. The following formula computes the break-even point in units:

$$\text{Break-even volume} = \frac{\text{Total fixed costs}}{\text{Sales price per unit} - \text{Variable cost per unit}}$$

For example, suppose that Trilex Manufacturing Company estimates its fixed costs for producing its line of small appliances at $390,00. The variable costs (including materials, direct labor, and factory overhead) amount to $12.10 per unit, and the selling price per unit is $17.50. Trilex computes its contribution margin this way:

$$\text{Contribution margin} = \text{Price per unit} - \text{Variable cost per unit}$$
$$= \$17.50 \text{ per unit} - \$12.10 \text{ per unit}$$
$$= \$5.40 \text{ per unit}$$

Trilex's break-even volume is as follows:

$$\text{Break-even volume (units)} = \frac{\text{Total fixed costs}}{\text{Per unit contribution margin}}$$
$$= \frac{\$390,000}{\$5.40 \text{ per unit}}$$
$$= 72,222 \text{ units}$$

To convert this number of units to break-even sales dollars, Trilex simply multiplies it by the selling price per unit:

$$\text{Break-even sales} = 72,222 \text{ units} \times \$17.50 = \$1,263,889$$

Trilex could compute the sales required to produce a desired profit by treating the profit as if it were a fixed cost:

$$\text{Sales (units)} = \frac{\text{Total fixed costs} + \text{Desired net income}}{\text{Per unit contribution margin}}$$

For example, if Trilex wanted to earn a $60,000 profit, its required sales would be:

$$\text{Sales (units)} = \frac{\$390,000 + \$60,000}{5.40} = 83,333 \text{ units}$$

Constructing a Break-Even Chart

The following outlines the procedure for constructing a graph that visually portrays the firm's break-even point (that point where revenues equal expenses).

Step 1 *On the horizontal axis, mark a scale measuring sales volume in dollars (or in units sold or some other measure of volume).* The break-even chart for the Magic Shop shown in Figure 8 uses sales volume in dollars because it applies to all types of businesses, products, and services.

Step 2 *On the vertical axis, mark a scale measuring income and expenses in dollars.*

Step 3 *Draw a fixed expense line intersecting the vertical axis at the proper dollar level parallel to the horizontal axis.* The area between this line and the horizontal axis represents the firm's fixed expenses. On the break-even chart for the Magic Shop shown in Figure 8, the fixed expense line is drawn horizontally beginning at $177,375 (point A). Because this line is parallel to the horizontal axis, it indicates that fixed expenses remain constant at all levels of activity.

FIGURE 8
Break-Even Chart, the
Magic Shop

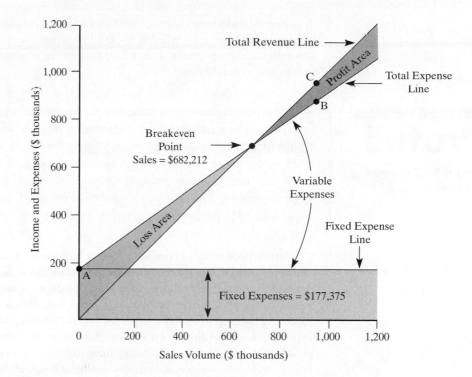

Step 4 *Draw a total expense line that slopes upward beginning at the point at which the fixed cost line intersects the vertical axis.* The precise location of the total expense line is determined by plotting the total cost incurred at a particular sales volume. The total cost for a given sales level is found by the following formula:

Total expenses = Fixed expenses + Variable expenses
expressed as a percentage of sales × Sales level

Arbitrarily choosing a sales level of $950,000, the Magic Shop's total costs would be as follows:

$$\text{Total expenses} = \$177,375 + (0.74 \times \$950,000)$$
$$= \$880,375$$

Thus, the Magic Shop's total cost is $880,375 at a net sales level of $950,000 (point B). The variable cost line is drawn by connecting points A and B. The area between the total cost line and the horizontal axis measures the total costs the Magic Shop incurs at various levels of sales. For example, if the Magic Shop's sales are $850,000, its total costs will be $806,375.

Step 5 *Beginning at the graph's origin, draw a 45-degree revenue line showing where total sales volume equals total income.* For the Magic Shop, point C shows that sales = income = $950,000.

Step 6 *Locate the break-even point by finding the intersection of the total expense line and the revenue line.* If the Magic Shop operates at a sales volume to the left of the break-even point, it will incur a loss because the expense line is higher than the revenue line over this range. This is shown by the triangular section labeled "Loss Area." However, if the firm operates at a sales volume to the right of the break-even point, it will earn a profit because the revenue line lies above the expense line over this range. This is shown by the triangular section labeled "Profit Area."

Using Break-Even Analysis

Break-even analysis is a useful planning tool for entrepreneurs, especially when approaching potential lenders and investors for funds. It provides an opportunity for integrated analysis of sales volume, expenses, income, and other relevant factors. Break-even analysis is a simple, preliminary screening device for the entrepreneur faced with the business start-up decision.

It is easy to understand and use. With just a few calculations, an entrepreneur can determine the minimum level of sales needed to stay in business as well as the effects of various financial strategies on the business. It is a helpful tool for evaluating the impact of changes in investments and expenditures.

ENTREPRENEURIAL
Profile

Fergus McCann and LimoLiner

Before launching LimoLiner, a company that provides luxury bus service with full amenities aimed at businesspeople traveling between downtown Boston and midtown Manhattan, entrepreneur Fergus McCann calculated his venture's break-even point. Knowing that it would take a while to build a solid base of customers, McCann determined that to break even his buses had to be only half-full on each one-way trip. A LimoLiner trip is priced at $89, which is $20 less than Amtrak's Acela Express and $120 less than a full-fare airline ticket. Satisfied that he would be able to generate at least $483 per one-way trip within a short time of opening, McCann launched LimoLiner.[34]

Break-even analysis does have certain limitations. It is too simple to use as a final screening device because it ignores the importance of cash flows. In addition, the accuracy of the analysis depends on the accuracy of the revenue and expense estimates. Finally, the assumptions pertaining to break-even analysis may not be realistic for some businesses. Break-even calculations make the following assumptions: fixed expenses remain constant for all levels of sales volume; variable expenses change in direct proportion to changes in sales volume; and changes in sales volume have no effect on unit sales price. Relaxing these assumptions does not render this tool useless, however. For example, the owner could employ nonlinear break-even analysis using a graphical approach.

IN THE ENTREPRENEURIAL
SPOTLIGHT

Rising to the Challenge . . . and Beyond the Break-Even Point

Guy Gottenbusch, owner of the Servatii Pastry Shop & Deli in Cincinnati, Ohio, was feeling the pinch from two sides. The cost of the flour, eggs, and other products he used in his baking were cutting into his shop's profits, and, at the same time, customers were cutting back their spending, choosing smaller, less expensive items from his line of baked goods and sandwiches. Having come from a long line of bakers, Gottenbusch knew well the dangers of allowing his business, which sells specialty items such as Vienna tortes and delicate mousses as well as more common fare such as bagels and muffins, to slip below its break-even point. "My overhead was totally fixed, and I knew if I lost my sales, I would lose profitability," he says.

With the help of a group of advisors from the Manufacturing Extension Partnership, Gottenbusch began to reinvent his business to ensure its profitability and survival. His first move was to increase sales by targeting new groups of customers. Gottenbusch worked with a local trade association to supply food to a few local hospitals, believing that patients and visitors would jump at the chance to purchase something more than the junk food found in most vending machines. "I realized there was a lot of potential volume and a captive audience," says Gottenbusch. That move led him to another important

decision: to begin making his baked goods free of trans fats. Not only did the entry into hospitals introduce Servatii's pastry products to new customers, it increased sales significantly. Servatii's products now are in 10 Cincinnati hospitals, and hospitals account for 10 percent of the company's sales. "Now I'm thinking about florists and even funeral homes," says Gottenbusch.

Gottenbusch also wanted to drive more traffic to his retail store. "It was time to be aggressive in getting more volume," he says. To accomplish that, he developed several new products that were unconventional, including a popular pumpkin pretzel, to attract customers' attention. He also received a patent on a pretzel stick with special grooves in it that allow a person to bite off small bits more easily. Selling for just 55 cents each, the pretzel sticks are just one-third the price of a traditional pretzel. To introduce customers to the new item, Gottenbusch offered free in-store samples and handed out free pretzel sticks at a local ballgame. The new pretzel stick was a hit with customers (Servatii sold 12,000 of them on Christmas Eve alone), and many customers who came in for the pretzel sticks purchased other items in the store as well. Gottenbusch realized that the pretzel stick appealed to value-seeking customers, and he began selling mixed plates of bite-sized pastries of various types and flavors, another move that proved to be very popular. Gottenbusch's new product idea also benefited Servatii because it is a distinctive product that sets the bakery apart from others.

To address escalating costs, Gottenbusch approached other bakers in the area and formed a purchasing association. Because the association's purchasing power is greater than that of any single member, it has been able to negotiate lower prices on items ranging from flour and butter to shortening and milk. "Some bakeries were paying as much as $30 a bag for flour, [but] we never got above $20," says Gottenbusch.

Gottenbusch also took advantage of one benefit of a recession: lower real estate costs. He negotiated a lease on a storefront in an upscale outdoor mall in Kentucky at a rate well below the normal market rate. That success has inspired Gottenbusch to hunt for other potential locations for new Servatii shops in upscale neighborhoods that he would not have been able to afford in the past.

1. Why is it important for an entrepreneur to know his or her company's break-even point?
2. What steps can an entrepreneur take when his or her business slips below its break-even point?

Sources: Adapted from Anjali Cordeiro, "Sweet Returns," *Wall Street Journal*, April 23, 2009, p. R6; Servatii Pastry Shop & Deli, *www.servatiipastryshop.com/Default.aspx*.

Chapter Review

1. Understand the importance of preparing a financial plan.
   - Launching a successful business requires an entrepreneur to create a solid financial plan. Not only is such a plan an important tool in raising the capital needed to get a company off the ground, but it also is an essential ingredient in managing a growing business.
   - Earning a profit does not occur by accident; it takes planning.
2. Describe how to prepare the basic financial statements and use them to manage a small business.
   - Entrepreneurs rely on three basic financial statements to understand the financial conditions of their companies:
     1. *The balance sheet.* Built on the accounting equation: Assets = Liabilities + Owner's equity (capital), it provides an estimate of the company's value on a particular date.
     2. *The income statement.* This statement compares the firm's revenues against its expenses to determine its net income (or loss). It provides information about the company's bottom line.
     3. *The statement of cash flows.* This statement shows the change in the company's working capital over the accounting period by listing the sources and the uses of funds.
3. Create projected financial statements.
   - Projected financial statements are a basic component of a sound financial plan. They help the manager plot the company's financial future by setting operating objectives and by analyzing the reasons for variations from targeted results. Also, the small business in search of start-up funds will need these pro forma statements to present to prospective lenders and investors. They also assist in determining the amount of cash, inventory, fixtures, and other assets the business will need to begin operation.
4. Understand basic financial statements through ratio analysis.
   - The 12 key ratios described in this chapter are divided into 4 major categories: liquidity ratios, which show the small firm's ability to meet its current obligations; leverage ratios, which tell how much of the company's financing is provided by owners and how much by creditors; operating ratios, which show how effectively the firm uses its resources; and profitability ratios, which disclose the company's profitability.
   - Many agencies and organizations regularly publish such statistics. If there is a discrepancy between the small firm's ratios and those of the typical business, the owner should investigate the reason for the difference. A below average ratio does not necessarily mean that the business is in trouble.
5. Explain how to interpret financial ratios.
   - To benefit from ratio analysis, the small company should compare its ratios to those of other companies in the same line of business and look for trends over time.

- When business owners detect deviations in their companies' ratios from industry standards, they should determine the cause of the deviations. In some cases, such deviations are the result of sound business decisions; in other instances, however, ratios that are out of the normal range for a particular type of business are indicators of what could become serious problems for a company.
6. Conduct a break-even analysis for a small company.
   - Business owners should know their firm's break-even point, the level of operations at which total revenues equal total costs; it is the point at which companies neither earn a profit nor incur a loss. Although just a simple screening device, break-even analysis is a useful planning and decision-making tool.

Discussion Questions

1. Why is it important for entrepreneurs to develop financial plans for their companies?
2. How should a small business manager use the ratios discussed in this chapter?
3. Outline the key points of the 12 ratios discussed in this chapter. What signals does each give a business owner?
4. Describe the method for building a projected income statement and a projected balance sheet for a beginning business.
5. Why are pro forma financial statements important to the financial planning process?
6. How can break-even analysis help an entrepreneur planning to launch a business? What information does it give an entrepreneur?

One significant advantage Business Plan Pro offers is the efficient creation of pro forma (projected) financial statements, including the balance sheet, profit and loss statement, and cash flows statement. Once you enter the revenues, expenses, and other relevant figures in the step-by-step tables, your financial statements are done! This can save time, and the format is one that is commonly recognized and respected by bankers and investors. The simplicity of this process also enables you to create "what if" scenarios based on various levels of anticipated revenues and expenses simply by saving versions of your business plan under unique file names.

On the Web

Go to *http://www.bplans.com/business_calculators/* or use the links titled "Finance" and "Business Calculators" on the Companion Web site (*www.pearsonhighered.com/scarborough*) under the "Business Plan Resource" tab. You will find a collection of online tools, including a break-even calculator. Open this tool and enter the information it requests—the average per unit revenue, the average per unit cost, and the anticipated monthly fixed costs. This tool will calculate your break-even point in units and revenue. Change the data and observe the difference the changes make in the break-even point. What does this tell you about the level of risk that you may experience based on the most realistic financial projections you can make?

In the Software

Select a sample plan that you found interesting. Go to the "Financial Plan" section and look at the financial statements that are contained in the business plan. Notice how the statements are organized. Month-to-month detail is provided for at least the first year, with annual totals for subsequent years. In addition, note the associated tables and graphics that appear within the financial plan. Graphics can be excellent tools for communicating information about financial trends and comparisons.

Click the "Resources" icon at the top of your screen within Business Plan Pro. Then scroll down to "Research" and find the "Free Industry Profile" link. This information may help to compare your company's key ratios to industry averages. You can also get this information from *RMA Annual Statements Studies,* Dun & Bradstreet, trade associations, and other sources. This portion of your plan will help to prove the validity of your financial forecasts.

Building Your Business Plan

Review the information in the "Financial Plan" section of the business plan. Add "Important Assumptions" to this section as you deem necessary. This is a good place to make notes and comments to test or further research any of these assumptions. If it is a start-up business, estimate the costs that you expect to incur to launch the business. The "Investment Offering" option may appear in the menu, based on your choice in the Plan Wizard, and you can complete that information. Review your information for your break-even analysis and the financial statements including your profit and loss, cash flow, and balance sheet statements.

This chapter identifies 12 key business ratios. Based on your projections, calculate each of these ratios and compare them to industry standard ratios. Most, if not all, of these ratios are available through Business Plan Pro's "Ratio" section, the final topic in the "Financial Plan" section.

RATIO ANALYSIS

	Projected Ratio	Industry Ratio	Variance
1. Current ratio			
2. Quick ratio			
3. Debt-ratio			
4. Debt to net worth ratio			
5. Times interest earned			
6. Average inventory turnover ratio			
7. Average collection period ratio			
8. Average payable period ratio			
9. Net sales to total assets ratio			
10. Net profit on sales ratio			
11. Net profit to assets ratio			
12. Net profit to equity ratio			

If you notice significant differences in these comparisons, determine why those variances exist. Does this tell you something about the reality of your projections, or is this just due to the stage and differences of your business compared to the larger industry? These ratios can be excellent tools to help you question, test, and validate your assumptions and projections. Good business planning, solid projections, and a thorough analysis of these ratios can help launch a viable business with greater probability of success.

Endnotes

1. Benjamin B. Gaunsel, "Toward a Framework of Financial Planning in New Venture Creation," presented at United States Association for Small Business and Entrepreneurship Annual Meeting, January 2005, Palm Springs, California, *www.sbaer.uca.edu/research/usasbe/2005/pdffiles/papers/25.pdf*.
2. Eileen Davis, "Dodging the Bullet," *Venture*, December 1988, p. 78.
3. C. J. Prince, "Number Rustling," *Entrepreneur*, March 2003, pp. 43–44.
4. Norm Brodsky, "Our Irrational Fear of Numbers," *Inc.*, January–February 2009, p. 33.
5. Mike Hogan, "Pocket Books," *Entrepreneur*, March 2006, pp. 42–43.
6. Norm Brodsky, "The Magic Number," *Inc.*, September 2003, pp. 43–46.
7. Jay Goltz, "Surviving the Recession," *FSB*, February 2009, pp. 26–27.
8. Geoff Colvin, "How to Manage Your Business in a Recession," *Fortune*, January 19, 2009, p. 91.
9. "When the Going Gets Tough, the Tough Don't Skimp on the Ad Budgets," *Knowedge@Wharton*, November 26, 2008, *http://knowledge.wharton.upenn.edu/article.cfm?articleid=2101*.
10. Jared Sandberg, "Counting Pizza Slices, Cutting Water Cups—You Call This a Budget?" *Wall Street Journal*, January 21, 2004, p. B1.
11. Diedrich Von Soosten, "The Roots of Financial Destruction," *IndustryWeek*, April 5, 1993, pp. 33–34.
12. Lori Ioannou, "He's Preaching the Power of Thrift," *Fortune*, October 30, 2000, p. 208[P].
13. Sarah E. Needleman, "Dial-a-Mattress Retailer Blames Troubles on Stores, Executive Team," *Wall Street Journal*, June 14, 2009, pp. B1, B6; "Dial-a-Mattress, in Bankruptcy, Plans Sale to a Rival," *New York Times*, March 25, 2009, *www.nytimes.com/2009/03/25/business/25mattress.html*.
14. Peter Lattman and Lauren A. E. Schuker, "MGM Recasts Leadership in Bid to Dig Out of Debt," *Wall Street Journal*, August 19, 2009, pp. B1, B2; Brett Pulley and Kelly Riddell, "MGM Said to Seek $3.7 Billion Debt Restructuring, Forbearance," *Bloomberg*, September 25, 2009, *www.bloomberg.com/apps/news?pid=20601087&sid=aPV.ZqDG6FRY*.
15. "Analyzing Creditworthiness," *Inc.*, November 1991, p. 196.
16. Rachel Dodes, Ann Zimmerman, and Jeffrey McCracken, "Retailers Brace for Major Change," *Wall Street Journal*, December 27, 2008, *online.wsj.com/article/SB123033610871336369.html*; Jonathan Stempel, "Goody's Retailer Files Bankruptcy, Will Liquidate," *Reuters*, January 14, 2009, *www.reuters.com/article/idUSN1444200220090114*.
17. Jill Andresky Fraser, "Giving Credit to Debt," *Inc.*, November 2000, p. 125.
18. Cliff Banks, "New Ways to Move Used Cars," *Ward's Dealer Business*, November 1, 2005, *http://wardsdealer.com/ar/auto_new_ways_move/*; Alex Taylor III, "Survival on Dealer's Row," *Fortune*, March 31, 2008, p. 24.
19. Ilan Mochari, "Give Credit to the Small Business Owner," *Inc.*, March 2001, p. 88.
20. Jim Mueller, "Understanding the Cash Conversion Cycle," *Investopedia*, July 12, 2006, *www.investopedia.com/articles/06/cashconversioncycle.asp*.
21. William C. Dunkelberg and Holly Wade, *NFIB Small Business Economic Trends*, NFIB Research Foundation, December 2009, pp. 6, 18.
22. "Slow Sales Cited in Tweeter Closing," *Chicago Tribune*, November 6, 2008, *http://archives.chicagotribune.com/2008/nov/06/business/chi-thu-brf4-tweeter-nov06*.

23. Darren Dahl, "The Truth About Profits," *Inc.*, October 2009, pp. 91–96.

24. Neil Parmar, "Crafty Ways Restaurants Cut Costs," *SmartMoney*, October 2, 2009, *www.smartmoney.com/spending/rip-offs/ crafty-ways-restaurants-cut-costs/*; Paul Frumkin, "NYC Restaurateurs Face Fierce Competition, Price Pressures," *Nation's Restaurant News*, November 13, 2006, pp. 1, 43–46.

25. Pat Croce, "Taking Your Own Pulse," *FSB*, December 2003/January 2004, p. 36.

26. Joshua Hyatt, "Planes, Trains, and . . . Buses," *FSB*, February, 2004, p. 20.

27. Neil Parmar, "Crafty Ways Restaurants Cut Costs," *SmartMoney*, October 2, 2009, *www.smartmoney.com/spending/rip-offs/ crafty-ways-restaurants-cut-costs/*.

28. Dirk Smillie, "What Recession?" *Forbes*, August 11, 2008, p. 64.

29. "STR Reports U.S. Hotel Performance for Week Ending 5 December 2009," *Hospitality.net*, December 14, 2009, *www.hospitalitynet.org/ news/154000320/4044710.html*; Terrie Lloyd, "Hotel Occupancies Fall Below Breakeven, eBiz News from Japan," *Japan Inc.*, August 3, 2009, *www.japaninc.com/terries_take_528*.

30. Norm Brodsky, "The Magic Number," *Inc.*, September 2003, pp. 43–46.

31. William F. Doescher, "Taking Stock," *Entrepreneur*, November 1994, p. 64.

32. Ibid.

33. Kris Hudson, "Red Roof Inn Defaults," *Wall Street Journal*, June 24, 2009, p. B8.

34. "LimoLiner," *Executive Travel*, June 25, 2009, *www. executivetravelmagazine.com/page/LimoLiner*; Joshua Hyatt, "Planes, Trains, and . . . Buses," *FSB*, February, 2004, p. 20.

Managing Cash Flow

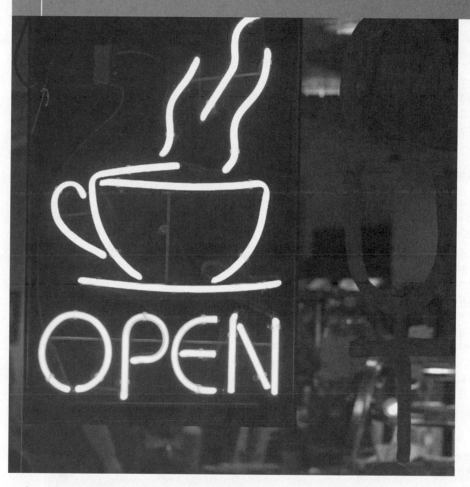

Learning Objectives

Upon completion of this chapter, you will be able to:

1 Explain the importance of cash management to the success of a small business.

2 Differentiate between cash and profits.

3 Understand the five steps in creating a cash budget and use them to build a cash budget.

4 Describe the fundamental principles involved in managing the "big three" of cash management: accounts receivable, accounts payable, and inventory.

5 Explain the techniques for avoiding a cash crunch in a small company.

In ordinary times, cash is merely king. When sales slump and costs rise, cash claims a far more grandiose title: emperor of the universe.

—Mark Henricks

Business isn't difficult—be sure the incomings are greater than the outgoings.

—A wise Vermonter

From Chapter 8 of *Effective Small Business Management: An Entrepreneurial Approach*, 10/e. Norman M. Scarborough.

Cash—a four-letter word that has become a curse for many small businesses. Lack of this valuable asset has driven countless small companies into bankruptcy. Unfortunately, many more firms will become failure statistics because their owners have neglected the principles of cash management that can spell the difference between success and failure. One small business consultant says that "one of the most serious mistakes business owners make is trying to run their businesses without cash flow projections. This is like driving along on the freeway at 70 miles per hour with a blindfold on. It's not a question of whether you are headed for an accident. It's a question of how serious the accident will be and whether or not you will survive it."[1]

Developing cash forecasts is important for every small business, but it is essential for new businesses because early sales levels usually do not generate sufficient cash to keep the company afloat. Too often, entrepreneurs launch their companies with insufficient cash to cover their start-up costs and the cash flow gap that results while expenses outstrip revenues. The result is business failure. Controlling the financial aspects of a business with the profit-planning techniques is immensely important; however, by themselves, these techniques are insufficient to achieve business success. Entrepreneurs are prone to focus on their companies' income statements—particularly sales and profits. The balance sheet and the income statement, of course, show an important part of a company's financial picture, but it is just that: only part of the total picture. It is entirely possible for a business to have a solid balance sheet and to make a profit and still go out of business by *running out of cash*. Even if a company's revenue exceeds its expenses for a given period, the cash flow from that revenue may not arrive in time to pay the company's cash expenses. Managing cash effectively requires an entrepreneur to look beyond the "bottom line" and focus on what keeps a company going—cash.

Cash Management

1. Explain the importance of cash management to the success of a small business.

Managing cash flow is a struggle for many business owners. In fact, research by the National Federation of Independent Businesses (NFIB) shows that managing cash flow consistently ranks among the top 10 problems that small business owners face.[2] Surveys by American Express OPEN Small Business Monitor show similar concerns: cash flow management ranks as the number one issue facing small business owners.[3] Figure 1 shows the most common cash flow problems that business owners encounter.

Cash management involves forecasting, collecting, disbursing, investing, and planning for the cash a company needs to operate smoothly. Managing cash is a matter of timing—gaining control over when a company collects cash and when it pays it out. Managing cash is an important task because cash is the most important, yet least productive, asset that a small business owns. "The more cash a business can accumulate and add to its surplus, the greater is its strength and stability," says one cash management guide aimed at entrepreneurs.[4] A business must have enough cash to meet its obligations as they come due, or it will experience bankruptcy. Creditors, employees, and lenders expect to be paid on time, and cash is the required medium of exchange.

Operating a business without cash flow projections is like driving at 70 miles an hour while wearing a blindfold. Not a good idea!

Source: Tom Wood\Alamy Images

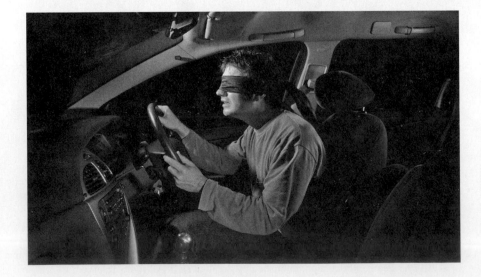

FIGURE 1
Cash Flow Concerns

Source: American Express
OPEN Small Business Monitor
April 15, 2009.

In a recent survey, 57 percent of small business owners report experiencing cash flow problems. The most common problems they encounter are as follows:

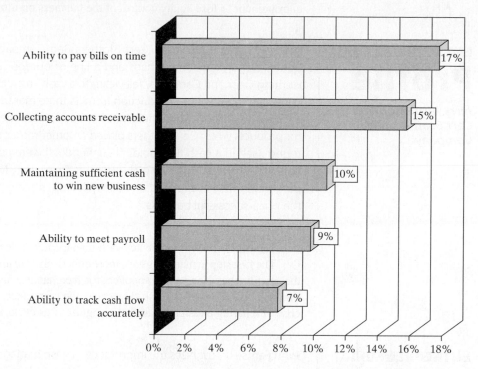

Proper cash management permits entrepreneurs to meet the cash demands of their businesses, to avoid retaining unnecessarily large cash balances, and to stretch the profit-generating power of each dollar their companies own. Entrepreneurs must have the discipline to manage cash flow from their first day of operation.

ENTREPRENEURIAL
Profile

H. J. Heinz and the
H. J. Heinz Company

Shortly after H. J. Heinz and two partners launched their first food business in 1875, their company's rapidly growing sales outstripped their start-up capital, and the business ran out of cash. A local newspaper called the entrepreneurs a "trio in a pickle." After the company failed, Heinz personally was liable for $20,000, a huge sum in that day. Undaunted, Heinz learned from his mistakes and launched a second food company the very next year. In this venture, he added the product that would eventually make him famous—ketchup—and with the help of careful cash management the H. J. Heinz Company has become one of the largest food companies in the world.[5]

Although cash flow problems afflict companies of all sizes and ages, young businesses are more prone to suffer cash shortages because they act like "cash sponges," soaking up every available dollar and then some. The reason for this is that their cash-generating "engines" have not had the opportunity to "rev up" to full speed and cannot generate sufficient power to produce the cash necessary to cover rapidly climbing expenses.

Owners of fast-growing businesses also must pay particular attention to cash management because the greatest potential threat to cash flow occurs when a company is experiencing rapid growth. If a company's sales are rising, the owner also must hire more employees, expand plant capacity, develop new products, increase the sales force and customer service staff, build inventory, and incur other drains on the firm's cash supply. However, collections from the increased sales often slip as a company grows, and the result is a cash crisis.

Unfortunately, many small business owners do not engage in cash planning. One study of 2,200 small businesses found that 68 percent performed no cash flow analysis at all![6] The result is that many successful, growing, and profitable businesses fail because they become insolvent; they do not have adequate cash to meet the needs of a growing business with a booming sales volume. The head of the NFIB says that many small business owners "wake up one day to find that the price of success is no cash on hand. They don't understand that if they're successful, inventory and receivables will increase faster than profits can fund them."[7] The resulting cash crisis may force an entrepreneur to lose equity control of the business or, ultimately, to declare bankruptcy and close.

ENTREPRENEURIAL
Profile
Jerry Michelson and Cerf Brothers Bag Company

After 94 years in business, Cerf Brothers Bag Company, a family-owned business that made duffle, cargo, and storage bags and a line of outdoor gear under the brand names Hideaway Hunting Gear and Camp Inn, fell victim to a cash crisis. In an attempt to lower its costs, the company shifted most of its production from its three manufacturing operations in the United States to factories in Asia. When these vendors accelerated their collection terms, insisting on payment for products when Cerf Brothers placed an order rather than after it was delivered, the company found itself in a cash flow bind. "[Our vendors] were asking us to pay for goods 3 to 5 months before we would be paid by our customers," says Jerry Michelson, the company's CEO. The company's cash flow evaporated and debt piled up, forcing its owners to declare bankruptcy and sell the once-successful business.[8]

Table 1 describes the five key cash management roles every entrepreneur must fill.

The first step in managing cash more effectively is to understand the company's **cash flow cycle**—the time lag between paying suppliers for merchandise and receiving payment from customers (see Figure 2). The longer this cash flow cycle, the more likely the business owner is to encounter a cash crisis. Preparing a cash forecast that recognizes this cycle, however, helps avoid a crisis.

ENTREPRENEURIAL
Profile
John Fernsell and Ibex Outdoor Clothing

John Fernsell recognizes the importance of cash management because of the length of his company's cash flow cycle. Fernsell, a former stockbroker, is the founder of Ibex Outdoor Clothing, a company that makes outdoor clothing from high-quality European wool. Sales are growing rapidly, but cash is a constant problem because of Ibex's lengthy cash flow cycle. Fernsell orders wool from his European suppliers in February and pays for it in June. The wool then goes to garment makers in California, who ship finished clothing to Ibex in July and August, when Fernsell pays for the finished goods. Ibex ships the clothing to retailers in September and October but does not get paid until November, December, and sometimes January! Ibex's major cash outflows are from June to August, but its cash inflows during those months are virtually nil, making it essential for Fernsell to manage the company's cash balances carefully.[9]

TABLE 1 Five Cash Management Roles of the Entrepreneur

Role 1: Cash finder. This is your first and foremost responsibility. You must make sure there is enough capital to pay all present (and future) bills. This is not a one-time task; it is an ongoing job.

Role 2: Cash planner. As cash planner, you make sure your company's cash is used properly and efficiently. You must keep track of its cash, make sure it is available to pay bills, and plan for its future use. Planning requires you to forecast your company's cash inflows and outflows for the months ahead with the help of a cash budget (discussed later in this chapter).

Role 3: Cash distributor. This role requires you to control the cash needed to pay the company's bills and the priority and the timing of those payments. Forecasting cash disbursements accurately and making sure the cash is available when payments come due is essential to keeping the business solvent.

Role 4: Cash collector. As cash collector, your job is to make sure your customers pay their bills on time. Too often, entrepreneurs focus on pumping up sales while neglecting to collect the cash from those sales. Having someone in your company responsible for collecting accounts receivable is essential. Uncollected accounts drain a small company's pool of cash very quickly.

Role. 5: Cash conserver. This role requires you to make sure your company gets maximum value for the dollars it spends. Whether you are buying inventory to resell or computer systems to keep track of what you sell, it is important to get the most for your money. Avoiding unnecessary expenditures is an important part of this task. The goal is to spend cash so that it produces a return for the company.

Source: Based on Bruce J. Blechman, "Quick Change Artist," *Entrepreneur,* January 1994, pp. 18–21.

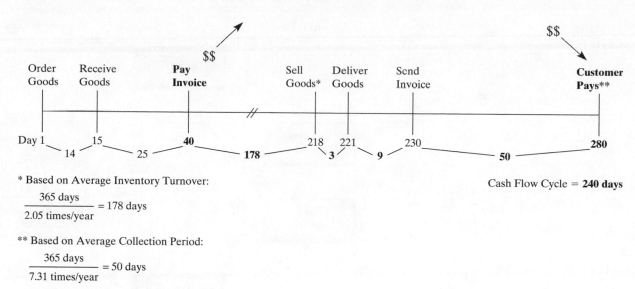

* Based on Average Inventory Turnover:

$$\frac{365 \text{ days}}{2.05 \text{ times/year}} = 178 \text{ days}$$

** Based on Average Collection Period:

$$\frac{365 \text{ days}}{7.31 \text{ times/year}} = 50 \text{ days}$$

Cash Flow Cycle = **240 days**

FIGURE 2 The Cash Flow Cycle

The next step in effective cash management is to begin whittling down the length of the cash flow cycle. Reducing the cycle from 240 days to, say, 180 days would free up incredible amounts of cash that the company whose cash flow cycle is illustrated in Figure 2 could use to finance growth and dramatically reduce its borrowing costs. What steps do you suggest the owner of this business take to reduce the cycle's length?

Cash and Profits Are Not the Same

2. Differentiate between cash and profits.

When analyzing cash flow, entrepreneurs must understand that cash and profits are not the same. Both are important financial concepts for entrepreneurs, but they measure very different aspects of a business. **Profit** (or net income) is the difference between a company's total revenue and its total expenses. It is an accounting concept designed to measure how efficiently a business is operating. In contrast, cash is the money that is readily available to use in a business. **Cash flow** measures a company's liquidity and its ability to pay its bills and other financial obligations on time by tracking the flow of cash into and out of the business over time. Many factors determine a company's cash flow, including its sales patterns, the timing of its accounts receivable and accounts payable, its inventory turnover rate, its debt repayment schedule, and its schedule of capital expenditures (e.g., fixtures, equipment, facilities expansion, and others).

Figure 3 shows the flow of cash through a typical small business. Decreases in cash occur when a business purchases, on credit or for cash, goods for inventory or materials for use in production. The company sells the goods either for cash or on credit. When it takes in cash or collects accounts receivable, a company's cash balance increases. Notice that purchases for inventory and production *lead* sales; that is, these bills typically must be paid *before* sales materialize. However, collection of accounts receivable *lags* behind sales; that is, customers who purchase goods on credit may not pay until a month or more later.

As important as earning a profit is, no business owner can pay creditors, employees, and lenders in profits; these payments require *cash*! "Cash flow is more important than earnings," says Evan Betzer, founder of a financial services firm.[10] A company can operate in the short run with a net loss showing on its income statement, but if its cash flow becomes negative, the business is in trouble. It can no longer pay suppliers, meet payroll, pay its taxes, or pay any other bills. In short, the business is out of business!

Preparing a Cash Budget

3. Understand the five steps in creating a cash budget and use them to build a cash budget.

The need for a reliable cash forecast arises because in every business the cash flowing in is rarely "in sync" with the cash flowing out. This uneven flow of cash creates periodic cash surpluses and deficits, making it necessary for entrepreneurs to track the flow of cash through their businesses

FIGURE 3
Cash Flow

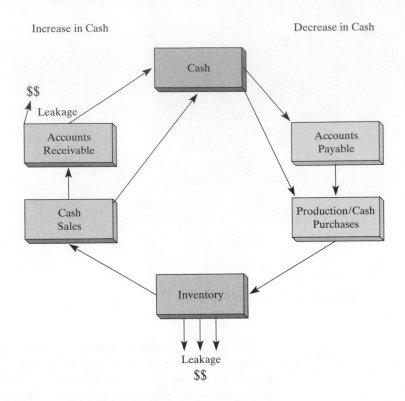

so they can project realistically the pool of cash that is available throughout the year. Many owners operate their businesses without knowing the pattern of their cash flows, believing that the process is too complex or time consuming. In reality, entrepreneurs simply cannot afford to ignore cash management. They must ensure that an adequate, but not excessive, supply of cash is on hand to meet their companies' operating needs.

How much cash is enough? What is suitable for one business may be totally inadequate for another, depending on each company's size, sales, collections, expenses, and other factors. Entrepreneurs should prepare a **cash budget**, which is nothing more than a "cash map," showing the amount and the timing of the cash receipts and the cash disbursements week-by-week or month-by-month. Entrepreneurs use it to predict the amount of cash they will need to cover expenses, operate smoothly, and grow the business over time, making it a valuable tool in managing a company successfully.

Typically, a small business should prepare a projected monthly cash budget for at least 1 year and quarterly estimates 1 or 2 years beyond that. To be effective, a cash budget must cover all seasonal sales fluctuations. The more variable a company's sales pattern, the shorter its planning horizon should be. For example, a firm whose sales fluctuate widely over a relatively short time frame might require a weekly cash budget rather than a monthly one. The key to managing cash flow successfully is to monitor not only the amount of cash flowing into and out of a company but also the *timing* of those cash flows.

Regardless of the time frame selected, a cash budget must be in writing for an entrepreneur to visualize a company's cash position. Creating a written cash plan is not an excessively time-consuming task and can help the owner avoid unexpected cash shortages, a situation that can cause a business to fail. One financial consultant describes "a client who won't be able to make the payroll this month. His bank agreed to meet the payroll for him—but banks don't like to be surprised like that," he adds.[11] Preparing a cash budget helps business owners avoid unpleasant surprises such as that. It also tells owners whether they are keeping excessive amounts of cash on hand. Computer spreadsheets such as Excel and Lotus 1-2-3 make the job fast and easy to complete and allow for instant updates and "what if" analyses.

A cash budget is based on the cash method of accounting, which means that cash receipts and cash disbursements are recorded in the forecast only when the cash transaction is expected to take place. For example, credit sales to customers are not reported until the company expects to receive the cash from them. Similarly, purchases made on credit are not recorded until the owner expects to pay them. Because depreciation, bad debt expense, and other noncash items involve no cash transfers, they are omitted entirely from the cash budget.

A cash budget is nothing more than a forecast of a company's cash inflows and outflows for a specific time period, and it will never be completely accurate. However, it does give a small business owner a clear picture of a company's estimated cash balance for the period, pointing out where external cash infusions may be required or where surplus cash balances may be available for investing. A good cash budget serves as an early warning system for cash flow challenges. In addition, by comparing actual cash flows with projections, an entrepreneur can revise his forecast so that future cash budgets will be more accurate.

ENTREPRENEURIAL

Profile

Michael Koss and Koss Corporation

Michael Koss, president and CEO of Koss Corporation, a manufacturer of stereo headphones, now emphasizes cash flow management after his company's brush with failure. In the 1980s, Koss Corporation expanded rapidly—so rapidly, in fact, that its cash flow couldn't keep pace. Debt climbed, and the company filed for reorganization bankruptcy. Emergency actions saved the business, and today Koss manages with the determination never to repeat the same mistakes. "I look at cash every single day," he says. "That is absolutely critical."[12]

Formats for preparing a cash budget vary depending on the pattern of a company's cash flow. Table 2 shows a monthly cash budget for a small retail store over a 4-month period. Each

TABLE 2 Cash Budget for Small Department Store

Assumptions:

Cash balance on December 31 = $12,000

Minimum cash balance desired = $10,000

Sales are 75% credit and 25% cash.

Credit sales are collected in the following manner:

- 60% collected in the first month after the sale.
- 30% collected in the second month after the sale.
- 5% collected in the third month after the sale.
- 5% are never collected.

Sales Forecasts Are as Follows:	Pessimistic	Most Likely	Optimistic
October (actual)		$300,000	
November (actual)		350,000	
December (actual)		400,000	
January	$120,000	150,000	$175,000
February	160,000	200,000	250,000
March	160,000	200,000	250,000
April	250,000	300,000	340,000

The store pays 70% of sales price for merchandise purchased and pays for each month's anticipated sales in the preceding month.

Rent is $2,000 per month.

An interest payment of $7,500 is due in March.

A tax prepayment of $50,000 must be made in March.

A capital addition payment of $130,000 is due in February.

Utilities expenses amount to $850 per month.

Miscellaneous expenses are $70 per month.

Interest income of $200 will be received in February.

Wages and salaries are estimated to be

January—$30,000

February—$40,000

March—$45,000

April—$50,000

(continued)

TABLE 2 Continued

Cash Budget—Pessimistic Sales Forecast

	Oct.	Nov.	Dec.	Jan.	Feb.	Mar.	Apr.
Cash Receipts:							
Sales	$300,000	$350,000	$400,000	$120,000	$160,000	$160,000	$250,000
Credit Sales	225,000	262,500	300,000	90,000	120,000	120,000	187,500
Collections:							
60%—1st month after sale				$180,000	$ 54,000	$ 72,000	$ 72,000
30%—2nd month after sale				78,750	90,000	27,000	36,000
5%—3rd month after sale				11,250	13,125	15,000	4,500
Cash Sales				30,000	40,000	40,000	62,500
Interest				0	200	0	0
Total Cash Receipts				$300,000	$197,325	$154,000	$175,000
Cash Disbursements:							
Purchases				$112,000	$112,000	$175,000	$133,000
Rent				2,000	2,000	2,000	2,000
Utilities				850	850	850	850
Interest				0	0	7,500	0
Tax Prepayment				0	0	50,000	0
Capital Addition				0	130,000	0	0
Miscellaneous				70	70	70	70
Wages/Salaries				30,000	40,000	45,000	50,000
Total Cash Disbursements				$144,920	$284,920	$280,420	$185,920
End-of-Month Balance:							
Cash (beginning of month)				$ 12,000	$167,080	$ 79,485	$ 10,000
+Cash Receipts				300,000	197,325	154,000	175,000
−Cash Disbursements				144,920	284,920	280,420	185,920
Cash (end of month)				167,080	79,485	(46,935)	(920)
Borrowing/Repayment				0	0	56,935	10,920
Cash (end of month [after borrowing])				$167,080	$ 79,485	$ 10,000	$ 10,000

Cash Budget—Most Likely Sales Forecast

	Oct.	Nov.	Dec.	Jan.	Feb.	Mar.	Apr.
Cash Receipts:							
Sales	$300,000	$350,000	$400,000	$150,000	$200,000	$200,000	$300,000
Credit Sales	225,000	262,500	300,000	112,000	150,000	150,000	225,000
Collections:							
60%—1st month after sale				$180,000	$ 67,500	$ 90,000	$ 90,000
30%—2nd month after sale				78,750	90,000	33,750	45,000
5%—3rd month after sale				11,250	13,125	15,000	5,625
Cash Sales				37,500	50,000	50,000	75,000
Interest				0	200	0	0
Total Cash Receipts				$307,500	$220,825	$188,750	$215,625
Cash Disbursements:							
Purchases				$140,000	$140,000	$210,000	$175,000
Rent				2,000	2,000	2,000	2,000
Utilities				850	850	850	850
Interest				0	0	7,500	0
Tax Prepayment				0	0	50,000	0
Capital Addition				0	130,000	0	0
Miscellaneous				70	70	70	70
Wages/Salaries				30,000	40,000	45,000	50,000
Total Cash Disbursements				$172,920	$312,920	$315,420	$227,920

TABLE 2 Continued

	Oct.	Nov.	Dec.	Jan.	Feb.	Mar.	Apr.
End-of-Month Balance:							
Cash [beginning of month]				$ 12,000	$146,580	$ 54,485	$ 10,000
+Cash Receipts				307,500	220,825	188,750	215,625
−Cash Disbursements				172,920	312,920	315,420	227,920
Cash (end of month)				146,580	54,485	(72,185)	(2,295)
Borrowing/Repayment				0	0	82,185	12,295
Cash (end of month [after borrowing])				$146,580	$ 54,485	$ 10,000	$ 10,000

Cash Budget—Optimistic Sales Forecast

	Oct.	Nov.	Dec.	Jan.	Feb.	Mar.	Apr.
Cash Receipts:							
Sales	$300,000	$350,000	$400,000	$175,000	$250,000	$250,000	$340,000
Credit Sales	225,000	262,500	300,000	131,250	187,500	187,500	255,000
Collections:							
60%—1st month after sale				$180,000	$ 78,750	$112,500	$112,500
30%—2nd month after sale				78,750	90,000	39,375	56,250
5%—3rd month after sale				11,250	13,125	15,000	6,563
Cash Sales				43,750	62,500	62,500	85,000
Interest				0	200	0	0
Total Cash Receipts				$313,750	$244,575	$229,375	$260,313
Cash Disbursements:							
Purchases				$175,000	$175,000	$238,000	$217,000
Rent				2,000	2,000	2,000	2,000
Utilities				850	850	850	850
Interest				0	0	7,500	0
Tax Prepayment				0	0	50,000	0
Capital Addition				0	130,000	0	0
Miscellaneous				70	70	70	70
Wages/Salaries				30,000	40,000	45,000	50,000
Total Cash Disbursements				$207,920	$347,920	$343,420	$269,920
End-of-Month Balance:							
Cash [beginning of month]				$ 12,000	$117,830	$ 14,485	$ 10,000
+Cash Receipts				313,750	244,575	229,375	296,125
−Cash Disbursements				207,920	317,920	343,120	269,920
Cash (end of month)				117,830	14,485	(99,560)	36,205
Borrowing/Repayment				0	0	109,560	0
Cash (end of month [after borrowing])				$117,830	$ 14,485	$ 10,000	$ 36,205

monthly column should be divided into two sections—estimated and actual (not shown)—so that subsequent cash forecasts can be updated according to actual cash transactions. There are five steps to creating a cash budget:

1. Determining an adequate minimum cash balance
2. Forecasting sales
3. Forecasting cash receipts
4. Forecasting cash disbursements
5. Estimating the end-of-month cash balance

Step 1: Determining an Adequate Minimum Cash Balance

What is considered an excessive cash balance for one small business may be inadequate for another, even if the two firms are in the same industry. Some suggest that a company's cash balance should equal at least one-fourth of its current liabilities, but this simple guideline does not work for all small businesses. The most reliable method of deciding cash balance is based on past experience. Past operating records should indicate the proper cash cushion needed to cover any unexpected expenses after all normal cash outlays are deducted from the month's cash receipts. For example, past records may indicate that it is desirable to maintain a cash balance equal to 5 days' sales. Seasonal fluctuations may cause a company's minimum cash balance to change. For example, the desired cash balance for a retailer in December may be greater than in June.

Step 2: Forecasting Sales

The heart of the cash budget is the sales forecast. It is the central factor in creating an accurate picture of a company's cash position because sales ultimately are transformed into cash receipts and cash disbursements. For most businesses, sales constitute the primary source of the cash flowing into the business. Similarly, sales of merchandise require entrepreneurs to use cash to replenish inventory. As a result, the cash budget is only as accurate as the sales forecast from which it is derived; an accurate sales forecast is essential to producing a reliable cash flow forecast.

For an established business, the sales forecast can be based on past sales, but entrepreneurs must be careful not to be excessively optimistic in projecting sales. Economic swings, increased competition, fluctuations in demand, and other factors can drastically alter sales patterns. A good cash budget must reflect the seasonality of a company's sales. Simply deriving a realistic annual sales forecast and then dividing it by 12 does *not* produce a reliable monthly sales forecast. Most businesses have sales patterns that are "lumpy" and not evenly distributed throughout the year. For instance, Super Bowl Sunday is the single largest revenue-generating day of the year for most pizzerias (and ranks second only to Thanksgiving as the largest food consumption day). In addition, as much as 25 percent of the sales at companies that supply exotic dancers for parties occur on Super Bowl Sunday.[13] GourmetGiftBaskets.com, a company that sells a variety of gift baskets (and that now holds the record for the world's largest cupcake, a 1,224-pound gargantuan) experiences this highly concentrated sales pattern. "We do 40 percent to 50 percent of our business in a 25-day window [during the holiday season]," says CEO Ryan Abood.[14] Highly seasonal sales patterns can make managing cash flow a challenge for entrepreneurs.

Ryan Abood (right), CEO of GourmetGiftBaskets.com, says that 40 to 50 percent of his company's sales occur within a 25-day window during the holiday season. Abood is receiving a certificate for the world's largest cupcake.

Source: Jeffrey R. Abood/Chuck Whitman/Whitman Photograph

LESSONS FROM THE STREET-SMART → entrepreneur

A Short Season

Bruce Zoldan, CEO of Phantom Fireworks, is monitoring the heavy rush of customer traffic at the Phantom Fireworks outlet in Youngstown, Ohio. In the 3-week period leading up to July 4, the small chain of fireworks stores will face a heavy flood of customers pouring through its doors from 7 AM until midnight, all of them looking for the ingredients for a brilliant Fourth of July fireworks celebration. During this 3-week burst of activity, Phantom Fireworks sells more than 25 million pounds of fireworks, and sales at any one of its 41 stores often reach $400,000 a day. After the peak Independence Day holiday, however, sales at many Phantom stores typically plummet to just $5,000 a day. That's when the real work for Zoldan and his staff begins. "We have 11 months of logistics for 1 month of sales," he says. Not only does gearing up for a 1-month sales blitz require lots of advance planning, it also demands some clever cash management techniques. Even

though sales are concentrated in just 1 month of the year, Phantom Fireworks expenses continue year-round.

"A seasonal business is infinitely more difficult to manage than most other businesses," says Les Charm, who teaches entrepreneurship at Babson College. How can business owners whose companies face highly seasonal sales patterns manage the uneven cash flow? The Street-Smart Entrepreneur offers the following tips:

■ *Be financially disciplined.* Seasonal business owners must establish a realistic budget, stick to it, and avoid the temptation to spend lavishly when cash flow is plentiful. Teevan McManus, owner of the Coronado Surfing Academy in San Diego, failed to heed this advice in his first year of business. "I burned through everything I made in the summer and was living off of my business line of credit before the next season came around," he recalls. "I barely made it to the next June."

- *Manage your time and your employees' time carefully.* During the busy season, employees may be working overtime to serve the rush of customers; during the off season a business owner may cut back to 20-hour workweeks or operate with a skeleton crew.
- *Use permanent employees sparingly.* Many owners of seasonal businesses use a small core of permanent employees and then hire part-time workers or student interns during their busy season. Planning for the right number of seasonal employees and recruiting them early ensures that a business will be able to serve its customers properly.
- *Put aside cash in a separate account that you use only for the lean months of your seasonal business.* Creating a separate account imposes a degree of discipline and discourages excessive spending when a company is flush with cash.
- *Maximize your productivity in the off season.* Use the slow season to conduct market research, perform routine maintenance and repairs, revise your Web site, and stay in touch with customers. Steve Kopelman's company, HauntedHouse.com, earns all of its $2.6 million in annual revenue in a 6-week period leading up to Halloween. Starting in November, Kopelman surveys his customers so that he can refine his marketing efforts for the next season and solicit suggestions for improvement. He visits trade shows to look for the latest technology and gadgets to keep his haunted houses fresh and exciting for his customers. Kopelman also negotiates leases on properties for the next season and studies his competition by visiting every haunted house Web site that he can find.
- *Use the off season to reconnect with customers.* The off season is the ideal time to catch up on all of the small but important customer service tasks that you do not have time to perform during the height of the busy season. The owner of one small company increased his company's annual sales and reduced customer turnover by 75 percent when he set up one-on-one meetings with clients during the slow season with the purpose of discovering their needs and getting feedback about how his company could serve them better.
- *Keep inventory at minimal levels during the off season.* As you will learn in this chapter, holding inventory unnecessarily merely ties up valuable cash.
- *Offer off-peak discounts.* Off-peak discounts may generate some revenue during slow periods.
- *Consider starting a complementary seasonal business.* Jan Axel, founder of Delphinium Design Landscaping in South Salem, New York, sees her business slow down considerably during the winter and decided to launch a holiday decorating service that generates cash flow when landscape sales evaporate.
- *Create a cash flow forecast.* Perhaps one of the most important steps that seasonal business owners can take is to develop a forecast of their companies' cash flow. Doing so allows them to spot patterns and trends and to make plans for covering inevitable cash shortages. Make sure that you include a pessimistic or worst-case scenario in your cash forecast.
- *Establish a bank line of credit.* The line of credit should be large enough to cover at least 3 months' worth of expenses. Use your cash flow forecast to show the banker how and when your company will be able to repay the loan. "[A good cash forecast] shows the banker that you know exactly where the peaks and valleys are and what your cash needs are," says one banker.

Sources: Based on "Make the Most of the Slow Season," *Marketing Profs*, May 28, 2009, pp. 1–2; Rich Mintzer, "Running a Seasonal Business," *Entrepreneur*, March 16, 2007, *www.entrepreneur.com/management/operations/article175954.html*; Gwendolyn Bounds, "Preparing for the Big Bang," *Wall Street Journal*, June 29, 2004, pp, B1, B7; Sarah Pierce, "Surviving a Seasonal Business," *Entrepreneur*, July 15, 2008, *www.entrepreneur.com/startingabusiness/businessideas/article195680.html*; Dan Kehrer, "10 Steps to Seasonal Success," *Business.com*, May 2006, *www.business.com/directory/advice/sales-and-marketing/sales/10-steps-to-seasonal-success/*; Amy Barrett, "Basics for Seasonal Business Owners," *BusinessWeek*, April 16, 2008, *www.businessweek.com/magazine/content/08_64/s0804058908582.htm?chan=smallbiz_smallbiz+index+page_best+of+smallbiz+magazine.*

ENTREPRENEURIAL
Profile

Ann Cummings and Peter Watson and Newcastle's Pudding Lady

When Ann Cummings and her brother Peter Watson purchased Newcastle's Pudding Lady, a business in Newcastle, Australia, that makes pudding, a traditional Australian Christmas dessert similar to fruitcake, one of their goals was to extend the company's sales season beyond the few weeks leading up to the holiday season. Cummings says that the business was "cash negative for months and months" as sales dwindled after Christmas but expenses continued. Cummings and Watson extended the company's product line with ChocFusions and FruitFusions (chocolate- and fruit-based desserts) and puddings made without flour for people with gluten allergies. "We took out the flavors that made the pudding a Christmas treat and put in a range of different flavors," says Cummings. New packaging also helped customers to associate the products with celebrations other than Christmas. Although Christmas remains the company's busiest season, Newcastle's Pudding Lady has reduced the seasonality of its sales and has added a cash budget and financial discipline to its recipe.[15]

Several quantitative techniques for forecasting sales, which are beyond the scope of this text (e.g., linear regression, multiple regression, time series analysis, and exponential smoothing), are available to owners of existing businesses with established sales patterns. These methods allow business owners to extrapolate past and present sales trends to arrive at a fairly accurate sales forecast.

The task of forecasting sales for a new firm is difficult but not impossible. For example, an entrepreneur might conduct research on similar firms and their sales patterns in the first year of operation to come up with a forecast. Local chambers of commerce and industry trade associations also collect such information. Publications such as RMA's *Annual Statement Studies,* which profiles financial statements for companies of all sizes in more than 750 industries, also is a useful tool. Other potential sources that may help predict sales include Census Bureau reports, newspapers, radio and television customer profiles, polls and surveys, and local government statistics. Talking with owners of similar businesses (outside the local trading area, of course) can provide entrepreneurs with realistic estimates of start-up sales. Table 3 gives an example of how one entrepreneur used a variety of marketing information to derive a sales forecast for his first year of operation in the automotive repair business.

No matter what techniques entrepreneurs use to forecast cash flow, they must recognize that even the best sales estimates will be wrong. Many financial analysts suggest that entrepreneurs create *three estimates*—an optimistic, a pessimistic, and a most likely sales estimate—and then make a separate cash budget for each forecast (a very simple task with a computer spreadsheet). This dynamic forecast enables entrepreneurs to determine the range within which their sales and cash flows will likely fall as the year progresses. By using the forecast that most closely reflects their sales patterns, entrepreneurs can project their companies' cash flow more accurately.

Step 3: Forecasting Cash Receipts

As noted earlier, sales constitute the major source of cash receipts. When a company sells goods and services on credit, the cash budget must account for the delay between the sale and the actual collection of the proceeds. Remember: You cannot spend cash you haven't collected yet! For instance, a company might not collect the cash from a sale in February until March or April (or even later), and the cash budget must reflect this delay. To project accurately a firm's cash receipts, entrepreneurs must analyze their companies' accounts receivable to determine the collection pattern. For example, an entrepreneur may discover that 20 percent of sales are for cash, 50 percent are paid in the month following the sale, 20 percent are paid 2 months after the sale, 7 percent after 3 months, and 3 percent are never collected. In addition to cash and credit sales, a cash budget must include any other cash the company receives, such as interest income, rental income, dividends, and others.

TABLE 3 Forecasting Sales for a Business Start-Up

Robert Adler wants to open a repair shop for imported cars. The trade association for automotive garages estimates that the owner of an imported car spends an average of $485 per year on repairs and maintenance. The typical garage attracts its clientele from a trading zone (the area from which a business draws its customers) with a 20-mile radius. Census reports show that the families within a 20-mile radius of Robert's proposed location own 84,000 cars, of which 24 percent are imports. Based on a local market consultant's research, Robert believes he can capture 9.9 percent of the market this year. Robert's estimate of his company's first year's sales are as follows:

Number of cars in trading zone	84,000 autos
× Percent of imports	×24%
= Number of imported cars in trading zone	20,160 imports
Number of imports in trading zone	20,160
× Average expenditure on repairs and maintenance	× $485
= Total import repair sales potential	$9,777,600
Total import repair sales potential	$9,777,600
× Estimated share of market	× 9.9%
= Sales estimate	$967,982

Robert Adler can convert this annual sales estimate of $967,982 into monthly sales estimates for use in his company's cash budget.

Some small business owners never discover the hidden danger in accounts receivable until it is too late for their companies. Receivables act as cash sponges, tying up valuable dollars until an entrepreneur collects them.

ENTREPRENEURIAL
Profile

Mary and Phil Baechler and Baby Jogger Company

When Mary and Phil Baechler started Baby Jogger Company to make strollers that would enable parents to take their babies along on their daily runs, Mary was in charge of the financial aspects of the business and watched its cash flow closely. As the company grew, the couple created an accounting department to handle its financial affairs. Unfortunately, the financial management system could not keep up with the company's rapid growth and failed to provide the necessary information to keep its finances under control. As inventory and accounts receivable ballooned, the company headed for a cash crisis. To ensure Baby Jogger's survival, the Baechlers were forced to reduce their workforce by half. Then they turned their attention to the accounts receivable and discovered that customers owed the business almost $700,000! In addition, most of the accounts were past due. Focusing on collecting the money owed to their company, the Baechlers were able to steer clear of a cash crisis and get Baby Jogger back on track.[16]

Figure 4 demonstrates how vital it is to act promptly once an account becomes past due. Notice how the probability of collecting an outstanding account diminishes the longer the account is delinquent. Table 4 illustrates the high cost of failing to collect accounts receivable on time.

Step 4: Forecasting Cash Disbursements

Most owners of established businesses have a clear picture of a company's pattern of cash disbursements. In fact, many cash payments, such as rent, salaries, loan repayments, and insurance premiums, are fixed amounts due on specified dates. The key factor in forecasting disbursements for a cash budget is to *record them in the month in which they will be paid, not when the debt or obligation is incurred*. Of course, the number and type of cash disbursements varies with each particular business, but the following disbursement categories are standard: purchases of inventory or raw materials, wages and salaries, rent, taxes, loan repayments, interest, marketing and selling expenses, Internet and Web site expenses, utility expenses, and miscellaneous expenses.

When preparing a cash budget, one of the worst mistakes entrepreneurs can make is to underestimate cash disbursements, which can result in a cash crisis. To prevent this, wise entrepreneurs cushion their cash disbursements, assuming they will be higher than expected. This is particularly important for entrepreneurs opening new businesses. In fact, some financial analysts recommend that people starting new businesses make the best estimates of their companies' cash

FIGURE 4
Collecting Delinquent Accounts

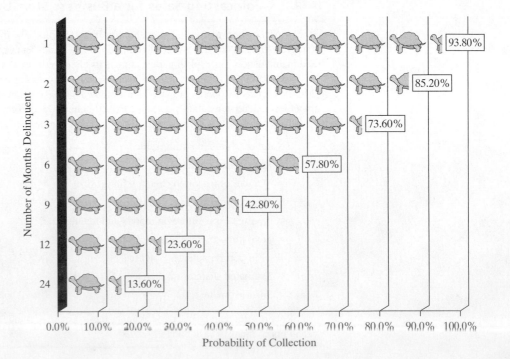

TABLE 4 Managing Accounts Receivable

Are your customers who purchase on credit paying late? If so, these outstanding accounts receivable probably represent a significant leak in your company's profits. Regaining control of these late payers will likely improve your company's profits and cash flow.

Slow-paying customers, in effect, are borrowing money from your business interest free! They are using your money without penalty while you forgo opportunities to put it to productive use in your company or to place it in interest-bearing investments. Exactly how much are poor credit practices costing you? The answer may surprise you.

The first step is to compute the company's average collection period ratio, which tells the number of days required to collect the typical account receivable. Then you compare this number to your company's credit terms. The following example shows how to calculate the cost of past-due receivables for a company whose credit terms are "net 30":

Average collection period	65 days
Less: credit terms	30 days
Excess in accounts receivable	35 days
Average daily sales of $21,500* × 35 days excess	$752,500
Normal rate of return on investment	10%
Annual cost of excess	$75,250

If your business is highly seasonal, quarterly or monthly figures may be more meaningful than annual ones.

*Average daily sales $= \dfrac{\text{Annual sales}}{365} = \dfrac{\$7,487,500}{365} = \$21,500$

disbursements and then add another 25 to 50 percent of that total as a contingency, recognizing that business expenses often run higher than expected. When setting up his company's cash budget, one entrepreneur included a line called "Murphy," an additional amount each month to account for Murphy's Law ("What can go wrong, will go wrong").

Sometimes business owners have difficulty developing initial forecasts of cash receipts and cash disbursements. One of the most effective techniques for overcoming the "I don't know where to begin" hurdle is to make a *daily* list of the items that generated cash (receipts) and those that consumed it (disbursements).

ENTREPRENEURIAL
Profile

Susan Bowen and Champion Awards

Susan Bowen, CEO of Champion Awards, a T-shirt screen printer with $9 million in annual sales, tracks the cash that flows into and out of her company every day. Focusing on keeping the process simple, Bowen sets aside a few minutes each morning to track updates from the previous day on four key numbers:

Accounts receivable: (1) What was billed yesterday? (2) How much was actually collected?
Accounts payable: (3) What invoices were received yesterday? (4) How much in total was paid out?

If Bowen observes the wrong trend—more new bills than new sales or more money going out than coming in—she makes immediate adjustments to protect her cash flow. The benefits produced (not the least of which is the peace of mind knowing no cash crisis is looming) more than outweigh the 10 minutes she invests in the process every day. "I've tried to balance my books every single day since I started my company in 1970," says Bowen.[17]

Step 5: Estimating the End-of-Month Cash Balance

To estimate a company's final cash balance for each month, entrepreneurs first must determine the cash balance at the beginning of each month. The beginning cash balance includes cash on hand as well as cash in checking and savings accounts. The cash balance at the *end* of one month becomes the *beginning* balance for the following month. Next the owner simply adds to that balance the projected total cash receipts for the month and then subtracts projected total cash disbursements to obtain the end-of-month balance before any borrowing takes place. A positive balance indicates that the business has a cash surplus for the month, but a negative balance shows a cash shortage will occur unless the entrepreneur is able to collect, raise, or borrow additional cash.

Normally, a company's cash balance fluctuates from month to month, reflecting seasonal sales patterns. These fluctuations are normal, but entrepreneurs must watch closely any increases and decreases in the cash balance over time. A trend of increases indicates that the small firm has ample cash that could be placed in some income-earning investment. In contrast, a pattern of cash decreases should alert the owner of an impending cash crisis.

Preparing a cash budget not only illustrates the flow of cash into and out of the small business, but it also allows a business owner to *anticipate* cash shortages and cash surpluses. By planning cash needs ahead of time, an entrepreneur is able to do the following:

■ Increase the amount and the speed of cash flowing into the company.
■ Reduce the amount and the speed of cash flowing out of the company.
■ Develop a sound borrowing and repayment program.
■ Impress lenders and investors with a plan for repaying loans or distributing dividends.
■ Reduce borrowing costs by borrowing only when necessary.
■ Take advantage of money-saving opportunities, such as economic order quantities and cash discounts.
■ Make the most efficient use of the cash available.
■ Finance seasonal business needs.
■ Provide funds for expansion.
■ Improve profitability by investing surplus cash.

The message is simple: Managing cash flow means survival for a business. Businesses tend to succeed when their owners manage cash effectively. Entrepreneurs who neglect cash flow management techniques are likely to see their companies fold; those who take the time to manage their cash flow free themselves of worrying about their companies' solvency to focus on what they do best: taking care of their customers and ensuring their companies' success.

The "Big Three" of Cash Management

4. Describe the fundamental principles involved in managing the "big three" of cash management: accounts receivable, accounts payable, and inventory.

It is unrealistic for entrepreneurs to expect to trace the flow of every dollar through their businesses. However, by concentrating on the three primary causes of cash flow problems, they can dramatically lower the likelihood of experiencing a devastating cash crisis. The "big three" of cash

▶ E N T R E P R E N E U R S H I P   **IN ACTION** ▶

Rowena's Cash Budget

Rowena Rowdy had been in business for slightly more than 2 years, but she had never taken the time to develop a cash budget for her company. Based on a series of recent events, however, she knew the time had come to start paying more attention to her company's cash flow. The business was growing fast, with sales more than tripling from the previous year, and profits were rising. However, Rowena often found it difficult to pay all of the company's bills on time. She didn't know why exactly, but she knew that the company's fast growth was requiring her to incur higher levels of expenses.

Last night, Rowena attended a workshop on managing cash flow sponsored by the local chamber of commerce. Much of what the presenter said hit home with Rowena. "This fellow must have taken a look at my company's financial records before he came here tonight," she said to a friend during a break in the presentation. On her way home from the workshop, Rowena decided that she would take the presenter's advice and develop a cash budget for her business. After all, she was planning to approach her banker about a loan for her company, and she knew that creating a cash budget would be an essential part of her loan request. She started digging for the necessary information, and this is what she came up with:

Current cash balance	$10,685
Sales pattern	63% on credit and 37% in cash
Collections of credit sales	61% in 1 to 30 days;
	27% in 31 to 60 days;
	8% in 61 to 90 days;
	1% never collected (bad debts)

| | Sales Forecasts: | | |
	Pessimistic	Most Likely	Optimistic
January (actual)	—	$24,780	—
February (actual)	—	$20,900	—
March (actual)	—	$21,630	—
April	$19,100	$23,550	$25,750
May	$21,300	$24,900	$27,300
June	$23,300	$29,870	$30,000
July	$23,900	$27,500	$29,100
August	$20,500	$25,800	$28,800
September	$18,500	$21,500	$23,900

Utilities expenses	$950 per month
Rent	$2,250 per month
Truck loan	$427 per month

The company's wages and salaries (including payroll taxes) estimates are:

April	$3,550		July	$6,255
May	$4,125		August	$6,060
June	$5,450		September	$3,525

The company pays 66 percent of the sales price for the inventory it purchases, an amount that it actually pays in the following month. (Rowena has negotiated "net 30" credit terms with her suppliers.)

Other expenses include:

Insurance premiums	$1,200, payable in April and September
Office supplies	$125 per month
Maintenance	$75 per month
Uniforms/cleaning	$80 per month
Office cleaning service	$85 per month
Internet and computer service	$225 per month
Computer supplies	$75 per month
Advertising	$450 per month
Legal and accounting fees	$250 per month
Miscellaneous expenses	$95 per month

A tax payment of $3,140 is due in June.

Rowena has established a minimum cash balance of $1,500.

If Rowena must borrow money, she uses her line of credit at the bank, which charges interest at an annual rate of 10.25 percent. Any money that Rowena borrows must be repaid the next month.

1. Help Rowena put together a cash budget for the 6 months beginning in April.
2. Does it appear that Rowena's business will remain solvent, or could the company be heading for a cash crisis?
3. What suggestions can you make to help Rowena improve her company's cash flow?

management are accounts receivable, accounts payable, and inventory. When it comes to managing cash flow, entrepreneurs' goals should be to accelerate their companies' accounts receivable and to stretch out their accounts payable. As one company's chief financial officer states, the idea is to "get the cash in the door as fast as you can, cut costs, and pay people as late as possible."[18] Business owners also must monitor inventory carefully to avoid tying up valuable cash in an excess inventory. Figure 5 illustrates the interaction of the "big three" (inventory, accounts receivable, and accounts payable) in a company's cash conversion cycle and a measure for each one (days' inventory outstanding, days sales' outstanding, and days' payable outstanding).

**FIGURE 5
The Cash Conversion
Cycle**

*Cash Conversion Cycle = Day's Inventory + Day's Sales Outstanding – Day's Payable Outstanding

Accounts Receivable

Selling merchandise and services on credit is a necessary evil for most small businesses. Many customers expect to buy on credit, and entrepreneurs extend it to avoid losing customers to competitors. However, selling to customers on credit is expensive; it requires more paperwork, more staff, and *more cash* to service accounts receivable. In addition, because extending credit is, in essence, lending money, the risk involved is higher. Every business owner who sells on credit encounters customers who pay late or, worst of all, who never pay at all.

**ENTREPRENEURIAL
Profile**

*Aaron Leventhal and
Hero Arts*

Aaron Leventhal, CEO of Hero Arts, a Richmond, California-based company that sells inks, rubber stamps, and other items to both small independent and large chain arts-and-crafts stores, was forced to draw on a previously untapped $100,000 line of credit when his customers began stretching out payments on their credit purchases. Because of customers' slow payments, "we've had more trouble managing our cash flow than in any year in the history of the company," says Leventhal, who had to extend a personal loan of $250,000 "when cash flow really got tight."[19]

According to a recent survey by Decipher Inc. and software publisher Intuit, the average small business has $1,500 in past due accounts receivable per month. The same survey also reports an average of $1,900 in bad debt losses each year for the typical small business, which adds up to a total annual loss of $42 billion for all small businesses![20] As you can imagine, this revenue leakage can be the source of severe cash flow problems for a small business. Much like a leak in a water pipe, revenue leakages from undisciplined collection procedures can become significant over time and cause serious damage. One expert estimates that revenue leakages rob companies of 2 percent of their sales. Health care and Web service providers, for instance, typically lose 5 to 10 percent of their revenues each year.[21]

Selling on credit is a common practice in business. "Extending credit is a [double]-edged sword," says Robert Smith, president of his own public relations firm in Rockford, Illinois. "I give credit so more people can afford my publicity services. I also have people who still owe me money—and who will probably never pay."[22]

Because so many entrepreneurs sell on credit, an assertive collection program is essential to managing a company's cash flow. A credit policy that is too lenient can destroy a business's cash flow, attracting nothing but slow-paying and "deadbeat" customers. In contrast, a carefully designed credit policy can be a powerful selling tool, attracting customers and boosting cash flow. "A sale is not a sale until you collect the money," warns the head of the National Association of Credit Management. "Receivables are the second most important item on the balance sheet. The first is cash. If you don't turn those receivables into cash, you're not going to be in business very long."[23]

**ENTREPRENEURIAL
Profile**

*Tamarack Resort and
Petra, Inc.*

When the Tamarack Resort, an upscale ski resort in the scenic high country of Idaho, filed for bankruptcy protection, the company owed $22 million in unpaid bills, many of them to small businesses. For example, Tamarack owed Petra, Inc., a small construction firm based in nearby Meridian, Idaho, $1.5 million that it never paid. The unpaid debts created cash flow problems for many small companies, including Petra, forcing them to scale back their operations and lay off workers.[24]

HOW TO ESTABLISH A CREDIT AND COLLECTION POLICY. The first step in establishing a workable credit policy that preserves a company's cash flow is to screen customers carefully before granting credit. Unfortunately, few small businesses conduct any kind of credit investigation before selling to a new customer. According to one study, nearly 95 percent of small firms that sell on credit sell to anyone who wants to buy.[25] If a debt becomes past due and a business owner has gathered no information about the customer, the odds of collecting the account are virtually nil.

The first line of defense against bad debt losses is a detailed credit application. Before selling to any customer on credit, a business owner should have the customer complete a customized application designed to provide the information needed to judge the potential customer's creditworthiness. At a minimum, this credit profile should include the following information about customers:

- Name, address, social security number, and telephone number
- Form of ownership (proprietorship, S corporation, LLC, corporation, etc.) and number of years in business
- Credit references (e.g., other suppliers), including contact names, addresses, and telephone numbers
- Bank and credit card references

After collecting this information, entrepreneurs should use it to check the potential customer's credit references. The savings from lower bad debt expenses can more than offset the cost of using a credit reporting service. Entrepreneurs can use the services of companies such as Dun & Bradstreet (D&B, *www.dnb.com*), Experian *(www.experian.com)*, Equifax *(www. equifax.com)*, TransUnion *(www.transunion.com)*, Veritas Credit Corporation *(www.veritas-usa.com)*, and KnowX *(www.knowx.com)* to gather credit information on potential customers. For entrepreneurs who sell to other business, D&B offers many useful services, including a Small Business Risk Account Score, a tool for evaluating the credit risk of new businesses. The National Association of Credit Management *(www.nacm.org)* is another important source of credit information because it collects information on many small businesses that other reporting services ignore. The cost to check a potential customer's credit at reporting services such as these ranges from around $5 to $100, a small price to pay when a small business is considering selling thousands of dollars worth of goods or services to a new customer. Before Terri Wilson, a top executive at OE Construction, agrees to do any work as a subcontractor, she conducts a credit check on the contractor to see how promptly the contractor pays its bills. She also gathers information about the company's owner, financial manager, and the volume of work it does to gauge the credit risk it poses to OE Construction.[26]

The next step involves establishing a firm written credit policy and letting every customer know in advance the company's credit terms. The credit agreement must be in writing and should specify a customer's credit limit (which usually varies from one customer to another, depending on their credit ratings) and any deposits required (often stated as a percentage of the purchase price). It should state clearly all of the terms the business will enforce if the account goes bad, including interest, late charges, attorney's fees, and others. Failure to specify these terms in the contract means they *cannot* be added later after problems arise. When will you send invoices? How soon is payment due: immediately, 30 days, 60 days? Will you offer early payment discounts? Will you add a late charge? If so, how much? The credit policies should be as tight as possible but remain within federal and state credit laws. According to the American Collectors Association, if a business is writing off more than 5 percent of sales as bad debts, the owner should tighten its credit and collection policy.[27]

The third step in an effective credit policy is to send invoices promptly because customers rarely pay before they receive their bills. Unfortunately, a recent study reports that 20 percent of small business owners forget to send invoices or to follow up on past due invoices.[28] The sooner a company sends invoices, the sooner its customers will pay them. Manufacturers and wholesalers should make sure invoices are en route to customers as soon as the shipments go out the door (if not before). Service companies should keep track of billable hours daily or weekly and bill as often as the contract or agreement with the client permits. Computerized billing software makes managing accounts receivable much easier, but only 34 percent of small businesses use these programs.[29] Some businesses also use **cycle billing**, in which a company bills a portion of its credit customers each day of the month to smooth out uneven cash receipts.

Bob Dempster, cofounder of American Imaging, Inc., a distributor of X-ray tubes, once handled receivables the same way most entrepreneurs do: When customers ignored the "net 30" terms on invoices, he would call them around the 45th day to ask what the problem was. Payments usually would trickle in within the next 2 weeks, but by then 60 days had elapsed, and American Imaging's cash flow was always strained. Then Dempster decided to try a different approach. Now he makes a "customer relations call" on the 20th day of the billing period to determine whether the customer is satisfied with the company's performance on the order. Before closing, he reminds the customer of the invoice due date and asks if there will be any problems meeting it. Dempster's proactive approach to collecting receivables has cut his company's average collection period by at least 15 days, improved cash flow, and increased customer satisfaction![30]

When an account becomes overdue, entrepreneurs must take *immediate* action. The longer an account is past due, the lower is the probability of collecting it. As soon as an account becomes overdue, many business owners send a "second notice" letter requesting immediate payment. If that fails to produce results, the next step is a telephone call. A better system is to call the customer the day after the payment is due to request payment. If the customer cannot pay the entire amount, get him or her to commit to a schedule of smaller payments. If that fails, collection experts recommend the following:

- Send a letter from the company's attorney.
- Turn the account over to a collection agency.
- Hire a collection attorney.

Collection agencies collect more than $40 billion annually for businesses.[31] Although collection agencies and attorneys take a portion of any accounts they collect (typically around 30 percent), they are often worth the price. According to the American Collector's Association, only 5 percent of accounts over 90 days delinquent will be paid voluntarily.[32]

Business owners must be sure to abide by the provisions of the federal Fair Debt Collection Practices Act, which prohibits any kind of harassment when collecting debts (e.g., telephoning repeatedly, issuing threats of violence, telling third parties about the debt, or using abusive language). The primary rule in dealing with past-due accounts is "Never lose your cool." Even if the debtor launches into an X-rated tirade when questioned about an overdue bill, the *worst* thing a collector can do is respond out of anger. Keep the call strictly business, and begin by identifying yourself, your company, and the amount of the debt. Ask the creditor what he or she intends to do about the past-due bill.

TECHNIQUES FOR ACCELERATING ACCOUNTS RECEIVABLE. Although "net 30" credit terms are common, nearly 40 percent of small business owners say that collecting accounts receivable takes more than 30 days.[33] Entrepreneurs can rely on a variety of techniques to speed cash inflow from accounts receivable:

- Speed up orders by having customers e-mail or fax them to you.
- Send invoices when goods are shipped rather than a day or a week later; consider e-mailing or faxing invoices to reduce "in transit" time to a minimum. For small monthly and per-transaction fees, Pat Jackson, an executive at Jackson Comfort Heating and Cooling Systems in Northfield, Ohio, equips her 22 field workers with Bluetooth-enabled devices that can accept credit card payments on the job site. "It's one of the best things we've done by far," says Jackson. "It's speeded up our cash inflow."[34]
- Indicate in conspicuous print or color the invoice due date and any late payment penalties imposed. (Check with an attorney to be sure all finance charges comply with state laws.) One study by Xerox Corporation found that highlighting the "balance due" section of invoices increased the speed of collection by 30 percent.[35]
- Include a telephone number and a contact person in your organization in case the customer has a question or a dispute about an invoice.
- Respond quickly and accurately to customers' questions about their bills

- Allow customers to use multiple payment methods, including checks, credit cards, PayPal, money orders, and cash.
- Restrict the customer's credit until past-due bills are paid. Salespeople should know which of their customers are behind in their payments. If not, they will continue to sell (most likely on credit) to those delinquent customers!
- Deposit customer checks and credit card receipts daily.
- Identify the top 20 percent of your customers (by sales volume), create a separate file system for them, and monitor them closely. Twenty percent of the typical company's customers generate 80 percent of all accounts receivable.
- Ask customers to pay a portion of the purchase price up front. Tired of chasing late payers after completing their public relations projects, Mike Clifford, founder of Clifford Public Relations, began checking potential clients' credit ratings and requiring an up-front payment of one-third of the cost of a job. Clifford also instituted a monthly billing system that tracks billable hours and related expenses. Since implementing the new system, Clifford has not experienced a single past-due account.[36]
- Watch for signs that a customer may be about to declare bankruptcy. Late payments from previously prompt payers and unreturned phone calls concerning late payments usually are the first clues that a customer may be heading for bankruptcy. If that happens, creditors typically collect only a small fraction, on average just 10 percent, of the debt owed.[37] Cynthia McKay, owner of a Le Gourmet Gift Basket franchise, lost thousands of dollars when five of her corporate clients filed for bankruptcy within a 10-month period. "That money is a weekly payroll for several employees," says McKay.[38]
- If a customer does file for bankruptcy, the bankruptcy court notifies all creditors with a "Notice of Filing" document. If an entrepreneur receives one of these notices, he or she should create a file to track the events surrounding the bankruptcy and take action immediately. To have a valid claim against the debtor's assets, a creditor must file a proof-of-claim form with the bankruptcy court within a specified time, often 90 days. (The actual time depends on which form of bankruptcy the debtor declares.) If, after paying the debtor's secured creditors, any assets remain, the court will distribute the proceeds to unsecured creditors who have legitimate proof-of-claim.
- Consider using a bank's lockbox collection service (located near customers) to reduce mail time on collections. In a **lockbox** arrangement, customers send payments to a post office box the bank maintains. The bank collects the payments several times each day and deposits them immediately into the company account. The procedure sharply reduces processing and clearing times from the usual 2 to 3 days to just hours, especially if the lockboxes are located close to the company's biggest customers' business addresses. The system can be expensive to operate and is most economical for companies with a high volume of large checks (at least 200 checks each month).
- Track the results of the company's collection efforts. Managers and key employees (including the sales force) should receive a weekly report on the status of the company's outstanding accounts receivable.

Another strategy that small companies, particularly those selling high-priced items, can use to protect the cash they have tied up in receivables is to couple a security agreement with a financing statement. This strategy falls under Article 9 of the Uniform Commercial Code (UCC), which governs a wide variety of business transactions, from the sale of goods to security interests. A **security agreement** is a contract in which a business selling an asset on credit gets a security interest in that asset (the collateral), protecting the company's legal rights in case the buyer fails to pay. To get the protection it seeks in the security agreement, the seller must file a financing statement called a UCC-1 form with the proper state or county office (a process the UCC calls "perfection"). The UCC-1 form gives notice to other creditors and to the general public that the seller holds a secured interest in the collateral named in the security agreement. The UCC-1 form must include the name, address, and signature of the buyer; a description of the collateral; and the name and address of the seller. If the buyer declares bankruptcy, the small business that sells the asset is not *guaranteed* payment, but the filing puts its claim to the asset ahead of those of unsecured creditors. A small company's degree of safety on a large credit sale is much higher with a security agreement and a properly-filed financing statement than if it did not file the security agreement.

IN THE ENTREPRENEURIAL
SPOTLIGHT Watch Those Accounts Receivable!

When Randy Ringer developed the cash flow forecasts for the business plan he created for Verse Group, a New York City–based marketing and branding company, he assumed that the company's clients would pay their invoices in 30 days. As Ringer and his business partner learned more about the industry, however, they discovered that companies in their industry typically did not see any cash flow until 60 or more days after completing a job and billing the client. They quickly revised their business plan and increased the minimum cash balance they would keep on hand from 3 months' worth of expenses to 6 months' worth. They also established a policy that requires clients to prepay a portion of any project that requires Verse Group to pay substantial up-front costs. Their industry's collection patterns "have changed the way we do business," says Ringer.

Do you know the typical collection pattern for accounts receivable for the industry in which you are about to launch a business? Not knowing this important number could create significant cash flow problems for your company and even cost you your business. The following table shows the day's payable outstanding (DPO) ratio (which is calculated by dividing 365 days per year by the industry's average collection period ratio) for a variety of industries.

Days' Payables Outstanding by Industry

Industry	DPO	Industry	DPO
Aerospace and defense	29.5	Industrial technology	26.5
Airlines	16.5	Industrial diversified	28.1
Apparel retailers	22.4	Land transportation	28.0
Auto manufacturers	49.9	Machinery makers	39.6
Auto parts and suppliers	38.3	Medical devices	17.5
Biotechnology	15.8	Medical supplies	20.2
Building materials	26.3	Newspaper publishers	14.0
Chemicals, commodity	29.6	Oil drilling	32.1
Chemicals, specialty	30.0	Oil secondary	37.9
Clothing, fabrics	27.6	Other food	19.5
Communications technology	30.0	Other industrial and commercial services	16.0
Computer makers	38.7	Other oil equipment and services	32.8
Consumer and household services	10.7	Other recreational services	16.8
Containers and packaging	33.3	Other specialty retailers	27.0
Distributors	39.4	Paper and forest	23.0
Drug retailers	27.3	Pharmaceuticals	18.0
Electrical components	33.1	Pipelines	41.2
Food producers	19.9	Restaurants	13.2
Food retailers	16.5	Retailers, broadline	27.5
Footwear	21.6	Semiconductors	22.8
Health care providers	12.2	Soft drinks	18.0
Heavy construction	28.4	Software	10.8
Home construction	19.3	Steel	26.6
Home furniture	18.1	Telecom operators	21.1
Household products, nondurable	25.5	Trucking	13.2

Note that a customer in the software industry with a DPO of 16 days would raise a red flag, but a customer in the pipeline business with a DPO 36 days is paying its bills faster than the industry average.

What can entrepreneurs who operate businesses in industries characterized by longer payment periods do to protect their companies' cash flow? The following tips will help:

■ **Increase your company's cash reserves.** Just as Randy Ringer did, entrepreneurs should plan to keep more cash on hand from the beginning to avoid being caught short. In addition, smart entrepreneurs establish a line of credit with a bank or other lending institution just in case they encounter a cash crisis. Note: The time to establish a line of credit is well *before* you need it!

- **Establish your company's credit and collection policy, tell your customers about it, and stick to it as closely as possible.** Doing so gives you more leverage when customers fall behind on their payments, as some inevitably will.

- **Avoid problem customers from the outset.** By screening credit customers carefully, small businesses can steer clear of those who are not likely to pay their bills on time or at all. "Businesses want the next order so desperately that they become more vulnerable to being taken advantage of by deadbeats," says one business expert. Always take the time to check potential credit customers' credit rating before granting them credit.

- **Monitor accounts receivable regularly—daily, if necessary.** Before Mike Edwards, founder of 5 Stones Group, a film production company based in Columbus, Ohio, starts a project, he creates contracts that requires clients to pay one-third of the price up front, one-third at mid-project, and one-third on completion. Still, to keep his company's cash flow positive, Edwards and his wife Tiffany, who manages 5 Stones Group's finances, have to monitor clients' accounts closely. "If the client says that [he] will make a payment next Friday, you have to call next Friday," he says. "You have to continually track payments."

- **Consider offering discounts for early payment.** These discounts, called cash discounts, will reduce a small company's total revenue, but that cost often is more than offset by speeding up the flow of cash inflows.

- **If customers still won't comply with your terms, consider raising prices.** That's what Mitch Miller, president of Dynamic Computer Solutions of Topeka (DCST), a computer systems integrator that generates $3 million in annual sales, did when several of his long-time customers decided to pay their invoices in 45 days instead of the 20 days in DCST's selling terms. Although a few clients mentioned the price increase, none left. "You have to be bold," says Miller.

1. Why is it so important for small companies to monitor their accounts receivable? What are the implications for companies that fail to do so?
2. Contact a local entrepreneur whose company sells goods or services on credit. Ask him or her to explain the company's credit and collection policy. Are slow-paying customers a problem? How does the company deal with customers whose accounts are past due?
3. Why are some entrepreneurs hesitant to take bold actions to collect the money that customers owe them?

Sources: Based on Randy B. Hecht, "Pay Me," *Entrepreneur*, July 2009, pp. 48–52; Christina Salerno, "How to Get Customers to Pay Up," *BNET*, March 7, 2009, *www.bnet.com/2403-13240_23-276588.html;* "Managing Credit, Receivables, and Collections," *IOMA*, December 2006, p. 4; Amy Feldman, "The Cash-Flow Crunch," *Inc.*, December 2005, pp. 51–52.

Accounts Payable

The second element of the "big three" of cash management is accounts payable. The timing of payables is just as crucial to proper cash management as the timing of receivables, but the objective is exactly the opposite. An entrepreneur should strive to stretch out payables as long as possible *without damaging the company's credit rating*. Paying late could cause suppliers to begin demanding prepayment or C.O.D. terms, which severely impair a company's cash flow. Sandeep Sood, CEO of Monsoon Company, a software maker in Berkeley, California, says that his customers have slowed their payments to an average of 70 days (compared to the company's "net 40" terms). The resulting strain on the company's cash flow has forced Sood to stretch out payments to his vendors and suppliers to 40 days from the normal 30 days.[39]

Small business owners should regulate their payments to vendors and suppliers to their companies' advantage. Ideally, a company purchases an item on credit, sells it, and collects payment for it before the company must pay the supplier's invoice. In that case, the vendor's credit terms amount to an interest-free loan. That is exactly the situation that Dell Inc., the fast-growing computer maker, puts itself in. Its high inventory turnover ratio of 52 times a year coupled with its ability to negotiate favorable credit terms with its suppliers and to collect customers' payments quickly means that the company enjoys an enviable cash conversion cycle of *negative* 33 days. On average, Dell collects payments from its customers and gets to use that cash before having to pay its suppliers 33 days later (see Figure 6)![40] Unfortunately, the typical small business experiences the opposite situation, paying its accounts payable in 40 days and collecting its accounts receivable in 59 days, which makes managing cash flow all the more important.[41]

*Cash Conversion Cycle = Day's Inventory + Day's Sales Outstanding – Day's Payable Outstanding =
7 + 32 – 72 = –33 days

Even when the cash flow timing isn't ideal, efficient cash managers benefit by setting up a payment calendar each month that allows them to pay their bills on time and to take advantage of cash discounts for early payment.

Nancy Dunis, CEO of Dunis & Associates, a Portland, Oregon, marketing firm, recognizes the importance of controlling accounts payable. "Our payables must be functioning just right to keep our cash flow running smoothly," says Dunis. She has set up a simple five-point accounts payable system:

1. **Set scheduling goals.** Dunis strives to pay her company's bills 45 days after receiving them and to collect all her receivables within 30 days. Even though "it doesn't always work that way," her goal is to make the most of her cash flow.
2. **Keep paperwork organized.** Dunis dates every invoice she receives and carefully files it according to her payment plan. "This helps us remember when to cut the check," she says, and, "it helps us stagger our payments over days or weeks," significantly improving the company's cash flow.
3. **Prioritize.** Dunis cannot stretch out all of her company's creditors for 45 days; some demand payment sooner. Those suppliers are at the top of the accounts payable list.
4. **Be consistent.** "Companies want consistent customers," says Dunis. "With a few exceptions," she explains, "most businesses will be happy to accept 45-day payments, so long as they know you'll always pay your full obligation at that point."
5. **Look for warning signs.** Dunis sees her accounts payable as an early warning system for cash flow problems. "The first indication I get that cash flow is in trouble is when I see I'm getting low on cash and could have trouble paying my bills according to my staggered filing system," she says.[42]

Business owners should verify all invoices before paying them. Some unscrupulous vendors send out invoices for goods they never shipped, knowing that many business owners will simply pay the bill without checking its authenticity. Someone in the company—for instance, the accounts payable clerk—should have the responsibility of verifying every invoice received. In a common scam targeting small businesses, the accounts payable clerk at one company caught a bogus invoice for $322 worth of copier paper and toner it never ordered nor received.[43]

Generally, taking advantage of cash discounts vendors offer benefits a small company. A cash discount (e.g., "2/10, net 30"—take a 2 percent discount if you pay the invoice within 10 days; otherwise, total payment is due in 30 days) offers a price reduction if the owner pays an invoice early. The savings the discount provides usually exceeds the cost of giving up the use of a company's cash by paying early.

Jeff Schreiber, owner of Hansen Wholesale, a company that distributes home products, is in the habit of taking advantage of the cash discounts vendors offer his company. In one year alone, Schreiber, whose company generates $3.5 million in annual sales, saved $15,000. "Your money works better if you take advantage of the discounts," says Schreiber.[44]

Clever cash managers also negotiate the best possible credit terms with their suppliers. Almost all vendors grant their customers trade credit, and entrepreneurs should take advantage of it. However, because trade credit is so easy to get, entrepreneurs must be careful not to abuse it, putting their businesses in a precarious financial position. Favorable credit terms can make a tremendous difference in a firm's cash flow. Table 5 shows the same most likely cash budget (from Table 2) with one exception: Instead of purchasing on C.O.D. terms (Table 2), the owner has negotiated "net 30" payment terms (Table 5). Notice the drastic improvement in this small company's cash flow that results from the improved credit terms.

If owners do find themselves financially strapped when payment to a vendor is due, they should avoid making empty promises that "the check is in the mail." Instead, they should discuss openly the situation with the vendor. Most suppliers are willing to work out payment terms for extended credit. One small business owner who was experiencing a cash crisis claims:

> One day things got so bad I just called up a supplier and said, "I need your stuff, but I'm going through a tough period and simply can't pay you right now." They said they wanted to keep me as a customer, and they asked if it was okay to bill me in 3 months. I was dumbfounded: They didn't even charge me interest.[45]

Entrepreneurs also can improve their firms' cash flow by scheduling controllable cash disbursements so that they do not come due at the same time. For example, paying employees every 2 weeks (or every month) rather than every week reduces administrative costs and gives the business more time to use its cash. Owners of fledgling businesses may be able to conserve cash by hiring

TABLE 5 Cash Budget: Most Likely Sales Forecast After Negotiating "Net 30" Trade Credit Terms

	Jan.	Feb.	Mar.	Apr.
Cash Receipts:				
Sales	$150,000	$200,000	$200,000	$300,000
Credit Sales	112,500	150,000	150,000	225,000
Collections:				
60%—1st month after sale	$180,000	$ 67,500	$ 90,000	$ 90,000
30%—2nd month after sale	78,750	90,000	33,750	45,000
5%—3rd month after sale	11,250	13,125	15,000	5,625
Cash Sales	37,500	50,000	50,000	75,000
Interest	0	200	0	0
Total Cash Receipts	$307,500	$220,825	$188,750	$215,625
Cash Disbursements:				
Purchases[a]	$105,000	$140,000	$140,000	$210,000
Rent	2,000	2,000	2,000	2,000
Utilities	850	850	850	850
Interest	0	0	7,500,	0
Tax Prepayment	0	0	50,000	0
Capital Addition	0	130,000	3	0
Miscellaneous	70	70	70	70
Wage/Salaries	30,000	40,000	45,000	50,000
Total Cash Disbursements[a]	$137,920	$312,920	$245,420	$262,920
End-of-Month Balance:				
Cash (beginning of month)[a]	$ 12,000	$181,580	$ 89,485	$ 32,815
+Cash Receipts	307,500	220,825	188,750	215,625
−Cash Disbursements[a]	137,920	312,920	245,420	262,920
Cash (end of month)[a]	181,580	89,485	32,815	(14,480)
Borrowing	0	0	0	24,480
Cash (end of month [after borrowing])[a]	$181,580	$ 89,485	$32,815	$ 10,000

[a]After negotiating "net 30" trade credit terms.

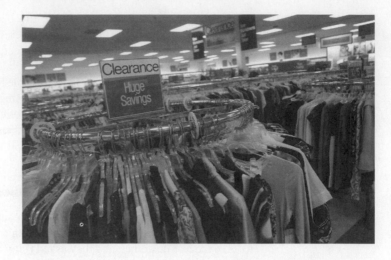

Excess inventory ties up a company's valuable cash and often requires a company to sell it at significant discounts.

Source: © Jeff Greenberg/Alamy

part-time employees or by using freelance workers rather than full-time, permanent workers. Scheduling insurance premiums monthly or quarterly rather than annually also improves cash flow.

Inventory

Carrying too much inventory increases the chances that a business will run out of cash. Although inventory represents the largest investment for many businesses, many entrepreneurs manage it haphazardly. As a result, the typical small business not only has too much inventory but also too much of the wrong kind of inventory! Because inventory is illiquid, it can quickly siphon off a company's pool of available cash. Managing inventory requires entrepreneurs to play a balancing game. "In good times, you never want to lose a sale by running out of an item," says Jay Goltz, owner of several retail stores. "But if you're not vigilant when sales are slow, that mentality can fill your warehouse and empty your checking account."[46]

Small businesses need cash to grow and to survive, which is difficult to do if they have money tied up in excess inventory, which yields a zero rate of return. "The cost of carrying inventory is expensive," says one small business consultant. "A typical manufacturing company pays 25 percent to 30 percent of the value of the inventory for the cost of borrowed money, warehouse space, materials handling, staff, lift-truck expenses, and fixed costs. This shocks a lot of people. Once they realize it, they look at inventory differently."[47] Tracking inventory consistently enables a business owner to avoid purchasing or manufacturing goods unnecessarily. Experienced entrepreneurs often maintain different levels of inventory for different items depending on how critical they are to the company's operation and on how quickly they can be replenished. For instance, the owner of one small landscape company knew that hardwood mulch was one of his best-selling items in the spring, but he refused to purchase excessive amounts of it because his primary supplier was nearby and could deliver mulch within a few hours of receiving an order.

Marking down items that don't sell keeps inventory lean and allows it to turn over frequently. Even though volume discounts lower inventory costs, large purchases may tie up the company's valuable cash. Wise business owners avoid overbuying inventory, recognizing that excess inventory ties up valuable cash unproductively. In fact, only 20 percent of a typical business's inventory turns over quickly, which means that owners must watch constantly for stale items.[48]

In addition to the cost of the inventory itself, the activities required to purchase, store, monitor, and control inventory are themselves costly. Efficient cash management calls for a business to commit just enough cash to inventory to meet demand. Paring down the number of suppliers enables a business to gain more bargaining power, minimize paperwork, and perhaps earn quantity discounts. Scheduling inventory deliveries at the latest possible date prevents premature payment of invoices. Finally, given goods of comparable quality and price, entrepreneurs should purchase goods from those suppliers who are best at making fast, frequent deliveries to keep inventory levels low.

Monitoring the big three of cash management can help every business owner avoid a cash crisis while making the best use of available cash. According to one expert, maximizing cash flow involves "getting money from customers sooner; paying bills at the last moment possible; consolidating money in a single bank account; managing accounts payable, accounts receivable, and inventory more effectively; and squeezing every penny out of your daily business."[49]

Avoiding the Cash Crunch

5. Explain the techniques for avoiding a cash crunch in a small company.

Nearly every small business has the potential to improve its cash position with little or no investment. The key is to make an objective evaluation of a company's financial policies, searching for inefficiency in its cash flow and ways to squeeze more cash out of their operations. Young firms cannot afford to waste resources, especially one as vital as cash. By utilizing these tools, the small business manager can get maximum benefit from the company's pool of cash.

Barter

Bartering, the exchange of goods and services for other goods and services, is an effective way to conserve cash. An ancient concept, bartering has remained an important cash preservation tool, especially during recessions. More than 500 barter exchanges (up from just 40 in 1980) operate across the United States, catering primarily to small- and medium-sized businesses, and many of them operate online. The dollar value of bartering transactions among companies in North America totals more than $12 billion each year, with businesses trading everything from accounting services and computers to carpet and meals.[50] Nearly one-fourth of small companies in the United States use bartering as a cash management strategy, but more business owners turn to bartering during economic recessions.[51] These entrepreneurs use bartering to buy much needed materials, equipment, and supplies—*without using cash*. The president of one barter exchange estimates that business owners can save "between $5,000 and $150,000 in yearly business costs."[52] In addition to conserving cash, companies using bartering can transform slow-moving and excess inventory into much-needed goods and services. Often business owners who join barter exchanges find new customers for the products and services they sell.

Of course, there is a cost associated with bartering, but the real benefit is that entrepreneurs "pay" for products and services at their wholesale cost of doing business and get credit in the barter exchange for the retail price. In a typical arrangement, businesses accumulate trade credits when they offer goods or services through the exchange. Then they can use their trade credits to purchase other goods and services from other members of the exchange.

ENTREPRENEURIAL
Profile

Tony Romano and Marcello's Pasta Grill

Tony Romano, owner of Marcello's Pasta Grill in Tempe, Arizona, and a member of the Arizona Trade Exchange, barters an average of $2,000 per week through the exchange. Romano says that bartering allows him to pay for most of his restaurant's monthly expenses—from laundry services to fire extinguisher maintenance—without having to spend valuable cash. Since joining the exchange, Romano also has seen restaurant traffic increase by 10 percent and has landed catering jobs from other exchange members.[53]

Tony Romano, owner of Marcello's Pasta Grill.

Source: Lisa Romano

The typical exchange charges a one-time membership fee that ranges from $250 to $800 and a 5 to 10 percent transaction fee (usually split evenly between the buyer and the seller) on every deal. Some exchanges also charge a monthly fee of $10 to $30. The exchange acts as a barter "bank," tracking the balance in each member's account and sending monthly statements summarizing account activity.

Rather than join a barter exchange, many enterprising entrepreneurs choose to barter on an individual basis. The natural place to start is with the vendors, suppliers, and customers with whom a company normally does business.

Trim Overhead Costs

High overhead expenses can strain a small company's cash supply to the breaking point. Frugal small business owners can trim their overhead in a number of ways.

WHEN PRACTICAL, LEASE INSTEAD OF BUY. Of the $850 million that U.S. businesses spend annually on productive assets, 27 percent is obtained through leases.[54] By leasing automobiles, computers, office equipment, machinery, and other assets rather than buying them, entrepreneurs conserve valuable cash. The value of such assets is not in *owning* them but in *using* them. Leasing is popular among entrepreneurs because of its beneficial effects on a company's cash flow; a study by the Equipment Leasing Association found that 80 percent of U.S. businesses use leasing as a cash management strategy.[55] Leasing also gives business owners maximum flexibility when acquiring equipment and protection against the risk of purchasing assets that become obsolete quickly.

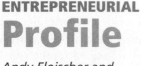

ENTREPRENEURIAL Profile

Andy Fleischer and Alabanza Corporation

Andy Fleischer, chief financial officer of Web hosting business Alabanza Corporation, recently switched from purchasing the company's servers to leasing them. Not only does leasing conserve the fast-growing company's precious cash, but it also enables it to keep its technology up-to-date, a vital factor given the nature of Alabanza's business. "In the past, we bought large blocks of servers up front," explains Fleischer. Leasing, however, allows Alabanza to spread the payment terms over 36 months, freeing up sizeable amounts of cash the company can use elsewhere.[56]

Although total lease payments often are greater than those for a conventional loan, most leases offer 100 percent financing, which means the owner avoids the large capital outlays required as down payments on most loans. In addition, leasing is an "off-the-balance-sheet" method of financing; the lease is considered an operating expense on the income statement, not a liability on the balance sheet. Thus, leasing conserves not only a company's cash flow but also its borrowing capacity. Leasing companies typically allow businesses to stretch payments over a longer time than those of a conventional loan. Lease agreements also are flexible; entrepreneurs can customize their lease payments to coincide with the seasonal fluctuations in their companies' cash balances.

Entrepreneurs can choose from two basic types of leases: operating leases and capital leases. At the end of an **operating lease**, a business turns the equipment back over to the leasing company with no further obligation. Businesses often lease computer and telecommunications equipment through operating leases because it becomes obsolete so quickly. At the end of a **capital lease**, a business may exercise an option to purchase the equipment, usually for a nominal sum. Table 6 compares the characteristics of leasing, borrowing, and paying cash for business assets.

AVOID NONESSENTIAL OUTLAYS. Smart entrepreneurs spend cash only when it is necessary. By forgoing costly ego indulgences such as ostentatious office equipment, first-class travel, and flashy company cars, business owners can make efficient use of their companies' cash. Before putting scarce cash into an asset, every business owner should put the decision to the acid test by asking, "What will this purchase add to the company's ability to compete and to become more successful?"

LOOK FOR SIMPLE WAYS TO CUT COSTS. Allowing expenses to creep up over time is a common tendency in any business, but smart entrepreneurs are always on the lookout for ways to cut costs and to operate more efficiently. One useful technique is to sit down with employees periodically with a list of company expenses and brainstorm ways the company can conserve cash without endangering product quality or customer service. Ideas might range from installing more energy-efficient equipment to adding more fuel-efficient cars to the company fleet.

TABLE 6 Lease, Borrow, or Pay Cash?

When faced with the need to purchase equipment, many entrepreneurs wonder whether they should lease the asset, borrow the money, or use the company's available cash to purchase it. The following table describes the key features of each option.

Feature	Lease	Borrow	Cash
Time frame	Monthly payments made over life of lease	Monthly payments made over life of loan	No monthly payments; total payment made at time of purchase
Actual cost	Current value of all future lease payments	Cost of equipment plus interest on loan	Cost of equipment plus opportunity cost of investing cash up front
Initial cost	Small (sometimes no) down payment	Substantial down payment often required	Entire purchase price of equipment
Impact on company's borrowing capacity	None. Leasing is an "off-the-balance-sheet" method of financing	Reduced borrowing capacity	None. Company incurs no additional liabilities.
Risk of obsolescence	Low. In an operating lease, company returns equipment to lessor at end of lease	High. Company owns the equipment after repaying the loan	High. Company owns the equipment up front
Tax implications	Lease payments are a deductible business expense	Interest payments on loan are a deductible business expense; company depreciates equipment over time	Company depreciates equipment over time
Impact on cash flow	Moderate. Company must make monthly lease payments	Moderate. Company must make monthly loan payments	Significant. Company pays entire purchase price up front. Cash is no longer available for other uses

Source: Based on "Leasing Gives You More IT Bang for Your Buck," Small and Medium Businesses: Hewlett Packard, HP.com, *http://h20330www3.hp.com/news_article.php?topiccode=20061212.*

ENTREPRENEURIAL
Profile

Christine Specht and Cousins Subs

Christine Specht, second-generation owner of Cousins Subs, a submarine sandwich franchise in Menomonee Falls, Wisconsin, recently introduced a system designed to reduce its locations' energy consumption by installing timers on lights, energy-efficient bulbs, programmable thermostats, and water-conserving devices. Specht also has reduced the volume of printed materials the company sends to franchisees and employees by establishing an intranet that hosts manuals, training materials, and other guides. The company's emphasis on efficiency has lowered operating costs without sacrificing quality or service.[57]

Entrepreneurs must be careful to avoid making across-the-board spending cuts to conserve cash, however. Doing so is a risky strategy because the owner runs the risk of cutting expenditures that literally drive the business. One common mistake during business slowdowns is cutting marketing and advertising expenditures. "As competitors pull back," says one advisor, "smart marketers will keep their ad budgets on an even keel, which is sufficient to bring increased attention to their products."[58] The secret to success is cutting nonessential expenditures. "If the lifeblood of your company is marketing, cut it less," advises one advertising executive. "If it is customer service, that is the last thing you want to cut back on. Cut from areas that are not essential to business growth."[59]

NEGOTIATE FIXED LOAN PAYMENTS TO COINCIDE WITH YOUR COMPANY'S CASH FLOW CYCLE. Many banks allow businesses to structure loans so that they can skip specific payments when their cash flow ebbs to its lowest point. Negotiating such terms gives businesses the opportunity to customize their loan repayments to their cash flow cycles. For example, Ted Zoli, president of Torrington Industries, a construction-materials supplier and contracting business, consistently uses "skipped payment loans" in his highly seasonal business. "Every time we buy a piece of construction machinery," he says, "we set it up so that we're making payments for 8 or 9 months, and then skipping 3 or 4 months during the winter."[60]

BUY USED OR RECONDITIONED EQUIPMENT. Many shrewd entrepreneurs purchase used or reconditioned equipment, especially if it is "behind-the-scenes" machinery. Some even buy their office furniture at flea markets and garage sales! One restaurateur saved significant amounts of cash in the start-up phase of his business by purchasing used equipment from a restaurant equipment broker.

ENTREPRENEURIAL
Profile
Stephanie Brock and HiveLive

Stephanie Brock, chief financial officer of HiveLive, a 30-employee Web software company in Boulder, Colorado, recently purchased used telephone headsets for the company's sales representatives for half the cost of new ones. When the company needed another router, Brock found a used one for 25 percent less than a new one. "We are always looking for refurbished, used equipment because we are a start-up company and we need to save money where we can," she says.[61]

HIRE PART-TIME EMPLOYEES AND FREELANCE SPECIALISTS WHENEVER POSSIBLE. Hiring part-timers and freelancers rather than full-time workers saves on both the cost of salaries and employee benefits. Robert Ross, president of Xante Corporation, a maker of laser printer products, hires local college students for telemarketing and customer support positions, keeping his recruiting, benefits, and insurance costs low.

OUTSOURCE. Many entrepreneurs conserve valuable cash by outsourcing certain activities to businesses that specialize in performing them rather than hiring someone to do them in-house (or doing the activities themselves). In addition to saving cash, outsourcing enables entrepreneurs to focus on the most important aspects of running their businesses.

USE E-MAIL OR FAXES RATHER THAN MAIL. Whenever appropriate, entrepreneurs should use e-mails or faxes rather than mail to communicate with customers, suppliers, and others to reduce costs.

USE CREDIT CARDS TO MAKE SMALL PURCHASES. Using a credit card to make small purchases from vendors who do not offer credit terms allows entrepreneurs to defer payment for up to 30 days. Entrepreneurs who use this strategy must be disciplined, however, and pay off the entire credit card balance each month. Carrying a credit card balance from month to month exposes an entrepreneur to annual interest rates of 15 to 25 percent—*not* a cash conserving technique!

ESTABLISH AN INTERNAL SECURITY AND CONTROL SYSTEM. Too many owners encourage employee theft by failing to establish a system of controls. Reconciling the bank statement monthly and requiring special approval for checks over a specific amount, say $1,000, help to minimize losses. Separating record-keeping and check-writing responsibilities, rather than assigning them to a single employee, offers more protection.

DEVELOP A SYSTEM TO BATTLE CHECK FRAUD. According to the American Collectors Association, Americans write about 1.7 million bad checks each day, totaling more than $50 million per day in bad check losses for U.S. businesses. About 70 percent of all "bounced" checks occur because 9 out of 10 customers fail to keep their checkbooks balanced; the remaining 30 percent of bad checks are the result of fraud. Companies lose more than $13 billion per year because of forged or fraudulent checks.[62] The most effective way to battle bad or fraudulent checks is to subscribe to an electronic check-approval service. The service works at the cash register, and approval takes about a minute. The fee a small business pays to use the service depends on the volume of checks. For most small companies, charges range from a base of $25 to $100 plus a percentage of the cleared checks' value.

CHANGE YOUR SHIPPING TERMS. Changing a company's shipping terms from "F.O.B. (free on board) buyer," in which the seller pays the cost of freight, to "F.O.B. seller," in which the buyer absorbs all shipping costs, improves cash flow.

SWITCH TO ZERO-BASED BUDGETING. **Zero-based budgeting (ZBB)** primarily is a shift in the philosophy of budgeting. Rather than build the current year's budget on increases from the previous year's budget, ZBB starts from a budget of zero and evaluates the necessity of every item. The idea is to start the budget at zero and review all expenses, asking whether each one is necessary.

START SELLING GIFT CARDS. Prepaid gift cards can be a real boost to a small company's cash flow. Customers pay for the cards up front, but the typical recipient does not redeem the gift card until later, sometimes much later, giving the company the use of the cash during that time. Gift cards are appropriate for many businesses, especially those in the retail or service sectors.

ENTREPRENEURIAL
Profile

*Eva Sztupka-Kerschbaumer
and ESSpa Kozmetika
Organic Skin Care*

Eva Sztupka-Kerschbaumer, owner of a day spa in Pittsburgh, Pennsylvania, found her company in a cash bind but needed $14,000 to replace two facial steamers and a microdermabrasion machine. To get the cash she needed, Sztupka-Kerschbaumer sent e-mails to her 8,000 customers, offering them discounted gift cards in return for payment up front. "This way, I lock in my customer base, purchase equipment, and get the cash flow," she says.[63]

INVEST SURPLUS CASH. Because of the uneven flow of receipts and disbursements, a company will often temporarily have more cash than it needs—for a week, month, quarter, or even longer. When this happens, most small business owners simply ignore the surplus because they are not sure how soon they will need it. They believe that relatively small amounts of cash sitting around for just a few days or weeks are not worth investing. However, this is not the case. Small business owners who put surplus cash to work *immediately* rather than allowing it to sit idle soon discover that the yield adds up to a significant amount over time. This money can help ease the daily cash crunch during business troughs. "Your goal . . . should be to identify every dollar you don't need to pay today's bills and to keep that money invested to improve your cash flow," explains a consultant.[64]

However, when investing surplus cash, an entrepreneur's primary objective should *not* be to earn the highest yield (which usually carries with it high levels of risk); instead, the focus should be on the safety and the liquidity of the investments. The need to minimize risk and to have ready access to the cash restricts an entrepreneur's investment options to just a few such as money market accounts, zero balance accounts, and sweep accounts. A **money market account** is an interest-bearing account offered by a variety of financial institutions, ranging from banks to mutual funds. Money market accounts pay interest while allowing depositors to write checks (most have minimum check amounts) without tying their money up for a specific time. After surviving a cash crisis shortly after launching their branding and communications company, Jaye Donaldson and her partner Chester Makoski now keep enough cash invested in a money market account to cover at least 3 to 6 months' of expenses.[65]

A **zero balance account** is a checking account that technically never has any funds in it but is tied to a master account. The company keeps its money in the master account, where it earns interest, but it writes checks on the ZBA. At the end of the day, the bank pays all of the checks drawn on the ZBA; then it withdraws enough money from the master account to cover them. ZBAs allow a company to keep more cash working during the float period, the time between a check being issued and its being cashed. A **sweep account** automatically "sweeps" all funds in a company's checking account above a predetermined minimum into an interest-bearing account, enabling it to keep otherwise idle cash invested until it is needed to cover checks.

BE ON THE LOOKOUT FOR EMPLOYEE THEFT. Because small business owners often rely on informal procedures for managing cash (or no procedures at all) and often lack proper control procedures, they are likely to become victims of theft, embezzlement, and fraud by their employees. The Association of Certified Fraud Examiners estimates that U.S. companies lose 5 percent of their annual revenue to fraud by employees. The median loss suffered by small businesses is $155,000. The most common methods employees use to steal from small businesses are check tampering and fraudulent billing schemes. Alarmingly, the typical fraud

IN THE ENTREPRENEURIAL
SPOTLIGHT A Cash Flow Dilemma

Lance Redmond stared out the window of his office and into the park along the river below. It was a beautiful fall day, and the sun reflected off the water, creating a beautiful hue of colors that magnified the brilliant reds, yellows, and oranges of the trees' leaves. One question stuck in Redmond's mind: What should he do with the check he had just received as an up-front payment from a large customer for a job the customer wanted Redmond's company to do? In light of the fact that Redmond's company, Stallion Manufacturing, a maker of industrial equipment, did not have the cash to meet a payroll due in just 20 days, the answer seemed simple: Cash the check.

The situation was much more complex than that, however. Redmond knew that his company was not capable of doing the job the customer was requesting. The scope of the job required engineering skills, equipment, and financing that Stallion Manufacturing simply did not have. Yet, here was the answer to his company's latest cash flow crisis. Redmond had never missed a payroll before, although he had come close on several occasions. He knew that if he could not give his 41 employees their paychecks on time some of them would very likely leave the company to work elsewhere. With sales at the 4-year-old company growing so fast, he could not afford to lose any of his most skilled and experienced employees.

If he cashed the check, he could use the money to meet payroll, and none of his employees would be aware that the company had narrowly escaped another cash crisis. He could even talk with managers from the company that wanted the work, pretending to consider the opportunity to complete the job. Of course, he'd eventually have to return the $42,000 check to the customer, but this would buy him enough time to collect other accounts customers owed Stallion.

Redmond called a meeting to talk about the situation with his top managers. The chief financial officer, Sandy Camanetti, suggested they cash the check, meet with the managers from the company, and bluff, pretending to consider accepting the job.

"But we *know* we can't do the job," said Jill Sanchez, Stallion's director of marketing. "What if they find out? Do we want to risk losing a large, valuable customer that we've had for a long time?"

Later that evening at dinner, Redmond happened to see an old friend who also ran his own business and whose opinion he respected. "Got a minute?" Redmond asked his friend, pulling back a chair at the table. "I have a situation I'd like to discuss with you. I need your input."

"Sure," his friend said. "Have a seat. What's up?"

Redmond explained the scenario, pushed back from table, and said, "There you have it. What should I do?"

1. Assume the role of Lance Redmond's friend. What advice would you offer him? Explain your reasoning.
2. Explain the ethical dimensions of Redmond's situation.
3. What other recommendations can you make to Redmond for resolving this problem? Develop a list of at least three suggestions that would help Redmond manage his company's cash flow more effectively.

lasts 18 months before the owner discovers it, most often after another employee tips off the owner to the theft.[66] One source of the problem is the typical entrepreneur's attitude that "we're all family here; no one would steal from family."

KEEP YOUR BUSINESS PLAN CURRENT. Before approaching any potential lender or investor, a business owner must prepare a solid business plan. Smart owners keep their plans up-to-date in case an unexpected cash crisis forces them to seek emergency financing. Revising the plan annually also forces the owner to focus on managing the business more effectively.

Conclusion

Successful owners run their businesses "lean and mean." Trimming wasteful expenditures, investing surplus funds, and carefully planning and managing the company's cash flow enable them to compete effectively in a hostile market. The simple but effective techniques covered in this chapter can improve every small company's cash position. One business writer says, "In the day-to-day course of running a company, other people's capital flows past an imaginative CEO as opportunity. By looking forward and keeping an analytical eye on your cash account as events unfold (remembering that if there's no real cash there when you need it, you're history), you can generate leverage as surely as if that capital were yours to keep."[67]

Chapter Review

1. Explain the importance of cash management to the success of a small business.
   - Cash is the most important but least productive asset the small business has. Entrepreneurs must maintain enough cash to meet a company's normal operating requirements (plus a reserve for emergencies) without retaining excessively large, unproductive cash balances.
   - Without adequate cash, a small business will fail.
2. Differentiate between cash and profits.
   - Cash and profits are not the same. More businesses fail for lack of cash than for lack of profits.
   - Profits, the difference between total revenue and total expenses, are an accounting concept. Cash flow represents the flow of actual cash (the only thing businesses can use to pay bills) through a business in a continuous cycle. A business can be earning a profit and be forced out of business because it runs out of cash.
3. Understand the five steps in creating a cash budget and use them to build a cash budget.
   - The cash budgeting procedure outlined in this chapter tracks the flow of cash through the business and enables the owner to project cash surpluses and cash deficits at specific intervals.
   - The five steps in creating a cash budget are as follows: determining an adequate minimum cash balance, forecasting sales, forecasting cash receipts, forecasting cash disbursements, and determining the end-of-month cash balance.
4. Describe the fundamental principles involved in managing the "big three" of cash management: accounts receivable, accounts payable, and inventory.
   - Controlling accounts receivable requires business owners to establish clear, firm credit and collection policies and to screen customers before granting them credit. Sending invoices promptly and acting on past-due accounts quickly also improve cash flow. The goal is to collect cash from receivables as quickly as possible.
   - When managing accounts payable, an entrepreneur's goal is to stretch out payables as long as possible without damaging the company's credit rating. Other techniques include: verifying invoices before paying them, taking advantage of cash discounts, and negotiating the best possible credit terms.
   - Inventory frequently causes cash headaches for small business managers. Excess inventory earns a zero rate of return and ties up a company's cash unnecessarily. Owners must watch for stale merchandise.
5. Explain the techniques for avoiding a cash crunch in a small company.
   - Trimming overhead costs by bartering, leasing assets, avoiding nonessential outlays, using zero-based budgeting, and implementing an internal control system boost a firm's cash flow position.
   - Investing surplus cash maximizes a company's earning power. The primary criteria for investing surplus cash are security and liquidity.

Discussion Questions

1. Why must small business owners concentrate on effective cash flow management?
2. Explain the difference between cash and profit.
3. Outline the steps involved in developing a cash budget.
4. How can an entrepreneur launching a new business forecast sales?
5. Outline the basic principles of managing a small firm's receivables, payables, and inventory.

6. How can bartering improve a company's cash position?

7. Alan Ferguson, owner of Nupremis, Inc., a Web-based application service provider, says, "We lease our equipment and technology because our core business is deploying it, not owning it." What does he mean? Is leasing a wise cash management strategy for small businesses? Explain.

8. What steps should business owners take to conserve cash in their companies?

9. What should a small business owner's primary concern be when investing surplus cash?

10. Fritz Maytag, owner of Anchor Steam, says, "Just because you are the best around doesn't mean that you have to franchise or even expand. You can stay as you are and have a business that's profitable and rewarding and a great source of pride." Do you agree? Do you think that most entrepreneurs would agree? Explain.

Managing cash flow is a task that many entrepreneurs initially ignore—until they face a cash crisis. Cash is the resource that sustains a company, enabling it to grow and survive. Without cash, a business fails. Creating a cash flow forecast and using it to manage your company is critical. As this chapter points out, cash and profit are not the same, and there are aspects of understanding cash flow that are nonintuitive. In addition to being a valuable planning tool, your cash flow statement can help you assess the future health and potential of your venture. We will review the cash flow aspects of your plan and determine what you can learn from that cash flow statement. This is one step to assess how financially realistic your plan is based on the information that you have provided to date.

On the Web

Go to the Companion Web site at *www.pearsonhighered.com/scarborough* and review the links associated. These online resources may offer additional information regarding the cash flow statement and the role it will play in your business plan.

In the Software

Review the information that you have regarding your sales forecast and the expense information in your projected profit and loss statement. Change any numbers that you have determined to be unrealistic. Now go to the "Financial Statement" section of the plan and look at your "Projected Cash Flow Statement." Do any of these months show a negative cash flow? If this is the case, based on your projections, you do not have an adequate cash cushion. The lowest, most negative amount indicates the minimal amount of additional cash your business needs. Make sure your projections are realistic and that you have adequate cash to make it through this negative period. Advanced planning is your best opportunity to avoid bankruptcy. Conversely, are there months where your projections indicate an excess amount of cash? If so, have plans to use this cash to its best ability when that time comes.

Save any changes you have made in your plan. Assume that this version of your plan represents your "most likely" outcome based on realistic expense and revenue projections. Now create two additional "what if" scenarios—one using a pessimistic forecast and another using an optimistic forecast. Save this same file under a new name, for example, with the words "pessimistic" or "optimistic" after the file name. This will enable you to make changes in your plan and assess what that does to your cash flow. For example, lower your revenues by 25 percent. What does that do to your cash flow? Increase your expenses by 25 percent. What impact does that have regarding the amount of cash you will need to get through the most negative cash flow months? If you are extending credit to your customers, increase the accounts receivable lag time by 15 days, from 30 to 45 days, for example. What does your cash flow statement look like now? Make the changes that could paint a potentially negative picture for your venture and save the plan under the new "pessimistic" file name. Close that plan and open your original so we can start with your "most likely" scenario again.

Save your original under an "optimistic" file name. If you are planning to extend credit, decrease the number of collection days by seven. What does that change do to your cash flow? Increase your revenues by 15 percent. Decrease your projected expenses by 15 percent. Working through these scenarios can help test and validate your numbers and prepare you for contingencies as your plan becomes a reality. The goal is to create three scenarios that will provide a best, worst, and most likely view of your business.

Building Your Business Plan

Review the data that affects your cash flow statement. Are there revisions you need to make based on your pro forma cash flow statement? What are some of the most significant cash demands of your business? Is it due to cash tied up in inventory? Is it your payroll? Are rent or lease expenditures disproportionately high based on your projected revenues? Can you take steps to reduce or better control these expenditures as you build your revenue stream? Once you have answered these questions, again determine whether you have adequate cash for your venture after allowing for potential cost overrun or revenues below your projections.

Endnotes

1. Philip Campbell, "Cash Flow Projections Made Easy," *Inc.*, *www.inc.com/resources/finance/articles/20041001/cashprojection.html*.

2. Bruce D. Phillips and Holly Wade, *Small Business Problems and Priorities*, National Federation of Independent Businesses, June 2008, pp. 12–15.

3. Matt Hantz and Alex Della Rocca, "American Express OPEN Economic Pulse," February 2010, p. 4.

4. *Managing Cash: The Small Business Owners' Guide to Financial Control*, MasterCard Worldwide, p. 4.

5. Mike Hofman, "Archive," *Inc.*, January 2002, p. 104.

6. "Are You Ready for the Major Leagues?" *Inc.*, February 2001, p. 106.

7. Daniel Kehrer, "Big Ideas for Your Small Business," *Changing Times*, November 1989, p. 58.

8. Rick Desloge, "Cerf Brothers Grandchildren Can't Hold On," *St. Louis Business Journal*, November 13, 2009, *http://stlouis.bizjournals.com/stlouis/stories/2009/11/16/story2.html;* "Cerf Bros. Files for Bankruptcy, Puts Itself Up for Sale," *8264.net*, November 12, 2009, *www.8264.net/html/Sports_News/International_Sports_Industry/200911/12-6877.html*.

9. Daniel Lyons, "Wool Gatherer," *Forbes*, April 16, 2001, p. 310.

10. Jason Leopold, "Enron but Not Forgotten," *Entrepreneur*, January 2003, p. 63.

11. Douglas Bartholomew, "4 Common Financial Mistakes . . . and How to Avoid Them," *Your Company*, Fall 1991, p. 9.

12. Karen M. Kroll, "Ca$h Wears the Crown," *Industry Week*, May 6, 1996, pp. 16–18.

13. Sam Walker, "Wardrobe Malfunctions, Inc.," *Wall Street Journal*, February 2, 2007, pp. W1, W12.

14. Kasey Wehrum, "Never Again," *Inc.*, November 2009, p. 28.

15. Ann Cummings, "Newcastle's Pudding Lady, on Running a Seasonal Business," *Dynamic Business*, January 22, 2007, *www.dynamicbusiness.com/articles/articles-entrepreneur-profile/ann-cummings-newcastles-pudding-lady-on-running-a-seasonal-business.html*.

16. Douglas Bartholomew, "4 Common Financial Mistakes . . . and How to Avoid Them," *Your Company*, Fall 1991, p. 9.

17. Jill Andresky Fraser, "Monitoring Daily Cash Trends," *Inc.*, October 1992, p. 49.

18. George Anders, "Truckers Trials: How One Firm Fights to Save Every Penny as Its Profits Plummet," *Wall Street Journal*, April 13, 1982, pp. 1, 22.

19. Serena Ng and Cari Tuna, "Big Firms Are Quick to Collect, Slow to Pay," *Wall Street Journal*, August 31, 2009, *http://online.wsj.com/article/SB125167116756270697.html*.

20. "2009 Fact Sheet: Intuit Billing Manager 'Get Paid Survey' Results," Intuit, November 13, 2008, p. 1.

21. Mark Henricks, "Losing Stream," *Entrepreneur*, September 2003, pp. 77–78.

22. C. J. Prince, "Give 'Em Credit," *Entrepreneur*, April 2004, pp. 59–60.

23. Michael Selz, "Big Customers' Late Bills Choke Small Suppliers," *Wall Street Journal*, June 22, 1994, p. B1.

24. Christina Salerno, "How to Get Customers to Pay Up," *BNET*, March 18, 2009, *www.bnet.com/2403-13240_23-276588.html;* Alyson Oüten, "Creditors Try to Force Tamarack into Bankruptcy," *KTVB.com*, December 14, 2009, *www.ktvb.com/news/Creditors-try-to-force-Tamarack-into-bankruptcy-79261737.html*.

25. Richard G. P. McMahon and Scott Holmes, "Small Business Financial Practices in North America: A Literature Review," *Journal of Small Business Management*, April 1991, p. 21.

26. Raymund Flandez, "Three Best Ways to Make Sure Customers Pay," *Wall Street Journal*, November 13, 2009, *http://online.wsj.com/article/SB10001424052748703683804574533482721614374.html?mod=WSJ_FinancingAndInvesting_LEFTTopHeadlines*.

27. Howard Muson, "Collecting Overdue Accounts," *Your Company*, Spring 1993, p. 4.

28. "2009 Fact Sheet: Intuit Billing Manager 'Get Paid Survey' Results," Intuit, November 13, 2008, p. 1.

29. "2009 Fact Sheet: Intuit Billing Manager 'Get Paid Survey' Results," Intuit, November 13, 2008, p. 1.

30. Kimberly Stansell, "Tend to the Business of Collecting Your Money," *Inc.*, March 2, 2000, *www2.inc.com/search/17568.html;* Frances Huffman, "Calling to Collect," *Entrepreneur*, September 1993, p. 50.

31. "Collections Information," ACA International, *www.acainternational.org/publications-collections-information-5431.aspx*.

32. "Time Shrinks Value of Debts," *Collection*, Winter 1992, p. 1.

33. "Intuit Survey Finds Small Business Owners Struggling to Get Paid," *PowerHomeBiz*, November 13, 2008, *www.powerhomebiz.com/News/112008/intuit.htm*.

34. Raymund Flandez, "Three Best Ways to Make Sure Customers Pay," *Wall Street Journal*, November 13, 2009, *http://online.wsj.com/article/SB10001424052748703683804574533482721614374.html?mod=WSJ_FinancingAndInvesting_LEFTTopHeadlines*.

35. Elaine Pofeldt, "Collect Calls," *Success*, March 1998, pp. 22–24.

36. "Make Them Pay!" *Inc.*, August 2003, p. 50.

37. John Gorham, "Revenge of the Lightweight," *Forbes*, March 6, 2000, p. 54.

38. C. J. Prince, "Vulture Capital," *Entrepreneur*, February 2003, pp. 47–48.

39. Serena Ng and Cari Tuna, "Big Firms Are Quick to Collect, Slow to Pay," *Wall Street Journal*, August 31, 2009, *http://online.wsj.com/article/SB125167116756270697.html*.

40. "Dell Inc: Key Ratios," *Morningstar*, February 19, 2009, *http://quicktake.morningstar.com/stocknet/efficiencyratios10.aspx?symbol=dell*.

41. Serena Ng and Cari Tuna, "Big Firms Are Quick to Collect, Slow to Pay," *Wall Street Journal*, August 31, 2009, *http://online.wsj.com/article/SB125167116756270697.html*.

42. Jill Andresky Fraser, "How to Get Paid," *Inc.*, March 1992, p. 105.

43. "Copier Toner Scam," Mid-South Better Business Bureau, February 13, 2006, *www.midsouth.bbb.org/newsrelease.html?newsid=83&newstype=1;* Elizabeth Olson, "When the Check in the Mail Is a Bill," *New York Times*, April 22, 2004, p. C5; "Protect Your Business from Phony Invoices," *GSA Business*, December 4, 2000, p. 28.

44. Crystal Detamore-Rodman, "Cash In, Cash Out," *Entrepreneur*, June 2003, pp. 53–54.

45. William G. Shepherd, Jr., "Internal Financial Strategies," *Venture*, September 1985, p. 68.

46. Jay Goltz, "Surviving the Recession," *FSB*, February 2009, p. 27.

47. Roberta Maynard, "Can You Benefit from Barter?" *Nation's Business*, July 1994, p. 6.

48. "33 Ways to Increase Your Cash Flow and Manage Cash Balances," *The Business Owner*, February 1988, p. 8.

49. Jeffrey Lant, "Cash Is King," *Small Business Reports*, May 1991, p. 49.

50. Andrew M Kaikati and Jack G. Kaikati, "Let's Make a Deal," *Wall Street Journal*, January 25, 2010, p. R8.

51. Justin Martin, "Fair Trade," *FSB*, June 2009, pp. 76–79; "Entrepreneurs Say Managing Through Recession Makes Them Sharper Business Owners," *American Express OPEN Small Business Monitor*, April 15, 2009, *http://home3.americanexpress.com/corp/pc/2009/mtr.asp*.

52. Richard J. Maturi, "Collection Dues and Don'ts," *Entrepreneur*, January 1992, p. 328.

53. Julie Jargon, "In Lean Times, Restaurants Barter for Trade Services," *Wall Street Journal*, December 3, 2009, p. B6.

54. "Overview of the Equipment Leasing and Finance Industry," Equipment Leasing Association, *www.elaonline.com/research/overview.cfm*.

55. "Overview of the Equipment Leasing and Finance Industry," Equipment Leasing Association, *www.elaonline.com/research/overview.cfm*.

56. Bob Violino, "What's the Deal?" *CFO-IT*, Spring 2004, pp. 15–18.

57. Christine Specht, "Cash Falling Through the Cracks?" *Franchising World*, April 2009, *www.franchise.org/Franchise-News-Detail.aspx?id=45070*.

58. Roger Thompson, "Business Copes with the Recession," *Nation's Business*, January 1991, p. 20.

59. Roger Thompson, "Business Copes with the Recession," *Nation's Business*, January 1991, p. 20.

60. Bruce G. Posner, "Skipped Loan Payments," *Inc.*, September 1992, p. 40.

61. Rachael King, "How to Buy Used Tech Gear Cheap," *BusinessWeek*, February 13, 2009, *www.businessweek.com/magazine/content/09_62/s0902042477247.htm*.

62. Michael Russell, "Fraud—Check Fraud Statistics," *Ezine@articles*, January 20, 2006, *http://ezinearticles.com/?Fraud—Check-Fraud-Statistics&id=131847*.

63. Diana Ransom, "Innovative Ways to Reel in Cash," *Wall Street Journal*, June 26, 2009, *http://online.wsj.com/article/SB124603061762161137.html*.

64. Jill Andresky Fraser, "Better Cash Management," *Inc.*, May 1993, p. 42.

65. C. J. Prince, "Money to Burn?" *Entrepreneur*, July 2004, pp. 51–52.

66. *2010 ACFE Report to the Nation on Occupational Fraud and Abuse*, Association of Certified Fraud Examiners (Austin, Texas: 2010), pp. 4–5, 15–16.

67. Robert A. Mamis, "Money In, Money Out," *Inc.*, March 1993, p. 103.

Building a Guerrilla Marketing Plan

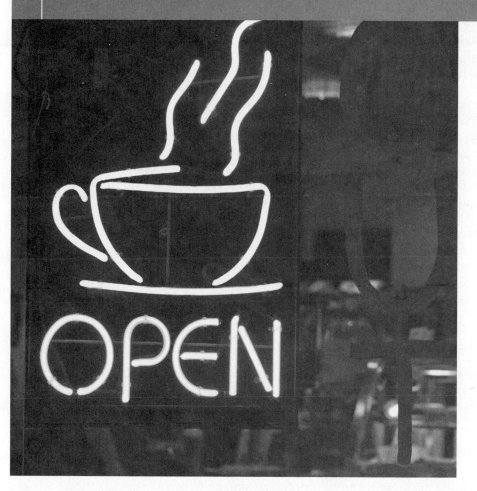

Learning Objectives

Upon completion of this chapter, you will be able to:

1 Describe the components of a guerrilla marketing plan and explain the benefits of preparing one.

2 Explain how small businesses can pinpoint their target markets.

3 Explain how to determine customer needs through market research and describe the tools that entrepreneurs use to conduct market research.

4 Describe the guerrilla marketing strategies on which a small business can build a competitive edge in the marketplace.

5 Discuss the "four Ps" of marketing—product, place, price, and promotion—and their role in building a successful marketing strategy.

In a small company, one person's hunch can be enough to launch a new product. In a big company, the same concept is likely to be buried in committee for months.

—Al Ries

This may seem simple, but you need to give customers what they want, not what you think they want. If you do this, people will keep coming back.

—John Ilhan

To be effective, a solid business plan must contain both a financial plan and a marketing plan. Like the financial plan, an effective marketing plan includes forecasts and analysis but from a different perspective. Rather than focus on cash flow, net income, and owner's equity, the marketing plan concentrates on a company's target customers, their buying power, and their buying behavior.

This chapter is devoted to creating an effective marketing plan, which is an integral part of a total business plan. Before producing computer-generated spreadsheets with financial projections, entrepreneurs must determine what to sell, to whom and how often, on what terms and at what price, and how to get the product or service to the customer. In short, a marketing plan identifies a company's target customers and describes how it will attract and keep them. The process does not have to be complex. Figure 1 explains how to build a seven-sentence marketing strategy.

Creating a Guerrilla Marketing Plan

1. Describe the components of a guerrilla marketing plan and explain the benefits of preparing one.

Marketing is the process of creating and delivering desired goods and services to customers and involves all of the activities associated with winning and retaining loyal customers. The secret to successful marketing is to understand what the company's target customers' needs, demands, and wants are before competitors can; to offer them the products and services that will satisfy those needs, demands, and wants; and to provide those customers with quality, service, convenience, and value so that they will keep coming back. The marketing function cuts across the entire organization, affecting every aspect of its operation—from finance and production to hiring and purchasing.

Marketing strategies are not just for giant corporations competing in international markets; small companies require effective marketing strategies as much as their largest rivals do. A recent study of small businesses by research firm Hurwitz and Associates reports a positive correlation between small companies that are experiencing increases in revenue and their expenditures on marketing.[1] Because their entire marketing budgets may be nothing more than rounding errors on larger competitors' marketing budgets, however, small companies must develop creative approaches and invest their marketing dollars wisely to reach their target customers. By developing **guerrilla marketing strategies**—unconventional, low-cost, creative techniques—small companies can wring as much or more "bang" from their marketing bucks as their larger rivals.

FIGURE 1
A Seven-Sentence Marketing Strategy

Source: Adapted from Alan Lautenslager, "Write a Creative Marketing Plan in Seven Sentences," *Entrepreneur*, April 24, 2006, *www.entrepreneur.com/marketing/marketingideas/guerrillamarketing columnistallautenslager/article159486. html.* Reprinted with permission of Entrepreneur Media, Inc.

Building a successful marketing plan does not have to be complex. One marketing expert says that entrepreneurs can create the foundation of a marketing plan with just seven sentences:

1. What is the purpose of your marketing?
2. Who is your target market?
3. What is your niche?
4. What are the benefits and competitive advantage?
5. What is your company's identity?
6. What tactics, strategies, and weapons will you use to carry out your marketing?
7. How much money will you spend on your marketing; in other words, what is your marketing budget?

Answering these seven questions will give you an outline of your company's marketing plan. Implementing a successful marketing plan boils down to two essentials:

1. Having a thorough understanding of your target market, including what customers want and expect from your company and its products and services.
2. Identifying the obstacles that stand in your way of satisfying customers (competitors, barriers to entry, outside influences, budgets, knowledge, and others) and eliminating them.

© Mike Baldwin / Cornered

BALDWIN

"It used to be all about truth and justice. Now, mostly I fight for market share."

ENTREPRENEURIAL
Profile

Steve Lichtman and Fitness Together

The importance of guerrilla marketing hit Steve Lichtman, owner of four franchised Fitness Together centers near Boston, Massachusetts, after he spent $7,000 to send a direct mail ad to 20,000 households in his trading area. The results were unimpressive; the campaign generated just enough new business to pay for itself. Lichtman realized that "we had to be a lot more strategic and creative" in the company's marketing efforts. He worked with his management team to define the company's value proposition, "One client, one trainer, one goal," which involves offering customized, one-on-one personal training sessions in small, suite-like settings, before looking for the most effective ways to communicate that message to customers. As part of his guerrilla marketing strategy, Lichtman formed a partnership with a local child care provider to provide parents with child care during their workouts. He also began building a network of contacts with local health care providers and has conducted exercise programs for rehab patients. To raise his company's visibility in the local community, Lichtman launched a "Lunch and Learn" program aimed at local businesses in which he talks with employees about health, nutrition, and exercise. Fitness Together also sends electronic newsletters with articles of interest to customers and potential customers and has a Facebook page. The company's Web site includes testimonials (some in the form of short videos) from satisfied customers. Lichtman's most comprehensive guerrilla marketing tactic was to organize a cooperative advertising program with other Fitness Together franchisees in New England. The franchisees pool their resources to purchase advertising in traditional media such as cable television ads and billboards at discounted prices.[2]

A marketing plan focuses the company's attention on the customer and recognizes that satisfying the customer is the foundation of every business. Indeed, the customer is the central player in the cast of every business venture. According to marketing expert Ted Levitt, the primary purpose of a business is not to earn a profit; instead, it is "to create and keep a customer. The rest, given reasonable good sense, will take care of itself."[3] Every area of the business must practice putting the customer first in planning and actions. A **guerrilla marketing plan** should accomplish four objectives:

1. It should pinpoint the target markets the small company will serve.
2. It should determine customer needs, wants, and characteristics through market research.

3. It should analyze a company's competitive advantages and build an effective, cost-efficient marketing strategy around them.

4. It should help create a marketing mix that meets customer needs and wants.

This chapter focuses on building a customer orientation into these four objectives of the small company's marketing plan.

Market Diversity: Pinpointing the Target Market

2. Explain how small businesses can pinpoint their target markets.

One of the first steps in building a marketing plan is identifying a small company's **target market**, the group of customers at whom the company aims its products and services. The more a business learns from market research about its local markets, its customers, and their buying habits and preferences, the more precisely it can focus its marketing efforts on the group(s) of prospective and existing customers who are most likely to buy its products or services.

Blane Nordahl, one of the most successful cat burglars ever (until he was caught), specialized in stealing only the finest sterling silver. What made Nordahl so difficult for police to catch was his meticulous market research that allowed him to target exactly the right homes to rob. Nordahl used local libraries and publications such as the *duPont Registry* and *Sotheby's Previews* to identify and learn about upscale neighborhoods. Then he would scout out the most likely "old money" homes in those neighborhoods, carefully selecting his targets to maximize his take and to minimize the likelihood of getting caught. Nordahl's systematic approach to selecting his target market worked for more than 15 years, netting him millions of dollars' worth of ill-gotten gain before a footprint left in a hasty exit allowed police to nab him. "Of all the burglars I've ever gone up against," says one police officer, "he is absolutely the best."[4]

Although Nordahl used a creative marketing approach to achieve illegal gain, small businesses can use a similar approach to make their marketing strategies more successful. Unfortunately, most marketing experts contend that the greatest marketing mistake that small businesses make is failing to define clearly the target market they will serve. Failing to pinpoint their target markets is especially ironic because small firms are ideally suited to reaching market segments that their larger rivals overlook or consider too small to be profitable. Why, then, do so many small businesses fail to pinpoint their target markets? Because identifying, defining, and researching a target market requires market research and a marketing plan, both of which involve hard work! The result is that these companies follow a sales-driven rather than a customer-driven marketing strategy. To be customer driven, an effective marketing strategy must be based on a clear, well-defined understanding of a company's target customers.

While attending college at the University of Illinois in Champaign, Scott Gittrich worked for a pizza franchise and stayed on after graduating, eventually working his way up to the role of operations manager. In 1991, Gittrich, 28, left to create his own pizza company, Toppers Pizza. He built the company on three simple principles: good pizza made from scratch, good service, and a unique atmosphere. (The company's core values include "live with integrity, have fun, build something special, bring it . . . with passion, and give customers what they want.") He opened the first Toppers in the town he knew best, Champaign, Illinois, and targeted college students. Today, the company, which boasts 25 stores in 4 states, has expanded its target market to include young people between the ages of 18 and 34, but college students remain the company's core customers. Although some restaurants are in suburban areas, most Toppers outlets are located within easy reach of colleges and universities, and they stay open until 3 AM to accommodate the nontraditional dining habits of their target customers. The company's menu, which ranges from pizza and grinders to wings and its signature Topperstix, is designed with its target market in mind. Pizza choices include Mac 'N Cheese and a Hangover Helper, all of which come with little green army men and hot peppers. Toppers' stores look less like traditional restaurants and more like urban cafés with couches, coffee tables, and flat-screen TVs. Even the company's ads, which sound like witty conversations between friends, are aimed at college students. Gittrich, whose goal is to build a national chain of 500 stores by 2020, tries to wrap his company's brand in the "fun and festive."[5]

A "one-size-fits-all" approach to marketing no longer works because the mass market is rapidly disappearing. The population of the United States, like that of many countries, is becoming increasingly diverse. The mass market that dominated the business world 35 years ago has been replaced by an increasingly fragmented market of multicultural customers whose purchasing power is growing rapidly (see Figure 2). In fact, Hispanics, African Americans, Asian Americans, and other minorities now make up 34 percent of the U.S. population.[6] The nation's increasingly diverse population offers businesses of all sizes tremendous marketing opportunities if they target specific customers, learn how to reach them, and offer goods and services designed specifically for them. To be successful, entrepreneurs must be in tune with the multicultural nature of the modern marketplace. Small businesses that take the time to recognize, understand, and cater to the unique needs, experiences, and preferences of these multicultural markets (and their submarkets) will reap immense rewards. The key to success is learning about those target customers' unique, needs, wants, and preferences.

The most successful businesses have well-defined portraits of the customers they are seeking to attract. From market research, they know their customers' income levels, ages, lifestyles, buying patterns, education levels, likes and dislikes, and even their psychological profiles. At successful companies, the target customer permeates the entire business—from the merchandise the company purchases and the ads it uses to the layout and décor of the store. Successful businesses have an advantage over their rivals because the images they have created for their companies appeal to their target customers, and that's why they prosper. Without a clear picture of its target market, a small company tries to reach almost everyone and usually ends up appealing to almost no one.

FIGURE 2
Changes in Multicultural Population and Purchasing Power, 2009–2014

Source: Jeffrey M. Humphreys, "The Multicultural Economy 2009," *Georgia Business and Economic Conditions*, Volume 69, Number 3, Third Quarter 2009, Selig Center for Economic Growth, University of Georgia, pp. 3, 13, 14.

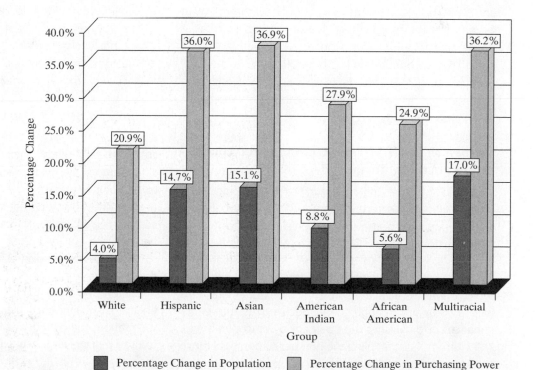

Make the Most of Your Marketing Efforts

Entrepreneurs must be clever guerrilla marketers if they are to compete with their larger rivals. The best small companies use their size and their closeness to their customers to their advantage. The Street-Smart Entrepreneur offers the following tips to entrepreneurs.

Capture Customers' and Potential Customers' Attention

Effective guerrilla marketers are not like wallflowers at a junior high school dance; they capitalize on every opportunity—and even create opportunities—to promote their businesses, often using their employees' daily routines as part of the show. At Beecher's Handmade Cheese in Seattle's Pike Place Market, customers watch employees in a glass-enclosed factory busily making gourmet cheese. Although the Pike's Place Market location generates just 10 percent of the company's sales (the bulk of its sales come through grocery stores and specialty markets), owner Kurt Dammeier says that the combination factory/retail store/restaurant is an important marketing tool for Beecher's. The cheese-making process captures customers' attention; reinforces the fact that the company's products include the freshest, finest ingredients; and reminds them that Beecher's takes an old-fashioned, artisanal approach to producing cheese. "There's just something about the open viewing format and the play-by-play cheese-making action that draws you in and makes you want to eat (and buy) cheese," says one happy customer. Having reached full capacity at its Seattle factory, Beecher's Handmade Cheese is opening a similar factory/store/marketing project in New York City.

Ensure that *All* of Your Company's "Touch Points" Are on Target

"Touch points" are the opportunities for a company to interact with its customers or potential customers and include everything from a salesperson dealing face-to-face with a customer in a store or a customer shopping on the company's Web site to a potential customer reading a company blog or downloading a free white paper on a topic of interest. It is the sum of customers' interactions with a company through these touch points that either enhances or diminishes the power of a company's brand. The Internet has multiplied the number of potential touch points, but do your company's touch points enhance or harm its customer relationships?

1. *List every touch point your company has with its customers and potential customers.* Include online, digital, and face-to-face interactions.
2. *Identify what you want customers or potential customers to do at each touch point.* This is the call to action. Do you want them to make a purchase? Learn more about the quality of your company's products? See you and your business as an expert in the field?
3. *Test each touch point for quality, call to action, and customer experience—from the customer's perspective.* Review every touch point to determine whether customers can do what they want to do (and what you want them to do!) easily, without confusion, quickly, and conveniently. For example, if a customer clicks through to the company's Web site after receiving an e-mail about a special sale, does the touch point take them to the appropriate landing page where they can easily make a purchase? If not, the touch point needs to be repaired.
4. *Make the necessary changes to improve the quality and customer experience of your company's touch points.* One of the best ways to learn how to improve your company's touch points is to get feedback from actual customers, asking them for advice on how to improve their experience. By improving the quality of your company's touch points, you will be able to increase sales, improve customer retention, and transform customers into active promoters of your business.

Offer Customers More Than They Expect

The best guerrilla marketers strive for more than mere customer satisfaction; their goal is to achieve customer *astonishment* by giving their customers more than they expect. Pat & Oscar's, a chain of successful restaurants that provides hearty, homemade, family-style meals, offers customers a 110 percent guarantee that they will be satisfied with the quality of their meals and their dining experience. If a customer is dissatisfied, the restaurant will refund the full price of the meal plus 10 percent. The guarantee not only provides a tangible signal that Pat & Oscar's stands behind its quality and customer service, but it also tells them about the confidence the company has in its ability to provide a stellar dining experience.

Treat Your Customers as Lifetime Investments

At Zane's Cycles in Branford, Connecticut, founder Chris Zane sets his company apart from the competition by offering free lifetime service on every bicycle he sells and 90-day price protection. The store also includes a cappuccino bar that provides free beverages for customers. "I'll give you lifetime service, guarantee you the lowest price, and fix you a cappuccino," says Zane. The company also charges nothing for any part that costs less than $1. Before purchasing a bicycle, customers can test it out on the company's test course.

Some people say that Zane's practices don't make sense and suggest that he is "giving away the store." The clever guerrilla marketer, however, sees the big picture. He has tracked data over the years and knows that the lifetime value of the average Zane customer (the gross revenue that a single customer generates over time) is $12,500. Compared to the lifetime value of his customers, the cost of the "freebies" that Zane offers is negligible. "My customers are valuable, and I treat them that way," says Zane. The message is clear: "We started with the belief, 'the only difference between us and our competition is the service that we offer,'" he says. "If you don't feel that we are living up to our mission, let us know and we'll fix it immediately." One of the leading companies in the industry, Zane's has achieved an amazing average growth rate of 25 percent per year since its founding in 1980!

Don't Ignore Negative Word of Mouth

The best guerrilla marketers recognize that no company can satisfy every customer. When negative word of mouth happens, they deal with it and learn from it. A recent study by the London School of Economics reports that to generate a 1 percent increase in its sales growth rate, a company must produce a 6.8 percent *increase* in its positive word-of-mouth.

To achieve that same 1 percent increase in its sales growth rate, a company also could *reduce* its negative word of mouth by just 2.4 percent. "Reducing negative comments could grow revenue by 300 percent [compared to] increasing positive comments," concludes the study. How can companies reduce negative word of mouth among its customers?

1. *Set up a process that allows customers to voice their complaints and frustrations and monitor it regularly.* Company blogs, Web sites, Facebook pages, and other social media are excellent tools for collecting both positive and negative customer feedback.

2. *When something goes wrong, admit the mistake and then fix it—fast.* Customers know that no company is perfect. When a company makes a mistake, owns up to it, and then fixes it promptly, it can win a loyal customer for life.

3. *Incorporate lessons from your company's mistakes into developing new and better processes and training.* Smart companies learn from their mistakes and use them to get better.

Sources: Based on Rebecca Marx, "Beecher's Handmade Cheese Is Opening a Cheese Factory in Manhattan Because 'New Yorkers Are Cheese Crazy,'" *Village Voice*, April 5, 2010, *http://blogs.villagevoice.com/ forkintheroad/archives/2010/04/cheese_factory.php;* "Beecher's Handmade Cheese to Open in NYC in 2011," Pacific Northwest Cheese Project, March 31, 2010, *http://pnwcheese.typepad.com/cheese/2010/03/beechers-to-expand-to-nyc-in-2011.html;* Paul Schwartz, "How Your Digital Touch Points Are Harming Your Customer Relationships," *Customer U*, April 28, 2009, *http://customeru.wordpress.com/2009/04/28/how-your-digital-touch-points-are-harming-customer-relationships/;* Valerie Killifer, "Enhancing the Customer Experience," *Fast Casual*, June 8, 2009, *www.fastcasual.com/ article.php?id=14737&na=;* Donna Fenn, "Treat Your Customers Like Lifetime Investments," *BNET*, March 8, 2010, *http://blogs.bnet.com/ smb/?p=106;* "When Word of Mouth Goes South," *Marketing Profs: Get to the Point,* December 12, 2008, pp. 1–2; Paul Marsden, Alain Samson, and Neville Upton, "Advocacy Drives Growth," *London School of Economics,* September 13, 2005, p. 1.

Determining Customer Needs and Wants Through Market Research

3-A. Explain how to determine customer needs through market research.

The changing nature of the U.S. population is a potent force that is altering the business landscape. Shifting patterns in age, income, education, race, and other population characteristics (which are the subject of demographics) have a major impact on companies, their markets, and the way they do business with their customers. Entrepreneurs who recognize demographic, social, and cultural trends as they emerge have the opportunity to differentiate their companies from the competition in meaningful ways. Those who fail to spot important trends and adjust their strategies accordingly run the risk of their companies becoming competitively obsolete as their target customers pass them by. How can entrepreneurs spot these significant trends?

■ Read a variety of current publications, including those that might ordinarily be outside of your areas of interest. Reading industry-related publications also allows you to identify significant trends that affect your business directly.

- Watch the top 10 television shows (at least periodically). They are great indicators of customers' attitudes and values and give valuable insight into the products and services they are interested in buying. AMC's hit series *Mad Men*, a show about the advertising industry set in the early 1960s, proved to be a major influence on men's and women's fashions, home décor, eyeglasses, and other aspects of life.
- See the top 10 movies. They also influence consumer behavior. After Tommy Lee Jones and Will Smith donned Ray-Ban sunglasses in the original *Men in Black*, sales of the company's sunglasses skyrocketed.
- Look to the past. Like clothing styles, some trends are recycled from the past. Organic food? That's what your grandparents ate! Gabriela Hernandez drew her inspiration for the line of retro makeup that her company, Bésame Cosmetics, sells from the classic colors and styles used by celebrity icons of the 1940s, such as Grace Kelly and Audrey Hepburn.[7]
- Talk to at least 100 customers each year to find out what they are buying and why. Ask them about other features they would like or other problems you could help them solve. "When in doubt, go to your customers," says veteran entrepreneur and author Norm Brodsky. "They will tell you what they want and lead you to solutions you'd never come up with on your own. Just about every successful new initiative I've taken in business has come from listening to customers."[8]
- Sensitize yourself to trend-tracking. Be on the lookout for emerging trends every day by stepping outside of your normal routine and noticing what's happening around you.
- Monitor social networking sites for evidence of emerging trends. The discussions of people who gather online can reveal significant shifts in attitudes and interests.

For entrepreneurs, the key to success is to align their businesses with as many demographic, social, and cultural trends as possible. Staying on trend means staying in synchronization with the market as it shifts and changes over time. The more trends a business converges with, the more likely it is to be successful. Conversely, a business moving away from significant trends in society is in danger of losing its customer base.

By performing some basic market research, entrepreneurs can detect key demographic, social, and cultural trends and zero in on the needs, wants, preferences, and desires of their target customers. Indeed, every business can benefit from a better understanding of its market, customers, and competitors. **Market research** is the vehicle for gathering the information that serves as the foundation for the marketing plan. It involves systematically collecting, analyzing, and interpreting data pertaining to the small company's market, customers, and competitors. Businesses

Hit television shows such as *Mad Men* often influence customers' buying habits.

Source: Alamy Images

320

face the challenge of reaching the highly fragmented markets that have emerged today, and market research can help them. Market research allows entrepreneurs to answer questions such as: Who are my customers and potential customers? To which age group(s) do they belong? What is their income level? Where do they live? Do they rent or own their own homes? What features are they looking for in the products or services I sell? How often do they buy these products or services? What models, styles, colors, or flavors do they prefer? What radio stations do they listen to? Which Web sites do they visit? What factors are most important to their buying decisions? How do the strengths of my product or service serve their needs and wants? What hours do they prefer to shop? How do they perceive my business? Which advertising media are most likely to reach them? How do customers perceive my business versus competitors? This information is an integral part of developing an effective marketing plan.

When marketing its goods and services, a small company must avoid mistakes because there is little margin for error when funds are scarce and budgets are tight. Small businesses simply cannot afford to miss their target markets, and market research can help them zero in on the bull's eye. This usually requires conducting market research up front, *before* launching a company. One of the worst—and most common—mistakes entrepreneurs make is *assuming* that a market exists for their products or services. The time to find out whether customers are likely to buy a product or a service is *before* investing thousands of dollars to launch it! Market research can tell entrepreneurs whether a sufficient customer base exists and how likely those customers are to buy their products and services.

ENTREPRENEURIAL
Profile
Jeff Harvey and Burgerville

Burgerville, a family-owned chain of hamburger restaurants based in Vancouver, Washington, recently set up a 24-foot-long mobile food truck nicknamed "Nomad" in a waterfront park in Portland, Oregon, to explore the market potential of possible new locations and to test customer interest in the company's products before committing to opening permanent stores. Burgerville CEO Jeff Harvey says that it cost the company $100,000 to outfit the truck, less than 10 percent of the cost of building a free-standing restaurant.[9]

In addition to collecting and analyzing demographic data about their target customers, entrepreneurs can learn a great deal by actually observing, mingling with, and interviewing customers as they shop.

Market research for a small business can be informal; it does *not* have to be time consuming, complex, or expensive to be valuable. Many entrepreneurs are discovering the speed, the convenience, and the low cost of conducting market research over the Web. Online surveys, customer opinion polls, and other research projects are easy to conduct, cost virtually nothing, produce quick responses, and help companies connect with their customers. Insight Express, an online market research firm, estimates that an online survey costs just 20 percent of what it costs to conduct a mail survey and only 10 percent of what it costs for a telephone survey.[10] With Web-based surveys, businesses can get real-time feedback from customers, often using surveys they have designed themselves. Web sites such as Survey Monkey (*www.surveymonkey.com*) and Zoomerang (*www.zoomerang.com*) allow entrepreneurs to conduct low-cost (in some cases free) online surveys of existing or prospective customers. One comparison study of online and mail surveys reports that response rates are higher for online surveys than for mail surveys.[11]

ENTREPRENEURIAL
Profile
Jay Burton and Local Motors

Jay Burton, cofounder of Local Motors, a Wareham, Massachusetts-based company that builds and sells cars on a micro scale, decided to start by building just one type of car, which was developed through an online collaboration of car enthusiasts, engineers, and (of course) potential customers. "It's like microbrewing for cars," says Burton. "We're not just selling the car; we're selling the experience." Local Motors sponsors online contests with prizes of up to $10,000 for its registered contributors, who generated important design ideas that the company incorporated into its first car, the Rally Fighter. Burton and the company's 10 employees decide which of the features that members of the Local Motors community suggest to incorporate into the company's designs and how to implement them in practical, cost-effective ways.[12]

3-B. Describe the tools that entrepreneurs use to conduct market research.

How to Conduct Market Research

The marketing approach that companies of all sizes strive to achieve is **individualized** (or **one-to-one**) **marketing**, a system of gathering data on individual customers and then developing a marketing plan designed specifically to appeal to their needs, tastes, and preferences. Its goal is not only to attract customers but also to keep them and to increase their purchases. In today's society, in which many people feel isolated and transactions are impersonal, one-to-one marketing gives a business a competitive advantage. Companies following this approach know their customers, understand how to give them the value they want, and, perhaps most important, know how to make them feel special. The goal is to treat each customer as an individual.

ENTREPRENEURIAL
Profile

Ritz-Carlton

The Ritz-Carlton hotel group uses a centralized computer network called Mystique that tracks its guests' preferences and spending habits with the company and provides information to all of the hotels in the chain so that they can offer guests individual attention. When a guest checks in, the desk clerk will know, for instance, that he or she prefers a queen-size bed with foam pillows, a stock of Le Bleu bottled water in the minibar, and a glass of orange juice and a copy of the *Wall Street Journal* with breakfast. Offering these "extras" without requiring the customer to ask for them makes hotel guests feel as though the hotel is catering specifically to their unique needs and preferences.[13]

Individualized marketing requires business owners to gather and assimilate detailed information about their customers. Fortunately, owners of even the smallest companies now have access to affordable technology that creates and manages computerized databases, allowing them to develop close, one-to-one relationships with their customers. Much like gold nuggets waiting to be discovered, significant amounts of valuable information about customers and their buying habits are hidden *inside* many small businesses, tucked away in computerized databases. For most business owners, collecting useful information about their customers and potential new products and markets is simply a matter of sorting and organizing data that are already floating around somewhere in their companies. "Most companies are data rich and information poor," claims one marketing expert.[14] The key is to mine these data and turn them into useful information that allows the company to "court" its customers with special products, services, ads, and offers that appeal most to them.

Entrepreneurs have at their disposal two basic types of market research: primary and secondary. *Primary research* is data that you collect and analyze yourself. *Secondary research* includes data that have already been compiled and are available often at a very reasonable cost or even free. Primary research techniques include the following:

■ *Customer surveys and questionnaires.* Keep them short. Word your questions carefully so that you do not bias the results, and use a simple ranking system (e.g., a 1-to-5 scale, with 1 representing "unacceptable" and 5 representing "excellent"). Test your survey for problems on a small number of people before putting it to use. Web surveys are inexpensive, easy to conduct, and provide feedback fast. Femail Creations, a mail-order company that sells clothing, accessories, and gifts to women, uses Web surveys to gather basic demographic data about its customers and to solicit new product ideas as well. Customer responses have led to profitable new product lines for the small company.[15]

■ *Social media.* Small companies have discovered that social media such as Facebook, Twitter, Yelp, and others are easy, inexpensive, and effective tools for gathering customer feedback. The owners of Liberty Market, a popular restaurant and food store in Gilbert, Arizona, routinely send Tweets to their regular customers after they visit to find out about their dining experience. Not only do the entrepreneurs receive useful feedback and suggestions for improvement, but they also stay close to their core customers.[16]

■ *Focus groups.* Enlist a small number of customers to give you feedback on specific issues in your business—quality, convenience, hours of operation, service, and so on. Listen carefully for new marketing opportunities as customers or potential customers tell you what is on their minds. Once again, consider using the Web; one small bicycle company conducts 10 online focus groups each year at virtually no cost and gains valuable marketing information from them.

- *Daily transactions.* Sift as much data as possible from existing company records and daily transactions—customer warranty cards, personal checks, frequent-buyer clubs, credit applications, and others.
- *Other ideas.* Set up a suggestion system (for customers and employees) and use it. Establish a customer advisory panel to determine how well your company is meeting customers' needs. Talk with suppliers about trends they have spotted in the industry. Contact customers who have not bought anything in a long time and find out why. Contact people who are not customers and find out why. Teach employees to be good listeners and then ask them what they hear.

Secondary research, which is usually less expensive to collect than primary data, includes the following sources:

- *Business directories.* To locate a trade association, use *Business Information Sources* (University of California Press) or the *Encyclopedia of Associations* (Gale Research). To find suppliers, use *The Thomas Register of American Manufacturers* (Thomas Publishing Company) or *Standard & Poor's Register of Corporations, Executives, and Industries* (Standard & Poor's Corporation). *The American Wholesalers and Distributors Directory* includes details on more than 18,000 wholesalers and distributors.
- *Direct mail lists.* You can buy mailing lists for practically any type of business. *The Standard Rate and Data Service (SRDS) Directory of Mailing Lists* (Standard Rate and Data) is a good place to start looking.
- *Demographic data.* To learn more about the demographic characteristics of customers in general, use *The Statistical Abstract of the United States* (U.S. Government Printing Office). Profiles of more specific regions are available in *The State and Metropolitan Data Book* (U.S. Government Printing Office). *The Sourcebook of Zip Code Demographics* (CACI, Inc.) provides detailed breakdowns of the population in every zip code in the country. *Sales and Marketing Management's Survey of Buying Power* (Bill Communications) has statistics on consumer, retail, and industrial buying.
- *Census data.* The Bureau of the Census publishes a wide variety of reports that summarize the wealth of data found in its census database, which is available at most libraries and at the Census Bureau's Web site (www.census.gov).
- *Forecasts.* The *U.S. Global Outlook* traces the growth of 200 industries and gives a 5-year forecast for each one. Many government agencies, including the Department of Commerce, offer forecasts on everything from interest rates to the number of housing starts. A government librarian can help you find what you need.
- *Market research.* Someone may already have compiled the market research you need. *The FINDex Worldwide Directory of Market Research Reports, Studies, and Surveys* (Cambridge Information Group) lists more than 10,600 studies available for purchase. Other directories of business research include *Simmons Study of Media and Markets* (Simmons Market Research Bureau, Inc.) and the *A.C. Nielsen Retail Index* (A.C. Nielsen Company).
- *Articles.* Magazine and journal articles pertinent to your business are a great source of information. Use the *Reader's Guide to Periodical Literature*, the *Business Periodicals Index* (similar to the *Reader's Guide* but focuses on business periodicals), and *Ulrich's Guide to International Periodicals* to locate the ones you need.
- *Local data.* Your state Department of Commerce and your local Chamber of Commerce will very likely have useful data on the local market of interest to you. Call to find out what is available.
- *The Web.* Most entrepreneurs are astounded at the marketing information that is available on the Web. Using one of the search engines, you can gain access to a world of information—literally!

Thanks to advances in computer hardware and software, data mining, once available only to large companies with vast computer power, is now possible for even very small businesses. **Data mining** is a process whereby business owners use computer software that uses statistical analyses, database technology, and artificial intelligence to find hidden patterns, trends, and connections in data. Business owners can then use the information generated to make better marketing decisions and predictions about their customers' behavior. Entrepreneurs can gain incredible marketing power by using data mining to find relationships among the many components of a data set, to identify

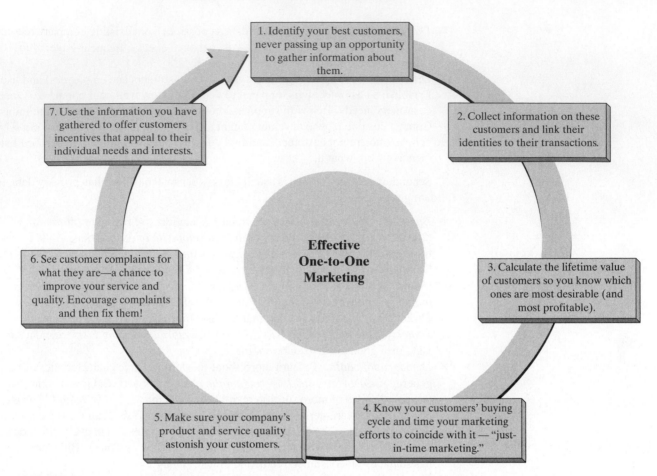

FIGURE 3
How to Become an Effective One-to-One Marketer

Source: Based on Susan Greco, "The Road to One-to-One Marketing," *Inc.*, October 1995, pp. 56–66.

clusters of customers with similar buying habits, and to predict customers' buying patterns. Popular data mining software packages include Clementine, DataScope Pro, GoldMine, and MineSet.

For an effective individualized marketing campaign to be successful, business owners must collect and mine three types of data:

1. *Geographic.* Where are my customers located? Do they tend to be concentrated in one geographic region?
2. *Demographic.* What are the characteristics of my customers (e.g., age, education levels, income, sex, marital status, and many other features).
3. *Psychographic.* What drives my customers' buying behavior? Are they receptive to new products or are they among the last to accept them? What values are most important to them?

Figure 3 explains how to become an effective individualized marketer.

Plotting a Guerrilla Marketing Strategy: Building a Competitive Edge

4. Describe the guerrilla marketing strategies on which a small business can build a competitive edge in the marketplace.

Small companies simply do not have the resources to devote to marketing that their larger rivals do. According to a recent Small Business Attitudes and Outlook Survey by Constant Contact, 70 percent of small business owners say that the biggest challenge they face is marketing their companies effectively with limited resources.[17] Marketing a small company effectively requires entrepreneurs to rely on guerrilla marketing strategies, those that use creative, low-cost marketing techniques that hit home with their target customers. Independent bookstores have discovered that large chains use their buying power to get volume discounts and undercut the independents' prices. Individual shop owners are finding new ways, such as special ordering, adult reading groups, educational classes, children's story hours, newsletters, autograph parties, and targeting unique niches to differentiate themselves and to retain loyal customers. These entrepreneurs are finding that the best way to gain a competitive advantage is to create value by giving customers what they really want that they cannot get elsewhere.

Successful businesses often use the special advantages they have to build a competitive edge over their larger rivals. Their close contact with the customer, personal attention, focus on service, and organizational and managerial flexibility provide a solid foundation from which to build a towering competitive edge in the market. Small companies can exploit their size to become more effective than their larger rivals at **relationship marketing** or **customer relationship management (CRM)**—developing, maintaining, and managing long-term relationships with customers so that they will want to keep coming back to make repeat purchases. CRM puts the customer at the center of a company's thinking, planning, and action and shifts the focus from a product or service to customers and their needs and wants. CRM requires business owners to take the following steps:

- Collect meaningful information about existing customers and compile it in a database.
- Mine the database to identify the company's best and most profitable customers, their needs, and their buying habits. In most companies, a small percentage of customers account for the majority of sales and profits. These are the customers on whom a business should focus its attention and efforts.
- Focus on developing lasting relationships with these customers. This often requires entrepreneurs to "fire" some customers that require more attention, time, and expense than they generate in revenue for the business. Failure to do so reduces a company's return on its CRM effort.
- Attract more customers who fit the profile of the company's best customers.

Business owners are discovering that even though they may be providing their customers with satisfactory service and value, many of their customers do not remain loyal, choosing instead to buy from other companies. Businesses that provide poor customer service are in grave danger. Hepworth, a consulting firm that specializes in customer retention, measures its clients' **revenue at risk**, which calculates the sales revenue a company stands to lose by measuring the percentage of customers who would leave because of poor service. According to Verde Group, another company that has conducted extensive research on customer satisfaction, the typical North American company is at risk of losing 21 percent of its customers because of high levels of dissatisfaction. What is more alarming is that more than 40 percent of customers who experience a customer service problem never tell the company about it, and 70 percent of customers defect because of a problem that, if the company knew about it, would have been easy to fix.[18] Today, earning customers' loyalty requires businesses to take customer focus and service to unprecedented levels, and that requires building long-term relationships with customers.

Guerrilla Marketing Principles

To be successful guerrilla marketers, entrepreneurs must be as innovative in creating their marketing strategies as they are in developing new product and service ideas. The following 16 guerrilla marketing principles can help business owners develop a competitive edge: niche-picking, generating publicity, entertailing, connecting with their customers, building a consistent branding strategy, embracing social networking, starting a blog, creating online videos, emphasizing their uniqueness, focusing on customers' needs, retaining existing customers, emphasizing quality, paying attention to convenience, concentrating on innovation, dedicating themselves to service, and emphasizing speed.

FIND A NICHE AND FILL IT. Many successful small companies choose their niches carefully and defend them fiercely rather than compete head-to-head with larger rivals. A niche strategy allows a small company to maximize the advantages of its smallness and to compete effectively even in industries dominated by giants. Focusing on niches that are too small to be attractive to large companies or in which entrepreneurs have unique expertise are common recipes for success among thriving small companies.

► ENTREPRENEURSHIP IN ACTION ►

Love and Therapy . . . for Your Favorite Jeans

Ever have the heart-breaking experience of having to retire that favorite pair of jeans—the ones that are broken in, so comfortable, and fit just right—because they have become so worn out and sport so many holes that you risk violating some cities' decency ordinances? If so, Denim Therapy, a New York City–based company started in 2006 by Karla Shuftan and Francine Rabinovich, may be the answer! The entrepreneurs emphasize that they do not merely patch worn jeans; they reweave them. For just $7 an inch, Denim Therapy will repair holes and worn hems by weaving new threads into the damaged area. Skilled reweavers begin repairing each hole with a fusable fabric that covers the hole before reweaving thread carefully selected to match the surrounding fabric in an embroidery machine. The average repair costs about $42 and takes 2 weeks.

Where others saw holes and frayed hems, Shuftan and Rabinovich saw opportunity. "It's hard to find the perfect pair of jeans," says Rabinovich, "but once you have them, you don't want to give them up." For denim devotees whose jeans are on the verge of the point of no return, Denim Therapy offers rebirth. "We offer a unique reconstructive repair with exceptional service and a whole lot of love," says Rabinovich.

Currently, the company repairs about 400 pairs of jeans per month. Rabinovich and Shuftan have purchased ads on Google but rely mostly on word of mouth. Several fashion and lifestyle magazines and television stations have reported Denim Therapy's story, resulting in some much needed publicity, but the entrepreneurs' goal is to build Denim Therapy into a strong brand that is recognized as the go-to service for jean repairs. The question is: What is the best way to achieve that on a very limited marketing budget?

1. Is Denim Therapy's situation—more marketing need than marketing budget available—typical for small businesses? Explain.
2. What steps can entrepreneurs faced with the situation in question 1 take to market their companies' products and services?
3. What recommendations can you make to Rabinovich and Shuftan about building Denim Therapy into a well-known brand on a limited budget?
4. Work with a small team of your classmates in a brainstorming session to devise a guerrilla marketing plan for Denim Therapy.

Sources: Based on Shivani Vora, "A Repair Shop for Ripped Jeans," *Inc.*, March 2010, p. 112; "The Buzz," Denim Therapy, *http://denimtherapy.com*.

ENTREPRENEURIAL
Profile

Alysa Binder and Dan Wiesel and Pet Airways

Pet Airways cofounder Alysa Binder and Zoe, the Jack Russell terrier who inspired her owners to start the company.

Source: Dave Weaver\AP Wide World Photos

Alysa Binder and her husband Dan Wiesel came up with the idea for their niche business after an unsatisfactory experience that involved loading their beloved Jack Russell terrier, Zoe, into the cargo hold of a jet for their cross-country move to Florida. The couple created Pet Airways, a Delray Beach, Florida-based company that specializes in flying pets safely and securely in the cabin of a 50-passenger airplane outfitted with carriers where reclining seats for humans would normally be. With fares starting at just $149, the company caters to vacationers, people who are relocating, those who are rescuing or adopting pets, and others who want a more secure method of travel for their pets. Nearly 1 million pets fly on airlines each year. "Instead of trying to convince human airlines to treat pets better, [we thought] 'why not start an airline just for pets?'" says Binder. "Everything we do is for the individual 'pawsengers.'" Pets receive a preflight organic meal and walk, and an onboard certified pet attendant checks the pets every 15 minutes. Pet Airways currently flies out of 9 regional airports but plans to expand service to 25 cities across the United States and Canada.[19]

"Small business is uniquely positioned for niche marketing," says marketing expert Phil Kotler. "If a small business sits down and follows the principles of targeting, segmenting, and differentiating, it doesn't have to collapse to larger companies."[20]

USE THE POWER OF PUBLICITY. **Publicity** is any commercial news covered by the media that boosts sales but for which a small company does not pay. Publicity has power; because it is from an unbiased source, a news feature about a company or a product that appears in a newspaper or magazine has more impact on people's buying decisions than an advertisement does. Exposure in any medium raises a company's visibility and boosts sales, and, best of all, publicity is free! It does require some creativity and effort, however. Entrepreneurs generate publicity in a multitude of ways, ranging from sponsoring a seminar and supporting a charity to writing an article for publication and creating an offbeat contest.

ENTREPRENEURIAL
Profile

*Nathan Handwerker
and Nathan's Famous
Frankfurters*

Contestants compete in Nathan's Famous Frankfurter's annual hot dog eating contest at Coney Island, where the company was founded in 1916.

Source: Stan Honda\Getty Images, Inc. AFP

Founded in 1916 by Nathan Handwerker, Nathan's Famous Frankfurters sponsors its popular hot dog eating contest every July 4 on New York's Coney Island. Contestants vying for the title attempt to eat as many hot dogs as they can in just 12 minutes. (The record, held by Joey Chestnut, is 68 hot dogs). Conducted every year since 1916, the contest has become so popular that more than 30,000 spectators gather at the company's original location and 1.5 million households watch it live on ESPN, generating huge amounts of publicity for the company![21]

DON'T JUST SELL; ENTERTAIN. Numerous surveys have shown that consumers are bored with shopping and that they are less inclined to spend their scarce leisure time shopping than ever before. Winning customers today requires more than low prices and wide merchandise selection; increasingly, businesses are adopting strategies based on **entertailing**, the notion of drawing customers into a store by creating a kaleidoscope of sights, sounds, smells, and activities, all designed to entertain—and, of course, sell (think Disney). The primary goal of entertailing is to catch customers' attention and engage them in some kind of entertaining experience so that they shop longer and buy more goods or services. Entertailing involves "making [shopping] more fun, more educational, more interactive," says one retail consultant.[22] Research supports the benefits of entertailing's hands-on, interactive, educational, approach to selling; one study reports that, when making a purchase, 34 percent of consumers are driven more by emotional factors such as fun and excitement than by logical factors such as price and convenience.[23] Entertailing's goal, of course, is not only to entertain but also to sell.

ENTREPRENEURIAL
Profile

*Navin Megji and Feature
and Laura Howe and
Matrushka Construction*

Navin Megji, founder of Feature, a chic clothing boutique located on San Vincente Boulevard in Brentwood, California, relies heavily on entertailing to draw customers to her store. "There's not a lot of walk-in traffic," she explains, which means making her store a destination all the more important. Megji has hosted after-hours trunk shows, "meet the designer" events with the designers of her funky clothing and accessory lines, and cupcake and cocktail parties. The $200 she spends on drinks and food for each event "is a minimal cost for the amount of business it brings in," says Megji.

Laura Howe, owner of Matrushka Construction, another clothing and accessories boutique located on Los Angeles's famous Sunset Boulevard, has been using entertailing as a guerrilla marketing strategy since she opened her shop in 2003. Howe, who designs and builds many of the garments she sells, has hosted performances by dance troupes, art shows, movie nights, fashion shows, and a unique T-Construction night at which customers design their own T-shirts by choosing various pieces and have them sewn together on the spot. "Customers [enjoy] feeling like they are part of something," she says. "That energy really translates because people feel like there's more going on."[24]

CONNECT WITH CUSTOMERS ON AN EMOTIONAL LEVEL. Some of the most powerful marketers are those companies that have a clear sense of who they are, what they stand for, and why they exist. Defining their vision for their companies in a meaningful way is one of the most challenging tasks facing entrepreneurs. That vision stems from the beliefs and values of the entrepreneur and is reflected in a company's culture, ethics, and business strategy. Although it is intangible, this vision is a crucial ingredient in a successful guerrilla marketing campaign. Once this vision is firmly planted, guerrilla marketers can use it to connect with their customers. Harley-Davidson, the maker of classic motorcycles with that trademark throaty rumble, has established an emotional connection with its customers that many other businesses only dream of. Clint Harris of Buckeye Lake, Ohio, was such a devoted fan of the motorcycle maker that when he died, he had a replica of his motorcycle (complete with his and his wife's biker nicknames, Heavy and Ruffy, engraved on it) made to serve as a headstone.[25]

Companies that establish deeper relationships with their customers rather than one based merely on making a sale have the capacity to be exceptional guerrilla marketers. These businesses win because customers receive an emotional boost every time they buy the company's product or service. Companies connect with their customers emotionally by supporting causes that are important to their customer base, sponsoring events that are of interest to their customers, taking exceptional care of their customers, and making it fun and enjoyable to do business with them.

ENTREPRENEURIAL Profile

Missy Park and Title Nine

When she was a collegiate athlete in the 1980s, Missy Park was disheartened by the absence of athletic gear made specifically for women. "We wore men's shorts," says the former Yale basketball player. "There was no women's basketball shoe. Jog bras didn't even exist." Spotting a business opportunity, Park launched a mail-order company that sold women's athletic apparel from the garage of her Emeryville, California, home in 1989. Today, Park's business, Title Nine, is a multimillion-dollar company with 15 retail stores, a popular Web site, and thousands of loyal customers. Park finds many ways to connect with her company's customers. Title Nine's catalog and Web site feature "real women" as models (they include an architect, a nurse, and a teacher), inspirational profiles of customers, and a candid blog called "Missy's Musings" written by Park herself. Title Nine also organizes numerous athletic events, including hikes, bicycling tours, and a Mother's Day run, that are designed to transform regular customers into friends and ambassadors for the business.[26]

BUILD A CONSISTENT BRANDING STRATEGY. Establishing an emotional bond with its customers is the first step to building a successful brand. Branding involves creating a distinct identity for a business and requires a well-coordinated effort at every touch point a company has with its customers. A brand represents a company's "personality," and entrepreneurs should spell out their companies' brand strategy in the business plan. In an age where companies find standing out from the crowd of competitors increasingly difficult, branding strategies have taken on much greater importance. The foundation of a successful brand is providing a quality product or superior customer service that meets or, preferably, *exceeds* customers' expectations. One way to do this is by defining exactly how your company's product or service solves a problem your customers face, preferably in a unique fashion, and communicating it to your customers. Green Mountain Coffee Roasters in Waterbury, Vermont, has built a strong brand by not only creating a better cup of coffee but also by doing its part to create a better world by embracing environmental sustainability and organic growing methods and supporting local communities through charitable donations. Although entrepreneurs lack the resources to invest in building a brand that Coca-Cola and Google do (Coca-Cola's brand alone is estimated to be worth more than *$70 billion*), they can take steps to add value to their companies' images through branding. One important step is to develop consistent logos, letterheads, graphics, packaging, and décor that serve as visual ambassadors for the company, communicating its desired image, values, and personality at a glance. Caribou Coffee, the nation's second largest chain of coffee stores, recently introduced a brand makeover built around the theme "Life is short. Stay awake for it."[27]

Another aspect of creating a successful brand is to transform existing customers into evangelists for the company and its products by keeping them happy. Convincing celebrities to endorse a brand also helps.

ENTREPRENEURIAL
Profile

Jim Amos and Tasti D-Lite

When Tasti D-Lite, a popular chain that sells frozen dairy desserts that taste like ice cream but contain fewer calories and less fat, opened its first store in Nashville, Tennessee, country music star Taylor Swift posted an enthusiastic message on Twitter that garnered attention for the company. "We're getting a Tasti D-Lite in Nashville," she tweeted. "YES!!" CEO Jim Amos also wanted to encourage the company's less famous customers to promote Tasti D-Lite online and invested in a computerized checkout system that automatically posts tweets to the accounts of members of the company's loyalty program (who earn points toward free treats with each purchase, Tweet, or Facebook post). "Word-of-mouth marketing has always been extremely important to this company, but Twitter has the capacity to increase word-of-mouth discussions exponentially," says Amos.[28]

EMBRACE SOCIAL NETWORKING. Social networking sites such as Facebook, LinkedIn, and Twitter allow companies and their customers to interact in ways that were not possible before, and smart entrepreneurs are using those sites to their advantage. Globally, online users now spend an average of 5 hours and 28 minutes per month on social networking sites, and small businesses are increasingly making connections with customers on those sites.[29] One recent study reports that companies that are highly engaged in social media significantly outperform in both revenues and profits those companies that are less engaged.[30]

Despite the popularity and potential profitability of social networking sites, however, only 24 percent (up from 12 percent the previous year) of small business owners use social media to attract new customers or to connect with existing ones.[31] Although sites such as Facebook and Twitter are better known for their social applications, they can also be powerful—and inexpensive—marketing tools for small companies. More than 40 percent of companies using social networking sites report landing at least one customer from their efforts (see Figure 4). Because implementing an effective social marketing strategy demands a significant investment of time (50 percent of business owners who use social media report that doing so demands more time than they had expected), some entrepreneurs outsource their social marketing efforts to companies that specialize in social media.[32]

Twitter, with nearly 20 million visitors to its Web site each year (many of them accessing the site from a mobile device), has become a popular social networking site where users post timely messages ("Tweets") consisting of no more than 140 characters.[33] Just 9 percent of small businesses use Twitter as a marketing tool, but the number of Twitter business users is growing

FIGURE 4
Acquiring Customers via Social Media

Source: The State of Inbound Marketing 2010, HubSpot, p. 11. www.hubspot.com/Portals/53/docs/resellers/reports/state_of_inbound_marketing.pdf.

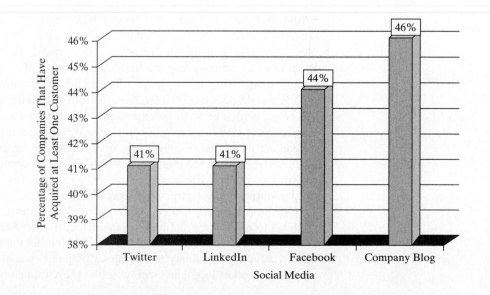

rapidly.[34] According to research by HubSpot, businesses that use Twitter generate twice as many sales leads as companies that do not.[35] Small companies use Twitter to listen to feedback from their customers or to update them about special events, sales, and promotions.

ENTREPRENEURIAL
Profile

Candace Nelson and Sprinkles

Sprinkles, a small chain of gourmet cupcake stores, uses "whisper" Tweets to attract customers to its stores.

Source: Jenny Brown/WENN.com/Newscom

Sprinkles, a small chain of gourmet cupcake stores that Candace Nelson started in 2005 in Beverly Hills, California, posts clever "whisper" Tweets about twice a week that include a code word such as "raspberry" or "peanut butter." Customers (typically limited to the first 25) who visit one of the company's eight stores and whisper the magic word receive a free cupcake. The Tweets have been very successful because they not only produce immediate results ("Within minutes of posting, we get customers in our store redeeming our promotions," says a Sprinkles manager), but they also keep the company's name in customers' minds.[36]

Another social media site, Facebook, remains popular among college students, but 63.3 percent of its more than 400 million users (70 percent of whom live outside the United States) are over the age of 25.[37] Because its online volume of traffic is immense, Facebook offers several business-oriented features, including a survey tool that allows business users to conduct market research and an option that lets businesses create Facebook pages ("public profiles") that they can use to connect with potential customers, post photographs, and promote events. In addition to reaching potential customers, establishing a business presence on social networking sites increases a company's visibility because search engines are able to locate social network pages.

ENTREPRENEURIAL
Profile

Peter Morse and James Store

Shortly after launching a Web site, the James Store, a women and children's clothing store founded in 1947 in Granville, Ohio, began using Facebook to "build relationships and communicate with customers both locally, around the country, and around the world," says Peter Morse, the company's marketing director. "So many people use Facebook that it was important for the James Store to be there." The James Store rewards its fans with coupons that are available only on its Facebook page. The coupons "drove new fans to our Facebook page, which in turn drove foot traffic to the store," says Morse. The company also uses Twitter to post Tweets that automatically become updates on its Facebook page. A recent Tweet about a sale on Vera Bradley bags generated orders from customers across the United States.[38]

START A BLOG. A Web log ("blog") is a frequently updated online personal journal that contains a writer's ideas on a multitude of topics with links to related sites. The proliferation of blogs has been stupendous; everyone from teenagers to giant corporations has created blogs. BlogPulse, a company that tracks blogs, estimates that 127 million blogs exist online, with 42,000 more being added daily.[39] Research by the University of Massachusetts Dartmouth, reports that 45 percent of the *Inc.* 500, the fastest-growing small companies in the United States, use blogs, compared to 39 percent of all small businesses.[40] The most successful small business blogs are not just remakes of a company's Web site with thinly veiled marketing messages but instead are those that tell interesting stories from the perspective of an industry (and company) insider. The key to successful business blogging is to create a blog that provides useful industry information but that also is entertaining. Web sites such as Ninjablogsetup, Word Press, Blogger, or LiveJournal make it easy for entrepreneurs to start blogging.

Business blogging can be an effective part of a guerrilla marketing strategy, enabling entrepreneurs to reach large numbers of potential customers very economically. Blogs help to establish a business owner as an expert in the field, attract the attention of potential customers, and boost a company's visibility and its sales. Companies post their blogs, promote them on their Web sites and on other blogs, and then watch as the viral nature of the Web takes over with visitors posting comments and e-mailing their friends about the blog. In fact, many small companies allow customers to contribute to their blogs, offering the potential for one of the most valuable marketing tools: unsolicited endorsements from satisfied users. Blogging's informal dialogue is an ideal match for small companies, whose cultures and style tend to be informal.

Blogs can serve many business purposes, including keeping customers updated on new products, enhancing customer service, and promoting the company. Increasingly, they are becoming mainstream features on business Web sites. If monitored regularly, blogs also can give entrepreneurs keen insight into customers' viewpoints and preferences in ways that few other techniques can. One business writer says that blogs are "like never-ending focus groups."[41] Creating a blog is not risk-free, however. Companies must be prepared to deal with negative feedback from some visitors.

CREATE ONLINE VIDEOS. Video hosting sites such as YouTube give creative entrepreneurs the opportunity to promote their businesses at no cost by creating videos that feature their company's products and services in action. Unlike television ads, uploading a video to YouTube costs nothing, and in some cases the videos reach millions of potential customers. Internet users watch 31 billion videos online each month (YouTube is the most popular viewing venue), and the average online viewer watches 12.2 hours of video per month.[42] The Pew Internet and American Life Project reports that 62 percent of adult Internet users have watched videos online.[43] Online videos do not have to be of professional quality to be effective; in fact, some of the most successful videos boast a distinctive "amateur" look.

The goal is to increase awareness of a company, drive traffic to its Web site or store, and increase sales. To market their companies successfully on YouTube, entrepreneurs should:

- *Think "edutainment."* Some of the most successful online videos combine both educational content and entertainment. FrontPoint Security, a McLean, Virginia-based company that makes home security systems that customers can install themselves, created a series of video tutorials that showed how their systems work and how install them in just 2 minutes. The videos were downloaded thousands of times, and FrontPoint managers have seen a 250 percent increase in the number of sales leads generated by its Web site.[44]
- *Be funny.* A common denominator among many successful online videos is humor. For businesses, the key is to link the humor in the video to the company's product or service and its customer benefits.

ENTREPRENEURIAL
Profile

Steve Aylsworth and Jet Luxury Resorts

To promote its services, Jet Luxury Resorts, a company that markets vacation rentals at Las Vegas hotels and condominiums, created a video called "The Bright Side of Life" that features a virile, bare-chested young man surrounded by beautiful women living it up in a Las Vegas penthouse. The end of the video reveals that the entire sequence is just part of a geriatric man's dream. The video, which runs slightly longer than 1 minute, has been downloaded nearly 250,000 times and won a spot on "The World's Funniest Commercials." Steve Aylsworth, chief operating officer of Jet Luxury Resorts, says, "We wanted to achieve two things: increase sales and increase our brand recognition." After the video caught on, the company saw a 50 percent increase in its Web traffic and a 20 percent increase in sales.[45]

- *Post videos on multiple social media sites.* Customers are more likely to see a video when a company makes it available on multiple social media sites. Mike Matuska, owner of Big Plush, an online store that sells more than 600 types of stuffed animals, created a homemade video about an 18-foot stuffed snake on top of a car and used TrafficGeyser to automatically post it to more than 100 video-sharing sites. He also posted it to his Facebook, Twitter, and MySpace accounts. Big Plush's simple, low-cost video has received more than 250,000 hits![46]
- *Focus on a point of differentiation.* "Differentiate your [company] with a video that shows the 'obvious' ('We make a lot of bubble gum') in a fun and visually powerful way," says one entrepreneur who specializes in video production. "Your competitors, meanwhile, are still trying to sell [using] stock statements or cliché slogans ('We care about quality' or 'Our customers are important to us'). Customers will see your company as cutting edge, fun, innovative, and personable because of your willingness to put faces behind what you build."[47] It's the ideal video recipe for small businesses.

Percentage of Small Business Owners Who Say They...

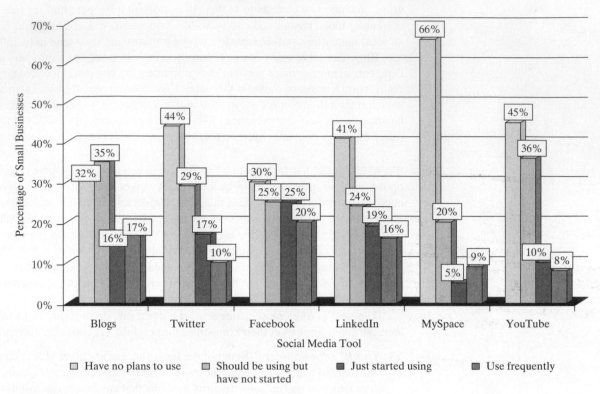

FIGURE 5
Small Business and Social Media Usage

Source: Constant Contact Small Business Attitudes Outlook Survey, June 18, 2009.

■ *Keep it short.* The average online video is 4 minutes long.[48] For a video to produce maximum benefit, it should be between 1 and 3 minutes long. Short videos are more viral than long ones.

Figure 5 shows how owners of small companies view the use of these social media tools.

STRIVE TO BE UNIQUE. One of the most effective guerrilla marketing tactics is to create an image of uniqueness for your business. Entrepreneurs can achieve a unique place in the market in a variety of ways, including through the products and services they offer, the marketing and promotional campaigns they use, the store layouts they design, and the business strategies they employ. The goal is to stand out from the crowd; few things are as uninspiring to customers as a "me-too" business that offers nothing unique.

ENTREPRENEURIAL
Profile

Bill Mason and Paleo-Bond

In 1992, paleontologist Bill Mason started Paleo-Bond, a company whose unique product line serves as its point of differentiation. Paleo-Bond sells a line of stabilizers and adhesives that are designed to prepare, preserve, and display fossils. Some of the company's bonding agents act as super-strong glues, bonding giant dinosaur bones to one another; others actually penetrate the fossil, filling tiny cracks and fissures. Paleo-Bond also sells a product that coats meteorites (which have high iron content) to prevent them from corroding. The St. Paul, Minnesota-based company generates $1 million in annual sales.[49]

FOCUS ON THE CUSTOMER. Many companies have lost sight of the most important component of every business: the customer. Businesses finally are waking up to the true costs of poor customer relations. A study by market research firm Genesys reports that businesses in the United States lose $83 billion in sales each year in abandoned sales or defections to competitors because of poor customer service.[50] The Retail Customer Dissatisfaction Study, conducted by the Jay H. Baker Retailing Initiative at the University of Pennsylvania and consulting firm Verde Group, reports that:

- Seventy-one percent of customers in the United States have defected to a competing business because of a poor customer service experience with a company.[51]
- For every complaint that a company receives from a customer, 17 other complaints exist, but the company never hears about them.
- Thirty-one percent of dissatisfied customers tell family members, friends, and colleagues about their negative experience with a company.
- Six percent of those people tell their "horror stories" to six or more people.
- Negative word of mouth has exponential power. For every 100 customers who have a negative experience with a business, the company stands to lose 32 to 36 current customers or potential customers.[52]

Because most of a company's sales come from existing customers, no business can afford to alienate them.

The most successful small businesses have developed a customer orientation and have instilled an attitude of customer satisfaction throughout the company. Companies with world-class customer attitudes set themselves apart by paying attention to the little things.

ENTREPRENEURIAL
Profile

Donna Flanagin and Flanagin's Bulk Mail

When customers with children enter Flanagin's Bulk Mail, a company in Valparaiso, Indiana, that specializes in mailing lists and bulk mail services, owner Donna Flanagin offers the children crayons and a coloring sheet so that they can create pictures that she displays on the front door. Flanagin sends children their drawings with a card on their birthdays. "It costs virtually nothing," observes Bruce Jones, director of the Disney Institute, "yet it reminds the parents and grandparents about her business and helps make a connection with her customers."[53]

How do these companies focus so intently on their customers? They follow basic principles:

- When you create a dissatisfied customer, fix the problem fast. One study found that, given the chance to complain, 95 percent of customers will buy again if a business handles their complaints promptly and effectively.[54] The worst way to handle a complaint is to ignore it, to pass it off to a subordinate, or to let a lot of time slip by before dealing with it.
- *Encourage* customer complaints. You can't fix something if you don't know it's broken, but once you know, be sure to fix it!
- Ask employees for feedback on improving customer service. A study by Technical Assistance Research Programs (TARP), a customer service research firm, found that frontline service workers can predict nearly 90 percent of the cases that produce customer complaints.[55] Put that expertise to work by involving frontline employees in process improvement efforts. Emphasize that *everyone* is part of the customer satisfaction team.
- Get total commitment to superior customer service from top managers and allocate resources appropriately.
- Allow managers to wait on customers occasionally. It's a great dose of reality. Dell CEO Michael Dell and his team of top managers meet periodically with the company's major customers to get a better understanding of how to serve their needs more effectively.[56]
- Develop a service theme that communicates your attitude toward customers. Customers want to feel they are getting something special.
- Reward employees "caught" providing exceptional service to customers. At ScriptSave, a company that manages prescription-drug benefit programs, managers hand out Bravo Bucks that are redeemable for gifts to employees who excel in providing superior customer service.[57]
- Carefully select and train everyone who deals with customers. According to the Genesys study of customer satisfaction, the most important factor in providing a satisfying customer service experience is competent sales and customer service representatives.[58] Smart entrepreneurs view training for what it is: an investment rather than an expense.
- *Never* let rude employees work with customers. Charlie Horn, CEO of ScriptSave, requires all customer service representatives to go through 3 weeks of training before taking their first telephone call from a customer. Each representative also gets an additional 60 hours of classroom training in customer service techniques.[59]

IN THE ENTREPRENEURIAL
SPOTLIGHT The Ultimate Question

John Ratliff, CEO of Appletree Answering Services, a Wilmington, Delaware-based company that operates 12 call centers, is a successful, fast-growing small company. With annual revenues exceeding $12 million, Appletree employees answer 70,000 telephone calls in a typical day for its customers, who include doctors and lawyers, for whom it provides messaging services, and companies of all sizes, for which it provides after-hours service support. "Our customers depend on our services every day," says Ratliff. "That puts us on a hyper-track for both good and bad customer experiences."

To measure the quality of customers' experience with Appletree, Ratliff turned to a simple measure called the Net Promoter Score (NPS). Developed by Fred Reichheld, a consultant for Bain and Company, the NPS asks customers just two questions:

1. How likely are you to recommend our company to friends and colleagues?
2. If you would not recommend us, why not?

On question 1, which Reichheld calls "the Ultimate Question," the NPS uses a 1 (not at all likely) to 10 (highly likely) scale. Customers who respond with nines and tens are considered "promoters" those who score a company with sevens and eights are "passives." Any customer who rates a company below a seven is considered to be a "detractor." To calculate its NPS, a company subtracts the percentage of detractors from the percentage of promoters. For example, a company that has 60 percent promoters, 25 percent passives, and 15 percent detractors has an NPS of 45 (60% − 15% = 45%).

Reichheld says that the NPS is a nearly ideal measure of a company's reputation in the marketplace and its ability to attract new customers and to retain existing ones. The average NPS for companies in the United States is 11, with promoters just barely outnumbering detractors. Most companies achieve promoter scores between 10 and 20, but the best businesses score a commanding 75 to 90. (Motorcycle maker Harley-Davidson has an NPS of 81, restaurant chain Chick-Fil-A scores a 79, and online retailer Amazon receives a 73.) Research by Bain and Company shows that companies that achieve the highest long-term profitable growth rates have NPS scores that are twice the industry average. "At small, fast-growing companies, more than half of new business comes from referrals, not advertising," explains Reichheld. "Our research reveals that in most industries, the firms with the highest NPS scores have the strongest profits and healthiest growth." NPS leaders outgrow their competitors by an average of 2.5 times.

According to research by Bain, 80 percent of managers believe that their companies provide superior customer service, but only 8 percent of their customers agree. "Most customers of the average firm—more than two-thirds—are either passive about the company or are downright detractors," Reichheld explains. "Once you find out who they are and why they're ticked off, you can take [corrective] action." NPS is an effective measure because it forces everyone in the company to focus on creating satisfied customers. "If customers are willing to promote you, that's the clearest indication of loyalty," says Reichheld.

NPS surveys are ideal for small businesses. They are easy and inexpensive to administer by telephone, mail, e-mail, or in person. Response rates also tend to be high—20 to 30 percent compared to 10 percent or less for traditional surveys—because, unlike most customer satisfaction surveys, the NPS survey takes only moments to complete. Every quarter, Appletree surveys all of its 5,600 customers and has a consistent response rate of 20 percent. The results are easy to tally, and entrepreneurs can communicate them to everyone in the company in an easy-to-understand way. Ratliff makes sure that every employee knows Appletree's NPS as soon as the results are tallied. To use the NPS effectively, small companies should:

- Show employees how their actions affect the company's NPS; empower frontline employees to take the necessary steps to improve customer satisfaction.
- Align incentives with NPS: NPS improvements = Increased profits = Employee bonuses and rewards.
- Recognize the employees or departments that produce the highest NPS; determine the best practices in the company and make them the foundation for training others.

When Appletree conducted its initial NPS survey, the company scored a rather unimpressive 26, which Ratliff says provided an important wake-up call. A consistent customer complaint was the inability to resolve billing issues in just a single call. Ratliff responded by empowering Appletree's service representatives to resolve customers' billing problems and allowing them to waive computer-generated late fees. The NPS survey also told Ratliff that the company's most satisfied customers raved about the way the company was able to customize its answering services to their specific needs. Building on that positive feedback, Ratliff standardized the process so that every new customer receives a customized "welcome experience." The changes are working. In its latest NPS survey, Appletree's NPS climbed to 56. The benefits to the company have marched in step with the improvements in its NPS. Customer referrals have increased by 200 percent, and the customer retention rate, sales, and profits have increased as well.

1. Is the NPS an effective way to measure customer satisfaction? What are the advantages and the disadvantages of using the NPS to measure customer satisfaction?
2. What benefits does calculating the NPS provide to a small company?

3. Select two companies in your area, one that you consider to offer superior customer service and one that does not. Select a (preferably random) sample of customers of each company and ask them to answer the NPS survey's questions. Tally the results. What conclusions can you draw from your analysis? What recommendations would you make to the business's owner?

Sources: Based on Justin Martin, "Get Customers to Sell for You," *FSB*, May 2008, *http://money.cnn.com/2008/05/21/smallbusiness/customers_ sell_for_you.fsb/index.htm;* Darren Dahl, "Would You Recommend Us?" *Inc.*, September 2006, pp. 40–42; Russ Banham, "Angry and Bored? You Must Be a Customer," *CFO*, July 2006, pp. 62–67; Scott Thurm, "One Question, and Plenty of Debate," *Wall Street Journal*, December 4, 2006, p. B3; "Measuring Your Net Promoter Score," The Ultimate Question, *www.theultimatequestion.com/theultimatequestion/measuring_netpromoter. asp?groupCode=2.*

RETAIN EXISTING CUSTOMERS. Loyal, long-term customers are the bedrock of every business. High customer retention rates translate into superior financial performance. Studies by the Boston Consulting Group show that companies with high customer retention rates produce above-average profits and superior growth in market share.[60] Increasing a company's retention rate by just 2 percent has the same impact as cutting expenses by 10 percent![61]

Because about 20 to 30 percent of a typical company's customers account for about 70 to 80 percent of its sales, it makes more sense to focus resources on keeping the best (and most profitable) customers than to spend them trying to chase "fair weather" customers who will defect to any better deal that comes along. Suppose that a company increases its customer base by 20 percent each year, but it retains only 85 percent of its existing customers. Its effective growth rate is just 5 percent per year [20% − (100% − 85%) = 5%]. If this same company can raise its customer retention rate to 95 percent, its net growth rate *triples* to 15 percent [20% − (100% − 95%) = 15%].[62]

Shrewd entrepreneurs recognize that the greatest opportunity for new business often comes from existing customers.

ENTREPRENEURIAL Profile

Faryl Robin Morse and Faryl Robin LLC

During a recent economic downturn, Faryl Robin LLC, a New York City–based company that sells stylish women's shoes priced between $170 and $350 a pair online and through retailers, began offering long-time customers longer credit terms as a reward for their loyalty. Faryl Robin, with annual sales of $4.5 million, also reduced the size of its minimum orders, allowing its retail customers to place orders as small as just nine pairs of shoes. Founder Faryl Robin Morse also began spending more time in her customers' stores, helping them sell shoes and training their staffs on sales techniques. The result: the company retained its customer base and saw sales increase 20 percent. Without the focus on customer retention, says Morse, "it is possible [that] we would have lost some customers."[63]

Although winning new customers keeps a company growing, keeping existing ones is essential to success. Research shows that repeat customers spend 67 percent more than new customers. In addition, attracting a new customer actually costs the typical business *seven to nine times* as much as selling to an existing one.[64] Table 1 shows the high cost of lost customers and the steps entrepreneurs can take to improve their customer retention rates.

The formula for marketing success is simple (but sometimes difficult to practice): Retain existing customers, enhance relationships with them, and attract new customers like them. In other words, entrepreneurs are better off asking, "How can we improve customer value and service to encourage our existing customers to do more business with us?" rather than "How

TABLE 1 The High Cost of Lost Customers

If you lose . . .	Spending $5 weekly	Spending $10 weekly	Spending $50 weekly	Spending $100 weekly	Spending $200 weekly	Spending $300 weekly
1 customer a day	$94,900	$189,800	$949,000	$1,898,000	$3,796,000	$5,694,000
2 customers a day	189,800	379,600	1,898,000	3,796,000	7,592,000	11,388,000
5 customers a day	474,500	949,000	4,745,000	9,490,000	18,980,000	28,470,000
10 customers a day	949,000	1,898,000	9,490,000	18,980,000	37,960,000	56,940,000
20 customers a day	1,898,000	3,796,000	18,980,000	37,960,000	75,920,000	113,880,000
50 customers a day	4,745,000	9,490,000	47,450,000	94,900,000	189,800,000	284,700,000
100 customers a day	9,490,000	18,980,000	94,900,000	189,800,000	379,600,000	569,400,000

When entrepreneurs understand the actual cost of losing a customer, they see their existing customers in a different way. What steps can business owners take to improve their customer retention rates?

1. *Contact your company's best customers regularly.* Identify the customers that account for 75 to 80 percent of your company's sales and call them (better yet, visit them) at least once every quarter.

2. *Keep your company's name in front of your customers.* You can accomplish this by consistently advertising, sending useful newsletters or e-mails, sponsoring workshops, seminars, or special events, or visiting customers to learn how your company can serve them better.

3. *Reward existing customers, especially long-time customers, with special deals exclusively for them.* It might be a special sale or a bonus discount.

4. *Surprise existing customers by giving them something extra.* In Louisiana, locals call it a lagniappe ("lan-yap"), a small gift that a merchant gives to a customer. Send loyal customers a special gift or include an extra "bonus" in their next order. It does not have to be expensive to be effective. For instance, when customers make a sizeable purchase at Wilson Creek Outfitters, a fly fishing shop in Morganton, North Carolina, the owner includes a dozen flies in the order for free. The cost of the lagniappe is minimal, but the goodwill and loyalty it garners is significant.

5. *Keep track of your customers and their needs.* Take the time to build a database of your customers, their contact information, and other relevant information about them and their needs.

6. *Don't take your company's customers for granted.* Your competitors are trying to lure them away; don't give them a reason to go! Avoid the tendency to become so inwardly focused that your company forgets about the importance of its customers.

Sources: Based on Customer Service Institute, 1010 Wayne Avenue, Silver Spring, Maryland, 20910; Rhonda Abrams, "Strategies: Make Customer Retention Priority," *USA Today*, May 29, 2009, *www.usatoday.com/money/smallbusiness/columnist/abrams/2009-05-29-customer-retention_N.htm*.

can we increase our market share by 10 percent?" One way that small companies can entice current customers to keep coming back is with a loyalty program (e.g., a car wash offering a punch card that gives customers one free wash after they purchase nine washes). Perhaps the most effective way for a business to build customer loyalty is to sell quality products and to offer outstanding customer service. A study by Forrester Research shows that a good customer experience correlates to customers' willingness to make repeat purchases from a company, reluctance to switch to a competing company, and likelihood of recommending the company to friends and colleagues.[65]

DEVOTION TO QUALITY. In this intensely competitive global business environment, quality goods and services are a prerequisite for success—and even survival. According to one marketing axiom, the worst of all marketing catastrophes is to have great advertising and a poor-quality product. Customers have come to expect and demand quality goods and services, and those businesses that provide them consistently have a distinct competitive advantage.

ENTREPRENEURIAL
Profile

John Stollenwerk and Allen Edmonds Shoe Corporation

Founded in 1922, shoemaker Allen Edmonds has resisted the temptation to move its production out of the United States to offshore locations, where costs are lower, choosing instead to focus on making quality men's footwear in the United States. In factories in Wisconsin and Maine, highly skilled craftsmen continue to build Allen Edmonds shoes, which sell for $200 to $400 a pair, by hand, following a 212-step process. "It's all about the shoes," says CEO John Stollenwerk. "I believe that Allen Edmonds can make them better and serve customers faster in the United States."[66]

FIGURE 6
The Quality DMAIC Process

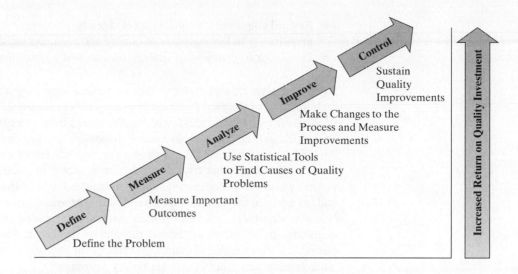

Control
Sustain Quality Improvements

Improve
Make Changes to the Process and Measure Improvements

Analyze
Use Statistical Tools to Find Causes of Quality Problems

Measure
Measure Important Outcomes

Define
Define the Problem

Increased Return on Quality Investment

Today, quality is more than just a slogan posted on the company bulletin board; world-class companies treat quality as a strategic objective—an integral part of the company culture. This philosophy is called **total quality management (TQM)**—quality not just in the product or service itself but also in *every* aspect of the business and its relationship with the customer and in continuous improvement in the quality delivered to customers. Companies achieve continuous improvement by using statistical techniques to discover problems, determine their causes, and solve them; then they must incorporate what they have learned into improving the process. The ultimate goals of TQM are to avoid quality problems, reduce cycle time (the time between a customer's order and delivery of the finished product), reduce costs, and continuously improve the process. TQM's focus on continuous improvement is built on the define, measure, analyze, improve, and control (DMAIC) process illustrated in Figure 6.

Companies on the cutting edge of the quality movement are developing new ways to measure quality. Manufacturers were the first to apply TQM techniques, but retail, wholesale, and service organizations have seen the benefits of becoming champions of quality. They are tracking customer complaints, contacting "lost" customers, and finding new ways to track the cost of quality and their return on quality (ROQ). ROQ recognizes that although any improvement in quality may improve a company's competitive ability, only those improvements that produce a reasonable rate of return are worthwhile. In essence, ROQ requires managers to ensure that the quality improvements they implement will more than pay for themselves. Using basic quality principles, Allen Edmonds recently invested more than $1.5 million to redesign its Port Washington, Wisconsin, factory using principles of lean manufacturing (which focus on maximizing value for customers and minimizing waste), a move that not only improved quality but also increased worker productivity.[67]

Companies successful in capturing a reputation for top-quality products and services follow certain guidelines to "get it right the first time":

- Build quality into the process; don't rely on inspection to obtain quality.
- Emphasize simplicity in the design of products and processes; it reduces the opportunity for errors to sneak in.
- Foster teamwork and dismantle the barriers that divide disparate departments.
- Establish long-term ties with select suppliers; don't award contracts on low price alone.
- Provide managers and employees the training needed to participate fully in the quality improvement program.
- Empower workers at all levels of the organization; give them authority and responsibility for making decisions that determine quality.
- Get managers' commitment to the quality philosophy. Otherwise, the program is doomed. Describing his role in his company's TQM philosophy, one CEO says, "People look to see whether you just talk about it or actually do it."[68]
- Rethink the processes the company uses to get its products or services to customers. Employees at Analog Devices redesigned its production process and significantly lowered the defect rate on its silicon chips, saving $1.2 million a year.[69]

- Reward employees for quality work. Ideally, employees' compensation is linked clearly and directly to key measures of quality and customer satisfaction.
- Develop a company-wide strategy for constant improvement of product and service quality.

ATTENTION TO CONVENIENCE. Ask customers what they want from the businesses they deal with and one of the most common responses is "convenience." In this busy, fast-paced world of dual-career couples and lengthy commutes to and from work (the average commute time is now 25.1 minutes), consumers have more disposable income but less time in which to enjoy it. Anything a business can do to enhance convenience for its customers gives it an edge. Several studies have found that customers rank easy access to goods and services at the top of their purchase criteria. Unfortunately, many businesses fail to deliver adequate levels of convenience, and, as a result, they fail to attract and retain customers. Some companies make it a chore to do business with them, almost as if their owners have created an obstacle course for customers to negotiate. In an effort to defend themselves against a few unscrupulous customers, these businesses have created elaborate procedures for exchanges, refunds, writing checks, and other basic transactions that frustrate legitimate customers.

Successful companies go out of their way to make it easy for customers to do business with them. Many restaurants have created online tools and social networking applications that give customers the convenience and the speed of placing their meal orders online. Domino's Pizza recently celebrated crossing the $1 billion level in online sales.[70] Other restaurateurs enhance customer convenience by placing their restaurants on wheels and driving them to their customers.

ENTREPRENEURIAL
Profile

Mark Manguera,
Caroline Shin-Manguera,
and Roy Choi and Kogi
Korean BBQ

Mark Manguera, Caroline Shin-Manguera, and Roy Choi, cofounders of Kogi Korean BBQ in Los Angeles, also operate four food trucks that comb the greater Los Angeles area, selling their upscale menu of spicy pork tacos, kimchi quesadillas, short rib sliders, kogi dogs, and other items to hungry patrons. Drivers use Twitter to tell more than 50,000 followers about Chef Choi's daily specials and the trucks' schedules. On a typical night, as many as 800 people queue up at each truck every time they stop (usually several times each evening), and although most items on the menu are between $2 and $4, customers spend an average of nearly $20.[71]

Many small companies have had success by finding simple ways to make it easier for customers to do business with them. How can entrepreneurs boost the convenience levels of their businesses? By conducting a "convenience audit" from the customer's point of view to get an idea of its ETDBW ("Easy To Do Business With") index:

- Is your business located near your customers? Does it provide easy access?
- Are your business hours suitable to your customers? Should you be open evenings and weekends to serve them better?
- Would customers appreciate pickup and delivery service? The owner of a restaurant located near a major office complex installed a Web site and a fax machine to receive orders from busy office workers; a crew of employees delivered lunches to the workers at their desks!
- Does your business provide a sufficient number of checkout stations so that shoppers do not have to stand in long lines to make their purchases? Does your company make it easy for customers to make purchases on credit or with credit cards?
- Are you using technology to enhance customer convenience? At Stop & Shop, a grocery chain in New England, customers can save valuable time (and money) with the EasyShop, a handheld computer that scans items as customers place them in their carts and keeps a running total of their purchases. The device makes grocery shopping more efficient by displaying each shopper's buying history by aisle and notifying shoppers when the orders they have placed with the deli or seafood department are ready to pick up. Since introducing EasyShop, both sales and customer loyalty at Stop & Shop have increased.[72]
- Are your employees trained to handle business transactions quickly, efficiently, and politely? Waiting while rude, poorly trained employees fumble through routine transactions destroys customer goodwill.
- Do your employees use common courtesy when dealing with customers?

- Does your company offer "extras" that make customers' lives easier? With a phone call to Hoyt Hanvey Jewelers, a small jewelry and gift store in Clinton, South Carolina, customers in need of a special gift simply specify how much they want to spend, and the owner takes care of the rest—selecting the gift, wrapping it, and shipping it. All customers have to do is pay the invoice when it arrives in the mail.
- Can you adapt existing products to make them more convenient for customers? When J.M. Smucker Company began test-marketing a premade, frozen peanut butter and jelly sandwich with no crust, CEO Tim Smucker was amazed at the results. The sandwiches, called Uncrustables, generated $20 million in sales, and Smucker added them to its product line.[73]
- Does your company handle telephone calls quickly and efficiently? Long waits "on hold," transfers from one office to another, and too many rings before answering signal customers that they are not important. Jerre Stead, CEO of Ingram Micro Inc., a distributor of computer products, expects every telephone call to the company to be answered within 3 seconds![74]

CONCENTRATION ON INNOVATION. Innovation is the key to future success. Markets change too quickly and competitors move too fast for small companies to stand still and remain competitive; they must constantly innovate. Because of their organizational and managerial flexibility, small businesses often can detect and act on new opportunities faster than large companies. Innovation is one of the greatest strengths of entrepreneurs, and it shows up in the new products, unique techniques, and unusual approaches they introduce. A recent study by the Product Development and Management Association of the top performing companies across more than 400 industries revealed that new products accounted for 49 percent of profits, more than twice as much as their less innovative competitors.[75] Because product life cycles are growing shorter, innovation, even incremental innovation that makes small improvements in existing products, is essential to long-term business success.

Innovation is an important source of competitive advantage for small companies in any industry, not just those in high-tech sectors.

ENTREPRENEURIAL Profile

Juan Hinestroza and Abby Liebman and Abbey Rachel

Abbey Liebman, a senior in Cornell University's Apparel Design program, used technology developed by Juan Hinestroza, a professor of Fiber Science, to create a solar-powered dress that generates enough electricity to safely power and even charge a cell phone or an iPod. Hinestroza and a team of researchers developed a simple process for permanently coating cotton threads with semiconductor polymers and nanoparticles that allow the threads to conduct electricity as easily as metal wire yet maintain their softness and flexibility. Part of Liebman's Abbey Rachel line of clothing, the dress incorporates 12 flexible solar cells into its seams and a small USB charger located in a hidden pocket at the waist. With "traditional cotton fabrics becoming fully conductive, [there are] a myriad of applications of wearable electronics," says Hinestroza.[76]

There is more to innovation than spending megadollars on research and development. How do small businesses manage to maintain their leadership role in innovating new products and services? They use their size to their advantage, maintaining their speed and flexibility much like a martial arts expert does against a larger opponent.

To be an effective innovator, an entrepreneur should:

- *Make innovation a strategic priority in the company by devoting management time and energy to it.*
- *Measure the company's innovative ability.* Tracking the number of new products or services introduced and the proportion of sales that products younger than 5 years old generate can be useful measures of a company's ability to innovate.
- *Set goals and objectives for innovation.* Establishing targets and rewarding employees for achieving them can produce amazing results.
- *Encourage new product and service ideas among employees.* Workers have many incredible ideas, but they will only lead to new products or services if someone takes the time to listen to them.

■ *Listen to customers.* A study by management consulting firm Grant Thornton reports that customers are the primary source (41 percent) of innovations for companies globally, outranking employees, R&D teams, and managers.[77] A telephone call from the owner of a children's hair salon led Damon Carson, owner of Kiddie Rides, to a new market for the fiberglass figures his company makes for the children's rides that sit in shopping malls and centers: fun chairs for kids to sit in while they get their hair cut. Carson now actively seeks customer feedback as a source of new ideas for his company.[78]

■ *Study existing products and services to see how you can improve them.* Many innovations are the result of improving the performance of something that already exists.

■ *Always be on the lookout for new product and service ideas.* They can come to you (or to anyone inside or outside the company) at any time. Victor and Janie Tsao, founders of Linksys Inc., a company that has become a leader in the market for affordable wireless routers and hubs study exactly what customers want networking technology to do and then roll out products rapidly to meet those needs. Linksys' size and flexibility are major competitive weapons. "We launch a new product a week," says one top manager. "By the time our competitors realize what's going on, we're already at work on the next one."[79]

■ *Keep a steady stream of new products and services flowing.* Even before sales of her safety-handle children's toothbrush took off, Millie Thomas, founder of RGT Enterprises, had developed other children's products using the same triangular-shaped handle, including a crayon holder, paintbrushes, and fingernail brushes.[80]

Table 2 describes a screening device for testing the viability of new product ideas.

DEDICATION TO SERVICE AND CUSTOMER SATISFACTION. Small companies have discovered that providing superior personalized customer service can be a powerful strategic weapon against their larger rivals in whose stores customers often are ignored and have to serve themselves. Small companies that lack the financial resources of their larger rivals have discovered that offering exceptional customer service is one of the most effective ways to differentiate themselves and to attract and maintain a growing customer base. "It doesn't take money to [provide] good customer service," says the head of one retail company. "It takes a commitment."[81] Unfortunately, the level of service in most companies is poor. A study by Accenture shows that 67 percent of customers globally had switched at least one service provider within the last year because of poor customer service. The study also reports that an alarming 42 percent of global customers say that the quality of customer service they receive from companies is terrible, poor, or fair.[82]

TABLE 2 Testing the Viability of a New Product Idea

Testing the viability of new product ideas in their early stages of development can help entrepreneurs avoid expensive product failures later—after they have already invested significant amounts of cash in developing and launching them. The Chester Marketing Group, Inc., of Washington Crossing, Pennsylvania, has developed the following test to determine the viability of a new product idea at each stage in the product development process. To calculate a new product idea's score, entrepreneurs simply multiply the score for each criterion by its weight and then add up the resulting weighted scores. For a product to advance to the next stage in the development process, its score should be at least 16.

Criterion	Score			Weight	Weighted Score
Extent of target market need	Below average 1	Average 2	Above average 3	2	
Potential profitability	Below average 1	Average 2	Above average 3	2	
Likely emergence of competition	Below average 1	Average 2	Above average 3	1	
Service life cycle	Below average 1	Average 2	Above average 3	1	
Compatibility with company strengths	Below average 1	Average 2	Above average 3	2	
				Total	

Source: Roberta Maynard, "Test Your Product Idea," *Nation's Business*, October 1997, p. 23.

Successful businesses recognize that superior customer service is only an intermediate step toward the goal of customer satisfaction. They concentrate on providing customers with quality, convenience, and service as their customers define those terms. Certainly, the least expensive—and the most effective—way to achieve customer satisfaction is through friendly, personal service. Numerous surveys of customers in a wide diversity of industries, from manufacturing and services to banking and high technology, conclude that the most important element of service is "the personal touch." Indeed, a study conducted by market research firm NFO WorldGroup found that friendly service, not the food, is the primary reason customers return to a restaurant![83] Whatever the nature of the business, calling customers by name, making attentive, friendly contact, and truly caring about customers' needs and wants are more essential than any other factor, even convenience, quality, and speed!

How can a company achieve stellar customer service and satisfaction?

Hire the Right Employees. The key ingredient in the superior service equation is *people*. There is no substitute for friendly, courteous sales and service representatives. A customer service attitude requires hiring employees who believe in and embrace customer service. When it comes to the impact of customer retention on a company's profitability, a responsive, customer-centric employee is worth many times the value of an employee who provides average (or, worse yet, below average) customer service. "You hire people for their inherent skill," says Gary Danko, owner of a restaurant that recently won a prestigious customer service award. "You can teach them the mechanics."[84]

Train Employees to Deliver Superior Service. According to customers, the single most important factor in providing good customer service is having knowledgeable employees who are well informed, polite, and friendly.[85] Successful businesses train every employee who deals directly with customers; they don't leave the art of customer service to chance. Superior service companies devote 1 to 5 percent of their employees' work hours to training, concentrating on how to meet, greet, and serve customers. "Employees must be trained to instinctively provide good service," says John Tschol, founder of the Service Quality Institute.[86]

Listen to Customers. The best companies constantly listen to their customers and respond to what they hear! This allows them to keep up with customers' changing needs and expectations. The only way to find out what customers really want and value is to ask them. Businesses rely on a number of techniques including surveys, focus groups, telephone interviews, comment cards, suggestion boxes, toll-free hotlines, and regular one-on-one conversations with customers (perhaps the best technique).

ENTREPRENEURIAL
Profile

Marie Moody and Stella & Chewy's

Marie Moody, founder of Stella & Chewy's, a company that makes an all-natural line of premium frozen pet food, changed the freezing process to reduce the formation of ice crystals on the product and the company's packaging in response to customer feedback. After making the changes, Stella & Chewy's sales skyrocketed from $500,000 to more than $5 million in just 2 years.[87]

Define Superior Service. Based on what customers say, managers and employees must decide exactly what "superior service" means in the company. Such a statement should (1) be a strong statement of intent, (2) differentiate the company from others, and (3) have value to customers. Deluxe Corporation, a printer of personal checks, defines superior service quite simply: "Forty-eight hour turnaround; zero defects."

Set Standards and Measure Performance. To be able to deliver on its promise of superior service, a business must establish specific standards and measure overall performance against them. Satisfied customers should exhibit at least one of three behaviors: loyalty (increased customer retention rate), increased purchases (climbing sales and sales per customer), and resistance to rivals' attempts to lure them away with lower prices (market share and price tolerance).[88] Companies must track performance on these and other service standards and reward employees accordingly.

Examine Your Company's Service Cycle. What steps must a customer go through to get your product or service? Business owners often are surprised at the complexity that has seeped into their customer service systems as they have evolved over time. One of the most effective techniques is to work with employees to flowchart each component in the company's service cycle, including everything a customer has to do to get your product or service. The goal is to look for steps and procedures that are unnecessary, redundant, or unreasonable and eliminate them.

Empower Employees to Offer Superior Service. One of the most important variables in employees delivering superior service is whether they perceive they have permission to do so. The goal is to push decision making down the organization to the employees who have contact with customers. This includes giving them the freedom to circumvent company policy if it means improving customer satisfaction. At Ritz-Carlton Hotels, every employee is authorized to spend up to $2,000 to resolve a customer's complaint.[89] If frontline workers don't have the power to solve disgruntled customers' problems, they quickly become frustrated and the superior service cycle breaks down. To be empowered, employees need knowledge and information, adequate resources, and managerial support.

Use Technology to Provide Improved Service. The role of technology is not to create a rigid bureaucracy but to free employees from routine clerical tasks, giving them more time and better tools to serve customers more effectively. Ideally, technology gives workers the timely information they need to help their customers and the freedom to serve them. To boost customer service, Best Buy's Geek Squad, a response team that provides 24-hour support for home and business computers and networks, issues smart phones to its agents. Agents use the phones to find directions to customers' homes and businesses, pull up technical information on the computers they are repairing, store handwritten notes on the work they have done, and connect wirelessly with the entire IT system at company headquarters. The high-tech phones allow service agents not only to offer better customer service faster but also to complete the entire transaction on the spot by submitting billing or credit card information.[90]

Reward Superior Service. What gets rewarded gets done. Companies that want employees to provide stellar service must offer rewards for doing so.

Get Top Managers' Support. The drive toward superior customer service will fall far short of its target unless top managers support it fully. Success requires more than just a verbal commitment; it calls for managers' involvement and dedication. Periodically, managers should spend time in customer service positions to maintain contact with customers and frontline employees in order to understand the challenges of providing good service.

Give Customers an Unexpected (and Pleasant) Surprise. Companies can make a lasting, favorable impression on their customers by providing them with an unexpected surprise periodically. The surprise does not have to be expensive to be effective. For instance, every morning, Julian Niccolini, co-owner of New York's famous Four Season's restaurant, scours the newspaper, clipping articles that his best customers would find interesting or helpful.[91] Cast members at Disney's theme parks are empowered to hand out "magic moments" to guests of their choice. The moment might be a ride on a float in a Disney parade, a special visit from a Disney princess, or a night's stay in a special suite in Cinderella's Castle.

EMPHASIS ON SPEED. We live in a world of instantaneous expectations. Technology that produces immediate results at the click of a mouse and allows for real-time communication has altered our sense of time and space. Speed reigns. Customers now expect companies to serve them at the speed of light! In such a world, speed has become a major competitive weapon. With their smaller, nimbler, more flexible organizations, small companies have a natural advantage in speed over large companies, which are burdened with lumbering bureaucracies and a self-absorbed culture.

World-class companies recognize that reducing the time it takes to provide a service or to develop, design, manufacture, and distribute a product reduces costs, improves quality, and increases market share. One study by McKinsey and Company found that high-tech products that come to market on budget but 6 months late will earn 33 percent less profit over 5 years. Bringing the product out on time but 50 percent over budget cuts profits just 4 percent![92] Service companies also know that they must build speed into their business systems if they are to satisfy their impatient, time-sensitive customers.

This philosophy of speed is called **time compression management (TCM)**, and it involves three aspects: (1) speeding new products to market, (2) shortening customer response time in manufacturing and delivery, and (3) reducing the administrative time required to fill an order. Studies show plenty of room for improvement; most businesses waste 85 to 99 percent of the time it takes to produce products or services without ever realizing it![93] Although speeding up the manufacturing process is a common goal, companies using TCM have learned that manufacturing takes only 5 to 10 percent of the total time between taking an order and getting the product into the customer's hands. The rest is consumed by clerical and administrative tasks. The primary opportunity for TCM lies in its application to the administrative process.

Companies relying on TCM to help them turn speed into a competitive edge should:

- "Reengineer" the entire process rather than attempt to do the same things in the same way, only faster.
- Study every phase of the business process, whether it involves manufacturing, shipping, administration, or some other function, looking for small improvements that speed up the entire process.
- Create cross-functional teams of workers and give them the power to attack and solve problems. In world-class companies, product teams include engineers, manufacturers, salespeople, quality experts—even customers.
- Share information and ideas across the company. Easy access to meaningful information can speed a company's customer response time.
- Set aggressive goals for time reduction and stick to the schedule. Some companies using TCM have been able to reduce cycle time from several weeks to just a few hours!
- Instill speed in the culture. At Domino's Pizza, kitchen workers watch videos of the fastest pizza makers in the country.
- Use technology to find shortcuts wherever possible. Rather than build costly, time-consuming prototypes, many time-sensitive businesses use computer aided design and computer assisted manufacturing (CAD/CAM) to speed product design and testing.

ENTREPRENEURIAL
Profile

Apple Computer and the iPod

Speed can be a source of significant competitive advantage, something that Apple Computer knows well. When it introduced the first iPod in 2001, it quickly dominated the market for MP3 players. Rather than wait for competitors to introduce new versions with improvements, Apple set out to make its own iPods obsolete by introducing new models to replace existing ones and doing it quickly. Recognizing that speed to market was a key to maintaining its market share, Apple has taken just 8 months to introduce each of the last eight iPod models, compared to 2 years for the first six models.[94]

IN THE ENTREPRENEURIAL
SPOTLIGHT This Shop Has Gone to the Dogs

Godfrey's Welcome to Dogdom, a pet boutique located in Mohnton, Pennsylvania, is not your ordinary pet store. Because Godfrey's is a delight to all of its customers' (both human and canine) senses, the store has become what every retailer strives for: a destination shop. Barb Emmett is the founder of the business, and from his favorite spot by the main counter, Jackson Godfrey, one of her three beloved Golden retrievers, is the store's OG, "official greeter." "Godfrey's is not a 'transactional' retail business," says Emmett. "We are an experiential business." Godfrey's sees the world from a dog's point of view and stocks a full line of dog-related products, ranging from essentials such as specialty foods, health-related products, and pet-care items to luxuries such as hand-cast stone sculptures, cast-bronze statues, dog apparel, and healthy fresh-baked dog biscuits in a multitude of flavors. "Our focus is on solutions to our customers' problems and issues with their dogs and is not based on commodity price and product selling," says Emmett.

Located in a barn originally built in 1867, the shop sits on four acres that include a spa and grooming center, two play parks, a canine learning center, an obstacle course, and a wading pool. In the works is a wellness center that focuses on alternative therapies such as acupuncture and therapeutic touch. The shop, which is always clean, well-organized, and fresh smelling, clearly is aimed at dog lovers and grabs them emotionally as soon as they walk in the door. As customers wend their way through the store's labyrinth, they find that each room has its own theme: a converted kitchen features food products, former bedrooms house displays of dog beds and duvets, a bathroom includes grooming and bathing products, and a "whining and dining room" contains dog-themed home décor items.

Pamela Danzinger, a retail consultant and author of a book, *Shopping: Why We Love It and How Retailers Can Create the Ultimate Customer Experience*, honored Godfrey's by naming it a "Shop That Pops." According to Danzinger, "Retailers face the same challenge: Shoppers are demanding more than just a selection of merchandise at a reasonable price. They want their shopping experiences and the stores that they frequent to really pop with special features that involve the customer, build their curiosity, and give off a contagious energy." Godfrey's delivers all of this and more. Emmett and her employees make a point to learn the names of their customers and their dogs, many of whom have their photographs on a store wall. She sends customers a regular newsletter chock full of useful information for dog owners and notices about upcoming store events. A dish on the counter is filled with complimentary dog treats, and owners can always find a free cup of coffee at Godfrey's. Customers can book their pets for a doggie play group or schedule family time with their pets at one of the store's play parks. Godfrey's also offers obedience courses, workshops, and seminars. Topics range from pet first aid and canine nutrition to animal communication and canine Reiki. Special events such as a Valentine's Day Whine and Dine Brunch, a Pooch Smooch Easter photography session, and a Howl-o-ween Pawrade and Pawty keep customers and their beloved pets coming back to Godfrey's. The store also serves a collection point for the local Animal Rescue League.

What sets Godfrey's Welcome to Dogdom apart from other pet stores? It boils down to the interaction of the following factors:

- Opportunities for high levels of customer involvement and interaction.
- A retail environment that evokes shoppers' curiosity with its unique layout and selection of merchandise.
- A store that creates a contagious air of excitement for people who love their dogs and treat them like members of the family rather than just pets—"a kind of pet utopia for dogs and their owners," says Emmett.
- A synergistic convergence of atmosphere, store design, and merchandise that creates a special place for customers and their dogs.
- A retail concept based on meaningful values. "I want to provide quality pet products and services that can enhance the lives of pets and their owners," says Emmett.
- A price–value model that customers understand and support.
- A friendly store that is welcoming, friendly, and gives customers and their pets a reason to return. "Our greatest strength is in creating an emotional bond with our customers," Emmett says.

Emmett has created a store with "soul" that engages customers on many different levels, creates a fun, festive atmosphere, and has a mission that goes far beyond merely selling pet products. The result has been many entrepreneurial awards, a growing base of loyal customers, and increased sales and profits. "The focus for retailing success in the future is not so much what you sell but how you sell it," says Danzinger.

1. Is it necessary for a company to spend large amounts of money to transform a store into a destination of choice for customers? Explain.
2. Select a retail shop with which you are familiar, perhaps one near your college or university. Work with a team of fellow students to brainstorm ways that the shop can apply the factors that Barb Emmett has used to make Godfrey's a destination store.

Sources: Based on Pam Danzinger, "A Shop That Pops: How Godfrey's, A Pet Boutique, Creates the Ultimate Customer Experience," Unity Marketing, Shops That Pop, *www.shopsthatpop.com/cms/Home_Page/White_Papers_Articles.php*; Pam Danzinger, "Does Your Shop Pop?" Unity Marketing, Shops That Pop, *www.shopsthatpop.com/cms/Home_Page/White_Papers_Articles.php*; Jon Fassnacht, "Shops That Pop," *Reading Eagle*, November 12, 2006, pp. C1–C2; Carole Simpson, "A Pooch's Paradise," *Reading Eagle*, August 9, 2004, p. D7; "Events," Godfrey's Welcome to Dogdom, *www.godfreysdogdom.com/events.asp.*

The Marketing Mix

5. Discuss the "four Ps" of marketing—product, place, price, and promotion—and their role in building a successful marketing strategy.

Implementing a marketing strategy requires entrepreneurs to determine how they will use the "four Ps" of marketing—product, place, price, and promotion. These four elements are self-reinforcing and, when coordinated, increase the sales appeal of a product or service. Entrepreneurs must integrate these elements into a coherent strategy to maximize the impact of their product or service on the consumer. All four Ps must reinforce the image of the product or service the company presents to the potential customer. One longtime retailer claims, "None of the modern marvels of computerized inventory control and point-of-sale telecommunications have replaced the need for the entrepreneur who understands the customer and can translate that into the appropriate merchandise mix."[95]

Product

The product itself is an essential element in marketing. Products can have form and shape, or they can be services with no physical form. Products travel through various stages of development. The **product life cycle** (see Figure 7) measures these stages of growth, and these measurements enable the company's management to make decisions about whether to continue selling the product, when to introduce new follow-up products, and when to introduce changes to an existing product. The length of a product's life cycle depends on many variables, including the type of product. Fashion clothing may have a product life cycle of just a few weeks, but a video game console's life cycle typically lasts about 4 years.[96] Products that are more stable, such as appliances, may take years to complete a life cycle. Product life cycles are growing shorter, however. The life cycle for golf equipment has shrunk over the past decade from 3 or 4 years to less than 1 year today.[97]

In the *introductory stage*, marketers present their product to potential consumers. Initial high levels of acceptance are rare. Generally, new products must break into existing markets and compete with established products. Advertising and promotion help the new product gain recognition among potential customers, who must get information about the product and the needs it can satisfy. The cost of marketing a product at this level of the life cycle is usually high, because small businesses must overcome customer resistance and inertia. Therefore, profits are generally low, or even negative, at the introductory stage.

After the introductory stage, the product enters the *growth and acceptance stage*. In this stage, customers begin to purchase the product in large enough numbers for sales to rise and profits to increase. Products that reach this stage, however, do not necessarily become successful. If in the introductory or the growth stage the product fails to meet consumer needs, it does not generate adequate sales volume and eventually disappears from the marketplace. For successful products, sales and profit margins continue to rise through the growth stage.

In the *maturity and competition stage*, sales volume continues to rise, but profit margins peak and then begin to fall as competitors' enter the market. Normally, this causes a reduction in the product's selling price to meet competitors' prices and to hold its share of the market.

Sales peak in the *market saturation stage* of the product life cycle and give the marketer fair warning that it soon will be time to introduce a new product innovation.

The final stage of the product life cycle is the *product decline stage*. Sales continue to drop, and profit margins fall drastically. However, when a product reaches this stage of the cycle, it does

FIGURE 7
The Product Life Cycle

not mean that it is doomed to failure. Products that have remained popular are always being revised. No company can maintain its sales position without product innovation and change. Although Radio Flyer, a company started in 1917 by immigrant cabinet maker Antonio Pasin (and managed by his grandsons, Robert and Paul), still sells the classic all-metal, rubber-wheeled red wagon that made the company famous, it has introduced several models for twenty-first-century children. The Ultimate Family Wagon includes five-way flip-and-fold seats, storage compartments, cup holders (two for kids and two for adults), a tray table, and a sun canopy. Radio Flyer's latest prototype, the Cloud 9, includes enough updates to appear on *Pimp My Ride*. The high-tech wagon features reclining upholstered seats with five-point safety harnesses; cup holders; fold-out storage compartments; foot brakes; a digital handle that tracks temperature, time, distance, and speed; a slot for an MP3 player; and stereo speakers. These innovations are designed to draw new generations of children to the classic toy.[98]

Understanding the product life cycle helps a business owner plan the introduction of new products to the company's product line. Too often, companies wait too late into the life cycle of one product to introduce another. The result is that they are totally unprepared when a competitor produces a "better mousetrap" and their sales decline. The ideal time to develop new products is early on in the life cycle of the current product (see Figure 8). Waiting until the current product is in the saturation or decline stages is like living on borrowed time.

Place

Place (or method of distribution) has grown in importance as customers expect greater service and more convenience from businesses. Because of this trend, mail-order houses, home shopping channels, home shopping parties, and the Web, offering the ultimate in convenience—shopping at home—have experienced booming sales in recent years. In addition, many traditionally stationary businesses have added wheels, becoming mobile animal clinics, computer repair shops, and dentist offices.

Any activity involving movement of goods to the point of consumer purchase provides place utility. Place utility is directly affected by the marketing channels of distribution, the path that goods or services and their titles take in moving from producer to consumer.

ENTREPRENEURIAL
Profile

Mitch Low and Redbox Automated Retail

Despite a decidedly low-tech approach, Redbox Automated Retail has become a fierce competitor in the movie rental business with its pervasive distribution strategy. The company offers new release DVD rentals for just $1 per night through a ubiquitous network of 22,000 self-service kiosks that are conveniently located in grocery and convenience stores and selected Walmart, Walgreens, and McDonald's locations. Each kiosk holds 630 DVDs, representing up to 200 of the latest movie releases that customers select with a touch screen and a debit or credit card. Despite their humble appearance, Redbox kiosks contain an element of technology. Connected to the company's main computer system, each kiosk contains a sophisticated inventory control system that determines how many copies of each new movie to stock based on past performance of similar movies at that location. Customers also can go online to reserve movies at their nearby Redbox. "That's the most interesting part—where technology meets old-fashioned field distribution," says Redbox president Mitch Low.[99]

FIGURE 8
**Time Between
Introductions of Products**

Channels typically involve a number of intermediaries who perform specialized functions that add valuable utility to the goods or service. Specifically, these intermediaries provide time utility (making the product available when customers want to buy it) and place utility (making the product available where customers want to buy it).

For consumer goods, there are four common channels of distribution:

1. *Manufacturer to consumer.* In some markets, producers sell their goods or services directly to consumers. Services, by nature, follow this channel of distribution. Dental care and haircuts, for example, go directly from creator to consumer.
2. *Manufacturer to retailer to consumer.* Another common channel involves a retailer as an intermediary. Many clothing items, books, shoes, and other consumer products are distributed in this manner.
3. *Manufacturer to wholesaler to retailer to consumer.* This is the most common channel of distribution for consumer goods. Prepackaged food products, hardware, toys, and other items are commonly distributed through this channel.
4. *Manufacturer to wholesaler to wholesaler to retailer to consumer.* A few consumer goods (e.g., agricultural goods and electrical components) follow this pattern of distribution.

Two channels of distribution are common for industrial goods:

1. *Manufacturer to industrial user.* The majority of industrial goods are distributed directly from manufacturers to users. In some cases, the goods or services are designed to meet the user's specifications.
2. *Manufacturer to wholesaler to industrial user.* Most expense items (paper clips, paper, rubber bands, cleaning fluids) that firms commonly use are distributed through wholesalers. For most small manufacturers, distributing goods through established wholesalers and agents is often the most effective route. With their limited resources, entrepreneurs sometimes have to rely on nontraditional distribution channels and use their creativity to get their products into customers' hands.

Price

Almost everyone agrees that the price of the product or service is a key factor in the decision to buy. Price affects both sales volume and profits, and without the right price, both sales and profits will suffer. The right price for a product or service depends on three factors: (1) a small company's cost structure, (2) an assessment of what the market will bear, and (3) the desired image the company wants to create in its customers' minds.

For many small businesses, nonprice competition, focusing on factors other than price, is a more effective strategy than trying to beat larger competitors in a price war. Nonprice competition, such as free trial offers, free delivery, lengthy warranties, and money-back guarantees, intends to play down the product's price and stress its durability, quality, reputation, or special features.

Promotion

Promotion involves both advertising and personal selling. Advertising communicates to potential customers through some mass medium the benefits of a good or service. Personal selling involves the art of persuasive sales on a one-to-one basis.

The goals of a small company's promotional efforts are to create a brand image, to persuade customers to buy, and to develop brand loyalty. Promotion can take many forms and is put before the public through a variety of media.

ENTREPRENEURIAL
Profile

*Sandeep Sood and
Monsoon Company*

In a clever guerrilla marketing campaign, Sandeep Sood, president of Monsoon Company, a Berkeley, California-based software development consulting company with $2 million in annual sales, sent a unique direct mail ad to its recession-weary customers. The ad, handwritten on 5-by-7-inch pieces of pasteboard torn from old boxes, said, "OK, this is a lame way to save money. Call us about smarter ways to save on software design and development." Sood says that customers' response to the promotion was tremendous.[100]

Like Sood, entrepreneurs often must find ways to use low-cost guerrilla tactics to create promotions that get their companies noticed by both local and national media. "Creative Use of Advertising and Promotion," is devoted to creating an effective advertising and promotion campaign for a small company.

Chapter Review

1. Describe the components of a guerrilla marketing plan and explain the benefits of preparing one.
   - A major part of the entrepreneur's business plan is the marketing plan, which focuses on a company's target customers and how best to satisfy their needs and wants. A solid marketing plan should pinpoint the specific target markets the company will serve, determine customer needs and wants through market research, analyze the firm's competitive advantages and build a marketing strategy around them, and create a marketing mix that meets customer needs and wants.

2. Explain how small businesses can pinpoint their target markets.
   - Sound market research helps the owner pinpoint his target market. The most successful businesses have well-defined portraits of the customers they are seeking to attract.

3. Explain how to determine customer needs through market research and describe the tools that entrepreneurs use to conduct market research.
   - Market research is the vehicle for gathering the information that serves as the foundation of the marketing plan. Good research does not have to be complex and expensive to be useful.

4. Describe the guerrilla marketing strategies on which a small business can build competitive edge in the marketplace.
   - When plotting a marketing strategy, owners must strive to achieve a competitive advantage, some way to make their companies different from and better than the competition. Successful small businesses rely on 16 guerrilla marketing principles to develop a competitive edge: niche-picking, generating publicity, entertailing, connecting with their customers, building a consistent branding strategy, embracing social networking, starting a blog, creating online videos, emphasizing their uniqueness, focusing on customers' needs, retaining existing customers, emphasizing quality, paying attention to convenience, concentrating on innovation, dedicating themselves to service, and emphasizing speed.

5. Explain the "four Ps" of marketing—product, place, price, and promotion—and their role in building a successful marketing strategy.
   - The marketing mix consists of the "4 Ps":
     Product. Entrepreneurs should understand where in the product life cycle their products are.
     Place. The focus here is on choosing the appropriate channel of distribution and using it most efficiently.
     Price. Price is an important factor in customers' purchase decisions, but many small businesses find that nonprice competition can be profitable.
     Promotion. Promotion involves both advertising and personal selling.

Discussion Questions

1. What is a marketing plan? What lies at its center?
2. What objectives should a marketing plan accomplish?
3. How can market research benefit a small business owner? List some possible sources of market information.
4. Does market research have to be expensive and sophisticated to be valuable? Explain.
5. Why is it important for small business owners to define their target markets as part of their marketing strategies?
6. What is a competitive edge? How might a small company gain a competitive edge?
7. Describe how a small business owner could use the following sources of a competitive advantage: niche-picking, generating publicity, entertailing, connecting with their customers, building a consistent branding strategy, embracing social networking, starting a blog, creating online videos,

emphasizing their uniqueness, focusing on customers' needs, retaining existing customers, emphasizing quality, paying attention to convenience, concentrating on innovation, dedicating themselves to service, and emphasizing speed.

8. Explain the concept of the marketing mix. What are the four Ps?

9. List and explain the stages in the product life cycle. How can a small firm extend its product's life?

10. With a 70 percent customer retention rate (average for most U.S. firms according to the American Management Association) every $1 million of business in 2005 will grow to more than $4 million by the year 2015. If you retain 80 percent of your customers, the $1 million will grow to a little over $6 million. If you can keep 90 percent of your customers, that $1 million will grow to more than $9.5 million. What can the typical small business do to increase its customer retention rate?

Incorporate the marketing concepts from the chapter along with those as you continue to build your business plan. The marketing section of your plan will add greater depth to your situation analysis and offer additional insight into your business strategy. For most business plans, 25 to 35 percent of the plan is devoted to the marketing plan, emphasizing the importance of this information. Your business plan should describe how you determined that a market exists for the products or services of your business, identify the market segments you are targeting, establish the unique selling proposition to differentiate your products and services, and describe how you will reach the market and motivate customers to purchase.

On the Web

The Internet is a great place to begin conducting market research. In addition to the resources it offers, the Web can also help determine which form of market research is most suitable for your plan. Your market research should provide specific information about your target market and the key factors that influence customers' buying decisions. Your business plan will benefit from even the most elementary market research and, if it does not provide new information, that research may validate what you already know.

The Internet can also help you identify your industry's trade associations. Assess the information that is available on their Web sites. Does the industry association have publications available? Does it sponsor seminars and workshops? What benefits does it provide to its members? What does it cost to join the association? Industry associations can be a valuable source of market research.

As this chapter mentions, excellent data that can assist with your plan is available through U.S. government Web sites, including the following:

- Small Business Administration (SBA): *www.sba.gov*
- Small Business Development Center (SBDC): *www.sba.gov/sbdc*
- U.S. Census Bureau: *www.census.gov*
- U.S. Department of Commerce: *www.trade.gov*
- U.S. Chamber of Commerce: *www.uschamber.com*

For example, the U.S. Census Bureau's Web site at *www.census.gov* provides a menu of available demographic reports that includes detailed information on various cities, towns, industries, county-specific economic surveys, business patterns for specific zip codes, and others.

Private market research sources are plentiful on the Web as well. Although most provide this information for a fee, many sites offer preliminary information at no cost. One example is geocluster data called PRIZM, an acronym for Potential Rating Index by Zip Markets. This market data, available from Claritas Inc., offers descriptions of consumers by zip code beyond that of traditional demographic data. PRIZM data classifies U.S. neighborhoods into 62 distinct lifestyle groups based on education, affluence, family life cycle, urbanization, mobility, race, and ethnicity. You can look up PRIZM information by going to *www.claritas.com/MyBestSegments* and clicking on the "Zip Code Look-Up" tab at the top. Enter your zip code into the search window for your results and you may be impressed by what you find—all at no cost. Other market research information is available through sites such as Zap Data at *www.zapdata.com*. Here you will find industry data reports with preliminary information, also available at no charge. This information, sorted by Standard Industry Classification (SIC) code, tracks how many companies are in the industry, their average sales, the number of employees, the company size, and their locations.

Online magazines, newspapers, and other publications offer an efficient way to search for articles and other information related to your business and the industry in which it operates. Many industry-specific magazines publish statistical editions and market reviews at regular intervals. Search the indexes to identify published information that might help the marketing section of your business plan. You may find an index listing for an article that includes forecasts for your industry or addresses industry economics or trends. You can also contact magazine editorial departments for additional information using the information on their Web sites.

In the Software

Review some of the sample business plans that have been the most helpful to date. Review the marketing section of these plans and note the type and depth of market information they include. This information is essential to establish a solid understanding of the market your business will serve and to use as the basis for developing and validating your strategy. Now go to each of the following sections in your business plan:

Your Company. Review the work that you began in the "Your Company" section of your business plan. As you review that information, does it capture a marketing focus? Does this section place the necessary emphasis on building lasting customer relationships? Add to and edit your work to reflect this critical perspective.

What Are You Selling? Make certain this section presents the goods and services you are selling to your customer. It must concisely communicate the value that your customers will realize by doing business with your company and the benefits they receive from your company's products and services.

Service Summary. Think about the unique nature of the services your business provides. How will your services offer more customer benefits than those of your competitors? How will your services be superior and provide meaningful value to your customers that will enhance their loyalty? Address these questions in this section of your plan.

Your Market. Add information that you have gleaned from your marketing research to describe your market in as much detail as possible.

Target Market Segment. Review the chapter concepts regarding target marketing. Use those concepts to help you develop a clear picture of your target customers. You should incorporate these profiles into this section to describe your target market segment.

Competition. A detailed and thorough discussion and analysis of each of your company's current and potential competitors is critical. The business plan must demonstrate that you have evaluated this critical factor and can identify, in realistic and practical terms, how your business will compete successfully. Demonstrate your knowledge of how customers make purchasing decisions and how your proposed venture can gain their business. Be honest and objective as you describe your competitors' strengths and weaknesses. Discuss the customer appeal, pricing strategies, advertising

campaigns, and the products and services your competitors offer.

Competitive Edge. Based on that information, review the "Competitive Edge" section of your plan. What unique attributes does your business offer that will provide real or perceived benefits for your customers? Make sure you capture those thoughts in this section. Be as detailed as possible and explain your strategies to create this advantage. Incorporate material from your marketing and sales plan that will show how these strategic advantages support your sales forecast.

The Sales Forecast. Is that forecast realistic? Is your company's cost of goods accurate? Go to the narrative section of the sales forecast and explain the numbers in the sales forecast. Include any assumptions on which you have developed your sales forecast. Explain why your sales are projected to change over time. Include any key events that may affect your sales and how and why they will influence the sales forecast. Finally, as you evaluate your numbers and the assumptions that support them, ask yourself if they are realistic. Developing financial forecasts using published statistics from sources such as RMA's *Annual Statement Studies* (*www.rmahq.org*), market research, industry studies, and other sources lends credibility to your plan. Once again, you will find links at the Companion Web site (*www.pearsonhighered.com/scarborough*) to information that may be helpful.

Marketing Plan Summary. A marketing strategy should present a clear link to forecasts of sales revenue. Use a detailed analysis and explanation of all assumptions on which the analysis rests. Your company's product, pricing, distribution, and promotion plans combined should produce a unified marketing strategy.

Building Your Business Plan

Continue to build your business plan with the new information you have acquired. Step back to assess whether you have a solid understanding of your market and whether your business plan effectively communicates that understanding.

Endnotes

1. Sanjeev Aggarwal and Laurie McCabe, *Small Business Marketing Health Check* (Newton, MA: Hurwitz and Associates, 2009), p. 5.
2. Sean McFadden, "Healthy Strategy: Lifestyle Fitness Corp. Owner Gets Strategic with Marketing," *Boston Business Journal*, March 31, 2009, *www.bizjournals.com/boston/stories/2009/03/30/smallb1.html*.
3. Howard Fana Shaw, "Customer Care Checklist," *In Business*, September–October 1987, p. 28.
4. Lynn Rosellini, "The High Life of Crime," *U.S. News & World Report*, November 20, 2000, pp. 76–77.
5. Jane Burns, "Executive Q & A: Toppers Pizza Founder Scott Gittrich on Pie Appeal," *Wisconsin State Journal*, February 27, 2010, *http://host.madison.com/wsj/business/article_67993bac-2336-11df-85c6-001cc4c002e0.html*; Kayla Bunge, "Pizza with Pizzazz: Toppers Finds Success In Wisconsin," *Janesville Gazette Extra*, September 14, 2009, *http://gazettextra.com/news/2009/sep/14/pizza-pizzazz-toppers-finds-success-wisconsin/*; Toppers, *www.toppers.com/#/intro/*.
6. Les Christie, "Census: U.S. Becoming More Diverse," *CNN Money*, May 14, 2009, *http://money.cnn.com/2009/05/14/real_estate/rising_minorities/index.htm*.
7. Sara Wilson, "Capitalize on Nostalgia," *Entrepreneur*, March 2009, p. 94.
8. Norm Brodsky, "My First Year," *Inc.*, April 2009, p. 34.
9. Allan Brettman, "Burgerville Goes Mobile with Food Truck," *The Oregonian*, July 22, 2009, *www.oregonlive.com/business/index.ssf/2009/07/burgerville_setting_up_mobile.html*; Karlene Lukovitz, "Taking Burgerville to the Streets," *Marketing Daily*, July 31, 2009, *www.mediapost.com/publications/?fa=Articles.showArticle&art_aid=110672*.
10. Kim Komando, "Three Reasons to Use Online Customer Surveys," Microsoft Small Business Center, *www.microsoft.com/smallbusiness/resources/marketing/market_research/3_reasons_to_use_online_customer_surveys.mspx*.

11. Damon Brown, "Online Customer Surveys for Small Business," *Inc. Technology*, December 2006, *http://technology.inc.com/internet/articles/200612/onlinesurveys.html*.

12. Kelly K. Spors, "The Customer Knows Best," *Wall Street Journal*, July 13, 2009, p. R5; Jesse Noyes, "Micro Motor Plants," *Boston Business Journal*, March 7, 2008, *http://boston.bizjournals.com/boston/stories/2008/03/10/story2.html*.

13. Avery Johnson, "Hotels Take 'Know Your Customer' to New Level," *Wall Street Journal*, February 7, 2006, pp. D1, D3.

14. Shari Caudron, "Right on Target," *Industry Week*, September 2, 1996, p. 45.

15. Angela Garber Wolf, "Million-Dollar Questionnaire," *Small Business Computing*, January 2002, pp. 47–48.

16. Samuel Axon, "How Small Businesses Are Using Social Media for Real Results," *Mashable*, March 22, 2010, *http://mashable.com/2010/03/22/small-business-social-media-results/*.

17. "70 Percent of Small Businesses Anticipate Growth in 2009 According to Survey," Constant Contact, June 18, 2009, *www.constantcontact.com/about-constant-contact/press/press_2009_0618_2.jsp*.

18. "Converting Customer Dissatisfaction into Loyalty and Profits at Cornerstone of New Boulder Business," Verde Group, October 3, 2005, *http://verdegroup.ca/default.asp?action=article&ID=36*.

19. Donnell Alexander, "It's a Bird. It's a Plane. It's a . . . Bird on a Plane?" *Entrepreneur*, August 2009, p. 15; "Our Story," Pet Airways, *www.petairways.com/content/our-story*.

20. Roberta Maynard, "Rich Niches," *Nation's Business*, November 1993, p. 41.

21. "Nathan's Famous Fourth of July International Hot Dog Eating Contest," Nathan's Famous Frankfurters, *www.nathansfamous.com/PageFetch/getpage.php?pgid=38*.

22. Dale D. Buss, "Entertailing," *Nation's Business*, December 1997, p. 18.

23. Ibid., pp. 12–18.

24. Susan Carpenter, "Fashion Sellers Turn Shopping into an Event," *Los Angeles Times*, October 18, 2009, *http://articles.latimes.com/2009/oct/18/image/ig-shoputainment18*.

25. Beth Kowitt, "True Obsessions," *Fortune*, May 11, 2009, pp. 84–91.

26. Sara Wilson, "Getting Personal," *Entrepreneur*, March 2006, p. 71; "About Us" Title Nine, *www.titlenine.com/category/who+are+we/meet+our+model+athletes.do*.

27. Mark Brandau, "Caribou's Brand Makeover," *Nation's Restaurant News*, March 2, 2010, *www.nrn.com/breakingNews.aspx?id=379916*.

28. Max Chafkin, "Tell Your Friends About Us: How to Get Twitter Endorsements," *Inc.*, March 2010, pp. 108–110.

29. "SocNet Usage Rises in February," *Marketing Charts,* March 24, 2010, *www.marketingcharts.com/interactive/socnet-usage-rises-in-feb-12346/nielsen-soc-network-usage-feb-10-mar-2010jpg/*.

30. "Social Media Engagement Directly Linked to Financial Success," *Marketing Charts*, July 21, 2009, *www.marketingcharts.com/interactive/social-media-engagement-directly-linked-to-financial-success-9858/*.

31. "Social Media Adoption by U.S. Small Businesses Doubles Since 2009," Robert H. Smith School of Business, University of Maryland, February 16, 2010, *www.rhsmith.umd.edu/news/releases/2010/021610.aspx*.

32. Matt McGee, "More Small Businesses Using Social Media," *Small Business Search Marketing*, February 24, 2010, *www.smallbusinesssem.com/more-small-businesses-using-social-media/2847/*.

33. "Marketers Adopt Emerging Channels," Marketing Charts, March 19, 2010, *www.marketingcharts.com/direct/marketers-adopt-emerging-channels-12344/*.

34. "9% of SMBs Currently Use Twitter to Market Their Businesses, According to BIA/Kelsey," BIA/Kelsey, October 21, 2009, *www.kelseygroup.com/press/pr091021.asp*.

35. "More Than 100 Twitter Followers Boost B2C Leads," *Marketing Charts*, April 19, 2010, *www.marketingcharts.com/direct/more-than-100-twitter-followers-boost-b2c-leads-12625/*.

36. Nancy Luna and Mike Fujiwara, "Local Eateries Tweet Like Crazy, but Does It Work?" *Orange County Register*, September 1, 2009, *www.ocregister.com/articles/twitter-218861-shah-beach.html;* "About Us," Sprinkles, *www.sprinkles.com/about/food_philosophy.html*.

37. Peter Corbett, "Facebook Demographics and Statistics Report 2010," January 4, 2010, iStrategyLabs, *www.istrategylabs.com/2010/01/facebook-demographics-and-statistics-report-2010-145-growth-in-1-year/;* Shel Holtz, "6 Questions to Ask Before Launching a Facebook Fan Page," *www.ragan.com/ME2/Audiences/dirmod.asp?sid=&nm=*

&type=MultiPublishing&mod=PublishingTitles&mid=5AA50C55146B4C8C98F903986BC02C56&tier=4&id=080BA062985C4E6C91AF7E507A91E9E9&AudID=3FF14703FD8C4AE98B9B4365B978201A.

38. Jennifer Schiff, "Social Network Marketing Meets Small Business," *Small Business Computing*, July 6, 2009, *www.smallbusinesscomputing.com/biztools/article.php/382829*.

39. "BlogPulse Stats," BlogPulse, March 24, 2010, *www.blogpulse.com/*.

40. Nora Ganim Barnes and Eric Mattson, "Social Media in the 2009 *Inc.* 500: New Tools and Trends," University of Massachusetts Dartmouth Center for Marketing Research, 2010, *www.umassd.edu/cmr/studiesresearch/socialmedia2009.pdf;* "Small Business Success Index Results: January 2010," Network Solutions, *http://growsmartbusiness.com/research-library/#social_media*.

41. John Nardini, "Create a Blog to Boost Your Business," *Entrepreneur*, September 27, 2005, *www.entrepreneur.com/article/0,4621,323598,00.html*.

42. "Online Video Viewing Reaches Record High 31 Billion," *Marketing Charts*, January 7, 2010, *www.marketingcharts.com/interactive/online-video-viewing-reaches-record-high-31b-11573/*.

43. Mary Madden, "The Audience for Online Video-Sharing Sites Shoots Up," Pew Research Center, July 29, 2009, *www.pewinternet.org/Reports/2009/13—The-Audience-for-Online-VideoSharing-Sites-Shoots-Up.aspx*.

44. April Joyner, "Show Us What You Can Do," *Inc.*, February 2010, pp. 81–82.

45. Raymund Flandez, "Three Best Ways to Make a Viral Video," *Wall Street Journal*, September 25, 2009, *http://online.wsj.com/article/SB10001424052970204488304574435020939186220.html*.

46. Raymund Flandez, "Three Best Ways to Make a Viral Video," *Wall Street Journal*, September 25, 2009, *http://online.wsj.com/article/SB10001424052970204488304574435020939186220.html;* Josh Catone, "5 Important Web Video Lessons for Small Business Owners," *Mashable*, November 14, 2009, *http://mashable.com/2009/11/14/small-business-video/*.

47. Russ Riendeau and Adrian Dinu, "The Power of Video in Business Marketing," *Sales and Marketing*, December 7, 2009, *www.salesandmarketing.com/msg/content_display/marketing/e3i6328aaffeb014c1320964b1bd19440b0*.

48. "Online Video Viewing Reaches Record High 31 Billion," *Marketing Charts*, January 7, 2010, *www.marketingcharts.com/interactive/online-video-viewing-reaches-record-high-31b-11573/*.

49. Kasey Wehrum, "Behind the Scenes," *Inc.*, July–August 2009, pp. 20–21.

50. Jack Loechner, "Poor Customer Service Costs Companies $83 Billion Annually," *Media Post*, February 18, 2010, *www.mediapost.com/publications/?fa=Articles.showArticle&art_aid=122502*.

51. Ibid.

52. "Beware of Dissatisfied Customers: They Like to Blab," *Knowledge@Wharton*, March 8, 2006, *http://knowledge.wharton.upenn.edu/article.cfm?articleid=1422*.

53. Carmine Gallo, "How Disney Works to Win Repeat Customers," *BusinessWeek*, December 1, 2009, *www.businessweek.com/smallbiz/content/nov2009/sb20091130_866423.htm*.

54. "Encourage Customers to Complain," *Small Business Reports*, June 1990, p. 7.

55. Dave Zielinski, "Improving Service Doesn't Require a Big Investment," *Small Business Reports*, February 1991, p. 20.

56. Brian Caulfield, "How to Win Customer Loyalty," *Business 2.0,* March 1, 2004, pp. 77–78.

57. Susan Greco, "Fanatics," *Inc.*, April 2001, pp. 36–48.

58. Loechner, "Poor Customer Service Costs Companies $83 Billion Annually."

59. Greco, "Fanatics," pp. 36–48.

60. Patricia Sellers, "Companies That Serve You Best," *Fortune*, May 31, 1993, p. 75.

61. Robert B. Tucker, "Earn Your Customers' Loyalty," Economics Press Techniques, Strategies, and Inspiration for the Sales Professional, *www.epic.co/SALES/selltips.htm#earn_loyalty*.

62. William A. Sherden, "The Tools of Retention," *Small Business Reports*, November 1994, pp. 43–47.

63. Anjali Cordeiro, "In Tough Times, Companies Coddle Their Regulars," *Wall Street Journal*, June 23, 2009, p. B4.

64. Richard Stone, "Retaining Customers Requires Constant Contact," *Small Business Computing*, January 11, 2005, *www.smallbusinesscomputing.com/biztools/print.pho/3457221*.

65. Bruce D. Temkin, William Chu, and Steven Geller, "Customer Experience Correlates to Loyalty," Forrester Research, February 17,

2009, *www.forrester.com/rb/Research/customer_experience_correlates_to_loyalty/q/id/53794/t/2;* Bruce D. Temkin, "Customer Experience Correlates to Loyalty," *Customer Experience Matters,* February 18, 2009, *http://experiencematters.wordpress.com/2009/02/18/customer-experience-correlates-to-loyalty/.*

66. Patricia Neale, "John Ratzenberger's 'Made in America' Season Premiere Features Allen Edmonds Shoe Corporation," Company Press Release, November 21, 2005, *www.allenedmonds.com/wcsstore/AllenEdmonds/about/Made%20in%20America%20PR%2011.21.05.pdf.*

67. Ibid.

68. Rahul Jacobs, "TQM: More Than a Dying Fad," *Fortune,* October 18, 1993, p. 67.

69. Ibid.

70. Brett Thorn, "Domino's Passes $1 Billion in Online Sales," *Nation's Restaurant News,* February 10, 2010, *www.nrn.com/article.aspx?id=379316.*

71. Howie Kahn, "The 10 Best Food Trucks in America," *GQ,* September 2009, *www.gq.com/food-travel/restaurants-and-bars/200908/best-food-trucks-van-leeuwen-new-york-seattle-los-angeles-slideshow#slide=3;* Jessica Gelt, "Kogi Korean BBQ, a Truck Brought to You by Twitter," *Los Angeles Times,* February 11, 2009, *www.latimes.com/theguide/restaurants/la-fo-kogi11-2009feb11,0,4560062.story;* "About," Kogi Korean BBQ, *http://kogibbq.com/about/.*

72. Giselle Tsirulnik, "Stop & Shop Helps Consumers Save Time, Money with Mobile," *Mobile Marketer,* September 1, 2009, *www.mobilemarketer.com/cms/news/commerce/4067.html.*

73. Emily Nelson, "Marketers Push Individual Portions and Families Bite," *Wall Street Journal,* July 23, 2002, pp. A1, A6.

74. Lucy McCauley, "Measure What Matters," *Fast Company,* May 1999, p. 100.

75. Mike Doherty, "The Best vs. the Rest," Innovation.net, November 1, 2004, *http://venture2.typepad.com/innovationnet/2004/11/the_best_vs_the.html.*

76. "Cotton Is the Fabric of Your Lights . . . Your iPod . . . Your MP3 Player . . . Your Cell Phone," *NanoWerk,* March 9, 2010, *www.nanowerk.com/news/newsid=15228.php;* Leslie Katz, "Solar Dress Charges Your MP3 Player," *CNet News,* March 10, 2010, *http://news.cnet.com/8301-17938_105-10466417-1.html.*

77. *Innovation: The Key to Future Success?* Grant Thornton International Ltd., September 2009, pp. 2–3.

78. Gwen Moran, "Power to the People," *Entrepreneur,* June 2006, pp. 21–24.

79. Matthew Maier, "Home Sweet Home Networking," *Business 2.0,* February 2003, pp. 23–24.

80. Roberta Maynard, "The Heat Is On," Nation's Business, October 1997, pp. 14–23.

81. Greco, "Fanatics," p. 38.

82. *High Performance in the Age of Customer Centricity,* Accenture 2008 Global Customer Satisfaction Report, Accenture, pp. 3–5.

83. Richard Gibson, "Can I Get a Smile with My Burger and Fries?" *Wall Street Journal,* September 23, 2003, p. D6.

84. Janet Adamy, "A Menu of Options," *Wall Street Journal,* October 30, 2006, p. B6.

85. *High Performance in the Age of Customer Centricity,* Accenture 2008 Global Customer Satisfaction Report, Accenture, p. 16.

86. Debbie Salinsky, "Insanely Great Customer Service," *Success,* September 2000, p. 61.

87. Marie Moody, "How to Profit from Complaints," *FSB,* December 2009, *http://money.cnn.com/2009/12/23/smallbusiness/profiting_from_customer_complaints.fsb/index.htm.*

88. Thomas A. Stewart, "After All You've Done for Your Customers, Why Are They Still NOT HAPPY?" *Fortune,* December 11, 1995, pp. 178–182; Gile Gerretsen, "Special Tools Are Used by Super Markets," *Upstate Business,* June 14, 1998, p. 4.

89. Peter Sanders, "Takin' Off the Ritz—A Tad," *Wall Street Journal,* June 23, 2006, pp. B1, B3; Brian Caulfield, "How to Win Customer Loyalty," *Fortune,* March 1, 2004, pp. 77–78.

90. Elena Malykhina, "Pocket PCs on a Mission," *Information Week,* February 20, 2006, p. 60.

91. "Don't Hate the Playa," *Get to the Point,* November 12, 2009, pp. 1–2.

92. Brian Dumaine, "How Managers Can Succeed Through Speed," *Fortune,* February 13, 1989, pp. 54–59.

93. Mark Henricks, "Time Is Money," *Entrepreneur,* February 1993, p. 44.

94. Kerry A. Dolan, "Speed: the New X Factor," *Forbes,* December 26, 2005, pp. 74–77; Fred Vogelstein, "Mastering the Art of Disruption," *Fortune,* February 6, 2006, pp. 23–24.

95. Stanley J. Winkelman, "Why Big Name Stores Are Losing Out," *Fortune,* May 8, 1989, pp. 14–15.

96. Jeffrey M. O'Brien, "Wii Will Rock You," *Fortune,* June 4, 2007, *http://money.cnn.com/magazines/fortune/fortune_archive/2007/06/11/100083454/index.htm.*

97. Brett Nelson, "Fore!-Boding," *Forbes,* April 14, 2003, p. 60.

98. Jeremy Bradley, "Classic Radio Flyer Wagon Updated for 2.0 World," *CNN,* December 24, 2008, *www.cnn.com/2008/TECH/12/24/radio.flyer.wagon/index.html;* Lucas Mearian, "Opinion: Radio Flyer Is Pimpin' Its Wagons," *Computer World,* October 27, 2008, *www.computerworld.com/s/article/9118086/Opinion_Radio_Flyer_is_pimpin_its_wagons.*

99. Farhad Manjoo, "Box Tops," *Fast Company,* July–August 2009, p. 57; "Redbox and Flextronics Celebrate the Production of 25,000 Redbox DVD Rental Kiosks," Redbox, May 6, 2010, *http://redboxpressroom.com/releases/PressRelease_Flextronics_050610.html#*

100. Jeff Wuorio, "How to Ramp Up Marketing in a Downturn," *Entrepreneur,* July 2009, pp. 55–57.

Creative Use of Advertising and Promotion

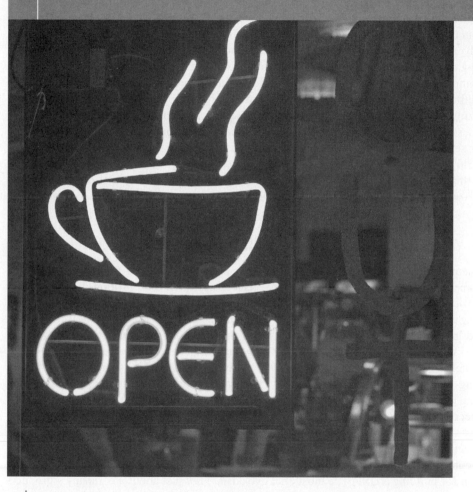

Learning Objectives

Upon completion of this chapter, you will be able to:

1. Define your company's unique selling proposition (USP).
2. Explain the differences among promotion, publicity, personal selling, and advertising.
3. Describe the advantages and disadvantages of the various advertising media.
4. Identify four basic methods for preparing an advertising budget.
5. Describe practical methods for stretching an entrepreneur's advertising budget.

Advertising is salesmanship mass produced. No one would bother

to use advertising if he could talk to all of his prospects face-to-

face. But he can't.

—Morris Hite

The man who stops advertising to save money is like the man who

stops the clock to save time.

—Anonymous

Advertising is not just a business expense; it is an investment in a company's future. Without a steady advertising and promotional campaign, a small business's customer base soon dries up. Advertising can be an effective means of increasing sales by telling customers about a business and its goods or services, by improving the image of the firm and its products, and by persuading customers to purchase its goods or services. A mega-budget is not a prerequisite for building an effective advertising campaign. With a dose of creativity and ingenuity, a small company can make its voice heard above the clamor of its larger competitors—and stay within a limited budget! A company's promotional strategy, which comprises advertising, publicity, and personal selling, must deliver the same clear, consistent, and compelling message about the business and its products or services. Customers respond best to a positive message that is delivered consistently by each component of the strategy. One goal of a company's promotional strategy is to create brand equity, which is measured by customer loyalty and customers' willingness to pay a premium for its products and services.

Developing an effective advertising program has become more challenging for business owners recently. Because of media overflow, overwhelming ad clutter, increasingly fragmented audiences, a plethora of advertising options, and more skeptical consumers, companies have had to become more innovative and creative in their advertising campaigns. Rather than merely turning up the advertising volume on their campaigns, companies are learning to change their frequencies, trying out new approaches in different advertising media.

A company's promotional efforts must differentiate its products and services from those of competitors. Some of the most effective advertisers have enhanced their brand loyalty by emphasizing in their promotional strategies the unique customer benefits that their products or services provide. For example, Nordstrom department stores are defined by friendly customer service, Volvo is known for automotive safety, and FedEx is recognized for guaranteed overnight delivery. One of the first steps is to carefully and thoughtfully define the message that a company's promotional campaign will emphasize by defining its *unique selling proposition*.

Define Your Company's Unique Selling Proposition (USP)

1. Define your company's unique selling proposition (USP).

Entrepreneurs should build their advertising messages on a **unique selling proposition (USP)**, a key customer benefit or a product or service that sets it apart from its competition. To be effective, a USP must actually *be* unique—something the competition does not (or cannot) provide—and compelling enough to encourage customers to buy. One technique is to replace your company's name and logo in one of your advertisements with those of your top competitor. Does the ad still make sense? If so, the ad is not based on your company's unique selling proposition! Unfortunately, many business owners never define their companies' USPs, and the result is an uninspiring "me-too" message that cries out "buy from us" without offering customers any compelling reasons to do so.

A successful USP answers the critical question every customer asks: "What's in it for me?" A successful USP should express in no more than 10 words what a business can do for its customers. Can your product or service save your customers time or money, make their lives easier or more convenient, improve their self-esteem, or make them feel better? If so, you have the foundation for building a USP. The most effective ads are *not* just about a company's products and services; instead, they focus on the company's customers and how its products and services can improve their lives.

The most effective USPs are simple, concrete, believable, emotional, and easy to communicate to prospective customers. The best way to identify a meaningful USP is to describe the primary benefits a product or service offers customers and then to list other secondary benefits it provides. Most businesses have no more than three primary benefits. Smart entrepreneurs look beyond the physical characteristics of their products or services, recognizing that sometimes the most powerful foundation for a USP is the *intangible* or *psychological* benefit a product or service offers customers—for example, safety, security, acceptance, status, prestige, and others. The key is to identify a gap that customers typically experience and then explain how your company's product or service can fill it. Before creating advertisements, entrepreneurs should develop a brief list of the facts that support the company's USP—for example, 24-hour service; a fully trained, experienced staff; industry awards won; and others. The final step is to consolidate the gap-filling benefits the company offers into a single statement, the USP.

Customers already appreciate the shopping convenience that Zappos, the online shoe company, offers; however, the potential gap that customers may experience is "What if the shoes don't fit or aren't comfortable?" Zappos eliminates those concerns with its USP: "365 day return policy, free shipping both ways." The result is that Zappos, which founder Tony Hseih recently sold to Amazon.com, has a base of 8 million customers and annual sales that exceed $1 billion![1]

The USP becomes the heart of a company's advertising message because it has the ability to cut through all of the advertising clutter. For instance, the owner of a quaint New England bed and breakfast came up with a four-word USP that captures the essence of the escape her business offers guests from their busy lives: "Delicious beds, delicious breakfasts." Sheila Paterson, cofounder of Marco International, a marketing consulting firm, says her company's USP is "Creative solutions for impossible marketing problems."[2]

By focusing a company's advertising message on these top benefits and the facts that support them, entrepreneurs can communicate their USPs to their target audiences in meaningful, attention-getting ways. Building a firm's marketing message around a USP spells out for customers the benefits they can expect if they buy the company's product or service and why they should do business with a company rather than with its competition. However, a company must be able to *deliver* on its USP; otherwise, the advertising effort is futile!

Table 1 describes a six-sentence advertising strategy designed to create powerful ads that focus on a USP.

Creating a Promotional Strategy

2. Explain the differences among promotion, publicity, personal selling, and advertising.

The terms *advertising* and *promotion* are often confused. **Promotion** is any form of persuasive communication designed to inform consumers about a product or service and to influence them to purchase these goods or services. It includes publicity, personal selling, and advertising.

Publicity

Publicity is any commercial news covered by the media that boosts sales but for which the small business does not pay. "[Publicity] is telling your story to the people you want to reach—namely the news media, potential customers, and community leaders," says the head of a public relations firm. "It is not haphazard . . . It requires regular and steady attention."[3] Publicity has power; because it is from an unbiased source, a news feature about a company or a product appearing in a newspaper or magazine has more impact on people's buying decisions than an advertisement does. Exposure in any medium raises a company's visibility and boosts sales, and, best of all, publicity is free! It does require some creativity and effort, however.

TABLE 1 A Six-Sentence Advertising Strategy

Does your advertising deliver the message you want to the audience you are targeting? If not, try stating your strategy in six sentences:

1. *Primary purpose.* What is the primary purpose of this ad? "The purpose of Rainbow Tours' ads is to get people to call for or download a free video brochure."
2. *Primary benefit.* What USP can you offer customers? "We will stress the unique and exciting places our customers can visit."
3. *Secondary benefits.* What other key benefits support your USP? "We will also stress the convenience and value of our tours and the skill and experience of our tour guides."
4. *Target audience.* At whom are we aiming the ad? "We will aim our ads at adventurous male and female singles and couples, 21 to 34, who can afford our tours."
5. *Audience reaction.* What response do you want from your target audience? "We expect our audience to download or call to request our video brochure."
6. *Company personality.* What image do we want to convey in our ads? "Our ads will reflect our innovation, excitement, conscientiousness, and our warm, caring attitude toward our customers."

Source: Adapted from Jay Conrad Levinson, "The Six-Sentence Strategy," *Communication Briefings,* December 1994, p. 4. Reprinted by permission from Communication Briefings. ©Briefing Media Group LLC.

Profile

Jody Hall and Vérité Coffee

After working at Starbucks for 12 years, Jody Hall saw firsthand the value of publicity and decided to emphasize it when she launched her own Seattle-based coffee shop, Vérité Coffee. In addition to selling coffee, Hall included a unique gourmet cupcake bakery in her store, which has generated articles in both the *Los Angeles Times* and *Food & Wine* magazine. During elections, Hall hands out free cupcakes to voters, advertising the offer in local papers with catchy slogans such as "Legalize Frostitution." Hall also generated publicity for Vérité Coffee by donating 1,000 cupcakes to the local zoo for an elephant's birthday party and to auctions at local schools. Her efforts have paid off; Vérité Coffee generates sales of more than $1 million, and several local supermarkets have approached her about carrying her company's products.[4]

The following tactics can help entrepreneurs stimulate publicity for their companies:

- *Write an article that will interest your customers or potential customers.* One investment advisor writes a monthly column for the local newspaper on timely topics such as "Retirement Planning," "Minimizing Your Tax Bill," and "How to Pay for College." Not only do the articles help build her credibility as an expert, but they also have attracted new customers to her business.
- *Sponsor an event designed to attract attention.* Even local events, for which sponsorships can be quite inexpensive, garner press coverage for sponsors.
- *Involve celebrities "on the cheap."* Few small businesses can afford to hire celebrities as spokespersons for their companies. Some companies have discovered other ways to get celebrities to promote their products, however. For instance, when Karen Neuburger, owner of Karen Neuburger's Sleepwear, learned that Oprah Winfrey is a "pajama connoisseur," she sent the talk show host a pair of her pajamas. The move paid off; Neuburger has appeared on Oprah's popular television show on three separate occasions.[5]
- *Contact local TV and radio stations and offer to be interviewed.* Many local news or talk shows are looking for guests to talk about topics of interest to their audiences (especially in January and February). Even local shows can reach new customers.
- *Publish a newsletter.* With a personal computer and desktop publishing software, any entrepreneur can publish a professional-looking newsletter. Freelancers can offer design and editing advice. Use the newsletter to reach present and potential customers.
- *Contact local business and civic organizations and offer to speak to them.* A powerful, informative presentation can win new business. (Be sure your public speaking skills are up to par first! If not, consider joining Toastmasters.)
- *Offer or sponsor a seminar.* Teaching people about a subject you know a great deal about builds confidence and goodwill among potential customers. The owner of a landscaping service and nursery offers a short course in landscape architecture and always sees sales climb afterwards!
- *Write news releases and fax or e-mail them to the media.* The key to having a news release picked up and printed is finding a unique angle on your business or industry that would interest an editor. Keep it short, simple, and interesting. E-mail press releases should be shorter than printed ones—typically four or five paragraphs rather than one or two pages—and they should include a link to the company's Web site.

Profile

Richard Mori and Mori Books

When New Hampshire switched to a new toll road system, the state declared all outstanding highway toll tokens worthless. Sensing a public relations opportunity, Richard Mori, owner of Mori Books in Amherst, offered to redeem the outdated tokens at double their face value for up to half the price of any book in his store and sent out press releases announcing the deal. Within days, newspapers and television and radio stations across New Hampshire were featuring Mori's business. The exposure led to a 25 percent increase in sales.[6]

- *Volunteer to serve on community and industry boards and committees.* You can make your town a better place to live and work and raise your company's visibility at the same time.
- *Sponsor a community project or support a nonprofit organization or charity.* Not only will you be giving something back to the community, but you will also gain recognition,

goodwill, and, perhaps, customers for your business. Appearance Plus, a dry cleaning business in Cincinnati, Ohio, received the equivalent of thousands of dollars worth of advertising from the publicity generated by its Coats for Kids campaign. Customers donated winter coats and blankets, which the company cleaned for free and then distributed to the needy.[7]

- *Promote a cause.* By engaging in **cause marketing**, entrepreneurs can support and promote a nonprofit cause or charity that is important to them and raise the visibility of their companies in the community at the same time. The key is choosing a cause that is important to your customers. One marketing expert offers the following formula for selecting the right cause: Mission statement + personal passion + customer demographics = ideal cause.[8] REI, a retailer of outdoor gear, generates goodwill among its customers and publicity for its business by donating both money and employees' time to worthy outdoor nonprofit programs such as Big City Mountaineers, which leads wilderness adventures for urban teens, and conservation causes such as the Continental Divide Trail Alliance and the Leave No Trace Center for Outdoor Ethics.[9]

IN THE ENTREPRENEURIAL
SPOTLIGHT One Small Company's 10 Seconds of Fame

Netflix revolutionized the video rental industry with its "keep a video as long as you want with no late fee" policy and its fast, convenient delivery. Lloyd Lapidus and Greg Pippo, the founders of Bag Borrow or Steal (now called Avelle) applied that same philosophy to the $5 billion women's handbag industry, allowing fashionistas to keep pace with rapid changes in designer handbag styles and avoid the guilt associated with buying them and shortly retiring them to the back of the closet. Lapidus and Pippo recognized that designer bags are as much status symbols for women as sleek sports cars are for men, but that trendy bags have a very short fashion life. The entrepreneurs also saw an increased desire for luxury goods among shoppers, even those whose budgets do not match their high-end tastes. Writers call the trend "masstige," prestige for the masses, and companies such as Bag Borrow or Steal that lease exclusive merchandise make it affordable. One reporter says, "The devil may wear Prada, but she can also borrow it—and exchange it—through Bag Borrow or Steal."

Launched in 2004 in Seattle, Washington, Bag Borrow or Steal offers women unlimited access to more than 4,000 styles of bags from more than 100 designers, including Louis Vuitton, Gucci, Fendi, Jimmy Choo, Vera Wang, Coach, Balenciaga, and others, for as little as $13 per week. Fashion divas lease upscale designer bags, many of which sell for thousands of dollars, for a few days, a week, a month, or even longer at a fraction of their selling prices. For instance, customers can lease a Louis Vuitton clutch that sells for $1,300 for just $65 a week. A beige Chanel bag that sells for $3,500 rents for $120 per week. Bag Borrow or Steal refurbishes all bags to like-new condition

before leasing them. A customer who falls in love with a particular bag also can purchase it at a discount. Customers who pay a $10 monthly fee to become members earn discounts on bag rental rates (insurance and postage extra).

For the first 4 years of its existence, Bag Borrow or Steal experienced a solid, if not stellar, growth rate. Mike Smith, CEO of the 75-employee company, then learned that Hollywood movie producer/writer/director Michael Patrick King had incorporated a line about Bag Borrow or Steal into the script of *Sex and the City: The Movie*, the original film based on the hit HBO series of the same name. In the scene, Louise (played by Jennifer Hudson), the assistant to Carrie Bradshaw (played by Sarah Jessica Parker), has an affinity for high-end handbags and admits that she does not buy them; instead, she rents them from Bag Borrow or Steal. Companies often pay millions of dollars for product placement or a mention like the one in the 10-second scene from *Sex and the City*, but Bag Borrow or Steal paid nothing. Smith says that the small company could not have been able to afford that kind of publicity. Executives at New Line Cinema, the movie studio that produced the film, contacted Smith and Chief Marketing Officer Jody Watson 6 months before the film's release, which gave the small company enough time to maximize the benefit of the publicity that was coming its way.

On its Web site, Bag Borrow or Steal offered visitors the opportunity to watch the movie trailer, launched a YouTube sweepstakes to win tickets to the premiere, and created a "Sex and the City" shop in which customers could browse through handbags inspired by the four main characters in

Sex and the City: The Movie, mentioned Bag Borrow or Steal, a small company that leases designer handbags to women. The company's 10 seconds of fame resulted in its customer base tripling.

Source: Bobby Bank\Getty Images-WireImage.com

the film. Visitors could take a quiz to discover which of the movie's characters they were most like—and then shop for bags connected to that character. Bag Borrow or Steal also added a new line of sunglasses and jewelry to its line of rental merchandise. "Companies don't get a gift like this every day," says Watson.

After the release of *Sex and the City: The Movie*, which grossed more than $415 million worldwide, membership at Bag Borrow or Steal tripled to 1.5 million customers. Despite ramping up its inventory in the weeks before the film's release, demand for rental bags was so overwhelming that Bag Borrow or Steal had to place some customers on waiting lists. For 7 straight days following the release, the small company set sales records. Magazines and television networks across the country featured stories on the small company. "It's a Cinderella story for us," says Watson.

1. Bag Borrow or Steal was fortunate enough to have an opportunity for top-tier publicity fall in its lap. What steps can entrepreneurs take to garner publicity for their small companies?
2. Select a small business with which you are familiar. Work with a team of your classmates to generate ideas for generating publicity for the company.

Sources: Based on Simona Covel, "Bag Borrow Or Steal Lands the Role of a Lifetime," *Wall Street Journal*, May 27, 2008, p. B7; Wendy Kaufman, "Women Turn to Online Rentals for Handbags," *National Public Radio*, December 5, 2005, *www.npr.org/templates/story/story. php?storyId=5038856;* Stuart Elliott, "'Sex and the City' and Its Lasting Female Appeal," *New York Times*, March 17, 2008, *www.nytimes.com/ 2008/03/17/business/media/17adco.html;* "Bag Borrow or Steal," Hambrick Group, *www.hambrickgroup.com/clientListBagBorrow.html;* Lauren Folino, "Fashion Entrepreneurs Capitalizing on High-End Rentals," *Inc.*, December 4, 2009, *www.inc.com/news/articles/2009/12/designer-fashion-rental.html.*

Personal Selling

Advertising often marks the beginning of a sale, but personal selling usually is required to close the sale. **Personal selling** is the personal contact between salespeople and potential customers that comes from sales efforts. Effective personal selling gives a small company an advantage over its larger competitors by creating a feeling of personal attention. Personal selling deals with the salesperson's ability to match customer needs to the company's goods and services. Top salespeople:

- *Are enthusiastic and are alert to opportunities.* Star sales representatives demonstrate deep concentration, high energy, and drive.
- *Are experts in the products or services they sell.* They understand how their product lines or services can help their customers.

■ *Concentrate on their best accounts.* They focus on customers with the greatest sales potential first. They understand the importance of the 80/20 rule: Approximately 80 percent of their sales comes from about 20 percent of their customers.

■ *Plan thoroughly.* On every sales call, the best representatives act with a purpose to close the sale.

■ *Use a direct approach.* They get right to the point with customers.

■ *Approach the sales call from their customers' perspectives.* They have empathy for their customers and know their customers' businesses and their needs. Rather than sell the features of a product or service, they emphasize the benefits those features offer their customers.

■ *Offer proof of the benefits their product or service provides.* The best salespeople provide tangible evidence such as statistics, facts, and testimonies from other customers about how their product or service will benefit the customer.

■ *Are good listeners.* They ask questions and listen. By listening, sales representatives are able to identify customers' "hot buttons," key issues that drive their purchase decisions. "Questions are the key to selling," says one experienced salesperson. "Nobody ever listened themselves out of a sale!"[10]

■ *Use past success stories.* They encourage customers to express their problems and then present solutions using examples of past successes.

■ *Leave sales material with clients.* The material gives the customer the opportunity to study company and product literature in more detail.

■ *See themselves as problem solvers, not just vendors.* Their perspective is "How can I be a valuable resource for my customers?" In fact, smart salespeople take the time to ask their existing customers, "Is there anything I am not doing that I could be doing to serve you better?" A study by Cahners Research found that sales representatives who understand the business needs and pressures that their customers face are 69 percent more likely to close a sale.[11]

■ *Measure their success not just by sales volume but by customer satisfaction.* The key to sustaining sales for the long term is to build a corps of satisfied customers.

One extensive study found that just 20 percent of all salespeople have the ability to sell and are selling the "right" product or service and that that 20 percent make 80 percent of all sales. The study also concluded that 55 percent of sales representatives have "absolutely no ability to sell"; the remaining 25 percent have sales ability but are selling the wrong product or service.[12]

A study by Cahners Research found that it takes an average of 5.12 sales calls to close a deal.[13] Common causes of sales rejections include the representative's failure to determine customers' needs, talking too much, and neglecting to ask for the order. Given the high cost of making a sales call (an average of nearly $400), those missed opportunities are quite costly. Figure 1 shows how sales representatives spend their time. (Note that they spend less than 25 percent of their time engaged in active selling!)

FIGURE 1
How Sales Representatives Spend Their Time

Source: Pace Productivity Inc., 2008.

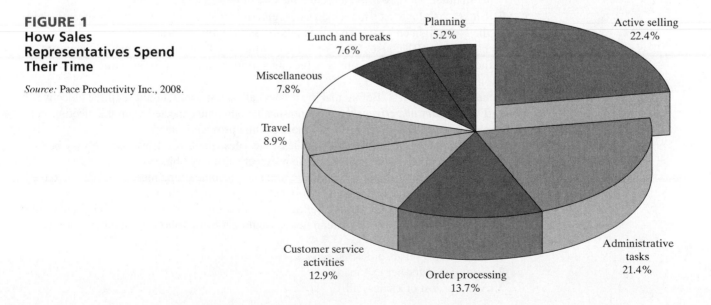

Entrepreneurs can improve their sales representatives' "closing averages" by following some basic guidelines:

- *Hire the right people.* A successful sales effort starts well before a sales representative calls on a potential customer. The first step is hiring capable salespeople who demonstrate empathy for customers, are motivated, persistent, and focused.
- *Train sales representatives.* Too often, business owners send sales representatives out into the field with little or no training and then wonder why they cannot produce. Training starts with teaching salespeople every aspect of the products or services they will be selling before moving on to teach them how to build relationships with customers. Training must also include the two most important selling skills of all: listening to the customer and closing the sale. Many business owners find that role playing exercises are an effective sales training technique.
- *Develop a selling system.* To be successful, sales representatives must develop an effective selling system. To build a winning selling system, entrepreneurs can take the following steps:
    1. *Prepare.* The best sales representatives know that what they do *before* they make a sales call significantly influences their success. In fact, the top complaint about sales representatives among buyers is a salesperson who is unprepared. Unfortunately, according to a study by Knowledge Anywhere, nearly 63 percent of sales representatives spend less than 20 minutes preparing for a sales call.[14] Smart salespeople take the time to research their customers (most often using the Internet) and to learn about the companies where their customers work.
    2. *Approach.* Establish rapport with the prospect. Customers seldom buy from salespeople they dislike or distrust.
    3. *Interview.* Get the prospect to do most of the talking; the goal is to identify his or her needs, preferences, and problems. The key is to *listen* and then to ask follow-up questions that help determine exactly what the customer wants. Norm Brodsky, founder of six companies, including a highly successful records storage business, says, "When I call on a prospect for the first time, I don't even talk about our company. I spend the whole visit just trying to learn all I can about the people I'm dealing with. I look to build rapport and understand how the customer likes to do business."[15]
    4. *Demonstrate, explain, and show.* Make clear the features and benefits of your product or service and point out how they meet the prospect's needs or solve his problems.
    5. *Validate.* Prove the claims about your product or service. If possible, offer the prospect names and numbers of other satisfied customers (with their permission, of course). Testimonials really work.
    6. *Negotiate.* Listen for objections from the prospect. Objections can be the salesperson's best friend; they tell him or her what must be "fixed" before the prospect will commit to an order. The key is to determine the *real* objection and confront it.
    7. *Close.* Ask for a decision. Good sales representatives know when the prospect flashes the green light on a sale. They stop talking and ask for the order.
- *Be empathetic.* The best salespeople look at the sale from the customer's viewpoint, not their own! Doing so encourages the sales representative to stress *value* to the customer.
- *Set multiple objectives.* Before making a sales call, salespeople should set three objectives:
    1. *The primary objective* is the most reasonable outcome expected from the meeting. It may be to get an order or to learn more about a prospect's needs.
    2. *The minimum objective* is the very least the salesperson will leave with. It may be to set another meeting or to identify the prospect's primary objections.
    3. *The visionary objective* is the most optimistic outcome of the meeting. This objective forces the salesperson to be open-minded and to shoot for the top.
- *Monitor sales efforts and results.* Selling is just like any other business activity and must be controlled. At a minimum, entrepreneurs should know the following numbers for their companies:
    1. Actual sales versus projected sales
    2. Sales generated per call made
    3. Average cost of a sales call

4. Total sales costs

5. Sales by product, salesperson, territory, customer, and so on

6. Profit contribution by product, salesperson, territory, customer, and so on

Advertising

Advertising is any sales presentation that is nonpersonal in nature and is paid for by an identified sponsor. A company's target audience and the nature of its message determine the advertising media it will use. However, the process does not end with creating and broadcasting an ad. Entrepreneurs also must evaluate an ad campaign's effectiveness. Did it accomplish the objectives it was designed to accomplish? Immediate-response ads can be evaluated in a number of ways. For instance, a business owner can include coupons that customers redeem to get price reductions on products and services. Dated coupons identify customer responses over certain time periods. Some firms use "hidden offers," statements hidden somewhere in an ad that offer customers special deals if they mention an ad or bring in a coupon from it. For example, Scott Fiore, owner of the Herbal Remedy, an all-natural pharmacy in Littleton, Colorado, uses a "bring this ad in for 10 percent off" message in his print ads so he can track each ad's success rate and adjust his advertising expenditures accordingly.

Business owners can also gauge an ad's effectiveness by measuring the volume of store traffic generated. Effective advertising should increase store traffic, which boosts sales of advertised and nonadvertised items. Of course, if an advertisement promotes a particular bargain item, the owner can judge its effectiveness by comparing sales of the items to preadvertising sales levels. Remember: The ultimate test of an ad is whether it increases sales!

Ad tests enable entrepreneurs to determine the most effective methods of reaching their target customers. An owner can design two different ads (or use two different media or broadcast times) that are coded for identification and see which one produces more responses. For example, a business owner can use a split run of two different ads in a local newspaper; that is, he can place one ad in part of the paper's press run and another ad in the remainder of the run. Then he can measure the response level to each ad to compare its effectiveness. Table 2 offers 12 tips for creating an effective advertising campaign.

The remainder of this chapter will focus on selecting advertising media, developing an advertising plan, and creating an advertising budget. Figure 2 illustrates the characteristics of a successful ad.

Selecting Advertising Media

3. Describe the advantages and disadvantages of the various advertising media.

Entrepreneurs quickly discover that a wide array of advertising media are available, including newspapers, magazines, radio, television, direct mail, the Web, as well as many specialty media. One of the most important decisions an entrepreneur must make is which media to use to disseminate the company's message. The medium used to transmit the message influences the customer's perception—and reception—of it. The right message broadcast in the wrong medium will miss its mark. Before selecting the vehicle for the message, entrepreneurs should consider several important questions:

■ *How large is my company's trading area?* How big is the geographic region from which the firm will draw its customers? The size of this area influences the choice of media.

■ *Who are my target customers and what are their characteristics?* Determining a customer profile often points to the appropriate medium to use to get the message across most effectively.

■ *With which media are my target customers most likely to interact?* Until he knows who his target audience is, a business owner cannot select the proper advertising media to reach it.

■ *What budget limitations do I face?* Every business owner must direct the firm's advertising program within the restrictions of its operating budget. Certain advertising media cost more than others.

■ *Which media do my competitors use?* Is it helpful for a business owner to know the media his competitors use, although he should *not* automatically assume that they are

TABLE 2 12 Tips for Effective Advertising

1. *Plan more than one advertisement at a time.* An advertising campaign is likely to be more effective if it is developed from a comprehensive plan for a specific time period. A piecemeal approach produces ads that lack continuity and a unified theme.

2. *Set long-run advertising objectives.* One cause of inadequate planning is the failure to establish specific objectives for the advertising program. If an entrepreneur never defines what is expected from advertising, the program is likely to lack a sense of direction.

3. *Use advertisements, themes, and vehicles that appeal to diverse groups of people.* Although personal judgment influences every business decision, business owners cannot afford to let bias interfere with advertising decisions. For example, you should not use a particular radio station simply because you like it. What matters is whether the company's target customers listen to the station.

4. *View advertising expenditures as investments not as expenses.* In an accounting sense, advertising is a business expense, but money spent on ads tends to produce sales and profits over time that might not be possible without advertising. An effective advertising program generates more sales than it costs. You must ask, "Can I afford *not* to advertise?"

5. *Use advertising that is different from your competitors' advertising.* Some managers tend to "follow the advertising crowd" because they fear being different from their competitors. "Me-too" advertising frequently is ineffective because it fails to create a unique image for the firm. Don't be afraid to be different!

6. *Choose the media vehicle that is best for your business even if it's not "number one."* It is not uncommon for several media within the same geographic region to claim to be "number one." Different media offer certain advantages and disadvantages. Entrepreneurs should evaluate each according to its ability to reach their target audiences most effectively.

7. *Consider using someone else as the spokesperson on your TV and radio commercials.* Although being your own spokesperson may lend a personal touch to your ads, the commercial may be seen as nonprofessional or "homemade." The ad may detract from the company's image rather than improve it.

8. *Limit the content of each ad.* Some entrepreneurs think that to get the most for their advertising dollar, they must pack their ads full of facts and illustrations. Overcrowded ads confuse customers and are easy to ignore. Simple, well-designed ads that focus on your USP are much more effective.

9. *Devise ways of measuring your ads' effectiveness that don't depend on just two or three customers' responses.* Measuring the effectiveness of advertising is an elusive art at best. But the opinions of a small unrepresentative sample of customers, whose opinions may be biased, is not a reliable gauge of an ad's effectiveness. The techniques described earlier offer objective measurements of an ad's ability to produce results.

10. *Don't simply drop an ad because nothing happens immediately.* Some ads are designed to produce immediate results, but many ads require more time because of the lag effect they experience. One of advertising's rules is: It's not the size; it's the frequency. The head of one advertising agency claims, "The biggest waste of money is stop-and-start advertising." With advertising, patience is essential, and entrepreneurs must give an advertising campaign a reasonable time to produce results. One recent study concluded that sales increases are most noticeable 4 to 6 months after an advertising campaign begins. One advertising expert claims that successful advertisers "are not capricious ad-by-ad makers; they're consistent ad campaigners."

11. *Emphasize the benefits that the product or service provides to the customer.* Too often, ads emphasize only the features of the products or services a company offers without mentioning the benefits they provide customers. Customers really don't care about a product's or service's "bells and whistles"; they are much more interested in the *benefits* those features can give them! Their primary concern is "What's in it for me?"

12. *Evaluate the cost of different advertising medium.* Remember the difference between the absolute and relative cost of an ad. The medium that has a low absolute cost may actually offer a high relative cost if it does not reach your intended target audience. Evaluate the cost of different media by looking at the cost per thousand customers reached. Remember: No medium is a bargain if it fails to connect you with your intended customers.

Sources: Adapted from Sue Clayton, "Advertising," *Business Start-Ups*, December 1995, pp. 6–7; *Marketing for Small Business*, The University of Georgia Small Business Development Center: Athens, Georgia, 1992, p. 69; "Advertising Leads to Sales," *Small Business Reports*, April 1988, p. 14; Shelly Meinhardt, "Put It in Print," *Entrepreneur*, January 1989, p. 54; Danny R. Arnold and Robert H. Solomon, "Ten 'Don'ts' in Bank Advertising;" *Burroughs Clearing House*, vol.16, no. 12, September 1980, pp. 20–24, 43; Howard Dana Shaw, "Success with Ads," *In Business*, November–December 1991, pp. 48–49; Jan Alexander and Aimee L. Stern, "Avoid the Deadly Sins in Advertising;" *Your Company*, August/September 1997, p. 22.

the best choice. An approach that differs from the traditional one may produce better results.

■ *How important is repetition and continuity of my advertising message?* Generally, an ad becomes effective only after it is repeated several times, and many ads must be continued for some time before they produce results. Some experts suggest that an ad must be run at least six times in most mass media before it becomes effective.

■ *How does each medium compare with others in its audience, its reach, and its frequency?* Audience measures the number of paid subscribers a particular medium attracts. This is called *circulation* in most print media, such as newspapers and magazines.

FIGURE 2
Characteristics of a Successful Ad

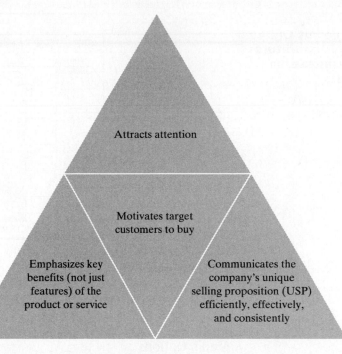

FIGURE 2
Characteristics of a Successful Ad

Reach is the total number of people exposed to an ad at least once in a period of time, usually 4 weeks. **Frequency** is the average number of times a person is exposed to an ad in that same time period.

■ *What does the advertising medium cost?* The entrepreneur must consider two types of advertising costs: absolute and relative. **Absolute cost** is the actual dollar outlay a business owner must make to place an ad in a particular medium for a specific time period. An even more important measure is an ad's **relative cost**, the ad's cost per potential customer reached. Relative cost is most often expressed as **cost per thousand (CPM)**, the cost of the ad per 1,000 customers reached. Suppose an entrepreneur decides to advertise his product in one of two newspapers in town. The *Sentinel* has a circulation of 21,000 and charges $1,200 for a quarter-page ad. The *Independent* has a circulation of 18,000 and charges $1,300 for the same space. Reader profiles of the two papers suggest that 25 percent of *Sentinel* readers and 37 percent of *Independent* readers are potential customers. Using this information, the entrepreneur computes the following relative costs:

	Sentinel	Independent
Circulation	21,000	18,000
Percentage of readers who are potential customers	× 25%	× 37%
Potential customers reached	5,250	6,660
Absolute cost of ad	$1,200	$1,300
Relative cost of ad (CPM)	$1,200/5,250 = .22857, or $228.57 per thousand potential customers reached	$1,300/6,660 = .19520, or $195.20 per thousand potential customers reached

Although the *Sentinel* has a larger circulation and a lower absolute cost for running the ad, the *Independent* offers this entrepreneur a better advertising deal because of its lower cost per thousand potential customers (CPM) reached. It is important to note that this technique does not give a reliable comparison across media; it is a meaningful comparison only *within* a single medium. Differences among the format, presentation, and coverage of ads in different media are so vast that cross-comparisons are not meaningful.

FIGURE 3
Traditional Versus Online Advertising Expenditures by Small Businesses in Local Markets

Source: Based on *The Local Commerce Monitor*, The BIA/Kelsey Group, 2009.

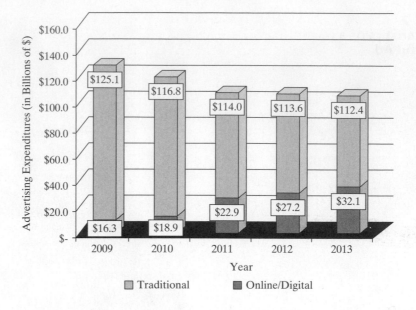

Media Options

The world of advertising is undergoing seismic changes. The lines that once separated the various advertising media are now blurring. Features that once were unique to a specific medium now operate across multiple media. Video, once the distinctive signature of television, now appears on companies' Web sites, in e-mail ads, on YouTube, on smart phones, and other devices. Traditional methods of advertising are not as effective as they once were because of increased advertising clutter, the growth in the time that customers spend online, and intense competition for buyers' attention. Small businesses are steadily shifting their advertising expenditures away from traditional media such as newspapers, television, direct mail, radio, magazines, and directories toward digital media such as e-mail campaigns, search engines, online and mobile device ads, and others (see Figure 3). According to *The Local Commerce Monitor* by BIA/Kelsey, 77 percent of small businesses now use digital or online advertising media, compared to 69 percent that use traditional advertising media.[16]

Entrepreneurs are looking to supplement or even replace traditional methods of advertising with inexpensive online tools and innovative, sometimes offbeat, techniques that capture buyers' attention.

Choosing advertising media is no easy task because each has particular advantages, disadvantages, and costs. Figure 4 gives a breakdown of U.S. business advertising expenditures by medium. Let's examine the features of various advertising media.

FIGURE 4
Advertising Expenditures by Medium

Source: Advertising Age, McCann-Erickson Inc., 2009.

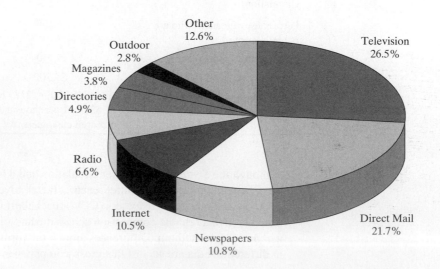

WORD-OF-MOUTH ADVERTISING. Perhaps the most effective and certainly the least expensive form of advertising is **word-of-mouth advertising** whereby satisfied customers recommend a business to friends, family members, and acquaintances. Unsolicited testimonials are powerful; because they are impartial, they score high on importance and credibility among potential customers. According to the Media Myth and Realities survey, 47 percent of U.S. consumers say that advice from family members and friends is a significant source of information about the products and services they buy.[17]

The best way for a company to generate positive word-of-mouth advertising is to provide superior quality and service, giving customers a reason to talk about the company in a positive way. A stellar experience leads to loyal customers who become walking advertisements for the company. In an age of social networking, the quality of the experience customers have with a business has more impact than any form of advertising. Word-of-mouth advertising can make or break a business because *dissatisfied* customers also speak out against businesses that treat them poorly. To ensure that the word-of-mouth advertising a company generates is positive, business owners must actually do what they want their customers to say they do.

ENTREPRENEURIAL Profile

Shelly Hwang and Young Lee and Pinkberry

When Shelly Hwang and Young Lee opened Pinkberry, a shop that sells all-natural, nonfat yogurt in West Hollywood, California, in a location that was less than ideal, they knew that they would have to rely on word-of-mouth advertising to build a customer base. Their yogurt, which comes in plain and green tea flavors with 18 toppings, ranging from kiwi and mango to fruity pebbles and carob chips, is served in a modern environment with upscale Italian furniture, Scandinavian light fixtures, and hip European music. Everything about Pinkberry resonates with the entrepreneurs' target customers, and the result was rampant word-of-mouth advertising. "When residents tasted the yogurt, their mouths were like machine guns," says Lee. "They talked about it; they brought their friends. Business has been just phenomenal from the first month." Word-of-mouth advertising has been so effective for Pinkberry that Hwang and Lee are planning to open other locations in California, Arizona, New York, and Texas.[18]

A customer endorsement is an effective way of converting the power of word of mouth to an advertising message. Of course, unpaid and unsolicited endorsements are the most valuable. Online, those endorsements often come from customer-generated product reviews. Today, customers tend to rely more on customer reviews for information about a product or service than on the company's own descriptions.[19] The lesson: Make sure that your Web site includes a section for customer endorsements and reviews.

The Holy Grail of word-of-mouth advertising is "buzz." Buzz occurs when a product is hot and everyone is talking about it. From the mood rings of the 1970s to Apple's iPods, buzz drives the sales of many products. The Internet has only magnified the power of buzz to influence a product's sales. Buzz on the Web has become a powerful force in influencing the popularity of a firm's products or services. What can business owners do to start a buzz about their companies or their products or services? Sometimes buzz starts on its own, leaving a business owner struggling to keep up with the fury it creates. More often than not, however, business owners can give it a nudge by creating interest, mystique, and curiosity in a product or service. Creating buzz does not have to be expensive, but it does require being different. Consider the following tips:

■ *Make your business buzz-worthy.* If your company has nothing to set it apart, customers have no incentive to create buzz about it. Does your company sell a novel product, have a unique marketing approach, offer stellar customer service, use a wacky logo, or anything else that can set it apart? If so, that can be the basis for buzz.

■ *Promote your company to "influencers" in your market.* Influencers are high-profile customers who are on the front edge of every trend. They are the first to wear the hottest athletic shoe, master the coolest video game, or make the hippest restaurant their new hangout; they also are willing to tell their friends. Promoting your company's products and services to influencers increases the likelihood that your company will be the subject of buzz.

■ *Make it easy for satisfied customers to spread the word about your company.* Ask customers periodically to tell a friend about your business and their positive experience with it. Put a "tell-a-friend" link on every page of your company's Web site. Reward customers who refer customers to your business by offering them something special in return.

Entrepreneur Lauren Luke uses YouTube videos to create buzz for her line of cosmetics, By Lauren Luke.

Source: TLA/Newscom

- *Use the Web to encourage viral marketing and amplify your company's word-of-mouth advertising.* One of the easiest ways to accomplish this is through e-mail because it is so easy for people to pass along to their friends. Another technique is to publicize news about your company on a blog and to include links to your company's Web site. Entrepreneurs also can use social media sites such as Facebook, Twitter, and others to engage customers and encourage buzz.
- *Tap into the power of YouTube.* Video-oriented Web sites such as YouTube, which draws 96.1 million unique viewers per month, can be a powerful tool for creating buzz for a company's products and services.[20] Videos on YouTube often become viral and are an important source of buzz for small companies.

ENTREPRENEURIAL
Profile

Laura Luke and By Lauren Luke

Thanks to the makeup tutorials that Lauren Luke began posting on YouTube to help her sell makeup on eBay, the 28-year-old single mother has become one of the United Kingdom's most popular YouTube stars, with 68 million views and 277,000 subscribers. In addition to the practical makeup tips Luke offers, the unscripted, unedited, genuine nature of her videos (viewers often hear her three dogs snoring in the background or her son watching cartoons) resonates with women of all ages—from preteens to octogenarians. Although not professionally trained, Luke's appeal is her knowledge, sincerity, and girl-next-door looks. "I'm definitely not a makeup artist," she says. "I've had no professional training. I'm more everybody's best friend they'd love to have in their bedroom playing makeup and giving tips." Building on her YouTube popularity, Luke now has her own line of cosmetics, By Lauren Luke. She also writes a popular newspaper column, has published a book, and has even helped develop a video game, Super Model Makeover by Lauren Luke.[21]

SPONSORSHIPS AND SPECIAL EVENTS. Although sponsorships and special events are a relatively new promotional medium for small companies, a growing number of small businesses are finding that sponsoring special events attracts a great deal of interest and provides a lasting impression of the company in customers' minds. As customers become increasingly harder to reach through any single advertising medium, companies of all sizes are finding that sponsoring special events—from wine tastings and beach volleyball tournaments to fitness walks and barbeque festivals—is an excellent way to reach their target audiences. North American businesses spend nearly $17 billion a year on event sponsorships.[22]

The costs of sponsorships vary and can meet a variety of budgets. Sponsoring a hole at a charitable golf outing may cost as little as $100, but landing the name of your business or product on the hood of a car driven by a NASCAR racer may reach as much as $7 million. Sponsorships and participation in special events can be very cost-effective if the entrepreneur supports events where attendees are potential customers. Local festivals and events gain the sponsor a great deal of positive public relations. Support for charity functions enhances the sponsor's community image, boosts sales, and often attracts new customers.

ENTREPRENEURIAL
Profile

George Cigale and Tutor.com

George Cigale, CEO of Tutor.com, a company based in New York City that sells online educational services, invests a significant portion of the company's promotional budget as a sponsor for the American Library Association's annual conference. Because public libraries are one of the company's primary customers, the conference gives Cigale and his employees the opportunity to spend quality time with an important group of their target customers. The sponsorship costs Tutor.com $10,000, and Cigale spends an additional $50,000 on travel and lodging for employees to attend and to sponsor a breakfast for the more than 300 librarians who attend the event. The sponsorship has paid off for Tutor.com. A librarian that Cigale met at the conference hired the company to create a pilot program for the California library system, a job that has generated $3 million a year in revenue.[23]

Small companies do not have to rely on other organizations' events to generate advertising opportunities; they can create their own special events. The owner of Quadrille Quilting in North Haven, Connecticut, partnered with the owners of two other quilting shops to create Shop Hops, an event in which customers buy "passports" to all three stores that entitle them to refreshments and special prizes. The first Shop Hop, which took place on a Super Bowl weekend, generated an entire month's sales in just one day for Quadrille Quilting.[24]

Creativity and uniqueness are essential ingredients in any special event promotion, and entrepreneurs excel at those. The following tips will help entrepreneurs get the greatest promotional impact from event sponsorships:

- *Do not count on sponsorships for your entire advertising campaign.* Sponsorships are most effective when they are part of a coordinated advertising effort. Most sponsors spend no more than 10 percent of their advertising budgets on sponsorships.
- *Look for an event that is appropriate for your company and its products and services.* The owner of a small music store in an upscale mountain resort sponsors a local jazz festival every summer during the busy tourist season and generates lots of business among both residents and tourists. Ideally, an event's audience should match the sponsoring company's target audience. Otherwise, the sponsorship will be a waste of money.
- *Research the event and the organization hosting it before agreeing to become a sponsor.* How well attended is the event? What is the demographic profile of the event's visitors? Is it well organized?
- *Try to become a dominant (or, ideally, the only) sponsor of the event.* A small company can be easily lost in a crowd of much larger companies sponsoring the same event. If sole sponsorship is too expensive, make sure that your company is the only one from its industry sponsoring the event.
- *Clarify the costs and level of participation required for sponsorship up front.* Doing so avoids unexpected surprises that can break a small company's advertising budget.
- *Get involved.* Do not simply write a check for the sponsorship fee and then walk away. Find an event that is meaningful to you, your company, and its employees and take an active role in it. Your sponsorship dollars will produce a higher return if you do.

In some cases the line between advertising and publicity has become blurry. In recent years, entrepreneurs have begun to explore new methods of getting their products or services in front of their target customers in a more subtle fashion. Many companies are engaged in product placement strategies in which their products or services appear in television shows, movies, video games, and other media that their target customers are likely to see.

ENTREPRENEURIAL
Profile

NeuroLogica

After the portable CT scanner made by NeuroLogica, a small company in Danvers, Massachusetts, appeared on the 300th episode of *ER,* traffic to its Web site increased 60 percent. The company also received 10 inquiries from hospital administrators who had seen the $330,000 machine on the television show, far above the normal two or three inquiries each month. The scanner also became the topic of discussion on several *ER*-related blogs, and fans of the show posted video clips on YouTube. "I was shocked to see how much exposure we received," says NeuroLogica's director of sales, David Webster. "My friends in the industry could not believe that we did not pay for it."[25]

Product placement is effective because it relies on highly sophisticated yet subtle brand exposure. One of the earliest and most successful cases of product placement occurred in the 1982 movie classic *E.T.: The Extra-Terrestrial*, in which the main character (E.T., the alien) discovers an affinity for Reese's Pieces. After the movie's premiere, sales of Reese's Pieces increased 65 percent![26]

TELEVISION. In advertising dollars spent, television ranks first in popularity of all media. Although the cost of national TV ads precludes their use by most small businesses, local spots can be an extremely effective means of broadcasting a small company's message. A 30-second commercial on network television may cost more than $500,000 (a 30-second spot during the Super Bowl sells for $2.5 million to $3 million, up from $600,000 in 1987), but a 30-second spot on local cable television, which now is in 61.5 percent U.S. homes, may go for as little as $10 in small markets.[27]

ENTREPRENEURIAL
Profile

Jason Apfel and FragranceNet.com

Jason Apfel launched FragranceNet.com, an online retailer of brand name fragrances and beauty products, in 1995. "At first, we just had an 800 number that customers could call to order fragrances over the phone," he says. "Then the Internet came along." An early Internet adopter, Apfel initially set up a static Web page designed to prompt customers to call the company's toll-free number and was amazed at the results. "The phone started ringing off the hook," he recalls. Apfel then set up an e-commerce site and, in 2001, began using search engine marketing with tools such as Google AdWords. "We've seen a 20 percent year-on-year increase in our conversion rate," says Apfel. In 2007, looking to expand the company's customer base, Apfel turned to television, a medium that FragranceNet.com had used before without much success. This time, however, Apfel used Google TV Ads to decide which cable networks across the nation to use and which programs to target while placing caps on costs. Apfel used the tool to locate programs that were relevant to the company's product line and that attracted the highest concentrations of its target customers. "We don't have $20 million to throw at a campaign and hope it works," he says. After the cable television ads ran, FrangranceNet.com saw a 35 percent increase in the number of visitors to its Web site and a corresponding increase in sales.[28]

Television advertising offers a number of distinct advantages:

- *Broad coverage.* Television ads provide extensive coverage of a sizeable region, and they reach a significant portion of the population. Television reaches 90.2 percent of adults every day, exceeding the reach of all other major advertising media.[29] In fact, the average household spends 8 hours and 14 minutes each day tuned in to television.[30] The typical adult sees 26 commercial breaks a day, for a total of 73 minutes of advertisements.[31]
- *Ability to focus on a target audience.* Because many cable channels focus their broadcasting in topical areas—from home and garden or food to science or cartoons—cable television

offers advertisers the ability to reach specific target markets much as radio ads do. Because an inverse relationship exists between time spent in television viewing and education level, television ads overall are more likely to reach people with lower educational levels.

- *Visual advantage.* The primary benefit of television is its capacity to present the advertiser's product or service visually. With TV ads, entrepreneurs are not limited to mere descriptions of a product or service; instead, they can demonstrate their uses and show firsthand their advantages. For instance, a small retail store selling a hydraulic log splitter can design a television commercial to show how easily the machine works. The ability to use sight, sound, and motion makes TV ads a powerful selling tool.
- *Flexibility.* Television ads can be modified quickly to meet the rapidly changing conditions in the marketplace. Advertising on TV is a close substitute for personal selling. Like a sales representative's call, television commercials can use "hard sell" techniques, attempt to convince through logic, appeal to viewers' emotions, persuade through subtle influence, or use any number of other strategies. In addition, advertisers can choose the length of the spot (30-second ads are most common), its time slot, and even the program during which to broadcast the ad.
- *Design assistance.* Few entrepreneurs have the skills to prepare an effective television commercial. Although professional production firms might easily charge $50,000 to produce a commercial, the television station from which an entrepreneur purchases air time often will help to design and produce an ad very inexpensively.

Television advertising also has several disadvantages:

- *Brief exposure.* Most television ads are on the screen for only a short time and require substantial repetition to achieve the desired effect. One of the realities is that television viewers often avoid or ignore the commercial messages.
- *Clutter.* By the age of 65, the average person has seen more than 2 million television commercials, and more ads are on the way![32] With so many television ads beaming across the airwaves, a small company's advertising message easily can become lost in the shuffle.
- *"Zapping" and "zipping."* "**Zappers**," television viewers who flash from one channel to another during commercials, and "**zippers**," those who use digital video recording devices such as TiVo to fast-forward through commercials, pose a real threat to TV advertisers. Zapping can cut deeply into an ad's reach, and 36 percent of U.S. households now own a DVR device (compared to just 12.3 percent in 2007).[33] One study reported that 85 percent of DVR users zip through all or most commercials when watching a show.[34] Zapping and zipping prevent TV advertisers from reaching the audiences they hope to reach.
- *Fragmented audience.* As the number of channels available proliferates, the question of where to advertise becomes more difficult to answer. The average household in the United States now receives 130 television channels, up from just 33 in 1990![35] This dramatic increase in the number of channels available has fragmented the audience that an ad run on a single channel reaches.
- *Costs.* TV commercials can be expensive to create. A professionally done 30-second ad (the most common length of a television ad) can cost several thousand dollars to develop, even before an entrepreneur purchases airtime. Advertising agencies and professional design firms offer design assistance—sometimes at hefty prices—leading many small business owners to hire less expensive freelance ad designers or turn to the stations on which they buy air time for help with their ads. Table 3 offers some suggestions for developing creative television commercials.

Using Television Creatively. Although television ads are not affordable for every small business, many entrepreneurs have found creative ways to use the power of television advertising without spending a fortune. Two popular methods include infomercials and home shopping networks. **Infomercials** (also called **direct-response television**) come in two lengths: short form, which are 2- to 3-minute pitches, and long form, 30-minute full-length television commercials packed with information, testimonials, and a sales pitch asking for an immediate response. The length of these ads allows entrepreneurs to demonstrate and explain their products in detail and to show customers the benefits of using them, a particularly important consideration for a new or complex product. Producing and airing a half-hour infomercial can be expensive, often costing $300,000 to $1 million, depending on its production quality, format, content, celebrity involvement, and

TABLE 3 Guidelines for Creative TV Ads

- **Keep it simple.** Avoid confusing the viewer by sticking to a simple concept.
- **Have one basic idea.** The message should focus on a single, important benefit to the customer. Why should people buy from your business?
- **Make your point clear.** The customer benefit should be obvious and easy to understand.
- **Make it unique.** To be effective, a television ad must reach out and grab the viewer's attention. Take advantage of television's visual experience.
- **Get viewers' attention.** Unless viewers watch the ad, its effect is lost.
- **Involve the viewer.** To be most effective, an ad should portray a situation to which the viewer can relate. Common, everyday experiences are easiest for people to identify with.
- **Use emotion.** The most effective ads evoke an emotion from the viewer—a laugh, a tear, or a pleasant memory.
- **Consider production values.** Television offers vivid sights, colors, motions, and sounds. Use them to your advantage!
- **Prove the benefit.** Television allows an advertiser to prove a product's or service's customer benefit by actually demonstrating it.
- **Identify your company well and often.** Make sure your store's name, location, and product line stand out. The ad should portray your company's image.

Source: Adapted from *How to Make a Creative Television Commercial*, Television Bureau of Advertising.

broadcast schedule. Short-form infomercials cost about $15,000 to $20,000 to produce. Because most infomercials ask for an immediate response from viewers, entrepreneurs can gauge their success at landing customers, sometimes within minutes of airing them and almost always within 1 week. Products such as the ShamWow, Snuggie, and PedEgg have reached millions of units in sales with the help of infomercials.

ENTREPRENEURIAL
Profile
Roger Fredericks and Fredericks Golf

Roger Fredericks, founder of Fredericks Golf has used 30-minute infomercials to sell instructional golf DVDs since 2005. Aired on the Golf Channel, Fredericks' infomercials typically generate $3,000 in sales for every $1,000 that he spends. Fredericks says that his company has sold $7 million in golf DVDs and that the infomercials have made him a celebrity, giving him opportunities to speak at golf clinics and conferences across the country and filling his instructional classes 6 months in advance.[36]

Only 1 in 10 products that rely on infomercials succeeds.[37] To become an infomercial star, a product should meet the following criteria:

- Be unique and of good quality.
- Solve a common problem.
- Be easy to use and easy to demonstrate.
- Appeal to a mass audience.
- Have an "aha! factor" that makes customers think "What a great idea!"

Shopping networks such as QVC and the HSN, which reach nearly 100 million homes, offer entrepreneurs another route to television. Time on these networks is free, but getting a product accepted is difficult; only a small percentage of the products reviewed by QVC or HSN are featured on the show. Shopping networks look for high-quality products that have "demonstration appeal" and are typically priced between $15 and $50 (although there are exceptions). Landing a product on one of these networks may be a challenge, but entrepreneurs who do often sell thousands of units in a matter of minutes.

ENTREPRENEURIAL
Profile
Sean "Diddy" Combs and Sean John and HSN

Entrepreneur Sean "Diddy" Combs recently set a new sales record on HSN when he appeared on the network 3 weeks before Christmas with a line of scents from his Sean John line of fragrances, including one for women. Viewer response was so overwhelming that Combs sold the entire collection of 5,600 units at $60 each in just 15 minutes.[38]

RADIO. Radio permits advertisers to reach specific audiences over large geographic areas. By choosing the appropriate station, program, and time for an ad, a small company can reach virtually any target market.

Radio advertising offers several advantages:

- *Extensive reach.* Radio's nearly universal presence gives advertisements in this medium a major advantage. Nearly every home and car in the United States is equipped with a radio, which means that radio ads receive a tremendous amount of exposure in the target market. Although the myriad of entertainment options available has reduced the time that customers spend with all advertising media, the average adult spends 18.5 hours each week listening to the radio. According to the Radio Advertising Bureau, radio reaches 71 percent of adults each day and 93 percent of customers each week![39]

- *Audience delivery.* Radio commercial breaks retain on average 92 percent of the lead-in listening audience, which means fewer commercial zappers than television ads experience.[40]

- *Market segmentation.* Radio advertising is flexible and efficient because advertisers can choose stations aimed at a specific market within a broad geographic region. Radio stations design their formats to appeal to specific types of audiences. (Ever notice how the stations you listen to are not the same ones your parents listen to?) AM stations, which once ruled the airways, now specialize mainly in "talk formats" such as call-in, news, religion, sports, and automotive shows. On the FM dial, country, urban contemporary, classical, classic rock, rhythm and blues, Hispanic, and "oldies" stations have listener profiles that give entrepreneurs the ability to pinpoint practically any advertising target.

- *Flexibility and timeliness.* Radio commercials have short closing times and can be changed quickly. Small firms that sell seasonal merchandise or advertise special sales or events can change their ads on short notice to match changing market conditions.

- *Friendliness.* Radio ads are more "active" than ads in printed media because they use the spoken word to influence customers. Vocal subtleties used in radio ads are impossible to convey through printed media. Spoken ads can suggest emotions and urgency, and they lend a personalized tone to the message.

Radio advertisements also have some disadvantages:

- *Poor listening.* Radio's intrusiveness into the public life almost guarantees that customers will hear ads, but they may not listen to them. Listeners are often engaged in other activities while the radio is on and may ignore the message.

- *Need for repetition.* Listeners usually do not respond to radio ads after a single exposure to them. Radio ads must be broadcast repeatedly to be effective. Consistency in radio ads is the key to success.

- *Limited message.* Radio ads are limited to 1 minute or less, which requires that business owners keep their messages simple, covering only one or two points. In addition, radio spots do not allow advertisers to demonstrate their products or services. Although listeners can hear the engine purr, they can't see the car; spoken messages can only describe the product or service.

Buying Radio Time. Business owners can zero in on a specific advertising target by using the appropriate radio station. Stations follow various formats—from rap to rhapsodies—to appeal to specific audiences. Radio advertising time is usually sold in 15-, 30-, and 60-second increments. Many radio stations now offer 5-second spots called "adlets" and even super-short 1- or 2-second "blinks" that are designed to increase the awareness of a brand among listeners.

Fixed spots are guaranteed to be broadcast at the times specified in the owner's contract with the station. Preemptible spots are cheaper than fixed spots, but the advertiser risks being preempted by an advertiser willing to pay the fixed rate for a time slot. Floating spots are the least expensive, but the advertiser has no control over broadcast times. Many stations offer package plans, using flexible combinations of fixed, preemptible, and floating spots. Table 4 offers a guide to producing effective radio copy.

Radio rates vary depending on the time of day the ads are broadcast and, like television, there are prime-time slots known as drive-time spots. Although exact hours may differ from station to station, the following classifications are common (listed in descending order of cost):

Class AA: Morning drive time—6 A.M. to 10 A.M.

Class A: Evening drive time—4 P.M. to 7 P.M.

TABLE 4 Guidelines for Effective Radio Copy

■ *Mention the business often.* This is the single most important and inflexible rule in radio advertising. Also make sure listeners know how to find your business. If the address is complicated, use landmarks.

■ *Stress the benefit to the listener.* Don't say "Dixon's has new fall fashions." Say "Dixon's fall fashions make you look fabulous."

■ *Use attention-getters.* One key to a successful radio ad is grabbing listeners' attention from the start and holding it. Radio gives the options of music, sound effects, and unusual voices. Crack the barrier with sound.

■ *Zero in on your audience.* Know to whom you're selling. Radio's selectivity attracts the right audience. It's up to you to communicate in the right language.

■ *Keep the copy simple and to the point.* Don't try to impress listeners with vocabulary. "To be or not to be" may be the best-known phrase in the language . . . and the longest word has just three letters.

■ *Sell early and often.* Don't back into the selling message. At most, you've got 60 seconds. Make the most of them. Don't be subtle.

■ *Write for the ear.* Forget the rules of grammar; write conversationally.

■ *Prepare your copy.* Underline words you want to emphasize so that the announcer knows how the ad should read.

■ *Triple space.* Type clean, legible copy. Make sure the announcer rehearses the ad.

■ *Use positive action words.* Use words such as *now* and *today*, particularly when you're writing copy for a sale. Radio has qualities of urgency and immediacy. Take advantage of them by including a time limit or the date the sale ends.

■ *Put the listener in the picture.* Radio's theater of the mind means you don't have to talk about a new car. With sounds and music, you can put the listener behind the wheel.

■ *Focus the spot on getting a response.* Make it clear what you want the listener to do. Don't try to get a mail response. Use phone numbers or a Web site address only, and repeat the number or Web address at least three times. End the spot with the phone number or the Web address.

■ *Don't stay with a loser.* Direct-response ads produce results right way—or not at all. Don't stick with a radio spot that is not generating sales. Change it.

Sources: Kim T. Gordon, "Turn It Up," *Entrepreneur*, January 2004, pp. 80–81; *Radio Basics*, Radio Advertising Bureau.

Class B: Home worker time—10 A.M. to 4 P.M.

Class C: Evening time—7 P.M. to Midnight

Class D: Nighttime—Midnight to 6 A.M.

Some stations may have different rates for weekend time slots.

NEWSPAPERS. Traditionally, the local print newspaper has been the medium that most small companies rely on to get their messages across to customers. Both the circulation and the number of newspapers in the United States are declining, however, and the share of advertising dollars the medium attracts has fallen below 11 percent. However, newspapers provide several advantages to small business advertisers:

■ *Targeted geographic coverage.* Newspapers are geared to a specific geographic region, and they reach potential customers across all demographic classes. Local newspapers, in particular, provide extensive coverage of a company's immediate trading area.

■ *Flexibility.* A business can change its newspaper advertisements on very short notice. Entrepreneurs can select the size of the ad, its location in the paper, and the days on which it runs. For instance, auto repair shops often advertise their tune-up specials in the sports section on weekends, and party shops display their ads in the entertainment section as the weekend approaches.

■ *Timeliness.* Papers almost always have very short closing times, the publication deadline prior to which the advertising copy must be submitted. Many newspapers allow advertisers to submit their copy as late as 24 hours before the ad runs.

■ *Communication potential.* Newspaper ads can convey a great deal of information by employing attractive graphics and copy. Properly designed, they can be very effective in attracting attention and persuading readers to buy.

■ *Low costs.* Newspapers normally offer advertising space at low absolute cost and, because of their blanket coverage of a geographic area, at low relative cost as well.

■ *Prompt responses.* Newspaper ads typically produce a relatively quick customer response. A newspaper ad is likely to generate sales the very next day, and advertisers who use coupons can track the response to an ad. This advantage makes newspapers an ideal medium for promoting special events such as sales, grand openings, or the arrival of a new product.

■ *Popularity of free newspapers.* Most communities have at least one free (to readers) newspaper, and their reach can be significant, an important consideration for advertisers. Studies show that 60 percent of consumers say that they read a free paper at least once a week.[41]

Newspaper advertisements also have disadvantages:

■ *Wasted readership.* Because newspapers reach a wide variety of people, at least a portion of an ad's coverage is wasted on readers who are not potential customers. This nonselective coverage makes it more difficult for newspapers to reach specific target markets than ads in other media.

■ *Reproduction limitations.* The quality of reproduction in newspapers is limited, especially when it is compared with that of magazines and direct mail. Recent technology advances, however, are improving the quality of reproduction in newspaper ads.

■ *Lack of prominence.* One frequently cited drawback of newspapers is that they carry so many ads that a small company's message might be lost in the crowd. The typical newspaper is 62 percent advertising. This disadvantage can be overcome by increasing the size of the ad or by adding color to it. Color can increase the reading of ads by as much as 80 percent over black-and-white ads. Studies show that two-color ads do "pull" better than black-and-white ones, but only by a small margin.[42] The *real* increase in ad recall and response comes from using full four-color ads. Bold headlines, illustrations, and photographs also increase an ad's prominence.

■ *Proper ad placement in the newspaper can increase an ad's effectiveness.* The best locations are on a right-hand page, near the right margin, above the half-page mark, or next to editorial articles. The most-read sections in the typical newspaper are the front page and the comics.

■ *Declining readership.* Newspaper circulation as a percentage of U.S. households has dropped from 98 percent in 1970 to less than 40 percent today as readers have migrated to the Internet.[43] In fact, more people now get national and international news from the Internet than from a newspaper.[44] Print newspaper ads are more effective with older adults and those with higher education and income. They are less effective with younger adults; studies show that just 32 percent of adults aged 18 to 34 read a daily newspaper.[45]

■ *Short ad life.* The typical newspaper is soon discarded and, as a result, an ad's life is extremely short. Business owners can increase the effectiveness of their ads by giving them greater continuity. Spot ads can produce results, but maintaining a steady flow of business requires some degree of continuity in advertising.

Buying Newspaper Ads. Newspapers typically sell ad space by lines and columns or inches and columns. For instance, a 4-column × 100-line ad occupies four columns and 100 lines of space 14 lines = 1 column inch. For this ad, a business owner pays the rate for 400 lines. If the newspaper's line rate is $3.50, this ad would cost $1,400 (400 lines × $3.50 per line). Most papers offer discounts for bulk, long-term, and frequency contracts and full-page ads. Advertising rates vary from one paper to another, depending on factors such as circulation and focus. Entrepreneurs should investigate the circulation statements, advertising rates, and reader profiles of a newspaper to see how well it matches the company's target audience before selecting one as an advertising medium.

INTERNET ADVERTISING. Just as the Internet has become a common tool for conducting business, it also has become a popular medium for advertisers. Internet advertising is growing rapidly because advertisers recognize that that is where their target customers are spending more of their time and because advertisers can track the effectiveness of their advertising campaigns. By 2013, U.S. companies are expected to spend $37.2 billion on online advertising (see Figure 5).

The blurring line between television and the Internet provides opportunities for small businesses to reach customers with inexpensive video ads. The Web's multimedia capabilities make it an ideal medium for companies to demonstrate their products and services with full motion, color, and sound and to get customers involved in the demonstration. Businesses that normally use direct mail can bring the two-dimensional photos and product descriptions in their print catalogs to life in video, avoid the expense of mailing them, and attract new customers that traditional mailings might miss.

FIGURE 5
U.S. Online Advertising
Spending as a
Percentage of Total
Advertising Spending

Source: eMarketer, April 2009.

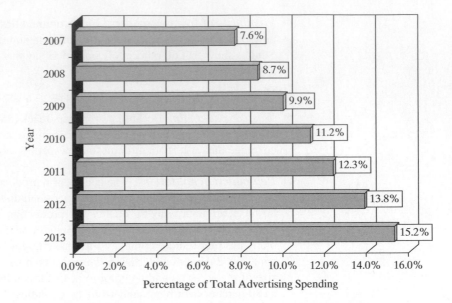

ENTREPRENEURIAL
Profile

*Wendy Chatelain
and Antoine's*

The fifth-generation owners of Antoine's, the legendary New Orleans restaurant founded in 1840, recently decided to branch out from the print and radio ads they had relied on for many years and create on online video. Working with online video production company TurnHere, Wendy Chatelain, sales and marketing manager of the nation's oldest family-owned restaurant, created a short video starring one of Antoine's third-generation waiters and featuring the famed restaurant's rich history and outstanding menu, including its flaming baked Alaska dessert. The ad, which Antoine's posted on its online Yellow Pages ad, its Web site, and on YouTube, cost just $1,000 to shoot, edit, and upload. The ad's results—300 new customers in just 1 month—exceeded Chatelain's expectations.[46]

Online advertisements take five basic forms: banner ads, display ads, contextual ads, pay-per-click ads, and e-mail ads. **Banner ads** are small rectangular ads that reside on Web sites, much like roadside billboards, touting a company's product or service. When site visitors click the banner ad, they go straight to the advertiser's homepage. One measure of a banner ad's effectiveness is the number of impressions it produces. An **impression** occurs every time an ad appears on a Web page, whether or not the user clicks on the ad to explore it. Another common way of judging the effectiveness of banner ads is the **click-through rate**, which is calculated by dividing the number of times customers actually click on the banner ad by the number of impressions for that ad. For instance, if an ad is displayed 1,000 times and 12 customers actually click the ad and go to the advertiser's Web site, the ad's click-through rate is 1.2 percent ($12 \div 1,000$). Banner ads suffer from a very low click-through rate—less than 0.5 percent compared to an average click-through rate of 15 percent for search engines.[47] The cost of a banner ad to an advertiser depends on the number of prospects who actually click on it.

Banner ads do not have to be expensive to be effective. Many small business owners increase the exposure their banner ads receive by joining a banner exchange program, which is similar to an advertising cooperative. In a banner exchange program, member companies can post their banners on each other's sites. These programs work best for companies selling complementary products or services. For instance, a small company that sells gourmet food products over the Web could exchange banner ads with a company that uses the Web to sell fine wines or upscale kitchen tools and appliances.

The primary disadvantage of banner ads is that Web users can easily ignore them. These ads have become such a part of the landscape of the Web that users tend to ignore them. Web designers search for the best page placement for banner ads and the "bells and whistles" that will attract browsers and encourage them to click through.

A form of Web advertising that is more difficult to ignore is **display ads**, which include both pop-up, interstitial ads, and contextual ads. A **pop-up ad** appears spontaneously in a separate window, blocking the site behind it. It is designed to grab consumers' attention for the few nanoseconds it takes them to close the window. One danger of such ads is that Internet users do not like them, perceiving them as an annoying intrusion. A slight variation on this ad is the "pop-under" ad, which immediately goes behind the active screen but stays open until the browser window is closed. An **interstitial ad** is an ad page that appears for a short time before a user-requested page appears. These ads are also called transition ads, splash pages, and flash pages.

Contextual ads are ads on Web sites that are correlated to a particular user's interests or on-line behavior. For instance, a user searching for sports information might see an ad for athletic shoes or T-shirts, and one searching for vitamins might see an ad for green tea or herbal remedies. To catch the attention of Web users, many advertisers, particularly those companies that aim their products at young customers, are using video ads rather than traditional display ads.

Pay-per-click ads require companies to bid on top-ranking search engine listings using key words that they expect Internet users to type into a search engine when they are interested in purchasing a particular product or service. The higher a company's bid is for a key word, the more prominent is the location of its ad on the results that the search engine returns. Companies pay for an ad only when a prospect actually clicks on it. Entrepreneurs who advertise on the Internet should consider making pay-per-click ads a part of their advertising strategies. Compete's Online Shopper Intelligence Study found that 61 percent of Internet shoppers use a search engine as their first stop for locating the products and services they are interested in purchasing.[48] According to a study by Goldstein Group Communications, companies allocate 11 percent of their marketing budgets to search engine marketing and landing highly placed spots on popular search engines.[49] Google, Yahoo!, and Bing are the leading search engines, and advertisers who want to increase the odds of reaching their target audiences should advertise on all three.

To calculate the maximum amount a company can afford to bid on a key word, use the following formula:

$$\text{Maximum keyword bid} = \text{Conversion rate} \times \text{Profit per sale}$$

Online conversion rates vary by industry, but the average conversion rate is about 3.2 percent. That means that for every 1,000 visitors to a company's site, 32 of them actually make a purchase. For a company that has a conversion rate of 3.2 percent and an average profit per order of $12, the maximum amount the owner should bid on a key word is:

$$\text{Maximum keyword bid} = 3.2\% \times \$12 = 38.4 \text{ cents}$$

Used properly, pay-per-click ads can drive customers to a company's Web site even before the search engines discover it and include it in their search results. Pay-per-click ads also allow advertisers to test the effectiveness of different ads by running several variations at once (e.g., one version might include a discounted price and another might include a free accessory).

These ads are efficient because advertisers pay for an ad only when a customer actually clicks on it. **Click fraud**, which occurs when a person or a computer program generates ad clicks even though they have no interest in the advertiser's product or service, is a danger to entrepreneurs who use pay-per-click ads. The click fraud rate on search engines ranges from 13 to 18 percent, with an average of 14.7 percent.[50]

E-mail is the most common application on the Internet, and e-mail advertising capitalizes on that popularity. The Radicati Group estimates that Internet users have more than 3.1 billion e-mail accounts![51] **E-mail advertising**, whereby companies broadcast their advertising messages by e-mail, is growing rapidly because it is effective and inexpensive. E-mail advertising takes two forms: permission e-mail and spam. As its name suggests, **permission e-mail** involves sending e-mail ads to customers with their permission; **spam** is unsolicited commercial e-mail. The Radicati Group also estimates that despite modern antispam technology, 19 percent of all delivered e-mail messages are spam.[52] Because most e-mail users see spam as a nuisance, they often view companies that use it in a negative fashion. Smart entrepreneurs do *not* rely on spam in their marketing strategies. Permission e-mail, however, can be an effective and money-saving advertising tool. Permission e-mail messages often produce very high response rates. According to Epsilon, a marketing services company, the average open rate for e-mail ads is 22 percent, and the average click-through rate is 5.9 percent.[53]

Building an e-mail address list simply requires attention to the basics of marketing. The goal is to encourage potential buyers to share their e-mail addresses. The reward may be a white paper report, a one-time discount, a special offer, a special report, a sweepstakes entry, or a drawing for a prize. Once a small company obtains potential customers' e-mail addresses, the next step is to send messages that are useful and interesting to them. The message must be geared to their interests and should highlight the product's unique selling proposition. Many companies have success with e-mail ad campaigns that produce immediate results and are very inexpensive to conduct.

ENTREPRENEURIAL
Profile

Josh Molinari and Anthony Green and Fajita Grill

When Josh Molinari and Anthony Green launched Fajita Grill, a quick-serve restaurant that sells fresh Southwestern-style food at two locations in Oswego and Fulton, New York, they wanted to build a large base of loyal customers as fast as possible and could not afford to wait for word-of-mouth advertising to take effect. Marketing director Abby Weaver experimented with traditional advertising media but had only limited success, which prompted her to turn to e-mail ads. She worked with e-mail marketing company Constant Contact to build an e-mail list of nearly 3,300 customers and to create clever ad campaigns that tell customers about special events, remind them of the benefits of their "Frequent Eater" cards, and offer discount coupons. "I can e-mail a coupon at 10 A.M., and by 11:30 there are people in line, coupon in hand," says Weaver. In addition to the high (and measurable) response rate, Weaver enjoys the flexibility and speed of e-mail ad campaigns. "I don't need a designer," she says. "I don't have to wait for a printer or the Postal Service to get it delivered. I can hit 'send' at 10 A.M. and watch how many people open the e-mail and where they click on the Fajita Grill Web site." Because of the informational reports that Weaver receives after each ad goes out, Fajita Grill constantly fine-tunes its e-mail campaign and has an impressive e-mail ad open rate of 43.8 percent.[54]

LESSONS FROM THE STREET-SMART ➤ entrepreneur

E-Mail Ads That Produce Results

When John and Jennifer Nugent opened the Colorado Wine Company in Pasadena, California, their goal was to remove much of the mystique and highbrow attitude that some people associate with wine. "We wanted to create an environment where anyone, no matter what level of wine knowledge they had, could enter the store, receive personal service and recommendations, try a sip or two of the daily selections at the bar, and leave feeling more comfortable and educated about wine," says Jennifer. The store, which also features a wine bar, specializes in wines, sakes, Champagnes, and beers from around the world, most of which are priced at $25 or less. To drive business to their store, the Nugents created a whimsical e-mail newsletter that covers a multitude of topics in an engaging manner. In addition to describing wine specials and arrivals and offering profiles of the wineries that supply the company, the newsletter includes fun topics such as "wine paraphernalia that makes us uncomfortable and/or scared" and invitations to upcoming wine tastings such as the popular "White Trash" tasting that pairs various wines with cheap convenience food. One recent newsletter, titled "Beans Don't Burn on the Grill, the Nearness of You, and What Pairs Best with a Roman Candle?" invited customers to attend a 1980's theme music night at the shop.

The Nugents use the newsletter to reinforce the casual, fun image of the store, to foster a sense of community among its customers, and to build a connection with them. "We're a small shop, and people like to visit because it's like a living room," says John. "We want the newsletter to feel the same way." The number of newsletter subscribers has increased from just a few hundred to several thousand and continues to grow rapidly. "After a broadcast, we usually spend half the next day returning e-mail," says John.

Businesses spend $2 billion a year on e-mail marketing campaigns and experts expect that number to grow by an impressive 18.5 percent each year for the next 5 years. What makes e-mail marketing appealing, especially to entrepreneurs, is that it is inexpensive, measurable, and it works! According to a study by the Direct Marketing Association, every $1 that companies spend on e-mail marketing produces a return of $45.06. Entrepreneurs who want to reproduce the success that the Colorado Wine Company has created using an e-mail advertising campaign should consider the following tips from The Street-Smart Entrepreneur:

Make a concerted effort to collect customers' (and potential customers') e-mail addresses.

Every contact that anyone in your company has with a customer presents an opportunity to collect another e-mail address. Seize them! Ensure that everyone in the company understands the importance of building an accurate and reliable e-mail list.

Make sure the e-mail's subject line is short, meaningful, and to-the-point.

Without the right subject line, e-mail recipients may never open the e-mail. One rule of thumb suggests that the subject line should not exceed 40 characters, including spaces. The best subject lines suggest the product's or service's USP. For example, "Fresh lunch FAST—just $5.99!" in the subject line of an e-mail expresses several product features to potential customers. Other subject line words that result in responses include "new," "save," "you," "instant," and "free."

Make sure your e-mails' look and feel are consistent with your company's overall image.

Every component of a company's advertising campaign should have a look and feel that is consistent with its brand, even though the ads may appear in many diverse media. The design of a company's e-mail ads should rely on the same colors, themes, slogans, and look as its ads in other media.

Send e-mails when customers are most likely to make their purchases.

Proper timing of e-mail ads can improve customer response rates dramatically. Friday is the day of the week on which recipients are most likely to read e-mails. January, July, August, and December are the months in which customers are least likely to pay attention to e-mail ads (although there are exceptions). A study by marketing research firm Atlas reports that lunch time and the late evening were the times of day that resulted in the highest response rates to e-mail ads in general. Companies must time their e-mail ads to correspond to their customers' demand for their products and services.

Write copy that produces the results you seek.

Start by concentrating on one idea. Before writing any copy, develop a mental picture of your target customer. Give him or her a name and try to envision how your company's product or service can benefit him or her. This will help you keep your ad copy focused on the USP you put in the subject line of the e-mail. When appropriate, consider including an endorsement from an existing customer (perhaps with a photo) to add credibility to your claims. Be sure to provide clearly visible links to your company's Web site at several places in the e-mail ad, including at the top and the bottom of the page. Always include a prominent call to action: How do you want the customer to respond?

Incorporate social networking links and video into e-mails.

Adding "Become a fan on Facebook" or "Follow us on Twitter" links to e-mails encourages customers to engage your company in other media and to promote it to their friends. The E-mail Marketing Trends Survey reports that 53.8 percent of small business owners say that including video in e-mails increases their company's click-through and open rates. Buttons that allow customers to download videos, forward them to friends, or post them on their Facebook pages encourage the viral nature of the Web to expand their advertising efforts many times over.

Use value-added items to increase your campaign's response rate.

In the typical inbox, there are dozens (if not more) of messages competing for the person's attention. One way to boost your campaign's response rate is to offer recipients something of value—for example, a coupon, a newsletter, or a white paper. Betsy Harper, CEO of Sales and Marketing Search, an executive search firm that specializes in sales and marketing positions, says that publishing a monthly e-mail newsletter that includes hiring trends and tips has improved her company's visibility, reputation, and sales. Recently, says Harper, "within 2 minutes (literally!) of sending our e-mail newsletter, I got an e-mail from a fellow in New York. He asked me to call him right away about filling a senior sales position. We talked, signed an agreement to work together the very next day, and started the search. We finished the search in record time and received a $22,000 fee."

Always comply with the CAN-SPAM Act.

The CAN-SPAM Act, a law that sets the rules for commercial e-mail, establishes requirements for commercial messages, gives recipients the right to opt out of e-mails, and spells out tough penalties for violators.

Sources: Based on: "E-mail Success Stories: How 11 Companies Are Pushing the (Electronic) Envelope," *Marketing Profs*, 2009, pp. 3–4; Lisa Barone, "E-mail Marketing Success Is About Relevance," *Small Business Trends*, June 18, 2009, *http://smallbiztrends.com/2009/06/email-marketing-success.html*; Peter Prestipino and Mike Phillips, "E-mail Marketing's Future . . . Right Now," *Website*, November 2009, pp. 26–29; Michelle Keegan, "Real Life Small Business Newsletter Tips," Constant Contact, *www.constantcontact.com/learning-center/hints-tips/volume10-issue2.jsp*; Gail Goodman, "Writing Compelling Promotional Copy," Constant Contact, *www.constantcontact.com/learning-center/hints-tips/ht-2006-07.jsp*; David Kesmodel, "More Marketers Place Web Ads by Time of Day," *Wall Street Journal*, June 23, 2006, pp. B1, B3; Ivan Levison, "Five Common E-mail Mistakes and How to Avoid Them," *Levison Letter*, vol. 17, no. 2, April 2002, *www.levison.com/email-advertising.htm*; "You've Got the Power," *Marketing Profs*, vol. 1, no. 23, May 22, 2008; 2010 E-mail Marketing Trends Survey, GetResponse, 2010, *www.getresponse.com/documents/core/reports/2010_Email_Marketing_Trends_Survey.pdf*, p. 5.

MAGAZINES. Another advertising medium available to the small business owner is magazines. Today, customers have more than 20,600 magazine titles from which to choose. Magazines have a wide reach, and their readers tend to be more educated and have higher incomes than consumers of other advertising media, such as television.[55]

Magazines offer several advantages for advertisers:

- *Long life spans.* Magazines have a long reading life because readers tend to keep them longer than other printed media. Few people read an entire magazine at one sitting. Instead, most pick it up, read it at intervals, and come back to it later. The result is that each magazine ad has a good chance of being seen several times.
- *Multiple channels of engagement.* More than 15,200 magazines have associated Web sites, which gives them the ability to engage customers across two channels. Magazine Web site usage is growing faster than Web usage overall.[56]
- *Multiple readership.* The average magazine has a readership of 3.9 adults, and each reader spends about 1 hour and 33 minutes with each copy. Many magazines have a high "pass-along" rate; they are handed down front reader to reader. For instance, the in-flight magazines on jets reach many readers in their lifetimes.
- *Target marketing.* Within the past 20 years, magazines have become increasingly focused. Advertisers can select magazines aimed at customers with specific interests—from wooden boats and black-and-white photography to container gardening and body-building. By selecting the appropriate special-interest periodical, small business owners can reach those customers with a high degree of interest in their goods or services. Once business owners define their target markets, they can select magazines whose readers most closely match their customer profiles. For instance, *House and Garden* magazine reaches a very different audience than *Rolling Stone.*
- *Ad quality.* Magazine ads usually are of high quality. Photographs and drawings can be reproduced very effectively, and high-quality color ads are readily available. In fact, consumers rank magazine ads ahead of ads in all other media on creating a positive impression.[57] Advertisers can choose the location of their ads in a magazine and can design creative ads that capture readers' attention. The most effective locations for magazine ads are the back cover, the inside front cover, and the inside back cover. Multiple page spreads also increase ad recall among readers.[58]

Magazines also have several disadvantages:

- *Costs.* Magazine advertising rates vary according to their circulation rates; the higher the circulation, the higher the rate. Thus, local magazines, whose rates are often comparable to newspaper rates, may be the best bargain for small businesses.
- *Long closing times.* Another disadvantage of magazines is the relatively long closing times they require. For a weekly periodical, the closing date for an ad may be several weeks before the actual publication date, making it difficult for advertisers to respond quickly to changing market conditions.
- *Lack of prominence.* Another disadvantage of magazine ads arises from their popularity as an advertising vehicle. The effectiveness of a single ad may be reduced because of a lack of prominence; 46.2 percent of the typical magazine content is devoted to advertising.[59] Proper ad positioning, therefore, is critical to an ad's success. Research shows that readers "tune out" right-hand pages and look mainly at left-hand pages.
- *Declining circulation rates.* Circulation rates for most magazines have declined over the last decade. According to the Pew Research Center for the People and the Press, 23 percent of adults say they are regular magazine readers, down from 33 percent in 1994.[60]

SPECIALTY ADVERTISING. As advertisers have shifted their focus to "narrowcasting" their messages to target audiences and away from "broadcasting," specialty advertising has grown in popularity. This category includes all customer gift items such as pens, shirts, caps, and umbrellas that are imprinted with a company's name, address, telephone number, Web site, and slogan. Specialty items are best used as reminder ads to supplement other forms of advertising and help to create goodwill among existing and potential customers.

Specialty advertising offers several advantages:

- **Reaching select audiences.** Advertisers have the ability to reach specific audiences with well-planned specialty items.
- **Personalized nature.** By carefully choosing a specialty item, business owners can "personalize" their advertisements. When choosing advertising specialties, business owners should use items that are unusual, related to the nature of the business, and meaningful to customers. For instance, a small software company generated a great deal of recognition by giving existing and potential customers flash memory sticks imprinted with its company logo and Web address.
- **Versatility.** The rich versatility of specialty advertising is limited only by the business owner's imagination. Advertisers print their logos on everything from pens and golf balls to key chains and caps.

The following are the disadvantages of specialty advertising:

- **Potential for waste.** Unless entrepreneurs choose the appropriate specialty item for their businesses, they will be wasting time and money.
- **Cost.** Some specialty items can be quite expensive. In addition, some owners have a tendency to give advertising materials to anyone—even to those people who are not potential customers. Proper distribution of give-away items is an important aspect of enhancing the effectiveness of and controlling the cost of specialty advertising.

POINT-OF-PURCHASE ADS. In-store advertising has become popular as a way of reaching the customer at a crucial moment—the point of purchase. Research suggests that consumers make 74 percent of all buying decisions at the point of sale.[61] Self-service stores are especially well suited for in-store ads because they remind people of the products as they walk the aisles. These in-store ads are not just simple signs or glossy photographs of the product in use. Some businesses use in-store music interspersed with household hints and, of course, ads. Another technique involves shelves that contain tiny devices that sense when a customer passes by and triggers a prerecorded sales message. Some self-service stores use floor graphics, point-of-purchase ads that transform their floors into advertising space.

OUT-OF-HOME ADVERTISING. Out-of-home, or outdoor, advertising is one of the oldest forms of advertising in existence. Archeological evidence shows that merchants in ancient Egypt chiseled advertising messages on stone tablets and placed them along major thoroughfares. Out-of-home advertising remains popular today; advertisers spend nearly $6 billion on this medium annually.[62] The United States is a highly mobile society, and out-of-home advertising takes advantage of this mobility. Out-of-home advertising is popular among small companies, especially retailers, because well-placed ads serve as reminders to shoppers that the small business is nearby and ready to serve their needs. Very few small businesses rely solely on out-of-home advertising; instead, they supplement other advertising media with out-of-home ads such as billboards and transit ads. With a creative out-of-home ad campaign, a small company can make a big impact with only a small budget.

ENTREPRENEURIAL
Profile

*Rob Bennett and
Bennett Infinity*

Rob Bennett, owner of Bennett Infinity in Lehigh Valley, Pennsylvania, saw his inventory of luxury cars building up and knew that he had to do something to attract customers and boost sales. Although Bennett never had used out-of-home advertising, he realized that the medium was ideal for reaching his target audience: upscale, well-educated professionals who enjoy driving. Research showed that although these buyers are affluent, they are value-conscious in their purchases. Bennett launched an outdoor ad campaign that emphasized the low monthly lease payments that were available on the most popular luxury models, concentrating the ads in upscale areas near his dealership. In the first 4 weeks, Bennett Infinity's sales jumped from an average of just two cars per week to seven cars per week! The initial campaign was such a hit that Bennett conducted a follow-up ad campaign that proved to be even more successful.[63]

Innovative out-of-home ads remind shoppers that a small business is nearby, ready to serve their needs.

Source: Outdoor Advertising Association of America, Inc.

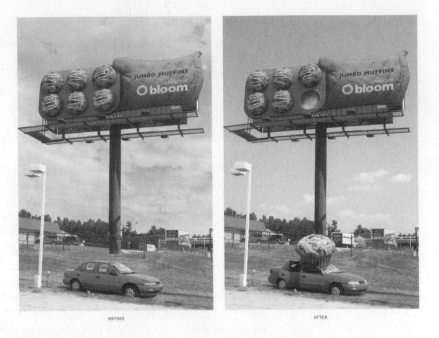

BEFORE · AFTER

Outdoor advertising offers certain advantages to a small business:

- **High exposure.** Out-of-home advertising offers a high-frequency exposure, especially among people who commute to work. The average one-way commute to work in the United States is just over 25 minutes.[64] Most people tend to follow the same routes in their daily travels, and billboards are there waiting for them when they pass by.

Source: www.CartoonStock.com

© Mike Baldwin / Cornered

"Then, for some reason, sales dropped right off."

- **Broad reach.** The typical billboard reaches an adult 29 to 31 times each month. The nature of outdoor ads makes them effective devices for reaching a large number of potential customers within a specific area. Not only has the number of cars on the road increased, but the number of daily vehicle trips people take has also climbed. In addition, the people outdoor ads reach tend to be younger, wealthier, and better educated than the average person.

- *Attention-getting.* The introduction of new technology such as 3-D, fiber optics, digital and LCD displays, and other creative special effects to out-of-home advertising has transformed billboards from flat, passive signs to innovative, attention-grabbing promotions that passersby cannot help but notice.
- *Flexibility.* Advertisers can buy out-of-home advertising units separately or in a number of packages. Through its variety of graphics, design, and unique features, outdoor advertising enables a small advertiser to match his or her message to the particular audience.
- *Cost efficiency.* Out-of-home advertising offers one of the lowest costs per thousand customers reached of all advertising media. The CPM for out-of-home ads is $2.26, compared to $4.54 for radio, $5.50 for newspaper ads, $6.98 for magazine ads, and $5.99 to $10.25 for television commercials.[65]

Out-of-home ads also have several disadvantages:

- *Brief exposure.* Because billboards are immobile, the reader is exposed to the advertiser's message for only a short time—typically only 1 or 2 seconds. As a result, the message must be short and to the point.
- *Limited ad recall.* Because customers often are zooming past out-of-home ads at high speed, they are exposed to an advertising message very briefly, which limits their ability to retain the message.
- *Legal restrictions.* Outdoor billboards are subject to strict regulations and to a high degree of standardization. Many cities place limitations on the number and type of signs and billboards allowed along the roadside. More than a dozen cities have banned digital billboards in the name of traffic safety.[66]
- *Lack of prominence.* A clutter of billboards and signs along a heavily traveled route tends to reduce the effectiveness of a single ad that loses its prominence among the crowd of billboards.

Using Out-of-Home Ads. Consumers are spending more time in their cars than ever before (18.5 hours per week), and out-of-home advertising is an effective way to reach them.[67] Technology has changed the face of out-of-home advertising dramatically in recent years. Computerized printing techniques that render truer, crisper, and brighter colors; billboard extensions; and three-dimensional effects have improved significantly the quality of standard billboards (known as posters or bulletins in the industry). New vinyl surfaces accept print-quality images and are extremely durable. Digital billboards, giant computer screens that rotate messages every 6 to 10 seconds, allow companies to create vibrant, eye-catching ads that really capture viewers' attention at reasonable cost.

Because the outdoor ad is stationary and the viewer is in motion, a small business owner must pay special attention to its design. An outdoor ad should:

- Allow viewers to identify the product and the company clearly and quickly.
- Use a simple background. The background should not compete with the message.
- Rely on large illustrations that jump out at the viewer.
- Include clear, legible fonts. All lowercase or a combination of uppercase and lowercase letters works best. Very bold or very thin typefaces become illegible at a distance. Select simple fonts that are easy to read from a distance.
- Use black-and-white designs. Research shows that black-and-white outdoor ads are more effective than color ads. If color is important to the message, pick color combinations that contrast both hue and brightness—for example, black on yellow.
- Emphasize simplicity. Short copy and short words are best. Don't try to cram too much onto a billboard. Because of their brief window of exposure, ads with just 3 to 5 words are most effective, and ads containing more than 10 words are ineffective.
- Use illumination so that passersby can read them at night. By using illuminated billboards, advertisers can increase the reach of outdoor ads by 16 percent.[68]
- Be located on the right-hand side of the highway.

Two of the latest trends in outdoor advertising are Internet-connected digital boards and billboards that send messages to customers' cell phones. With digital billboards, ad content is virtually unlimited; advertisers can include eye-catching graphics and streaming media in their ads. (Giant digital billboards, called spectaculars, are common in New York's Times Square, where much of the traffic includes pedestrians, whose travel speeds are slower than cars.) Digital billboard ads, which cost between $1,200 and $10,000 per month, offer advertisers great flexibility. For instance, a restaurant could change the messages it displays to advertise its breakfast offerings in the morning, lunch specials at mid-day, and dinner menu in the afternoon and evening.

The latest outdoor ads include a computer chip that interacts with a cell phone's Web browser, which enables advertisers to send messages to passersby's cell phones. For instance, a movie theater's smart billboard could send messages stating starting times for feature films it is running to interested customers' cell phones.

TRANSIT ADVERTISING. A variation of out-of-home advertising is transit advertising, which includes advertising signs on the inside and outside of the public transportation vehicles such as trains, buses, and subways throughout the country's urban areas. The medium is likely to grow as more cities look to public transit systems to relieve traffic congestion.

Transit ads offer a number of advantages:

- *Wide coverage.* Transit advertising offers advertisers mass exposure to a variety of customers. The message literally goes to where the people are.
- *Repeat exposure.* Transit ads provide lengthy and repeated exposure to a message, particularly for inside cards, the ads that appear inside the vehicle.
- *Low cost.* Even small businesses with limited budgets can afford transit advertising.
- *Flexibility.* Transit ads come in a wide range of sizes, numbers, and duration. With transit ads, an owner can select an individual market or any combination of markets across the country.

Transit ads also have several disadvantages:

- *Generality.* Although entrepreneurs can choose the specific transit routes on which to advertise, they cannot target a particular segment of the market through transit advertising as effectively as they can with other media. The effectiveness of transit ads depends on the routes that public vehicles travel and on the people they reach, which, unfortunately, the advertiser cannot control. Overall, transit riders tend to be young, affluent, and culturally diverse.
- *Limited appeal.* Unlike many media, transit ads are not beamed into the potential customer's residence or business. The result is that customers cannot keep them for future reference.
- *Brief message.* Transit ads do not permit advertisers to present a detailed description or a demonstration of the product or service for sale. Although inside ads have a relatively long exposure (the average ride lasts 22.5 minutes), outside ads must be brief and to the point.

DIRECT MAIL. Direct mail has long been a popular method of direct marketing and includes tools such as letters, postcards, catalogs, discount coupons, brochures, and other items that are mailed to homes or businesses. The earliest known catalogs were printed by fifteenth-century printers. Although Internet sales have surpassed direct mail catalog sales, companies still sell virtually every kind of product imaginable through direct mail, from Christmas trees and lobsters to furniture and clothing (the most popular mail-order purchase). Nearly 20,000 U.S. companies send 20 billion direct mail catalogs to stay-at-home shoppers, who purchase $102 billion in goods each year.[69]

Direct mail offers some distinct advantages to entrepreneurs:

- *Flexibility.* An advantage of direct mail is that businesses can tailor the message to the target audience. Rather than send a blanket mail blast to 100,000 addresses, advertisers can target 5,000 high-potential customers with a mailing. An advertiser's presentation to customers can be as simple or as elaborate as necessary. One custom tailor shop achieved a great deal of success with fliers it mailed to customers on its mailing list when it included a swatch of material from the fabric for the upcoming season's suits. With direct mail, the tone of the message can be personal, creating a positive psychological effect. In addition, advertisers control the timing of their campaigns, sending ads when they are most appropriate.
- *Reader attention.* With direct mail, an advertiser's message does not have to compete with other ads for the reader's attention. Most people enjoy getting mail, and the U.S.

Postal Service estimates that 85 percent of households open and read daily some or all of the direct mail that they receive.[70] Unlike many e-mail messages, direct mail gets a recipient's undivided attention at least for a moment. If the message is on the mark and sent to the right audience, direct mail ads can be a powerful advertising tool.

■ *Rapid feedback.* Direct mail advertisements produce quick results. In most cases, an ad will generate sales within 3 or 4 days after customers receive it. Business owners should know whether a mailing has produced results within a relatively short time period.

■ *Measurable results and testable strategies.* Because they control their mailing lists, direct marketers can readily measure the results their ads produce. In addition, direct mail allows advertisers to test different ad layouts, designs, and strategies (often within the same "run") to see which one "pulls" the greatest response. The best direct marketers are always fine-tuning their ads to make them more effective. Table 5 offers guidelines for creating direct mail ads that really work.

■ *Effectiveness.* The right message targeted at the right mailing list can make direct mail one of the most efficient forms of advertising. Direct mail to the right people produces results.

Direct-mail ads also suffer from several disadvantages:

■ *Inaccurate mailing lists.* The key to the success of the entire mailing is the accuracy of the customer list. Using direct mail ads with a poor mailing list is a guaranteed waste of money. Experienced direct mail marketers cite the 60-30-10 rule, which says that 60 percent of a campaign's success depends on the quality of the list, 30 percent on the offer, and 10 percent on the creativity of the ad.[71] Make sure the mailing list you use is accurate and up-to-date.

■ *Clutter.* The average household in the United States receives about 900 pieces of direct mail each year.[72] With that volume of direct mail, it can be difficult for an advertisement to get customers' attention.

■ *High relative costs.* Relative to the size of the audience reached, the cost of designing, producing, and mailing an advertisement via direct mail is high. Rising paper and postage costs pose real threats to companies that use direct mail. However, if a mailing is well planned and properly executed, it can produce a high percentage of returns, making direct mail one of the least expensive advertising methods in terms of results.

■ *High throwaway rate.* Often called junk mail, direct-mail ads become "junk" when an advertiser selects the wrong audience or broadcasts the wrong message. According to the Direct Mail Association, the average response rate for a direct mail campaign is 3.7 percent.[73] By supplementing traditional direct-mail pieces with toll-free (800) numbers, links to Web sites, and carefully timed follow-up phone calls, companies have been able to increase their response rates.

How to Use Direct Mail. The key to a direct mailing's success is the right mailing list. Even the best direct-mail ad will fail if sent to the "wrong" customers. Owners can develop lists themselves, using customer accounts, telephone books, city and trade directories, and other sources, including companies that sell complementary but not competing products, professional organizations' membership lists, business or professional magazines' subscription lists, and mailing list brokers who sell lists for practically any need. Advertisers can locate list brokers through *The Direct Marketing List Source* from the Standard Rate and Data Service found in most public libraries. In a world in which the average U.S. adult receives 41 pounds of direct mail each year, the key to success with a direct mail campaign is to get your ad noticed, and the right mailing list is the ideal starting point.

ENTREPRENEURIAL
Profile

Michael Greco and Dartmouth Pharmaceuticals

Dartmouth Pharmaceuticals, launched in 1991 as a maker of cold and allergy medications, developed a line of all-natural skin and nail care products called Elon Essentials, but annual sales were a measly $5,000. To pump up sales, CEO Michael Greco decided to send direct mail ads to dermatologists. To increase the probability that the busy doctors would look at the ads, Greco sent them by priority mail. The direct mail campaign helped Dartmouth increase sales of its Elon Essentials line to more than $1.5 million in just a few years, and the company is now gearing up to add a national sales force to sell its products.[74]

TABLE 5 Guidelines for Creating Direct Mail Ads That Really Work

In many industries, a successful direct mail campaign is one that produces a response rate of at least 2.5 percent, which means that *97.5 percent* of the customers who received the ad did *not* respond to it! What steps can entrepreneurs take to improve the results of their direct mail campaigns?

Realize that repetition is one key to success.

Experts estimate that customers must receive at least three direct mail pieces per month from a business before they really notice the ad.

Provide meaningful incentives.

Direct mail succeeds by getting prospects to respond to a written offer. To do that, a direct mail ad must offer potential customers something of value—a free sample, a special price, a bonus gift, or anything that a company's target customers value. Twenty percent of prospects who do not open the direct mail ads they receive say that they have no reason to open them. Make sure your offer gives them a reason!

Write copy that will get results.

Try the following proven techniques:

- Promise readers your most important benefit in the headline or first paragraph.
- Use short "action" words and paragraphs and get to the point quickly.
- Make the copy look easy to read with lots of "white space."
- Use eye-catching words such as *free, you, save, guarantee, new, profit, benefit, improve*, and others.
- Consider using computerized "handwriting" somewhere on the page or envelope; it attracts attention.
- Forget grammatical rules; write as if you were speaking to the reader.
- Repeat the offer three or more times in various ways.
- Back up claims and statements with proof and endorsements whenever possible.
- Ask for the order or a response.
- Ask attention-getting questions such as "Would you like to lower your home's energy costs?" in the copy.
- Use high-quality copy paper and envelopes (those with windows are best) because they stand a better chance of being opened and read. Brown envelopes that resemble government correspondence work well.
- Envelopes that resemble bills almost always get opened.
- Address the envelope to an individual, not "Occupant."
- Avoid mailing labels, which shout "direct mail ad piece." The best campaigns print addresses directly on the envelopes.
- Use stamps if possible. They get more letters opened than metered postage.
- Use a postscript (P.S.)—always; they are the most often read part of a printed page. Make sure the P.S. contains a "hook" that will encourage the recipient to read on. This is the perfect place to restate the offer's unique selling proposition.
- Include a separate order form that passes the following "easy" test:
  - *Easy to find.* Consider using brightly colored paper or a unique shape.
  - *Easy to understand.* Make sure the offer is easy for readers to understand. Marketing expert Paul Goldberg says, "Confuse 'em and you lose 'em."
  - *Easy to complete.* Keep the order form simple and unconfusing.
  - *Easy to pay.* Direct mail ads should give customers the option to pay by whatever means is most convenient.
  - *Easy to return.* Including a postage-paid return envelope (or at a minimum a return envelope) will increase the response rate.
- **Build and maintain a quality mailing list over time.** The right mailing list is the key to a successful direct mail campaign. You may have to rent lists to get started, but once you are in business use every opportunity to capture information about your customers. Constantly focus on improving the quality of your mailing list.

Test your campaigns and track their results.

"Testing is everything," says the founder of a company that used direct mail ads as part of a marketing strategy that led his company to $10 million in annual sales. Monitoring the response rate from each mailing is essential for knowing which ads and which lists actually produce results.

Sources: Adapted from *What's in the Mailbox? The Impact of One-to-One Marketing on Consumer Response*, Winterberry Group, January 2007, p. 7; "Direct Mail Tips for Manufacturers' Letters," Koch Group, *www.kochgroup.com/directmail.html;* Kim T. Gordon, "Copy Right," *Business Start-Ups*, June 1998, pp. 18–19; Paul Hughes, "Profits Due," *Entrepreneur*, February 1994, pp. 74–78; "Why They Open Direct Mail, " *Communications Briefings*, December 1993, p. 5; Ted Lammers, "The Elements of Perfect Pitch," *Inc.*, March 1992, pp. 53–55: "Special Delivery," *Small Business Reports*, February 1993, p. 6; Gloria Green and James W. Peltier, "How to Develop a Direct Mail Program," *Small Business Forum*, Winter 1993/1994, pp. 30–45; Susan Headden, "The Junk Mail Deluge," *U.S. News & World Report*, December 8, 1997, pp. 40–48; Joanna L. Krotz, "Direct-Mail Tips for Sophisticated Marketers," Microsoft Small Business Center, *www.microsoft.com/smallbusiness/resources/marketing/customer_service_acquisition/direct_mail_tips_for_sophisticated_marketers.mspx.*

DIRECTORIES. Directories may seem old-fashioned compared to newer high-tech tools, but both are valuable ways for businesses to reach commercial or industrial customers. Directories are an important medium for reaching those customers who have already made purchase decisions. The directory simply helps these customers locate the specific product or service they have decided to buy. Directories include telephone books, industrial guides, buyer guides, annuals, catalog files, and yearbooks that list various businesses and the products they sell.

Directories offer several advantages to advertisers:

- *Prime prospects.* Directory listings reach customers who are prime prospects because they have already decided to purchase an item. The directory just helps them find what they are looking for.
- *Long life.* Directory listings usually have long lives. A typical directory may be published annually.

However, there are certain disadvantages to using directories:

- *Lack of flexibility.* Listings and ads in many directories offer only a limited variety of design features. Business owners may not be as free to create unique ads as in other printed media.
- *Ad clutter.* In many directories, ads from many companies are clustered together so closely that no single ad stands out from the rest.
- *Obsolescence.* Because directories are commonly updated only annually, some of their listings become obsolete. This is a problem for a small firm that changes its name, location, or phone number.

When choosing a directory, the small business owner should evaluate several criteria:

- *Completeness.* Does the directory include enough listings that customers will use it?
- *Convenience.* Are the listings well organized and convenient? Are they cross-referenced?
- *Evidence of use.* To what extent do customers actually use the directory? What evidence of use does the publisher offer?
- *Age.* Is the directory well established and does it have a good reputation?
- *Circulation.* Do users pay for the directory or do they receive complimentary copies? Is there an audited circulation statement?

TRADE SHOWS. Trade shows provide manufacturers and distributors with a unique opportunity to advertise to a preselected audience of potential customers who are inclined to buy. Thousands of trade shows take place each year, and carefully evaluating and selecting the right shows can produce profitable results for a business owner. Trade show success does *not* depend on how much an exhibitor spends; instead, success is a function of planning, preparation, and follow-up.

Trade shows offer the following advantages:

- *A natural market.* Trade shows bring together buyers and sellers in a setting in which exhibitors can explain and demonstrate their products. Comparative shopping is easy, and the buying process is efficient for customers.
- *Pre-selected audience.* Trade exhibits attract potential customers with a genuine interest in the goods or services on display. There is a high probability that trade show attendees will make a purchase. A study by Exhibit Surveys reports that 53 percent of trade show attendees plan to purchase at least one of the products on display within 1 year.[75]
- *New customer market.* Trade shows offer exhibitors a prime opportunity to reach new customers and to contact people who are not accessible to sales representatives.
- *Cost advantage.* As the cost of making a field sales call continues to escalate, companies are realizing that trade shows are an economical method of generating leads and making sales presentations.

However, trade shows do have certain disadvantages:

- *Increasing costs.* The cost of exhibiting at trade shows is rising. Registration fees, travel and setup costs, sales salaries, and other expenditures may be a barrier to some small firms.
- *Wasted effort.* A poorly planned exhibit ultimately costs the small business more than its benefits are worth. Too many firms enter exhibits in trade shows without proper preparation, and they end up wasting their time, energy, and money on unproductive activities.

To avoid these disadvantages, entrepreneurs should:

- Research trade shows to find the ones that will put you in front of the best prospects for your product or service.
- Establish objectives for every trade show. Do you want to generate 100 new sales leads, make new product presentations to 500 potential customers, or make $5,000 in sales?
- Communicate with key potential customers *before* the show; send them invitations or invite them to stop by your booth for a special gift.
- Plan your display with your target audience in mind and make it memorable. Be sure your exhibit shows your company and its products or services in the best light. Do everything to maximize the visibility of your exhibit and keep the display neat.
- Staff your booth with knowledgeable salespeople. Attendees appreciate meeting face-to-face with knowledgeable and friendly staff.
- Do something to attract a crowd to your booth. Demonstrate your product or service so that customers can see it in action, sponsor a drawing for a prize, or set up an interactive display. Drawing a crowd creates "buzz" for your company among attendees.
- Learn to distinguish between serious customers and "tire-kickers."
- Make it easy for potential customers to get information about your company and its products and services. Distribute literature that clearly communicates the benefits of your products or services.
- Project a professional image at all times. Salespeople who man the booth should engage prospects in conversation and should ask qualifying questions.
- Follow up promptly on sales leads. The most common mistake trade show participants make is failing to follow up on the sales leads the show generated. If you are not going to follow up leads, why bother to attend the show in the first place?

Few small businesses rely on a single advertising medium to communicate their advertising messages to potential customers, choosing instead to employ **cross-channel advertising strategies** whereby they communicate with potential customers using a variety of media. For instance, Gary Lindsey, head of marketing at The Parent Company, a consumer product business that targets young parents, says that although the company is primarily Web-based, it relies heavily on direct mail catalogs and e-mail marketing to drive sales. "There's real return on investment from those catalogs," says Lindsey. "People love shopping on the Internet, but there is something powerful when you combine print and Internet."[76]

> ► ENTREPRENEURSHIP **IN ACTION** ►

A "Gorilla" Marketing Strategy

Located halfway between Los Angeles and Las Vegas on a desolate stretch of highway just off of Interstate 15 near the famous Route 66, passersby might mistake Peggy Sue's 50's Diner as just another kitschy restaurant aimed at tourists. But there's far more to this small business than meets the eye. The diner was originally built in 1954 with just three booths and nine counter stools, but in 1987 Champ and Peggy Sue Gabler took over and began revitalizing the diner and its advertising strategy. They expanded the original diner to a 60-seat restaurant. Thanks to family recipes from Peggy Sue's grandmother and great 1950s music, the diner became a popular destination for local residents, truck drivers, passing tourists, and soldiers from a nearby military post.

By the early 1990s, Peggy Sue's was generating $280,000 in annual sales, a respectable figure given that the economy was experiencing a recession. The Gablers decided that the diner could do much better, however, and invested $600,000 from their own savings and an SBA-guaranteed loan to quadruple the diner's capacity and add a juke-boxed theme façade, a 3,000-square-foot 50's-style five-and-dime store, soda and ice cream fountains, a pizza parlor, and a large collection of 1950s memorabilia. Upon entering the diner, visitors can learn about their futures from a Magic Elvis Fortune Telling Machine, where "The King tells all." Waitresses dress in real waitress uniforms and are prone to call their guests "Hon." The menu, which includes breakfast, lunch, and dinner, features items such as the Buddy Holly bacon cheeseburger, a Mickey Mouse

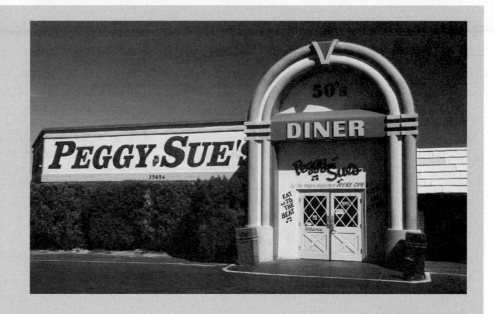

The juke-boxed themed facade of Peggy Sue's 50's Diner invites customers to step back to a simpler time.

Source: ©America/Alamy

club sandwich, the Fabian French dip, and the Fats Domino meat loaf special.

The Gablers ramped up their advertising, renting space on billboards along nearby highways and launching a radio advertising campaign. Within 2 years, sales had increased to nearly $1 million. Sales have continued to grow steadily, reaching $3 million a year. Recently, however, sales have remained flat, and the Gablers decided once again that it was time to shake things up. Champ rented a large billboard just outside of Las Vegas that cost $1,600 more per month than any of Peggy Sue's other billboard locations. "Big casinos pay top dollar to advertise in that area," he says. "And here is our [billboard], saying nothing more than our name and 'Hungry? 90 miles.'" The Gablers also added a "dinersaur" park next to the restaurant, complete with larger-than-life dinosaur sculptures made of sheet metal that cost $40,000 to build and install. A 12-foot-tall sheet metal statue of King Kong also is part of the diner's "gorilla" marketing strategy. "Forty thousand cars a day

pass the back of our property [on Interstate 15]," says Champ. "We're not sure how long it will take to get a return on our new monsters, but they have created another marketing strategy in trying times."

1. Visit the Web site of Peggy Sue's 50's Diner (*www.peggysuesdiner.com*) and use a search engine to locate visitors' photos of the diner and its "dinersaur" park. Evaluate the advertising plan that the Gablers have developed for the diner.

2. Are there other advertising media and techniques described in this chapter that you would suggest the Gablers consider using to boost Peggy Sue's 50's Diner's sales and profits? Explain.

Sources: Based on Maggie Overfelt, "Gorilla Marketing," *FSB*, June 2008, pp. 49–50; "About Us, Peggy Sue's 50's Diner" *www.peggysuesdiner.com;* Spencer Cross, "Because You Know You've Always Wondered . . . Yermo's 'Peggy Sue's 50's Diner' Isn't Half Bad," *Los Angeles Met Blogs*, November 25, 2008, *http://la.metblogs.com/2008/11/25/because-you-know-youve-always-wonderedyermos-peggy-sues-50s-diner-isnt-half-bad/.*

How to Prepare an Advertising Budget

4. Identify four basic methods for preparing an advertising budget.

One of the most challenging decisions confronting a small business owner is how much to spend on advertising. The amount entrepreneurs want to spend and the amount they can afford to spend usually differ significantly. Entrepreneurs can use the following four methods to create an advertising budget: *what-is-affordable, matching competitors, percentage of sales,* and *objective and task.*

With the what-is-affordable method, business owners see advertising as a luxury. They view it completely as an expense rather than as an investment that generates sales and profits in the future. As the name implies, entrepreneurs who use this method spend whatever their companies can afford on advertising. Too often, business owners determine their advertising budgets after they have funded all of the other budget items. The result is an advertising budget that is inadequate for getting the job done. This method also fails to relate the marketing communications budget to the marketing communications objective.

Another approach is to match the advertising budget of the company's competitors, either in a flat dollar amount or as a percentage of sales. This method assumes that a company's advertising needs and strategies are the same as those of its competitors, which is rarely the case. Although competitors' actions can be helpful when establishing a floor for marketing communications expenditures, relying on this technique can lead to blind imitation instead of a budget suited to a small company's circumstances.

The most commonly used method of establishing an advertising budget is the simple percentage-of-sales approach. This method relates advertising expenditures to actual sales results. Tying advertising expenditure to sales rather than to profits creates greater consistency in advertising because most companies' sales tend to fluctuate less than profits. One rule of thumb for establishing an advertising budget is spending 10 percent of projected sales the first year of business, 7 percent the second year, and at least 5 percent in each successive year. Relying totally on broad rules like these can be dangerous, however. They may not be representative of a small company's advertising needs.

The objective-and-task method is the most difficult and least used technique for establishing an advertising budget. It also is the method most often recommended by advertising experts. With this method, an entrepreneur links advertising expenditures to specific business objectives. The objective-and-task method builds up an advertising budget from the bottom up by analyzing what it will cost to accomplish an entrepreneur's business objectives. For example, suppose that an entrepreneur wants to boost sales of a particular product 10 percent by attracting local college students. He may determine that a nearby rock radio station would be the best advertising medium to use. Then he must decide on the number and frequency of the ads and estimate their costs. Entrepreneurs follow this process for each advertising objective.

Once they establish their advertising objectives and budgets, many entrepreneurs find it useful to use a calendar to plan the timing of their advertising campaigns and expenditures across the year. Figure 6 illustrates three common advertising scheduling strategies.

FIGURE 6
Advertising Scheduling Strategies

Continuous—Small business spends its advertising budget consistently across time. Ideal for companies whose products or services are in demand year-round—e.g., grocery stores and drug stores.

Flighting—Small business concentrates its ad expenditures in carefully timed batches. Ideal for companies that experience peaks and valleys in the demand for their products or services—e.g., vacation rental companies.

Pulsing—Small business makes some expenditures consistently across the year but concentrates the rest of its ad expenditures in carefully timed pulses. Ideal for companies that must keep their names in front of customers year-round but experience peaks and valleys in the demand for their products or services—e.g., landscape services.

How to Advertise Big on a Small Budget

5. Describe practical methods of stretching a small business owner's advertising budget.

The typical small business does not have the luxury of an unlimited advertising budget. Most cannot afford to hire a professional ad agency. This does not mean, however, that a small company should assume a second-class advertising posture. Most advertising experts say that, unless a small company spends more than $10,000 to $15,000 a year on advertising, it probably doesn't need an ad agency. For most, hiring freelance copywriters and artists on a per-project basis is a much better bargain. With a little creativity and a dose of ingenuity, small business owners can stretch their advertising dollars and make the most of what they spend. Four useful techniques are cooperative advertising, shared advertising, stealth advertising, and publicity.

COOPERATIVE ADVERTISING. With **cooperative advertising**, a manufacturing company shares the cost of advertising with a retailer if the retailer features its products in those ads. Both the manufacturer and the retailer get more advertising per dollar by sharing expenses. Cooperative advertising not only helps small businesses stretch their advertising budgets, but it also offers another source of savings: the free advertising packages that many manufacturers supply to retailers. These packages usually include photographs and illustrations of the product as well as professionally prepared ads to use in different media.

SHARED ADVERTISING. With **shared advertising**, a group of similar businesses forms a syndicate to produce generic ads that allow the individual businesses to dub in local information. The technique is especially useful for small businesses that sell relatively standardized products or services such as legal assistance, autos, and furniture. Because the small firms in the syndicate pool their funds, the result usually is higher-quality ads and significantly lower production costs.

STEALTH ADVERTISING. Guerrilla marketing principles are offbeat, low-cost techniques for marketing a small company's goods and services. In advertising, these techniques are called **stealth advertising**, which includes innovative ads that do not necessarily look like traditional ads and often are located in unexpected places. Ads now appear on electrical outlets in airport terminals, on eggs (gently printed directly onto the shells with lasers), clothes hangers from laundries, in urinals in public restrooms (using a device called Wizmark that plays sounds and pictures when a guest arrives), and other unusual places.[77] One consumer products company achieved success with a campaign that involved painting manhole covers in New York City to look like steaming hot cups of coffee. Bamboo Lingerie attracted a great deal of attention for its brand by stenciling on New York City sidewalks the message "From here it looks like you could use some new underwear" and its name and logo.[78]

OTHER WAYS TO SAVE. Other cost-saving suggestions for advertising expenditures include the following:

- *Repeat ads that have been successful.* In addition to reducing the cost of ad preparation, repetition may create a consistent image in a small firm's advertising program.
- *Use identical ads in different media.* If a billboard has been an effective advertising tool, an owner should consider converting it to a newspaper or magazine ad or a direct mail flier.
- *Hire independent copywriters, graphic designers, photographers, and other media specialists.* Many small businesses that cannot afford a full-time advertising staff buy their advertising services à la carte. They work directly with independent specialists and usually receive high-quality work that compares favorably with that of advertising agencies without paying a fee for overhead.
- *Concentrate advertising during times when customers are most likely to buy.* Some small business owners make the mistake of spreading an already small advertising budget evenly—and thinly—over a 12-month period. A better strategy is to match advertising expenditures to customers' buying habits.

Chapter Review

1. Define your company's unique selling proposition (USP).
   - Branding a company's products or services depends on communicating the correct *unique selling proposition* (USP), a key customer benefit or a product or service that sets a business apart from its competition.
   - The USP answers the customer's ultimate question: "What's in it for me?"
2. Explain the differences among promotion, publicity, personal selling, and advertising.
   - Promotion is any form of persuasive communication designed to inform consumers about a product or service and to influence them to purchase these goods or services. It includes publicity, personal selling, and advertising.
   - Publicity is any commercial news covered by the media that boosts sales but for which the business does not pay.
   - Personal selling is the personal contact between salespeople and potential customers that comes from sales efforts.
   - Advertising is any sales presentation that is nonpersonal in nature and is paid for by an identified sponsor. A company's target audience and the nature of its message determine the advertising media it will use.
3. Describe the advantages and disadvantages of various advertising media.
   - The medium used to transmit an advertising message influences the customer's perception—and reception—of it.
   - Media options include word-of-mouth, sponsorships and special events, television, radio, newspapers, the Internet, magazines, specialty advertising, point-of-purchase ads, out-of-home advertising, transit advertising, direct mail, directories, and trade shows.
4. Identify four basic methods for preparing an advertising budget.
   - Establishing an advertising budget presents a real challenge to the small business owner.
   - The four basic methods of preparing an advertising budget are what is affordable, matching competitors, percentage of sales, and objective and task.
5. Describe practical methods for stretching a business owner's advertising budget.
   - Despite their limited advertising budgets, small businesses do not have to take a second-class approach to advertising. Three techniques that can stretch a small company's advertising dollars are cooperative advertising, shared advertising, and stealth advertising.

Discussion Questions

1. What are the three elements of promotion? How do they support one another?
2. What factors should a small business manager consider when selecting advertising media?
3. What is a unique selling proposition? What role should it play in a company's advertising strategy?
4. One company sent an e-mail that stated the following USP: "Combining the strategy, business processes, implementation, and technical support skills of a CRM systems integrator with the data management, analytic, and marketing skills of a database marketing service provider to deliver and operate a close-looped marketing and sales environment." How do you rate the effectiveness of this USP? Explain. What are the characteristics of an effective USP?

5. Review the advantages and disadvantages of the following advertising media:
   a. Word of mouth
   b. Sponsorships and special events
   c. Television
   d. Radio
   e. Newspapers
   f. Internet advertising
   g. Magazines
   h. Specialty advertising
   i. Direct mail
   j. Out-of-home advertising
   k. Transit advertising
   l. Directories
   m. Trade shows

6. Assume you are a small business owner who has an advertising budget of $1,500 to invest in a campaign promoting a big July 4th "blowout" sale. Where would you be most likely to invest your advertising budget if you were trying to reach customers in the 25–45 age range with higher than average disposable income who are likely to be involved in boating activities in a local resort town? Explain. How would you generate free publicity to extend your advertising budget?

7. What are fixed spots, preemptible spots, and floating spots in radio advertising?

8. Describe the characteristics of an effective out-of-home advertisement.

9. Briefly outline the steps in creating an advertising plan. What principles should the small business owner follow when creating an effective advertisement?

10. Describe the common methods of establishing an advertising budget. Which method is most often used? Which technique is most often recommended? Why?

11. What techniques can small business owners use to stretch their advertising budgets?

12. Use a search engine to locate the most recent "E-mail Marketing Trends Survey." Using the information in it, work with a team of your classmates to select a local small business with which you are familiar to design an effective e-mail advertising campaign. What are the advantages and the disadvantages of using e-mail as an advertising medium?

A coordinated and consistent advertising and promotion effort is essential to an entrepreneur's success. Companies that fail to maintain a high profile among their target customers are soon forgotten. As an entrepreneur, your job is to leverage the advertising and promotion ideas from the chapter. Review the concepts and company examples in the chapter to determine whether they provide insight and ideas that may work to promote your business. How do you anticipate promoting your business? Which advertising media do you plan to use? Why?

On the Web

If you anticipate using the Web to promote your business, you will want to invest time to determine how best to do that. Search for similar businesses on the Internet. Identify three favorite sites. Note the appearance, layout, and navigation tools on these sites. What do you find attractive? What do you find distracting? Use this to develop ideas about how your site should look and what it should accomplish for your business.

In the Software

Determine how much you plan to invest in your advertising and promotional activities. Will you use newspapers, radio, television, sponsorships, or other media? What role will publicity play in promoting your business? Include estimates of the cost of your advertising and promotional activities in your business plan. Once again, reviewing sample plans may help to get ideas of where you want to invest your advertising budget. You also will need to do some additional research to help determine how much your advertising and promotional efforts are going to cost. Once you have come up with some preliminary figures, go to the marketing section and develop your unique selling proposition. Review other information to test for consistency throughout the plan.

Building Your Business Plan

Continue to build your business plan with the new information you have acquired. Step back to assess whether you have a solid understanding of your market and whether your business plan effectively communicates that understanding.

Endnotes

1. Larry Dignan, "5 Looming Questions About the Amazon-Zappos Deal," ZDNet, July 23, 2009, *www.zdnet.com/blog/btl/5-looming-questions-about-the-amazon-zappos-deal/21591*.
2. Lin Grensing-Pophal, "Who Are You?" *Business Start-Ups*, September 1997, pp. 38–44.
3. Meg Whittemore, "PR on a Shoestring," *Nation's Business*, January 1991, p. 31.
4. Sara Wilson, "Learning from the Best: Coffee 101," *Entrepreneur*, March 2006, p. 64.
5. Debra Phillips, "Fast Track," *Entrepreneur*, April 1999, p. 42.
6. Elaine Appleton Grant, "A Token Strategy," *Inc.*, May 2006, *www.inc.com/magazine/20060501/priority-promos.html*.
7. Joanna L. Krotz, "'Cause Marketing' Tips: Boost Business by Giving Back," Microsoft Small Business Center, *www.microsoft.com/smallbusiness/resources/marketing/advertising_branding/cause_marketing_tips_boost_business_by_giving_back.mspx*.

8. Peggy Linial, "Small Business and Cause Related Marketing: Getting Started," Cause Marketing Forum, *www.causemarketingforum.com/framemain.asp?ID=189*.
9. Catharine Livingston and Gordy Megrose, "Adventure Altruism: Giving Large," *Outside Online*, January 2006, *http://outside.away.com/outside/altruism.html*.
10. Barry Farber, "Sales Shape-Up," *Entrepreneur*, August 2006, p. 72.
11. Barbara K. Mednick, "Behavior Counts in Sales," *Minneapolis St. Paul Star Tribune*, May 28, 2004, *www.startribune.com/working*.
12. "Most Salespeople Can't Sell," *Small Business Reports*, September 1990, p. 10.
13. Eric Anderson and Bob Trinkle, *Outsourcing the Sales Function: The Real Cost of Field Sales* (Mason, OH: Thomson Publishing, 2005), p. 8.
14. "Salespeople Don't Prep Enough for Calls," *Sales & Marketing Management's Performance Newsletter*, December 12, 2005, p. 2.

15. Norm Brodsky, "Keep Your Customers," *Inc.*, September 2006, pp. 57–58.

16. Steve Marshall, "Local Commerce Monitor Wave XIII," BIA/Kelsey, August 2009, *www.kelseygroup.com/research/local-commerce-monitor.asp*.

17. "Survey Reveals Media Channel Lines Continue to Blur," Media Myth and Realities, Ketchum, January 12, 2009, *www.ketchum.com/media_myths_and_realities_2008_survey_news_release*.

18. Sara Wilson, "All Systems Yo," *Entrepreneur*, February 2007, p. 38; "About Us," Pinkberry, *www.pinkberry.com*.

19. Dave Kissel, "Shaping the 90 Percent," *Media Myths and Realities*, Ketchum Perspectives, 2009, *http://ketchumperspectives.com/archives/2009_i1/90percent.php*.

20. "Online Video Viewership Rises 1.3%," Marketing Charts, April 10, 2010, *www.marketingcharts.com/direct/online-video-viewership-rises-13-12779/nielsen-online-brands-unique-viewers-mar-10-apr-2010jpg/*.

21. Maria Ricapito, "Lauren Luke's Next Project," *Vanity Fair*, March 3, 2010, *www.vanityfair.com/online/beauty/2010/03/lauren-lukes-next-project.html;* Deborah Song, "Putting Her Best Face Forward," *Entrepreneur*, August 28, 2009, *www.entrepreneur.com/startingabusiness/successstories/article203188.html*.

22. Ryan McCarthy, "Blessed Events: How to Make a Sponsorship Pay Off," *Inc.*, April 2008, pp. 48–50.

23. Solano Avenue Events and News, *www.solanoavenueassn.org/scut_past/scut04_7.html*.

24. Kim T. Gordon, "Tips for Event Sponsorship," *Entrepreneur*, March 2006, *www.entrepreneur.com/magazine/entrepreneur/2006/march/83672.html*.

25. Adam Bluestein, "Prime-Time Exposure," *Inc.*, March 2008, pp. 66–68.

26. "And Now a Word from Our Sponsor . . ." Media Awareness Network, *www.media-awareness.ca/english/resources/educational/teachable_moments/word_from_our_sponsor.cfm*.

27. "TV Basics," Television Bureau of Advertising, 2010, *www.tvb.org/rcentral/mediatrendstrack/tvbasics/12_ADS-Natl.asp;* Emily Fredrix, "Super Bowl Ad Prices Dip, But Still Pricey," *CBS News*, January 11, 2010, *www.cbsnews.com/stories/2010/01/11/sportsline/main6082591.shtml*.

28. "Sweet Smell of Success," Google AdWords, *www.google.com/adwords/tvads/success/fragrancenet.html*.

29. "Adults Reached Yesterday by Major Media," Television Bureau of Advertising, *www.tvb.org/nav/build_frameset.aspx*.

30. "Consumers Allocate High Percentage of Total Daily Media Hours to Television," Television Bureau of Advertising, *www.tvb.org/nav/build_frameset.aspx*.

31. "TV Viewers Watch Commercials," *Marketing Charts*, May 14, 2010, *www.marketingcharts.com/television/tv-viewers-watch-commericals-12877/*.

32. "Television and Health," *The Sourcebook for Teaching Science*, *www.csun.edu/science/health/docs/tv&health.html*.

33. Andrew Hayes, "Increased DVR Usage Is Good News for Marketing Research Companies," Bernett Research, May 4, 2010, *www.bernett.com/Bernett-Marketing-Research-Blog/?Tag=DVR%20Usage*.

34. Darren Murph, "DVR Owners Do Indeed Skip Ads, Study Affirms," Switched, August 7, 2008, *www.switched.com/2008/08/07/dvr-owners-do-indeed-skip-ads-study-affirms/*.

35. "TV Universe Expands, Share of Channels Tuned Does Not," *Media Daily News*, July 21, 2009, *www.mediapost.com/publications/?fa=Articles.showArticle&art_aid=110159*.

36. Shelly Banjo, "As Seen (Often) on TV," *Wall Street Journal*, May 11, 2009, *http://online.wsj.com/article/SB10001424052970204475004574126820963295620.html*.

37. Ibid.

38. Ismael AbduSalaam, "Diddy Breaks Record with Shopping Channel Appearance," *AllHipHop*, December 2, 2009, *http://allhiphop.com/stories/news/archive/2009/12/02/22051224.aspx*.

39. *Radio Marketing Guide*, Radio Advertising Bureau, 2009, *www.rab.com/public/marketingGuide/rabRmg.html*.

40. Ibid.

41. "Advertisers Chase News Consumers," *Sales and Marketing Management's Manage Smarter Newsletter*, March 5, 2007, p. 1.

42. "What Makes Products Sell?" *Communication Briefings,* July 1997, p. 6.

43. Martin Langeveld, "Newspapers Take a Bus Plunge: Circulation Plummets 10.6%," *Nieman Journalism Lab*, October 26, 2009, *www.niemanlab.org/2009/10/newspapers-take-a-bus-plunge-circulation-plummets-10-6-percent/*.

44. "Internet Overtakes Newspapers as News Outlet," The Pew Research Center for the People and the Press, December 23, 2008, *http://people-press.org/report/479/internet-overtakes-newspapers-as-news-source*.

45. The State of the News Media: An Annual Report on American Journalism, Project for Excellence in Journalism, 2009, *www.stateofthemedia.org/2009/narrative_newspapers_audience.php*.

46. Evelyn Nussenbaum, "Instant Infomercials," *FSB*, December 2008–January 2009, pp. 37–38.

47. Ralph F. Wilson, "Use Banner Ads to Promote Your Web Site," *Web Marketing Today*, March 9, 2009, *www.wilsonweb.com/articles/bannerad.htm;* "Study: Click-Through Rates Lower Than Expected," *Marketing Vox*, February 27, 2009, *www.marketingvox.com/study-click-through-rates-lower-than-expected-043342/*.

48. "Online Shoppers Rely on Search Engines," *Marketing Charts*, February 23, 2010, *www.marketingcharts.com/interactive/online-shoppers-rely-on-search-engines-12056/*.

49. "Marketing Budget Survey: How Do I Plan for 2010?" Goldstein Group Communications, Solon, OH, 2009, p. 2.

50. *Click Fraud Report, Q1 2010*, Click Forensics, April 2010, p. 3.

51. E-mail Security Market, 2010–2014, Executive Summary, Radicati Group, Palo Alto, CA, 2010, pp. 2–3.

52. E-mail Security Market, 2010-2014, Executive Summary, Radicati Group, Palo Alto, CA, 2010, pp. 2–3.

53. Q3 2009 North America E-mail Trends and Benchmarks Results, Epsilon, Irving, TX, December 2009, p. 2.

54. "Innovative Southwestern Restaurant Sizzles," Constant Contact, *www.constantcontact.com/email-marketing/customer-examples/fajita-grill.jsp*.

55. *The Magazine Handbook*, Magazine Publishers of America (New York: Author, 2009), pp. 8, 9, 57.

56. Ibid., pp. 7, 10.

57. Ibid., p. 31.

58. *The Magazine Handbook: A Comprehensive Guide 2006/07*, Magazine Publishers of America (New York: Author, 2007) p. 23.

59. *The Magazine Handbook* (2009), p. 13.

60. *The State of the News Media 2009: An Annual Report on American Journalism*, Pew Project for Excellence in Journalism, *www.stateofthemedia.org/2009/narrative_magazines_audience.php?media=9&cat=2*.

61. POPAI Library, Point-of-Purchase Advertising International, *www.popai.com/Content/NavigationMenu/Resources/Research/Research.htm*.

62. "Facts & Figures," Outdoor Advertising Association of America, *www.oaaa.org/marketingresources/factsandfigures.aspx*.

63. "Case Studies: Bennett Infiniti Inc.," Outdoor Advertising Association of America, *www.oaaa.org/images/upload/research/200312916163668014966.pdf*.

64. American Fact Finder, U.S. Census Bureau, *http://factfinder.census.gov/servlet/ADPTable?_bm=y&-geo_id=01000US&-qr_name=ACS_2005_EST_G00_DP3&-gc_url=null&-ds_name=&-_lang=en&-redoLog=false*.

65. "U.S. Advertising CPM, by Media," *eMarketer*, February 2009, *www.emarketer.com/Results.aspx?N=785*.

66. Larry Copeland, "More Cities Ban Digital Billboards," *USA Today*, March 24, 2010, *www.usatoday.com/news/nation/2010-03-22-visual-soup_N.htm*.

67. *Arbitron National In-Car Study* (New York: 2009), p. 5.

68. *Arbitron National In-Car Study* (New York: December 2003), p. 2, *www.oaaa.org/pdf/Incarstudy_summary.pdf*.

69. Hamilton Davison, "The U.S. Catalog Mailing Industry—Today and Tomorrow," American Catalog Mailers Association, January 31, 2008, pp. 3, 8.

70. "Staying Power," *Direct Mail News*, December 1, 2008, pp. 17–19.

71. "Direct Mail Tips for Manufacturers' Letters," Koch Group, *www.kochgroup.com/directmail.html*.

72. "Advertising Mail and the Environment," Mail Moves America, December 15, 2008, *www.mailmovesamerica.org/environmentmyth.php*.

73. Amanda Ferrante, "New DMA Response Rate Study Shows E-mail Still Strong for Conversion Rates," *DemandGen*, March 16, 2009, *www.demandgenreport.com/home/archives/feature-articles/183-new-dma-response-rate-study-shows-email-still-strong-for-conversion-rates.html*.

74. "Success Stories: Dartmouth Pharmaceuticals," U.S. Postal Service, *www.usps.com/directmail/dartmouthpharmaceuticals.htm;* "Company Info," Dartmouth Pharmaceuticals, *www.ilovemynails.com/elonhome.html*.

75. Skip Cox, "The Unique Value of Exhibitions in Accelerating the Sales Process," Exhibition Surveys, presented at the Exhibition and Convention Executives Forum, June 15, 2006, *www.exhibitsurveys.com/files/File/whitepapers/AcceleratingSalesProcess.pdf*.

76. "'Dead Tree Medium' No Longer: For Many Marketers, Print Outperforms Digital," *Knowledge@Wharton*, March 19, 2008, *http://knowledge.wharton.upenn.edu/article.cfm?articleid=1919&CFID=19193179&CFTOKEN=81243060&jsessionid=a830557b30537714f7f0107e5da2e19272f2*.

77. Max Chafkin, "Ads and Atmospherics: Outdoor Campaigns Are Suddenly Hip," *Inc.*, February 2007, pp. 39–41; Jennifer Pollack, "Can Your Banner Ad Do This?" *Fast Company*, July–August 2006, p. 51; Sara Wilson, "Hawking on Eggshells," *Entrepreneur*, February 2007, p. 75.

78. Steven Heller, "Going Overground," *Metropolis,* March 14, 2007, *www.metropolismag.com/cda/story.php?artid=2557*.

Pricing and Credit Strategies

Learning Objectives

Upon completion of this chapter, you will be able to:

1 Explain why pricing is both an art and a science.
2 Discuss the relationships among pricing, image, competition, and value.
3 Describe effective pricing strategies for both new and existing products and services.
4 Explain the pricing techniques used by retailers.
5 Explain the pricing techniques used by manufacturers.
6 Explain the pricing techniques used by service firms.
7 Describe the impact of credit on pricing.

Price is what you pay. Value is what you get.

—Warren Buffett

The real price of everything, what everything really costs to the

man who wants to acquire it, is the toil and trouble of acquiring it.

—Adam Smith

Pricing: A Creative Blend of Art and Science

One of the most challenging, yet most important, decisions entrepreneurs must make involves pricing their products and services. Studies by the consulting firm Accenture indicate that increasing prices by just 1 percent can produce an 11 percent increase in a company's profit, a result that is much greater than that produced by a comparable 1 percent decrease in costs.[1] "There's nothing you can do as quickly to improve profitability—and nothing you can do as quickly to destroy profitability—as change your pricing," says one consultant who specializes in pricing.[2] Prices that are too high can drive customers away and hurt a small company's sales. Pricing products and services too low, a common tendency among first-time entrepreneurs, robs a business of its ability to earn a profit, leaves customers with the impression that the business's goods and services are of inferior quality, and threatens the business's long-term success.

ENTREPRENEURIAL
Profile

*Ilana Eberson:
The NYC Business
Networking Group*

Ilana Eberson, founder of the NYC Business Networking Group, a New York City–based business networking company, wondered why her young company was struggling financially, given her $50 per hour fee. When she worked with a consultant to determine how much of her time she donated to her clients without charge (including free follow-up work, travel time, and support services), Eberson discovered that her hourly fee was closer to $7 per hour! She tightened her pricing policy, turned down jobs from potential customers who balked at her prices, eliminated the money-losing practices that she had fallen into, and, in the process, turned around her company.[3]

Determining the most appropriate price for a product or service requires entrepreneurs to consider how the following factors interact to provide clues about the proper price to charge:

- The total cost associated with providing the product or service
- Target customers' characteristics, including their buying power and their perceptions of the product or service
- The current and anticipated market forces that determine supply and demand
- The pricing strategies of competitors and their competitive behavior
- The company's anticipated sales volume and the impact of that production volume on unit cost
- The entrepreneur's desired image for the company and customers' expectations regarding product or service quality and price
- Normal cycles or seasonality in the market
- Customers' sensitivity to price changes
- Psychological factors that influence customers' perceptions of price and quality
- Substitute products or services that are available to customers
- Traditional and expected credit terms and discount policies

Notice that some of the factors, such as costs and competitors' prices, are relatively easy to quantify, but others, such as customers' sensitivity to price changes and desired image, are much less tangible. This is where the creative blending of art and science comes into play that leads to a final pricing decision. In pure economic terms, **price** is the monetary value of a good or service; it is a measure of what a customer must give up to obtain a good or service. For shoppers, price is a reflection of value. Customers often look to a product's or service's price for clues about value. Consider the following examples, which illustrate the sometimes puzzling connection between price and perceived value:

- From a tiny shop in Florence, Italy, Stefano Bemer handcrafts some of the finest shoes in the world. Bemer, who decided to enter the shoemaking business when the cobbler in his small town died, makes both ready-to-wear and custom shoes for customers around the globe. Materials range from the mundane (traditional leather) to the exotic (shark, ostrich, stingray, crocodile, toad, and hippopotamus). Prices for a pair of ready-to-wear shoes range from $1,200 to $2,600, and a pair of custom shoes, which require between 38 and 45 hours of work and two fittings, sells for $3,350 to $4,100. Despite these lofty prices, Bemer has a waiting list of customers and delivery times of 2 to 3 months.[4]

Shoemaker Stefano Bemer, whose handmade shoes sell for $1,200 to $4,100 per pair.

Source: Laif

■ For sporting clays shooters and hunters, the ultimate in gear is a custom-made shotgun. Companies such as Holland & Holland, Boss, William Evans, and Purdey offer some of the finest custom shotguns in the world. Skilled craftsmen who specialize in particular components build each part of the gun, which is a one-of-a-kind work of art. "It's built completely for you, not anybody else," says one appreciative customer. At Purdey, building a shotgun to a customer's measurements and specifications requires dozens of artisans and at least 2 years. The company makes just 80 to 90 guns per year. Purdey's over-and-under (the arrangement of the barrels) models start at $110,000, but custom engraving (e.g., a photorealistic etching of a dog or bird in flight), gold inlays, special woods, checkering, and other features easily can add another $100,000 to the price. "When I shoot with my Purdey, I feel like an orchestra conductor waving my baton," says one customer, who owns six Purdeys and has two more under construction.[5]

As you can see, setting higher prices sometimes can *increase* the appeal of a product or service ("If you charge more, you must be worth it").

Entrepreneurs must develop a keen sensitivity to both the psychological and economic impact of their pricing decisions. A product's or service's price must exceed the cost of providing it, and it must be compatible with customers' perceptions of value. "Pricing is not just a math problem," says one business writer. "It's a psychology test."[6] The psychology of pricing is an art much more than it is a science. It focuses on creating value in the customer's mind but recognizes that value is what the customer perceives it to be. At the outset, the goal is not necessarily to determine the ideal *price*, but an ideal *price range*. This **price range** is the area between the **price floor** that is established by a company's total cost to produce the product or provide the service and the **price ceiling**, which is the most the target customers are willing to pay (see Figure 1). The final price within this range depends on the image the company wants to create in the minds of its customers.

FIGURE 1
Acceptable Price Range

Price Ceiling ("What will the market bear?")

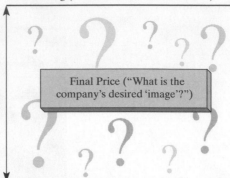

Acceptable
Price
Range

Final Price ("What is the company's desired 'image'?")

Price Floor ("What are the company's costs?")

The price floor depends on a company's cost structure, which can vary considerably from one business to another, even though they may be in the same industry. Although their cost structures may be different from their competitors', many entrepreneurs play follow-the-leader with their prices, simply charging what their competitors do on similar or identical products or services. Although this strategy simplifies the pricing decision, it can be very dangerous. Determining the price floor for a product or service requires entrepreneurs to have access to timely, accurate information about the cost of producing or selling a product or providing a service.

The price ceiling depends on entrepreneurs' ability to understand their customers' characteristics and buying behavior, the benefits that the product or service offers customers, and the prices of competing products. The best way to learn about customers' buying behavior is to conduct ongoing market research and to spend time with customers, listening to the feedback they offer. Small companies with effective pricing strategies tend to have a clear picture of their target customers and how their companies' products and services fit into their customers' perception of value. A company that begins losing valued customers who complain that its prices are too high has bumped into the price ceiling, and the owner should consider cutting prices.

An entrepreneur's goal is to position the company's prices within this acceptable price range that falls between the price floor and the price ceiling. The final price that entrepreneurs set depends on the desired image they want to create for their products or services: discount (bargain), middle-of-the road (value), or prestige (luxury). A prestige pricing strategy is not necessarily better or more effective than a no-frills, value pricing strategy. What matters most is that the company's pricing strategy matches the image the owner wants to create for the product or service.

Entrepreneurs often find themselves squeezed by rising operating and raw material costs but are hesitant to raise prices because they fear losing customers. Businesses faced with rising operating and raw material costs should consider the following strategies:

- *Communicate with customers.* Let your customers know what's happening. Danny O'Neill, owner of The Roasterie, a wholesale coffee business that sells to upscale restaurants, coffeehouses, and supermarkets, operates in a market in which the cost of raw material and supplies can fluctuate wildly due to forces beyond his control. When coffee prices nearly doubled in just 3 months, O'Neill was able to pass along the rising costs of his company's raw material to customers without losing a single one. He sent his customers a six-page letter and copies of newspaper articles about the increases in coffee prices. The approach gave the Roasterie credibility and helped show customers that the necessary price increases were beyond his control.[7]
- *Rather than raise the price of the good or service, include a surcharge.* Price increases tend to be permanent, but if higher costs are the result of a particular event (e.g., a hurricane that disrupted the nation's ability to process oil and resulted in rapidly rising fuel costs), a company can include a temporary surcharge. If the pressure on its costs subsides,

the company can eliminate the surcharge. When fuel prices began climbing rapidly, John Bunch, owner of a fishing guide service in St. James City, Florida, added a $50 fuel surcharge to his charter boat fishing rates, which start at $375 for 4 hours.[8]

■ *Rather than raise prices, consider eliminating customer discounts, coupons, and "freebies."* Eliminating discounts, coupons, and other freebies is an invisible way of raising prices that can add significantly to a small company's profit margin. Borders, the large bookstore chain, recently restructured its generous discount program because it had begun to cut too deeply into the company's profitability. Loyal customers still earn discounts (as do loyal customers at Borders' competitors), but the discounts are smaller and expire faster.[9]

■ *Offer products in smaller sizes or quantities.* As food costs soared, many restaurants introduced "small plates," reduced portions that enabled them to keep their prices in check. In the quick-service sector, mini-burgers billed as "fun food" and offered in bundles became a popular item on many menus.

■ *Focus on improving efficiency everywhere in the company.* Although raw materials costs may be beyond a business owner's control, other costs within the company are not. One way to cope with the effects of a rapid increase in costs is to find ways to cut costs and to improve efficiency in other areas. These improvements may not totally offset higher raw materials costs, but they can dampen their impact. Rather than raise prices, the owners of Jen-Mor Florists, a family-run flower shop in Dover, Delaware, decided to cut the number of deliveries to the edge of their territory to just one per day to reduce the company's delivery expenses.[10]

■ *Consider absorbing raw material cost increases to keep accounts with long-term importance to the company.* Saving a large account might be more important than keeping pace with rising costs. Companies that absorb the rising cost of raw materials often find ways to cut costs in other areas and to operate more efficiently.

■ *Emphasize the value your company provides to customers.* Unless a company reminds them, customers can forget the benefits and value its products offer. "If you provide great value to your customers, a little price increase isn't going to scare them away," says Elizabeth Gordon, a small business consultant.[11]

■ *Raise prices incrementally and consistently rather than rely on large periodic increases.* Companies that raise prices incrementally are less likely to experience resistance due to customers' sticker shock.

■ *Shift to less expensive raw materials, if possible.* When seafood and beef prices increased, many restaurants added more chicken dishes to their menus. When gold prices tripled within a 4-year period, jeweler John Christian, based in Austin, Texas, began creating more designs in silver and gold, all-silver, and even steel to keep costs and prices under control. The company also launched a separate line of products called Carved Creations priced well below the average $750 price for the John Christian line. Within 2 years, Carved Creations accounted for 30 percent of the company's sales.[12]

■ *Anticipate rising materials costs and try to lock in prices early.* It pays to keep tabs on raw materials prices and to be able to predict cycles of inflation. Entrepreneurs who can anticipate rising prices may be able to make purchases early or lock in long-term contracts before prices take off. After Hurricane Katrina devastated the Gulf Coast and disrupted the production of gasoline, fuel prices skyrocketed both for motorists and for airlines. Because Southwest Airlines had locked in contracts for fuel at pre-Katrina prices, the low-cost carrier was able to post impressive profits even though the rest of the industry's fuel cost had climbed 57 percent.[13]

Three Powerful Pricing Forces: Image, Competition, and Value

Price Conveys Image

2. Discuss the relationships among pricing, image, competition, and value.

A company's pricing policy can be a powerful tool for establishing a brand and for creating a desired image among its target customers. Whether they are seeking an image of exclusivity or one that reflects bargain basement deals, companies use price to enhance their brands. Some companies emphasize low prices, whereas others establish high prices to convey an image of quality, exclusivity, and prestige, all of which appeal to a particular market segment. For example, price reflects the notion of perceived value nowhere better than in the Swiss watch industry. Companies such as Bulgari, Rolex, Cartier, Patek Philippe, Blanepain, and Corum are legendary brands of ultrapremium handmade watches that sell from $5,000 to $395,000. Bulgari created a limited edition of just 24 ASIOMA Multi-Complications Tourbillon watches and priced them at $134,000 each.[14] Manufactured by Maîtres du Temps, is one of the most complex watches in the world, featuring nearly 700 moving parts (it weighs nearly half a pound), and sells for $395,000.[15] Some of these timepieces keep time no better than an inexpensive quartz-driven watch, but their owners are buying more than just a watch. Owning one of these watches is a mark of financial success. Value for some products does not reside solely in their superior technical performance but in their scarcity and uniqueness and the resulting image ("wow" factor) they create for the buyer. Although entrepreneurs must recognize the extremely limited market for ultraluxury items such as these, the ego-satisfying ownership of limited-edition watches, shoes, handbags, cars, jewelry, and other items is the psychological force that supports a premium price strategy.

Too often, small companies underprice their products and services, believing that low prices are the only way they can gain an advantage in the marketplace. According to management consulting firm McKinsey and Company, 80 to 90 percent of the pricing mistakes that companies make involve setting prices that are too low.[16] Companies that fall into this trap fail to recognize the extra value, convenience, service, and attention that they give their customers—things that many customers are willing to pay extra for. These entrepreneurs forget that price is just *one* element of the marketing mix and that for many customers it is not the most important factor. A study by Accenture reports that 73 percent of customers in the United States say that they have switched service providers because of poor service; only 47 percent say they have switched because another company offered lower prices.[17]

The secret to setting prices properly is understanding a company's target market, the customer groups at which it aims its goods or services. Target market, business image, and price are closely related.

ENTREPRENEURIAL
Profile

Jan Ryde: Hästens

Hästens, a fifth-generation family-owned business founded in Kopping, Sweden, and owned by Jan Ryde, has been making beds that are renowned for their quality, comfort, and durability since 1852. Hästens beds, which are made from all-natural materials, including cotton, horsehair, flax, down, and wool (no foam, no latex, no chemicals), take 4 days to construct by hand and are designed to last at least 30 years. The springs are made from heat-treated steel and are mounted in individual fabric pockets so that they move independently of one another and conform to the curves of a person's body without affecting the surrounding springs. To prove the durability of its beds, Hästens tests them under conditions that they are likely to encounter (kids using them as trampolines) as well as those they are not (dragging them down dirt roads). Aimed at upscale customers who are connoisseurs of the finest life has to offer, Hästens beds range in price from $3,500 for the Naturally model to $70,000 for the King Vividus. Its most popular model is the 2000T, which sells for $27,500.[18]

Competition and Prices

An important part of setting appropriate prices is tracking competitors' prices regularly; however, the prices that competitors are charging is just *one* variable in the pricing mix (and often not the most important one at that). When setting prices, entrepreneurs should take into account their competitors' prices, but they should *not* automatically match or beat them. Businesses that offer customers extra quality, value, service, or convenience can charge higher prices as long as customers recognize the "extras" they are getting. In other words, companies that successfully implement a differentiation strategy can charge higher prices for their products and services.

ENTREPRENEURIAL
Profile

Sarah Lurie:
Iron Core Kettlebells

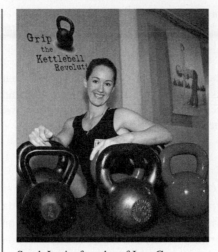

Sarah Lurie, founder of Iron Core Kettlebells

Source: Jack Smith/New York Times-Maps and Graphics

After spending 8 years as a Wall Street trader, Sarah Lurie returned to college in Arizona to finish her degree. While in school, Lurie discovered kettlebells, a traditional Russian technique of using iron weights in a swinging motion, and incorporated them into her exercise and bodybuilding routine. (A kettlebell looks like a bowling ball with a suitcase handle attached and weighs from 9 to 88 pounds.) After earning a master's degree in economics, she used $50,000 of her personal savings and a business credit card to launch Iron Core Kettlebells gym, a facility devoted to the unusual exercise equipment, in San Diego. Over time, the costs of operating her business increased, and Lurie knew that it was time to raise prices. Since opening, she had kept a close eye on her competitors' prices but recognized that her gym offered customers something unique: short, intense workouts with unusual equipment that produce impressive results. Lurie, a certified Russian Kettlebell Challenge Instructor, author of *Kettlebells for Dummies,* and the star of a series of kettlebell exercise videos, confidently raised her prices 30 percent. Only a handful of customers left because of the price increase. Lurie, who has opened a second Iron Core location, says, "If you're providing such great value to your customers that they can't live without you, a little price increase isn't going to scare them away."[19]

Two factors are vital to determining the effects of competition on a small firm's pricing policies: the location of the competitors and the nature of the competing goods. In most cases, unless a company can differentiate the quality and the quantity of extras it provides, it must match the prices charged by nearby competitors for identical items. For example, if a self-service station charges a nickel more for a gallon of gasoline than the self-service station across the street charges, customers will simply go across the street to buy. Without the advantage of a unique business image—quality of goods sold, value of service provided, convenient location, favorable credit terms—a small company must match local competitors' prices or lose sales. Before matching any competitor's price change, however, entrepreneurs should consider their rivals' strategies. The competition may be establishing its prices using a unique set of criteria and a totally different strategy.

The nature of competitors' goods also influences a small company's pricing policies. Entrepreneurs must recognize those products that are direct substitutes for those they sell and strive to keep prices in line with them. For example, the local sandwich shop should consider the hamburger restaurant, the taco shop, and the roast beef shop as competitors because they all serve fast foods. Although none of them offer the identical menu of the sandwich shop, they are all competing for the same quick-meal dollar.

Whenever possible, entrepreneurs should avoid head-to-head price competition with other firms that can more easily offer lower prices because of their lower cost structures. Most locally owned drugstores cannot compete with the prices of large national drug chains. However, many local drugstores operate successfully by using nonprice competition by offering personal service, free delivery, credit sales, and other extras that the chains have eliminated. Nonprice competition can be an effective strategy for a small business in the face of larger, more powerful enterprises, because there are many dangers in experimenting with prices. For instance, price shifts cause fluctuations in sales volume that the small firm may not be able to tolerate. In addition, frequent price changes may damage the company's image and its customer relations.

One of the deadliest games a small business can get into with competitors is a price war. Price wars eradicate profit margins, force companies out of business, and scar an entire industry for years. The retail book industry has been marred by price wars. Although dominated by large retailers such as online giant Amazon.com and chain stores such as Barnes & Noble, the industry is home to more than 23,000 small, independent booksellers whose annual sales average just $1.5 million. In an attempt to gain market share, Walmart, with annual sales of more than $400 billion, launched a price war, offering new-release books that normally sell between $28 and $35 for just $8.99, a price that Amazon.com quickly matched. Because publishers sell the books to retailers for $14 to $17.50, the price war eliminated profit margins on books for both giant retailers. The battle between the retail leviathans also had a devastating effect on the entire industry, particularly locally owned, independent booksellers, some of whom were forced to close because they could not one compete with prices that were below their costs![20]

Price wars usually begin when one competitor believes that it can achieve a higher volume through lower price or that it can exert enough pressure on competitors' profits to drive them out of business. In most cases, entrepreneurs overestimate the power of price cuts to increase sales sufficiently to improve net profitability.

ENTREPRENEURIAL
Profile
McDonald's

McDonald's infamous "Campaign 55," in which it planned to lower the price of a different sandwich to 55 cents each month, launched another volley in an ongoing fast-food price war that no company seemed to be winning. The 55-cent price was a throwback to the prices in 1955, the year McDonald's was founded. The company kicked off the campaign by selling Big Macs (which cost around 40 cents to make) for 55 cents and hoped to increase store traffic and boost sales on other menu items enough to offset the lower margin on the sandwich. Unfortunately, the increased traffic never materialized, and same-store sales fell 6 percent from the year before. In less than 2 months, amid complaints from its franchisees, McDonald's abandoned the promotion.[21]

In a price war, a company may cut its prices so severely that it is impossible to achieve the volume necessary to offset the lower profit margins. If a company that has a 25 percent gross profit margin cuts prices by 10 percent, it would have to *triple* its sales volume just to break even. Even when price cuts work, their effects are often temporary. Customers lured by the lowest price usually have almost no loyalty to a business. The lesson: The best way to survive a price war is to stay out of it by emphasizing the unique features, benefits, and value your company offers its customers!

Focus on Value

Ultimately, the "right" price for a product or service depends on one factor: the value that it provides customers. There are two aspects of value, however. Entrepreneurs may recognize the *objective* value of their products and services, which is the price customers would be willing to pay if they understood perfectly the benefits that a product or service delivers for them. Unfortunately, few, if any, customers can see a product or a service's true objective value; instead, they see only its *perceived* value, which determines the price they are willing to pay for it. "Customers see value in more than product and price," says Jim Barnes, a business owner, consultant, and author. "They spend where they believe they get the best total value, and that does not mean always opting for the lowest price." Small companies that find creative ways to add value to their products and services—for instance, by making it easy for customers to buy from them (Barnes calls these "I'll-look-after-that-for-you" moments), impressing them with stellar service, and providing unexpected extras (such as an electronics retailer consolidating a customer's various remote controls into one when installing a new television)—do not have to resort to price cuts as often as companies that fail to do these things. By offering extra value, these companies encourage their customers to look beyond mere price to determine value. "We must offer the customer something that allows us to earn the prices we charge," concludes Barnes. "We must go above and beyond, creating new and different forms of value that will compensate for the pressure on customers to obtain more for less."[22]

Businesses that underprice their products and services or that run constant sales and discount price promotions may be short-circuiting the value proposition they are trying to communicate to their customers. Customers may respond to price cuts, but companies that rely on them to boost sales risk undermining the perceived value of their products and services. In addition, once customers grow accustomed to buying products and services during special promotions, the habit can be difficult to break. They simply wait for the next sale. Many retailers now face this problem as customers accustomed to buying items on sale postpone buying them until the next special sale arrives. The result has been fluctuating sales and a diminished value of those stores' brands.

In some economic conditions, companies have little choice but to offer lower-priced products. Techniques that companies can use to increase customers' perception of value, and essentially lower their prices with less risk of diminishing their brands, include offering coupons and rebates that are not as closely connected to the product as direct price cuts. Limited-time discounts used

© Mike Baldwin / Cornered

"I'm getting the fire-breathing dragon with wings. He wanted $200, but I talked him down to fifty bucks."

sparingly also increase sales without causing long-term damage to a brand. Another strategy that some companies have used successfully is to launch a **fighter brand**, a less expensive, no-frills version of a company's flagship product that is designed to confront lower-priced competitors head-on, satisfy the appetites of value-conscious customers, and preserve the image of the company's premium product. Rather than lower the price of its Pentium computer chip, Intel introduced the lower-cost Celeron chip to stave off rival AMD's line of value-priced chips.

The good news is that companies can influence customers' perceptions of value through marketing and other efforts. "The price you get for a product is a function of what it's truly worth—and how good a job you do communicating that value to the end user," says one entrepreneur.[23] Indeed, setting a product's or a service's price is another way a company can communicate value to its customers. For most shoppers, three reference points define a fair price: the price they have paid for the product or service in the past, the prices competitors charge for the same or similar product or service, and the costs a company incurs to provide the product or service. The price that customers have paid in the past for an item serves as a baseline reference point, but people often forget that inflation causes a company's costs to rise from year to year. Therefore, it is important for business owners to remind customers periodically that they must raise prices to offset the increased cost of doing business. "Over time, costs always go up," says Norm Brodsky, owner of a successful document storage company. "I'd rather raise prices a little every year or with every new contract than be forced to demand a big increase down the road."[24]

As we have seen already, companies often find it necessary to match competitors' prices on the same or similar items unless they can establish a distinctive image in customers' minds. One of the most successful strategies for companies facing direct competition is to differentiate their products or services by adding value for customers and then charging for it. For instance, a company might offer faster delivery, a longer product warranty, extra service, or something else that adds value to an item for its customers and allows the business to charge a higher price.

Perhaps the least understood of the three reference points is a company's cost structure. Customers often underestimate the costs businesses incur to provide products and services, whether it is a simple cotton T-shirt on a shelf in a beachfront shop or a life-saving drug that may have cost hundreds of millions of dollars and many years to develop. They forget that business owners must make or buy the products they sell, market them, pay their employees, and cover a host of other operating expenses, ranging from health care to legal fees.

LESSONS FROM THE STREET-SMART → entrepreneur

Enhancing Your Company's Pricing Power

As the economy slowed in a recent recession, businesses of all sizes and across a myriad of industries began offering price discounts to encourage customers to buy their goods and services. Fast-casual restaurants such as Applebee's and Ruby Tuesday offered a selection of dinner specials priced at two for $20. Quick-service restaurants expanded their value menus and introduced bundled items at rock-bottom prices. Subway's $5 footlong sandwiches were a hit, appealing to a broad base of customers.

Many of these companies then realized that they had created a challenging problem: How do we raise prices when the economy improves? Once customers become accustomed to value deals, how does a business change customers' perceptions of the relationship between price and value? The following pricing-power matrix can help:

The horizontal axis of the matrix measures the extent to which customers view a product or service as a necessity or as a discretionary purchase. The vertical axis describes a product's or service's level of uniqueness, which ranges from an undifferentiated commodity to a completely unique item. Where on the matrix does your company's product or service fall?

The best quadrant for a company to operate in is the upper-left corner, a unique necessity, a situation in which customers have a high need for a product or service that is unique and highly differentiated from competing products

and services. An individual's favorite brand of shampoo or the blades that fit a person's razor are good examples. These products have the greatest degree of pricing power, even during economic downturns.

The lower-right quadrant is discretionary commodities. With a discretionary commodity, a company's products or services are very similar to those of competitors and customers do not have to have them or can postpone their purchases of them, at least for a while. The airline industry finds itself in this unenviable position because many customers can choose alternative methods of travel, postpone their trips, or choose a less expensive flight on a competing airline.

The remaining two quadrants offer in-between positions of pricing power. In the lower-left corner are products and services that, although necessities, offer little opportunity for differentiation. Light bulbs and lumber are good examples, and companies that produce them often end up matching competitors' prices because customers see them as the same.

The upper-right quadrant contains products and services that are unique but highly discretionary; customers simply do not have to have them. Companies that operate in this sector do not have maximum pricing power. Luxury cars such as Rolls-Royce are good examples. During a recent economic downturn, for instance, Rolls-Royce introduced the $245,000 Ghost, a smaller, more "affordable" car (at least compared to the rest of its line, including the $380,000 Phantom) that is, in the Rolls-Royce tradition, built by hand. It offers amenities such as night-vision

The Pricing-Power Matrix

cameras, inch-thick lamb's wool carpet, and a cashmere head liner. Apple, which is also located in this quadrant, recently cut the price of its entry-level iPhone in half and introduced a next-generation model to maintain sales in the face of competing smartphones and more frugal customers.

Companies have the ability to move from one quadrant to a more desirable one by executing the proper strategy. The following questions can help entrepreneurs to determine their strategic options to increase their pricing power:

1. Can you offer a product or service that your customers consider a necessity? Doing so enhances a small company's pricing power.

2. Can you offer an "affordable luxury"? Even in austere economic conditions, customers often are willing to splurge on small luxuries such as gourmet chocolates, premium ice cream, and luxury muffins. These affordable luxuries give companies a great deal of pricing power.

3. What steps can you take to differentiate your company's products or services from those of competitors? The greater the degree of differentiation of a company's products and services, the less price sensitive customers tend to be and the more pricing power a company has.

4. Can you offer customers something that will save them money? If so, your company has the ability to increase its pricing power.

5. Can you reduce the role of price in customers' buying decisions by, for example, offering superior customer service? Most small companies have the ability to de-emphasize the role that price plays in customers' buying decisions.

Sources: Based on Geoff Colvin, "Yes, You Can Raise Prices," *Fortune*, March 2, 2009, p. 20; Sara Wilson, "When to Lower Your Price Point," *Entrepreneur*, April 2009, pp. 28–29; Hannah Elliott, "Stealth Wealth," *Forbes*, January 18, 2010, p. 62; Dan Neil, "Rolls Royce Builds a Real Car," *Wall Street Journal*, April 10–11, 2010, p. W6; Yukari Iwatani Kane, "To Sustain iPhone, Apple Halves Price," *Wall Street Journal*, June 9, 2009, p. B1.

Pricing Strategies and Tactics

3. Describe effective pricing strategies for both new and existing products and services.

The number of variations in pricing strategies and tactics is limitless. The wide variety of options is exactly what allows entrepreneurs to be so creative with their pricing. This section will examine some of the more commonly used tactics under a variety of conditions. Pricing always plays a critical role in a firm's overall strategy; pricing policies must be compatible with a company's total marketing plan.

New Product Pricing: Penetration, Skimming, or Sliding

Most entrepreneurs approach setting the price of a new product with a great deal of apprehension because they have no precedent on which to base their decisions. If a new product's price is too high, it is in danger of failing because of low sales volume. However, if its price is too low, the product's sales revenue might not cover costs. Establishing a price that is too low is far more dangerous. Not only does the company forego revenues and profits, but it also limits the product's perceived value in the eyes of its target customers.

When pricing any new product, an entrepreneur must satisfy three objectives:

1. ***Get the product accepted.*** No matter how unique a product is, its price must be acceptable to a company's potential customers. The price a company can charge depends, in part, on the type of product it introduces:
   - **Revolutionary products** are so new that they transform an industry. Companies that introduce these innovative products usually have the ability to charge prices that are close to the price ceiling, although they may have to educate customers about the product's benefits.
   - **Evolutionary products** involve making enhancements and improvements to products that are already on the market. Companies that introduce these products do not have the ability to charge premium prices unless they can use the enhancements they have made to differentiate their products from those of competitors. Establishing a price that is too low for an evolutionary product can lead to a price war.
   - **Me-too products** are products that companies introduce just to keep up with competitors. Because they offer customers nothing new or unique, me-too products offer companies the least amount of pricing flexibility. Achieving success with these products means focusing on cost control and targeting the right market segments.

2. ***Maintain market share as competition grows.*** If a new product is successful, competitors will enter the market, and a small company must work to expand or at least maintain its market share. Continuously reappraising a product's price in conjunction with special advertising and promotion techniques helps the company maintain market share.

3. *Earn a profit.* A small company must establish a price for the new product that is higher than its cost. Entrepreneurs should not introduce a new product at a price below cost because it is much easier to lower the price than to increase it once the product is on the market. Pricing their products too low is a common and often fatal mistake for new businesses; entrepreneurs are tempted to underprice their products and services when they enter a new market to ensure its acceptance.

Entrepreneurs have three basic strategies to choose from in establishing a new product's price: penetration, skimming, and life cycle pricing.

PENETRATION. When a company introduces a new product into a market in which customers are price sensitive, a **penetration pricing strategy** enables the business to build market share quickly and establish itself as the market leader. In other words, it sets the price just above total unit cost to develop a wedge in the market and quickly achieve a high volume of sales. The resulting low profit margins may discourage other competitors from entering the market with similar products.

A penetration pricing strategy is ideal when introducing relatively low-priced goods into a market in which no elite segment and little opportunity for differentiation exists. This strategy works best when customers' switching costs (the cost of switching to a lower-priced competitor's product) is high (e.g., video game consoles). Penetration pricing also works when a company's competitors are locked into high cost structures that result from the channels of distribution they use, labor agreements, or other factors. For instance, since its inception Southwest Airlines has relied on its lower cost structure to compete with older, "legacy" carriers by emphasizing low prices.

Entrepreneurs must recognize that penetration pricing is a long-range strategy; until a company achieves customer acceptance for the product, profits are likely to be small. When a young college student launched a carpet cleaning business to help pay for his education, he decided to be the low-cost provider in his area. Although he landed plenty of work for his part-time business, he found that his company generated very little profit after deducting the expenses of doing business. Realizing that his customers would be willing to pay more for quality work, he raised his prices and began earning a reasonable profit.[25]

A danger of a penetration pricing strategy is that it attracts customers who know no brand loyalty. Companies that garner customers by offering low introductory prices must wonder what will become of their customer bases if they increase their prices or if a competitor undercuts their prices. If a penetration pricing strategy succeeds and the product achieves mass-market penetration, sales volume increases, economies of scale result in lower unit cost, and the company earns attractive profits. The objective of the penetration strategy is to achieve quick access to the market to generate high sales volume as soon as possible.

SKIMMING. A **skimming pricing strategy** often is used when a company introduces a unique product into a market with little or no competition. Sometimes a company uses this tactic when introducing a product into a competitive market that contains an elite group that is willing and able to pay a premium price. A company sets a higher-than-normal price in an effort to quickly recover the initial developmental and promotional costs of the product. The idea is to set a price well above the product's total unit cost and to promote the product heavily to appeal to the segment of the market that is not sensitive to price. This pricing tactic often reinforces the unique, prestigious image of a company and projects a high quality picture of the product. A skimming strategy works well when a company has a mature product, loyal customers, a reputation for quality, and few competitors.

ENTREPRENEURIAL
Profile

Sylvie Chantecaille:
Chantecaille

When Sylvie Chantecaille, owner of the cosmetic company that bears her name, launched a new biodynamic lifting cream aimed at female baby boomers who are fighting the aging process, she priced the product at $295 for 1.7 ounces. "Can we really sell it for that much?" Chantecaille recalls thinking as she pondered her pricing decision. Her concern was unfounded; her company sells more than 20,000 units of the special cream each year through exclusive department stores, such as Neiman Marcus and Barneys New York, and small, upscale cosmetic shops. Encouraged by customers' response, Chantecaille recently introduced a 1.7 ounce Nano Gold Energizing Cream that sells for $420.[26]

LIFE CYCLE PRICING. A variation of the skimming pricing strategy is **life cycle pricing**. Using this technique, the firm introduces a product at a high price. Then, as the product moves through its life cycle, the company relies on technological advances, the learning curve effect, and economies of scale to lower its cost and to reduce the product's price faster than its competitors can. By beating other businesses in a price decline, the company discourages competitors and, over time, becomes a high-volume producer. High-definition television sets are a prime example of a product introduced at a high price that quickly cascaded downward as companies forged important technological advances and took advantage of economies of scale. When they were first introduced in 1998, high-definition TVs sold for $10,000; today, high-definition sets that have more features are priced at $500 or less. Life cycle pricing assumes that competition will emerge over time. Even if no competition arises, companies almost always lower the product's price to attract a larger segment of the market. In a sliding strategy, the initial high price contributes to the rapid return of start-up or development costs and generates a pool of funds to finance expansion and technological advances.

Table 1 offers useful tips for avoiding common pricing mistakes.

Pricing Techniques for Established Products and Services

Entrepreneurs have a variety of pricing techniques or tactics available to them to apply to established products and services.

ODD PRICING. Although studies of consumer reactions to prices are mixed and generally inconclusive, many entrepreneurs use the technique known as **odd pricing**. They set prices that end in odd numbers (frequently 5, 7, or 9), because they believe that an item selling for $12.69 appears to be much cheaper than an item selling for $13.00. Psychological techniques such as odd pricing are designed to appeal to certain customer interests, but research on their effectiveness is mixed. Some studies show no benefits from using odd pricing, but others have concluded that the technique can produce significant increases in sales.

TABLE 1 Tips for Avoiding Pricing Mistakes

Tip #1. Be careful with cost-plus pricing. When companies base their prices on costs rather than on customers' perception of value, the result is almost always prices that are either too low or too high.

Tip #2. Recognize that "me-too" pricing gives a company no pricing power. A much better strategy is to differentiate your company's products or services by creating additional value for customers or by targeting market niches.

Tip #3. Realize that you cannot achieve the same profit margin across every product line your company sells. The profit margin for paper clips is likely to be quite different from the profit margin for printers.

Tip #4. Recognize that your customer base is made up of different customer segments and that some of them are more sensitive to price than others. Even if a company sells a single product or service, its value proposition differs among its different customer segments. That means that by adding extra value to its offerings aimed at customers who are willing to pay for it, a company can charge higher prices.

Tip #5. Do not put off raising prices out of fear of a customer backlash. If your costs of providing a product or service go up and you never raise prices, your profit margins shrink until you can no longer stay in business. Perpetually absorbing cost increases by holding prices the same is the pricing equivalent of sticking your head in the sand. The outcome is certain: business failure.

Tip #6. Do not compensate sales representatives solely on sales volume. Doing so encourages them to sell at any price, particularly low prices that destroy the company's profitability. Create profit-based incentives for your sales force.

Tip #7. Avoid launching a price war. As you learned in this chapter, no one "wins" a price war, and one can devastate an industry's profits for years.

Tip #8. Realize that although discounts have their place in a company's pricing strategy, they can be as addictive as drugs. "Companies that get hooked on discounts do little more than drive down their value proposition, sometimes past the point of no return," says one pricing consultant. If you decide to use discounts, use them sparingly, briefly, and creatively.

Tip #9. Recognize that some customers are more valuable to your business than others. Customers who always demand the lowest prices and the highest level of service often are a company's least profitable customers. Do not waste a disproportionate amount of time and energy catering to them; instead, identify your company's most profitable customers, focus on serving them well, and attract more customers like them.

Tip #10. Remember that price is just one variable in the sales equation. Costs, customers' perception of value, and image are important factors as well. Use them!

Sources: Based on "Eradicate Pricing Errors," *Sales & Marketing Management*, August 5, 2009, p. 1; Steve McKee, "How to Discount (If You Insist)," *BusinessWeek*, August 14, 2009, *www.businessweek.com/smallbiz/content/aug2009/sb20090814_425078.htm*.

PRICE LINING. **Price lining** is a technique that greatly simplifies the pricing function. Under this system, the manager stocks merchandise in several different price ranges or price lines. Each category of merchandise contains items that are similar in appearance, quality, cost, performance, or other features. Many lined products appear in sets of three—good, better, and best—at prices designed to satisfy different market segment needs and incomes. Apple revised pricing for its industry-leading iTunes music downloads, moving from a flat 99 cents per song to a lined pricing strategy, with songs available for 69 cents, 99 cents, or $1.29. Price lining can boost a store's sales because it makes goods available to a wide range of shoppers, simplifies the purchase decision for customers, and allows them to keep their purchases within their budgets.

DYNAMIC PRICING. For many businesses, the pricing decision has become more challenging because the Web gives customers access to incredible amounts of information about the prices of items ranging from cars to computers. Increasingly, customers are using the Web to find the lowest prices available. To maintain their profitability, companies have responded with **dynamic (or customized) pricing**, in which they set different prices on the same products and services for different customers using the information they have collected about their customers. Rather than sell their products at fixed prices, companies using dynamic pricing rely on fluid prices that may change based on supply and demand and on which customer is buying or when a customer makes a purchase. For instance, a first-time customer making a purchase at an online store may pay a higher price for an item than a regular customer who shops there frequently pays for that same item.

Dynamic pricing is not a new concept. The standard practice in ancient bazaars involved merchants and customers haggling until they came to a mutually agreeable price, which meant that different customers paid different prices for the same goods. Although the modern version of dynamic pricing often involves sophisticated market research or the Internet, the goal is the same: to charge the right customer the right price at the right time. For example, travelers can use Priceline and similar Web sites to purchase last minute airline tickets at significant discounts (e.g., a round-trip ticket from New York to Los Angeles for just $250 rather than for the full-fare price of $750). Travelers benefit from lower prices, and the airlines are able to generate revenue from seats that otherwise would have gone unsold.

LEADER PRICING. **Leader pricing** is a technique in which the small retailer marks down the customary price (i.e., the price consumers are accustomed to paying) of a popular item in an attempt to attract more customers. The company earns a much smaller profit on each unit because the markup is lower, but purchases of other merchandise by customers seeking the leader item often boost sales and profits. In other words, the incidental purchases that consumers make when shopping for the leader item boosts sales revenue enough to offset a lower profit margin on the leader. Grocery stores often use leader pricing. For instance, during the holiday season, stores often use turkeys as a price leader, knowing that they will earn higher margins on the other items shoppers purchase with their turkeys.

GEOGRAPHIC PRICING. Small businesses whose pricing decisions are greatly affected by the costs of shipping merchandise to customers across a wide range of geographic regions frequently employ one of the **geographic pricing** techniques. For these companies, shipping costs constitute a substantial portion of the cost of doing business and often cut deeply into already narrow profit margins. One type of geographic pricing is **zone pricing**, in which a company sells its merchandise at different prices to customers located in different territories. For example, a manufacturer might sell at one price to customers east of the Mississippi and at another to those west of the Mississippi. The U.S. Postal Service's parcel post charges are a good example of zone pricing. A small business must be able to show a legitimate basis (e.g., difference in selling or transportation costs) for the price discrimination or risk violating Section 2 of the Clayton Act.

Another variation of geographic pricing is the **uniform delivered pricing**, a technique in which a company charges all of its customers the same price regardless of their location, even though the cost of selling or transporting merchandise varies. The company calculates freight charges for each region in which it sells and combines them into a uniform fee. The result is that local customers subsidize the firm's charge for shipping merchandise to distant customers.

A final variation of geographic pricing is **F.O.B. factory**, in which the small company sells its merchandise to customers on the condition that they pay all shipping costs. Using this technique, a company can set a uniform price for its product and let each customer cover the freight cost.

DISCOUNTS. Many small businesses use **discounts**, or **markdowns**, reductions from normal list prices, to move stale, outdated, damaged, or slow-moving merchandise. A seasonal discount is a price reduction designed to encourage shoppers to purchase merchandise before an upcoming season. For instance, many retail clothiers offer special sales on winter coats in late summer. Some companies grant discounts to special groups of customers, such as senior citizens or college students, to establish a faithful clientele and to generate repeat business. One study suggests that for items other than luxury goods, placing discount signs close to merchandise displays and promoting dollar discounts rather than percentage discounts increases the probability of making a sale.[27]

As tempting as discounts are to businesses when sales are slow, they also carry risks. Because price is an important signal of quality and image to customers, businesses that turn to discounts too often create the impression that they may be lowering their quality standards, thereby diluting the value of their brand and image in the marketplace. "For the sake of a short-term increase in sales, you can wreck the long-term value of your brand," says Rafi Mohammed, author of *The Art of Pricing*.[28] Many restaurants, from quick-service chains to fast-casual outlets, relied heavily on price discounts in an attempt to attract customers during a recent recession. For many, however, the increased traffic that the discounts generated failed to offset the impact of price cuts, resulting in the same lower total revenues they were trying to avoid. In addition, when the economy improved, many restaurants had difficulty weaning customers from their discount price expectations. "They've trained customers to eat $5 footlong sandwiches," says one industry analyst about a popular chain's discounts.[29] As the economy improved, restaurants reduced their use of discount coupons and introduced new, higher-priced menu items.[30]

Recent research suggests that using a **steadily decreasing discount (SDD)**, a limited duration discount that declines over time, is superior to a standard (hi-lo) discount, a common tactic in which a company offers frequent discounts off of its standard prices. When one company used a hi-lo discount of 20 percent for 3 days before returning the items to full price, sales increased by 75 percent. For the same items, a steadily decreasing discount of 30 percent the first day, 20 percent the second day, and 10 percent the third day (which yielded an average discount of 20 percent), produced an increase in sales of 200 percent. The researchers conclude that the SDD is more effective because it creates a sense of urgency, especially among wary or indecisive customers.[31]

Multiple unit pricing is a promotional technique that offers customers discounts if they purchase in quantity. Many products, especially those with a relatively low unit value, are sold using multiple pricing. For example, instead of selling an item for 50 cents, a small company might offer five for $2.

BUNDLING. Many small businesses have discovered the marketing benefits of **bundling**, grouping together several products or services, or both, into a package that offers customers extra value at a special price. Rather than cut into their already thin profit margins with price discounts during a recent recession, some restaurants used a bundling strategy, offering customers value-priced groupings of items. Dairy Queen (DQ) introduced its Sweet Deals menu, which offers customers a choice of nine items—two for $3, three for $4, and four for $5. Within just a few months, sales had increased, and the Sweet Deals menu accounted for 7 percent of the company's sales. More important, DQ's BrandIndex score, a rating that tracks customers' perceptions of a company's value, had increased by 1.7 percentage points and was among the industry's highest.[32]

Optional-product pricing involves selling the base product for one price but selling the options or accessories at a much higher percentage markup. Automobiles are often sold at a base price with each optional price separately. In many cases, the car is sold with some of the options bundled together.

ENTREPRENEURIAL
Profile

*Don and Joseph
Saladino: Drive 495*

Drive 495, an upscale fitness and golf center in New York's SoHo District started by brothers Don and Joseph Saladino, offers three simulation bays where urban golfers can practice their swings on 31 famous courses from around the world, including Pebble Beach and St. Andrews. Drive 495 uses optional-product pricing; standard 1-year memberships start at $5,000, an annual membership with unlimited golf and fitness lessons costs $25,000, and a lifetime membership with unlimited lessons for 1 year is $100,000.[33]

Captive-product pricing is the granddaddy of all pricing tactics, in which the basic product is useless without the appropriate accessories. King Gillette, the founder of the company that manufactures Gillette razors, taught the business world that the *real* money is not in the razor (the product) itself, but in the blades (the accessory). Today, we see the same pricing strategy used by Nintendo and other electronic game system manufacturers that have a very small profit margin on the product but substantially higher margins on the game cartridges. When Nintendo launched its popular Wii game system, the company's strategy was to sell a simpler game system with games that players could enjoy without having to invest dozens of hours to learn them. This strategy enabled Nintendo to introduce its game system at a price of just $249, well below the $500 price tag on Sony's PlayStation 3 and Microsoft's $400 Xbox 360. Nintendo's real money-maker, however, is the games that it sells to Wii owners, which are priced at $50 each (still below the $60 price tag on most PlayStation games). Nintendo's pricing strategy worked, and sales of Wii stations and games outstripped those of Sony's and Microsoft's products.[34]

By-product pricing is a technique in which the revenues from the sale of by-products allow a firm to be more competitive in its pricing of the main product. For years, owners of sawmills considered bark chips to be a nuisance. Today they package them and sell them as ground cover to homeowners, gardeners, and landscapers. Zoos across the globe offer one of the most creative examples of byproduct pricing, packaging once-worthless exotic animal droppings and marketing it as fertilizer under the clever name "Zoo Doo."

SUGGESTED RETAIL PRICES. Many manufacturers print suggested retail prices on their products or include them on invoices or in wholesale catalogs. Small business owners frequently follow these suggested retail prices because doing so eliminates the need to make a pricing decision. Nonetheless, following prices established by a distant manufacturer may create problems for the small firm. For example, a haberdasher may try to create a high-quality, exclusive image through a prestige pricing policy, but manufacturers may suggest discount outlet prices that are incompatible with the small firm's image. Another danger of accepting the manufacturer's suggested price is that it does not take into consideration a small company's cost structure or competitive situation. A recent controversial U.S. Supreme Court decision overturned a nearly 100-year-old ruling and allows manufacturers to set and enforce minimum prices that retailers must charge for the manufacturer's products as long as doing so does not reduce competition. However, more than 30 states are considering passing new antitrust laws that explicitly ban all minimum price agreements in an attempt to preempt the court's decision.[35]

FOLLOW-THE-LEADER PRICING. Some businesses make no effort to be price leaders in their immediate geographic areas and simply follow the prices that their competitors establish. Maintaining a follow-the-leader pricing policy may not be healthy for a small business because it robs the company of the opportunity to create a distinctive image in its customers' eyes.

A small company's pricing strategy must be compatible with its marketing objectives, its marketing mix, and its cost structure. In addition, the pricing strategy must be consistent with the competitive realities of the marketplace and the shifting forces of supply and demand. The forces that shape the pricing decision can change rapidly and, therefore, a company's pricing strategy is never completely fixed. Pricing decisions must take into account a company's cost, the special value the product or service creates for buyers, and the pricing tactics of competitors.

The underlying forces that dictate how a business prices its goods or services vary greatly among industries. The next three sections will investigate pricing techniques used in retailing, manufacturing, and service firms.

IN THE ENTREPRENEURIAL

SPOTLIGHT When the Price Is *Not* Right

When the economy slowed, Jason Robbins, CEO of ePromos Promotional Products, a New York City–based company that sells a variety of promotional products, corporate gifts, and trade show giveaways, resisted using discounts to sustain the 10-year-old company's sales growth. "We always wanted to be the service leader," explains Robbins.

"Our fear was that once you get people hooked on cheap prices, they wouldn't pay full price again." However, after reaching $25 million in annual sales, the company's revenue began declining rapidly. "Everything just froze," says Robbins. He and his team of employees began considering price cuts to kick-start sales. The principal question was,

"How can we use discounts judiciously to rejuvenate sales without sending a signal to customers that our company is just another low-price competitor?"

Robbins eventually decided to offer a limited-time $50 discount to first-time buyers and to mark down prices on 3,000 of the 13,000 items that ePromos sells. To minimize the impact on the company's 25 percent gross profit margin, however, Robbins reduced the prices only on those items on which the company received rebates from manufacturers for meeting sales goals. Robbins also understood the power of offering free shipping for increasing sales at online companies and offered customers free shipping. Even though sales were down for the year, the pricing moves halted the free-fall in the company's revenue, and ePromos weathered the storm far better than many of its competitors. "We believe we maintained our position as a high-service competitor and didn't damage our reputation," Robbins says.

By refusing to engage in a price war with competitors and offering limited discounts only on certain items, Robbins was able to generate sales without portraying his company as a discount seller. When his company's sales began to decline due to a faltering economy, Robbins knew that he had to re-evaluate ePromos' pricing strategy. What are the signs that mean it is time to consider changing your company's pricing strategy?

1. *Unit sales growth slows or declines.* When sales volume stalls or declines, the market may be saturated, the economy may be struggling, competitors could be stealing away your customers, or your prices are out of line with customers' perceived value of your products and services.

2. *Discounts fail to increase sales.* The reason that companies offer price discounts is to increase sales, ideally by a greater percentage than the discount. If a discount fails to produce results, continuing to offer it is a recipe for disaster. "Price cutting usually is not the best strategy for a small business—especially a business that serves a target market that cares more about value and service than paying the lowest possible price," explains one business writer. "Not only does discounting generally fail to help you acquire

new customers, but it may also result in your making less money from the customers you already have."

3. *Competitors introduce new products or services.* Innovations by competitors can change—sometimes dramatically—the price–value equation in the market. "If the competition has leapfrogged you on value, you may not be able to maintain your current pricing strategy," explains one pricing expert.

4. *Low-cost competitors enter the market.* When a market is experiencing high growth, it often attracts new entrants. If those new competitors have lower cost structures and utilize penetration pricing strategies, their entry can muddle the entire industry's pricing structure. When faced with this situation, some companies engage in a price war, but others take different approaches, such as introducing fighter brands or moving into less-price-sensitive niche markets.

5. *Gross profit margin declines.* "Creating a Solid Financial Plan," that a company's gross profit margin equals (Sales − Cost of goods sold) ÷ Sales. The only ways to repair a gross profit margin that is too low is to either reduce the company's cost of goods sold or to increase its prices.

1. Explain the dangers of using discounting as a pricing strategy for increasing sales.

2. Use the Web to research price wars. What conditions usually prompt price wars? What impact do price wars have on an industry and the companies in it? What are the typical outcomes in a price war?

3. Many small companies compete successfully without focusing on providing the lowest prices, even in industries in which customers view product or service prices as important purchasing criteria. What tactics do these companies use to compete successfully without relying on the lowest prices?

Sources: Based on Ryan McCarthy, "Pricing: How Low Can You Really Go?" *Inc.*, March 2009, pp. 91–92; Vincent Ryan, "The Price Is Wrong," *CFO*, December 2009, p. 52; Rosalind Resnick, "Hold the Line on Price," *Washington Post*, March 9, 2009, *www.washingtonpost.com/wp-dyn/content/article/2009/03/11/AR2009031103668.html*; "About Us." ePromos. *www.epromos.com/AboutePromos/AboutUs.jsp.*

Pricing Techniques for Retailers

4. Explain the pricing techniques used by retailers.

Because retail customers have become more price conscious and the Internet has made prices more transparent, retailers have changed their pricing strategies to emphasize value. This value–price relationship allows for a wide variety of highly creative pricing and marketing practices. Delivering high levels of recognized value in products and services is one key to retail customer loyalty. To justify paying a higher price than those charged by competitors, customers must perceive a company's products or services as giving them greater value.

Markup

The basic premise of a successful business operation is selling a good or service for more than it costs to produce it. The difference between the cost of a product or service and its selling price is called **markup** (or **markon**). Markup can be expressed in dollars or as a percentage of either cost or selling price:

$$\text{Dollar markup} = \text{Retail price} - \text{Cost of the merchandise}$$

$$\text{Percentage (of retail price) markup} = \frac{\text{Dollar markup}}{\text{Retail price}}$$

$$\text{Percentage (of cost) markup} = \frac{\text{Dollar markup}}{\text{Cost of unit}}$$

For example, if a man's shirt costs $15, and the manager plans to sell it for $25, the markup is as follows:

$$\text{Dollar markup} = \$25 - \$14 = \$11$$

$$\text{Percentage (of retail price) markup} = \frac{\$11}{\$25}$$

$$= 44\%$$

$$\text{Percentage (of cost) markup} = \frac{\$11}{\$14}$$

$$= 78.6\%$$

The cost of merchandise used in computing markup includes not only the wholesale price of the merchandise but also any incidental costs (e.g., selling or transportation charges) that the retailer incurs.

Once entrepreneurs have a financial plan in place, including sales estimates and anticipated expenses, they can compute their companies' initial markup. The **initial markup** is the *average* markup required on all merchandise to cover the cost of the items, all incidental expenses, and a reasonable profit.

$$\text{Initial markup} = \frac{\text{Operating expenses} + \text{Reductions} + \text{Profits}}{\text{Net sales} + \text{Reductions}}$$

Operating expenses are the cost of doing business, such as rent, utilities, and depreciation; reductions include markdowns, special sales, employee discounts, and the cost of stockouts. For example, if a small retailer forecasts sales of $980,000, operating expenses of $540,000, and $24,000 in reductions, and she expects a profit of $58,000, the initial markup percentage is:

$$\text{Initial markup percentage} = \frac{\$540,000 + \$24,000 + \$58,000}{\$980,000 + \$24,000}$$

$$= 62\%$$

Any item in the store that carries a markup of at least 62 percent covers costs and meets the owner's profit objective. Any item that carries a markup less than 62 percent reduces the company's net income.

Once an entrepreneur determines the initial markup percentage, he or she can compute the appropriate retail price to achieve that markup using the following formula:

$$\text{Retail price} = \frac{\text{Dollar cost}}{(1 - \text{Initial markup percentage})}$$

For instance, applying the markup 62 percent to an item that cost the retailer $17.50 gives the following retail price:

$$\text{Retail price} = \frac{\$17.50}{(1 - 62\%)} = \$45.99$$

The owner establishes a retail price of $45.99 for the item using a 62 percent markup.

Finally, a retailer must verify that the computed retail price is consistent with the company's overall image. Is the final price congruent with the company's strategy? Is it within an acceptable price range? How does it compare with the prices charged by competitors? Perhaps most important, are the customers willing and able to pay this price?

Pricing Techniques for Manufacturers

5. Explain the pricing techniques used by manufacturers.

For manufacturers, the pricing decision requires the support of accurate, timely accounting records. The most commonly used pricing technique for manufacturers is **cost-plus pricing**. Using this method, manufacturers establish a price composed of direct materials, direct labor, factory overhead, selling and administrative costs, plus the desired profit margin. Figure 2 illustrates the components of cost-plus pricing.

The primary advantage of the cost-plus pricing method is its simplicity. Given the proper cost accounting data, computing a product's final selling price is relatively easy. In addition, because this technique adds a profit onto the top of the firm's costs, a manufacturer is likely to achieve the desired profit margin. This strategy does not encourage manufacturers to use their resources efficiently, however. Because manufacturers' cost structures vary so greatly, cost-plus pricing also fails to consider the competition adequately. Finally, cost-plus pricing fails to recognize the important relationships among price, value, and image. "The price that consumers are willing to pay has little to do with manufacturing costs," says pricing expert Rafi Mohammed. He says that a better pricing strategy is to capture "the value of a product, not simply mark up its costs."[36] Despite its drawbacks, the cost-plus method of establishing prices remains prominent in industries such as construction and printing.

Direct Costing and Pricing

One requisite for a successful pricing policy in manufacturing is a reliable cost accounting system that can generate timely reports to determine the costs of processing raw materials into finished goods. The traditional method of product costing is called **absorption costing** because all manufacturing and overhead costs are absorbed into the finished product's total cost. Absorption costing includes direct materials and direct labor, plus a portion of fixed and variable factory overhead costs, in each unit manufactured. Full-absorption financial statements are used in published annual reports and in tax reports and are very helpful in performing financial analysis. However, full absorption statements are of little help to a manufacturer when determining prices or the impact of price changes.

A more useful technique for managerial decision making is **variable** (or **direct**) **costing**, in which the cost of the products manufactured includes only those costs that vary directly with the quantity produced. In other words, variable costing encompasses direct materials, direct labor, and factory overhead costs that vary with the level of the company's output of finished goods. Factory overhead costs that are fixed (e.g., rent, depreciation, and insurance) are *not* included in the costs of finished items. Instead, they are considered to be expenses of the period.

A manufacturer's goal when establishing prices is to discover the cost combination of selling price and sales volume that exceeds the variable costs of producing a product and contributes enough to cover fixed costs and earn a profit. Full-absorption costing clouds the true relationships among price, volume, and costs by including fixed expenses when calculating unit cost. Direct costing, however, yields a constant unit cost of the product no matter what the volume of production is. The result is a clearer picture of the price–volume–costs relationship.

FIGURE 2
Components of Cost-Plus Pricing

TABLE 2 Full-Absorption Versus Direct-Cost Income Statement

Full-Absorption Income Statement

Sales Revenue		$ 790,000
Cost of Goods Sold		
Materials	250,500	
Direct Labor	190,200	
Factory Overhead	120,200	560,900
Gross Profit		$ 229,100
Operating Expenses		
General & Administrative	66,100	
Selling	112,000	
Other	11,000	
Total Operating Expenses		189,100
Net Income (before taxes)		$ 40,000

Direct-Cost Income Statement

Sales Revenue (100%)		$ 790,000
Variable Costs		
Materials	250,500	
Direct Labor	190,200	
Variable Factory Overhead	13,200	
Variable Selling Expenses	48,100	
Total Variable Costs (63.5%)		502,000
Contribution Margin (36.5%)		288,000
Fixed Costs		
Fixed Factory Overhead	107,000	
Fixed Selling Expenses	63,900	
General and Administrative	66,100	
Other Fixed Expenses	11,000	
Total Fixed Expenses (31.4%)		248,000
Net Income (before taxes)(5.1%)		$ 40,000

The starting point for establishing product prices is the direct-cost income statement. As Table 2 indicates, the direct-cost statement yields the same net income as does the full-absorption income statement. The only difference between the two statements is the format. The full-absorption statement allocates costs such as advertising, rent, and utilities according to the activity that caused them, but the direct-cost income statement separates expenses into fixed and variable costs. Fixed expenses remain constant regardless of the production level, but variable expenses fluctuate according to production volume.

When variable costs are subtracted from total revenues, the result is the manufacturer's **contribution margin**, the amount remaining that contributes to covering fixed expenses and earning a profit. Expressing this contribution margin as a percentage of total revenue yields the firm's contribution percentage. Computing the contribution percentage is a critical step in establishing prices through the direct-costing method. This manufacturer's contribution percentage is 36.5 percent, which is calculated as follows:

$$\text{Contribution percentage} = 1 - \frac{\text{Variable expenses}}{\text{Revenues}}$$

$$= 1 - \frac{\$502,000}{\$790,000} = 36.5\%$$

Computing a Break-Even Selling Price

A manufacturer's contribution percentage tells what portion of total revenue remains after covering variable costs to contribute toward meeting fixed expenses and earning a profit. This manufacturer's contribution percentage is 36.5 percent, which means that variable costs absorb 63.5 percent of total revenues. In other words, variable costs represent 63.5 percent $(1.00 - 0.365 = 0.635)$ of the product's selling price. Suppose that this manufacturer's variable costs include the following:

Material	$2.08/unit
Direct labor	$4.12/unit
Variable factory overhead	$0.78/unit
Total variable cost	$6.98/unit

The minimum price at which the manufacturer would sell the item is $6.98. Any price below that would not cover variable costs. To compute the break-even selling price for his product, an entrepreneur uses the following equation:

$$\text{Break-even selling price} = \frac{\text{Profit} + \left(\begin{array}{c}\text{Variable cost} \\ \text{per unit}\end{array} \times \begin{array}{c}\text{Quantity} \\ \text{produced}\end{array}\right) + \begin{array}{c}\text{Total} \\ \text{fixed cost}\end{array}}{\text{Quantity produced}}$$

To break even, the manufacturer assumes $0 profit. Suppose that its plans are to produce 50,000 units of the product and that fixed costs will be $110,000. The break-even selling price is as follows:

$$\text{Break-even selling price} = \frac{\$0 + (\$6.98/\text{unit} \times 50,000 \text{ units}) + \$110,000}{50,000 \text{ units}}$$

$$= \frac{\$459,000}{50,000 \text{ units}}$$

$$= \$9.18 \text{ per unit}$$

Thus, $2.20 ($9.18/unit − $6.98/unit) of the $9.18 break-even price goes toward meeting fixed production costs. But suppose the manufacturer wants to earn a $50,000 profit. Then the required selling price is calculated as follows:

$$\text{Selling price} = \frac{\$50,000 + (6.98/\text{unit} \times 50,000 \text{ units}) + \$110,000}{50,000 \text{ units}}$$

$$= \frac{\$509,000}{50,000 \text{ units}}$$

$$= \$10.18/\text{unit}$$

Now the manufacturer must decide whether customers will purchase 50,000 units at $10.18. If the manufacturer thinks they won't, managers must decide either to produce a different, more profitable product or lower the selling price by lowering either its cost or its profit target. Any price above $9.18 will generate some profit, although less than that desired. In the short run, the manufacturer could sell the product for less than $9.18 if competitive factors dictate, but *not* below $6.98 because a price below $6.98 would not cover the variable costs of production.

Because the manufacturer's capacity in the short run is fixed, pricing decisions should be aimed at using resources most efficiently. The fixed cost of operating the plant cannot be avoided, and the variable costs can be eliminated only if the firm ceases to offer the product. Therefore, the selling price must be at least equal to the variable costs (per unit) of making the product. Any price above that amount contributes to covering fixed costs and providing a reasonable profit.

Of course, over the long run the manufacturer cannot sell below total costs and continue to survive. A product's selling price must cover total product costs—both fixed and variable—and generate a reasonable profit.

▶ ENTREPRENEURSHIP IN ACTION ▶

Guitars and Pearls: A Lesson in Pricing

Founded in 1833, C. F. Martin & Company is the oldest guitar maker in the world. Now in its sixth generation of family ownership, the company's acoustic guitars have a reputation for being among the highest quality, best sounding instruments on the market, and many stars—past and current, ranging from the King of Rock and Roll, Elvis Presley; the Singing Cowboy, Gene Autry; to Sting and Steve Miller—play nothing but a Martin. The company makes 52,000 guitars each year. Although employees use modern equipment in the manufacturing process, much of the work performed in the 300 steps required to build a guitar at 60 different workstations is done by the hands of highly skilled and experienced workers. Workers hand tune each guitar to make sure that its sound is just right. Prices for the most popular Martin guitars range from $2,000 to $3,000, but the company makes highly specialized limited edition models such as the D-100 Deluxe made of Brazilian rosewood, which sells for $110,000.

When a faltering economy caused consumers to pull back their spending and Martin's sales to decline, CEO Chris Martin was hesitant to reduce the company's prices because he feared diluting the company's reputation as a maker of fine guitars. "We needed something so we wouldn't have to lay people off," he says. To devise a strategy for dealing with declining sales, Chris Martin looked back at the company's rich history and took note of how his great-grandfather managed to get Martin through the Great Depression: He introduced a lower-cost guitar made of mahogany without any inlay or frills and priced it at $20 to $30, a fraction of the price of the company's standard model that had beautiful wood, fancy inlays, and lots of features. The moderately priced models played an important role in the company's ability to survive the Depression and carried the company until the economy became stronger and Martin began producing its higher-end guitars once again.

In 2009, Martin introduced the Series 1 guitar, a solid wood guitar (no laminates) that, like its Depression-era predecessor, lacks inlays and extra features and sells for less than $1,000, which is considered a "sweet spot" in the industry. "For the money, they're very good instruments," says one long-time Martin retailer. "It was really smart of Martin to come out with [the Series 1] in the current economy. They are filling a niche quite well." Indeed, the company sold out of its entire first production run of 8,000 Series 1 guitars within 1 month. Production costs are considerably lower for the Series 1 because "we have fewer man-hours in each instrument," says Chris Martin. The strategy was successful because Martin could produce Series 1 guitars using the same basic production process and already had a network of distributors in place to sell them.

Although Jeremy Shepherd, founder of Pearl Paradise, an online retailer of pearls, is in a completely different industry, he faces many of the same challenges that Chris Martin did. As the economy slowed, Shepherd noticed that sales of high-end pearl jewelry began to decline. He had built his company by selling high-quality pearl necklaces and bracelets priced between $1,000 and $5,000. About 40 percent of the company's sales occurred during the last

Chris Martin is the sixth generation CEO of C. F. Martin & Company, a company that makes quality guitars, most of which are priced between $2,000 and $3,000. Martin is pictured holding his daughter, Claire Francis Martin, perhaps the seventh generation CEO of the company.

Source: Tim Shaffer/New York Times-Maps and Graphics

quarter of the year. As the crucial Christmas season drew near, Shepherd noticed that although traffic on the company's Web site had increased, the company's sales had declined. Customers were purchasing fewer high-end items, opting instead for pearl jewelry priced at less than $1,000. Shepherd and his employees began discussing their options for getting the company's sales back on track.

1. Visit the Web sites of C. F. Martin & Company (*www.martinguitar.com*) and Pearl Paradise (*www.pearlparadise.com*). Search online for more information on these companies. How are the two companies similar, particularly with regards to the

quality of the products they sell and the pricing strategies they use?

2. What course of action do you recommend that Shepherd take to improve sales at Pearl Paradise without damaging his company's reputation as a retailer of quality pearl jewelry and an expert in pearls? Explain.

Sources: Based on Timothy Appel, "Guitar Maker Revives No-Frills Act from the '30s," *Wall Street Journal*, July 6, 2009, pp. B1–B2; Ryan McCarthy, "Prices: How Low Can You Really Go?" *Inc.*, March 2009, pp. 91–92; "Famous Martin Owners," C. F. Martin & Company, *www.martinguitar.com/artists/famous.php*.

Pricing Techniques for Service Businesses

6. Explain the pricing techniques used by service firms.

Service businesses must establish their prices on the basis of the materials used to provide the service, the labor employed, an allowance for overhead, and a profit. As in a manufacturing operation, a service firm must have a reliable and accurate accounting system to track the total costs of providing the service. Most service firms base their prices on an hourly rate, usually the actual number of hours required to perform the service. For most firms, labor and materials constitute the largest portion of the cost of the service. To establish a reasonable and profitable price for service, the small business owner must know the cost of materials, direct labor, and overhead for each unit of service. Using these basic cost data and a desired profit margin, an owner of a small service firm can determine the appropriate price for the service.

Consider a simple example for pricing a common service—television repair. Ned's TV Repair Shop uses the direct-costing method to prepare an income statement for exercising managerial control (see Table 3). Ned estimates that he and his employees spend about 9,250 hours in the actual production of television repair service. The total cost per productive hour for Ned's TV Repair Shop is as follows:

$$\text{Total cost per hour} = \frac{\$104,000 + 68,000}{9,250 \text{ hours}} = \$18.59/\text{hour}$$

Now Ned must add in an amount for his desired profit. He expects a net operating profit margin of 18 percent on sales. To compute the final price, he uses the following equation:

$$\text{Price per hour} = \text{Total cost per productive hour} \div (1 - \text{net profit target as \% of sales})$$

$$= \$18.59 \div (1 - .18)$$

$$= \$22.68/\text{hour}$$

TABLE 3 Direct-Cost Income Statement, Ned's TV Repair Shop

Sales Revenue		$199,000
Variable Expenses		
Labor	52,000	
Materials	40,500	
Variable Factory Overhead	11,500	
Total Variable Expenses		104,000
Fixed Expenses		
Rent	2,500	
Salaries	38,500	
Fixed Overhead	27,000	
Total Fixed Expenses		68,000
Net Income		$ 27,000

A price of $22.68 per hour will cover Ned's costs and generate the desired profit. Smart service shop owners compute the cost per production hour at regular intervals throughout the year because they know that rising costs can eat into their profit margins very quickly. Rapidly rising labor costs and materials prices dictate that the service firm's price per hour be computed even more frequently. As in the case of the retailer and the manufacturer, Ned must evaluate the pricing policies of competitors and decide whether his price is consistent with the firm's image.

Of course, the price of $22.68 per hour assumes that all jobs require the same amount of materials. If this is not a valid assumption (and it probably is not), Ned must recalculate the price per hour without including the cost of materials.

$$\text{Cost per productive hour} = \frac{\$172,000 - \$40,500}{9,250 \text{ hours}}$$

$$= \$14.22/\text{hour}$$

Adding in the desired 18 percent net operating profit on sales yields:

$$\text{Price per hour} = \$14.22/\text{hour} \div (1-.18)$$

$$= \$17.34/\text{hour}$$

Under these conditions Ned would charge $17.34 per hour plus the actual cost of materials used and a markup on the cost of materials. For instance, a repair job that takes 4 hours to complete would have the following price:

Cost of service (4 hours × $17.34/hour)	$ 69.36
Cost of materials	$ 41.00
Markup on materials (60%)	$ 24.60
Total price	$134.96

Because services are intangible, their pricing offers more flexibility than do tangible products. One danger that entrepreneurs face is pricing their services too low because prospective customers' perceptions of a service are influenced heavily by its price. In other words, establishing a low price for a service actually may harm a service company's sales!

ENTREPRENEURIAL Profile

Reid Carr: Red Door Interactive

Reid Carr, founder of Red Door Interactive, a San Diego–based company that specializes in Web services, prices each project that his company takes on by estimating the number of hours it will take to complete, multiplying that number by an hourly rate, and then including some "wiggle room" for unforeseen cost overruns. If the flow of work slows, Carr allows his employees to work on pro bono projects to raise the visibility of his company and to show the quality of work his employees create. "Pro bono work is free advertising," explains Carr.[37]

The Impact of Credit on Pricing

7. Describe the impact of credit on pricing.

In today's business environment, linking a company's pricing strategy with its credit strategy has become essential because many customers expect to "pay with plastic" rather than with cash. Consumers crave convenience when they shop, and one of the most common conveniences they demand is the ability to purchase goods and services on credit. Small businesses have three options for selling to customers on credit: credit cards, installment credit, and trade credit.

Credit Cards

Nearly 181 million Americans have credit cards. The average credit card holder has 4.4 credit cards but uses only two of them regularly. Shoppers use credit cards for more than 20 billion transactions a year to purchase nearly $2 trillion worth of goods and services annually.[38] The message

Shoppers purchase nearly $2 trillion worth of goods and services using credit cards each year. Accepting credit and debit cards increases a small company's customer base and leads to higher sales.

Source: Deklofenak/Shutterstock

is clear: Customers expect to make purchases with credit cards, and small companies that fail to accept credit cards run the risk of losing sales to competitors who do. Research shows that customers who use credit cards make purchases that are 112 percent higher than if they had used cash.[39] Accepting credit cards broadens a small company's customer base and closes sales that it would lose if customers had to pay in cash.

Companies that accept credit cards incur additional expenses for offering this convenience, however. Businesses must pay to use the system—typically 1 to 6 percent of total credit card charges, which they, in turn, must factor into the prices of their products or services. They also pay a transaction fee of 5 to 50 cents per charge (the average fee is 10 cents) and must purchase or lease equipment to process transactions. Fees operate on a multistep process. On a $100 Visa or MasterCard purchase at a typical business, a processing bank buys the credit card slip from the retailer for $97.71. The processing bank collects a processing fee of 40 cents and sells the slip to the bank that issued the card for about $98.11. The remaining $1.89 discount is called the interchange fee, which is what the processing bank passes along to the issuing bank. The prices entrepreneurs charge must reflect the higher costs associated with credit card transactions.

DEBIT CARDS. Consumers in the United States carry more than 507 million debit cards that act as electronic checks, automatically deducting the purchase amount immediately from a customer's checking account. Shoppers conduct more than 36 billion debit card transactions each year.[40] As customers' use of debit cards grows, small businesses also are equipping their stores to handle debit card transactions. The equipment is easy to install and to set up, and the cost to the company is negligible. The payoff can be big, however, in the form of increased sales and decreased losses from bad checks.

E-COMMERCE AND CREDIT CARDS. When it comes to online business transactions, the most common method of payment is the credit card. Internet vendors are constantly challenged by the need to provide secure methods of transacting business in a safe environment. Many shoppers are suspicious of online transactions for reasons of security and privacy. Therefore, online merchants must be sure to ensure their customers' privacy and the security of their credit card transactions by using computer encryption software.

Online merchants also face another obstacle: credit card fraud. Because they lack the face-to-face contact with their customers, online merchants face special challenges to avoid credit card fraud. According to a study by the Merchant Risk Council, online merchants lose 1.2 percent of their annual revenue, about $3.3 billion, to fraud each year.[41] Because small and mid-sized companies are less likely than large businesses to use high-tech online fraud detection tools, they are more likely to be victims of e-commerce fraud.[42] The following steps can help online merchants reduce the probability that they will become victims of credit card fraud:

- Use an address verification system (AVS) to compare every customer's billing information on the order form with the billing information in the bank or credit card company's records.
- Require customers to provide the CVV2 number from the back of the credit card. Although crooks can get access to this number, it can help screen out some fraudulent orders.
- Check customers' Internet Protocol (IP) addresses. If an order contains a billing address in California, but the IP address from which the order is placed is in China, chances are that the order is fraudulent.
- Monitor activity on the Web site with the help of a Web analytics software package. Many packages are available, and analyzing log files can help online entrepreneurs to pinpoint the sources of fraud.
- Verify large orders. Large orders are a cause for celebration, but only if they are legitimate. Check the authenticity of large orders, especially if the order is from a first-time customer.
- Post notices on the Web site that your company uses antifraud technology to screen orders. These notices make legitimate customers feel more confident about placing their orders and crooks trying to commit fraud tentative about running their scams.
- Contact the credit card company or the bank that issued the card. If you suspect that an order may be fraudulent, contact the company *before* processing it. Taking this step could save a small company thousands of dollars in losses.[43]

Installment Credit

Small companies that sell big-ticket consumer durables—major appliances, cars, and boats—frequently rely on installment credit. Because very few customers can purchase these items in a single lump-sum payment, small businesses finance them over time. The time horizon may range from just a few months up to 25 or more years. Most companies require the customer to make an initial down payment for the merchandise and then finance the balance for the life of the loan. The customer repays the loan principal plus interest on the loan. One advantage of installment loans for a small business is that the owner retains a security interest as collateral on the loan. If the customer defaults on the loan, the owner still holds the title to the merchandise. Because installment credit absorbs a small company's cash, many entrepreneurs rely on financial institutions such as banks and credit unions to provide the installment credit. When a business has the financial strength to "carry its own paper," the interest income from the installment loan contract often yields more than the initial profit on the sale of the product. For some businesses, such as auto dealerships and furniture stores, financing is an important source of revenue and profit.

Trade Credit

Many small companies, especially those that sell to other businesses, offer their customers trade credit; that is, they create customer charge accounts. The typical small business invoices its credit customers monthly. To speed collections, some offer cash discounts if customers pay their balances early; others impose penalties on late payers. Before deciding to use credit as a competitive weapon, the small business owner must make sure that the company's cash position is strong enough to support that additional pressure.

Trade credit can be a double-edged sword. Small businesses must be willing to grant credit to purchasers to get and keep their business, but they must manage credit accounts carefully to make sure that their customers pay in full and on time.

Chapter Review

1. Explain why pricing is both an art and a science.
   - Pricing requires a knowledge of accounting to determine the firm's cost; strategy to understand competitors' behaviors; and psychology to understand customers' behaviors.

2. Discuss the relationships among pricing, image, competition, and value.
- Company pricing policies offer potential customers important information about the firm's overall image. Accordingly, when developing a marketing approach to pricing, business owners must establish prices that are compatible with what their customers expect and are willing to pay. Too often, small business owners *underprice* their goods and services, believing that low prices are the only way they can achieve a competitive advantage. They fail to identify the extra value, convenience, service, and quality they give their customers—all things many customers are willing to pay for.
- An important part of setting appropriate prices is tracking competitors' prices regularly; however, what the competition is charging is just one variable in the pricing mix. When setting prices, business owners should take into account their competitors' prices, but they should not automatically match or beat them. Businesses that offer customers extra quality, value, service, or convenience can charge higher prices as long as customers recognize the "extras" they are getting. Two factors are vital to studying the effects of competition on the small firm's pricing policies: the location of the competitors and the nature of the competing goods.

3. Describe effective pricing strategies for both new and existing products and services.
- Pricing a new product is often difficult for the small business owner, but it should accomplish three objectives: getting the product accepted, maintaining market share as the competition grows, and earning a profit.
- Three major pricing strategies are generally used to introduce new products into the market: penetration, skimming, and sliding down the demand curve.
- Pricing techniques for existing products and services include odd pricing, price lining, leader pricing, geographic pricing, opportunistic pricing, discounts, multiple pricing, bundling, and suggested retail pricing.

4. Explain the pricing techniques used by retailers.
- Pricing for the retailer means pricing to move merchandise. Markup is the difference between the cost of a product or service and its selling price.
- Some retailers use retail price, but others put a standard markup on all their merchandise; more frequently, they use a flexible markup.

5. Explain the pricing techniques used by manufacturers.
- A manufacturer's pricing decision depends on the support of accurate cost-accounting records. The most common technique is cost-plus pricing, in which the manufacturer charges a price that covers the cost of producing a product plus a reasonable profit. Every manufacturer should calculate a product's break-even price, the price that produces neither a profit nor a loss.

6. Explain the pricing techniques used by service firms.
- Service firms often suffer from the effects of vague, unfounded pricing procedures and frequently charge the going rate without any idea of their costs. A service firm must set a price based on the cost of materials used, labor involved, overhead, and a profit. The proper price reflects the total cost of providing a unit of service.

7. Describe the impact of credit on pricing.
- Offering customer credit enhances a small company's reputation and increases the probability, speed, and magnitude of customers' purchases. Small firms offer three types of customer credit: credit cards, installment credit, and trade credit (charge accounts).

Discussion Questions

1. Stuart Frankel, a Subway franchisee, came up with the idea for Subway's "$5 footlong" to combat slow weekend sales at his restaurants. It was such a hit that Subway introduced the idea to all of its 33,000 outlets, and in 1 year it generated $3.8 billion in sales. One marketing consultant asks, "Is the $5 footlong just a flash in the pan, or is it a function of consumer price points and price elasticity that affect all markets?" What do you think?

2. What does the price of a good or service represent to the customer? Why is a customer orientation to pricing important?

3. How does pricing affect a small firm's image?

4. What competitive factors must the small firm consider when establishing prices?

5. Describe the strategies a small business could use when setting the price of a new product. What objectives should the strategy seek to achieve?

6. Define the following pricing techniques: odd pricing, price lining, leader pricing, geographic pricing, and discounts.

7. Why do many small businesses use the manufacturer's suggested retail price? What are the disadvantages of this technique?

8. What is markup? How is it used to determine prices?

9. What is follow-the-leader pricing? Why is it risky?

10. What is cost-plus pricing? Why do so many manufacturers use it? What are the disadvantages of using it?

11. Explain the difference between full-absorption costing and direct costing. How does absorption costing help a manufacturer determine a reasonable price?

12. Explain the techniques a small service firm can use to set an hourly price.

13. What is the relevant price range for a product or service?

14. What advantages and disadvantages does offering trade credit provide to a small business?

15. What are the most commonly used methods to purchase online using credit? What accounts for consumer uncertainty when giving credit card information online as opposed to via the telephone?

16. What advantages does accepting credit cards provide a small business? What costs are involved?

Determining an "ideal" price for a product or service is challenging. Setting a price that is too low can generate high sales volume but also can reduce profit margins and possibly impede the company's ability to generate a positive cash flow. Setting a price that is too high may send potential customers to competitors, and sales may never materialize. Pricing is both an art and a science. The first step is to determine what it costs to provide your product or service to customers; the second step is to establish a price that covers total costs, generates a profit, and creates the desired image for your business. Setting the price of your products and services and knowing your company's break-even point is a fundamental element of your business plan. Resources and information are available within Business Plan Pro that may help you better understand the impact that pricing will have on your business.

On the Web

Conduct some competitive pricing research on the Web. Search for products and services that are similar to those that you are offering and list their price points. Check to see that you are making parallel comparisons of these products. For example, are you considering the entire price, which may include shipping, handling, complementary products, and other attributes that will influence the final price to the customer? Do you consider these businesses to be direct competitors? If not, why?

What does this information tell you about your price point? Is your price strategy consistent with your business strategy?

In the Software

Open your business plan and locate the "Break-Even" section under "Financial Plan." Follow the instructions and enter the information that will enable you to determine your break-even point. This will require you to have estimated figures for your fixed costs, variable costs, and prices. Once you have entered that information, look at the break-even point shown in units and revenue. Is this break-even point realistic? How long would you expect it would take to reach your break-even point? Is this time frame acceptable? Now increase your price by 10 percent. How does this change your break-even point? The software is an excellent tool to experiment with your break-even by entering different price points and costs to see the impact price will have on the break-even point when you will begin making a profit.

Building Your Business Plan

Go to the "Sales Forecast" table under the "Sales Strategy" section. An optional wizard will appear that you may select to help you through the process, or you can enter your information directly on the worksheet. If you have not done so yet, enter your price information in that section. Work through the rest of the table as you estimate your direct unit costs. The instructions and examples will assist you through that process.

Endnotes

1. Christopher T. Heun, "Dynamic Pricing Boosts Bottom Line," *Information Week*, October 29, 2001, *www.informationweek.com/story/showArticle.jhtml?articleID=6507202*.
2. Vincent Ryan, "Price Fixing," *CFO*, December 2009, p. 50.
3. Norm Brodsky, "Rule No. 1: Never Work for Chump Change," *Inc.*, March 2010, pp. 31–32.
4. Gary Walther, "The Sole of Stefano Bemer," *Forbes Life*, October 27, 2008, pp. 56–57.
5. Eric Arnold, "Aim High," *Forbes*, December 28, 2009, p. 86.
6. Howard Scott, "The Tricky Art of Raising Prices," *Nation's Business*, February 1999, p. 32.
7. Rick Bruns, "Tips for Coping with Rising Costs of Key Commodities," *Fast Company*, December 1997, pp. 27–30.
8. Rick Brooks, "More Businesses Slap on Fuel Fees," *Wall Street Journal*, May 4, 2006, pp. D1, D2; GiddyUp Fishing Charters, *www.captgiddyup.net/*.
9. Jeffrey A. Trachtenberg, "Borders Slashes Buyer Rewards, Cuts Discounts," *Wall Street Journal*, March 28, 2007, pp. D1, D4.
10. "Gas Prices Could Affect the Price of Pizzas, Flowers," *Greenville News*, April 29, 2006, p. 3A.

11. C. J. Prince, "Is the Price Right," *Entrepreneur*, November 2008, *www.entrepreneur.com/magazine/entrepreneur/2008/november/198068.html*.
12. Malika Zouhali-Worrall, "Ring in the Profits," *FSB*, December 2009/January 2010, p. 15.
13. Kate Dubose Tomassi, "Southwest Best Prepared for Rising Fuel Prices," *Forbes*, July 19, 2006, *www.forbes.com/markets/2006/07/19/southwest-airlines-markets06.html*.
14. Stacy Meichtry, "What Your Time Is Really Worth," *Wall Street Journal*, April 7–8, 2007, pp. P1, P4, and P5; Adam McCollum, "The Big Time," *Forbes Life*, September 18, 2006, *http://members.forbes.com/fyi/2006/0918/114.html*.
15. Adam McCollum, "Maîtres du Temps Chapter One," *Forbes Life*, October 27, 2008, p. 33.
16. Michael V. Marn, Eric V. Roegner, and Craig C. Zawada, "Pricing New Products," *McKinsey Quarterly*, Number 3, 2003, *www.mckinseyquarterly.com/article_abstract.aspx?ar=1329&l2=16&l3=19&srid=190&gp=0*.
17. Barbara Lyon, "Customer Service, Not Price, Remains Top Cause of Customer Churn, Accenture Study Finds," Accenture, November 18, 2008, *http://newsroom.accenture.com/article_print.cfm?article_id=4769article_id=4769*.
18. Greg Hardesty, "Luxury Mattress Is the Stuff of Dreams," *Greenville News*, August 15, 2009, p. 3D; "History," Hästens, *www.hastens.com/en/THE-EXPERIENCE/History/*.
19. C. J. Prince, "Is the Price Right?" *Entrepreneur*, November 2008, p. 55; Erin Chambers, "Career Reinvention: Wall Street Trader Turned Fitness Guru," *Wall Street Journal*, May 8, 2008, *http://online.wsj.com/article/SB121018652707174445.html*; "Our Story," Iron Core, *www.ironcorekettlebells.com/story/*.
20. "ABA Asks Department of Justice to Investigate Bookseller Price Wars," *Bookselling This Week*, October 22, 2009, *http://news.bookweb.org/news/aba-asks-department-justice-investigate-bestseller-price-wars*; Veronica G. Rodriguez, "Bookstores," Small Business Development Center National Information Clearing House, May 2007, pp. 1–5.
21. Richard Gibson, "Big Price Cut at McDonald's Seems a McFlop," *Wall Street Journal*, May 9, 1997, pp. B1, B2; Richard Gibson, "Prices Tumble on Big Macs, but Fries Rise," *Wall Street Journal*, April 25, 1997, pp. B1, B2; Cliff Edwards, "Some McDonald's Franchisees Quietly Boosting Prices to Offset Cost of Promotion," *Greenville News*, April 26, 1997, p. 8D.
22. Jim Barnes, "Stop Cutting Prices! Retain Customers with Four Types of Experiential Value," Customer Think, April 24, 2009, *www.customerthink.com/article/retain_customers_with_four_types_experiential_value*.
23. Allison Stein Wellner, "Is It Time to Raise Prices?" *Inc.*, June 2005, p. 80.
24. Norm Brodsky, "Dealing with Cost Hikes," *Inc.*, August 2005, p. 49.
25. Gladys Edmunds, "Price Is Right? Not If It's Too Low," *USA Today*, June 8, 2005, *www.usatoday.com/money/smallbusiness/columnist/edmunds/2005-06-08-price_x.htm*.
26. Lisa Sefcik, "About Chantecaille," *Live Strong*, October 4, 2009, *www.livestrong.com/article/25297-chantecaille/*; Rachel Dodes and Cheryl Lu-Lien Tan, "What Price Beauty? Costly Face Creams Lift Prices, Spirits," *Wall Street Journal*, December 19, 2006, pp. A1, A12.
27. "New Study on Retail Discounting: What Works for Some Products Might Be a Bust for Others," Kelley School of Business, Indiana University, November 18, 2009, *http://info.kelley.iu.edu/news/page/normal/12630.html*.
28. Josh Hyatt, "And in This Corner, the Price-Fighter," *CFO*, December 2008, p. 29.
29. Lisa Baertlein, "Subway's $5 Deal a Hard Habit to Break," *Reuters*, September 17, 2009, *www.reuters.com/article/idUSTRE58G6NG20090917*.
30. "NPD: Restaurants Likely to Wean Customers Off Discounts/Deals," *Fast Casual*, May 20, 2010, *www.fastcasual.com/article.php?id=18348*.
31. "Don't Let This One Get Away," *Get to the Point: Customer Insight*, January 20, 2010, pp. 1–2.
32. Mark Brandeau, "Chains Mull Benefits of Value Menus, Combo Deals," *Nation's Restaurant News*, February 23, 2009, *www.nrn.com/breakingNews.aspx?id=363398&menu_id=1368*.
33. "City Swingers," *Forbes Life*, September 2006, p. 30; "Swing Set," *Men's Vogue*, April 2007, *www.mensvogue.com/health/regimen/articles/2007/04/drive_495*.
34. Hiroshi Suzuki, "Nintendo's Japan Wii Sales Double Those of Sony PlayStation 3," *Bloomberg News*, April 2, 2007, *www.bloomberg.com/apps/news?pid=conewsstory&refer=conews&tkr=NTDOY:US&sid=a_A5anLn.xE8*; Brian Bremmer, "Will Nintendo's Wii Strategy Score?" *Business Week*, September 20, 2006, *www.businessweek.com/globalbiz/content/sep2006/gb20060920_163780.htm*; Kathleen Sanders and Matt Casamassina, "U.S. Wii Price, Launch Date Revealed," *IGN Entertainment*, September 13, 2006, *http://wii.ign.com/articles/732/732669p1.html*; "Playing a Different Game," *Economist*, October 26, 2006, *www.economist.com/business/displaystory.cfm?story_id=8080787*.
35. Joseph Pereira, "State Law Targets 'Minimum Pricing,'" *Wall Street Journal*, April 28, 2009, p. D1.
36. Rafi Mohammed, "Apple's iPad Can Capitalize on Fragmented Marketplace," *The Wrap*, February 8, 2010, *www.thewrap.com/blog-entry/apples-ipad-can-capitalize-fragmenting-marketplace-14006*.
37. David Worrell, "Time Well Spent," *Entrepreneur*, June 2006, p. 63.
38. Ben Woolsey and Matt Schulz, "Credit Card Statistics, Industry Facts, Debt Statistics," *CreditCards.com*, May 13, 2010, *www.creditcards.com/credit-card-news/credit-card-industry-facts-personal-debt-statistics-1276.php#issuervolume*.
39. "Credit Counseling Statistics," Consumer Credit Counseling Service, *http://creditcounselingbiz.com/credit_counseling_statistics.htm*.
40. Ben Woolsey and Matt Schulz, "Credit Card Statistics, Industry Facts, Debt Statistics," *CreditCards.com*, May 13, 2010, *www.creditcards.com/credit-card-news/credit-card-industry-facts-personal-debt-statistics-1276.php#issuervolume*.
41. "Merchant Risk Council Announces Annual e-Commerce Fraud Survey Results," Merchant Risk Council, March 10, 2010, *www.merchantriskcouncil.org/index.cfm?fuseaction=Feature.showFeature&FeatureID=137*.
42. "Merchants Hit Back at E-Commerce Fraud," CyberSource, November 17, 2009, *www.cybersource.com/news_and_events/view.php?page_id=1798*.
43. Michael Bloch, "Preventing Credit Card Chargebacks—Anti-Fraud Strategies," Taming the Beast, *www.tamingthebeast.net/articles2/card-fraud-strategies.htm*.

E-Commerce and Entrepreneurship

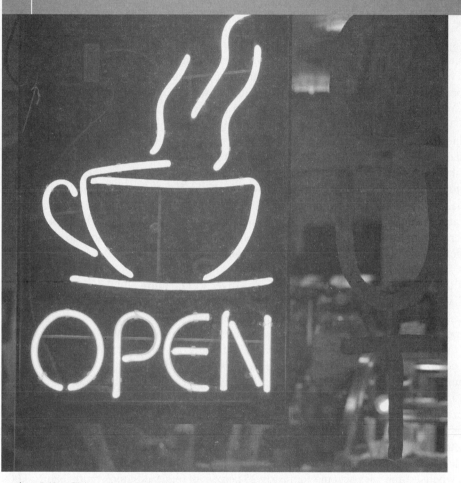

Like China, the Internet is a huge new market. It's up to you to figure out what to do with it: use it as a prospecting tool, make connections with people, add value for your existing customers.

—Larry Chase

In the mental geography of e-commerce, distance has been eliminated. There is only one economy and one market.

—Peter Drucker

Learning Objectives

Upon completion of this chapter, you will be able to:

1 Describe the benefits of selling on the World Wide Web.
2 Understand the factors an entrepreneur should consider before launching into e-commerce.
3 Explain the 10 myths of e-commerce and how to avoid falling victim to them.
4 Explain the basic strategies entrepreneurs should follow to achieve success in their e-commerce efforts.
5 Learn the techniques of designing a killer Web site.
6 Explain how companies track the results from their Web sites.
7 Describe how e-businesses ensure the privacy and security of the information they collect and store from the Web.

E-commerce is creating a new economy, one that is connecting producers, sellers, and customers via technology in ways that have never been possible before. The result is a new method of doing business that is turning traditional methods of commerce and industry on their heads. Companies that ignore the impact of the Internet on their markets run the risk of becoming as relevant to customers as the rotary-dial telephone. The most successful small companies are embracing the Internet, not as merely another advertising medium or marketing tool, but as a mechanism for transforming their companies and changing *everything* about the way they do business. As these companies discover new, innovative ways to use the Internet and communications technology to connect with their suppliers and to serve their customers better, they are creating a new industrial order. In short, e-commerce has launched a revolution. Just as in previous revolutions in the business world, some old players are ousted, and new leaders emerge. The winners are discovering new business opportunities, new ways of serving their customers, and new methods of organizing and operating their businesses.

Perhaps the most visible changes are occurring in the world of retailing. Although e-commerce will not replace traditional retailing, no retailer, from the smallest corner store to industry giant Walmart, can afford to ignore the impact of the Web on their businesses. Companies can take orders at the speed of light from anywhere in the world and at any time of day. The Internet enables companies to collect more information on customers' shopping and buying habits than any other medium in history. This ability means that companies can focus their marketing efforts like never before—for instance, selling garden supplies to customers who are most likely to buy them and not wasting resources trying to sell to those who have no interest in gardening. The capacity to track customers' Web-based shopping habits allows companies to personalize their approaches to marketing and to realize the benefits of individualized (or one-to-one) marketing. Ironically, the same Web-based marketing approach that allows companies to get so personal with their customers also can make shopping extremely impersonal. Entrepreneurs who set up shop on the Web will likely never meet their customers face-to-face or even talk to them. Yet those customers, who can live anywhere in the world, visit the online store at all hours of the day or night and expect to receive individual attention. Making a Web-based marketing approach succeed requires a business to strike a balance, creating an e-commerce strategy that capitalizes on the strengths of the Web while meeting customers' expectations of convenience and service.

In this fast-paced world of e-commerce, size doesn't matter as much as speed and flexibility do. One of the Web's greatest strengths is its interactive, social nature and the ability to provide companies with instantaneous customer feedback, giving them the opportunity to learn and to make necessary adjustments. Businesses, whatever their size, that are willing to experiment with different approaches to reaching customers and are quick to learn and adapt will grow and prosper; those that cannot will fall by the wayside. The Internet continues to create a new industrial order, and companies that fail to adapt to it will soon become extinct.

E-commerce is redefining even the most traditional industries, such as the pizza business. Both Papa John's and Domino's have long since passed the $1 billion mark in online pizza sales. Online pizza sales are growing so fast that it took Papa John's 7 years to reach its first billion in online sales but only 2 years to achieve its second billion. Andy Freitas, a Papa John's franchisee in Washington, DC, says that in two of his outlets online sales account for more than 50 percent of total sales. On a recent Super Bowl Sunday (the busiest single day in the pizza business), Domino's, where online sales account for nearly 25 percent of total sales, took more than 160,000 orders online, and more than 1,000 customers *per minute* were placing online orders just before kickoff. Pizza Hut, the largest pizza chain in the United States, generates online sales of $2 billion a year.[1]

High-volume, low-margin commodity products tend to be best suited for selling on the Web. Although the most popular items purchased online vary from one country to another, the items that customers purchase most often online are computer hardware, clothing, and consumer electronics.[2] However, companies can—and do—sell practically anything over the Web, from antiques and pharmaceuticals to popcorn and drug-free urine.

Companies of all sizes are establishing a presence on the Web because that's where their customers are. The number of Internet users worldwide now stands at more than 1.9 billion, up from only 361 million at the end of 2000.[3] In the United States, people spend an average of 13.2 hours per week on the Internet (not including reading and sending e-mail, which adds 4.5 hours), nearly as much as they do watching television (14.0 hours per week).[4] Figure 1 shows how people in various countries compare in their time spent online.

FIGURE 1
Time Spent Online by Country (Hours per Week)

Source: Brian McRoberts, George H. Terhanian, Ken Allredge, and Carla Keppler, "Understanding the Role of the Internet in the Lives of Consumers: Digital Influence Index," Fleishman-Hillard and Harris Interactive, June 2010, p. 8.

Consumers have adopted the Internet much more quickly than any other major innovation in the past. The Internet reached an audience of 50 million people in just 4 years, compared to 38 years for radio and 13 years for television. One of the Internet's most popular sites, Facebook, reached 50 million users in just 2 years.[5] Online sales now account for 7 percent of total retail sales in the United States, and experts forecast that they will reach $249 billion in 2014, which amounts to a 10 percent annual growth rate. In addition, Jupiter Research predicts that online research will influence 53 percent of total purchases by 2014, up from 27 percent in 2005 (see Figure 2).[6] Although the rapid growth rate of online sales will not last indefinitely, the Web represents a tremendous opportunity for both online and off-line sales that small businesses cannot afford to ignore.

Benefits of Selling on the Web

1. Describe the benefits of selling on the World Wide Web.

Although a Web-based sales strategy does not guarantee success, small companies that have established Web sites realize many benefits, including the following:

- ■ *The opportunity to increase revenues and attract new customers.* For many small businesses, launching a Web site is the equivalent of opening a new sales channel. Companies that launch e-commerce efforts soon discover that their sites are generating additional sales from new customers.
- ■ *The ability of brick-and-mortar retailers to drive online customers into their stores and increase sales there.* Owners of retail stores have discovered that setting up a Web site leads not only to increased online sales, but also to higher in-store sales. Some retailers offer customers the convenience of ordering products online and then picking them up in the store.

FIGURE 2
U.S. Online and Web-Influenced Retail Sales 2009–2014 (in Billions of $)

Source: Forrester Research Web Influenced Retail Sales Forecast, 2009.

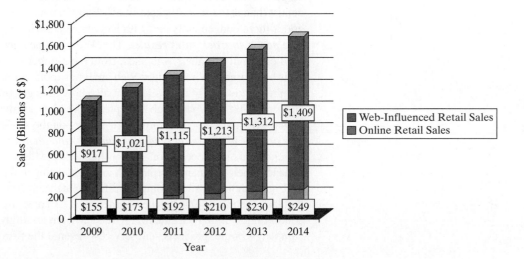

- *The ability to expand their reach into global markets.* The Web is the most efficient way for small businesses to sell their products to the millions of potential customers who live outside the borders of the United States.

- *The ability to remain open 24 hours a day, 7 days a week.* More than half of all retail sales occur after 6 P.M., when many traditional stores close. Extending the hours a brick-and-mortar store remains open can increase sales, but it also takes a toll on the business owner and the employees. With a Web site up and running, customers never have to worry about whether an online store is "open."

- *The capacity to use the Web's interactive nature to enhance customer service.* Although selling on the Web can be highly impersonal because of the lack of human interaction, companies that design their sites properly can create an exciting, interactive experience for their online visitors. Customers can contact a company at any time of the day, control the flow of information they get, and, in some cases, interact with company representatives in real time. In addition, technology now allows companies to "personalize" their sites to suit the tastes and preferences of individual customers.

- *The power to educate and to inform.* Far more than most marketing media, the Web gives entrepreneurs the power to educate and to inform customers. Women and members of Generation Y, especially, crave product information before they make purchases. The Web allows business owners to provide more detailed information to visitors than practically any other medium.

- *The ability to lower the cost of doing business.* The Web is one of the most efficient ways of reaching both new and existing customers. Properly designed and promoted, a Web site can reduce a company's cost of generating sales leads, providing customer support, and distributing marketing materials. For instance, sending customers an e-mail newsletter is much less expensive than paying the printing and postage costs of sending the same newsletter by "snail mail."

- *The capacity to improve the efficiency of purchasing and inventory control processes.* The Internet also has the potential to improve the efficiency of small companies' purchasing and inventory-control processes. In a study by BuyerZone, an online marketplace for business purchasing, more than 75 percent of small business owners say that using the Internet in their purchasing decisions allows them to save both money and time when making buying decisions.[7] By integrating its Web site and its inventory-control system, a company also can shorten its sales cycle and reduce its inventory costs. Linking its Web orders directly to suppliers enables a business to cut purchasing costs even more.

- *The ability to spot new business opportunities and to capitalize on them.* E-commerce companies are poised to give customers just what they want when they want it. As the number of dual-career couples rises and the amount of available leisure time shrinks, consumers are looking for ways to increase the convenience of shopping, and the Web is fast becoming the solution they seek. Increasingly, customers view shopping as an unpleasant chore that cuts into already scarce leisure time, and they are embracing anything that reduces the amount of time they must spend shopping. (One study of New York shoppers by Visa reports that 42 percent of people prefer to clean their bathrooms and 18 percent would rather visit the dentist than stand in a checkout line![8]) Entrepreneurs who tap into customers' need to buy goods more conveniently and with less hassle are winning the battle for market share.

- *The power to track sales results.* The Web gives businesses the power to track virtually any kind of activity on their Web sites, from the number of visitors to the click-through rates on their banner ads. With modern Web analytics tools, entrepreneurs can track not only the number of visitors to their sites, but also how they got there, how they maneuver around the site, and what they buy. Web entrepreneurs can experiment with different designs and layouts for their sites to determine their impact on the site's sales.

- *The opportunity to build credibility and a brand identity among customers.* Many entrepreneurs who operate off-line businesses have discovered that launching a Web site enhances their company's reputation among existing and potential customers. A well-designed Web site can help a small company differentiate itself from its competitors, especially those that lack Web sites. One business writer says, "A company that neglects its Web site may be committing commercial suicide. A Web site is increasingly becoming the gateway to a company's brand, products, and services—even if the firm does not sell online."[9]

ENTREPRENEURIAL
Profile

*Jesse and Anne Heap:
Pink Cake Box*

Anne Heap, co-owner of Pink Cake Box Bakery, works on an edible high-heel shoe that is part of a custom-made cake.

Source: Mike Derer/AP Wide World Photos

In 2005, Jesse and Anne Heap launched Pink Cake Box, a bakery in Denville, New Jersey, that specializes in custom-made cakes, cupcakes, and cookies. They immediately set up a Web site and started a blog that now reach tens of thousands of customers each month. Recognizing that the Web was a powerful yet low-cost way to connect with their customers, the Heaps devoted significant effort during start up to building a meaningful online presence. Still, "I don't think we realized how critical the Web would become to our business," admits Jesse. "It's been crucial to building the business and driving customer growth. The majority of our customers originate through the Web." The Pink Cake Box blog also has been an integral part of the company's success. "To differentiate ourselves, we used our blog to promote our cakes and offer customers and cake enthusiasts a constant stream of new cakes, contests, and videos," says Anne, the company's cake designer and pastry chef. "Our goal was to stay connected to our customers and to foster strong brand recognition." The rich content of the Pink Cake Box Web site, which includes photographs and videos of many of the company's astonishing cakes (which start at $250), customer testimonials, information about cake-making classes, and a link to the blog, has produced a site that is highly visible in search engines and that brings in customers. "The blog receives upwards of 120,000 unique visitors per month and drives a large percentage of our orders," says Jesse. The Heaps are developing plans to launch a retail shop and international versions of their Web site and blog. "It takes time to build a strong Web presence," says Jesse, "but once you gain momentum, the site's popularity will sustain your business."[10]

Source: www.CartoonStock.com

"Ya, right. Who needs a Web presence. I'll just compete in the global economy from here."

Factors to Consider Before Launching into E-Commerce

2. Understand the factors an entrepreneur should consider before launching into e-commerce.

Despite the many benefits the Web offers, not every small business owner has embraced e-commerce. According to a study by advertising and marketing firm Ad-ology, just 54 percent of small companies have Web sites, nearly double the percentage that were operating online in 2007.[11] Even more surprising, 46 percent of small business owners in a Discover Small Business Watch survey say that not every company needs a Web site![12] Why are so many small companies hesitant to use the Web as a business tool? For many entrepreneurs, the key barrier is not knowing where or how to start an e-commerce effort, whereas for others cost concerns are a major issue. Other roadblocks include the fear that customers will not use the Web site and the problems associated with ensuring online security.

Whatever the size of their companies, entrepreneurs are realizing that establishing a presence on the Web is no longer a luxury. "A Web site is your ticket to get into the game," says the CEO of one high-tech company. "If you don't have one, you might as well not even name your business."[13] Indeed, business owners who are not at least considering creating a Web presence or integrating the Web creatively into their operations are putting their companies at risk. However, before launching an e-commerce effort business owners should consider the following important issues:

- How a company exploits the Web's interconnectivity and the opportunities it creates to transform relationships with its suppliers and vendors, its customers, and other external stakeholders is crucial to its success.
- Web success requires a company to develop a plan for integrating the Web into its overall strategy. The plan should address issues such as site design and maintenance, creating and managing a brand name, marketing and promotional strategies, sales, and customer service.
- Developing deep, lasting relationships with customers takes on even greater importance on the Web. Attracting customers on the Web costs money, and companies must be able to retain their online customers to make their Web sites profitable.
- Creating a meaningful presence on the Web requires an ongoing investment of resources— time, money, energy, and talent. Establishing an attractive Web site brimming with catchy photographs of products is only the beginning.
- Measuring the success of its Web-based sales effort is essential to remaining relevant to customers whose tastes, needs, and preferences are always changing.

Doing business on the Web takes more time and energy than many entrepreneurs think. Answering the following questions helps entrepreneurs make sure they are ready to do business on the Web and avoid unpleasant surprises in their e-commerce efforts:

- What exactly do you expect a Web site to do for your company? Will it provide information only, reach new customers, increase sales to existing customers, generate sales from foreign customers, improve communication with customers, enhance customer service, or reduce your company's cost of operation?
- How much can you afford to invest in an e-commerce effort?
- What rate of return do you expect to earn on that investment?
- How long can you afford to wait for that return?
- How well suited are your products and services to sell on the Web?
- How will the "back office" of your Web site work? Will you tie your Web site directly into your company's inventory-control system?
- How will you handle order fulfillment? Can your current fulfillment system handle the increase in volume you are expecting?
- What impact, if any, will your Web site have on your company's traditional channels of distribution?
- What mechanism will your site use to ensure secure customer transactions?
- How will your company handle customer service for the site? What provisions will you make for returned items?
- How do you plan to promote the site to draw traffic to it?
- What information will you collect from the visitors to your site? How will you use it? Will you tell visitors how you intend to use this information?
- Have you developed a privacy policy? Have you posted that policy on your company's Web site for customers?
- Have you tested your site with real, live customers to make sure that it is easy to navigate and easy to order from?
- How will you measure the success of your company's Web site? What objectives have you set for the site?

IN THE ENTREPRENEURIAL
SPOTLIGHT
An E-Commerce Strategy That Fits

Warren Bennett had always enjoyed wearing fine suits, but his appreciation for a fine-fitting suit became the genesis of a business idea when he purchased several custom-made wool suits from the Tulsi Tailoring Family while performing volunteer work at a small school in Nepal. When Bennett returned to his home in the United Kingdom, he reconnected with an old school friend, David Hathiramani, who also appreciated well-made suits. The duo decided to combine their engineering and software training to create A Suit That Fits (ASTF), a company whose goal is to combine technology and fine tailoring to give customers custom-made suits at off-the-rack prices. Bennett and Hathiramani tested their business idea at the Hampstead Market, a small street market in London, and within 20 minutes had sold two suits. Recognizing that their idea had potential, they quickly created a Web site (*www.asuitthatfits.com*) and used credit cards to cover the start-up costs of their business.

To achieve the ideal fit, customers can go to one of the company's 22 measuring and fitting centers across the United Kingdom, have a tailor come to them for a custom fitting if they live in or around London, or use an innovative online measurement wizard that allows them to input their exact measurements. The Web-based Style Wizard offers customers complete control over the details of their suits—from the type of pockets to the color of the buttons—even if they cannot meet with a tailor in person. It also allows them to narrow the more than 40 billion possible suit combinations to the exact specifications they want. Nearly 85 percent of the company's existing customers go online to reorder. The suits—both men's and women's—are made in Kathmandu, Nepal, by a small group of expert tailors, with final adjustments made in London. Suit prices start at just £200 (about $310) an incredible bargain for a hand-tailored garment.

The fast-growing company now employs more than 30 people in London and 85 in Nepal. A Suit That Fits reflects the founders' ethical values and operates in a socially responsible manner. The company makes a concerted effort to live up to its mission statement: "A Suit That Fits believes in building long-term relationships through responsible business—achieving commercial success while incorporating ethical values and respect for people, communities, and the environment." The company's tailors in Nepal receive salaries that are 50 percent above the national average and receive incentive bonuses.

ASTF also donates 5 percent of its production costs to a school in Kathmandu, recently providing funding for a new science lab and a computer lab. At its London operation, ASTF works hard to keep employees engaged, providing them with a dedicated place to socialize and an "ideas wall," where anyone can post innovative ideas and suggestions for improvement. Bennett and Hathiramani also hold weekly team meetings to share information with their employees and to listen to their concerns. ASTF also donates sample suits to two charities in London that help homeless men find work.

The young entrepreneurs behind ASTF maximize the cost advantages that operating on the Web and sourcing their products to their connections in Nepal provide them. They also recognize the importance of using guerrilla marketing techniques, including using social networking sites such as Facebook and Twitter, to promote their business. "We want to think strategically about how we use social media and develop a consistent tone of voice across all customer touch points," says Hathiramani. ASTF usually ranks at the top on Google searches for "tailored suits." The company also has made suits for British celebrities and for Sultan Kosen, the world's tallest man, who stands 8 feet, 1 inch tall.

With its e-commerce strategy in place, ASTF, which generates nearly $3.1 million in annual sales, has a bright future. The company recently won Dell's Global Small Business Excellence Award, which awards $50,000 worth of Dell products and services to small companies that use technology in innovative ways to improve the customer experience and to grow. In just 3 years, ASTF has more than 20,000 customers, and the founders' goal is to use their Web site to add another 15,000 customers, most of them outside the United Kingdom, within 1 year. "We'll be putting our Dell prize to work to streamline productivity, reach more customers around the world, foster innovation, and build an infrastructure that can support our long-term growth," says Bennett. "The possibilities are endless."

1. How does the Internet allow small companies such as A Suit That Fits to achieve rapid growth and sales success so quickly? Do you think the company would have been as successful as it is without its e-commerce strategy? Explain.

2. Several competitors have entered the market, trying to duplicate ASTF's strategy. What steps do you

recommend Bennett and Hathiramani take to maintain their competitive advantage? How can they connect with their customers more effectively? What challenges does a company that makes tailor-made suits face by conducting a significant portion of its business online?

Sources: Based on "A Suit That Fits Business Income Doubles," *Telegraph*, January 19, 2010, *www.telegraph.co.uk/finance/businessclub/sales/7028017/*

A-Suit-That-Fits-business-income-doubles.html; Dan Martin, "British Start-Up Named World's Best Small Business," *Business Zone*, December 17, 2009, *www.businesszone.co.uk/topic/business-trends/tailoring-start-named-worlds-best-small-business*; "Label Spotlight: A Suit That Fits.com," *Commerce with a Conscience*, January 21, 2010, *www.commercewithaconscience.info/2010/01/21/label-spotlight-a-suit-that-fits/*; "2009 U.K. Winner: A Suit That Fits," Dell Entrepreneur Excellence Award, Dell Inc., September 2009, *www.dellhero.com/uk/country-winner.asp*; Dan Martin, "Back to the Floor: A Small Business in Action," *Business Zone*, April 13, 2010, *www.businesszone.co.uk/topic/business-trends/back-floor-small-business-action/27689*.

Ten Myths of E-Commerce

3. Explain the 10 myths of e-commerce and how to avoid falling victim to them.

Although many entrepreneurs have boosted their businesses with e-commerce, setting up shop on the Web is no guarantee of success. Scores of entrepreneurs have plunged unprepared into the world of e-commerce only to discover that there is more to it than merely setting up a Web site and waiting for the orders to start pouring in. Make sure that you do not fall victim to one of the following e-commerce myths.

Myth 1. If I Launch a Site, Customers Will Flock to It

Some entrepreneurs think that once they set up their Web sites, their expenses end there. Not true! Without promotional support, no Web site will draw enough traffic to support a business. With an estimated 600 billion Web pages already in existence and the number of new Web documents growing by 6 million per day, getting a site noticed has become increasingly difficult. Experts estimate that only about half of the Web's content is indexed and therefore retrievable by search engines.[14] Merely listing a site with popular Web search engines cannot guarantee that Web users will find a small company's site. Just like traditional retail stores seeking to attract customers, virtual companies have discovered that drawing sufficient traffic to a Web site requires promotion—and lots of it! "No one will know you're on the Web unless you tell them and motivate them to visit," explains Mark Layton, owner of a Web-based distributor of computer supplies and author of a book on e-commerce.[15]

Entrepreneurs with both physical and virtual stores must promote their Web sites at every opportunity by printing their URLs on everything related to their physical stores—on signs, in print and broadcast ads, in store windows, on shopping bags, on merchandise labels, and anywhere else their customers might see it. Virtual shop owners should consider buying ads in traditional advertising media as well as using banner ads, banner exchange programs, and cross-marketing arrangements with companies selling complementary products on their Web sites. Other techniques include creating some type of interactivity with customers, such as a Web-based newsletter, posting a video about the company's products on YouTube, writing articles that link to the company's site, hosting a chat room that allows customers to interact with one another and with company personnel, incorporating a bulletin board or customer-generated reviews, establishing a blog, or sponsoring a contest. For instance, one small pet store has had success promoting both its Web site and its retail store with Howl-O-Ween, an online photo contest featuring people's dogs dressed in Halloween costumes.

Blogs are easy to create, but they require regular updating with fresh content to attract visitors. BlogPulse, a company that tracks blogs, estimates that the Web hosts more than 143 million blogs.[16] Blogs with fresh, entertaining content and a soft-sell approach can be an effective way to draw potential customers to a company's Web site. Podcasts, video versions of blogs, are another attention-getting tool for a small company's Web site.

ENTREPRENEURIAL
Profile
Andrew Lock: GotBiz.TV

Andrew Lock, who launched a Web-based television business, GotBiz.TV, from his Utah home, got his start with a podcast aimed at entrepreneurs called "Help! My Business Sucks!" With a blend of clever humor, sharp wit, and business know-how, Lock's 10-minute podcasts offer entrepreneurs useful advice on a variety of topics. More than 100,000 viewers from around the world tune into Lock's online broadcast each week.[17]

The key to promoting a Web site successfully is networking, building relationships with customers, bloggers, social media, trade associations, online directories, and other Web sites a company's customers visit. "You need to create relationships with the businesses and people with whom you share common customers," says Barbara Ling, author of a book on e-commerce. "Then you need to create links between sites to help customers find what they are looking for."[18]

Myth 2. Online Customers Are Easy to Please

Customers who shop online today tend to be experienced Internet users whose expectations for their online shopping experiences are high and continue to rise. Experienced online shoppers tend to be unforgiving, quickly clicking to another site if their shopping experience is subpar or if they cannot find the products and information they want. Because Web shoppers are becoming more discriminating, companies are finding that they must improve their Web sites to attract and keep their customers.

To be successful online marketers, small companies must create Web sites with the features that appeal to experienced Web shoppers, such as simple navigation, customer reviews, rock-solid security, and quick access to product information, videos, and blogs. Many small businesses outsource most (sometimes all) of the activities associated with conducting business online to companies that specialize in e-commerce services. These companies prefer to focus on their core competencies—product design, marketing, extending a brand, manufacturing, and others—and hire other companies whose core competencies reside in e-commerce to handle Web site design, hosting, order processing, and order fulfillment ("pick, pack, and ship"). Rather than make constant investments in technology that may not produce a reasonable return, these small companies preserve their capital and their energy and focus them on the aspects of business that they do best. Other entrepreneurs prefer to keep the design and operation of their Web sites in house.

Myth 3. Making Money on the Web Is Easy

Promoters who hawk "get-rich-quick" schemes on the Web lure many entrepreneurs with the promise that making money on the Web is easy. It isn't. Doing business online can be quite lucrative, but it takes time and requires an up-front investment. As hundreds of new Web sites spring up every day, getting a company's site noticed requires more effort and marketing muscle than ever before.

Entrepreneurs engaging in e-commerce recognize the power that the Internet gives customers. Pricing, for example, is no longer as simple as it once was for companies. Auction sites such as eBay and Priceline.com mean that entrepreneurs can no longer be content to take into account only local competitors when setting their own prices. With the Web, price transparency is now the rule of the day. With a few mouse clicks, customers can compare the prices of the same or similar products and services from companies across the globe. In this wired and connected economy, the balance of power has shifted to customers, and new business models recognize this fact.

Myth 4. Privacy Is Not an Important Issue on the Web

The Web allows companies to gain access to almost unbelievable amounts of information about their customers. Many sites offer visitors "freebies" in exchange for information about themselves. Companies then use this information to learn more about their target customers and how to market to them most effectively. Concerns over the privacy of and the use of this information have become the topic of debate by many interested parties, including government agencies, consumer watchdog groups, customers, and industry trade associations.

Companies that collect information from their online customers have a responsibility to safeguard their customers' privacy, to protect it from unauthorized use, and to use it responsibly. That means that businesses should post a privacy statement on their Web sites, explaining to customers how they intend to use the information they collect. One of the surest ways to alienate online customers is to experience a security breach that allows their personal information to be stolen, to abuse the information collected from them by selling it to third parties, or to spam customers with unwanted solicitations. A recent survey by PayPal and comScore reports that 21 percent of online shoppers have abandoned their shopping carts because of security concerns.[19] BBBOnLine offers a useful resource center (*www.bbbonline.org/UnderstandingPrivacy/PMRC/*) that is designed to help small business owners who want to establish or upgrade their Web site's privacy policies.

Businesses that publish privacy policies and then adhere to them build trust among their customers, an important facet of doing business on the Web. According to John Briggs, director of e-commerce for the Yahoo! Network, customers "need to trust the brand they are buying and believe that their online purchases will be safe transactions. They need to feel comfortable that [their] personal data will not be sold and that they won't get spammed by giving their e-mail address. They need to know about shipping costs, product availability, and return policies up front."[20] Privacy *does* matter on the Web, and businesses that respect their customers' privacy will win their customers' trust. Trust is the foundation on which companies build the long-term customer relationships that are so crucial to Web success.

Myth 5. "Strategy? I Don't Need a Strategy to Sell on the Web! Just Give Me a Web Site, and the Rest Will Take Care of Itself."

Building a successful e-business is no different than building a successful brick-and-mortar business, and that requires a well-thought-out strategy. Building a strategy means that an entrepreneur must first develop a clear definition of the company's target audience and a thorough understanding of customers' needs, wants, likes, and dislikes. To be successful, a Web site must be appealing to the customers it seeks to attract just as a traditional store's design and décor must draw foot traffic. Before your Web site can become the foundation for a successful e-business, you must create it with your target audience in mind.

One goal of developing a strategy is to set a business apart from its competitors. The same is true for creating a strategy for conducting business online. It is just as important, if not more important, for an online business to differentiate itself from the competition if it is to be successful. Unlike customers in a retail store, who must exert the effort to go to a competitor's store if they cannot find what they want, online customers only have to make a mouse click or two to go to a rival Web site. Therefore, competition online is fierce, and to succeed a company must have a sound strategy.

ENTREPRENEURIAL
Profile
Nick Swinmurn: Zappos

Zappos, the largest online shoe retailer, founded in 1999 by Nick Swinmurn after a frustrating and fruitless trip to a local mall in search of shoes, offers online customers a huge selection of shoes, including dress and athletic shoes for men and women, extra-wide shoes for hard-to-fit feet, and even "vegetarian" shoes made from materials other than leather. Zappos' strategy is simple: offer customers the greatest variety and selection of shoes possible to gain an edge over brick-and-mortar stores that are limited in the stock that they can carry and offer stellar customer service. Zappos, now owned by Amazon.com, stocks more than 90,000 styles in a wide array of sizes of more than 500 brands for a total inventory of nearly 2 million pairs of shoes. As part of Zappos' commitment to customer service, the company offers free expedited shipping (even on shoes that customers return) and a sophisticated warehouse system that provides shoppers real-time information on the availability of any particular shoe. Tony Hsieh, CEO and majority owner, says that Zappos' focus on its customers (evidenced by its free-shipping policy, which costs more than $100 million annually) is the reason that 65 percent of Zappos shoppers are repeat customers. Its strategy is working. The Las Vegas–based company reached $1 billion in sales in just 10 years.[21]

Myth 6. The Most Important Part of Any E-Commerce Effort Is Technology

Although understanding the technology of e-commerce is an important part of the formula for success, it is *not* the most crucial ingredient. What matters most is the ability to understand the underlying business and to develop a workable business model that offers customers something of value at a reasonable price while producing a reasonable return for the company. The entrepreneurs who are proving to be most successful in e-commerce are those who know how their industries work inside and out and then build an e-business around that knowledge. They know that they can hire Web designers, database experts, and fulfillment companies to create the technical aspects of their online businesses, but that nothing can substitute for a solid understanding of their industry, their target market, and the strategy needed to pull the various parts together. The key is seeing the Web for what it really is: another way to reach and serve customers with an effective business model and to minimize the cost of doing business.

Tony Hsieh, CEO of Zappos, the online shoe retailer, has created collaborative relationships with the company's vendors and suppliers using the Web, including giving them information that most retailers would never share about sales, inventory levels, and profits. Vendors work in tandem with Zappos' buyers via the Internet to manage inventory and generate sales and "have complete visibility into our business," says Fred Mossler, head of the company's merchandising team. "The benefits we've reaped from building relationships with our vendors are endless," he says. "They help us plan our business and make sure that we have enough of the right product at the right time. They help procure inventory on hot-selling items. Sometimes they provide unique items that can be found only on Zappos. They work closely with our marketing team to plan the right campaigns."[22]

Unfortunately, many entrepreneurs tackle e-commerce by focusing on technology first and then determine how that technology fits their business idea. "If you start with technology, you're likely going to buy a solution in search of a problem," says Kip Martin, program director of META Group's Electronic Business Strategies. Instead, he suggests, "Start with the business and ask yourself what you want to happen and how you'll measure it. *Then* ask how the technology will help you achieve your goals. Remember: Business first, technology second."[23]

Myth 7. On the Web, Customer Service Is Not as Important as It Is in a Traditional Retail Store

The Web offers shoppers the ultimate in convenience. With just a few mouse clicks, people can shop for practically anything anywhere in the world and have it delivered to their doorsteps within days. In fact, 78 percent of online customers say that they prefer shopping online because it is more convenient than other shopping methods.[24] As convenient as online shopping is, customers still expect high levels of service. Unfortunately, many e-commerce companies treat customer service as an afterthought, an attitude that costs businesses in many ways, including lost customers and a diminished public image. In one study, 79 percent of shoppers who had experienced a frustrating online shopping experience reported that they were not likely to return to the online store. The study also revealed 27 percent of shoppers said that they were less likely to shop at the retailer's physical store.[25]

The average conversion rate for e-commerce sites is just 3.2 percent.[26] In other words, out of 1,000 visitors to the typical company's Web site, just 32 of them actually make a purchase! Sites that are difficult to navigate, slow to load, offer complex checkout systems, or confuse shoppers will turn customers away quickly, never to return. Online merchants must recognize that customer service is just as important (if not more so) on the Web as it is in traditional brick-and-mortar stores.

There is plenty of room for improvement in customer service on the Web. Research by PayPal and comScore shows that 45 percent of Web shoppers who fill their online shopping carts abandon them without checking out and that the average value of the goods in their carts is $109.[27] The most common reasons for leaving a site without purchasing include the following: (1) shipping and handling charges were too high (46 percent), (2) the customer was simply comparison shopping (37 percent), (3) the total cost of the items was higher than the customer anticipated (36 percent), and (4) the customer wanted to either look for a coupon or to make the purchase off-line (27 percent). Even more alarming is the fact that 47 percent of the owners of e-businesses do not know their sites' shopping cart abandonment rate.[28]

When customers do abandon their online shopping carts, companies often can close a significant percentage of those sales by sending a prompt follow-up e-mail designed to win back the customer. One survey by Listrak, an e-mail marketing company, reports that just 11 percent of e-commerce companies send follow-up e-mails to customers who have abandoned their shopping carts.[29] The benefits from doing so can be significant, however. A study by Experian CheetahMail indicates that follow-up e-mails to customers who abandon their carts produce 20 times the transaction rates and revenue of their traditional e-mail marketing campaigns.[30]

Profile

Rockler Woodworking and Hardware

Rockler Woodworking and Hardware, founded in 1954, sells specialty hardware, tools, and woodworking products through its 30 retail stores, a catalog, and its Web site (*www.rockler.com*), which the company has been operating since 1996. Recognizing the potential that abandoned online shopping carts represented, Rockler began sending automated e-mails to shoppers who left their carts without checking out. The e-mails, which contain no incentives (45 percent of companies that send follow-up e-mails offer some kind of incentive), recaptured so many of the company's lost sales that the initiative now accounts for 2 percent of Rockler's total sales![31]

The lesson for e-commerce entrepreneurs is simple: Devote time, energy, and money to developing a functional mechanism for providing superior customer service. Those who do will build a sizeable base of loyal customers who will keep coming back. Perhaps the most significant actions online companies can take to bolster their customer service efforts are to provide a quick, intuitive online checkout process, create a well-staffed and well-trained customer response team, offer a simple return process, and provide an easy order-tracking process so customers can check the status of their orders at any time.

LESSONS FROM THE **STREET-SMART** ➤ entrepreneur

How to Reduce Your Company's Shopping Cart Abandonment Rate

Nearly half of all online shoppers abandon their shopping carts without completing their transactions. This chapter points out the reasons customers abandon their carts. Sometimes they are merely window shopping or just change their minds, but, more often than not, the cause has more to do with a company's Web site, purchase process, or perceived lack of security or customer service. E-commerce entrepreneurs can reduce the likelihood that customers will leave their companies' Web sites frustrated and unlikely to return by taking the following tips from the Street-Smart Entrepreneur:

■ Consider providing free shipping if a customer's order exceeds some minimum purchase. Research by Wharton professor David Bell shows that companies that want to fill relatively few orders should establish higher free-shipping thresholds; firms that want customers to visit regularly—perhaps so that they can sell ads on their site—should use lower shipping thresholds. More than 60 percent of online retailers say that providing free shipping (with conditions) is their most successful marketing tool.

■ If you do not offer free shipping, provide multiple shipping methods and be sure to include a table that shows shoppers the cost of each shipping option— and do it early in the checkout process.

■ Label the cart button "add to cart" rather than "buy now" or "purchase." "Buy now" and similar language creates in customers' minds the impression that their decision is irreversible. The reality is that the

average delay between a customer's first visit to a site and the final purchase is 33 hours and 54 minutes.

■ Reassure customers that their personal information is safe and that their transaction is secure. Security concerns cause 21 percent of Web shoppers to abandon their carts. Many customers look for sites that have been certified as secure by a reliable third-party service such as the Better Business Bureau, VeriSign, TRUSTe, McAfee, and others. Make sure that shoppers feel secure from their first click on your site.

■ Make sure that your site presents an image of credibility. E-businesses must communicate their trustworthiness by providing highly visible privacy policies, customer satisfaction guarantees, exchange and return policies, and contact information. For small companies, including a telephone number and a physical address are important. Photographs of the owners and employees help, too.

■ Reduce the number of steps required to complete the checkout process. Just as in regular retail stores, online customers appreciate a quick, efficient checkout process that is as simple as possible. A convoluted checkout process is an invitation to customers to abandon their shopping carts.

■ Once shoppers have filled their carts, make sure that the "checkout" button is easy to find. Label it clearly and put it in a prominent location.

■ Include a progress indicator on each checkout page. Clearly numbering the steps in the process and letting customers know where they are in that process improves customer-retention rates during checkout.

- Provide a link back to the items in the customers' shopping cart. This allows customers to return to the product page to make sure they have selected the correct item without losing their place in the checkout process.

- Allow customers to see whether an item is in stock on the product page. Customers become frustrated when they learn that an item is out of stock *after* having clicked through most or all of the checkout process.

- Include product photos in the shopping cart. Research shows that simply including product photos increases a company's conversion rate by as much as 10 percent.

- Make it easy for customers to change the contents of their shopping carts. The cart page should allow customers to change quantities, colors, sizes, and other options or to delete an item from the cart (believe it or not!) with just one mouse click.

- Give customers the option of calling to resolve problems they encounter during checkout. A toll-free line enables a company to track the number of problem-solving calls, which can point out flaws in the design of the Web site or the checkout process.

- Make it easy for customers to pay for their online purchases. Credit cards are the most popular online payment method (55 percent of all transactions), but many small online merchants do not generate enough revenue to justify the costs of gaining credit card merchant status. If a small company's credit card sales are no more than $250 per month, a credit card company charges about 35 percent of each transaction, compared to just 3 to 5 percent of monthly credit card sales of at least $7,500 per month. Electronic payment services such as Google's Checkout or PayPal, which is owned by eBay, allow customers to send payments to anyone with an e-mail address through their checking accounts or their credit cards. Customers who sign up for the free service can use their PayPal accounts to buy products online conveniently, and PayPal charges the company making the sale a fee that ranges from 1.9 to 2.9 percent of the transaction, depending on its monthly transaction volume. When a merchant signs on with PayPal, it simply adds PayPal's "Buy Now" button to its site, which customers click to pay with their PayPal accounts.

Kurt Denke and Pam Moore launched Blue Jeans Cable, a company that sells high-quality video and audio cables and connectors as a part-time, home-based, eBay business. Sales grew quickly, and in 2002 the copreneurs decided to launch their own Web site, but they needed a low-cost, convenient, and secure payment-processing system. "We looked at all kinds of payment processing solutions," recalls Denke. "The initial fees to set up a merchant [account] and payment processing gateway were just too much." Denke and Moore settled on PayPal, which charges no up-front or monthly fees, offers very competitive processing rates, and provides a free shopping cart tool. The couple frequently download their merchant sales report and analyze it to understand better their customers' buying habits. Denke and Moore's home-based business has "exceeded our wildest expectations," says Denke. Sales are rising fast, and 95 percent of Blue Jeans Cable's sales are processed through PayPal.

- Encourage user reviews and reward customers who provide them. User reviews can be an important selling tool online. When shoppers read about the positive experiences that customers have had with a company, they are more likely to make purchases.

- Incorporate a short survey of randomly chosen customers who abandon their shopping carts. The results can help you to improve their online shopping experience and lower your cart abandonment rates.

Sources: Based on Terry Jukes, "8 Best Practices for Reducing Shopping Cart Abandonment," E-Marketing and Commerce, February 12, 2009, *www.emarketingandcommerce.com/article/8-best-practices reducing shopping-cart-abandonment/1*; Bryan Eisenberg, "20 Tips to Minimize Shopping Cart Abandonment, Part 1," ClickZ, August 8, 2003, pp. 1–2; Bryan Eisenberg, "20 Tips to Minimize Shopping Cart Abandonment, Part 2," ClickZ, August 15, 2003, pp. 1–2; "Reasons Why Web Site Visitors Abandoned Their Shopping Carts," SeeWhy, June 3, 2010, *http://seewhy.com/blog/2010/06/03/reasons-why-website-visitors-abandoned-their-shopping-carts/*; "Digital Window Shopping: The Long Journey to 'Buy'" (Santa Clara, CA: McAfee, 2009), pp. 3–4; "Customer Case Study: Blue Jeans Cable," PayPal, 2006, *www.paypal.com/en_US/pdf/bluejeanscableCaseStudy.pdf*; Sally Lowery, "Got the Shopping Cart Blues?" Bronto Software Inc., 2009.

Myth 8. Flashy Web Sites Are Better Than Simple Ones

Businesses that fall into this trap pour significant amounts of money into designing flashy Web sites with all of the "bells and whistles." The logic is that to stand out on the Web a site really has to sparkle. That logic leads to a "more is better" mentality when designing a site. On the Web, however, "more" does *not* necessarily equate to "better." A Web site that performs efficiently and loads quickly is essential to online retail success. Although fancy graphics, photographs, music, bright colors, and spinning icons can attract attention, sites filled with "cornea gumbo" are distracting, slow to download, and generally ineffective. Sites that download slowly usually never have the chance to sell because customers click to another site. A study by Forrester Research and Akamai concludes that the new threshold for Web site download times is just 2 seconds and that 40 percent of online shoppers will wait no longer than 3 seconds for a Web site to load before moving on to another site.[32] A study by TagMan, a company that specializes in digital tracking and reporting, reports that a 1-second delay in a Web page loading results in 10 percent of users abandoning the page. "Businesses do not understand the impact of poor site performance," warns Brian Walker, an analyst at Forrester Research. "Customers not only will bail out on a session or a [shopping] cart, but they also may not return." Walker points out that the company's research shows that more than 25 percent of customers are less likely to shop at a company's brick-and-mortar store if they have a bad experience online.[33] The lesson: Keep the design of your site simple so that pages download in no more than 2 or 3 seconds and make sure that it performs effectively.

Myth 9. It's What's Up Front That Counts

Designing an attractive Web site is important to building a successful e-business. However, designing the back office, the systems that take over once a customer places an order on a Web site, is just as important as designing the site itself. If the behind-the-scenes support is not in place or cannot handle the traffic from the Web site, a company's entire e-commerce effort will come crashing down. Although e-commerce can lower many costs of doing business, it still requires a basic infrastructure somewhere in the channel of distribution to process orders, maintain inventory, fill orders, and handle customer service. Many entrepreneurs hoping to launch virtual businesses are discovering the need for a "click-and-mortar" approach to provide the necessary infrastructure to serve their customers. "The companies with warehouses, supply-chain management, and solid customer service are going to be the ones that survive," says Daryl Plummer, head of the Gartner Group's Internet and New Media division.[34]

To customers, a business is only as good as its last order, and many e-companies are not measuring up. Many small e-tailers' Web sites do not offer real-time inventory lookup, which gives online shoppers the ability to see whether an item they want to purchase is actually in stock. In addition, many have not yet linked their Web sites to an automated back office, which means that processing orders takes longer and that errors are more likely. As software to integrate Web sites with the back office becomes easier to use and more affordable, more small businesses will use them to offer these features.

ENTREPRENEURIAL
Profile

David Cox: Fragrances of Ireland

Fragrances of Ireland, a small company founded in 1983 in the village of Kilmacanogue, Ireland, by Brian Cox and Donald Pratt, sells a line of Irish perfumes, colognes, soaps, and toiletries across Ireland, the United Kingdom, Canada, and the United States. The fast-growing company sells its products in more than 300 stores in Ireland and the United Kingdom and on its Web site (*www.perfume.ie*) but was falling farther behind on its deliveries as volume increased. Current owner David Cox was struggling to manage the company's inventory because reports were inaccurate and outdated. Cox turned to Webgistix, an order fulfillment company, which helped the company implement a Web-based order fulfillment system that allows managers to view orders, check inventory levels, and generate customized reports anytime. Fragrances of Ireland's new system has enabled the company to gain control of its inventory and to speed up delivery times by getting orders out the same day that customers place them.[35]

Web-based entrepreneurs often discover that the greatest challenge their businesses face is not necessarily attracting customers on the Web but creating a workable order fulfillment strategy. Order fulfillment involves everything required to get goods from a warehouse into a customer's hands and includes order processing, warehousing, picking and packing, shipping, and billing. Some entrepreneurs choose to handle order fulfillment in-house with their own employees, whereas others find it more economical to hire specialized fulfillment houses to handle these functions. **Virtual order fulfillment** (or drop-shipping) suits many e-tailers perfectly. When a customer orders a product from its Web site, the company forwards the order to its wholesaler or distributor, which then ships the product to the customer with the online merchant's label on it.

Although e-tailers avoid the risks and problems associated with managing inventory, they lose control over delivery times and service quality. In addition, for some small businesses, finding a fulfillment house willing to handle a relatively small volume of orders at a reasonable price can be difficult. Major fulfillment providers that focus on small companies include Amazon.com, FedEx, UPS, DHL, ShipWire, Webgistix, and WeFulfillIT.com.

Myth 10. It's Too Late to Get on the Web

A common myth, especially among small business owners, is that those companies that have not yet moved onto the Web have missed a golden opportunity. One Internet entrepreneur who has launched two multimillion-dollar companies, compares e-commerce to the California gold rush in the mid-nineteenth century, "The [e-commerce] landscape looks like California must have looked in 1850. The gold rush is over, and the easy money is gone. However, much more gold was mined in California after 1850 than before; so it is with e-commerce. Enormous opportunities are still available online to those smart enough to take advantage of them."[36] The reality is that e-commerce is still very young, and companies are still figuring out how to succeed on the Web. For every e-commerce site that exists, many others have failed. An abundance of online business opportunities exists for those entrepreneurs insightful enough to spot them and clever enough to capitalize on them.

One fact of e-commerce that has emerged is the importance of speed. Companies doing business on the Web have discovered that those who reach customers first often have a significant advantage over their slower rivals. "The lesson of the Web is not how the big eat the small, but how the fast eat the slow," says a manager at a venture capital firm specializing in Web-based companies.[37] Succumbing to this myth often leads entrepreneurs to make a fundamental mistake once they finally decide to go online: They believe they have to have a "perfect" site before they can launch it. Few businesses get their sites "right" the first time. In fact, the most successful e-commerce sites are constantly changing, removing what does not work and adding new features to see what does. Successful Web sites are much like a well-designed flower garden, constantly growing and improving, yet changing to reflect the climate of each season. Their creators worry less about creating the perfect site at the outset than about getting a site online and then fixing it, tweaking it, and updating it to meet changing customer demands.

Strategies for E-Success

4. Explain the basic strategies entrepreneurs should follow to achieve success in their e-commerce efforts.

The typical Internet user in the United States spends an average of 13.2 hours a week online, almost as much time as the average person spends each week watching television. However, converting these Web users into paying customers requires a business to do more than merely set up a Web site and wait for the hits to start rolling in. Doing business from a Web site is like setting up shop on a dead-end street or a back alley. You may be ready to sell, but no one knows you are there! Building sufficient volume for a site takes energy, time, money, creativity, and, perhaps most important, a well-defined strategy. Many entrepreneurs choose to start their e-commerce efforts small and simply and then expand them as sales grow and their needs become more sophisticated. Others make major investments in creating full-blown, interconnected sites at the outset. The cost of e-commerce varies significantly, depending on the options that an entrepreneur chooses. Following are some guidelines for building a successful Web strategy for a small e-company.

Focus on a Niche in the Market

Like Curly, the crusty old trail boss in the movie *City Slickers*, who said that the secret to happiness was "one thing," many small businesses are finding success on the Web by focusing on one thing. Rather than try to compete head-to-head with the dominant players on the Web who have the resources and the recognition to squash smaller competitors, smart entrepreneurs focus on serving market niches. Smaller companies' limited resources usually are better spent serving niche markets than trying to be everything to everyone. The idea is to concentrate on serving a small corner of the market the giants have overlooked. Niches exist in every industry and can be highly profitable, given the right strategy for serving them. A niche can be defined in many ways, including by geography, by customer profile, by product, by product usage, and many others.

Like Curly, the crusty trail boss in *City Slickers* who said that the secret to happiness was "one thing," many small companies are finding success online by focusing on one thing—a market niche.

Source: Photos 12/Alamy Images

ENTREPRENEURIAL
Profile

James Hughes:
Caledonian Creations

James Hughes launched Caledonian Creations, a company that specializes in making leather goods such as sporrans (the pouch worn from the belt on the front of a kilt), straps, kilt belts, and Celtic bags, when he was in his early twenties after his business plan helped him win financing from the Prince's Scottish Business Trust, a fund established by the Prince of Wales to help young people in the United Kingdom launch businesses. One disadvantage of a focus strategy is being so narrowly focused that attracting a large enough customer base can be a challenge. Without the power of the Web, it is unlikely that Caledonian Creations, with its highly specialized product line, would be able to survive from its location in Drymen, Scotland![38]

The Web allows small businesses to attract niche customers that would have been impossible to reach in sufficient volume without it. Because of its broad reach, the Web is the ideal mechanism for implementing a focus strategy because small companies can reach large numbers of customers with a common interest.

Develop a Community

On the Web, competitors are just a mouse click away. To attract customers and keep them coming back, e-companies have discovered the need to offer more than just quality products and excellent customer service. Many seek to develop a community of customers with similar interests, the nucleus of which is their Web site. The idea is to increase customer loyalty by giving customers the chance to interact with other like-minded visitors or with experts to discuss and learn more about topics they are passionate about. E-mail lists, chat rooms, customer polls ("What is your favorite sports drink?"), blogs, guest books, and message boards are powerful tools for building a community of visitors at a site because they give visitors the opportunity to have conversations about products, services, and topics that interest them.

Small businesses that are most successful at building a community enlist their most passionate customers as company evangelists. Companies that successfully create a community around their Web sites turn their customers into loyal fans who keep coming back and, better yet, invite others to join them.

Attract Visitors by Giving Away "Freebies"

One of the most important words on the Internet is "free." Many successful e-merchants have discovered the ability to attract visitors to their sites by giving away something free and then selling them something else. One e-commerce consultant calls this cycle of giving something away and then selling something "the rhythm of the Web."[39] The "freebie" must be something that customers value, but it does *not* have to be expensive nor does it have to be a product. In fact, one of the most common giveaways on the Web is *information*. (After all, that's what most people on the Web are after!) Creating a free online or e-mail newsletter with links to your company's site, of course, and to others of interest is one of the most effective ways of drawing potential customers to a site. Meaningful content presented in a clear, professional fashion is a must. Experts advise keeping online newsletters short—no more than about 600 words.

ENTREPRENEURIAL
Profile

Catherine Bean and Megan Murphy: Bella of Cape Cod

Catherine Bean and Megan Murphy started Bella ("Beautiful, Eclectic, Lovely, Luscious, and Affordable") of Cape Cod in 2004 by selling affordable, fashionable jewelry at home parties. The stay-at-home moms soon realized that the number of jewelry parties they could host was limited by their time, their schedules, and the short New England tourist season. They came up with the creative solution of holding Web-based virtual parties hosted by their online customers. To make their idea work, they needed an inexpensive yet effective way to promote their online parties to customers. Bean and Murphy created a newsletter packed with interesting stories about their jewelry, tips on how to care for it and wear it, and, of course, promotions about their parties and products. The virtual parties were a big hit with customers, and each party resulted in more customers on the company's contact list, which has grown from 1,500 people to nearly 8,100. The e-mail newsletter's open rate is an impressive 30 percent, and Bella's sales, especially in the "off season," have increased significantly.[40]

Make Creative Use of E-Mail, but Avoid Becoming a "Spammer"

Used properly and creatively, e-mail can be an effective, low cost way to build traffic on a Web site. E-commerce companies cite e-mail as the most effective marketing technique (89 percent), followed by pay-per-click searches (80 percent) and search engine optimization (53 percent).[41] E-mail **click-through rates**, the percentage of recipients who open an e-mail and click the link to the company's Web site, average 6.0 percent.[42] Marketing e-mails sent on Wednesdays have the highest combination of open and click-through rates (see Figure 3). A survey by eROI shows that the best time of day to send marketing e-mails is mid-day, from 10 A.M. to 2 P.M.[43]

Just as with newsletters, an e-mail's content should offer something of value to recipients. Customers welcome well-constructed permission e-mail that directs them to a company's site for information or special deals, unlike unsolicited and universally despised e-mails known as spam. Unfortunately, getting legitimate e-mails noticed has become more challenging for business

FIGURE 3
E-Mail Open and Click-Through Rates by Day of the Week

Source: eROI, 2007.

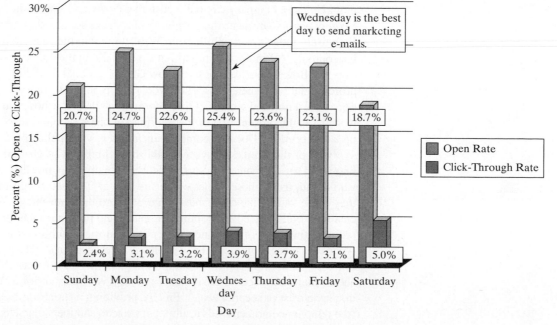

TABLE 1 Does Your E-Mail Measure Up to the Anti-Spam Test?

1. Is the content of your e-mail appropriate for your audience? Are recipients likely to be interested in the offers or articles you are sending? The biggest problem with sales-oriented e-mails and the primary cause of low open and click-through rates is irrelevant content.
2. Does the e-mail offer something of value to recipients—an invitation to a special sale, a free newsletter filled with useful information, or something similar? Sending frivolous e-mails that pack little or no value to customers is one surefire way to send your company's click-through rate plummeting.
3. Has your e-mail provider been blacklisted by spam-screening tools?
4. Have the recipients on your e-mail list opted into your e-mail list? Trolling Internet user lists for e-mail addresses is *not* an acceptable way to build a recipient list.
5. Does the subject line include your company's name? Is the subject line accurate and not misleading? Do *not* include "$$$" in the subject line, as so many spam messages do.
6. Is the e-mail readable? Some e-mails sent in HTML format can appear garbled and unreadable on some computers.
7. Is the frequency of the e-mail appropriate? Customers do not appreciate being hammered by 20 e-mails from a company in 1 week.
8. Is the timing of your e-mail appropriate? Monday mornings, when people are returning to work from the weekend and their inboxes are full of messages, is *not* the best time to send an e-mail.
9. Can recipients opt out of your e-mail list if they choose to?
10. Does the e-mail contain your company's valid mailing address? In 2003, Congress passed the CAN-SPAM Act, which did not ban spam but put limitations on how marketers can use e-mail as part of their marketing tools. This is one of the act's requirements.

owners because spam is on the rise. Symantec, a company that provides online security and software services, estimates that 89.8 percent of all e-mails sent are spam.[44]

Companies often collect visitors' e-mail addresses when they register to receive a "freebie." To be successful at collecting a sufficient number of e-mail addresses, a company must make clear to customers that they will receive messages that are meaningful to them and that the company will not sell e-mail addresses to others (which should be part of its posted privacy policy). Once a company has a customer's permission to send information in additional e-mail messages, it has a meaningful marketing opportunity to create a long-term customer relationship. Table 1 includes a spam test to which every company should submit its e-mail campaigns.

Make Sure Your Web Site Says "Credibility"

Many studies have concluded that trust and security issues are the leading inhibitors of online shopping. Unless a company can build customers' *trust* in its Web site, selling is virtually impossible. Visitors begin to evaluate the credibility of a site as soon as they arrive. In fact, one study says that Web users judge the credibility of a Web site within the first one-twentieth of a second (50 milliseconds)![45] "Windows of opportunity, especially in the online environment, close very quickly," says Jay Bower, president of Crossbow Group, a digital marketing company.[46] Does the site look professional? Are there misspelled words and typographical errors? If the site provides information, does it note the sources of that information? If so, are those sources legitimate? Are they trustworthy? Is the presentation of the information fair and objective, or is it biased? Has the site been updated recently? Does the company include a privacy policy posted in an obvious place?

One of the simplest ways to establish credibility with customers is to use brand names they know and trust. Whether a company sells nationally recognized brands or its own well-known private brand, using those names on its site creates a sense of legitimacy. People buy brand names they trust, and online companies can use that to their advantage. Another effective way to build customer confidence is by joining an online seal program such as TRUSTe or BBBOnLine. The online equivalent of the Underwriter Laboratories stamp or the Good Housekeeping Seal of Approval, these seals mean that a company meets certain standards concerning the privacy of customers' information and the resolution of customer complaints. A survey by *Consumer Reports* shows that 71 percent of customers say that it is important for a Web site they purchase from to display a trust or security seal.[47] Finally, providing a street address, an e-mail address, and a toll-free telephone number sends a subtle message to shoppers that a legitimate business is behind the

Web site. Many small companies include photographs of their brick-and-mortar stores and of their founders and employees to combat the Web's anonymity and to let shoppers know that they are supporting a friendly small business.

Consider Forming Strategic Alliances

Most small companies seeking e-commerce success lack the brand and name recognition that larger, more established companies have. Creating that sort of recognition on the Web requires a significant investment of both time and money, two things that most small companies find scarce. If building name recognition is one of the keys to success on the Web, how can small companies with their limited resources hope to compete? One option is to form strategic alliances with bigger companies that can help a small business achieve what it could not accomplish alone. One expert says, "The question is no longer, 'Should I consider an alliance?' Now the questions are 'What form should the alliance take?' and 'How do I find the right partner?'"[48]

One of the simplest ways to begin forging alliances online is through an **affiliate marketing program**. Also known as *referral* or *associate marketing*, this technique involves an online merchant paying a commission to another online business (the affiliate) for directing customers to the merchant's Web site. As social media have become more important, affiliate marketing has slipped in its popularity. According to the Affiliate Marketing Survey Report, just 15 percent of online merchants say that affiliate marketing drives a high volume of sales for their businesses.[49] Still, Forrester Research predicts that affiliate marketing revenues will increase from $1.9 billion in 2009 to $4 billion in 2014.[50]

Make the Most of the Web's Global Reach

The Internet has reduced dramatically the cost of launching a global business initiative; even the tiniest of businesses can engage in international business with a well-designed Web site. Still, despite the Web's reputation as an international marketplace, many Web entrepreneurs fail to utilize its global reach. Nearly 90 percent of the 1.9 billion people around the world who use the Internet live outside the United States. Only 27.7 percent of Web users speak English.[51] It does not make sense for entrepreneurs to limit their Web sites to just a small percentage of the world because of a language barrier. A top manager at Travelocity, a travel-planning Web site, says that whenever his company adds country-specific features to its site, sales in that country typically double![52]

ENTREPRENEURIAL
Profile
Diane Irvine: Blue Nile

At Blue Nile, a leading online retailer of diamonds and fine jewelry, global sales have proved to be the company's engine for growth, displaying far greater increases than domestic sales. Sales in foreign countries took off after Blue Nile created country-specific versions of its Web site with a local currency payment option in 35 nations. CEO Diane Irvine says that Blue Nile was able to expand at a very low cost without building stores or warehouses abroad. "It's all about the technology," she says.[53]

E-companies seeking to draw significant sales from foreign markets must design their sites with customers from other lands and cultures in mind. A common mechanism is to include several "language buttons" on the opening page of a site that take customers to pages in the language of their choice. Companies trying to establish a foothold in foreign markets by setting up Web sites dedicated to them run the same risk that companies setting up physical locations there do: offending international visitors by using the business conventions and standards they are accustomed to using in the United States. Business practices, even those used on the Web that are acceptable, even expected, in the United States, may be taboo in other countries. Color schemes can be important, too. Selecting the "wrong" colors and symbols on a site targeting people in a particular country can hurt sales and offend visitors. A little research into the subtleties of a target country's culture and business practices can save a great deal of embarrassment and money! Creating secure, simple, and reliable payment methods for foreign customers also increases sales.

When translating the content of their Web pages into other languages, entrepreneurs must use extreme caution. This is *not* the time to pull out their notes from an introductory Spanish course and begin their own translations. Hiring professional translation and localization services to convert a company's Web content into other languages minimizes the likelihood of a company unintentionally offending foreign customers.

Promote Your Web Site Online and Off-Line

E-commerce entrepreneurs have to use every means available—both online and off-line—to promote their Web sites and to drive traffic to them. Cross-promotions in which a physical store promotes the Web site and the Web site promotes the physical store can boost sales in both venues. In addition to using traditional online techniques, such as registering with search engines, creating banner ads, and joining banner exchange programs, Web entrepreneurs must promote their sites off-line as well. Ads in other media such as direct mail or newspapers that mention a site's URL will bring customers to it. It is also a good idea to put the company's Web address on *everything* a company publishes, from its advertisements and letterhead to shopping bags and business cards. A passive approach to generating Web site traffic is a recipe for failure. Entrepreneurs who are as innovative at promoting their e-businesses as they are at creating them can attract impressive numbers of visitors to their sites.

ENTREPRENEURIAL
Profile

Ling Valentine:
Ling's Cars

Ling Valentine, founder of Ling's Cars, and the military truck she uses to promote her company's Web site.

Source: LingsCars.com

Ling Valentine, owner of Ling's Cars, one of the most successful car-leasing operations in the United Kingdom, purchased a used six-wheel military truck and had her husband build a fake nuclear missile on top of it imprinted with her company's Web address, Lingscars.com, to promote her site. Ling uses the truck and missile as a movable billboard, placing it on busy highways, where millions of drivers see it every year. "My nuclear missile truck brings in loads of visitors every time I park it next to a motorway," says Valentine.[54]

Use Web 2.0 Tools to Attract and Retain Customers

The social aspects of the Internet that are evident on sites such as Facebook and Twitter have become part of companies' e-commerce efforts. Known as enterprise 2.0, these online selling techniques recognize that shoppers, especially young ones, expect to take a proactive role in their shopping experience by writing (and reading) product reviews, asking questions, posting comments in blogs, and engaging in other interactive behavior. According to the Pew Internet & American Life Project, 69 percent of adult Internet users have watched online videos, 33 percent read blogs, and 46 percent participate in social networking sites.[55] Simply inviting customers to post product reviews on a site can boost sales. A global study by Nielsen reports that 70 percent of online shoppers say that they trust customer reviews that are posted online when making a purchase decision, second only to reviews from people that they know (90 percent).[56]

Small businesses are responding to the opportunity to connect with their customers online by adding the following social media to their e-commerce strategies:

- **Mashups.** A **mashup** is a Web site or an application that combines content from multiple sources into a single Web service. For example, Twitzu is a mashup that allows users to manage invitations and responses to events. They invite their Twitter followers to an event—the grand opening of a new location, for example—and then receive responses from guests on Twitzu.
- **Really Simple Syndication (RSS). Really Simple Syndication** is an application that allows subscribers to aggregate content from their favorite Web sites into a single feed that is delivered automatically whenever the content is updated. RSS is ideal for companies whose customers are information junkies. "[RSS] is a must-have for any company Web site or blog because it allows people to track current news via their RSS feeds," says Louis Columbus, an expert on using social media.[57]

■ **Social networking.** Many small businesses attract potential customers to their Web sites by adding a social networking component that allows visitors to engage in "conversation" with one another through bulletin boards, blogs, and links to social Web sites such as Facebook and Twitter. Tony Hsieh, CEO of online shoe retailer Zappos, uses his Twitter account to update more than 14,000 followers on news about the company and its products.[58] Other companies are finding that enabling customers to post their favorite products to their MySpace and Facebook profiles increases sales.

ENTREPRENEURIAL
Profile

Gina Drennon: Feather Your Nest

Gina Drennon, owner of Feather Your Nest, a specialty shop in Eureka Springs, Arkansas, that sells a unique collection of handmade and vintage gifts and decorations, has made her business stand out from the competition by actively engaging customers in a variety of online social media. Shoppers can find Feather Your Nest on Facebook and Twitter and can learn about what's happening behind the scenes by reading Drennon's blog. "I've seen our Web stats increase, followers increase, interactions increase, and most important, sales increase," she says. "I've made many meaningful connections with bloggers and magazine editors that have featured our products and our store, which brings us huge amounts of attention that you really cannot put a price on. At least half of the national press we've received is due to contacts we've made over social media."[59]

■ **Wikis.** A **wiki** is a dynamic collection of Web pages that allows users to add to or edit their content. The most popular wiki is Wikipedia, the user-created online encyclopedia for which users provide the content. Some companies use wikis to encourage customers to participate in the design of their products, a process called **co-creation**.

■ **Widgets.** Another tool that small companies use to attract attention on the Web is **widgets** (also known as *gadgets*), which are low-cost applications that appear like small television screens on Web sites, blogs, or computer desktops and perform specific functions. Entrepreneurs can create their own widgets or purchase them from developers and customize them, adding their own names, brands, and logos. Customers and visitors can download the widget to their desktops or perhaps post it to their own blogs or Facebook pages, where other Web users will see it. A popular widget not only drives customers to a site but can also improve a company's ranking on major search engines. "It's a great way to continually remind people that you exist," says Ivan Pope, CEO of widget developer Snipperoo.[60] Pizza retailer Papa John's developed a widget that allows customers to order a pizza from almost anywhere, including a Facebook page, a YouTube video, a Google search—even a cell phone.[61]

Develop an Effective Search Engine Optimization (SEO) Strategy

Because of the growing popularity of search engines among Internet shoppers, Web search strategies have become an essential part of online companies' promotion strategies. Because the sheer number of Web pages is overwhelming, it is no surprise that Internet shoppers use search engines extensively. A study by Compete shows that search engines are the most common tool that online shoppers use to find the products and services they want; 61 percent of shoppers say that they always or often use search engines when shopping online.[62] As a result, companies are devoting more of their marketing budgets to search engine listings that are focused on landing their Web sites at or near the top of the most popular search engines. For a company engaged in e-commerce, a well-defined search marketing strategy is an essential part of its overall marketing strategy.

One of the biggest challenges facing e-commerce entrepreneurs is maintaining the effectiveness of their search engine marketing strategies. Because the most popular search engines are constantly updating and refining their algorithms, the secretive formulas and methodologies search engines use to find and rank the results of Web searches, Web entrepreneurs also must evaluate and refine constantly their search strategies. Allan Keiter, owner of MyRatePlan.com, a company that helps customers compare cellular phone plans, traditionally had relied on natural listings on the search engine giant Google to direct customers to his company's Web site. His company almost always appeared in the top 10 results list for customers looking for information on calling plans. Then Google engineers changed the algorithm used to produce search results, and MyRatePlan.com virtually disappeared from its search results. Keiter watched helplessly as his company's revenues plunged by 20 percent.[63]

A company's Web search strategy must recognize the two basic types of search engine results: natural or organic listings and paid or sponsored listings. **Natural (or organic) listings** often arise as a result of "spiders," powerful programs search engines use to crawl around the Web, analyzing sites for keywords, links, and other data. Based on what they find, spiders index Web sites so that a search engine can display a listing of relevant Web sites when a person enters a keyword in the engine to start a search. Some search engines use people-powered searches rather than spider-powered ones to assemble their indexes. With natural listings, an entrepreneur's goal is to get his or her Web site displayed at or near the top of the list of search results. **Search engine optimization (SEO)** involves managing the content, keywords, titles, tags, features, and design of a Web site so that it appears at or near the top of Internet search results. The reason that SEO is so important: iProspect reports that 68 percent of search engine users click a link to a site that appears on the first page of the search results.[64] "The difference between being seen on page one and page two of search results can mean thousands, even millions, of dollars for a business in revenue," says Martin Falle, CEO of SEO Research, a search engine marketing company.[65] A useful resource for entrepreneurs is SEO Book, a search engine optimization site (*www.seobook.com*) that offers both free tools and more than 100 training modules on a variety of SEO topics for a fee.

Companies can use the following tips to improve their search placement results:

- Conduct brainstorming sessions to develop a list of keywords and phrases that searchers are likely to use when using a search engine to locate a company's products and services and then use those words and phrases on your Web pages. Usually, simple terms are better than industry jargon.
- Use Google's AdWords Keyword Tool to determine how many monthly searches users conduct globally and locally for a keyword or phrase. More specific, lower-volume keywords and phrases usually produce higher search rankings because they provide potential customers the more focused results they are seeking.
- Use relevant keywords in the title tags (meta tags, which are limited to 25 characters) and headlines of your Web pages. Most search engines are geared to pick them up. For best results, you should focus each page of your site on one specific keyword or phrase, which should appear in the page's title. Placing keywords in these critical locations can be tedious, but it produces better search results for the companies that take the time to do it.
- Visit competitors' sites for keyword ideas, but avoid using the exact phrases. Simply right-clicking a competitor's Web page and choosing "View Source" will display the keywords used in the meta tags on the site.
- Ask customers which words and phrases they use when searching for the products and services the company sells.
- Use data analysis tools to review Web logs to find the words and phrases (and the search engines) that have brought visitors to the company's Web site.
- Check blogs and bulletin boards related to the company's products and services for potential key terms.
- Don't forget about misspellings; people often misspell the words they type into search engines. Include them in your list.
- Hire services such as Wordtracker that monitor and analyze Web users' search engine tendencies.
- Block irrelevant results with "negative keywords," those that are excluded in a search.
- Place links to your Web site on high-profile Web sites. Search engines rank sites that have external links to high-volume sites higher than those that do not. John W. Tuggle, founder of Learn Guitar Now, an online company that sells guitar instruction, benefits from having one of the leading guitar makers, Gibson Guitars, post links to his Web site and several of his tutorial videos on its site. Before going online, Tuggle made just $19,000 a year giving guitar lessons and had to work a second job. With his online business, Tuggle now earns $100,000 a year, "and it just keeps going up," he says.[66]
- Start a blog. Well-written blogs not only draw potential customers to your site, but they also tend to attract links from other Web sites. Blogs also allow entrepreneurs to use keywords strategically and frequently, which moves their sites up in search engine rankings.

■ Post videos on your site. In addition to uploading them to video sites such as YouTube, companies can wait for organic listings to appear or they can submit their videos to search engines for listing. Forrester Research estimates that a properly submitted video is 50 times more likely to achieve a first-page listing on Google than any text-based page.[67]

Because organic listings can take months to materialize, many e-commerce companies rely on paid listings, which give them an immediate presence in search engines. **Paid, or sponsored, listings** are short text advertisements with links to the sponsoring company's Web site that appear on the results pages of a search engine when a user types in a keyword or phrase. Entrepreneurs use paid search listings to accomplish what natural listings cannot. Fortunately, just five search engines—Google, Yahoo!, Microsoft Bing, AOL, and Ask.com—account for 99 percent of the searches conducted in the United States.[68] Google, the most popular search engine with nearly 72 percent of all searches, displays paid listings as "sponsored links" at the top and down the side of each results page, and Yahoo! shows "sponsored results" at the top and the bottom of its results pages. Advertisers bid on keywords to determine their placement on a search engine's results page. On Google, an ad's placement in the search results is a function of the ad's relevance (determined by a quality score of 1 to 10 that Google assigns) and the advertiser's bid on the keyword. The ad that gets the most prominent placement (at the top) of the search engine's results page when a user types in that keyword on the search engine is the one with the highest combination of quality score and bid price. An advertiser pays only when a shopper clicks through to its Web site from the search engine. For this reason, paid listings also are called *pay-for-placement, pay-per-click,* or *pay-for-performance ads.* At one popular search engine, the average bid for keywords in its paid listings is 40 cents, but some words can bring as much as $100!* For small e-commerce companies, the average cost for a pay-per-click keyword has risen from 39 cents in 2004 to 52 cents today.[69] Although paid listings can be expensive, they allow advertisers to evaluate their effectiveness using the statistical reports the search engine generates. Pay-per-click advertisers can control costs by geo-targeting their ads, having them appear only in certain areas, and by setting a spending limit per day.

Using generic terms results in large numbers of searches but often produces very small conversion rates and very little in sales; normally, entrepreneurs get better results bidding on more precise, lower volume keywords. Rather than compete with much larger companies for 5 or 10 common keywords, a more effective strategy is to bid on 200 less popular keywords.

ENTREPRENEURIAL Profile

Tomima Edmark: Andra Group Inc.

Tomima Edmark, CEO of Andra Group Inc., a business that sells lingerie at HerRoom.com and men's underwear at HisRoom.com, has seen the return on her company's paid listings increase by at least 100 percent since shifting to this strategy. Andra Group now bids on about 36,000 keywords, including more specific terms, up from 12,000 words before. "For example, 'bra' is a generic term, and there's a ton of traffic on it, but not high conversion," says Edmark. "We have been able to find specific phrases with 'bra' in them [such as specific brands and sizes] that turned our bra campaign profitable."[70]

One problem facing companies that rely on paid listings to generate Web traffic is **click fraud**, which occurs when a company pays for clicks that are generated by someone with no interest in or intent to purchase a product or service. "Clickbots," programs that can generate thousands of phony clicks on a Web site, are a common source of click fraud. Experts estimate that the pay-per-click fraud rate is between 15 and 17.5 percent.[71] Web analytics software can help online merchants detect click fraud, which can be quite costly. Large numbers of visitors who leave within seconds of arriving at a site, computer IP addresses that appear from all over the world, and pay-per-click costs that rise without any corresponding increase in sales are clues that a company is a victim of click fraud.

---

*An online merchant's cost per sale = cost per click ÷ merchant's conversion rate. For example, a merchant with a 1 percent conversion rate who submits a keyword bid of 10 cents per click is paying $10 per sale ($0.10 ÷ 0.01 = $10).

IN THE ENTREPRENEURIAL
SPOTLIGHT   A "Gilt"-Free Shopping Experience

It is noon on a typical weekday, and customers are waiting to pounce on the discounted merchandise as soon as the sale kicks off, eager to snap up a great deal on clothing from designers such as Rodarte, Derek Lam, Christian Louboutin, and others, because they know the best bargains go very quickly. Designer sample sales typically are by invitation only, and fashionistas work their list of contacts to finagle invitations to these private events, where they can purchase luxury brand merchandise at discounts of 50 to 70 percent. Shoppers line up around the block for the semi-annual Barneys Warehouse Sale in New York City and, because all sales are final, often strip down to their underwear between the racks to try on a $3,000 dress marked down to $600.

This particular sample sale has a different twist, however, because more than 100,000 customers will be attending, making this the most crowded store in the city. Except that there is no store. Gilt Groupe, founded in 2007 by Alexis Maybank and Alexandra Wilkis Wilson (who are known inside the company as A&A), runs "flash sales" entirely online. Access to Gilt's Web site is by invitation only (which gives it an air of exclusivity, exactly what the designers whose items are sold there are looking for), but, because the site has limited access, none of the sales or merchandise shows up in online searches. Landing an invitation to join is much easier than scoring an invitation to a brick-and-mortar New York sample sale, however. One of Gilt's 2 million customers (75 percent of whom are women) can issue an invitation or interested shoppers can contact the company's customer service department to receive one.

On its Web site, Gilt hosts about 70 sales each week and runs each one for just 36 hours before taking all of the merchandise down. "Whereas a department store might move a certain amount of product in a season, we can do it in 36 hours," says Amanda Graber, Gilt's public relations manager. The speed of the sales and the discreetness with which the company conducts them appeal to designers, some of whom were initially reluctant to offer their merchandise through Gilt. Thanks to the site's tremendous success and rapid growth rate, that reluctance has withered. "I have so many brands banging down our door, that I have to say 'no,'" says Wilkis Wilson. Gilt also boasts an incredible sell-through rate, the proportion of a designer's inventory that customers actually purchase. In the typical department store, the sell-through rate is about 65 percent across a 12-week season; at Gilt, the sell-through rate typically is 92 percent, which means Gilt customers tend to pick the virtual racks clean! "Most online shopping mirrors brick-and-mortar stores," says Susan Lyne, Gilt's CEO. "They're

not taking advantage of what's uniquely possible online, the heightened sense of entertainment and competition. A big part of the Gilt promise is discovery: You come every day, and it's new every day." Recently, an ostrich feather jacket from Alessandro Dell'Aqua, originally priced at $3,175, sold for $618. Normally priced at $2,420, a Marc Jacobs leather bomber jacket sold for $548. Generating sales totally online means that Gilt has a tremendous cost advantage over its brick-and-mortar rivals, which incur the expense of operating physical locations.

Maybank and Wilkis Wilson have been friends since they were students at Harvard, where they met in a Portuguese class. After completing Harvard Business School, Maybank learned the ropes of e-commerce at eBay and AOL, and Wilkis Wilson embarked on a career as a merchandising executive at luxury brands Bulgari and Louis Vuitton. The two had been discussing ideas for starting a business and told Kevin Ryan, former CEO of DoubleClick and now a venture capitalist, about their ideas. According to Ryan, his "eureka" moment occurred one day when he saw a long line of women waiting in line to get into a Marc Jacobs sale on New York's 18th Street. "If there are 200 women who are willing to stand in this line," he recalls thinking, "that means that in the United States there are probably hundreds of thousands. But they don't live in New York, they're busy right now, and they just can't do that. We can bring the sale to them." The skills, experience, and networks of the three proved to be the ideal launching pad for Gilt Groupe. Ryan, who knew of a French company called Vente Privée that had achieved success in Europe with online designer fashion sales, invested some seed capital, and the Web site went live in late 2007.

Sales at Gilt have grown very rapidly. When Maybank and Wilkis Wilson launched the site, there were just 15,000 members, most of whom came through their network of contacts. Today, Gilt boasts more than 2 million members—and growing. Just 2 years after start-up, sales had reached $170 million, and 1 year later they were pushing $500 million. Gilt's success has convinced design houses to create clothing specifically for the site rather than merely selling overstocked merchandise. The company now works with more than 700 brands and has launched other sites such as Jettsetter, which offers travel deals; Gilt Fuse, which offers lower-priced brands such as American Apparel; and Gilt Man, which sells men's clothing. Since launching the Gilt Man site, the company's revenue from menswear has tripled. Some early Gilt members complain that the company has moved away from its original concept, including many brands whose names they do not recognize.

The Gilt Web site has a decidedly upscale look, with muted colors and no flashing "sale" signs and appeals to the company's target customers: upscale shoppers who are "aspirational" luxury buyers, people who are eager to purchase designer goods but cannot afford to pay full price for them. The key is to make sure that customers feel as though they are getting access to bargains that are not available to just anyone. The site also provides shoppers with extensive product descriptions and simple photographs of merchandise. "We deliver an incredible amount of information about the product," says Lyne, "and we have a direct line to our customers every day." The company also offers an iPad application for shoppers.

Gilt's management team is exploring an initial public offering for the company, which was valued at $400 million in its latest round of venture capital financing. Challenges do exist, however. "This is a pretty easy market to enter," admits Lyne, "but the operational aspects of it are incredibly complex. We change out the store every night. Receiving, sale preparation, and shipping and fulfillment are incredibly complex." Lyne is focusing on the company's e-commerce strategy. "We have to be thinking about what the Internet makes possible," she says. "Can we do something that drives the next wave of excitement in e-commerce? We need to get better at personalization. We need to be able to offer you different sales than we might offer somebody in Minneapolis or your mother."

1. What advantages does operating solely online offer Gilt Groupe? What are the disadvantages?
2. What advice can you offer the Gilt Groupe's management team as they continue to develop their e-commerce strategy? What steps can they take to stay connected to their customers and to keep their customers coming back?

Sources: Based on Mary Jo A Pham, "Gilt Groupe's Haute Sample Sales Expand," *Fortune*, June 25, 2010, *http://tech.fortune.cnn.com/2010/06/25/gilt-groupe-brings-you-the-online-sample-sale/*; Lauren Sherman, "By Invitation Only," *Forbes*, February 25, 2008, *www.forbes.com/forbes/2008/0225/070.html*; Andrew Rice, "What's a Dress Worth?" *New York Magazine*, February 24, 2010, *http://nymag.com/fashion/10/spring/63807/*.

Gilt Groupe founders Alexis Maybank (center) and Alexandra Wilkis Wilson (right) with CEO Susan Lyne (left).

Source: Ben Baker/Redux Pictures

Designing a Killer Web Site

5. Learn the techniques of designing a killer Web site.

Web users are not a patient lot. They sit before their computers, their fingers poised on their mouse buttons, daring any Web site to delay them with files that take too long to load. Slow-loading sites or sites that are confusing and poorly designed cause Web users to move on faster than a bolt of lightning can strike. With more than 234 million Web sites online and more added every day, how can an entrepreneur design a Web site that will capture and hold potential customers' attention long enough to make a sale? What can they do to keep customers coming back on a regular basis? There is no surefire formula for stopping online customers in their tracks, but the following suggestions will help.

Decide How to Bring Your Site to Life

Entrepreneurs who are not technologically savvy often turn to e-commerce hosting companies that provide one-stop services, including site design, built-in shopping carts, security filters, Web analytics, and, in some cases, credit card processing. Many of these services offer customizable templates that allow entrepreneurs to update and modify their sites very easily using "wizards." Other entrepreneurs choose to hire Web site designers to create a customized Web site or build their own sites. Whatever option they choose, entrepreneurs must pay a monthly hosting fee, which can be a flat amount, an amount per transaction, or a percentage of sales. When it comes

**FIGURE 4 (a)
Percentage of Adult
Internet Users.**

Source: "Generations Online in 2009,"
Pew Internet and American Life
Project, 2009.

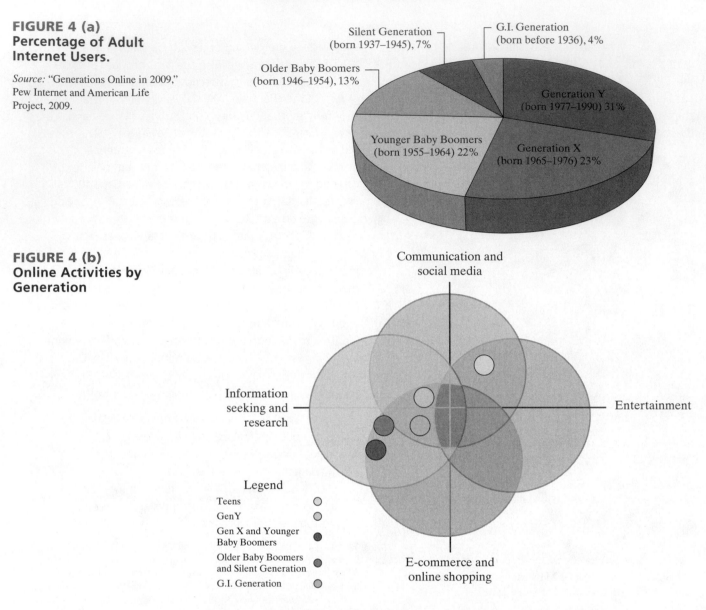

**FIGURE 4 (b)
Online Activities by
Generation**

to e-commerce, the lesson for entrepreneurs is this: Focus your efforts on the core competencies that your company has developed, whether they reside in "traditional" business practices or on-line, and outsource all of the other aspects of doing business online to companies that have the expertise to make your e-commerce business successful.

Start with Your Target Customer

Before creating their Web sites, entrepreneurs must paint a clear picture of their target customers. Only then are they ready to design a site that will appeal to their customers. The goal is to create a design in which customers see themselves when they visit. Creating a site in which customers find a comfortable fit requires a careful blend of market research, sales know-how, and aesthetics. The challenge for a business on the Web is to create the same image, style, and ambiance in its online presence as in its off-line stores. Figure 4 shows the percentage of adults online by generation and the type of online experiences they seek.

Give Customers What They Want

Although Web shoppers are price conscious, they rank fast, reliable delivery high on their list of criteria in their purchase decisions. Studies also show that shoppers look for a large selection of merchandise available to them immediately. Remember that the essence of the selling on the Web is providing *convenience* to customers. A well-designed Web site is intuitive, leading customers to a series of actions that are natural and result in a sale. Sites that allow them to shop whenever

FIGURE 5

Features That Make U.S. Shoppers More Likely to Buy from a Web Site

Factors that Web shoppers say are most important when they are deciding whether to purchase from a Web site.

Source: Revolutionizing Web Site Design: The New Rules of Usability, Oneupweb, 2010, p. 11.

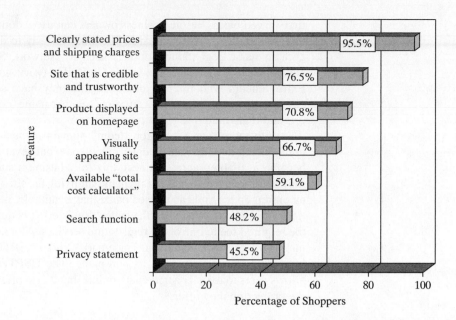

they want, to find what they are looking for easily, and to pay for it conveniently and securely will keep customers coming back. Clear photographs of merchandise with a feature that allows customers to rotate the image, change colors, and zoom in increase sales. Furniture maker Herman Miller's Web site not only makes it easy for shoppers to browse and to buy its products, but the site also offers research on the benefits of ergonomic designs and allows visitors to try various furniture layouts in rooms created with a special 3D design tool.[72] One of the reasons Amazon.com has become the largest online retailer is that its five-point strategy is designed to give online shoppers exactly what they want: low prices, wide selection, product availability, shopping convenience, and extensive information about the products it sells.[73]

Figure 5 shows the factors that Web shoppers say are most important when they are deciding whether to buy from a Web site.

Select an Intuitive Domain Name

Choose a domain name that is consistent with the image you want to create for your company and register it. Entrepreneurs should never underestimate the power of the right domain name or Universal Resource Locator (URL), which is a company's address on the Internet. It not only tells online shoppers where to find a company, but it also should suggest something about the company and what it does. Even the casual Web surfer could guess that the "toys.com" name belongs to a company selling children's toys. (It does; it belongs to eToys, Inc., which also owns "etoys.com," "e-toys.com," and several other variations of its name.) The ideal domain name should be:

- *Short.* Short names are easy for people to remember, so the shorter a company's URL is, the more likely potential customers are to recall it.
- *Memorable.* Not every short domain name is necessarily memorable. Some business owners use their companies' initials as their domain name (e.g., "*www.sbfo.com*" for Stanley Brothers Furniture Outlet). The problem with using initials for a domain name is that customers rarely associate the two, which makes a company virtually invisible on the Web.
- *Indicative of a company's business or business name.* Perhaps the best domain name for a company is one that customers can guess easily if they know the company's name. For instance, mail-order catalog company L.L.Bean's URL is "*www.llbean.com*," and New Pig, a maker of absorbent materials for a variety of industrial applications, uses "*www.newpig.com*" as its domain name. (The company carries this concept over to its toll-free number, which is 1-800-HOT-HOGS.)
- *Easy to spell.* Even though a company's domain name may be easy to spell, it is usually wise to buy several variations of the correct spelling simply because some customers are not likely to be good spellers!

Just because entrepreneurs come up with the perfect URL for their companies' Web sites does not necessarily mean that they can use it. Domain names are given on a first-come, first-served basis. Before business owners can use a domain name, they must ensure that someone else has not already taken it. The simplest way to do that is to go to one of the accredited domain name registration services such as Network Solutions (*www.networksolutions.com*), NetNames (*www.netnames.com*), or Go Daddy (*www.godaddy.com*) to conduct a name search. Entrepreneurs who find the domain name they have selected already registered to someone else have two choices: They can select another name, or they can try to buy the name from the original registrant.

With more than 82 million ".com" domain names currently registered, finding a relevant, unregistered domain name can be a challenge, but several new top-level domain names recently became available: .aero (airlines), .biz (any business site), .coop (business cooperatives), .info (any site), .museum (museums), .name (individuals' sites), and .pro (professionals' sites).[74] Once an entrepreneur finds an unused name that is suitable, he or she must register it (plus any variations of it)—and the sooner, the better! Registering is quite easy: Simply submit a form and pay the required fee to one of the registration services. Although not required, registering the domain name with the U.S. Patent and Trademark Office (USPTO) at a cost of $275 provides maximum protection for a company's domain name. The USPTO's Web site (*www.uspto.gov*) not only allows users to register a trademark online, but it also offers useful information on trademarks and the protection they offer.

Make Your Web Site Easy to Navigate

Research shows that the leading factor in convincing online shoppers to make a purchase from a Web site is its ease of navigation. The starting point for evaluating a site's navigability is to conduct a user test. Find several willing shoppers, sit them in front of a computer, and watch them as they cruise through the company's Web site to make a purchase. It is one of the best ways to get meaningful, immediate feedback on the navigability of a site. Watching these test customers as they navigate the site also is useful. Where do they pause? Do they get lost in the site? Are they confused by the choices the site gives them? Is the checkout process too complex? Are the navigation buttons from one page of the site to another clearly marked, and do they make sense? "Eighty percent of visitors will leave [a Web site] if they can't find what they are looking for after three pages," says Bryan Eisenberg, an e-commerce consultant.[75]

Successful Web sites recognize that shoppers employ different strategies to make a purchase. Some shoppers want to use a search tool, others want to browse through product categories, and still others prefer a company to make product recommendations. Effective sites accommodate all three strategies in their design.

Add Wish List Capability

Giving customers the ability to create wish lists of products and services they want and then connect other people to those lists not only boosts a company's sales but also increases its visibility.

Create a Gift Idea Center

Online retailers have discovered that one of the most successful tools for improving their conversion rates is to offer a gift idea center. A gift idea center is a section of a Web site that includes a variety of gift ideas where shoppers can browse for ideas based on price, gender, or category. Gift idea centers can provide a huge boost for e-tailers, particularly around holidays because they offer creative suggestions for shoppers looking for the perfect gift. Other variations of this approach that have proved to be successful for e-commerce entrepreneurs include suggested items pages, bargain basement sale pages, and featured sale pages.

Build Loyalty by Giving Online Customers a Reason to Return to Your Web Site

Just as with brick-and-mortar retailers, e-tailers that constantly have to incur the expense of attracting new customers find it difficult to remain profitable because of the extra cost required to acquire customers. One of the most effective ways to encourage customers to return to a site is to establish an incentive program that rewards them for repeat purchases. "Frequent buyer" programs that offer discounts or points toward future purchases, giveaways such as T-shirts emblazoned with a company's logo, or special sales only for loyal customers are common elements of incentive programs. Incentive programs that are properly designed with a company's target customer in mind really work.

Establish Hyperlinks with Other Businesses, Preferably Those Selling Products or Services That Complement Yours

Listing the Web addresses of complementary businesses on your company's site and having them list your site's address on their sites offers customers more value and can bring traffic to your site that you otherwise would have missed. For instance, the owner of a site selling upscale kitchen gadgets should consider a cross-listing arrangement with sites that feature gourmet recipes, wines, and kitchen appliances.

Include an E-Mail Option, an Address, and a Telephone Number on Your Site

Customers appreciate the opportunity to communicate with your company, and you should give them many options for doing so. If you include e-mail access on your site, however, be sure to respond to it promptly. Nothing alienates customers faster than a company that is slow to respond or fails to respond to their e-mail messages. Also be sure to include an address and a toll-free telephone number for customers who prefer to write or call with their questions. Unfortunately, many companies either fail to include their telephone numbers on their sites or bury them so deeply within the sites' pages that customers never find them.

Offer Shoppers Online Order Tracking

Give shoppers the ability to track their orders online. Many customers who order items online want to track the progress of their orders. One of the most effective ways to keep a customer happy is to send an e-mail confirmation that your company received the order and another e-mail notification when you ship the order. The shipment notice should include the shipper's tracking number and instructions on how to track the order from the shipper's site. Order and shipping confirmations instill confidence in even the most Web-wary shoppers.

Offer Web-Only Specials

Give Web customers a special deal that you don't offer in any other advertising piece. Change your specials often (weekly, if possible) and use clever "teasers" to draw attention to the offer. Regular special offers available only on the Web give customers an incentive to keep visiting a company's site.

Look for Opportunities to Up-Sell and Cross-Sell

Sales clerks in brick-and-mortar retail stores quickly learn the art of up-selling, recommending more upscale products, and cross-selling, offering, for example, a customer who purchases a shirt the opportunity to purchase a matching tie as well. Online merchants can use the same tactic by displaying recommended items on product pages. Men's clothing retailer Jos. A Bank (*www.josabank.com*) employs this sales strategy extremely well when a customer places an item in a shopping cart by displaying a list of "matching apparel" on the product page.

Use the Power of Social Media

Make it easy for customers to connect with your company on social media such as Facebook, Twitter, and others by including social media sharing links and links to your company's social media pages on your Web site. Social media can be a powerful marketing tool.

Use Customer Testimonials

Customer testimonials about a company and its products and services lend credibility to a site, but the testimonials must be genuine and believable.

ENTREPRENEURIAL
Profile
Charlie and Eddie Bakhash: American Pearl

American Pearl, a company that sells pearls from its Fifth Avenue showroom in New York City and its Web site (*www.americanpearl.com*), reinforces the owners' extensive knowledge of and dedication to pearls with a Web page dedicated to customer testimonials. Explaining the importance of the testimonial page, Eddie Bakhash, whose father, Charlie, started the company in 1950, says, "We understand that purchasing an expensive strand of pearls for a loved one on the Internet can require courage." The highly successful company also instills confidence in customers by offering an unconditional 30-day, money-back guarantee.[76]

Follow a Simple Design

Catchy graphics and photographs are important to snaring customers, but designers must choose them carefully. Designs that are overly complex take a long time to download, and customers are likely to move on before they appear. The Web Site Garage (*http://thewebsitegarage.com*), a Web site maintenance company, offers companies a free 21-point inspection of their Web sites and a report that describes problems ranging from slow download speeds to search engine optimization and their potential solutions.

Specific design tips include:

- Avoid clutter, especially on your site's homepage. "The homepage is like a store's display window, minus the mannequins," explains a report on proper Web design.[77] The best designs are simple and elegant with a balance of both text and graphics. "The minimalist approach makes a site appear more professional," says one design expert.[78]
- Use less text on your site's homepage, landing pages, and initial product or service pages. Although including detailed, text-heavy content deeper in your site is acceptable and even desirable, incorporating too much text early on dissuades customers. Allow customers to drill down to more detailed product and service descriptions.
- Avoid huge graphic headers that must download first, prohibiting customers from seeing anything else on your site as they wait (or, more likely, *don't* wait). Use graphics judiciously so that the site loads quickly; otherwise, impatient customers will abandon the site.
- Include a menu bar at the top of every page that makes it easy for customers to find their way around your site.
- Make the site easy to navigate by including easy-to-follow navigation buttons at the bottom of pages that enable customers to return to the top of the page or to the menu bar. This avoids "the pogo effect," where visitors bounce from page to page in a Web site looking for what they need. Without navigation buttons or a site map page, a company runs the risk of customers getting lost in its site and leaving. Organizing a Web site into logical categories also helps.
- Minimize the number of clicks required for a customer to get to any particular page in the site. Long paths increase the likelihood of customers bailing out before they reach their intended destination.
- Incorporate meaningful content in the site that is useful to visitors, well organized, easy to read, and current. The content should be consistent with the message a company sends in the other advertising media it uses. Although a Web site should be designed to sell, providing useful, current information attracts visitors, keeps them coming back, and establishes a company's reputation as an expert in the field.
- Include a "frequently asked questions" (FAQ) section. Adding a searchable FAQ section to a site can reduce dramatically the number of telephone calls and e-mails customer service representatives must handle. FAQ sections typically span a wide range of issues—from how to place an order to how to return merchandise—and cover topics customers most often want to know about.
- Be sure to include privacy and return policies as well as product guarantees the company offers.
- Avoid fancy typefaces and small fonts because they are too hard to read.
- Be vigilant for misspelled words, typographical errors, and formatting mistakes; they destroy a site's credibility in no time and send customers fleeing to competitors' sites.
- Don't put small fonts on "busy" backgrounds; no one will read them!
- Use contrasting colors of text and graphics. For instance, blue text on a green background is nearly impossible to read.
- Be careful with frames. Using frames that are so thick that they crowd out text makes for a poor design.
- Test the site on different Web browsers and on different size monitors. A Web site may look exactly the way it was designed to look on one Web browser and be a garbled mess on another. Sites designed to display correctly on large monitors may not view well on small ones.
- Use your Web site to collect information from visitors, but don't tie up customers with a tedious registration process. Most will simply leave the site never to return. Offers for a free e-mail newsletter or a contest giveaway can give visitors enough incentive to register with a site.
- Incorporate a search function that allows shoppers to type in the items they want to purchase. Unlike in-store shoppers, who might browse until they find the item, online shoppers usually

want to go straight to the products they seek. Ideally, the search function acknowledges common misspellings of key terms, avoiding the dreaded "No Results Found" message.

- Include company contact information and an easy-to-find customer service telephone number.
- Avoid automated music that plays continuously and cannot be cut off.
- Make sure the overall look of the site is consistent and appealing. "When a site is poorly designed, lacks information, or cannot support customer needs, that [company's] reputation is seriously jeopardized," says one expert.[79]
- Remember: Simpler usually is better.

Assure Customers That Online Transactions Are Secure

If you are serious about doing business on the Web, make sure that your site includes the proper security software and encryption devices. Computer-savvy customers are not willing to divulge their credit card numbers on sites that are not secure. E-commerce companies should avoid storing their customers' credit card information (even though one-third of small companies do).[80] With attacks from hackers increasingly prevalent, the risk is just too high.

Post Shipping and Handling Charges Up Front

A common gripe among online shoppers is that some e-tailers fail to reveal their shipping and handling charges early in the checkout process. Responsible online merchants keep shipping and handling charges reasonable and display them early on in the buying process—before shoppers add items to a cart. When customers' orders qualify for free shipping, the site should automate this step rather than require customers to input a free shipping code.

Create a Fast, Simple Checkout Process

One sure-fire way to destroy an online company's conversion rate is to impose a lengthy, convoluted checkout process that requires customers to wade through pages of forms to fill out just to complete a purchase. When faced with a lengthy checkout process, customers simply abandon a site and make their purchases elsewhere. E-commerce experts suggest that the top performing sites require a maximum of five clicks to check out, but the fewer the steps required for customers to check out, the more successful will be the site at generating sales.[81]

Confirm Transactions

Order-confirmation e-mails, which a company can generate automatically, let a customer know that the company received the online order and can be an important first line of defense against online fraud. If the customer claims not to have placed the order, the company can cancel it and report the transaction and the credit card information as suspicious. Order confirmation e-mails should include shipping information and a tracking number that allows customers to view the status of their orders.

Keep Your Site Fresh

Customers want to see something new when they visit stores, and they expect the same when they visit virtual stores as well. Regularly add new content such as videos, blogs, customer testimonials, or information-rich articles to your site. Delete any hyperlinks that have disappeared, and keep the information on your Web site current. One sure way to run off customers on the Web is to continue to advertise your company's "Christmas Special" in August! Fresh information and new specials keep customers coming back.

Test Your Site Often

Smart e-commerce entrepreneurs check their sites frequently to make sure they are running smoothly and are not causing customers unexpected problems. A good rule of thumb is to check your site at least monthly—or weekly if its content changes frequently.

Consider Hiring a Professional Designer

Pros can do it a lot faster and better than you can. However, don't give designers free rein to do whatever they want to with your site. Make sure it meets your criteria for an effective site that can sell.

Entrepreneurs must remember that on the Web every company, no matter how big or how small, has the exact same screen size for its site. What matters most is not the size of your company, but how you put that screen size to use.

▶ E N T R E P R E N E U R S H I P **IN ACTION** ▶

In Need of a Web Site Makeover

While attending Stanford University, Brian Spaly began using a girlfriend's sewing machine to alter his pants so that they fit better. Soon, Spaly's friends were asking for good-fitting pants of their own. Spaly and his roommate Andy Dunn spotted a business opportunity and launched Bonobos, an online company that sells pants that fit well with the help of a proprietary curved waistband that follows the body's natural shape and "some magic in the seat" that makes them "comfortable but not frumpy." Bonobos sells its pants only online (*www.bonobos.com*) at prices that range from about $110 to $200.

Bonobos is committed to customer service, and the company's Web site emphasizes convenience. "We hate shopping, too," explains one page. "You have to do it on your free time at the expense of things you actually enjoy." The company offers free shipping and the most accommodating return policy in the business: "any pant, any time, any reason." Bonobos even pays for the return shipping. The company generates about $170,000 in sales each month, but Spaly and Dunn believe that a redesigned Web site can generate a higher level of sales. A group of e-commerce experts reviewed Bonobos' Web analytics and discovered some interesting trends.

Finding Us

Typically, about half of the traffic on a company's Web site comes from search engines, with the remainder split evenly among referrals, affiliate sites, and direct traffic; that is, customers who type in the company's Web address. Bonobos, however, generates just 21 percent of its traffic from search engines and 50 percent from referring Web sites. About 25 percent of the company's customers go directly to its Web site. Bonobos invests a great deal of energy in generating publicity, but the analytics report suggests that the company is not scoring high placement in search engine results. The report shows that "Bonobos" is one of the most common keywords that customers use. Very few customers find the company by searching for "men's pants" or "pants that fit."

Conversion Rate

Like most e-commerce companies, Bonobos' conversion rate fluctuates from week to week. The Web analytics report shows that the site's current conversion rate typically falls between 1.8 and 3.0 percent, which is below average. Many factors influence a company's conversion rate, but Spaly and Dunn are convinced that theirs should be higher.

Shopping Cart Abandonment

Bonobos' shopping cart abandonment rate is 63 percent. One analyst points out that the site's checkout process asks for a coupon code early in the process and suspects that many customers abandon their carts to search for a discount coupon. Many of them never return to complete their transactions. The team of experts points out that if Bonobos could lower its cart abandonment rate by 10 percent, sales would increase by $20,000 per month.

Page Views and Bounce Rate

Web analytics show that the typical visitor to the Bonobos site views on average eight pages. However, the site's bounce rate, the percentage of visitors that leave the site after viewing just one page, is nearly 33 percent, well above the 20 percent that the experts consider "good." The bounce rate is one measure of the quality of a guest's visit. High bounce rates indicate that a site's landing pages simply are not relevant to visitors. If Bonobos can reduce its bounce rate to 20 percent, sales would increase by $10,000 per month. A high bounce rate coupled with a high number of page views per visit suggests that shoppers are not finding the products that they are looking for.

Navigation and Shopping

The team of experts questions the site's use of quirky names for various types of pants such as Snapdragons, Jive Cats, and Cracker Jacks on the homepage. To be effective, the online shopping experience must be intuitive, allowing customers to easily find the items they seek. "They should make it easier for a visitor to figure out where to find corduroy pants or weekend wear," says one expert. "A new customer is not going to know what 'Snapdragons' means." Improving the site's navigation and simplifying the shopping process can lead to greatly increased sales.

Global Reach

One of the greatest advantages to small companies that operate online is the ability to expand their reach globally at a low cost. Although Bonobos generates most of its sales from customers across North America, the site receives a considerable amount of traffic from shoppers in Australia. Bonobos can ship its pants internationally just as easily as it can locally, but the existing site lacks the ability to be customized for foreign customers and cultures. For instance, a customer in North America is most likely to use a search engine to look for "pants," but a shopper in Australia would use the term "trousers."

1. What suggestions can you make for improving Bonobos' search engine optimization (SEO) strategy?
2. Visit the Bonobos Web site and spend a few minutes exploring it. Work with a small team of your classmates to develop a list of ideas for improving the site. Review each of the points described in this feature and incorporate specific suggestions for improving each area.

Source: Based on Max Chafkin, "Improving Your Sense of Style," *Inc.,* November 2008, pp. 35–37.

Tracking Web Results

6. Explain how companies track the results from their Web sites.

Web sites offer entrepreneurs a treasure trove of valuable information about how well their sites are performing—if they take the time to analyze it. **Web analytics**, tools that measure a Web site's ability to attract customers, generate sales, and keep customers coming back, help entrepreneurs to know what works—and what doesn't—on their sites. Online companies that use Web analytics have an advantage over those that do not. Their owners can review the data collected from their customers' Web site activity, analyze them, make adjustments to the Web site, and then start the monitoring process over again to see whether the changes improve the site's performance. In other words, Web analytics give entrepreneurs the ability to apply the principles of continuous improvement to their sites. In addition, the changes these e-business owners make are based on facts (the data from the Web analytics) rather than on mere guesses about how customers interact with a site. A variety of Web analytics software packages are available, but effective ones offer the following types of information:

- *Commerce metrics.* Basic analytics such as sales revenue generated, number of items sold, which products are selling best (and which are not), and others.
- *Visitor segmentation measurements.* These measurements provide entrepreneurs valuable information about online shoppers and customers, including whether they are return customers or new customers, how they arrived at the site (e.g., via a search engine or a pay-per-click ad), which search terms they used (if they used a search engine), and others.
- *Content reports.* This information tells entrepreneurs which products customers are looking for and which pages they view most often (and least often), how they navigate through the site, how long they stay, which pages they are on when they exit, and more. Using this information, an entrepreneur can get an idea of how effective the site's design is.
- *Process measurements.* These metrics help entrepreneurs to understand how their Web sites attract visitors and convert them into customers. Does the checkout process work smoothly? How often do shoppers abandon their carts? At what point in the process do they abandon them? These measures can lead to higher conversion rates for an online business.

Other common measures of Web site performance include the following:

- **Recency** is the length of time between a customer's visits to a Web site. The more frequently customers visit a site, the more likely they are to become loyal customers.
- The **click-through rate (CTR)** is the proportion of people who see a company's online ad and actually click on it to reach the company's Web site. Each time an ad is displayed is called an impression; therefore:

$$\text{CTR} = \text{Number of clicks} \div \text{Number of impressions}$$

For instance, if a company's ad is displayed 500 times in 1 day and 12 people clicked it, the CTR is $12 \div 500 = .024$, or 2.4 percent.
- The **cost per acquisition (CPA)** is the cost a company incurs to generate each purchase (or customer registration):

$$\text{CPA} = \text{Total cost of acquiring a new customer} \div \text{Number of new customers}$$

For example, if a company purchases an advertisement in an e-magazine for $200, and it yields 15 new customers, then the cost of acquisition is $200 \div 15 = \$13.33$.

- The **conversion** (or **browse-to-buy**) **rate** is the proportion of visitors to a site who actually make a purchase. It is one of the most important measures of Web success and is calculated as follows:

Conversion rate = Number of customers who make a purchase ÷ Number of visitors to the site

Conversion rates vary dramatically across industries but usually range from 1 to 4 percent. The average conversion rate is 3.2 percent.[82] In other words, out of every 1,000 people who visit a Web site, on average, 32 of them actually make a purchase.

Ensuring Web Privacy and Security

Privacy

The Web's ability to track customers' every move naturally raises concerns over the privacy of the information companies collect. E-commerce gives businesses access to tremendous volumes of information about their customers, creating a responsibility to protect that information and to use it wisely. The potential for breaching customers' privacy is present in any e-business. To make sure they are using the information they collect from visitors to their Web sites legally and ethically and safeguarding it adequately, companies should take the following steps:

TAKE AN INVENTORY OF THE CUSTOMER DATA COLLECTED. The first step to ensuring proper data handling is to assess exactly the type of data the company is collecting and storing. How are you collecting the information? Why are you collecting it? How are you using it? Do visitors know how you are using the data? Should you get their permission to use the data in this way? Do you use all of the data you are collecting?

DEVELOP A COMPANY PRIVACY POLICY FOR THE INFORMATION YOU COLLECT. A **privacy policy** is a statement explaining the type of information a company collects online, what it does with that information, and the recourse customers have if they believe the company is misusing the information. *Every* online company should have a privacy policy, but many do not. A survey by TRUSTe, a provider of Internet privacy services, reports that 56 percent of small business's Web sites have no privacy policy. Of the small companies that do have privacy policies, 35 percent of the owners say that they simply cut the privacy policy from another company's Web site and pasted it onto their own.[83]

Several online privacy firms, including TRUSTe (*www.truste.org*), BBBOnline (*www.bbbonline.com*), and BetterWeb (*www.betterweb.com*), offer Web "seal programs," the equivalent of a Good Housekeeping seal of privacy approval. To earn a privacy seal of approval, a company must adopt a privacy policy, implement it, and monitor its effectiveness. Many of these privacy sites also provide online policy wizards, automated questionnaires that help e-business owners create comprehensive privacy statements.

POST YOUR COMPANY'S PRIVACY POLICY PROMINENTLY ON YOUR WEB SITE AND FOLLOW IT. Creating a privacy policy is not sufficient; posting it in a prominent place on the Web site (accessible from every page on the site) and then abiding by it make a policy meaningful. Whether a company has a privacy policy posted prominently often determines whether customers will do online business with it. A study by Carnegie Mellon University reports that shoppers are more likely to purchase from online merchants that have sound privacy policies and post them.[84] One of the worst mistakes a company can make is to publish its privacy policy online and then fail to follow it. Not only is this unethical, but it also can lead to serious damage awards if customers take legal action against the company.

Security

Concerns about security and fraud present the greatest obstacles to the growth of e-commerce. A study by Harris Interactive reports that 45 percent of Web users have terminated an order or abandoned a shopping cart because of security fears.[85] Indeed, cybercrime has become big business, costing consumers and companies $5.8 billion annually.[86] Determining the extent of online security breaches is difficult because many companies never report breaches of computer security to authorities. Every company with a Web site—no matter how small—is a potential target for hackers and others seeking to cause harm. Hackers and attackers have become more sophisticated, which makes Web site security a top priority for *every* company doing business online. In a recent WhiteHat Security study of 1,659 Web sites that researchers considered "serious" about security, 75 percent had at least one serious point of vulnerability that hackers could exploit.[87]

A company doing business on the Web faces two conflicting goals: to establish a presence on the Web so that customers can have access to its site and the information maintained there and to preserve a high level of security so that the business, its site, and the information it collects from customers are safe from hackers and intruders intent on doing harm. Companies have a number of safeguards available to them, but hackers with enough time, talent, and determination usually can beat even the most sophisticated safety measures. If hackers manage to break into a system, they can do irreparable damage—stealing programs and sensitive customer data, modifying or deleting valuable information, changing the look and content of sites, or crashing sites altogether. In the largest data breach to date, hackers broke into the database at one retail company and stole information that included more than 45 million debit and credit card numbers.[88] Web-hosting company Network Solutions discovered that despite layers of protection, hackers had breached the transaction data of more than 4,300 of its merchant Web sites, which exposed the credit card data of 574,000 shoppers.[89] In addition to the actual losses these scams cause, another real danger is that scams such as these erode customers' confidence in e-commerce, posing real threats to every online entrepreneur.

Security threats are real for companies of every size, and entrepreneurs must contend with that reality. To minimize the likelihood of invasion by hackers and viruses, e-companies rely on several tools, including virus detection software, intrusion detection software, and firewalls. The most basic level of protection is **virus detection software**, which scans computer drives for viruses, nasty programs written by devious hackers that are designed to harm computers and the information they contain. The severity of viruses ranges widely, from relatively harmless programs that put humorous messages on a user's screen to those that erase a computer's hard drive or cause the entire system to crash. Because hackers are *always* writing new viruses to attack computer systems, entrepreneurs must keep their virus detection software up-to-date and run it often. An attack by one virus can bring a company's entire e-commerce platform to a screeching halt in no time! One virus that was sent by e-mail with the subject line "I love you" infected computer systems across the globe, leaving companies with an estimated $15 billion in damages and downtime.

Intrusion detection software is essential for any company doing business on the Web. These packages constantly monitor the activity on a company's network server and sound an alert if they detect someone breaking into the company's computer system or if they detect unusual network activity. Intrusion detection software not only detects attempts by unauthorized users to break into a computer system while they are happening, but it also traces the hacker's location. Most packages also have the ability to preserve a record of the attempted break-in that will stand up in court so that companies can take legal action against cyber-intruders. Web security companies such as McAfee provide software such as ScanAlert that scans a small business's Web site daily to certify that it is "Hacker Safe." Online companies using the software are able to post a certification mark signifying that their sites are protected from unauthorized access.

A **firewall** is software that operates between the Internet and a company's computer network that allows authorized data from the Internet to enter a company's network and the programs and data it contains but keeps unauthorized data, such as viruses, spyware, and other malware out. The equivalent of the lock on a small company's front door, a firewall serves as the lock on its computer network's front door. Establishing a firewall is essential for any company operating on the Web, but entrepreneurs must make sure that their firewalls are set up properly. Otherwise, they are useless! Even with all of these security measures in place, it is best for a company to run its Web site on a separate server from the network that runs the business. If hackers break into the Web site, they still do not have access to the company's sensitive data and programs.

Increasing the security of a computer system requires using properly installed security tools, perhaps in multiple layers, and making sure that they function properly and are up-to-date. Even though 65 percent of small businesses store customer data on their computer systems, only 53 percent of small companies check their virus detection software and firewalls weekly to ensure that they are up-to-date (and 11 percent *never* check them).[90] The National Cyber Security Alliance (*http://staysafeonline.org*) and the Computer Security Institute (*www.gocsi.com*) offer articles, information, and seminars to help business owners maintain computer security. *Information Security Magazine* (which can be found at *http://searchsecurity.techtarget.com*) also offers helpful advice on maintaining computer security.

In e-commerce, just as in traditional retailing, sales do not matter unless a company gets paid! On the Web, customers demand transactions they can complete with ease and convenience, and the simplest way to allow customers to pay for e-commerce transactions is with credit cards. From a Web customer's perspective, however, one of the most important security issues is the security of his or her credit card information. To ensure the security of their customers' credit card information, online retailers typically use **secure sockets layer (SSL) technology** to encrypt customers' transaction information as it travels across the Internet. By using secure shopping cart features from storefront-building services or Internet service providers, even the smallest e-commerce stores can offer their customers secure online transactions.

Processing credit card transactions requires a company to obtain an Internet merchant account from a bank or financial intermediary. Setup fees for an Internet merchant account typically range from $500 to $1,000, but companies also pay monthly access and statement fees of between $40 and $80 plus a transaction fee of 10 to 60 cents per transaction. Once an online company has a merchant account, it can accept credit cards from online customers.

Online credit card transactions also pose a risk for merchants; online companies lose $3.3 billion a year to online payment fraud each year, 1.2 percent of their sales revenue (see Figure 6), about half of it from **chargebacks**, online credit card transactions that customers dispute.[91] Good customer service minimizes the number of legitimate chargebacks. Illegitimate chargebacks usually are the result of thieves stealing credit card numbers and then using them to make online purchases. Unlike credit card transactions in a retail store, those made online ("card not present" transactions) involve no signatures, and Internet merchants incur the loss (and usually a fine from the credit card company) when a customer disputes the transaction.

ENTREPRENEURIAL
Profile

Jamon Robinson: Sun Tints, Inc.

Jamon Robinson, president of Sun Tints, Inc., a company that sells automotive accessories online and from a store in Bountiful, Utah, was frustrated that 1 out of every 100 online purchases resulted in a chargeback. In an effort to combat the problem, Robinson signed up with BadCustomer.com, a Web site (*www.badcustomer.com*) that allows merchants to search for customers who have a history of chargebacks before completing a credit card sale. In the first 3 months of using the service, Robinson refused several credit card transactions and did not have any chargebacks.[92]

FIGURE 6
Losses to Online Fraud

Source: "Online Fraud Report: 11th Annual Edition," Cybersource Corporation, Mountain View, California: 2010, p. 4.

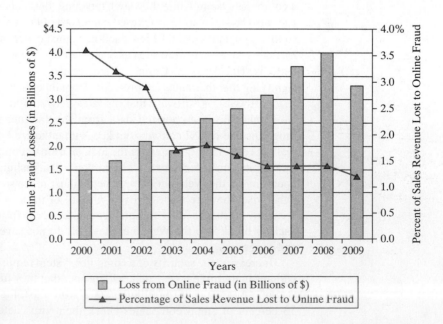

One way to prevent fraud is to ask customers for their card verification value (CVV, CID, or CVV2), the three-digit number above the signature panel on the back of the credit card, as well as their card number and expiration date. Online merchants also can subscribe to a real-time credit card processing service that authorizes credit card transactions, but the fees can be high. Sending confirmation e-mails that include the customer's shipping information after receiving an order also reduces the likelihood of a chargeback. In addition, using a shipper that provides the ability to track shipments so online merchants can prove that the customer actually received the merchandise can help minimize the threat of payment fraud.

Chapter Review

1. Describe the benefits of selling on the World Wide Web.
   - The opportunity to increase revenues
   - The ability to expand their reach into global markets
   - The ability to remain open 24 hours a day, 7 days a week
   - The capacity to use the Web's interactive nature to enhance customer service
   - The power to educate and to inform
   - The ability to lower the cost of doing business
   - The ability to spot new business opportunities and to capitalize on them
   - The power to track sales results
2. Understand the factors an entrepreneur should consider before launching into e-commerce.
   - How a company exploits the Web's interconnectivity and the opportunities it creates to transform relationships with its suppliers and vendors, its customers, and other external stakeholders is crucial to its success.
   - Web success requires a company to develop a plan for integrating the Web into its overall strategy. The plan should address issues such as site design and maintenance, creating and managing a brand name, marketing and promotional strategies, sales, and customer service.
   - Developing deep, lasting relationships with customers takes on even greater importance on the Web. Attracting customers on the Web costs money, and companies must be able to retain their online customers to make their Web sites profitable.
   - Creating a meaningful presence on the Web requires an ongoing investment of resources—time, money, energy, and talent. Establishing an attractive Web site brimming with catchy photographs of products is only the beginning.
   - Measuring the success of Web-based sales efforts is essential to remaining relevant to customers whose tastes, needs, and preferences are always changing.
3. Explain the 10 myths of e-commerce and how to avoid falling victim to them.
   - Myth 1. If I launch a site, customers will flock to it.
   - Myth 2. Online customers are easy to please.
   - Myth 3. Making money on the Web is easy.
   - Myth 4. Privacy is not an important issue on the Web.
   - Myth 5. "Strategy? I don't need a strategy to sell on the Web! Just give me a Web site, and the rest will take care of itself."
   - Myth 6. The most important part of any e-commerce effort is technology.
   - Myth 7. On the Web, customer service is not as important as it is in a traditional retail store.
   - Myth 8. Flashy Web sites are better than simple ones.
   - Myth 9. It's what's up front that counts.
   - Myth 10. It's too late to get on the Web.
4. Explain the basic strategies entrepreneurs should follow to achieve success in their e-commerce efforts.
   - Consider focusing on a niche in the market.
   - Develop a community of online customers.
   - Attract visitors by giving away "freebies."
   - Make creative use of e-mail, but avoid becoming a "spammer."
   - Make sure your Web site says "credibility."

- Consider forming strategic alliances with larger, more established companies.
- Make the most of the Web's global reach.
- Promote your Web site online and off-line.

5. Learn the techniques of designing a killer Web site.
   - Select a domain name that is consistent with the image you want to create for your company and register it.
   - Be easy to find.
   - Give customers want they want.
   - Establish hyperlinks with other businesses, preferably those selling products or services that complement yours.
   - Include an e-mail option and a telephone number on your site.
   - Give shoppers the ability to track their orders online.
   - Offer Web shoppers a special all their own.
   - Follow a simple design for your Web page.
   - Assure customers that their online transactions are secure.
   - Keep your site up-to-date.
   - Consider hiring a professional to design your site.

6. Explain how companies track the results from their Web sites.
   - Web sites offer entrepreneurs a treasure trove of valuable information about how well their sites are performing—if they take the time to analyze it. Web analytics, tools that measure a Web site's ability to attract customers, generate sales, and keep customers coming back, help entrepreneurs to know what works—and what doesn't—on their sites.

7. Describe how e-businesses ensure the privacy and security of the information they collect and store from the Web.
   - To make sure they are using the information they collect from visitors to their Web sites legally and ethically, companies should take the following steps:
     - Take an inventory of the customer data collected.
     - Develop a company privacy policy for the information you collect.
     - Post your company's privacy policy prominently on your Web site and follow it.
   - To ensure the security of the information they collect and store from Web transactions, companies should rely on virus and intrusion detection software and firewalls to ward off attacks from hackers.

Discussion Questions

1. How has the Internet and e-commerce changed the ways companies do business?
2. Explain the benefits a company earns by selling on the Web.
3. Discuss the factors entrepreneurs should consider before launching an e-commerce site.
4. What are the 10 myths of e-commerce? What can an entrepreneur do to avoid them?
5. What strategic advice would you offer an entrepreneur about to start an e-company?
6. What design characteristics make for a successful Web page?
7. Explain the characteristics of an ideal domain name.
8. Describe the techniques that are available to e-companies for tracking results from their Web sites. What advantages does each offer?
9. What steps should e-businesses take to ensure the privacy of the information they collect and store from the Web?
10. What techniques can e-companies use to protect their banks of information and their customers' transaction data from hackers?
11. How can online entrepreneurs evaluate the effectiveness of their Web sites?
12. When Matt Buchan and Alex Garcia purchased a struggling hair salon in Seattle, Washington, their turnaround strategy included using the Internet as a key component of their business and marketing strategies. What advice can you offer these entrepreneurs for integrating the Web into their hair salon to enhance their customers' experience?

The Internet has transformed the way entrepreneurs operate, giving them the ability to sell their goods and services 24/7 and to reach customers around the world. Web-based businesses can connect with suppliers, provide higher levels of customer service, understand and respond to customer's preferences, and gain insight into their customers' online buying behavior to improve the experience. One of the initial questions asked in the initial Business Plan Pro wizard relates to your business Web site. What was your response to that question— yes or no? Use the contents of this chapter to review your decision. Think about the online presence that you would like your business to have. Is your Web site going to be an information only site, or do you plan to have a robust online store that is capable of conducting e-commerce? As you look through the list of the 10 myths mentioned in this chapter, ask yourself if you have fallen prey to any of these myths. What benefits do you expect to realize from your online presence?

On the Web

If you are planning to create a Web site that is for information-only purposes, go to sites that accomplish that goal. For example, you may want to visit *www.epinions.com*. Note the layout and navigation of the site and how it presents this information. If you plan to have a dynamic online store, Amazon.com's site was a pioneer in the evolution of online shopping. Go to *www.amazon.com* and take a fresh look at the site's attributes. What attributes on the site make it simple, efficient, and "safe" for new and returning buyers? Identify those qualities and explore how your site might also benefit from those attributes.

In the Software

Open your plan in Business Plan Pro and go to the "Web Summary" section. If you will create a Web site, click "View" and "Wizard" and change that decision. Business Plan Pro will update the outline of your business plan by adding a "Web Summary" section. Read the instructions within the software and click the sample plan link in the

upper right-hand section of the instructions. Add content to this section. The following questions may help you as you build your e-commerce strategy:

- Have you registered a URL for your business? If not, how will you begin the process to secure and register a Web address?
- How would you assess the general level of comfort that your target market has with the Web? For example, are they a technologically savvy group that uses the Web as a part of their daily life, or is this group an older audience that is just learning how to leverage the power of the Web?
- List the objectives you hope to realize through your Web site.
- Is your site going to have an online store? If so, explore how to implement credit card or other online payment options. What are the costs associated with the method of accepting payments online that you have chosen?
- Who will design and update the site? Will you or someone in your organization, or will you outsource that work?
- How will you measure, track, and assess the performance of your site, and how often will that occur?
- Are you going to incorporate Web analytics tools and resources that may help you to measure your Web site's performance?
- Does your business plan demonstrate that you have planned and budgeted for your Web site based on the required resources to design, launch, and maintain your site?

Building Your Business Plan

The additions you have made regarding your Web site may be significant or minimal. Step back and review the information that you have captured in your plan to date. With these additions, does your plan continue to tell a consistent and coherent story about your business? Review and edit other sections that may be affected by your additions to the Web section. Some of those sections may include areas that relate to marketing promotions, communications, expenses, and revenues.

Endnotes

1. Bret Thorn, "Domino's Passes $1 Billion in Online Sales," *Nation's Restaurant News*, February 10, 2010, *www.nrn.com/article/dominos-passes-1-billion-online-sales*; "Pizza Hut Expects $2 Billion in Online Sales," I4UNews, April 20, 2010, *www.i4u.com/article33268.html*; Karl Flinders, "Web Takes a Bigger Slice of Domino's," February 16, 2010, *Computer Weekly, www.computerweekly.com/Articles/2010/02/16/240320/Web-takes-a-bigger-slice-of-Domino39s-Pizza.htm*; "Papa John's Surpasses $1 Billion in Online Pizza Sales," Fresh News, May 8, 2008, *www.freshnews.in/papa-johns-surpasses-1-billion-in-online-pizza-sales-26218*; "Online Ordering Leader Papa John's First to Surpass $2 Billion in Online Sales," *QSR*, May 3, 2010, *www.qsrmagazine.com/articles/wire/story/20100503006043en*.

2. Erick Schonfeld, "Forrester Forecast: Online Retail Sales Will Grow to $250 Billion by 2014," TechCrunch, March 8, 2010, *http://techcrunch.com/2010/03/08/forrester-forecast-online-retail-sales-will-grow-to-250-billion-by-2014/*.

3. "Internet Usage Statistics: The Internet Big Picture," Internet World Stats, 2009, *www.internetworldstats.com/stats.htm*.

4. Brian McRoberts, George H. Terhanian, Ken Allredge, and Carla Keppler, *Understanding the Role of the Internet in the Lives of Consumers: Digital Influence Index*, Fleishman-Hillard and Harris Interactive, June 2010, p. 8.

5. "Living in Exponential Times," Get to the Point: Marketing Inspiration, *Marketing Profs*, May 11, 2009, pp. 1–2.

6. Erick Schonfeld, "Forrester Forecast: Online Retail Sales Will Grow to $250 Billion by 2014," TechCrunch, March 8, 2010, *http://techcrunch.com/2010/03/08/forrester-forecast-online-retail-sales-will-grow-to-250-billion-by-2014/*; Don Davis, "Consumers Will Buy or Research Online Half of Purchases by 2014, Forrester Says," *Internet Retailer*, March 31, 2010, *www.internetretailer.com/2010/03/31/consumers-will-buy-or-research-online-half-of-purchases-by-2014*.

7. "Business Purchasing Survey Shows 93 Percent of Small Businesses Value Internet for Research over Online Purchasing," BuyerZone, *www.buyerzone.com/corporate/about_buyerzone/pr051705.html*.

8. Nick Timiraos, "Facts," *Wall Street Journal*, December 23–24, 2006, p. A7.

9. "A Perfect Market," *Economist*, May 15, 2004, p. 4.

10. Kelly Heyboer, "Baking and Blogging: Speaking with Extreme Baker and Pink Cake Blogger Anne Heap," *Star Ledger*, March 4, 2009, *http://blog.nj.com/jerseyblogs/2009/03/baking_and_blogging_speaking_w. html*; Matt McGee, "A Small Marketing Success Story: Pink Cake Box," Search Engine Land, March 13, 2008, *http://searchengineland .com/a-small-business-marketing-success-story-pink-cake-box-13567*.

11. "Small Business Marketing Forecast 2010," Ad-ology, November 2009, p. 17.

12. Denise O'Berry, "Yes, You Do Need a Web Site for Your Small Business," *All Business*, December 17, 2009, *www.allbusiness.com/company-activities-management/company-structures-ownership/13624856-1.html*.

13. Lauren Simonds, "Web Sites: They're Not Just for E-Commerce," *Small Business Computing*, February 15, 2007, *www.smallbusinesscomputing .com/news/article.php/3660186.*

14. Frank Fortunato, "Search Engine Strategy Expo Exposes Valuable Tips," *E-Commerce Guide*, May 1, 2007, *www.ecommerce-guide.com/solutions/article.php/3675066*.

15. Robert McGarvey, "Connect the Dots," *Entrepreneur*, March 2000, pp. 78–85.

16. "BlogPulse Stats," BlogPulse, July 9, 2010, *www.blogpulse.com*.

17. Kristin Ladd, "Help! My Business Sucks!" *Entrepreneur*, September 3, 2009, *www.entrepreneur.com/startingabusiness/successstories/article203244.html*; Richard Markosian, "Rage Against Businesses That Suck," *Utah Stories*, September 21, 2009, *www.utahstories.com/help-my-business-sucks.html*.

18. Claire Tristram, "Many Happy Returns," *Small Business Computing*, May 1999, p. 73.

19. *Digital Window Shopping: The Long Journey to 'Buy,'* McAfee, Santa Clara, California: 2009, p. 3.

20. "Survival of the Fastest," *Inc. Technology*, No. 4, 1999, p. 57.

21. Fred Mossler and Tony Hsieh, "A Lesson from Zappos: Follow the Golden Rule," *Harvard Business Review*, June 4, 2010, *http://blogs.hbr.org/cs/2010/06/a_lesson_from_zappos_follow_th.html*; "The Zappos Story," Zappos.com, *www.zappos.com/about.zhtml*; Sidra Durst, "Shoe In," *Business 2.0*, December 2006, p. 54; "Beyond Their Years," *Entrepreneur*, November 2003, *www.entrepreneur.com/article/0,4621,311420,00.html*; "Zappos.com on Pace to More Than Double Sales This Year," *Internet Retailer*, November 3, 2003, *www.internetretailer.com/dailynews.asp?id=10577*; Jane Bennett Clark, Robert Frick, Sean O'Neill, Ronaleen Roha, and Alison Stevenson, "Point Click Buy," *Kiplinger's*, June 2003, pp. 90–93.

22. Fred Mossler and Tony Hsieh, "A Lesson from Zappos: Follow the Golden Rule," *Harvard Business Review*, June 4, 2010, *http://blogs.hbr.org/cs/2010/06/a_lesson_from_zappos_follow_th.html*.

23. Steve Bennett and Stacey Miller, "The E-Commerce Plunge," *Small Business Computing*, February 2000, p. 50.

24. John Horrigan, "Online Shopping," February 13, 2008, Pew Internet and American Life Project, *www.pewinternet.org/Reports/2008/Online-Shopping.aspx?r=1*.

25. "Akamai Reveals 2 Seconds as the New Threshold of Acceptability for E-Commerce Web Page Response Time," Akamai, September 14, 2009, *www.akamai.com/html/about/press/releases/2009/press_091409.html*.

26. Fiona Swerdlow, "2009 State of Retailing Online: Marketing Report," Shop.org, May 5, 2009, *http://blog.shop.org/2009/05/05/2009-state-of-retailing-online-marketing-report/*.

27. Melissa Campanelli, "Abandonment Issues," *E-Marketing and Commerce*, June 24, 2009, *www.emarketingandcommerce.com/blog/abandonment-issues*.

28. "Why Do We Abandon Shopping Carts?" Vovici, January 2006, *www.vovici.com/efm-innovation/reference/website-visitors/shopping-cart-abandonment-survey.asp*.

29. "E-mail Service Provider Listrak Conducts 'Shop and Abandon' Cart Study Using Internet Retailer 500 List," Listrak, August 13, 2009, *www.listrak.com/News/Listrak-Conducts-Abandon-Cart-Study/*.

30. "The Remarketing Report: Benchmark Data and Analysis on Connecting Web Behavior to E-mail Marketing," Experian CheetahMail, January 2010, p. 2.

31. "Case Studies: Rockler Automated Cart Abandonment Program Drives 2% of Sales," Blue Hornet Digital River, *www.bluehornet.com/case-studies/full/rockler*; "E-mail Service Provider Listrak Conducts 'Shop and Abandon' Cart Study Using Internet Retailer 500 List," Listrak, August 13, 2009, *www.listrak.com/News/Listrak-Conducts-Abandon-Cart-Study/*.

32. "Akamai Reveals 2 Seconds as the New Threshold of Acceptability for E-Commerce Web Page Response Times," Akamai, September 14, 2009, *www.akamai.com/html/about/press/releases/2009/press_091409.html*; Kristina Knight, "Study: Consumers Abandon Slow-Loading Web Sites," *BizReport*, April 27, 2010, *www.bizreport.com/2010/04/study_consumers_abandon_slow_loading_websites.html#*; "TagMan Solves Slow Page Load/Audience Loss Problems with Introduction of New TagMan ServerTags," TagMan, May 10, 2010, *http://blog.tagman.com/2010/05/tagman-solves-slow-page-loadaudience-loss-problems-with-introduction-of-new-tagman-servertags/*.

33. "Web Site Performance Management," *Internet Retailer*, July 1, 2010, *www.internetretailer.com/2010/07/01/web-site-performance-management*.

34. Fred Vogelstein, "A Cold Bath for Dot-Com Fever," *U.S. News & World Report*, September 13, 1999, p. 37.

35. "The World Is Discovering Fragrances of Ireland Through Webgistix," Webgistix, Olean, New York, *www.webgistix.com/success_FOI.pdf*.

36. Greg Howlett, "Trade PPV for VLV: Visitor Lifetime Value Metric Makes Money," *E-Commerce Guide*, May 23, 2007, *www.ecommerce-guide.com/solutions/building/article.php/3679441*.

37. Bronwyn Fryer and Lee Smith, ".com or Bust," *Forbes Small Business*, December 1999–January 2000, p. 41.

38. "History," Caledonian Creations, *www.caledoniancreations.co.uk/company/history.htm*.

39. Ralph F. Wilson, "The Five Mutable Laws of Web Marketing," *Web Marketing Today*, April 1, 1999, *www.wilsonweb.com/wmta/basic-principles.htm*, pp. 1–7.

40. "Bella of Cape Cod Offers a Lot of Bling for the Buck," Constant Contact, *www.constantcontact.com/email-marketing/customer-examples/bella-of-cape-cod.jsp*.

41. "E-Commerce Spending Will Rise 11% to $156 Billion This Year, Study Says," *Internet Retailer*, May 5, 2009, *www.internetretailer.com/2009/05/05/e-commerce-spending-will-rise-11-to-156-1-billion-this-year-s*.

42. "Epsilon Q4 2009 E-mail Trends and Benchmarks," Epsilon, Irving, Texas: February 2010, p. 2.

43. "Use of Testing in E-mail Marketing," eROI, 2009, p. 5; "Q3 E-mail Marketing Statistics," eROI, January 2008, p. 1.

44. "State of Spam and Phishing," Symantec, June 2010, p. 1.

45. Gitte Lindgaard, Gary Fernandes, Cathy Dudek, and J. Brown, "Attention Web Designers: You Have 50 Milliseconds to Make a Good Impression," *Journal of Behaviour and Information Technology*, March 2006, p. 115.

46. David Port, "How to Make Your Web Site Really Sell," *Entrepreneur*, September 2009, p. 84.

47. Phil Hochmuth, "Trust Marks: What's Behind the Label Counts," Yankee Group, Boston, Massachusetts: 2009, p. 3.

48. Jan Gardner, "10 Ideas for Growing Business Now," *Inc.*, October 29, 2001, *www2.inc.com/search/23629.html*.

49. "Affiliate Marketing Survey Report," e-Consultancy, 2008, *www.slideshare.net/econsultancy/affiliate-marketing-survey-report-2008-presentation-594947*.

50. Peter Figueredo, "Best-Kept Secrets of Affiliate Marketing Success," iMedia Connection, January 15, 2010, *www.imediaconnection.com/content/25634.asp*.

51. "The Top Ten Languages Used in the Internet," *Internet World Stats*, July 9, 2010, *www.internetworldstats.com/stats7.htm*.

52. Dylan Tweney, "Think Globally, Act Locally," *Business 2.0*, November 2001, pp. 120–121.

53. Don Davis, "Survivor: E-retail," *Internet Retailer*, April 2009, *www.internetretailer.com/2009/04/01/survivor-e-retail*; "Blue Nile Announces First Quarter 2010 Financial Results," Blue Nile, Inc., May 6, 2010, *www.internetworldstats.com/stats7.htm*.

54. Patrick Altoft, "5 Killer Ways to Promote Your Web Site Offline," Blogstorm, January 7, 2008, *www.blogstorm.co.uk/5-killer-ways-to-promote-your-website-offline/*; "Interview with 'Dragon Eater' Ling Valentine," Self Made Minds, January 31, 2008, *http://selfmademinds .com/200801/interview-with-dragon-eater-ling-valentine/*.

55. Kristin Purcell, "The State of Online Video," Pew Internet and American Life Project, June 3, 2010, *www.pewinternet.org/Reports/ 2010/State-of-Online-Video.aspx*; Aaron Smith, "New Numbers for Blogging and Blog Readership," Pew Internet and American Life Project, July 22, 2008, *www.pewinternet.org/Commentary/2008/ July/New-numbers-for-blogging-and-blog-readership.aspx*; "Adults on Social Network Sites," Pew Internet and American Life Project, October 8, 2009, *www.pewinternet .org/Infographics/Growth-in-Adult-SNS-Use-20052009.aspx*.

56. "Global Advertising: Consumers Trust Real Friends and Virtual Strangers the Most," NielsenWire, July 7, 2009, *http://blog. nielsen.com/nielsenwire/consumer/global-advertising-consumers-trust-real-friends-and-virtual-strangers-the-most/print/*.

57. Louis Columbus, "Is Social Networking and Asset or a Liability for Your Company?" *CRM Buyer*, September 2, 2008, *www.crmbuyer.com/ story/64352.html*.

58. Jessica E. Vascellaro, "Twitter Goes Mainstream," *Wall Street Journal*, October 27, 2008, pp. R1, R8.

59. Erica Swallow, "5 Small Business Social Media Success Stories," *Mashable*, June 2, 2010, *http://mashable.com/2010/06/02/small-business-social-media-success-stories/*.

60. Dan Briody, "Puppy Power," *Inc.*, November 2007, pp. 55–56.

61. Steve Coomes, "Pizza Chains 'Fan' Sales Flames by Adding Widgets to Social Networking Sites," *Nation's Restaurant News*, November 20, 2008, *www.nrn.com/article/pizza-chains-fan-sales-flames-adding-widgets-social-networking-sites*.

62. Jack Loechner, "Search Engines: The Shopper's Aid," Center for Media Research: Research Brief, March 4, 2010, *www.mediapost.com/ publications/?fa=Articles.printFriendly&art_aid=123651*.

63. Justin Martin, "Get Right with Google," *FSB*, September 2006, pp. 70–78.

64. "iProspect Blended Search Results Study," iProspect, April 2008, p. 13.

65. James A. Martin, "Search Engine Optimization: SEO Tips for Small Business," *Small Business Computing*, September 29, 2009, *www.smallbusinesscomputing.com/buyersguide/article.php/3841381/ Search-Engine-Optimization-SEO-Tips-for-Small-Business.htm*.

66. Ibid.

67. Nate Elliot, "The Easiest Way to a First-Page Ranking on Google," *Forrester Blogs*, January 8, 2009, *http://blogs.forrester.com/interactive_ marketing/2009/01/the-easiest-way.html*.

68. "Top Search Engines for 2010," SEO Consultants Directory, July 2, 2010, *www.seoconsultants.com/search-engines/*.

69. Justin Martin, "Get Right with Google," *FSB*, September 2006, pp. 70–78; "E-Commerce Spending Will Rise 11% to $156 Billion This Year, Study Says," *Internet Retailer*, May 5, 2009, *www.internetretailer .com/2009/ 05/05/e-commerce-spending-will-rise-11-to-156-1-billion-this-year-s*.

70. "Lingerie e-Retailer Andra Group Uncovers Customers Ready to Buy," *Internet Retailer*, April 30, 2009, *www.internetretailer.com/ 2009/04/30/lingerie-e-retailer-andra-group-uncovers-customers-ready-to-buy*.

71. "Click Fraud Rises in Q1 2010," *Marketing Charts*, May 21, 2010, *www.marketingcharts.com/direct/click-fraud-rises-in-q1-2010-12972/*.

72. Herman Miller, *www.hermanmiller.com*; "Design Matters," *Fortune Tech Guide*, 2001, pp. 183–188.

73. "Santa's Helpers," *Economist,* May 15, 2004, pp. 5–8.

74. Max Chafkin, "Where Have All the Words Gone?" *Inc.*, July–August 2009, pp. 23–24.

75. Christopher Saunders, "How Do I: Attract and Keep Customers?" *E-Commerce Guide*, June 8, 2004, *www.ecommerce-guide.com/ news/article.php/3365551*.

76. "About Us," American Pearl, *www.americanpearl.com/aboutus.html*.

77. *Revolutionizing Web Site Design: The New Rules of Usability*, OneupWeb, Traverse City, Michigan: 2010, p. 11.

78. Melissa Campanelli, "The Right Stuff," *Entrepreneur*, April 2007, p. 54.

79. Carol Stavraka, "There's No Stopping E-Business. Are You Ready?" *Forbes*, December 13, 1999, Special Advertising Section.

80. "2009 National Cyber Security Alliance/Symantec Small Business Study," National Cyber Security Alliance, 2009, pp. 3–4.

81. James Maguire, "The 'Mystery Shopping' Report," *E-Commerce Guide*, February 21, 2006, *www.e-commerce-guide.com/solutions/ customer_relations/article.php/3586441*.

82. Fiona Swerdlow, "2009 State of Retailing Online: Marketing Report," Shop.org, May 5, 2009, *http://blog.shop.org/2009/05/05/2009-state-of-retailing-online-marketing-report/*.

83. "How to Reduce Shopping Cart Abandonment," TRUSTe, San Francisco: 2009, p. 3.

84. "Online Shoppers Will Pay Extra to Protect Privacy, Study Shows," PhysOrg.com, June 6, 2007, *www.physorg.com/news100357431.html*.

85. "Digital Window Shopping: The Long Journey to 'Buy,'" McAfee, Santa Clara, California: 2009, p. 5.

86. Methusela Cebrian Ferrer, "State of the Internet 2009: A Report on the Ever-Changing Threat Landscape," CA Internet Business Security Unit, CA Technologies, Islandia, New York: 2010, p. 1.

87. "WhiteHat Web Site Security Statistics Report, 9th Edition," WhiteHat Security, Santa Clara, California: Spring 2009, p. 5.

88. Larry Greenemeier, "Largest Data Breach Ever," *Information Week*, April 2, 2007, p. 21.

89. Pankaj Kumar, "E-Commerce Data Security 2010: Learning from 2009's Debacles," *CRMBuyer*, January 18, 2010, *www.crmbuyer. com/story/69129.html?wlc=1278516295*.

90. "2009 National Cyber Security Alliance/Symantec Small Business Study," National Cyber Security Alliance, 2009, pp. 3–4.

91. "Online Fraud Report, 11th Annual Edition," Cybersource Corporation, Mountain View, California: 2010, p. 4.

92. Emily Maltby, "Shady Shoppers Beware," *Wall Street Journal*, November 24, 2009, *http://online.wsj.com/article/ SB10001424052748704533904574548210301039526.html#*.

Sources of Equity Financing

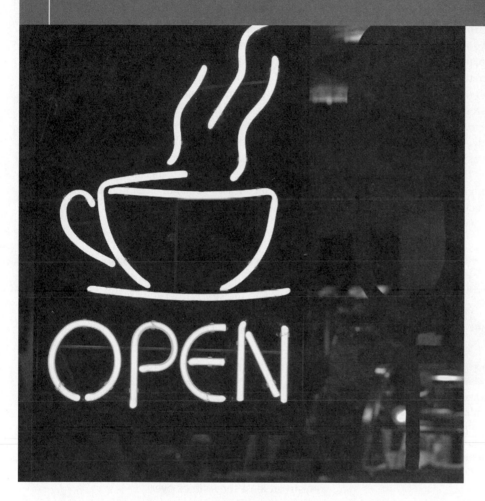

All it takes to start a company is one hundred thousand dollars . . .

and no "sense."

—Guy Jones, founder of River Runner Outdoor Center

The key for entrepreneurs is to find investors who are going to add

value to the company as it goes along.

—Rod Nelson

Learning Objectives

Upon completion of this chapter, you will be able to:

1 Explain the differences among the three types of capital small businesses require: fixed, working, and growth.

2 Describe the various sources of equity capital available to entrepreneurs, including personal savings, friends and relatives, angels, partners, corporations, venture capital, and public stock offerings.

3 Describe the process of "going public," as well as its advantages and disadvantages.

4 Explain the various simplified registrations, exemptions from registration, and other alternatives available to entrepreneurs who want to sell shares of equity to investors.

Raising the money to launch a new business venture has always been a challenge for entrepreneurs. Capital markets rise and fall with the stock market, overall economic conditions, and investors' fortunes. These swells and troughs in the availability of capital make the search for financing look like a wild roller-coaster ride. Entrepreneurs, especially those in less glamorous industries or those just starting out, soon discover the difficulty of finding outside sources of financing. Many banks shy away from making loans to start-ups, venture capitalists are looking for ever-larger deals, private investors have grown cautious, and a public stock offering remains a viable option for only a handful of promising companies with good track records and fast-growth futures. The result has been a credit crunch for entrepreneurs looking for small to moderate amounts of start-up capital. Entrepreneurs and business owners who need between $100,000 and $3 million are especially hard hit because of the vacuum that exists at that level of financing.

In the face of this capital crunch, businesses' need for capital has never been greater. When searching for the capital to launch their companies, entrepreneurs must remember the following "secrets" to successful financing:

- *Choosing the right sources of capital for a business can be just as important as choosing the right form of ownership or the right location.* It is a decision that will influence a company for a lifetime; therefore, entrepreneurs must weigh their options carefully and understand the consequences of the deal before committing to a particular funding source. Avoid the tendency to jump at the first check that comes your way; instead, consider the long-term impact on your business of accepting that check.
- *The money is out there; the key is knowing where to look.* Entrepreneurs must do their homework *before* they set out to raise money for their ventures. Understanding which sources of funding are best suited for the various stages of a company's growth and then taking the time to learn how those sources work are essential to success.
- *Creativity counts.* To find the financing their businesses demand, entrepreneurs must use as much creativity in attracting financing as they did in generating the ideas for their products and services.

ENTREPRENEURIAL
Profile

Drue Kataoka and Svetlozar Kazanjiev: Aboomba

As Drue Kataoka (left) and Svetlozar Kazanjiev planned their wedding, they drew inspiration from traditional wedding registries to create the world's first start-up registry to finance the launch of their business, Aboomba.

Source: Gary Reyes/Newscom

When Drue Kataoka and Svetlozar Kazanjiev began planning their wedding, they took a different approach to their wedding registry. Rather than list the typical household appliances that appear on most wedding registries, the couple created "The World's First Start-up Registry," listing items to help them launch their e-commerce site called Aboomba. They took elements from their business plan, such as "feed an engineer for a day ($273.97)," "Red Bull for a week ($52.41)," and "Amazon EC2 Cloud Web hosting for a week ($134.40)," and incorporated them into their start-up registry. Guests and others responded to the creative approach to raising capital, providing the couple with every item on their start-up registry at least three times over.[1]

- *The Internet puts vast resources of information that can lead to financing at entrepreneurs' fingertips.* The Internet often offers entrepreneurs, especially those looking for relatively small amounts of money, the opportunity to discover sources of funds that they otherwise might miss. The Web site created for this text (*www.pearsonhighered.com/scarborough*) provides links to many useful sites related to raising both start-up and growth capital. The Internet also provides a low-cost, convenient way for entrepreneurs to get their business plans into potential investors' hands anywhere in the world. When searching for sources of capital, entrepreneurs must not overlook this valuable tool!
- *Be thoroughly prepared before approaching potential lenders and investors.* In the hunt for capital, tracking down leads is tough enough; don't blow a potential deal by failing to be ready to present your business idea to potential lenders and investors in a clear, concise, convincing way. That, of course, requires a solid business plan.

■ *Looking for "smart" money is more important than looking for "easy" money.* Some entrepreneurs have little difficulty attracting investors' money. However, easy money is not always smart money. Even though it may be easy to acquire, money from the wrong investor can spell disaster for a small company. Entrepreneurs cannot overestimate the importance of making sure that the "chemistry" among themselves, their companies, and their funding sources is a good one. Too many entrepreneurs get into financial deals because they needed the money to keep their businesses growing only to discover that their plans do not match those of their financial partners.

ENTREPRENEURIAL
Profile

Brian Carlton: New Breed Wireless

When Brian Carlton launched CEIG, a company that sells content and applications for mobile phones under the brand name New Breed Wireless, he accepted an offer from a private investor who put up $400,000, payable in two installments, in exchange for 25 percent of the company. The relationship was rocky from the beginning, and the investor made clear his expectations of the company's performance. When CEIG missed one benchmark 1 year into the deal, the investor refused to invest the second installment, and Carlton was forced to scramble for money to keep the company afloat. "That investor didn't understand how technology businesses grow," says Carlton, whose company ultimately received the remaining $200,000 from the investor. Wiser for the experience, Carlton has revised his capital searching strategy, relying on smaller amounts of money and screening carefully every potential investor. With his new approach, Carlton has raised $1.1 million from 25 investors and has retained 75 percent of the equity in his business.[2]

■ *Plan an exit strategy.* Although it may seem peculiar for entrepreneurs to plan an exit strategy for investors when they are seeking capital to *start* their businesses, doing so increases their chances of closing a deal. Investors do not put their money into a business with the intent of leaving it there indefinitely. Their goal is to get their money back—along with an attractive return on it. Entrepreneurs who fail to define potential exit strategies for their investors reduce the likelihood of getting the capital their companies need to grow.

Rather than rely primarily on a single source of funds as they have in the past, entrepreneurs must piece together capital from multiple sources, a method known as **layered financing**. They

ENTREPRENEURIAL
Profile

Martin Eberhard, Marc Tarppening, and Elon Musk: Tesla Motors

Elon Musk, CEO of Tesla Motors, poses with one of the company's high performance electric cars in New York City's Times Square following Tesla Motors' initial public offering.

Source: Mark Lennihan/AP Wide World Photos

Founded in 2003 by Silicon Valley engineers Martin Eberhard and Marc Tarppening and PayPal founder Elon Musk, Tesla Motors, a Palo Alto, California-based maker of sleek, high-performance electric cars, has relied on layered financing from a variety of sources to produce its first two all-electric cars, the Roadster and the Model S. The Roadster, which goes from zero to 60 miles per hour in just 3.7 seconds and travels 245 miles between charges, sells for $100,000. The Model S, a seven-passenger hatchback capable of hitting 60 miles per hour in 5.5 seconds, sells for about $50,000. To launch their company (which is named after Nikola Tesla, the inventor of alternating current), the cofounders invested some of their own money and turned to private investors, a "who's who" list of Silicon Valley entrepreneurs, including Google founders Sergey Brin and Larry Page, for capital. As it grew, the company also attracted millions of dollars of financing from a number of venture capital companies. Daimler, the parent company of Mercedes-Benz invested $50 million in return for 9 percent of the company's stock. Tesla also received a low-interest $465 million loan from the Department of Energy after being recognized as one of the nation's leading electric vehicle research companies. Because of the huge capital investment required to build a successful automotive company, Tesla's founders knew that an initial public offering (IPO) of the company's stock was necessary. Seven years after its launch, the company, which had not yet earned an annual profit, conducted a successful IPO that raised more than $226 million. Musk, now Tesla's CEO, already is developing plans for new models, including a crossover SUV, a delivery van, and a pickup truck.[3]

have discovered that raising capital successfully requires them to cast a wide net to capture the financing they need to launch their businesses. Much like assembling a patchwork quilt from using fabric from many different sources, financing a small business often requires entrepreneurs to find capital from many different sources.

For most entrepreneurs, raising the money to start or expand their businesses is a challenge that demands time, energy, creativity, and a measure of luck. "Raising money is a marathon, not a sprint," says one entrepreneur who has raised $4 million for her 4-year-old company.[4] This chapter and the next one will guide you through the myriad of financing options available to entrepreneurs, focusing on both sources of equity (ownership) and debt (borrowed) financing.

IN THE ENTREPRENEURIAL
SPOTLIGHT The Hunt for Capital

While majoring in business at the University of Arizona, Sean Conway, who suffers from attention deficit hyperactivity disorder (ADHD), had difficulty listening to lectures and taking notes simultaneously. Conway noticed that many students experienced the same problem, and he and Justin Miller, a junior at the University of Arizona, recognized a business opportunity. They decided to launch Notehall (www.notehall.com), a Web site that serves as a marketplace for students to buy and sell class notes and study guides, first targeting students on their campus. Their goal, however, was to harness the power of the Web and take the concept to other campuses around the world. Conway and Miller started Notehall with $70,000 from Conway's inheritance and Miller's bar mitzvah money.

To access class notes, users purchase credits through the site's virtual currency system and spend them to download files (100 credits cost $3; lecture notes cost 25 credits; and a complete study guide costs 100 credits). Students who post notes and study guides receive a commission (25 cents on lecture notes and $1 on a study guide) when they are downloaded. Notehall generates revenue by taking a commission on each download. "With the time it takes to make a study guide, let alone study, you can go to Notehall and find someone who's already made a study guide," says one enthusiastic user at the University of Arizona.

One year into business, the company was out of cash, and the 20-something entrepreneurs had no more money to invest. Conway convinced his grandfather to contribute $17,000 for marketing, which helped the young company reach nearly 8,000 students at the University of Arizona while Conway pitched the business to angel investors and venture capital firms. No one was interested in investing.

Desperate for capital, Conway submitted his business plan to DreamIt Ventures, an entrepreneurial boot camp in Philadelphia funded by four economic development organizations that provides promising entrepreneurs with office space, advisors, and the opportunity to meet potential lenders and investors. Notehall was one of just 10 companies selected to participate in DreamIt for the summer. Conway's boot camp experience paid off. By the end of the program, Conway had convinced investors to put $500,000 into Notehall.

Conway's next move was to apply to become a contestant on ABC's Shark Tank, a television show that gives entrepreneurs the opportunity to pitch their business ideas to five angel investors who ask questions and then decide to invest or pass on each business opportunity. The show's producers accepted Notehall, and after a few tense minutes of grilling from the angel investors, Conway and D. J. Stephan, the company's marketing officer, struck a deal with investor Barbara Corcoran for $90,000 in exchange for 25 percent of Notehall.

Conway has expanded the management team at Notehall and has created an advisory board composed of both academicians and businesspeople. The company now reaches 33 colleges and generates sales of $900,000, up from just $40,000 in the previous year. Conway knows that to continue to expand, Notehall will need more capital to fuel its growth.

1. How typical is Notehall's struggle to raise capital? What advice can you give to an entrepreneur such as Sean Conway about raising capital to start a business? Which sources of funding do you recommend and in what sequence? Explain.

2. Is it ethical for students to make money selling notes taken from a professor's lecture? Critics of Notehall claim that some students may not have enough money to purchase notes on Notehall, which might put them at a disadvantage compared to those who can afford to purchase notes. Do you agree? Explain.

3. Visit the Web site for ABC's Shark Tank at http://abc.go.com/shows/shark-tank and watch an episode. (You can find Sean Conway and

Notehall cofounders (left to right) Justin Miller, Sean Conway and Fadi Chalfoun.

Source: NoteHall, 340 Bryant Street, Suite #104, San Francisco, CA 94107 (650)276-0409

D. J. Stephan's pitch for Notehall on episode 108.) At the site, you can also read more about the entrepreneurs who appear on the show and their businesses. Do you agree with the angels' decisions? In which of the businesses, if any, would you invest? What criteria did you use to evaluate each opportunity? What does this experience teach you about pitching your own idea to potential investors?

Sources: Based on Emily Maltby, "Need Funding? Better Get Creative," *Wall Street Journal*, October 15, 2009, p. B5; "America's Best Young Entrepreneurs: Notehall," *Bloomberg's Business Week*, *http://images.businessweek.com/ss/09/10/1009_entrepreneurs_25_and_under/18.htm*; "About Us," Notehall, *www.notehall.com/index/about*; Hank Stephenson, "Study Buddy," *Tucson Weekly*, May 7, 2009, *www.tucsonweekly.com/tucson/study-buddy/Content?oid=1180388*.

Planning for Capital Needs

1. Explain the differences among the three types of capital small businesses require: fixed, working, and growth.

Becoming a successful entrepreneur requires one to become a skilled fund-raiser, a job that usually requires more time and energy than most business founders anticipate. In start-up companies, raising capital can easily consume as much as one-half of the entrepreneur's time and can take many months to complete. Most entrepreneurs are seeking less than $1 million (indeed, most need less than $100,000), which may be the toughest money to secure. Where to find this seed money depends, in part, on the nature of the proposed business and on the amount of money required. For example, the creator of a computer software firm would have different capital requirements than the founder of an ice cream shop. Although both entrepreneurs might approach some of the same types of lenders or investors, each would be more successful targeting specific sources of funds best suited to their particular financial needs and businesses.

Capital is any form of wealth employed to produce more wealth. It exists in many forms in a typical business, including cash, inventory, plant, and equipment. Entrepreneurs need three different types of capital.

Fixed Capital

Fixed capital is needed to purchase a business's permanent or fixed assets, such as buildings, land, computers, and equipment. Money invested in these fixed assets tends to be frozen because it cannot be used for any other purpose. Typically, large sums of money are involved in purchasing fixed assets, and credit terms usually are lengthy. Lenders of fixed capital expect the assets purchased to improve the efficiency, and thus the profitability, of the business and to create improved cash flows that ensure repayment.

Working Capital

Working capital represents a business's temporary funds; it is the capital used to support a company's normal short-term operations. Accountants define working capital as current assets minus current liabilities. The need for working capital arises because of the uneven flow of cash into and out of the business due to normal seasonal fluctuations. Credit sales, seasonal sales swings, or unforeseeable changes in demand create fluctuations in *any* small company's cash flow. Working capital normally is used to buy inventory, pay bills, finance credit sales, pay wages and salaries, and take care of any unexpected emergencies. Lenders of working capital expect it to produce higher cash flows to ensure repayment at the end of the production/sales cycle.

Growth Capital

Growth capital, unlike working capital, is not related to the seasonal fluctuations of a small business. Instead, growth capital requirements surface when an existing business is expanding or

TABLE 1 Equity Capital Sources at Various Stages of Company Growth

Characteristics	Start-Up	Early	Expansion	Profitability
	Business is in conceptual phase and exists only on paper.	Business is developing one or more products or services but is not yet generating sales.	Business is selling products or services and is generating revenue and is beginning to establish a customer base.	Company has established a customer base and is profitable.

Possible Sources of Funding	Likelihood of using each source: H = Highly likely; P = Possible; U = Unlikely			
Personal savings	H	H	H	H
Retained earnings	U	U	U	H
Friends and relatives	H	H	P	P
Angel investors	H	H	P	U
Partners	H	H	P	U
Corporate venture capital	P	H	H	H
Venture capital	U	P	H	H
Initial public offering (IPO)	U	U	P	H
Regulation S-B Offering	U	U	P	H
Small Company Offering Registration (SCOR)	U	P	P	H
Private placements	U	P	P	H
Intrastate offerings (Rule 147)	U	P	P	H
Regulation A	U	P	P	H

changing its primary direction. For example, a small manufacturer of silicon microchips for computers saw his business skyrocket in a short time period. With orders for chips rushing in, the growing business needed a sizable cash infusion to increase plant size, expand its sales and production workforce, and buy more equipment. During times of such rapid expansion, a growing company's capital requirements are similar to those of a business start-up. Like lenders of fixed capital, growth capital lenders expect the funds to improve a company's profitability and cash-flow position, thus ensuring repayment.

Although these three types of capital are interdependent, each has certain sources, characteristics, and effects on the business and its long-term growth that entrepreneurs must recognize. Table 1 shows the various stages of a company's growth and the sources of capital most suitable in each stage.

Sources of Equity Financing

2. Describe the various sources of equity financing available to entrepreneurs, including personal savings, friends and relatives, angels, partners, corporations, venture capital, and public stock offerings.

Equity capital represents the personal investment of the owner (or owners) in a business and is sometimes called *risk* capital because the investor assumes the primary risk of losing his or her funds if the business fails. For instance, private investor Victor Lombardi lost the $3.5 million he invested in a start-up called NetFax, a company that was developing the technology to send faxes over the Internet. However, when NetFax's patent application stalled, the company foundered. Just 3 years after its launch, NetFax ceased operations, leaving Lombardi's investment worthless.[5]

If a venture succeeds, however, founders and investors share in the benefits, which can be quite substantial. The founders of and early investors in Yahoo!, Sun Microsystems, FedEx, Intel, and Microsoft became multimillionaires when the companies went public and their equity investments finally paid off. To entrepreneurs, the primary advantage of equity capital is that it does not have to be repaid like a loan does. Equity investors are entitled to share in the company's earnings (if there are any) and usually to have a voice in the company's future direction.

The primary disadvantage of equity capital is that the entrepreneur must give up some—perhaps *most*—of the ownership in the business to outsiders. Although 50 percent of something is better than 100 percent of nothing, giving up control of your company can be disconcerting and dangerous. Many entrepreneurs who give up majority ownership in their companies in exchange for equity capital find themselves forced out of the businesses they started! Entrepreneurs are most likely to give up more equity in their businesses in the start-up phase than in any other.

We now turn our attention to nine common sources of equity capital.

Personal Savings

The *first* place entrepreneurs should look for start-up money is in their own pockets. It's the least expensive source of funds available! Entrepreneurs apparently see the benefits of self-sufficiency; the most common source of equity funds used to start a small business is the entrepreneur's pool of personal savings, a technique known as **bootstrapping**. The Global Entrepreneurship Monitor (GEM) study reports that in the United States, the average cost to start a business is $70,200 and that the typical entrepreneur provides 67.9 percent of the initial capital requirement.[6]

Lenders and investors *expect* entrepreneurs to put their own money into a business start-up. If an entrepreneur is not willing to risk his or her own money, potential investors are not likely to risk their money in the business either. Furthermore, failure to put up sufficient capital of their own means that entrepreneurs must either borrow excessive amounts of capital or give up significant shares of ownership to outsiders to fund their businesses properly. Excessive borrowing in the early days of a business puts intense pressure on its cash flow, and becoming a minority shareholder may dampen a founder's enthusiasm for making a business successful. Neither outcome presents a bright future for the company involved. Using their own money at start up allows entrepreneurs to minimize the debt their companies take on and to retain control of their companies' future.

Because they are not able to attract capital from outside sources, entrepreneurs often must bootstrap their companies, launching them with little or no money. It takes creativity, boldness, and a certain degree of brashness and moxie, but it works.

ENTREPRENEURIAL
Profile

Vlad Shmunis and Vlad Vendrow: RingCentral

In 2003, Vlad Shmunis and Vlad Vendrow cofounded RingCentral, a company that uses cloud computing to offer small companies sophisticated Internet-based voice and fax services that require no special hardware or software, by bootstrapping it with their own money. By targeting small companies with services that were once available only to large corporations with sophisticated phone systems, such as virtual receptionists, call forwarding, multiple extensions, and transcribing voice mail into e-mail, for as little as $10 per month, their company grew quickly. "Customers were happy and recommended [our service] to their friends," says Shmunis, who earlier had launched a company called Ring Zero Systems. "We were always growing." Like most bootstrappers, the founders focused on keeping their costs low. "We ran this business out of a 1,000-square-foot office with 10 people," Shmunis says. "We kept building and building." Within 3 years, RingCentral had 20,000 customers, and its capital requirements were outstripping the company's ability to meet them. Only then did Shmunis and Vendrow look for outside financing. RingCentral negotiated two rounds of investments totaling $24 million from venture capital companies, but Shmunis and Vendrow maintained control of their company.[7]

Friends and Family Members

Although most entrepreneurs look to their own bank accounts first to finance a business, few have sufficient resources to launch their businesses alone. After emptying their own pockets, entrepreneurs should look to friends and family members who might be willing to invest in a business venture. Because of their relationships with the founder, these people are most likely to invest.

ENTREPRENEURIAL
Profile

*Dave and Catherine
Cook: myYearbook*

While flipping through their high school yearbooks, 17-year-old Dave Cook said to his 15-year-old sister, Catherine, "This is 2005. Why is anyone buying yearbooks anymore?" Soon they envisioned a social networking Web site where young people could post photos, stories, and other memorabilia. Over dinner one evening, the budding entrepreneurs described their idea to their older brother Geoff, who had started his own Internet company while in college in 1997 and sold it in 2002. "As soon as I heard the idea, I thought it was very cool and put in $250,000," says Geoff, who is now the company's CEO. "We got another $250,000 from an angel investor whom I had worked with on my previous company." In just 6 weeks, the Cooks used the money to launch myYearbook; hire staff (including programmers in India); set up headquarters in quaint New Hope, Pennsylvania; and market the company's Web site (*www.myyearbook.com*). Within months of the site's launch, thousands of teenagers had signed up as members. myYearbook has since landed $17.1 million in two rounds of venture capital to finance its rapid growth. The site has more than 20 million members worldwide, is one of the 30 most-trafficked Web sites, and generates annual sales of more than $20 million. myYearbook recently launched a new service, Chatter, which allows users to play games and connect with other users in their immediate geographic areas.[8]

The GEM study of entrepreneurial trends across the globe reports that family members and friends are the biggest source of external capital used to launch new businesses. Investments from family and friends are an important source of capital for entrepreneurs, but the amounts invested typically are small, often no more than just a few thousand dollars. Across the globe, the average amount that family members and friends invest in start-up businesses averages just $3,000.[9] In the United States alone, family members and friends invest an average of $27,715 in a typical small business start-up for an astonishing total of $100 billion per year![10]

Investments (or loans) from family and friends are an excellent source of seed capital and can get a start-up far enough along to attract money from private investors or venture capital companies. Inherent dangers lurk in family business investments and loans, however. A recent study reports a default rate of 14 percent on business loans from family and friends, compared to a default rate of 1 percent for bank loans.[11] Unrealistic expectations or misunderstood risks have destroyed many friendships and have ruined many family reunions. To avoid problems, an entrepreneur must honestly present the investment opportunity and the nature of the risks involved to avoid alienating friends and family members if the business fails. Smart entrepreneurs treat family members and friends who invest in their companies in the same way they would treat business partners. Some investments in start-up companies return more than friends and family members ever could have imagined. In 1995, Mike and Jackie Bezos invested $300,000 into their son Jeff's start-up business, Amazon.com. Today, Mike and Jackie own 6 percent of Amazon.com's stock, and their shares are worth billions of dollars![12]

Table 2 offers suggestions for structuring family and friendship financing deals.

Angels

After dipping into their own pockets and convincing friends and relatives to invest in their business ventures, many entrepreneurs still find themselves short of the seed capital they need. Frequently, the next stop on the road to business financing is private investors. These **private investors** (or **angels**) are wealthy individuals, often entrepreneurs themselves, who invest in business start-ups in exchange for equity stakes in the companies. Alexander Graham Bell, inventor of the telephone, used angel capital to start Bell Telephone in 1877. More recently, companies such as Google, Facebook, Apple, Starbucks, Amazon.com, and Costco relied on angel financing in their early years to finance growth.

In many cases, angels invest in businesses for more than purely economic reasons (often because they have experience and a personal interest in the industry), and they are willing to put money into companies in the earliest stages (often before a company generates any revenue), long before venture capital firms jump in. Angel financing is ideal for companies that have outgrown the capacity of investments from friends and family but are still too small to attract the interest of venture capital companies. For instance, after raising the money to launch Amazon.com from family and friends, Jeff Bezos turned to angels because venture capital firms were not interested in the business start-up. Bezos attracted $1.2 million from a dozen angels before landing $8 million from venture capital firms a year later.[13]

TABLE 2 Suggestions for Structuring Family and Friendship Financing Deals

Tapping family members and friends for start-up capital, whether in the form of equity or debt financing, is a popular method of financing business ideas. In a typical year, some 6 million individuals in the United States invest about $100 billion in entrepreneurial ventures. Unfortunately, these deals don't always work to the satisfaction of both parties. Even those that do can strain family relationships in the early, uncertain days of a company's tenuous existence. "[Family] relationships change when money enters the picture," says Meg Hirshberg, who with her husband, Gary, cofounded Stonyfield Farm. She recalls fretting over family gatherings at Thanksgiving in the now successful company's early days because her mother and her brothers had invested heavily in their start-up business, which Meg knew was a risky venture. "I knew that soon after our arrival, the conversation would turn to the fate of their cash," she says. "Their questions were sheathed in a kindness that barely covered the sharp blade of concern within. Profits? Not even close. Margins? Come on. Cash burn? Lots of that. I would sympathize with the turkey as slivers of explanations and excuses were sliced from our tender hides. In those early days, our carcass of a business felt cooked, too."

The following suggestions can help entrepreneurs avoid needlessly destroying family relationships and friendships:

- *Consider the impact of the investment on everyone involved.* Will it impose a hardship on anyone? Is the investor putting up the money because he or she wants to or because he or she feels obligated to? Can all parties afford the loan if the business folds? Convincing Aunt Sally to invest her retirement nest egg in a high-risk start-up is not the best financing strategy. Lynn McPhee used $250,000 from family members to launch Xuny, a Web-based clothing store. "Our basic rule of thumb was, if [the investment is] going to strap someone, we won't take it," she says.
- *Keep the arrangement strictly business.* The parties should treat all loans and investments in a business-like manner, no matter how close the friendship or family relationship, to avoid problems down the line. If the transaction is a loan exceeding $10,000, it must carry a rate of interest at least as high as the market rate; otherwise the IRS may consider the loan a gift and penalize the lender.
- *Educate "naïve" investors.* Family members and friends usually invest in a business because of their relationships with the founder, not because they understand the business itself. Take the time to explain to potential investors the basics of the business idea, how it will make money, and the risks associated with investing in it.
- *Settle the details up front.* Before any money changes hands, both parties must agree on the details of the deal. How much money is involved? Is it a loan or an investment? How will the investor cash out? How will the loan be paid off? What happens if the business fails?
- *Never accept more than investors can afford to lose.* No matter how much capital you may need, accepting more than family members or friends can afford to lose is a recipe for disaster—and perhaps financial hardship or even bankruptcy for the investors. In the early days of Stonyfield Farm, Meg Hirshberg was frightened because she knew that her mother had invested far more in the company than she could afford to lose. "I was terrified of how our potential failure might affect her retirement and her relationship with Gary and me," she recalls. Although Hirshberg's fears proved to be unfounded, they caused her much grief.
- *Create a written contract.* Don't make the mistake of closing a financial deal with just a handshake. The probability of misunderstandings skyrockets! Putting an agreement in writing demonstrates the parties' commitment to the deal and minimizes the chances of disputes from faulty memories and misunderstandings.
- *Treat the money as "bridge financing."* Although family and friends can help you launch your business, it is unlikely that they can provide enough capital to sustain it over the long term. Sooner or later, you will need to establish a relationship with other sources of capital if your company is to grow. Consider money from family and friends as a bridge to take your company to the next level of financing.
- *Develop a payment schedule that suits both the entrepreneur and the lender or investor.* Although lenders and investors may want to get their money back as quickly as possible, a rapid repayment or cash-out schedule can jeopardize a fledgling company's survival. Establish a realistic repayment plan that works for the parties without putting excessive strain on the young company's cash flow.
- *Have an exit plan.* Every deal should define exactly how investors will "cash out" their investments.
- *Keep everyone informed.* Entrepreneurs should keep investors informed about the company's progress, its successes and failures, and the challenges it faces. Investors want to know both good news and bad news.

Sources: Based on Meg Cadoux Hirshberg, "Brother Can You Spare a Dime?" *Inc.*, November 2009, pp. 45–46; Jenny McCune, "Tips for Feud-Free Financing from Friends and Family," *Bankrate*, July 24, 2000, *www.bankrate.com/brm/news/biz/Capital_borrowing/20000724.asp*; Andrea Coombes, "Retirees as Venture Capitalists," CBS.MarketWatch.com, November 2, 2003, *http://netscape.marketwatch.com/news/story.asp?dist=feed&siteid= netscape&guid={1E1267CD-32A4-4558-9F7E-40E4B7892D01}*; Paul Kvinta, "Frogskins, Shekels, Bucks, Moolah, Cash, Simoleans, Dough, Dinero: Everybody Wants It. Your Business Needs It. Here's How to Get It," *Smart Business*, August 2000, pp. 74–89. Alex Markels, "A Little Help from Their Friends," *Wall Street Journal*, May 22, 1995, p. R10; Heather Chaplin, "Friends and Family," *Your Company*, September 1999, p. 26.

FIGURE 1
Angel Financing

Source: Center for Venture Financing, Whittemore School of Business, University of New Hampshire, *www.unh.edu/cvr*.

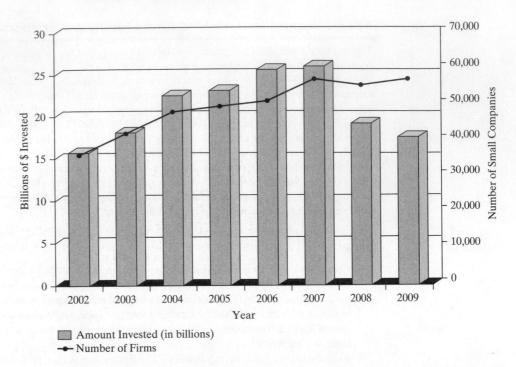

Angels are a primary source of capital for companies in the start-up stage through the growth stage, and their role in financing small businesses is significant. The Center for Venture Research at the University of New Hampshire estimates that nearly 260,000 angels invest $17.6 billion a year in 57,000 small companies, most of them in the start-up phase (see Figure 1).[14] Angels invest as much money in small companies as venture capital firms, but they put it into 20 times as many companies as venture capital firms. Because the angel market is so fragmented and, in many cases, built on anonymity, we may never get a completely accurate estimate of its investment in business start-ups. However, experts concur on one fact: Angels are a vital source of equity capital for small businesses.

Angels fill a significant gap in the seed capital market. They are most likely to finance start-ups with capital requirements in the $10,000 to $2 million range, well below the $3 million to $10 million minimum investments most professional venture capitalists prefer. Because they invest in the earliest stages of a business, angels also tolerate risk levels that would make venture capitalists shudder. In fact, 52 percent of angels' investments lose money, returning less than the angels' original investment. The potential for investing in big winners exists as well; 7 percent of angels' investments produce a return of more than 10 times their original investments.[15]

Lewis Gersh, an experienced angel investor, says that out of 10 companies that an angel invests in, 5 will fail, 2 will break even, and 2 will return two to three times the original investment. Just 1 company out of 10 will produce a significant return, "which means that every one of them has to have the potential of being a home run," says Gersh. Most angels consider a "home run" investment to be one that results in a return of 10 to 30 times the original investment in 5 to 7 years, somewhat lower than the returns that venture capital firms expect.[16] One angel investor, a retired entrepreneur, says that of the 31 companies he has invested in, "more than half have gone under, but four were home runs, returning 25 times my investment. The others gave me a small return or at least some of my money back."[17] Angel financing is important because angels often finance deals that venture capitalists will not consider.

ENTREPRENEURIAL
Profile

Shan Sinha and Alex DeNeui: Docverse

Chris Dixon, a serial entrepreneur and angel investor, has put money into 23 start-up companies. Although not all of them have been successful, some of Dixon's investments have been home runs, including Skype and Postini. Dixon also was an early investor in Docverse, a company whose software simplifies Web-based collaboration on Microsoft Office documents. Microsoft veterans Shan Sinha and Alex DeNeui launched Docverse in 2007 and attracted nearly $2 million from Dixon and other angel investors to build the company before selling it to Google for $25 million, producing an impressive return for themselves and their angel investors.[18]

Because angels prefer to maintain a low profile, the real challenge lies in *finding* them. Most angels are seasoned entrepreneurs themselves; on average, angel investors have founded 2.7 companies and have 14.5 years of entrepreneurial experience. They also are well educated; 99 percent have college degrees. Research also shows that 88 percent of angel investors are men (their average age is 57 years) who have been investing in promising small companies for 9 years. The typical angel invests an average of $50,000 in a company that is at the seed or start-up growth stages and makes an investment in one company per year.[19] The average time required to close an angel financing deal is 67 days.[20] Angels accept 14.5 percent of the investment proposals they receive.[21] When evaluating a proposal, angels look for a qualified management team ("We invest in people," says one angel), a business with a clearly defined niche, the potential to dominate the market, and a competitive advantage. They also want to see market research that proves the existence of a sizable and profitable customer base.

Because angels frown on "cold calls" from entrepreneurs they don't know, locating them boils down to making the right contacts. Asking friends, attorneys, bankers, stockbrokers, accountants, other business owners, and consultants for suggestions and introductions is a good way to start. "Angels are more likely to invest in a company that was referred to them by someone they know and trust," says Marianne Hudson, director of the angel initiative at the Kauffman Foundation.[22] Networking is the key. Angels almost always invest their money locally, so entrepreneurs should look close to home for them—typically within a 50- to 100-mile radius. Angels also look for businesses they know something about, and most expect to invest their knowledge, experience, and energy as well as their money in a company. In fact, the advice and the network of contacts that angels bring to a deal can sometimes be as valuable as their money!

ENTREPRENEURIAL
Profile
Rich Aberman and Bill Clerico: WePay

When Rich Aberman and Bill Clerico started WePay, an online payment service that allows groups ranging from fraternities to owners of fantasy sports teams to collect, manage, and spend money, they relied on angel investor Max Levchin to help them build out their system and keep it secure. Chafkin, who cofounded online payment company PayPal, "built the PayPal fraud system," says Clerico. "That's why we aggressively sought him out." WePay raised $1.65 million in capital from angel investors.[23]

Angel investing has become more sophisticated, with investors pooling their resources to form angel networks and angel capital funds, dubbed *super angels*, that operate like mini versions of professional venture capital firms and draw on the investors' skills, experience, and contacts to help the start-ups in which they invest succeed. Veteran angel investor Mike Maples operates Floodgate, a super-angel fund that manages $35 million in angel capital and invests between $250,000 and $1 million in promising start-ups, including Twitter and Digg.[24]

Today, more than 300 angel capital networks operate in cities of all sizes across the United States (up from just 10 in 1996), with as many operating in other countries.[25] Entrepreneurs can find angel networks in their areas with the help of the Angel Capital Association's directory (*www.angelcapitalassociation.org*). With the right approach, an entrepreneur can attract more money and a larger network of advisors from an angel capital group than from individual investors. The typical angel capital group has 44 members, who invest $1.77 million each year in 6.3 companies, on average.[26]

ENTREPRENEURIAL
Profile
Hans Severiens: Band of Angels

In 1994, Hans Severiens, a professional investor, created the Band of Angels, a group of about 130 angels (mostly Silicon Valley millionaires) who meet monthly in Portola Valley, California, to listen to entrepreneurs pitch their business plans. The Band of Angels reviews about 50 proposals each month before inviting a handful of entrepreneurs to make brief presentations at its monthly meeting. Interested members often team up with one another to invest in the businesses they consider most promising. The Band of Angels' average investment is $890,000, which usually nets the investors between 15 and 20 percent of a company's stock. Since its inception, the Band of Angels has invested more than $186 million in more than 200 promising young companies, most of them in the high-tech sector, including Symantec and Logitech. Nine of the companies have made initial public offerings, and 45 of them have been acquired by larger companies.[27]

Angels are an excellent source of "patient money," often willing to wait 5 to 7 years or longer to cash out their investments. They earn their returns through the increased value of the business, not through dividends and interest. For example, more than 1,000 early investors in Microsoft Inc. are now millionaires, and the original investors in Genentech Inc. (a genetic engineering company) have seen their investments increase more than 500 times.[28] Angels' return-on-investment targets tend to be lower than those of professional venture capitalists. Although venture capitalists shoot for 60 to 75 percent returns annually, angel investors usually settle for 20 to 50 percent (depending on the level of risk involved in the venture). A study by the Kauffman Foundation reports that the average return on angels' investments in small companies is 2.6 times the original investment in 3.5 years, which is the equivalent of an annual 27 percent internal rate of return.[29] Angel investors typically purchase 15 to 30 percent ownership in a small company, leaving the majority ownership to the company founder(s). They look for the same exit strategies that venture capital firms look for: either an initial public offering or a buyout by a larger company.

The accompanying Lessons from the Street-Smart Entrepreneur feature offers useful tips for attracting angel financing.

LESSONS FROM THE STREET-SMART → entrepreneur

Tips for Attracting Angel Financing

John White and John Bellaud understand the importance of capital to a small business and know firsthand how hard raising capital can be for a small company. White and Bellaud are in the process of raising $14 million for their company, Joy Berry Enterprises, Inc., which distributes the works of Joy Berry, a popular author of more than 250 children's books. Berry's books, which teach children about responsibility and proper behavior through stories, music, and multimedia, have sold more than 85 million copies. White and Bellaud want to consolidate all of Berry's books in one publishing house with marketing muscle. They raised $600,000 from angel investors in the company's early days, but turbulence in the financial markets has squeezed the flow of capital to a trickle. White and Bellaud managed to scrape together $3 million in another round of angel investments, enough to license Berry's books and get them on the market, but they still need $11 million to secure intellectual property rights and implement their marketing plan.

Although they are an important source of small business financing, angels can be extremely difficult to locate. You won't find them listed under "angels" in the Yellow Pages of the telephone directory. Patience and persistence—and connections—pay off in the search for angel financing, however. How does an entrepreneur who needs financing find an angel to help launch or expand a company and make the deal work? Take the following tips from the Street-Smart Entrepreneur:

- *Start looking for potential investors early—before you need the money.* Finding private investors takes a lot longer than most entrepreneurs think. Starting early is one key to success.

- *Have a business plan ready.* Once you find potential private investors, don't risk them losing interest while you put together a business plan. Have the plan ready to go *before* you begin your search.

- *Don't expect to raise all of the money at once.* Entrepreneurs often get capital for their businesses in fits and spurts. In one 2-year period, Joy Berry Enterprises raised money in five different rounds, sometimes in amounts as small as $200,000.

- *Look close to home.* Most angels prefer to invest their money locally, so conduct a thorough search for potential angels within a 50- to 100-mile radius of your business.

- *Canvass your industry.* Angels tend to specialize in particular industries, usually ones they know a lot about.

- *Recognize that, in addition to the money they invest, angels also want to provide their knowledge and expertise.* Indeed, angels' experience and knowledge can be just as valuable as their money *if* entrepreneurs are willing to accept it.

- *Remember that angels invest for more than just financial reasons.* Angels want to earn a good return on the money they invest in businesses, but there's usually more to it than that. Angels often invest in companies for personal reasons.

- *Emphasize the skills and experience of the management team.* Angels, like venture capitalists, invest in people, not just good ideas.

- *Join local philanthropic organizations, chambers of commerce, nonprofit organizations, and advisory* boards so that you can meet potential angels. Potential investors often are involved in these organizations.

- *Ask business professionals such as bankers, lawyers, stockbrokers, accountants, and others for names of potential angels.* They know people who have the money and the desire to invest in business ventures.
- *Network, network, network.* Finding angel financing initially is a game of contacts—getting an introduction to the right person from the right person.
- *Investigate the investors and their past deals.* Never get involved in a deal with an angel you don't know or trust. Be sure you and your investors have a common vision of the business and the deal.
- *Summarize the details of the deal in a letter of intent.* Although a letter of intent is not legally binding, it outlines the basic structure of the deal and exposes the most sensitive areas of negotiation so that there are no surprises. What role, if any, will the angel play in running the business? Angels can be a source of valuable help, but some entrepreneurs complain of angels' meddling.
- *Talk about the risks up front.* Some entrepreneurs do everything they can to disguise the risks associated with their businesses from potential investors. Smart entrepreneurs disclose the risks early on. Don't dwell on the downside, but be honest about the risk of the investment.
- *Keep the deal simple.* The simpler the deal is, the easier it will be to sell to potential investors. Probably the simplest way to involve angels is to sell them common stock.
- *Be prepared to "pay to pitch."* Many angel networks charge entrepreneurs a few hundred dollars to pitch their ideas to a group of angels. If you have your pitch ready and can get before the right group of potential investors, your money is well spent.

- *Nail down the angels' exit path.* Angels make their money when they sell their ownership interests. Ideally, the exit path should be part of structuring the deal. Will the company buy back the angels' shares? Will the company go public so the angels can sell their shares on the market? Will the owners sell out to a larger company? What is the time frame for doing so?
- *Avoid intimidating potential investors.* Most angels are turned off by entrepreneurs with an attitude of "I have someone else who will do the deal if you don't." In the face of such coercion, many private investors simply walk away from the deal.
- *Always be truthful.* Overpromising and underdelivering will kill a deal and spoil future financing opportunities.
- *Develop alternative financing arrangements.* Never back an angel into a corner with "take this deal or leave it." Have alternative plans prepared in case the investor balks at the outset.
- *Don't take the money and run.* Investors appreciate entrepreneurs who keep them informed—about how their money is being spent and the results it shows. Prepare periodic reports for them.
- *Stick to the deal.* It is tempting to spend the money where it is most needed once it is in hand. Resist! If you promised to use the funds for specific purposes, do it. Nothing undermines an angel's trust as quickly as violating the original plan.
- *Don't forget to "make the ask."* After pitching your idea to a potential angel investor, remember to ask for the investment. Otherwise, you're sure to be turned down.

Sources: Based on Rosalind Resnick, "The Art (and Journey) of Raising Funds," *Wall Street Journal*, July 13, 2010, *http://online.wsj.com/article/ NA_WSJ_PUB:SB10001424052748704288204575363052617468556.html*; David E. Gumpert, "Confessions of an Angel Investor," November 14, 2007, *Bloomberg Business Week*, November 14, 2007, *www.businessweek.com/ smallbiz/content/nov2007/sb20071114_582315.htm*.

Partners

Entrepreneurs can take on partners to expand the capital base of a business.

ENTREPRENEURIAL
Profile

Lan Tran Cao: Viet Café

After spending nearly 30 years in various IT jobs for major corporations, Lan Tran Cao decided to return to her first love—cooking. Raised in Saigon, Cao started cooking for the 13 members of her family when she was just 12 and then went on to study the art of cooking in France. Cao used her experience starting restaurants (she launched two of them while in college in Sydney, Australia) to open Viet Café in downtown Manhattan. She used money from her savings to finance most of the start-up costs of the restaurant, which serves traditional Vietnamese dishes such as lemongrass chicken rolls and roast lacquered duck. Starting a restaurant in New York City is extremely expensive, however, and Cao needed more capital. She decided to bring in a partner, who owns 30 percent of Viet Café, but Cao is both the chef and the CEO of the company.[30]

Before entering into any partnership arrangement, however, entrepreneurs must consider the impact of giving up some personal control over operations and of sharing profits with others. Whenever entrepreneurs give up equity in their businesses (through whatever mechanism), they run the risk of losing control over it. As the founder's ownership in a company becomes increasingly diluted, the probability of losing control of its future direction and the entire decision-making process increases.

Corporate Venture Capital

Large corporations are in the business of financing small companies. Today, about 13 percent of all venture capital deals involve corporate venture capital. The average investment that large corporations make in small companies is $3.52 million, an amount that represents 7.4 percent of total venture capital investments.[31] Approximately 300 large corporations across the globe, including Intel, Motorola, Cisco Systems, Chevron, Comcast, Nokia, UPS, Best Buy, and General Electric, have venture capital divisions that invest on average a total of $2.1 billion a year in young companies, most often those in the product development and sales growth stages. The large companies are looking not only for financial returns from the small companies in which they invest, but also for innovative products that can benefit them. Young companies get a boost from the capital injections large companies give them, but they also stand to gain many other benefits from the relationship. The right corporate partner may share technical expertise, distribution channels, marketing know-how, and provide introductions to important customers and suppliers. Another intangible yet highly important advantage that an investment from a large corporate partner gives a start-up is credibility, often referred to as "market validation." Doors that otherwise would be closed to a small company magically open when the right corporation becomes a strategic partner.

Foreign corporations also are interested in investing in small U.S. businesses. Often these corporations are seeking strategic partnerships to gain access to new technology, new products, or access to lucrative U.S. markets. In return, the small companies they invest in benefit from the capital infusion as well as from their partners' international experience and extensive network of connections. "What's most difficult for start-ups is finding customers and establishing a brand, but Intel Capital can help," says Arvind Sodhani, head of Intel's venture capital division, one of the largest and most active venture capital companies in the world.[32] Figure 2 shows recent trends in corporate venture capital.

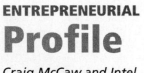

ENTREPRENEURIAL Profile

Craig McCaw and Intel Capital: Clearwire

In 2006, Intel Capital invested $600 million in Clearwire, a wireless broadband communications and networking company that was founded in 2003 by Craig McCaw. Intel's leading investment attracted venture capital investments from other corporations, including Motorola. In 2007, Clearwire made an initial public offering of 24 million shares of its stock at $25 per share and raised $600 million in capital. In 2008, Intel made a follow-on investment of $1 billion in Clearwire. Since 1991, Intel has invested more than $9 billion in more than 1,000 promising young companies not only in the United States but also in 45 countries around the world whose products or services align with its strategy.[33]

Venture Capital Companies

Venture capital companies (VCs) are private, for-profit organizations that raise money from investors to purchase equity positions in young businesses they believe have high-growth and high-profit potential, producing annual returns of 300 to 500 percent over 5 to 7 years. More than 700 venture capital firms operate across the United States today, investing in promising small companies in a variety of industries (see Figure 3). Companies in California's Silicon Valley and Boston's high-tech corridor attract about half of all venture capital investments.[34] Some colleges and universities have created venture funds designated to invest in promising businesses started by their students, alumni, faculty, and others. Business schools at the University of Michigan, the University of Maryland, the University of North Dakota, Cornell University, and, in a joint venture called the University Venture Fund, the University of

FIGURE 2
Corporate Venture Capital

Source: PricewaterhouseCoopers MoneyTree Report, 2010.

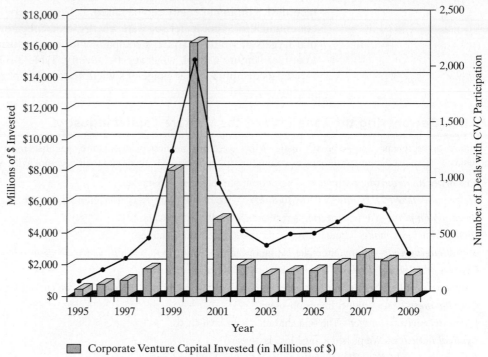

Corporate Venture Capital Invested (in Millions of $)
Number of Deals with Corporate Venture Capital Participation

Pennsylvania, Brigham Young University, the University of Utah, and Westminster College operate venture capital funds that are comanaged by students, faculty, and sometimes professional venture capitalists.[35]

Venture capital firms, which provide about 7 percent of all funding for private companies, have invested billions of dollars in high-potential small companies over the years, including notable businesses such as Apple, Microsoft, Intel, and Outback Steakhouse. Clearwire, the wireless communications company, tops the list of companies backed by venture capital with a

FIGURE 3
Venture Capital Financing

Source: PricewaterhouseCoopers MoneyTree Report, 2009.

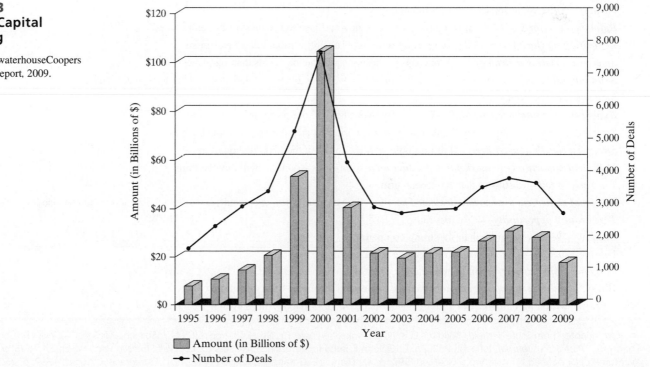

Amount (in Billions of $)
Number of Deals

record $1.3 billion of equity capital raised.[36] Although companies in high-tech industries such as communications, computer software, energy, medical care, and biotechnology are the most popular targets of venture capital, a company with extraordinary growth prospects has the potential to attract venture capital, whatever its industry. Table 3 offers a humorous look at how venture capitalists decipher the language of sometimes overly optimistic entrepreneurs.

TABLE 3 Deciphering the Language of the Venture Capital Industry.

By nature, entrepreneurs tend to be optimistic. When screening business plans, venture capitalists must make an allowance for entrepreneurial enthusiasm. Here's a dictionary of phrases commonly found in business plans and their accompanying venture capital translations.

Exploring an acquisition strategy—Our current products have no market.

We're on a clear P2P (pathway to profitability)—We're still years away from earning a profit.

Basically on plan—We're expecting a revenue shortfall of 25 percent.

Internet business model—Potentially bigger fools have been identified.

A challenging year—Competitors are eating our lunch.

Considerably ahead of plan—Hit our plan in 1 of the last 3 months.

Company's underlying strength and resilience—We still lost money, but look how we cut our losses.

Core business—Our product line is obsolete.

Currently revising budget—The financial plan is in total chaos.

Cyclical industry—We posted a huge loss last year.

Entrepreneurial CEO—He is totally uncontrollable, bordering on maniacal.

Facing challenges—Our sales continue to slide, and we have no idea why.

Facing unprecedented economic, political, and structural shifts—It's a tough world out there, but we're coping the best we can.

Highly leverageable network—No longer works but has friends who do.

Ingredients are there—Given 2 years, we might find a workable strategy.

Investing heavily in R&D—We're trying desperately to catch the competition.

Limited downside—Things can't get much worse.

Long sales cycle—Yet to find a customer who likes the product enough to buy it.

Major opportunity—It's our last chance.

Niche strategy—A small-time player.

On a manufacturing learning curve—We can't make the product with positive margins.

Passive investor—Someone who phones once a year to see if we're still in business.

Positive results—Our losses were less than last year.

Refocus our efforts—We've blown our chance, and now we have to fire most of our employees.

Repositioning the business—We've recently written off a multimillion-dollar investment.

Selective investment strategy—The board is spending more time on yachts than on planes.

Solid operating performance in a difficult year—Yes, we lost money and market share, but look how hard we tried.

Somewhat below plan—We expect a revenue shortfall of 75 percent.

Expenses were unexpectedly high—We grossly overestimated our profit margins.

Strategic investor—One who will pay a preposterous price for an equity share in the business.

Strongest fourth quarter ever—Don't quibble over the losses in the first three quarters.

Sufficient opportunity to market this product no longer exists—Nobody will buy the thing.

Too early to tell—Results to date have been grim.

A team of skilled, motivated, and dedicated people—We've laid off most of our staff, and those who are left should be glad they still have jobs.

Turnaround opportunity—It's a lost cause.

Unique—We have no more than six strong competitors.

Volume-sensitive—Our company has massive fixed costs.

Window of opportunity—Without more money fast, this company is dead.

Work closely with the management—We talk to them on the phone once a month.

A year in which we confronted challenges—At least we know the questions even if we haven't got the answers.

Sources: Adapted from Scott Herhold, "When CEOs Blow Smoke," *e-company*, May 2001, pp. 125–127; Suzanne McGee, "A Devil's Dictionary of Financing," *Wall Street Journal*, June 12, 2000, p. C13; John F. Budd Jr., "Cracking the CEO's Code," *Wall Street Journal*, March 27, 1995, p. A20; "Venture-Speak Defined," *Teleconnect*, October 1990, p. 42; Cynthia E. Griffin, "Figuratively Speaking," *Entrepreneur*, August 1999, p. 26.

POLICIES AND INVESTMENT STRATEGIES. VCs usually establish stringent policies to govern their overall investment strategies.

Investment Size and Screening. The average venture capital firm's investment in a small company is $7.8 million. Depending on the size of the venture capital company and its cost structure, minimum investments range from $50,000 to $5 million. Investment ceilings, in effect, do not exist. Most firms seek investments in the $3 million to $10 million range to justify the cost of screening the large number of proposals they receive.

In a normal year, VCs invest in only 3,500 of the nearly 30 million small businesses in the United States! The venture capital screening process is *extremely* rigorous. The typical venture capital company invests in less than 1 percent of the business plans it receives. According to the Global Entrepreneurship Monitor, only about 1 in 1,000 businesses in the United States attracts venture capital during its existence.[37] The typical venture capital firm receives about 1,100 business plans each year. For every 100 business plans that the average venture capital firm receives, 90 of them are rejected immediately because they do not match the firm's investment criteria or requirements. The firm conducts a thorough due diligence investigation of the remaining 10 companies and typically invests in only 1 of them. The average time required to close a venture capital deal is 80 days, slightly longer than the time required to complete angel financing.[38]

Ownership. Most venture capitalists prefer to purchase ownership in a small business through common stock or convertible preferred stock. Although some venture capital firms purchase less than 50 percent of a company's stock, it is not uncommon for others to buy a controlling share of a company, leaving its founders with a minority share of ownership. Entrepreneurs must weigh the positive aspects of receiving needed financing against the disadvantages of owning a smaller share of the business. "Would you rather have 80 percent of a company worth zero or 50 percent of a company worth $500 million?" asks a partner at one venture capital firm.[39]

Stage of Investment. Most venture capital firms invest in companies that are either in the early stages of development (called early stage investing) or in the rapid-growth phase (called expansion stage investing); few invest in businesses that are only in the start-up phase (see Figure 4). According to the Global Entrepreneurship Monitor, only 1 in 10,000 entrepreneurs

FIGURE 4
Venture Capital by Stage of Company Growth

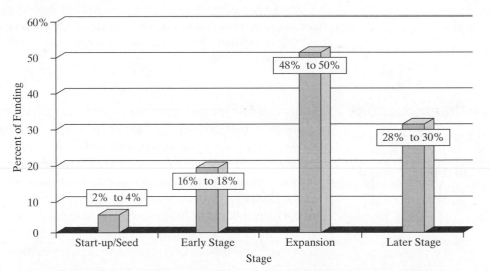

Start-up/Seed—This is the initial stage in which companies are just beginning to develop their ideas into products or services. Typically, these businesses have been in existence less than 18 months and are not yet fully operational.

Early Stage—These companies are refining their initial products or services in pilot tests or in the market. Even though the product or service is available commercially, it typically generates little or no revenue. These companies have been in business less than 3 years.

Expansion Stage—These companies' products or services are commercially available and are producing strong revenue growth. Businesses at this stage may not be generating a profit yet, however.

Later Stage—These companies' products or services are widely available and are producing ongoing revenue and, in most cases, positive cash flow. Businesses at this stage are more likely to be generating a profit. Sometimes these businesses are spin-offs of already established successful private companies.

worldwide receives venture capital funding at start up.[40] About 96 to 98 percent of all venture capital goes to businesses in the early, expansion, and later stages, although some venture capital firms are showing more interest in companies in the start up phase because of the tremendous returns that are possible by investing then.[41] Most venture capital firms do not make just a single investment in a company. Instead, they invest in a company over time across several stages, where their investments often total $10 to $15 million or more. To fuel its fast growth, Gilt Groupe, a company that conducts online sample sales of luxury branded merchandise to its members at discounts up to 70 percent, has landed $83 million in venture capital in three rounds of financing in just 3 years.[42]

Advice and Contacts. In addition to the money they invest, venture capital companies provide the small companies in their portfolios with management advice and access to valuable networks of contacts of suppliers, employees, customers, and other sources of capital. One of their goals in doing so is to strengthen the companies in which they have invested, thereby increasing their value. Former NBA star David Robinson's company, Admiral Capital Group, recently invested in Centerplate, an event catering business that focuses on sports venues, and plans to use his network of contacts to help the company expand, particularly into professional basketball events.[43]

Control. In exchange for the financing they receive from venture capitalists, entrepreneurs must give up a portion of their businesses, sometimes surrendering a majority interest and control of its operations. Most venture capitalists prefer to let the founding team of managers employ its skills to operate a business *if* they are capable of managing its growth. However, most venture capitalists join the boards of directors of the companies they invest in or send in new managers or a new management team to protect their investments. The term sheets they negotiate often include the right to determine the CEO. In other words, venture capitalists are *not* passive investors! A study of new business ventures by Harvard professor Noam Wasserman reports that only half of the companies' founders were in the CEO position after 3 years and that the likelihood of a founder being replaced increases significantly after a company receives capital from outside investors, especially venture capitalists.[44]

Some venture capitalists serve only as financial and managerial advisors, whereas others take an active role managing the company—recruiting employees, providing sales leads, choosing attorneys and advertising agencies, and making daily decisions—which can cause friction with the founding entrepreneur(s). The majority of these active venture capitalists say they are forced to step in because the existing management team lacked the talent and experience to achieve growth targets.

ENTREPRENEURIAL
Profile

Jason Brown: Cotton Comfort

As Jason Brown learned, a common complaint among entrepreneurs who accept venture capital is that their investors push too hard for too much growth too soon. Brown was just 26 years old when a group of venture capitalists offered to invest $5 million in Cotton Comfort, a small chain of clothing stores he had launched at age 20. He gave up 46 percent of his company in exchange for the capital investment and the investors' experience. Brown says that the venture capitalists pushed him to grow the company too fast, and when the economy slowed Cotton Comfort ran out of cash and folded. "I was too young to know that my job was to listen to what the VCs had to say but to know that they had only a chapter out of the novel of understanding about my business," says Brown, who went on to launch two more successful businesses.[45]

Investment Preferences. Venture capital funds are larger, more professional, and more specialized than they were 25 years ago. As the industry grows, more venture capital funds are focusing their investments in niches—everything from information technology services to biotechnology. Some will invest in almost any industry but prefer companies in particular stages, including the start-up phase. Traditionally, however, only about 2 to 4 percent of the companies receiving venture capital financing are in the start-up (seed) stage, when entrepreneurs are forming a company or developing a product or service. Most of the start-up businesses that attract venture capital today are in the biotechnology, software, IT services, energy, and medical device industries.

WHAT VENTURE CAPITALISTS LOOK FOR. Entrepreneurs must realize that it is very difficult for any small business, especially start-ups, to pass the intense screening process of a venture capital company and qualify for an investment. Two factors make a deal attractive to venture capitalists: high returns and a convenient (and profitable) exit strategy. "VCs spend a lot of time boiling down the characteristics of successful companies to their essence: team, market, and product," says David Pakman, an entrepreneur turned venture capitalist.[46] When evaluating potential investments, venture capitalists look for the following features.

Competent Management. Attracting venture capital takes more than just a good idea; it requires a management team that can transform an idea into a viable business. Venture capitalists believe in the adage "Money follows management." To them, the most important ingredient in the success of any business is the ability of the management team. They are looking for a team of managers that shares the same vision for the company and have the experience and the ability to make that vision a reality. "Our business is about investing in people who can get it done," explains Steve Domenik of venture capital fund Sevin Rosen. "The [business] idea is almost secondary."[47] From a venture capitalist's perspective, the ideal management team has experience, managerial skills, commitment, and the ability to build effective teams.

Competitive Edge. Investors are searching for some factor that will enable a small business to set itself apart from its competitors. This distinctive competence may range from an innovative product or service that satisfies unmet customer needs to a unique marketing or R&D approach. It must be something with the potential to make the business a leader in its field.

Growth Industry. Hot industries attract profits—and venture capital. Most venture capital funds focus their searches for prospects in rapidly expanding fields because they believe the profit potential is greater in these areas. Venture capital firms are most interested in young companies in industries that have enough growth potential to become at least $100 million businesses within 3 to 5 years. Venture capitalists know that most of the businesses they invest in will flop, so their winners have to be *big* winners.

Viable Exit Strategy. Venture capitalists not only look for promising companies with the ability to dominate a market, but they also want to see a plan for a feasible exit strategy, ideally to be executed within 3 to 5 years. A recent study by the National Venture Capital Association reports that the number one factor that venture capitalists say creates a nonfavorable environment for venture capital is difficulty in achieving successful exits.[48] Venture capital firms realize the return on their investments when the companies they invest in either make an initial public offering or sell out to a larger business. For instance, Dell recently purchased Equallogic, a company that developed highly efficient network data storage solutions for businesses, for $1.4 billion, creating a handsome payout for Equallogic's three founders and the venture capital companies that had invested in it. Paula Long, Peter Haden, and Paul Koning started Equallogic in Haden's attic in 2003, and within 3 years its sales had increased from $492,000 to more than $100 million.[49] "If your vision is to run a company and hand it over to your kids, VC funding is out of the question," says Mike Simon, CEO of LogMeIn, Inc., a software company that has raised $20 million in capital, half of it from venture capital firms.[50]

Intangible Factors. Some other important factors considered in the screening process are not easily measured; they are the intuitive, intangible factors the venture capitalist detects by gut feeling. This feeling might be the result of the small firm's solid sense of direction, its strategic planning process, the chemistry of its management team, or a number of other factors.

ENTREPRENEURIAL

Profile

Ofer Raz and Hod Fleishman: GreenRoad

In 2003, Ofer Raz and Hod Fleishman launched GreenRoad, a company whose software helps companies and individuals improve driving habits, reduce collisions, improve fuel economy, and reduce vehicle operating costs, and quickly realized that their company would require a significant investment to capitalize on the market opportunity that lay before it. The duo estimates that the cost of vehicle crashes in the United States alone is $235 billion, and that 90 percent of all crashes are the result of driver behavior. Their subscription-based service provides real-time feedback and driver coaching and is designed to reduce those costs and save lives by improving drivers' behavior. Customers who use the company's technology (including Ryder, Ericsson,

T-Mobile, LeFleur Transportation, and others) typically reduce the number of crashes by 50 percent and fuel consumption and emissions by up to 10 percent. After pitching their idea to many venture capital firms, Raz and Fleishman have received $42.5 million in financing across three rounds. Venture capitalists were impressed with the experience of the management team that Raz and Fleishman had assembled, the company's fast growth, and the size of the potential market. Representatives from the venture capital firms hold five of GreenRoad's board seats, but the company has the capital it needs to support continued R&D, product innovation, and a more concentrated sales and marketing effort.[51]

Despite its many benefits, venture capital is not suitable for every entrepreneur. "VC money comes at a price," warns one entrepreneur. "Before boarding a one-way money train, ask yourself if this is the best route for your business and personal desires because investors are like department stores the day after Christmas—they expect a lot of returns in a short period of time."[52]

IN THE ENTREPRENEURIAL
SPOTLIGHT A Mint of an Idea

At age 25, Aaron Patzer held masters degrees in computer science and electrical engineering from Princeton and had a full-time job as a software engineer for an electronic design automation company. Like many young people, Patzer was creating a household budget and tracking his spending using one of the best-selling money management programs on the market, but he grew increasingly frustrated by its complexity, lack of flexibility, and inability to give him real-time information. "There's got to be a better way to do this," he recalls thinking. Convinced that he could create a money management tool that would be simple to use, Patzer, who says that his father read the *Wall Street Journal* to him as a toddler, quit his job and spent 14 hours a day for the next 7 months writing the software to drive Mint.com, an online financial planning Web site that allows users to create budgets, track their spending, and compare their spending habits to other people with similar lifestyles. In the early days, he financed the company out of his personal savings but realized that building a real business would take more cash than he had available.

Patzer pitched his business plan to a dozen angel investors and to some of the top venture capital firms in Silicon Valley, but none of them were interested in investing money in an unproven start-up. "Every single VC told me that I would fail because no one would trust a start-up with their financial information," he says. Despite the negative feedback, Patzer persisted in his quest for capital, eventually getting the opportunity to make a presentation about Mint.com to Josh Kopelman, cofounder of venture capital firm First Round Capital, at a networking event for entrepreneurs. "I had a server running on a laptop in the

trunk of my car," recalls the always-prepared Patzer. "I ran out and got the laptop and fired up a demo."

Kopelman was impressed with the demonstration and asked Patzer to send him a business plan. Reading it, Kopelman says that he spotted "a really big market and someone who had really thought it out. [Patzer] saw an opportunity to solve a really big pain point for customers." Ten days later, First Round Capital, which, unlike most venture capital firms, focuses on small companies in the start-up and seed stages, invested $325,000 in Mint.com and lined up another $725,000 from other early stage VCs Felicis Ventures and Soft Tech VC. In less than 1 year, Mint.com had attracted 400,000 users, a signal of the success that was to come.

First Round Capital member Rob Hayes, who had extensive product development experience at Palm, joined the Mint.com board, and Kopelman became a board advisor. Guidance from Hayes, Kopelman, and others helped CEO Patzer avoid many mistakes that start-up companies make and to quickly resolve others. After Mint.com won the top award at a technical conference, a surge in traffic to its Web site caused the company's servers to crash, and engineers at Mint.com traced the problem to a flaw in its database technology. That evening, drawing on his extensive network of contacts, Kopelman contacted an executive at Mint.com's database provider and asked him to help solve the problem. "We were able to resolve the issue within 24 hours because of the connections Josh had," says Patzer.

As Mint.com continued to grow and its capital requirements increased, First Round Capital was there to help, investing more of its own money in subsequent rounds of venture capital for a total of more than $2.5 million and connecting Patzer and the management team with other venture capital firms. Patzer continued to rely on Kopelman, Hayes, and other advisors to help him navigate the challenges of building a company, and within 2 years Mint.com had 1.5 million users and was tracking $200 billion in transactions. Just 3 years after starting Mint.com, Patzer and his venture capital investors sold the company to Intuit, the leading producer of money management software for $170 million, producing an impressive rate of return for Patzer, First Round Capital, and all of the company's investors. Kopelman says that the Mint.com deal produced the highest return of any investment that First Round Capital has made. Patzer says that he is "eternally grateful" to Kopelman, Hayes, and First Round Capital. "They took a risk on a 25-year-old kid who didn't have a whole lot of experience," he says. His advice for other young entrepreneurs? "Stone-cold, iron-willed determination," he says. "It's going to be long hours and a lot of hard work, but if you have confidence in your product, you will succeed."

1. Early stage venture capital was an essential ingredient in Mint.com's success. Yet only 2 to 4 percent of all venture capital goes to companies in the seed and start-up phases. Why?
2. Suppose that an entrepreneur with a fast-growing business tells you that he has the opportunity to acquire an investment from a venture capital company and wants your advice. What questions would you ask him before offering him advice?
3. Refer to question 2. Explain the advantages and disadvantages that entrepreneurs experience when they accept venture capital.

Sources: Based on Spencer E. Ante, "Mint.com: Nurtured by SuperAngel VCs," *Bloomberg Business Week*, September 15, 2009, *www.businessweek.com/technology/content/sep2009/tc20090915_065038.htm*; Rieva Lesonsky, "Entrepreneurship: The Next Generation, Aaron Patzer, 29," *All Business*, June 2010, *www.allbusiness.com/banking-finance/banking-lending-credit-services-electronic/14562114-1.html*; "30 Under 30" America's Coolest Young Entrepreneurs, *Inc.*, 2008, *www.inc.com/30under30/2008/profile/5-patzer.html*; "Intuit to Acquire Mint.com," Mint.com, September 14, 2009, *www.mint.com/press/intuit-to-acquire-mint-com/*.

Public Stock Sale ("Going Public")

3. Describe the process of "going public," as well as its advantages and disadvantages.

In some cases, small companies can "go public" by selling shares of stock to outside investors. In an **initial public offering (IPO)**, a company raises capital by selling shares of its stock to the general public for the first time. A public offering is an effective method of raising large amounts of capital, but it can be an expensive and time-consuming process filled with regulatory nightmares. "An IPO can be a wonderful thing," says one investment banker, "but it's not all sweetness and light."[53] Once a company makes an initial public offering, *nothing* will ever be the same again. Managers must consider the impact of their decisions not only on the company and its employees but also on shareholders and the value of their stock.

Going public isn't for every business. In fact, most small companies do not meet the criteria for making a successful public stock offering. Since 2001, the average number of companies that make initial public offerings each year is 139, and only about 20,000 companies in the United States—less than 0.5 percent of the total—are publicly held. Few companies with less than $25 million in annual sales manage to go public successfully. It is extremely difficult for a start-up company with no track record of success to raise money with a public offering. Instead, investment bankers who underwrite public stock offerings typically look for established companies with the following characteristics:

- Consistently high growth rates.
- High profit potential. Strangely enough, profitability at the time of the IPO is not essential; since 2001, 47 percent of companies making IPOs had negative earnings.[54]
- Three to 5 years of audited financial statements that meet or exceed SEC standards. After the Enron and WorldCom scandals, investors are demanding impeccable financial statements.
- A solid position in a rapidly growing industry. In 1999, the median age of companies making IPOs was 4 years; today, it is 15 years.[55]
- A sound management team with experience and a strong board of directors.

Figure 5 shows the trend in the number of IPOs and the amount of capital raised.

FIGURE 5
IPOs

Source: Thomson Financial
Securities Data.

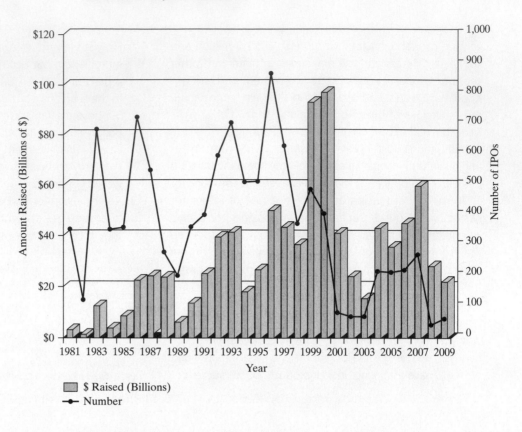

Entrepreneurs who are considering taking their companies public should first consider carefully the advantages and the disadvantages of an IPO. The *advantages* include the following:

ABILITY TO RAISE LARGE AMOUNTS OF CAPITAL. The biggest benefit of a public offering is the capital infusion the company receives. Since 2001, the average IPO has raised $250 million for the issuing company. After going public, the corporation has the cash to fund R&D projects, expand plant and facilities, repay debt, or boost working capital balances without incurring the interest expense and the obligation to repay that comes with debt financing. For instance, when Ancestry.com, the Web site that helps people research family histories and create family trees, went public, the sale of 7.4 million shares at $13.50 per share generated $100 million for the company (before subtracting the expenses of making the offering).[56]

IMPROVED CORPORATE IMAGE. All of the media attention a company receives during the registration process makes it more visible. In addition, becoming a public company in some industries improves its prestige and enhances its competitive position, one of the most widely recognized, intangible benefits of going public.

IMPROVED ACCESS TO FUTURE FINANCING. Going public boosts a company's net worth and broadens its equity base. Its improved stature and financial strength make it easier for the firm to attract more capital—both equity and debt—and to grow.

ATTRACTING AND RETAINING KEY EMPLOYEES. Public companies often use stock-based compensation plans to attract and retain quality employees. Stock options and bonuses are excellent methods for winning employees' loyalty and for instilling a healthy ownership attitude among them. Employee stock ownership plans (ESOPs) and stock purchase plans are popular recruiting and motivational tools in many small corporations, enabling them to hire top-flight talent they otherwise would not be able to afford.

USING STOCK FOR ACQUISITIONS. A company whose stock is publicly traded can acquire other businesses by offering its own shares rather than cash. Acquiring other companies with shares of stock eliminates the need to incur additional debt. When search engine giant Google purchased YouTube, the small company that popularized online video, for $1.65 million (Google's largest acquisition to date), it used Google stock rather than cash to complete the transaction. YouTube founders Chad Hurly, Steve Chen, and Jawed Karim had been considering an IPO for YouTube, but Google's offer was attractive enough to change their minds.[57]

LISTING ON A STOCK EXCHANGE. Being listed on an organized stock exchange, even a small regional one, improves the marketability of a company's shares and enhances its image. When a company's stock trades on an organized exchange, it has more clout in its market. Most small companies' stocks, however, do not qualify for listing on the nation's largest exchanges—the New York Stock Exchange (NYSE) and the American Stock Exchange (AMEX). However, the AMEX offers a market for small-company stocks, The Emerging Company Marketplace. Most small companies' stocks are traded on either the National Association of Securities Dealers Automated Quotation (NASDAQ) system's National Market System (NMS) and its emerging small-capitalization exchange or one of the nation's regional stock exchanges. The most popular regional exchanges include the Midwest (MSE), Philadelphia (PHLX), Boston (BSE), and Pacific (PSE).

The *disadvantages* of going public include the following:

DILUTION OF FOUNDER'S OWNERSHIP. Whenever entrepreneurs sell stock to the public, they automatically dilute their ownership in their businesses. Most owners retain a majority interest in the business, but they may still run the risk of unfriendly takeovers years later after selling more stock.

LOSS OF CONTROL. If enough shares are sold in a public offering, the company founder risks losing control of the company. If a large block of shares falls into the hands of dissident stockholders, they could vote the existing management team (including the founder) out.

LOSS OF PRIVACY. Taking their companies public can be a big ego boost for owners, but they must realize that their companies are no longer solely theirs. Information that was once private must be available for public scrutiny. The initial prospectus and the continuous reports filed with the Securities and Exchange Commission (SEC) disclose a variety of information about the company and its operations—from financial data and raw material sources to legal matters and patents to *anyone*—including competitors. Entrepreneurs who decide not to take their companies public most often cite the loss of privacy and loss of control as the primary reasons.

REGULATORY REQUIREMENTS AND REPORTING TO THE SEC. Operating as a publicly held company is expensive, especially since Congress passed the Sarbanes-Oxley Act in 2002. The SEC traditionally has required publicly held companies to file periodic reports with it, which often requires a more powerful accounting system, a larger accounting staff, and greater use of attorneys and other professionals. Created in response to ethical fiascoes involving Enron and WorldCom, Sarbanes-Oxley was designed to improve the degree of internal control and the level of financial reporting by publicly held companies. Critics contend that the cost of complying with the law is overbearing and point to Sarbanes-Oxley as one reason the number of IPOs has plunged. According to an SEC study, the median cost of complying with Sarbanes-Oxley to public companies with market values of less than $75 million is $365,900 per year.[58]

ENTREPRENEURIAL Profile

Paymaxx and CompuPay

The high cost of regulatory compliance dissuades many potential companies from going public. Paymaxx, founded in 1991, became one of the largest payroll provider companies in the United States, and the fast-growing company was considering an IPO to acquire the capital necessary to fuel its growth. Its founders made an abrupt U-turn in their plans when they discovered the cost of complying with Sarbanes-Oxley, choosing instead to sell the company to a larger payroll processing company, CompuPay.[59]

FILING EXPENSES. A public stock offering usually is an expensive way to generate funds to finance a company's growth. For the typical small company, the cost of a public offering is about 15 percent of the capital raised. On small offerings, costs can eat up as much as 40 percent of the capital raised, whereas on larger offerings, those above $25 million, only 10 to 12 percent will go to cover expenses. Once an offering exceeds $15 million, its relative issuing cost drops. The largest cost is the underwriter's commission, which is typically 6.5 to 7 percent of the proceeds on offerings less than $10 million and 13 percent on those over that amount. Critics claim that the underwriting fees that U.S. investment banks charge are the highest in the world, which, when combined with the reporting requirements of the Sarbanes-Oxley Act, dissuade companies, particularly small ones, from making IPOs in the United States. Research by Grant Thornton shows a decline in the proportion of small-company IPOs in recent years. From 1991 to 1997, IPOs that generated less than $50 million accounted for nearly 80 percent of all IPOs; today, that percentage had dropped to just 28 percent.[60]

ACCOUNTABILITY TO SHAREHOLDERS. The capital that entrepreneurs manage and risk is no longer just their own. The managers of a publicly held firm are accountable to the company's shareholders. Indeed, the law requires that managers recognize and abide by a relationship built on trust. Profit and return on investment become the primary concerns for investors. If the stock price of a newly public company falls, shareholder lawsuits are inevitable. Investors whose shares decline in value often sue the company's managers for fraud and the failure to disclose in the IPO prospectus the potential risks of their investments.

ENTREPRENEURIAL
Profile

Vonage

When VoIP provider Vonage went public, the offering price of its shares was $17, and the company set aside 13.5 percent of the 31.25 million shares it was offering for its customers. However, when Vonage shares fell to $14.85 on its first day of trading and then plummeted in the months that followed, more than 10,000 customers filed a lawsuit against Vonage, claiming that the company made false and misleading statements about its financial condition during the IPO. As part of its agreement with the issue's underwriters, Vonage had to pay $11.7 million to cover the cost of the shares for which disgruntled customers refused to pay when the stock price fell.[61]

PRESSURE FOR SHORT-TERM PERFORMANCE. In privately held companies, entrepreneurs are free to follow their strategies for success, even if those strategies take years to produce results. When a company goes public, however, entrepreneurs quickly learn that shareholders are impatient and expect results immediately. In publicly held companies, quarterly results matter. Founders are under constant pressure to produce short-term results, which can have a negative impact on a company's long-term strategy. The U.S. Chamber of Commerce has called the emphasis on the short term "one of the biggest threats to America's competitiveness."[62] David Klock, who took his once publicly held company Comp Benefits private, says, "I am glad we're private because [it gives us] the ability to make investments that may take two or three quarters to give a good return. That's difficult to do as a public company."[63]

LOSS OF FOCUS. As impatient as they can be, entrepreneurs often find the time demands of an IPO frustrating and distracting. Managing the IPO takes time away from managing the company. Working on an IPO can consume as much as 75 percent of top managers' time, robbing them of their ability to manage the business effectively. "The most common mistake [in an IPO] is the failure to understand the amount of time and effort that is required and the amount of distraction from the primary business," says one IPO expert.[64]

TIMING. Many factors that are beyond the company's control, such as declines in the overall stock market, economic recessions, industry shakeups, and potential investors' jitters, can quickly slam shut a company's "window of opportunity" for an IPO even after top managers have spent months and many thousands of dollars working on the offering. After 5 months of work with its lead underwriter, Credit Suisse, Smile Brands Group, a company that provides

"HUNTING AND GATHERING ISN'T VERY PROFITABLE. LET'S INVENT IPOs."

support services to dental practices, withdrew its proposed $132 million IPO, citing volatile and deteriorating market conditions that hampered the company's ability to sell its stock within the projected $16 to $18 price range.[65]

THE REGISTRATION PROCESS. Taking a company public is a complicated, bureaucratic process that usually takes several months to complete. Many experts compare the IPO process to running a corporate marathon, and both the company and its management team must be in shape and up to the grueling task. Making an IPO requires a coordinated effort from a team of professionals, including company executives, an accountant, a securities attorney, a financial printer, and at least one underwriter. The key steps in taking a company public follow.

Choose the Underwriter

The single most important ingredient in making a successful IPO is selecting a capable **underwriter** (or **investment banker**). The underwriter serves two primary roles: helping to prepare the registration statement for the issue and promoting the company's stock to potential investors. The underwriter works with company managers as an advisor in preparing the registration statement that must be filed with the SEC, promoting the issue in a road show, pricing the stock, and providing after-market support. Once the registration statement is finished, the underwriter's primary job is selling the company's stock through an underwriting syndicate of other investment bankers it develops.

ENTREPRENEURIAL

Profile

Allen and Eugene Stoltzfus and John Fairfield: Rosetta Stone

Rosetta Stone, a company founded in 1992 by Allen and Eugene Stoltzfus and John Fairfield that sells software that allows people to learn foreign languages using pictures and sounds in context rather than translations, recently made an initial public offering. The company, whose shares now trade on the New York Stock Exchange under the symbol "RST," selected Morgan Stanley and William Blair as its lead underwriters to manage the offering of 6.25 million shares at $18 per share (above the initial estimate of $15 to $17 per share) that generated $112 million to fuel the company's global expansion plans.[66]

Negotiate a Letter of Intent

To begin an offering, the entrepreneur and the underwriter must negotiate a **letter of intent**, which outlines the details of the deal. The letter of intent covers a variety of important issues, including the type of underwriting, its size and price range, the underwriter's commission, and any warrants and options included. It almost always states that the underwriter is not bound to the offering until it is executed—usually the day before or the day of the offering. However, the letter usually creates a binding obligation for the company to pay any direct expenses the underwriter incurs relating to the offer.

491

There are two types of underwriting agreements: firm commitment and best effort. In a **firm commitment agreement**, the underwriter agrees to purchase all of the shares in the offering and resell them to investors. This agreement *guarantees* that the company will receive the required funds, and most large underwriters use it. In a **best efforts agreement**, the underwriter merely agrees to use its best efforts to sell the company's shares and does not guarantee the company will receive the needed financing. The managing underwriter acts as an agent, selling as many shares as possible through the syndicate. Some best effort contracts are all or nothing—if the underwriter cannot sell all of the shares, the offering is withdrawn. Another version of the best efforts agreement is to set a minimum number of shares that must be sold for the issue to be completed. These methods are riskier because the company has no guarantee of raising the required capital.

The company and the underwriter must decide on the size of the offering and the price of the shares. To keep the stock active in the aftermarket, most underwriters prefer to offer a *minimum* of 400,000 to 500,000 shares. A smaller number of shares inhibits sufficiently broad distribution. Most underwriters recommend selling 25 to 40 percent of the company in the IPO. To keep interest in the issue high, the underwriter usually recommends an initial price between $10 and $20 per share, although some companies stock is priced higher. The underwriter establishes an estimated price range for the company's IPO in the underwriting agreement, but it does not establish the final price until the day before the offering takes place. Depending on anticipated demand for the company's shares, the condition of the market, and other factors, the actual price may be outside the estimated range. Since 2001, 55 percent of companies' offerings have been within the underwriter's estimated price range; 17 percent of them actually came in above the range.[67] For instance, in an IPO that generated $226 million for Tesla Motors, the maker of high-performance electric cars, lead underwriters estimated the offering price to be $14 to $16 per share, but because of strong demand for the issue, the actual offering price was $17 per share.[68]

Most letters of intent include a **lock-up agreement** that prevents the sale of insider shares, those owned by directors, managers, founders, employees, and other insiders, for 12 to 36 months. The sale of these shares early in a company's public life could send negative signals to investors, eroding their confidence in the stock and pushing its price downward.

Prepare the Registration Statement

After a company signs the letter of intent, the next task is to prepare the **registration statement** to be filed with the SEC and the prospectus to be distributed to potential investors. These documents describe both the company and the stock offering and disclose information about the risks of investing. It includes information on the use of the proceeds, the company's history, its financial position, its capital structure, the risks it faces, its managers, and many other details. The statements are extremely comprehensive and may take months to develop. To prepare them, entrepreneurs must rely on their team of IPO professionals.

File with the SEC

When the statement is finished (with the exception of pricing the shares, proceeds, and commissions, which cannot be determined until just before the issue goes to market), the company officially files the statement with the SEC and awaits the review of the Division of Corporate Finance. The division sends notice of any deficiencies in the registration statement to the company's attorney in a comment letter. The company and its team of professionals must address all of the deficiencies noted in the comment letter and prepare an amended registration statement. Finally, the company files the revised registration statement, along with a pricing amendment (giving the price of the shares, the proceeds, and the underwriter's commission).

Wait to Go Effective

While waiting for the SEC's approval, the managers and the underwriters are busy. The underwriters are building a syndicate of other underwriters who will market the company's stock. (No sales can be made prior to the effective date of the offering, however.) The SEC also limits the publicity and information a company may release during this **quiet period** (which officially starts when the company reaches a preliminary agreement with the managing underwriter and ends 90 days after the effective date).

Securities laws do permit a **road show**, a gathering of potential syndicate members sponsored by the managing underwriter. Its purpose is to promote interest among potential underwriters in the IPO by featuring the company, its management, and the proposed deal. The managing underwriter and key company officials barnstorm major cities such as New York, Boston, San Francisco, Chicago, Los Angeles, and sometimes foreign cities such as London and Hong Kong at a grueling pace. Company executives often make presentations to stockbrokers and institutional investors in two or three cities a day for 2 to 4 weeks. During the road show for Unica Corporation, a company that sells enterprise marketing management software, top managers courted potential underwriters in 12 cities in just 14 days! Their efforts were exhausting but productive: Unica sold 4.8 million shares of its stock and raised $48 million.[69]

On the last day before the registration statement becomes effective, the company signs the formal underwriting agreement. The final settlement, or closing, takes place a few days after the effective date for the issue. At this meeting the underwriters receive their shares to sell and the company receives the proceeds of the offering.

Typically, the entire process of going public takes from 60 to 180 days, but it can take much longer if the issuing company is not properly prepared for the process.

Meet State Requirements

In addition to satisfying the SEC's requirements, a company also must meet the securities laws in all states in which the issue is sold. These state laws (or "blue sky" laws) vary drastically from one state to another, and the company must comply with them.

Simplified Registrations and Exemptions

4. Explain the various simplified registrations, exemptions from registration, and other alternatives available to entrepreneurs wanting to sell shares of equity to investors.

The IPO process described previously (called an S-1 filing) requires maximum disclosure in the initial filing and costly compliance with federal regulations, discouraging most small businesses from using it. Fortunately, the SEC allows several exemptions from this full-disclosure process for small businesses. Many small businesses that go public choose one of these simplified options the SEC has designed for small companies. The SEC has established a number of simplified registration statements and exemptions from the registration process:

REGULATIONS S-B AND S-K. In 2009, the SEC eliminated Regulation S-B but transferred many of its provisions into Regulation S-K, a simplified registration process for small companies seeking to make initial or subsequent public offerings. Not only does this regulation simplify the initial filing requirements with the SEC, but it also reduces the ongoing disclosure and filings required of companies by giving them "smaller reporting company" status. Its primary goals are to open the doors to capital markets to smaller companies by cutting the paperwork and the costs of raising capital. To be eligible for the simplified registration process under Regulation S-K, a company must have annual revenues of less than $50 million or have outstanding publicly held stock ("public float") worth no more than $75 million. The goal of Regulation S-K's simplified registration requirements is to enable smaller companies to go public without incurring the expense of a full-blown registration.

REGULATION D (RULES 504, 505, AND 506). Regulation D rules minimize the expense and the time required to raise equity capital for small businesses by simplifying or eliminating the requirement for registering the offering with the SEC, which often takes months and costs many thousands of dollars. Under Regulation D, the whole process typically costs less than half of what a traditional public offering costs. The SEC's objective in creating Regulation D was to give small companies the same access to equity financing that large companies have via the stock market while bypassing many of the same costs and filing requirements. A Regulation D offering requires only minimal notification to the SEC. Offerings made under Regulation D do impose limitations and demand certain disclosures, but they only require a company to file a simple form (Form D) with the SEC within 15 days of the first sale of stock. Form D consists of fill-in-the-blank questions about the company, the issue, the use of the proceeds, and other pertinent matters.

Rule 504 is the most popular of the Regulation D exemptions because it is the least restrictive. It allows a company to sell shares of its stock to an unlimited number of investors without regard to their experience or level of sophistication. A business also can make multiple offerings under Rule 504 as long as it waits at least 6 months between them. However, Rule 504 does place a cap of $1 million in a 12-month period on the amount of capital a company can raise. Ligatt

Security International, a small cyber-security company in Norcross, Georgia, recently raised $147,000 under Rule 504 to finance its expansion.[70]

A Rule 505 offering has a higher capital ceiling ($5 million) than Rule 504 in a 12-month period but imposes more restrictions (no more than 35 nonaccredited investors, no advertising of the offer, and more stringent disclosure requirements).

Rule 506 imposes no ceiling on the amount that can be raised, but most companies that make Rule 506 offerings raise between $1 million and $50 million in capital. Like a Rule 505 offering, it limits the issue to no more than 35 nonaccredited investors and prohibits advertising the offer to the public. There is no limit on the number of accredited investors, however. Rule 506 also requires detailed disclosure of relevant information, but the extent depends on the size of the offering.

SECTION 4(6). Section 4(6) covers private placements and is similar to Regulation D, Rules 505 and 506. It does not require registration on offers up to $5 million if they are made only to accredited investors.

INTRASTATE OFFERINGS (RULE 147). Rule 147 governs intrastate offerings, those sold only to investors in a single state by a company doing business in that state. To qualify, a company must be incorporated in the state in which it makes the offering, conduct a significant percentage of its business in that state, and make offers and sales of the issue only to residents of that state. There is no ceiling on the amount of the offering, but only residents of the state in which the issuing company operates can invest. The maximum number of shareholders is 500, and a company's asset base cannot exceed $10 million.

REGULATION A. Regulation A, although currently not used often, allows an exemption for public stock offerings up to $5 million over a 12-month period. Regulation A imposes few restrictions, but it is more costly than the other types of exempted offerings because it requires a company to file a registration statement with the SEC (although its requirements are simpler than those for an S-1 offering). A Regulation A offering allows a company to sell its shares directly to investors.

A small company can sell its stock under Rule 504 of Regulation D, Rule 147, or Regulation A using a Small Corporate Offering Registration (SCOR) by also registering the offering at the state level. The ceiling on a SCOR offering is $1 million (except in Texas, where there is no limit), and the issuing price of the stock must be at least $1 per share. Before selling its stock, a company must file Form U-7, a disclosure document that resembles a business plan but also serves as a state securities offering registration, a disclosure document, and a prospectus. A company must register the offering in every state in which it will sell its stock to comply with the states' blue sky laws, although current regulations allow simultaneous registration in multiple states. Entrepreneurs using SCOR may advertise their companies' offerings and can sell them directly to any investor with no restrictions and no minimums.

DIRECT STOCK OFFERINGS. Many of the simplified registrations and exemptions discussed previously give entrepreneurs the power to sidestep investment bankers and sell their companies' stock offerings directly to investors and, in the process, save themselves thousands of dollars in underwriting fees. By going straight to Main Street rather than through underwriters on Wall Street, entrepreneurs cut out the underwriter's commission, many legal expenses, and most registration fees. Entrepreneurs willing to handle the paperwork requirements and to market their own shares can make direct public offerings (DPOs) for about 6 percent of the total amount of the issue, compared with 15 percent for a traditional stock offering, and raise as much or more money as a private placement generates.

**ENTREPRENEURIAL
Profile**

*Gary Steszewski:
CityMade, Inc.*

CityMade, Inc., a company founded in 1999 that specializes in the sale of local gift items ranging from apparel and food to beverages and sports merchandise that are made in particular cities, recently launched a direct public offering. The company prepared its SCOR offering with the help of Direct Public Offerings Services, a company in Niagara Falls, New York, that helps small businesses make DPOs, and is offering 375,000 shares of common stock at $2 per share. With a minimum purchase of just $300, the DPO is aimed at small investors, many of whom are loyal customers. CityMade, which currently operates in 12 cities, including Boston, New York City, and Washington, DC plans to use the $750,000 of equity capital from the DPO to expand into 100 new cities within the next 5 years. "CityMade has positioned itself for aggressive growth over the next 3 years," says CityMade's president, Gary Steszewski. "We doubled our sales to $1.3 million in 3 years and project sales will more than double in the next 2 years."[71]

The Internet has opened a new avenue for direct public offerings and is one of the fastest-growing sources of capital for small businesses. Much of the Internet's appeal as a fund-raising tool stems from its ability to reach large numbers of prospective investors very quickly and at a low cost. Companies that make direct stock offerings on the Internet most often make them under either Regulation A or Regulation D and usually generate between $300,000 and $4 million for the company.

Direct public offerings work best for companies that have a single product or related product lines, a base of customers who are loyal to the company, good name recognition, and annual sales between $3 million and $25 million. The first company to make a successful DPO over the Internet was Spring Street Brewing, a microbrewery founded by Andy Klein. Klein raised $1.6 million in a Regulation A offering in 1996. Companies that make successful direct public offerings of their stock over the Web must meet the same standards as companies making stock offerings using more traditional methods. Experts caution Web-based fund seekers to make sure that their electronic prospectuses meet SEC and state requirements. Table 4 provides a brief quiz to help entrepreneurs determine whether their companies would be good candidates for a DPO.

Foreign Stock Markets

Some foreign stock markets offer entrepreneurs access to equity funds more readily than U.S. markets. The London Stock Exchange's AIM (Alternative Investment Market) is geared to small companies with its lower costs and less extensive reporting and regulatory requirements. "Smaller deals can get done on the AIM," says one securities attorney. "They're cheaper, and there are fewer requirements. The deals I've seen there could not have been done here." Similarly, stock exchanges in Canada (Toronto and Vancouver), Germany, Korea, Hong Kong, and Singapore are attracting small U.S. companies that are hungry for capital. These foreign exchanges encourage equity listings of small companies because the cost of offerings is about half that in the United States.

TABLE 4 Is a Direct Public Offering for You?

Drew Field, an expert in direct public offerings, has developed the following 10-question quiz to help entrepreneurs decide whether their companies are good candidates for a DPO.

1. Does your company have a history of consistently profitable operations under the present management?
2. Is your company's management team honest, socially responsible, and competent?
3. In 10 words or fewer, can you explain the nature of your business to laypeople who are new to investing?
4. Would your company excite prospective investors, making them want to share in its future?
5. Does your company have natural affinity groups, such as customers with strong emotional loyalty?
6. Do members of your natural affinity groups have discretionary cash to risk for long-term gains?
7. Would your company's natural affinity groups recognize your company's name and consider your offering materials?
8. Can you get the names, addresses, and telephone numbers of affinity group members, as well as some demographic information about them?
9. Can a high-level company employee spend half-time for 6 months as a DPO project manager?
10. Does your company have—or can you obtain—audited financial statements for at least the last 2 fiscal years?

The more questions you can answer with "yes," the more likely it is that a direct public offering could work for your company.

Sources: Drew Field Direct Public Offers, "Screen Test for a Direct Public Offering," *www.dfdpo.com/screen.htm*; Stephanie Gruner, "Could You Do a DPO?" *Inc.*, December 1996, p. 70.

▶ ENTREPRENEURSHIP IN ACTION ▶

Three Twins Ice Cream: We Need to Build a Factory

Neil Gottlieb spent several years working in corporate finance at Gap and Levi's, but his entrepreneurial aspirations finally lured him to start his own company. The Cornell University graduate was considering returning to graduate school but, remembering the delicious fresh orange sherbet his mother made in the family kitchen, he was inspired to start Three Twins Ice Cream in San Rafael, California. Having heard that the Business Planning Class at San Francisco's Renaissance Entrepreneurship Center was known as "The Mini MBA Program," Gottlieb enrolled and began developing the business plan for launching Three Twins Ice Cream, the name for which was inspired by his twin brother and sister-in-law, who also is a twin. Based on the research gathered for his business plan, Gottlieb was confident that a market existed for rich, premium ice cream made with all-natural, organic ingredients.

After graduating from the class, Gottlieb invested the $70,000 he had been saving since he began delivering newspapers as a boy and opened the first Three Twins Ice Cream store in a San Rafael shopping center. Manning the shop alone, Gottlieb worked 166 days in a row. He made ice cream every morning, sold it in the shop during the day, and cleaned up and did paperwork in the evenings. In addition to selling ice cream in the retail shop, Gottlieb sold pints of Three Twins Ice Cream to local restaurants, cafés, small retail outlets, and even farmers' markets, building name recognition for the brand and his small company. He made the ice cream from a carefully formulated mix that he purchased for $15 per gallon from a local organic dairy. Similar mixes made from nonorganic ingredients would have cost just $4 per gallon, but Gottlieb adhered to his company's "organic only" strategy. To be certified organic, "All of your inputs—the milk, cream, sugar, and flavorings—have to be organic," he explains. "Even the chemicals you use to clean and sanitize equipment have to be organic. You have to keep records of sanitation and production so you can show for any batch that you are in compliance."

The company's first store became a success, and Gottlieb opened two more retail stores, one in Napa Valley and one in San Francisco's Haight-Ashbury district. He pitched his company's ice cream to Whole Foods, and the upscale grocer began selling Three Twins Ice Cream at one of its San Francisco stores. Despite Gottlieb's success with retail stores and a growing wholesale business, his goal was to transform Three Twins Ice Cream into a national brand. "We don't want to be an artisanal brand selling $8 pints of ice cream," he says. "We want to be a national brand that sells really good ice cream." To realize that goal, however, Gottlieb knew that he had to build his own factory, where he could produce large quantities of ice cream at lower cost and expand the range of flavors the company offered. Currently, Three Twins has the ability to produce about 50,000 pints of ice cream per year.

Gottlieb began creating plans for a 4,200-square-foot certified-organic factory at a cost of about $2 million that would be capable of producing 2 million pints of ice cream per year. "The economics of the company are not sustainable without the factory," he says. Gottlieb found an ideal site in nearby Petaluma, California, and approached several lenders, but banks were embroiled in their own financial crisis and were not interested in making a large loan to a small start-up company. "No one's lending money right now," says Gottlieb. Financial projections show that once the factory is up and running, Three Twins could reduce the cost of making its ice cream enough to reduce its retail prices from $7 to $8 per pint to $5 per pint.

Gottlieb realizes that borrowing money from traditional lenders is not a likely prospect in the near future and that he must turn to alternative sources of financing.

1. Work with a small team of your classmates to brainstorm ideas for financing alternatives for Three Twins Ice Cream's capital needs.
2. Refer to question 1. Rank the list of financing sources that you have developed in order of priority. Briefly explain the advantages and the disadvantages of each.
3. What tips can you offer Gottlieb before he approaches the sources of financing you have listed?
4. Assuming that you have the financial means to invest in a small company, would you invest in Three Twins Ice Cream? Explain. If so, what questions would you ask before investing?

Sources: Based on Jessica Bernstein, "Sweet Success for Three Twins Ice Cream," *Marin Independent Journal*, July 5, 2010, *http://dailyme.com/story/2010070500001093/sweet-success-twins-ice-cream.html*; Loralee Stevens, "Organic Ice Cream Maker Three Twins Adds Production Plant," *North Bay Business Journal*, April 26, 2010, *www.northbaybusinessjournal.com/20581/organic-ice-cream-maker-three-twins-adds-production-plant/*; "Neal Gottlieb of Three Twins Ice Cream," Renaissance Entrepreneurship Center, 2010, *www.rencenter.org/index.php?option=com_content&view=article&id=222:neal-gotlieb&catid=41:general&Itemid=108*; Paul Jones, "Terra Linda Ice Cream Shop Opens Factory," *Marinscope Newspapers*, May 5, 2010, *www.marinscope.com/articles/2010/05/05/news_pointer/news/doc4be0d603d2f58277165007.txt*.

ENTREPRENEURIAL

Profile

Jay Shaw and Ray Ruff:
NetDimensions

Founded in 1999 by Jay Shaw and Ray Ruff with the help of angel investors, NetDimensions has grown steadily into a global provider of performance, knowledge, and learning management systems to corporate human resource management departments. Needing capital for product development, working capital, and marketing, managers considered an initial public offering in the United States, but the cost of making a relatively small issue and the subsequent cost of complying with Sarbanes-Oxley caused them to turn to London's Alternative Investment Market, which lists more than 1,000 small companies. (The average market capitalization of the companies listed on AIM is $59 million, compared to $1.2 billion for companies that are listed on the NASDAQ OMX.) The company, then with annual sales of $3.5 million, made an IPO that raised £3 million ($4.75 million), netting the company £2.32 million ($3.68 million) after the expenses of the offering. Today NetDimensions, which is listed under the symbol "NETD" on AIM, has offices around the globe and serves more than 800 clients, many of them *Fortune* 500 companies.[72]

Securing capital to launch or to expand a small business is no easy task. However, entrepreneurs who understand the equity funding options that are available and are prepared to go after them stand a much better chance of getting the financing they seek than those who don't.

Chapter Review

1. Explain the differences among the three types of capital small businesses require: fixed, working, and growth.
   - Capital is any form of wealth employed to produce more wealth. Three forms of capital are commonly identified: fixed capital, working capital, and growth capital.
   - Fixed capital is used to purchase a company's permanent or fixed assets; working capital represents the business's temporary funds and is used to support the business's normal short-term operations; growth capital requirements surface when an existing business is expanding or changing its primary direction.

2. Describe the various sources of equity capital available to entrepreneurs, including personal savings, friends and relatives, angels, partners, corporations, venture capital, and public stock offerings.
   - The most common source of financing a business is the owner's personal savings. After emptying their own pockets, the next place entrepreneurs turn for capital is family members and friends. Angels are private investors who not only invest their money in small companies, but also offer valuable advice and counsel to them. Some business owners have success financing their companies by taking on limited partners as investors or by forming an alliance with a corporation, often a customer or a supplier. Venture capital companies are for-profit, professional investors looking for fast-growing companies in "hot" industries. When screening prospects, venture capital firms look for competent management, a competitive edge, a growth industry, and important intangibles that will make a business successful. Some owners choose to attract capital by taking their companies public, which requires registering the public offering with the SEC.

3. Describe the process of "going public," as well as its advantages and disadvantages.
   - Going public involves: (1) choosing an underwriter, (2) negotiating a letter of intent, (3) preparing the registration statement, (4) filing with the SEC, and (5) meeting state requirements.
   - Going public offers the advantages of raising large amounts of capital, better access to future financing, improved corporate image, and gaining listing on a stock exchange. Disadvantages include dilution of the founder's ownership, loss of privacy, the burden of reporting to the SEC, filing expenses, and accountability to shareholders.

4. Explain the various simplified registrations and exemptions from registration available to small businesses wanting to sell securities to investors.
   - Rather than go through the complete registration process, some companies use one of the simplified registration options and exemptions available to small companies: Regulations S-B and S-K, Regulation D (Rule 504), Regulation D (Rule 505 and Rule 506) Private Placements, Section 4(6), Rule 147, Regulation A, Small Corporate Offering Registration (SCOR), direct stock offerings, and foreign stock markets.

Discussion Questions

1. Why is it so difficult for most small business owners to raise the capital needed to start, operate, or expand their ventures?
2. What is capital? List and describe the three types of capital a small business needs for its operations.
3. Define *equity financing*. What advantage does it offer over debt financing?
4. What is the most common source of equity funds in a typical small business? If an owner lacks sufficient equity capital to invest in the firm, what options are available for raising it?
5. What guidelines should entrepreneurs follow if friends and relatives choose to invest in their businesses?
6. What is an angel investor? Assemble a brief profile of the typical private investor. How can entrepreneurs locate potential angels to invest in their businesses?
7. What advice would you offer an entrepreneur on how to strike a deal with a private investor and avoid problems?
8. What types of businesses are most likely to attract venture capital? What investment criteria do venture capitalists use when screening potential businesses? How do these compare to the typical angel's criteria?
9. How do venture capital firms operate? Describe their procedure for screening investment proposals.
10. Summarize the major exemptions and simplified registrations available to small companies wanting to make public offerings of their stock.

A business plan is an important instrument in the search for capital; therefore, one of the most common motivations for creating a business plan is to secure equity financing. The business plan can be an excellent communication tool to convince investors of a business's stability and convey its potential earning power. A business plan adds credibility to your vision and the investments that others may make in it. Think about the financial needs of your company. Do you need start-up funding beyond the amount that you can provide? Is your business going to need working capital? Does your business need additional financing for growth? If you have the need to raise capital for any purpose, your business plan can help you clarify those needs and formulate a strategy for raising capital.

Review some sample plans in Business Plan Pro and note the financial sections in them. If you are creating a start-up plan, you may want to review the following sample plans: Elsewares Promotional, Westbury Storage, Inc., and Southeast Health Plans. If you are going to be searching for financing for an ongoing business, these plans may be of interest: Coach House Bed & Breakfast, The Daily Perc, and Bioring SA. These diverse plans present financial information in ways that may give you ideas how to best communicate your company's financial needs and potential. Use approaches that fit your plan as you consider the elements that potential investors will find enticing so that they will want to learn more about the growth and earning potential of your business. Leverage each aspect of the financial section—the break-even analysis, projected profit and loss, projected cash flow, projected balance sheet, and business rations—to prove your company's attractiveness as an investment opportunity.

On the Web

If you need start-up or growth capital for your venture, visit the Companion Web Site at *www.pearsonhighered.com/scarborough* for this chapter and review these equity financing options. Determine whether these sources may be useful to you as you explore financing opportunities. You will also find additional information regarding bootstrap and nontraditional funding.

In the Software

Open your plan in Business Plan Pro and go to the "Financial Plan" section. You may want to begin this section by providing an overview of your financial situation and needs. State your assumptions about the existing financial environment. Your assumptions will help to identify general facts upon which you are basing your plan, such as anticipated economic conditions, short-term interest rates, long-term interest rates, expected tax rates, personnel expenses, cash expenses, sales on credit, and others. Let the software lead you through this section.

Next consider which of the following sources you plan to use as a source of equity capital:

- Friends and family members
- Private investors or "angels"
- Partners
- Corporate venture capitalist
- Venture capital companies
- Public stock sale
- Simplified registrations and exemptions

Building Your Business Plan

One of the most valuable aspects of developing the financial section of your business plan is to determine the amount of capital your business will need and to describe the use of that capital in the business. In addition, you must consider the implications of accepting capital from outside investors. There always are costs associated with using other people's money; make sure that you know what they are in your situation. Keep in mind that potential investors will also be assessing the qualifications of your management team, the industry's growth potential, the proposed exit strategy, and other factors as they assess the financial stability and potential of your business venture. A business plan is an effective way to expand your equity financing options and to help you strike a deal with the options that are best for your situation.

Endnotes

1. Jennifer Wang, "Dearly Beloved, Please Send Cash," *Entrepreneur*, December 2009, p. 76.
2. Elizabeth Holmes, "Show Me the Money—Maybe," *Wall Street Journal*, June 25, 2007, p. R6.
3. Antonio Perez, "U.S. Venture Capital Investments at Two-Year High," *Epoch Times*, July 18, 2010, *www.theepochtimes.com/n2/content/view/39423/99999999/1/1/*; Ben Oliver, "The Man Behind Tesla," *CAR*, March 5, 2010, p. 113; Mara Lemos-Stein, "Tesla Motors Files for IPO—So Much for Profits," *Wall Street Journal*, January 29, 2010, *http://blogs.wsj.com/venturecapital/2010/01/29/tesla-motors-files-for-ipo-so-much-for-the-profits/*; "Tesla History," Edmunds, *www.edmunds.com/tesla/history.html*; "About Tesla," Tesla Motors, *www.teslamotors.com/about*.
4. Mark Henricks, "The Money Market," *Entrepreneur*, July 2006, p. 72.
5. Silva Sansoni, "Burned Angels," *Forbes*, April 19, 1999, pp. 182–185.
6. *Global Entrepreneurship Monitor: National Entrepreneurship Assessment—United States of America, 2004–2005 Executive Report*, Global Entrepreneurship Research Association, 2006, p. 23.
7. Sramana Mitra, "Bootstrapped SaaS Gains Critical Mass," *Forbes*, April 16, 2010, *www.forbes.com/2010/04/15/bootstrap-medallia-krawler-intelligent-technology-saas.html*; Patrick Hoge, "Ringtones in the Cloud," *Portfolio*, June 9, 2010, *www.portfolio.com/industry-news/technology/2010/06/09/startup-ringcentral-aims-internet-phone-service-at-small-businesses*; Dalia Fahmy, "Financing, with Strings Attached," *New York Times*, January 29, 2009, *www.nytimes.com/2009/01/29/business/smallbusiness/29sbiz.html*.
8. "Social Media: An Interview with the Co-founder and CEO of myYearbook," ThinkEquity LLC, March 8, 2010, pp. 1–3; Neil Glassman, "myYearbook's Celebrity Chatter Launches with Miley Cyrus, Rihanna, Lady Gaga, and More," *Social Times*, June 11, 2010, *www.socialtimes.com/2010/06/myyearbook-celebrity-chatter/*; Henricks, "The Money Market," pp. 69–74; Sara Wilson, "Most Likely to Succeed," *Entrepreneur*, May 2007, p. 41.
9. *Global Entrepreneurship Monitor 2006 Financing Report*, Global Entrepreneurship Research Association, 2006, p. 8.
10. *Global Entrepreneurship Monitor: National Entrepreneurship Assessment—United States of America, 2004–2005 Executive Report*, Global Entrepreneurship Research Association, 2006, p. 22.
11. Stephen L. Rosenstein, "Use Caution with Family Loans for Your Business," *Baltimore Sun*, August 10, 2008, *www.baltimoresun.com/business/bal-bz.ml.biztip10aug10,cs-bearstoday,6345879.column*.
12. Paul Kvinta, "Frogskins, Shekels, Bucks, Moolah, Cash, Simoleans, Dough, Dinero: Everybody Wants It. Your Business Needs It. Here's How to Get It," *Smart Business*, August 2000, pp. 74–89.
13. Pamela Sherrid, "Angels of Capitalism," *U.S. News & World Report*, October 13, 1997, pp. 43–45.
14. Wright, "Angel Investor Market Holds Steady in 2009 but Changes Seen in Types of Deals UNH Center for Venture Research Finds."
15. Robert Wiltbank and Warren Boeker, "Returns to Angel Investors in Groups," Angel Capital Education Foundation, November 2007, *www.angelcapitaleducation.org/dir_downloads/resources/RSCH_-_ACEF_-_Returns_to_Angel_Investor_in_Groups.pdf*.
16. "Raising Funds," *Inc.*, November 2008, pp. 69–70.
17. Jeanne Lee, "Building Wealth," *FSB*, June 2006, p. 43.
18. Tomio Geron, "Filling Vacuum Left by VCs, 'Super Angels' Show Growing Influence," *VentureWire*, April 28, 2010, *www.fis.dowjones.com/article.aspx?ProductIDFromApplication=32&aid=DJFVW0002010042 8e64s00002&r=Rss&s=DJFVW*; Ira Sager, Kimberly Weisul, and Spencer Ante, "Tech Investing: How Smart Is the Smart Money?" *Bloomberg Business Week*, February 25, 2010, *http://images.businessweek.com/ss/10/02/0225_angel_investors/2.htm*.
19. Robert E. Wilbank and Warren Boeker, "Angel Performance Project," Angel Capital Education Foundation, November 2007, *www.angelcapitalassociation.org/dir_downloads/resources/RSCH_-_ACEF_-_Returns_to_Angel_Investors_PPT.pdf*; Wright, "Angel Investor Market Holds Steady in 2009 but Changes Seen in Types of Deals UNH Center for Venture Research Finds."
20. "What Is the Average Closing Time to Receive Financing?" *Jian Business Power Tools*, *www.jian.com/library-of-business-information/f252/venture-capital/what-is-the-average-closing-time-it-takes-between-receiving-a.php*.
21. Wright, "Angel Investor Market Holds Steady in 2009 but Changes Seen in Types of Deals UNH Center for Venture Research Finds."
22. Henricks, "The Money Market," p. 72.
23. Tomio Geron, "'Super Angels' Rise to Fore," *Wall Street Journal*, May 6, 2010, *http://online.wsj.com/article/SB1000142405274870442350457521279 2672226992. html?KEYWORDS=Super+Angels+Rise+to+Fore&mg=com-wsj*.
24. Ibid.; Bambi Francisco Roizen, "How to Get Funded by Super Angel Mike Maples," *Vator News*, May 13, 2010, *http://vator.tv/news/2010-05-13-how-to-get-funded-by-super-angel-mike-maples*.
25. "FAQ: The Value of Angel Investors and Angel Groups," Angel Capital Association, 2009, p. 1.
26. "ACA Member Landscape: 2009 Different Than 2008 (and Not)," Angel Capital Association, April 16, 2009, pp. 2, 3, and 7.
27. "Vital Statistics," Band of Angels, *www.bandangels.com*; Bonnie Azab Powell, "Angel Investors Fill Void Left by Risk Capital," *New York Times*, July 6, 2001, p. 28; Loren Fox, "Heaven Can't Wait," *Business 2.0*, March 20, 2001, pp. 123–124; Anne Ashby Gilbert, "Small Stakes in Small Business," *Fortune*, April 12, 1999, p. 162[H]; Sherrid, "Angels of Capitalism," pp. 43–45; John Heylar, "The Venture Capitalist Next Door," *Fortune*, November 13, 2000, pp. 293–312.
28. Bruce J. Blechmna, "Step Right Up," *Entrepreneur*, June 1993, pp. 20–25.
29. Wiltbank and Boeker, "Returns to Angel Investors in Groups."
30. Anne Fisher, "Changing Course," *Fortune*, November 27, 2006, p. 278.
31. *Corporate Venture Capital Group Investment Analysis 1995 Through Q1 2010*, National Venture Capital Association, 2010, p. 1.
32. "Intel Capital Featured in TopCapital," Intel, May 28, 2009, *www.intel.com/capital/news/releases/090528_2.htm*.
33. "Intel Capital Featured in TopCapital," Intel, May 28, 2009, *www.intel.com/capital/news/releases/090528_2.htm*; *Key Steps Before Talking to Venture Capitalists*, Intel Capital, 2009, p. 3; Stephen Lawson, "Clearwire IPO Jumps Up on Opening," *Network World*, March 8, 2007, *www.networkworld.com/news/2007/030807-clearwire-ipo-jumps-up-on.html*; Scott Austin, "The Top 10 Richest Venture-Backed

Companies of All Time," *Wall Street Journal,* June 1, 2010, *http://blogs.wsj.com/venturecapital/2010/06/01/the-top-10-richest-venture-backed-companies-of-all-time/.*

34. "Investments by Region," PricewaterhouseCoopers MoneyTree Survey, Q1 2010, *www.pwcmoneytree.com/MTPublic/ns/nav.jsp?page=region.*

35. David Worrell, "School Ties," *Entrepreneur,* November 2006, pp. 88–90.

36. Austin, "The Top 10 Richest Venture-Backed Companies of All Time."

37. William D. Bygrave with Mark Quill, *Global Entrepreneurship Monitor: 2006 Financing Report,* Global Entrepreneurship Research Association, 2006, p. 23.

38. Dee Power and Brian E. Hill, "Venture Capital Survey," *The Capital Connection,* 2008, *www.capital-connection.com/survey-close.html.*

39. Sharon Kahn, "The Venture Game," *FSB,* May 2009, pp. 60–95.

40. Mabel Brecrick-Okereke, "Report to U.N. Cautions that Focus on Venture Capital Can Hinder Entrepreneurial Economy," United Nations Association of the United States of America, *http://unusa.school.aol.com/newsroom/NewsReleases/ean_venture.asp*; Cara Cannella, "Where Seed Money Really Comes From," *Inc.,* August 2003, p. 26.

41. PricewaterhouseCoopers MoneyTree Survey, *www.pwcmoneytree.com/MTPublic/ns/nav.jsp?page=stage*; National Venture Capital Association, *www.nvca.org.*

42. Anthony Tjan, "Changing Fashion: An Interview with Gilt Groupe Founder Alexandra Wilkis Wilson," *Harvard Business Review,* March 5, 2010, *http://blogs.hbr.org/tjan/2010/03/on-a-recent-trip-to.html*; Colleen Debaise, "Luanching Gilt Groupe, A Fashionable Enterprise," *Wall Street Journal,* July 16, 2010, *http://online.wsj.com/ article/SB10001424052748703792704575366842447271892.html.*

43. Jason Del Ray, "The Ticker," *Inc.,* September 200, p. 30.

44. Dan Bigman, "On the Hunt," *Forbes,* August 3, 2009, pp. 56–59; Michael J. Roberts and Noam T. Wasserman, "The Founding CEO's Dilemma: Stay or Go?" *Working Knowledge,* August 15, 2005, *http://hbswk.hbs.edu/item/4948.html.*

45. Dalia Fahmy, "Financing, With Strings Attached," *New York Times,* January 29, 2009, *www.nytimes.com/2009/01/29/business/smallbusiness/29sbiz.html.*

46. David Pakman, "Why Mint Matters: A Message to Entrepreneurs About Products," *Pakman's Blog: Disruption,* March 2, 2009, *http://dpakman.wordpress.com/2009/03/02/why-mint-matters-a-message-to-entrepreneurs-about-products/.*

47. Tracy T. Leteroff, "In Full Bloom," *Entrepreneur,* July 2006, p. 78.

48. *Results from the 2010 Global Venture Capital Survey,* National Venture Capital Association and Deloitte, July 13, 2010, p. 14.

49. Benjamin Kepple, "Equallogic Founders to be Honored," *New Hampshire Union Leader,* May 14, 2008, *www.unionleader.com/article.aspx?headline=EqualLogic+founders+to+be+honored&articleId=775baed8-e07f-4d16-ba43-45d2f75034fe.*

50. Henricks, "The Money Market," p. 72.

51. Gwen Moran, "Toward Safer, Greener Roads," *Entrepreneur,* May 2010, p. 65; "GreenRoad Company Overview," GreenRoad Technologies, *www.greenroad.com/company_overview.html.*

52. Dave Pell, "What's Old Is New Again," *FSB,* July/August 2000, p. 122.

53. Kvinta, "Frogskins, Shekels, Bucks, Moolah, Cash, Simoleans, Dough, Dinero," p. 87.

54. Jay Ritter, "Some Factoids About the 2009 IPO Market," University of Florida, April 14, 2010, p. 15.

55. Ibid., p. 8.

56. "Ancestry.com IPO Trades Higher," *Street Insider,* November 5, 2009, *www.streetinsider.com/Hot+List/Ancestry.com+(ACOM)+IPO+Trades+Higher/5079090.html*; "Ancestry.com Inc.," Hoover's IPO Central, 2010, *www.hoovers.com/company/Ancestrycom_Inc/rrcrkxi-1.html.*

57. Kevin Delaney, "Google Looks to Boost Ads with YouTube," *Wall Street Journal,* October 10, 2006, p. B1.

58. Tony Taylor, "A Going (Public) Concern," *GSA Business,* February 20, 2006, p. 15.

59. "CompuPay and PayMaxx Finalize Agreement," CompuPay, June 24, 2005, *www.compupay.com/about_compupay.cfm?subpage=426*; Lynn Stephens and Robert C. Schwartz, "The Chilling Effects of Sarbanes-Oxley: Myth or Reality?" *CPA Journal,* June 2006, *www.nysscpa.org/cpajournal/2006/606/infocus/p14.htm.*

60. David Weild and Edward Kim, *Market Structure Is Causing the IPO Crisis—and More,* Grant Thornton, June 2010, p. 10.

61. Darren Dahl, "Assessing Vonage's Grim IPO," *Inc.,* August 2006, p. 26; Shawn Young, "Vonage Customers Withholf Payment for IPO Shares," *Wall Street Journal,* August 2, 2006, p. B1; Shawn Young and Randy Smith, "How Vonage's High Profile IPO Stumbled on the Stock Market," *Wall Street Journal,* June 3–4, 2006, pp. A1, A6.

62. Joseph McCafferty, "The Long View," *CFO,* May 2007, p. 48.

63. Tim Reason, "Off the Street," *CFO,* May 2003, p. 58.

64. Joanna L. Ossinger, "Stock Answers," *Wall Street Journal,* June 25, 2007, p. R6.

65. Clare Baldwin, "NewPage, Smile Brands Withdraw IPOs as Stocks Sink," Fox Business, May 25, 2010, *www.foxbusiness.com/personal-finance/2010/05/25/update-newpage-smile-brands-withdraw-ipos-stocks-sink/*; "IPO Withdrawals—U.S.," IPO Home, Renaissance Capital, *www.renaissancecapital.com/IPOHome/Press/IPOWithdrawals.aspx.*

66. Andrew Ross Sorkin, "Rosetta Stone IPO Prices Above Estimate Range," *New York Times,* April 16, 2009, *http://dealbook.blogs.nytimes.com/2009/04/16/rosetta-stone-ipo-prices-above-estimate-range/*; "Our History," Rosetta Stone, *www.rosettastone.com/global/history.*

67. "IPO Pricings Compared to Range," IPO Home, Renaissance Capital, *www.renaissancecapital.com/ipohome/news/Tesla-Motors-prices-IPO-at-$17.00-above-the-range-8215.html.*

68. "Tesla Motors Prices at $17, Above the Range," IPO Home, Renaissance Capital, July 22, 2010, *www.renaissancecapital.com/ipohome/news/Green-Dot-sells-more-shares-and-prices-at-$36-above-the-range-8288.html.*

69. David M. Katz, "A Tough Act to Follow," *CFO,* March 2006, pp. 65–72; Unica Corporation, IPO Home, *www.ipohome.com/common/ipoprofile.asp?ticker=UNCA.*

70. Form D: Ligatt Security International, March 23, 2010, *http://attrition.org/errata/charlatan/gregory_evans/ligatt04/LIGATT-SEC-Form-D.pdf.*

71. Aria Munro, "New York's CityMade, Inc. Announces Direct Public Offering," *eNewsChannels,* April 16, 2009, *http://enewschannels.com/2009/04/16/enc6687_151018.php*; "CityMade Direct Public Offering," CityMade, *www.citymade.com/dpo.php.*

72. "NetDimensions Announces Intention to Float on AIM," NetDimensions, *www. netdimensions.com/company/view-news.php?NewsId=43*; "First Day of Dealings on AIM and Placing," *www.netdimensions.com/company/view-news.php?NewsId=44NetDimensions*; Chee Sing Chan, "Beating the Dotcom Bust," *Computerworld Hong Kong,* June 2010, p. 26; "Corporate Fact Sheet," NASDAQ OMX, 2009, p. 1; "Market Statistics," London Stock Exchange, June 2010, p. 2.

Sources of Debt Financing

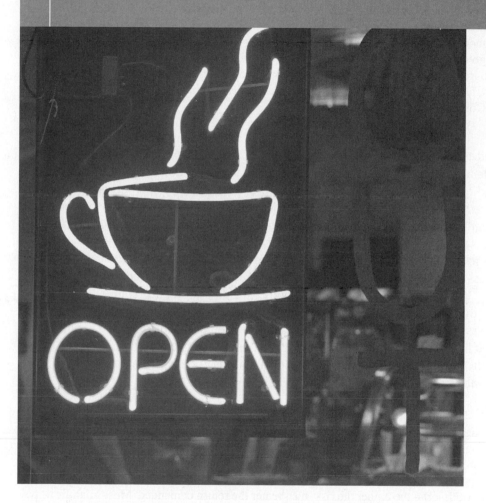

Learning Objectives

Upon completion of this chapter, you will be able to:

1. Describe the various sources of debt capital and the advantages and disadvantages of each.
2. Explain the types of financing available from nonbank sources of credit.
3. Identify the sources of government financial assistance and the loan programs these agencies offer.
4. Describe the various loan programs available from the Small Business Administration.
5. Discuss state and local economic development programs.
6. Discuss methods of financing growth and expansion internally with bootstrap financing.
7. Explain how to avoid becoming a victim of a loan scam.

Always borrow from pessimists. They never expect to get it back.

—Anonymous

The best source of money is not to need it.

—Therese Flaherty

From Chapter 15 of *Effective Small Business Management: An Entrepreneurial Approach*, 10/e. Norman M. Scarborough.

Debt financing involves the funds that a small business owner borrows and must repay with interest. Small companies in the United States rely heavily on debt capital to start and feed their growing businesses. The U.S. Small Business Administration (SBA) estimates that lenders make $700 billion worth of loans of less than $1 million to small companies each year. Add to that amount loans from family members and friends and credit card borrowing, and total small business borrowing approaches $1 trillion a year.[1] Lenders of capital are more numerous than investors, but small business loans can be just as difficult (if not more difficult) to obtain, especially given the recent turbulence in the financial markets. Small businesses are facing a credit crunch; the crises on Wall Street have severely limited credit on Main Street. A recent survey by the National Federation of Independent Businesses (NFIB) reports that just 50 percent of small business owners who attempted to borrow money received at least most of the capital they sought, down from 89 percent just 3 years before.[2] The NFIB also reports that capital spending by small businesses, which is fueled by their access to financing, is hovering just above a 35-year low.[3] When entrepreneurs do not have access to credit, they cannot make capital investments, and their companies do not grow as fast, hire as many employees, and generate as much in sales—and the entire economy suffers.

The government's attempt to increase the availability of credit through the Troubled Asset Relief Program (TARP), which the Treasury Department launched at the pinnacle of the financial meltdown, failed to improve access to credit, especially for small companies, according to a report from the Congressional Oversight Panel.[4]

ENTREPRENEURIAL
Profile

Frank and Ingrid Brown: The Villager

Frank and Ingrid Brown, owners of The Villager, a gallery in Auburn, Alabama, that sells affordable artwork from more than 150 artists from across the United States, needed capital to expand their business, which currently has 20 employees. They approached a bank for a loan backed by a guarantee from the U.S. Small Business Administration's 7(a) loan program, but the bank rejected their application. The Browns then applied for the maximum $35,000 loan through America's Recovery Capital (ARC) loan program, which Congress passed in response to the banking crisis as a way to provide financing to viable but struggling small companies. After completing volumes of paperwork, the Browns received a loan, but for just $14,000. "We couldn't get any answers for why we didn't get the full amount," says Frank, who says that the small loan was hardly worth the effort required to complete the application process. The Browns also are frustrated because their local bank extended their business a $10,000 line of credit, just 20 percent of the amount they had requested. "People like us hire people," says Frank, "but without the capital it needs to grow, The Villager isn't bringing on new staffers."[5]

Although entrepreneurs who borrow capital maintain complete ownership of their businesses, they must carry it as a liability on the balance sheet as well as repay it with interest at some point in the future. In addition, because lenders consider small businesses to be greater risks than bigger corporate customers, small companies must pay higher interest rates because of the risk–return trade-off—the higher the risk, the greater the return demanded. Most small firms pay the **prime rate**, the interest rate banks charge their most creditworthy customers, *plus* two or more percentage points. Still, the cost of debt financing often is lower than that of equity financing because debt financing does not require entrepreneurs to dilute their ownership interest in the company.

The need for debt capital can arise from a number of sources, but financial experts identify the following reasons business owners should consider borrowing money:[6]

- *Increasing the company's workforce and/or inventory to boost sales.* Sufficient working capital is the fuel that feeds a company's growth.
- *Gaining market share.* Businesses often need extra capital as their customer bases expand and they incur the added expense of extending credit to customers.
- *Purchasing new equipment.* Financing new equipment that can improve productivity, increase quality, and lower operating expenses often takes more capital than a growing company can generate internally.

- *Refinancing existing debt.* As companies become established, they can negotiate more favorable borrowing terms compared to their start-up days, when entrepreneurs take whatever money they can get at whatever rate they can get. Replacing high-interest loans with loans carrying lower interest rates improves cash flow significantly.

- *Taking advantage of cash discounts.* Suppliers sometimes offer discounts to customers who pay their invoices early. "Purchasing, Quality Management, and Vendor Analysis," business owners should take advantage of cash discounts in most cases.

- *Buying the building in which the business is located.* Many entrepreneurs start out renting the buildings that house their businesses; however, if location is crucial to their success, it may be wise to purchase the location.

- *Establishing a relationship with a lender.* If a business has never borrowed money, taking out a loan and developing a good repayment and credit history can pave the way for future financing. Smart business owners know that bankers who understand their businesses play an integral role in their companies' ultimate success.

- *Retiring debt held by a "nonrelationship" creditor.* Entrepreneurs find that lenders who have no real interest in their companies' long-term success or do not understand their businesses can be extremely difficult to work with. They prefer to borrow money from lenders who are willing to help them achieve their business mission and goals.

- *Foreseeing a downturn in business.* Establishing access to financing before a business slowdown hits insulates a company from a serious cash crisis and protects it from failure.

Entrepreneurs seeking debt capital face an astounding range of credit options varying greatly in complexity, availability, and flexibility. Not all of these sources of debt capital are equally favorable, however. By understanding the various sources of capital—both commercial and government lenders—and their characteristics, entrepreneurs can greatly increase the chances of obtaining a loan.

Figure 1 shows the financing strategies that small business owners use for their companies. We now turn to the various sources of debt capital.

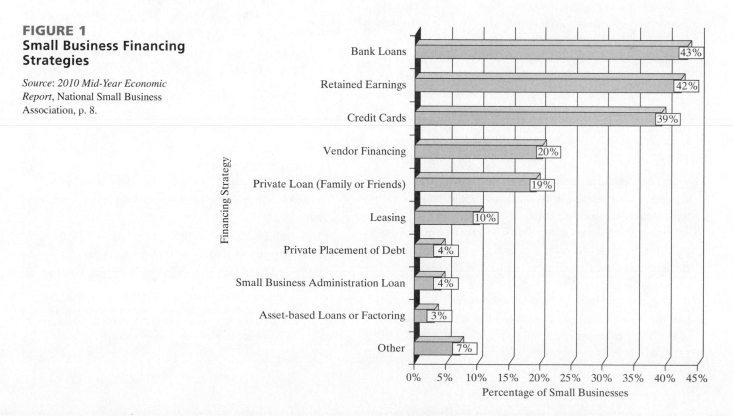

FIGURE 1
Small Business Financing Strategies

Source: 2010 Mid-Year Economic Report, National Small Business Association, p. 8.

IN THE ENTREPRENEURIAL
SPOTLIGHT   A Tale of Two Borrowers

Aaron's Automotive

Tari Dudley had a plan to open a woman-friendly auto repair shop in Fort Worth, Texas, and operate it with her son-in-law, Aaron Phelps, who had owned a swimming pool cleaning business. Dudley had $47,000 in collateral, including a $30,000 certificate of deposit, and an excellent credit rating. Neither Dudley nor Phelps had operated a repair shop before, but Phelps had worked on cars all of his life and recently had returned to school to become a certified mechanic.

However, when Dudley applied for a $250,000 loan at the bank where she had been a customer for 24 years, the loan officer did not bother to hand her an application; instead, he wrote her name and phone number on a small adhesive note. "That was it," says Dudley, who suspects that the loan officer threw away the note as soon as she left the bank. She then applied for a loan at two community banks, both of which were impressed with her plan for an auto repair shop aimed at women. After 3 weeks, however, both rejected Dudley's loan request.

Like many entrepreneurs, Dudley is caught square in the middle of a severe credit crunch. Government officials are encouraging banks to lend money; bankers say they want to lend money but claim that government policies discourage them from doing so.

After striking out at banks, Dudley turned to a private investor, who promised to put up $30,000 but later backed out. Undeterred by the inability to get capital, Dudley and Phelps decided to forge ahead with their repair shop, confident that it would be successful. Dudley emptied her 401(k) retirement account and invested the severance pay she received from her former job, and Phelps and his wife contributed their savings account. They also scaled back their start-up costs, holding off on the purchase of an $80,000 piece of diagnostic equipment until their business becomes cash flow positive. They opened their repair shop, Aaron's Automotive ("the woman-friendly shop") with two employees and rely on a credit card with a $12,000 limit to cover their monthly deficits. They charge $80 per hour for labor, an amount that is below what most auto dealerships in the area charge. Customers are beginning to discover the business, but Dudley and Phelps do not have the money to advertise. "We're keeping our head above water," says Dudley. As the entrepreneurs fill small bags with candy, business cards, and pens bearing the Aaron's Automotive logo to deliver to prospective customers, Dudley says, "It's all about cash flow. I can't put out a big sign because we don't have the money. I can't advertise. So we're putting candy in bags."

Gorman Mechanical

Michael Mushegan, a graduate of the University of Arizona with a degree in finance, wanted to purchase Gorman Mechanical, a company in Azle, Texas, that installs and services commercial and residential heating and air conditioning units in the Dallas–Fort Worth area. Mushegan was familiar with the industry because he had grown up in it; his family operated a similar business in Arizona. Mushegan applied for a loan to purchase Gorman Mechanical, which had been in business for nearly 10 years and was profitable, at the bank where he was a customer. When the loan officer did not ask detailed questions about the business, the loan, and how he would use the money, Mushegan knew that his chances of getting financing were slim. Then he learned about SBA-guaranteed loans and discovered that a large bank, Wells Fargo, was one of the most active SBA lenders in the nation. Mushegan applied for an SBA-backed loan at Wells Fargo. "[Bankers told me] that industry experience is crucial and that my credit rating was outstanding, which also was extremely important," he says.

With an SBA loan guarantee, Wells Fargo approved Mushegan's loan application. After putting up 15 percent of the purchase price using his own money and investments from family, he took over Gorman Mechanical and became a business owner for the first time.

1. One of these businesses received a bank loan and the other did not. Describe the differences between the two companies that led to one entrepreneur receiving the financing he needed and the other one failing to qualify for a loan.
2. What steps would you have recommended to Tari Dudley to increase the probability of qualifying for a loan?
3. Suppose that Dudley had approached you for help after being turned down by three banks. What other sources of capital would you have suggested she use?

Source: Based on Barry Shlacter, "Small Businesses Continue to Feel Lending Pinch," *Fort Worth Star-Telegram*, December 27, 2009, *www.finreg21.com/news/small-businesses-continue-feel-lending-pinch-4.*

Sources of Debt Capital

Commercial Banks

1. Describe the various sources of debt capital and the advantages and disadvantages of each.

Commercial banks are the very heart of the financial market, providing the greatest number and variety of loans to small businesses. Commercial banks provide 50 percent of the dollar value of all loans to small businesses.[7] For small business owners, banks are lenders of *first* resort, especially as their companies grow. The typical loan amount is small; more than 88 percent of all small business bank loans are for less than $100,000 (see Figure 2). The average micro business loan (those less than $100,000) is $6,820, and the average small business loan (those between $100,000 and $1 million) is $245,775.

ENTREPRENEURIAL
Profile

Blanca and Robert Welborn: Med-National

Med-National, a company founded in 1987 by Blanca and Robert Welborn in San Antonio, Texas, that provides medical and dental services to the Department of Defense, applied for a $300,000 loan from several local banks with which the company had done business in the past. The company needed the financing to hire 20 doctors, dentists, and support staff to secure two contracts with the U.S. Army. Even though Med-National generates nearly $6 million in annual sales, has been profitable since its inception, and has an excellent credit rating, the banks refused the loan request. After nearly a year, the Welborn's persistence finally paid off when they secured the $300,000 loan they needed from one of the nation's largest small business lenders, Wells Fargo. Despite the Welborn's success, lack of access to credit has slowed their company's growth. "If we could borrow money more easily, we would be hiring even more people," says Robert.[8]

Banks tend to be conservative in their lending practices and prefer to make loans to established small businesses rather than to high-risk start-ups. Small companies that are less than 3 years old are as much as 50 percent less likely to receive loans or lines of credit than older, more established businesses.[9] Because start-ups are so risky, bankers prefer to make loans to companies that have successful track records. Banks are concerned with a small company's operating past and scrutinize its records to project its position in the immediate future. They also want proof of a company's stability and its ability to generate adequate cash flows that ensure repayment of the loan. If they do make loans to a start-up venture, banks like to see significant investment from the owner, sufficient cash flows to repay the loan, ample collateral (such as compensating balances)

FIGURE 2
Commercial Bank Loans to Small Businesses by Size of Loan

Source: The Small Business Economy: A Report to the President, 2009, p. 74.

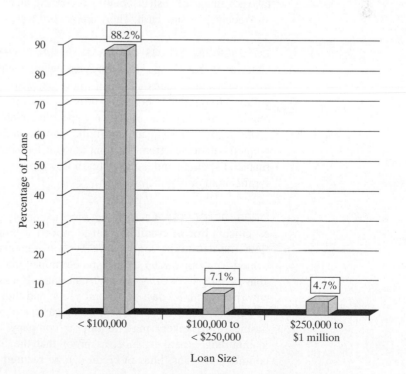

to secure it, or an SBA guarantee to insure it. Entrepreneurs should not overlook small community banks (those with less than $10 billion in assets) for loans. These small banks, which make up 98.7 percent of U.S. banking institutions, account for 52 percent of the dollar volume of all small business loans.[10] They also tend to be "small business–friendly" and are more likely than their larger counterparts to customize the terms of their loans to the particular needs of small businesses, offering, for example, flexible payment terms to match the seasonal pattern of a company's cash flow or interest-only payments until a piece of equipment begins generating revenue.

When evaluating a loan application, banks focus on a company's capacity to create positive cash flow because they know that's where the money to repay their loans will come from. The first question in most bankers' minds when reviewing an entrepreneur's business plan is "Can this business generate sufficient cash to repay the loan?" Even though they rely on collateral to secure their loans, the last thing banks want is for a borrower to default, forcing them to sell the collateral (often at "fire sale" prices) and use the proceeds to pay off the loan. *That's* why bankers stress cash flow when analyzing a loan request, especially for a business start-up. "Cash is more important than your mother," jokes one experienced borrower.[11]

Banks, as well as many other lenders, also require that entrepreneurs sign a personal guarantee for any loan they make to small businesses. By making a personal loan guarantee, an entrepreneur is pledging that he or she will be personally liable for repaying the loan in the event that the business itself cannot repay the loan. In the eyes of the law a sole proprietor or a general partner and the business are one and the same; therefore, for them, personal loan guarantees are redundant. However, because the owners of S corporations, corporations, and LLCs are separate from their businesses, they are not automatically responsible for the company's debts. Once the owners of these businesses sign a personal loan guarantee, however, they become liable for their companies' loans. (It is as if these individuals have "cosigned" the loan with the business.) Working with a partner, Rosalind Resnick launched NetCreations, an Internet marketing company, using money from various sources, including bank loans. The bank "required us to provide personal guarantees for [NetCreation's] credit line and equipment lease—loans that totaled $2 million," says Resnick. "It wasn't until our company went public that the bank let us off the hook [for those loans]."[12]

Short-Term Loans

Short-term loans, extended for less than 1 year, are the most common type of commercial loan banks make to small companies. These funds typically are used to replenish the working-capital account to finance the purchase of inventory, boost output, finance credit sales to customers, or take advantage of cash discounts. As a result, an owner repays the loan after converting inventory and receivables into cash. There are several types of short-term loans.

COMMERCIAL LOANS (OR TRADITIONAL BANK LOANS). The basic short-term loan is the commercial bank's specialty. Business owners typically repay the loan, which often is unsecured because secured loans are much more expensive to administer and maintain, as a lump sum within 3 to 6 months. In other words, the bank grants a loan to the small business owner without requiring him or her to pledge any specific collateral to support the loan in case of default. The owner repays the total amount of the loan at maturity. Sometimes the interest due on the loan is prepaid—deducted from the total amount borrowed. Until a small business is able to prove its financial strength and liquidity (cash flow) to the bank's satisfaction, it will probably not qualify for this kind of commercial loan.

LINES OF CREDIT. One of the most common requests entrepreneurs make of banks is to establish a **line of credit**, a short-term loan with a preset limit that provides much needed cash flow for day-to-day operations. With a commercial (or revolving) line of credit, business owners can borrow up to the predetermined ceiling at any time during the year quickly and conveniently by writing themselves a loan. Banks set up lines of credit that are renewable for anywhere from 90 days to several years, and they usually limit the open line of credit to 40 to 50 percent of a firm's present working capital, although they may lend more for highly seasonal businesses. Bankers may require a company to rest its line of credit during the year, maintaining a zero balance, as proof that the line of credit is not a perpetual crutch. Like commercial loans, lines of credit can be secured or unsecured. Small lines of credit often are unsecured, and large ones usually are secured by accounts receivable, inventory, equipment, or other business assets. A business typically pays a small handling fee (1 to 2 percent of the maximum amount of credit) plus interest on the amount borrowed—usually prime-plus-three points or more. Because banks prefer the security of established businesses, securing a line of credit can be difficult for some small companies, especially new ones. A study by the National Federation of Independent Businesses reports that the most difficult type of loan for small business owners to obtain is a line of credit; only 37.6 percent of the small companies that apply receive one.[13]

ENTREPRENEURIAL
Profile

Brad Glaberson: Cucina Fresca, Inc.

Brad Glaberson, founder of Cucina Fresca, Inc., a specialty foods company in Seattle, Washington, switched from the bank he had used for 10 years when his banker eliminated his company's $70,000 line of credit and converted the existing $38,000 balance to a term loan. Glaberson approached Foundation Bank, a small community bank in Seattle, and offered loan officers a tour of his operations, monthly financial reports, and access to all of his company's financial records as part of his loan application. Foundation Bank extended Cucina Fresca a $102,000 line of credit, which Glaberson used to launch a new product line called Lazy Lasagna.[14]

Table 1 shows one method for determining how large a line of credit a small company should seek.

FLOOR PLANNING. Floor planning is a form of financing frequently employed by retailers of "big-ticket items" that are easily distinguishable from one another (usually by serial number), such as automobiles, recreational vehicles, boats, and major appliances. For example, Thrifty

TABLE 1 How Large Should Your Line of Credit Be?

Determining how large a small company's line of credit should be is an important step for a growing business. As a company's sales grow, so will its inventory and accounts receivable balances, both of which tie up valuable cash. To avoid experiencing a cash crisis, many growing companies rely on a line of credit. How large should that line of credit be? The following formulas will help you answer that question:

$$\frac{\text{Average collection}}{\text{period ratio}} + \frac{\text{Average inventory}}{\text{turnover ratio}} - \frac{\text{Average payable}}{\text{period ratio}} = \frac{\text{Cash}}{\text{flow cycle}}$$

Cash flow cycle $\times$ Average daily sales $-$ Forecasted annual profit $=$ Line of credit requirement

Example: Suppose that Laramie Corporation has an average collection period ratio of 49 days and an average inventory turnover ratio of 53 days. The company's average payable period is 39 days, its annual sales are $5,800,000, and its net profit margin is 6.5 percent. What size line of credit should Laramie seek?

Average collection period ratio	49 days
Average inventory turnover ratio	53 days
Total	102 days
Minus average payable period ratio	39 days
Cash flow cycle	63 days
Annual sales	$5,800,000
Average daily sales (annual sales ÷ 365 days)	$ 15,890
Cash flow cycle	63 days
Times average daily sales	$ 15,890
Equals	$1,001,096
Minus forecasted profit (annual sales × net profit margin)	377,000
Equals line of credit requirement	$ 624,096

Laramie Corporation should seek a line of credit of $624,000.

Source: Adapted from George M. Dawson, "It Figures," *Entrepreneur Start-Ups*, December 2000, p. 27.

Car Sales makes a floor-plan financing program available to the network of franchised dealers that sell the used cars that are taken out of service from its Thrifty Car Rental system. Bombadier Capital, the provider of the floor plan, finances Thrifty Car Sales dealers' purchases of automobiles from Thrifty Car Rental and maintains a security interest in each car by holding its title as collateral.[15] Dealers pay interest on the loan monthly and repay the principal as the cars are sold. The longer a floor-planned item sits in inventory, the more it costs a business owner in interest expense. Banks and other floor planners often discourage retailers from using their money without authorization by performing spot checks to verify prompt repayment of the principal as items are sold.

Intermediate and Long-Term Loans

Banks primarily are lenders of short-term capital to small businesses, although they will make certain intermediate and long-term loans. Intermediate and long-term loans are extended for 1 year or longer and are normally used to increase fixed- and growth-capital balances. Commercial banks grant these loans for starting a business, constructing a plant, purchasing real estate and equipment, and other long-term investments. Loan repayments are normally made monthly or quarterly.

TERM LOANS. Another common type of loan banks make to small businesses is a **term loan**. Typically unsecured, banks grant these loans to businesses whose past operating history suggests a high probability of repayment. Some banks make only secured term loans, however. Term loans impose restrictions (called **covenants**) on the business decisions an entrepreneur makes concerning the company's operations. For instance, a term loan may set limits on owners' salaries, prohibit further borrowing without the bank's approval, or maintain certain financial ratios. An entrepreneur must understand all of the terms attached to a loan before accepting it.

INSTALLMENT LOANS. These loans are made to small firms for purchasing equipment, facilities, real estate, and other fixed assets. When financing equipment, a bank usually lends the small business from 60 to 80 percent of the equipment's value in return for a security interest in the equipment. The loan's amortization schedule typically coincides with the length of the equipment's usable life. When financing real estate (commercial mortgages), banks typically will lend up to 75 to 80 percent of the property's value and will allow a lengthier repayment schedule of 10 to 30 years.

CHARACTER LOANS. Banking regulatory changes intended to create jobs by increasing the credit available to small- and medium-sized companies now allow banks to make **character loans**. Rather than requiring entrepreneurs to prove their creditworthiness with financial statements, evaluations, appraisals, and tax returns, banks making character loans base their lending decisions on the borrower's reputation and reliability (i.e., "character").

The Lessons from the Street-Smart Entrepreneur feature describes how small business owners can maintain positive relationships with their bankers.

LESSONS FROM THE STREET-SMART ➤ entrepreneur

How to Maintain a Positive Relationship with Your Banker

Too often, entrepreneurs communicate with their bankers only when they find themselves in a tight spot and needing money. Unfortunately, that's not the best way to manage a working relationship with a bank. "Businesspeople have a responsibility to train their bankers in their businesses," says one lending advisor. "A good banker will stay close to the business, and a good business will stay close to the banker." A good banking relationship has the power to influence in a significant way the success of a small business.

How can business owners develop and maintain positive relationships with their bankers? The first step is picking the right bank and the right banker. Some banks are not terribly enthusiastic about making small business loans, whereas others target small businesses as their primary customers. Entrepreneurs should visit several banks—both small community banks and large national banks—and talk with a commercial loan officer about their banking needs and the bank's products and services. After finding the right banker, the entrepreneur must focus on maintaining effective communication. The best strategy is to keep bankers informed—of *both good news and bad*.

Karyn Korteling started her restaurant, Pastabilities, in downtown Syracuse, New York, when the city's downtown revitalization efforts were just underway. She knew that a quality restaurant located downtown could be successful by appealing to the 30,000 people who worked in the area. The menu of delicious pastas, pizzas, salads, and specialty dishes struck a chord with the lunch crowd, and soon Pastabilities also became a gathering spot for people heading out for a night on the town. Pastabilities has grown from a one-room lunch spot into a full-blown restaurant with three dining rooms, a full-service bar, and seasonal outdoor dining in a quaint plaza. Ready to add a second location but needing financing to make the move, Korteling has been meeting with her banker for several months to discuss the company's financial performance and expansion plans. She keeps her banker informed about the progress of her company (such as how she has trained her management team so that she can split her time between two locations) as well as the challenges it faces. She also asks for advice on some issues. "The more they know about you and your business, the better," she says.

What else can entrepreneurs do to manage their banking relationships?

- *Understand the factors that influence a banker's decision to lend money.* Bankers *want* to lend money to businesses; that's how they generate a profit. However, they want to lend money to businesses they believe offer a very high probability of repaying their loans on time. Bankers look for companies that are good credit risks and have clear plans for success.

- *Invite the banker to visit your company.* An on-site visit gives the banker the chance to see exactly what a company does and how it does it. It's also a great opportunity to show the bank where and how its money is put to use.

- *Make a good impression.* A company's physical appearance can go a long way toward making either a positive (or a negative) impression on a banker. Lenders appreciate clean, safe, orderly work environments and view sloppily maintained facilities (such as spills, leaks, and unnecessary clutter) as negatives.

- *Send customer mailings to the banker as well.* "Besides the numbers, we try to give our bankers a sense of our vision for the business," says Mitchell Goldstone, president of Thirty-Minute Photos Etc. Goldstone sends customer mailings to his bankers "so they know we're thinking about opportunities to generate money."

- *Send the banker samples of new products.* "I try to make my banker feel as if he's a partner," says Drew Santin, president of a product-development company. "Whenever we get a new machine, I go out of my way to show the banker what it does."

- *Show off your employees.* Bankers know that one of the most important components of building a successful company is a dedicated team of capable employees. Giving bankers the opportunity to visit with employees and ask them questions while touring a company can help alleviate fears that they are pumping their money into a high-risk "one-person show."

- *Know your company's assets.* Almost always interested in collateral, bankers will want to judge the quality of your company's assets—property, equipment, inventory, accounts receivable, and others. Be sure to point them out. "As you walk the lender through your business," says one experienced banker, "it's always a good idea to identify assets the banker might not think of."

- *Be prepared to personally guarantee any loans the bank makes to your business.* Even though many business owners choose the corporate form of ownership for its limited liability benefits, some are surprised when a banker asks them to make personal guarantees on business loans. It's a common practice, especially on small business loans.

- *Keep your business plan up-to-date and make sure your banker gets a copy of it.* Bankers lend money to companies that can demonstrate that they will use the money wisely and productively. They also want to make sure that the company offers a high probability of repayment. The best way to provide bankers with that assurance is with a solid business plan.

- *Know how much money you need and how you will repay it.* When a banker asks "How much money do you need?" the correct answer is not "How much can I get?"

1. What advantages do entrepreneurs gain by communicating openly with their bankers?
2. Why do so few entrepreneurs follow Karyn Korteling's example when dealing with their bankers?
3. What are the consequences of an entrepreneur failing to communicate effectively with a banker?

Sources: Based on Emily Maltby, "Uptick Catches Entrepreneurs by Surprise," *Wall Street Journal*, December 8, 2009, p. B7; Keith Lowe, "Keep Your Banker Informed," *Entrepreneur*, April 1, 2002, *www.entrepreneur.com/article/0,4621,298380,00.html*; David Worrell, "Attacking a Loan," *Entrepreneur*, July 2002, *www.entrepreneur.com/article/0,4621,300734,00.html*; Maggie Overfelt, "How to Raise Cash During Crunch Time," *FSB*, March 2001, pp. 35–36; Jenny McCune, "Getting Banks to Say 'Yes'," Bankrate.com, March 19, 2001, *www.bankrate.com/brm/news/biz/Capital_borrowing/20001319a.asp*; Joan Pryde, "Lending a Hand with Financing," *Nation's Business*, January 1998, pp. 53–59; Joseph W. May, "Be Frank with Your Bank," *Profit*, November/December 1996, pp. 54–55; "They'll Up Your Credit If . . ." *Inc.*, April 1994, p. 99; Jane Easter Bahls, "Borrower Beware," *Entrepreneur*, April 1994, p. 97; Jacquelyn Lynn, "You Can Bank on It," *Business Start-Ups*, August 1996, pp. 56–61; Stephanie Barlow, "Buddy System," *Entrepreneur*, March 1997, pp. 121–125; Carlye Adler, "Secrets from the Vault," *FSB*, June 2001, p. 33.

Nonbank Sources of Debt Capital

2. Explain the types of financing available from nonbank sources of credit.

Although they are usually the first stop for entrepreneurs in search of debt capital, banks are not the only lending game in town. We now turn our attention to other sources of debt capital that entrepreneurs can tap to feed their cash-hungry companies.

Asset-Based Lenders

Asset-based lenders, which are usually smaller commercial banks, commercial finance companies, or specialty lenders, allow small businesses to borrow money by pledging otherwise idle assets such as accounts receivable, inventory, or purchase orders as collateral. This form of financing works especially well for manufacturers, wholesalers, distributors, and other companies with significant stocks of inventory, accounts receivable, equipment, real estate, or other assets. Even unprofitable companies whose income statements could not convince loan officers to make traditional loans can get asset-based loans. Because asset-based lenders focus more on collateral than on a company's credit rating, these cash-poor but asset-rich companies can use normally unproductive assets—accounts receivable, inventory, equipment, and purchase orders—to finance rapid growth and the cash crises that often accompany it. Even large companies such as Levi Strauss, Goodyear, and Rite Aid rely on asset-based loans.[16]

Like banks, asset-based lenders consider a company's cash flow, but they are much more interested in the quality of the assets pledged as collateral. The amount a small business can borrow through asset-based lending depends on the **advance rate**, the percentage of an asset's value that a lender will lend. For example, a company pledging $100,000 of accounts receivable might negotiate a 70 percent advance rate and qualify for a $70,000 asset-based loan. Advance rates can vary dramatically depending on the quality of the assets pledged and the lender. Because inventory is an illiquid asset (i.e., hard to sell), the advance rate on inventory-based loans is quite low, usually 10 to 50 percent. Steven Melick, CEO of the Sycamore Group, an e-business software developer, gets an 85 percent advance rate on his company's loans from GE Capital by pledging high-quality accounts receivable as collateral.[17] The most common types of asset-based financing are discounting accounts receivable, inventory financing, and purchase order financing.

DISCOUNTING ACCOUNTS RECEIVABLE. The most common form of secured credit is accounts receivable financing. Under this arrangement, a small business pledges its accounts receivable as collateral; in return, the lender advances a loan against the value of approved accounts receivable. The amount of the loan tendered is not equal to the face value of the accounts receivable, however. Even though the lender screens the firm's accounts and accepts only qualified receivables, it makes an allowance for the risk involved because some receivables will be uncollectible. A small business usually can borrow an amount equal to 55 to 85 percent of its receivables, depending on their quality. Generally, lenders do not accept receivables that are past due.

When the University of Alabama received an invitation recently to play for a national championship in football, Weezabi LLC, a three-person company in Birmingham, Alabama, had to scramble to produce 60,000 Crimson Tide T-shirts. Unable to qualify for traditional financing, the tiny company, one of just a few licensed to produce Alabama merchandise, turned to asset-based financing for the capital it needed to purchase and print the T-shirts. "If it [weren't] for that loan, we would have missed the boat on all of this hot-market stuff," says owner Seth Chapman.[18]

INVENTORY FINANCING. Here, a small business loan is secured by its inventory of raw materials, work in process, or finished goods. If an owner defaults on the loan, the lender can claim the firm's inventory, sell it, and use the proceeds to satisfy the loan (assuming the bank's claim is superior to the claims of other creditors). Because inventory usually is not a highly liquid asset and its value can be difficult to determine, lenders are willing to lend only a portion of its worth, usually no more than 50 percent of the inventory's value. Most asset-based lenders avoid inventory-only deals; they prefer to make loans backed by inventory *and* more secure accounts receivable.

PURCHASE ORDER LOANS. Small companies that receive orders from large customers can use those purchase orders as collateral for loans. The customer places an order with a small business, which needs financing to fill the order. The small business pledges the future payment from the order as security for the loan, and the lender verifies the credit rating of the customer (not the small business) before granting the short-term loan, which often carries annual interest rates of 40 percent or more. Borrowers usually repay the loan within 60 days.

Sales at Slider the UNscooter, a Simi Valley, California-based company that sells ride-on scooters, were outstripping the company's cash flow, but because the company was less than 2 years old, lenders were not willing to extend traditional financing. Owner George Tarrab landed orders from several major retailers but needed financing to manufacture the scooters to fill them. He turned to a lender that specializes in purchase order financing, which provided $200,000 in financing. Even though UNscooter incurred large fees on the purchase order loans, Tarrab says that the loan allowed his company to fill the orders, free up cash for marketing, and attract other high-volume customers. Even though most experts advise using purchase order loans as a last resort, Tarrab had little choice. "We had to get creative," he says.[19]

Asset-based financing is a powerful tool. A small business that could obtain a $1 million line of credit with a bank would be able to borrow as much as $3 million by using accounts receivable as collateral. It is also an efficient method of borrowing because entrepreneurs borrow only the money they need, when they need it. Asset-based borrowing is an excellent just-in-time method of borrowing, one that often is available within just hours. As bank credit has tightened, its popularity has increased.

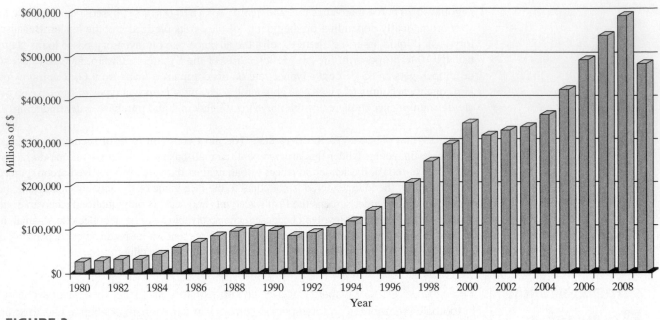

FIGURE 3
Asset-Based Loans

Source: Commercial Finance Association.

However, asset-based loans are more expensive than traditional bank loans because of the cost of originating and maintaining them and the higher risk involved. To ensure the quality of the assets supporting the loans they make, lenders often monitor borrowers' assets, perhaps as often as weekly, making paperwork requirements on these loans intimidating, especially to first-time borrowers. Rates usually run from 2 to 8 percentage points (or more) above the prime rate. Because of this rate differential, small business owners should not use asset-based loans over the long term; their goal should be to establish their credit through asset-based financing and then to move up to a line of credit. Figure 3 shows the trend in asset-based borrowing since 1980.

Trade Credit

Because of its ready availability, trade credit is an extremely important source of financing to most entrepreneurs. In fact, 60 percent of small businesses use trade credit as a source of financing.[20] Trade credit involves convincing vendors and suppliers to sell goods and services without requiring payment up front. When banks refuse to lend money to a small business because they see it as a poor credit risk, an entrepreneur may be able to turn to trade credit for capital. Getting vendors to extend credit in the form of delayed payments (e.g., "net 30" credit terms) usually is much easier for small businesses than obtaining bank financing. Essentially, a company receiving trade credit from a supplier is getting a short-term, interest-free loan for the amount of the goods purchased.

Vendors and suppliers usually are willing to finance a small business owner's purchase of goods from 30 to 90 days, interest free. The key to maintaining trade credit as a source of funds is establishing a consistent and reliable payment history with every vendor.

ENTREPRENEURIAL
Profile

Ed and Jennifer Foy:
eFashion Solutions

In 2000, Ed and Jennifer Foy started eFashion Solutions, a company that provides e-commerce solutions for branded, well-known companies in the apparel, entertainment, and specialty retail industries, in Secaucus, New Jersey. The company performs a full range of services, including purchasing, merchandising, Web site design, marketing, business intelligence, customer service, order management, and order fulfillment for its clients. As their company grew, the Foys raised $24 million in equity capital and used a variety of traditional bank financing to support its operations. When the company's regular lender shut off access to credit because of the financial crisis, the Foys began using trade credit from their vendors. eFashion Solutions has been able to negotiate "net 60" credit terms with some vendors but takes advantage of cash discounts from other vendors that range from 1 to 10 percent for early payment.[21]

Equipment Suppliers

Most equipment suppliers encourage business owners to purchase their equipment by offering to finance the purchase over time. This method of financing is similar to trade credit but with slightly different terms. Usually, equipment vendors offer reasonable credit terms with only a modest down payment and the balance financed over the life of the equipment (often several years). In some cases, the vendor repurchases equipment for salvage value at the end of its useful life and offers the business owner another credit agreement on new equipment. Start-up companies often use trade credit from equipment suppliers to purchase equipment and fixtures such as counters, display cases, refrigeration units, machinery, and the like. It pays to scrutinize vendors' credit terms, however; they may be less attractive than those of other lenders.

Commercial Finance Companies

When denied bank loans, small business owners often look to commercial finance companies for the same types of loan. Commercial finance companies are second only to banks in making loans to small businesses and, unlike their conservative counterparts, are willing to tolerate more risk in their loan portfolios.[22] For instance, Chris Lehnes, a top manager at CIT Small Business Lending, says that his company regularly makes loans to small businesses with debt to equity ratios of 10:1 (10 times as much debt as equity), a situation that would send most bankers scurrying back to their vaults.[23] Of course, like banks, finance companies' primary consideration is collecting their loans, but finance companies tend to rely more on obtaining a security interest in some type of collateral, given the higher risk loans that make up their portfolios. Because commercial finance companies depend on collateral to recover most of their losses, they do not always require a complete set of financial projections of future operations as most banks do. However, this does *not* mean that they neglect to evaluate carefully a company's financial position, especially its cash balance, before making a loan. "We're looking at the projected cash flow—the ability of the business to repay us," says CIT's Lehnes. "We put a lot of weight on what the business has done in the past couple of years."[24]

Approximately 150 large commercial finance companies, such as AT&T Small Business Lending, UPS Capital, GE Capital Solutions, CIT Small Business Lending, and others, make a variety of loans to small companies, ranging from asset-based loans and business leases to construction and SBA loans. Dubbed "the Wal-Marts of finance," commercial finance companies usually offer many of the same credit options as commercial banks do, including intermediate and long-term loans for real estate and fixed assets as well as short-term loans and lines of credit.

ENTREPRENEURIAL

Profile

Connie Kalitta: Kalitta Air

Connie Kalitta started Kalitta Air, an air cargo carrier, in 2000, and the company grew quickly to become a leading company in the air cargo market. Three years later, Kalitta wanted to expand his company to reach global markets, which required larger aircraft with greater cruising ranges. Kalitta turned to GE Capital, which provided the company with long-term financing for two Boeing 747-400 freighters, allowing the company to gain significant market share in air shipments to Asia.[25]

Finance companies offer small business borrowers faster turnaround times, longer repayment schedules, and more flexible payment plans than traditional lenders, all valuable benefits to cash-hungry small companies. However, because their loans are subject to more risks, finance companies charge higher interest rates than commercial banks. Their most common methods of providing credit to small businesses are asset-based—accounts receivable financing and inventory loans. Rates on loans from commercial finance companies are higher than those at banks—as high as 15 to 30 percent (including fees), depending on the risk a particular business presents and the quality of the assets involved. Because many of the loans they make are secured by collateral (usually the business equipment, vehicle, real estate, or inventory purchased with the loan), finance companies often impose more onerous reporting requirements, sometimes requiring weekly (or even daily) information on a small company's inventory levels or accounts receivable balances. However, entrepreneurs who cannot secure financing from traditional lenders because of their short track records, less-than-perfect credit ratings, or fluctuating earnings often find the loans they need at commercial finance companies.

ENTREPRENEURIAL
Profile

*Mariusz Kolodziej:
Hudson Bakery*

In 1994, Mariusz Kolodziej left his native Poland and moved to New York City, where he opened Hudson Bakery, a small commercial bakery. Soon some of New York's finest restaurants and hotels were serving his breads, baguettes, rolls, Panini, and focaccias, and the company's reputation for distinctive, high-quality products and excellent service—and its sales—grew rapidly. In 2003, using a combination of retained earnings, bank financing, and loans and leases from a commercial finance company, Kolodziej moved production into a 50,000-square-foot bakery in North Bergen, New Jersey. Later, he opened a second bakery near Philadelphia to serve restaurants and hotels in that city. GE Capital provided Hudson Bakery with a $1.5 asset-based lease that enabled Kolodziej to acquire the equipment to outfit its new commercial bakeries.[26]

Savings and Loan Associations

Savings and loan associations (S&Ls) specialize in loans for real property. In addition to their traditional role of providing mortgages for personal residences, S&Ls offer financing on commercial and industrial property. In the typical commercial or industrial loan, the S&L will lend up to 80 percent of the property's value with a repayment schedule of up to 30 years. Minimum loan amounts are typically $50,000, but most S&Ls hesitate to lend money for buildings specially designed for a particular customer's needs. S&Ls expect the mortgage to be repaid from the company's future profits.

Stock Brokerage Houses

Stockbrokers also make loans, and many of them offer loans to their customers at lower interest rates than banks. These **margin loans** carry lower rates because the collateral supporting them—the stocks and bonds in the customer's portfolio—is of high quality and is highly liquid. Moreover, brokerage firms make it easy to borrow. Usually, brokers set up a line of credit for their customers when they open a brokerage account. To tap that line of credit, a customer simply writes a check or uses a debit card. Typically, a margin loan does not have a fixed repayment schedule; the debt can remain outstanding indefinitely, as long as the market value of the borrower's portfolio of collateral meets minimum requirements. Aspiring entrepreneurs can borrow up to 50 percent of the value of their stock portfolios, up to 70 percent of their bond portfolios, and up to 90 percent of the value of their government securities.

Using stocks and bonds as collateral on a loan can be risky. Brokers typically require a 30 percent cushion on margin loans. If the value of the borrower's portfolio drops, the broker can make a **margin call**; that is, the broker can call the loan and require the borrower to provide more cash and securities as collateral. Recent swings in the stock market have translated into margin calls for many entrepreneurs, requiring them to repay a significant portion of their loan balances within a matter of days—or hours. If an account lacks adequate collateral, the broker can sell some of the customer's portfolio to pay off the loan.

Insurance Companies

For many small businesses, life insurance companies can be an important source of business capital. Insurance companies offer two basic types of loans: policy loans and mortgage loans. **Policy loans** are extended on the basis of the amount of money paid through premiums into the insurance policy; with a policy loan, a business owner serves as his or her own bank, borrowing against the money accumulated in the investment portion of an insurance policy. It usually takes about 2 years for an insurance policy to accumulate enough cash surrender value to justify a loan against it. Once the cash value accumulates in a policy, an entrepreneur may borrow up to 95 percent of that value for any length of time. Interest is levied annually, but the entrepreneur determines the repayment rate, or repayment may be deferred indefinitely. However, the amount of insurance coverage is reduced by the amount of the loan. Policy loans typically offer very favorable interest rates, sometimes below the prime rate. Only insurance policies that build cash value—those that combine a savings plan with insurance coverage—offer the option of borrowing. These include whole life (permanent insurance), variable life, universal life, and many corporate-owned life insurance policies. Term life insurance, which offers only pure insurance coverage, has no borrowing capacity.

Insurance companies make **mortgage loans** on a long-term basis on real property worth a minimum of $500,000. They are based primarily on the value of the real property being purchased. The insurance company will extend a loan of up to 75 or 80 percent of the real estate's value and will allow a lengthy repayment schedule over 25 or 30 years so that payments do not strain the firm's cash flows excessively. Many large real estate developments such as shopping malls, office buildings, and theme parks rely on mortgage loans from insurance companies.

Credit Unions

Credit unions, nonprofit financial cooperatives that promote saving and provide loans to their members, are best known for making consumer and car loans. However, many are also willing to lend money to their members to launch businesses, especially since many banks have restricted loans to higher-risk start-ups. The first credit union in the United States was chartered in New Hampshire in 1909.[27] Today, more than 7,500 federally and state-chartered credit unions operate in the United States, and many of them make business loans, usually in smaller amounts than commercial banks typically make. In fact, the average credit union business loan is $181,000, but some credit unions have made business loans in the millions of dollars.[28] Because credit unions are exempt from federal income tax, they often charge lower interest rates than banks.

Today credit unions make more than $33.4 billion in small business loans to their members, nearly triple the $12.3 billion in small business loans they made in 2004.[29] Lending practices at credit unions are very much like those at banks, but they are subject to restraints that banks are not. For instance, credit unions are prohibited from making business loans that total more than 12.25 percent of their assets (a cap that Congress is considering increasing to 25 percent). Recent changes in legislation, however, exempt certain business loans from that limitation. In another move that favors entrepreneurs, the SBA recently opened its 7(a) loan programs to credit unions, providing even more avenues for entrepreneurs seeking financing. The Export-Import Bank also is exploring ways to work with credit unions that want to provide export financing to small businesses. Increasingly, entrepreneurs are turning to credit unions to finance their businesses' capital needs.

ENTREPRENEURIAL
Profile
Gladys and Eustace Kumanja: Queen Bee Beauty Supply

Gladys and Eustace Kumanja immigrated to the United States from Kenya in 1996 with the dream of one day opening a business of their own. Their dream became a reality when the Kumanjas opened Queen Bee Beauty Supply in Smyrna, Delaware, with the help of a $250,000 business loan from the American Spirit Federal Credit Union. Initially, the Kumanjas approached three commercial banks, but their applications were denied because the banks said that they lacked sufficient capital and business experience. The loan from the credit union, the result of the 2009 American Recovery and Investment Act designed to stimulate the economy, is supported by a 90 percent guarantee from the SBA.[30]

Entrepreneurs searching for a credit union near them can use the online database at the Credit Union National Association's Web site (*www.cuna.org*).

Bonds

Bonds, which are corporate IOUs, have always been a popular source of debt financing for large companies, but few small business owners realize that they can also tap this valuable source of capital. Although the smallest businesses are not viable candidates for issuing bonds, a growing number of small companies are finding the funding they need through bonds when banks and other lenders say no. Because of the costs involved, issuing bonds usually is best suited for companies generating annual sales between $5 million and $30 million and have capital requirements between $1.5 million and $10 million. Although they can help small companies raise much needed capital, bonds have certain disadvantages. The issuing company must follow the same regulations that govern businesses selling stock to public investors. Even if the bond issue is private, the company must register the offering and file periodic reports with the SEC.

Convertible bonds, bonds that give the buyer the option of converting the debt to equity by purchasing the company's stock at a fixed price in the future, have become more popular for small companies. In exchange for offering the option to convert the bond into stock, the small company issuing the convertible bonds gets the benefit of paying a lower interest rate on the bond than on a traditional bond. The conversion feature is valuable only if the company is successful and its value increases over time.

Small manufacturers needing money for fixed assets with long repayment schedules have access to an attractive, relatively inexpensive source of funds in **industrial development revenue**

bonds (IDRBs). To issue IDRBs, a company must work with a local or state government agency, which issues the bonds on the company's behalf. The company, not the government entity, is responsible for repaying both the principal and the interest on the bond issue. Typically, the amount of money companies that issue IDRBs seek to raise is at least $2 million, but some small manufacturers have raised as little as $500,000 using a mini-bond program that offers a simple application process and short closing times. Each government entity has its own criteria, such as job creation, expansion of the tax base, and others that companies must meet to be eligible to issue mini-bonds. NGK Spark Plugs, a company founded in 1936 that produces spark plugs for automotive, marine, motorcycle, and small engines, issued $15 million in industrial revenue bonds with the help of the West Virginia Economic Development Agency to build an 85,000 square-foot factory in Sissonville, West Virginia, that created 80 new jobs.[31]

To open IDRBs up to even smaller companies, some states pool the industrial bonds of several small companies too small to make an issue alone. By joining together to issue composite industrial bonds, companies can reduce their issuing fees and attract a greater number of investors. The issuing companies typically pay lower interest rates than they would on conventional bank loans.

Private Placements

We saw how companies can raise capital by making private placements of their stock (equity). Private placements are also available for debt instruments. A private placement involves selling debt to one or a small number of investors, usually insurance companies or pension funds. Private placement debt is a hybrid between a conventional loan and a bond. At its heart, it is a bond, but its terms are tailored to the borrower's individual needs, as a loan would be.

Privately placed securities offer several advantages over standard bank loans. First, they usually carry fixed interest rates, rather than the variable rates banks often charge. Second, the maturity of private placements is longer than most bank loans: 15 years rather than 5. Private placements do not require hiring expensive investment bankers. Finally, because private investors can afford to take greater risks than banks, they are willing to finance deals for fledgling small companies.

ENTREPRENEURIAL
Profile
Mark Benioff:
Salesforce.com

Entrepreneur Mark Benioff started Salesforce.com, a company that provides customer relationship management applications to more than 72,500 businesses, in his apartment in San Francisco in 1999. The company, now a leader in the field of enterprise cloud computing, recently closed a $500 million private debt placement of 5-year notes that are convertible to company stock to fund its rapid growth and acquisitions of smaller companies.[32]

Small Business Investment Companies (SBICs)

The Small Business Investment Company program was started after Russia's successful launch of the first space satellite, Sputnik, in 1958. Its goal was to accelerate the United States' position in the space race by funding high-technology start-ups. Created by the 1958 Small Business Investment Act, **small business investment companies (SBICs)** are privately owned financial institutions that are licensed and regulated by the SBA. In a unique public–private partnership, the 307 SBICs operating across the United States use a combination of private capital and federally guaranteed debt to provide long-term venture capital to small businesses. In other words, SBICs operate like any other venture capital firm, but, unlike traditional venture capital firms, they use private capital and borrowed government funds to provide both debt and equity financing to small businesses.

Since 1958, SBICs have provided $57.2 billion in long-term debt and equity financing to more than 107,000 small businesses, adding many thousands of jobs to the U.S. economy.[33] Most SBICs prefer later-round financing over funding raw start-ups. Because of changes in their financial structure made a few years ago, however, SBICs now are better equipped to invest in start-up companies. On average, about 30 percent of SBIC investments go to companies that are less than 2 years old.[34] Funding from SBICs helped launch companies such as Apple, Federal Express, Whole Foods Market, Sun Microsystems, Outback Steakhouse, and Build-A-Bear Workshop.

SBICs must be capitalized privately with a minimum of $5 million, at which point they qualify for up to three dollars in long-term SBA loans for every dollar of private capital invested in small businesses, up to the ceiling of $150 million. As a general rule, SBICs may provide financial assistance only to small businesses with a net worth of less than $18 million and average after-tax earnings of $6 million during their past 2 years. However, employment and total annual sales standards vary from industry to industry. SBICs are limited to a maximum investment or loan amount of 30 percent of their private capital to a single client.

Operating as government-backed venture capitalists, SBICs provide both debt and equity financing to small businesses. Currently, the average amount of SBIC financing in a company is $649,000.[35] Because of SBA regulations affecting the financing arrangements an SBIC can offer, many SBICs extend their investments as loans with an option to convert the debt instrument into an equity interest later. Most SBIC loans are between $100,000 and $5 million. Although their interest rates can be high, the loan term is longer than most banks allow. Borrowers typically do not make installment payments; instead, the loan is due at an agreed-upon date. When they make equity investments, SBICs are prohibited from obtaining a controlling interest in the companies in which they invest (no more than 49 percent ownership). The most common methods of SBIC financing are straight debt instruments (24.5 percent), debt instruments combined with equity investments (29.8 percent), and equity-only investments (45.7 percent).[36]

ENTREPRENEURIAL
Profile

Mike Tie and Philip Williams: Paramount Building Solutions

Paramount Building Solutions, a company formed in Tempe, Arizona, in 2003 by Mike Tie and Philip Williams, provides janitorial services to leading retailers in the grocery and "big box" categories. To finance their expansion plans for their company, Tie and Williams worked with LaSalle Capital Group, a Chicago-based SBIC with an investment pool of $128 million. Using capital from LaSalle, Paramount expanded its footprint by acquiring Janitorial Management Services, a similar company that serves large retail customers in 14 states. Paramount, which recently received the Portfolio Company of the Year award from the National Association of Small Business Investment Companies, now has thousands of service locations across the United States. "In partnership with LaSalle and our other investors, we have grown Paramount from a small start-up business to a leading national player in the janitorial services industry," says Tie, the company's CEO.[37]

Small Business Lending Companies (SBLCs)

Small business lending companies (SBLCs) make only intermediate and long-term SBA-guaranteed loans. They specialize in loans that many banks would not consider and operate on a nationwide basis. For instance, most SBLC loans have terms extending for at least 10 years. The maximum interest rate for loans of 7 years or longer is 2.75 percent above the prime rate; for shorter-term loans, the ceiling is 2.25 percent above prime. Another feature of SBLC loans is the management expertise that SBLCs offer the companies to which they make loans. Corporations own most of the nation's SBLCs, which gives them a solid capital base.

Federally Sponsored Programs

Federally sponsored lending programs have suffered from budget reductions in the last several years. Current trends suggest that the federal government is reducing its involvement in the lending business, but many programs are still quite active and some are actually growing.

Economic Development Administration (EDA)

3. Identify the sources of government financial assistance and the loan programs these agencies offer.

The Economic Development Administration (EDA), a branch of the Commerce Department, offers a variety of grants, loan guarantees, and loans to create new businesses and to expand existing businesses in areas with below-average income and high unemployment. Focusing on economically distressed communities, the EDA finances long-term investment projects needed to stimulate economic growth and to create jobs by making loan guarantees. The EDA guarantees up to 80 percent of business loans between $750,000 and $10 million. Entrepreneurs apply for loans through private lenders, for whom an EDA loan guarantee significantly reduces the risk of lending. Start-up companies must supply 15 percent of the guaranteed amount in the form of equity, and established businesses must make equity investments of at least 15 percent of the guaranteed amount. Small businesses can use the loan proceeds for a variety of purposes, including supplementing working capital, purchasing equipment, buying land, and renovating buildings.

EDA business loans are designed to help replenish economically distressed areas by creating or expanding small businesses that provide employment opportunities in local communities. To qualify for a loan, a business must be located in a disadvantaged area and its presence must directly benefit local residents. Some communities experiencing high unemployment or suffering from the effects of devastating natural disasters have received EDA Revolving Loan Fund (RLF) grants to create loan pools for local small businesses. The EDA provides grants to a state or local agency, which makes loans at or below market rates to small companies that otherwise have difficulty borrowing money. Currently, 578 revolving loan funds with a capital base of $852 million are in operation. Loan amounts range from as little as $1,000 to more than $1 million, but most fall between $25,000 and $175,000.[38]

ENTREPRENEURIAL **Profile** *Leroy Shatto: Shatto Milk Company*	Tired of struggling to survive in the traditional dairy industry, Leroy Shatto, owner of Shatto Milk Company, wanted to differentiate his company by shifting to producing all-natural, hormone-free milk that the company would market to customers directly in old-fashioned glass bottles. Shatto used the revolving loan fund at the Mo-Kan Regional Council in St. Joseph, Missouri, to revamp his entire dairy operation and now produces high-quality, hormone-free milk. The SBA recently named Shatto Missouri's Small Business Owner of the Year.[39]

The EDA's Trade Adjustment Assistance for Firms (TAAF) program provides financial assistance to manufacturers and service companies that have been affected adversely by imports. Small companies work with one of 11 Trade Adjustment Assistance Centers to receive grants that cover 50 to 75 percent of the cost of projects (from market research and product development to e-commerce and inventory control) that are aimed at improving the company's competitive position. For instance, a family-owned business that produces a line of food items recently received a grant that allowed it to implement a lean manufacturing system, install sophisticated computer software that enables it to track production batches and inventory, and train workers. Because of the grant, the company has added 50 employees and has increased its sales by 20 percent.[40]

Department of Housing and Urban Development (HUD)

The Department of Housing and Urban Development (HUD) sponsors several loan programs to assist qualified entrepreneurs in raising needed capital. Community Development Block Grants (CDBGs) are extended to cities and towns that, in turn, lend or grant money to entrepreneurs to start small businesses that will strengthen the local economy. Grants are aimed at cities and towns in need of revitalization and economic stimulation. Some grants are used to construct buildings and plants to be leased to entrepreneurs, sometimes with an option to buy. Others are earmarked for revitalizing a crime-ridden area or making start-up loans to entrepreneurs or expansion loans to existing business owners. No ceilings or geographic limitations are placed on CDBG loans and grants, but projects must benefit low- and moderate-income families.

HUD also makes loan guarantees through its Section 108 provision of the Community Block Development Grant program. The agency has funded more than 1,200 projects since its inception in 1978. These loan guarantees allow a community to transform a portion of CDBG funds into federally guaranteed loans large enough to pursue economic revitalization projects that can lead to the renewal of entire towns. For instance, the city of Greenville, South Carolina, used Section 108 funds to renovate a public market designed to serve as an anchor in its West End section that was targeted for revitalization. Since its construction, 16 small businesses have located in the market, creating new jobs and stimulating economic growth in the area, and a new stadium modeled after Boston's Fenway Park is home to the local minor league baseball team.[41]

U.S. Department of Agriculture's Rural Business and Cooperative Program and Business Program

The U.S. Department of Agriculture (USDA) provides financial assistance to certain small businesses through its Rural Business-Cooperative Service (RBS). The RBS program is open to all types of businesses (not just farms) and is designed to create nonfarm employment opportunities in rural areas—those with populations below 50,000 and not adjacent to a city where densities exceed 100 people per square mile. Entrepreneurs in many small towns, especially those with populations below 25,000, are eligible to apply for loans through the RBS program, which makes almost $900 million in loan guarantees each year.

The RBS does make a limited number of direct loans to small businesses, but the majority of its activity is in loan guarantees. Through its Business and Industry (B&I) Guaranteed Loan Program, the RBS will guarantee as much as 80 percent of a commercial lender's loan up to $25 million (although actual guarantee amounts are almost always far less, usually between $200,000 and $1 million) for qualified applicants. Entrepreneurs apply for loans through private lenders, who view applicants with loan guarantees favorably because the agency's guarantee reduces the lender's risk dramatically.

ENTREPRENEURIAL
Profile

Jasch and Kathleen Hamilton: Diamond Organics

Founded in 1998 by copreneurs Jasch and Kathleen Hamilton with the help of a $298,000 B&I loan guarantee from the USDA, Diamond Organics has become the largest online supplier of organic foods in the United States from its location in tiny Moss Landing, California. To fuel the company's current growth spurt and to launch a prepared food line called Kathleen's Kitchen, CEO Kathleen Hamilton is relying on another B&I guarantee of $2.9 million for a loan from Excel National Bank.[42]

To make a loan guarantee, the RBS requires much of the same documentation as most banks and most other loan guarantee programs. Because of its emphasis on developing employment in rural areas, the RBS requires an environmental impact statement describing the jobs created and the effect the business has on the area. The RBS also makes grants available to businesses and communities for the purpose of encouraging small business development and growth.

Small Business Innovation Research (SBIR) Program

Started as a pilot program by the National Science Foundation in the 1970s, the Small Business Innovation Research (SBIR) program has expanded to 11 federal agencies, ranging from NASA to the Department of Defense. The total SBIR budget across all 11 agencies is more than $2 billion annually. These agencies award cash grants or long-term contracts to small companies that want to initiate or to expand their research and development (R&D) efforts. SBIR grants give innovative small companies the opportunity to attract early stage capital investments *without* having to give up significant equity stakes or taking on burdensome levels of debt.

The SBIR process includes three phases. Phase I (project feasibility) grants, which determine the feasibility and commercial potential of a technology or product (called "proof of concept"), last for up to 6 months and have a ceiling of $100,000. Phase II (prototype development) grants, designed to develop the concept into a specific technology or product, run for up to 24 months and have a ceiling of $750,000. Approximately 40 percent of all phase II applicants receive funding. Phase III is the commercialization phase, in which the company pursues commercial applications of the research and development conducted in phases I and II and must use private or non-SBIR federal funding to bring a product to market.

Competition for SBIR funding is intense; only 17 percent of the small companies that apply receive funding. So far, nearly 108,400 SBIR awards totaling more than $25.2 billion (26 percent in phase I and 74 percent in phase II) have gone to more than 16,000 small companies, which traditionally have had difficulty competing with big corporations for federal R&D dollars. The government's dollars have been well invested. Nearly 45 percent of small businesses receiving phase II SBIR awards have achieved commercial success with their products.[43]

ENTREPRENEURIAL
Profile

AeroTech Research, Inc.

AeroTech Research, Inc., a small company in Newport Beach, Virginia, received phase I and II grants from NASA to develop its Turbulence Prediction and Warning System (TPAWS) that improves pilots' awareness of weather conditions that create turbulence so that they can avoid it. Air turbulence is a problem for both military and commercial flights and is the leading cause of injuries in the airline industry. Turbulence has actually ripped engines from airplanes, broken wings, and caused passengers great anxiety. With the help of the SBIR grants, AeroTech created an enhanced radar warning system that alerts pilots to turbulence hotspots well in advance so that they can fly around them. AeroTech has installed TPAWS on more than 120 Delta commercial jets and is marketing the system to other airlines, both domestic and foreign.[44]

The Small Business Technology Transfer Program

The Small Business Technology Transfer (STTR) program complements the SBIR program. Whereas SBIR focuses on commercially promising ideas that originate in small businesses, the STTR allows small companies to exploit the commercially promising ideas that originate in universities, federally funded R&D centers, and nonprofit research institutions. Researchers at these institutions can join forces with small businesses to spin off commercially promising ideas while remaining employed at their research institutions. Five federal agencies award grants in two of three phases (up to $100,000 in phase I and up to $500,000 in phase II) to these research partnerships. The STTR's annual award budget is approximately $2 billion.

▶ E N T R E P R E N E U R S H I P   IN ACTION ▶

Where Do We Turn Now?

Tina Bean started Five Star Feeds, a business that sells live-stock feed, pet food, and gardening supplies, in Port Arthur, Texas, in 2001 and has operated it at a profit since then. Bean applied for a business expansion loan at her bank and received $800,000, which she used to more than double the size of her store. With the expansion completed, she needs $150,000 to purchase the inventory—more pet supplies, jeans, boots, and Western-style clothing—to fill it, but the bank is balking at making the loan. The loan officer's response is "We'll cross that bridge when we get there," says Bean. "Well, I'm there. I can't open the store if I don't have anything to put in it." Until she can get the capital she needs to purchase the inventory, Bean says she is stuck.

Like Tina Bean, Matt and Marnie Brannon have been running their business, Midwest Fiat, for several years. Their company, located in Columbus, Ohio, sells vintage Italian car parts online and operates a service and restoration shop for Fiat autos. Matt started the business as a hobby, but it grew into a full-time business for him and his wife in 2004. "Our revenues have grown each year," he says, pointing out the company's excellent credit rating and its track record of success. The Brannons have the opportunity to purchase one of their main competitors, a move that would quadruple the company's revenue, expand its product line, and enable it to move into a larger space. "We need a loan to help us make the purchase and sustain the operating capital needed for the first 6 months of the expansion, which includes hiring five employees."

Until now, the Brannons have never borrowed money for their business, choosing instead to allow it to grow organically, using its earnings to fund its growth. "With a solid business plan and all of the documentation, financials, and records needed for the loan, we approached a national bank," says Matt. "The loan officer [said] it would be a slam dunk," he recalls. "In fact, he encouraged us to increase the request from $110,000 to $125,000." A month later, the loan officer contacted the Brannons and told them that the bank had denied their loan request. "He encouraged us to pursue a home-equity line of credit, but that would give us only half the amount we would need," says Matt. The Brannons have applied for a loan at two small community banks. "They're asking questions," he says. "I'm optimistic but nervous. They are taking a long time to make a decision, and we are on borrowed time at this point, having already missed the deadline our competitor gave us to take the offer."

1. What other sources of financing do you recommend Tina Bean and Matt and Marnie Brannon turn to for the financing they need for their businesses?
2. The Brannons had never borrowed money for their business before the opportunity to purchase a competitor suddenly emerged. What steps can entrepreneurs take to make sure that they have financing arrangements in place when such opportunities arise?

Sources: Based on Peter S. Goodman, "Credit Tightens for Small Businesses," *New York Times*, October 13, 2009, *www.nytimes.com/2009/10/13/business/smallbusiness/13lending.html*; Emily Maltby, "SOS: Send Loans Now," *CNNMoney*, July 27, 2009, *http://money.cnn.com/galleries/2009/smallbusiness/0903/gallery.loan_woes.smb/index.html.*

Small Business Administration (SBA)

4. Describe the various loan programs available from the Small Business Administration.

The Small Business Administration (SBA) has several programs designed to help finance both start-up and existing small companies that cannot qualify for traditional loans because of their thin asset bases and their high risk of failure. In its nearly 60 years of operation, the SBA has helped 20 million small companies through a multitude of programs get the financing they need for start up or for growth by making or guaranteeing $211 billion in loans.[45] In the wake of the upheaval in the financial markets, banks have tightened their lending standards, and many small businesses cannot qualify for loans. Although SBA loan programs account for less than 10 percent of all small business lending, tight credit conditions make them all the more important for small companies in search of capital.[46] "SBA programs help newer businesses and businesses that don't have a lot of collateral," says an executive at a bank that makes SBA-guaranteed loans.[47] About 35 percent of SBA-backed loans go to start-up companies.[48]

The SBA's $90.5 billion loan portfolio makes it the largest single financial backer of small businesses in the nation.[49] The SBA does *not* actually lend money to entrepreneurs directly; instead, entrepreneurs borrow money from a traditional lender (About 4,500 lenders in the United States make SBA loans), and the SBA guarantees a percentage of the loan to the lender in case the borrower defaults. To be eligible for SBA backing, a business must be within the agency's criteria that define a small business. In addition, some types of businesses, such as those engaged in gambling, pyramid sales schemes, or real estate investment, among others, are ineligible for SBA loans. The loan application process can take from 3 days to many months, depending on how well prepared the entrepreneur is and which bank is involved.

Express Programs

To speed up processing times, the SBA has created three "express" programs that give entrepreneurs responses to their loan applications within 36 hours.

THE SBA*EXPRESS* PROGRAM. With the SBA*Express* Program, participating lenders use their own loan procedures and applications to make loans of up to $350,000 to small businesses, streamlining the application process for SBA loan guarantees. Because the SBA guarantees up to 50 percent of the loan, banks are often more willing to make smaller loans to entrepreneurs who might otherwise have difficulty meeting lenders' standards. Lenders can charge up to 6.5 percent above the prime interest rate on SBA*Express* loans below $50,000 and up to 4.5 percent above prime on loans greater than $50,000. Loan maturities on these loans typically are 7 years. Mike Robillard, president of San Antonio Clippers in San Antonio, Texas, used an SBA*Express* loan to add two locations to his Sports Clips hair salon franchise operation. Robillard needed growth capital quickly to secure the best locations, a key to success in his industry. "We had to start laying out money quickly to lock down those locations," he says.[50]

PATRIOT EXPRESS PROGRAM. The SBA recently piloted the **Patriot Express Program**, which is designed to assist some of the nation's 25 million veterans and their spouses who want to become entrepreneurs. The loan ceiling is $500,000, and the SBA guarantees up to 90 percent (normally 85 percent) of the loan amount in case the borrower defaults. Like SBA*Express* loans, the turnaround time on loan applications is just 36 hours. Patriot Express loans carry interest rates that range from 2.25 to 4.75 percent above the prime interest rate. The average Patriot Express loan is $82,000.[51]

ENTREPRENEURIAL
Profile

*Jenny Housely:
Sorpresas Moments
of Celebration*

Jenny Housely, a military veteran, started Sorpresas Moments of Celebration, a business in Augusta, Georgia, that hosts birthday parties and other celebrations and offers preschool fine arts classes, with the help of a $25,000 loan guarantee from the Patriot Express Program. Even though she was armed with a business plan and assistance from a local Small Business Development Center, Housely still found attracting start-up capital to be a challenge. "It is difficult to get money from anyone because we are a new business," she says. Backed by the Patriot Express Program guarantee, Housely was able to acquire the loan from a Florida lender and start her company.[52]

COMMUNITY*EXPRESS* **PROGRAM.** In 1999, working with the National Community Reinvestment Coalition, the SBA created the Community*Express* loan program, which provides loans to entrepreneurs in communities that have experienced economic distress [those that are identified under the SBA's Historically Underutilized Business Zones (HUBZones) and the Community Reinvestment Act] and who are viewed as high-risk borrowers. The maximum loan amount is $250,000, with an SBA guarantee of 90 percent (normally 85 percent), and turnaround times on loan requests can be as fast as 36 hours. Community*Express* loans account for 9 percent of all SBA loans, up from just 1 percent in 2002.[53] Approximately 70 percent of Community*Express* loans go to minority entrepreneurs, and 40 percent go to start-up companies. Like Patriot Express loans, Community*Express* loans carry interest rates that range from 2.25 to 4.75 percent above the prime interest rate. The average Community*Express* loan is $27,000.[54] Recipients of Community*Express* loans also receive training and consulting services for their businesses.

SBA Loan Programs

7(A) LOAN GUARANTY PROGRAM. The SBA works with local lenders (both bank and nonbank) to offer a variety of loan programs designed to help entrepreneurs who cannot get capital from traditional sources to gain access to the financing they need to launch and grow their businesses. By far the most popular SBA loan program is the 7(A) **loan guaranty program** (see Figure 4), which makes partial guarantees on loans up to $2 million to small businesses. Private lenders actually extend these loans to companies, but the SBA guarantees them in case the borrower defaults. Normally, the SBA guarantees 85 percent of loans up to $150,000 and 75 percent of loans above $150,000 up to the loan guarantee ceiling of $1,500,000. However, as part of the American Recovery and Reinvestment Plan, the SBA temporarily increased its guarantees to 90 percent (up to the $1.5 million guarantee cap) and eliminated all of the loan processing fees, which range from 2 percent to 3.75 percent. After Gary Skrla lost his corporate job, he secured an $879,000 loan from Seattle, Washington-based Fortune Bank with the help of a 7(a) guarantee to open Ace Hardware in Silver Lake, Washington. Skrla saved nearly $20,000 due to the elimination of the fees on the SBA's loan guarantees.[55]

The SBA does not actually lend any money to small businesses; it merely acts as an insurer, guaranteeing the lender a certain level of repayment in case the borrower defaults on the loan. Because the SBA assumes most of the credit risk, lenders are more willing to consider riskier deals that they normally would refuse.

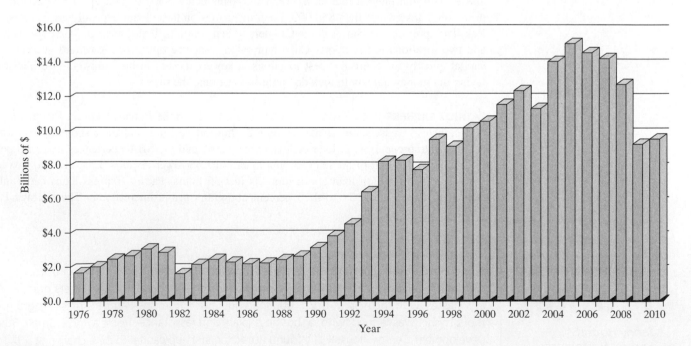

FIGURE 4
SBA 7(A) Guaranteed Loans

Source: U.S. Small Business Administration.

Profile

Anamika Khanna and Tim Volkem: Kasa Indian Eatery

Anamika Khanna and Tim Volkem, founders of Kasa Indian Eatery.

Source: Kasa Indian Eatery

Anamika Khanna, a former brand manager for Kraft Foods, and Tim Volkem, a former attorney, used two SBA-guaranteed 7(a) loans totaling $700,000 and $300,000 of their money to open two Indian restaurants in San Francisco, California, in just 2 years. They used the first loan to start Kasa (which means "Royal Meal" in Sanskrit) Indian Eatery in the city's Castro neighborhood and a year later received a second SBA-guaranteed loan to open another location in the Marina district. The popular restaurants, which feature a menu built around recipes from Khanna's grandmother and the kati roll, a flaky, flatbread sandwich filled with fresh, high-quality ingredients, now employ 30 people.[56]

Qualifying for an SBA loan guarantee requires cooperation among the entrepreneur, the participating bank, and the SBA. The participating bank determines the loan's terms and sets the interest rate within SBA limits. Contrary to popular belief, SBA guaranteed loans do *not* carry special deals on interest rates. An entrepreneur negotiates interest rates with the participating bank, with a ceiling of prime plus 2.25 percent on loans of less than 7 years and prime plus 2.75 percent on loans of 7 to 25 years. Interest rates on loans of less than $25,000 can go up to prime plus 4.75 percent. The average interest rate on SBA-guaranteed loans is prime plus 2 percent (compared to prime plus 1 percent on conventional bank loans). The SBA normally assesses a one-time guaranty fee of between 2.5 and 3.5 percent for all loan guarantees, depending on the loan amount.

In a recent 5-year period, the SBA provided 7(a) guarantees on loans to an average of nearly 77,000 small businesses per year that would have had difficulty getting loans without the help of the SBA guarantee. The average 7(a) loan is $174,000, and the average duration of an SBA loan is 12 years—longer than the typical commercial small business loan. In fact, longer loan terms are a distinct advantage of SBA loans. At least half of all bank business loans are for less than 1 year. By contrast, SBA real estate loans can extend for up to 25 years (compared to just 10 to 15 years for a conventional loan), and working capital loans have maturities of 7 years (compared with 2 to 5 years at most banks). These longer terms translate into lower payments, which are better suited for young, fast-growing, cash-strapped companies.

Profile

Ted Clarke and Pat Easter: Jet Stream Car Wash

Ted Clarke and Pat Easter, former fighter pilots and squadron mates in the Navy, became commercial airline pilots after their military careers, but both men wanted to own their own business. With the help of a 25-year SBA-guaranteed 7(a) loan from Business Loan Express, Clarke and Easter constructed Jet Stream Car Wash, a touchless car wash, in Bonney Lake, Washington, that operates 24 hours a day.[57]

THE CAPLINE PROGRAM. In addition to its basic 7(a) loan guarantee program (through which the SBA makes about 70 percent of its loans), the SBA provides guarantees on small business loans for start up, real estate, machinery and equipment, fixtures, working capital, exporting, and restructuring debt through several other methods. Approximately two-thirds of all SBA loan guarantees are for machinery and equipment or working capital. The **CAPLine Program** offers short-term capital to growing companies seeking to finance seasonal buildups in inventory or accounts receivable under five separate programs, each with maturities of up to 5 years: seasonal line of credit (provides advances against inventory and accounts receivable to help businesses weather seasonal sales fluctuations), contract line of credit (finances the cost of direct labor and materials costs associated with performing contracts), builder's line of credit (helps small contractors and builders finance labor and materials costs), standard asset-based line of credit (an asset-based revolving line of credit for financing short-term needs), and small asset-based line of credit (an asset-based revolving line of credit up to $200,000). CAPLine is aimed at helping cash-hungry small businesses by giving them a credit line to draw on when they need it. These loans are what small companies need most because they are so flexible, efficient, and, unfortunately, so hard for small businesses to get from traditional lenders.

SECTION 504 CERTIFIED DEVELOPMENT COMPANY PROGRAM. Established in 1980, the SBA's Section 504 program is designed to encourage small businesses to purchase fixed assets, expand their facilities, and create jobs. Section 504 loans provide long-term financing at fixed rates to small companies to purchase land, buildings, or equipment. Because they are designated for fixed asset purchases that provide basic business infrastructure to small companies that otherwise might not qualify, 504 loans are intended to serve as a catalyst for economic development. Three lenders play a role in every 504 loan: a bank, the SBA, and a **certified development company (CDC).** A CDC is a nonprofit organization licensed by the SBA and designed to promote economic growth in local communities. Some 270 CDCs now operate across the United States and make more than 9,000 504 loans in an average year. An entrepreneur generally is required to make a down payment of just 10 percent of the total project cost. The CDC puts up 40 percent at a low, long-term, fixed rate, supported by an SBA loan guarantee in case the entrepreneur defaults. The bank provides long-term financing at market rates for the remaining 50 percent, which also is supported by an SBA guarantee. The major advantages of Section 504 loans are their fixed rates and terms, their 10- to 20-year maturities, and the low down payment required.

<table>
<tr><td>

ENTREPRENEURIAL

Profile

John Fernandez:
Daystar Desserts

</td><td>

Despite a 10-year track record of success in business, John Fernandez, CEO of Daystar Desserts, a company in Ashland, Virginia, that makes cheesecakes and other desserts, struck out with three banks when he applied for a loan to fulfill a contractual obligation to purchase the building that his company had been renting for 5 years. Daystar, with 54 employees and $15 million in annual sales, was in solid financial shape, but a crumbling real estate market and turmoil in the financial markets stymied the company's attempts to secure a $2 million loan. Fernandez turned to the SBA's 504 loan program, and, with the agency's loan guarantee, Village Bank extended Daystar a $2 million loan. Because the loan came under the America's Recovery Capital program, Fernandez saved nearly $60,000 in loan fees. Fernandez, a trained chef, started Daystar in his home in 1998; today, the company is one of the leading suppliers of cakes in the Northeast.[58]

</td></tr>
</table>

As attractive as they are, 504 loans are not for every business owner. The SBA imposes several restrictions on 504 loans:

- For every $50,000 ($100,000 for small manufacturers) the CDC lends, the project must create at least one new job or achieve a public policy goal such as rural development, expansion of exports, minority business development, and others.
- Machinery and equipment financed must have a useful life of at least 10 years.
- The borrower must occupy at least two-thirds of a building constructed with the loan, or the borrower must occupy at least half of a building purchased or remodeled with the loan.
- The borrower must qualify as a small business under the SBA's definition and must not have a tangible net worth in excess of $7 million or have an average net income in excess of $2.5 million after taxes for the preceding 2 years.

Because of strict equity requirements, existing small businesses usually find it easier to qualify for 504 loans than do start-ups. The average 504 loan is $586,000.[59]

MICROLOAN PROGRAM. The majority of entrepreneurs require less than $100,000 to launch their businesses. Indeed, research suggests that most entrepreneurs require less than $50,000 to start their companies. Unfortunately, loans of that amount can be the most difficult to get. Lending these relatively small amounts to entrepreneurs starting businesses is the purpose of the SBA's Microloan Program. Called **microloans** because they range from just a hundred dollars to as much as $35,000, these loans have helped thousands of people take their first steps toward entrepreneurship. Banks typically have shunned loans in such small amounts because they considered them to be unprofitable. In 1992, the SBA began funding microloans at 96 private, nonprofit lenders in 44 states in an attempt to "fill the void" in small loans to start-up companies, and the program has expanded from there. Since its inception, the SBA Microloan Program has made loans totaling more than $407 million to nearly 35,000 entrepreneurs![60]

Today, more than 170 authorized lenders make SBA backed microloans. The average size of a microloan is $13,550, with a maturity of 3 years (the maximum term is 6 years), and interest rates that range between 8 and 13 percent. Lenders' standards are less demanding than those on conventional loans; in fact, about 37 percent of all microloans go to business start-ups.[61] All microloans are made as installment loans through nonprofit intermediaries such as Trickle Up and ACCION International that are approved by the SBA. The typical microloan recipient is a small company with five or fewer employees and collateral that bankers shun for traditional loans, for example, earthworms from a fish bait farmer in Ohio or a Minnesota grocery store's frozen fish inventory.[62] Although microloans are available to anyone, the SBA hopes to target those entrepreneurs who have the greatest difficulty getting start-up and expansion capital: women, minorities, and people with low incomes.

ENTREPRENEURIAL
Profile
*Michael Golata
and Sam's Club*

Retailer Sam's Club, a division of Walmart, is working with a nonbank SBA lender, Superior Financial Group, to offer its small business members microloans of up to $25,000 through the SBA. "Access to capital is a major pain point for our [small business] members," says Catherine Corley, vice-president of membership. Michael Golata, a contractor for UPS who delivers emergency medical equipment to hospitals, had the opportunity to expand his business by bringing other delivery drivers into his business. Golata found a used Sprinter van for $12,500 and applied to two local banks for a loan, but both rejected his loan application. A commercial finance company was willing to lend him the money, but Golata balked at the 21 percent interest rate and $450 monthly payments. He learned about the microloans that Sam's Club was offering with Superior Financial Group and applied online for a $10,000 loan. The next day, Superior approved his loan with a 7.25 percent interest rate over 10 years. "I thought I was dreaming," says Golata, whose business with UPS immediately increased from $3,000 a week to $8,000.[63]

LOANS INVOLVING INTERNATIONAL TRADE. For small businesses going global, the SBA has the **Export Express Program**, which, like other express programs, offers quick turnaround times on applications for guarantees of 75 to 85 percent on loans up to $250,000 to help small companies develop or expand their export initiatives. Loan maturities range from 5 to 25 years, depending on the purpose of the loan.

The SBA also offers the **Export Working Capital (EWC) Program**, which is designed to provide working capital to small exporters by providing loan guarantees of 90 percent of the loan amount up to $1.5 million. The SBA works in conjunction with the Export-Import Bank to administer this loan guarantee program. Applicants file a one-page loan application, and the response time normally is 10 days or less. Small businesses must use loan proceeds to finance small business exports.

ENTREPRENEURIAL
Profile
*James Dixon:
Thomasville Lumber
Company*

After a fire destroyed the Coastal Lumber Company's sawmill in Thomasville, Alabama, former employee James Dixon worked with a local bank to secure an Export Working Capital loan of $1 million to reopen the mill as Thomasville Lumber, purchase raw materials, and begin exporting lumber. Thomasville Lumber produces more than 20 million board feet of yellow pine lumber annually and exports 80 to 90 percent of it to Spain, Western Europe, Japan, and the Caribbean. The company, with export sales that exceed $10 million, employs more than 70 workers and received the Governor's Trade Excellence Award.[64]

The **International Trade Loan Program** is for small businesses that are engaging in international trade or that are being adversely affected by competition from imports. The SBA allows global entrepreneurs to combine loans from the Export Working Capital Program with those from the International Trade Program for a maximum guarantee of $1.75 million. The loan ceiling is $2 million, and maturities run up to 25 years.

DISASTER ASSISTANCE LOANS. As their name implies, **disaster assistance loans** are made to small businesses devastated by financial or physical losses from hurricanes, earthquakes, floods, tornadoes, and other disasters. Business physical disaster loans are designed to help companies repair or replace damage to physical property (buildings, equipment, inventory, etc.) caused by the disaster, and economic injury loans provide working capital for businesses throughout the disaster period. For businesses, the maximum disaster loan usually is $2 million, but Congress often raises

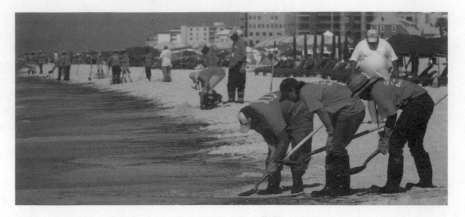

Workers clean up oil from the Deepwater oil spill in the Gulf of Mexico along a beach in Alabama. The SBA extended disaster loans to many small companies that suffered losses as a result of the spill.

Source: AP Photo/Dave Martin

that ceiling when circumstances warrant. Disaster loans carry below-market interest rates and long payback periods. Loans that exceed $14,000 require the entrepreneur to pledge some kind of collateral, usually a lien on the business property. In the aftermath of the Deepwater oil spill that dumped more than 200 million gallons of oil into the Gulf of Mexico, shutting down commercial and recreational fishing and decimating the tourist industry, the SBA granted disaster assistance loans to small businesses that suffered financial losses.[65]

State and Local Loan Development Programs

5. Discuss state and local economic development programs.

Just when many federally funded programs are facing cutbacks, state-sponsored loan and development programs are becoming more active in providing funds for business start-ups and expansions. Many states have decided that their funds are better spent encouraging small business growth rather than "chasing smokestacks"—trying to entice large businesses to locate in their boundaries. These programs come in many forms, but they all tend to focus on developing small businesses that create the greatest number of jobs and economic benefits. Entrepreneurs who apply for state and local funding must have patience and be willing to slog through some paperwork, however.

Although each state's approach to economic development and job growth is unique, one common element is some kind of small business financing program: loans, loan guarantees, development grants, venture capital pools, and others. One approach many states have had success with is **capital access programs (CAPs)**. First introduced in 1986 in Michigan, 22 states now offer CAPs that are designed to encourage lending institutions to make loans to businesses that do not qualify for traditional financing. Under a CAP, a bank and a borrower each pay an up-front fee (a portion of the loan amount) into a loan-loss reserve fund at the participating bank, and the state matches this amount. The reserve fund, which normally ranges from 6 to 14 percent of the loan amount, acts as an insurance policy against the potential loss a bank might experience on a loan and frees the bank to make loans that it otherwise might refuse. One study of CAPs found that 55 percent of the entrepreneurs who received loans under a CAP would not have been granted loans without the backing of the program.[66]

Even cities and small towns have joined in the effort to develop small businesses and help them grow. More than 7,500 communities across the United States operate **revolving loan funds (RLFs)** that combine private and public funds to make loans to small businesses, often at below-market interest rates. As money is repaid into the funds, it is loaned back out to other entrepreneurs. Full Spectrum Solutions, a company that produces a line of high-quality energy- and cost-saving light fixtures, recently received a $200,000 loan from the Jackson County (Mississippi) Economic Development Corporation's revolving loan fund. Full Spectrum used the loan to purchase the equipment and machinery and to hire new workers to manufacture its Everlast® Induction Lighting System.[67]

In addition to RLFs, more than 1,000 communities across the United States have created **community development financial institutions (CDFIs)** that designate at least some of their loan portfolios for entrepreneurs and small businesses. CDFIs operate through a variety of mechanisms, including microenterprise loan funds, community development loan funds, and others, and provide loans to people who do not meet traditional lenders' criteria. Because the loans that they make are higher risk, the interest rates that CDFIs charge are higher than those charged by traditional lenders.

ENTREPRENEURIAL
Profile

Anthony Viggiano: Autotether

When Anthony Viggiano's friend nearly died in a boating accident, he created a device called the Autotether that makes boating safer. Autotether is a wireless lanyard that automatically shuts off a boat's ignition if the driver falls overboard. The system also protects up to three passengers by sounding an alarm if one of them falls overboard. Because it is wireless and allows a boat's operator and passengers to move about freely, the Autotether offers significant improvements over standard kill switches. To accommodate growing demand for the product, Viggiano received a $250,000 loan from a CDFI, the Connecticut Development Authority, which provided Autotether with critical working capital and allowed the young company to hire 16 more employees.[68]

IN THE ENTREPRENEURIAL
SPOTLIGHT Alternative Sources of Financing

Although banks tend to be lenders of first resort for small businesses, accounting for the greatest volume of loans to small businesses, they are not the only lending game in town, as the following profiles illustrate.

Heart to Heart Gifts

Yi Ping Lai's business, Heart to Heart Gifts, an online store based in San Diego, California, sells toys, costumes, party decorations, and accessories priced from $6 to $100 for girls up to age 6. Recently, the company's sales passed the $1 million mark. Even though a recession caused sales to decline by nearly 50 percent, Yi says that the company remained profitable. Yet her bank cancelled Heart to Heart's $55,000 line of credit, saying that Yi and her company had become high credit risks. After many meetings with her bankers, Yi was able to get the line of credit reestablished, but only for $20,000. Yi is developing a new product line that will increase her company's sales, but without adequate financing her efforts are hampered. "I need that cash flow for my business," she says. Finally, Yi turned to a nonprofit community development corporation in San Diego, where a loan officer helped her obtain a $35,000 line of credit.

Lake Powell Furniture

Kip and Melissa Bennett became the owners of Lake Powell Furniture, a small furniture store in Page, Arizona, in 2003. Within a few years, their hard work paid off; sales had increased so much that the business had outgrown its existing location. Kip had spotted an ideal location for their store on a busy corner in downtown Page, and the building was for sale. All he needed was the financing to purchase the building and transform it into a furniture store. Kip began approaching banks about commercial property loans and found one willing to make a $500,000 loan. Unfortunately, the bank was a victim of the crisis in the financial markets, and Kip lost the $7,000 that he had put into the loan application.

At the recommendation of another business owner in Page, Kip approached Mercantile Commercial Capital, a nonbank lender that specializes in SBA 504 loans, which are designed to help small business owners purchase fixed assets such as buildings and equipment. Within a few months, the Bennetts received a $500,000 loan from Mercantile backed by an SBA guarantee. Despite an economic slowdown, they say that sales are on track to match their best year ever, an outcome that they say would not have been possible without their new, larger store.

Jackson Pianos

Joseph Jackson, owner of Jackson Pianos LLC, in St. Louis, Missouri, a company that tunes, repairs, refurbishes, and sells pianos, has seen his company's sales increase by 35 percent within the last year to exceed $500,000. His company has outgrown its existing space, but Jackson is having difficulty getting a loan to expand his business into a larger building. Jackson's bank rejected his loan application even though he has an excellent personal credit score and his company is profitable. He then turned to two large banks, but they also rejected his applications, saying that his company's cash flow was insufficient and that he should have more money tucked away in accounts. Even when Jackson reduced his loan request from $300,000 to $90,000, both banks again refused. "We've already missed our chance on a few buildings because of this," he says.

1. What advice can you offer business owners when banks refuse their loan applications?
2. Assume the role of consultant to Joe Jackson, owner of Jackson Pianos. What advice can you offer him about getting the financing he needs to support his company's expansion?

Sources: Based on Nick Carey, "Small U.S. Firms Face Credit Squeeze as Crisis Drags," *Reuters*, October 11, 2009, *www.reuters.com/article/idUSN1111766420091012*; "Start-up Stories: 'How We Got the Cash,'" *CNNMoney*, April 27, 2009, *http://money.cnn.com/galleries/2009/smallbusiness/0904/gallery.how_entrepreneurs_got_bank_loans.smb/2.html*; Emily Maltby, "Real Collateral Damage," *Wall Street Journal*, July 22, 2010, pp. B1, B6.

Internal Methods of Financing

6. Discuss methods of financing growth and expansion internally with bootstrap financing.

Small business owners do not have to rely solely on financial institutions and government agencies for capital. Instead, the business itself has the capacity to generate capital. Perhaps the least expensive form of capital is the company's retained earnings, the portion of its profits that the owner keeps in the company. Another method of "generating capital" is never to use it in the first place by managing the business frugally. Other types of **bootstrap financing** are available to virtually every small business and include factoring, leasing rather than purchasing equipment, and using credit cards.

Factoring Accounts Receivable

Rather than carry credit sales on its own books (some of which may never be collected), a small business can sell outright its accounts receivable to a factor. A **factor** buys a company's accounts receivable and pays for them in two parts. The first payment, which the factor makes immediately, is for 50 to 80 percent of the accounts' agreed-upon value, which is typically discounted at a rate of 3 to 5 percent of the value of the invoice. The factor makes the second payment of 15 to 18 percent, which makes up the balance less the factor's service fees, when the original customer pays the invoice. Because factoring is a more expensive type of financing than loans from either banks or commercial finance companies, many entrepreneurs view factors as lenders of last resort. However, for businesses that cannot qualify for those loans, factoring may be the only choice!

Begun by American colonists to finance their cotton trade with England, factoring has become an important source of capital for many small businesses that depend on fast billing turnaround across a multitude of industries ranging from hardware stores and pharmacies to pest control firms and staffing agencies (see Figure 5). Factoring deals are either with recourse or without recourse. Under deals arranged with recourse, a small business owner retains the responsibility for customers who fail to pay their accounts. The business owner must take back these uncollectible invoices. Under deals arranged without recourse, however, the owner is relieved of the responsibility of collecting them. If customers fail to pay their accounts, the factor bears the loss. Because the factoring company assumes the risk of collecting the accounts, it normally

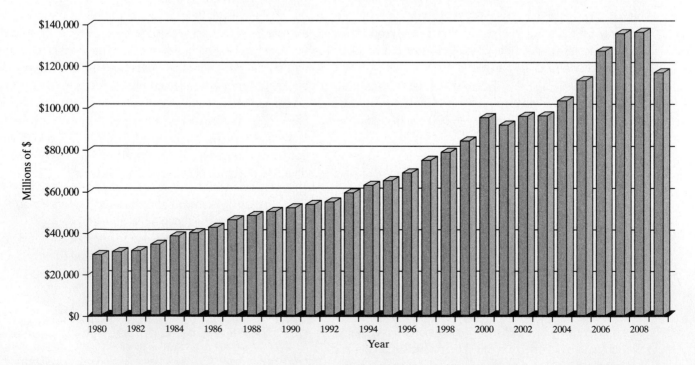

FIGURE 5
Factoring Volume

Source: "Annual Asset-Based Lending and Factoring Surveys 2009," Commercial Finance Association, May 17, 2010, p. 15.

screens the firm's credit customers, accepts those judged to be creditworthy, and advances the small business owner a portion of the value of the accounts receivable. Factors will discount anywhere from 2 to 40 percent of the face value of a company's accounts receivable, depending on a small company's:

- Customers' financial strength, credit ratings, and their ability to pay their invoices on time.
- Industry and its customers' industries because some industries have a reputation for slow payments.
- History and financial strength, especially in deals arranged with recourse.
- Credit policies.

The discount rate on deals without recourse usually is higher than on those with recourse because of the higher level of risk they carry for the factor.

Although factoring is more expensive than traditional bank loans (a 2 percent discount from the face value of an invoice due in 30 days amounts to an annual interest rate of 24.5 percent), it is a source of quick cash and is ideally suited for fast-growing companies, especially start-ups that cannot qualify for bank loans. "Factoring provides a business with immediate cash for accounts receivable because a business can sell receivables as soon as they are generated," explains the head of one factoring operation.[69] Small companies that sell to government agencies and large corporations, both famous for stretching out their payments for 60 to 90 days or more, also find factoring attractive because they collect the money from the sale (less the factor's discount) much faster. Taylor Pershing, CEO of a staffing company that provides employees for hospitals, relies on factoring as a source of financing. His company incurs payroll expenses for 50 employees up front but does not collect from its clients until later and uses factoring to fill the cash gap. "We sometimes wait 30, 60, or 90 days to get paid," he says. "Without factoring, I'd need at least $500,000 in cash on hand or a similar-sized revolving credit line to meet payroll."[70]

Leasing

Leasing is another common bootstrap financing technique. Today, small businesses can lease virtually any kind of asset—from office space and telephones to computers and heavy equipment. By leasing expensive assets, a small business owner is able to use them without tying up valuable capital for an extended period of time. In other words, entrepreneurs can reduce the long-term capital requirements of their businesses by leasing equipment and facilities, and they are not investing their capital in depreciating assets. Also, because no down payment is required and because the cost of the asset is spread over a longer time (lowering monthly payments), the company's cash flow improves.

Credit Cards

Unable to find financing elsewhere, many entrepreneurs have launched their companies using the fastest and most convenient source of debt capital available: credit cards! Because they cannot get financing anywhere else, many entrepreneurs launch their companies by charging their start-up expenses to credit cards. It is a common financing technique; nearly 58 percent of entrepreneurs use credit cards to cover the costs of starting their businesses, a significant increase from the 16 percent who used credit cards for start-ups in 1993.[71] Filmmaker Spike Lee financed one of his first movies, *Do the Right Thing*, with credit cards and launched his career as a director. Putting business start-up costs on credit cards charging 20 percent or more in annual interest is expensive, risky, and can lead to severe financial woes, however. A study by Robert Scott of Monmouth University and the Kauffman Foundation reports that taking on credit card debt reduces the likelihood that a start-up company will survive its first 3 years of operation. Every $1,000 increase in credit card debt results in a 2.2 percent increase in the probability that a company will fail.[72]

Unfortunately, some determined entrepreneurs have no other choice but to finance their companies with credit cards. Credit cards are a ready source of temporary financing that can carry a company through the start-up phase until it begins generating positive cash flow, but entrepreneurs must use them judiciously.

ENTREPRENEURIAL
Profile

Shannon Cumberland:
Rosy Rings

Shannon Cumberland launched Rosy Rings in her kitchen by maxing out five credit cards.

Source: Shannon Cumberland/Rosy Rings

Shannon Cumberland launched Rosy Rings, a company that sells handmade botanical candles, in her Denver, Colorado, kitchen by maxing out five credit cards. For Cumberland, the high-risk move paid off. Rosy Rings, now with more than $2 million in annual sales, manufactures more than 250,000 candles each year that are sold online and in 1,800 retail stores across the United States.[73]

Where *Not* to Seek Funds

7. Explain how to avoid becoming a victim of a loan scam.

Entrepreneurs searching for capital must be wary of con artists whose targets frequently include financially strapped small businesses. The swindle usually begins when the con artist scours an area for "DEs"—desperate entrepreneurs—in search of quick cash injections to keep their businesses going. Usually, the scam involves advance fees and follows one of two patterns (although a number of variations exist). Under one scheme, scammers guarantee a small business owner a loan from a nonexistent bank with false credentials. The con artist tells the owner that loan processing will take time and that in the meantime the owner must pay a percentage of the loan amount as an advance fee. Of course, the loan never materializes, and the small business owner loses the deposit, sometimes several thousands of dollars.

Another common scam begins with a "loan broker" who promises a capital-hungry small business owner an SBA loan if the owner pays a small processing fee. Again, the loan never appears, and the small business owner loses his or her deposit. Other scammers charge entrepreneurs excessive fees to help them apply for SBA loan guarantees.

Unfortunately, schemes by con artists preying on unsuspecting business owners who are in need of capital are more common when credit tightens. Scams most commonly involve the SBA's smallest loan programs, such as the SBA*Express* and Microloan programs. The Internet has made crooks' jobs easier. On the Web, they can establish a legitimate-looking presence, approach their targets anonymously, and vanish instantly—all while avoiding mail fraud charges if they happen to get caught. These con artists move fast, cover their trails well, and are extremely smooth. The best protection against such scams is common sense and remembering the adage, "If it sounds too good to be true, it probably is." Experts offer the following advice to business owners:

- Be suspicious of anyone who approaches you—unsolicited—with an offer for "guaranteed financing."
- Watch out for red flags that indicate a scam: "guaranteed" loans, up-front fees, and unsolicited pitches over the Web.
- Conduct a thorough background check on any lenders, brokers, or financiers with whom you intend to do business. Is the lender registered to do business in your state? Does the Better Business Bureau have a record of complaints against the company?
- Make sure you have an attorney review all loan agreements before you sign them.
- *Never* pay advance fees for financing, especially on the Web, unless you have verified the lender's credibility.

Chapter Review

1. Describe the various sources of debt capital and the advantages and disadvantages of each.
   - Commercial banks offer the greatest variety of loans, although they are conservative lenders. Typical short-term bank loans include commercial loans, lines of credit, discounting accounts receivable, inventory financing, floor planning, and character loans.
2. Explain the types of financing available from nonbank sources of credit.
   - Asset-based lenders allow small businesses to borrow money by pledging otherwise idle assets, such as accounts receivable, inventory, or purchase orders, as collateral.

- Trade credit is used extensively by small businesses as a source of financing. Vendors and suppliers commonly finance sales to businesses for 30, 60, or even 90 days.
- Equipment suppliers offer small businesses financing similar to trade credit, but with slightly different terms.
- Commercial finance companies offer many of the same types of loans that banks do, but they are more risk oriented in their lending practices. They emphasize accounts receivable financing and inventory loans.
- Savings and loan associations specialize in loans to purchase real property—commercial and industrial mortgages—with payback terms of up to 30 years.
- Stock brokerage houses offer loans to prospective entrepreneurs at lower interest rates than banks because they have high-quality, liquid collateral—stocks and bonds in the borrower's portfolio.
- Insurance companies provide financing through policy loans and mortgage loans. Policy loans are extended to the owner against the cash surrender value of insurance policies. Mortgage loans are made for large amounts and are based on the value of the land being purchased.
- Small business investment companies (SBICs) are privately owned companies licensed and regulated by the SBA that qualify for SBA loans to be invested in or loaned to small businesses.
- Small business lending companies (SBLCs) make only intermediate and long-term loans that are guaranteed by the SBA.

3. Identify the various federal loan programs aimed at small businesses.
   - The Economic Development Administration, a branch of the Commerce Department, makes loan guarantees to create and expand small businesses in economically depressed areas.
   - The Department of Housing and Urban Development extends grants (such as Community Development Block Grants) to cities that, in turn, lend and grant money to small businesses in an attempt to strengthen the local economy.
   - The Department of Agriculture's Rural Business-Cooperative Service loan program is designed to create nonfarm employment opportunities in rural areas through loans and loan guarantees.
   - The Small Business Innovation Research Program involves 11 federal agencies that award cash grants or long-term contracts to small companies wanting to initiate or to expand their research and development (R&D) efforts.
   - The Small Business Technology Transfer Program allows researchers at universities, federally funded R&D centers, and nonprofit research institutions to join forces with small businesses and develop commercially promising ideas.

4. Describe the various loan programs available from the Small Business Administration.
   - SBA loan activity is in the form of loan guarantees rather than direct loans. Popular SBA programs include the SBA*Express* Program, the Patriot Express Program, the Community*Express* Program, the 7(a) loan guaranty program, the CAPLine Program, the Microloan Program, the 504 Certified Development Company Program, several export loan programs, and the disaster loan program.

5. Discuss state and local economic development programs.
   - In an attempt to develop businesses that create jobs and economic growth, most states offer small business financing programs, usually in the form of loans, loan guarantees, and venture capital pools.
   - Many state and local loan and development programs, such as capital access programs and revolving loan funds, complement those sponsored by federal agencies.

6. Discuss valuable methods of financing growth and expansion internally with bootstrap financing.
   - Small business owners may also look inside their firms for capital. By factoring accounts receivable, leasing equipment instead of buying it, and using credit cards, owners can stretch their supplies of capital.

7. Explain how to avoid becoming a victim of a loan scam.
   - Entrepreneurs hungry for capital for their growing businesses can be easy targets for con artists running loan scams. Entrepreneurs should watch out for promises of "guaranteed" loans, up-front fees, and offers that seem too good to be true.

Discussion Questions

1. What role do commercial banks play in providing debt financing to small businesses? Outline and briefly describe the major types of short-term, intermediate, and long-term loans commercial banks offer.

2. What is trade credit? How important is it as a source of debt financing to small firms?

3. Explain how asset-based financing works. What is the most common method of asset-based financing? What are the advantages and disadvantages of using this method of financing?

4. What function do SBICs serve? How does an SBIC operate? What methods of financing do SBICs rely on most heavily?

5. Briefly describe the loan programs offered by the following:
   a. Economic Development Administration
   b. Department of Housing and Urban Development
   c. Department of Agriculture
   d. Local development companies

6. Explain the purpose and the methods of operation of the Small Business Innovation Research Program and the Small Business Technology Transfer Program.

7. Which of the SBA's loan programs accounts for the majority of its loan activity? How does the program work?

8. Explain the purpose and the operation of the SBA's Microloan Program.

9. How can a firm employ bootstrap financing to stretch its current capital supply?

10. What is a factor? How does the typical factor operate? Explain the advantages and the disadvantages of factoring. What kinds of businesses typically use factors?

Many entrepreneurs are reluctant to give up a percentage of ownership in their companies that equity capital requires and turn instead to debt capital as a source of funds. Almost every lending institution expects to see a quality business plan. A business plan adds credibility and is testimony that you have invested thought and time in your business idea. If you need debt capital for your venture, a business plan can help you clarify how much money you will need, formulate a financing strategy for acquiring the funds, and communicate to potential lenders why you are worth the risk.

On the Web

If you need start-up or growth capital for your venture, visit the Companion Web site at *www.pearsonhighered.com/scarborough* and review some equity financing options. Determine whether these sources may be useful as you explore financing opportunities. You will also find additional information regarding bootstrap and nontraditional funding.

Sample Plans

You should review sample plans in Business Plan Pro for companies that are seeking debt financing. Lenders will want to confirm that you have a sound business or business idea, that you are motivated enough to make the business successful, and that you will be able to make your payments on time! They also will want to know about any collateral that you have to bring to the table. Use each aspect of the financial section—the break-even analysis, projected profit and loss, projected cash flow, projected balance sheet, and business ratios—to tell your company's financial story to your lending audience.

In the Software

Open your plan in Business Plan Pro and go to the "Financial Plan" section. Your assumptions will state anticipated economic conditions, current short-term and long-term interest rates, expected tax rates, personnel expenses, cash expenses, sales on credit, or any areas that you hope to develop and confirm through further research. You will then assess the type and amount of debt financing that you will need. Will this be short- or long-term financing? Work through the finance section and review the numbers in your break-even point calculation, balance sheet, projected profit and loss statement, and cash flow forecast. This section also will enable you to review industry ratios and to compare them to your company's anticipated performance. These ratio comparisons may be helpful for lenders. Make certain this section clearly tells your financial story. Providing relevant information that will be meaningful to the potential lenders who will review your plan is critical.

Building Your Business Plan

The business plan will help to assess the amount of debt financing needed, describe the use of these funds, and make certain that you can live with the financial consequences of these decisions. This "financial road map" helps you to analyze your funding options. Expect potential lenders to review your pro forma statements and, like investors, to assess the qualifications of your management team, the industry's growth potential, your proposed exit strategy, and other factors as they assess the financial stability of your venture.

Endnotes

1. Mara Der Hovanesian, "Tapped Out?" *BusinessWeek*, Winter 2007, *www.businessweek.com/magazine/content/07_09/b4023443.htm*.

2. William J. Dennis, *Small Business Credit in a Deep Recession*, National Federation of Independent Businesses, February 2010, pp. 8–9.

3. Melissa Sharp, "Small Business Optimism Declines in June," National Federation of Independent Businesses, July 13, 2010, *www.nfib.com/press-media/press-media-item?cmsid=52004*.

4. Emily Maltby, "Bailout Missed Main Street, New Report Says," *Wall Street Journal*, May 14, 2010, p. B6.

5. Catherine Clifford, "Small Business Loans: 410 Billion Evaporates," *CNNMoney*, November 17, 2009, *http://money.cnn.com/2009/11/16/smallbusiness/small_business_loans_evaporate/*.

6. Cynthia E. Griffin, "Something Borrowed," *Entrepreneur*, February 1997, p. 26; Business Lenders Inc., *www.businesslenders.com/q&a.htm*.

7. *The Small Business Credit Crunch and the Impact of the TARP*, Congressional Oversight Panel, May 2010, p. 13.

8. Peter S. Goodman, "Credit Tightens for Small Businesses," *New York Times*, October 13, 2009, *www.nytimes.com/2009/10/13/business/smallbusiness/13lending.html*.

9. Conor Dougherty and Pu-Wing Tam, "Start-ups Chase Cash as Funds Trickle Back," *Wall Street Journal*, April 1, 2010, p. B1.

10. *Small Business and Micro Business Lending in the United States for Data Years 2007–2008*, U.S. Small Business Administration, Office of Advocacy, May 2009, p. 6.

11. Daniel M. Clark, "Banks and Bankability," *Venture*, September 1989, p. 29.

12. Rosalind Resnick, "Loan Woes," *Entrepreneur*, April 2007, p. 96.

13. Dennis, Jr., *Small Business Credit in a Deep Recession*, p. 1.

14. Emily Maltby, "Tightening the Credit Screws," *Wall Street Journal*, May 17, 2010, *http://online.wsj.com/article/NA_WSJ_PUB:SB10001424052748704784904575111250456800076.html*.

15. "Thrifty Names President of Thrifty Car Sales; Announces Strategic Alliances with Bank of America, APCO, Manheim, and Others," Dollar Thrifty Automotive Group, February 8, 2005, *www.dtag.com/phoenix.zhtml?c=71946&p=irol-newsArticle&ID=27723&highlight=*.

16. Tim Reason, "Borrowing Big Time," *CFO*, November 2003, pp. 87–94.

17. Juan Hovey, "Want Easy Money? Look for Lenders Who Say Yes," *FSB*, November 2000, pp. 41–44.

18. Kyle Stock, "Asset-Based Lending Grows in Popularity," *Wall Street Journal*, February 2, 2010, p. B5.

19. Carol Tice, "Can a Purchase Order Loan Keep Your Business Growing?" *Entrepreneur*, June 17, 2010, *www.entrepreneur.com/money/financing/article207058.html*.

20. Rebel Cole, *Bank Credit, Trade Credit, or No Credit: Evidence from the Surveys of Small Business Finances*, U.S. Small Business Administration, Office of Advocacy, June 2010, p. 21.

21. Emily Maltby, "Vendors Can Help Financing," *Wall Street Journal*, February 18, 2010, p. B5; Ina Steiner, "eFashion Solutions Powers Brands on eBay, Fashion Vault, Amazon.com," Auction Bytes, July 8, 2010, *www.auctionbytes.com/cab/abn/y10/m07/i08/s01*.

22. *Small Business and Micro Business Lending in the United States 2005*, p. 6.

23. David Worrell, "The Other Colors of Money," *Entrepreneur*, July 2004, p. 67.

24. Ibid.

25. "Case Studies: Kalitta Air," GE Capital, *www.gecapital.com/en/case-study-kalitta-air.html*.

26. "Customer Success Story: Hudson Bakery," GE Capital, *www.hudsonbread.com/media.html*; "Tactical Conquest," Hudson Bakery, *www.hudsonbread.com/media.html*.

27. John R. Walter, "Not Your Father's Credit Union," *Economic Quarterly*, Federal Reserve Bank of Richmond, Vol. 92, No. 4, Fall 2006, pp. 353–377.

28. Jorina Fontelera, "Where to Go When Banks Say No," *ThomasNet News*, June 9, 2009, *http://news.thomasnet.com/IMT/archives/2009/06/where-to-go-when-banks-say-no-alternative-funding-sources-for-entrepreneurs.html*.

29. *2009 Yearend Statistics for Federally Insured Credit Unions*, National Credit Union Administration, p. 7.

30. Chris Branch, "Delaware Business: Loan Big for Beauty Shop, Credit Union," *Delaware Online*, July 17, 2010, *www.delawareonline.com/article/20100717/BUSINESS/7170317/Delaware-business-Loan-big-for-beauty-shop-credit-union*.

31. "NGK Overview," NGK Spark Plugs, *www.ngksparkplugs.com/About_nGK/index.asp?mode=nml*; *West Virginia Economic Development Agency Annual Report 2008*, West Virginia Economic Development Agency, p. 9; "Success Stories," West Virginia Department of Commerce, *www.wvcommerce.org/business/successstories/default.aspx*.

32. Steven E. F. Brown, "Salesforce Wraps Up $500 Million Private Placement," *San Francisco Business Times*, January 19, 2010, *http://sanfrancisco.bizjournals.com/sanfrancisco/stories/2010/01/18/daily29.html*; "Company Milestones," Salesforce.com, *www.salesforce.com/company/co_milestones.jsp*.

33. "America's Small Business Partners," National Association of Small Business Investment Companies, *www.nasbic.org*.

34. "History and Current Highlights," National Association of Small Business Investment Companies, *www.nasbic.org/?page=SBIC_Program_History*.

35. "SBIC Program Overview," National Association of Small Business Investment Companies, January 23, 2009, p. 2.

36. Ibid.

37. "Paramount 2009 Portfolio Company of the Year Award from NASBIC," Paramount Building Solutions, November 11, 2009, *www.paramountbldgsol.com/about/pressRelease.cfm?preID=16*; "Paramount Building Solutions Named Portfolio Company of the Year," LaSalle Capital Group, November 2009, *www.lasallecapitalgroup.com/PDFs/NASBIC-award.pdf*.

38. Economic Development Administration Fiscal Year 2009 Annual Report, Economic Development Administration, *www.eda.gov/PDF/EDA%20FY%202009%20Annual%20Report.pdf*.

39. "Revolving Loan Fund Innovative Practices: Mo-Kan Regional Council Revolving Loan Fund," *EDA Update*, September 2009, Vol. 2, No. 9, *www.planning.org/eda/newsletter/2009/sep.htm#4*.

40. "Trade Adjustment Assistance for Firms Case Studies," U.S. Economic Development Administration, *www.lasallecapitalgroup.com/PDFs/NASBIC-award.pdf*.

41. "Section 108 Case Studies," U.S. Department of Housing and Urban Development, *www.hud.gov/offices/cpd/communitydevelopment/programs/108/casestudies.cfm*.

42. *USDA Rural Development Progress Report 2009*, U.S. Department of Agriculture, pp. 22–23.

43. Charles Wessner, "An Assessment of the SBIR Program," National Research Council, *http://books.nap.edu/openbook.php?record_id=11989&page=12*, pp. 91–107.

44. "SBIR/STTR Hallmarks of Success Videos: AeroTech Research Inc.," NASA Small Business Innovation Research Program, *http://sbir.nasa.gov/SBIR/video/aerotech.html*; "Steering Aircraft Clear of Choppy Air," *Tech Briefs*, January 1, 2006, *www.techbriefs.com/content/view/1238/118/*; "NASA Selects AeroTech to Quantify Benefits of Advanced Weather Avoidance Systems for Aircraft," *Federal Circle*, August 5, 2010, *http://thefederalcircle.com/nasa-selects-aerotech-to-quantify-benefits-of-advanced-weather-avoidance-systems-for-aircraft/*.

45. *Summary of Performance and Financial Information 2009 Fiscal Year*, U.S. Small Business Administration, February 22, 2010, p. 5.

46. Emily Maltby, "A Credit Crunch That Lingers," *Wall Street Journal*, June 21, 2010, *http://online.wsj.com/article/NA_WSJ_PUB:SB10001424052748704852004575257970246239874.html*.

47. Diana Ransom, "Status Report: Small Business Lending," *Wall Street Journal*, September 23, 2009, *http://online.wsj.com/article/NA_WSJ_PUB:SB125372460362634601.html*.

48. "2009 Recovery Act: Helping Small Business Start, Grow, and Succeed—Q&A for Small Business Owners," U.S. Small Business Administration, p. 2.

49. *Summary of Performance and Financial Information 2009 Fiscal Year*, U.S. Small Business Administration, February 22, 2010, p. 3.

50. Julie Monahan, "Quick Fix," *Entrepreneur*, April 2004, p. 27.

51. Michelle Samaad, "Patriot Express's $500 Million in Loans Helps Returning Military," *Credit Union Times*, July 1, 2010, *www.cutimes.com/News/2010/7/Pages/Patriot-Express-500-Million-in-Loans-Helps-Returning-Military-.aspx*.

52. Tim Rausch, "Federal Program Provides Loans for Small Businesses," *Augusta Chronicle*, October 18, 2009, *http://chronicle.augusta.com/stories/2009/10/18/bus_552290.shtml*.

53. Raymund Flandez, "SBA Loan Cap Hits Minority Owners," *Wall Street Journal*, December 9, 2008, pp. B1, B7.

54. "The SBA's 7(a) Loan Program: A Flexible Tool for Commercial Lenders," *Community Development Insights*, Washington, D.C.: U.S. Department of the Treasury, September 2008, *www.occ.treas.gov/cdd/Insights-SBAs7(a).pdf*, p. 3.

55. "Success Story: Ace Hardware of Silver Lake," *Summary of Performance and Financial Information, 2009 Fiscal Year*, U.S. Small Business Administration, p. 21.

56. Tom Abate, "Small Business Facing Credit Crunch," *San Francisco Chronicle*, January 21, 2010, *www.sfgate.com/cgi-bin/article.cgi?f=/c/a/2010/01/20/BUOL1BKH26.DTL*; Joan M. Lang, "Kasa Indian Eatery," *Restaurant Business*, June 2009, p. 26.

57. "Spotlight on Success: Navy Pilots Aim for Business Success on Land," *BLX Lending Report*, Vol. 1, No. 1, *www.blxonline.com/Files/Public/BLX-Success-Story-Jet-Stream-Car-Wash.pdf*.

58. "Starved for Financing: Is There Relief in Sight for U.S. Small Businesses?" *Knowledge@Wharton*, October 28, 2009, *www.knowledgeatwharton.com.cn/index.cfm?fa=viewArticle&articleID=2135&languageid=1*; John Reid Blackwell, "Daystar Desserts CEO Chef Shares Recipe for Survival," *Richmond Times-Dispatch*, September 13, 2009, *www2.timesdispatch.com/business/2009/sep/13/cake13_20090912-192805-ar-30606/*.

59. Summary of Performance and Financial Information Fiscal Year 2009, Small Business Administration, *www.sba.gov/idc/groups/public/documents/sba_homepage/serv_aboutsba_perf_summ.pdf*, p.8.

60. "Microloan Program," U.S. Small Business Administration, *www.sba.gov/financialassistance/borrowers/guaranteed/mlp/index*.

61. *SBA Microloan Program: FY 2007*, Women Impacting Public Policy, *www.wipp.org/news_details.asp?story_id=204&memberonly=False*.

62. Gwendolyn Bounds, "Risky Businesses May Find Loans Even Scarcer," *Wall Street Journal*, April 13, 2004, p. B8.

63. Mae Anderson, "Sam's Club Will Offer Small Business Loans," *MSNBC*, July 6, 2010, *www.msnbc.msn.com/id/38103657/*; Stephanie Clifford, "Retailers Devise Novel Ways to Revive Sales," *New York Times*, July 4, 2010, *www.nytimes.com/2010/07/05/business/05loan.html*.

64. Brian Davis, "Lumber Company Builds Small Town Employment," Alabama International Trade Center, *www.aitc.ua.edu/success-stories*, p. 1; Arthur McLean, "Thomas Lumber Honored by Governor," *Thomasville Times*, March 29, 2007, *www.thethomasvilletimes.com/news/2007-03-29/Front_Page/Thomasville_Lumber_honored_by_Gov.html*.

65. Carol Chastang, "SBA Administrator Offers Economic Injury Assistance to Louisiana Small Businesses Affected by Deepwater BP Oil Spill," U.S. Small Business Administration, May 6, 2010, pp. 1–2.

66. Ziona Austrian and Zhongcai Zhang, "An Inventory and Assessment of Pollution Control and Prevention Financing Programs," Great Lakes Environmental Finance Center, Levin College of Urban Affairs, Cleveland State University, *www.csuohio.edu/glefc/inventor.htm#sba*.

67. "Full Spectrum Solutions Growing Green," Enterprise Group of Jackson, *www.enterprisegroup.org/economic-development-corporation*, p. 1.

68. "Success Stories: CDA Helps CT Businesses," Connecticut Development Authority, *www.ctcda.com/successStories/newsView.asp?NewsID=52*; "About Us," Autotether, *www.autotether.com/at/index.php?option=com_content&view=article&id=67&Itemid=81*.

69. Sean P. Melvin, "Hidden Treasure," *Entrepreneur*, February 2002, pp. 56–58.

70. "Success Stories," Keystone Capital, *www.keystonefactoring.com/success-stories/*.

71. Raymond J. Keating, *Credit Cards and Small Business: The Benefits, Opportunities, and Policy Debate*, Small Business and Entrepreneurship Council, March 2009, p. 11; Robert Scott, *The Use of Credit Card Debt by New Firms*, The Kauffman Firm Survey, August 2009, p. 2.

72. Robert Scott, *The Use of Credit Card Debt by New Firms*, The Kauffman Firm Survey, August 2009, pp. 2, 4.

73. Linda Dishman, "Play Your Cards Right," *Entrepreneur*, November 9, 2009, *www.entrepreneur.com/money/financing/article203940.html*.

Location, Layout, and Physical Facilities

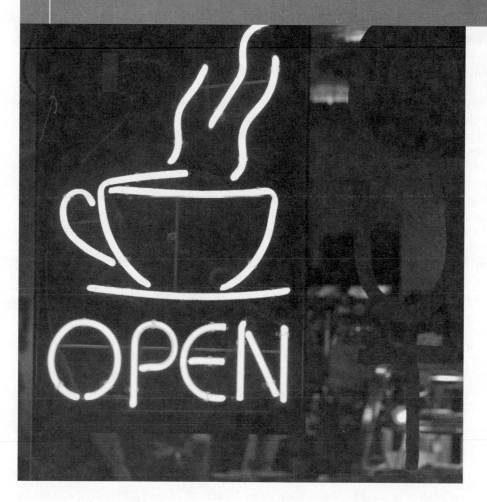

The more alternatives, the more difficult the choice.

—Abbe' D'Allanival

Choices are the hinges of destiny.

—Pythagoras

Learning Objectives

Upon completion of this chapter, you will be able to:

1 Explain the stages in the location decision.

2 Describe the location criteria for retail and service businesses.

3 Outline the basic location options for retail and service businesses.

4 Explain the site selection process for manufacturers.

5 Discuss the benefits of locating a start-up company in a business incubator.

6 Describe the criteria used to analyze the layout and design considerations of a building, including the Americans with Disabilities Act.

7 Explain the principles of effective layouts for retailers, service businesses, and manufacturers.

From Chapter 16 of *Effective Small Business Management: An Entrepreneurial Approach*, 10/e. Norman M. Scarborough.

1. Explain the stages in the location decision.

Few decisions that entrepreneurs make have as lasting and as dramatic an impact on their businesses as the choice of a location. Entrepreneurs who choose their locations wisely—with their customers' preferences and their companies' needs in mind—can establish an important competitive advantage over rivals who choose their locations haphazardly. Because the availability of qualified workers, tax rates, infrastructure, traffic patterns, quality of life, and many other factors vary from one site to another, the location decision is an important one that influences the growth rate and the ultimate success of a company. Thanks to widespread digital connectivity, mobile computing, extensive cellular coverage, and affordable air travel, entrepreneurs have more flexibility when choosing a business location than ever before.

The characteristics that make for an ideal location often vary dramatically from one company to another due to the nature of their business. In the early twentieth century, companies looked for ready supplies of water, raw materials, or access to railroads. For instance, West Virginia once was home to a thriving glassmaking industry because it provided entrepreneurs with ample supplies of quality sand (a key raw material), natural gas for heating glass furnaces, and inexpensive river transportation to get finished products to market.[1] Today, businesses are more likely to look for sites that are close to universities and offer high-speed Internet access and accessible interstate highways and airports. In fact, one study concluded that the factors that made an area most suitable for starting and growing small companies included access to dynamic universities, an ample supply of skilled workers, a nearby airport, a temperate climate, and a high quality of life.[2]

The key to finding a suitable location is identifying the characteristics that can give a company a competitive edge and then searching out potential sites that meet those criteria. For example, businesses that depend on face-to-face contact with customers must identify locations that attract high volumes of well-qualified walk-in customers. Although online sales continue to increase steadily, brick-and-mortar stores still dominate consumer sales, accounting for 93 percent of all retail sales.[3] One reason for the staying power of physical locations is the appeal of their real-world presence. An inviting physical location enables people to touch, feel, and experience the products and services a business offers. Potential buyers can pick up merchandise, try it on, and compare it side-by-side with other items. An optimal location also provides a gathering place where people can share experiences and one-on-one exchanges. The ability to look someone in the eye and ask questions or watch a demonstration appeals to human nature and provides a powerful sales tool for the business. Investing time in collecting and analyzing the data relevant to choosing a location pays off in increased customer traffic, higher sales, and greater efficiencies.

ENTREPRENEURIAL
Profile

Tony and John Calamunci: Johnny's Lunch

When Tony and John Calamunci began selling franchises based on the family-owned diner that their grandfather, Johnny Colera, started in Jamestown, New York, in 1936 (and that their parents still operate), they realized that opening outlets in areas in which large concentrations of their target customers lived was essential to their success. They hired an experienced franchise veteran, George Goulson, and worked with Pitney-Bowes' MapInfo to use the latest geospatial technology to determine the ideal locations for their restaurants, which sell budget-priced meals such as hot dogs, hamburgers, onion rings, and milkshakes. The Calamuncis started by defining their target customers, which they discovered includes people in the lower-middle to upper-middle income bracket who fall between the ages of 16 and 24 or over 60. Using the MapInfo software, they identified 72 types of neighborhoods that best matched the demographic and psychographic profile of Johnny's Lunch customers. The next step was to find locations that matched the 72 prototype neighborhoods. They identified 4,500 areas across the United States that held large concentrations of potential Johnny's Lunch customers (most of whom lived within 1 mile of the proposed location) and would be good locations for restaurants. "These models increase our ability to pick 'home-run' locations and avoid the site mistakes that can cripple a budding franchise," says Goulson. Johnny's Lunch is launching its franchising effort in and around Toledo, Ohio, which Goulson says is a microcosm of the United States. "Small restaurant owners like us can use location intelligence to prevent mistakes that could cripple franchising plans from the start. They can't afford not to invest in location intelligence."[4]

The location decision process resembles an inverted pyramid. The first level of the decision is the broadest, requiring an entrepreneur to select a particular region of the country. Then an entrepreneur must select the right state, then the right city, and, finally, the right site within the city (see Figure 1). The "secret" to selecting the ideal location lies in knowing the factors that are most important to a company's success and then finding a location that satisfies as many of them as possible, particularly those that are most critical. For instance, one of the most important location factors for high-tech companies is the availability of a skilled labor force, and their choice of location reflects this. If physically locating near customers is vital to a company's success, an entrepreneur's goal is to find a site that makes it most convenient for his or her target customers to do business with the company!

Selecting the Region

The first step in selecting the best location is to focus on selecting the right region. This requires entrepreneurs to look at the location decision from the "30,000-foot level," as if he or she were in an airplane looking down. In fact, in the early days of their companies, Sam Walton, founder of retail giant Walmart, and Ray Kroc, who built McDonald's into a fast-food legend, actually used private planes to survey the countryside for prime locations for their stores.

Which region of the country has the characteristics necessary for a new business to succeed? Above all, entrepreneurs must place their customers first when considering a location. As the experience of Johnny's Lunch suggests, facts and statistics, not speculation, lead entrepreneurs to the best locations for their businesses. Common requirements may include rapid growth in the

FIGURE 1
The Location Decision

Source: From Dale M. Lewison and M. Wayne DeLozier, *Retailing* (Columbus, OH: Merrill/Macmillan Publishing, 1984), p. 341.

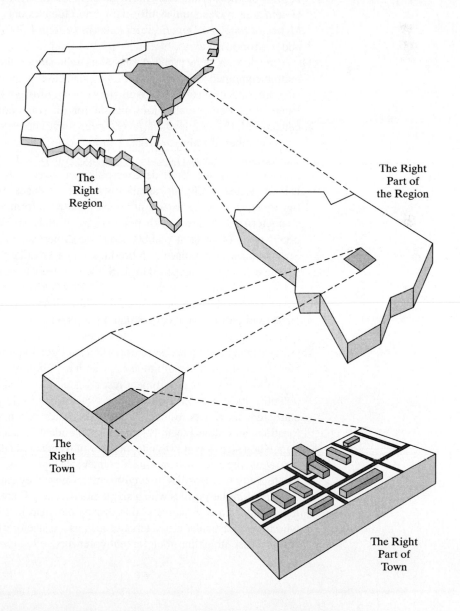

The Right Region

The Right Part of the Region

The Right Town

The Right Part of Town

population of a certain age group, rising disposable incomes, the existence of necessary infrastructure, a nonunion environment, and low costs. At the broadest level of the location decision, entrepreneurs prefer to locate in regions of the country that are experiencing substantial growth. Every year many popular business publications prepare reports on the various regions of the nation—which ones are growing, which are stagnant, and which are declining. Studying shifts in population and industrial growth gives entrepreneurs an idea of where the action is—and isn't. Questions to consider include: How large is the population? How fast is it growing? What is the makeup of the overall population? Which segments are growing fastest? Slowest? What is the trend in the population's income? Is it increasing or decreasing? Are other businesses moving into the region? If so, what kinds of businesses? Generally, entrepreneurs want to avoid dying regions; they simply cannot support a broad base of potential customers. A small company's customers are the people, businesses, and industries in an area, and if it is to be successful it must choose a location that is convenient to its customers.

One of the first stops entrepreneurs should make when conducting a regional evaluation is the U.S. Census Bureau. It provides a number of excellent sources of basic demographic and population data, including the *U.S. Statistical Abstract* and the *County and City Data Book*. The *U.S. Statistical Abstract* provides entrepreneurs looking for the right location with a multitude of helpful information, from basic population characteristics and projections to poverty rates and energy consumption. Each state also publishes its own statistical abstract, which provides the same type of data for its own population. The *County and City Data Book* contains useful statistics on the populations of all of the nation's 3,142 counties and 12,175 cities with populations of 25,000 or more (and even more data for cities with populations that exceed 100,000). *USA Counties* provides similar information and focuses only on the nation's counties. The *State and Metropolitan Area Data Book* includes more than 1,500 data items for individual states, counties, and metropolitan areas.

In addition to the print versions of its publications, the Census Bureau makes most of the information contained in its vast and valuable databases available to entrepreneurs researching potential sites through its easy-to-use Web site (*www.census.gov*). Entrepreneurs can use this Web site to locate vital demographic information for different potential locations, such as age, income, education level, employment level, occupation, ancestry, commuting times, housing data (house value, number of rooms, mortgage or rent status, number of vehicles owned, and so on), and many other characteristics. The Census Bureau's American FactFinder site (*http://factfinder.census.gov*) provides easily accessible demographic fact sheets and maps on nearly every community in the United States, including small towns. The Census Bureau's American Community Survey (*www.census.gov/acs/www/*) provides detailed information on the demographic and economic characteristics of areas with populations of at least 250,000 and of other selected areas with populations of at least 65,000. Both the American FactFinder and the American Community Survey allow entrepreneurs to produce easy-to-read, customizable maps of the information they generate in their searches. The U.S. Census Bureau also offers the Zip Code Tabulation Areas (ZCTA) Web site (*www.census.gov/geo/ZCTA/zcta.html*), which organizes the wealth of census data by zip code. The database of 33,178 ZCTAs across the United States allows users to create tables and plot maps of census data by zip code. With a little practice, entrepreneurs can prepare customized reports on the potential sites they are considering. These Web-based resources give entrepreneurs instant access to important site-location information that only a few years ago would have taken many hours of intense research to compile!

A variety of nongovernment resources also are available that can help entrepreneurs research potential locations. ZoomProspector (*www.zoomprospector.com*) is a useful Web site that gives entrepreneurs access to much of the same information that large companies use when selecting locations and allows them to search for the ideal location using a multitude of factors, including population size, job growth rate, number of patents issued, venture capital invested, education level, household incomes, and proximity to interstate highways, railroads, and airports. Once entrepreneurs locate a city that matches their customer profiles, they can find other cities across the United States that have similar profiles with a single mouse click. Entrepreneurs who are considering a particular region can create "heat maps" that display the areas that have the highest concentrations of people who have a particular characteristic, such as a bachelor's degree or the highest household incomes. Another useful online tool for entrepreneurs, ePodunk (*www.epodunk.com*), provides in-depth census-based information on more than 46,000 towns and cities of all sizes around the United States. ZIPskinny (*www.zipskinny.com*) is a Web site that provides census profiles and comparison communities using zip codes.

ENTREPRENEURIAL
Profile
Sharon Chan: Laurus Construction

Laurus Construction, a company in Costa Mesa, California, that builds and renovates commercial and residential buildings, uses ZoomProspector to identify potential new markets to enter. Managers use profiles of existing towns where the company has had success to spot other towns with similar characteristics. "I'm able to figure out which communities to rule out and which to pursue," says Vice President Sharon Chan. "It's almost like having a marketing company on tap."[5]

The Population Reference Bureau (*www.prb.org*) provides a detailed breakdown of the most relevant data collected from the most recent census reports. Its DataFinder database includes 244 variables for the United States and 132 variables for 210 other nations. The site also includes helpful articles that discuss the implications of the changing demographic and economic profile of the nation's (and the world's) population, such as the impact of aging baby boomers on business and the composition of the U.S. workforce.

Other helpful resources merit mention as well. *Demographics USA* is a useful publication that provides market surveys on various U.S. demographic segments. It provides information on demographic groups' purchasing power, retail sales by type of merchandise, employment and payroll data, and forecasts of economic conditions at both the zip code and the county level. The buying power indices in *Demographics USA* indicate an area's purchasing potential for economy products, mid-priced products, and premium products. It also reports consumers' spending on particular types of products and services, such as apparel, entertainment, and appliances. Entrepreneurs can use *Demographics USA* to analyze the level of competition in a particular area, assess the sales potential of a particular location, compare consumers' buying power across a dozen categories, and more.

Lifestyle Market Analyst, a four-part annual publication, matches population demographics with lifestyle interests. Section 1 provides demographics and lifestyle information for 210 "Designated Market Areas" across the United States. Section 2 gives demographic and geographic profiles of 77 lifestyle interests that range from avid readers and dieters to wine aficionados and pet owners. Section 3 describes the dominant lifestyle interests for each of the 210 market areas. Section 4 provides comparisons of other activities that correspond with each lifestyle interest. Entrepreneurs can use *Lifestyle Market Analyst* to determine, for example, how likely members of a particular market segment are to own a dog, collect antiques, play golf, own a vacation home, engage in extreme sports, invest in stocks or bonds, or participate in a host of other activities.

Other sources of demographic data include the *Survey of Buying Power*, the *Editor and Publisher Market Guide*, *The American Marketplace: Demographics and Spending Patterns*, *Rand McNally's Commercial Atlas and Marketing Guide*, and *Site Selection* magazine. The *Survey of Buying Power*, having recently undergone the most extensive overhaul in its 80-year history, provides statistics, rankings, and projections for every county and media market in the United States, with demographic groups segmented by age, race, city, county, and state. This publication, now available only online (*www.surveyofbuyingpower.com*), also includes current information on retail spending and forecasts for each spending category. The data are divided into 323 metro markets, as defined by the Census Bureau, and 210 media markets, which are television or broadcast markets defined by Nielsen Media Research. The *Survey* also includes several unique statistics. Effective buying income (EBI) is a measure of disposable income, and the buying power index (BPI), for which the *Survey* is best known, is a unique measure of spending power that takes population, EBI, and retail sales into account to determine a market's ability to buy goods and services.

The *Editor and Publisher Market Guide* is similar to the *Survey of Buying Power* but provides additional information on markets. The *Editor and Publisher Market Guide* includes detailed economic and demographic information, ranging from population and income statistics to information on climate and transportation networks for all 3,096 counties in the United States and more than 1,600 key cities in both the United States and Canada.

The American Marketplace: Demographics and Spending Patterns provides useful demographic information in eight areas: education, health, income, labor force, living arrangements, population, race and ethnicity, and spending and wealth. Most of the tables in the text are derived from government statistics, but *The American Marketplace* also includes a discussion of the data in each table as well as a forecast of future trends. Many users say the primary advantage of *The American Marketplace* is its ease of use.

The *Commercial Atlas and Marketing Guide* provides data on more than 120,000 places in the United States, many of which are not available through Census reports. This guide, which includes two volumes, one an index and the other the actual guide, provides 11 economic indicators for every major geographic market; tables showing population trends, income, buying power, trade, and manufacturing activity; and large cross-reference maps. Its format makes it easy to collect large amounts of valuable data on any region in the country (and specific areas within a region).

Site Selection magazine (*www.siteselection.com*) is another useful resource that helps entrepreneurs determine the ideal location for their companies. Issues contain articles that summarize incentive programs offered by various states, profiles of each region of the country, and the benefits of locating in different states.

The task of analyzing various potential locations—gathering and synthesizing data on a wide variety of demographic and geographic variables—is one ideally suited for a computer. In fact, a growing number of entrepreneurs are relying on geographic information systems (GIS), powerful software programs that combine map drawing with databases, to pinpoint the ideal location for their businesses. GIS packages allow users to search through virtually any database and plot the results on a map of the country, an individual state, a specific city, or even a single city block. The visual display highlights what otherwise would be indiscernible business trends. For instance, entrepreneurs can use GIS software to plot their existing customer base on a map with colors representing the different population densities. Then they can zoom in on those areas with the greatest concentration of customers, mapping a detailed view of zip code borders or even city streets. GIS street files originate in the U.S. Census Department's TIGER (Topographically Integrated Geographic Encoding Referencing) file, which contains map information broken down for every square foot of each Metropolitan Statistical Area (MSA). TIGER files contain the name and location of every street in the country and detailed block statistics for the 345 largest urban areas. In essence, TIGER is a massive database of geographic features such as roads, railways, and political boundaries across the entire United States that, when linked with mapping programs and demographic databases, gives entrepreneurs incredible power to pinpoint existing and potential customers on easy-to-read digital maps. Many states and counties across the United States now provide GIS files online that allow entrepreneurs to identify sites that meet certain location criteria for their businesses.

The Small Business Administration's Small Business Development Center (SBDC) program also offers location analysis assistance to entrepreneurs. These centers, numbering more than 1,100 nationwide, provide training, counseling, research, and other specialized assistance to entrepreneurs and existing business owners on a wide variety of subjects—all at no charge! (To locate the SBDC nearest you, contact the SBA office in your state or go to the SBA's Small Business Development Center locator page at *www.sba.gov/aboutsba/sbaprograms/sbdc/sbdclocator/SBDC_ LOCATOR.html*.)

For entrepreneurs interested in demographic and statistical profiles of international cities, Euromonitor International (*www.euromonitor.com*) and the Organization for Economic Development and Cooperation (OECD; *www.oecd.org*) are excellent resources.

Once an entrepreneur has identified the best region of the country, the next step is to evaluate the individual states in that region.

Selecting the State

Every state has an economic development office to recruit new businesses. Even though the publications produced by these offices will be biased in favor of locating in that state, they still are excellent sources of information and can help entrepreneurs assess the business climate in each state. Some of the key issues to explore include the laws, regulations, and taxes that govern businesses and incentives or investment credits the state may offer to businesses locating there. Table 1 shows the Small Business and Entrepreneurship Council's list of the most friendly and

TABLE 1 Most and Least Friendly States for Small Businesses

States Most Friendly to Small Businesses	States Least Friendly to Small Businesses
1. South Dakota	42. Hawaii
2. Nevada	43. Minnesota
3. Texas	44. Massachusetts
4. Wyoming	45. Rhode Island
5. Washington	46. Maine
6. Florida	47. Vermont
7. South Carolina	48. New York
8. Colorado	49. California
9. Alabama	50. New Jersey
10. Virginia	51. District of Columbia

Source: Raymond J. Keating, *Small Business Survival Index 2009: Ranking the Policy Environment for Entrepreneurship Across the Nation*, 14th Annual Edition, Small Business and Entrepreneurship Council, Oakton, Virginia, December 2009, p. 22.

least friendly states for small businesses, a ranking that evaluates 36 factors, including a variety of taxes, health care costs, regulatory costs, and others.

Other factors to consider when selecting a location include proximity to markets, proximity to raw materials, wage rates, quantity and quality of the labor supply, general business climate, and tax rates.

PROXIMITY TO MARKETS. Locating close to the markets they plan to serve is critical to manufacturers, especially when the cost of transporting finished goods is high relative to their value. Locations near customers offer a competitive advantage. Service firms often find that proximity to their clients is essential. If a business is involved in repairing equipment used in a specific industry, it should be located where that industry is concentrated. The more specialized a business, or the greater the relative cost of transporting the product to the customer, the more likely it is that proximity to the market will be of importance in the location decision.

ENTREPRENEURIAL **Profile** *IKEA*	IKEA, a Swedish maker of stylish, low-priced furniture with more than 300 stores in 35 countries (including 38 in the United States), recently opened its first U.S. manufacturing plant in Danville, Virginia, a location that gives the company convenient and inexpensive access to its distribution centers in Georgia, Maryland, and New Jersey and to its U.S. customers. Until IKEA opened the factory in Danville, the company had to ship goods to the United States from factories in Eastern Europe, which wiped out the cost advantages of operating factories in low-cost areas. "This kind of lightweight furniture is cheap to make, and transportation is a huge part of the overall cost," says one top manager.[6]

PROXIMITY TO NEEDED RAW MATERIALS. A business that requires raw materials that are difficult or expensive to transport may need a location near the source of those raw materials. For example, fish-process plants benefit from locating close to ports. Some companies locate close to the source of raw materials because of the cost of transporting heavy low-value materials over long distances. The Oil-Dri Corporation of America, founded by Nick Jaffe during the Great Depression, has two factories that make its Cat's Pride brand kitty litter located near major deposits of fuller's earth, the material from which the product is made.[7] For products in which bulk or weight is not a factor, locating close to suppliers can facilitate quick deliveries and reduce inventory-holding costs. The value of products and materials, their cost of transportation, and their unique functions interact to determine how close a business must be to its sources of supply.

WAGE RATES. Existing and anticipated wage rates provide another measure for comparison among states. Wages can sometimes vary from one state or region to another, significantly affecting a company's cost of doing business. For instance, according to the Bureau of Labor Statistics, the average hourly compensation for workers (including wages and benefits) ranges from a low of $24.72 in the South to a high of $32.13 in the Northeast.[8] Wage rate differentials within geographic regions can be even more drastic. When reviewing wage rates, entrepreneurs must be sure to measure the wage rates for jobs that relate to their particular industries or companies. In addition to surveys by the Bureau of Labor Statistics (*www.bls.gov*), local newspaper ads can give entrepreneurs an idea of the pay scale in an area. In addition, entrepreneurs can obtain the latest wage and salary surveys with an e-mail or telephone call to the local chambers of commerce for cities in the region under consideration. Entrepreneurs should study not only prevailing wage rates but also *trends* in rates. How does the rate of increase in wage rates compare to those in other states? Another factor influencing wage rates is the level of union activity in a state. How much union organizing activity has the state seen within the last 2 years? Is it increasing or decreasing? Which industries have unions targeted in the recent past?

LABOR SUPPLY. Business owners should know how many qualified people are available in the area to do the work required in the business. Some states attempt to attract industry with the promise of cheap labor. Unfortunately, businesses locating in those states may find unskilled, low-wage laborers who can be difficult to train. The size of an area's labor pool and the education, skills, and ability of its members determine a company's ability to fill jobs with qualified workers at reasonable wages. "The single biggest reason why anyone is moving companies is access to talent," says Tim Nitti, co-owner of location strategy company KLG.[9]

Knowing the exact nature of the labor needed and preparing job descriptions and job specifications in advance helps business owners determine whether there is a good match between their companies and the available labor pool. Checking educational statistics in the state to determine the number of graduates in relevant fields of study provides an idea of the local supply of qualified workers. This type of planning results in entrepreneurs finding locations with a steady source of quality workers.

ENTREPRENEURIAL
Profile
Tarran Pitschka: Wicked Quick

The idea for Tarran Pitschka's clothing line, Wicked Quick, came to him while he was standing between two funny cars at the starting line at the Pomona Speedway in California, but he chose to locate his company in Portland, Oregon. One of the principal reasons for Pitschka choosing Portland is the city's pool of talent. "This is one of the central spots in the world to draw on talent for the apparel business," he says. "There are so many creative people. I can get anything I want designed and made."[10]

Economists have long known that businesses thrive when they congregate in one place. "Companies that operate in clusters have greater access to talent," explains Jeffrey Grogan, partner at the Monitor Group, a Boston strategy consulting firm. They also serve as fertile ground for start-ups. For instance, North Carolina's Research Triangle, an area defined by the surrounding communities of Raleigh, Durham, and Chapel Hill, has become a Mecca for companies in high-tech industries, such as computer software, semiconductors, communications, pharmaceuticals, and biotech, because of the area's pool of highly skilled labor. Major colleges such as Duke University, the University of North Carolina, and North Carolina State University funnel talented graduates trained in fields such as virtual reality and market research into local companies. The resulting cluster of high-tech companies also leads to many business start-ups as employees leave to start their own companies, creating a hotbed of entrepreneurial activity.

BUSINESS CLIMATE. Assessing the business climate provides important information about the environment. What is the state's overall attitude toward this type of business? Has the state passed laws that impose restrictions on the way a company can operate? Does the state impose a corporate income tax? Is there an inventory tax? Does the state offer small business support programs or financial assistance to entrepreneurs? Some states have created environments that are "entrepreneur-friendly" based on these factors.

John and Tullaya Akins, owners of the Bangkok Cuisine Thai Restaurant in Sandpoint, Idaho, wanted to open a second Asian-themed restaurant. The copreneurs had selected a brick building in Sandpoint's downtown district that had housed a bicycle shop but changed their minds when they learned that the city would impose an impact fee (to tap into the city's water and sewer systems and to cover fire and police protection) of $26,000 to convert the building into a 45-seat restaurant. "That's make or break for us," says John. "We are shopping for a location in Ponderay (a nearby town with minimal impact fees) and the surrounding area that is more business friendly. It's too bad. We love this community."[11]

TAX RATES. Another important factor entrepreneurs must consider is the tax burden states impose on businesses and individuals. Income taxes may be the most obvious tax states impose on both business and individual residents, but entrepreneurs also must evaluate the impact of payroll taxes, sales taxes, property taxes, and specialized taxes on the cost of their operations. Currently, seven states impose no income tax on their residents, but state governments always impose taxes of some sort on businesses and individuals.[12] In some cases, states offer special tax rates or are willing to negotiate fees in lieu of taxes for companies that create jobs and stimulate the local economy.

When professional basketball player and entrepreneur LeBron James left the Cleveland Cavaliers to join the Miami Heat, many factors influenced the decision, including the states' tax rates. James owns several businesses, including LRMR Marketing, a sports marketing company, and King James Inc., the company that manages James' endorsements (which at $200 million to date outweigh his NBA earnings of $68 million). King James Inc. generates $28 million a year in endorsement revenue, and because Florida imposes no income tax James saves at least $1.8 million annually on his business income alone![13]

Source: Johnny Louis/Newscom

INTERNET ACCESS. Fast and reliable Internet access is another important factor in the location decision. Internet access through cable, DSL, or T1 lines is essential for high-tech companies and those engaging in e-commerce. Even those companies that may not do business over the Web use the Internet as a daily business tool for e-mail and information access. Companies that fall behind in high-tech communications soon find themselves at a severe competitive disadvantage.

TOTAL OPERATING COSTS. When scouting a state in which to locate a company, an entrepreneur must consider the total cost of operating a business there. For instance, a state may offer low utility rates, but its labor costs and tax rates may be among the highest in the nation. To select the ideal location, entrepreneurs must consider the impact of a state's total cost of operation on their business ventures. The state evaluation matrix in Table 2 provides a handy tool designed to help entrepreneurs determine which states best suit the most important location criteria for their companies. This same matrix can be adapted to analyze individual cities as well.

The next phase of the location selection process concentrates on selecting the best city.

TABLE 2 State Evaluation Matrix

Location Criterion	Weight 10 = High 1 = Low	Score 5 = High 1 = Low	State Weighted Score (Weight × Score) Florida	Georgia	South Carolina
Quality of labor force		1 2 3 4 5			
Wage rates		1 2 3 4 5			
Union activity		1 2 3 4 5			
Energy costs		1 2 3 4 5			
Tax burden		1 2 3 4 5			
Educational/training assistance		1 2 3 4 5			
Start-up incentives		1 2 3 4 5			
Quality of life		1 2 3 4 5			
Availability of raw materials		1 2 3 4 5			
Other		1 2 3 4 5			
Other		1 2 3 4 5			
Total score					

*Assign to each location criterion a weight that reflects its relative importance (10 high to 1 low). Then score each state on a scale of 1 (low) to 5 (high). Calculate the weighted score (weight × score) for each state. Finally, add up the total weighted score for each state. The state with the highest total weighted score is the best location for your business.

IN THE ENTREPRENEURIAL
SPOTLIGHT A Total Transformation

The sound of diners' muffled conversations and clinking silverware and plates reverberate through the Mission Restaurant in Syracuse, New York, but the sounds that once occupied this space once were quite different. For more than a century, visitors to this building were more likely to hear choirs singing hymns and pastors preaching sermons. The building that houses Steve Morrison's restaurant, which specializes in fresh Pan-American cuisine, was home to the Syracuse Wesleyan Methodist Church, which was built in the 1840s and was an important stop on the Underground Railroad that helped slaves escape to freedom in the northern United States and Canada from 1831 to 1863. Today the bustling restaurant serves fresh, homemade Mexican, Southwestern, and South American specialty dishes to customers in a unique setting that sets it apart from its competition.

Like Steve Morrison, some small business owners are establishing their businesses in locations that once served other purposes. Transforming a church into a restaurant poses some unique engineering and design challenges, but there are benefits as well, including using the building's history as part of the restaurant's marketing strategy. In 2007, real estate developer Dick Friedman purchased the Charles Street Jail in Boston, which was built in 1851 as a model of modern jail reform. Built in the shape of a cross with four wings extending from a central, octagonal rotunda that stands 90 feet tall, the granite structure was hidden by brick walls and barbed wire for many years until it closed in 1990. After a $150 million renovation, the building is now home to the luxurious Liberty Hotel. It is conveniently situated in Boston's Beacon Hill neighborhood, providing guests with easy access to the amenities of downtown Boston, including shopping, entertainment, and dining. Transforming a prison into a luxury hotel "is not for the faint of heart," says Friedman, "but I think it was worth it."

The plush hotel is a unique combination of historic preservation and contemporary design even though guest rooms, with their floor-to-ceiling windows, flat-screen TVs, private bars, and luxurious beds, have almost nothing in common with the former cells that occupied the building. Yet the designers made sure to retain small touches of the building's "jailness." "We kept a variety of the jail's original cell doors and bars," says architect Gary Johnson. Designers also kept a portion of one of the original catwalks in the rotunda. In addition to 300 guest rooms, including 10 luxury suites with views of the Charles River, the hotel is home to meeting rooms, a grand ballroom, a restaurant, and a bar. The bar, Alibi, is located in the portion of the jail where intoxicated arrestees spent time sobering up and includes fully restored cell blocks with original iron-bar doors and a beautiful blue stone floor. In the restaurant, Clink, waitstaff wear uniforms adorned with hand-stenciled inmate numbers. Rather than use "Do not disturb" signs, guests hang signs that say "Solitary" on their doors. The hotel has become a popular spot for visitors to Boston and generates annual sales of $40 million.

Mary Liz Curtin and Stephen Scannell opened their furniture and gift shop, Leon and Lulu LLC (the business is named after the couple's cat, Leon Redbone Johnson, and their 120-pound Rottweiler, Lulu), in a building that once was a popular roller skating rink and Motown concert venue in Clawson, Michigan. They purchased the building for $750,000 in 2005 and spent $225,000 on renovation, keeping its original flooring, benches, trophy cases, scoreboard and signs. "We get letters from people who thank us for keeping the history alive," says Curtin. On weekends and during special events, employees skate through the store's aisles, offering drinks and cookies to shoppers. The store, with its eclectic collection of merchandise, generates sales of $2 million per year.

1. What are the advantages and the disadvantages of transforming historic buildings, such as the ones described here, into new business locations?
2. Work with several of your classmates to select a historic building in your area and outline a plan for transforming it into a space that is suitable for a business (or businesses). How would you incorporate the building's history into the business's marketing plan?

Sources: Based on Sarah E. Needleman, "Entrepreneurs Make Use of Odd Spaces," *Wall Street Journal*, May 4, 2010, p. B5; Ann Coppola, "Lockdown Luxury," *Corrections*, September 24, 2007, *www.corrections.com/articles/16699-lockdown-luxury;* "About Us," Mission Restaurant, *www.themission restaurant.com;* "Quick Facts," Liberty Hotel, *www.libertyhotel.com/quick_facts/index.html;* "History," Leon and Lulu, *www.leonandlulu.com/history.*

The former Charles Street Jail is now the luxurious Liberty Hotel in downtown Boston.

Source: Michael Dwyer/Almay Images

The lobby of the Liberty Hotel retains some of the jail's original features and adds to the hotel's unique prison theme.

Source: CB2/ZOB/Newscom

Selecting the City

A company's location should match the market for its products or services, and assembling a demographic profile tells an entrepreneur how well a particular site measures up to his or her target market's profile. Entrepreneurs should consider a variety of factors when selecting a city.

ENTREPRENEURIAL
Profile

*Larry Reinstein:
Fresh City*

Fresh City, a Needham, Massachusetts-based chain of 16 fast-casual restaurants that features a fresh, healthy menu, considers the population density and the education and income levels of an area when scouting potential locations. "We find that the better educated the consumer is, the more apt they are to be our kind of guest," says CEO Larry Reinstein. Fresh City has located its restaurants in communities with high concentrations of well-educated, high-income people in and around Boston and plans to open restaurants in Herndon, Virginia, just outside of Washington, D.C., which recently was named one of the healthiest cities in the United States.[14]

POPULATION TRENDS. Analyzing over time the lists of "best cities for business" compiled annually by many magazines reveals one consistent trend: Successful small companies in a city tend to track a city's population growth. In other words, more potential customers means that a small business has a better chance of success. Detroit, Michigan, once home to a thriving automotive industry, has seen its population shrink from a peak of 1.85 million in 1950 to just 800,000 people. Vacant commercial and residential properties account for 40 square miles of the city's total area of 139 square miles. Since 1999, median household income has declined 25 percent, creating a difficult environment for entrepreneurs.[15] Seattle, Washington, in contrast, is home to a large and growing population of highly educated young people; 43 percent of the city's population is between the ages of 20 and 44, the prime time for entrepreneurial activity. The city's diverse high-tech sector, convenient access to some of the most beautiful natural areas anywhere, availability of venture capital, and concentration of top medical centers, colleges, and universities make it a magnet for entrepreneurs. In 1975, two young entrepreneurs, Bill Gates and Paul Allen, launched a company called Microsoft in Seattle, which one location expert describes as "a high-tech and lifestyle Mecca."[16]

An entrepreneur should know more about a city and its various neighborhoods than do the people who live there. By analyzing population trends and other demographic data, an entrepreneur can examine a city in detail, and the location decision becomes more than "a shot in the dark." Studying the characteristics of a city's residents, including population sizes and density, growth trends, family size, age breakdowns, education, income levels, job categories, gender, religion, race, and nationality, gives entrepreneurs the facts they need to make an informed location decision. For example, with basic census data, entrepreneurs can determine the value of the homes in an area, how many rooms they contain, how many bedrooms they contain, what percentage of the population owns their homes, and the amount residents' monthly rental or mortgage payments are. Imagine how useful such information would be to someone about to launch a home accessories store!

POPULATION DENSITY. The number of people per square mile can be another important factor in determining the optimal business location. In many of the older cities in the eastern United States, people live or work in very high-density areas. Businesses that depend on high traffic volume benefit by locating in high-density areas.

Knowing the population density within a few miles of a potential location gives entrepreneurs a clear picture of whether a city can support their businesses. It can also help them develop the appropriate marketing strategies to draw customers. Fitness club owners have discovered that population density is one of the most important factors in selecting a suitable location. Experience has taught them that customers are willing to drive or walk only so far to visit a fitness club. Information on population density and other important demographic characteristics is available from the publications mentioned earlier in this chapter and from market research companies.

COMPETITION. For some retailers locating near competitors makes sense because similar businesses located near one another may serve to increase traffic flow to both. This location strategy works well for products for which customers are most likely to comparison shop. For instance, in many cities, auto dealers locate next to one another in a "motor mile," trying to create a shopping magnet for customers. The convenience of being able to shop for dozens of brands of cars all within a few hundred yards of one another draws customers from a sizable trading area. Locating near competitors is a common strategy for restaurants as well. Of course, this strategy has limits. Overcrowding of businesses of the same type in an area can create an undesirable impact on the profitability of all competing firms.

Studying the size of the market for a product or service and the number of existing competitors helps an entrepreneur determine whether he or she can capture a sufficiently large market share to earn a profit. Again, census reports can be a valuable source of information. *County Business Patterns* gives a breakdown of businesses in manufacturing, wholesale, retail, and service categories and estimates companies' annual payrolls and number of employees broken down by county. *Zip Code Business Patterns* provides the same data as *County Business Patterns,* except it organizes the data by zip code. The *Economic Census*, which is produced for years that end in "2" and "7," gives an overview of the businesses in an area—their sales (or other measure of output), employment, payroll, and form of organization. It covers eight industry categories, including retail, wholesale, service, manufacturing, construction, and others, and provides statistics not only at the national level, but also by state, MSA, county, places with 2,500 or more inhabitants, and zip code. The *Economic Census* is a useful tool for helping entrepreneurs determine whether the areas they are considering as a location are already saturated with competitors.

CLUSTERING. Some cities have characteristics that attract certain industries, and, as a result, companies tend to cluster there. **Clusters** are geographic concentrations of interconnected companies, specialized suppliers, distribution networks, and service providers that are present in a region.[17] According to Harvard professor Michael Porter, clusters are important because they allow companies in them to increase their productivity and to gain a competitive edge. For instance, with its highly trained, well-educated, and technologically literate workforce, Austin, Texas, has become a draw for high-tech companies. Home to Dell Inc. and HP, Austin offers many small technology companies exactly what they need to succeed.

When the concentration of companies in a city reaches the tipping point, other businesses in those industries tend to spring up there as well. Once a symbol of declining manufacturing in the Rust Belt, Cleveland, Ohio, is now home to a cluster of biomedical companies that have banded together to form an organization called BioEnterprise. Anchored by a network of superb medical institutions, including the Cleveland Clinic, Case Western University, University Hospitals, and Summa Health Systems, the biomedical cluster provides a world-class knowledge base and access to venture capital. BioEnterprise has created or recruited more than 100 biomedical companies and has helped them land nearly $1 billion in financing.

ENTREPRENEURIAL
Profile
Jerry Silver: LucCell

Jerry Silver, president of LucCell, a small company that emerged from research at Case Western University, is counting on Cleveland's biomedical cluster to help it grow. LucCell is on the cutting edge of photogenetics, which uses light to change DNA, and already has raised $500,000 in start-up funding. The company's genetically engineered "bio-light switches" might someday trigger malfunctioning brain or spinal cord cells and revolutionize the treatment of disorders ranging from Parkinson's disease to paralysis.[18]

COMPATIBILITY WITH THE COMMUNITY. One of the intangibles that can be determined only by a visit to an area is the degree of compatibility a business has with the surrounding community. In other words, a small company's image must fit in with the character of a town and the needs and wants of its residents.

ENTREPRENEURIAL
Profile
Joe Masher: Bow Tie Cinemas

Bow Tie Cinemas, a fourth-generation family-owned business, recently opened a 17-screen multiplex theater in Richmond, Virginia, the largest theater complex the company has ever opened. When selecting locations for its theaters, Bow Tie looks for communities that are consistent with its image, which involves bringing style and elegance back to the theater experience and providing patrons with superb movie presentations and service. Chief operating officer Joe Masher says that the chain looks for cities with active arts, medical, and educational communities. "Richmond was a perfect storm for all three," he says.[19]

LOCAL LAWS AND REGULATIONS. Before selecting a particular site within a city, small business owners must explore the local zoning laws to determine whether there are any ordinances that would place restrictions on business activity or that would prohibit establishing a business altogether. **Zoning** is a system that divides a city or county into small cells or districts to control the use of land, buildings, and sites. Its purpose is to contain similar activities in suitable locations. For instance, one section of a city may be zoned industrial to house manufacturing operations, whereas another section may be zoned commercial for retail businesses. An entrepreneur must explore the zoning regulations to make sure the site qualifies. In addition to limiting the activities that can take place at a site, zoning also may control the hours of operation, parking requirements, noise limitations, and size of the businesses located there. In some cases, an entrepreneur may appeal to the local zoning commission to rezone a site or to grant a **variance,** a special exception to a zoning ordinance. This tactic is risky, potentially time consuming, and could be devastating if the board disallows the variance.

TRANSPORTATION NETWORKS. Manufacturers and wholesalers in particular must investigate the quality of local transportation systems. If a company receives raw materials or ships finished goods by rail, is a location with rail access available in the city under consideration? What kind of highway access is available? Are there any plans in the future for major construction that might impact the desired location? Will transportation costs be reasonable? Does the transportation infrastructure allow for efficient distribution? The availability of loading and unloading zones may be an important feature for a product-based business location.

POLICE AND FIRE PROTECTION. Does the community in which you plan to locate offer adequate police and fire protection? An absence of adequate police and fire protection will result in higher insurance costs and increased risks for the owner.

COST OF UTILITIES AND PUBLIC SERVICES. Some entity that provides water and sewer services, trash collection, and other utilities should serve the location. Streets should be in good repair with adequate drainage. Not having these services in place translates into higher costs for a business over time.

INCENTIVES. Some cities and counties offer financial and other incentives to encourage businesses that will create jobs to locate within their borders. These incentives range from job training for workers and reduced tax rates to financial grants and loans.

ENTREPRENEURIAL
Profile
Mitch Butler and Steven White: Image Vision Labs

Mitch Butler and Steven White launched their software company, Image Vision Labs, from a corner table in a Starbucks in Plano, Texas. When they were looking for a permanent location for their company, however, the business partners selected the nearby small town of Anna, where they were lured by a $110,000 economic development grant from the town (its first) and a low-interest $100,000 loan from a revolving loan program that Anna funded with a grant from the U.S. Department of Agriculture. Image Vision Labs, which uses artificial intelligence and visual-recognition technology to help companies block objectionable content from being viewed on their networks, already has hired 10 people from Anna, a town of fewer than 2,000 residents, most of whom traditionally have had to commute to other areas for work.[20]

QUALITY OF LIFE. A final consideration when selecting a city is the quality of life it offers. Entrepreneurs have the freedom and the flexibility to locate their companies in cities that suit not only their business needs but also their personal preferences. When choosing locations for their companies, entrepreneurs often consider factors such as cultural events, outdoor activities, entertainment opportunities, safety, and the city's "personality." Cities that offer comfortable weather, cultural events, colleges and universities, museums, outdoor activities, concerts, unique restaurants, and an interesting nightlife have become magnets for entrepreneurs looking to start companies. Cities such as Austin, Boston, Seattle, San Francisco, Washington, Dallas, Minneapolis, Portland, Boulder, and others have become incubators for creativity and entrepreneurship as educated young people drawn by the cities' quality of life have moved in.

ENTREPRENEURIAL
Profile
*Joshua Onysko:
Pangea Organics*

Joshua Onysko, founder of Pangea Organics, a company that markets a line of all-natural skin care products, had lived on the east coast and in Jackson Hole, Wyoming, but chose to locate his business in Boulder, Colorado. Personally, Onysko was attracted to the outdoor activities, including world-class ski slopes, available in Boulder. Professionally, he knew that the quality of life in Boulder and the nearby University of Colorado would allow him to attract the high-quality, skilled workforce that he needed to build his company. When he was ready to fill three new sales and marketing jobs, Onysko received more than 300 applications. Boulder also proved to be a business-friendly town with a strong entrepreneurial presence. Onysko credits his choice of location for playing a major role in Pangea's success; the company now generates annual sales of more than $7 million.[21]

Not only can a location in a city offering a high quality of life away from the workplace be attractive to an entrepreneur, but it also allows businesses to attract and retain a quality workforce. According to a study of the importance of location on recruiting employees conducted by the Human Capital Institute, the three most important factors in attracting talent are job opportunities, a clean and safe community, and an affordable cost of living.[22]

The Final Site Selection

Successful entrepreneurs develop a site evaluation system that is both detailed and methodical. Each type of business has different evaluation criteria, and experience has taught successful entrepreneurs to analyze the facts and figures behind each potential location in search of the best possible site. A manufacturer may need to consider access to customers, raw materials, suppliers, labor, and suitable transportation. Service firms need access to customers but can generally survive in lower-rent areas, whereas a retailer's prime consideration is customer traffic. The one element common to all three is the need to locate where customers want to do business.

The site location decision draws on the most precise information available on the makeup of the area. Using the sources of published statistics described earlier in this chapter, an entrepreneur can develop valuable insights regarding the characteristics of people and businesses in the immediate community. After narrowing the list of potential locations using statistics, entrepreneurs must visit each site for a firsthand view of its suitability. Many sites that look good "on paper" may be unsuitable because of other factors. On-site visits to potential locations are essential because they allow entrepreneurs to evaluate each site's intangible aspects.

Rental or lease rates are an important factor when choosing a site. The location with the lowest rental rate may not be the best deal, however. "Cheap" rental rates often indicate second-class locations (and the resulting poor revenues they generate). Of course, entrepreneurs must be sure that the rent or lease payments for a particular location fit comfortably into their companies' financial structure.

ENTREPRENEURIAL
Profile
Gino Circiello: Gino's

Gino's, an Italian restaurant that Gino Circiello opened on New York City's Lexington Avenue in 1945, proudly stuck to its mid-twentieth-century roots, much to the delight of its loyal customers. The restaurant, famous for its never-changing menu, moderate prices, and tomato-red wallpaper adorned with 314 leaping zebras, recently closed after the building's owner raised Gino's rent by $8,000 to more than $30,000 per month.[23]

Many businesses are downsizing their outlets to lower their start-up and operating costs and to allow for a greater number of location options that are not available to full-sized stores. Many quick-service restaurants are placing smaller, less expensive outlets in locations that cannot support a full-sized store and are finding that sales per square foot exceed those of traditional outlets.[24] Doughnut retailer Krispy Kreme is experimenting with its Neighborhood Shop and Kremery, small shops that are one-third the size of its regular "factory stores" that make and sell doughnuts on site. The smaller stores, which are located near factory stores that supply the doughnuts, allow the company to take its products to more customers by placing them in convenient locations that are not capable of housing a much larger traditional store. In a similar move,

Baskin-Robbins is using a similar concept called BR Express to set up shops in small spaces in airports and on college campuses.[25] Retailers and restaurateurs have discovered that these non-traditional locations can generate three to five times more traffic than locations in shopping centers and malls.

Finally, an entrepreneur must be careful to select a site that creates the right impression for a business in the customers' eyes. A company's location speaks volumes about a company's "personality."

IN THE ENTREPRENEURIAL

SPOTLIGHT We'll Bring Our Location to You

Joshua Henderson, a chef who once cooked at the Avalon Hotel in Beverly Hills, is one of the few entrepreneurs who does not worry about whether his restaurant's location is suitable. If he finds business to be too slow in one locale, he simply moves to another one in just minutes. Henderson is one of a growing number of restaurateurs who operate food trucks that travel to different locations in a city, set up shop, serve hungry customers, and move on. Once shunned as nothing more than lowly lunch trucks slinging second-rate hash and bland sandwiches, these mobile eateries are a far cry from their forebears, offering gourmet cuisine equivalent to that offered in Michelin-starred restaurants, but at far lower prices. Henderson, owner of Skillet Street Food, operates two trucks that serve about 200 lunches each per day, generating sales of $400,000 per year.

Articles in popular food magazines and television shows such as the Food Network's *The Great Food Truck Race* are feeding the food-truck trend. A sluggish economy that led customers to look for less expensive dining options also has played a role in the trucks' popularity. New York's popular Rickshaw Dumpling Truck, whose dumpling recipes were created by Anita Lo, chef at Manhattan's upscale Annisa in Greenwich Village, sells six duck dumplings with sauce for just $6.50. In San Francisco, a skewer of escargot in puff pastry sells for $2 at the Spencer on the Go truck operated by Laurent Katgley, who owns Chez Spencer, an upscale French restaurant. At Hudson's on the Bend, a wild game restaurant in Austin, Texas, the average check is $75. However, when owner and chef Jeff Blank rolled out his food truck, The Mighty Cone, he priced his menu so that the average check is less than $10. Although a struggling economy caused sales at Hudson's on the Bend to decline by 25 percent, sales at The Mighty Cone, which specializes in fried chicken, shrimp, and avocado coated with a mixture of almonds, sesame seeds, corn-flakes, and chili flakes, filled the gap and allowed Blank to hire extra staff.

Start-up costs for a mobile restaurant range from $20,000 to $160,000 (or more, depending on the truck's setup), far below the cost of opening a full-service restaurant in a fixed location, especially in a large city. Kenny Lao, owner of the Rickshaw Dumpling Bar in New York's Chelsea district, was looking for a location in midtown Manhattan in which to open a second dumpling restaurant but was discouraged by the high rental rates of $200 to $300 per square foot. Restaurant owners know that high rental rates increase their fixed costs, which, in turn, increase their break-even points and make it more difficult to earn a profit. Lao was not willing to take that risk and instead chose to spend $150,000 to outfit the Rickshaw Dumpling Truck.

Many food truck operators find that their mobile restaurants give them a great deal of flexibility. In addition to their regular lunch runs, restaurateurs can dispatch them to street fairs, community festivals, or the campuses of large businesses or even rent them out for weddings and private events. Paul Shenkman, owner of Sam's Chowder House near San Francisco, recently launched Sam's ChowderMobile. "With Sam's ChowderMobile, we can bring a 'mobile seafood shack' with outstanding food right to companies at their locations," says Shenkman. "We can even hold lobster clambakes right on the beach or at your home or office."

To market their mobile restaurants, entrepreneurs often turn to social media, such as Facebook and Twitter, sending out tweets to their followers announcing the trucks' locations, and on their Web sites. Kogi, a popular Korean barbecue restaurant in Culver City, California, operates four Kogi trucks and uses Twitter to alert more than 70,000 loyal customers to the day's specials and the trucks' locations and routes.

Ordinances, regulations, and zoning laws that govern the licensing and operation of food trucks vary significantly from one city to another and sometimes pose significant barriers to mobile restaurateurs. In Seattle, food vendors can park their trucks only on private property, but many other cities sell permits that allow them to park in most public parking spots. In Los Angeles, food vendors must pay an annual licensing fee of $695 and buy a permit for

$340. In addition, trucks that stop in one spot for more than 2 hours must demonstrate that customers have access to a restroom that meets safety codes. Sacramento's city ordinances make operating a mobile food truck impractical. Mobile food vendors cannot stay in one commercial area for more than 30 minutes and cannot operate after 6 P.M. from November to March. Randall Selland, owner of gourmet restaurants The Kitchen and Ella Dining Room and Bar, was inspired by mobile vendors at a street food festival in San Francisco to launch his own food truck. However, Sacramento's restrictive regulations have put his plans on hold. Portland, Oregon, in contrast, welcomes mobile food vendors and counts more than 200 of them in operation. Bo Kwon, owner of Koi Fusion PDX, a food truck that sells Korean tacos, spent $90,000 outfitting his truck. Kwon has been so successful that he plans to put a second one on the road and, eventually, open a restaurant. "With this economy, [food trucks] have become an outlet for a lot of chefs," he says.

1. What advantages do food trucks have over stationary restaurants? Disadvantages?
2. Do you think that a mobile food truck would be successful in your community? If so, what kind of food truck? Explain your reasoning.

Sources: Based on Katy McLaughlin, "Food Truck Nation," *Wall Street Journal*, June 5, 2009, pp. W1, W4; Lisa Jennings, "Vendors Drive Traffic but Rev Up Operator Aggression," *Nation's Restaurant News*, June 8, 2009, *www.nrn.com/article/vendors-drive-traffic-rev-operator-aggression*; Lisa Jennings, "ChowderMobile Joins Growing Fleet of Food Trucks," *Nation's Restaurant News*, June 17, 2009, *www.nrn.com/article/chowdermobile-joins-growing-fleet-food-trucks;* Chris Macias, "Sacramento Says No to Hot New Food Trend," *Sacramento Bee*, August 23, 2010, *www.sacbee.com/2010/08/23/2975917/sacramento-says-no-to-hot-new.html.*

Location Criteria for Retail and Service Businesses

2. Describe the location criteria for retail and service businesses.

Few decisions are as important for retailers and service firms than the choice of a location. Because their success depends on a steady flow of customers, these businesses must locate their businesses with their target customers' convenience and preferences in mind. This section presents some of the important location criteria for retail and service businesses.

Trade Area Size

Every retail and service business should determine the extent of its **trading area,** the region from which a business can expect to draw customers over a reasonable time span. The primary variables that influence the scope of the trading area are the type and the size of the business. If a retail store specializes in a particular product line and offers a wide selection and knowledgeable salespeople, it may draw customers from a great distance. In contrast, a convenience store with a general line of merchandise has a small trading area because it is unlikely that customers will drive across town to purchase items that are available within blocks of their homes or businesses. As a rule, the larger the store, the greater its selection, and the better its service, the broader is its trading area. Businesses that offer a narrow selection of products and services tend to have smaller trading areas. For instance, the majority of a massage therapist's clients live within 3 to 5 miles of the location, with a secondary tier of clients who live within 5 to 10 miles. Clients who are willing to travel more than 15 minutes for a session are rare.[26]

The following environmental factors also influence trading area size.

RETAIL COMPATIBILITY. Shoppers tend to be drawn to clusters of related businesses. That is one reason shopping malls, lifestyle centers, and outlet shopping centers are popular destinations for shoppers and are attractive locations for retailers. The concentration of businesses pulls customers from a larger trading area than a single free-standing business does. Retail compatibility describes the benefits a company receives by locating near other businesses selling complementary products and services. Clever retailers choose their locations with an eye on the surrounding mix of businesses. For instance, grocery store operators prefer not to locate in shopping centers with movie theaters, offices, and fitness centers, all businesses whose customers occupy parking spaces for extended time periods. Drugstores, nail salons, and ice cream parlors have proved to be much better shopping center neighbors for grocers.

DEGREE OF COMPETITION. The size, location, and activity of competing businesses also influence the size of the trading area. If a business will be the first of its kind in a location, its trading area might be extensive. However, if the area already has multiple stores nearby that are direct competitors, its trading area is diminished significantly. Market saturation is a problem for businesses in many industries, ranging from fast-food restaurants to convenience stores.

TRANSPORTATION NETWORK. The transportation networks are the highways, roads, and public service routes that presently exist or are planned. An inconvenient location reduces the business's trading area. Entrepreneurs should check to see whether the transportation system works smoothly and is free of barriers that might prevent customers from reaching their store. Is it easy for customers traveling in the opposite direction to cross traffic? Do signs and lights allow traffic to flow smoothly?

PHYSICAL, CULTURAL, OR EMOTIONAL BARRIERS. Physical barriers may be parks, rivers, lakes, or any other obstruction that hinders customers' access to the area. Locating on one side of a large park may reduce the number of customers who will drive around it to get to the store. In urban areas, new immigrants tend to cluster together, sharing a common culture and language. These trading areas are defined by cultural barriers, where inhabitants patronize only the businesses in their neighborhoods. The Little Havana section of Miami or the Chinatown sections of San Francisco, New York, and Los Angeles are examples. One powerful emotional barrier is safety. If high-crime areas exist around a site, potential customers may not travel through the area to reach the business. The leaders of many large cities are focusing their efforts on reducing crime and eliminating barriers to potential shoppers.

POLITICAL BARRIERS AND CREATIONS OF LAW. Political barriers are creations of law. County, city, or state boundaries—and the laws within those boundaries—are examples. State tax laws sometimes create conditions in which customers cross to border states to save money. For instance, North Carolina imposes one of the lowest cigarette taxes in the country, and shops located near the state line do a brisk business in the product selling to customers from bordering states.

Entrepreneurs should evaluate the characteristics of a trading area thoroughly; the matrix in Table 3 is a helpful tool for conducting an analysis. Once entrepreneurs rank each factor in relative importance and assign a score on the 1 to 5 scale, they simply multiply the two values to get a score for each characteristic. Adding up the scores produces a total score. (Higher is better.)

TABLE 3 Retail Trading Area Analysis

Characteristics	Relative Importance 1 = Low, 10 = High	Trading Area Score 1 = Major Disadvantage, 5 = Major Advantage	Area A	Area B
	1 2 3 4 5 6 7 8 9 10	1 2 3 4 5		
Population size and density				
Per capita disposable income				
Total disposable income				
Educational levels of the population				
Age distribution				
Number and size of existing competitors				
Strength of existing competitors				
Level of market saturation				
Population growth projections				
Ease of access				
Other:				
Total score				

Customer Traffic

Perhaps the most important screening criterion for a potential retail and a service location is the number of potential customers passing by the site during business hours. To be successful, a business must be able to generate sufficient sales to surpass its break-even point, and doing that requires an ample volume of traffic. One of the key success factors for a convenience store, for instance, is a high-traffic location with easy accessibility. Entrepreneurs should know the traffic counts (pedestrian and auto) at the sites they are considering. Shoeshine stands and kiosks in airports are examples of service businesses that benefit from the high volume of potential customers who pass by.

Adequate Parking

If customers cannot find convenient and safe parking, they are not likely to stop in the area. Many downtown areas have lost customers because of inadequate parking. Although shopping malls typically average 5 parking spaces per 1,000 square feet of shopping space, many central business districts get by with 3.5 spaces per 1,000 square feet. Customers generally will not pay to park if parking is free at shopping centers or in front of competing stores. Even when a business provides free parking, some potential customers may not feel safe on the streets, especially after dark. Many large city business districts become virtual ghost towns at the end of the business day. A location where traffic vanishes after 6 P.M. may not be as valuable as mall and shopping center locations that mark the beginning of the prime sales at 6 P.M.

Expansion Potential

A location should be flexible enough to provide for expansion if success warrants it. Failure to consider this factor can force a successful business to open a second store when it would have been more advantageous to expand at its original location.

Visibility

No matter what a retailer sells or how well it serves customers' needs, it cannot survive without visibility. Highly visible locations simply make it easy for customers to make purchases. A site lacking visibility puts a company at a major disadvantage before it even opens its doors. In a competitive marketplace, customers seldom wish to search for a business when equally attractive alternatives are easy to locate.

Some service businesses, however, can select sites with less visibility if the majority of their customer contacts are by telephone, fax, or the Internet. For example, customers usually contact plumbers by telephone; so rather than locating close to their customer bases, plumbers have flexibility in choosing their locations. Similarly, businesses that work at their customers' homes, such as swimming pool services, can operate from their homes and service vans.

The Index of Retail Saturation

The **index of retail saturation (IRS)** is a measure of the potential sales per square foot of store space for a given product within a specific trading area. This measure combines the number of customers in a trading area, their purchasing power, and the level of competition. The index is the ratio of a trading area's sales potential for a particular product or service to its sales capacity:

$$IRS = \frac{C \times RE}{RF}$$

where:

C = Number of customers in the trading area

RE = Retail expenditures (the average dollar expenditure per person for the product in the trading area)

RF = Retail facilities (the total square feet of selling space allocated to the product in the trading area)

This computation is an important one for any retailer to make. Locating in an area already saturated with competitors results in dismal sales volume and often leads to failure.

To illustrate the IRS, suppose that an entrepreneur looking at two sites for a sports store finds that he needs sales of $175 per square foot to be profitable. Site 1 has a trading area with 25,875 potential customers, each of whom spends an average of $42 on sports gear annually; the only competitor in the trading area has 6,000 square feet of selling space. Site 2 has 27,750 potential customers spending an average of $43.50 on sports gear annually; two competitors occupy 8,400 square feet of space. The IRS of site 1 is:

$$\text{IRS} = \frac{25{,}875 \times 42}{6{,}000}$$

$$= \$181.12 \text{ sales potential per square foot}$$

The IRS of site 2 is:

$$IRS = \frac{27{,}750 \times 43.50}{8{,}400}$$

$$= \$143.71 \text{ sales potential per square foot}$$

Although site 2 appears to be more favorable on the surface, site 1 is the better location according to the index; site 2 fails to meet the minimum standard of $175 per square foot.

Reilly's Law of Retail Gravitation

Reilly's Law of Retail Gravitation, a classic work in market analysis published in 1931 by William J. Reilly, uses the analogy of gravity to estimate the attractiveness of a particular business to potential customers. The ability to draw customers is directly related to the extent to which customers see it as a "destination" and is inversely related to the distance customers must travel to reach the business. Reilly's model also provides a way to estimate the trade boundary between two market areas by calculating the "break point" between them. The break point between two primary market areas is the boundary between the two where customers become indifferent about shopping at one or the other. The key factor in determining this point of indifference is the size of the communities. If two nearby cities have the same population sizes, then the break point lies halfway between them. The following is the equation for Reilly's Law:[27]

$$BP = \frac{d}{1 + \sqrt{P_b/P_a}}$$

where:

BP = Distance in miles from location A to the break point

d = Distance in miles between locations A and B

P_a = Population surrounding location A

P_b = Population surrounding location B

For example, if city A and city B are 22 miles apart, and city A has a population of 22,500 and city B has a population of 42,900, the break point, according to Reilly's law is:

$$BP = \frac{22}{1 + \sqrt{42{,}900/22{,}500}} = 9.2 \text{ miles}$$

The outer edge of city A's trading area lies about 9 miles between city A and city B. Although only a rough estimate, this simple calculation using readily available data can be useful for screening potential locations.

Location Options for Retail and Service Businesses

3. Outline the basic location options for retail and service businesses

Retail and service business owners can locate in seven basic areas: the central business district (CBD), neighborhoods, shopping centers and malls, near competitors, inside large retail stores, outlying areas, and at home. According to the International Council of Shopping Centers, the average cost to lease space in a shopping center is about $17 per square foot. At regional malls, lifestyle centers, and power centers, rental rates typically range from $20 to $25 per square foot. In central business locations, the average cost is between $35 and $45 per square foot (although rental rates can vary significantly in either direction of that average, depending upon the city).[28]

Central Business District

The **central business district (CBD)** is the traditional center of town—the downtown concentration of businesses established early in the development of most towns and cities. Entrepreneurs derive several advantages from a downtown location. Because businesses are centrally located, they attract customers from the entire trading area of the city. In addition, small businesses benefit from the traffic generated by other stores clustered in the downtown district. However, locating in a CBD does have certain disadvantages. Intense competition, high rental rates, traffic congestion, and inadequate parking facilities characterize some CBDs.

Beginning in the 1950s, many cities experienced difficulty in preventing the decay of their older downtown business districts as residents moved to the suburbs and began shopping at newer, more convenient shopping centers and malls. Today, however, many CBDs are experiencing rebirth as cities restore them to their former splendor and shoppers return. Many customers find irresistible the charming atmosphere that traditional downtown districts offer with their rich mix of stores, their unique architecture and streetscapes, and their historic character. Cities have begun to reverse the urban decay of their downtown business districts through proactive revitalization programs designed to attract visitors and residents alike to cultural events by locating major theaters and museums in the downtown area. In addition, many cities are providing economic incentives to real estate developers to build apartment and condominium complexes in the heart of the downtown area. Vitality is returning as residents live and shop in the once nearly abandoned downtown areas. The "ghost-town" image is being replaced by both younger and older residents who love the convenience and excitement of life at the center of the city.

ENTREPRENEURIAL Profile

Bill and Sam Cass: Nymbol's Secret Garden of Imagination

Bill Cass and his wife Sam left their jobs designing shoes for Nike and moved to Langley, a small town on Washington's Whidbey Island, where they opened Nymbol's Secret Garden of Imagination in the scenic town's central business district. The Casses decided to open their unique shop, which sells an array of puppets, costumes, masks, jewelry, and other unique items, after visiting Langley, known as Washington's "Most Beautiful Waterfront Town," on a family vacation. Their shop benefits from its location near other interesting retail stores that together draw impressive numbers of customers, particularly during the busy tourist season.[29]

Neighborhood Locations

Small businesses that locate near residential areas rely heavily on the local trading areas for business. For example, many grocers and convenience stores located just outside residential subdivisions count on local clients for successful operation. One study of food stores found that the majority of the typical grocers' customers live within a 5-mile radius. The primary advantages of a neighborhood location include relatively low operating costs and rents and close contact with customers.

Shopping Centers and Malls

Until the early twentieth century, central business districts were the primary shopping venues in the United States. As cars and transportation networks became more popular in the 1920s, shopping centers began popping up outside cities' central business districts. Then, in October 1956, the nation's first shopping mall, Southdale, opened in the Minneapolis, Minnesota, suburb of Edina. Designed by Victor Gruen, the fully enclosed mall featured 72 shops anchored by 2 competing department stores (a radical concept at the time), a garden courtyard with a goldfish pond, an aviary, hanging plants, and artificial trees. With its multilevel layout and parking garage, Southdale was a huge success and forever changed the way Americans would shop.[30] Today, shopping centers and malls are a mainstay of the American landscape. Because many different types of stores operate under one roof, shopping malls give meaning to the term "one-stop shopping." In a typical month, nearly 191 million adults visit malls or shopping centers, which generate $2.25 trillion in annual sales.[31]

There are eight types of shopping centers (see Table 4).

NEIGHBORHOOD SHOPPING CENTERS. The typical neighborhood shopping center is relatively small, containing from 3 to 12 stores and serving a population of up to 40,000 people who live within a 10-minute drive. The anchor store in these centers is usually a supermarket or a drugstore. Neighborhood shopping centers typically are straight-line strip malls with parking available in front and primarily serve the daily shopping needs of customers in the surrounding area.

COMMUNITY SHOPPING CENTERS. A community shopping center contains from 12 to 50 stores and serves a population ranging from 40,000 to 150,000 people. The leading tenant often is a large department or variety store, a super drugstore, or a supermarket. Community shopping centers sell more clothing and other soft goods than do neighborhood shopping centers. Of the eight types of shopping centers, community shopping centers take on the greatest variety of shapes, designs, and tenants.

POWER CENTERS. A power center combines the drawing strength of a large regional mall with the convenience of a neighborhood shopping center. Anchored by several large specialty retailers, such as warehouse clubs, discount department stores, or large specialty stores, these centers target older, wealthier baby boomers, who want selection and convenience. Anchor stores usually account for 80 percent of power center space, compared with 50 percent in the typical community shopping center. Just as in a shopping mall, small businesses can benefit from the traffic generated by anchor stores, but they must choose their locations carefully so that they are not overshadowed by their larger neighbors.

THEME OR FESTIVAL CENTERS. Festival shopping centers employ a unifying theme that individual stores display in their décor and sometimes in the merchandise they sell. Entertainment is a common theme for these shopping centers, which often target tourists. Many festival shopping centers are located in urban areas and are housed in older, sometimes historic, buildings that have been renovated to serve as shopping centers.

OUTLET CENTERS. As their name suggests, outlet centers feature manufacturers' and retailers' outlet stores selling name-brand goods at a discount. Unlike most other types of shopping centers, outlet centers typically have no anchor stores; the discounted merchandise they offer draws sufficient traffic. Most outlet centers are open-air and are laid out in strips or in clusters, creating small "villages" of shops.

LIFESTYLE (OR TOWN) CENTERS. Typically located near affluent residential neighborhoods where their target customers live, lifestyle centers are designed to look less like shopping centers and malls and more like the busy streets in the central business districts that existed in towns and cities in their heyday. Occupied by many upscale national chain specialty stores such as Talbot's, Pier 1 Imports, Jos. A. Bank Clothiers, and others, these centers combine shopping convenience and entertainment ranging from movie theaters and open-air concerts to art galleries and people-watching. "Lifestyle centers create a shopping-leisure destination that's an extension of customers' personal lifestyles," says one industry expert.[32] The typical lifestyle center generates between $400 and $500 in sales per square foot compared to $381 in sales per square foot in traditional malls.[33] Lifestyle centers are among the most popular types of shopping centers being built today. The first lifestyle center, The Shops of Saddle Creek, opened in Germantown, Tennessee, in 1987. Today, more than 400 lifestyle centers operate across the United States.[34]

REGIONAL SHOPPING MALLS. The regional shopping mall serves a large trading area, usually from 5 to 15 miles or more in all directions. These enclosed malls contain from 50 to 100 stores and serve a population of 150,000 or more living within a 20- to 40-minute drive. The anchor is typically one or more major department stores, with smaller specialty stores occupying the spaces between the anchors. Clothing is one of the popular items sold in regional shopping malls.

SUPER-REGIONAL SHOPPING MALLS. A super-regional mall is similar to a regional mall but is bigger, containing more anchor stores and a greater variety of shops selling deeper lines of merchandise. Its trade area stretches up to 25 or more miles. Canada's West Edmonton Mall, the largest mall in North America, with more than 800 stores and 100 restaurants, is one of the most famous super-regional malls in the world. In addition to its abundance of retail shops, the mall contains an ice skating rink, a water park, an amusement park, miniature golf courses, and a 21-screen movie complex.

When evaluating a mall or shopping center location, an entrepreneur should consider the following questions:

- Is there a good fit with other products and brands sold in the mall or center?
- Who are the other tenants? Which stores are the anchors that will bring people into the mall or center?

TABLE 4 Types of Shopping Centers

Type of Shopping Center	Concept	Square Footage (including anchors)	Acreage	Typical Anchor Number	Typical Anchor Type	Anchor Ratio (%)[a]	Primary Trade Area (miles)[b]
Malls							
Regional center	General and fashion merchandise; mall (typically enclosed)	480,000–800,000	40–100	2 or more	Full-line department store; junior department store; mass merchant; discount department store; fashion apparel	50–70	5–15
Super-regional center	Similar to regional center but offers more variety	>800,000	60–120	3 or more	Full-line department store; junior department store; mass merchant; fashion apparel	50–70	5–25
Open-Air Centers							
Neighborhood center	Convenience	30,000–150,000	3–15	1 or more	Supermarket	30–50	3
Community center	General merchandise; convenience	100,000–350,000	10–40	2 or more	Discount department store; supermarket; drugstore; home improvement store; large specialty or discount apparel retailer	40–60	3–6
Lifestyle center	Upscale national chain specialty stores, dining, and entertainment in an outdoor setting	150,000–500,000, but can be larger or smaller	10–40	0–2	Not usually anchored in the traditional sense, but may include bookstore; large specialty retailers; multiplex cinema; small department store	0–50	8–12
Power center	Category-dominant anchors; few small business tenants	250,000–600,000	25–80	3 or more	Category killer; home improvement store; discount department store; warehouse club; off-price retailer	75–90	5–10
Theme/festival center	Leisure; tourist-oriented; retail and service	80,000–250,000	5–20	Unspecified	Restaurants; entertainment	N/A	25–75
Outlet center	Manufacturers' outlet stores	50,000–400,000	10–50	N/A	Manufacturers' outlet stores	N/A	25–75

[a] The share of a center's total square footage that is occupied by its anchors.
[b] The area from which 60 to 80 percent of the center's sales originate.
Source: International Council of Shopping Centers, New York.

- Demographically, is the center a good fit for your products or services? What are its customer demographics?
- How much foot traffic does the mall or center generate? How much traffic passes the specific site you are considering?
- How much vehicle traffic does the mall or center generate? Check its proximity to major population centers, the volume of tourists it draws, and the volume of drive-by freeway traffic. A mall or center that scores well on all three is more likely to be a winner.
- What is the mall's vacancy rate? What is the turnover rate of its tenants?
- How much is the rent and how is it calculated? Most mall tenants pay a base amount of rent plus a small percentage of their sales above a specified level.
- Is the mall or center successful? How many dollars in sales does it generate per square foot? Compare its record against industry averages. The International Council of Shopping Centers (*www.icsc.org*) is a good source of industry information.

A mall location is no guarantee of business success, however. Malls have been under pressure lately, and many weaker ones (known as "greyfields") have closed or have been redeveloped. The basic problem is an oversupply of mall space; there is 22.5 square feet of mall retail space for every person in the United States! Another problem is that many malls are showing their age; in fact, 85 percent of the malls in the United States are more than 20 years old.[35] In addition, the demographic makeup of an area's shoppers often changes over time, creating a new socioeconomic customer base that may or may not be compatible with a small company's target customer profile. As a result, many malls have undergone extensive renovations to emphasize "entertailing," adding entertainment features to their existing retail space in an attempt to generate more traffic. For instance, in addition to its 520 retail shops and 60 restaurants, Minneapolis's Mall of America, the second largest mall in the United States (located only a few miles from Southdale, the nation's first mall), includes a Nickelodeon Universe amusement park at its center, a 1.2 million gallon aquarium, a flight simulator, and a 14-screen movie complex in its 4.2 million square feet of space.[36]

Source: www.CartoonStock.com

Near Competitors

One of the most important factors in choosing a retail or service location is the compatibility of nearby stores with the retail or service customer. For example, stores selling high-priced goods such as cars or merchandise that requires comparisons, such as antiques, find it advantageous to locate near competitors to facilitate comparison shopping. Locating near competitors might be a key factor for success in businesses that sell goods that customers compare on price, quality, color, and other factors.

Although some business owners avoid locations near direct competitors, others see locating near rivals as an advantage. For instance, restaurateurs know that successful restaurants attract other restaurants, which, in turn, attract more customers. Many cities have at least one "restaurant row," where restaurants cluster together; each restaurant feeds customers to the others.

Locating near competitors has its limits, however. Clustering too many businesses of a single type into a small area ultimately will erode their sales once the market reaches the saturation point. As the number of gourmet coffee shops has exploded in recent years, many have struggled to remain profitable, often competing with three or four similar shops, all within easy walking distance of one another. When an area becomes saturated with competitors, the stores cannibalize sales from one another, making it difficult for all to survive.

Inside Large Retail Stores

Rather than compete against giant retailers, some small business owners are cooperating with them, locating their businesses inside the larger company's stores. These small companies offer products that the large retailers do not and benefit from the large volume of customer traffic the large stores attract. The world's largest retailer, Walmart, is host to several small businesses, including franchisees of fast-food chains Subway and McDonald's and medical clinics and banks. These stores within a store reap the benefits of the large volume of traffic from the more than 200 million people who shop at Walmart each year.

Outlying Areas

Generally, it is not advisable for a small business to locate in a remote area because accessibility and traffic flow are vital to retail and service success, but there are exceptions. Some companies have transformed their remote locations into part of their identities. Cabela's, a chain of 30 sporting goods stores founded in 1961 by brothers Dick and Jim Cabela, has had great success with stores in rather remote locations such as Kearny, Nebraska, and Mitchell, South Dakota. The extensive breadth and depth of Cabela's product line and its reputation for "entertailing" give potential customers a compelling reason to travel to the stores.

An entrepreneur should consider the cost of a location (its rental or lease expense) in light of its visibility to potential customers. If a less expensive location is difficult for customers to find and has a low traffic count, a business located there will have to spend a disproportionate amount of money on promotion. Consequently, a superior, highly visible location may offer lower total operating cost because of the traffic it generates. Many customers do not want to go exploring to find a business and, consequently, never bother to try.

Home-Based Businesses

For more than 15 million entrepreneurs, home is where the business is, and their numbers are swelling. One recent study from the SBA reports that 52 percent of all small companies are home-based and that more than 21 percent of home-based businesses generate more than $100,000 in annual revenue.[37] Many service businesses operate from entrepreneurs' homes. Because many service companies do not rely on customers to come to their places of business, incurring the expense of an office location is unnecessary. For instance, customers typically contact plumbers or exterminators by telephone, and the work is performed in customers' homes. Web-based and catalog retailers also operate from their homes.

ENTREPRENEURIAL
Profile
Billy Carmen: Wizard Industries

When an economic downturn forced Billy Carmen to downsize his specialty tools company, Wizard Industries, he decided to eliminate the office-warehouse he had been renting in Los Angeles and run the business from his home. Carmen decided to move to Sebastopol, California, a town whose ordinances are friendly to home-based businesses, allowing him, for example, to put a business sign outside his home and have customers' packages picked up for delivery.[38]

Choosing a home location has disadvantages. It may affect family life, interruptions are more frequent, the refrigerator is all too handy, work is always just a few steps away, and isolation can be a problem. Another difficulty some home-based entrepreneurs face involves zoning laws. As their businesses grow and become more successful, entrepreneurs' neighbors often begin to complain about the increased traffic, noise, and disruptions from deliveries, employees, and customers who drive through their residential neighborhoods to conduct business. A judge recently ordered Jennifer Spiegel to close her business, Spiegel Farms, a wedding and event venue located on Spiegel's 62-acre farm in Campobello, South Carolina, after neighbors complained that operating the business violated the zoning regulations in their residential neighborhood. Spiegel had operated the business from her farm for nearly 9 years and had hosted more than 340 weddings.[39]

The Location Decision for Manufacturers

4. Explain the site selection process for manufacturers.

The criteria for the location decision for manufacturers are very different from those of retailers and service businesses; however, the decision can have just as much impact on the company's success. In some cases, a manufacturer has special needs that influence the choice of a location. When one manufacturer of photographic plates and film was searching for a location for a new plant, it had to limit its search to those sites with a large supply of available fresh water, a necessary part of its process. In other cases, zoning ordinances dictate a company's location decision. If a manufacturer's process creates offensive odors or excessive noise, it may be even further restricted in its choices.

The type of transportation facilities required dictates the location of a plant in some cases. Some manufacturers may need a location on a railroad siding, whereas others may need only access to interstate highways. Some companies ship bulk materials by ship or barge and consequently require a facility convenient to a navigable river or lake. The added cost of using multiple shipping methods (e.g., rail-to-truck or barge-to-truck) can significantly increase shipping costs and make a location unfeasible for a manufacturer. Because water is expensive to transport, companies that produce bottled water must choose their locations carefully. Ideally, a site is close to large markets but not so close that pollutants from major metropolitan areas diminish the quality of the water source. Companies must find springs that provide good-tasting water and enough space to build a bottling plant nearby.[40]

As fuel costs escalate, the cost of shipping finished products to customers also influences the location decision for many manufacturers, forcing them to open factories or warehouses in locations that are close to their primary markets to reduce transportation costs.

Quallion LLC, a maker of lithium-ion batteries, recently built a $220 million factory near Los Angeles, California, because it offers easy, low-cost access to shipping ports that serve its customers, many of whom are located in the Far East. "One reason for our success is our close proximity to the ports of Los Angeles and Long Beach for shipping products in high volume," says Quallion president Paul Beach. "We have lower costs of transportation." Despite the burdens imposed by high operating costs and extensive government regulation, Southern California provides other critical inputs that Quallion requires, including a highly skilled pool of workers from which to draw and access to other high-tech firms.[41]

In some cases the perishability of the product dictates location. Vegetables and fruits must be canned in close proximity to the fields from which they are harvested. Companies that process and can fish must find locations at the water's edge. The ideal location is determined by quick and easy access to the perishable products.

Foreign Trade Zones

Created in 1934, foreign trade zones can be an attractive location for small manufacturers that engage in global trade and are looking to reduce or eliminate the tariffs, duties, and excise taxes they pay on the materials and parts they import and the goods they export. A **foreign trade zone** (see Figure 2) is a specially designated area in or near a U.S. customs port of entry that allows

FIGURE 2
How a Foreign Trade Zone (FTZ) Works

resident companies to import materials and components from foreign countries; assemble, process, manufacture, or package them; and then ship the finished product back out while either deferring, reducing, or eliminating tariffs and duties. As far as tariffs and duties are concerned, a company located in a foreign trade zone is treated as if it is located outside the United States. For instance, a maker of speakers can import components from around the world and assemble them at its plant located in a foreign trade zone. The company pays no duties on the components it imports or on the speakers it exports to other foreign markets. The only duties the manufacturer pays are on the speakers it sells in the United States. There are 256 foreign trade zones and 498 subzones, which are special foreign trade zones that are established for limited purposes, operating in the United States. The value of shipments into foreign trade zones has increased from $147 billion in 1998 to nearly $700 billion today.[42]

Empowerment Zones

Originally created to encourage companies to locate in economically blighted areas, **empowerment zones** offer businesses tax breaks on the investments they make within zone boundaries. Companies can get federal tax credits, grants, and loans for hiring workers living in empowerment zones and for investments they make in plant and equipment in the zones. Empowerment zones operate in both urban and rural areas, ranging from Los Angeles, California, to Sumter, South Carolina. Boston, Massachusetts has a technology-oriented business incubator located within a federal empowerment zone called TechSpace, which provides high-potential start-up businesses with a full-service facility featuring completely integrated information technology and business services.

Business Incubators

5. Discuss the benefits of locating a start-up company in a business incubator.

For many start-up companies, a business incubator may make the ideal initial location. A **business incubator** is an organization that combines low-cost, flexible rental space with a multitude of support services for its small business residents. The primary reason that communities establish incubators is to enhance economic development, create jobs, and diversify the local economy. The strategy works; 84 percent of the companies that graduate from incubators stay in the local community.[43]

ENTREPRENEURIAL
Profile

TechTown

TechTown, an incubator established by Wayne State University in 2000 in what once was a former GM building in Detroit, Michigan (engineers designed the original Chevrolet Corvette on the third floor), is home to more than 160 innovative start-up companies, most of which are high-tech companies concentrated in four industries: alternative energy, medical technology, logistics, and the Internet. Clean Emissions Fluids (CEF), one of TechTown's residents, has developed a computer-controlled fueling station that dispenses the appropriate mixture of biofuels and petroleum products to maximize a vehicle's efficiency. CEF, founded by former auto industry engineers Oliver Baer, Chris Channell, and Terri Teller, recently set up a small manufacturing operation in TechTown's newest building and has space to grow into as its sales increase. The incubator also has hosted more than 1,500 people with entrepreneurial dreams, many of them former auto industry employees, in a 10-week business start-up training program called FasTrac that is sponsored by the Kauffman Foundation.[44]

An incubator's goal is to nurture young companies during the volatile start-up period and to help them survive until they are strong enough to go out on their own. Most incubators (54 percent) are "mixed-use," hosting a variety of start-up companies, followed by incubators that focus on technology companies (see Figure 3).[45] The shared resources incubators typically provide their tenants include secretarial services, a telephone system, computers and software, fax machines, meeting space, and, sometimes, management consulting services and access to financing. Not only do these services save young companies money, but they also save them valuable time. Entrepreneurs can focus on getting their products and services to market rather than searching for the resources they need to build their companies. Many business incubators help their tenants gain access to capital; a survey by the National Business Incubation Association reports that 83 percent of incubators provide some kind of access to seed capital, ranging from help with obtaining federal grants to making connections with angel investors.[46]

The typical incubator has entry requirements that prospective residents must meet. Incubators also have criteria that establish the conditions a business must maintain to remain in the facility as well as the expectations for "graduation" into the business community. The typical start-up that lives in an incubator stays for an average of 3 years. More than 1,200 incubators operate across the United States, up from just 12 in 1980. Perhaps the greatest advantage of choosing to locate a start-up company in an incubator is a greater chance for success; according to the National Business Incubation Association, graduates from incubators have a success rate of 87 percent. Each year, business incubators help an estimated 27,000 start-up companies that provide full-time employment for more than 100,000 workers.[47]

Layout and Design Considerations

6. Describe the criteria used to analyze the layout and design considerations of a building, including the Americans with Disabilities Act.

Once an entrepreneur chooses the best location for his or her business, the next issue to address is designing the proper layout for the space to maximize sales (retail) or productivity (manufacturing or service). **Layout** is the logical arrangement of the physical facilities in a business that contributes to efficient operations, increased productivity, and higher sales. Planning for the most effective and efficient layout in a business environment can produce dramatic improvements in a company's operating effectiveness and efficiency. An attractive, effective layout can help a company's recruiting efforts, reduce absenteeism, and improve employee productivity and satisfaction. A recent U.S. Workplace Survey by global design firm Gensler reports that 90 percent of employees believe that better workplace design and layout improves their performance and productivity and the company's competitiveness, yet only 50 percent of workers say that their work environment encourages innovation.[48] The changing nature of work demands that workspace design also changes. Although many jobs require the ability to focus on "heads down," individual tasks, collaboration with coworkers is becoming a more significant component of work even when workers are scattered across the globe and "meet" virtually. An effective workspace

FIGURE 3
Business Incubators by Industry

Source: National Business Incubation Association, Athens, Ohio, 2010.

must be flexible enough to accommodate and encourage both types of work. Increasingly, work is becoming more complex, team-based, technology dependent, and mobile; workspaces must change to accommodate these characteristics. The study by Gensler concludes that top performing companies have workspaces that are more effective than those of average companies, particularly for collaboration. Gensler also reports that employees at top performing companies spend 23 percent more time collaborating with their coworkers than do employees at average companies.[49]

When creating a layout, managers must consider its impact on space itself (comfort, flexibility, size, and ergonomics), the people who occupy it (type of work, special requirements, need for interaction, tasks performed), and the technology they use (communication, Internet access, and equipment).[50] The following factors have a significant impact on a space's layout and design.

Size and Adaptability

A building must offer adequate space and be adaptable to accommodate a business's daily operations. If space is restrictive at the outset of operations, efficiency will suffer. There must be room enough for customers' movement, inventory, displays, storage, work areas, offices, and restrooms. Haphazard layouts undermine employee productivity and can create organizational chaos. A business that launches in a location that is already overcrowded may find it limits its potential. The unfortunate result is that an owner may be required to make a premature and costly move to a new location.

As a business expands, a lack of adequate room or an inefficient configuration may limit future growth. Some businesses wait too long before moving into larger quarters, and they fail to plan their new space arrangements properly. To avoid this problem, experts recommend that new business owners plan their space requirements 1 to 2 years ahead and update the estimates every 6 months. When preparing the plan, entrepreneurs should include the expected growth in the number of employees, manufacturing, selling, or storage space requirements, and the number and location of branches to be opened.

ENTREPRENEURIAL
Profile
Gravity Tank

At Gravity Tank, a small design-strategy firm in Chicago, a layout that encourages collaboration is essential because employees often work together on project teams for several months. Designers came up with a flexible layout that includes work bays that can be reconfigured quickly and easily by moving lightweight dividers made from cardboard that hang from an overhead grid. Cork bulletin boards (which also serve as dividers) allow employees to share ideas easily, and the furnishings in each bay have built-in power outlets, Ethernet cables, and trays of office supplies, giving employees easy access to all of the tools they need to work. Employees have the flexibility they need in an office space, and Gravity Tank created the entire space for just $20,000.[51]

External Appearance

The physical appearance of a building determines the first impression that customers have of a business and contributes significantly to establishing its identity in customers' minds. Therefore, a building's appearance must be consistent with the entrepreneur's desired image for the business. Retailers, in particular, must recognize the importance of creating the proper image for their stores and how their shops' layout and physical facilities influence this image. In many ways, the building's appearance sets the tone for the customer's quality and service expectations. The appearance should reflect the "personality" of the business. Should the building project an exclusive image or an economical one? Is the atmosphere informal and relaxed, or it is formal and businesslike? Externally, the storefront, its architectural style and color, signs, entrances, and general appearance, give important clues to customers about a business's image. For example, a glass front enables a retail business to display merchandise easily and to attract potential customers' attention. Passersby can look in and see attractive merchandise displays or, in some cases, dedicated employees working.

Communicating the right signals through layout and physical facilities is an important step in attracting a steady stream of customers. Retail consultant Paco Underhill advises merchants to "seduce" passersby with their storefronts. "The seduction process should start a minimum of 10 paces away," he says. "A store's interior architecture is fundamental to the customer's experience—the stage upon which a retail company functions."[52]

Williams-Sonoma, an upscale retailer of kitchenware, seduces passersby with window displays that look more like someone's kitchen than a retail shop. Stores in the chain change their eye-catching displays frequently to reflect the foods of the season. The goal is to sell and make customers feel welcome and to put them in a positive frame of mind. "If you have a positive feeling," says Julie Irwin, marketing professor at the University of Texas at Austin, "you're going to associate it with everything you see." Once inside a Williams-Sonoma store, an array of aromas rising from freshly-baked foods or hot beverages also lure customers and encourage them to stay, which increases the probability that they make a purchase.[53]

The following tips help entrepreneurs to create displays that sell:

- *Keep displays simple.* Simple, uncluttered arrangements of merchandise draw the most attention and have the greatest impact on potential customers.
- *Keep displays clean and up-to-date.* Dusty, dingy displays or designs that are outdated send the wrong message to customers.
- *Promote local events.* Small companies can show their support of the community by devoting part of the display window to promote local events.
- *Change displays frequently.* Customers don't want to see the same merchandise every time they visit a store. Experts recommend changing window displays at least quarterly. Businesses that sell fashionable items, however, should change their displays at least twice a month, if not weekly.
- *Get expert help, if necessary.* Some business owners have no aptitude for design! In that case, their best bet is to hire a professional to design window and in-store displays. If a company cannot afford a professional designer's fees, the entrepreneur should check with the design departments at local colleges and universities. There might be a faculty member or a talented student willing to work on a freelance basis.
- *Appeal to all of a customer's senses.* Effective displays engage more than one of a customer's senses. Who can pass up a bakery case of freshly baked, gooey cinnamon buns with their mouth-watering aroma wafting up to greet passersby?
- *Contact the companies whose products you sell to see whether they offer design props and assistance.* These vendors may offer additional insight and are aware of industry trends and competitor tactics.

Entrances

All entrances to a business should invite customers in. Wide entryways and attractive merchandise displays that are set back from the doorway can draw customers into a business. A store's entrance should catch passing customers' attention and draw them inside. "That's where you want somebody to slam on the brakes and realize they're going someplace new," says retail consultant Paco Underhill.[54] Retailers with heavy traffic flows such as supermarkets or drugstores often install automatic doors to ensure smooth traffic flow into and out of their stores. Retailers should remove any barriers that interfere with customers' easy access to the storefront. Broken sidewalks, sagging steps, mud puddles, and sticking or heavy doors not only create obstacles that might discourage potential customers, but they also create legal hazards for a business if they cause customers to be injured.

The Americans with Disabilities Act

The **Americans with Disabilities Act (ADA),** passed in July 1990, requires most businesses to make their facilities available to physically challenged customers and employees. In addition, the law requires businesses with 15 or more employees to accommodate physically challenged candidates in their hiring practices. Most states have similar laws, many of them more stringent than the ADA, that apply to smaller companies as well. The rules of the these state laws and the ADA's Title III are designed to ensure that mentally and physically challenged customers have equal access to a firm's goods or services. For instance, the act requires business owners to remove architectural and communication barriers when "readily achievable." The ADA allows flexibility in how a business achieves this equal access, however. For example, a restaurant either could provide menus in Braille or could offer to have a staff member read the menu to blind customers. A small dry cleaner might not be able to add a wheelchair ramp to its storefront without incurring significant expense, but the owner could comply with the ADA by offering curbside pickup and delivery services for disabled customers at no extra charge.

Although the law allows a good deal of flexibility in retrofitting existing structures, buildings that were occupied after January 25, 1993, must be designed to comply with all aspects of the law. For example, buildings with three stories or more must have elevators; anywhere the floor level changes by more than one-half inch, an access ramp must be in place. In retail stores, checkout aisles must be wide enough—at least 36 inches—to accommodate wheelchairs. Restaurants must have 5 percent of their tables accessible to wheelchair-bound patrons.

Complying with the ADA does not necessarily require businesses to spend large amounts of money. The Justice Department estimates that more than 20 percent of the cases customers have filed under Title III involved changes the business owners could have made at no cost, and another 60 percent would have cost less than $1,000![55] In addition, companies with $1 million or less in annual sales or with 30 or fewer full-time employees that invest in making their locations more accessible to all qualify for a tax credit. The credit is 50 percent of their expenses between $250 and $10,500. Businesses that remove physical, structural, and transportation barriers for disabled employees and customers also qualify for a tax deduction of up to $15,000.

The ADA also prohibits any kind of employment discrimination against anyone with a physical or mental disability. A physically challenged person is considered to be "qualified" if he or she can perform the essential functions of the job. The employer must make "reasonable accommodation" for a physically challenged candidate or employee without causing "undue hardship" to the business. Most businesses have found that making these reasonable accommodations for customers and employees has created a more pleasant environment and offer additional conveniences for all.

Signs

One of the lowest-cost and most effective methods of communicating with customers is a business sign. Signs communicate what a business does, where it is, and what it is selling. The United States is a very mobile society, and a well-designed, well-placed sign can be a powerful vehicle for reaching potential customers.

A sign should be large enough for passersby to read from a distance, taking into consideration the location and speed of surrounding traffic arteries. To be most effective, the message should be short, simple, and clear. A sign should be legible in both daylight and at night; proper illumination is a must. Contrasting colors and simple typefaces are best. The most common problems with business signs are that they are illegible, poorly designed, improperly located, poorly maintained, and have color schemes that are unattractive or hard to read.

Before investing in a sign, an entrepreneur should investigate the local community's sign ordinance. In some cities and towns, local regulations impose restrictions on the size, location, height, and construction materials used in business signs.

Interiors

Designing a functional, efficient interior layout demands research, planning, and attention to detail. Retailers in particular have known for a long time that their stores' layouts influence their customers' buying behavior. Retailers such as Cabela's, Barnes & Noble, and Starbucks use layouts that encourage customers to linger and spend time (and money). Others, such as Lowe's, Aldi, and Walmart, reinforce their discount images with layouts that communicate a warehouse environment, often complete with pallets, to shoppers. Luxury retailers such as Tiffany and Company, Coach, and Nordstrom create opulent layouts in which their upscale customers feel comfortable.

Technology has changed drastically the way employees, customers, and the environment interact with one another, but smart entrepreneurs realize that they can influence the effectiveness of those interactions with well-designed layouts. The result can be a boost to a company's sales and profits. For instance, as their customers' needs and expectations have changed, retailers have modified the layouts of their stores to meet those needs. Because shoppers are busier than ever and want an efficient shopping experience (particularly men), many retail stores have moved away from the traditional departments (e.g., shoes, cosmetics, men's suits) and are organizing their merchandise by "lifestyle categories," such as sports, women's contemporary, men's business casual, and others. These displays expose customers to merchandise that they otherwise might have missed and make it easier for them to, say, put together an entire outfit without having to roam from one department to another.

Designing an effective layout is an art and a science. **Ergonomics,** the science of adapting work and the work environment to complement employees' strengths and to suit customers' needs, is an integral part of a successful design. For example, chairs, desks, and table heights that allow people to work comfortably help employees perform their jobs faster and more easily. Design experts claim that improved lighting, better acoustics, and proper climate control benefit the company as well as employees. An ergonomically designed workplace can improve workers' productivity significantly and lower days lost due to injuries and accidents. A study for the Commission of Architecture and the Built Environment and the British Council for Offices reports that simple features such as proper lighting reduce absenteeism by 15 percent and increase productivity between 2.8 and 20 percent.[56]

Unfortunately, many businesses fail to incorporate ergonomic design principles into their layouts, and the result is costly. Every year, 1.8 million workers experience injuries related to repetitive motion or overexertion. The most frequent and most expensive workplace injuries are musculoskeletal disorders (MSDs), which cost U.S. businesses at least $15 billion in workers' compensation claims each year. According to the Occupational Safety and Health Administration (OSHA), MSDs account for 29.4 percent of all lost-workday injuries and illnesses and one-third of all workers compensation claims.[57] Workers who spend their days staring at computer monitors (a significant and growing proportion of the workforce) often are victims of MSDs.

The most common MSD is carpal tunnel syndrome (CTS), which occurs when repetitive motion causes swelling in the wrist that pinches the nerves in the arm and hand. Studies by the Bureau of Labor Statistics estimate that 3.7 percent of U.S. workers suffer from carpal tunnel syndrome and that the average worker with CTS loses 23 workdays, costing companies more than $2 billion per year.[58] The good news for employers, however, is that preventing injuries, accidents, and lost days does *not* require spending thousands of dollars on ergonomically correct solutions. Most of the solutions to MSDs are actually quite simple and inexpensive, ranging from installing equipment that eliminates workers' repetitive motions to introducing breaks during which workers engage in exercises designed by occupational therapists to combat MSDs.

When planning store, office, or plant layouts, business owners usually focus on minimizing costs. Although staying within a budget is important, minimizing injuries and enhancing employees' productivity with an effective layout should be the overriding issues. Many exhaustive studies have concluded that changes in office design have a direct impact on workers' performance, job satisfaction, and ease of communication. In a reversal of the trend toward open offices separated by nothing more than cubicles, businesses are once again creating private offices in their workspaces. Many businesses embraced open designs, hoping that they would lead to greater interaction among workers. Many companies, however, have discovered that most office workers need privacy and quiet surroundings to be productive. Rather than encourage teamwork, open offices leave workers distracted, frustrated, and less productive—just like the characters in the Dilbert cartoon strip. "Open offices do lead to more unstructured communication, but those same offices can lead to problems of [employee] concentration," says Babson College's Tom Davenport, whose research shows that workplace design has a direct impact on white-collar workers' performances and productivity.[59]

When evaluating an existing building's interior, an entrepreneur must be sure to determine the integrity of its structural components. Are the building's floors sufficiently strong to hold the business's equipment, inventories, and personnel? Strength is an especially critical factor for manufacturing firms that use heavy equipment. When multiple floors exist, are the upper floors anchored as solidly as the primary floor? Is the floor space adequate for safe and efficient movement of goods and people?

Floors and walls must be both functional and attractive. On the functional side, walls and ceilings should be fireproof and soundproof. Are the colors of walls and ceilings compatible, and do they create an attractive atmosphere for customers and employees? For instance, many high-tech companies use bright, bold colors in their designs because they appeal to their young employees. In contrast, more conservative companies, such as accounting firms and law offices, decorate with more subtle, subdued tones because they convey an image of trustworthiness and honesty. Upscale restaurants that want their patrons to linger over dinner use deep, luxurious tones and soft lighting to create the proper ambiance. Fast-food restaurants, in contrast, use strong, vibrant colors and bright lighting to encourage customers to get in and out quickly, ensuring the fast table turnover they require to be successful.

For many businesses, a drive-through window adds another dimension to the concept of customer convenience and is a relatively inexpensive way to increase sales. In the quick-service restaurant business, drive-through windows are an essential design component, accounting for 70 percent of sales, an increase from 60 percent in 2002.[60] Although drive-through windows are staples at fast-food restaurants and banks, they can add value for customers in other businesses as well, including drugstores, hardware stores, and even wedding chapels.

Lighting, Scent, and Sound

Retailers can increase sales by engaging all of customers' senses. Retail behavioral expert Paco Underhill, founder of Envirosell, a market research company, says that most of customers' unplanned purchases come after they touch, taste, smell, or hear something in a store. For example, stores that sell fresh food will see sales increase if they offer free samples to customers. "If somebody doesn't try 'em, they're not going to buy 'em," quips Underhill.[61] Lighting, scent, and sound are particularly important.

LIGHTING. Good lighting allows employees to work at maximum efficiency. Proper lighting is measured by the amount of light required to do a job properly with the greatest lighting efficiency. In a retail environment, proper lighting should highlight featured products and encourage customers to stop and look at them. "The lighting and the atmosphere created with the lighting really makes your store more spectacular," says the president of a design firm that specializes in restaurants and retail stores.[62] Efficiency also is essential because lighting consumes 24 percent of the total energy used in the typical commercial building.[63] Technological advances are increasing the popularity and lowering the cost of light-emitting diode (LED) lighting. LEDs use just 20 percent of the electricity of incandescent lights and 50 percent of compact fluorescent lights, and the best LED bulbs last 20 to 25 times longer than comparable incandescent bulbs.[64] LEDs also generate less heat, which reduces business's cooling costs.

Lighting provides a good return on investment given its overall impact on a business. Few people seek out businesses that are dimly lit because they convey an image of untrustworthiness. The use of natural light gives a business an open and cheerful look and can boost sales. A series of studies by energy research firm Heschong Mahone Group reports that stores using natural light experience sales that are 40 percent higher than those of similar stores using fluorescent lighting.[65] Similarly, a study by office furniture maker Haworth reports that employees who work in more natural environments (with natural light and external views) exhibit less job stress, more job satisfaction, and fewer ailments.[66]

SCENT. Research shows that scents can have a powerful effect in retail stores. The Sense of Smell Institute reports that the average human being can recognize 10,000 different aromas and can recall scents with 65 percent accuracy after 1 year, a much higher recall rate than visual stimuli produce. In one experiment, Eric Spangenberg of Washington State University diffused a subtle scent of vanilla into the women's department of a store and rose maroc into the men's department, he discovered that sales nearly doubled. He also discovered that if he switched the scents, sales in both departments fell well below their normal averages.[67]

Many companies—from casinos to retail stores—are beginning to understand the power of using scent as a marketing tool to evoke customers' emotions. Almost every bakery uses a fan to push the smell of fresh-baked breads and sweets into pedestrian traffic lanes, tempting them to sample some of their delectable goodies. "Smell has a greater impact on purchasing than everything else combined," says Alan Hirsch of the Smell & Taste Treatment & Research Foundation. "If something smells good, the product is perceived as good."[68] Thomas Pink, a company founded in 1984 by brothers James, Peter, and John Mullen in London that sells premium shirts, blouses, and ties, uses a signature "line-dried linen" scent in its 20 stores in the United States and others around the world.[69] Sony infuses its Style Stores with a blend of vanilla, orange, and cedar that is designed to make women shoppers feel more at ease.[70]

SOUND. Background music can be an effective merchandising tool if the type of music playing in a store matches the demographics of its target customers. Abercrombie & Fitch plays loud, upbeat music with a rhythmic beat that creates a nightclub-like atmosphere for its youthful customers, but Victoria's Secret uses classical music in its stores to reinforce an upscale image for its brand.[71] Research shows that music is a stimulant to sales because it reduces resistance; warps shoppers' sense of time, causing them to stay in the store longer; and helps to produce a positive mental association between the music and the store's intended image.[72] One rule seems clear for retail soundscapes: Slow is good. Because people's biorhythms often mirror the sounds around them, a gently meandering mix of classical music or soothing ambient noise encourages shoppers to slow down and relax. Classical music, in particular, makes shoppers feel affluent and boosts sales more than other types of music.[73] "If customers are moving less quickly," says shopping psychologist Tim Dennison, "they're more likely to engage with a product and make a purchase." The growing competition for the attention of time-pressed shoppers forces businesses to focus more on the total sensory experience they provide. "Retailers will have to make their stores more stimulating," says Dennison.[74]

Environmentally Friendly Design

Businesses are designing their buildings in more environmentally friendly ways not only because it is the right thing to do, but also because it saves money. In addition to saving energy (and the planet), companies that create well-planned, environmentally friendly designs see employee productivity increase by 3.5 to 10 percent.[75] Companies are using recycled materials; installing high-efficiency lighting, fixtures, and appliances; and incorporating LEED (Leadership in Energy and Environmental Design) principles into construction and renovation.

ENTREPRENEURIAL
Profile

Joey Terrell: Denny's

Joey Terrell, a Denny's franchisee, recently built a new restaurant in Joliet, Illinois, that incorporates an environmentally friendly design. "It's one of the few LEED-certified restaurants in the country," says Terrell, who estimates that the restaurant saves $20,000 in utility costs alone per year. In addition to the operating savings it generates, the restaurant also cost $40,000 less to build than a traditional Denny's restaurant. Denny's is now incorporating many of the features in Terrell's restaurant into the design of its new outlets.[76]

▶ ENTREPRENEURSHIP **IN ACTION** ▶

Sneakerhead Heaven

For more than 30 years, Barry Pener has been managing Man of Fashion, a chain of 35 well-known stores that sell fashionable urban clothing and shoes founded by his grandfather in St. Louis, Missouri. In 2005, Pener noticed a new type of customer in his stores—sneakerheads, people (mostly men) who see sneakers as more than mere footwear and treat them as if they were works of art. Pener talked with his Nike sales representative, who confirmed the emerging trend. The sales representative told Pener about high-end sneaker stores in Los Angeles and New York City and suggested that he open a similar store in his Midwestern location. Pener flew to New York City to visit the stores, learn about their customers, and get ideas for opening his own high-end store in St. Louis. While there, he learned that sneakerheads tend to be

men between the ages of 18 and 34 who spend anywhere from $80 to $500 for a pair of upscale shoes from makers such as Nike, Puma, and Adidas. He also spotted a men's clothing store in New York City's funky SoHo district whose design caught his eye by creating a unique, exclusive look—the exact look that he wanted for his store aimed at sneakerheads.

Pener contacted the architectural firm that created the New York store's design and explained his plan to owner Carol Tobin. Several weeks later, Tobin pitched an unusual, counterintuitive idea for Pener's new store, which he had decided to name RSole. Rather than use a bold, in-your-face design, Tobin's idea was to create an "anonymous" storefront, one that would enhance its image of exclusivity. The theory is that an obscure storefront attracts elite shoppers. Pener loved the idea even though he knew that building a customer base would take more time. In the end, the wait would be worthwhile.

For his first RSole store, Pener secured a good location in St. Louis near the Washington University campus, and Tobin began transforming the space into something that looked more like an art gallery or a museum than a traditional shoe store. "They wanted to exhibit these sneakers they considered works of art in a way that would really emphasize the beauty, detail, and design of the sneakers," she says. The interior of the store is black, which makes the displays of colorful shoes "pop" and lends an air of sophistication and exclusivity to the store. Tobin also installed innovative lighting designs. "Black sucks up light," she says, "so we had to focus light intelligently. We installed fixtures at indirect angles in the walls and on the ceiling to add drama and draw attention to the shoes." Special, highly efficient LED lighting in the walls, some of which are recessed to create a "moving geometry," make displays of shoes look as though they are floating. The design also incorporates LED squares in the floor to define different selling areas and to create an entertaining, visually appealing element that guides customers through the store. The system, which borrows elements of theater lighting, allows employees to adjust the color and the intensity of the light the squares emit. "The LED squares direct people along certain paths, like emergency lighting," says Tobin.

Cash registers are located at the back of the store to create the image of a gallery, and Plexiglas panels "float" above the floor, creating displays and shelving that are unique and create a feeling of motion. "We wanted something exciting, something where the audio-visual component was alive so people weren't just seeing moving lights, but they were hearing music, maybe seeing a video of some music star doing something with the sneakers," Tobin explains. The panels along one wall are mounted on rods that allow them to rotate 360 degrees and lock at any position, giving employees the ability to vary the store layout. "We wanted [customers] to feel that there was movement and flexibility in the store," says Tobin.

The storefront uses an opaque film to coat the window glass that is interrupted by clear "peep holes" to pique customers' curiosity and encourage them to peer into the store from the street. "We opened, and I was really nervous," says Pener, because customer traffic was light. Three months later, however, customers had discovered the store. RSole was generating lots of buzz, particularly among its sneakerhead target customers, and foot traffic increased significantly. "Sneakerheads claim the store as their own and want to be associated with it," says Pener. RSole also received a marketing boost when celebrities such as Ted Ginn, Jr., of the Miami Dolphins and local hip-hop star Murphy Lee began shopping there. RSole sells more than 2,000 pairs of sneakers a month, and Pener recently opened a second location in Memphis, Tennessee. Pener credits his stores' unique layout and design with much of the success. "Without that, it would have been just another shoe store," he says.

1. What risks did Pener take by using a counterintuitive, gallery-like design in his RSole store? What was the payoff?
2. Use the Internet to conduct some basic research on sneakerheads. Is there a city in your state that you think would be a good location for an RSole store? Explain.
3. What role does the design of RSole's stores play in their success? Does RSole's unique interior design create the image for the store that Pener was seeking? Explain.

Sources: Based on Mina Kimes, "Secret Kicks," *FSB*, May 2009; Erin M. Loewe, "Shoe Envy," *All Business*, April 1, 2007, *www.allbusiness.com/ retail-trade/miscellaneous-retail/4165891-1.html.*

Layout: Maximizing Revenues, Increasing Efficiency, and Reducing Costs

7. Explain the principles of effective layouts for retailers, service businesses, and manufacturers.

The ideal layout depends on the type of business and on the entrepreneur's strategy for gaining a competitive edge. Retailers design their layouts with the goal of maximizing sales revenue; manufacturers design theirs to increase efficiency and productivity and to lower costs.

Layout for Retailers

Retail layout is the arrangement of merchandise in a store. A retailer's success depends, in part, on well-designed floor displays. Paco Underhill, retail consultant and author of *Why We Buy: The Science of Shopping*, calls a store's interior design "the stage on which a retail company functions."[77] Unfortunately, according to Underhill, most retailers do not consider what customers want to experience when designing their spaces.[78]

A retail layout should pull customers into the store and make it easy for them to locate merchandise; compare price, quality, and features; and ultimately make a purchase. In addition, a floor plan should take customers past displays of other items that they may buy on impulse. Research shows that 66 percent of all buying decisions are made once a customer enters a store, which means that the right layout can boost sales significantly. One study reports that 78 percent of general market shoppers make impulse purchases. Shoppers are heavily influenced by in-store displays, especially end-cap displays, those at the ends of aisles.[79]

Retailers have always recognized that some locations within a store are superior to others. Customer traffic patterns give the owner a clue to the best location for the highest gross margin items. Merchandise purchased on impulse and convenience goods should be located near the front of the store. Items people shop around for before buying and specialty goods attract their own customers and should not be placed in prime space. Prime selling space should be restricted to products that carry the highest markups.

Retail store layout evolves from a clear understanding of customers' buying habits. If customers come into the store for specific products and have a tendency to walk directly to those items, placing complementary products in their path increases sales. Observing customer behavior helps business owners to identify "hot spots," where merchandise sells briskly, and "cold spots," where it may sit indefinitely. By experimenting with factors such as traffic flow, lighting, aisle size, music type and audio levels, signs, and colors, an owner can discover the most productive store layout. For instance, one of the hot spots in a Barnes & Noble bookstore during the busy holiday season is the "Christmas table" at the front of the children's department. The table, which holds between 75 and 125 titles, draws consistent traffic and is the most desired spot for a book aimed at children.[80]

Business owners should display merchandise as attractively as their budgets allow. Customers' eyes focus on displays, which tell them the type of merchandise the business sells. It is easier for customers to relate to one display than to a rack or shelf of merchandise. Open displays of merchandise can surround the focal display, creating an attractive selling area. Retailers can boost sales by displaying together items that complement each other. For example, displaying ties near dress shirts or handbags next to shoes often leads to multiple sales.

Spacious displays provide shoppers an open view of merchandise and reduce the likelihood of shoplifting. An open, spacious image is preferable to a cluttered appearance. Display height is also important because customers won't buy what they cannot see or reach. When planning in-store displays, retailers should remember the following:

- **Make products easy to reach.** The average man is 68.8 inches tall, and the average woman is 63.6 inches tall. The average person's normal reach is 16 inches, and the extended reach is 24 inches. The average man's standing eye level is 62 inches from the floor, and the average woman's standing eye level is 57 inches from the floor.[81] Placing merchandise on very low or very high shelves discourages customers from making purchases. For example, putting hearing aid batteries on bottom shelves where the elderly have trouble getting to them or placing popular children's toys on top shelves where little ones cannot reach them hurts sales of these items. Walgreen's recently remodeled its store shelves to make products easier to reach.[82]
- **Shoppers prefer wide aisles.** One study found that shoppers, especially women, are reluctant to enter narrow aisles in a store. Narrow aisles force customers to jostle past one another, creating what experts call the "butt-brush factor." Open aisles allow customers to shop comfortably and encourage them to spend more time in a store.[83]
- **Placing shopping baskets in several areas around a store can increase sales.** Seventy-five percent of shoppers who pick up a basket buy something, compared to just 34 percent of customers who do not pick up a basket.[84] Smart retailers make shopping baskets available to customers throughout the store, not just at the entrance.
- **Make it easy to locate merchandise.** Making shoppers hunt for the items they want to buy lowers the probability that they will purchase an item and that they will return to a particular store. Easy-to-read signs, clearly marked aisles, and displays of popular items located near the entrance make it easy for shoppers to find their way around a store.

- **Whenever possible, allow customers to touch the merchandise.** Customers are much more likely to buy items if they can pick them up. The probability that customers who are shopping for clothing will make purchases increases if they try on the garments. Therefore, having friendly sales representatives who offer to "start a dressing room" for customers who pick up articles of clothing pays off.[85]

Retailers should separate the selling and nonselling areas of a store and should never waste prime selling space with nonselling functions such as storage, receiving, office, and fitting areas. Although nonselling activities are necessary for a successful retail operation, they should not take precedence and occupy valuable selling and merchandising space. Many retailers place their nonselling departments in the rear of the building, recognizing the value of each foot of space in a retail store and locating their most profitable items in the best-selling areas. Entrepreneurs should use at least 80 percent of available retail space for selling and merchandising.

The various areas within a small store's interior space are not equal in generating sales revenue. Certain areas contribute more to revenue than others. The value of store space depends on floor location in a multistory building, location with respect to aisles and walkways, and proximity to entrances. Space values decrease as distance from the main entry-level floor increases. Selling areas on the main level contribute a greater portion to sales than do those on other floors because they offer greater exposure to customers than either basement or higher-level locations. Therefore, main-level locations carry a greater share of rent than other levels.

The layout of aisles in the store has a major impact on the customer exposure that merchandise receives. Items located on primary walkways should be assigned a higher share of rental costs and should contribute a greater portion to sales revenue than those displayed along secondary aisles. Space values also depend on the spaces' relative position to the store entrance, which serves as the "landing strip" for shoppers. A critical moment occurs when shoppers walk into a store as they slow down, try to orient themselves, and expand their peripheral vision to get a panoramic view of the retail spaces. An effective layout allows them to familiarize themselves with the retail landscape as quickly as possible.

ENTREPRENEURIAL Profile

Old Navy

Clothing retailer Old Navy recently created a new layout for its stores using a "racetrack" layout in which the primary aisle starts at the store's entrance and loops through the entire store in a circular, square, or rectangular pattern. The goal of a racetrack layout is to expose customers to as much merchandise as possible and to encourage them to browse through other merchandise displayed on smaller "rabbit trails" that branch off of the main aisle. The new Old Navy layout also includes dressing rooms, a children's play area, and cash registers located in the center of the store and a "fundamentals" wall that displays low-priced items.[86]

Most American shoppers turn to the right when entering a store and will move around it counterclockwise.[87] That makes the front right-hand section of a retail store the "retail sweet spot." Retailers should put their best selling and highest profit margin items in this prime area. Only about one-fourth of a store's customers will go more than halfway into the store. Therefore, the farther away an area is from the entrance, the lower its value. Using these characteristics, Figure 4 illustrates space values for a typical small-store layout.

Understanding the value of store space ensures proper placement of merchandise. The items placed in the high-rent areas of the store should generate adequate sales and contribute enough profit to justify their high-value locations. The decline in value of store space from front to back of the shop is expressed in the 40-30-20-10 rule. This rule assigns 40 percent of a store's rental cost to the front quarter of the shop, 30 percent to the second quarter, 20 percent to the third quarter, and 10 percent to the final quarter. Each quarter of the store should contribute the same percentages of its sales revenue; if not, the business owner should reevaluate the store's layout.

FIGURE 4
The Space Value for a Small Store

For example, suppose that the owner of a small retail store anticipates $520,000 in sales this year. Each quarter of the store should generate the following sales volume:

Front quarter	$520,000 × 0.40 = $208,000
Second quarter	$520,000 × 0.30 = $156,000
Third quarter	$520,000 × 0.20 = $104,000
Fourth quarter	$520,000 × 0.10 = $ 52,000
Total	**$520,000**

LESSONS FROM THE STREET-SMART ▶ entrepreneur

Creating a Layout and Design That Really Sells

Sephora, launched in 1993 as a French perfume chain, has stormed the makeup market in the United States, forcing other makeup retailers to change their tactics. For years, women shopping for makeup had two choices: drugstores that offered products in tightly sealed packages or department stores that required a hovering salesperson whose sales commission was tied to particular brands. Spotting an opportunity, managers at Sephora decided to break out of the traditional mold for marketing makeup, offering more than 13,000 products in one store and giving customers the freedom to explore and sample various types of makeup. Women can try lipsticks, eyeliners, blushes, and other products from more than 250 brands on their own, or they can ask for assistance from one of Sephora's highly trained sales associates.

The Street-Smart Entrepreneur offers business owners the following lessons learned by studying the factors behind Sephora's success.

Recognize that design and layout really are important, especially for retailers.

Customers look for visual cues to determine the character of a business. Your company's design and layout should reinforce the image you seek to create in your customers' minds. "The Sephora retail concept is rooted in aesthetics, presenting our clients with the most unique product assortment, store design, and client services," says Joey Manues, the company's store director. "Our locations became our advertising."

Make sure that your storefront offers a clean, inviting look that invites customers to enter.

Despite stocking more than 13,000 products, Sephora stores are always neat and orderly. The unspoken message Sephora sends to customers is clear: We offer a large selection of products, but they are always easy to find. Displays organize fragrances in alphabetical order and cosmetics by brand. Large storefront windows allow passersby to have a bird's-eye view of the store instantly and to see the breadth and depth of its product line.

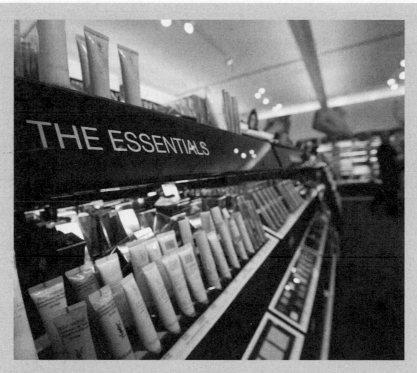

Sephora's layout sends a clear signal to its customers: We offer an extensive selection of products, but they are easy to find.

Source: Wilfredo Lee/AP Wide World Photos

Create displays that "pop" to draw customers into your store.

Sephora stores showcase makeup and cosmetics in minimalist display cases that allow the vivid colors and appealing shapes of the products to draw customers in. The lipstick bar sparkles with more than 365 eye-popping colors, ranging from lavender and gold to blue and green, organized by hue. Strategically placed mirrors, cotton swabs, and makeup remover encourage customers to experiment—and buy.

Avoid pressuring customers.

Some businesses impose pushy salespeople on customers the moment they step into a store, a technique that turns off many customers and sends them bolting toward the exit. Sephora allows customers to browse at their own pace without pressure from a salesperson, which encourages them to linger. Some customers spend an hour or more trying out different products until they find those that are just right for them. Typically, the longer a customer stays, the more she buys.

Offer stellar customer service from well-trained employees.

Sephora does not abandon customers and leave them to fend for themselves. When a customer asks for assistance, sales associates are ready to bolt into action. Borrowing a page from Disney, Sephora calls its sales associates "cast members" and refers to the sales floor as "on stage." Cast members are highly trained, each one having completed a rigorous course of study on skin and hair care and general beauty that the company calls the Science of Sephora (S.O.S.) offered at Sephora University. Cast members offer customers free makeovers in scheduled appointments in specially designed staging areas.

Enhance your brand with visual cues.

All of Sephora's stores use the same color palette: black, white, and red. A red carpet welcomes customers at the entrance, and black-and-white floor tiles punctuate the stores' interior. The color theme also extends to the exterior, where bold black-and-white striped columns make storefronts stand out. Cast members dress in black designer tunics and slacks and wear no jewelry or makeup other than red lipstick and either red or clear nail polish—again reinforcing the brand with color. They also wear a single black glove, which serves as the ideal backdrop for displaying products (much like jewelers use black velvet backdrops to make their jewelry sparkle).

Make creative use of nonselling space to sell.

Sephora stores include beauty studios, where cast members offer customers a variety of 10-minute mini-classes on beauty tips and trends. Tutorials include topics such as

"Conceal and Reveal," "Day to Night," "Smoky Eye," and "A Clean Start." Beauty studios occupy space that Sephora could devote to product displays, but the way the company creatively uses this nonselling space actually generates sales that the company might not otherwise have made.

Sephora's success demonstrates the power of a store's layout and design. "Every aspect of the stores from their architectural layout and interior design to the background music to the customer experience is designed to reinforce a shopping experience that emphasizes freedom, exploration, discovery, and a personal definition of beauty," says CEO Daniel Richard.

Sources: Based on Leilani Salter, "Mississippi Just Got More Beautiful with Sephora Opening at Renaissance," *Mississippi Digital Daily*, May 10, 2010, *www.msdigitaldaily.com/3/Lifestyles/CAT5/Mississippi%20just%20got%20more%20beautiful%20with%20Sephora%20opening%20at%20Renaissance/1805/default.aspx;* "Sephora: Liberating Beauty Products," *Bloomberg Business Week*, January 25, 2006, *www.businessweek.com/innovate/content/jan2006/id20060125_183621.htm.*

Layout for Manufacturers

Manufacturing layout decisions take into consideration the arrangement of departments, workstations, machines, and stock-holding points within a production facility. The general objective is to arrange these elements to ensure a smooth workflow (in a production area) or a particular traffic pattern (in a service area).

Manufacturing facilities have come under increased scrutiny as firms attempt to improve quality, decrease inventories, and increase productivity through facilities that are integrated, flexible, and controlled. Facility layout has a dramatic effect on product mix, product processing, materials handling, storage, control, and production volume and quality. Some manufacturers are using 3-D simulation software (based on the same technology as the 3-D video games people play) to test the layout of their factory and its impact on employees and their productivity *before* they ever build them. The highly realistic simulations tell designers how well a particular combination of people, machinery, and environment interacts with one another. The software can identify potential problem areas, such as layouts that force workers into awkward positions that would cause injuries, equipment designs that cause workers to reach too far for materials, and layouts that unnecessarily add extra time to the manufacturing process by requiring extra materials handling or unneeded steps.[88]

FACTORS IN MANUFACTURING LAYOUT. The ideal layout for a manufacturing operation depends on several factors, including the following:

- *Type of product.* Product design and quality standards, whether the product is produced for inventory or for order, and physical properties, such as the size of materials and products' special handling requirements, susceptibility to damage, and perishability
- *Type of production process.* Technology used, types of materials handled, means of providing a service, and processing requirements in terms of number of operations involved and amount of interaction between departments and work centers
- *Ergonomic considerations.* To ensure worker safety, to avoid unnecessary injuries and accidents, and to increase productivity
- *Economic considerations.* Volume of production; costs of materials, machines, workstations, and labor; pattern and variability of demand; and length of permissible delays
- *Space availability within facility itself.* To ensure the space will adequately meet current and future manufacturing needs

TYPES OF MANUFACTURING LAYOUTS. Manufacturing layouts are categorized either by the work flow in a plant or by the production system's function. The three basic types of layouts that manufacturers can use separately or in combination are product, process, and fixed position. They differ in their applicability of different levels of manufacturing volume.

Product Layouts. In a **product (or line) layout,** a manufacturer arranges workers and equipment according to the sequence of operations performed on the product. Conceptually, the flow is an unbroken line from raw materials input to finished goods. This type of layout is applicable to rigid-flow, high-volume, continuous or mass-production operations or when the product is highly standardized. Automobile assembly plants, paper mills, and oil refineries are examples of product layouts. Product layouts offer the advantages of lower materials handling costs; simplified tasks that can be done with low-cost, lower-skilled labor; reduced amounts of work-in-process inventory; and relatively simplified production control activities. All units are routed along the same fixed path, and scheduling consists primarily of setting a production rate. Disadvantages of product layouts include their inflexibility, monotony of job tasks, high fixed investment in specialized equipment, and heavy interdependence of all operations. A breakdown in one machine or at one workstation can idle the entire line. Such a layout also requires the owner to duplicate many pieces of equipment in the manufacturing facility; duplication can be cost-prohibitive for a small firm.

Process Layouts. In a **process layout,** a manufacturer groups workers and equipment according to the general function they perform, without regard to any particular product. Process layouts are appropriate when production runs are short, when demand shows considerable variation and the costs of holding finished goods inventory are high, or when the product is customized. Process layouts have the advantages of being flexible for doing customer work and promoting job satisfaction by offering employees diverse and challenging tasks. Its disadvantages are the higher costs of materials handling, more skilled labor, lower productivity, and more complex production control. Because the workflow is intermittent, each job must be individually routed through the system and scheduled at the various work centers, and its status must be monitored individually.

Fixed-Position Layouts. In a **fixed-position layout,** the bulk of the final product is assembled in one spot; materials do not move down a line as in a product layout. Workers and equipment go to the materials rather than having the materials flow down a line to them. Aircraft assembly shops and shipyards typify this kind of layout.

DESIGNING LAYOUTS. The starting point in layout design is determining how and in what sequence product parts or service tasks flow together. One of the most effective techniques is to create an overall picture of the manufacturing process using assembly charts and process flowcharts. Given the tasks and their sequence and knowledge of the volume or products that can be produced, an entrepreneur can analyze space and equipment needs.

ANALYZING PRODUCTION LAYOUTS. Although there is no general procedure for analyzing the numerous interdependent factors that enter into layout design, specific layout problems lend themselves to detailed analysis. Two important criteria for selecting and designing a layout are worker effectiveness and materials handling costs.

Designing layouts ergonomically so that they maximize workers' strengths is especially important for manufacturers. Creating an environment that is comfortable and pleasant for workers will pay big benefits over time in the form of higher productivity, lower absenteeism and tardiness, and fewer injuries. Designers must be sure that they match the environment they create to workers' needs rather than trying to force workers to adapt to the environment.

Manufacturers can lower materials handling costs by using layouts designed to automate product flow whenever possible and to minimize flow distances and times. The extent of automation depends on the level of technology and amount of capital available, as well as behavioral considerations of employees. Flow distances and times are usually minimized by locating sequential processing activities or interrelated departments in adjacent areas. The following features are important to a good manufacturing layout:

1. Planned materials flow pattern
2. Straight-line layout where possible
3. Straight, clearly marked aisles
4. Backtracking kept to a minimum
5. Related operations close together
6. Minimum of in-process inventory
7. Easy adjustment to changing conditions
8. Minimum materials handling distances
9. Minimum of manual handling
10. No unnecessary rehandling of material
11. Minimum handling between operations
12. Materials delivered to production employees quickly
13. Use of gravity to move materials whenever possible
14. Materials efficiently removed from the work area

15. Materials handling done by indirect labor
16. Orderly materials handling and storage
17. Good housekeeping

Chapter Review

1. Explain the stages in the location decision.
- The location decision is one of the most important decisions an entrepreneur will make, given its long-term effects on the company. An entrepreneur should look at the choice as a series of increasingly narrow decisions: Which region of the country? Which state? Which city? Which site?
- Demographic statistics are available from a wide variety of sources, but government agencies such as the U.S. Census Bureau have a wealth of detailed data that can guide an entrepreneur in selecting the best location.

2. Describe the location criteria for retail and service businesses.
- For retailers and many service businesses, the location decision is especially crucial. They must consider the size of the trade area, the volume of customer traffic, the number of parking spots, availability of room for expansion, and the visibility of a site.

3. Outline the basic location options for retail and service businesses.
- Retail and service businesses have seven basic location options: central business districts (CBDs), neighborhoods, shopping centers and malls, near competitors, inside large retail stores, outlying areas, and at home.

4. Explain the site selection process for manufacturers.
- A manufacturer's location decision is strongly influenced by local zoning ordinances. Some areas offer industrial parks designed specifically to attract manufacturers. Two crucial factors for most manufacturers are the accessibility to (and the cost of transporting) raw materials and the quality and quantity of available labor.

5. Discuss the benefits of locating a start-up company in a business incubator.
- Business incubators are locations that offer flexible, low-cost rental space to their tenants as well as business and consulting services. Their goal is to nurture small companies until they are ready to "graduate" into the larger business community. Many government agencies and universities offer incubator locations.

6. Describe the criteria used to analyze the layout and design considerations of a building, including the Americans with Disabilities Act.
- When evaluating the suitability of a particular building, an entrepreneur should consider several factors:
  - Size: Is the structure large enough to accommodate the business with some room for growth?
  - Construction and external appearance: Is the building structurally sound, and does it create the right impression for the business?
  - Entrances: Are they inviting?
  - Legal issues: Does the building comply with the Americans with Disabilities Act and, if not, how much will it cost to bring it up to standard?
  - Signs: Are they legible, well located, and easy to see?
  - Interior: Does the interior design contribute to your ability to make sales and is it ergonomically designed?
  - Lighting, scent, and sound: Is the lighting adequate to the tasks workers will be performing, and what is the estimated cost of lighting? Can the business use scents to stimulate sales? Is the background music the business use appropriate for its target audience?

7. Explain the principles of effective layout for retailers, service businesses, and manufacturers.
- Layout for retail store and service businesses depends on the owner's understanding of customers' buying habits. Some areas of a retail store generate more sales per square foot and are, therefore, more valuable than others.
- The goal of a manufacturer's layout is to create a smooth, efficient workflow. Three basic layout options exist: product, process, and fixed position. Two key considerations are worker productivity and materials handling costs.

Discussion Questions

1. How do most small business owners choose a location? Is this wise?
2. What factors should a manager consider when evaluating a region in which to locate a business? Where are such data available?
3. Outline the factors entrepreneurs should consider when selecting a state in which to locate a business.
4. What factors should a seafood-processing plant, a beauty shop, and an exclusive jewelry store consider in choosing a location?
5. What intangible factors might enter into the entrepreneur's location decision?
6. What are zoning laws? How do they affect the location decision?
7. What is the trade area? What determines a small retailer's trade area?
8. Why is it important to discover more than just the number of passersby in a traffic count?
9. What types of information can an entrepreneur collect from census data?
10. Why might a cheap location not be the best location?
11. What function does a small firm's sign serve? What are the characteristics of an effective business sign?
12. Explain the statement: "The portions of a small store's interior space are not of equal value in generating sales revenue." What areas are most valuable?
13. What are some of the major features that are important to a good manufacturing layout?

For many businesses, analyzing the value of a potential business site is critical. Owners of retail- or service-based companies usually want high-traffic locations for optimal exposure. Owners of manufacturing, repair, or storage businesses must address issues regarding the location's suitability for their specific needs. Selecting the wrong location places a company at a disadvantage before it ever opens for business. This chapter emphasizes that selecting the right location is crucial to any business venture.

On the Web

The Web offers valuable information regarding location information. "Building a Guerrilla Marketing Plan" was the PRIZM information from Claritas, Inc. (*www.claritas.com/MyBestSegments/Default.jsp*). This information identifies the most common market segments in your zip code and may be a way to validate whether your location is in proximity to your target customers. PRIZM has categorized American consumer markets based on demographic and customer segmentation profiling research data by zip code. A restaurant or a retail business, for example, will find that locating close to its target customers is a key success factor. Additional information, such as traffic counts and other location attributes, are important factors to include in your business plan.

In the Software

Open your business plan and go to the "Your Company" section. Here is where you will describe your ideal, potential, or existing location. If the location you have chosen possesses many of the positive attributes mentioned in the chapter, identify your location as a strength. If your location has negative characteristics, recognize it as a weakness and develop a plan to address how you will overcome the challenges your location presents. If you determine that your location is a critical component for the success of the business, you should assess your location under the "Keys to Success" section. Remember to include the expense for your location—rent, lease, or mortgage payments—into the financial section of your plan.

Building Your Business Plan

Selecting your location is an important strategic business decision for most business ventures. Your business plan will help you profile, describe, and ultimately decide on the most attractive business location available. Once you have secured a location, your plan can leverage that location's strongest attributes to optimize customer exposure, sales, and profits.

Endnotes

1. Betty Joyce Nash, "West Virginia Glass Houses," *Region Focus*, Winter 2009, pp. 43–46.

2. Mark Henricks, "Hot Spots," *Entrepreneur*, October 2005, pp. 68–74.

3. Erick Schonfeld, "Forrester Forecast: Online Retail Sales Will Grow to $250 Billion by 2014," TechCrunch, March 8, 2010, *http://techcrunch. com/2010/03/08/forrester-forecast-online-retail-sales-will-grow-to-250-billion-by-2014/.*

4. Karen E. Klein, "Finding the Perfect Location," *BusinessWeek*, March 24, 2008, *www.businessweek.com/smallbiz/content/mar2008/ sb20080324_098559.htm?chan=smallbiz_smallbiz+index+page_top+ small+business+stories;* Nora Parker, "Johnny's Lunch Plans Franchise Expansion with LI," *Directions Magazine,* October 8, 2007, *www.directionsmag.com/article.php?article_id=2569&trv=1;* Chris Knape, "New Diner Downtown Is Johnny on the Spot," *Grand Rapids Press,* May 12, 2008, p. B4.

5. Jessica Bruder, "The Right Moves," *FSB*, April 2009, p. 16.

6. Daniel Brooks, "New IKEA Factory Hums," *Region Focus*, Fall 2009, p. 2.

7. "Oil-Dri Corporation of America," *Funding Universe, www. fundinguniverse.com/company-histories/OilDri-Corporation-of-America-Company-History.html.*

8. "Employer Costs for Employee Compensation for the Regions," Bureau of Labor Statistics, March 2010, *www.bls.gov/ro4/ro4ecec.htm.*

9. Jacquelyn Lynn, "Location Is Key," *Entrepreneur*, November 2008, p. 26.

10. Jason Daily, "Where to Be an Entrepreneur," *Entrepreneur*, August 2009, p. 51.

11. Ralph Bartholdt, "Couple: High Fees Preventing Dream of Sandpoint Restaurant," *Bonner County Daily Bee*, August 5, 2010, *http://bonnercountydailybee.com/articles/2010/08/05/news/ doc4c5a57423fa76606867788.txt.*

12. "State Individual Income Taxes 2007," Taxadmin.org, *www.taxadmin.org/FTA/rate/ind_inc.html.*

13. Michael McCann, "LeBron James and His Big Decision: Thoughts on the Role of Endorsement Income Potential and State Income Taxes," *Sports Law Blog*, July 8, 2010, *http://sports-law.blogspot.com/2010/07/ lebron-james-and-his-big-decision.html.*

14. David Farkas, "Site Selection: Where Good Food Means the Most," *Chain Leader*, September 1, 2009, pp. 14–17.

15. Alex P. Kellogg, "Black Flight Hits Detroit," *Wall Street Journal*, June 5–6, 2010, pp, A1, A12; Alex P. Kellogg, "Detroit's Smaller Reality," *Wall Street Journal*, February 27–28, 2010, p. A3.

16. Sue Shellenbarger, "The Next Youth-Magnet Cities," *Wall Street Journal*, September 30, 2009, p. D1; Garth Stein, "Seattle Grace," *Fast Company*, May 2009, pp. 92–96.

17. "Clusters and Cluster Development," Institute for Strategy and Competitiveness, Harvard Business School, *www.isc.hbs.edu/ econ-clusters.htm.*

18. Austin Carr, "Fast Cities 2010: Venture Capital Mindset," *Fast Company*, May 2010, p. 87; John Mangels, "Biotech Start-up Hopes Light-Activated Nerve Cells Will Make It a Northeast Ohio Star," Cleveland.com, September 1, 2009, *http://blog.cleveland.com/metro/ 2009/09/biotech_startup_hopes_lightact.html.*

19. David Van Den Berg, "Cinemas Prosper During Recession," *Region Focus*, Winter 2009, p. 2.

20. Sarah Kerner, "Anna Awards First Economic Development Grant," *Collin County Business Press*, August 2, 2010, *www.ccbizpress.com/ display.php?id=4175.*

21. Matt Woolsey, "America's Top 25 Towns to Live Well," *Forbes*, May 4, 2009, *www.forbes.com/2009/05/04/towns-cities-real-estate-lifestyle-real-estate-top-towns.html.*

22. "Worker Relocation Worries," *Inside Training Newsletter*, November 29, 2007, p. 1.

23. Gay Telese, "BASTA," *New Yorker*, May 31, 2010, *www.newyorker.com/talk/2010/05/31/100531ta_talk_talese.*

24. Ron Ruggless, "BK Debuts Whopper Bar Concept, Eyes On-site Arena in Plan to Beef Up Growth," *Nation's Restaurant News*, *www.nrn.com/landingPage.aspx?menu_id=1424&coll_id=676&id=364528;* "BK to Debut Whopper Bar Next Year," *Nation's Restaurant News*, October 7, 2008, *www.nrn.com/breakingNews.aspx?id=359160.*

25. Molly Gise, "Krispy Kreme Debuts Smaller 'Neighborhood Shop' Concept," *Nation's Restaurant News*, August 3, 2009, *www.nrn.com/ article/krispy-kreme-debuts-smaller-neighborhood-shop-concept.*

26. Shannon Perez, "6 Tips to Finding the Perfect Location for Your Practice," MassageTherapy.com, *www.massagetherapy.com/articles/ index.php/article_id/1377.*

27. Matt Rosenberg, "About Reilly's Law of Retail Gravitation," About.com, *http://geography.about.com/cs/citiesurbangeo/a/ aa041403a.htm;* G. I. Thrall and J. C. del Valle, "The Calculation of Retail Market Areas: The Reilly Model," *GeoInfoSystems,* Vol. 7, No. 4, 1997, pp. 46–49.

28. "U.S. Mall Vacancy Average Hits 9 Percent in Second Quarter, Report Says," International Council of Shopping Centers, July 7, 2010, *www.icsc.org/apps/news_item.php?id=2642.*

29. Carolyn Tamler, "Meet Nymbol, the Nicest Bogart in Langley, Washington," *Whidbey Island Life Examiner*, July 8, 2010, *www.examiner.com/life-in-seattle/meet-nymbol-the-nicest-bogart-langley-washington.*

30. Paul Lukas, "Our Malls, Ourselves," *Fortune*, October 18, 2004, pp. 243–256.

31. "Industry Fun Facts," International Council of Shopping Centers, *www.icsc.org/srch/about/impactofshoppingcenters/Did_You_Know.pdf.*

32. Parija Bhatnagar, "Not a Mall. It's a Lifestyle Center," *CNN/Money*, January 12, 2005, *http://money.cnn.com/2005/01/11/news/fortune500/ retail_lifestylecenter/.*

33. Kris Hudson and Vanessa O'Connell, "Recession Turns Malls into Ghost Towns," *Wall Street Journal*, May 22, 2009, pp. A1, A10.

34. Tony Tagliavia, "Ground Broken on New 'Lifestyle' Mall," *Wood Television*, October 6, 2009, *www.woodtv.com/dpp/news/local/kent_ county/knapp_crossing_groundbreaking.*

35. Paul Lukas, "Our Malls, Ourselves." *Fortune*, October 18, 2004.

36. "Industry Fun Facts," International Council of Shopping Centers; "About Mall of America," Mall of America, *www.mallofamerica.com/ about_moa_faqs.aspx.*

37. "Frequently Asked Questions," Small Business Administration, Office of Advocacy, September 2009, p.1; Ying Lowrey, *Start-up Business Characteristics and Dynamics: A Data Analysis of the Kauffman Firm Survey*, Small Business Administration Office of Advocacy, August 2009, p. 20.

38. Raymund Flandez, "Entrepreneurs Pack Up and Go Home," *Wall Street Journal*, June 2, 2009, pp. B1, B6.

39. Lynne P. Shackleford, "Injunction Forbids Weddings at Farm," *Spartanburg Herald-Journal*, June 28, 2009, p. A1; Jennifer Phillips, "Judge Orders Spiegel Farms to Close," *Fox Carolina*, July 30, 2009, *www.foxcarolina.com/news/20223898/detail.html.*

40. Deborah Ball, "Bottled Water Pits Nestle vs. Greens," *Wall Street Journal*, May 25, 2010, pp. A1, A16.

41. Ron Starner, "The Price of Success," *Site Selection*, September 2009, *www.siteselection.com/features/2009/sep/California/.*

42. Elizabeth Whiteman, Marc Chittum, and Michael Masserman, "Foreign Trade Zones Record Increase in Shipments," International Trade Administration, *http://trade.gov/press/publications/newsletters/ ita_0110/shorttakes_0110.asp.*

43. "Business Incubation FAQ," National Business Incubation Association, *www.nbia.org/resource_center/bus_inc_facts/index.php.*

44. Sarah E. Needleman, "Entrepreneurs Find New Way to Grow," *Wall Street Journal*, May 22, 1020, p. B5; Michael V. Copeland, "Making Detroit High Tech," *Fortune*, March 1, 2010, pp. 29–30; Nitasha Tiku and April Joyner, "Where Great Ideas Are Born," *Inc.*, May 2010, 44–47.

45. "Business Incubation FAQ," National Business Incubation Association.

46. "What Is Business Incubation?" National Business Incubation Association, March 31, 2006, *www.nbia.org/resource_center/ what_is/index.php.*

47. "Business Incubation FAQ," National Business Incubation Association.

48. *The Gensler Design + Performance Index: The U.S. Workplace Study*, Gensler Inc., October 22, 2008, p. 12.

49. "Workplace Design = Job Performance?" *Inside Training*, October 29, 2008, p. 1.

50. *The Integrated Workplace*, Office of Governmentwide Policy, Office of Real Property, Washington, DC: 2008, pp. 8–9.

51. Michal Lev-Ram, "How to Make Your Workspace Work Better," *Business 2.0*, November 2006, pp. 58–60.

52. Laura Tiffany, "The Rules of . . . Retailing," *Business Start-Ups*, December 1999, p. 106; Paul Keegan, "The Architect of Happy Customers," *Business 2.0*, August 2002, pp. 85–87.

53. Elizabeth Razzi, "Retailers' Siren Song," *Kiplinger's Personal Financial Magazine*, November 2000, pp. 130–134.

54. Tiffany, "The Rules of . . . Retailing," p. 106.

55. "Educational Kit," President's Committee on Employment of People with Disabilities, *www50.pcepd.gov/pcepd/archives/pubs/ek99/wholedoc.htm#decisions*.

56. Brian Amble, "Poor Workplace Design Damages Productivity," *Management-Issues*, May 23, 2006, *www.management-issues.com/2006/8/24/research/poor-workplace-design-damages-productivity.asp*.

57. "Injuries, Illnesses, and Fatalities," Bureau of Labor Statistics, U.S. Department of Labor, November 12, 2009, p. 1; "Proposal for an Ergonomics Program Standard," Occupational Health and Safety Administration, *www.osha-slc.gov/ergonomics-standard/ergo-faq.html*.

58. "Carpal Tunnel Syndrome," The National Women's Health Information Center, Department of Health and Human Services, *www.womenshealth.gov/faq/carpal-tunnel-syndrome.cfm*.

59. Linda Tischler, "Death to the Cubicle!" *Fast Company*, June 2005, pp, 29–30.

60. Mike Hughlett, "Drive-Throughs Done Right Ring up Returns," *Chicago Tribune*, November 28, 2008, *www.chicagotribune.com/business/chi-fri-drive-throughs-1128-nov28,0,4729183.story*.

61. "Paco Underhill: Shopping Scientist," *CBC News*, November 7, 2000, *www.cbc.ca/consumers/market/files/home/shopping/index.html*.

62. "The Five Guys Mistake," *QSR Magazine*, August 2010, *www.qsrmagazine.com/articles/second_location/144/fiveguys-1.phtml*.

63. Tiffany Meyers, "Waste Not," *Entrepreneur*, February 2008, p. 75.

64. Michael V. Copeland, "The Light Bulb Goes Digital," *Fortune*, February 8, 2010, pp. 33–38.

65. Jennifer Alsever, "Showing Products in a Better Light," *Business 2.0*, September 2005, p. 62.

66. Josh Gould, "Sustainable Workplace Design Creates Innovation Opportunities," *Buildings*, July 2009, *www.buildings.com/tabid/3413/ArticleID/8617/Default.aspx*.

67. *Dollars and Sense: The Impact of Multi-Sensory Marketing*, 4Imprint, 2009, p. 3, *http://info.4imprint.com/wp-content/uploads/blue-paper-sensory-marketing.pdf*.

68. Suzanne Hoppough, "What's That Smell?" *Forbes*, October 2, 2006, p. 76.

69. Ibid.

70. James Vlahos, "Scent and Sensibility," *New York Times*, September 9, 2007, *http://query.nytimes.com/gst/fullpage.html?res=9D07EFDC1E3AF93AA3575AC0A9619C8B63&sec=&spon=&pagewanted=2*.

71. *Dollars and Sense: The Impact of Multi-Sensory Marketing*, 4Imprint.

72. Colleen Bazdarich, "In the Buying Mood? It's the Muzak," *Business 2.0*, March 2002, p. 100.

73. Nadine Heintz, "Play Bach, Boost Sales," *Inc.*, January 2004, p. 23.

74. Theunis Bates, "Volume Control," Time.com, August 2, 2007, *www.time.com/time/printout/0,8816,1649304,00.html*.

75. Josh Gould, "Sustainable Workplace Design Creates Innovation Opportunities," *Buildings*, July 2009, *www.buildings.com/tabid/3413/ArticleID/8617/Default.aspx*.

76. Joey Terrell, "How I Turned My Denny's Green," *Entrepreneur*, January 2010, p. 100.

77. Paul Keegan, "The Architect of Happy Customers," *Business 2.0*, August 2002, pp. 85–87.

78. Russell Boniface, "I Spy a Shopper," *AIArchitect*, June 23, 2006, *www.aia.org/aiarchitect/thisweek06/0623/0623paco.cfm*.

79. "Survey: 43 Percent of Shoppers Rely on Lists," *Retail Shopping Experience*, August 19, 2010, *www.retailcustomerexperience.com/article/139799/Survey-43-percent-of-customers-rely-on-shopping-lists*.

80. Jeffrey A, Trachtenberg, "How a Children's Book Got a Christmas Break," *Wall Street Journal*, December 5, 2005, pp. B1, B5.

81. Tom Stevens, "Practice People," *IndustryWeek*, March 17, 1997, pp. 33–36.

82. Judy Sharpton, "I Love It When I'm Right," *Green Profit*, April 15, 2010, *www.ballpublishing.com/greenprofit/ViewArticle.aspx?articleid=17755*.

83. Zach Dundas, "The Butt-Brush Factor," *Willamette Weekly*, December 15, 2004, *http://wweek.com/story.php?story=5822*.

84. Paul Keegan, "The Architect of Happy Customers," *Business 2.0*, August 2002, pp. 85–87; Kenneth Labich, "This Man Is Watching You," *Fortune*, July 19, 1999, pp. 131–134.

85. Keegan, "The Architect of Happy Customers," pp. 85–87.

86. Rachel Tobin Ramos, "Old Navy Stores Go Under the Knife," *Atlanta Journal Constitution*, March 17, 2010, *www.ajc.com/business/old-navy-stores-go-378109.html*.

87. Boniface, "I Spy a Shopper."

88. "Release Me," *Entrepreneur*, January 1998, pp. 48–49.

Supply Chain Management

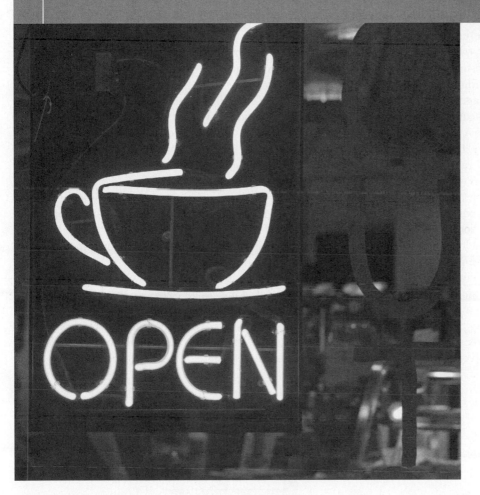

Learning Objectives

Upon completion of this chapter, you will be able to:

1 Understand the components of a purchasing plan.

2 Explain the principles of total quality management (TQM) and Six Sigma and their impact on quality.

3 Conduct economic order quantity (EOQ) analysis to determine the proper level of inventory.

4 Differentiate among the three types of purchase discounts that vendors offer.

5 Calculate a company's reorder point.

6 Develop a vendor rating scale.

7 Describe the legal implications of the purchasing function.

Without the right goods, sales are impossible.

—Anonymous

Quality in a product or service is not what the supplier puts in. It is what the customer gets out and is willing to pay for. Customers pay only for what is of use to them and gives them value. Nothing else constitutes quality.

—Peter Drucker

From Chapter 17 of *Effective Small Business Management: An Entrepreneurial Approach*, 10/e. Norman M. Scarborough.

This chapter discusses the activities involved in managing a small company's supply chain—purchasing, quality management, and vendor analysis. Although none of these is the most glamorous or exciting job an entrepreneur undertakes, they form an important part of the foundation that supports every small business. When entrepreneurs begin producing products or providing services, they quickly learn how much their products or services depend on the quality of the components and services they purchase from their suppliers. Today, success depends on higher levels of collaboration among the businesses that make up a company's supply chain. "Many businesses still regard the supply chain as the back end of their businesses, but the modern supply chain has a much bigger contribution to make," concludes one study of supply chain management. "It can help companies differentiate themselves from the competition and achieve greater sustainable growth."[1] Today, thriving companies operate as part of a seamless network of alliances and partnerships with customers, suppliers, and distributors. For many businesses, the quality of the supply chain determines their ability to satisfy their customers and to compete effectively. "Competition is not really company vs. company," says one expert, "but supply chain vs. supply chain."[2] In other words, supply chain management has become an important strategic issue rather than merely a tactical matter for companies. Several studies have found that companies that utilize best practice supply chain management tools outperform those with average supply chains. Top performing companies saw their revenues grow more than twice as fast and earn 33 percent more profit, while carrying one-third less inventory.[3]

Managing the supply chain has become more challenging, however, because the globalization of business makes supply chains longer and adds layers of complexity to supply chain activities. A recent study by FM Global and CFO Research Services reports that 67 percent of CFOs say that purchasing production inputs from foreign suppliers is at least "somewhat common" in their companies, and 62 percent say that global sourcing activity will increase over the next 3 years. Nearly 40 percent of these executives report that their companies' global purchasing patterns increase the level of risk in the supply chain.[4] Figure 1 shows the greatest risks that companies face in their supply chains. Purchasing goods and services from companies scattered across the globe means that entrepreneurs must manage the elements of their supply chains much more closely to avoid disruptions, inventory shortages, or, at the other extreme, excess inventories that they must discount to sell.

U.S. companies spend more than $20 trillion on goods and services each year, and small and medium-size businesses account for 45 percent of that total.[5] Selecting the right vendors and designing a fast and efficient supply chain influences a small company's ability to produce and sell quality products and services at competitive prices. These decisions have far-reaching effects for a business as well as a significant impact on its bottom line. Depending on the type of business involved, the purchasing function can consume anywhere from 25 to 85 cents of each dollar

FIGURE 1
Supply Chain Risks

of sales. By shaving just 2 percent off of its cost of goods sold, a typical small company can increase its net income by more than 25 percent! A study of various industries by IBM determined that to match the bottom-line impact of a $1 savings in purchasing, a company must increase its sales revenue by an average of 19.7 percent.[6] To realize these savings, however, entrepreneurs must create a purchasing plan, establish well-defined measures of product or service quality, and select vendors and suppliers using a set of relevant, objective criteria.

When a company's supply chain breaks down, the result can be devastating in both immediate and future costs, such as recalling dangerous or defective products and lost sales from customers who turn to substitute products. Some of those lost customers never return, and, worse yet, the company's name and reputation are tarnished forever. For instance, Robert's American Gourmet, a company founded in 1986 by Robert Ehrlich that produces snack foods aimed at health-conscious customers, was forced to recall two of its snacks, Veggie Booty and Super Veggie Tings Crunchy Corn Sticks, after the FDA linked them to a salmonella outbreak that sickened 60 people in 19 states. An analysis traced the salmonella to a spray-on vegetable seasoning that a supplier imported from China. The products, which had accounted for more than 12 percent of the company's sales, were off of store shelves for 3 months, and Robert's American Gourmet's sales declined during the recall and for months afterward.[7]

Both manmade and natural disasters pose a threat to companies' supply chains. In a study of companies across a variety of industries conducted by the Aberdeen Group, 82 percent of managers say that their companies had experienced a supply disruption or outage within the previous 2 years.[8] Automakers BMW and Nissan were among the many companies whose supply chains were disrupted by the eruption of the Eyjafjallajökull volcano in Iceland. Nissan interrupted production at its Japanese factories of three models, the Cube, the Murano, and the Rogue, because the volcanic eruption halted cargo flights from a European supplier of air pressure sensors. BMW slowed production at three German plants and its sole North American plant in Greer, South Carolina, because the ash cloud prevented flights carrying supplies of transmissions. BMW scrambled to find alternative shipping routes but, in the meantime, the company lost many days of production of some of its most popular models, including the X5 and X6.[9] Minimizing problems from disruptions in a company's supply chains as a result of disasters and unexpected events requires a sound purchasing plan.

Creating a Purchasing Plan

1. Understand the components of a purchasing plan.

Purchasing involves the acquisition of needed materials, supplies, services, and equipment of the right quality, in the proper quantities, for reasonable prices, at the appropriate time, and from the right vendor. A major objective of purchasing is to acquire enough (but not too much) stock to ensure smooth, uninterrupted production or sales and to see that the merchandise is delivered on time. A purchasing plan must identify a company's quality requirements, its cost targets, and the criteria for determining the best supplier, considering such factors as reliability, service, delivery, and cooperation.

ENTREPRENEURIAL
Profile

McCormick and Company

McCormick and Company, a business that sells spices ranging from allspice to turmeric, literally spans the globe to purchase from hundreds of suppliers the raw materials it requires for its product line. For more than 100 years, company buyers have traveled to Uganda and Madagascar for vanilla; to China and Nigeria for ginger; to Yugoslavia and Albania for sage; and to India, Turkey, Pakistan, and Syria for cumin seed. McCormick makes significant investments to find suppliers that can deliver quality materials in a timely manner and engages in extensive testing and security practices to ensure the quality and the safety of the raw materials it purchases.[10]

A purchasing plan is closely linked to the other functional areas of managing a small business: production, marketing, sales, engineering, accounting, finance, and others. A purchasing plan should recognize this interaction and help integrate the purchasing function into the total organization. A small company's purchasing plan should focus on the five key elements of purchasing: quality, quantity, price, timing, and vendor selection (see Figure 2).

FIGURE 2
Components of a
Purchasing Plan

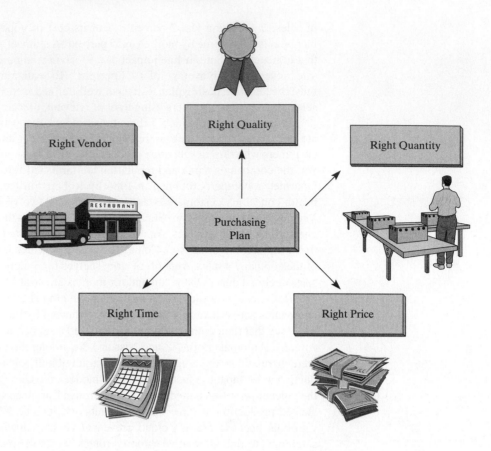

Quality

Not long ago businesses saw quality products and services as luxuries for customers who could afford them. Many companies mistakenly believed that producing or purchasing high-quality products and services was too costly. Today, business owners understand that quality goods and services are absolutely *essential* to remaining competitive. The benefits that companies earn by creating quality products, services, and processes come not only in the form of fewer defects, but also in lower costs, higher productivity, and higher customer retention rates. W. Edwards Deming, one of the founding fathers of the modern quality movement, always claimed that higher quality resulted in lower costs. Internally, companies with a quality focus report significant improvements in work-related factors such as increased employee morale, lower employee turnover, and enhanced quality of work life. Benefits such as these can result in a significant competitive advantage over rivals of *any* size.

Total quality companies believe in and manage with the attitude of continuous improvement, a concept the Japanese call *kaizen*. The kaizen philosophy holds that small improvements made continuously over time accumulate into a radically reshaped and improved process. When defective items do occur, managers and employees who are engaged in continuous improvement do not simply rework or repair them. Instead, they see defective items as an opportunity to improve the entire process. Their goal is to identify the root cause of the defects and to change the entire process so that the same problem does not occur again. Kaizen also encourages managers to focus on improving the entire system, not just its individual components. World-class organizations in the twenty-first century have made continuous improvement a fundamental element of their competitive strategies.

Quality has an impact on both costs and revenues. Improved quality leads to less scrap and rework time, lower warranty costs, and increased worker productivity. On the revenue side of the equation, quality improves the firm's reputation, attracts customers, and often allows a firm to charge higher prices. The bottom-line impact of quality is increased profitability.

Tools for Ensuring Quality: Lean Principles, 5S Principles, Six Sigma, and Total Quality Management

LEAN PRINCIPLES. Originally applied to manufacturing, Lean principles also have produced significant quality improvements in both the retail and service sectors. The fundamental idea behind the Lean philosophy is to eliminate waste in a company's activities, whether they are in manufacturing, distribution, inventory control, customer service, human resources, or other areas, and to make a company lean (and efficient) in its operation. Lean is built on five principles:

1. *Value.* Companies must create products and services that add value from the customer's perspective.
2. *Value stream.* Businesses must identify the essential steps that allow them to create an efficient production or service workflow.
3. *Flow.* Companies must eliminate every step in the value stream that adds no value or creates delays, bottlenecks, and wasted effort. The goal is to create a smoothly flowing, efficient process that produces value for customers.
4. *Pull.* Companies produce only when customer demand pulls products and services through the system. Attempting to push them through the system results in inefficiency in the form of excess inventory, costs, and waste. Customer demand, the "pull" in the system, drives the entire supply chain.
5. *Perfection.* Companies should strive for perfection by eliminating waste and inefficiency everywhere it arises and by providing exactly the products and services customers want.

The principles of Lean are aimed at eliminating seven wastes. Figure 3 (a) shows the seven wastes in a manufacturing environment, and Figure 3 (b) shows the seven wastes in a service operation. Some experts have added an eighth waste to both lists: underutilization of people. Some companies treat their workers as if they know very little. World-class companies see their employees as a valuable source of ideas, creativity, and solutions, and they create systems that capture their employees' knowledge and apply it to the process of continuous improvement.

FIGURE 3 (a)
Seven Wastes of Manufacturing

7. Defects. Products that fail to meet the customer's definition of quality are extremely expensive. "Small" defects often result in huge costs down the line.

1. Overproduction. Interferes with a smooth flow of goods and clouds a company's view of what customers really want.

2. Waiting time. Products that wait for the work cycle to be completed increase cost and create waste and inefficiency.

6. Unnecessary motion. A production system that requires employees to make unnecessary motions to complete a job is inefficient and can lead to injuries.

3. Transportation. The unnecessary movement of products between processes is a common source of waste and inefficiency.

5. Inventory. Storing inventory to which no one is adding value increases costs and masks flaws in the production system.

4. Overprocessing. Processing products beyond customers' standards absorbs resources unnecessarily and produces little value.

FIGURE 3 (b)
Seven Wastes
of Service

7. Defects. Flaws in the service process (poor service, incorrect billing, missing items in a shipment) are extremely costly to repair and result in lost customers.

1. Duplication. Systems that require employees to replicate prior steps (e.g., re-entering order information) increase costs and are inefficient.

2. Delay. Customers who must wait for service are indicative of an inefficient system.

6. Unnecessary motion. Improperly designed workspaces and poor ergonomics impede employees' ability to serve customers efficiently and effectively.

3. Lost opportunities. Companies that miss the opportunity to retain existing customers (customer retention rate) or to gain new ones (increases in sales) eventually fail.

5. Inventory. Companies that run out of the products necessary to provide the service lose sales and alienate customers.

4. Unclear communication. Confusion over how to use a product or service or employees who constantly address customers' questions suggest that the system needs improvement.

IN THE ENTREPRENEURIAL
SPOTLIGHT Lean Works Anywhere

Innovation always has been a key ingredient at Capel Incorporated, the oldest and largest privately owned rug manufacturer in the United States. Founded by Leon Capel, Sr., in 1917 in Troy, North Carolina, the company actually began life as the Gee-Haw Plowline Company, a manufacturer of plow lines used to guide mules and horses in the fields. Within a few years, the introduction of the motorized tractor made Capel's plow line business obsolete, but his ability to innovate saved the company. Capel used the materials from the plow lines to create a continuous yarn, which he then spun into the world's first continuous-yarn braided rug. Leon's sons eventually took over the family business and added their own innovations, including an air table that spun rugs as they were braided, minimizing the amount of manual handling and increasing workers' productivity. They also opened the company's first retail stores, which now number 11.

Capel is now in the hands of third-generation owner Richard Capel, who has introduced important innovations of his own. Perhaps Richard's most important contribution has been introducing Lean principles to the business, an idea that was inspired after he attended a workshop sponsored by North Carolina State University's Industrial Extension Service on the Toyota Production System, on which many of the Lean principles are based.

Richard started with the company's manufacturing process, introducing workers to Lean principles and teaching them to spot the seven wastes. He set up a system to encourage employee ideas and solutions to production problems and established a "pull" system in which customer demand rather than production capacity determines production. Richard implemented a kanban inventory system that triggers orders for more materials only when they are needed, a move that allowed Capel to cut its investment in inventory while increasing the availability of materials.

The results of Capel's early efforts at Lean were impressive. With these basic changes, the company reduced its costs by $890,000 annually. Sales also increased because Capel could process and deliver customers' orders much faster and much more efficiently, which produced a total economic benefit to the company of more than $2 million. Performance improved so much that Capel began offering a Zip Ship program that allows 1-day turnaround on some orders.

Everyone at Capel was so impressed with the results of implementing Lean in the company's manufacturing process that managers decided to apply them to the corporate office. One of the first processes Lean teams addressed was setting up customer accounts, which took weeks to complete because of paperwork, credit checks, database setup, and other activities. The first step was to create a Value Stream Map (VSM), a Lean tool that displays every step required in a process. Mapping the account creation process enabled a team of employees to identify waste, inefficiency, and bottlenecks, just as it did when applied to manufacturing processes. "Once you visualize the problem areas, only then can you begin to resolve them," says Steve Laton, one of the members of the Lean team. The VSM helped the team identify the "ideal flow," which removed the non-value-added steps in the process. The new lean process creates customer accounts within 24 hours.

Buoyed by their success with Lean principles, Capel and his employees are developing plans to apply them in other areas of the business. "Lean works anywhere," says Richard.

1. What lessons can other small companies learn from Capel's experience of applying Lean principles?
2. Do you agree with Richard Capel's statement, "Lean works anywhere"? Explain.
3. Use the Internet to research Value Stream Mapping. Work with a local business owner to map one of the company's processes. Do you spot inefficiencies? How can you redesign the process to create the "ideal flow"?

Source: Based on "Capel Rugs of Troy Weaves Continuous Improvement," Industrial Extension Service, North Carolina State University, January 2010, *www.ies.ncsu.edu/_library/docs/capelrugs_lean.cfm.*

5S PRINCIPLES. Often used in conjunction with Lean, the 5S principles are simple but effective ways to improve quality by organizing the employees' work environment. The 5Ss are:

1. *Sort.* Companies sort items in the workplace into two categories—necessary and unnecessary—and eliminate everything that is unnecessary.
2. *Straighten.* Companies arrange the tools, equipment, and materials employees need to do their jobs in the most efficient manner, minimizing wasted motion and effort.
3. *Shine.* Once organized, employees keep their workspaces neat and clean.
4. *Systematize.* Businesses strive for continuous improvement in sorting, straightening, and shining by standardizing best-practice processes.
5. *Sustain.* Companies sustain their drive toward continuous improvement by encouraging the involvement of all employees, self-discipline, and creating a performance measurement system.

ENTREPRENEURIAL
Profile

Bill Vogel: Vogel Wood Products

Bill Vogel, CEO of Vogel Wood Products, a Monona, Wisconsin-based maker of wood and laminate cabinetry, fixtures, and office systems for home and commercial use, knew that his 15-employee company was operating well below peak efficiency. "We were putting in tons of overtime to get orders out the door," he says. Vogel knew that competition in the industry was becoming fiercer and that his company had to undergo dramatic changes to gain a competitive edge. With the help of the Wisconsin Manufacturing Extension Partnership, Vogel and his employees embarked on a quality improvement journey using Lean manufacturing and 5S principles. The goal was to get every employee involved and to create a culture in which the customer comes first. The first step was to map the company's existing processes, including those in manufacturing, assembly, and the front office, so that they could identify areas of inefficiency and waste. Employees then focused on using 5S principles to create a clean, organized, and efficient workplace. "With Lean and 5S, the goal is to work more effectively, not harder," says Vogel. One team of employees came up with the idea of placing tools on carts that employees could move from one work station to another, reducing time wasted searching for the right tool. The changes allowed employees to identify and eliminate bottlenecks in the production process that Vogel says "unlocked the flow" of work. The company has reaped many benefits from the changes. In addition to improved employee morale, Vogel Wood Products cut its cycle time (the time from receiving an order to delivering it to the customer) in half, reduced its work-in-process inventory by 70 percent, reduced overtime and labor costs by more than 6 percent, and increased its profits by 4 percent. "The principles of Lean are simple," says sales manager Denita Ward. "The trick is to step back to see where basic changes can be made that result in real improvements."[12]

SIX SIGMA. Six Sigma relies on data-driven statistical techniques to improve the quality and the efficiency of any process and to increase customer satisfaction. The quality threshold that Six Sigma programs set is high: just an average of 3.4 defects per 1 million opportunities! Although initially used by large corporations, Six Sigma can be adapted to work in small businesses as well. The four key tenets of Six Sigma are:

1. *Delight customers with quality and speed.* Six Sigma recognizes that the customer's needs come first. The goal is to produce products that are of the highest quality in a process that is efficient and fast.
2. *Constantly improve the process.* Six Sigma builds on the concept of continuous improvement. According to W. Edwards Deming, most quality problems are the result of the *process* (which management creates) rather than the *employees* (who work within the process that management builds). The goal is to reduce the variation of the process, which is measured by the standard deviation (denoted by the Greek letter sigma).
3. *Use teamwork to improve the process.* Six Sigma counts on teams of employees working together to improve a process. People working together to share their knowledge can generate better solutions to quality problems than individuals can.
4. *Make changes to the process based on facts, not guesses.* To improve a process, employees must have quantifiable measures of results (e.g., quality of output) and of the process itself (e.g., how the process operated to produce those results).[11]

Table 1 explains the DMAIC process upon which the Six Sigma approach is built. For small companies, the goal of this process is to understand their core business processes better so that managers and employees can work together to make significant improvements to them over time.

TOTAL QUALITY MANAGEMENT. Under the total quality management (TQM) philosophy, companies define a quality product as one that conforms to predetermined standards that satisfy customers' demands. That means getting *everything*—from delivery and invoicing to installation and follow-up—right the first time. Although these companies know that they may never reach their targets of perfect quality, they never stop striving for perfection, recognizing that even a 99.9 percent level of quality is not good enough (see Table 2). The businesses that have effectively implemented these programs understand that the process involves a total commitment from strategy to practice and from the top of the organization to the bottom.

Rather than trying to inspect quality into products and services after they are completed, TQM instills the philosophy of doing the job right the first time. Although the concept is simple, implementing such a process is a challenge that requires a very different kind of thinking and very

TABLE 1 The Six Sigma DMAIC Approach

Principle	Process Improvement Technique
Define	Identify the problem.
	Define the requirements.
	Set the goal for improvement.
Measure	Validate the process problem by mapping the process and gathering data about it.
	Refine the problem statement and the goal.
	Measure current performance by examining the relevant process inputs, steps, and output to establish a baseline.
Analyze	Develop a list of potential root causes.
	Identify the vital few.
	Use data analysis tools to validate the cause-and-effect connections between root causes and the quality problem.
Improve	Develop potential solutions to remove root causes by making changes to the process.
	Test potential solutions and develop a plan for implementing those that are successful.
	Measure the results of the improved process.
Control	Establish standard measures for the new process.
	Establish standard procedures for the new process.
	Review performance periodically and make adjustments, as needed.

Source: Adapted from Andrew Spanyi and Marvin Wurtzel, "Six Sigma for the Rest of Us," *Quality Digest*, July 2003. Reprinted with permission.

TABLE 2 Why 99.9 Percent Quality Isn't Good Enough

Most companies willingly accept a certain percentage of errors and defects. Usually the range is 1 to 5 percent. In some companies, errors and defects are regarded as a routine part of daily operations. However, quality consultants say that even 99.9 percent isn't good enough.

What would be the result if some things were done right only 99.9 percent of the time? Consider the implications:

- Two unsafe landings at Chicago's O'Hare Airport per day.
- 16,000 lost pieces of mail per hour.
- 200,000 incorrectly filled drug prescriptions per year.
- 5,000 incorrect surgical procedures performed each week.
- 22,000 checks deducted from the wrong accounts every hour.
- 1,314 telephone calls misdirected every minute.
- 14 babies delivered to the wrong parents each day.
- 2,488,200 magazines published with the wrong covers every year.

If you are in the unlucky one-tenth of 1 percent, the error affects you 100 percent. In addition, unless a company strives for 100 percent product or service quality, there is little chance that it will ever achieve 99.9 percent quality.

Sources: Based on Lieca Brown, "Sigma Management," *Point of Beginning*, August 2001, p. 6; *On the Job Performance* (Chicago: Dartnell Corporation, 1997), p. 3; San Marino, "Is Good Enough' Good Enough?" *IndustryWeek*, February 3, 1997, p. 22.

different culture than most organizations are comfortable with. Because the changes TQM requires are so significant, patience is a must for companies adopting the philosophy. Consistent quality improvements rarely occur overnight. Yet, too many small business managers think, "We'll implement TQM today and tomorrow our quality will soar." TQM is *not* a "quick-fix," short-term program that can magically push a company to world-class-quality status overnight. Because it requires such fundamental, often drastic, changes in the way a company does business, TQM takes time both to implement and to produce results. Patience is a must. Although some small businesses that use TQM begin to see some improvements within just a matter of weeks, the *real* benefits take longer to realize. It takes at least 3 or 4 years before TQM principles gain acceptance among employees, and as many as 8 years are necessary to fully implement TQM in a company.

To implement TQM successfully, a small business owner must rely on these fundamental principles:

- *Employ benchmarking to achieve quality outcomes.* **Benchmarking** is the process of identifying world-class processes or procedures other companies (often in other industries) currently are using and building quality standards around these for your business. This search for best practices is ongoing. As part of their quality initiative, employees at Scotsman Ice Systems, a small company in Fairfax, South Carolina, that makes high-end commercial and residential ice machines and refrigerators, benchmark production processes of other manufacturing companies. To make sure that they do not miss anything, they have developed a benchmarking booklet that contains a list of key questions to take with them on benchmarking trips.[13]
- *Shift from a management-driven culture to a participative, team-based one.* Two basic tenets of TQM are employee involvement and teamwork. Business owners must be willing to push decision-making authority down the organization to where the real experts are. Teams of employees working together to identify and solve problems can be a powerful force in an organization of any size. Experience with TQM has taught entrepreneurs that the combined knowledge and experience of workers is much greater than that of only one person. Tapping into the problem-solving capabilities of the team produces profitable results.
- *Modify the reward system to encourage teamwork and innovation.* Because the team, not the individual, is the building block of TQM, companies often have to modify their compensation systems to reflect team performance. Traditional compensation methods pit one employee against another, undermining any sense of cooperation. Often they are based on seniority rather than on how much an employee contributes to the company. Compensation

589

systems under TQM usually rely on incentives, linking pay to performance. However, rather than tying pay to individual performance, these systems focus on team-based incentives. Each person's pay depends on whether the entire team (or, sometimes, the entire company) meets a clearly defined, measurable set of performance objectives.

- *Train workers constantly to give them the tools they need to produce quality and to upgrade the company's knowledge base.* One of the most important factors in making long-term, constant improvements in a company's processes is teaching workers the philosophy and the tools of TQM. Admonishing employees to "produce quality" or offering them rewards for high quality is futile unless a company gives them the tools and know-how to achieve that end. Managers must be dedicated to making their companies "learning organizations" that encourage people to upgrade their skills and give them the opportunities and incentives to do so. The most successful companies spend anywhere from 1 to 5 percent of their employees' time on training, most of it invested in workers, not managers. To give employees a sense of how the quality of their job fits into the big picture, many TQM companies engage in **cross-training,** teaching workers to do other jobs in the company.

- *Train employees to measure quality with the tools of statistical process control (SPC).* The only way to ensure gains in quality is to measure results objectively and to trace the company's progress toward its quality objectives. That requires teaching employees how to use statistical process control techniques such as fishbone charts, Pareto charts, control charts, and measures of process capability.* Without knowledgeable workers using these quantitative tools, TQM cannot produce the intended results.

- *Use Pareto's Law to focus TQM efforts.* One of the toughest questions managers face in companies embarking on TQM for the first time is "Where do we start?" The best way to answer that fundamental question is to use Pareto's Law (also called the 80/20 Rule), which states that 80 percent of a company's quality problems arise from just 20 percent of all causes. By identifying this small percentage of causes and focusing quality improvement efforts on them, a company gets maximum return for its effort. This simple yet powerful rule forces workers to concentrate resources on the most significant problems first, where payoffs are likely to be biggest, and helps build momentum for successful TQM effort.

- *Share information with everyone in the organization.* Asking employees to make decisions and to assume responsibility for creating quality necessitates that the owner share information with them. Employees cannot make sound decisions consistent with the company's initiative if managers are unwilling to give them the information they need to make those decisions.

- *Focus quality improvements on astonishing the customer.* The heart of TQM is customer satisfaction—better yet, customer astonishment. Unfortunately, some companies focus their quality improvement efforts on areas that never benefit the customer. Quality improvements with no customer focus (either internal or external customers) are wasted.

- *Don't rely on inspection to produce quality products and services.* The traditional approach to achieving quality was to create a product or service and then to rely on an army of inspectors to "weed out" all of the defects. Not only is such a system a terrible waste of resources (consider the cost of scrap, rework, and no-value-added inspections), but it gives managers no opportunity for continuous improvement. The only way to improve a process is to discover the cause of poor quality, fix it (the sooner the better), and learn from it so that workers can *avoid* the problem in the future. Using the statistical tools of the TQM approach allows a company to learn from its mistakes with a consistent approach to constantly improving quality.

- *Avoid using TQM to place blame on those who make mistakes.* In many firms, the only reason managers seek out mistakes is to find someone to blame for them. The result is a culture based on fear and the unwillingness of workers to take chances to innovate. The goal of TQM is to improve the processes in which people work, *not* to lay blame on

---

*To learn more about total quality management and the tools of statistical quality control, look in modern statistics or operations management textbooks or visit the following Web sites: *http://deming.eng.clemson.edu/pub/den/deming_map.htm* and *http://search.bnet.com/search/Total+Quality+Management.html?t=13&s=0&o=0.*

workers. Searching out "the guilty party" doesn't solve the problem. The TQM philosophy sees each problem that arises as an opportunity for improving the company's system.

■ *Strive for continuous improvement in processes as well as in products and services.* There is no finish line in the race for quality. A company's goal must be to improve the quality of its processes, products, and services constantly, no matter how high it currently stands!

Many of these principles are evident in quality guru W. Edwards Deming's 14 points, a capsulized version of how to build a successful TQM approach (see Table 3).

Implementing a TQM program successfully begins at the top. If the owner or chief executive of a company doesn't actively and visibly support the initiative, the employees who must make it happen will never accept it. TQM requires change: change in the way a company defines quality, in the way it sees its customers, in the way it treats employees, and in the way it sees itself. Successful implementation also involves modification of the organization's culture.

Quantity: The Economic Order Quantity (EOQ)

3. Conduct economic order quantity (EOQ) analysis to determine the proper level of inventory.

The typical small business has its largest investment in inventory. However, an investment in inventory is not profitable because dollars spent return nothing until the inventory is sold. In a sense, a small company's inventory is its largest non-interest-bearing investment. Entrepreneurs must focus on controlling this investment and on maintaining proper inventory levels.

TABLE 3 Deming's 14 Points

Total quality management cannot succeed as a piecemeal program or without true commitment to its philosophy. W. Edwards Deming, the man most visibly connected to TQM, drove home these concepts with his 14 points, the essential elements for integrating TQM successfully into a company. Deming's message was straightforward. Companies must transform themselves into customer-oriented, quality-focused organizations in which teams of employees have the training, the resources, and the freedom to pursue quality on a daily basis. The goal is to track the performance of a process, whether manufacturing a clock or serving a bank customer, and to develop ways to minimize variation in the system, eliminate defects, and spur innovation. The 14 points are as follows:

1. *Constantly strive to improve products and services.* This requires total dedication to improving quality, productivity, and service—continuously.
2. *Adopt a total quality philosophy.* There are no shortcuts to quality improvement; it requires a completely new way of thinking and managing.
3. *Correct defects as they happen,* rather than relying on mass inspection of end products. Real quality comes from improving the process, not from inspecting finished products and services. At that point, it's too late. Statistical process control charts help workers detect when a process is producing poor-quality goods or services. Then they can stop it, make corrections, and get the process back on target.
4. *Don't award business on price alone.* Rather than choosing the lowest-cost vendor, businesses should work toward establishing close relationships with the vendors who offer the highest quality.
5. *Constantly improve the system of production and service.* Managers must focus the entire company on customer satisfaction, measure results, and make adjustments as necessary.
6. *Institute training.* Workers cannot improve quality and lower costs without proper training to erase old ways of doing things.
7. *Institute leadership.* The supervisor's job is not to boss workers around; it is to lead. The nature of the work is more like coaching than controlling.
8. *Drive out fear.* People often are afraid to point out problems because they fear the repercussions. Managers must encourage and reward employee suggestions.
9. *Break down barriers among staff areas.* Departments within organizations often erect needless barriers to protect their own turf. Total quality requires a spirit of teamwork and cooperation across the entire organization.
10. *Eliminate superficial slogans and goals.* These only offend employees because they imply that workers could do a better job if they would only try.
11. *Eliminate standard quotas.* They emphasize quantity over quality. Not everyone can move at the same rate and still produce quality.
12. *Remove barriers to pride of workmanship.* Most workers want to do quality work. Eliminating "de-motivators" frees them to achieve quality results.
13. *Institute vigorous education and retraining.* Managers must teach employees the new methods of continuous improvement, including statistical process control techniques.
14. *Take demonstrated management action to achieve the transformation.* Although success requires involvement of all levels of the organization, the impetus for change must come from the top.

These 14 interrelated elements contribute to a chain-reaction effect. As a company improves its quality, costs decline, productivity increases, the company gains additional market share due to its ability to provide high-quality products at competitive prices, and the company and its employees prosper.

Source: Deming, W. Edwards, *Out of the Crisis*, pp. 23–24, © 2000 Massachusetts Institute of Technology, by permission of The MIT Press.

ENTREPRENEURIAL
Profile

Peter Nygard: Nygard International

A few years ago, Peter Nygard, founder of Nygard International, a women's clothing manufacturer in Toronto, Ontario, was concerned about the high and increasing level of inventory in his warehouse. The company's inventory had ballooned to its highest level ever, and what concerned Nygard even more than the amount of stock was the imbalance of the inventory. Nygard was overstocked with out-of-style fashions but was running short of items that were popular. To solve the inventory problem, Nygard developed a purchasing plan designed to create a more efficient flow of goods from "the sheep and the silkworms to the consumer," he says. Nygard invested in software that tracked both actual and forecasted sales of specific products, and he shifted the company's ordering, manufacturing, shipping, and selling operations online. The company cut its manufacturing costs by one-third and reduced the time required to fill a customer's order from 3 weeks to just 1 day! Nygard estimates that making these changes in the company's supply chain has added about $10 million a year to his company's bottom line. In addition, he says, "We can gather information and make decisions based on what is actually selling with the snap of a finger as opposed to philosophizing or assuming."[14]

A primary objective of this portion of the purchasing plan is to generate an adequate turnover of merchandise by purchasing proper quantities. Tying up capital in extra inventory limits a company's working capital and exerts pressure on its cash flows. Also, a business risks the danger of being stuck with spoiled or obsolete merchandise, an extremely serious problem for many small businesses. Excess inventory also takes up valuable selling space that could be used for items with higher turnover rates and more profit potential. However, maintaining too little inventory can be extremely costly. An owner may be forced to reorder merchandise too frequently, escalating total inventory costs. In addition, inventory stockouts occur when customer demand exceeds a company's supply of merchandise, causing customer ill will. Persistent stockouts are inconvenient for customers, and many customers eventually abandon the store to shop elsewhere. Manufacturers that run out of inventory must shut down temporarily and incur huge costs. For instance, Toyota, which operates an extremely lean production process, was forced to shut down production when the factory that supplies all of its brake shoes was damaged by an earthquake. The supply shortage cost Toyota an estimated $200 million in revenue.[15] Carrying either too much or too little inventory both are expensive mistakes that lead to serious problems in other areas of the business.

The goal is to maintain enough inventory to meet customer orders and to satisfy production needs but not so much that storage costs and inventory investments are excessive. The analytical techniques used to calculate **economic order quantities (EOQs)** help business owners to determine the amount of inventory to purchase in an order or to produce in a production run to minimize total inventory costs. To compute the economic order quantity, a small business owner must first determine the three principal elements of total inventory costs: the cost of the units, the holding (or carrying) cost, and the setup (or ordering) cost.

Cost of Units

The cost of the units is simply the number of units demanded for a particular time period multiplied by the cost per unit. Suppose that a small manufacturer of lawnmowers forecasts demand for the upcoming year to be 100,000 mowers. He needs to order enough wheels at $4.15 each to supply the production department. He computes:

$$\text{Total annual cost of units} = D \times C$$

where:

$$D = \text{Annual demand (in units)}$$

$$C = \text{Cost of a single unit (\$)}$$

In this example,

$$D = 100{,}000\,\text{mowers} \times 4\,\text{wheels per mower} = 400{,}000\,\text{wheels}$$

$$C = \$4.15\,\text{per wheel}$$

$$
\begin{aligned}
\text{Total annual cost of units} &= D \times C \\
&= 400{,}00\,\text{wheels} \times \$4.15 \\
&= \$1{,}660{,}000
\end{aligned}
$$

Holding (Carrying) Costs

An excessive inventory investment ties up a large amount of a company's cash unproductively in the form of holding costs. The typical costs of holding inventory include the costs of storage, insurance, taxes, interest, depreciation, damage or spoilage, obsolescence, and pilferage. The expense involved in physically storing the items in inventory is usually substantial, especially if inventories are large. An entrepreneur may have to rent or build additional warehousing facilities, pushing the cost of storing the inventory even higher. The company also may incur expenses in transferring items into and out of inventory. The cost of storage also includes the expense of operating the facility (e.g., heating, lighting, refrigeration), as well as the depreciation, taxes, and interest on the building. Most small business owners purchase insurance on their inventories to shift the risk of fire, theft, flood, and other disasters to an insurer. The premiums paid for this coverage also are included in the cost of holding inventory. In general, the larger a company's average inventory, the greater is its storage cost. For most companies, holding costs for an item range from 15 to 35 percent of its actual cost.

Depreciation costs represent the reduced value of inventory over time. Some businesses experience rapidly depreciating inventory. For example, an auto dealership's inventory is subject to depreciation because it must sell models left over from the previous year at reduced prices.

Spoilage, obsolescence, and pilferage also add to the costs of holding inventory. Some small firms, especially those that deal in trendy merchandise, assume an extremely high risk of obsolescence. For example, a fashion merchandiser with a large inventory of the latest styles may be left with worthless merchandise when styles change. In addition, unless the entrepreneur establishes sound inventory control procedures, the business will suffer losses from employee theft and shoplifting.

Let us return to the lawnmower manufacturer example to illustrate the cost of holding inventory:

$$\text{Total annual holding (carrying) costs} = \frac{Q}{2} \times H$$

where:

$$Q = \text{Quantity of inventory ordered}$$

$$H = \text{Holding cost per unit per year}$$

TABLE 4 Holding (Carrying) Costs

If Q Is . . .	$Q/2$, Average Inventory, Is . . .	$Q/2 \times H$, Holding Cost, Is . . .
500	250	$312.50
1,000	500	625.00
2,000	1,000	1,250.00
3,000	1,500	1,875.00
4,000	2,000	2,500.00
5,000	2,500	3,125.00
6,000	3,000	3,750.00
7,000	3,500	4,375.00
8,000	4,000	5,000.00
9,000	4,500	5,625.00
10,000	5,000	6,250.00

The greater the quantity ordered, the greater is the inventory carrying costs. This relationship is shown in Table 4, assuming that the cost of carrying a single unit of inventory for 1 year is $1.25.

Setup (Ordering) Costs

The various expenses incurred in actually ordering materials and inventory or in setting up the production line to manufacture them determine the setup or ordering costs of a product. The costs of obtaining materials and inventory typically include preparing purchase orders; analyzing and choosing vendors; processing, handling, and expending orders; receiving and inspecting items; and performing all of the required accounting and clerical functions. Even if the small company produces its own supply of goods, it encounters most of these same expenses. Ordering costs are usually relatively fixed, regardless of the quantity ordered.

Setup or ordering costs are found by multiplying the number of orders made in a year (or the number of production runs in a year) by the cost of placing a single order (or the cost of setting up a single production run). In the lawnmower manufacturing example, the annual requirement is 400,000 wheels per year and the cost to place an order is $9.00, and the ordering costs are as follows:

$$\text{Total annual stepup (ordering) costs} = \frac{D}{Q} \times S$$

where:

$$D = \text{Annual demand}$$
$$Q = \text{Quantity of inventory ordered}$$
$$S = \text{Setup (ordering) costs for a single run (or order)}$$

The greater the quantity ordered, the smaller the number of orders placed. This relationship is shown in Table 5, assuming an ordering cost of $9.00 per order.

TABLE 5 Setup Cost

If Q is . . .	D/Q, Number of Orders per Year, Is . . .	$D/Q \times S$, Setup (Ordering) Cost, Is . . .
500	800	$7,200.00
1,000	400	3,600.00
5,000	80	720.00
10,000	40	360.00

Solving for EOQ

If carrying costs were the only expense involved in obtaining inventory, the business owner would purchase the smallest number of units possible in each order to minimize the cost of holding the inventory. For example, if the lawnmower manufacturer purchased just four wheels per order, carrying cost would be minimized:

$$\text{Carrying cost} = \frac{Q}{2} \times H$$

$$= \frac{4}{2} \times \$1.25$$

$$= \$2.50$$

but the ordering cost would be outrageous:

$$\text{Ordering cost} = \frac{D}{Q} \times S$$

$$= \frac{400,000}{4} \times \$9$$

$$= \$900,000$$

Obviously this is not the small manufacturer's ideal inventory solution.

Similarly, if ordering costs were the only expense involved in procuring inventory, the business owner would purchase the largest number of units possible in order to minimize the ordering cost. In our example, if the lawnmower manufacturer purchased 400,000 wheels per order, ordering cost would be minimized:

$$\text{Ordering cost} = \frac{D}{Q} \times S$$

$$- \frac{400,000}{400,000} \times \$9$$

$$= \$9$$

but carrying cost would be tremendously high:

$$\text{Carrying cost} = Q \times H$$

$$= \frac{400,000}{2} \times \$1.25$$

$$= \$250,000$$

A quick inspection shows that neither of those solutions minimizes the total cost of the manufacturer's inventory. Total cost is composed of the cost of the unit, carrying cost, and ordering costs:

$$\text{Total cost} = (D \times C) + \left(\frac{Q}{2} \times H \right) + \left(\frac{D}{Q} \times S \right)$$

These costs are illustrated in Figure 4. Notice that as the quantity ordered increases, the ordering costs decrease and the carrying costs increase.

The EOQ formula simply balances the ordering cost and the carrying cost of the small business owner's inventory so that total costs are minimized. Table 6 summarizes the total costs for various values of Q for our lawnmower manufacturer.

As Table 6 and Figure 4 illustrate, the EOQ formula locates the minimum point on the total cost curve, which occurs where the cost of carrying inventory ($Q/2 \times H$) equals the cost of ordering inventory ($D/Q \times S$). As we have seen, if a small business places the smallest number of orders possible each year, its ordering cost is minimized, but its carrying cost is maximized.

FIGURE 4
Economic Order Quantity

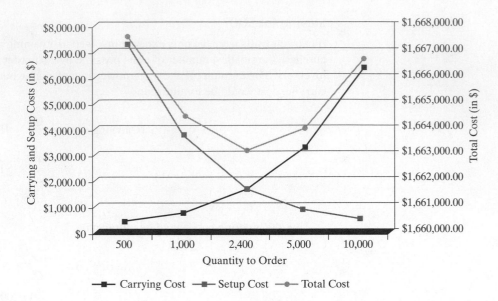

Conversely, if the company orders the smallest number of units possible in each order, its carrying cost is minimized, but its ordering cost is maximized. Total inventory cost is minimized when carrying cost and ordering cost are balanced.

Let us return to our lawnmower manufacturer and compute its economic order quantity, EOQ, using the following formula:

$$S = \$9.00 \text{ per order}$$

$$C = \$1.55 \text{ per wheel}$$

$$EOQ = \sqrt{\frac{2 \times D \times S}{H}}$$

$$= \sqrt{\frac{2 \times 400{,}000 \times \$9.00}{\$1.25}}$$

$$= 2{,}400 \text{ wheels}$$

To minimize total inventory cost, the lawnmower manufacturer should order 2,400 wheels at a time. Furthermore,

$$\text{Number of orders per year} = \frac{D}{Q}$$

$$= \frac{400{,}000}{2{,}400}$$

$$= 166.67 \text{ orders}$$

TABLE 6 Economic Order Quantity and Total Cost

If Q is ...	$D \times C$, Cost of Units, Is ...	$Q/2 \times H$, Carrying Cost, Is ...	$D/Q \times S$, Ordering Cost, Is ...	TC, Total Cost, Is ...
500	$1,660,000	$312.50	$7,200.00	$1,667,512.50
1,000	1,660,000	625.00	3,600.00	1,664,225.00
2,400	**1,660,000**	**1,500.00**	**1,500.00**	**1,663,000.00**
5,000	1,660,000	3,125.00	720.00	1,663,845.00
10,000	1,660,000	6,250.00	360.00	1,666,610.00

This manufacturer will place approximately 167 orders this year at a minimum total cost of $1,663,000, computed as follows:

$$\text{Total cost} = (D \times C) + \left(\frac{Q}{2} \times H\right) + \left(\frac{D}{Q} \times S\right)$$

$$= (400,000 \times \$4.15) + (2,400/2 \times \$1.25) + (400,000/2,400 + \$9.00)$$

$$= \$1,660,000 + \$1,500 + \$1,500$$

$$= \$1,663,000$$

Economic Order Quantity with Usage

The preceding EOQ model assumes that orders are filled instantaneously; that is, fresh inventory arrives all at once. Because that assumption does not hold true for many small manufacturers, it is necessary to consider a variation of the basic EOQ model that allows inventory to be added over time rather than instantaneously. In addition, a manufacturer is likely to be taking items from inventory for use in the assembly process over the same time period. For example, the lawn-mower manufacturer may be producing blades to replenish his supply, but at the same time assembly workers are reducing the supply of blades to make finished mowers. The key feature of this version of the EOQ model is that inventories are used while inventories are being added.

Using the lawnmower manufacturer as an example, we can compute the EOQ for the blades. To make the calculation, we need two additional pieces of information: the usage rate for the blades, U, and the factory's capacity to manufacture the blades, P. Suppose that the maximum number of lawnmower blades the company can manufacture is 480 per day. We know from the previous illustration that annual demand for mowers is 100,000 units (therefore, 100,000 blades). If the plant operates 5 days per week for 50 weeks (250 days), its usage rate is

$$U = \frac{100,000 \text{ units per year}}{250 \text{ days}} = 400 \text{ units per day}$$

It costs $325 to set up the blade manufacturing line and $8.71 to store one blade for 1 year. The cost of producing a blade is $24.85. To compute EOQ, we modify the basic formula:

$$\text{EOQ} = \sqrt{\frac{2 \times D \times S}{H \times \left(1 - \dfrac{U}{P}\right)}}$$

For the lawnmower manufacturer,

$$D = 100,000 \text{ blades}$$

$$S = \$325 \text{ per production run}$$

$$H = \$8.71 \text{ per blade per year}$$

$$U = 400 \text{ blades per day}$$

$$P = 480 \text{ blades per day}$$

$$\text{EOQ} = \sqrt{\frac{2 \times 100,000 \times \$325}{8.71 \times \left(1 - \dfrac{400}{480}\right)}}$$

$$= 6,691.50 \text{ blades} = 6,692 \text{ blades}$$

Therefore, to minimize total inventory cost, the lawnmower manufacturer should produce 6,692 blades per production run. In addition,

$$\text{Number of production runs per year} = \frac{D}{Q}$$

$$= \frac{100,000 \text{ blades}}{6,692 \text{ blades/run}}$$

$$= 14.9 \approx 15 \text{ runs}$$

The manufacturer will make 15 production runs during the year at a total cost of:

$$\text{Total cost} = (D \times C) + \left(\left(1 - \frac{U}{P}\right) \times \frac{Q}{2} \times H\right) + \left(\frac{D}{Q} \times S\right)$$

$$= (100{,}000 \times \$24.85) + \left(\left(1 - \frac{400}{480}\right) \times \frac{6{,}692}{2} \times \$8.71\right) + \left(\frac{100{,}000}{6.692} \times \$325\right)$$

$$= \$2{,}485{,}000 + \$4{,}857 + \$4{,}857$$

$$= \$2{,}494{,}714$$

Business owners must remember that the EOQ analysis is based on estimations of cost and demand. The final result is only as accurate as the input used. Consequently, this analytical tool serves only as a guideline for decision making. The final answer may not be the ideal solution because of intervening factors, such as opportunity costs or seasonal fluctuations. Knowledgeable entrepreneurs use EOQ analysis as a starting point in making a decision and then use managerial judgment and experience to produce a final ruling.

Price

For the typical small business owner, price is always a substantial factor when purchasing inventory and supplies. In many cases, an entrepreneur can negotiate price with potential suppliers on large orders of frequently purchased items. In other instances, perhaps when an entrepreneur purchases small quantities of items infrequently, he or she must pay list price. The typical entrepreneur shops around before ordering from the supplier that offers the best price. However, this does not mean that a business owner should always purchase inventory and supplies at the lowest price available. The best purchase price is the lowest price at which the owner can obtain goods and services *of acceptable quality*. As quality guru W. Edwards Deming said, "Price has no meaning without a measure of the quality being purchased."[16] Companies that are lured by low prices on key products or components from suppliers in foreign countries sometimes discover that shipping costs, customs fees, and the additional costs and challenges of coordinating long-distance shipments more than offset the goods' lower prices.

Recall that one of Deming's 14 points is *"Don't award business on price alone."* Without proof of quality, an item with the lowest initial price actually may produce the *highest* total cost. Deming condemned the practice of constantly switching suppliers in search of the lowest initial price because it increases the variability of a process and lowers its quality. Instead, he recommended that businesses establish long-term relationships built on mutual trust and cooperation with a single supplier.

When evaluating a supplier's price, small business owners must consider not only the actual price of goods and services, but also the selling terms accompanying them. In some cases, the selling terms can be more important than the price itself. Sometimes a vendor's terms might include some type of purchase discount. Vendors typically offer three types of discounts: trade discounts, quantity discounts, and cash discounts.

4. Differentiate among the three types of purchase discounts that vendors offer.

TRADE DISCOUNTS. Trade discounts are established on a graduated scale and depend on a small firm's position in the channel of distribution. In other words, trade discounts recognize the fact that manufacturers, wholesalers, and retailers perform a variety of vital functions at various stages in the channel of distribution and compensate them for providing these needed activities. Figure 5 illustrates a typical trade discount structure.

QUANTITY DISCOUNTS. Quantity discounts are designed to encourage businesses to order large quantities of merchandise and supplies. Vendors are able to offer lower prices on bulk purchases because the cost per unit is lower than for handling small orders. Quantity discounts normally exist in two forms: noncumulative and cumulative. Noncumulative quantity discounts are granted only if a certain volume of merchandise is purchased in a single order. For example, a wholesaler may offer small retailers a 3 percent discount only if they purchase 10 gross of Halloween masks in a single order. Table 7 shows a typical noncumulative quantity discount structure. Cumulative quantity discounts are offered if a firm's purchases from a particular vendor exceed a specified quantity or dollar value over a predetermined time period. The time frame

FIGURE 5
Trade Discount Structure

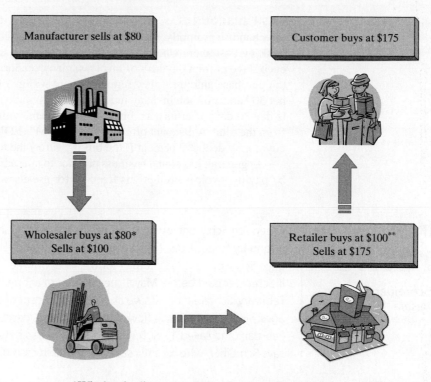

*Wholesale discount = 54% of suggested retail price.
** Retail discount = 43% of suggested retail price.

varies, but one year is most common. For example, a manufacturer of appliances may offer a small business a 3 percent discount on subsequent orders if its purchases exceed $10,000 per year.

Some small business owners who normally buy in small quantities and are unable to qualify for quantity discounts can earn such discounts by joining buying groups, purchasing pools, or buying cooperatives.

ENTREPRENEURIAL
Profile

Blue Hawk Cooperative

Blue Hawk Cooperative is an organization that allows small, independent heating, ventilation, and air conditioning (HVAC) dealers to earn discounts on items they purchase from more than 100 vendors. Founded in 2005 by Dan Bleier, owner of Able Distributors, an HVAC dealer in Chicago, Illinois, Blue Hawk provides quantity discounts to its 230 members (who have nearly 1,100 locations) by combining their purchasing power into one entity. Bleier started Blue Hawk as a way for his family-owned distributorship and other independent HVAC dealers to compete effectively with large chain stores whose volume purchases earned them significant discounts (and hence the ability to offer low prices). "We didn't have the volume to get the manufacturer rebates they could," he says. With the help of the cooperative, members receive discounts on their purchases of items ranging from electric motors to refrigerants. "Our Blue Hawk affiliation has boosted our buying power, enhanced our supplier relationships, and increased our customer satisfaction," says Don Chmura, vice president of purchasing for Refrigeration and Electric Supply Company, a distributor with eight locations in Little Rock, Arkansas.[17] According to the National Cooperative Business Association, more than 700 purchasing cooperatives like Blue Hawk operate in the United States.[18]

TABLE 7 Noncumulative Quantity Discount Structure

Order Size	Price
1–1,000 units	List price
1,001–5,000 units	List price – 2%
5,001–10,000 units	List price – 4%
10,001 units and above	List price – 6%

CASH DISCOUNTS. Cash discounts are offered to customers as an incentive to pay for merchandise promptly. Many vendors grant cash discounts to avoid being used as an interest-free bank by customers who purchase merchandise and then fail to pay by the invoice due date. To encourage prompt payment of invoices, many vendors allow customers to deduct a percentage of the purchase amount if they remit payment within a specified time. Cash discount terms "2/10, net 30" are common in many industries. This notation means that the total amount of the invoice is due 30 days after its date, but if the bill is paid within 10 days the buyer may deduct 2 percent from the total. A discount offering "2/10, EOM" (EOM means "end of month") indicates that the buyer may deduct 2 percent if the bill is paid by the tenth of the month after the purchase.

In general, it is sound business practice to take advantage of cash discounts. The money saved by paying invoices promptly is freed up for use elsewhere.

ENTREPRENEURIAL
Profile

Jeff Schreiber: Hansen Wholesale

When Jeff Schreiber, owner of Hansen Wholesale, a small distributor of home products, attended a January trade show, he purchased $40,000 of ceiling fans from a manufacturer. The contract gave Schreiber until July to pay for the fans, but the manufacturer also included a cash discount: If Schreiber paid before May 1, he could earn a 3 percent discount on the purchase. By paying in February, Schreiber could save another 1.5 percent of the purchase price. For Schreiber, who manages his company's cash flow meticulously, the decision was an easy one; he paid the invoice in February and saved $1,800. "Your money works better if you take advantage of the discounts," says Schreiber, who recently saved $15,000 in cash discounts for his company in just 1 year.[19]

Businesses incur an implicit (opportunity) cost of forgoing a cash discount. By failing to take advantage of a cash discount, a business owner is, in effect, paying an annual interest rate to retain the use of the discounted amount for the remainder of the credit period. For example, suppose the Print Shop receives an invoice for $1,000 from a vendor offering a cash discount of 2/10, net 30. Figure 6 illustrates this situation and shows how to compute the cost of forgoing the cash discount. Actually, it costs the Print Shop $20 to retain the use of its $980 for an extra 20 days. Translating this into an annual interest rate:

$$I = P \times R \times T$$

where

$$I = \text{Interest (\$)}$$
$$P = \text{Principle (\$)}$$
$$R = \text{Rate of interest (\%)}$$
$$T = \text{Time (number of days/360)}$$

To compute R, the annual interest rate,

$$R = \frac{I}{P \times T}$$

FIGURE 6
A Cash Discount

TABLE 8 Cost of Forgoing Cash Discounts

Cash Discount Terms	Cost of Forgoing Cash Discounts (Annually)
2/10, net 30	36.735%
2/30, net 60	34.490%
2/10, net 60	13.693%
3/10, net 30	55.670%
3/10, net 60	22.268%

In our example,

$$R = \frac{\$20}{980 \times \frac{20}{360}}$$

$$= 36.735\%$$

The cost to the Print Shop of forgoing the cash discount is 36.735 percent per year! If there is $980 available on day 10 of the trade credit period, the entrepreneur should pay the invoice unless he is able to earn more than 36.735 percent on that money. If the entrepreneur does not have $980 on day 10 but can borrow it at less than 36.735 percent, he should do so to take advantage of the cash discount. Table 8 summarizes the cost of forgoing cash discounts offering various terms.

Although it is a good idea for business owners to take advantage of cash discounts, it is not a wise practice to stretch accounts payable to suppliers beyond the payment terms specified on the invoice. Letting payments become past due destroys the trusting relationship a small company has built with its vendors.

Timing—When to Order

5. Calculate a company's reorder point.

Timing the purchase of merchandise and supplies is also a critical element of a purchasing plan. Entrepreneurs must schedule delivery dates so that their companies do not lose customer goodwill from stockouts. In addition, they must concentrate on maintaining proper control over the firm's inventory investment without tying up an excessive amount of working capital. There is a trade-off between the cost of running out of stock and the cost of carrying additional inventory.

When planning delivery schedules for inventory and supplies, owners must consider the **lead time** for an order, the time gap between placing an order and receiving it. In general, business owners cannot expect instantaneous delivery of merchandise. As a result, managers must plan reorder points for inventory items with lead times in mind. To determine when to order merchandise for inventory, entrepreneurs must calculate the reorder point for key inventory items. Developing a reorder point model involves determining the lead time for an order, the usage rate for the item, the minimum level of stock allowable, and the economic order quantity (EOQ). The **lead time** for an order is the time gap between placing an order with a vendor and actually receiving the goods. It may be as little as a few hours or as long as several weeks to process purchase requisitions and orders, contact the supplier, receive the goods, and add them to the company's inventory. Obviously, owners who purchase from local vendors encounter shorter lead times than those who rely on distant suppliers.

ENTREPRENEURIAL
Profile

Seth Murray: Belle Baby Carriers

Seth Murray, founder of Belle Baby Carriers, opted to use local vendors and service companies to supply the components of his company's simple, comfortable baby carrier to ensure the quality of his product, which has proved popular with celebrities such as Jessica Alba, Julia Roberts, and Angelina Jolie. Murray considered outsourcing the components to suppliers in China but instead chose suppliers "within 30 miles" of his Boulder, Colorado, location. Although his company's costs are somewhat higher, Belle Baby Carriers places orders with local vendors as they come in, a practice that conserves cash, keeps inventory levels low, and allows the company to operate using Lean principles. In the meantime, Murray's competitors must pay for and wait for the arrival of large containers from Asia and deal with shipping costs and customs regulations. "We have a just-in-time mentality," says Murray. "We have constant communications with our suppliers, and we don't have to worry about shipping costs and import duties."[20]

Business owners can determine the usage rate for a particular product from past inventory and accounting records. They must estimate the speed at which the supply of merchandise will be depleted over a given time. The anticipated usage rate for a product determines how long the supply will last. For example, if an entrepreneur projects that she will use 900 units in the next 6 months, the usage rate is five units per day (900 units/180 days). The simplest reorder point model assumes that the firm experiences a linear usage rate; that is, depletion of the firm's stock continues at a constant rate over time.

Business owners must determine the minimum level of stock allowable. If a firm runs out of a particular item (i.e., incurs stockouts), customers soon lose faith in the business and begin to shop elsewhere. To avoid stockouts, many firms establish a minimum level of inventory greater than zero. In other words, they build a cushion, called **safety stock,** into their inventories in case demand runs ahead of the anticipated usage rate. If that occurs, the owners can dip into the safety stock to fill customer orders until a shipment of goods arrives.

To compute the reorder point for an item, the owner must combine this inventory information with the product's EOQ. The following example illustrates the reorder point technique:

$$L = \text{Lead time for an order} = 5\,\text{days}$$
$$U = \text{Usage rate} = 5\,\text{units per day}$$
$$S = \text{Safety stock (minimum level)} = 75\,\text{units}$$
$$\text{EOQ} = \text{Economic order quantity} = 540\,\text{units}$$

The formula for computing the reorder point is:

$$\text{Reorder point} = (L \times U) + S$$

In this example,

$$\text{Reorder point} = (5\,\text{days} \times 18\,\text{units/day}) + 75\,\text{units}$$
$$= 165\,\text{units}$$

This business owner should order 540 more units when inventory drops to 165 units. Figure 7 illustrates the reorder point situation for this small business.

The simple reorder technique makes assumptions that may not be valid in particular situations. First, the model assumes that the firm's usage rate is constant, but for most small businesses demand varies daily. Second, the model assumes that lead time for an order is constant when, in fact, few vendors deliver precisely within lead time estimates. Third, in this model, the owner never taps safety stock; however, late deliveries or accelerated demand often force owners to dip into their inventory reserves. More advanced models relax some of these assumptions, but the simple model can be a useful inventory guideline for making inventory decisions in a small company.

Another popular reorder point model assumes that the demand for a product during its lead time is normally distributed (see Figure 8). The area under the normal curve at any given point represents the probability that a particular demand level will occur. Figure 9 illustrates the application of this normal distribution to the reorder point model *without* safety stock. The model

FIGURE 7
Reorder Point Model

FIGURE 8
Demand During Leading

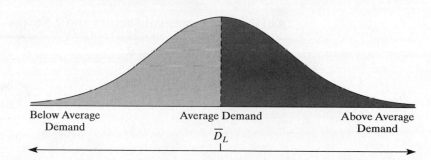

Below Average Demand Average Demand $\overline{D}_L$ Above Average Demand

recognizes that three different demand patterns can occur during a product's lead time. Demand pattern 1 is an example of below-average demand during lead time; demand pattern 2 is an example of average demand during lead time; and demand pattern 3 is an example of an above-average demand during lead time.

If the reorder point for this item is normal for the product during lead time, 50 percent of the time demand will be below average (note that 50 percent of the area under the normal curve lies below average). Similarly, 50 percent of the time demand during lead time will exceed the average, and the firm will experience stockouts (note that 50 percent of the area under the normal curve lies above average).

To reduce the probability of inventory shortage, a business owner can increase the reorder point above $\overline{D}_L$ (average demand during the lead time). But how much should the owner increase the reorder point? Rather than attempt to define the actual costs of carrying extra inventory versus the costs of stockouts (remember the trade-off described earlier), this model allows the small business owner to determine the appropriate reorder point by setting a desired customer level. For example, the owner may want to satisfy 95 percent of customer demand for a product during lead time. This service level determines the amount of increase in the reorder point. In effect, these additional items serve as a safety stock:

$$\text{Safety stock} = SLF \times SD_L$$

where:

$$SLF = \text{Service level factor (the appropriate Z score)}$$

$$SD_L = \text{Standard deviation of demand during lead time}$$

Table 9 shows the appropriate service level factor (Z score) for some of the most popular target customer service levels.

FIGURE 9
Reorder Point Without Safety Stock

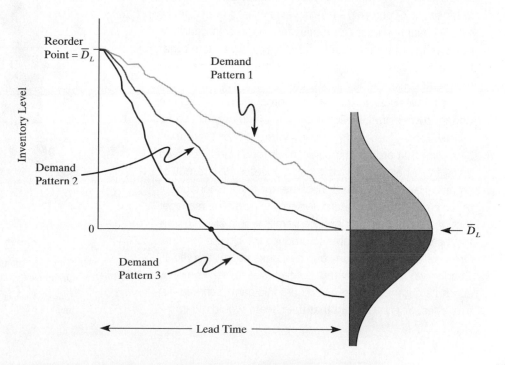

TABLE 9 Service Level Factors and Z Scores

Target Customer Service Level	Z Score*
99%	2.33
97.5%	1.96
95%	1.645
90%	1.275
80%	0.845
75%	0.675

*Any basic statistics book provides a table of areas under the normal curve, which gives the appropriate Z score for any service level factor.

► ENTREPRENEURSHIP IN ACTION ►

Supply Chain Risk

Fifty years ago, business was more localized than it is today, and companies had more control over their supply chains and faced less risk of supply interruptions. If one supplier failed to deliver goods or materials, a company usually could find a nearby supplier to fill the order with very little delay. Today, a global economy means that supply chains are longer and more complex; companies all across the globe buy and sell products to other businesses, and the logistics of those deliveries must be choreographed as carefully as an elaborate dance. A glitch at any point in the process often causes ripples—and problems—throughout the remainder of the chain. Natural disasters, labor strikes, dangerous ingredients, faulty products, political instability, terrorism, piracy, and a host of other problems threaten companies' supply chains. A recent study by McKinsey and Company reports that 77 percent of executives say that the amount of supply chain risk their companies face has increased in the last 5 years. More than half of these executives admit that their companies have not addressed the factors that pose the greatest risk to their supply chains.

Just 2 weeks away from a major production run, Gigi Lee Chang, owner of Plum Organics (www.plumorganics.com), a New York City–based company with sales of more than $1 million that produces organic meals for children, received a call from her supplier of organic cheese. "We're out of organic parmesan cheese because there's a shortage of organic milk," the representative told Chang. The manager *thought* that a shipment of organic milk would arrive in time for the company to be able to produce the cheese for Plum Organics' production run, but he could not guarantee it. Chang was concerned and contacted another company about its organic cheese, but its organic parmesan had not fully aged. She was afraid that the cheese would affect the

taste of the finished product. She had a choice to make: Count on her regular supplier to get the shipment of organic milk and come through with the cheese or use the less-than-fully-aged parmesan from the other company. "You try to ask questions to figure out what the risk is, and when you make your bet, hopefully it's going to turn out," she says.

Julie Allison, owner of Eyebobs (*www.eyebobs.com*), a 10-employee company in Minneapolis, Minnesota, that markets stylish reading glasses, understands the importance of managing her company's supply chain. Allison travels to Italy, France, and China at least three times a year

Gigi Lee Chang, founder of Plum Organics.

Source: Amanda Edwards/Getty Images, Inc.-Liaison

to visit Eyebob's suppliers. When working with a new supplier, she tests the quality of the product and the supplier's delivery by placing small orders. To keep costs—and product prices—in check, Allison has introduced glasses with frames made from materials other than plastic, which is adversely affected by increases in petroleum prices. Eyebobs sells reading glasses with frames made from metal and bamboo. "The risks change," says Allison. "Every day you're learning something new."

1. Suppose that Gigi Lee Chang asks you to make a recommendation on the decision she faces

concerning the delivery of the organic cheese for her company's production run. What do you tell her? Explain your reasoning.

2. What steps can Chang and Allison take to manage the risks in the supply chains for their businesses?

Sources: Based on Denise Paulonis and Sabrina Norton, "Managing Global Supply Chains: McKinsey Global Survey Results," *The McKinsey Quarterly*, August 2008, *www.mckinseyquarterly.com/McKinsey_Global_Survey_Results_Managing_global_supply_chains_2179;* Chris Penttila, "Risky Business," *Entrepreneur*, November 2008, pp. 17–18; Russ Banham, "Reducing Disruption in the Global Supply Chain," *Wall Street Journal*, April 21, 2009, p. A12.

Figure 10 shows the shift to a normally distributed reorder point model with safety stock. In this case, the manager has set a 95 percent customer service level; that is, the manager wants to meet 95 percent of the demand during lead time. The normal curve in the model without safety stock (from Figure 9) is shifted up so that 95 percent of the area under the curve lies above the zero inventory level. The result is a reorder point that is higher than the original reorder point by the amount of the safety stock:

$$\text{Reorder point} = \bar{D}_L + (SLF \times SD_L)$$

where

$\bar{D}_L$ = Average demand during lead time (original reorder point)

SLF = Service level factor (the appropriate Z score)

SD_L = Standard deviation of demand during lead time

FIGURE 10
Reorder Point with Safety Stock

To illustrate, suppose that the average demand for a product during its lead time (1 week) is 325 units with a standard deviation of 110 units. If the desired service level is 95 percent, the service level factor (from Table 9) would be 1.645. The reorder point is:

$$\text{Reorder point} = 325 + (1.645 \times 110) = 325 + 181 = 506 \text{ units}$$

Figure 11 illustrates the shift from a system without safety stock to one with safety stock for this example. With a reorder point of 325 units ($\bar{D}_L$), this small business owner will experience inventory shortages during the lead time 50 percent of the time. With a reorder point of 506 units (i.e., a safety stock of 181 units), the business owner will experience inventory stockouts during the lead time only 5 percent of the time.

Managing the Supply Chain: Vendor Analysis and Selection

6. Develop a vendor rating scale.

Businesses have discovered that managing their supplies chains for maximum effectiveness and efficiency not only can increase their profitability but also can provide them with an important competitive advantage in the marketplace. Proper **supply chain management (SCM)** enables companies to reduce their inventories, get products to market much faster, increase quality, and

FIGURE 11
Shift from a No-Safety Stock System to a Safety Stock System

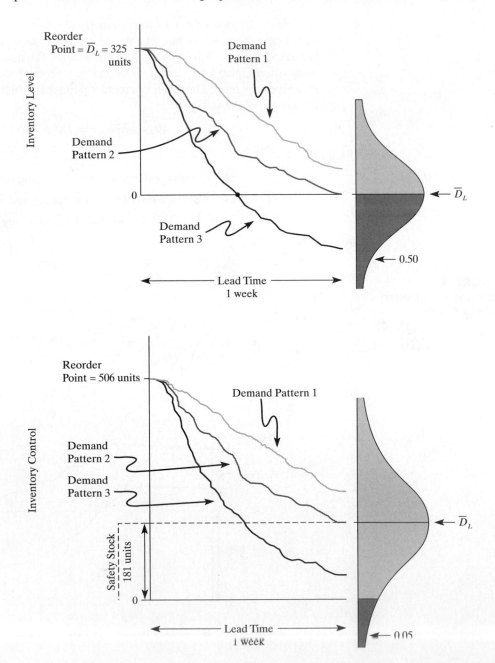

improve customer satisfaction. SCM requires businesses to forge long-term partnerships with reliable suppliers rather than to see vendors merely as "someone trying to sell me something." Doing so can produce an impressive payoff; experts note that implementing a successful SCM system yields an average savings of 15 percent by controlling unnecessary spending, negotiating lower prices, maintaining lower inventory levels, and reducing waste and inefficiency in the purchasing process, all of which save companies vast amounts of money.[21]

Companies are learning that to make SCM work they must share information with their suppliers and make their entire supply chains transparent to everyone involved in them. In the early days, that meant linking suppliers and companies as if they were parts of a single business on private data networks using electronic data interchange (EDI), which allowed companies and vendors to exchange orders and invoices electronically. The Internet takes EDI a step further. Web-based supply chain management, or **e-procurement**, allows companies to share information concerning production plans, shipment schedules, inventory levels, sales forecasts, and actual sales on a real-time basis with their vendors, enabling the companies to make instant adjustments to their orders and delivery schedules. Many studies have found a correlation between the amount of information shared among supply chain members and the efficiency of the entire chain. Costs are significantly lower for retailers, wholesalers, and manufacturers when they are connected in a supply chain network with open communication.[22]

With e-procurement, companies are connected via the Web to their customers and to their suppliers, which allows them to respond rapidly to changing buyer preferences by modifying in real time the inventory they purchase. In turn, suppliers can make the fast adjustments in production scheduling to produce the items that customers actually are buying. Companies "are starting to understand that the 'supply' side of the supply chain isn't worth a hill of beans if the 'demand' side is disconnected," says one industry expert.[23] A study by the consulting firm Aberdeen Group reports that companies that use e-procurement to connect seamlessly the members of their supply chains are able to reduce the prices that they pay for their purchases by 7 percent and cut the delivery time for their orders by 67 percent.[24] With these systems, valuable information flows from the small business selling suits to customers up the supply chain all the way to the sheep shearer harvesting wool!

A Web-based SCM process works like this: Software at a retail store captures data from sales as they happen and looks for underlying trends for use in calculating quantities of which products to purchase in the future. For instance, SCM software at a retail store may notice that sales of black low-rise jeans are selling more briskly than anticipated and forecasts the quantity of jeans the store should order. That information then goes up the supply chain to the jean maker. Taking into account delivery times and manufacturing speed, the software helps the jean maker create a detailed production plan for cutting, sewing, and shipping the garments on time. The software determines how much fabric the jean maker must have to produce the required number of black low-rise jeans and orders it from the textile producer. The software can track everything from the location of the raw materials in the production process to the quality of the finished product for everyone in the supply chain. "Supply chain analytics boost the bottom line because they produce greater efficiency, less scrap, better quality, and lower production costs and improve the top line through greater customer satisfaction," says a top manager at IDC, a research company that has studied the impact of SCM on companies' performance. "This is basic business made better."[25]

To function smoothly, a small company's supply chain should follow the "triple A's": agile, adaptable, and aligned.[26] An *agile* supply chain is one that is fast, flexible, and responsive to changes in demand. Agile supply chains are able to deal with the inevitable disruptions and fluctuations by creating strong partnerships with suppliers, adequate but not excessive levels of safety stock, contingency plans for catastrophic events, and an information system that provides everyone in the chain with timely information. Companies that sell products such as fashion merchandise or video games that have unpredictable demand, high costs associated with stockouts (and the resulting lost sales), and require large end-of-season markdowns to move leftover items require an agile supply chain. Companies that sell basic products such as groceries and cosmetics that have predictable demand, carry low profit margins, and require small end-of-season markdowns require supply chains that are lean and efficient. An *adaptable* supply chain is one that changes as a company's needs change and is able to accommodate a small company's growth. Adaptable supply chains are predictive and are able to anticipate changes in companies' buying and selling processes and help them to adapt to the changes in real time. A supply chain is properly *aligned* when all companies in it work together as a team to improve the chain's performance for the benefit of the entire group. In the past, some companies were hesitant to share information with the businesses in their supply chains. Success today requires that companies not only share information seamlessly but that they also synchronize their efforts to maximize efficiency throughout the entire chain. Agile, adaptable, aligned supply chains reduce costs and improve performance by increasing the speed at which companies get products into customers' hands, reducing excess inventory, and decreasing the use of price markdowns that erode companies' profit margins.

ENTREPRENEURIAL
Profile

Seven Eleven Japan

Seven Eleven Japan (SEJ), the Japanese division of the convenience store chain, operates a supply chain characterized by the triple A's. SEJ uses real-time point-of-sale terminals in its stores that track sales constantly and monitor inventory levels. Satellite connections link stores with vendors, distribution centers, and shipping companies so that every element in the supply chain has access to relevant, timely information. The system is so agile that SEJ delivers products to its store three times a day and reconfigures their arrangement on shelves to appeal to different customer groups at different times. SEJ's supply chain proved its adaptability when an earthquake rocked a major city, closing roadways and eliminating normal distribution routes. To deliver the products its customers needed in the midst of a crisis, SEJ employed helicopters and motorcycles to navigate around the gridlock. SEJ aligns its suppliers' interests with its own by allowing them to make deliveries without requiring store managers to verify the contents of every delivery.[27]

If a company's supply chain is to conform to the triple A's, it must be built on the foundation of reliable vendors that can supply it with quality merchandise, equipment, supplies, and services at reasonable prices in a timely manner. Finding the right vendors sometimes can be a challenge.

ENTREPRENEURIAL
Profile

Matthew Accarrino: SPQR

Some small business owners hire "foragers" to track down hard-to-find specialty items that the typical supply chain misses. When Matthew Accarrino, now head chef at SPQR, an upscale restaurant in San Francisco, worked at a famous restaurant outside of Rome, Italy, he and his staff visited local farmers for freshly picked ingredients for that evening's meals. "You differentiate yourself not only through cooking but also by accessing products that are unique to your restaurant," he says. Accarrino relies on that same philosophy at SPQR, but his busy schedule requires him to hire foragers to locate certain unique, hard-to-find items for the menu. Forager Erin Littlestar is the sustainability and sourcing manager (her nickname is the "sourceress") for Sweetgreen, a small chain of fast-casual restaurants in Washington, D.C. "I'm systematically going through the menu and looking at what's there that could be better," she says. She has tracked down a farmer who provides "a dozen different varieties of dates" and cream that is so good that the pastry chef churns her own butter with it.[28]

Selecting the right vendors or suppliers for a business has an impact well beyond simply obtaining goods and services at the lowest cost. Although searching for the best price is always an important factor, successful small business owners must consider other factors in vendor selection, such as reliability, reputation, quality, support services, speed, and proximity.

Vendor Certification

To add objectivity to the vendor selection process, many firms are establishing vendor certification programs, agreements to give one supplier the majority of their business if that supplier meets rigorous quality and performance standards. Today, businesses of all sizes and types are establishing long-term "partnering" arrangements with vendors that meet their certification standards. When creating a vendor certification program, entrepreneurs should remember the three Cs: *commitment, communication,* and *control. Commitment* to consistently meeting the company's quality standards must be paramount. No company can afford to do business with vendors that cannot meet its quality targets. Second, a company must establish two-way *communication* with vendors. Communication implies trust, and trust creates working relationships that are long-term and mutually beneficial. Treating suppliers like partners can reveal ways to boost quality and lower costs for both parties. Finally, a company must make sure that its vendors and suppliers have in place the *controls* that enable them to produce quality results and to achieve continuous improvements in their processes. In today's competitive marketplace, entrepreneurs expect all vendors to demonstrate that they operate processes built on continuous improvement.

Creating a vendor certification program requires entrepreneurs to develop a vendor rating scale that allows them to evaluate the advantages and disadvantages of each potential vendor. The scale allows entrepreneurs to score potential vendors on a measurement of the purchasing criteria that are most important to their companies' success. The first step to developing a scale is to determine the criteria that are most important to selecting a vendor (e.g., price, quality, prompt delivery). The next step is to assign weights to each criterion to reflect its relative importance. The third step involves developing a grading scale for comparing vendors on the criteria. Developing a usable scale requires that the owner maintain proper records of past vendor performances. Finally, the owner must compute a weighted total score for each vendor and select the vendor that scores the highest on the set of criteria. Consider the following example. Bravo Bass Boats, Inc., is faced with choosing from among several suppliers of a critical raw material. The company's owner has decided to employ a vendor rating scale to select the best vendor using the following procedure.

Step 1   *Determine important criteria.* The owner of Bravo has selected the following criteria:

         Quality
         Price
         Prompt delivery
         Service
         Assistance

Step 2   *Assign weights to each criterion to reflect its relative importance.*

Criterion	Weight
Quality	35
Price	30
Prompt delivery	20
Service	10
Assistance	5
Total	100

Step 3   *Develop a grading scale for each criterion.*

Criterion	Grading Scale
Quality	$\dfrac{\text{Number of acceptable lots from Vendor X}}{\text{Total number of lots from Vendor X}}$
Price	$\dfrac{\text{Lowest quoted price of all vendors}}{\text{Price offered by Vendor X}}$
Prompt Delivery	$\dfrac{\text{Number of on-time deliveries from Vendor X}}{\text{Total number of deliveries from Vendor X}}$
Service	A subjective evaluation of the quality of service offered by each vendor
Assistance	A subjective evaluation of the advice and assistance provided by each vendor

Step 4   *Compute a weighted score for each vendor.*

Criterion	Weight	Grade	Weighted Score (weight × grade)
Vendor 1			
Quality	35	9/10	31.5
Price	30	12.50/13.00	28.8
Prompt delivery	20	10/10	20.0
Service	10	8/10	8.0
Assistance	5	5/5	5.0
Total weighted score			93.3
Vendor 2			
Quality	35	8/10	28.0
Price	30	12.50/13.50	27.8
Prompt delivery	20	8/10	16.0
Service	10	8/10	8.0
Assistance	5	4.5	4.0
Total weighted score			83.8
Vendor 3			
Quality	35	7/10	24.5
Price	30	12.50/12.50	30.0
Prompt delivery	20	6/10	12.0
Service	10	7/10	7.0
Assistance	5	1/5	1.0
Total weighted score			74.5

Using this analysis of the three suppliers, Bravo should purchase the majority of this raw material from Vendor 1.

This vendor analysis procedure assumes that business owners have a working knowledge of their supplier network. Start-up companies seldom will, however. Owners of start-up companies must find suppliers and gather data to conduct a vendor analysis. One of the best ways to do that is to ask potential vendors for references. In some cases, industry trade associations have knowledge regarding the integrity of suppliers or vendors. Other sources for information on vendors include trade association and shows, the local chamber of commerce, and publications such as *McRAE's Blue Book* (*www.macraesbluebook.com*), which includes information on more than 1,000,000 industrial companies with more than 40,000 product listings, and the *Thomas Register of American Manufacturers* (*www.thomasnet.com*), which lists more than 67,000 industrial product categories. Both of these sources provide lists of products and services and the names, addresses, telephone numbers, and ratings of their manufacturers. Entrepreneurs whose product lines have an international flair may look to the *Thomas Global Register* for information on companies throughout the world dealing in practically every type of product or service. Web sites such as Alibaba (*www.alibaba.com*), Worldwide Brands (*www.worldwidebrands.com*), and Panjiva (*www.panjiva.com*) also are valuable tools that help entrepreneurs locate reliable suppliers across the globe for practically any product.

The Final Decision

Once business owners identify potential vendors and suppliers, they must decide which one (or ones) to do business with. Entrepreneurs should consider the following factors before making the final decision about the right supplier.

How to Manage Supply Chain Risk

Many small firms pay prices for goods and services that are too high and they find their purchasing options limited by a lack of competent suppliers. The broader the base of potential suppliers a business has, the more supply flexibility and security it has and the greater is its ability to get the best prices on its purchases. Use the following tips from the Street-Smart Entrepreneur to build meaningful, long-term relationships with the best suppliers:

1. *Establish your company's critical criteria for selecting a vendor.* What characteristics must the ideal vendor have? You must know up front what you are looking for in a vendor.

2. *Research thoroughly prospective vendors before you purchase anything from them.* The Internet is a useful tool for conducting a preliminary screening analysis.

3. *Interview prospective vendors with the same level of intensity that you interview prospective employees.* Both relationships influence how successful a company is at achieving quality objectives. "It's not easy to put aside the time," says James Walker, president of Octagon Research Solutions, a 60-person software company, "but for us, it's all about whether we can have a good relationship with [our vendors.]" Use the criteria you established in step 1 to establish a list of questions to ask potential vendors.

4. *Be assertive.* Ask tough questions and be a knowledgeable buyer. Don't allow suppliers to do their typical "sales pitches" before you have time to ask your questions.

5. *Check potential vendors' credit ratings.* Judging a potential vendor's financial strength and stability is important. Dealing with a vendor that is undergoing financial woes creates unnecessary complications for business owners.

6. *Get referrals.* Ask all potential vendors to supply a list of referrals of businesses that they have served over the last 5 years or more. Then make the necessary contacts.

7. *Visit potential vendors' businesses.* The best way to judge a vendor's ability to meet your company's needs is to see the operation firsthand. Nancy Connolly, president of Lasertone Corporation, a maker of copier and laser toner, insists on "a personal meeting between me and the president of the company," she says, before establishing a relationship with a vendor. The goal is to judge the level of the potential vendor's commitment to meeting Lasertone's needs.

8. *Evaluate potential suppliers' plans for dealing with risks and interruptions in their own supply chains.* Remember that if your vendor's supply of materials is interrupted, your supply also will be interrupted.

9. *Don't fixate on price.* Look for value in what they sell. If your only concern is lowest price, vendors will push their lowest-priced (and often lowest-quality) product lines.

10. *Ask "What if?"* The real test of a strong vendor--customer relationship occurs when problems arise. Smart entrepreneurs ask vendors how they will handle particular types of problems when they arise.

11. *Attend trade shows.* Work the room. A visit to a trade show is not a vacation; it's business. Find out whether the next booth has a valuable new vendor who has the potential to increase your company's profitability.

12. *Don't forget about local vendors.* Because of their proximity, local vendors can sometimes provide the fastest service. Solving problems often is easier because local vendors can make on-site service calls.

13. *Test a vendor before committing completely.* Susan Gilbert, owner of Café in the Park, a restaurant in San Diego, says, "Inventory is cash flow. When I'm dealing with a vendor, I need to know how quickly they can deliver, how quickly I can turn over the inventory, and keep it all tight." Rather than place an order for 100 Danish pastries with a new vendor, for instance, Gilbert starts with an order of a few dozen pastries to judge the vendor's performance.

14. *Find an appropriate balance between sole sourcing, which offers the benefits of economies of scale, and multisourcing, which reduces the risk of interrupted supplies.* Recall that a common strategy uses Pareto's Law, the 80/20 Rule.

15. *Work with the vendors.* Tell your suppliers what you like and don't like about their products and service. In many cases, they can resolve your concerns. Most vendors want to build long-term relationships with their customers. Give them a chance to do so.

16. *Do unto others . . .* Treat your vendors well. Be selective, but pay on time and treat them with respect.

1. Why do so many firms focus solely on selecting vendors that offer the lowest prices? What are the dangers of doing so?
2. Develop a list of 10 questions you would ask a potential vendor on a product you select.

Sources: Based on Nancy Germond, "Supply Chain Risk Management a Must as Global Sourcing Intensifies," *All Business*, June 11, 2010, *www.allbusiness.com/company-activities-management/management-risk-management/14609006-1.html*; Kelly L. Frey, "Selecting a Vendor: RFPs and Responses to RFPs," Baker, Donelson, Bearman, Caldwell, and Berkowitz, *www.bakerdonelson.com/Documents/Selecting%20a%20Vendor.pdf*; Allison Stein Wellner, "Finding the Right Vendor," *Inc.*, July 2003, pp. 88–95; Jan Norman, "How to Find Suppliers," *Business Start-ups*, October 1998, pp. 44–47; *Physical Risks to the Supply Chain: A View from Finance*, CFO Research Services and FM Global, February 2009, pp. 6–7.

NUMBER OF SUPPLIERS. One important question entrepreneurs face is "Should I buy from a single supplier or from several different sources?" Concentrating purchases at a single supplier (or sole sourcing) results in special attention from the supplier, especially if orders are substantial. Second, a business may be able to negotiate quantity discounts if its orders are large enough. Finally, a small company can cultivate a closer, more cooperative relationship with the supplier. Suppliers are more willing to work with companies that prove to be loyal customers. The result of this type of partnership can be better-quality goods and services. Stratsys, a company that makes plastic prototypes for the aerospace, automotive, and medical industries, purchases some of its most important raw materials from a single source. Company managers admit that doing so involves risk, but they believe that their company produces better quality products by eliminating the variability that multiple sources of supply would introduce into their production process.[29]

However, using a single vendor also has disadvantages. A company can experience shortages of critical materials if its only supplier suffers a catastrophe, such as bankruptcy, a fire, a strike, or a natural disaster.

ENTREPRENEURIAL
Profile
Caterpillar Inc.

Caterpillar Inc. narrowly avoided a devastating worldwide shutdown of its factories when a tornado severely damaged the sole plant in Oxford, Mississippi, that manufactures the steel cylinder couplings that link hydraulic hoses on almost every piece of equipment the company makes. Managers quickly took steps to get the damaged factory back online, scoured their warehouses for existing couplings, and transferred production to several new suppliers, including a metal-working company in Ontario, Canada, that had surplus capacity from a slowdown in the auto industry. The close call caused managers to add machinery in several of its factories that can produce couplings in an emergency.[30]

To offset the risks of sole sourcing, many companies rely on the 80/20 Rule. They purchase 80 percent of their supplies from their premier supplier and the remaining 20 percent from several "backup" vendors. Although this strategy may require a compromise on getting the lowest prices, it removes the risk of sole sourcing and lets a company's premier suppliers know that they have competition.

RELIABILITY. Business owners must evaluate a potential vendor's ability to deliver adequate quantities of quality merchandise when it is needed. One common complaint small businesses have against their suppliers is late delivery. Late deliveries or shortages cause lost sales and create customer ill will. Large customers often take precedence over small ones when it comes to service.

PROXIMITY. A supplier's physical proximity is an important factor when choosing a vendor. The cost of transporting merchandise can increase significantly the total cost of merchandise to a buyer. Foreign manufacturers also require longer delivery times, and because of the distance that shipments must travel, a hiccup anywhere in the distribution channel often results in late deliveries. In addition, entrepreneurs can solve quality problems more easily with nearby suppliers than with distant vendors.

ENTREPRENEURIAL
Profile
*Jamey Bennett:
LightWedge*

When Jamey Bennett decided to start a company to sell the LightWedge, an idea he came up with when he was 17, he looked to foreign manufacturers to produce the sheet of clear acrylic that contained light-emitting diodes that softly illuminate a page, allowing one to read in bed without disturbing a sleeping partner. With orders in hand from bookseller Barnes & Noble and catalog retailer Levenger, Bennett purchased equipment and tooling for a factory in China's Guangdong Province. Things ran smoothly for a few months until Bennett introduced a LightWedge designed for paperbacks. The factory ignored Bennett's repeated requests to modify the original design, and he switched production to another Chinese factory where things quickly got worse. Bennett ordered 5,000 LightWedges, but only 2,000 arrived—4 months late—and many had lenses that were so scratched or marred by "some kind of mysterious goop" that they were unusable. Because of the problems, LightWedge lost an estimated $1.5 million in sales, and Bennett decided that it was time to bring production back to the United States. Today, a factory in Newport News, Virginia, manufactures the LightWedge, and although costs are 20 percent higher than they were in China, Bennett knows that he will get quality products delivered on time.[31]

Despite potential problems such as the ones that Jamey Bennett encountered, outsourcing purchases of materials and components to foreign manufacturers, particularly to those in Asia, Eastern Europe, and Mexico, is a growing trend. Even though the risks and complications of using foreign suppliers are substantial, many companies cannot resist the lure of the low prices they offer. In China, for example, the typical factory worker earns slightly more than $1 per hour, compared to wages that are 20 to 30 times that in the United States and Western Europe. Yet the poor transportation infrastructure in China can increase the cost and the complexity of getting a product to market. Many companies from toy manufacturers to drug makers also have experienced quality problems with Chinese suppliers.

SPEED. How fast can a supplier deliver products to your business? A speedy supply chain can be a competitive advantage for a company.

ENTREPRENEURIAL
Profile
Zara

Zara, a popular clothing chain owned by Spanish company Inditex, is known for its tightly controlled supply chain that zips the latest fashions at very affordable prices (the average item sells for $27) to its stores in 73 countries. The company's high-tech logistics system gets the latest designer styles from the drawing board to store shelves in less than 2 weeks, compared to an industry average of 9 months![32]

A successful retail operation depends on a smoothly functioning supply chain that is transparent, agile, adaptable, and aligned with members' best interests.

Source: Archimage/Alamy Images

SERVICES. Entrepreneurs must evaluate the range of services vendors offer. Do salespeople make regular calls, and are they knowledgeable about their product line? Will sales representatives assist in planning store layout and in creating attractive displays? Will the vendor make convenient deliveries on time? Is the supplier reasonable in making repairs on equipment after installation and in handling returned merchandise? Are sales representatives able to offer useful advice on purchasing and other managerial functions? Is the supplier willing to take the time to help you solve problems that inevitably will crop up?

ENTREPRENEURIAL
Profile

PayCycle

CPA Charles Ross uses payroll services company PayCycle to handle the payroll function for his own business as well as for many of his small business clients. PayCycle won Ross as a loyal customer after he discovered that he had entered a client's payroll information incorrectly, creating a problem that PayCycle remedied quickly. It was Friday afternoon, and the client's W-2 forms had to go out the following Monday, which meant that PayCycle had to recalculate an entire year's payroll. Even though it required almost a full day's work for someone at PayCycle over a weekend, the payroll service fixed the problem, and the forms went out on schedule on Monday. That level of service explains why Ross is a lifelong customer and why 90 percent of PayCycle's customers refer new customers to the company.[33]

COLLABORATION. The goal is to find a supplier that is eager to join forces with the intent of building a long-term partnership with your company. Other small companies make ideal candidates.

ENTREPRENEURIAL
Profile

Center for Systems Management and Technovative Marketing

When NASA approached Scott Fischer, president of the Center for Systems Management (CSM), a Vienna, Virginia, company that provides training and consulting services for corporations and government agencies, about creating a video for an internal marketing campaign, Fischer knew that the job was beyond his company's ability. Wanting the chance to expand his work with the space agency, Fischer began looking for a company with which he could partner to create the video. He had to work quickly because NASA needed the video in just 45 days. Fischer and a team of employees selected Technovative Marketing, a seven-person marketing firm headed by Harriet Donnelly. Donnelly worked on the video herself and attended every meeting that Fischer had with NASA officials. (Donnelly assigns both a staff person and a senior manager to every Technovative project to make sure that clients always have two points of contact.) Because of the partnership that CSM and Technovative Marketing forged, the project turned out to be a huge success. NASA has enlisted CSM for similar projects, and, in turn, CSM is partnering with Technovative Marketing.[34]

PRICE NEGOTIATIONS. Small firms usually must pay market or list price for items that they purchase infrequently. This is not the case for goods purchased on a regular basis and that are essential components or supplies. An entrepreneur should have no hesitation about attempting to purchase the critical goods or services it needs at the best price and terms of sale. The terms of sale, as mentioned previously, can be a significant factor in the final price that the entrepreneur pays.

Legal Issues Affecting Purchasing

7. Describe the legal implications of the purchasing function.

When a small business purchases goods for a supplier, ownership passes from seller to buyer. But when do title and risk of loss to the goods pass from one party to the other? The answer is important because any number of things can happen to the merchandise after a customer orders it but before a company delivers it. When small business owners order merchandise and supplies from their vendors, they should know when the ownership of the merchandise—and the risk associated with it—shifts from supplier to buyer.

IN THE ENTREPRENEURIAL SPOTLIGHT

A (Supply) Chain Is Only as Strong as Its Weakest Link

Zoran Corporation is a designer of the chips that go into many of the electronic gizmos that are so prevalent today, including smartphones, digital cameras, television sets, printers, DVDs, DVRs, and others. Based in Sunnyvale, California, the company sits squarely in the middle of a complex supply chain that can be extremely challenging to manage because companies are hesitant to share sensitive sales information with other businesses. Sometimes Zoran does not know how customers use its specialized video- and audio-processing chips. One batch that the company thought was going into DVD players ended up in digital picture frames. Most of Zoran's customers are the anonymous factories located in Asia that produce consumer electronics for global giants such as Toshiba, Samsung, Sony, and many others.

Zoran does not actually manufacture the chips it designs. Instead the company subcontracts manufacturing to dozens of companies, such as Taiwan Semiconductor Manufacturing Company (TSMC), that specialize in chip-making. TSMC, in turn, purchases equipment used to etch circuits and bake chemicals onto semiconductors from companies such as Applied Materials in Santa Clara, California. Customer demand for electronic devices drives the entire supply chain, however. Thin profit margins and the rapid decline in the value of electronic components demand that companies keep their inventories lean and manage their supply chains carefully.

The accompanying figure shows how lengthy modern supply chains can be. Electronics retailers such as Best Buy place orders with Toshiba for DVD players 6 weeks before the items are to be stocked on stores' shelves, but the length and the complexity of the global supply chain means that acquiring all of the components and assembling them into finished players often takes as long as 12 weeks. Toshiba then places an order for the DVD players with the contract factories in Asia (many of which are in China), which, in turn, place orders for chips they need with Zoran. Zoran then orders its subcontractors, including TSMC, to make the chips to supply the orders from the contract factories in Asia.

Life of a DVD Player | How the tech supply chain makes the world's gadgets

❶	❷	❸	❹	❺	❻	❼
Minnesota-based **Best Buy** decides how many DVD players it wants, orders from Toshiba ...	**Toshiba** tells factories-for-hire in China to crank up production ...	Those Chinese **factories-for-hire** order chips from Zoran Corp ...	**Zoran** tells its own subcontractors, including TSMC, to get busy making more chips ...	**TSMS,** in Taiwan, buys factory equipment from Applied Materials ...	In California, **Applied Materials** shops for specialty machine-tool services ...	Machine-tool firm **D&H Manufacturing** — at the end of the chain—mills aluminum blocks for Applied.

To produce the chips, TSMC and other factories order equipment and machinery from Applied Materials, which orders parts from machine tool shops such as D&H Manufacturing, a small precision machining company in Fremont, California. Hiccups at any point in the supply chain often ricochet through the entire chain, disrupting the smooth flow of goods from producer to consumer. For instance, an anticipated decrease in demand due to an economic slowdown led Best Buy to reduce the number of DVD players it ordered, which caused TSMC to cut back production in its factories to just 35 percent utilization and idle thousands of workers. Applied Materials, an equipment supplier to those factories, saw its sales plummet as well. Angelo Grestoni, owner of D&H Manufacturing, the machine shop, says that he was left holding a year's supply of some products rather than the normal 3 months' worth. "We've got millions of dollars of inventory we can't sell, and we're paying storage fees on it," he says.

1. What types of supply chain risks does Zoran face?
2. What steps can Zoran take to minimize the risks it faces?

Source: Based on Phred Dvorak, "Clarity Is Missing Link in Supply Chain," *Wall Street Journal,* May 18, 2009, pp. A1, A14.

Title

Before the Uniform Commercial Code (UCC) was enacted, the concept of title—the right to ownership of goods—determined where responsibility for merchandise fell. Today, however, the UCC has replaced the concept of title with three other concepts: identification, risk of loss, and insurable interest.

Identification

Before title can pass to the buyer, the goods must already be in existence and must be identifiable from all other similar goods. Specific goods already in existence are identified at the time the sales contract is made. For example, if Graphtech, Inc., orders a Model 477-X plotter, the goods are identified at the time the contract (oral or written) is made. Generic goods are identified when they are marked, shipped, or otherwise designated as the goods in the contract. For example, an order of fuel oil may not be identified until it is loaded into a transfer truck for shipment.

Risk of Loss

Risk of loss determines which party incurs the financial risk if the goods are damaged, destroyed, or lost while in transit. Risk of loss does *not* always pass with title. Three particular rules govern the passage of title and the transfer of risk or loss.

RULE 1: AGREEMENT. A supplier and a small business owner can agree to the terms under which title passes. Similarly, the two parties can agree (preferably in writing) to shift the risk of loss at any time during the transaction. In other words, any explicit agreement between buyer and seller determines when title and risk of loss will pass.

RULE 2: F.O.B. SELLER. Under a sales contract designated F.O.B. ("free on board") seller, title passes to the buyer as soon as the seller delivers the goods into the care of a carrier or shipper. In addition, an **F.O.B. seller contract** (also known as a **shipment contract**) requires that the buyer pay all shipping and transportation costs. For example, a North Carolina manufacturer sells 100,000 capacitors to a buyer in Ohio with terms "F.O.B. North Carolina." Under this contract, the Ohio firms pays all shipping costs, and title and risk of loss pass from the manufacturer as soon as the carrier takes possession of the shipment. If the goods are lost or damaged in transit, the buyer suffers the loss. Of course, the buyer can purchase insurance (see insurable interest below) and has legal recourse against the carrier if the carrier is at fault. If a contract is silent on shipping terms, the courts assume that the contract is a shipment contract (F.O.B. seller), and the buyer bears the risk of loss while the goods are in transit.

RULE 3: F.O.B. BUYER. A sales contract designated F.O.B. buyer requires that the seller deliver the goods to the buyer's place of business (or to a place that the buyer designates such as a warehouse). Title and risk of loss transfer to the small business when the goods are delivered to the business or to the designated destination. Also, an **F.O.B. buyer contract** (also called a **destination contract**) requires the seller to pay all shipping and transportation costs. In the example above, if the contract were "F.O.B. Ohio," the North Carolina manufacturer pays the cost of shipping the order, and title and risk of loss pass to the Ohio company when the shipment is delivered to its place of business. In this case, the seller bears any losses due to goods that are lost or damaged in transit.

Insurable Interest

Insurable interest ensures the right of either party to the sales contract to obtain insurance to protect against lost, damaged, or destroyed merchandise as long as that party has "sufficient interest" in the goods. In general, once goods are identified, the buyer has an insurable interest in them. The seller has a sufficient interest as long as the seller retains title to the goods. However, under certain circumstances both the buyer and the seller have insurable interests even after title has passed to the buyer.

Receiving Merchandise

Once the merchandise is received, the buyer must verify its identity and condition. When the goods are delivered, the owner should check the number of cartons unloaded against the carrier's delivery receipt to make sure that the shipment is complete. It is also a good idea to examine the boxes for damage; if shipping cartons are damaged, the carrier should note this on the delivery receipt. The owner should open all cartons immediately after delivery, inspect the merchandise for quality and condition, and check it against the invoices for discrepancies. If merchandise is damaged or faulty, the buyer should contact the supplier immediately and follow up with a written report. The owner should never destroy or dispose of damaged or flawed merchandise unless the supplier specifically authorizes it. Proper control techniques in receiving merchandise prevent the small business owner from paying for suppliers' and shippers' mistakes.

Selling on Consignment

Small business owners who lack the necessary capital to invest or are unwilling to assume the risk of investing in inventory may be able to sell goods on consignment. Selling on **consignment** means that the small business owner does not purchase the merchandise carried from the supplier (called the consignor); instead, the owner pays the consignor only for the merchandise actually sold. For providing the supplier with a market for his goods, the small business owner normally receives a percentage of the revenue on each item sold. The business owner (called the **consignee**) may return any unsold merchandise to the supplier (the **consignor**) without obligation. Under a consignment agreement, title and risk of loss do not pass to the consignee unless the contract specifies these terms. In other words, the supplier bears the financial costs of lost, damaged, or stolen merchandise. The small business owner who sells merchandise on a consignment basis realizes the following advantages:

- The owner does not have to invest money in these inventory items, but the merchandise on hand is available for sale.
- The owner does not pay the consignor until the item is sold.
- Because the consignment relationship is founded on the law of agency, the consignee never takes title to the merchandise and does not bear the risk of loss for the goods.
- The supplier normally plans and sets up displays for the merchandise and is responsible for maintaining them.

Before selling items on consignment, the small business owner and the supplier should create a written contract, which should include the following items:

- A list of items to be sold and their quantities
- Prices to be charged
- Location of merchandise in store
- Duration of contract
- Commission charged by the consignee
- Policy on defective items and rejects
- Schedule for payments to consignor
- Delivery terms and merchandise storage requirements
- Responsibility for items lost to pilferage and shoplifting
- Provision for terminating consignment contract

If managed properly, selling goods on consignment can be beneficial to both the consignor and the consignee.

Chapter Review

1. Understand the components of a purchasing plan.
   - The purchasing function is vital to every small business's success because it influences a company's ability to sell quality goods and services at reasonable prices. Purchasing is the acquisition of needed materials, supplies, services, and equipment of the right quality, in the proper quantities, for reasonable prices, at the appropriate time, and from the right suppliers.
2. Explain the principles of total quality management (TQM) and Six Sigma and their impact on quality.
   - The idea behind Lean principles is to eliminate waste in a company's activities using five principles: value, value stream, flow, pull, and perfection.

617

- 5S principles are simple but effective ways to improve quality in an organization:
  - Sort items into two categories, necessary and unnecessary, and eliminate everything that is unnecessary
  - Straighten and organize the tools employees use and their workspaces.
  - Shine all workspaces.
  - Systematize best-practice processes so that the company can apply them universally.
  - Sustain the drive toward continuous improvement.
- Six Sigma relies on quantitative tools to improve quality. At its core are four key tenets: Delight customers with quality and speed, constantly improve the process, use teamwork to improve the process, and make changes to the process based on facts, not guesses.
- Under the total quality management (TQM) philosophy, companies define a quality product as one that conforms to predetermined standards that satisfy customers' demands. The goal is to get delivery and invoicing to installation and follow-up right—the first time.
- To implement TQM successfully, a small business owner must rely on 10 fundamental principles: Shift from a management-driven culture to a participative, team-based one; modify the reward system to encourage teamwork and innovation; train workers constantly to give them the tools they need to produce quality and to upgrade the company's knowledge base; train employees to measure quality with the tools of statistical process control (SPC); use Pareto's Law to focus TQM efforts; share information with everyone in the organization; focus quality improvements on astonishing the customer; don't rely on inspection to produce quality products and services; avoid using TQM to place blame on those who make mistakes; and strive for continuous improvement in processes as well as in products and services.

3. Conduct economic order quantity (EOQ) analysis to determine the proper level of inventory.
   - A major goal of the small business is to generate adequate inventory turnover by purchasing proper quantities of merchandise. A useful device for computing the proper quantity is economic order quantity (EOQ) analysis, which yields the ideal order quantity, the amount that minimizes total inventory costs. Total inventory costs consist of the cost of the units, holding (carrying) costs, and ordering (setup) costs. The EO balances the costs of ordering and of carrying merchandise to yield minimum total inventory cost.

4. Differentiate among the three types of purchase discounts vendors offer.
   - Trade discounts are established on a graduated scale and depend on a small firm's position in the channel of distribution.
   - Quantity discounts are designed to encourage businesses to order large quantities of merchandise and supplies.
   - Cash discounts are offered to customers as an incentive to pay for merchandise promptly.

5. Calculate a company's reorder point.
   - There is a time gap between the placing of an order and actual receipt of the goods. The reorder point model tells the owner when to place an order to replenish the company's inventory.

6. Develop a vendor rating scale.
   - Creating a vendor analysis model involves four steps: Determine the important criteria (i.e., price, quality, prompt delivery, service, etc.); assign a weight to each criterion to reflect its relative importance; develop a grading scale for each criterion; and compute a weighted score for each vendor.

7. Describe the legal implications of the purchasing function.
   - Important legal issues involving purchasing goods involve title, or ownership of the goods; identification of the goods; risk of loss and when it shifts from seller to buyer; and insurable interests in the goods. The buyer and seller can have an insurable interest in the same goods at the same time.

Discussion Questions

1. What is purchasing? Why is it important for the small business owner to develop a purchasing plan?
2. What is TQM? How can it help small business owners achieve the quality goods and services they require?
3. One top manager claims that to implement total quality management successfully, "You have to change your company culture as much as your processes." Do you agree? Explain.
4. Visit the Web site of the National Institute of Standards and Technology (*www.quality.nist.gov*), the organization that grants the Malcolm Baldrige National Quality Award, the highest quality award in the United States. Research one of the companies that received the Baldrige Award and prepare a one-page summary of its quality initiative and the results that it produced.
5. List and briefly describe the three components of total inventory costs.
6. What is the economic order quantity? How does it minimize total inventory costs?
7. Should a small business owner always purchase products from the vendor with the lowest prices? Why or why not?
8. Briefly outline the three types of purchase discounts. Under what circumstances is each the best choice?
9. What is lead time? Outline the procedure for determining a product's reorder point.
10. Explain how an entrepreneur launching a company could locate suppliers and vendors.
11. What factors are commonly used to evaluate suppliers?
12. Explain the procedure for developing a vendor rating scale.
13. Explain briefly the three concepts that have replaced the concept of title. When do title and risk of loss shift under an FOB seller contract? An FOB buyer contract?
14. What should a small business owner do when merchandise is received?
15. Explain how a small business would sell goods on consignment. What should be included in a consignment contract?

Entrepreneurs can improve the quality of the products and services they offer, control the cost of purchasing or producing those products and services, and enhance the level of service that they provide their customers through effective management of supply chains. The issues of purchasing, quality management, and vendor analysis cut across all of the functions of an organization and, in many cases, play a significant role in determining a company's ability to compete successfully. If your business is product-based, supply chain management issues will represent a significant part of your business and your business plan. Supply chain management factors are an important part of a product-based business plan.

On the Web

The Companion Web site at *www.pearsonhighered.com/scarborough* offers additional information in the areas of supply chain management, including purchasing, quality management, and vendor analysis. Review these sites and determine whether these sources may be useful to you as you build your plan.

In the Software

Confirm that you have selected the "product" type of plan outline within Business PlanPro. You can do this by clicking on the "Plan Setup" icon and looking at the "Type of business" comments below. It will state, "I sell products" or "I sell services," depending on your choice. If you do sell products, select the proper choice to indicate whether you manufacture those products or purchase and resell them. The outline within Business PlanPro will automatically adjust to your choice. Complete the information in the "Product" section of your business plan. Make sure you also review your financial information regarding product and inventory expenses.

Building Your Business Plan

Once you have completed the "Product" section, step back and review your plan. By now, you have completed most of the sections in your plan, and it should tell a cohesive story about your business.

Endnotes

1. Gina Paglucia Morrison and Anca van Assendelft, *Charting a New Course: The Retail Merchandising-Supply Network*, IBM, November 1, 2006, p. 1.

2. Ian Mount and Brian Caulfield, "The Missing Link," *eCompany*, May 2001, p. 84.

3. Morrison and Assendelft, *Charting a New Course*, p. 1; "Rethinking the Purchasing Function," *McKinsey Quarterly Chart Focus Newsletter*, May 2008, p. 1.

4. *Physical Risks to the Supply Chain: The View from Finance*, CFO Research Services and FM Global, February 2009, p. 2.

5. "U.S. Commercial Spending Estimated at $20.3 Trillion in 2008," *Web CPA*, September 29, 2009, *www.webcpa.com/news/-51868-1.html*.

6. *Low-Cost Country Sourcing Can Benefit a Company's Bottom Line*, IBM, 2006, p. 6.

7. Helen Coster, "Tainted Booty," *Forbes*, April 21, 2008, pp. 84–86.

8. Beth Bacheldor, "Keeping Risks to a Minimum," *InformationWeek*, October 10, 2005, pp. 43–45.

9. Rudolph Bell, "Volcano Disrupts BMW Supply Chain to S.C," *The State*, April 20, 2010, *www.thestate.com/2010/04/20/1251405/ volcano-disrupts-bmw-supply-chain.html;* "Iceland Volcano: Nissan and BMW Suspend Some Production," *BBC News*, April 20, 2010, *http://news.bbc.co.uk/2/hi/8631676.stm*.

10. Randy Myers, "The Spice Trade," *CFO*, June 2007, p. 74.

11. Joelle Dick, Caroline Kvitka, Aaron Lazenby, and Rich Schwerin, "Four Keys to Lean Six Sigma," *Profit*, November 2004, p. 9.

12. "Vogel Wood Slices Through Lead Times with Lean Transformation," Wisconsin Manufacturing Extension Partnership, *www.wmep.org/ SuccessStories/vogel.aspx*.

13. Jill Jusko, "Scotsman Ice Systems: IW Best Plants Profile 2006," *IndustryWeek*, October 1, 2006, *www.industryweek.com/ ReadArticle.aspx?ArticleID=12682*.

14. Mount and Caulfield, "The Missing Link," p. 84.

15. Doug Bartholomew, "Supply Chains at Risk," *IndustryWeek*, October 1, 2006, *www.industryweek.com/ReadArticle.aspx?ArticleID=12713*.

16. W. Edwards Deming, *Out of the Crisis*, MIT Press: Cambridge, Massachusetts, 2000, p. 32.

17. Donna Abernathy, "Purchasing Cooperatives Give Small Business an Edge," Business Know-How, 2010, *www.businessknowhow.com/ money/purchasing-coop.htm;* Kelly Johnson and Suzette Rubio, "Blue Hawk Cooperative: The New Kid on the Block," *Supply House Times*, July 1, 2007, *www.supplyht.com/CDA/Articles/Feature_Article/ BNP_GUID_9-5-2006_A_1000000000000131400*; "Testimonials," Blue Hawk Cooperative, *www.bluehawk.coop/membertestimonia.html*.

18. "Co-Op Types," National Cooperative Business Association, *www.ncba.coop/ncba/about-co-ops/co-op-types*.

19. Crystal Detamore-Rodman, "Cash In, Cash Out," *Entrepreneur*, June 2003, *www.entrepreneur.com/magazine/entrepreneur/2003/ june/61916.html*.

20. David Worrell, "Paying for Quality over Quantity," *Entrepreneur*, October 2008, p. 53.

21. Connie Winkler, "Where Does the Money Go?" *CFO-IT*, Spring 2005, pp. 45–49.

22. "The Value of Sharing Information Up and Down the Supply Chain," *CIO*, January 28, 2005, *www.cio.com/article/1887/The_Value_ of_Sharing_Information_Up_and_Down_the_Supply_Chain/1*; Imam Baihaqi and Nicholas Beaumont, "Information Sharing in Supply Chains: A Literature Review and Research Agenda," Monash University Department of Management Working Paper Series, June 2005, *www.buseco.monash.edu.au/mgt/research/working- papers/2005/wp45-05.pdf*.

23. Bob Evans, "Supply Chains Hit Home (Sweet Home)," *InformationWeek*, February 7, 2007, p. 68.

24. Brian Nadel, "Show Me the Money," Special Advertising Feature in *Fortune*, April 3, 2006, pp. S1–S5.

25. Ian Mount and Brian Caulfield, "The Internet-Based Supply Chain," *eCompany*, May 2001, p 85.

26. Hau Lee, "The Three A's of Supply Chain Excellence," *Electronics Supply and Manufacturing*, October 1, 2004, *www.my-esm.com/ showArticle.jhtml?articleID=47903369*; Tracy Mayor, "The Supple Supply Chain," *CIO*, June 13, 2007, *www.cio.com/ article/119301/*.

27. Hau L. Lee, "The Triple-A Supply Chain," BNet, *www.bnet.com/cp/ the-triple-a-supply-chain/174992*.

28. Bret Thorn, "Search Party," *Nation's Restaurant News*, March 8, 2010, pp. 30–34.

29. Ian MacMillan, "A Few Good Suppliers," *CFO*, October 2004, p. 26.

30. Ilan Brat, "Rebulding After a Catastrophe," *Wall Street Journal*, May 19, 2008, pp. B1–B2.

31. John Turrettini, "Remade in America," *Forbes*, January 12, 2004, p. 190; "LightWedge," *Inc.*, September 2006, pp. 124–125.

32. Cecelie Rohwedder, "Zara Grows as Retail Rivals Struggle," *Wall Street Journal*, March 26, 2009, pp. B1, B5.

33. Michael Fitzgerald, "Turning Vendors into Partners," *Inc.*, August 2005, pp. 94–100.

34. Ibid.

Managing Inventory

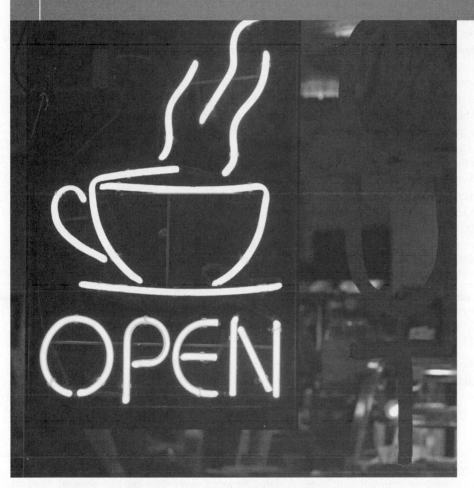

Learning Objectives

Upon completion of this chapter, you will be able to:

1 Explain the various inventory control systems and the advantages and disadvantages of each.
2 Describe how just-in-time (JIT) and JIT II inventory control techniques work.
3 Describe methods for reducing losses from slow-moving inventory.
4 Discuss employee theft and shoplifting and how to prevent them.

If a product isn't selling, I want to get it out of there because it's taking up space that can be devoted to another part of my line that moves. Besides, having a product languish on the shelves doesn't do much for our image.

—Norman Melnick, chairman of Pentech International

Honesty pays, but it doesn't seem to pay enough to suit some people.

—F. M. Hubbard

Supply chain management and inventory control are closely linked. This chapter will discuss various inventory control methods, how to move "slow" inventory items, and how to protect inventory from theft. An entrepreneur's goal is to maximize the value of a company's inventory while reducing both the cost and the risks of owning inventory. The issue is significant; the largest expenditure for many small businesses is in inventory: raw materials, work-in-process, or finished goods.

Although many business owners understand the dangers of carrying excess inventory, they face a constant battle to avoid the problem. A study by the Aberdeen Group reports that 70 percent of businesses rate themselves "average" or "below average" on inventory management.[1] In addition, 91 percent report that they are making changes to their businesses, such as improving sales forecasting, enhancing replenishment strategies, and increasing the level of cooperation with vendors, to improve their ability to manage inventory more effectively.[2] For years, businesses maintained high levels of inventory so that the manufacturing or sales processes ran smoothly. Managers now realize that inventory simply masks other problems that a company may have, such as poor quality, sloppy supply chain management, improper pricing, inadequate marketing, inefficient layout, low productivity, and others. Reducing the amount of inventory a company carries exposes these otherwise hidden problems; only then can managers and employees solve them.

Another reason that business owners are lowering inventory levels is the high cost of carrying excess inventory. U.S. businesses incur $357 billion in carrying costs each year (19.3 percent of the total value of the inventory they hold), the majority of it in the form of taxes, depreciation, insurance, and obsolescence.[3] Holding inventory requires renting or purchasing additional warehouse space, increasing labor costs, boosting borrowing, and tying up a company's valuable cash unnecessarily. Companies with lean inventory levels lower their costs of operation, and those savings go straight to the bottom line. The potential payoff for managing inventory efficiently is huge; companies that switch to lean inventory systems can increase their profitability by 20 to 50 percent.

The information age has made techniques such as just-in-time (JIT) inventory systems available to even the smallest of businesses. Internet-based networks that connect a company seamlessly with its suppliers have dramatically reduced the time for needed parts or material to arrive and the need to hold inventory. At the other end of the pipeline, a company's customers expect to have what they need when they need it. In today's competitive market, few customers will wait beyond a reasonable time for items they want. Managing inventory properly requires business owners to master an intricate balancing act, keeping enough inventory on hand to meet customers' expectations but maintaining inventory levels low enough to avoid incurring excessive costs.

Managing inventory effectively requires an entrepreneur to implement the following seven interrelated steps:

1. *Develop an accurate sales forecast.* The proper inventory level for each item is directly related to the demand for that item. A business cannot sell merchandise that it does not have; conversely, an entrepreneur does not want to stock inventory that customers will not buy.

ENTREPRENEURIAL
Profile

Dan Richardson:
Northway Sports

Dan Richardson, owner of Northway Sports, a retailer in East Bethel, Minnesota, that sells Polaris all-terrain vehicles (ATVs), snowmobiles, and motorcycles, says that he lost several sales of Polaris' most popular ATV because the manufacturer had not been able to deliver the units he had ordered 5 months before. When a recession hit, Polaris, like most manufacturers, slashed production to keep its inventory lean and to avoid putting pressure on its dealers to purchase products that they could not sell. Polaris' forecasts showed sluggish sales. Several months later, however, surging demand for the company's products caught managers by surprise, and Polaris was unable to fill its dealers' orders.[4]

2. *Develop a plan to make inventory available when and where customers want it.* Inventory will not sell if customers have a difficult time finding it. If a company is constantly running out of items customers expect to find, its customer base will dwindle over time as shoppers look elsewhere for those items. An important component of superior customer service is making sure adequate quantities of items are available when customers want them. Two ways of measuring this aspect of customer service include calculating the percentage of customer

orders that a company ships on time and the percentage of the dollar volume of orders that it ships on time. Tracking these numbers over time gives business owners sound feedback on how well they are managing their inventory levels from the customer's perspective.

Polaris, the maker of all-terrain vehicles, snowmobiles, and motorcycles, once used a system that required dealers to place large orders of inventory twice a year. However, when sales slowed, the "stack 'em high, watch 'em fly" system caused problems with dealers and at Polaris. Today, Polaris has switched to a system that allows dealers to order smaller quantities of inventory more frequently, which allows them to maintain leaner inventories and match supply with customer demand more effectively.[5]

3. *Build relationships with your most critical suppliers to ensure that you can get the merchandise you need when you need it.* Business owners must keep suppliers and vendors aware of how their merchandise is selling and communicate their needs to them. Vendors and suppliers can be an entrepreneur's greatest allies in managing inventory. Increasingly, the word that describes the relationship between world-class companies and their suppliers is *partnership*.

4. *Set realistic inventory turnover objectives.* Keeping in touch with their customers' likes and dislikes and monitoring their inventory enable owners to estimate the most likely buying patterns for different types of merchandise. One of the factors having the greatest impact on a company's sales, cash flow, and ultimate success is its inventory turnover ratio.

5. *Compute the actual cost of carrying inventory.* Many business owners do not realize how expensive carrying inventory actually is. Without an accurate cost of carrying inventory, it is impossible to determine an optimal inventory level. Carrying costs include items such as interest on borrowed money, insurance expenses associated with the inventory, inventory-related personnel expenses, obsolescence, and others. When new product introductions make existing products obsolete, companies must hold inventory to an absolute minimum. For instance, in the computer industry the onrush of new technology causes the value of a personal computer held in inventory to decline 1 percent each week! This gives computer makers big incentives to keep their inventories as lean as possible.

George Falzon, owner of G. Falzon & Company, a small jewelry store in Holliston, Massachusetts, watched the cost of holding inventory, particularly engagement rings and wedding bands, increase as the prices of precious metals soared. A weak economy demanded that Falzon avoid overinvesting in inventory, which is a common cause of cash crises, but potential customers expect to see a wide selection of items when shopping. Falzon developed a clever solution: He began stocking replicas of jewelry pieces made from plated silver and cubic zirconium rather than platinum, silver, gold, and diamonds. Because most engagement and wedding pieces are special orders, customers do not mind looking at the replicas. Falzon says that stocking the replicas saves him about $75,000 in inventory, which allows him to display four times as many styles of engagement rings and wedding bands.[6]

6. *Use the most timely and accurate information system the business can afford to provide the facts and figures necessary to make critical inventory decisions.* Computers and modern point-of-sale terminals that are linked to a company's inventory records enable business owners to know exactly which items are selling and which ones are not. The owner of a chain of baby products stores uses a computer network to link all of his stores to the computer at central headquarters. Every night after the stores close, the point-of-sale terminals in each store download the day's sales to the central computer, which compiles an extensive sales and inventory report. When he walks into his office every morning, the owner reviews the report and can tell exactly which items are moving fastest, which are moving slowest, and which are not selling at all. He credits the system with the company's above-average inventory turnover ratio and much of his chain's success.

7. *Teach employees how inventory control systems work so that they can contribute to managing the firm's inventory on a daily basis.* All too often, the employees on the floor have no idea of how the various information systems and inventory control techniques operate or interact with one another. Consequently, the people closest to the inventory contribute little to

controlling it. Well-trained employees armed with information can be one of an entrepreneur's greatest weapons in the battle to control inventory. Fast changes in product demand require inventory control systems that are capable of responding quickly, allowing entrepreneurs and their employees to make adjustments to inventory levels on the fly.

The goal is to find and maintain the proper balance between the cost of holding inventory and the requirements to have merchandise on hand when customers demand it. Either extreme can be costly. If entrepreneurs focus solely on minimizing cost, they will undoubtedly incur stockouts, lost sales, and customer ill will because they cannot satisfy their customers' needs. For instance, researchers studying inventory control systems at Bulgari, a jewelry manufacturer headquartered in Rome, Italy, discovered that stockouts of just one popular item had lowered the company's profits by 5 percent of sales.[7] At the other extreme, entrepreneurs who attempt to hold enough inventory to meet every peak customer demand will find that high inventory costs diminish their chances of remaining profitable. "There's a fine line between not having racks of clearance [merchandise] from leftover inventory and cutting to the bone," says one retail expert.[8] Walking this inventory tightrope is never easy, but the following inventory control systems can help business owners strike a reasonable balance between the two extremes.

Inventory Control Systems

1. Explain the various inventory control systems and the advantages and disadvantages of each.

Regardless of the type of inventory control system business owners choose, they must recognize the importance of **Pareto's Law** (or the **80/20 Rule**), which holds that about 80 percent of the value of a company's sales revenue is generated by 20 percent of the items in its inventory. Sometimes a company's best-selling items are its highest-priced items, but more often they are low-priced items that sell in high volume. Because most sales are generated by a small percentage of items, entrepreneurs should focus the majority of their inventory control efforts on this 20 percent. Observing this simple principle ensures that entrepreneurs will spend time controlling only the most productive—and, therefore, most valuable—inventory items. With this technique in mind, we now examine three basic types of inventory control systems: perpetual, visual, and partial.

IN THE ENTREPRENEURIAL
SPOTLIGHT
The Long Tail Theory: Is Pareto's Law Still Valid?

In 1896, Italian economist Vilfredo Pareto observed that 20 percent of people owned about 80 percent of wealth. Since then, Pareto's Law, or the 80/20 Rule, has been used to describe many aspects of business, including the idea that about 20 percent of a company's customers account for 80 percent of its sales. For instance, researchers in Japan analyzed nearly 100 million transactions and confirmed that 25 percent of convenience stores' customers account for 80 percent of their total sales. Pareto's Law also applies to a company's inventory: 80 percent of a company's sales come from only 20 percent of its products. The result is that managers focus their efforts on the "vital" 20 percent of items rather than the "trivial" remaining 80 percent.

Chris Anderson, editor of *Wired* magazine, claims that the Internet has the potential to limit the application

The New Marketplace

Source: Chris Anderson, "About Me," Long Tail, *www.longtail.com/about.html.*

of Pareto's Law because it allows businesses to sell efficiently low-volume items that exactly match the unique needs, wants, and interests of small groups of customers in niche markets. Anderson called his theory the Long Tail Theory, because the Internet allows customers to migrate down the tail of the distribution curve (see accompanying figure). If the Long Tail Theory is true, it has significant implications for business owners and the way they manage their inventory. Anderson says that the 80 percent of a company's products that Pareto's Law considers "trivial" have the potential on the Internet to rival the sales volume of the 20 percent that the Law considers "vital."

Researchers at the Sloan School of Management at the Massachusetts Institute of Technology recently studied several years of data at a private-label women's clothing company that sold the same merchandise through its catalog and its Internet-based store. Their analysis showed that catalog sales conformed perfectly to the 80/20 Rule; 20 percent of the items in the catalog accounted for 80 percent of catalog sales. However, Internet customers purchased a greater variety of products even though the online store offered the exact same selection of items at the same prices. (After the company's managers saw the study's results, they adjusted their marketing strategy, sending fewer catalogs to their top online customers.) When Suunto began selling its Vector altimeter watch online, the company planned to offer only its most popular black and green model, which made up the top 20 percent of its product mix. However, the company quickly discovered that customers wanted offbeat colors as well, including unusual shades such as champagne and yellow. At Amazon.com, sales of obscure book titles that brick-and-mortar bookstores do not even carry account for almost 40 percent of book sales. Tyler Smith, cofounder of Niche Retail, a company that helps small companies develop online strategies for reaching niches, says that for many of his customers, "There's no historical top 20 percent, and the top sellers move quickly and change." The Long Tail Theory demands that business owners always be on the lookout for new, obscure products aimed at niche markets and for ways to market these "less popular" items online.

In 1999, when Tony Hsieh became CEO of Zappos, the largest online retailer of shoes (now owned by Amazon.com), he was unsure of which sales pattern to expect. "I thought the 80/20 Rule might apply," he says. Instead, many customers turned to Zappos, which stocks more than 1.5 million pairs of shoes across more than 1,000 brands, for unique, hard-to-find styles and sizes. At Zappos, whose fulfillment centers are bigger than 17 football fields, the top 20 percent of products account for 50 percent of the company's sales; the remaining 80 percent of its products make up the other half of its sales. "It varies from brick-and-mortar quite a bit," says Hsieh.

1. Use the Internet to research the Long Tail Theory and its applications. Does the theory appear to be valid? Explain your reasoning.
2. What implications does the Long Tail Theory have for small companies that do business online?

Sources: Based on Susan Greco, "A World Without Best Sellers: Creating a 'Long Tail' Product Mix," *Inc.*, September 2007, pp. 47–52; Takayuki Mizuno, Masahiro Toriyama, Takao Terano, and Misako Takayasu, "Pareto Law of Expenditure of a Person in Convenience Stores," *Physica A*, Vol. 387, 2008, pp. 3931–3935; "About Me," Long Tail, *www.longtail.com/about.html*; Erik Brynjolfssen, Yu (Jeffrey) Hu, and Duncan Simester, "Goodbye Pareto Principle, Hello Long Tail: The Effect of Search Costs on the Concentration of Product Sales," Sloan School of Management, Massachusetts Institute of Technology, November 2007, pp. 1–40; Erick Schonfeld, "Poking Holes in the Long Tail Theory," *Tech Crunch*, July 2, 2008, *http://techcrunch.com/2008/07/02/poking-holes-in-the-long-tail-theory/*.

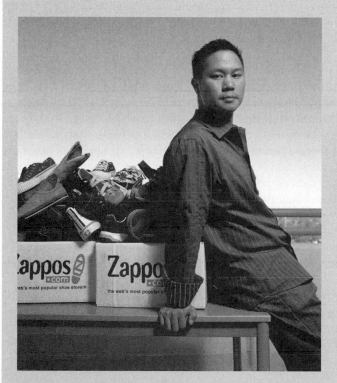

Tony Hsieh, CEO of Zappos. At Zappos, the top 20 percent of products account for 50 percent of the company's sales.

Source: Brad Swonetz/Redux Pictures

Perpetual Inventory Systems

Perpetual inventory systems are designed to maintain a running count of the items in inventory. Although a number of different perpetual inventory systems exist, they all have a common element: They keep a continuous tally of each item added to or subtracted from the firm's stock of merchandise. A typical manual system uses a perpetual inventory sheet that includes fundamental product information such as the item's name, stock number, description, economic order quantity (EOQ), and reorder point.

These perpetual inventory sheets are usually placed next to the merchandise in the warehouse or storage facility. Whenever a shipment is received from a vendor, the quantity is entered in the receipt column and added to the total. When the item is sold and taken from inventory, it is simply deducted from the total. As long as this procedure is followed consistently, an entrepreneur can determine quickly the number of each product on hand. Bar-coding the inventory allows the process to be done by handheld scanners that are tied directly to a computerized inventory control system. Automating the perpetual inventory system makes it more accurate and reliable, and when inventory levels drop to the reorder trigger point the system generates purchase orders to replenish the supply.

Although consistent use of the system yields accurate inventory counts at any moment, sporadic use creates problems. If managers or employees take items out of stock or place them in inventory without recording them, the perpetual inventory sheet yields incorrect totals and can foul up the entire inventory control system. Another disadvantage of this system is the cost of maintaining it. If not computerized, keeping perpetual inventory records for a large number of items and ensuring the accuracy of the system can be unreasonable. Therefore, these systems are used most frequently and most successfully in controlling high-dollar-volume items that require strict monitoring. Management must watch these items closely and ensure that inventory records are accurate.

Advances in computerized cash registers have overcome many of the disadvantages of using the basic perpetual inventory system. Small businesses now can afford computerized **point of sale (POS) systems** that perform all of the functions of a traditional cash register and maintain an up-to-the minute inventory count. Although POS systems are not new (major retailers have been using them for more than 30 years), their affordable prices are. Not so long ago, most systems required large investments in hardware and software. Today, small business owners can set up POS systems on personal computers for less than $1,000.

Combining a POS system with Universal Product Code (bar code) labels and high-speed scanners gives a small business a state-of-the-art checkout system that feeds vital information into its inventory control system. These systems rely on an inventory database; as items are rung up on the register, product information is recorded and inventory balances are adjusted. Using the system, business owners can tell how quickly each item is selling and how many items are in stock at any time. In addition, their inventory records are more accurate and are always current. They also can generate instantly a variety of reports to aid in making purchasing decisions. The system can be programmed to alert owners when the supply of a particular item drops below a predetermined reorder point or even to print automatically a purchase order to the EOQ indicated. Finally, modern POS systems allow business owners to generate an array of inventory reports instantly. Entrepreneurs can slice and dice data in a multitude of ways, which allows them to determine which items are selling the fastest and which are moving the slowest. Timely reports such as these give entrepreneurs the ability to make sound decisions about scheduling advertising, running special promotions, offering discounts, and arranging store displays. Computerized POS systems also make it possible for entrepreneurs to use a basic perpetual inventory system for a large number of items, a task that, if performed manually, would be virtually impossible.

Visual Inventory Control Systems

The most common method of controlling inventory in a small business is the **visual control system**, in which managers simply conduct periodic visual inspections to determine the quantity of various items they should order. This system suits businesses that stock a large number of low-value items with low-dollar volume. Unfortunately, this method is also the least effective for ensuring accuracy and reliability. Oversights of key items often lead to stockouts and resulting lost sales. The biggest disadvantage of the visual control system is its inability to detect and to foresee shortages of inventory items.

In general, a visual inventory control system works best in firms in which daily sales are relatively consistent, the entrepreneur is closely involved with the inventory, the variety of merchandise is small, and items can be obtained quickly from vendors. For example, small firms dealing in perishable goods use visual control systems very successfully, and rarely, if ever, rely on analytical inventory control tools. For these firms, shortages are less likely to occur under a visual system; when they do occur, they are not likely to create major problems. Entrepreneurs who rely on visual systems must be alert to shifts in customer buying patterns that alter required inventory levels.

Partial Inventory Control Systems

For small business owners with limited time and money, the most viable option for inventory management is a partial inventory control system. These systems rely on the validity of Pareto's Law, or the 80/20 Rule. For example, if a small business carries 5,000 different items in stock, roughly 1,000 of them account for about 80 percent of the firm's sales volume. Experienced business owners focus their inventory control efforts on those 1,000 items. Unfortunately, many owners seek to maintain tight control over the remaining 4,000 items, a frustrating and wasteful practice. Entrepreneur John Payne says that Pareto's Law applied to the consumer electronics business that he ran for years; about 75 percent of his company's sales came from just 20 percent of the items he carried in inventory.[9] Smart entrepreneurs design their inventory control systems with this principle in mind. One of the most popular partial inventory control systems is the ABC system.

THE ABC METHOD OF INVENTORY CONTROL. The ABC method focuses control efforts on that small percentage of items that accounts for the majority of the firm's sales. The typical **ABC system** divides a firm's inventory into three major categories:

A items account for a high dollar usage volume.

B items account for a moderate dollar usage volume.

C items account for low dollar usage volume.

The **dollar usage volume** of an item measures the relative importance of that item in a company's inventory. Note that value is *not* necessarily synonymous with high unit cost. In some instances, a high-cost item that generates only a small dollar volume can be classified as an A item. More frequently, however, A items are those that are low to moderate in cost and high volume by nature.

The initial step in establishing an ABC classification system is to compute the annual dollar usage volume for each product (or product category). **Annual dollar usage volume** is simply the cost per unit of an item multiplied by the annual quantity used. For instance, Florentina, the owner of a speaker shop, may find that she sold 190 pairs of a popular brand of speakers during the previous year. If the speakers cost her $75 per unit, their annual dollar usage volume would be as follows:

$$190 \times \$75 = \$14,250$$

The next step is to arrange the products in descending order on the basis of the computed annual dollar usage volume. Once so arranged, they can be divided into appropriate classes by applying the following rule:

A items: roughly the top 15 percent of the items listed

B items: roughly the next 35 percent

C items: roughly the remaining 50 percent

For example, Florentina's small retail shop is interested in establishing an ABC inventory control system to lower losses from stockouts, theft, and other hazards. Florentina has computed the annual dollar usage volume for the store's merchandise inventory, as shown in Table 1. (For simplicity, we show only 12 inventory items.)

The ABC inventory control method divides the firm's inventory items into three classes, depending on the items' value. Figure 1 graphically portrays the segmentation of the items listed in Table 1.

The purpose of classifying items according to their annual dollar usage volume is to establish the proper degree of control over each item held in inventory. Clearly, it is wasteful and inefficient to exercise the same level of control over C items and A items. Items in the A classification should be controlled under a perpetual inventory system, with as much detail as necessary. Analytical tools and frequent counts may be required to ensure accuracy, but the extra cost of tight control for these valuable items is usually justified. Managers should not retain a large supply of reserve or safety stock because doing so ties up excessive amounts of money in inventory, but they must monitor the stock closely to avoid stockouts and the lost sales that result.

Control of B items should rely more on periodic control systems and basic analytical tools such as EOQ and reorder point analysis. Managers can maintain moderate levels of safety stock for these items to guard against shortages and can afford monthly, or even bimonthly, merchandise inspections. Because B items are not as valuable to the business as A items, less rigorous control systems are required.

C items typically constitute a minor proportion of the small firm's inventory value and, as a result, require the least effort and expense to control. These items are usually large in number and small in total value. The most practical way to control them is to use uncomplicated records and procedures. Large levels of safety stock for these items are acceptable because the cost of carrying them is usually minimal. Substantial order sizes often enable the business to take advantage of quantity discounts without having to place frequent orders. The cost involved in using detailed

TABLE 1 Calculating Annual Dollar Usage Volume and an ABC Inventory Analysis for Florentina's

Item	Annual Dollar Usage Volume	% of Annual Dollar Usage
Paragon	$374,100	42.00
Excelsior	294,805	33.10
Avery	68,580	7.70
Bardeen	54,330	6.10
Berkeley	27,610	3.10
Tara	24,940	2.80
Cattell	11,578	1.30
Faraday	9,797	1.10
Humboldt	8,016	0.90
Mandel	7,125	0.08
Sabot	5,344	0.06
Wister	4,453	0.05
Total	$890,678	100.00

Classification	Items	Annual Dollar Usage	% of Total
A	Paragon, Excelsior	$668,905	**75.1**
B	Avery, Bardeen, Berkeley, Tara	175,460	**19.7**
C	Cattell, Faraday Humboldt Mandel, Sabot, Wister	46,313	**5.2**
Total		$890,678	**100.00**

FIGURE 1
ABC Inventory Control

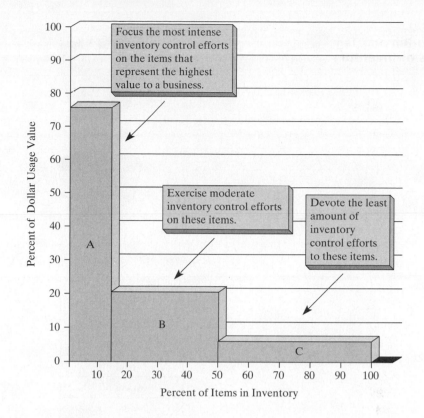

record keeping and inventory control procedures greatly outweighs the advantages gleaned from strict control of C items.

One practical technique for maintaining control over C items simply is the **two-bin system**, which keeps two separate bins full of material. The first bin is used to fill customer orders, and the second bin is filled with enough safety stock to meet customer demand during the lead time. When the first bin is empty, the owner places an order large enough to refill both bins with the vendor. During the lead time for the order, the manager uses the safety stock in the second bin to fill customer demand.

When storage space or the type of item makes a two-bin system impractical, an entrepreneur can use a **tag system**. Based on the same principles as the two-bin system, which is suitable for many manufacturers, the tag system applies to most retail, wholesale, and service firms. Instead of placing enough inventory to meet customer demand during lead time into a separate bin, the owner marks this inventory level with a brightly colored tag. When the supply is drawn down to the tagged level, the owner reorders the merchandise. Figure 2 illustrates the two-bin and tag systems of controlling C items.

In summary, business owners minimize total inventory costs when they spend time and effort controlling items that represent the greatest inventory value. Some inventory items require strict, detailed control techniques; other items simply do not justify the additional cost of tight controls. Because of its practicality, the ABC inventory system is commonly used in industry. In addition, the technique is easily computerized, speeding up the analysis and lowering its cost. Table 2 summarizes the use of the ABC control system.

Physical Inventory Count

Regardless of the type of inventory control system used, every small business owner must conduct a periodic physical inventory count. Even when a company uses a perpetual inventory system, the owner still must count the actual number of items on hand because errors inevitably occur. A physical inventory count allows owners to reconcile the actual amount of inventory in stock with the amount reported through the inventory control system. These

FIGURE 2
The Two-Bin and Tag Systems of Inventory Control

The Two-Bin System

Safety Stock

Reorder!   Safety Stock

Bin 1   Bin 2

The Tag System

| Model 101 |
| Model 101 |
| Model 101 |
| Model 101 |
| Model 101 |
| Model 101 |
| Model 101 |
| Model 101 |

Reorder!

| Model 101 |
| Model 101 |

counts give managers a fresh start when determining the actual number of items on hand and enable them to evaluate the effectiveness and the accuracy of their inventory control systems.

The typical method of taking inventory involves two employees; one calls out the relevant information for each inventory item, and the other records the count on a tally sheet. There are two basic methods of conducting a physical inventory count. One alternative is to take inventory at regular intervals. Many businesses take inventory at the end of the year. In an attempt to minimize counting, many managers run special year-end inventory reduction sales. This **periodic count** generates the most accurate measurement of inventory. The other method of taking inventory, called **cycle counting**, involves counting a number of items on a continuous cycle. Instead of waiting until year-end to tally the entire inventory of items, an entrepreneur counts a

TABLE 2 ABC Inventory Control Features

Feature	A Items	B Items	C Items
Level of control	Monitor closely and maintain tight control.	Maintain moderate control.	Maintain loose control.
Reorder point	Based on forecasted requirements.	Based on EOQ calculations and past experience.	When level gets low, reorder.
Record keeping	Keep detailed records of receipts and disbursements.	Use periodic inspections and control procedures.	No records required.
Safety stock	Keep low levels of safety stock.	Keep moderate levels of safety stock.	Keep high levels of safety stock.
Inspection frequency	Monitor schedule changes frequently.	Check on changes in requirements periodically.	Make few checks on requirements.

few types of items each day or each week and checks the numbers against the inventory control system. Performing a series of "mini-counts" each day or each week allows for continuous correction of mistakes in inventory control systems and detects inventory problems faster than an annual count does.

Once again, technology can make the job of taking inventory much easier for small business owners. Electronic data interchange (EDI) and Web-based systems enable business owners to track their inventories and to place orders with vendors quickly and with few errors by linking them to their vendors electronically. These systems often rely on handheld computer terminals equipped with scanning devices. An employee runs the scanning device across a bar code label on the shelf that identifies the inventory item. Then the employee counts the items on the shelf and enters that number using the number pad on the terminal. By linking the handheld terminal to a computer, the employee then downloads the physical inventory count into the company's inventory control software in seconds.

In the past, suppliers simply manufactured a product, shipped it, and then sent the customer an invoice. To place an order, employees or managers periodically estimated how many units of a particular item they needed and when they needed them. Today, however, in many EDI or Web-based supply chain management systems, the vendor is tied directly into a company's POS system, monitoring it constantly. When the company's supply of a particular item drops to a preset level, the vendor automatically sends a shipment to replenish its stock to an established level. Information that once traveled by mail (or was never shared at all), such as shipping information, invoices, inventory balances, sales, even funds, now travel instantly between businesses and their suppliers. The result is a much more efficient system of purchasing, distribution, and inventory control.

ENTREPRENEURIAL
Profile

Michael Fidenza: Ideal Supply Company

When one of Ideal Supply Company's top customers asked the small supplier of industrial pipes and valves to set up an EDI system, general manager Michael Fidenza decided that doing so would give his company an edge over its rivals. "Our industry is old-fashioned," says Fidenza. "We tend to lag behind the times." Ideal Supply not only forged an even closer relationship with its big customer, but it also reaped benefits from its suppliers. Because Ideal Supply was one of the few companies in the industry with EDI capability, Fidenza was able to negotiate higher discounts from Ideal Supply's suppliers because of increased efficiencies in the purchasing process. "One of our vendors offered us an extra 5 percent in discounts," he says. "Another plugs in an extra $10,000 worth of product with every $50,000 purchase—just because we're EDI." Ideal Supply has earned an impressive return on its original investment of $5,000 for EDI hardware and software. Today, 80 percent of the company's purchases and 15 percent of its sales are processed through its EDI system.[10]

Radio Frequency Identification Tags (RFID)

Inventory control systems that use bar codes to track the movement of inventory through the supply chain have been around for years. Increasingly, businesses are replacing their bar code systems with more flexible systems based on **radio frequency identification (RFID)** tags that are attached to individual items or to shipments and transmit data to a company's inventory management system. Each tag, which is about the size of a grain of sand, contains a tiny microchip that stores a unique electronic product code (EPC) and a tiny antenna. Because the tags use short-range radio frequencies, they can transmit information under almost any condition, avoiding the line-of-sight restrictions bar code systems experience. Once activated, the tags perform like talking bar codes and enable business owners to identify, count, and track the inventory items to which they are attached, providing them with highly accurate, real-time information constantly. When a shipment arrives at a warehouse or retail store, the RFID tags signal an inventory system reader, an object about the size of a coin that records the identity, the quantity, and characteristics of each item now in stock. The reader relays the information to a central inventory control system so that business owners can have access to all of this information online. Some stores have installed "smart" shelves equipped with readers that detect the identity and quantity of the items placed on them. When a customer makes a purchase, the smart shelf sends a message to the inventory control system, telling it to reduce the number on hand by the number of items the customer buys. In essence, RFID technology allows business owners to locate and track an item at any point in the supply chain—from the raw material stage to the finished product.

Other retailers use RFID technology to make inventory counts a breeze. Employees simply walk the aisles of the store holding a special reader that scans the RFID tags of the items on store shelves. At some stores, fully integrated RFID systems allow cashiers to ring up customers' purchases by scanning the contents of an entire shopping cart in just seconds, minimizing the time that customers have to stand in checkout lines. The cost of RFID tags continues to fall, from $1 per tag in 2000 to about five cents today. As costs decline further and the reliability of the tags improve, more businesses will be adopting the technology to improve the degree of control they have over their inventory.

ENTREPRENEURIAL
Profile
Serge Blanco

Serge Blanco, a French company that manufactures upscale sportswear, uses RFID technology to track the movement of products from its factories to its 40 retail stores and the 320 independent retailers that sell its clothing across Europe and the Middle East. The factories place an RFID tag on every garment they produce, which allows the company to monitor the location of each item of clothing in its distribution center and to make sure that each one is shipped to the right store at the right time. Once the garments arrive at its stores, RFID readers continue tracking them. For instance, at the Serge Blanco store in Toulon, France, employees take inventory counts of the entire store every hour using handheld RFID readers! When a customer makes a purchase, a POS terminal records the individual item sold before an employee removes the RFID tag. The system transmits sales reports to headquarters and to factories so that managers know exactly which items are selling (and therefore must be reordered) and which ones are languishing on store shelves. RFID readers in the store's dressing rooms identify which items customers try on but do not buy. Another reader near the store exit alerts employees when a garment with a tag still attached passes by, which helps reduce losses to theft. Managers say that the system has increased sales, reduced stockouts, lowered costs, and increased efficiency.[11]

LESSONS FROM THE STREET-SMART ➤ entrepreneur

Best Practices in Inventory Management

Many entrepreneurs have discovered the dangers of excess inventory. Not only does it tie up a company's valuable cash unnecessarily, but it also hides a host of other operating problems that a company has and needs to address. When it comes to managing inventory, small business owners often face four problems:

1. They have too much of some products.
2. They have too little of other products.
3. They don't know what they have in stock.
4. They know what they have in stock but cannot find it.

Addressing these four problems requires business owners to create a system of inventory management based on best practices. "Effective inventory management allows a distributor to meet or to exceed customers' expectations of product availability by maintaining the amount of each

item that will also maximize their company's net profit," says one expert. The following tips from the Street-Smart Entrepreneur about inventory management best practices help accomplish that goal:

- *Recognize the difference between your company's "stock" and its "stuff."* "Stock" is made up of the inventory that customers want and expect a company to have available. "Stuff" is everything else that is in the warehouse or stockroom and typically includes slow-moving items. The goal is to manage the stock in such a way that the company can meet customers' demand for items and make a profit and to get rid of everything else—the "stuff."
- *Set up an inventory management process that recognizes the value of your company's stock.* Remember that Pareto's Law, the 80/20 Rule, applies to many situations, particularly inventory control. About 20 percent of the items in a typical company's

inventory account for about 80 percent of its sales. The idea is to set up a system that exercises the greatest degree of control over the most valuable 20 percent of the company's items.

■ *Work with vendors and suppliers to keep the inventory of essential items as lean as possible.* Even companies that utilize just-in-time techniques find it necessary to carry inventory; however, they keep their levels of stock to a minimum. Look for suppliers that can meet your company's quality requirements and provide rapid deliveries on short notice. Sharing information with the members of your company's supply chain and connecting with them electronically are excellent ways to shorten the lead time on the items you order.

■ *Use computerized inventory control systems to monitor your company's stock.* Computerized inventory control systems that are linked to POS terminals allow entrepreneurs to know which items they have in stock at any time. The reports that these systems generate also help them to know which items are selling best and which items are not selling

Gary Peltz, second generation owner of Peltz Shoes, uses RFID labels to control inventory in his stores.

Source: Peltz Famous Brand Shoes

at all. This information leads to improved inventory decisions in the future and allows entrepreneurs to adjust their buying decisions on the fly. Gary Peltz, second-generation owner of Peltz Shoes, a family-run business with four locations in Florida, recently installed an RFID-based inventory control system. Each shoebox is tagged with a printed RFID label. To take inventory, employees simply push a mobile reader cart down the store's aisles. The cart captures the signals from every box on the sales floor and feeds the information to the store's computerized inventory management system. Because the system increased the company's ability to control its inventory, it paid for itself in just 1 year. The next step is to tie Peltz Shoes' POS terminals into the inventory control system to complete the sales loop.

■ *Track the inventory metrics that are most important to your company's success.* A business can improve only what it measures. Common metrics for inventory control include the inventory turnover rate (for the business as a whole and for individual products or product lines), gross profit margin, age of inventory, measures of overstock, customer order till rate, number of backorders, and many others.

■ *Organize your warehouse or stockroom to make it easy to find the items you need.* Organizing a warehouse or stockroom based on the knowledge of which items are in highest demand and which ones are seldom needed allows businesses to minimize the cost of filling orders. Placing the fastest-moving items in the most accessible location, preferably nearest the packing and shipping area, minimizes the time that employees spend walking around the warehouse or stockroom. Once again, computerized inventory control systems can help by printing the warehouse "address" of the items that employees must "pick" to fill orders.

■ *Get rid of the "stuff."* Eliminating unwanted or unnecessary inventory frees up valuable cash and simplifies the inventory management process. Possible ideas include:
  ■ Reducing the price of the items to get rid of them.
  ■ Offer incentives to salespeople to sell slow-moving "stuff."
  ■ Offer the items for sale at an online auction house.

Sources: Adapted from Jon Schreibfeder, *The First Steps to Achieving Effective Inventory Control,* Microsoft Business Solutions, *http://download. microsoft.com/download/b/f/3/bf334d7f-ad07-458e-a716-fdf46a0cf63c/ eimwp1_invcontrol.pdf;* "Inventory Best Practices," *The Bottom Line,* Manufacturing Extension Partnership, June 2003, pp. 1–2.

As Serge Blanco's experience suggests, the impact of RFID technology, which actually dates back to World War II, on inventory control is enormous. "This is an innovative technology similar to the Internet," says Mark Roberti, editor of *RFID Journal*. "You can now make any object smart."[12] International consulting firm McKinsey and Company estimates that once in use, RFID technology has the ability to increase companies' revenues by as much as 6 percent by improving the availability of items that customers want to buy and reducing the time and energy that staff spend looking for merchandise.[13]

Just-In-Time Inventory Control Techniques

Just-in-Time Techniques

2. Describe how just-in-time (JIT) and JIT II inventory control techniques work.

Many U.S. businesses have turned to a popular inventory control technique called **just-in-time (JIT)** to reduce costly inventories and turn around their financial fortunes. Until recently, these companies had accepted the following long-standing principles of manufacturing: Long production runs of standard items are ideal; machines should be up and running as much as possible; machines must produce a large number of items to justify long setup times and high costs; similar processes should be consolidated into single departments; tasks should be highly specialized and simplified; and inventories (raw materials, work-in-process, and finished goods) should be large enough to avoid emergencies such as supply interruptions, strikes, and breakdowns.

The just-in-time philosophy, however, views excess inventory as a blanket that masks problems and as a source of unnecessary costs that inhibit a firm's competitive position. Under a JIT system, materials and inventory flow smoothly through the production process without stopping. They arrive at the appropriate location just in time instead of becoming part of a costly inventory stockpile. Just-in-time is a philosophy that seeks to improve a company's efficiency. One key measure of efficiency is the level of inventory on hand; the lower the level of inventory, the more efficient is the production system.

The heart of the JIT philosophy is eliminating waste in whatever form it may take—time wasted moving work in process from one part of a factory to another, money wasted when employees must scrap or rework an item because of poor quality, cash tied up unnecessarily in excess inventory because of a poorly designed process, and many others. Refer to Figure 3, which illustrates the seven wastes that just-in-time, TQM, Six Sigma, and other continuous improvement strategies are designed to eliminate.

Companies using JIT successfully embrace a broader philosophy of continuous improvement ("kaizen"). These companies encourage employees to find ways to improve processes by simplifying them, making them more efficient, and redesigning them to make them more flexible. A cornerstone of the JIT philosophy is making waste in a company visible. The idea is that hidden waste is easy to ignore; visible waste gives everyone an incentive to eliminate it. Managers at a small company that manufactures fabrics for use in the papermaking industry set off an area in the middle of the production floor and put all of the wasted fabrics there on display. The not-so-subtle message was "help us find ways to reduce this waste." Within a matter of months, with the help of suggestions from both individuals and teams of employees, the pile of waste shrank dramatically.

In the past, only large companies could reap the benefits of computerized JIT and inventory control software, but now a proliferation of inexpensive programs designed for PCs gives small companies that ability. The most effective businesses know that what is required is not simply the technology, but the critical strategic alliances with suppliers who are themselves technologically sophisticated enough to interact on a real-time basis to deliver what is needed, when it is needed. The ultimate goal is to drive excess inventory to as close to zero as possible.

ENTREPRENEURIAL
Profile

Topshop

For British clothing retailer Topshop, now with three stores in the United States, a lean, just-in-time inventory control system is a key part of the company's strategy. Topshop has found a unique niche tucked between discount stores that sell cheap "fast fashion" and luxury retailers that sell pricey haute couture. Its most expensive items top out around $200, and its cutting-edge fashions have made its store popular with a broad demographic base, ranging from teens to women in their forties looking for the latest fashions. The company was struggling in the 1990s, when managers decided to stop competing on price and to "make a stand that we would become the fashion authority." To implement the new strategy of becoming a fashion destination, Topshop began working with its suppliers to speed deliveries of small batches of items to its stores, particularly its 90,000-square-foot flagship London store, which company buyers and designers see as a fashion laboratory. Three shipments of goods arrive each day at the London store, which means that merchandise turns over so quickly that many customers come back every week to see what is new. The London store allows managers to determine which items will sell best, and Topshop's supply chain is set up so that shipments arrive at its other outlets within 2 weeks, compared to 6 or 8 weeks at most clothing retailers. With Topshop's lean inventory, customers know that if they find an item that they like, they had better purchase it then. The result is that the flagship London store sees an average of 30,000 customers a day, half of whom make a purchase. Topshop says that it sells 30 pairs of panties ("knickers") per minute, 6,000 pairs of jeans per day, and 35,000 pairs of shoes per week. "It's mad," says a brand director. "The stock goes straight in and out the door."[14]

Advocates claim that when JIT is successfully implemented, companies experience five positive results:

1. Lower investment in inventory
2. Reduced inventory carrying and handling costs
3. Reduced cost from obsolescence of inventory
4. Lower investment in space for inventory and production
5. Reduced total manufacturing costs from the better coordination needed between departments to operate at lower inventory levels

Despite the many benefits JIT systems offer, they do carry risks. Any disruption in a company's supply chain, even for inexpensive, commonplace items, can cause the entire operation to come to a halt. Recently, nearly 70 percent of Japan's automobile production was paralyzed for several days after an earthquake damaged Riken Corporation, which supplies piston rings (which cost only $1.50 each) for all of the major Japanese automakers. Japanese carmakers rely heavily on the just-in-time philosophy, and they keep their inventories of parts extremely lean. Because piston rings are customized for each car model, automakers could not switch to alternate suppliers, and the interruption in the supply chain forced assembly plants to shut down temporarily.[15]

For JIT systems to be most productive, entrepreneurs must consider the human component of the equation as well. Two elements are essential:

1. *Mutual trust and teamwork.* Managers and employees view each other as equals, have a commitment to the organization and its long-term effectiveness, and are willing to work as a team to find and solve problems.
2. *Empowerment.* Effective organizations provide their employees with the authority to take action to solve problems. The objective is to have the problems dealt with at the lowest level and as quickly as possible.

JIT is most effective in repetitive manufacturing operations where companies traditionally have relied on holding significant levels of inventory, where production requirements can be forecasted accurately, and where suppliers and customers work together as partners throughout the supply chain. Experience shows that companies with the following characteristics have the greatest success with JIT:

- Reliable deliveries of all parts and supplies
- Short distance between customers and their vendors
- Consistently high quality of vendors' products
- Stable and predictable product demand that allows for accurate production schedules

Just-in-Time II Techniques

In the past, some companies that adopted JIT techniques discovered an unwanted side effect: increased hostility resulting from the increased pressure they put on their suppliers to meet tight and often challenging schedules. To resolve that conflict, many businesses have turned to an extension of JIT, just-in-time II (JIT II), which focuses on creating a close, harmonious relationship with a company's suppliers so that both parties benefit from increased efficiency. Lance Dixon, who created the JIT II concept when he was a manager at Bose Corporation, a manufacturer of audio equipment, sought to create a working environment that empowered the supplier within the customer's organization. To work successfully, JIT II requires suppliers and their customers to share what was once closely guarded information in an environment of trust and cooperation. Under JIT II, customers and suppliers work hand in hand, acting more like partners than mere buyers and sellers.

In many businesses practicing JIT II, suppliers' employees work onsite at the customer's plant, factory, or warehouse almost as if they were employees of the customer. These on-site workers are responsible for monitoring, controlling, and ordering inventory from their own companies. While at Bose, Dixon decided to try JIT II because it offered the potential to reduce significantly the company's inventory of materials and components, cut purchasing costs, and generate cost-cutting design and production tips from suppliers who understood Bose's process. This new alliance between suppliers and their customers formed a new supply chain that lowered costs at every one of its links. To protect against leakage of confidential information, Dixon had all of the employees from Bose's suppliers who worked in its plant sign confidentiality agreements. Dixon also put a ceiling on the amount each supplier's employee could order without previous authorization from Bose.[16]

Manufacturers are not the only companies benefiting from JIT II. In a retail environment, the concept is more commonly known as **efficient consumer response (ECR)**, but the principles are the same. Rather than build inventories of merchandise that might sit for months before selling (or worse, never sell at all), retailers that use ECR replenish their inventories constantly on an as-needed basis. Because vendors are linked electronically to the retailer's POS system, they can monitor the company's inventory and keep it stocked with the right merchandise mix in the right quantities. Both parties reduce the inventories they must carry and experience significant reductions in paperwork and ordering costs. JIT II and ECR techniques work best when two companies transact a significant amount of business that involves many different parts or products. Still, maintaining trust is the biggest barrier the companies must overcome.

IN THE ENTREPRENEURIAL SPOTLIGHT

Perry Ellis International: Integrated Inventory Control

Founded in 1969, Perry Ellis International, a Miami, Florida-based apparel company, has grown rapidly and now manages 27 different brands, including its namesake, Perry Ellis; Jantzen; Savane; Original Penguin; and others. The company manages a global supply network of more than 100 companies and distributes garments in 10 different clothing categories through 7 channels to a variety of regional, national, and international department stores and small independent specialty stores. Because Perry Ellis operates in the ever-changing fashion industry, the company must exercise tight control over its inventory to be successful. The company's inventory control system had evolved over time and was composed of a set of internally built components that were sagging under the company's fast growth. As a result, managers were not

getting timely inventory reports, one key to success in the fashion apparel business.

Working with software provider Oracle, Perry Ellis created an integrated business system that links stores, warehouses, headquarters, and suppliers and gives everyone in the supply chain timely access to information about inventory levels. For instance, suppliers of fabric for Perry Ellis shirts can see which types of shirts are selling best and adjust their production schedules accordingly. "Retailers and their suppliers [are] partnering closer than they ever have before by sharing demand information in a bidirectional way," says one industry analyst. "Retailers are sharing more transaction and consumer information to help manufacturers with their sales and operations planning activities. Suppliers are sharing supply chain event and inventory information to help retailers better understand the status of products and how they're filling the channel." The new, integrated inventory control system gives managers a real-time picture of the company's diverse inventory, whether it is in warehouses, in transit, or in stores. "We have small stores, so there's not much room for inventory," says Luis Paez, chief information officer for Perry Ellis. "Having the right inventory in the right place at the right time becomes critical because we can't have a lot of [merchandise on hand]."

To make sure that happens, the new system relies on sales feedback from each store and automatic allocations that determine which items need to be replaced and ensure that each store is always fully stocked with items that customers are buying. The result is fewer stockouts and higher levels of customer satisfaction. The new system is working: It has increased the company's sales by 15 to 20 percent. Perry Ellis' retail stores are not the only beneficiaries of the new inventory control system; its department store customers also are gaining better control over their Perry Ellis–branded merchandise. Perry Ellis representatives share inventory reports with department store buyers and managers about which items are selling and where and are able to offer suggestions on price adjustments. In other words, the company has become a resource to its retail customers, helping them sell more merchandise at better prices. The new system slices and dices information down to the individual store level and uses statistics and geographic information systems (GIS) data to generate reports that describe the groups of target customers that are driving sales of various products, allowing Perry Ellis and its retail customers to stock products with the greatest potential to sell in stores. "We work to have the right inventory at the right store at the right time for more than 12,000 stores," says Paez.

The new inventory control system at Perry Ellis enables the company and its department and specialty store customers to track ever-changing fashion trends and to respond to them quickly and efficiently—a must in the hotly competitive fashion world. "The ultimate goal of companies in the value chain is to become demand-driven," says an industry analyst. "Driven by a better understanding of what customers want and ultimately being able to translate that effectively into fulfilling the demand."

1. One key to the success of Perry Ellis' inventory control system is a supply chain that provides visibility of sales and inventory information for every business in the chain. Why are some companies hesitant to share sales and inventory data with their supply chain partners? What are the benefits of doing so?
2. What advantages does Perry Ellis reap by managing its inventory so carefully?

Source: Based on David A. Kelly, "Building a Seamless Retail System," *Profit*, August 2008, pp. 16–22.

Turning Slow-Moving Inventory into Cash

3. Describe methods for reducing losses from slow-moving inventory.

Managing inventory effectively requires a business owner to monitor the company's inventory turnover ratio and to compare it with that of other firms of similar size in the same industry. The inventory turnover ratio is calculated by dividing a company's cost of goods sold by its average inventory. This ratio expresses the number of times per year the business turns over its inventory. In most cases, the higher the inventory turnover ratio, the better the small firm's financial position will be. A very low inventory turnover ratio indicates that much of the inventory may be stale and obsolete or that the inventory investment is too large.

Because of the variability in demand and the cyclical nature of the market, auto dealers often struggle to maintain an adequate number of inventory turns and to keep the number of cars on their lots from ballooning, which drives up their operating costs. The longer a car sits on a dealer's lot, the greater is the cost of borrowing to pay for it. Auto companies consider 50 to 60 days' worth of cars to be an adequate inventory. When gasoline prices increase, however, dealers see large gas-guzzling SUVs languish on their lots, with inventories increasing to 100 days' worth. Inventories of fuel-efficient and hybrid models, however, fall to record lows. After one spike in gas prices, Toyota (which usually stocks 35 to 45 days' worth of inventory) reported that its Scion line, which it markets to young people, was down to 7.2 days' supply, and its hybrid Prius inventory stood at just 6 days' worth. Similarly, supply of its Fit was just 9 days.[17]

Slow-moving items carry a good chance of loss resulting from spoilage or obsolescence. Firms dealing in trendy fashion merchandise or highly seasonal items often experience losses as a result of being stuck with unsold inventory for long periods of time. Some small business owners are reluctant to sell these slow-moving items by cutting prices, but it is much more profitable to dispose of this merchandise quickly than it is to hold it in stock at regular prices.

Sales during the all-important holiday season at the Pants Store, a small chain of clothing stores near Birmingham, Alabama, were slower than owner Mickey Gee, whose father, Taylor, started the business in 1950, expected, leaving him with 20 percent more merchandise than normal. Gee used markdowns, some as much as 80 percent, to turn the slow-moving merchandise into cash. He also invested in an inventory control system that helps him identify which brands and which items are selling best (and which are not) in his four locations.[18]

A business owner who postpones marking down stale merchandise, fearing it will reduce profits and hoping that the goods will sell eventually at the regular price, is making a mistake. The longer the merchandise sits, the dimmer are the prospects of ever selling it, much less selling it at a profit. Pricing these items below regular price or even below cost is difficult, but it is much better than having valuable working capital tied up in unproductive assets.

The technique that Mickey Gee used, the markdown, is the most common technique for liquidating slow-moving merchandise. Not only is the markdown effective in eliminating slow-moving goods, but it also is a successful promotional tool. Advertising special prices on such merchandise helps a small business garner a larger clientele and contributes to establishing a favorable business image. Using special sales to promote slow-moving items helps create a functional program for turning over inventory more quickly. To get rid of a large supply of out-of-style neckties, one small business offered a "1-cent sale" to customers purchasing neckwear at the regular price. One retailer of stereos and sound equipment chooses an unusual holiday—President's Day—to sponsor an all-out blitz, including special sales, prices, and promotions to reduce its inventory. Other techniques that help eliminate slow-moving merchandise include the following:

- Creating middle-of-the-aisle display islands that attract customer attention
- Offering 1-day-only sales
- Giving quantity discounts for volume purchases
- Creating bargain tables with a variety of merchandise for customers to explore
- Using eye-catching lights and tickets marking sale merchandise
- Setting up an online store on eBay
- Using an inventory liquidation company to get rid of excess merchandise

As inventory control techniques become increasingly sophisticated and accurate, slow-moving inventory will never be "lost" in the supply chain. Aggressive methods of selling slower-moving inventory allow business owners to convert inventory into cash and to produce an acceptable inventory turnover ratio. The inventory management tools described in this chapter also play an important role in avoiding slow-moving merchandise. They highlight those items that are slow-moving, enabling business owners to avoid the mistake of ordering them again. In effect, this information on what *isn't* selling influences entrepreneurs' decisions about the merchandise they order in the future as much as information on those items that *are* selling well. The ability to avoid slow-moving items in the first place means that business owners can invest their working capital more effectively and produce faster inventory turnover ratios, lower costs, and higher profits.

Protecting Inventory from Theft

4. Discuss employee theft and shoplifting and how to prevent them.

Small companies are a big target for crime. Businesses lose nearly $92 million per day, about 5 percent of their total sales, to criminals, although the actual loss may be even greater because so many business crimes go unreported.[19] Whatever the actual loss is, its effect is staggering. If a company operates at a 5 percent net profit margin, it must generate an additional $20 in sales for every $1 lost to theft. Small companies are especially vulnerable because they often lack the sophistication to identify early on the illegal actions of employees or professional thieves and to implement controls to prevent theft and fraud. A study by the Association of Certified Fraud Examiners reports that small companies are the most frequent victims of theft and fraud and that the median loss for small companies is $155,000.[20] When a company has a small asset base, a loss from theft and fraud can be a crippling blow, threatening its very existence.

Many entrepreneurs believe that the primary sources of theft originate outside the business In reality, most firms are victimized by their own employees.

Employee Theft

Ironically, the greatest criminal threat to small businesses comes from the inside. Employee theft accounts for the greatest proportion of the criminal losses businesses suffer and cost companies $39.5 million per day.[21] Because employees have access to the inner workings of a business, they can inflict more damage than shoplifters. One study reports that dishonest employees steal, on average, 6.6 times more per incident than shoplifters.[22] Unfortunately, employee theft is more prevalent than ever. Tim Dimoff, president of SACS Consulting & Investigative Services Inc., which is based in Mogadore, Ohio, gives one reason for the increased prevalence. "I call the attitude employees take in the workplace 'entitlement,'" he says. "They justify in their minds that they are entitled to take things because they work so hard." Dimoff adds that some businesses all but encourage employee theft. How? By failing to file criminal charges against employees caught stealing. Many business owners do not want the negative publicity that results from prosecuting employee thieves. Others worry about the cost to the company to prosecute, how the time away from management will affect the organization, and the impact that the incident will have on employee morale. Often it is easier just to ask the guilty employee to leave.[23]

The median length of time it takes employers to catch an employee who is stealing is 18 months, and managers usually discover the theft when another employee tips them off.[24] How can thefts go undetected for so long? Most thefts occur when employees take advantage of the opportunities to steal that small business owners unwittingly give them. Typically, small business owners are so busy building their companies that they rarely even consider the possibility of employee theft—until disaster strikes.

In addition, many small companies do not have adequate financial, audit, and security procedures in place. Fewer than 30 percent of small companies use internal audit teams as a loss prevention tool, compared to nearly 83 percent of large companies. Even though tips from employees are the most common way of discovering employee theft and fraud, only 15 percent of small companies have installed antifraud hotlines for employees to report suspicious activities.[25] Add to this mix of lax control procedures the high degree of trust that most small business owners place in their employees, and you have a perfect recipe for employee theft.

ENTREPRENEURIAL
Profile
Berle Apparel Group

Berle Apparel Group, a family-owned manufacturer of men's trousers founded in 1946 in Charleston, South Carolina, recently discovered that a long-time employee had embezzled more than $600,000. The employee, who was the company's financial controller, diverted Berle's payroll tax payments to the Internal Revenue Service for more than 2 years by giving the IRS the impression that the company had gone out of business.[26]

What Causes Employee Theft?

Security experts estimate that 30 percent of workers pilfer small items from their employers and that 60 percent of employees will steal if given enough opportunity and motivation.[27] Employees steal from their companies for any number of reasons. Some may have a grudge against the company; others may have a drug, alcohol, or gambling addiction to support. Still others succumb to the temptation of an easy opportunity to steal because of a company's lack of proper controls. The Association of Certified Fraud Examiners reports that more than 85 percent of employees caught stealing have never been charged or convicted of a prior theft offense.[28]

Employees steal from the company for four reasons: need, greed, temptation, and opportunity. A business owner can control only temptation and opportunity. To minimize their losses to employee theft, business owners must understand how both the temptation and the opportunity to steal creep into their companies. The following are conditions that lead to major security gaps in small companies.

THE TRUSTED EMPLOYEE. The fact is that *any* employee can be a thief, although most are not. Slightly more than half of the workers who steal from their companies have been employed for less than 5 years, but long-time employees who steal cause more damage (median loss of $81,000 versus $260,000). Many entrepreneurs view their long-time employees almost as partners. This attitude, although not undesirable, can result in security breaches. Many owners refuse to believe that their most trusted employees present the greatest security threat, but these workers have the

639

greatest accessibility to keys, cash registers, records, and even safe combinations. Because of their seniority, these employees hold key positions and are quite familiar with operations, and they know where weaknesses in control and security procedures lie.

Michael and John Koss, second-generation owners of Koss Corporation, a Milwaukee, Wisconsin-based maker of stereo headphones, discovered that the company's vice president of finance had used her position to steal more than $31 million from the company over 6 years. She covered her theft for so long by inducing employees in the finance department to make fraudulent accounting entries that made her theft transactions appear to be legitimate. The employee, who had held her position at Koss for 18 years, used the money to finance purchases of cars, clothing, jewelry, home renovations, household furnishings, trips, and other personal expenditures.[29]

Business owners also should be wary of "workaholic" employees. Is this worker really dedicated to the company, or is he or she working so hard to cover up theft? Employee thieves are unwilling to take extended breaks from their jobs for fear of being detected. As long as a dishonest employee remains on the job, he or she can cover up theft. As a security precaution, business owners should require every employee to take vacations long enough so that someone else has to take over his or her responsibilities (at least 5 consecutive business days). Most schemes are relatively simple and require day-to-day maintenance to keep them going. Business failure records are filled with stories of firms in which the "ideal" employee turned out to be a thief. "In 90 percent of the cases in which people steal from their companies, the employer would probably have described this person, right up to the time the crime was discovered as a trusted employee," says one expert.[30]

DISGRUNTLED EMPLOYEES. Business owners also must monitor the performance of disgruntled employees. Employees are more likely to steal if they believe that their company treats them unfairly, and the probability of their stealing goes even higher if they believe that they themselves have been treated unfairly. Employees dissatisfied with their pay or their promotions may retaliate against an employer by stealing. Dishonest employees make up the difference between what they are paid and what they believe they are worth by stealing. Many believe pilfering is a well-deserved "perk."

ORGANIZATIONAL ATMOSPHERE. Many entrepreneurs unintentionally create an atmosphere that encourages employee dishonesty. Failing to establish formal controls and procedures invites theft. Nothing encourages dishonest employees to steal more than knowing they are unlikely to be caught. Four factors encourage employee theft:

1. The need or desire to steal (e.g., to support a habit or to cope with a sudden financial crisis)
2. A rationalization for the act (e.g., "They owe me this.")
3. The opportunity to steal (e.g., access to merchandise, complete control of financial functions)
4. The perception that there is a low probability of being caught (e.g., "Nobody will ever know.")

Owners must recognize that they set the example for security and honesty in the business. Employees place more emphasis on what owners *do* than on what they *say*. Entrepreneurs who install a complete system of inventory control and then ignore it are telling employees that security is unimportant. No one should remove merchandise, materials, or supplies from inventory without recording them properly. There should be no exceptions to the rules, even for bosses and their relatives. Managers should develop clear control procedures and establish penalties for violations. The single biggest deterrent (to employee theft) is a strong, top-down policy that is well communicated to all employees that theft will not be tolerated and that anyone caught stealing will be prosecuted—*no exceptions.*

Entrepreneurs must constantly emphasize the importance of security. Business owners must use every available opportunity to reduce employees' temptation to steal. One business owner relies on payroll inserts to emphasize to employees how theft reduces the funds available for growth, expansion, and higher wages. Another useful tool is a written code of ethics signed by every employee that spells out penalties for violations. Workers must understand that security is a team effort. Security rules and procedures must be reasonable, and owners must treat workers equitably. Unreasonable rules are no more effective—and may even be more harmful—than poorly enforced procedures. A work environment that fosters honesty at every turn serves as an effective deterrent to employee theft.

PHYSICAL BREAKDOWNS. Another major factor contributing to employee theft is weak physical security. The owner who pays little attention to the distribution of keys, safe combinations, and other entry devices is inviting theft. In addition, owners who fail to lock doors and windows or to install reliable alarm systems literally are leaving their businesses open to thieves both inside and outside the organization.

Open windows and unattended doors give dishonest employees a prime opportunity to slip stolen merchandise out of the plant or store. One security expert worked with a small manufacturing operation that was experiencing high levels of employee theft during the night shift. His investigation revealed that employees could exit the building through 14 different doors with little or no supervision. The company closed most of the exits, installed security cameras at those that remained open, and assigned managers to supervise the night shift. After implementing these simple changes, employee theft plummeted to nearly zero.[31]

Many businesses find that their profits go out with the trash, literally. When collecting trash, a dishonest employee may stash valuable merchandise in with the refuse and dump it in the receptacle. After the store closes, the thief returns to collect the loot. One drugstore owner lost more than $7,000 in merchandise in just 6 months through trash thefts.

IMPROPER CASH CONTROL. Many small business owners encourage employee theft by failing to implement proper cash control procedures. Without a system of logical, practical audit controls on cash, a firm will likely suffer internal theft. Dishonest employees quickly discover there is a low probability of detection and steal cash with impunity.

Cashiers clearly have the greatest accessibility to the firm's cash and, consequently, experience the greatest temptation to steal. The following scenario is all too common: A customer makes a purchase with the exact amount of cash and leaves quickly. The cashier fails to ring up the purchase and pockets the cash without anyone's knowledge. Some small business owners create a cash security problem by allowing too many employees to operate cash registers and handle customer payments. If a cash shortage develops, the owner is unable to trace responsibility.

A daily inspection of cash register transactions can point out potential employee theft problems. When transactions indicate an excessive number of voided transactions or no-sale transactions, the owner should investigate. A no-sale transaction could mean the register was opened to give a customer change or to steal cash. A large number of incorrect register transactions also are a sign of foul play. Clerks may be camouflaging thefts by voiding transactions, under-ringing sales amounts, or pretending to scan items at checkout without actually ringing them up (a problem known as "sweethearting").

ENTREPRENEURIAL
Profile
Famous Footwear

To cut its losses from theft Famous Footwear, a chain of retail shoe stores, recently installed a cash register monitoring system in every store. The system records every cash register transaction and looks for suspicious patterns. Within a short time, the monitoring system cut the company's unexplained inventory losses in half. When she learned about the new system, one store manager, convinced that she would soon be caught, admitted to stealing more than $2,000 in cash.[32]

Cash shortages and overages are also clues that alert managers to possible theft. All small business owners are alarmed by cash shortages, but few are disturbed by cash overages. However, cash discrepancies in either direction are an indication of inept cashiering or of poor cash controls. The manager who investigates all cash discrepancies can greatly reduce the opportunity for cashiers to steal.

Preventing Employee Theft

Many incidents of employee theft go undetected, and of those employees who are caught stealing, only a small percentage is prosecuted. The burden of dealing with employee theft falls squarely on the owner's shoulders. Although business owners cannot eliminate employee theft, they can reduce its likelihood by using some relatively simple procedures and policies that are cost-effective to implement.

SCREEN EMPLOYEES CAREFULLY. Statistics show that, on average, 1 out of every 28 employees is caught committing employee theft.[33] Perhaps a business owner's greatest weapon against crime is a thorough pre-employment screening process. The best time to weed out prospective criminals is before hiring them! One security company conducted an analysis of more than 19,000 applicants for retail jobs and rated 19.3 percent of them as "high risk" candidates for employee theft.[34] Although state and federal regulations prohibit employers from invading job applicants' privacy and from using discriminatory devices in the selection process, employers have a legitimate right to determine job candidates' integrity and qualifications. A comprehensive selection process and reliable screening devices greatly reduce the chances that an entrepreneur will hire a thief. Smart entrepreneurs verify the information applicants provide on their résumés because they know that some of them will either exaggerate or misrepresent their qualifications. A thorough background check with references and previous employers also is essential. (One question that sheds light on a former employer's feelings toward a former employee is "Would you hire this person again?")

Some security experts recommend the use of **integrity tests**, paper-and-pencil tests that offer valuable insight into job applicants' level of honesty. Business owners can buy integrity tests for $20 or less that have already been validated (to avoid charges of discrimination) and that they can score on their own. Because drug addictions drive many employees to steal, employers also should administer drug tests consistently to all job applicants. The most reliable drug tests cost the company from $35 to $50 each, a small price to pay given the potential losses that can result from hiring an employee with a drug habit. In addition, business owners should conduct criminal background checks on every candidate they are considering hiring.

CREATE AN ENVIRONMENT OF HONESTY. Creating an environment of honesty and integrity starts at the top of an organization. This requires business owners to set an impeccable example for everyone else in the company. In addition to creating a standard of ethical behavior, business owners should strive to establish high morale among workers. A positive work environment in which employees see themselves as an important part of the team is an effective deterrent to employee theft. Establishing a written code of ethics and having employees sign "honesty clauses" offers tangible evidence of a company's commitment to honesty and integrity.

ESTABLISH A SYSTEM OF INTERNAL CONTROLS. The basis for maintaining internal security on the job is establishing a set of reasonable internal controls designed to prevent employee theft. An effective system of checks and balances goes a long way toward deterring internal crime; weak or inconsistently enforced controls are an open invitation for theft. The most basic rule is to separate among several employees related duties that might cause a security breach if assigned to a single worker. For instance, owners should avoid letting the employee who issues checks reconcile the company's bank statement. Similarly, the person who orders merchandise and supplies should not be the one who also approves those invoices for payment. Spreading these tasks among a number of employees makes organizing a theft more difficult. The owner of a small retail art shop learned this lesson the hard way. After conducting an inventory audit, he discovered that more than $25,000 worth of art supplies was missing. The owner finally traced the theft to the company bookkeeper, who was creating fictional invoices and then issuing checks to herself for the same amount.

FIGURE 3
Behaviors Exhibited by Perpetrators of Employee Theft

Source: 2010 Report to the Nations on Occupational Fraud and Abuse, Association of Certified Fraud Examiners, Austin, Texas, p. 70.

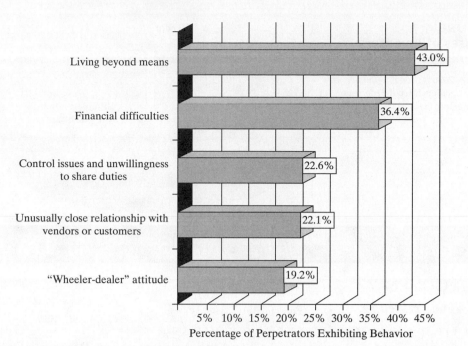

Business owners should insist that all company records be kept up-to-date. Sloppy record keeping makes theft difficult to detect. All internal documents—shipping, ordering, invoicing, and collecting—should be numbered. Missing numbers should arouse suspicion. One subtle way to test employees' honesty is to commit deliberate errors occasionally to see if employees detect them. If you send an extra case of merchandise to the loading dock for shipment, does the supervisor catch it, or does it disappear?

USE TECHNOLOGY TO REDUCE THEFT. Business owners can use a variety of technologies, often available at low cost, to minimize losses to employee theft and fraud. Kevin Donahue, owner of a Planet Beach franchise in McLean, Virginia, uses a security system that gives him access to his store's alarm system and security cameras from almost anywhere in the world over the Internet. "It gives me the ability to travel and manage my staff remotely," says Donahue, who paid $100 to install the system and pays a monthly fee of $39.[35]

WATCH FOR SIGNS OF EMPLOYEE THEFT. Research shows that employees who are stealing tend to exhibit certain behavior patterns (see Figure 3). Watch for them.

SET UP A HOTLINE. One of the most effective tools for preventing employee theft is to encourage employees to report suspicious activity. Perhaps the easiest way to encourage reporting it is to establish a hotline that allows employees to provide tips anonymously.

EMBRACE A ZERO TOLERANCE POLICY. Business owners should demonstrate zero tolerance for theft. They must adhere strictly to company policy when dealing with employees who violate the company's trust. When business owners catch an employee thief, the best course of action is to fire the perpetrator and to prosecute. Too often, owners take the attitude: "Resign, return the money, and we'll forget it." Letting thieves off, however, only encourages them to move on to other businesses where they will steal again. Prosecuting a former employee for theft is never easy, but it does send a clear signal about how the company views employee crime.

Notice in Figure 4 that although the primary cause of inventory shrinkage is employee theft, shoplifting also is a common problem.

FIGURE 4
Causes of Inventory Shrinkage

Source: 2010 National Retail Security Survey, National Retail Federation, Washington, D.C.

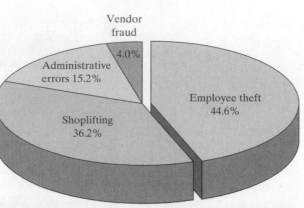

Vendor fraud 4.0%

Administrative errors 15.2%

Employee theft 44.6%

Shoplifting 36.2%

► E N T R E P R E N E U R S H I P **IN ACTION** ►

FOUL PLAY

The Trusted Employee

Like many business owners, Karin Wilson saw sales slide at Page and Palette Inc., the bookstore in Fairhope, Alabama, that she co-owns with her husband, during the last recession. By the time the all-important holiday season arrived, the store was running low on its inventory of books. However, cash flow at Page and Palette was extremely tight, and Wilson was unable to convince her book suppliers to extend the store additional credit. One week before Christmas, Wilson happened to see the company's credit card bill, which indicated the Page and Palette was months behind on its payments and was racking up huge fees and interest expenses. She began investigating and soon discovered evidence that the company's bookkeeper, who had a personal account with the same bank, had been using money from the company's account to pay her personal credit card bill.

Wilson was shocked because the bookkeeper was one of her most trusted employees. She also discovered that the bookkeeper had used money intended to pay publishers for the store's book orders to write checks to herself. Wilson says that the former employee used the money that she embezzled from Page and Palette to pay for a membership in a local golf club and for private school tuition for her child. Wilson estimates that the former employee took about $150,000 over two-and-a-half years and covered the theft by forging reports that made it look as though she had paid the company's vendors and credit card bills. Because the theft left the store in a cash bind, Wilson was unable to order a sufficient inventory of books, which ultimately cost the business as much as 20 percent of its annual revenue in lost sales. "She realized quickly how trusting we were," says Wilson.

Since discovering that she was a victim of employee theft, Wilson has changed the way she operates her business. She destroyed the stamp bearing her signature that the former employee used on business checks. Employees no longer have access to the company's credit cards; Wilson now approves every credit card purchase. She also has the company's bank statements sent to her home rather than to the business.

The Desperate Employee

Brandon Ansel, owner of a Roly Poly sandwich and Biggby Coffee franchise in Jackson, Michigan, noticed that one of the restaurant's employees failed to deposit money from the cash register into the company's bank account daily. Instead, he would wait 3 or 4 days to deposit the cash. When Ansel questioned the employee, the man said that he was so busy that he could not get to the bank on time. Eventually, the employee began stretching the time between deposits to 9 days, and Ansel suspected that the man was skimming cash from each day's receipts. When Ansel confronted the man, he admitted that he was having severe financial problems and had taken the money with the intent of repaying it. A member of the man's family approached Ansel and paid him $9,000, the amount the former employee admitted that he had taken. Ansel decided not to press charges against his former employee. Ansel says that he, too, has changed some of his operating procedures and admits that as a small business owner he feels more susceptible to employee theft because he lacks the systems that larger companies have to alert managers to signs of theft.

1. What factors led to the thefts at Page and Palette and the Roly Poly–Biggby Coffee franchise?
2. Do you agree with Brandon Ansel's view that small businesses are more vulnerable to employee theft because they lack the systems to detect the signs of theft? Explain.
3. Do you agree with the approach that Brandon Ansel took with the employee who stole from his company? Explain.
4. List at least five steps business owners can take to prevent employee theft.

Source: Based on Simona Covel, "Small Businesses Face More Fraud in Downturn," *Wall Street Journal*, February 19, 2009, p. B5.

Shoplifting

The most frequent business crime is shoplifting. In fact, research shows that 1 of every 11 adults in the United States has shoplifted.[36] Retail businesses in the United States lose an estimated $11.7 billion annually to shoplifters each year, and small businesses suffer a significant share of those losses.[37] Shoplifting takes an especially heavy toll on small businesses because they usually have the weakest lines of defense against shoplifters. Shoplifting losses, which ultimately are passed on to the consumer, account for approximately 3 to 4 percent of the average price tag.

TYPES OF SHOPLIFTERS. Anyone who takes merchandise from a store without paying for it, no matter what the justification, is a shoplifter. Shoplifters look exactly like other customers. They can be young children in search of a new toy or elderly people who are short of money. *Anyone* can be a shoplifter, given the opportunity, the ability, and the desire to steal. Police have apprehended people from all walks of life—including wealthy socialites and famous celebrities—for shoplifting.

Fortunately for small business owners, most shoplifters are amateurs who steal because the opportunity presents itself. Many steal on impulse, and the theft is the first criminal act. Many of those caught have the money to pay for their "five-finger discounts." Observant business owners supported by trained store personnel can spot potential shoplifters and deter many shoplifting incidents; however, they must understand the shoplifter's profile. Experts identify five types of shoplifters.

Juveniles. Juveniles account for approximately one-half of all shoplifters. Many juveniles steal as a result of peer pressure. Most have little fear of prosecution, assuming they can hide behind their youth. When owners detect juvenile shoplifters, they must not let sympathy stand in the way of good judgment. Many hard-core criminals began their careers as shoplifters, and small business owners who fail to prosecute the youthful offender do nothing to discourage a life of crime. Juvenile offenders should be prosecuted through proper legal procedures just as any adult shoplifter would be.

Impulse Shoplifters. Impulse shoplifters steal on the spur of the moment when they succumb to temptation. These shoplifters do not plan their thefts, but when a prime opportunity to shoplift arises, they take advantage of it. For example, a salesperson may be showing a customer several pieces of jewelry. If the salesperson is called away, the customer might pocket an expensive ring and leave the store before the employee returns.

The most effective method of fighting impulse shoplifting is prevention. To minimize losses, the owner should remove the opportunity to steal by implementing proper security procedures and devices.

Shoplifters sometimes work in teams. Here a girl shoplifts computer software while a partner obstructs employees' view of the theft.

Source: PhotoEdit, Inc.

© Mike Baldwin / Cornered

"The sign said buy one, get one free.
But I only needed one. The free one."

Shoplifters Supporting Other Criminal Behaviors. Shoplifters motivated to steal to support a drug or alcohol habit often are easy to detect because their behavior is usually unstable and erratic. One shoplifter recently apprehended was supporting a $100-a-day heroin habit by stealing small items from local retailers and then returning the merchandise for refunds. (The stores almost never asked for sales receipts.) Small business owners should exercise great caution in handling these shoplifters because they can easily become violent. Criminals deranged by drugs or alcohol might be armed and could endanger the lives of customers and employees if they are detained. It is best to let the police apprehend these shoplifters.

Kleptomaniacs. Kleptomaniacs have a compulsive need to steal even though they have little, if any, need for the items they shoplift. In many cases, these shoplifters could afford to purchase the merchandise they steal. Kleptomaniacs account for less than 5 percent of shoplifters, but their disease costs business owners a great deal. They need professional psychological counseling, and the owner only helps them by seeing that they are apprehended.

Professionals. A study by the National Retail Federation reports that 92 percent of businesses have been victims of professional shoplifters within the last year.[38] Professional shoplifters are individuals, groups, or gangs who steal merchandise in significant quantities as part of a criminal enterprise. These criminal operations rely on "boosters," people who are paid to steal merchandise from stores, and "fences," those who specialize in converting stolen goods into cash or drugs. Although professional shoplifters account for 32 percent of shoplifting incidents, the dollar impact of their thefts is disproportionately large. Losses to professional shoplifters are 54 times greater than the average shoplifting loss.[39] Police in Polk County, Florida, recently arrested 18 people who were part of a professional shoplifting ring that stole cosmetics, baby formula, over-the-counter drugs, and other items worth between $60 million and $100 million over a 5-year period. The thieves used specially made bags and purses with hidden compartments to conceal the stolen goods. "The thieves worked in pairs and in less than 3 minutes could walk out with as much as $4,000 in merchandise," says Sheriff Grady Judd. "They were so good that you could watch them steal and not be aware of what they were doing." The operation was so sophisticated that the thieves created schedules of the stores they would hit to avoid stealing from any one store too often and raising suspicion.[40]

Because professional shoplifters' business is theft, they are very difficult to detect and deter. Professional shoplifters tend to focus on expensive merchandise they can sell quickly to their fences, such as consumer electronics, appliances, guns, or jewelry. Usually the fences don't keep the stolen goods long, often selling them on online auction sites or at flea markets at a fraction of their value. Therefore, apprehending and prosecuting professional shoplifters is quite difficult. Police have apprehended professional shoplifters with detailed maps of a city's shopping districts, showing target stores and the best times to make a "hit." Furthermore, many professional shoplifters are affiliated with organized crime, and they are able to rely on their associates to avoid detection and prosecution. Table 4 provides some interesting facts about shoplifting.

DETECTING SHOPLIFTERS. Although shoplifters can be difficult to detect, business owners who know what to look for can spot them in action. Entrepreneurs must always be on the lookout for shoplifters, but they should be especially vigilant on Saturdays and around Christmas, when shoplifters can hide their thefts more easily in the frenzy of a busy shopping day.

Shoplifters can work alone or in groups. In general, impulse shoplifters prefer solitary thefts, whereas juveniles and professionals operate in groups. A common tactic for group shoplifters is for one member of the gang to create some type of distraction while other members steal the merchandise. Business owners should be wary of loud, disruptive groups that enter their stores.

TABLE 4 Shoplifting Facts

- Nearly $12 billion worth of goods are stolen from retailers each year. That's more than $1.3 million worth of merchandise per hour.
- There are approximately 27 million shoplifters (or 1 in 11 people) in the United States. More than 10 million people have been caught shoplifting in the last 5 years.
- Shoplifting affects more than the offender. It overburdens the police and the courts, adds to a store's security expenses, increases the cost of goods for legitimate shoppers, reduces sales tax dollars that go to communities, and hurts children and families.
- There is no such thing as a "typical" shoplifter. Anyone can be a shoplifter. Men and women shoplift about equally as often.
- Approximately 25 percent of shoplifters are kids. Fifty-five percent of adult shoplifters say they started shoplifting in their teens.
- Many shoplifters buy and steal merchandise in the same visit. Shoplifters commonly steal from $2 to $200 per incident, depending on the type of store and item(s) chosen.
- Shoplifting is often an impulse crime: 73 percent of adult and 72 percent of juvenile shoplifters don't plan to steal in advance.
- Eighty-six percent of kids say they know other kids who shoplift, and 66 percent say they hang out with those kids.
- Approximately 3 percent of shoplifters are "professionals" who steal solely for resale or profit as a business. These include drug addicts who steal to feed their habit, hardened professionals who steal as a lifestyle, and international shoplifting gangs who steal for profit as a business.
- Eighty-eight percent of retailers say that shoplifting losses from professional shoplifters has increased over the last 3 years.
- The majority of shoplifters are nonprofessionals who steal, not out of financial need or greed, but as a response to social and personal pressures in their lives.
- The excitement generated from "getting away with it" produces a chemical reaction that results in what shoplifters describe as an incredible "rush" or "high" feeling. Many shoplifters say that this high is their true reward rather than the merchandise itself.
- Drug addicts who have become addicted to shoplifting describe shoplifting as equally addicting as drugs.
- Even after getting caught, 57 percent of adults and 33 percent of juveniles say it is hard for them to stop shoplifting.
- Most nonprofessional shoplifters don't commit other types of crimes. They'll never steal an ashtray from your house and will return to you a $20 bill that you drop. Their criminal activity is restricted to shoplifting and, therefore, any rehabilitation program should be "offense specific" for this crime.
- The typical shoplifter steals an average of 1.6 times per week.

Sources: Information and statistics provided by the National Association for Shoplifting Prevention (NASP), *www.shopliftingprevention.org*; *2009 Organized Retail Crime Survey*, National Retail Federation, Washington, D.C., 2010, p. 5; Richard C. Hollinger and Amanda Adams, *2009 National Retail Security Survey*, University of Florida, pp. 9–10.

Solitary shoplifters are usually quite nervous. They avoid crowds and shy away from store personnel, preferring privacy to ply their trade. To make sure they avoid detection, they constantly scan the store for customers and employees. These shoplifters spend more time nervously looking around the store than examining merchandise. Also, they shop when the store is most likely to be understaffed, during early morning, lunch, or late evening hours. Shoplifters frequently linger in the same area for an extended time without purchasing anything. Customers who refuse the help of sales personnel or bring in large bags and packages (especially empty ones) also arouse suspicion.

Shoplifters have their own arsenal of tools to assist them in plying their trade. They often shop with booster boxes, shopping bags, umbrellas, bulky jackets, baby strollers, or containers disguised as gifts. These props often have hidden compartments that can be tripped easily, allowing the shoplifter to fill them with merchandise quickly.

Some shoplifters use specially designed coats with hidden pockets and compartments that can hold even large items. Small business owners should be suspicious of customers wearing out-of-season clothing (e.g., heavy coats in warm weather or rain gear on clear days) that could conceal stolen goods. Hooked belts also are used to enable the shoplifter to suspend items from hangers without being detected.

Another common tactic is "ticket switching," in which the shoplifter exchanges price tickets on items and pays a very low price for an expensive item. An inexperienced or unobservant cashier may charge $9.95 for a $30.00 item that the shoplifter remarked when no one was looking. A more elaborate scheme is one in which shoplifters create counterfeit bar codes that they paste over existing bar codes on packages so that when the item is scanned, it rings up at a much lower price. After 3 years, police finally nabbed a shoplifter who used this technique to steal more than $600,000 worth of toy LEGOs from dozens of stores in five western states. His phony bar codes caused $100 LEGO sets to ring up for just $19 at checkout counters. He then resold the LEGO sets at a markup on a Web site for toy collectors.[41]

One variation of traditional shoplifting techniques is the "grab-and-run" in which a shoplifter grabs an armload of merchandise located near an exit and then dashes out the door into a waiting getaway car. The element of surprise gives these thieves an advantage, and they are often gone before anyone in the store realizes what has happened.

DETERRING SHOPLIFTERS. The problem of shoplifting is worsening. Every year, business losses due to customer theft increase, and many companies are declaring war on shoplifting. Funds allocated for fighting shoplifting losses are best spent on *prevention*. By focusing on preventing shoplifting rather than on prosecuting violators after the fact, business owners take a strong stand in protecting their firms' merchandise. Of course, no prevention plan is perfect. When violations occur, owners must prosecute; otherwise the business becomes known as an easy target. Retailers say that when a store gets a reputation for being tough on shoplifters, thefts drop off.

Knowing what to look for dramatically improves a business owner's odds in combating shoplifting:

- *Watch the eyes.* Amateurs spend excessive time looking at the merchandise they're about to steal. Their eyes, however, are usually checking to see who (if anyone) is watching them.
- *Watch the hands.* Experienced shoplifters, like good magicians, rely on sleight of hand.
- *Watch the body.* Amateurs' body movements reflect their nervousness; they appear to be unnatural.
- *Watch the clothing.* Loose, bulky clothing is the uniform of the typical shoplifter.
- *Watch for devices.* Anything a customer carries is a potential concealing device.
- *Watch for loiterers.* Many amateurs must work up the nerve to steal.
- *Watch for switches.* Working in pairs, shoplifters will split duties; one will lift the merchandise, and, after a switch, the other will take it out of the store.

Store owners can take other steps to discourage shoplifting.

Train Employees to Spot Shoplifters. One of the best ways to prevent shoplifting is to train store personnel to be aware of shoplifters' habits and to be alert for possible theft. In fact, most security experts agree that alert employees are the best defense against shoplifters. Employees should look for nervous, unusual customers and monitor them closely. Shoplifters prefer to avoid sales personnel and other customers, and when employees approach them, shoplifters know they are being watched. Even when all salespeople are busy, an alert employee should approach the customer and say, "I'll be with you in a moment." Honest customers appreciate the clerk's politeness, and shoplifters are put off by the implied surveillance.

All employees should watch for suspicious people, especially those carrying the props of concealment. Employees in clothing stores must keep a tally of the items being taken into and out of dressing rooms. Some clothing retailers prevent unauthorized use of dressing rooms by locking them; customers who want to try on garments must check with a store employee first.

An alert cashier can be a tremendous boon to the store owner attempting to minimize shoplifting losses. A cashier who knows the store's general pricing policy and is familiar with the prices of many specific items is the best insurance against the ticket-switching shoplifter. A good cashier also should inspect all containers being sold; tool boxes, purses, briefcases, and other items can conceal stolen merchandise.

Employees should be trained to watch for group shoplifting tactics. A group of shoppers that enters the store and then disperses in all directions may be attempting to distract employees so that some gang members can steal merchandise. Sales personnel should watch closely the customer who lingers in one area for an extended time, especially one who examines a lot of merchandise but never purchases anything.

The sales staff should watch for customers who consistently shop during the hours when most employees are on breaks. Managers can help eliminate this cause of shoplifting by ensuring that their stores are well staffed at all times. Coordinating work schedules to ensure adequate coverage is a simple but effective method of discouraging shoplifting.

The cost of training employees to be alert to shoplifting "gimmicks" can be recouped many times over by preventing losses from retail theft. The local police department or chamber of commerce may be able to conduct training seminars for local small business owners and their employees, or security consulting firms might sponsor a training course on shoplifting techniques and protective methods. Refresher courses every few months can help keep employees sharp in spotting shoplifters.

Pay Attention to the Store Layout. A well-planned store layout also can be an effective obstacle in preventing shoplifting losses. Proper lighting throughout the store makes it easier for employees to monitor shoppers, whereas dimly lit areas give dishonest customers a prime opportunity to steal without detection. In addition, display cases should be kept low, no more than 3 or 4 feet high, so store personnel can have a clear view of the entire store. Display counters should have spaces between them; continuous displays create a barrier between customers and employees.

Business owners should keep small expensive items such as jewelry, silver, and accessories behind display counters or in locked cases with a sales clerk nearby. Valuable or breakable items also should be kept out of customer reach and should not be displayed near exits, where shoplifters can pick them up and quickly step outside. All merchandise displays should be neat and organized so that it will be noticeable if an item is missing.

Cash registers should be located so that cashiers have an unobstructed view of the entire store. Other protective measures include prominently posting signs describing the penalties involved for shoplifting and keeping unattended doors locked (within fire regulations). Exits that cannot be locked because of fire regulations should be equipped with noise alarms to detect any attempts at unauthorized exit.

Install Mechanical Devices. Another option business owners have in the attempt to reduce shoplifting losses is to install mechanical devices. A complete deterrence system can be expensive, but failure to implement one is usually more expensive. Tools such as two-way mirrors allow employees at one end of the store to monitor a customer at the other end, and one-way viewing windows enable employees to watch the entire store without being seen.

Other mechanical devices, such as closed-circuit TV cameras, convex wall mirrors, and peepholes, also help the owner protect the store from shoplifters. Not every small business can afford to install a closed-circuit camera system, but one clever entrepreneur got the benefit of such a system without the high cost. He installed one "live" camera and several "dummy" cameras that did not work. The cameras worked because potential shoplifters thought they were all live. Another high-tech weapon used against shoplifters is a mannequin named Anne Droid, which is equipped with a tiny camera behind one eye and a microphone in her nose!

An owner can deter ticket-switching shoplifters by using tamper-proof price tickets: perforated, gummed labels that tear away if a customer tries to remove them or price tags attached to merchandise by hard-to-break plastic strips. Some owners use multiple price tags concealed on items to deter ticket switchers. One of the most effective weapons for combating shoplifting is the electronic article surveillance (EAS) system, small tags that are equipped with electronic sensors that set off sound and light alarms if customers take them past a store exit. These tags are attached to the merchandise and can be removed only by employees with special shears. Owners using these electronic tags must make sure that all cashiers are consistent in removing them from items purchased legitimately; otherwise, they may be liable for false arrest or, at the very least, may cause customers embarrassment.

APPREHENDING SHOPLIFTERS. Despite all of the weapons business owners use to curtail shoplifting, the sad reality is that most of the time shoplifters are successful at plying their trade. Shoplifters say they are caught an average of only once in every 48 times they steal and that they are turned over to the police just 50 percent of the time. Of those shoplifters who do get caught, less than half are prosecuted. The chance that any shoplifter will actually go before a judge is about 1 in 100.[42] Building a strong case against a shoplifter is essential; therefore, small business owners must determine beforehand the procedures to follow once they detect a shoplifter. The store owner has to be certain that the shoplifter has taken or concealed the merchandise and has left the store with it. Although state laws vary, owners must do the following to make the charges stick:

1. *See* the person take or conceal the merchandise.
2. *Identify* the merchandise as belonging to the store.
3. *Testify* that it was taken with the intent to steal.
4. *Prove* that the merchandise was not paid for.

Most security experts agree that owners should never apprehend the shoplifter if they have lost sight of the suspect even for an instant. In that time, the person may have dumped the merchandise.

Another primary consideration in apprehending shoplifters is the safety of store employees. In general, employees should never directly accuse a customer of shoplifting and should never try to apprehend the suspect. The wisest course of action when a shoplifter is detected is to alert the police or store security personnel and let them apprehend the suspect. Apprehension *outside* the store is safest. This tactic strengthens the owner's case and eliminates unpleasant in-store scenes that upset other customers or that might be dangerous. Of course, if the stolen merchandise is very valuable, or if the criminal is likely to escape once outside, the owner may have no choice but to apprehend the shoplifter in the store.

Once business owners detect and apprehend a shoplifter, they must decide whether to prosecute. Many small business owners fail to prosecute because they fear legal entanglements or negative publicity. However, failure to prosecute encourages shoplifters to try again and gives the business the image of being an easy target. Of course, each case is an individual matter. For example, the owner may choose not to prosecute elderly or senile shoplifters or those who are mentally incompetent. But in most cases, prosecuting the shoplifter is the best option, especially for juveniles and first-time offenders. The business owner who prosecutes shoplifters consistently soon develops a reputation for toughness that most shoplifters hesitate to test. It is in the interest of every business owner to have that reputation.

Conclusion

Inventory control is one of those less-than-glamorous activities that business owners must perform if their businesses are to succeed. Although it doesn't offer the flash of marketing or the visibility of customer service, inventory control is no less important. In fact, business owners who invest the time and the resources to exercise the proper degree of control over their inventory soon discover that the payoff is huge!

Chapter Review

1. Explain the various inventory control systems and the advantages and disadvantages of each.
   - Inventory represents the largest investment for the typical small business. Unless properly managed, the cost of inventory will strain the firm's budget and cut into its profitability. The goal of inventory control is to balance the cost of holding and maintaining inventory with meeting customer demand.
   - Regardless of the inventory control system selected, business owners must recognize the relevance of the 80/20 Rule, which states that roughly 80 percent of the value of the firm's inventory is in about 20 percent of the items in stock. Because only a small percentage of items account for the majority of the value of the firm's inventory, managers should focus control on those items.
   - Three basic types of inventory control systems are available to the small business owner: perpetual, visual, and partial. Perpetual inventory control systems are designed to maintain a running count of the items in inventory. Although they can be expensive and cumbersome to operate by hand, affordable computerized point-of-sale (POS) terminals that deduct items sold from inventory on hand make perpetual systems feasible for small companies. The visual inventory system is the most common method of controlling merchandise in a small business. This system works best when shortages are not likely to cause major problems. Partial inventory control systems are most effective for small businesses with limited time and money. These systems operate on the basis of the 80/20 Rule.
   - The ABC system is a partial system that divides a firm's inventory into three categories depending on each item's dollar usage volume (cost per unit multiplied by quantity used per time period). The purpose of classifying items according to their value is to establish the proper degree of control over them. A items are most closely controlled by perpetual inventory control systems; B items use basic analytical tools; and C items are controlled by very simple techniques such as the two-bin system, the level control method, or the tag system.

2. Describe how just-in-time (JIT) and JIT II inventory control techniques work.
   - The just-in-time system of inventory control sees excess inventory as a blanket that masks production problems and adds unnecessary costs to the production operation. Under a JIT philosophy, the level of inventory maintained is the measure of efficiency. Materials and parts should not build up as costly inventory. They should flow through the production process without stopping, arriving at the appropriate location just in time.
   - JIT II techniques focus on creating a close, harmonious relationship with a company's suppliers so that both parties benefit from increased efficiency. To work successfully, JIT II requires suppliers and their customers to share what was once closely guarded information in an environment of trust and cooperation. Under JIT II, customers and suppliers work hand in hand, acting more like partners than mere buyers and sellers.

3. Describe methods for reducing losses from slow-moving inventory.
   - Managing inventory requires monitoring the company's inventory turnover ratio; slow-moving items result in losses from spoilage or obsolescence.
   - Slow-moving items can be liquidated by markdowns, eye-catching displays, or quantity discounts.

4. Discuss employee theft and shoplifting and how to prevent them.
   - Employee theft accounts for the majority of business losses due to theft. Most small business owners are so busy managing their companies' daily affairs that they fail to develop reliable security systems. Thus, they provide their employees with prime opportunities to steal.
   - The organizational atmosphere may encourage employee theft. The owner sets the organizational tone for security. A complete set of security controls, procedures, and penalties should be developed and enforced. Physical breakdowns in security invite employee theft. Open doors and windows, poor key control, and improper cash

controls are major contributors to the problem of employee theft. Employers can build security into their businesses by screening and selecting employees carefully. Orientation programs also help the employee to get started in the right direction. Internal controls, such as division of responsibility, spot checks, and audit procedures, are useful in preventing employee theft.

- Shoplifting is the most common business crime. Fortunately, most shoplifters are amateurs. Juveniles often steal to impress their friends, but prosecution can halt their criminal ways early on. Impulse shoplifters steal because the opportunity suddenly arises. Simple prevention is the best defense against these shoplifters. Alcoholics, vagrants, and drug addicts steal to supply some need and are usually easiest to detect. Kleptomaniacs have a compelling need to steal. Professionals are in the business of theft and can be very difficult to detect and quite dangerous.

- Three strategies are most useful in deterring shoplifters. First, employees should be trained to look for signs of shoplifting. Second, store layout should be designed with theft deterrence in mind. Finally, antitheft devices should be installed in the store.

Discussion Questions

1. Describe some of the incidental costs of carrying and maintaining inventory for the small business owner.
2. What is a perpetual inventory system? How does it operate? What are the advantages and disadvantages of using such a system?
3. What advantages and disadvantages does a visual inventory control system have over other methods?
4. For what type of business product line is a visual control system most effective?
5. What is the 80/20 Rule, and why is it important in controlling inventory?
6. Outline the ABC inventory control procedure. What is the purpose of classifying inventory items using this procedure?
7. Briefly describe the types of control techniques that should be used for A, B, and C items.
8. What is the basis for the JIT philosophy? Under what condition does a JIT system work best?
9. What is JIT II? What is its underlying philosophy? What risks does it present to businesses?
10. Outline the two methods of taking a physical inventory count. Why is it necessary for every small business manager to take inventory?
11. Why are slow-moving items dangerous to the small business? What can be done to liquidate them from inventory?
12. Why are small companies more susceptible to business crime than large companies?
13. Why is employee theft a problem for many small businesses? Briefly describe the reasons for employee theft.
14. Construct a profile of the employee most likely to steal goods or money from an employer. What four elements must be present for employee theft to occur?
15. Briefly outline a program that could help the typical small business owner minimize losses due to employee theft.
16. List and briefly describe the major types of shoplifters.
17. Outline the characteristics of a typical shoplifter that should arouse a small business manager's suspicions. What tools and tactics is a shoplifter likely to use?
18. Describe the major elements of a program designed to deter shoplifters.
19. How can proper planning of store layout reduce shoplifting losses?
20. What must an owner do to have a good case against a shoplifter? How should a suspected shoplifter be apprehended?

For many product-oriented businesses, inventory control represents a major investment. Unfortunately, many entrepreneurs fail to manage their inventory investments carefully, and this can lead to serious financial, managerial, and customer service problems. Fortunately, small companies can now afford to purchase inventory control systems that once were available only to large organizations.

Technological solutions supported by a sound inventory control system enable even the smallest companies to reap the benefits of maintaining proper inventory control systems.

On the Web

The Companion Web site at *www.pearsonhighered.com/ scarborough* offers a series of links that provide additional information regarding inventory control resources. Review these sites, specifically those that relate to your industry, and determine whether these sources may be useful to you as you build your plan.

In the Software

Review the "Products" section of your plan to make certain that you have included the inventory management issues discussed in this chapter. Does it describe how you plan to manage your inventory? What type of inventory control system will you use in your business? Is it perpetual, visual, or partial? Have you incorporated a description of that system into the plan?

Building Your Business Plan

Your business plan should describe your company's inventory control strategy. If inventory represents a significant investment for your business, you should invest the time required to develop this section of your plan and make sure that your financial forecasts capture this information as well. If you plan to purchase an inventory control system, be sure to include this as one of your expenses.

Endnotes

1. Sahir Anand and Chris Cunane, *Inventory Optimization: Retail Strategies for Eliminating Stockouts and Overstocks*, Aberdeen Group, May 2009, p. 4.
2. Nari Viswanathan, *Inventory Management: 3 Keys to Freeing Working Capital*, Aberdeen Group, May 2009, p. 4.
3. James A. Cooke, "Glimmers of Hope," State of Logistics Report, *Supply Chain Quarterly*, September 21, 2010, *www.supplychainquarterly.com/topics/State%20of%20Logistics%20Report/scq201005sol/*.
4. Joann S. Lublin, "Polaris, Maker of Sport Vehicles, Races to Catch Up with Business," *Wall Street Journal*, May 24, 2010, pp. B1–B2.
5. Ibid.
6. Simona Covel, "Looking for Cost Cuts in Lots of New Places," *Wall Street Journal*, October 16, 2008, p. B5.
7. "With Billions of Bytes of Customer Data, How Can Retailers Be 'Starved for Information?'" *Knowledge@Wharton*, August 2000, *http://pf.inc.com/articles/2000/08/20043.html*.
8. Pallavi Gogoi, "Retailers Pull Back, at a Cost," *Bloomberg Business Week*, August 7, 2008, *www.businessweek.com/bwdaily/dnflash/content/aug2008/db2008087_200562.htm?chan=top+news_top+news+index_news+++analysis*.
9. John Payne, "Pareto's Law—Your Formula for Success," *Ezine Articles*, January 25, 2005, *http://ezinearticles.com/?Paretos-Law—Your-Formula-For-Success&id=11091*.
10. Phaedra Hise, "Early Adoption Pays Off," *Inc.*, August 1996, p. 101.
11. Claire Swedburg, "Serge Blanco Store Takes Stock of RFID," *RFID Journal*, April 27, 2010, *www.rfidjournal.com/article/view/7561*.
12. Mark Henricks, "Tell and Show," *Entrepreneur*, April 2004, pp. 77–78.
13. Alex Niemeyer, Minsok H. Pak, and Sanjay Ramaswamy, "Smart Tags for Your Supply Chain," *McKinsey Quarterly*, No. 4, 2003, *www.mckinseyquarterly.com/article_page.aspx?ar=1347&L2=1&L3=26*.
14. Elizabeth Esfahani, "High Class, Low Price," *Business 2.0*, November 2006, pp. 74–76; Adam Smith, "How Topshop Changed Fashion," *Time*, May 24, 2007, *www.time.com/time/globalbusiness/article/0,9171,1625185,00.html*; "About Topshop," Topshop.com, *www.topshop.com/webapp/wcs/stores/servlet/StaticPageDisplay?storeId=12556&catalogId=19551&identifier=ts1%20about%20topshop*.
15. Amy Chozick, "A Key Strategy of Japan's Car Makers Backfires," *Wall Street Journal*, July 20, 2007, pp. B1, B5.
16. Mark Henricks, "On the Spot," *Entrepreneur*, May 1997, *www.entrepreneur.com/article/14178*.
17. Matthew Dolan, "Industry's Big Hope for Small Cars Fades," *Wall Street Journal*, March 23, 2009, p. B1; "Biggest by Default: Toyota May Be Number One, but It Still Faces Challenges," *Knowledge@Wharton*, February 4, 2009, *www.wharton.universia.net/index.cfm?fa=viewArticle&id=1666&language=english*; Neal E. Boudette, "Big Dealer to Detroit: Fix How You Make Cars," *Wall Street Journal*, February 9, 2007, pp. A1, A8; Sholnn Freeman, "Smaller Cars Enjoy New Chic," *Washington Post*, September 28, 2005, *www.washingtonpost.com/wp-dyn/content/article/2005/09/27/AR2005092701812.html*.
18. Dana Mattioli, "Little Shops Make Big Plays for the Holidays," *Wall Street Journal*, October 27, 2009, p. B5.
19. *2010 ACFE Report to the Nation on Occupational Fraud and Abuse*, Association of Certified Fraud Examiners, Austin, Texas, 2010, p. 4; Kathy Grannis, "Retail Fraud, Shoplifting Rates Decrease, According to National Retail Security Survey," National Retail Federation, June 15, 2010, *www.nrf.com/modules.php?name=News&op=viewlive&sp_id=945*.
20. *2010 ACFE Report to the Nation on Occupational Fraud and Abuse*, pp. 4–5, 29.
21. Grannis, "Retail Fraud, Shoplifting Rates Decrease, According to National Retail Security Survey."
22. "Theft Surveys," Jack L. Hayes International, Wesley Chapel, Florida, 2010, *www.hayesinternational.com/thft_srvys.html*.
23. Serri Pfeil, "Is There a Thief Among Us?" *Employment Review*, December 2000, pp. 37–38.
24. *2010 ACFE Report to the Nation on Occupational Fraud and Abuse*, pp. 14, 16.
25. *2010 ACFE Report to the Nation on Occupational Fraud and Abuse*, p. 39.
26. John P. McDermott, "Woman Charged in Fraud," *Charleston Post and Courier*, July 30, 2010, p. 7B; John P. McDermott, "Woman Pleads Guilty in Fraud," *Charleston Post and Courier*, September 17, 2010, *www.postandcourier.com/news/2010/sep/17/woman-pleads-guilty-in-fraud/*.
27. Nancy Germond, "Your Company Isn't Immune to Employee Theft," *All Business*, February 2, 2008, *www.allbusiness.com/crime-law-enforcement-corrections/crime-prevention/6623333-1.html*.
28. *2010 ACFE Report to the Nation on Occupational Fraud and Abuse*, p. 5.
29. "Koss Corp. Hires Chief Financial Officer," *Business Journal of Milwaukee*, January 18, 2010, *http://milwaukee.bizjournals.com/milwaukee/stories/2010/01/18/daily2.html*; Rich Kirchen, "Former Koss Exec Sachdeva Indicted on Six Counts," *Business Journal of Milwaukee*, January 20, 2010, *http://milwaukee.bizjournals.com/milwaukee/stories/2010/01/18/daily39.html*.
30. Robert T. Gray, "Clamping Down on Worker Crime," *Nation's Business*, April 1997, p. 44.
31. Scott Wescott, "Are Your Staffers Stealing?" *Inc.*, October 2006, pp. 33–35.
32. Calmetta Coleman, "Sticky Fingers," *Wall Street Journal*, September 8, 2000, pp. A1, A6.
33. "Theft Surveys," Jack L. Hayes International.
34. "Jack L. Hayes International Inc.'s 18th Annual Retail Theft Survey," 2006, *www.hayesinternational.com/thft_srvys.html*.
35. Raymund Flandez, "Stop That Thief," *Wall Street Journal*, June 12, 2008, *http://online.wsj.com/article/NA_WSJ_PUB:SB121322091260765769.html*.
36. Amanda C. Kooser, "Make the Cut?" *Entrepreneur*, February 2006, p. 26.
37. Grannis, "Retail Fraud, Shoplifting Rates Decrease, According to National Retail Security Survey."
38. *2009 Organized Retail Crime Survey*, National Retail Federation, Washington, D.C., 2010, p. 4.

39. Richard Hollinger and Lynn Langton, *2005 National Retail Security Survey Final Report*, University of Florida and the National Retail Federation, *www.crim.ufl.edu/research/srp/finalreport_2005.pdf*, pp. 27, 29.

40. *2009 Organized Retail Crime Survey*, National Retail Federation, pp. 3–4; "Operation 'Beauty Stop' Nabs 18 in $100 Million Theft Ring," WFTV, January 25, 2008, *www.wftv.com/news/15130764/detail.html*.

41. Ann Zimmerman, "As Shoplifters Use High-Tech Scams, Retail Losses Rise," *Wall Street Journal*, October 25, 2006, pp. A1, A12.

42. "Shoplifting Statistics," National Association for Shoplifting Prevention.

Staffing and Leading a Growing Company

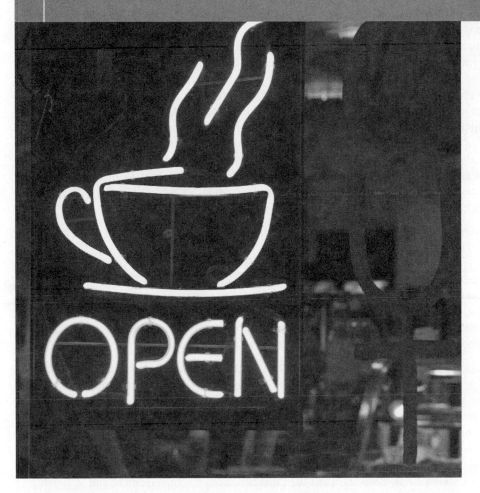

Learning Objectives

Upon completion of this chapter, you will be able to:

1 Explain the challenges involved in the entrepreneur's role as leader and what it takes to become a successful leader.

2 Describe the importance of hiring the right employees and how to avoid making hiring mistakes.

3 Explain how to build the kind of company culture and structure to support the company's mission and goals and to motivate employees to achieve them.

4 Understand the potential barriers to effective communication and describe how to overcome them.

5 Discuss the ways in which entrepreneurs can motivate their employees to achieve higher levels of performance.

The speed of the leader determines the rate of the pack.

—Anonymous

It doesn't make any difference whether the product is cars or cosmetics. A company is only as good as the people it keeps.

—Mary Kay Ash

From Chapter 19 of *Effective Small Business Management: An Entrepreneurial Approach*, 10/e. Norman M. Scarborough.

The Entrepreneur's Role as Leader

1. Explain the challenges involved in the entrepreneur's role as leader and what it takes to be a successful leader.

To be successful, an entrepreneur must assume a wide range of roles, tasks, and responsibilities, but none is more important than the role of leader. Some entrepreneurs are uncomfortable assuming this role, but they must learn to be effective leaders if their companies are to grow and reach their potential. **Leadership** is the process of influencing and inspiring others to work to achieve a common goal and then giving them the power and the freedom to achieve it. Without leadership ability, entrepreneurs—and their companies—never rise above mediocrity. Entrepreneurs can learn to be effective leaders, but the task requires dedication, discipline, and hard work. In the past, business owners often relied on an autocratic management style, one built on command and control. Today's workforce is more knowledgeable, has more options, is more skilled, and, as a result, expects a different, more sophisticated style of leadership. Companies that fail to provide that leadership are at risk of losing their best employees. Leaders of small companies must gather information and make decisions with lightning-fast speed, and they must give workers the resources and the freedom to solve problems and exploit opportunities as they arise. Effective leaders empower employees to act in the best interest of the business.

Until recently, experts compared a leader's job to that of a symphony orchestra conductor. Like the symphony leader, an entrepreneur made sure that everyone in the company was playing the same score, coordinated individual efforts to produce a harmonious sound, and directed the orchestra members as they played. The conductor (entrepreneur) retained virtually all of the power and made all of the decisions about how the orchestra would play the music, without any input from the musicians themselves. Today's successful entrepreneur, however, is more like the leader of a jazz band, which is known for its improvisation, innovation, creativity, and free-wheeling style. "The success of a small [jazz band] rests on the ability to be agile and flexible, skills that are equally central to today's business world," says Michael Gold, founder of Jazz Impact, a company that teaches management skills through jazz.[1] Business leaders, like the leaders of jazz bands, should exhibit the following characteristics:

- *Innovative.* Leaders must step out of their own comfort zones to embrace new ideas; they avoid the comfort of complacency.
- *Passionate.* One of entrepreneurs' greatest strengths is their passion for their businesses. Members of their team feed off of that passion and draw inspiration from it.
- *Willing to take risks.* "[Taking] risk is not an option in jazz or for any company that wants to be solvent 10 years from now," says Gold.[2]
- *Adaptable.* Although leaders must stand on a bedrock of resolute values, like jazz band leaders, they must adapt their leadership styles to fit the situation and the people involved.

Management and leadership are not the same; yet, both are essential to a company's success. Leadership without management is unbridled; management without leadership is uninspired. Leadership gets a small business going; management keeps it going. In other words, leaders are the architects of small businesses; managers are the builders.

Some entrepreneurs are good managers yet are poor leaders; others are powerful leaders but are weak managers. The best bet for the latter is to hire people with solid management skills to help them to execute the vision they have for their companies. Stephen Covey, author of *Principle-Centered Leadership*, explains the difference between management and leadership in this way:

Leadership deals with people; management deals with things. You manage things; you lead people. Leadership deals with vision; management deals with logistics toward that vision. Leadership deals with doing the right things; management focuses on doing things right. Leadership deals with examining the paradigms on which you are operating; management operates within those paradigms. Leadership comes first, then management, but both are necessary.[3]

Leadership and management are intertwined; one without the other means that a small business is going nowhere. Leadership is especially important for companies in the growth phase, when entrepreneurs are hiring employees (often for the first time) and must keep the company and everyone in it focused on its mission as growth tests every seam in the fabric of the organizational structure. At this stage, selling everyone in the company on the mission, goals, and objectives for which the leader is aiming is crucial to a business's survival and success. "People don't want to be managed," says one CEO. "They want to be led."[4] Effective leaders exhibit certain behaviors. They:

- *Create a set of values and beliefs for employees and passionately pursue them.* Employees look to their leaders for guidance when making decisions. True leaders focus attention on the principles, values, and beliefs on which they founded their companies.
- *Establish a culture of ethics.* One of the most important tasks facing leaders is to mold a highly ethical culture for their companies. They also must demonstrate the character and the courage necessary to stick to the ethical standards that they create—especially in the face of difficulty.
- *Define and then constantly reinforce the vision they have for the company.* Effective leaders have a clear vision of where they want their companies to go, and they concentrate on communicating that vision to those around them. Unfortunately, this is one area in which employees say their leaders could do a better job. Clarity of purpose is essential to a successful organization because people want to be a part of something that is bigger than they are; however, the purpose must be more than merely achieving continuous quarterly profits.
- *Respect and support employees.* To gain the respect of their employees, leaders must first respect those who work for them.
- *Set the example for employees.* Leaders' words ring hollow if they fail to "practice what they preach." Few signals are transmitted to workers faster than the hypocrisy of leaders who sell employees on one set of values and principles and then act according to a different set.
- *Create a climate of trust in the organization.* Leaders who demonstrate integrity soon win the trust of their employees, an essential ingredient in the success of any organization. Honest, open communication and a consistent pattern of leaders doing what they say they will do serve to build trust in a business. Research suggests that building trust among employees is one of the most important tasks of leaders, wherever they may work. Building trust demands that leaders rely on three "Cs": competence (the leader is able to get the job done), consistency (the leader's actions are reliable, whatever the situation), and caring (the leader demonstrates compassion for those he or she leads).[5] Employees at small businesses are more likely to trust their leaders than employees at large companies.[6]
- *Build credibility with their employees.* To be effective, leaders must have credibility with their employees, a sometimes challenging task for entrepreneurs, especially as their companies grow and they become insulated from the daily activities of their businesses. To combat the problem of losing touch with the problems their employees face as they do their jobs, many managers periodically return to the front line to serve customers. For instance, at Southwest Airlines top managers spend 1 day each quarter loading baggage onto planes, checking passengers onto flights, serving as flight attendants, and performing other frontline jobs.[7] The idea is that top managers will make better decisions about policies and procedures if they see firsthand the impact of those decisions on customers and frontline employees.
- *Focus employees' efforts on challenging goals and keep them driving toward those goals.* Effective leaders have a clear vision of where they want their companies to go, and they are able to communicate their vision to those around them. Leaders must repeatedly reinforce the goals they set for their companies.
- *Provide the resources employees need to achieve their goals.* Effective leaders know that workers cannot do their jobs well unless they have the tools they need. They provide workers with not only the physical resources they need to excel, but also the necessary intangible resources, such as training, coaching, and mentoring.
- *Communicate with employees.* Leaders recognize that helping workers to see the company's overarching goal is just one part of effective communication; encouraging employee feedback and then listening is just as vital. In other words, they know that communication is a two-way street.
- *Value the diversity of workers.* Smart business leaders recognize the value of their workers' varied skills, abilities, backgrounds, and interests. When channeled in the right direction, diversity can be a powerful weapon in achieving innovation and maintaining a competitive edge.

- *Celebrate workers' successes.* Effective leaders recognize that workers want to be winners and do everything they can to encourage top performance among their people. The rewards they give are not always financial; in many cases, a reward may be as simple as a handwritten congratulatory note.
- *Value risk-taking.* Effective leaders recognize that in a rapidly changing competitive environment, they must make decisions with incomplete information and be willing to take risks to succeed.
- *Understand that leadership is multidimensional.* Smart leaders know that there is no single "best" style of leadership. The dimensions of leadership change depending on the people participating, the conditions and circumstances of the situation, and the desired outcome.
- *Value new ideas from employees.* Successful leaders know that because employees work every day on the front lines of the business, they see ways to improve quality, customer service, and business systems.
- *Understand that success really is a team effort.* Small companies typically depend more on their founding entrepreneurs than on anyone else. After all, someone has to take responsibility for the toughest decisions. However, effective leaders understand that their roles are only a small piece of the entire company puzzle.

ENTREPRENEURIAL
Profile

*Larry McDonnell:
Waste Management*

Undercover Boss, a television series on CBS, features CEOs of companies ranging from Waste Management and Choice Hotels to White Castle and Hooters. The CEOs are disguised as new employees as they take on jobs on the front lines of their companies, where the "real work" is performed. In one episode, Larry McDonnell, CEO of Waste Management, cleans toilets and rides a garbage truck route. Along the way, he encounters hard-working people who do everything they can to help "the new guy" succeed and learns about the struggles workers face every day. In addition to seeing firsthand just how difficult many jobs can be, all of the CEOs had a superb refresher course in how important every worker's role is in the success of a company and how the policies that they and other senior managers create often make workers' jobs harder.

- *Encourage creativity among workers.* Rather than punish workers who take risks and fail, effective leaders are willing to accept failure as a natural part of innovation and creativity. They know that innovative behavior is the key to future success. They do everything they can to encourage creativity among workers.
- *Create an environment in which people have the motivation, the training, and the freedom to achieve the goals they have set.* Leaders know that *their* success depends on the success of their followers.
- *Become a catalyst for change.* With market and competitive climates changing so rapidly, entrepreneurs must reinvent their companies constantly. Although leaders must cling to the values and principles that form the bedrock of their companies, they must be willing to change, sometimes radically, the policies, procedures, and processes within their businesses. If a company is headed in the wrong direction, the leader's job is to recognize that and to get the company moving in the right direction. "No leader knows enough about the future to make the optimal decision every time, but it's better to set a clear course today and tackle problems that arise tomorrow," says Andy Grove, former CEO of Intel, the computer chip maker.[8]
- *Develop leadership talent.* Effective leaders look beyond themselves to spot tomorrow's leaders and take the time to help them grow into their leadership potential.
- *Maintain a sense of humor.* One of the most important tools a leader can have is a sense of humor. Without it, work can become dull and unexciting for everyone.
- *Behave with integrity at all times.* Real leaders know that they set the ethical tone in the organization. Even small lapses in a leader's ethical standards can have a significant impact on a company's ethical climate. Workers know they can trust leaders whose actions support their words. Similarly, they quickly learn not to trust leaders whose day-to-day dealings belie the principles they preach.
- *Keep an eye on the horizon.* Effective leaders are never satisfied with what they and their employees accomplished yesterday. They know that yesterday's successes are not enough to sustain their companies indefinitely. They see the importance of building and maintaining sufficient momentum to carry their companies to the next level.

Leading an organization, whatever its size, is one of the biggest challenges any entrepreneur faces. Yet, for an entrepreneur, leadership success is one of the key determinants of a company's success. Research suggests that there is no single "best" style of leadership; the style a leader uses depends, in part, on the situation at hand. Some situations are best suited for a participative leadership style, but in others an authoritarian style actually may be best. Research by Daniel Goleman and others suggests that today's workers tend to respond more to adaptive, humble leaders who are results-oriented and who take the time to cultivate other leaders in the organization.[9] The practice is known as **servant leadership**, a phrase coined by Robert Greenleaf in 1970. Servant leaders are servants *first* and leaders *second*, putting their employees and their employees' needs ahead of their own. They are more concerned about empowering others in the organization than they are at enhancing their own power bases. "Servant leadership is about getting people to a higher level by leading people at a higher level," says author Ken Blanchard.[10]

Entrepreneurs cannot bestow the mantle of "leader" on themselves. Managers may inherit their subordinates, but leaders have to *earn* their followers. An entrepreneur's employees determine whether he or she is worthy of leadership. *Without followers, there are no leaders.* Astute leaders know that their success depends on their employees' success. After all, the employees actually do the work, implement the strategies, and produce the results. Successful leaders establish an environment in which their followers can achieve success. Joe Tortorice, Jr., founder and CEO of Jason's Deli, a privately owned company with 219 restaurants in 28 states, says "People are looking for three things out of their leaders: direction, trust, and hope."[11]

To be effective, entrepreneurial leaders must perform four vital tasks:

- Hire the right employees and constantly improve their skills.
- Build an organizational culture and structure that allows both workers and the company to reach their potential.
- Communicate the vision and the values of the company effectively and create an environment of trust among workers.
- Motivate workers to higher levels of performance.

Hiring the Right Employees: The Company's Future Depends on It

2. Describe the importance of hiring the right employees and how to avoid making hiring mistakes.

The decision to hire a new employee is an important one for every business, but it is *especially* important for small businesses because the impact of a single hire on a small company is significant. "As an entrepreneur, every single hire is critical," says Stephen Fairley, CEO of the Rainmaker Institute, a business-coaching firm.[12] Every new employee a business owner hires determines the heights to which the company can climb—or the depths to which it will plunge. "Bad hires" can poison a small company's culture for years.

Hiring mistakes also are expensive. Although some employee turnover is healthy, high employee turnover rates cost companies billions of dollars annually. Employee turnover costs a company anywhere from one-half the value of an hourly worker's annual wages and benefits to 3 to 5 times the value of a manager's salary and benefits.[13] Consider a small business with 20 employees that has an employee turnover rate of 25 percent, the national average. Assuming that the employees earn wages that are consistent with the national average (about $39,200) and receive benefits that total 25 percent of their wages, the *minimum* turnover cost to the company is $122,500. The average turnover cost the company incurs is about $490,000!

Unfortunately, hiring mistakes in business are all too common. The culprit in most cases? The company's selection and hiring process. A recent survey by SurePayroll reports that 75 percent of business owners say that they have hired at least one employee they later wish they never had.[14] One study reported in the *Harvard Business Review* concludes that 80 percent of employee turnover is caused by bad hiring decisions.[15] Some small business owners invest more time and effort into deciding which copy machine to lease than which employee to hire for a key position.

The most common causes of a company's poor hiring decisions include:

- Managers who rely on candidates' descriptions of themselves rather than requiring candidates to demonstrate their abilities.
- Managers who fail to follow a consistent, evidence-based selection process. Forty-seven percent of managers admit that they make hiring decisions in 30 minutes or less,

and 44 percent of managers say that they rely on their intuition to make hiring decisions.

- Managers who fail to provide candidates with sufficient information about what the jobs for which they are hiring actually entail.[16]

As crucial as finding good employees is to a small company's future, it is no easy task because entrepreneurs face a labor shortage, particularly among knowledge-based workers. The severity of this shortage will worsen as baby boomers retire in increasing numbers and the growth rate of the U.S. labor force slows.

How to Hire Winners

Even though the importance of hiring decisions is magnified in small companies, small businesses are most likely to make hiring mistakes because they lack the human resources experts and the disciplined hiring procedures large companies have. In many small businesses, the hiring process is informal, and the results often are unpredictable. The following guidelines can help entrepreneurs to hire winners and avoid making costly hiring mistakes as they build their team of employees.

COMMIT TO HIRING THE BEST TALENT. Smart entrepreneurs follow the old adage, "A players hire A players; B players hire C players." They are not threatened by hiring people who may be smarter and more talented than they are. In fact, they recognize that doing so is the best way to build a quality team.

ELEVATE RECRUITING TO A STRATEGIC POSITION IN THE COMPANY. Assembling a quality workforce begins with a sound recruiting effort. By investing time and money at this crucial phase of the staffing process, entrepreneurs can generate spectacular savings down the road by hiring the best talent. The recruiting process is the starting point for building quality into a company. Recruiting is so important that many entrepreneurs choose to become actively involved in the process themselves. Visionary entrepreneurs *never* stop recruiting because top quality talent is hard to find and is extremely valuable. Tom Bonney, founder of CMF Associates, a fast-growing financial consulting firm in Philadelphia, knows that finding superior talent is essential to the success of his service business. "I never stop recruiting," he says. "Even if I don't have a need, I am always looking."[17]

Attracting a pool of qualified job candidates requires not only constant attention but also creativity, especially among smaller companies that often find it difficult to match the more generous offers large companies make. With a sound recruiting strategy and a willingness to look in new places, however, smaller companies *can* hire and retain high-caliber employees. The following techniques will help.

Look inside the company first. One of the best sources for top prospects is right inside the company itself. A policy of promotion from within serves as an incentive for existing workers to upgrade their skills and to produce results. In addition, an entrepreneur already knows the employee's work habits, and the employee already understands the company's culture. At Advanced Technology Institute (ATI), a research and development management company in North Charleston, South Carolina, more than 60 percent of all jobs are filled from within the company.[18]

Encourage employee referrals. To cope with the shortage of available talent, many companies are offering their employees (and others) bonuses for referring candidates who come to work and prove to be valuable employees. Employees serve as reliable screens because they do not want to jeopardize their reputations with their employer. Employee referrals from social networks such as LinkedIn, Facebook, and Twitter allow employers to tap into their employees' network of contacts. At Dixon Schwabl, an advertising and public relations firm in Victor, New York, 90 percent of the company's new hires come from employee referrals. The system works well; employee turnover is less than 3 percent.[19]

Use multiple channels to recruit talent. Although newspaper ads still top employers' list of job postings, many businesses are successfully attracting candidates through other media, particularly the Internet. Posting job listings on career-oriented sites such as Monster.com, Hotjobs.com, and others not only expands a small company's reach far beyond an ad in a local newspaper, but also is very inexpensive. Employers also are connecting with potential employees (not all of whom are actively seeking new jobs) through their employees' networks of contacts; company blogs; career sites, such as LinkedIn; and social media sites, such as Facebook and Twitter. In fact, nearly 75 percent of companies use career and social networking sites to recruit employees, and 58 percent of managers say that they have hired an employee whom they found through these sites.[20]

ENTREPRENEURIAL
Profile

Ronn Torossian:
5W Public Relations

Ronn Torossian, founder of 5W Public Relations in New York City, has recruited several employees using Facebook and Twitter. The 75-person public relations firm has a LinkedIn profile, a company Facebook page, a blog, and a Twitter account that it uses to publicize job openings. "Social media absolutely does work to recruit new hires," he says.[21]

Recruit on campus. For many employers, college and university campuses remain an excellent source of workers, especially for entry-level positions. After screening résumés, a recruiter can interview a dozen or more high-potential students in just 1 day. Companies must be sure that the recruiters they send to campuses are professional, polished, and prepared to represent the company well because 42 percent of students say that their impression of a recruiter is the primary determinant of their perception of a company.[22]

Forge relationships with schools and other sources of workers. Some employers have found that forging long-term relationships with schools and other institutions can provide a valuable source of workers. As colleges and universities begin to offer students more internship opportunities, a small business can gain greatly by hosting one or more students for a semester or for the summer. The company has an opportunity to observe the student's work habits and, if positive, sell the student on a permanent position on his or her graduation.

ENTREPRENEURIAL
Profile

Jeff Fissel and Wes
Cruver: KZO
Innovations

Jeff Fissel launched his software company, KZO Innovations, during his senior year at George Mason University in Fairfax, Virginia, and wanted to tap into the vast pool of talent that surrounded him. Start-up capital was scarce, however, and Fissel and his cofounder Wes Cruver knew that they would have difficulty paying salaries even to part-time employees. With the help of a professor, the entrepreneurs approached the university's career services office with a proposal for internships at KZO Innovations in which students could earn college credit and gain practical work experience. "The interns are happy, and we are relieved to have a solid workforce," says Fissel. Several of the company's current 20 employees began their careers at KZO Innovations as student interns.[23]

▶ E N T R E P R E N E U R S H I P **IN ACTION** ▶

Internships: Learning Experience or Cheap Labor

David, a communications major at a large university in the Northeast, wanted to strengthen his résumé and accepted an unpaid internship at a small communications firm where he was guaranteed that he would "be fully involved in all of the work that the agency was doing." Eager to take on challenging assignments and learn new job-related skills, David reported for work. Unfortunately, he did he not receive any meaningful assignments (hello, photocopier!), and his supervisor rarely spoke to him. Regular employees left him out of staff meetings and sessions

with clients, and the office was so unorganized that he never completed any real work.

Sarah, an intern at TOMS Shoes, a cross between a for-profit and nonprofit company founded by Blake Mycoskie that donates a pair of shoes to needy people for every pair it sells, has had an extremely positive and productive internship experience. A recent entry from her blog tells the story:

As the fifth week of our internship rolls around, the office is buzzing and the work is flowing steadily. We were promised on day 1 that we would be doing work that mattered at TOMS, not just typical intern grunt work—coffee runs and long hours at the copy machine. As the internship has continued to unfold, this promise has proved to be true. With several huge TOMS initiatives in the forefront, we have officially made the leap from "new interns" to marketers, graphic designers, event planners, online marketers, retail representatives, and more. What a rush!*

Like TOMS Shoes, small companies with their limited budgets can tap into a talented, highly motivated pool of workers at little or no cost through internship programs. "[Internships] were a natural fit," says Mycoskie. "College students were really drawn to what we were doing." Student interns benefit by gaining practical job experience and building a network of contacts, and many of them earn college credit for their internships. Some colleges require students to take on internships to qualify for graduation. Yet some people criticize unpaid internships, saying that companies are merely taking advantage of eager students who are willing to work for free just to gain work experience and industry connections. "[Internships] give companies an unfair business advantage," says Michael Tracy, an employment attorney. "It's the same as companies that pay people subminimum wage or that make people work unpaid overtime."

Shawn Graham, a successful author who worked an unpaid internship at a large financial services company while in college, is a proponent of requiring companies to pay their student interns, claiming that doing so makes interships much more practical for students. Graham says that he learned a great deal from his intership experience but it imposed a financial hardship.

I had to buy suits to wear at the office (full disclosure— my mom helped finance the suits as I was a poor college student) and pay bus fare a few days a week. In the grand scheme of things, I don't think paying an intern at least minimum wage would be a huge hit to the bottom lines of most companies.

The U.S. Department of Labor has said very little about internships until April 2010, when it issued the following six guidelines based on the Fair Labor Standards Act of 1938:

1. The internship, even though it includes actual operation of the facilities of the employer, is similar to training that would be given in an educational environment.
2. The internship experience is for the benefit of the intern.
3. The intern does not displace regular employees, but works under close supervision of existing staff.
4. The employer that provides the training derives no immediate advantage from the activities of the intern, and on occasion its operations may actually be impeded.
5. The intern is not necessarily entitled to a job at the conclusion of the internship.
6. The employer and the intern understand that the intern is not entitled to wages for the time spent in the internship.

Companies that violate the rules on internships are subject to fines from the U.S. Department of Labor and state labor agencies.

When Ari Goldberg launched StyleCaster, a Web site that mixes fashion news, clothing recommendations, and social networking, he relied on a contingent of unpaid student interns from top universities to provide content and articles for the site. Michelle Halpern, a recent graduate from Syracuse University, saw an internship at StyleCaster as a way to launch a career as a journalist. She borrowed money for living expenses from her parents and moved to New York City to work more than 40 hours a week at no pay. Her hard work paid off. Not only did she have the opportunity to attend New York Fashion Week and mingle with designers and fashion moguls, but she also received an offer for a full-time (paid!) job at StyleCaster, making her the sixth intern to move into employee status. "An internship is an easier way to get a foot in the door and make contacts," says Halpern.

1. Which of the following viewpoints do you support? (1) Unpaid internships are an ideal way for students to gain experience and make contacts. (2) Unpaid internships are simply a way for companies to get free labor. Explain.
2. Should companies be required to pay student interns the minimum wage? What impact, if any, would this requirement have on employers', particularly small companies', willingness to offer internships?

Sources: Based on Shawn Graham, "Legal Debates Aside, Companies Should Pay Interns," *Fast Company*, May 4, 2010, *www.fastcompany.com/1637926/ legal-debates-aside-companies-should-pay-interns*; Laurie Pike, "The Full-Time Non-Employee," *Entrepreneur*, April 2010, pp. 81–87; Mark Grabowski, "Debate: Internship Reform Only Hurts Students," *AOL News*, June 21, 2010, *www.aolnews.com/opinion/article/debate-the-feds-internship-crackdown-only-hurts-students/19522287*; Angus Loten, "Why Interns Are Good for Business," *Inc.*, February 25, 2010, *www.inc.com/internships/2008/internship-horror-stories.html*; Seth Fiegerman, "11 Internship Horror Stories," *MainStreet*, February 23, 2010, *www.mainstreet.com/ slideshow/career/worst-internships-america.*

*Reprinted with permission from TOMS Shoes.

Recruit "retired" workers. By 2016, nearly 35 percent of workers in the United States will be 55 or older, and in 2019 the youngest members of the Baby Boom generation will turn 55.[24] According to the American Association of Retired Persons (AARP), 70 percent of these baby boomers plan to continue working after reaching retirement age to maintain their lifestyles.[25] To avoid labor shortages, small businesses must be ready to hire them, perhaps as part-time employees. Kevin McGillivray, owner of KEM Group, a financial services and tax preparation service in Danvers, Massachusetts, needed help during the busy tax season. He placed an ad on the Web site *www.retirementjobs.com*, and within a few days he had hired a former corporate controller and a retired H&R Block employee.[26] With a lifetime of work experience and time on their hands and a strong work ethic, retired workers can be the ideal solution to many entrepreneurs' labor problems. One survey by WorldatWork, an international association of human resource professionals, reports that just 49.4 percent of employers proactively pursue older workers in their recruiting efforts.[27] Older employees can be a valuable asset to small firms.

Consider using offbeat recruiting techniques. To attract the workers they need to support their growing businesses, some entrepreneurs have resorted to creative recruiting techniques, such as the following:

- Sending young recruiters to mingle with college students on spring break
- Sponsoring a "job shadowing" program that gives students and other prospects the opportunity to observe firsthand the nature of the work and the work environment
- Inviting college seniors to a company tailgating party at a sports event
- Posting "what it's like to work here" videos created by current employees on YouTube and other video sites
- Launching a monthly industry networking meeting for local workers at Internet companies
- Hosting or joining a local job fair
- Keeping a file of all of the workers mentioned in the "People on the Move" column in the business section of the local newspaper and then contacting them a year later to see whether they are happy in their jobs[28]

Offer what workers want. Adequate compensation and benefits are important considerations for job candidates, but other, less tangible factors also weigh heavily in a prospect's decision to accept a job. To recruit effectively, entrepreneurs must consider what a McKinsey and Company study calls the "employee value proposition," the factors that would make the ideal employee want to work for their businesses. Flexible work schedules and telecommuting that allow employees to balance the demands of work and life can attract quality workers to small companies. In fact, a study by staffing firm Robert Half International reports that after salary and benefits, flexible work schedules and telecommuting were the most important incentives in attracting employees.[29]

CREATE PRACTICAL JOB DESCRIPTIONS AND JOB SPECIFICATIONS. Business owners must recognize that what they do *before* they ever start interviewing candidates for a position determines to a great extent how successful they will be at hiring winners. The first step is to perform a **job analysis**, the process by which a firm determines the duties and nature of the jobs to be filled and the skills and experience required of the people who are to fill them. Without a proper job analysis, a hiring decision is, at best, a coin toss. The first step in conducting a job analysis is to develop a **job description**, a written statement of the duties, responsibilities, reporting relationships, working conditions, and methods and techniques, as well as materials and equipment, used in a job. A results-oriented job description explains what a job entails and the duties the person filling it is expected to perform. A detailed job description includes a job title, job summary, duties to be performed, nature of supervision, the job's relationship to others in the company, working conditions, and definitions of job-specific terms.

Preparing job descriptions may be one of the most important parts of the hiring process because it creates a blueprint for the job. Without this blueprint, managers tend to hire the person with experience whom they like the best. Useful sources of information for writing job descriptions include the manager's knowledge of the job, the workers currently holding the job, and the *Dictionary of Occupational Titles (DOT),* which is available at most libraries. The *Dictionary of Occupational Titles,* published by the Department of Labor, lists more than 20,000 job titles and descriptions and serves as a useful tool for getting an entrepreneur started when writing job descriptions. In addition to traditional approaches, Web-based technologies offer new ways to share these job descriptions through online job sites and podcasts.

The second objective of a job analysis is to create a **job specification**, a written statement of the qualifications and characteristics needed for a job stated in terms such as education, skills, and experience. A job specification shows the business owner what kind of person to recruit and establishes the standards an applicant must meet to do the job well. In essence, it is a written "success profile" of the ideal employee. Does the person have to be a good listener, empathetic, well-organized, decisive, a "self-starter?" Should he or she have experience in Java programming? An entrepreneur about to hire a new employee who will be telecommuting from home, for instance, would look for someone with excellent communication skills, problem-solving ability, a strong work ethic, and the ability to use technology comfortably. One of the best ways to develop this success profile is to study the top performers currently working for the company and to identify the characteristics that make them successful. Table 1 provides an example that links the tasks for a sales representative's job (drawn from job description) to the traits or characteristics an entrepreneur identified as necessary to succeed in that job. These traits become the foundation for writing the job specification.

SCREEN RÉSUMÉS. The starting point for screening prospective employees is reviewing candidates' résumés. A survey by CareerBuilder reports that 48 percent of human resource managers say that they receive 25 résumés for each job opening. In addition, 38 percent of the managers say that they spend less than 1 minute reviewing a résumé, and 18 percent spend less than 30 seconds![30] Table 2 describes some unusual items lifted from actual résumés.

CHECK REFERENCES. Entrepreneurs should take the time to check *every* applicant's references. Although many entrepreneurs see checking references as a formality and pay little attention to it, others realize the need to protect themselves (and their customers) from hiring unscrupulous workers. A reference check is necessary because more than half of job seekers lie in their résumés, often by inflating their job titles.[31] A recent study by OfficeTeam reports that employers drop 21 percent of job applicants after they conduct reference checks.[32] Rather than rely only on the references that candidates list on their résumés, wise employers call an applicant's previous employers and talk to their immediate supervisors to get a clear picture of the applicant's job performance, character, and work habits.

TABLE 1 Linking Tasks from the Job Description to the Traits Needed to Perform the Job

Job Task	Trait or Characteristic
Generate new leads and close new sales.	Outgoing, strong communication skills, persuasive, friendly
Make 15 "cold calls" per week.	A self-starter, determined, optimistic, independent, confident
Analyze customer needs and recommend proper equipment.	Good listener, intuitive, patient, empathetic
Counsel customers about options and features required.	Organized, polished speaker, "other" oriented
Prepare and explain financial records; negotiate finance contracts.	Honest, mathematically oriented, comfortable with numbers, understands basics of finance, computer literate
Retain existing customers.	Relationship builder, customer focused

TABLE 2 Résumé Bloopers

All of the following résumé bloopers are real. Would you hire someone who committed these blunders?

- A job candidate listed God as one of her references (but, strangely enough, did not list a telephone number).
- A woman listed "alligator watching" as one of her hobbies.
- A man included "Master of Time and the Universe" as part of his work experience.
- One candidate's résumé was 24 pages long, and she had been in the workforce only 5 years.
- A candidate wrote that he was "looking for a full-time position with minimal time commitment."
- Under "Accomplishments," one man listed that he "finished eighth in his class of 10."
- An applicant claimed that "You will want me to be Head Honcho in no time."
- A job seeker claimed that he spoke "English and Spinach."
- Under "Qualifications," one woman explained that her "twin sister has an accounting degree."
- A candidate listed as skills, "written communication = 3 years; verbal communication = 5 years."
- Under education, one young applicant said, "I have a bachelorette degree in computers."
- One job applicant claimed that he had 28 dog years of experience in sales (4 human years, we assume).
- A candidate included a video with his résumé. The purpose of the video: to hypnotize the manager and persuade him to hire the man.
- One job candidate claimed that he possessed "demonstrated ability at multi-tasting."
- Under "Education," one applicant claimed to have "repeated courses repeatedly."

Sources: Based on "Hiring Managers Share Most Memorable Resume Mistakes in New CareerBuilder Survey," *CareerBuilder*, September 15, 2010, *www.careerbuilder.com/share/aboutus/pressreleasesdetail.aspx?id= pr586&sd=9/15/2010&ed=9/15/2010*; "Funny Resume Bloopers, But Don't Let This Happen to You," Do It Yourself, *www.doityourself.com/stry/ara_funnyresumebloop*; "150 Funniest Resume Mistakes, Bloopers, and Blunders Ever," Job Mob, *http://jobmob.co.il/blog/funniest-resume-mistakes/*.

ENTREPRENEURIAL Profile

Andy Levine: Development Counsellors International

Andy Levine, president of Development Counsellors International, now requires 12 references for the final stage of the interview process. "It can be pretty amusing when you ask for 12 references. Some candidates have an e-mail to us within an hour; some we never hear from again," says Levine. "When I call references, I start by trying to get them comfortable. I make it clear that what they say will not travel back to the person. Then I often ask, 'If you had to pick three words to describe this person, what are the first that come to mind?' It's very interesting, the picture that emerges after you've done eight or nine of these interviews."[33]

PLAN AN EFFECTIVE INTERVIEW. Once an entrepreneur knows what to look for in a job candidate, he or she can develop a plan for conducting an informative job interview. Too often, business owners go into an interview unprepared, and, as a result, they fail to get the information they need to judge the candidate's qualifications, qualities, and suitability for the job. A common symptom of failing to prepare for an interview is that the interviewer rather than the candidate does most of the talking. Effective interviewers spend about 25 percent of the interview talking and about 75 percent listening. Despite their popularity, interviews are less reliable in predicting job performance than samples of a candidate's work, job-knowledge tests, and peer ratings of past job performance.[34] The following tips improve the quality of the interview process:

- *Involve others in the interview process.* Solo interviews are prone to errors. A better process is to involve employees, particularly employees with whom the prospect would be working, in the interview process, either individually or as part of a panel.
- *Develop a series of core questions and ask them of every candidate.* Entrepreneurs will benefit if they rely on a set of relevant questions they ask in every interview. This will give the screening process consistency, and they can still customize each interview using impromptu questions based on an individual's responses.
- *Ask open-ended questions.* Open-ended questions demanding more than a "yes or no" response are most effective because they encourage candidates to talk about their work

experience in a way that will disclose the presence or the absence of the traits and characteristics entrepreneurs are seeking. Peter Bregman, CEO of Bregman Partners, a company that helps businesses implement change, says that one of the most revealing questions that an interviewer can ask candidates is "What do you do in your spare time?" To emphasize the importance of a candidate's hobbies, Bregman points to Captain C. B. "Sully" Sullenberger, the airline pilot who safely landed a disabled jet with 155 passengers on the Hudson River using skills that he learned from his hobby, flying gliders.[35]

- *Present hypothetical situations.* Building the interview around job-specific hypothetical situations gives the owner a preview of the candidate's actual work habits and attitudes. Rather than telling interviewers about what candidates might do, these scenarios give them insight into what candidates actually do (or have done) in job-related situations.

- *Probe for specific examples in the candidate's past work experience that demonstrate the necessary traits and characteristics.* A common mistake interviewers make is failing to get candidates to provide the detail they need to make an informed decision.

- *Inquire about recent successes and failures.* Smart interviewers look for candidates who describe them both with equal enthusiasm because they know that peak performers put as much into their failures as they do their successes and usually learn something valuable from their failures. Ask the candidates to provide examples of their successes and failures.

- *Create an informal setting.* Select a "non-interview" location that allows several employees to observe the candidate in an informal setting. Taking candidates on a plant tour or setting up a coffee break gives everyone a chance to judge a candidate's interpersonal skills and personality outside the formal interview process. These informal settings can be revealing. At Zappos, the online shoe store, recruiters often interview shuttle service drivers and administrative assistants to discover how job candidates treated them. "I want to know about that interaction," says recruiter Andrew Kovacs.[36]

Table 3 shows an example of some interview questions one manager uses to uncover the traits and characteristics he seeks in a top-performing sales representative.

Conducting the Interview

An effective interview contains three phases: breaking the ice, asking questions, and selling the candidate on the company.

BREAKING THE ICE. In the opening phase of the interview, the entrepreneur's primary goal is to create a relaxed environment. Icebreakers—questions about a hobby or special interest—get the

TABLE 3 Interview Questions for Candidates for a Sales Representative Position

Trait or Characteristic	Question
Outgoing, persuasive, friendly, a self-starter, determined, optimistic, independent, confident	How do you persuade reluctant prospects to buy? Can you give an example?
Good listener, patient, empathetic, organized, polished speaker, other-oriented	What would you say to a fellow salesperson who is getting more than her share of rejections and is having difficulty getting appointments?
Honest, customer-oriented, relationship builder	How do you feel when someone questions the truth of what you say? Can you give an example of how you handled this situation?

Other questions:

- If you owned a company, why would you hire yourself?
- If you were head of your department, what would you do differently? Why?
- How do you acknowledge the contributions of others in your department?

candidate to relax. These "icebreaker" questions also allow the interviewer an opportunity to gain valuable insight into the person. These questions generate little or no pressure and allow the interviewee to expound on something he or she knows a great deal about.

ASKING QUESTIONS. During the second phase of the interview, employers ask the questions from their question bank to determine the applicant's suitability for the job. Employers' primary job at this point is to *listen*. They also take notes during the interview to help them ask follow-up questions based on a candidate's comments and to evaluate a candidate after the interview is over. Experienced interviewers also pay close attention to a candidate's nonverbal clues, or body language, during the interview. They know that candidates may be able to say exactly what they want with their words but that the candidate's body language does not lie!

Some of the most valuable interview questions attempt to gain insight into the candidate's ability to reason, be logical, and be creative. In a **puzzle interview**, the goal is to determine how job candidates think by asking them offbeat, unexpected questions such as, "How would you weigh an airplane without scales?" "Why are manhole covers round?" or "How would you determine the height of a building using only a barometer?" At Zappos, interviewers ask candidates which superhero they would like to be and why.[37] Usually, the logic and creativity a candidate uses to derive an answer is much more important than the answer itself.

Another interview format is the **situational interview** in which the interviewer gives candidates a typical job-related situation (sometimes in the form of a role-playing exercise) and presents a series of open-ended questions to assess how the candidates might respond. One entrepreneur had a candidate deal with an "angry customer," who was played by a fellow interviewer. Studies show that situational interviews have a 54 percent accuracy rate in predicting future job performance, much higher than the 7 percent accuracy rate of the traditional interview.[38]

The **peer-to-peer interview** may provide a closer look at how prospective employees will get along with other staff. Applicants meet one-on-one with potential peers to ask questions about the job and the company. The employees share their assessment with the manager. This interview technique is becoming more common in companies, especially those in which work is team-based. "In a small organization, you're going to spend a lot of time together," says Michael Harris, an expert in peer-to-peer interviews. "It becomes even more important for the entrepreneur to share some of the [hiring] responsibility with employees."[39] Because employees are involved in the hiring process, they feel empowered and "buy into" the hiring process, which can be good for morale and productivity. Peer interviews also allow applicants to gain insight into an organization's culture.

ENTREPRENEURIAL
Profile

Rick Self: Advanced Technology Institute (ATI)

At Advanced Technology Institute (ATI), a research and development management company in North Charleston, South Carolina, managers conducted traditional 1- or 2-hour interviews. After making several bad hires, CEO Rick Self switched to peer-to-peer interviews that last at least half a day, involve several employees from all parts of the company, and include a lunch with employees from the department in which the applicant would work. The candidate's final interview is with the CEO. The goal is to judge how well applicants will fit into ATI's team-based work environment. "We're trying to find out what makes someone both good and happy to be here and then we bake that into a set of structured interviews," says Self.[40]

Managers should conduct training sessions with employees who will participate in the interviews to make certain that they know which questions are illegal and that keep their questions job-related.[41] The Equal Employment Opportunity Commission (EEOC) does not outlaw specific interview questions; rather, it recognizes that some questions can result in employment discrimination. If a candidate files charges of discrimination against a company, the burden of proof shifts to the employer to prove that all pre-employment questions were job related and non-discriminatory. Table 4 offers a quiz to help entrepreneurs understand the types of questions that are most likely to result in charges of discrimination.

TABLE 4 Is It Legal?

Legal	Illegal	Interview Question
❏	❏	1. Are you currently using illegal drugs?
❏	❏	2. Have you ever been arrested?
❏	❏	3. Do you have any children or do you plan to have children?
❏	❏	4. When and where were you born?
❏	❏	5. Is there any limit on your ability to work overtime or travel?
❏	❏	6. How tall are you? How much do you weigh?
❏	❏	7. Do you drink alcohol?
❏	❏	8. How much alcohol do you drink each week?
❏	❏	9. Would your religious beliefs interfere with your ability to do the job?
❏	❏	10. What contraceptive practices do you use?
❏	❏	11. Are you HIV positive?
❏	❏	12. Have you ever filed a lawsuit or worker's compensation claim against a former employer?
❏	❏	13. Do you have physical/mental disabilities that would interfere with doing your job?
❏	❏	14. Are you a U.S. citizen?

Answers: 1. Legal. 2. Illegal. Employers cannot ask about an applicant's arrest record, but they can ask if a candidate has ever been convicted of a crime. 3. Illegal. Employers cannot ask questions that could lead to discrimination against a particular group (e.g., women, physically challenged, etc.). 4. Illegal. The Civil Rights Act of 1964 bans discrimination on the basis of race, color, sex, religion, or national origin. 5. Legal. 6. Illegal. Unless a person's physical characteristics are necessary for job performance (e.g., lifting 100-pound sacks of mulch), employers cannot ask candidates such questions. 7. Legal. 8. Illegal. Notice the fine line between question 7 and question 8; this is what makes interviewing challenging. 9. Illegal. This question would violate the Civil Rights Act of 1964. 10. Illegal. What relevance would this have to an employee's job performance? 11. Illegal. Under the Americans with Disabilities Act, which prohibits discrimination against people with disabilities, people who are HIV positive or who have AIDS are considered "disabled." 12. Illegal. Workers who file such suits are protected from retribution by a variety of federal and state laws. 13. Illegal. This question would also violate the Americans with Disabilities Act. 14. Illegal. This question violates the Civil Rights Act of 1964.

The goal of the interview process is to find someone who is qualified to do the job well. By steering clear of questions about subjects that are peripheral to the job itself, employers are less likely to ask questions that will land them in court. Wise entrepreneurs ask their attorneys to review their bank of questions before using them in an interview. Table 5 describes a simple test for determining whether an interview question might be considered discriminatory.

SELLING THE CANDIDATE ON THE COMPANY. "A" players want to play for "A" teams. In the final phase of the interview, when employers have an attractive candidate, they should sell the benefits of working for the company. This phase begins by allowing the candidate to ask questions about the company, the job, or other issues. Experienced interviewers note the nature of these questions and the insights they give into the candidate's personality. This part of the interview offers employers a prime opportunity to explain to the candidate why the company is an attractive place to work. The best candidates will have other offers, and it is up to the entrepreneur to make sure they leave the interview wanting to work for the company. Finally, before closing the interview employers should thank the candidates and tell them what happens next. For example, "We will be contacting you about our decision within 2 weeks."

BACKGROUND CHECKS. Background checks are essential. In addition to turning up convictions for criminal activity, a background check can show whether a job candidate has been convicted of stealing from a previous employer. A check of a candidate's driving records will show convictions for DUI and other traffic violations. This information can save an entrepreneur thousands of dollars by avoiding a bad hire at a cost of $50 or less for a basic criminal records check. "A lot of times, employers argue that a background check is too expensive," says Zuni

TABLE 5 A Guide for Interview Questions

Small business owners can use the "OUCII" test as a guide for determining whether an interview question might be considered discriminatory:

- Does the question *Omit* references to race, religion, color, sex, or national origin?
- Does the question *Unfairly* screen out a particular class of people?
- Can you *Consistently* apply the question to every applicant?
- Does the question *Have* job-relatedness and business necessity?

Corkerton, president of Hilliard, Ohio-based RefCheck Information Services Inc. "But the litigation that comes as a result of not having done their due diligence and having been negligent in their hiring process can be far greater."[42]

A background check is a basic step in avoiding charges of negligent hiring, the failure to investigate the background of a prospective employee who proves to be dangerous to customers or other employees. For example, a Nebraska delivery driver for a pizza chain attacked a woman after delivering a pizza to her home. The employee had a previous sexual-assault conviction that a simple background check would have detected, preventing a tragedy, damage to the company's reputation, and the resulting litigation. A court ordered the pizza chain to pay the victim $175,000.[43]

Checking potential employees' social networking pages, such as those on Facebook and MySpace, also can provide a revealing look at the character of job candidates. A study by CareerBuilder reports that 22 percent of employers investigate job candidates' Facebook and MySpace pages and that one-third have discovered something there that caused them to reject a candidate.[44]

EMPLOYMENT TESTS. Although various state and federal laws have made using employment tests as screening devices more difficult in recent years, many companies find them quite useful. To avoid charges of discrimination, entrepreneurs must be able to prove that the employment tests they use are both valid and reliable. A **valid test** is one that measures what it is intended to measure: for example, aptitude for selling, creativity, integrity. A **reliable test** is one that measures consistently over time. Employers must also be sure that the tests they use measure aptitudes and factors that are job related. Many testing organizations offer ready-made tests that have been proved to be both valid and reliable. Entrepreneurs can use these tests safely. In today's environment, if a test has not been validated and proven to be reliable or is not job related, it is best not to use it.

ENTREPRENEURIAL Profile

Richard Linder: PCA Skin Inc.

PCA Skin Inc., a company based in Scottsdale, Arizona, that develops clinical skin care products, recently began using personality-based employment tests, and managers say that the tests, which take only 10 minutes to administer, have helped the company improve its hiring process. "We have had 65 candidates take the test," says CEO Richard Linder. The company has hired 17 new employees, and "so far, every hire we have made using the test has resulted in a successful placement."[45]

According to the U.S. Department of Labor, 75 percent of illegal drug users are employed, and those who are employed are most likely to work for small companies, which rely less on drug tests than large businesses.[46] In an attempt to avoid hiring illegal drug users, 84 percent of employers use pre-employment drug tests and 39 percent administer postemployment random drug tests.[47] Although administering drug tests adds expense to the hiring process, the cost is far less than that of the potential problems an employee with a drug habit causes. Employers who use drug tests should establish a policy and follow it consistently.

Experienced entrepreneurs do not rely on any one element in the employee-selection process. They look at the total picture painted by each part of a candidate's portfolio. They know that the hiring process provides them with one of the most valuable raw materials their companies count on for success—capable, hard-working people. They also recognize that hiring an employee is not a single event but the beginning of a long-term relationship.

IN THE ENTREPRENEURIAL
SPOTLIGHT   What a Great Place to Work!

New Belgium Brewing Company

"There's something wrong if making beer can't be fun," says Kim Jordan, CEO of New Belgium Brewing Company, the business she cofounded with her husband Jeff Lebesch in 1991. The idea for the company came to Lebesch while he was on a bicycle tour of Belgium, peddling his way through towns and villages that are famous for making superb, rich, boldly flavored craft beers. Inspired by his trip, Lebesch began brewing beer in his basement using dairy equipment that he modified for beer-making. Jordan became the tiny company's bottler, sales representative, distributor, marketing director, and financial manager.

Today, CEO Jordan works hard to make sure that her employees have fun while making New Belgium's unique line of craft beers, which includes Fat Tire (named after Lebesch's bicycle trip through Europe that inspired him to start the company), Skinny Dip (a seasonal beer for summer with a hint of lime), Mothership Wit Organic Wheat Beer (the company's first organic offering), and Blue Paddle (a Czech-inspired pilsner). She created an employee stock ownership plan in which every employee receives an ownership interest in the Fort Collins, Colorado-based company and a free custom bicycle after 1 year with the company. (New Belgium Brewing is an environmentally conscious company and encourages employees to follow its lead. The company has been using wind-powered electricity since 1999.) Employees now own one-third of the company. After 5 years with the company, every employee receives an all-expenses-paid trip to Belgium to learn about beer-making. Employees also receive two free six packs of beer each week. Jordan involves employees at all levels of the company when crafting New Belgium's strategic plan and budgets. "Operating a business in a way that is consistent with your values is particularly pleasing," says Jordan.

Daxko Inc.

One of David Gray's first goals when he became CEO of Daxko, a small company in Birmingham, Alabama, that provides software and technology services to nonprofits, was to reshape the company's culture. "I'm a big believer in corporate culture as a competitive advantage," Gray says. The transformation was successful; Daxko's culture more closely resembles those of companies in Silicon Valley than those in the traditional South. All new employees receive 15 paid vacation days, a free YMCA membership, and 6 weeks of paid parental leave. The company allocates $1,500 to each employee to spend on any kind of professional development activity they choose, and for every 7 years of service employees qualify for a 4-week paid sabbatical leave. To encourage interaction among employees and the creativity that it spawns, no one, including managers, has a private office. The company does have a work–play lounge that includes a 52-inch television and a Nintendo Wii. It is not uncommon to see employees on a break playing the latest video game or cheering on their "team" in a friendly Wii competition. "It's symbolic of a company that focuses on contributions instead of hours clocked," says one management consultant. Employees also connect with one another over the weekly free lunch, sometimes just to socialize and other times to discuss projects on which they are working. "It's pretty intense here," says product manager Saranda West. "Expectations for what I need to accomplish are clearly set, and if I can play Wii while doing it, that's even better."

1. Daxko's David Gray says, "I'm a big believer in corporate culture as a competitive advantage." Do you agree? Explain.
2. Why do company cultures like the ones at New Belgium Brewing Company and Daxko appeal to employees, particularly members of Generation X and Generation Y? Would you want to work for New Belgium Brewing or Daxko? Explain.

Sources: Based on Joseph V. Tirella, Malika Zouhali-Worrall, Alec Foege, David Koeppel, and Ian Mount, "Meet the New Boss," *FSB*, June 2009, pp. 63–68; "Our Story," New Belgium Brewing Company, *www.newbelgium .com/culture/our-story.aspx*; "About Daxko," Daxko, *http://daxko.com/ about-daxko/*.

Kim Jordan, CEO of New Belgium Brewing Company.

Source: New Belgium Brewing Company.

Building the Right Culture and Organizational Structure

Company culture is the distinctive, unwritten code of conduct that governs the behavior, attitudes, relationships, and style of an organization. It is the essence of "the way we do things around here." In many entrepreneurial companies, culture plays an important role in gaining a competitive edge. A company's culture has a powerful impact on the way people work together in a business, how they do their jobs, and how they treat their customers. Company culture manifests itself in many ways—from how workers dress and act to the language they use. At some companies, the unspoken dress code requires workers to wear suits and ties, but at many high-technology companies employees routinely show up in jeans, T-shirts, and flip-flops. In many companies, the culture creates its own language. At Disney theme parks, workers are not "employees"; they are "cast members." They do not merely go to work; their jobs are "parts in a performance." Customers are referred to as "guests." When a cast member treats someone to lunch, it's "on the mouse." Anything negative—such as a cigarette butt on a walkway—is "a bad Mickey," and anything positive is "a good Mickey."

An important ingredient in a company's culture is the performance objectives an entrepreneur sets and against which employees are measured. If entrepreneurs want integrity, respect, honesty, customer service, and other important values to be the foundation on which a positive culture can flourish, they must establish measures of success that reflect those core values. *Effective executives know that building a positive organizational culture has a direct, positive impact on the financial outcomes of an organization.* The intangible factors that comprise an organization's culture have an influence, either positive or negative, on the tangible outcomes of profitability, cash flow, return on equity, employee productivity, innovation and cost control. An entrepreneur's job is to establish a culture that creates a positive influence on the company's tangible outcomes. Companies that focus on creating a positive corporate culture have better financial performance than those that do not, according to the San Francisco-based Great Places to Work Institute.[48]

Sustaining a company's culture begins with the hiring process. Beyond the normal requirements of competitive pay and working conditions, the hiring process must focus on finding employees who share the values of the organization. "Companies are realizing that culture is as important as strategy and that they can't just look at the short term anymore," says Barbara Bilodeau, a manager at Boston-based Bain & Co.[49] Nurturing the right culture in a company can enhance a company's competitive position by improving its ability to attract and retain quality workers and by creating an environment in which workers can grow and develop. As a new generation of employees enters the workforce, companies are discovering that more relaxed, open cultures have an edge in attracting the best workers. These companies embrace nontraditional, fun cultures that incorporate concepts such as casual dress, team-based assignments, telecommuting, flexible work schedules, free meals, company outings, and many other unique options. Modern organizational culture relies on the following principles to create a productive, fun workplace:

- *Respect for the quality of work and a balance between work life and home life.* Modern companies recognize that their employees have lives away from work. These businesses offer flexible work schedules, part-time work, job sharing, telecommuting, sabbaticals, and conveniences such as on-site day care or concierge services that handle employees' errands. Work–life balance issues are becoming more important to employees, and companies that address them have an edge when it comes to recruiting and retaining a quality workforce. "Employers realize that by offering work–life programs, they are getting a lot in return in terms of productivity and commitment to the organization," says one consultant.[50]

ENTREPRENEURIAL Profile

Paul Graziani: Analytical Graphics, Inc.

Analytical Graphics, Inc. (AGI), a small company in Exton, Pennsylvania, that produces software for the space, defense, and intelligence industries, helps its employees balance the demands of work and life by providing three meals a day for employees and having a dry cleaning service make pickups and deliveries each week. AGI installed washers and dryers after younger workers said that they had trouble finding time to do laundry. CEO Paul Graziani says that increased workforce productivity more than offsets the costs of providing these perks.[51]

- *A sense of purpose.* These companies rely on a strong sense of purpose to connect employees to the company's mission. At motorcycle legend Harley-Davidson, employees are so in tune with the company's mission that some of them have tattoos of the company's name.

Achieving work-life balance: Paul Graziani, CEO of Analytical Graphics, Inc., says that increases in productivity more than offset the cost of installing washers and dryers for employees to use.

Source: AGI\Analytical Graphics, Inc.

■ *Diversity.* The U.S. workforce is becoming more diverse; by 2039, the majority of the workforce will consist of minorities. Companies with appealing cultures embrace cultural diversity in their workforces, actively seeking out workers with different backgrounds. They recognize that a workforce with a rich mix of cultural diversity gives their companies more talent, skills, and abilities from which to draw. Because the entire world is now a potential market for many small companies, having a workforce that looks, acts, and thinks like their customers, with all of their ethnic, racial, religious, and behavioral variety, is a strength. Figure 1 shows the composition of the U.S. workforce in 1995, 2010, and 2050.

■ *Integrity.* Employees want to work for a company that stands for honesty and integrity. They do not want to have to check their personal value systems at the door when they report to work. Indeed, many workers take pride in the fact they work for a company that is ethical and socially responsible.

■ *Participative management.* Modern managers recognize that employees expect a participative management style to be part of a company's culture. Today's workforce does not respond well to the autocratic management styles of the past. To maximize productivity and encourage commitment to accomplishing the company's mission, entrepreneurs must trust and empower employees at all levels of the organization to make decisions and to take the actions they must to do their jobs well.

■ *Learning environment.* Progressive companies encourage and support lifelong learning among their employees. They are willing to invest in their employees, improving their skills and helping them to reach their full potential. That attitude is a strong magnet for the best and brightest workers, who know that to stay at the top of their fields they must always be learning. Dealer.com, a small company in Burlington, Vermont, that provides online marketing services for the automotive industry, provides a multitude of training opportunities for its employees through uFuel, its online learning system. The company also offers its top performing employees a custom-designed MBA curriculum taught by professors at a local university.[52]

■ *A sense of fun.* Children laugh an average of 400 times a day; however, by the time a person reaches age 35 he or she laughs on average just 15 times a day.[53] At many successful small companies, the lines between work and play are blurred, and laughter is common. The founders of these businesses see no reason for work and fun to be mutually exclusive. In fact, they believe that a workplace that creates a sense of fun makes it easier to recruit quality workers and encourages them to be more productive and more customer-oriented. "Healthy and sustainable organizations focus on the fundamentals: quality, service, fiscal responsibility, leadership—but they didn't forget to add fun to that

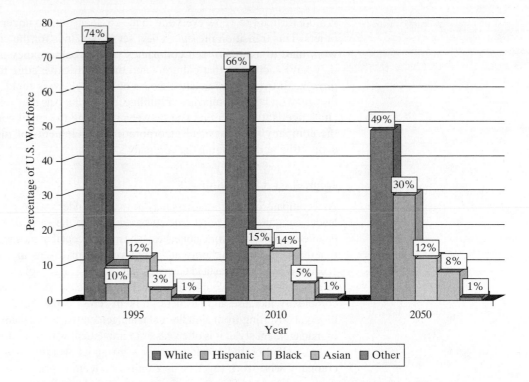

FIGURE 1
Racial and Ethnic Diversity of the U.S. Workforce: 1995, 2010, 2050

Sources: Bureau of the Census and the U.S. Equal Employment Opportunity Commission.

formula," says Leslie Yerkes, a consultant and author.[54] At Heinfeld, Meech, and Company, a CPA firm in Tucson, Arizona, the culture emphasizes excellence, honesty, teamwork, and respect in addition to fun. To relieve stress, employees participate in office "decathlons" that include events such as flying paper airplanes, playing paper football, and racing office chairs.[55]

■ *Engagement.* Employees who are fully engaged in their work take pride in making valuable contributions to the organization's success and derive personal satisfaction from doing so. Although engaged employees are a key ingredient in superior business performance, just 28 percent of employees in North America are fully engaged in their work, and 18 percent of them actually are disengaged.[56] What can managers do to improve employee engagement?

  ■ Constantly communicate the purpose and vision of the organization and why it matters.
  ■ Challenge employees to learn and advance in their careers and give them the resources and the incentives to do so.
  ■ Create a culture that encourages and rewards engagement.

Companies that build their cultures on these principles have an edge when it comes to attracting, retaining, and motivating workers. In other words, creating the right culture helps a small company compete more effectively.

No screening process is perfect, which is why small companies must make sure that every new hire is an appropriate fit with their culture. "Most [employee] turnover is from a lack of cultural match," says Julie Godshall Brown, president of Godshall and Godshall Personnel Consultants.[57]

ENTREPRENEURIAL
Profile

Tony Hsieh: Zappos

At Zappos, the online shoe retailer, new hires go through an extensive 4-week orientation and training program in which they learn everything from the importance of customer service to the company's 10 core values. About 1 week into the program, the company offers its new hires $1,500 to quit. This might sound like a crazy idea, but only 10 percent of new employees accept the offer. Zappos uses the "bonus" to ensure that the employees it hires are engaged and committed to the company and are a good fit with its unique culture.[58]

MANAGING GROWTH AND A CHANGING CULTURE. As companies grow, they often experience dramatic changes in their culture. Procedures become more formal, operations grow more widespread, jobs take on more structure, communication becomes more difficult, and the company's personality often begins to change. As more workers come on board, employees find it more difficult to know everyone in the company and to understand how their jobs connect with others. This transition presents a new set of demands for the entrepreneur. Unless entrepreneurs work hard to maintain their companies' unique culture, they may wake up one day to find that they have sacrificed that culture—and the competitive edge that went with it—in the name of growth. Entrepreneurs must be aware of the challenges rapid growth brings with it; otherwise, they may find their companies crumbling around them as they reach warp speed. An entrepreneur's challenge is to walk a fine line between retaining the small company traits that are the seeds of the company's success and incorporating the elements of infrastructure that are essential to supporting and sustaining the company's growth.

Team-Based Management

As a company grows, its success may lie in the founder's willingness to shift from a top-down, single-leader structure to one that is team-based. Unlike the early days of a company when the founder handled much of the work alone, he or she must accept that the magnitude and the complexity of work requires delegating authority and empowering employees to make decisions. Leaders who build successful teams understand that each team member has a role to play and that every role plays a part in a bigger picture. Companies are relying more on team-based job designs as competition and complexity increase and business problems cross departmental and geographic boundaries. Even though converting from a traditional management style to a team approach requires a major change in management style, it is often easier to implement with a small number of workers.

A **self-directed work team** is a group of workers from different functional areas of a company who work together as a unit. The team operates largely without supervision, making decisions and performing tasks that once belonged only to managers. Some teams may be temporary, attacking and solving a specific problem, but many are permanent components of an organization's structure. As their name implies, these teams manage themselves, performing such functions as setting work schedules, ordering raw materials, evaluating and purchasing equipment, developing budgets, hiring and firing team members, and solving problems. Teams function best in environments in which the work is interdependent and people must interact to accomplish their goals. The goal is to get people working together to serve customers better. Johnsonville Sausage, a privately owned company founded in 1945 and based in Sheboygan Falls, Wisconsin, uses a team-based structure rather than traditional departments. The company hires "members" rather than employees, and supervisors have the title of "coaches," a not-so-subtle reminder of the role the company expects them to fill.[59]

Managers in companies using teams are just as involved as before, but the nature of their work changes dramatically. Before teams, managers were bosses who made most of the decisions affecting their subordinates alone. They often hoarded information and power for themselves. In a team environment, managers take on the role of coaches. They empower those around them to make decisions affecting their work and share information with their workers. As facilitators, their job is to support and to serve the teams functioning in the organization and to make sure the teams produce results.

Companies have strong, competitive reasons for using team-based management. Businesses that use teams effectively report significant gains in quality, reductions in cycle time, lower costs, increased customer satisfaction, and improved employee motivation and morale. A team-based approach is not appropriate for every organization, however. Although teams have saved some companies from extinction, for others, the team approach has failed. A team-based management system is *not* easy to start. Switching from a traditional organizational structure to a team-based one is filled with potential pitfalls. A common criticism of teams is groupthink, a concept identified by Yale psychology professor Irving Janis in his classic book, *Victims of Groupthink*. Janis observed that **groupthink** sometimes leads groups to build a false sense of confidence that leads to unsound decisions that team members would not have made individually.[60] Years later, Jerry Harvey described another danger of group decisions that he called the **Abilene Paradox**, a situation in which a group makes a decision that is precisely the *opposite* of what its individual members want to do. What makes the difference? What causes teams to fail? The following errors are common in team-oriented environments:

- Assigning a team an inappropriate task, one in which the team members may lack the necessary skills to be successful (lack of training and support).
- Creating work teams but failing to provide the team with meaningful performance targets.

- Failing to deal with known underperformers and assuming that being part of a group will solve the problem; it doesn't.
- Failing to compensate the members of the team equitably.

To ensure the success of the teams approach, entrepreneurs must do the following:

- *Make sure that teams are appropriate for the company and the nature of the work.* A good starting point is to create a "map" of the company's work flow that shows how workers build a product or deliver a service. Is the work interdependent, complex, and interactive? If so, teamwork is likely to improve the company's performance.
- *Form teams around the natural work flow and give them specific tasks to accomplish.* Teams can be effective only if managers challenge them to accomplish specific, measurable objectives. They need targets to shoot for.
- *Provide adequate support and training for team members and leaders.* Team success requires a new set of skills. Workers must learn how to communicate, resolve conflict, support one another, and solve problems as a team. Smart managers see that team members get the training they need.
- *Involve team members in determining how their performances will be measured, what will be measured, and when it will be measured.* Doing so gives team members a sense of ownership and pride about the tasks they are accomplishing.
- *Make at least part of team members' pay dependent on team performance.* Companies that have used teams successfully still pay members individually, but they make successful teamwork a major part of an individual's performance review.

Figure 2 illustrates the four stages teams go through on their way to performing effectively and reaching set goals.

Communicating Effectively

Effective communication is the lifeblood of a successful company. It reinforces the organization's vision, connects employees to the business, fosters process improvement, facilitates change, and drives business results by changing employee behavior. An important and highly visible part of the entrepreneurs' role is to communicate the values, beliefs, and principles for which their

FIGURE 2
The Stages of Team Development

4. Understand the potential barriers to effective communication and describe how to overcome them.

businesses stand. Entrepreneurs also must help employees to understand the importance of their roles and how they fit into the "big picture" of the company's success. Studies confirm that effective communication makes a difference in a company's performance. Management consulting firm Towers Watson reports that the return on investment over the last 5 years in companies with the most effective communications is 47 percent higher than the return for those with the least effective communications. The study also found a strong correlation between a company's communication effectiveness and its employee engagement level and retention rate.[61]

Improving Communication

A leader's foremost job is to communicate the company's vision to everyone in the company and to empower employees to accomplish the vision within the framework of the company's culture. Much of what leaders do involves communication; indeed, leaders spend about 80 percent of their time participating in some form of communication. To some managers, communicating means only one thing: sending messages to others. Although talking to people both inside and outside the organization is an important part of an entrepreneur's job, so is encouraging communication throughout the company at all levels and across all functional areas. "Communicators are evolving from crafting the content [of the message] to facilitating the discussion," says Sharon McIntosh, director of global communications at PepsiCo.[62]

ENTREPRENEURIAL
Profile
Analytical Graphics

At Analytical Graphics, the company that creates software for the aerospace and defense industries, managers implemented a system that encourages communication among employees. Every Friday, the company hosts a lunch meeting for all employees that includes "Storytime," during which employees from various departments describe the projects they are working on, how their work depends on the work of other departments, and how their work affects the company's clients. In addition to improving communication among workers, Storytime also enhances the sense of teamwork throughout the company.[63]

BARRIERS TO EFFECTIVE COMMUNICATION. One of the most frustrating experiences for entrepreneurs occurs when they ask an employee to do something and nothing happens. Although entrepreneurs are quick to perceive the failure to respond as the employee's lack of motivation or weak work ethic, often the culprit is improper communication. The primary reasons employees usually don't do what they are expected to do have little to do with their motivation and desire to work. Instead, workers often fail to do what they need to do because:

- They don't know what to do.
- They don't know how to do it.
- They don't have the authority to do it.
- They get no feedback on how well or how poorly they are doing it.
- They are either ignored or punished for doing it right.
- They realize that no one ever notices even if they *are* doing it right.

The common thread running through all of these causes is poor communication between the entrepreneur and employee. What barriers to effective communication must entrepreneurs overcome?

- *Managers and employees don't always feel free to say what they really mean.* CEOs and top managers in companies of any size seldom hear the truth about problems and negative results from employees. This less-than-honest feedback results from the hesitancy of subordinates to tell "the boss" bad news. Over time, this tendency paralyzes the upward communication in a company.
- *Ambiguity blocks real communication.* The same words can have different meanings to different people, especially in modern companies, where the workforce is likely to be highly diverse. For instance, an entrepreneur may tell an employee to "take care of this customer's problem as soon as you can." The owner may have meant "solve this problem by the end of the day" but the employee may think that fixing the problem by the end of the week will meet the owner's request.
- *Information overload causes the message to get lost.* With information from mail, telephone, faxes, e-mail, face-to-face communication, and other sources, employees in

modern organizations are bombarded with messages. With such a large volume of information washing over workers, it is easy for some messages to get lost.

■ *Selective listening interferes with the communication process.* Sometimes people hear only what they want to hear, selectively tuning in and out on a speaker's message. The result is distorted communication.

■ *Defense mechanisms block a message.* When people are confronted with information that upsets them or conflicts with their perceptions, they immediately put up defenses. Defense mechanisms range from verbally attacking the source of the message to twisting perceptions of reality to maintain self-esteem.

■ *Conflicting verbal and nonverbal messages confuse listeners.* Nonverbal communication includes a speaker's mannerisms, gestures, posture, facial expressions, and other forms of body language. When a speaker sends conflicting verbal and nonverbal messages, research shows that listeners will believe the nonverbal message almost every time.

OVERCOMING COMMUNICATION BARRIERS. How can entrepreneurs overcome these barriers to become better communicators? The following tips will help:

■ *Clarify your message before you attempt to communicate it.* Identify exactly what you want the receiver to think and do as a result of the message and focus on getting that point across clearly and concisely.

■ *Use face-to-face communication whenever possible.* Although not always practical, face-to-face communication reduces the likelihood of misunderstandings because it allows for immediate feedback and nonverbal clues.

■ *Be empathetic.* Put yourself in the place of those who will receive your message, and develop it accordingly.

■ *Match your message to your audience.* An entrepreneur would be very unlikely to use the same words, techniques, and style to communicate his company's financial position to a group of industry analysts as he would to a group of workers on the factory floor.

■ *Be organized.* Effective communicators organize their messages so that their audiences can understand them easily.

■ *Encourage feedback.* Good leaders actively seek honest feedback from as many employees as possible. At computer chip maker Intel, managers routinely hold "skip-level meetings," in which managers meet with employees who are two levels down the organization. "It's a powerful tool for getting information," says Patricia Murray, the company's director of human resources.[64]

■ *Get out of the office and talk to employees.* Some of the most meaningful conversations managers have take place when they leave their offices to "wander" through the workplace. Management author Tom Peters calls it "MBWA, management by wandering around."

■ *Tell the truth.* The fastest way to destroy your credibility as a leader is to lie.

■ *Don't be afraid to tell employees about the business, its performance, and the forces that affect it.* Too often, entrepreneurs assume that employees don't care about such details. Employees *are* interested in the business that employs them and want to understand where it is headed and how it plans to get there.

Listening

When one thinks about communication, listening typically does not come to mind, yet listening is an essential part of the communication process. Entrepreneurs must listen to what employees on the front line are learning about customers' needs and demands. "The key to success and growth is getting employees to tell you what's really going on," says Vineet Nayar, CEO of HCL Technologies and author of *Employees First, Customers Second*.[65] The employees who serve customers are the *real* experts in the company's day-to-day activities. They are in closer contact with potential problems and opportunities at the operating level than anyone else in the company, particularly managers. According to a survey by VitalSmarts, more than 90 percent of employees say that they know early on when projects are destined to fail, and 78 percent say they are currently working on a doomed project. More than three-fourths of employees compare their failing projects to a "slow motion train wreck."[66] Managers who take the time to listen to their frontline employees avoid many of these train wrecks. In addition, by encouraging employees to develop creative solutions to problems and innovative ideas for capitalizing on opportunities and then listening to and acting on them, entrepreneurs can make their companies more successful.

At Best Buy, the Minneapolis, Minnesota-based electronics retailer, managers focus on communicating with employees rather than at them and use a variety of social media tools to help them. The company uses its intranet to conduct weekly employee polls on a multitude of topics and has built wikis that allow employees with common interests to build a storehouse of valuable knowledge. "Wiki has been a great source for local store employees to learn details about their specific location's business goals, see what the competition is up to, find information on company strategy, and learn and share best practices," says Andy Hokenson, the company's senior specialist for dialogue and intranet. Senior managers participate in online "town hall meetings," in which employees ask questions about anything. Best Buy's IdeaX site encourages employees to submit and discuss ideas for improving the company's operations; so far, employees have submitted more than 6,500 ideas. The centerpiece of the company's communication system is the Watercooler, an online discussion forum that encourages employees to engage one another and managers in meaningful conversations. Managers recently proved how important the Watercooler is when they reduced the discount on employee purchases. Hundreds of employees expressed concern and explained how the discount encourages them to try out products that they then recommend to customers. Managers got the message and reinstated the full employee discount.[67]

Improvements such as these depend on entrepreneurs' ability to listen. To improve listening skills, entrepreneurs can use the PDCH formula: identify the speaker's *purpose*, recognize the *details* that support that purpose, see the *conclusions* they can draw from what the speaker is saying, and identify the *hidden* meanings communicated by body language and voice inflections.

The Informal Communication Network: The "Grapevine"

Despite all of the modern communication tools available, the grapevine, the informal lines of communication that exist in every company, remains an important link in a company's communication network. The grapevine carries vital information—and sometimes rumors—through every part of the organization with incredible speed. The grapevine kicks into overdrive when the information in a company's formal communication network is scarce. It is not unusual for employees to hear about important changes in an organization through the grapevine well before official communication channels transmit the news. Research shows that up to 70 percent of all organizational communication comes by way of the grapevine, yet many top managers are not aware of the efficiency with which this informal communication channel operates.[68] Text and instant messaging and e-mail increase the speed at which the grapevine transmits informal communications, all under the radar of management.

Knowing that employees are connected through the grapevine allows entrepreneurs to send out ideas to obtain reactions without making a formal announcement. When management is in the loop, the grapevine can be an excellent source of informal feedback. Smart managers recognize the grapevine's existence and use it as a communication tool to both send and receive meaningful information.

Kim Seymour, founder and owner of Cravings, a Raleigh, North Carolina, retail company that sells trendy maternity clothing and accessories, appreciates the value of listening to the employee grapevine for feedback. Seymour seeks advice from employees who teach her about merchandising, marketing, and customer relations. One employee brings 9 years of experience as a retail manager, experience Seymour did not have when she started the company. "There's no way someone is going to be an expert in every aspect of running a business," says Seymour.[69]

The Challenge of Motivating Workers

5. Discuss the ways in which entrepreneurs can motivate their employees to achieve higher levels of performance.

Motivation is the degree of effort an employee exerts to accomplish a task; it shows up as excitement about work. Motivating workers to higher levels of performance is one of the most difficult and challenging tasks facing a small business manager. Few things are more frustrating to an entrepreneur than an employee with a tremendous amount of talent who lacks the desire to use it. This section discusses four aspects of motivation: empowerment, job design, rewards and compensation, and feedback.

Empowerment

One motivating principle is empowerment. **Empowerment** involves giving workers at every level of the organization the authority, the freedom, and the responsibility to control their own work, to make decisions, and to take action to meet the company's objectives. Research indicates that employees experience increased initiative and motivation when they are empowered. Empowerment affects their self-confidence and the level of tenacity they display when faced with setbacks. Empowered employees take responsibility for making decisions and following them through to completion; they feel energized and excited by what they do and are more likely to achieve mutually agreed-upon goals.[70] Empowerment complements the team-based management style discussed earlier.

Empowerment builds on what real business leaders already know: that the people in their organizations bring with them to work an amazing array of talents, skills, knowledge, and abilities. Workers are willing—even anxious—to put these to use; unfortunately, in too many businesses suffocating management styles and poorly designed jobs quash workers' enthusiasm and motivation. Enlightened entrepreneurs recognize their workers' abilities, develop them, and then give workers the freedom and the power to use them. Entrepreneurs who share information, responsibility, authority, and power soon discover that their success (and their companies' success) is magnified many times over.

When implemented properly, empowerment can produce impressive results, not only for the business, but also for newly empowered employees. For the business, benefits typically include significant productivity gains, quality improvement, more satisfied customers, improved morale, and increased employee motivation. For workers, empowerment offers the chance to do a greater variety of work that is interesting and challenging. Empowerment challenges workers to make the most of their creativity, imagination, knowledge, and skills.

Not every worker *wants* to be empowered, however. Some will resist, wanting only to "put in their 8 hours and go home." Companies that move to an empowerment philosophy will lose about 5 percent of their workforce because some employees simply are unwilling or are unable to make the change. Another 75 percent of the typical workforce will accept empowerment and thrive under it, and the remaining 20 percent will pounce on it eagerly because they want to contribute their talents and their ideas.

Empowerment works best when entrepreneurs:

- *Are confident enough to give workers all the authority and responsibility they can handle.* Initially, this may involve giving workers the power to tackle relatively simple assignments. As their confidence and ability grow, most workers are eager to take on additional responsibility.
- *Play the role of coach and facilitator.* Smart owners empower their workers and then get out of the way so they can do their jobs.
- *Recognize that empowered employees will make mistakes.* The worst thing an owner can do when empowered employees make mistakes is to hunt them down and punish them. That teaches everyone in the company to avoid taking risks and to always play it safe—something no innovative small business can afford.
- *Hire people who can blossom in an empowered environment.* Empowerment is not for everyone. Owners quickly learn that as costly as hiring mistakes are, such errors are even more costly in an empowered environment. Ideal candidates are high-energy self-starters who enjoy the opportunity to grow and enhance their skills.
- *Train workers continuously to upgrade their skills.* Empowerment demands more of workers than traditional work methods. Managers are asking workers to solve problems and make decisions they have never made before. To handle these problems well, workers need training, especially in effective problem-solving techniques, communication, teamwork, and technical skills.
- *Trust workers to do their jobs.* Once workers are trained to do their jobs, owners must learn to trust them to assume responsibility for their jobs. After all, they are the real experts; they face the problems and challenges every day.
- *Listen to workers when they have ideas, solutions, or suggestions.* Because they are the experts on the job, employees often come up with incredibly insightful, innovative ideas for improving them—*if* entrepreneurs give them the chance. Surveying employees, for example, can become a critical part of companies' efforts to bolster employees' commitment

to their jobs, a concept called **employee engagement.** Engaged workers are more willing to help bosses and coworkers solve problems, take initiative, promote the company outside of work, and offer ideas for improving the company. Failing to acknowledge or act on employees' ideas sends them a clear message: Your ideas really don't count.

■ *Recognize workers' contributions.* One of the most important tasks an entrepreneur can perform is to recognize positive employee performance. In *The Carrot Principle*, authors Adrian Gostick and Chester Elton say that recognition must be frequent, specific and timely, and, of course, deserved.[71] Some businesses reward workers with monetary awards; others rely on recognition and praise; still others use a combination of money and praise. Whatever system an owner chooses, the key to keeping a steady flow of ideas, improvements, suggestions, and solutions is to recognize the people who supply them.

ENTREPRENEURIAL
Profile

Container Store and Build-A-Bear

At the Container Store, a chain of retail stores that sell a complete line of storage and organization products and is a frequent resident on *Fortune*'s "Best Companies to Work For" list, founder Kip Tindell encourages store managers to recognize employees who do outstanding work. Brian Edison, manager of a Container Store near Dallas, Texas, puts handwritten sticky notes of congratulations for jobs well done on employees' lockers. At Build-A-Bear, a chain of retail stores that allows kids (and adults) to build their own stuffed animals, managers hand out handwritten "Atta-bear" notes of recognition when employees excel at their jobs. These spontaneous, real-time rewards have special meaning to the employees who receive them.[72]

■ *Share information with workers.* For empowerment to succeed, entrepreneurs must make sure workers get adequate information, the raw material for good decision making. Some companies have gone beyond sharing information to embrace **open-book management,** in which employees have access to *all* of a company's records, including its financial statements. The goal of open-book management is to enable employees to understand why they need to raise productivity, improve quality, cut costs, and improve customer service. Under open-book management, employees:

  ■ Review and learn to understand the company's financial statements and other critical numbers in measuring its performance.
  ■ Learn that a significant part of their jobs is making sure those critical numbers move in the right direction.
  ■ Have a direct stake in the company's success through profit sharing, ESOPs, or performance-based bonuses.

ENTREPRENEURIAL
Profile

Anthony and Elizabeth Wilder: Anthony Wilder Design/Build

At Anthony Wilder Design/Build, a residential architecture and construction company in Cabin John, Maryland, copreneurs Anthony and Elizabeth Wilder practice open-book management with their 30 employees. The Wilders teach their employees how to read the company's financial and operating reports so that they can understand how their work and their department's work directly affects the firm's financial performance. The Wilders also changed the incentive system they use so that every quarter employees receive a portion of the company's net income rather than bonuses for their individual performances. Before, says Elizabeth, "they didn't have a stake in the outcome. Now they can feel it, see it, quantify it." Every month, employees meet for breakfast to discuss business and to brainstorm ways to improve the company's performance.[73]

Job Design

A recent survey by the Conference Board shows that only 45 percent of employees are satisfied with their jobs, a significant decrease from 61 percent in 1987. In addition, only 36 percent of workers under the age of 25 say they are satisfied. The survey also reports that 51 percent of workers find their jobs interesting, down from 70 percent in 1987.[74] Managers have learned that the job itself and the way it is designed can make it more interesting and can be a source of satisfaction and motivation for workers. During the industrial age, work was organized on the

At Anthony Wilder Design/Build, copreneurs Anthony and Elizabeth Wilder practice open-book management with their 30 employees.

Source: Anthony Wilder Design/ Build, Inc.

principle of **job simplification**, which involves breaking the work down into its simplest form and standardizing each task. Assembly line operations are based on job simplification. The scope of workers' jobs is extremely narrow, resulting in impersonal, monotonous, and boring work that creates little challenge or motivation for workers. The result is apathetic, unmotivated workers who care little about quality, customers, or costs.

To break this destructive cycle, some companies have redesigned workers' jobs. The following strategies are common: job enlargement, job rotation, job enrichment, flextime, job sharing, and flexplace.

Job enlargement (or **horizontal job loading**) adds more tasks to a job to broaden its scope. For instance, rather than an employee simply mounting four screws in computers coming down an assembly line, a worker might assemble, install, and test the entire motherboard (perhaps as part of a team). The idea is to make the job more varied and to allow employees to perform a more complete unit of work.

Job rotation involves cross-training employees so they can move from one job in the company to others, giving them a greater number and variety of tasks to perform. As employees learn other jobs within an organization, both their skills and their understanding of the company's purpose and processes rise. Cross-trained workers are more valuable because they give a company the flexibility to shift workers from low-demand jobs to those where they are most needed. As an incentive for workers to learn to perform other jobs within an operation, some companies offer skill-based pay, a system under which the more skills workers acquire, the more they earn.

Job enrichment (or **vertical job loading**) involves building motivators into a job by increasing the planning, decision making, organizing, and controlling functions—traditionally managerial tasks—workers perform. The idea is to make every employee a manager—at least a manager of his or her own job.

To enrich employees' jobs, a business owner must build five core characteristics into them:

- *Skill variety* is the degree to which a job requires a variety of different skills, talents, and activities from the worker. Does the job require the worker to perform a variety of tasks that demand a variety of skills and abilities, or does it force him to perform the same task repeatedly?
- *Task identity* is the degree to which a job allows the worker to complete a whole or identifiable piece of work. Does the employee build an entire piece of furniture (perhaps as part of a team), or does he merely attach four screws?
- *Task significance* is the degree to which a job substantially influences the lives or work of others—employees or final customers. Does the employee get to deal with customers, either internal or external? One effective way to establish task significance is to put employees in touch with customers so they can see how customers use the product or service they make.
- *Autonomy* is the degree to which a job gives a worker the freedom, independence, and discretion in planning and performing tasks. Does the employee make decisions affecting his work, or must he rely on someone else (e.g., the owner, a manager, or a supervisor) to "call the shots?"

- *Feedback* is the degree to which a job gives the worker direct, timely information about the quality of his performance. Does the job give employees feedback about the quality of their work or does the product (and all information about it) simply disappear after it leaves the worker's station?

A study conducted by researchers at the University of New Hampshire and the Bureau of Labor Statistics concludes that employees of companies that use job enrichment principles are more satisfied than those who work in jobs designed using principles of simplification.[75]

Flextime is an arrangement under which employees work a normal number of hours but have flexibility about when they start and stop work. A recent study by the Families and Work Institute reports that 86 percent of employees say that a job that gives them the flexibility to balance work and family life is either very or extremely important.[76] Most flextime arrangements require employees to build their work schedules around a set of "core hours"—such as 10 A.M. to 2 P.M., but give them the freedom to set their schedules outside of those core hours. For instance, one worker might choose to come in at 7 A.M. and leave at 3 P.M. to attend her son's soccer game, and another may work from 11 A.M. to 7 P.M. Flextime not only raises worker morale, but it also makes it easier for companies to attract high-quality young workers who want rewarding careers without sacrificing their lifestyles. In addition, companies using flextime schedules experience higher levels of employee engagement and lower levels of tardiness, turnover, and absenteeism.

ENTREPRENEURIAL
Profile
Sarah Novotny: Blue Gecko

Blue Gecko, a Seattle-based company that provides database services and promises its customers a response to an emergency within 30 minutes no matter the time of day, uses technology to give its employees the flexibility to set their work schedules and locations. "Most of our work requires only an Internet connection and focus," says cofounder Sarah Novotny. Offering flextime helps her employees to keep their work and their lives in balance and to meet the company's 30-minute pledge to its customers. It also gives her company access to a larger pool of more qualified applicants.[77]

Flextime is becoming an increasingly popular job design strategy. A recent survey by Families and Work Institute found that 79 percent of the nation's workers have flexible schedules, up from 68 percent in 1998.[78] The number of companies using flextime is likely to continue to grow as companies find recruiting capable, qualified full-time workers more difficult and as technology makes working from a dedicated office space less important. Research shows that when considering job offers, candidates, particularly members of Generation Y, weigh heavily the flexibility of the work schedule companies offer.

Job sharing is a work arrangement in which two or more people share a single full-time job. For instance, two college students might share the same 40-hour-a-week job, one working mornings and the other working afternoons. Salary and benefits are prorated between the workers sharing a job. Because job sharing is a simple solution to the growing challenge of work–life balance, it is becoming more popular. Companies already using it are finding it easier to recruit and retain qualified workers. "Employers get the combined strengths of two people, but they only have to pay for one," says one hotel sales manager, herself a job sharer.[79]

Flexplace is a work arrangement in which employees work at a place other than the traditional office, such as a satellite branch closer to their homes or, in many cases, at home. Flexplace is an easy job design strategy for companies to use because of **telecommuting**. Using modern communication technologies such as iPads, smartphones, texting, e-mail, and laptop computers, employees have more flexibility in choosing where they work. Today, it is quite simple for workers to connect electronically to their workplaces (and to all of the people and the information there) from practically anywhere on the planet.

ENTREPRENEURIAL
Profile
Barfield, Murphy, Shank, and Smith

Employees at Barfield, Murphy, Shank, and Smith (BMSS), an accounting firm in Birmingham, Alabama, enjoy the benefits of flextime schedules, and many of them also telecommute. Jaclyn Collins, who has worked for the company since 2000, began telecommuting from her home office (which BMSS set up) in 2008 when her husband took a job in a community outside of Birmingham. During the hectic tax season, BMSS provides a valet, who runs errands for employees, and arranges for a laundry service to make pickups and deliveries twice a week. The result: an extremely low employee turnover rate of just 2 to 3 percent annually.[80]

According to a study by information technology provider CDW-G, 36 percent of private sector companies allow telecommuting, and 14 percent of private sector employees are telecommuters.[81] Telecommuting employees get the flexibility they seek and benefit from reduced commuting times and expenses, not to mention a less expensive wardrobe (bathrobes and bunny slippers compared to business suits and wingtips or high heels). Companies reap many benefits as well, including improved employee morale, less absenteeism, lower turnover, higher productivity, and more satisfied, more loyal employees. Studies show that telecommuting can reduce employee turnover by 20 percent and increase productivity between 15 and 20 percent.[82] Cisco Systems, a software provider, says that employees who telecommute show increased productivity, higher quality work, and more job satisfaction as a result of their ability to control their work–life balance.[83]

Before implementing telecommuting, entrepreneurs must address the following important issues:

- Does the nature of the work fit telecommuting? Obviously, some jobs are better suited for telecommuting than others.
- Have you selected the right employees for telecommuting? Telecommuting is not suitable for every job or for every worker. Experienced managers say that employees who handle it best are experienced workers who know their jobs well, are self-disciplined, and are good communicators.
- Can you monitor compliance with federal wage and hour laws for telecommuters? Generally, employers must keep the same employment records for telecommuters that they do for traditional office workers.
- Have you provided the necessary computer, communications, and ergonomically designed office equipment for employees to work offsite? Trying to "make do" with substandard equipment creates problems and frustration and undermines any telecommuting effort from the outset.
- Are you adequately insured? Employers should be sure that the telecommuting equipment that employees use in their homes is covered under their insurance policies.
- Can you keep in touch? Telecommuting works well as long as long-distance employees stay in touch with headquarters.
- Have you created an equitable telecommuting policy that defines under what conditions telecommuting is acceptable? One danger of telecommuting is that it can create resentment among employees who remain office-bound.

Rewards and Compensation

The rewards an employee receives from the job itself are intrinsic, but managers have a wide variety of extrinsic rewards to motivate workers at their disposal. The key to using rewards to motivate involves tailoring the reward system to the needs and characteristics of the workers. Effective reward systems tap into the values and issues that are important to people. Smart entrepreneurs take the time to learn what makes their employees "tick" and then build their reward system around those motivational factors. For instance, a technician making $30,000 a year may consider a chance to earn a $5,000 bonus to be a powerful motivator; an executive earning $200,000 a year may not.

Research by Globoforce, a Boston-based company that specializes in rewards and incentives, shows that small, frequent awards are more effective than periodic cash bonuses, which is good news for small companies that cannot always afford financial rewards. The study suggests that 80 to 90 percent of a company's employees should get some type of reward every year and that every week a company should be giving rewards to 5 percent of its employees (a concept known as continuous reinforcement). "Small awards all the time are a way to constantly touch people," he says. Jennifer Lepird, who works in the human resources department at software developer Intuit, recently spent several weeks and many long days integrating into Intuit's salary structure the employees at a company that Intuit had purchased. Her manager sent her a congratulatory e-mail thanking her for her quality work and a gift certificate worth $200. Lepird was thrilled. "The fact that somebody took the time to recognize the effort made the long hours just melt away," she says.[84]

One of the most popular rewards is money. Cash is an effective motivator—up to a point; its effects tend to be short-term. Many companies have moved to **pay-for-performance compensation systems**, in which employees' pay depends on how well they perform their jobs. In other words, extra productivity equals extra pay. By linking employees' compensation directly to the company's financial performance, an entrepreneur increases the likelihood that workers will achieve performance

Source: King Features Syndicate

targets that are in their best interest and in the company's best interest. A common application of the pay-for-performance concept is a **profit-sharing system**, in which a company shares a portion of its profit with the employees who work to produce it.

ENTREPRENEURIAL
Profile

Mike Rydin: Heavy Construction Systems Specialists

Heavy Construction Systems Specialists (HCSS), a company based in Sugarland, Texas, that develops software for the construction industry, has a profit-sharing system for its 106 employees as well as an employee stock purchase plan. In a recent year, CEO Mike Rydin says that HCSS employees received 22 percent of their base salaries through the profit-sharing system. All 106 employees also participate in the stock purchase plan, through which they own 30 percent of the company.[85]

Pay-for-performance systems work only when employees see a clear correlation between their performance and their pay. This offers an advantage for small companies when the employees can see a clearer impact their performance has on the company's profitability and ultimate success compared to their counterparts at large corporations. To be successful, however, pay-for-performance systems should meet the following criteria:

- *Performance-based.* Employees' incentive pay must be clearly and closely linked to their performances.
- *Relevant.* Entrepreneurs must set up the system so that employees see the connection between what they do every day on the job—selling to customers, producing a product, or anything else—and the rewards they receive under the system.
- *Simple.* The system must be simple enough so that employees understand and trust it. Complex systems that employees have difficulty understanding do not produce the desired results.
- *Equitable.* Employees must consider the system fair.
- *Inclusive.* The system should be inclusive. Entrepreneurs are finding creative ways to reward all employees, no matter what their jobs might be.

■ *Timely.* The company should make timely payouts to employees. A single annual payout is ineffective—employees have long since forgotten what they did to earn the incentive pay. The closer a reward payment is to the action that prompted it, the more effective it will be.

Money is not the only motivator entrepreneurs have at their disposal. Nonfinancial incentives can be more important sources of employee motivation. With a little creativity, small businesses can provide meaningful rewards that motivate employees without breaking the bank. Often the most meaningful motivating factors are the simplest—and least costly—ones, such as praise, recognition, respect, feedback, job security, and promotions. When an employee has done an exceptional job, an entrepreneur should be the first to recognize that accomplishment and to say "thank you." Praise is a simple and powerful motivational tool. "Praise is the most powerful driver of performance known to mankind," says Bob Nelson, a workplace consultant.[86] People enjoy getting praise and recognition; it is just human nature. As Mark Twain once said, "I can live for two months on a good compliment."

ENTREPRENEURIAL

Profile

Claire Prager: The Cheesecake Factory

The Cheesecake Factory, the Calabasas, California-based restaurant chain, produces a newsletter, "Slice," that recognizes employees' exceptional performances by including stories on workers who go the extra mile to take care of their customers or other employees. A recent issue told the story of an employee who drove to Los Angeles International Airport to deliver a credit card to a customer who had left it in the restaurant. Claire Prager, the company's talent manager, says that the employees who are featured in the newsletter become celebrities in their locations and that the stories are an important part of the company's culture, often inspiring other employees to go the extra mile.[87]

One sure way to kill high performance is failing to recognize the performance and the employees responsible for it. Failing to praise good work eventually conveys the message that the owner either doesn't care about exceptional performance or cannot distinguish between good work and poor work. In either case, through inaction, the manager destroys employees' motivation to excel.

Rewards do *not* have to be expensive to be effective, but they should be creative and should have a direct link to employee performance. Consider how the following rewards for exceptional performance both recognize the employee's contribution and build a positive organizational culture:

■ At Nugget Market, a supermarket chain based in Woodland, California, top managers showed their appreciation for employees' hard work by washing associates' cars.[88]

■ The AAA Fair Credit Foundation in Salt Lake City, Utah, involves all of its employees in rewarding excellent performance. Employees recognize the extra efforts and special accomplishments of their coworkers by recommending them for "Dollar Days." When an employee earns eight Dollar Days, he or she cashes them in for a day off.[89]

■ At Adec Group, a Greenville, South Carolina-based company that manages communications across multiple channels for large companies, owner June Wilcox treats employees to company-paid movie outings and baseball games—during office hours—when they complete challenging assignments.

Whatever system of rewards they use, entrepreneurs will be most successful if they match rewards to employees' interests and tastes. For instance, the ideal reward for one employee might be tickets to a sports event; to another, it might be tickets to a theatrical performance. The better entrepreneurs know their employees' interests and tastes, the more effective they will be at matching rewards with performance.

In the future, entrepreneurs will rely more on nonmonetary rewards—praise, recognition, letters of commendation, and others—to create a work environment where employees take pride in their work. Under this system, employees enjoy what they do and find their work challenging, exciting, and rewarding. The benefit to the company is that these employees are more likely to act like owners of the business themselves. The goal of nonmonetary rewards is to let employees know that every person is important and that the company notices, appreciates, and recognizes excellent performance.

Performance Feedback

Entrepreneurs not only must motivate employees to excel in their jobs, but also focus employees' efforts on the right business targets. Providing feedback on progress toward those targets can be a

Creating a Winning Workplace

John Sullivan, a store director for Nugget Market, a family-owned grocery chain founded in 1926 and based in Woodland, California, is proud that his employer is on *Fortune*'s list of the "100 Best Companies to Work For." "We have a wonderful relationship in the store," says Sullivan. "We really are a family. I know [my coworkers'] kids, their husbands and wives, I know their dogs' and cats' names, what classes they are taking in school and whether they got a flat on the way to work. The nice thing about this company is that the associates are empowered to do what it takes to make their guests (customers) happy and meet their needs. I'm excited to come to work every day."

Entrepreneurs strive to create a work environment that nurtures a culture like the one at Nugget Market. Not all are successful, but the ones who are find that a winning workplace gives their companies a significant competitive advantage. What are these companies doing right? The following lessons from the Street-Smart Entrepreneur offer meaningful insight into creating a winning workplace:

- *Select the right employees.* Mike's Carwash, based in Indianapolis, Indiana, uses an intense screening process, hiring just 1 out of 100 applicants. Candidates take two tests, one that measures math aptitude and one that provides insight into their personalities. At least two employees interview every candidate and look for strong logical and social skills as well as an attitude of customer service.

- *Provide stable employment.* Winning workplaces do everything they can to avoid layoffs. Doing so creates an implied contract of trust with employees. Wegman's, rated as one of the best grocery chains in the country, has never had a layoff since its founding in 1916. Employees return the company's loyalty by sticking around. Eleven percent of the Rochester, New York-based company's employees have tenure of 15 or more years.

- *Give employees incentives to stay.* High employee turnover rates are costly and result in lost potential and "brain drain." To keep their employees, a growing number of small companies share their financial success with their workers through profit-sharing plans or employee stock ownership plans (ESOPs). Michael and Jack Kennedy, owners of Railroad Associates Corporation, a company in

Hershey, Pennsylvania, that repairs railways, established an ESOP shortly after launching the company in 2000. Today, nonmanagerial employees own 40 percent of the company's stock and can qualify for bonuses of up to 50 percent of their regular pay for providing superior customer service, completing projects on time, and maintaining a good safety record. A recent study by the Cass Business School in London concludes that employee-owned businesses create jobs faster and typically outperform companies in which employees have no stake.

- *Offer training and advancement opportunities.* Winning workplaces invest in their employees. At Mike's Carwash, employees receive regular training on techniques for providing outstanding customer service. Every week, employees watch short videos that offer customer service tips and other job-related education and updates on company news and events. The company also offers tuition reimbursement of up to $2,500 annually for employees who want to continue their education.

- *Provide flexible work schedules.* Many employees face challenges as they attempt to balance the demands of work, family, and activities. Companies that provide flexible work schedules have an edge when it comes to attracting quality employees. At A Speaker for You, an event planning company in Louisville, Kentucky, employees set their own work and vacation schedules. "We have found that giving this kind of freedom to employees brings enhanced rewards to the company," says the company's president, Tim Green. "Employees have proven trustworthy over a long period of time. That is why we continue to grow."

- *Rely on innovative job design and participative management.* Many employees, especially young workers, want to join companies that offer a culture of participative management rather than a top-down, autocratic style. At Railroad Associates, owners Michael and Jack Kennedy have created a very flat organization structure with virtually no middle managers. They delegate the authority and the responsibility for making decisions and solving problems directly to their employees. The Kennedys also make sure that workers get plenty of training, in the classroom, online, and on the job, so that they are able to make good decisions.

Sources: Based on Kelly K. Spors, "Top Workplaces 2009," *Wall Street Journal*, September 28, 2009, pp. R4, R5; Ellen Galinsky, Shanny L. Peer, and Sheila Eby, *When Work Works: 2009 Guide to Bold New Ideas for*

Making Work Work, Families and Work Institute, 2009, pp. 37–38; "I Work for One of the 10 Best Companies," *Fortune*, 2010, *http://money.cnn.com/galleries/2010/fortune/1001/gallery.Bestcompanies_employees.fortune/5.html*; Sam Potter, "Employee Involvement Gets the Best," *Kipp Report*, September 7, 2010, *www.kippreport.com/2010/09/employee-involvement-gets-the-best/*.

powerful motivating force in a company. To strengthen the link between the entrepreneur's vision for the company and its operations, he or she must build a series of specific performance measures that serve as periodic monitoring points. For each critical element of the organization's performance—quality, financial performance, market position, productivity, employee development—he or she should develop specific measures that connect daily operational responsibilities with the company's overall strategic direction. These measures establish the benchmarks for measuring employees' performance and the company's progress. The adage "what gets measured and monitored gets done" is true in most organizations. An entrepreneur defines for everyone in the company what is most important by connecting the company's long-term strategy to its daily operations and measuring performance.

Providing feedback implies that entrepreneurs have established meaningful targets that serve as standards of performance for them, their employees, and the company as a whole. One characteristic successful people have in common is that they set goals and objectives—usually challenging ones—for themselves. Entrepreneurs are no different. Successful entrepreneurs usually set targets for performance that make them stretch to achieve, and then they encourage their employees to do the same. The result is that they keep their companies constantly moving forward.

For feedback to serve as a motivating force in a business requires entrepreneurs to follow the procedure illustrated in Figure 3, the feedback loop.

DECIDING WHAT TO MEASURE. The first step in the feedback loop is deciding what to measure. Every business has a set of numbers that are critical to its success, and these "critical numbers" are what entrepreneurs should focus on. Obvious critical numbers include sales, profits, profit margins, cash flow, and other standard financial measures. However, supporting these measurements is an additional set of critical numbers that are unique to a company's operations. In most cases, these are the numbers that actually drive profits, cash flow, and other financial measures—they are the company's *real* critical numbers.

DECIDING HOW TO MEASURE. Once an entrepreneur identifies his or her company's critical numbers, he or she must decide how to measure them. In some cases, identifying the critical

FIGURE 3
The Feedback Loop

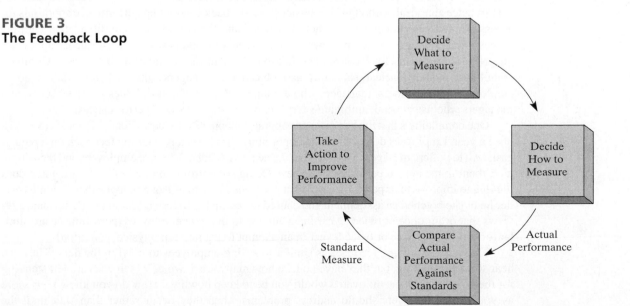

numbers defines the measurements owners must make, and measuring them simply becomes a matter of collecting and analyzing data. In other cases, the method of measurement is not as obvious—or as tangible. For instance, in some businesses social responsibility is a key factor, but how should managers measure their company's performance on such an intangible concept? One of the best ways to develop methods for measuring such factors is to use brainstorming sessions involving employees, customers, and even outsiders. For example, one company used this technique to develop a "fun index," which used the results of an employee survey to measure how much fun employees are having at work. The index is an indication of how satisfied they are with their work, the company, and their managers.

COMPARING ACTUAL PERFORMANCE AGAINST STANDARDS. In this stage of the feedback loop, the goal is to look for variances *in either direction* from company performance standards. In other words, opportunities to improve performance arise when there is a gap between "what should be" and "what is." The most serious deviations usually are those in which actual performance falls far below the standard. Entrepreneurs must focus their efforts on figuring out why actual performance is substandard. The goal is *not* to hunt down the guilty party (or parties) for punishment but to discover the cause of the poor performance and fix it. Managers should not ignore deviations in the other direction, however. If actual performance consistently exceeds the company's standards, it may be an indication that the standards are set too low.

TAKING ACTION TO IMPROVE PERFORMANCE. When managers or employees detect a performance gap, their next challenge is to decide on a course of action that will eliminate it. Typically, several suitable alternatives to solving a performance problem exist; the key is finding an acceptable solution that solves the problem quickly, efficiently, and effectively.

Performance Appraisal

One of the most common methods of providing feedback on employee performance is through **performance appraisal**, the process of evaluating an employee's actual performance against desired performance standards. Most performance appraisal programs strive to accomplish three goals:

1. To give employees feedback about how they are performing, which can be an important source of motivation
2. To provide entrepreneurs and employees the opportunity to create a plan for developing employee skills and abilities and for improving their performance
3. To establish a basis for determining promotions and salary increases

The primary purpose of performance appraisals is to encourage and to help employees improve their performance. Unfortunately, they can turn into uncomfortable confrontations that do nothing more than upset the employees, aggravate the entrepreneur, and destroy trust and morale. This may occur because the entrepreneur does not understand how to conduct an effective performance appraisal. Although U.S. businesses have been conducting performance appraisals for at least 75 years, most companies, their managers, and their employees are dissatisfied with the process. A survey by Salary.com shows that 60 percent of workers say that performance appraisals do not produce any useful feedback and fail to help them set meaningful objectives.[90] Common complaints include unclear standards and objectives, managers who lack information about employees' performances, managers who are unprepared or who lack honesty and sincerity, and managers who use general, ambiguous terms to describe employees' performances.

One complaint is that the performance appraisal happens only periodically: in most cases, just once a year. Employees do not have the opportunity to receive any ongoing feedback on a regular basis. All too often, managers save up all of the negative feedback to give employees and then dump it on them in the annual performance review. Doing so destroys employees' motivation and does *nothing* to improve their performance. What good does it do to tell an employee that 6 months earlier he or she botched an assignment and caused the company to lose a customer? Performance reviews that occur once or twice a year in an attempt to improve employees' performance are similar to working out once or twice a year in an attempt to get into top physical condition!

The lack of ongoing feedback is similar to asking employees to bowl in the dark. They can hear some pins falling, but they have no idea how many are down or which ones are left standing for the next frame. How motivated would you be to keep bowling? How do you know your score as you bowl? Managers should address problems when they occur rather than wait until the

▶ E N T R E P R E N E U R S H I P **IN ACTION** ▶

Spying or Protecting His Investment?

Ryan Elmore, owner of Pepper Jack's Neighborhood Grill, a neighborhood restaurant in Erie, Colorado, was confident that his employees were hard at work when he was away from the business. However, when Elmore installed a video surveillance system that allowed him to monitor the action in his restaurant online, he was shocked at what he saw. The restaurant manager who was on duty went home a few minutes after Elmore left, and cooks took shortcuts when they made the restaurant's signature fettuccine Alfredo. Employees took extended breaks, sat at tables and sent text messages, and doled out free dinners to their friends. "I couldn't believe it," says Elmore. "You may trust your employees, but you don't know what happens when you walk out the door."

Today, a networked video system is in place, and Elmore's 20 employees know that he is watching their performances even when he is away from the restaurant. Elmore can remotely view a customer's cash register receipt and call up the video of that transaction. He can determine whether employees are cleaning the restaurant when they are supposed to and whether they are smiling at customers and greeting them appropriately. He knows when meals arrive late at diners' tables and can detect employees who are eating unauthorized meals. Installation of the video system cost Elmore just $850 and a $160 monthly online subscription fee that gives him unlimited access to both live and archived video. The investment paid off quickly. While reviewing video, Elmore and his business partner, his wife Janel, noticed that the restaurant frequently was overstaffed. Adjusting employees' schedules to cover the busiest times alone saved the company $50,000 per year. The restaurant's food costs also declined 3 percent because servers stopped giving away

free meals to their friends. Overall, Elmore was able to reduce the company's annual operating costs by $100,000. "The technology has more than paid for itself," he says.

Elmore admits that, initially, he felt guilty about "spying" on his employees, but the results have diminished that concern. "I want to know where every dollar is going," he says. "This is my life. Everything I have is riding on this." Remote monitoring of their business gives the Elmores the ability to have more free time away from the restaurant without surrendering control over it. Elmore credits the video system with helping him identify and reward one of his best workers. While watching videos, he noticed that one kitchen staff was cleaning more often than usual. When he investigated, Elmore discovered that the kitchen manager had created a contest to motivate her employees. Elmore was impressed and promoted her.

1. How would you feel about working for a business that uses a video system to monitor employees at work? Explain. Why do business owners use monitoring systems?
2. "Most employees do not like to be monitored, and it may cause some resentment," says one employment attorney. Do you agree? Explain.
3. Use the Web to research video monitoring of employees and prepare a list of at least five recommendations to help companies avoid legal problems.
4. Can you suggest other ways besides video monitoring that employers like Elmore can use to encourage employees to do their jobs well when the boss is away?

Source: Based on Jennifer Alsever, "Being Big Brother," *FSB*, October 2008, pp. 43–45.

performance appraisal session. Continuous feedback, both positive and negative, is a much more effective way to improve employees' performance and to increase their motivation than once-a-year feedback in a performance appraisal session.

Performance appraisals require planning and preparation on the entrepreneur's part. The following guidelines can help an entrepreneur create a performance appraisal system that actually works:

- *Link the employee performance criteria to the job description discussed earlier in this chapter.* To evaluate an employee's performance effectively, a manager must fully understand the responsibilities of the employee's position.
- *Establish meaningful, job-related, measurable, and results-oriented performance criteria.* The criteria should describe behaviors and actions, not traits and characteristics. What kind of behavior constitutes a solid performance in the job? Criteria that are quantifiable, such as customer satisfaction scores, the percentage of on-time shipments, and other specific measurements, rather than subjective criteria, such as leadership potential, initiative, and problem-solving ability, form the foundation of a meaningful performance evaluation.

■ *Prepare for the appraisal session by outlining the key points you want to cover with employees.* Important points to include are employees' strengths and weaknesses and developing a plan for improving their performance.

■ *Invite employees to provide an evaluation of their own job performance based on the performance criteria.* In one small company, workers rate themselves on a one-to-five scale in categories of job-related behavior and skills as part of the performance appraisal system. Then they meet with their supervisor to compare their evaluations with those of their supervisor and discuss them.

■ *Be specific.* One of the most common complaints employees have about the appraisal process is that managers' comments are too general to be of any value. Offer the employees specific examples of their desirable or undesirable behavior.

■ *Keep a record of employees' critical incidents—both positive and negative.* The most productive evaluations are those based on managers' direct observation of their employees' on-the-job performance. These records also can be vital in case legal problems arise.

■ *Discuss employees' strengths and weaknesses.* An appraisal session is not the time to "unload" about everything employees have done wrong over the past year. Use it as an opportunity to design a plan for improvement and to recognize employees' strengths, efforts, and achievements.

■ *Incorporate employees' goals into the appraisal.* Ideally, the standard against which to measure employees' performance is the goals they have played a role in setting. Workers are more likely to be motivated to achieve—and buy into—goals that they have helped establish.

■ *Keep the evaluation constructive.* Avoid the tendency to belittle employees. Do not dwell on past failures. Instead, point out specific things they should do better and help them develop meaningful goals for the future and a strategy for getting there.

■ *Praise good work.* Avoid focusing only on what employees do wrong. Take the time to express your appreciation for hard work and solid accomplishments.

■ *Focus on behaviors, actions, and results.* Problems arise when managers move away from tangible results and actions and begin to critique employees' abilities and attitudes. Such criticism creates a negative tone for the appraisal session and undercuts its primary purpose.

■ *Avoid surprises.* If entrepreneurs are doing their jobs well, performance appraisals should contain no surprises for employees or the owner. The ideal time to correct improper behavior or slumping performance is when it happens, not months later. Managers should provide employees with continuous feedback on their performance and use the appraisal session to keep employees on the right track.

■ *Plan for the future.* Smart entrepreneurs use appraisal sessions as gateways to workers' future success. They spend only about 20 percent of the time discussing past performance; they use the remaining 80 percent of the time developing goals, objectives, and a plan for the future.

ENTREPRENEURIAL
Profile

Brian Roth: Trufast

Brian Roth, CEO of Trufast, a small maker of fasteners located in Bryan, Ohio, realized that his company's performance appraisal process was ineffective. "The only thing the review did was cover the previous 2 weeks of performance," he says. "Basically, it was worthless." Roth revamped the entire process to focus on more frequent feedback and rewards. At the end of every quarter, all 80 of the company's employees meet with their supervisors, who assign up to 25 points in each of four areas: initiative, aptitude, flexibility, and attitude. Employees who score at least 70 points earn incentive pay; the higher their scores, the greater the bonus amount. More than 90 percent of Trufast's employees receive some bonus. Roth says that the program has reduced employee turnover and produces a return on investment of between 15 and 18 percent. "My employees keep asking me when the next review is and what they need to know to score well on it," says Roth. "That tells me all I need to know."[91]

Some companies allow employees to evaluate each other's performance in **peer reviews** or evaluate their boss's performance in **upward feedback**. These are aspects of a technique called **360-degree feedback**. Peer appraisals can be especially useful because an employee's coworkers see his or her on-the-job performance every day. As a result, peer evaluations tend to be more accurate and more valid than those of some managers. In addition, they may capture behavior that managers miss. Disadvantages of peer appraisals include the following: potential retaliation against coworkers who criticize, the possibility that appraisals will be reduced to "popularity contests," and the refusal of some workers to offer any criticism because they feel uncomfortable evaluating others. Some bosses using upward feedback report similar problems, including personal attacks and extreme evaluations by vengeful subordinates.

Regardless of the technique, employee feedback should be honest, clear, and respectful. Entrepreneurs will benefit from developing effective feedback skills as they grow the business and delegate additional responsibilities to employees.

Chapter Review

1. Explain the challenges involved in the entrepreneur's role as leader and what it takes to be a successful leader.
   - Leadership is the process of influencing and inspiring others to work to achieve a common goal and then giving them the power and the freedom to achieve it.
   - Management and leadership are not the same; yet both are essential to a small company's success. Leadership without management is unbridled; management without leadership is uninspired. Leadership gets a small business going; management keeps it going.
2. Describe the importance of hiring the right employees and how to avoid making hiring mistakes.
   - The decision to hire a new employee is an important one for every business, but its impact is magnified many times in a small company. Every "new hire" an entrepreneur makes determines the heights to which the company can climb or the depths to which it will plunge.
   - To avoid making hiring mistakes, entrepreneurs should develop meaningful job descriptions and job specifications, plan and conduct an effective interview, and check references before hiring any employee.
3. Explain how to build the kind of company culture and structure to support the company's mission and goals and to motivate employees to achieve them.
   - Company culture is the distinctive, unwritten code of conduct that governs the behavior, attitudes, relationships, and style of an organization. Culture arises from an entrepreneur's consistent and relentless pursuit of a set of core values that everyone in the company can believe in. Small companies' flexible structures can be a major competitive weapon.
4. Understand the potential barriers to effective communication and describe how to overcome them.
   - Research shows that managers spend about 80 percent of their time in some form of communication; yet their attempts at communicating sometimes go wrong. Several barriers to effective communication include: managers and employees don't always feel free to say what they really mean; ambiguity blocks real communication; information overload causes the message to get lost; selective listening interferes with the communication process; defense mechanisms block a message; and conflicting verbal and nonverbal messages confuse listeners.
   - To become more effective communicators, entrepreneurs should: clarify their messages before attempting to communicate them; use face-to-face communication whenever possible; be empathetic; match their messages to their audiences; be organized; encourage feedback; tell the truth; and not be afraid to tell employees about the business, its performance, and the forces that affect it.
5. Discuss the ways in which entrepreneurs can motivate their workers to higher levels of performance.
   - Motivation is the degree of effort an employee exerts to accomplish a task; it shows up as excitement about work. Four important tools of motivation are empowerment, job design, rewards and compensation, and feedback.
   - Empowerment involves giving workers at every level of the organization the power, the freedom, and the responsibility to control their own work, to make decisions, and to take action to meet the company's objectives.

- Job design techniques for enhancing employee motivation include job enlargement, job rotation, job enrichment, flextime, job sharing, and flexplace.
- Money is an important motivator for many workers, but not the only one. The key to using rewards such as recognition and praise to motivate involves tailoring them to the needs and characteristics of the workers.
- Giving employees timely, relevant feedback about their job performance through a performance appraisal system can also be a powerful motivator.

Discussion Questions

1. What is leadership? What is the difference between leadership and management?
2. What behaviors do effective leaders exhibit?
3. Why is it so important for small companies to hire the right employees? What can entrepreneurs do to avoid making hiring mistakes?
4. What is a job description? A job specification? What functions do they serve in the hiring process?
5. Outline the procedure for conducting an effective interview.
6. What are some alternative techniques to traditional interviews?
7. What is company culture? What role does it play in a small company's success? What threats does rapid growth pose for a company's culture?
8. What mistakes do companies make when switching to team-based management? What might companies do to avoid these mistakes? Explain the four stages teams typically experience.

9. What is empowerment? What benefits does it offer workers? The company? What must a small business manager do to make empowerment work in a company?
10. Explain the differences among job simplification, job enlargement, job rotation, and job enrichment. What impact do these different job designs have on workers?
11. Is money the "best" motivator? How do pay-for-performance compensation systems work? What other rewards are available to small business managers to use as motivators? How effective are they?
12. Suppose that a mail-order catalog company selling environmentally friendly products identifies its performance as a socially responsible company as a "critical number" in its success. Suggest some ways for the owner to measure this company's "social responsibility index."
13. What is a performance appraisal? What are the most common mistakes managers make in performance appraisals? What should small business managers do to avoid making those mistakes?

This chapter discusses the importance of leadership, culture, organizational design, staffing, and managing the people who will work in your business. The "Management" section is where these issues are most often addressed within the business plan. This section of the plan captures the key information about your management team, including both its strengths and weaknesses. The management section of the business plan also addresses other personnel issues for your venture.

On the Web

Visit the Companion Web Site at *www.pearsonhighered.com/ scarborough* and review the links associated. You will find resources that address leadership issues, interviewing techniques, employee motivation programs, culture, organizational structure,

and other topics that you may find helpful. These resources may offer additional insight for the human resource and managerial aspects of your business that you may want to incorporate into your business plan.

In the Software

Review the management section of your business plan and make certain that it addresses the important management and personnel issues for your venture. Check to see that your plan includes the relevant concepts. Think about the business culture that you plan to build. Assess the leadership abilities of the current management team. Are additional managers or other positions needed? Have you accounted for new hires and the anticipated expenses associated with adding these employees? Does your plan address factors that will allow you to retain existing employees? How do you plan to motivate employees to achieve high levels of performance?

Endnotes

1. Michael Gold, "Jazzin' CEO," *Manage Smarter*, January 9, 2008, p. 1.
2. Ibid.
3. Francis Huffman, "Taking the Lead," *Entrepreneur*, November 1993, p. 101.
4. Sam Allman, "Leadership vs. Management," *Successful Meetings*, October 2009, p. 12.
5. Matthew E. May, "The 3 C's of Trust," Open Forum, September 24, 2010, *www.openforum.com/idea-hub/topics/the-world/article/the-3-cs-of-trust-matthew-e-may*.
6. "Trust in Managers in Short Supply," Right Management, May 27, 2010, *www.right.com/news-and-events/press-releases/item8361.aspx*.
7. Ryan Underwood, "The CEO Next Door," *Fast Company*, September 2005, pp. 64–66; Jeffrey Pfeffer, "A Field Day for Executives," *Business 2.0*, December 2004, p. 88.
8. Jeffrey Pfeffer, "Executive-in-Chief," *Business 2.0*, March 1, 2005, *http://money.cnn.com/magazines/business2/business2_archive/2005/03/01/8253107/index.htm*.
9. Dave Zielinski, "New Ways to Look at Leadership," *Presentations*, June 2005, pp. 26–33.
10. "What Is Servant Leadership? Ken Blanchard," Greenleaf Center for Servant Leadership, *www.greenleaf.org/whatissl/KenBlanchard.html*.
11. Sam Oches, "It's the Customers, Stupid. Or Is It?" *QSR Magazine*, September 16, 2010, *www.qsrmagazine.com/articles/exclusives/0910/employees-1.phtml*.
12. Chris Penttila, "Hire Away," *Entrepreneur*, June 2007, p. 20.
13. "The Real Cost of Employee Turnover," Rainmaker Group, *www.therainmakergroupinc.com/add.asp?ID=94*.
14. "SurePayroll Main Street Insights: Small Business Owners Wasting Big Money on Hiring Decisions," SurePayroll, June 16, 2009, *www.surepayroll.com/spsite/press/releases/2009/release061609.asp*.
15. David Meyer, "Nine Recruiting and Selection Tips to Ensure Successful Hiring," About.com, *http://humanresources.about.com/od/selectemployees/a/staff_selection_p.htm*.
16. "Hiring Decisions Miss the Mark 50% of the Time," Corporate Executive Board, October 24, 2008, *http://ir.executiveboard.com/phoenix.zhtml?c=113226&p=irol-newsArticle&ID=1205091&highlight=;* "2 Out of 3 Managers Still Fear a Hiring Decision They'll Regret," DDI, March 16, 2009, *www.ddiworld.com/about/pr_releases_en.asp?id=211*.
17. Chris Pentilla, "Talent Scout," *Entrepreneur*, July 2008, p. 19.
18. Kelly K. Spors, "Top Workplaces 2009," *Wall Street Journal*, September 28, 2009, pp. R1, R4.
19. Jennifer Wang, "10 Companies Getting It Right," *Entrepreneur*, March 2010, p. 83.
20. "Most Businesses Use Social Nets for Hiring," *eMarketer*, July 13, 2010, *www.emarketer.com/Article.aspx?R=1007811*.
21. Chris Penttila, "Build a Social Media Hiring Strategy," *Entrepreneur*, July 1, 2009, *www.entrepreneur.com/hiringcenter/article202466.html*.
22. Jennifer J. Salopek, "Recruiters Look to Be Big Man on Campus," *Workforce Management*, September 2010, p. 12.
23. Joel Holland, "More Than What You Paid For," *Entrepreneur*, June 2010, p. 86.
24. Mitra Toossi, "Labor Force Projections to 2016: More Workers in Their Golden Years," *Monthly Labor Review*, November 2007, p. 33.
25. *Staying Ahead of the Curve 2007: The AARP Work and Career Study*, American Association of Retired Persons, September 2008, p. 8.
26. Gary M. Stern, "Hiring Older Workers," *Small Business Review*, February 11, 2007, *http://smallbusinessreview.com/human_resources/hiring_older_workers/index.html*.
27. *The Real Talent Debate: Will Aging Boomers Deplete the Workforce?* WorldatWork, Scottsdale, Arizona, 2007, p. 12.
28. "Innovating Human Resources," *BrainReactions*, January 16, 2007, *www.brainreactions.com/whitepapers/brainreactions_hr_innovation_paper.pdf*, pp. 11–14; Christopher Caggiano, "Recruiting Secrets," *Inc.*, October 1998, pp. 30–42.
29. Amy Barrett, "Making Telecommuting Work," *BusinessWeek*, October 17, 2008, *www.businessweek.com/magazine/content/08_70/s0810048750962.htm?chan=smallbiz_smallbiz+index+page_best+of+small+biz+magazine*.
30. "Survey: Up to 25 Applications Reviewed per Job," *Workforce Management*, September 16, 2010, *www.workforce.com/section/news/article/survey-up-25-applications-reviewed-per-job.php*.
31. "Smart Questions for Your Hiring Manager," *Inc.*, February 2007, p. 47.
32. "Survey: 21 Percent of Job Seekers Dropped After Reference Checks," *Workforce Management*, June 23, 2010, *www.workforce.com/section/news/article/survey-21-percent-job-seekers-dropped-after-reference.php*.
33. Andy Levine, "Dig We Must," *Inc.*, August 2006, p. 97.
34. Dan Heath and Chip Heath, "Hold the Interview," *Fast Company*, June 2009, pp. 51–52.
35. Peter Bregman, "The Interview Question You Should Always Ask," *Harvard Business Publishing*, January 27, 2009, *http://blogs.harvardbusiness.org/cs/2009/01/the_interview_question_you_sho.html*.
36. Ed Frauenheim, "Serious Hiring Keeps Zappos in a Fun Mood," *Workforce Management*, September 14, 2009, p. 20.
37. Ibid.
38. Chris Penttila, "Testing the Waters," *Entrepreneur*, January 2004, pp 72–73.
39. Chris Penttila, "Peering In," *Entrepreneur*, January 2005, pp. 70–71.
40. Spors, "Top Workplaces 2009."
41. Penttila, "Peering In," p. 71.
42. Richard Slawsky, "Reducing Risk: The Search for Reputable Employees," QSRWeb.com, August 9, 2007, *www.qsrweb.com/article.php?id=8390&na=1*.
43. Ibid.
44. Vasanth Sridharan, "22% of Employers Check Your Facebook Profile When They Are Looking to Hire You. That's It?" *Business Insider*, September 11, 2008, *www.businessinsider.com/2008/9/22-of-employers-check-your-facebook-profile-when-they-re-looking-to-hire-you-that-s-it-*.
45. Emily Maltby, "To Find Best Hires, Firms Become Creative," *Wall Street Journal*, November 17, 2009, *http://online.wsj.com/article/SB10001424052748704538404574539971535489470.html*.
46. "Drug Free Work Week," U.S. Department of Labor, *www.dol.gov/asp/programs/drugs/workingpartners/DFWW-Introduction.asp*.
47. McGuire Woods, "But I Have a Prescription! . . . Drug Testing in the Age of Medical Marijuana," *Society of Human Resource Managers*, July 1, 2010, *www.shrm.org/LegalIssues/StateandLocalResources/Pages/ButIHaveaPrescription.aspx*.
48. Jessica Marquez, "Kindness Pays . . . Or Does It?" *Workforce*, June 25, 2007, pp. 40–49.
49. Ibid.
50. Julia Chang, "Balancing Act," *Sales & Marketing Management*, February 2004, p. 16.
51. Spors, "Top Workplaces 2009."
52. "Top Small Company Workplaces," *Inc.*, 2010, *www.inc.com/top-workplaces/2010/profile/dealercom-mark-bonfigli.html*.
53. Jody Urquhart, "Creating a Fun Workplace . . . 13 Ways to Have Fun at Work," I Do Inspire, *www.idoinspire.com/?q=node/15*.
54. Nichole L. Torres, "Let the Good Times Roll," *Entrepreneur*, November 2004, p. 57.
55. Jennifer Wang, "10 Top Companies Getting It Right," *Entrepreneur*, March 2010, p. 83.
56. Jennifer Robison, "Despite the Downturn, Employees Remain Engaged," *Gallup Management Journal*, January 14, 2010, *http://gmj.gallup.com/content/125036/despite-downturn-employees-remain-engaged.aspx#3*.
57. Noelle Coyle, "Fish or Cut Bait?" *Black Box*, Quarter 1, 2010, p. 60.
58. Tony Hsieh, "How Zappos Infuses Culture Using Core Values," *Harvard Business Review*, May 24, 2010, *http://blogs.hbr.org/cs/2010/05/how_zappos_infuses_culture_using_core_values.html*; Sam Narisi, "You Hired Them—Now Pay Them to Quit?" *HR Recruiting Alert*, June 16, 2008, *www.hrrecruitingalert.com/new-onboarding-twist-bribing-hires-to-quit/*.
59. George A. Wolf, Jean A. Talaga, and Laurent Bernard, "A Matter of Transparency," *All Business*, June 1, 2009, *www.allbusiness.com/company-activities-management/management-benchmarking/12368521-1.html*.
60. David Freedman, "The Idiocy of Crowds," *Inc.*, September 2006, pp. 61–62.

61. *Capitalizing on Effective Communication: How Courage, Innovation, and Discipline Drive Business Results in Challenging Times, Communication ROI Study Report 2009/2010*, Towers Watson, November 2009, pp. 2–3; "How to Communicate with Employees," *Inc.*, May 1, 2010, *www.inc.com/magazine/20100501/guidebook-how-to-communicate-with-employees.html*, p. 1.

62. "Employee Engagement," *Motiv8*, May 26, 2010, *www.motiv8comm.com/IdeasandTrends/index_may26.html*.

63. Spors, "Top Workplaces 2009."

64. Mina Kimes, "How Can I Get Candid Feedback from My Employees?" *Fortune*, April 13, 2009, p. 24.

65. Kathy Gurchiek, "U.S. Rank-and-File Workers Feel Undervalued by Managers," *Society for Human Resource Managers*, July 16, 2010, *www.shrm.org/Publications/HRNews/Pages/WorkersFeelUndervalued.aspx*.

66. "Doomed!" *Inside Training*, February 22, 2007, p. 1.

67. "Employee Engagement," *Motiv8*; Robert B. Tucker, "Listening to Employees Is a Best Buy," *Blogging Innovation*, March 11, 2010, *www.business-strategy-innovation.com/2010/03/listening-to-employees-is-best-buy.html*.

68. "I Heard It Through the Grapevine," American Management Association, November 21, 2005, *www.amanet.org/training/articles/I-Heard-It-Through-the-Grapevine.aspx*.

69. Chris Penttila, "Live and Learn: You May Be the Boss, But That Doesn't Mean You Can't Let Your Employees Teach You a Thing or Two," *Entrepreneur*, June 2004, pp. 36–39.

70. "Empowering Your Employees," BNET, *www.bnet.com/2410-13059_23-95573.html*.

71. Daniel Akst, "The Rewards of Recognizing a Job Well Done," *Wall Street Journal*, January 31, 2007, p. D9.

72. Paul Keegan, "Maxine Clark and Kip Tindell," *Fortune*, February 8, 2010, pp. 68–72.

73. Spors, "Top Workplaces 2009."

74. Sarah E. Needleman, "Business Owners Try to Motivate Employees," *Wall Street Journal*, January 14, 2010, p. B5; "Americans' Job Satisfaction Falls to Record Low," *USA Today*, January 6, 2010, *www.usatoday.com/money/workplace/2010-01-05-job-satisfaction-use_N.htm*.

75. Robert D. Mohr and Cindy Zoghi, "Is Job Enrichment Really Enriching?" U.S. Department of Labor, U.S. Bureau of Labor Statistics, Office of Productivity and Technology, Washington, DC: January 2006, pp. 13–15.

76. Ellen Galinsky, Shanny L. Peer, and Sheila Eby, *When Work Works: 2009 Guide to Bold New Ideas for Making Work Work*, Families and Work Institute, 2009, p. 1.

77. Ibid., pp. 37–38.

78. Ellen Galinsky, James T. Bond, Kelly Sakai, Stacy S. Kim, and Nicole Giuntoli, *2008 National Study of Employers*, Families and Work Institute, New York: May 2008, p. 6.

79. Carol Kleiman, "Job Sharing Working Its Way into Mainstream," *Greenville News*, August 6, 2000, p. 3G.

80. Spors, "Top Workplaces 2009."

81. Gerry Blackwell, "Telecommuting Trend Taking Off for Small Biz," *Small Business Computing*, September 22, 2008, *www.smallbusinesscomputing.com/news/article.php/3773076*.

82. Meredith Levinson, "Survey: Telecommuting Improves Productivity, Lowers Cost," *CIO*, October 7, 2008, *www.cio.com/article/453289/Telecommuting_Improves_Productivity_Lowers_Costs_New_Survey_Finds*; Harriet Hagestad, "New Ways to Work: Telecommuting and Job Sharing," *CareerBuilder*, June 23, 2006, *www.careerbuilder.com/JobSeeker/careerbytes/CBArticle.aspx?articleID=369&cbRecursionCnt=1&cbsid=49944662f7b64dc38639d9a3ef87dd18-204624985-R5-4*.

83. "Cisco Study Finds Telecommuting Significantly Increases Employee Productivity, Work–Life Flexibility, and Job Satisfaction," Cisco, June 25, 2009, *http://newsroom.cisco.com/dlls/2009/prod_062609.html*.

84. Telis Demos, "Motivate Without Spending Millions," *Fortune*, April 12, 2010, pp. 37–38.

85. Spors, "Top Workplaces 2009."

86. Kevin Gray, "Can't Pay Your Employees What You'd Like? Praise Them Instead," BNET, January 19, 2010, *www.bnet.com/article/cant-pay-your-employees-what-youd-like-praise-them-instead/385221*.

87. Lisa Bertagnoli, "How to Motivate Restaurant Employees," *Restaurants and Institutions*, December 1, 2009, *www.rimag.com/article/ca6710028.html?rssid=272*.

88. Milton Moskowitz, Robert Levering, and Christopher Tkaczyk, "100 Best Companies to Work For," *Fortune*, February 8, 2010, p. 77.

89. Galinsky et al., *When Work Works*, pp. 20–21.

90. Scott Westcott, "Putting an End to End-of-Year Reviews," *Inc.*, December 2007, pp. 58–59.

91. Ibid.

Management Succession and Risk Management Strategies in the Family Business

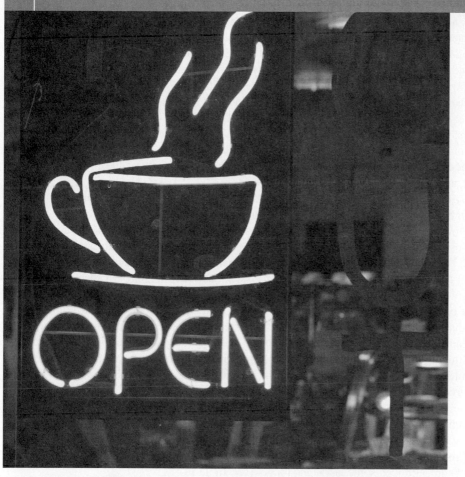

Learning Objectives

Upon completion of this chapter, you will be able to:

1 Explain the factors necessary for a strong family business.
2 Understand the exit strategy options available to an entrepreneur.
3 Discuss the stages of management succession.
4 Explain how to develop an effective management succession plan.
5 Understand the four risk management strategies.
6 Discuss the basics of insurance for small businesses.

When it works right, nothing succeeds like a family firm. The roots run deep, embedded in family values. The flash of the fast buck is replaced with long-term plans. Tradition counts.

—Eric Calonius

Walk sober off before the sprightlier age comes titt'ring on and shoves you from the stage.

—Alexander Pope

From Chapter 20 of *Effective Small Business Management: An Entrepreneurial Approach*, 10/e. Norman M. Scarborough.

Family Businesses

1. Explain the factors necessary for a strong family business.

Nearly 90 percent of all companies in the United States, about 26.4 million businesses, are family owned. Yet family-owned businesses, those in which family members control ownership and/or decision making, are often overlooked by the media, which focus most of their attention on the larger companies in our economy. In reality, family businesses generate 64 percent of the U.S. gross domestic product, account for 62 percent of all employment and 78 percent of job creation, and pay 65 percent of all wages.[1] Despite common perceptions, not all family businesses are small. The average annual sales of family businesses in the United States are about $36.5 million, and 33 percent of *Fortune* 500 companies are family businesses.[2] Globally, family-owned businesses account for 70 to 90 percent of world GDP.[3] Some of the best-known companies in the world are family-owned, including Ford Motor Company, Samsung, Hyundai, Sainsbury, Mars, and Walmart. In fact, Sam Walton's heirs own 43 percent (1.7 billion shares) of the stock in the world's largest company, Walmart, and those shares are worth an estimated $92 billion, an amount that exceeds the GDP of 161 countries in the world.[4]

When a family business works right, it is a thing of beauty. Family members share deeply rooted values that guide the company and give it a sense of harmony. Family members understand and support one another as they work together to achieve the company's mission. That harmony can produce a significant financial payoff. A study by Jim Lee of Texas A&M University–Corpus Christi shows that family-owned businesses are more profitable and experience faster employment and revenue growth over time than nonfamily businesses.[5] Another study of companies in the Standard & Poor's 500 Index by Ronald Anderson, David Reeb, and Sattar Mansi found that family firms outperformed their nonfamily counterparts on a variety of financial measures.[6] Other research comparing the financial performances of similar sets of family and nonfamily businesses has concluded that "firms controlled by the founding family have greater value, are operated more efficiently, and carry less debt than other firms."[7]

Family businesses also have a dark side, and it stems from their lack of continuity. Sibling rivalries, fights over control of the business, and personality conflicts often lead to nasty battles that can tear families apart and destroy once thriving businesses. Long-standing feuds can make family relationships difficult, and, when mixed with business decisions and the wealth family businesses can create, the result can be explosive. When Dhirubhai Ambani, founder of Reliance Industries Ltd., one of India's most successful companies, died without a will, his sons, Mukesh and Anil, battled over how to run the extensive business empire they took over. After years of personal and legal battles, the brothers entered into an agreement brokered by their mother that split the company into pieces so that each could operate his share of the business independently of the other. "Since their father's death, the brothers have been trying to outdo and undercut each other," says one observer.[8]

The stumbling block for most family businesses is management succession; 70 percent of first-generation businesses fail to survive into the second generation, and, of those that do survive, only 12 percent make it to the third generation. Just 3 percent of family businesses survive to the fourth generation and beyond.[9] The leading causes of family business failures are inadequate estate planning, failure to create a management succession plan, and lack of funds to pay estate taxes.[10] Just when they are ready to make the transition from one generation of leaders to the next, family businesses are most vulnerable. As a result, the average life expectancy of a family business is 24 years, although some last *much* longer (see Table 1).[11]

ENTREPRENEURIAL
Profile
Will Tuttle: Tuttle Farm

Will Tuttle, the 63-year-old patriarch of one of the oldest family businesses in the United States, Tuttle Farm in Dover, New Hampshire, recently announced that his generation will be the last to operate the farm. Founded in 1632 by John Tuttle with a land grant from England's King Charles II, Tuttle Farm has struggled with the encroachment of housing and commercial developments and the impact of a severe recession. Will Tuttle, who began helping his father on the farm at age 6, has listed the 134-acre farm for sale at $3.35 million. "This is a different business now," says Tuttle. "I don't see much opportunity for small farms to thrive."[12]

According to a study of family businesses across the globe by PriceWaterhouseCoopers, 27 percent of family business owners say that ownership of their companies will change hands within the next 5 years and 53 percent of the owners expect to pass their companies on to the next

TABLE 1 The World's Oldest Family Businesses.

William O'Hara, director of the Institute for Family Enterprise at Bryant College, and Peter Mandel have compiled a list of some of the world's oldest family businesses.

Company	Country	Nature of Business	Year Established
Hoshi Ryokan	Japan	Hotel	718
Château de Goulaine	France	Vineyard, museum, butterfly collection	1000
Fonderia Pontifica Marinelli	Italy	Bell foundry	1000
Barone Ricasoli	Italy	Wine and olive oil	1141
Barovier & Toso	Italy	Artistic glassmaking	1295
Hotel Pilgram Haus	Germany	Innkeeping	1304
Richard de Bas	France	High-quality paper maker	1326
Torrini Firenze	Italy	Goldsmiths	1369
Antinori	Italy	Wine	1385
Camuffo	Italy	Shipbuilding	1438
Baronnie de Coussergues	France	Wine	1495
Grazia Deruta	Italy	Ceramics	1500
Fabbrice D'Armi Beretta	Italy	Firearms production	1526
William Prym GmbH & Company	Germany	Copper, brass, haberdashery	1530
John Brooke & Sons	Great Britain	Textiles	1541
Codorniu	Spain	Wine	1551
Fonjallaz	Switzerland	Wine	1552

Source: William T. O'Hara and Peter Mandel, "The World's Oldest Family Companies," *Family Business,* *www.familybusinessmagazine.com/oldworld.html.*

generation of family members.[13] The best way to ensure the legacy of a family business and a successful transition from one generation of family owners to the next is to develop a succession plan for the company. Although business founders inevitably want their businesses to survive them and most intend to pass them on to their children, they do not always support their intentions by a plan to accomplish that goal. The study by PriceWaterhouseCoopers reports that 47 percent of family businesses have no succession plans in place (see Figure 1).[14] Another survey of family business owners by MassMutual Financial Group and Arthur Andersen reports that 19 percent had not engaged in any kind of estate planning other than creating a will.[15] For most family businesses, the greatest threat to survival comes from *within* the company rather than from outside it. Many entrepreneurs dream of their businesses continuing in the family but take no significant steps to make their dreams a reality.

David Bork, founder of the Aspen Family Business Conference, has identified several qualities that are essential to a successful family business: shared values, shared power, tradition, a willingness to learn, family behavior, and strong family ties.[16]

Shared Values

The first, and probably most overlooked, quality is a set of shared values. What family members value and believe about people, work, and money shapes their behavior toward the business. All members of a family business should talk openly to determine, in a nonjudgmental fashion, each one's values. Without shared values, it is difficult to create a sense of direction for a business.

To avoid the problems associated with conflicting values and goals, family business owners should consider taking the following actions:

- Make it clear to all family members that they are not required to join the business full-time. Family members' goals, ambitions, and talents should be foremost in their career decisions.
- Do not assume that a successor must come from within the family. Simply being born into a family does not guarantee that a person will make a good business leader.

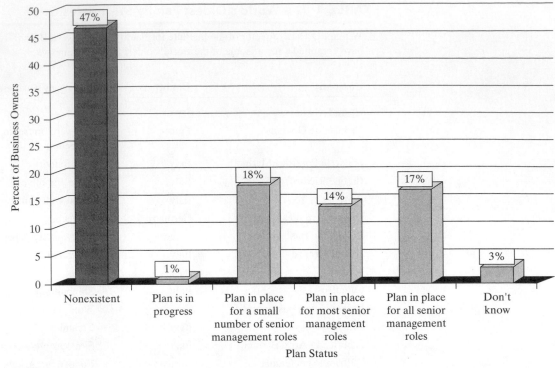

FIGURE 1
Status of Management Succession Plans in Small Businesses

Source: Kin in the Game, PriceWaterhouseCoopers Family Business Survey, 2010–2011, p. 22.

When Pierre Bellon stepped down as CEO of Sodexho, the food management services business his grandfather started in 1895, he named as his successor Michael Landel, the first nonfamily member to lead the company. Landel, a 26-year veteran of Sodexho, had held a variety of positions in the family-controlled business, and Bellon was confident that Landel was the right person to lead the company. "You have to be completely in line with the culture of the family, share the same values, and have very strong respect for what they have done," says Landel.[17]

■ Give family members the opportunity to work outside the business initially to learn first-hand how others conduct business. Working for others allows family members to develop knowledge, confidence, and credibility before stepping back into the family business.

Shared Power

Shared power is not necessarily equal power. Rather, shared power is based on the idea that family members allow those people with the greatest expertise, ability, and knowledge in particular areas to handle decisions in those areas. Dividing responsibilities along the lines of expertise is an important way of acknowledging respect for each family member's talents and abilities.

When Thad Garner invented a concoction of red peppers and vinegar called Texas Pete Hot Sauce during the Great Depression, he and his brothers, Harold and Ralph, built a business, T.W. Garner Food Company, around the product. Each assumed responsibilities in a different area of the company based on his talents and interests. Thad (known as "Mr. Texas Pete") took over the sales and marketing side of the business, while Harold managed its financial and operational aspects and Ralph handled production. Working together, the brothers built the company into a very successful business, selling millions of dollars' worth of Texas Pete a year.[18]

Tradition

Tradition is necessary for a family business because it serves to bond family members and to link one generation of business leaders to the next. However, founders must hold tradition in check when it becomes a barrier to change. The key is to select those traditions that provide a solid foundation for positive behavior while taking care not to restrict the future growth of the business. "The companies that are successful change their strategy after each generation," says Joachim Schwass, a professor of family business at Switzerland's IMD business school. "Bringing in the new generation and saying, 'Son, do as I did,' will not work."[19]

ENTREPRENEURIAL
Profile

*Maximilian Riedel:
Riedel Glas Austria*

Maximilian Riedel, head of North American operations for Austrian glassmaker Riedel, which for 300 years has been famous for its feather-light fine crystal wine glasses, is next in line to take control of the family business. Like his father and grandfather did, Maximilian created a new line of wine glasses that has become one of the company's best selling products. The eleventh-generation glassmaker created a sensation among oenophiles with his revolutionary stemless "O" series of wine tumblers that are designed to convey the nuances of the aroma and the flavor of wine. (The wine glass is "the messenger of the wine," he says.) Every business decision that Maximilian makes is steeped in 250 years of family business history, but already he has shown that he is willing to take bold steps to innovate and keep the family business in tune with the demands of the twenty-first century.[20]

A Willingness to Learn

A willingness to learn and grow is the hallmark of any successful firm, and it is essential to a family business. The family business that remains open to new ideas and techniques is likely to reduce its risk of obsolescence. The current generation of leadership must set the stage for new ideas involving the next generation in today's decisions. In many cases, a formal family council serves as a mechanism through which family members can propose new ideas. Perhaps more important than a family council is fostering an environment in which family members trust one another enough to express their ideas, thoughts, and suggestions openly and honestly. Open discussion of the merits of new ideas is a tradition that has proved valuable for many family businesses' ability to sustain their competitive advantages.

Behaving Like Families

Families that play together operate family businesses that are more likely to stay together. Time spent together outside the business creates the foundation for the relationships family members have at work. Too often, life in a family business can degenerate into nothing but day after day of work and discussions of work at home. In some cases, work is the only way some parents interact with their children. When a family adds activities outside the scope of the business, however, new relationships develop in a different arena. A family should not force members to "play together" but instead should create an environment that welcomes every member into fun family activities. Planned activities should be broad enough in scope to involve all family members. In time, trust, respect, openness, and togetherness lead to behavior that communicates genuine caring and concern for the well-being of each family member, and that spills over into the working relationship as well.

A Strong Family Support Network

According to a global survey of family business owners, the most important advantage family businesses have is the strong support network from family members (see Figure 2). Strong family ties grow from one-on-one relationships. Shared time conveys the message that the family business is *more* than just a business; it is a group of people who care for one another working together for a common goal. The bond that a family business creates among relatives can be strong and enduring. "There's a love and a trust and a respect that can be very powerful when they are brought into a business environment," says Ross Nager, director of a center for family businesses.[21]

The same emotions that hold family businesses together can also rip them apart if they run counter to the company's and the family's best interest. Emotions run deep in family businesses, and the press is full of examples of once successful companies that have been ruined by family

FIGURE 2
Advantages of the Family Business Model

Source: Thomas L. Kalaris, "Family Business: In Safe Hands?" *Barclays Wealth Insights*, 2009, p. 10.

feuds over who controls the company and how to run it. Conflict is a natural part of any business, but it can be especially powerful in family businesses because family relationships magnify the passions binding family members to the company (see Figure 3). Without a succession plan, those passions can explode into destructive behavior that can endanger the family business.

Exit Strategies

2. Understand the exit strategy options available to an entrepreneur.

Most family business founders want their companies to stay within their families, although in some cases maintaining family control is not practical. Sometimes no one in the next generation of family members has an interest in managing the company or has the necessary skills and experience to handle the job. Under these circumstances, the founder must look outside the family for leadership if the company is to survive. Whatever the case, entrepreneurs must confront their mortality and plan for the future of their companies. Having a solid management succession plan in place well before retirement is near is critical to success. Entrepreneurs should examine their options well before they decide to step down from the businesses they have founded. Three options are available to entrepreneurs who are planning to retire: sell to outsiders, sell to (nonfamily) insiders, or pass the business on to family members with the help of a management succession plan. We turn now to these three exit strategies.

FIGURE 3
Disadvantages of the Family Business Model

Source: Thomas L. Kalaris, "Family Business: In Safe Hands?" *Barclays Wealth Insights*, 2009, p. 11.

IN THE ENTREPRENEURIAL
SPOTLIGHT Parent–Child Inc.

Thanks to the Great Recession, family businesses are taking on a slightly different look. When passed from one generation to the next, family businesses often have family members from two, sometimes three, generations working side-by-side. As many parents in their 40s and 50s are experiencing layoffs and their college-graduate children struggle to find even part-time jobs, a new type of family business is becoming more popular: companies cofounded by parents and children. At first blush, parents and children cofounding companies sounds like a recipe for feuding and fighting, but doing so offers many benefits. Parents bring experience, a network of contacts, business acumen, and money to the deal. Their children contribute enthusiasm, energy, and a working knowledge of technology skills, Internet savvy, and social media know-how. The combination can work together to create a dynamic business that has real staying power.

Arian Mahmoodi demonstrated entrepreneurial tendencies as a child, and his father, Farzad, was not surprised when at age 14 Arian launched a business buying and reselling Nintendo games on Amazon. Arian operated the business from his bedroom in his family's home in Hannawa Falls, New York, and counted on his parents to drive him to the post office to mail the games he sold to customers. "I'd wake up and package the orders in the morning before school," he says.

Arian had dreams of a bigger company and used the profits from his business to launch SellYourOldiPhone.com, a Web site through which he buys used and often broken iPhones, refurbishes them, and then resells them. After Arian sent out his first e-mail blast promoting his company, hundreds of orders poured in, and he turned to his father, a professor of supply chain management at Clarkson University in Pottsdam, New York, for help. Farzad helped his son organize his business, and together they assigned unique tracking numbers to customers and their orders.

SellYourOldiPhone.com was so successful that Arian replicated his business model a year later and launched SellYourOldMacBook.com. Arian, then 17 and preparing for college, and Farzad had grown into distinct and complementary roles in their small businesses. Arian, the chief executive officer, is the "face" of the companies and manages the Web sites and customer service. He also is responsible for the companies' advertising and pricing. Farzad handles the companies' accounting and legal matters and manages the supply chain (of course!). He also monitors the flow of iPhones and MacBooks to and from the technicians who refurbish them and determines which international markets the companies enter.

The father–son duo purchase and resell about 30 devices each week, generating about $230,000 in sales per year. Arian's focus is on growing the businesses, and he has reinvested all of the companies' earnings back into the businesses, using them to buy more phones and computers. Farzad enjoys using the companies as a laboratory where he can test various supply chain ideas. When Arian goes to college, they plan to hire an employee to take over most of the day-to-day operations.

So far, father and son have gotten along well as business partners. The respect that each has for the other is readily apparent, but both admit that they have had disagreements. While participating in a 3-week academic program at Cornell University, Arian discovered a bargain on accessories such as chargers and phone cases and placed a large order without telling his father. "I got a call from my Dad," he says with a smile. "'What is this? We have all these boxes.' He wasn't too happy because he couldn't park in the garage."

Perhaps the biggest issue between the two is how fast their companies should grow. Arian wants the companies on the fast track, but his father is pushing for a slower rate of growth so that his son can enjoy his college experience. For now, at least, Arian is willing to listen to his father's advice. "We're in agreement at this time to keep it as is," he says.

1. Work with a classmate to brainstorm the advantages and the disadvantages of starting a family business with a parent.
2. Would you be willing to go into business with a parent? Explain.
3. What recommendations can you make to someone who is about to launch a business with a parent?

Source: Based on Colleen Debaise, Emily Maltby, and Sarah E. Needleman, "Parent and Child Inc.," *Wall Street Journal*, November 15, 2010, http://online.wsj.com/article/SB10001424052748703794104575546553171806306.html.

Selling to Outsiders

Selling a business to an outsider is no simple task. Done properly, it takes time, patience, and preparation to locate a suitable buyer, strike a deal, and make the transition. Advance preparation, maintaining accurate financial records, and timing are the keys to a successful sale. Too often, however, business owners, like some famous athletes, stay with the game too long, until they and their businesses are well past their prime. They postpone selling until the last minute when they reach retirement age or when they face a business crisis. Such a "fire sale" approach rarely yields the maximum value for a business.

A straight sale may be best for those entrepreneurs who want to step down and turn the reins of the company over to someone else. However, selling a business outright is not an attractive exit strategy for those who want to stay on with the company or for those who want to surrender control of the company gradually rather than all at once.

Family-owned Snyder's of Hanover, founded in 1909 and now the world's largest maker of pretzels, recently agreed to merge with Lance Inc., a Charlotte, North Carolina-based manufacturer of snack crackers. Snyder's product line and extensive distribution network in grocery stores nationwide provide a solid strategic fit with Lance, which has strongholds in delis, convenience stores, and small retail stores. Lance issued 32.7 million shares of common stock to Snyder's shareholders, most of whom are members of the founding family.[22]

The financial terms of a sale also influence the selling price of the business and the number of potential bidders. Does the owner want "clean, cash only, 100 percent at closing" offers, or is he or she willing to finance a portion of the sale? A 100 percent, cash-only requirement dramatically reduces the number of potential buyers. However, the owner can exit the business "free and clear" and does not incur the risk that the buyer may fail to operate the business profitably and be unable to complete the financial transition.

Selling to Insiders

When entrepreneurs have no family members to whom they can transfer ownership or who want to assume the responsibilities of running a company, selling the business to employees is often the preferred option. In most situations, the options available to owners are (1) sale for cash plus a note, (2) a leveraged buyout, and (3) an employee stock ownership plan (ESOP).

A SALE FOR CASH PLUS A NOTE. Whether entrepreneurs sell their businesses to insiders, outsiders, or family members, they often finance a portion of the sales price. The buyer pays the seller a lump-sum amount of cash up front and the seller holds a promissory note for the remaining portion of the selling price, which the buyer pays off in installments. Because of its many creative financial options, this method of selling a business is popular with buyers. They can buy promising businesses without having to come up with the total purchase price all at one time. Sellers also appreciate the security and the tax implications of accepting payment over time. They receive a portion of the sale up front and have the assurance of receiving a steady stream of income in the future. In addition, they can stretch their tax liabilities from the capital gains on the sale over time rather than having to pay them in a single year. In many cases, sellers' risks are lower because they may even retain a seat on the board of directors to ensure that the new owners are keeping the business on track.

LEVERAGED BUYOUTS. In a **leveraged buyout (LBO)**, managers and/or employees borrow money from a financial institution and pay the owner the total agreed-upon price at closing; then they use the cash generated from the company's operations to pay off the debt. The drawback of this technique is that it creates a highly leveraged business. Because of the high levels of debt they take on, the new management team has very little room for error. Too many management mistakes or a slowing economy has led many highly leveraged businesses into bankruptcy.

If properly structured, LBOs can be attractive to both buyers and sellers. Because they get their money up front, sellers do not incur the risk of loss if the buyers cannot keep the business operating successfully. The managers and employees who buy the company have a strong incentive to make sure the business succeeds because they own a piece of the action and some of their capital is at risk in the business. The result can be a highly motivated workforce that works hard and makes sure that the company operates efficiently.

ENTREPRENEURIAL
Profile

Jack Stack: Springfield Remanufacturing Corporation

In one of the most successful LBOs in history, Jack Stack and a team of 12 other managers purchased an ailing subsidiary of International Harvester in an attempt to save their jobs and those of the 120 employees they managed. The new company, Springfield Remanufacturing Corporation (SRC), which specializes in engine remanufacturing for the automotive, trucking, agricultural, and construction industries, began with an astronomically high debt-to-equity ratio of 89:1, but the team of motivated managers and employees turned the company around. Today, SRC has more than 1,200 employees and 26 divisions that range from automotive engines to home furnishings.[23]

EMPLOYEE STOCK OWNERSHIP PLANS (ESOPs). Unlike LBOs, **employee stock ownership plans (ESOPs)** allow employees and/or managers (that is, the future owners) to purchase the business gradually, which frees up enough cash to finance the venture's growth. With an ESOP, employees contribute a portion of their earnings over time toward purchasing shares of the company's stock from the founder until they own the company outright. (Although in leveraged ESOPs, the ESOP borrows the money to buy the owner's stock up front. Then, using employees' contributions, the ESOP repays the loan over time. Another advantage of a leveraged ESOP is that the principal and the interest the ESOP borrows to buy the business are tax deductible, which can save thousands or even millions of dollars in taxes.) Transferring ownership to employees through an ESOP is a long-term exit strategy that benefits everyone involved. The owner sells the business to the people he or she can trust the most—his or her managers and employees. The managers and employees buy a business they already know how to run successfully. In addition, because they own the company, the managers and employees have a huge incentive to see that it operates effectively and efficiently. One study of ESOPs in privately held companies found that they increased sales, employment, and sales per employee by 2.4 percent a year.[24] Figure 4 shows the trend in the number of ESOPs and the number of employee owners.

The third exit strategy available to company founders is transferring ownership to the next generation of family members with the help of a comprehensive management succession plan.

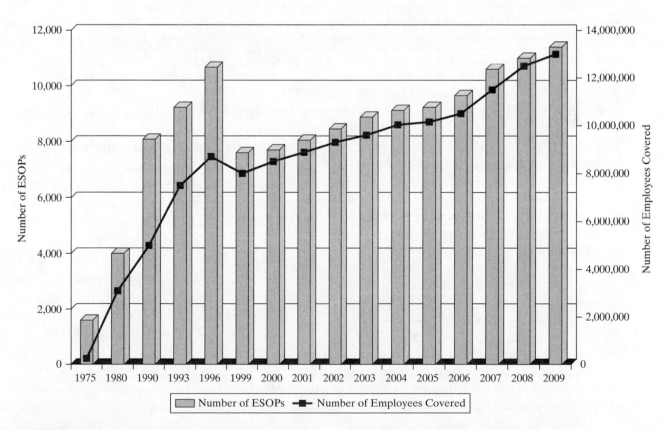

FIGURE 4
Employee Stock Ownership Plans

Source: "A Statistical Profile of Employee Ownership," National Center for Employee Ownership, 2010.

How to Set Up an ESOP

In 1978, long before people knew about the health benefits of whole-grain products, Bob Moore and his wife, Charlee, salvaged an abandoned 125-year-old flour mill and launched Bob's Red Mill Natural Foods, a company in Portland, Oregon, that produces a variety of products, from grain and flour to hot cereal and baking mixes. For Moore and his employees, the path was filled with challenges, including a fire that caused extensive damage to the old factory and the necessity of constantly investing in new equipment and technology. Moore expanded the company's reach to include customers in a handful of Western states, but the turning point came in 1993 when Moore brought in John Wagner as chief financial officer and co-owner. Together, Moore and Wagner focused on marketing the company's all-natural, whole-grain products at food and trade shows, where they garnered the attention of small health food stores, food distributors, and, eventually, grocery chains. "Now you can find our products in every province and state in North America and lots of places overseas," Moore says proudly.

Moore and Wagner launched a profit-sharing plan for their employees in 1995 and began sharing financial information with them weekly. They also conducted training sessions for employees on reading the company's financial statements. The training not only taught employees how to calculate their share of the company's profits but also enabled them to see exactly how the work they did every day affected the company's bottom line—and, therefore, their payouts.

As Moore passed the normal retirement age, employees began to wonder about their future, especially if Moore and Wagner decided to sell the company to a larger business. "Will we still have jobs?" they wondered. "Will the culture that we love so much change?"

Moore answered employees' lingering questions on his eighty-first birthday celebration. Moore and Wagner had decided not to sell Bob's Red Mill Natural Foods to a large company. Instead, they had created an employee stock ownership plan that would transfer ownership of the company to the 200 people whom they considered to be instrumental in its success. "It's been my dream all along to turn this company over to the employees, and to make that dream a reality is very, very special to me," says Moore. "This is the ultimate way to keep this business moving forward."

"The partners could have sold this company many times for a lot more money" says vice president of operations Dennis Vaughn, "but to them this company is about so much more than the money." After Moore announced the creation of the ESOP, he said modestly, "I thought some of them were going to kiss me. It went over very, very, very well." Roger Farnen, the company's quality assurance manager, says, "By creating the ESOP, Bob and the partners have fulfilled their ultimate quest for sharing success among all employees. Bob is passing the entrepreneurial torch on to his employees and is instilling in us that hard work provides rewards."

What steps should an entrepreneur who is interested in setting up an ESOP take? Consider the following advice from the Street-Smart Entrepreneur:

Step 1. Conduct a feasibility analysis to determine whether an ESOP is right for you and your company.

A company should be profitable and should have at least 20 employees to make an ESOP work. Creating the necessary plan documents and filing them with the proper government agencies costs about $10,000. A business valuation, which can range from $5,000 to $10,000 for a small company, is a necessity. Fixed costs of administering the ESOP run about $2,000 plus $20 to $30 per employee participant per year. A final consideration is whether the company will generate enough revenue to be able to repay the loan.

Step 2. Hire an attorney who specializes in ESOPs to help you develop a plan for creating and implementing an ESOP.

ESOPs can take many different forms, and an expert can help you determine the advantages and disadvantages of each one so that you can determine the one that is best for you and your company.

Step 3. Find the money to fund the ESOP.

About 75 percent of ESOPs are leveraged, which means that they borrow the money to purchase the owner's stock from the ESOP trust. Banks and other financial institutions usually find loans to ESOPs quite attractive.

Step 4. Establish a process to operate the ESOP.

Companies most often create an ESOP committee of managers and employees to provide guidance to the ESOP trust for managing the ESOP. The team also is responsible for communicating the details of the ESOP and the benefits of investing in it to company employees.

Barbara Gabel, who with her husband, Zach Zachowski, launched Zachary's Chicago Pizza in Oakland, California, in 1984, recently established an ESOP to transfer ownership of their business to their employees. "It's the ultimate exit strategy," says Gabel, referring to the benefits ESOPs provide both entrepreneurs and employees. Each year, employees at Zachary's receive an amount of stock that is equal to 25 percent of their salaries. General Manager J. P. LaRussa, who began working as a part-time dishwasher at Zachary's

the day it opened, says, "This breathes new life into the business in a very positive way."

Sources: Based on Karen E. Klein, "ESOPs on the Rise Among Small Businesses," *Bloomberg Business Week*, March 26, 2010, *www.businessweek.com/smallbiz/content/mar2010/sb20100325_591132.htm*; Theo Francis, "Inside Eileen Fisher's Employee Stock Plan," *Wall Street Journal*, January 22, 2007, pp. B1, B3; Alec Rosenberg, "Employees to Slice Up Zachary's Pizza," *Oakland Tribune*, June 27, 2003, *www.zacharys.com/news_oakland_tribune.html*; "ESOP Statistics," ESOP Association, *www.esopassociation.org/media/media_statistics.asp*; "How Small Is Too Small for an ESOP?" National Center for Employee Ownership, *www.nceo.org/library/howsmall.html*; "Steps to Setting up an ESOP," National Center for Employee Ownership, *www.nceo.org/library/ steps.html*.

Management Succession

3. Discuss the stages of management succession.

Experts estimate that between 2001 and 2017, $12 trillion in wealth will be transferred from one generation to the next, representing the greatest transfer of wealth in history and much of it funneled through family businesses.[25] Most of the family businesses in existence today were started after World War II, and many of the founders who have not yet transferred ownership to the next generation now are at or past retirement age and are ready to pass the torch of leadership. A recent study by the Alliance of Merger and Acquisition Advisors reports that 70 percent of business owners plan to transfer ownership of their businesses by 2020 but that 90 percent of them do not have an adequate succession plan in place.[26]

For a smooth transition from one generation to the next, family businesses need a succession plan. Without a succession plan, family businesses face an increased risk of faltering or failing in the next generation. Those businesses with the greatest probability of surviving are the ones whose owners prepare a succession plan well before it is time to transfer control to the next generation. Succession planning also allows business owners to minimize the impact of taxes on their businesses, their estates, and their successors' wealth as well and to avoid saddling the next generation of ownership with burdensome debt.

Why, then, do so many entrepreneurs postpone succession planning until it is too late? Many business founders hesitate to let go of their businesses because their personal identities are so wrapped up in their companies. Over time, a founder's identity becomes so intertwined in the business that, in the entrepreneur's mind, there is no distinction between the two. The attitude is "I am the company, and the company is me."

ENTREPRENEURIAL
Profile

Michael and Emily Powell: Powell's Books

When Michael Powell, who for 27 years had managed Powell's Books, the largest privately held chain of bookstores in the United States, reached age 66, he realized that it was time to begin transferring control of the company to his daughter, Emily, then 28, with the help of the 10-year transition plan he had created 7 years before. When Michael, who took over the family business from his father, talks about retiring from the company he built, however, he covers his face with his hands and his voice grows soft. "There are emotional issues in giving up control and ownership," he admits. "Half my brain says, 'Do it,' and the other half says, 'What are you doing?' This is business and family."[27]

Many entrepreneurs share Powell's feelings. According to a survey by the Monitor Group, less than 17 percent of business owners say that they expect to retire after leaving their businesses. (In fact, 45 percent say that they plan to start another company.)[28]

Another barrier to succession planning is that, in planning the future of the business, owners are forced to accept the painful reality of their own mortality. In addition, turning over the reins of a business they have sacrificed for, fretted over, and dedicated themselves to for so many years is extremely difficult to do—even if the successor is a son or daughter! Paul Snodgrass, son of the founder of Pella Products, a maker of apparel for work and outdoor activities, who accepted leadership of the company from his father, explains, "Dad loves you and wants you to take over the business, but he also put heart and soul into that business, and he's not going to let anybody screw it up—not even you."[29] Finally, many family business founders believe that controlling the business also gives them a degree of control over family members and family behavior.

Planning for management succession protects not only the founder's, successor's, and company's financial resources, but it also preserves what matters most in a successful business: its heritage and tradition. "Real succession planning involves developing a strategy for transferring the trust, respect, and goodwill built by one generation to the next," explains Andy Bluestone, who took over as president of the financial services company his father founded.[30] Management succession planning requires, first, an attitude of trusting others. It recognizes that other family members have a stake in the future of the business and want to participate in planning its future. Planning is an attitude that shows that decisions made with open discussion are more constructive than those without family input. Second, management succession is an evolutionary process and must reconcile an entrepreneur's inevitable anguish with the successors' desire for autonomy. Owners' emotional ties to their businesses usually are stronger than their financial ties. On the other side of the equation are the successors, who yearn to have the autonomy to run the business their way. These inherent conflicts can—and often do—result in skirmishes.

Succession planning reduces the tension and stress created by these conflicts by gradually "changing the guard." A well-developed succession plan is like the smooth, graceful exchange of a baton between runners in a relay race. The new runner still has maximum energy; the concluding runner has already spent his or her energy by running at maximum speed. The athletes never come to a stop to exchange the baton; instead, the handoff takes place on the move. The race is a skillful blend of the talents of all team members—an exchange of leadership so smooth and powerful that the business never falters, but accelerates, fueled by a new source of energy at each leg of the race.

Management succession involves a lengthy series of interconnected stages that begins very early in the life of the owner's children and extends to the point of final ownership transition (see Figure 5). If management succession is to be effective, it is necessary for the process to begin early in the successor's life (stage I). For instance, the owner of a catering business recalls putting his son to work in the family owned company at age 7. On weekends, the boy would arrive at dawn to baste turkeys and was paid in his favorite medium of exchange—doughnuts![31] In most cases, family business owners involve their children in their businesses while they are still in junior high or high school. In this phase, the tasks are routine, but the child is learning the basics of how the business operates. Young adults begin to appreciate the role the business plays in the life of the family. They learn firsthand about the values and responsibilities of running the company.

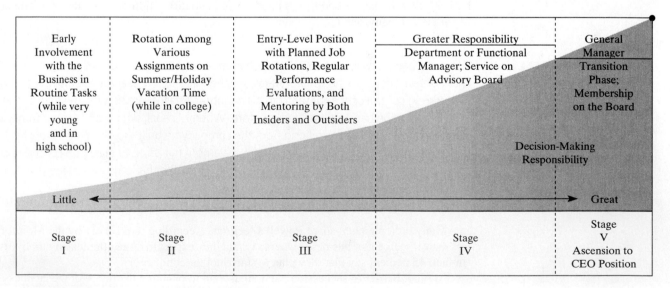

FIGURE 5
Stages in Management Succession

While in college, the successor moves to stage II of the continuum. During this stage, the individual rotates among a variety of job functions to both broaden his or her base of understanding of the business and to permit the parents to evaluate his or her skills. Upon graduation from college, the successor enters stage III. At this point, the successor becomes a full-time worker and ideally has already begun to earn the respect of coworkers through his behavior in the first two stages of the process. In some cases, the successor may work for a time outside of the family business to gain experience and to establish a reputation for competency that goes beyond "being the boss's kid." Stage III focuses on the successor's continuous development, often through a program designed to groom the successor using both family and nonfamily managers as mentors.

ENTREPRENEURIAL
Profile

*The Joyner Family:
C. Dan Joyner Realtors*

From the time that Danny Joyner was a young boy "helping" his father in the real estate business that the elder Joyner was building, he knew that he wanted to join his father's company. "I've always known that this is what I would do," says Danny, who joined the company full time after graduating from college. Danny heads the successful company's commercial real estate division, and Dan's two daughters and a son-in-law also work in the family business. With a succession plan in place and all of his children in leadership positions in the company, founder Dan Joyner says that the company is positioned to make a smooth transition into the second generation of ownership.[32]

As the successor develops his or her skills and abilities, he or she moves to stage IV, in which real decision-making authority grows rapidly. Stage IV of the succession continuum is the period when the founder makes a final assessment of the successor's competence and ability to take full and complete control over the firm. The skills the successor needs include the following:

- *Financial abilities.* Understanding the financial aspect of a business, what its financial position is, and the managerial implications of that position are crucial to success.
- *Technical knowledge.* Every business has its own body of knowledge, ranging from how the distribution system works to the trends shaping the industry, that an executive must master.
- *Negotiating ability.* Much of business, whether buying supplies and inventory or selling to customers, boils down to negotiating, and a business owner must be adept at it.
- *Leadership qualities.* Leaders must be bold enough to stake out the company's future and then give employees the resources, the power, and the freedom to pursue it.
- *Communication skills.* Business leaders must communicate the vision they have for their businesses; good listening skills also are essential for success as a top manager.
- *Juggling skills.* Business owners must be able to handle multiple projects effectively. Like a juggler, they must maintain control over several important assignments simultaneously.
- *Integrity.* To be an effective leader of a family business, a successor must demonstrate honesty and integrity in business dealings.
- *Commitment to the business.* It helps if a successor has a genuine passion for the business. Leaders who have enthusiasm for what they do create a spark of excitement throughout the entire organization.[33]

The final stage in the management succession process involves the ultimate transition of organizational leadership. It is during this stage that the founder's role as mentor is most crucial.

ENTREPRENEURIAL
Profile

*Laura Michaud: Beltone
Electronics Corporation*

Laura Michaud, who in 1980 became the third-generation owner of Beltone Electronics Corporation, a very successful maker of hearing aids that was founded in 1940, says that the training and mentoring that her father provided was key to her success to managing the family business. Her father insisted on an extensive training program that involved Michaud in all aspects of the company, including having her actually build a hearing aid. "You need to work in all areas of operations," says Michaud, who ran the company for 17 years before selling it to a larger company.[34]

Source: Wall Street Journal\Cartoon
Features Syndicate

"There has been a changing of the guard, Crampton."

In stage IV, the successor may become the organization's CEO, while the former CEO retains the title of chairman of the board. In other cases, the best solution is for the founder to step out of the business entirely and give the successor the chance to establish his or her own identity within the company. "Any leader's final legacy is building the next generation," says one business consultant.[35]

Developing a Management Succession Plan

4. Explain how to develop an effective management succession plan.

Families that are most committed to ensuring that their businesses survive from one generation to the next exhibit four characteristics: (1) They believe that owning the business helps achieve their families' missions. (2) They are proud of the values their businesses are built on and exemplify. (3) They believe that the business is contributing to society and makes it a better place to live. (4) They rely on management succession plans to assure the continuity of their companies.[36] Developing a management succession plan takes time and dedication, yet the benefits are well worth the cost. A sound succession plan enables a company to maintain its momentum and sense of purpose and direction.

It is important to start the planning process early, well before the founder's retirement. Succession planning is not the kind of activity an entrepreneur can do in a hurry, and the sooner an entrepreneur starts, the easier it will be. Unfortunately, too many entrepreneurs put it off until it is too late. "Very few privately owned businesses make it through several generations, and one reason is the failure of the senior generation to do any planning at all until it is too late in the game," says one expert.[37] Creating a succession plan involves the following steps.

Step 1: Select the Successor

The average tenure of the founder of a family business is 25 years.[38] Yet there comes a time for even the most dedicated founder to step down and hand the reins of the company to the next generation. Entrepreneurs should never assume that their children want to take control of the business, however. Above all, they should not be afraid to ask the question: "Do you really want to take over the family business?" Too often, children in this situation tell Mom and Dad what they want to hear out of loyalty, pressure, or guilt. It is critical to remember at this juncture in the life of a business that children do not necessarily inherit their parents' entrepreneurial skills and desires. By leveling with their children about the business and their options regarding a family succession, owners can know which heirs, if any, are willing to assume leadership of the business.

One of the worst mistakes entrepreneurs can make is to postpone naming a successor until just before they are ready to step down. One study by the Raymond Institute and MassMutual reports that 55 percent of family business owners age 61 or older have not yet designated a successor![39] The problem is especially acute when more than one family member works for the company and is interested in assuming leadership of it. Sometimes founders avoid naming successors because they don't want to hurt the family members who are not chosen to succeed them. However, both the business and the family will be better off if, after observing family members as they work in the business, the founder picks a successor based on skill and ability.

At age 79, Rupert Murdoch, CEO of News Corporation, had not yet named his successor even though two of his sons, Lachlan and James, have been involved in running the company. Lachlan resigned as the company's chief operating officer but remains on the board of directors; James has worked for News Corporation for 14 years in a variety of positions and is in charge of a division that accounts for 20 percent of the company's revenue. Although the elder Murdoch insists that he has no plans to retire, he says that he is confident that one of his children will emerge to succeed him as CEO. "Every parent likes to see that," he says.[40]

When naming a successor, merit is a better standard to use than gender or birth order. The key is to establish standards of performance, knowledge, education, and ability and then to identify the person who best meets those standards. As part of his company's succession plan, Joe De La Torre selected his daughter Gina to take over Juanita's Foods rather than his two sons because her financial skills and her ability to solve problems were what the company needed most.[41] Gina La Torre is part of a growing trend among family businesses; 34 percent of family business founders expect the next CEO to be a woman, quite a change from just a generation ago.[42]

After 60 years, Harry Vold, founder of Harry Vold Rodeo Company, a business based in Pueblo West, Colorado, that supplies rodeos with bucking broncos and bulls, turned over the reins of the family business to the youngest of his six children, Kirsten, when she was just 25 years old. Although Harry expected one of his children to take over the business, he was a bit surprised that Kirsten was the one who showed the greatest potential and stepped forward. Kirsten, too, was somewhat surprised. "I was going to be a lawyer, drive a sports car, and live in L.A.," she says with a laugh. After graduating from the University of Southern Colorado, Kirsten took a job in sports marketing but soon felt the tug of the family business and returned home to take an active role in managing it. Kirsten worked hard to prove herself in an industry that men tend to dominate. "She's earned their respect," says her mother proudly. Transferring control from one generation to the next taxed the skills, patience, and ability of both Harry and Kirsten. "It was a struggle, a power struggle, along the way," she says. "For both of us, but it built character for both of us." Harry is pleased with the way things worked out. "I was a bit surprised to begin with, but I'm not now," he says. "I am totally confident that she makes the right decisions. As far as I'm concerned, she's all the cowgirl I need."[43]

Step 2: Create a Survival Kit for the Successor

Once he or she identifies a successor, an entrepreneur should prepare a survival kit and then brief the future leader on its contents, which should include all of the company's critical documents (wills, trusts, insurance policies, financial statements, bank accounts, key contracts, corporate bylaws, and so forth). The founder should be sure that the successor reads and understands all of the relevant documents in the kit. Other important steps the owner should take to prepare the successor to take over leadership of the business include:

- Create a strategic analysis for the future. Working with the successor, the entrepreneur should identify the primary opportunities and the challenges facing the company and the requirements for meeting them.
- On a regular basis, share with the successor his or her vision of the business's future direction, describing key factors that have led to its success and those that will bring future success.
- Be open and listen to the successor's views and concerns.

- Teach and learn at the same time.
- Identify the industry's key success factors.
- Tie the key success factors to the company's performance and profitability.
- Explain the company's overall strategy and how it creates a competitive advantage.
- Discuss the values and philosophy of the business and how they have inspired and influenced past actions.
- Discuss the people in the business and their strengths and weaknesses.
- Describe the philosophy underlying the firm's compensation policy and explain why employees are paid what they are.
- Make a list of the firm's most important customers and its key suppliers or vendors and review the history of all dealings with the parties on both lists.
- Discuss how to treat these key players to ensure the company's continued success and its smooth and error-free ownership transition.
- Develop a job analysis by taking an inventory of the activities involved in leading the company. This analysis can show successors those activities on which they should be spending most of their time.
- Document as much process knowledge—"how we do things"—as possible. After many years in their jobs, business owners are not even aware of their vast reservoirs of knowledge. For them, making decisions is a natural part of their business lives. They do it effortlessly because they have so much knowledge and experience. It is easy to forget that a successor will not have the benefit of those years of experience unless the founder communicates it.
- Include an ethical will, a document that explains to the next generation of leaders the ethical principles on which the company operates. An ethical will gives company founders the chance to bequeath to their heirs not only a business, but also the wisdom and ethical lessons learned over a lifetime.

ENTREPRENEURIAL
Profile

Paul Weber: Webers Hamburgers

In 1963, Paul Weber started Webers Hamburgers, a small restaurant that has become a landmark, in Ontario, Canada, known for its fresh, tasty burgers. Targeting vacationers and city dwellers looking for an escape, Weber selected a location near the small town of Orillia, about 2 hours north of Toronto. On a typical Saturday during the peak summer season, Webers serves about 800 hamburgers per hour, a pace that tests the restaurant's systems and employees. Managing the family business is second-generation owner Paul Weber, Jr., who grew up working in the restaurant and took over the family business in 1989. Paul Jr. credits much of the company's success to the systems that his father established, refined, and documented over more than a quarter of a century. In fact, Webers continues to document for future generations every part of their business, including the order processing procedure and the techniques they use to entertain guests when lines stretch across the parking lot.[44]

Hungry customers line up, waiting to get into Webers Hamburgers in Orillia, Ontario.

Source: Angelo Cavalli/SuperStock

Step 3: Groom the Successor

The process by which business founders transfer their knowledge to the next generation is gradual and often occurs informally as they spend time with their successors. Grooming the successor is the founder's greatest teaching and development responsibility, and it takes time, usually 5 to 10 years.

ENTREPRENEURIAL
Profile

*Brian Tuberman:
SCTR Systems*

When the founder of SCTR Systems, a company created in 1967 that sells computerized retail systems to independent grocers, began looking for a successor (from outside the family, because none of his children were interested in taking over the family business) 12 years before he planned to retire, he recruited Brian Tuberman and immediately began grooming him to take over the company. Tuberman purchased the business from the founder in 2005 and credits the smooth transition of ownership to the lessons he learned from his mentor. "Everyone thought I was crazy to quit what I was doing to make plans for 12 years down the road," says Tuberman, "but the previous owner and I believed in each other and in the company and made it happen."[45]

To implement the succession plan, the founder must be:

- Patient, realizing that the transfer of power is gradual and evolutionary and that the successor should earn responsibility and authority one step at a time until the final transfer of power takes place.
- Willing to accept that the successor will make mistakes.
- Skillful at using the successor's mistakes as a teaching tool.
- An effective communicator and an especially tolerant listener.
- Capable of establishing reasonable expectations for the successor's performance.
- Able to articulate the keys to the successor's performance.

Teaching is the art of assisting discovery and requires letting go rather than controlling. When problems arise in the business, the founder should consider delegating some of them to the successor-in-training. The founder also must resist the tendency to wade in and fix the problem unless it is beyond the scope of the successor's ability. Most great teachers and leaders are remembered more for the success of their students than for their own success.

Step 4: Promote an Environment of Trust and Respect

Another priceless gift a founder can leave a successor is an environment of trust and respect. Trust and respect on the part of the founder and others fuel the successor's desire to learn and excel and build the successor's confidence in making decisions. Empowering the successor by gradually delegating responsibilities creates an environment in which all parties can objectively view the growth and development of the successor. Customers, creditors, suppliers, and staff members can gradually develop confidence in the successor. The final transfer of power is not a dramatic, wrenching change but a smooth, coordinated passage.

A problem for some founders at this phase is the meddling retiree syndrome, in which they continue to show up at the office after they have officially stepped down and get involved in business issues that no longer concern them. This tendency merely undermines the authority of the successor and confuses employees as to who really is in charge. Helen Dragas, who succeeded her father at the Dragas Company, a residential construction business, praises her father for handing the reins of the company over to her and then trusting her to handle them. "He gave me the authority and then he stepped back," she says of the successful transfer of leadership.[46]

Step 5: Cope with the Financial Realities of Estate and Gift Taxes

The final step in developing a workable management succession plan is structuring the transition to minimize the impact of estate, gift, and inheritance taxes on family members and the business. Entrepreneurs who fail to consider the impact of these taxes (which have been as high as 55 percent) may force their heirs to sell a successful business just to pay the estate's tax (commonly known as the "death tax") bill. Despite facing potentially large tax bills, 19 percent of senior generation owners have done no estate planning at all![47]

Profile

*Clayton Leverett:
Stillwater Farm*

Just a few hours after Clayton Leverett's son, Whit, was born, the young father began to wonder whether Whit would be able to retain the family's 150-year-old Stillwater Ranch, a cattle ranch in Llano, Texas, now in its fifth generation of family ownership. Estate taxes have cut deeply into the Leverett family's land holdings and cattle operations twice before. The family was forced to sell thousands of acres of valuable land to pay estate taxes when Clayton's grandmother died in 2006. When Clayton's father died later that same year, the family faced the estate tax a second time, and once again had to sell acreage and lay off employees. Clayton also had to take on a second job to pay the estate tax. "We will only be able to sell only so much [land] before the ranch becomes unprofitable and we are forced to sell the entire operation," explains a frustrated Clayton.[48]

Although Congress eliminated the estate tax for 2010 (see Table 2), the tax has not evaporated forever. (When George Steinbrenner, owner of the New York Yankees, died in 2010, the year Congress repealed the estate tax, his heirs paid no estate taxes. Had Steinbrenner died in 2009, however, his heirs would have faced a stiff tax bill of $500 million![49]) More than two-thirds of adults believe that that estate tax should remain extinct, and research supports this view. A study by Antony Davies of Duquesne University reports that for every 4.5 percent increase in the estate tax (the average increase in the tax since 1993), 6,000 small businesses are liquidated or absorbed into large companies. Conversely, Davies' research suggests that repealing the tax would create 100,000 new businesses that would employ 2 million workers with a total payroll of $80 billion.[50]

Entrepreneurs who fail to engage in proper estate planning will subject their family members to a painful tax bite when they inherit the business. Entrepreneurs should be actively engaged in estate planning no later than age 45; those who start businesses early in their lives or whose businesses grow rapidly may need to begin as early as age 30. A variety of options exist that may prove to be helpful in reducing the estate tax liability. Each operates in a different fashion, but their objective remains the same: to remove a portion of business owners' assets out of their estates so that when they die those assets will not be subject to estate taxes. Many of these estate planning tools need time to work their magic, so the key is to put them in place early on in the life of the business.

TABLE 2 Changes in the Estate and Gift Taxes

After years of complaints from family business owners, Congress finally overhauled the often punishing structures of estate and gift taxes. The federal estate tax is actually interwoven with the gift tax, but under the modified law the impact of the two taxes began to differ in 2004. Congress repealed the estate tax in 2010, but resurrected it in 2011! The following table shows the trends in the exemptions and the minimum tax rates for the estate and gift taxes:

Year	Estate Tax Exemption	Gift Tax Exemption	Maximum Tax Rate
2001	$675,000	$675,000	55%
2002	$1 million	$1 million	50%
2003	$1 million	$1 million	49%
2004	$1.5 million	$1 million	48%
2005	$1.5 million	$1 million	47%
2006	$2 million	$1 million	46%
2007	$2 million	$1 million	45%
2008	$2 million	$1 million	45%
2009	$3.5 million	$1 million	45%
2010	Tax repealed	$1 million	35% (gifts only)
2011	$5 million	$5 million	35%
2012	?	?	?

No matter how the federal laws governing estate taxes may change over the next few years, entrepreneurs whose businesses have been successful must not neglect estate planning. Even though the federal estate tax burden has eased somewhat (at least for a while), many states have *increased* their estate tax rates.

BUY-SELL AGREEMENT. One of the most popular estate planning techniques is the buy-sell agreement. A **buy-sell agreement** is a contract that co-owners often rely on to ensure the continuity of a business. In a typical arrangement, the co-owners create a contract stating that each agrees to buy the others out in case of the death or disability of one. That way, the heirs of the deceased or disabled owner can "cash out" of the business while leaving control of the business in the hands of the remaining owners. The buy-sell agreement specifies a formula for determining the value of the business at the time the agreement is to be executed. One problem with buy-sell agreements is that the remaining co-owners may not have the cash available to buy out the disabled or deceased owner. To resolve this issue, many businesses buy life and disability insurance for each of the owners in amounts large enough to cover the purchase price of their respective shares of the business. Without the support of adequate insurance policies, a buy-sell agreement offers virtually no protection.

ENTREPRENEURIAL
Profile

Junab Ali and Jay Uribe: Mobius Partners

Junab Ali and Jay Uribe, founders of Mobius Partners, a $25 million a year company that specializes in enterprise IT solutions, created a buy-sell agreement to protect themselves and their business in the event of the death or disability of a partner. Their agreement is supported by insurance policies on each partner, giving them the income security they need for their families and providing the remaining partner the financial resources to buy the shares of the missing partner.[51]

LIFETIME GIFTING. The owners of a successful business may transfer money to their children (or other recipients) from their estate throughout their lives. Current federal tax regulations allow individuals to make gifts of $13,000 per year, per parent, per recipient, that are exempt from federal gift taxes. Another benefit: Gift recipients do not have to pay taxes on the gift. For instance, husband-and-wife business owners could give $1.56 million worth of stock to their three children and their spouses over a period of 10 years without incurring any estate or gift taxes at all.

SETTING UP A TRUST. A **trust** is a contract between a grantor (the founder) and a trustee (generally a bank officer or an attorney) in which the grantor gives to the trustee legal title to assets (e.g., stock in the company), which the trustee agrees to hold for the beneficiaries (children). The beneficiaries can receive income from the trust, or they can receive the property in the trust, or both, at some specified time. Trusts can take a wide variety of forms, but two broad categories of trusts are available: revocable trusts and irrevocable trusts. A **revocable trust** is one that the grantor can change or revoke during his or her lifetime. Under present tax laws, however, the only trust that provides a tax benefit is an **irrevocable trust**, in which the grantor cannot require the trustee to return the assets held in trust. The value of the grantor's estate is lowered because the assets in an irrevocable trust are excluded from the value of that estate. However, an irrevocable trust places severe restrictions on the grantor's control of the property placed in the trust. Business owners use several types of irrevocable trusts to lower their estate tax liabilities:

Bypass Trust. The most basic type of trust is the bypass trust, which allows a business owner to put up to $3 million into trust naming his or her spouse as the beneficiary upon the owner's death. The spouse receives the income from the trust throughout his or her life, but the principal in the trust bypasses the surviving spouse's estate and goes to the couple's heirs free of estate taxes upon the spouse's death. A bypass trust is particularly useful for couples who plan their estates together. By leaving assets to one another in bypass trusts, they can make sure that their assets are taxed only once between them. However, entrepreneurs should work with experienced attorneys to create bypass trusts because the IRS requires that they contain certain precise language to be valid.

Irrevocable Life Insurance Trust (ILIT). This type of trust allows a business owner to keep the proceeds of a life insurance policy out of his or her estate and away from estate taxes, freeing up that money to pay the taxes on the remainder of the estate. To get the tax benefit, business owners must be sure that the business or the trust (rather than themselves) owns the insurance policy. The primary disadvantage of an irrevocable life insurance trust is that if the owner dies within 3 years of establishing it, the insurance proceeds *do* become part of the estate and *are* subject to estate taxes. Because the trust is irrevocable, it cannot be amended or rescinded once it is established. Like most trusts, ILITs must meet stringent requirements to be valid, and entrepreneurs should use experienced attorneys to create them.

Irrevocable Asset Trust. An irrevocable asset trust is similar to a life insurance trust except that it is designed to pass the assets in the parents' estate on to their children. The children do not have control of the assets while the parents are still living, but they do receive the income from those assets. Upon the parents' death, the assets in the trust go to the children without being subjected to the estate tax.

Grantor Retained Annuity Trust (GRAT). A grantor retained annuity trust (GRAT) is a special type of irrevocable trust and has become one of the most popular tools for entrepreneurs to transfer ownership of a business while maintaining control over it and minimizing estate taxes. Under a GRAT, an owner can put property in an irrevocable trust for a maximum of 10 years. While the trust is in effect, the grantor (owner) retains the voting power and receives the interest income from the property in the trust. At the end of the trust (not to exceed 10 years), the property passes to the beneficiaries (heirs). The beneficiaries are required to pay the gift tax on the value of the assets placed in the GRAT but pay no estate tax on them. However, the IRS taxes GRAT gifts according to their discounted present value because the heirs did not receive use of the property while it was in trust. The primary disadvantage of using a GRAT in estate planning is that if the grantor dies during the life of the GRAT, its assets pass back into the grantor's estate. These assets then become subject to the full estate tax.

Establishing a trust requires meeting many specific legal requirements and is not something business owners should do on their own. It is much better to hire experienced attorneys, accountants, and financial advisors to assist in creating them. Although the cost of establishing a trust can be high, the tax savings they generate are well worth the expense.

ESTATE FREEZE. An **estate freeze** attempts to minimize estate taxes by having family members create two classes of stock for the business: (1) preferred voting stock for the parents and (2) nonvoting common stock for the children. The value of the preferred stock is frozen, whereas the common stock reflects the anticipated increased market value of the business. Any appreciation in the value of the business after the transfer is not subject to estate taxes. However, the parent must pay gift tax on the value of the common stock given to the children. The value of the common stock is the total value of the business less the value of the voting preferred stock retained by the parent. The parents also must accept taxable dividends at the market rate on the preferred stock they own.

FAMILY LIMITED PARTNERSHIP. Creating a **family limited partnership (FLP)** allows business-owning parents to transfer their company to their children (thus lowering their estate taxes) while still retaining control over it for themselves. To create an FLP, the parents (or parent) set up a partnership among themselves and their children. The parents retain the general partnership interest, which can be as low as 1 percent, and the children become the limited partners. As general partners, the parents control both the limited partnership and the family business. In other words, nothing in the way the company operates has to change. Over time, the parents can transfer company stock into the limited partnership, ultimately passing ownership of the company to their children.

One of the principal tax benefits of an FLP is that it allows discounts on the value of the shares of company stock the parents transfer into the limited partnership. Because a family business is closely held, shares of ownership in it, especially minority shares, are not as marketable as those of a publicly held company. As a result, company shares transferred into the limited partnership are discounted at 20 to 50 percent of their full market value, producing a large tax savings for everyone involved. The average discount is 40 percent, but that amount varies based on the industry and the individual company involved. A business owner should consider an FLP as part of a succession plan "when there has been a buildup of substantial value in the business and the older generation has a substantial amount of liquidity," says one expert.[52]

Because of their ability to reduce estate and gift taxes, FLPs have become one of the most popular estate planning tools in recent years. However, a Tax Court ruling against a Texas entrepreneur who, 2 months before he died, established an FLP that contained both business and personal assets, cast a pall over the use of FLPs as estate planning tools. Another case, however, calmed estate planners' fears and reestablished the use of FLPs as legitimate estate planning tools as long as entrepreneurs create them properly. The following tips will help entrepreneurs establish an FLP that will withstand legal challenges:

- Establish a legitimate business reason other than avoiding estate taxes, such as transferring a business over time to the next generation of family members, for creating the FLP and document it on paper.
- Make sure all members of the FLP make contributions and take distributions according to a predetermined schedule. "Don't allow partners to use partnership funds to pay for personal expenses and do not time partnership distributions with personal needs for cash," says one attorney.[53]
- Do not allow members to put all of their personal assets (such as a house, automobiles, or personal property) into the FLP. Commingling personal and business assets in an FLP raises a red flag to the IRS.
- Maintain proper records for establishing and operating the FLP.
- Expect an audit of the FLP. The IRS tends to scrutinize FLPs; be prepared for a thorough audit.[54]

Gordon Van Tuinen founded West Michigan Uniform (WMU) in Holland, Michigan, in 1963 and managed it until he retired in 1983, when his son Ken took over as CEO. To transfer the family business to Ken and his four other children, Gordon relied on a variety of estate planning tools, including lifetime gifting and an estate freeze. Ken, who owns the majority of shares in WMU, is now engaged in planning to give control of the company to the third generation of family members with the goal of minimizing the impact of estate taxes. In addition to using lifetime gifting to transfer shares of the company to his three children, one of whom works in the business, Ken created three family limited partnerships that will allow the children to assume ownership of the company over time without incurring oppressive tax bills.[55]

Developing a succession plan and preparing a successor requires a wide variety of knowledge and skills, some of which the business founder will not have. That's why it is important to bring experts into the process when necessary. Entrepreneurs often call on their attorneys, accountants, insurance agents, and financial planners to help them build a succession plan that works best for their particular situations. Because the issues involved can be highly complex and charged with emotion, bringing in trusted advisors to help improves the quality of the process and provides an objective perspective.

Risk Management Strategies

5. Understand the four risk management strategies.

Insurance is an important part of creating a management succession plan because it can help business owners minimize the taxes on the estates they pass on to their heirs and can provide much needed cash to pay the taxes the estate does incur. However, insurance plays an important role in many other aspects of a successful business—from covering employee injuries to protecting against natural disasters that might shut a business down temporarily. When most small business owners think of risks such as these, they automatically think of insurance. However, insurance companies are the first to point out that insurance does not solve all risk problems. A more comprehensive strategy is risk management, which takes a proactive approach to dealing with the risks that businesses face daily. A survey by the National Federation of Independent Businesses shows that just 38 percent of small companies have an emergency preparedness plan for dealing with either a natural or manmade disaster.[56] At least 25 percent of small businesses that are forced to close after a major disaster never reopen; among small businesses that have no disaster plan, the percentage that never reopen jumps to 50 percent.[57] "Small companies often spend more time planning the company picnic than planning for an event that could put them out of business," says one insurance expert.[58] Dealing with risk successfully requires a combination of four risk management strategies: avoiding, reducing, anticipating, and transferring risk.

Avoiding risk requires a business to take actions to shun risky situations. For instance, conducting credit checks of customers decreases losses from bad debts. Wise managers know that they can avoid some risks simply by taking proactive management actions. Workplace safety improves when business owners implement programs designed to make all employees aware of the hazards of their jobs and how to avoid being hurt. Business owners who have active risk identification and prevention programs can reduce their potential insurance costs as well as create a safer, more attractive work environment for their employees. Because avoiding risk altogether usually is not practical, however, a strategy of reducing risk becomes necessary.

A risk-reducing strategy requires a company to take steps to lower the level of risk associated with a situation. Risk reduction strategies do not eliminate risk, but they lessen its impact. Even with avoidance and reduction strategies, the risk is still present; thus, losses can occur.

ENTREPRENEURIAL
Profile
George Pauli: Great Embroidery LLC

George Pauli, owner of Great Embroidery LLC in Mesa, Arizona, recently installed back-up generators for the two machines that he uses to stitch logos on 12 garments at a time. Pauli's business experiences power interruptions about six times a year, and before he installed the generators each incident cost him at least $120 in lost merchandise because the machines' needles could not resume exactly where they had left off when the power shut off.[59]

Risk anticipation strategies promote self-insurance. Knowing that some element of risk still exists, a business owner puts aside money each month to cover potential losses. Sometimes a self-insurance fund may not be large enough to cover the losses from a particular situation. When this happens, a business stands to lose despite the best efforts to anticipate risk, especially in the first few years before the fund is fully funded and able to cover large claims. Most businesses, therefore, include in their risk strategies some form of insurance to transfer risk.

ENTREPRENEURIAL
Profile
Racine Federated

Managers at Racine Federated, a small company in Racine, Wisconsin, that sells industrial instruments, machinery, and tools, grew tired of watching the cost of health care coverage for their 110 employees climb every year and decided to establish a self-insurance fund to cover employees' health care benefits. If employees' claims were low in a given year, Racine would save money over what it would have paid in insurance premiums. If several workers suffered catastrophic injuries or illnesses at once, however, the company could face a cash crisis. Recognizing that a self-insurance strategy alone could be risky, Racine purchased a "stop-loss" policy, which takes over payment if any individual employee's health care costs exceed $55,000 a year. Racine also hired a company to handle all of the insurance paperwork. In the 7 years since switching to self-insurance, Racine has saved $300,000 over the cost of the company's old insurance plan without reducing its coverage.[60]

George Pauli, owner of Great Embroidery LLC, installed back-up generators for his company as part of a risk reduction strategy.

Source: Andy DeLisle/Wonderful Machine

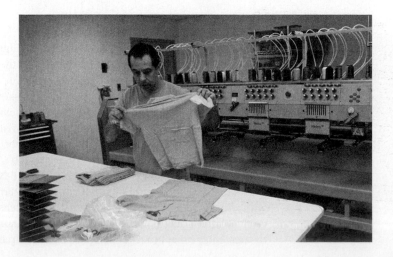

Self-insurance is not for every business owner, however. For businesses with fewer than 50 employees, self-insurance is usually not a wise choice because there is so much variation in the number and size of annual claims. Self-insuring also is time-consuming, requiring business owners to take a more active role in managing their companies' insurance needs. Companies using self-insurance should be financially secure with a relatively stable workforce and should see it as a long-term strategy for savings.

Risk transfer strategies depend on using insurance. Insurance is a risk transfer strategy because an individual or a business transfers some of the costs of a particular risk to an insurance company, which is set up to spread out the financial burdens of risk. During a specific time period, the insured business pays money (a premium) to an insurance carrier (either a private company or a government agency). In return, the carrier promises to pay the insured a certain amount of money in the event of a loss. Small companies across the United States are feeling the pinch of rapidly escalating insurance costs and are devising creative ways to control their insurance costs.

Captive insurance, which is a hybrid of self-insurance and risk transfer strategies, is a technique that large businesses have used for years that is gaining popularity among small businesses. To implement a captive insurance strategy, small companies band together to create their own insurance company and contribute enough capital to cover a defined level of risk. The group outsources the daily management of the insurance company to a business that specializes in that area and then purchases reinsurance to cover losses above the amount that they have contributed. Over time, if the group experiences no large losses, the excess capital paid into the insurance company goes back to the businesses as dividends. Currently, 27 states and the District of Columbia have passed legislation authorizing insurance captives.

ENTREPRENEURIAL
Profile
Dudley Miles:
J.D. Miles & Sons

Dudley Miles, CEO of J.D. Miles & Sons, a roofing contractor founded by his grandfather in 1910, was plagued by escalating insurance premiums that threatened his company's profitability. Working through Roof Connect, an industry association, Miles convinced 25 other roofing contractors to band together to create a captive insurance company. The small businesses agreed to self-insure losses up to $500,000 and purchased reinsurance to cover larger losses. They also adopted several risk reduction strategies such as quarterly safety inspections and random drug tests for employees. The result has been a reduction in the number of claims, improved safety records, and lower premiums than the members of the plan were paying before.[61]

The Basics of Insurance

6. Discuss the basics of insurance for small businesses.

Insurance is the transfer of risk from one entity (an individual, a group, or a business) to an insurance company. Without insurance, many of the products and services that businesses provide would be impossible because the risk of overwhelming financial loss would be too great given the litigious society in which we live. Yet many small business owners ignore their companies' insurance needs or buy insurance coverage for their companies but not enough to protect them from the most basic risks such as property damage, fire, theft, and liability. Home-based business owners, in particular, put their companies at risk. According to the Independent Insurance Agents & Brokers of America, 58 percent of home-based business owners lack adequate insurance to protect them against liability, property damage, or loss.[62]

To be insurable, a situation or hazard must meet the following requirements:

1. It must be possible to calculate the actual loss being insured. For example, it would probably not be possible to insure an entire city against fire because too many variables are involved. It is possible, however, to insure a specific building.
2. It must be possible to select the risk being insured. No business owner can insure against every potential hazard, but insurance companies offer a wide variety of policies. One company even offers an alien abduction policy ($150 a year for $150 million of coverage) and has actually paid one claim! Another offers werewolf insurance, but the policy pays only if the insured turns into a werewolf.[63] Famous insurer Lloyd's of London has insured

Entrepreneurs can buy insurance to protect themselves and their companies from almost any calamity. One insurance company actually offers werewolf insurance!

Source: Lon Chaney\Alamy

coffee taster Gennarro Pelliccia's tongue and taste buds for £10 million. Pelliccia, who samples coffees for Costa Coffee, says, "In my profession, my taste buds and sensory skills are crucial. My taste buds allow me to distinguish any defects, which enables me to protect and guarantee Costa's unique Mocha Italia blend." Lloyd's also once wrote a policy to insure the smile of actress America Ferrera, star of the television show *Ugly Betty*, for $10 million.[64]

3. There must be enough potential policyholders to assume the risk. A tightrope walker who specializes in walking between tall downtown buildings would have difficulty purchasing insurance because there are not enough people engaging in that activity to spread the risk sufficiently.

Perhaps the biggest barrier facing entrepreneurs is the difficulty of understanding the nature of the risks that they and their businesses face. The risk management pyramid (see Figure 6) helps entrepreneurs decide how they should allocate their risk management dollars. Begin by identifying the primary risks your company faces: for example, a fire in a manufacturing plant, a lawsuit from a customer injured by your company's product, a computer system meltdown, an earthquake, and so on. Then rate each event on three factors:

1. *Severity.* How much would the event affect your company's ability to operate?
2. *Probability.* How likely is the event to occur?
3. *Cost.* How much would it cost your company if the event occurred?

Rate the event on each of these three factors using a simple scale: A (high) to D (low). For instance, a small technology company might rate a fire in its offices as BDA. On the other hand, that same company might rank a computer system crash as ABA. Using the risk management pyramid, a business owner sees that the event rated ABA is higher on the risk scale than the event rated BDA. Therefore, this company would focus more of its risk management dollars on preventing a computer system crash than on protecting against an office fire.

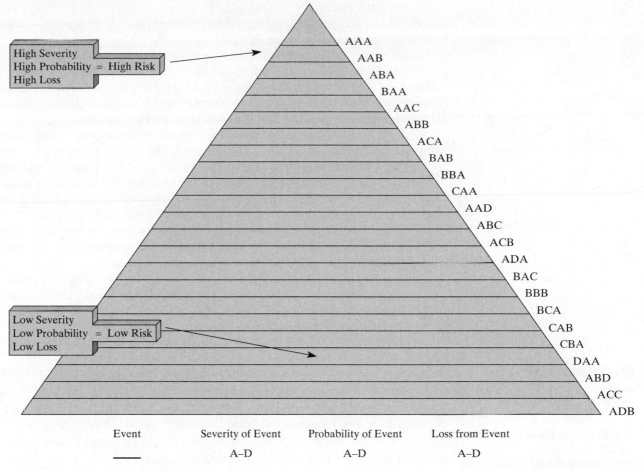

High Severity
High Probability = High Risk
High Loss

Low Severity
Low Probability = Low Risk
Low Loss

Event	Severity of Event	Probability of Event	Loss from Event
——	A–D	A–D	A–D

FIGURE 6
The Risk Management Pyramid

Types of Insurance

No longer is the cost of insurance an inconsequential part of doing business. Now the ability to get adequate coverage and to pay the premiums is a significant factor in starting and running a small business. Sometimes just *finding* coverage for their businesses is a challenge for entrepreneurs.

ENTREPRENEURIAL
Profile

Jane Reifert:
Incredible Adventures

For Incredible Adventures, a small Sarasota, Florida-based company that offers customers the opportunity to fly in a Russian MiG jet fighter; experience weightlessness; go to the edge of space; swim with sharks; or make a high-altitude, low-opening (HALO) sky dive; in addition to many other exciting adventures, purchasing insurance is a challenge. President Jane Reifert says that she spends as much time with lawyers and insurance agents as she does with customers. "You can insure people swimming in shark-infested waters, but you can't insure people inside shark cages," she says incredulously.[65]

A wide range of business, individual, and group insurance is available to small business owners, and deciding which ones are necessary can be difficult. Some types of insurance are essential to providing a secure future for the company; others may provide additional employee benefits. The four major categories of insurance are property and casualty insurance, life and disability insurance, health insurance and workers' compensation coverage, and liability insurance. Each category is divided into many specific types, each of which has many variations offered by insurance companies. Business owners should begin by purchasing a basic **business owner's policy (BOP)**, which typically includes basic property and casualty insurance and liability insurance coverage. BOPs alone are not sufficient to meet most small business owners' insurance needs, however. Entrepreneurs should start with BOPs and then customize their insurance coverage to suit their companies' special needs by purchasing additional types of coverage.

PROPERTY AND CASUALTY INSURANCE. Property and casualty insurance covers a company's tangible assets, such as buildings, equipment, inventory, machinery, signs, and others that might be damaged, destroyed, or stolen. Business owners should be sure that their policies cover the replacement cost of their property, not just its value at the time of the loss, even if this coverage costs extra. One business owner whose policy covered the replacement cost of his company's building was glad he had purchased the extra coverage when he suffered a devastating fire loss. When he began rebuilding, he discovered that the cost to comply with current building code regulations was much higher than merely replacing the previous structure.

Specific types of property and casualty insurance include property, surety, marine and inland marine, crime, liability, business interruption, motor vehicle, and professional liability insurance.

Property insurance protects a company's assets against loss from damage, theft, or destruction. It applies to automobiles, boats, homes, office buildings, stores, factories, and other items of property. Some property insurance policies are broadly written to include all of an individual's property up to some maximum amount of loss, whereas other policies are written to cover only one building or one specific piece of property, such as a company car. Many natural disasters, such as floods and earthquakes, are not covered under standard property insurance; business owners must buy separate insurance policies for those particular events.

Within the last decade, business owners across the United States have suffered billions of dollars in losses from natural disasters ranging from tornadoes and hurricanes to snow and ice storms. Many of the businesses that lacked proper insurance coverage were forced to close for good, and others are still struggling to recover.

ENTREPRENEURIAL
Profile

*The Brennan Family:
Ralph Brennan
Restaurant Group*

Even with adequate insurance, it took the Brennans, New Orleans' famous family of restaurateurs, more than a year to reopen the celebrated Commander's Palace after Hurricane Katrina severely damaged the historic Garden District building that housed it. Almost all of the interior of the building, which was constructed in 1880, had to be rebuilt because of water damage, and more than 80 percent of the kitchen equipment had to be replaced. Charlie Williamson, vice president of the Ralph Brennan Restaurant Group, says that the company's disaster preparation plan has grown from 2 pages before the hurricane to a 68-page booklet that covers not only operating plans but also technology and communications plans.[66]

A company's BOP may insure the buildings and contents of a factory for loss from fire or natural disaster, but the owner may also buy insurance, called extra expense coverage, to cover expenses that occur while the destroyed factory is being rebuilt. **Extra expense coverage** pays for the costs of temporarily relocating workers and machinery so that a business can continue to

After suffering damage from Hurricane Katrina, New Orleans' famous Commander's Palace restaurant is now fully restored. Even with adequate insurance coverage, the restoration took more than a year.

Source: © Angelo Cavalli/SuperStock

operate while it rebuilds or repairs its factory. A similar type of insurance, called **business interruption insurance**, covers business owners' lost income and ongoing expenses in case their companies cannot operate for an extended period of time. As devastating as interruptions can be to a small company, studies show that 55 percent of small business owners do not purchase business interruption coverage and that 63 percent of them do not know how the coverage works.[67] Even more alarming is the fact that 25 percent of businesses whose operations are interrupted by a disaster never reopen.[68]

ENTREPRENEURIAL Profile

Wendy Stevens: Alloy Design

Wendy Stevens, who owns Alloy Design, a business in Boyertown, Pennsylvania, that manufactures accessories and home decorations out of stainless steel, watched helplessly as more than 100 firefighters battled a blaze that ultimately claimed the building that housed her company. "I remember feeling huge waves of nausea and thinking, 'My business is gone,'" she says. "Everything was destroyed—equipment, inventory, paperwork. All that remained were two stone walls, a floor, and 20 years of designing, building, and selling my product." Fortunately, Stevens had good insurance coverage, including property and inventory insurance as well as business interruption insurance. One year after the fire, Stevens was back in business. "After losing everything, I've managed to bounce back with even better products and to expand into new markets. I'm now selling in four different countries."[69]

Machinery and equipment insurance is a common addition for many businesses and covers a wide range of problems with equipment such as production machinery, electrical systems, HVAC systems, and others. For instance, a restaurant that loses thousands of dollars' worth of food when a freezer breaks down would be covered for its loss under machinery and equipment insurance.

Auto insurance policies offer liability coverage that protects against losses resulting from injuries, damage, or theft involving the use of company vehicles. A typical BOP does not include liability coverage for automobiles; business owners must purchase a separate policy for auto insurance. The automobiles a business owns must be covered by a commercial policy, not a personal one.

Electronic data processing (EDP) insurance covers losses from the theft or loss of computers and data, the impact of computer viruses and computer system failures, intrusion by hackers, and invasion of customer information stored in company databases. EDP insurance has become more important as businesses have moved their operations online and engage in increasing volumes of e-commerce. Thomas Shipley, whose company sells business accessories, generates 30 percent of his sales from the company's Web site. Shipley purchased an EDP policy that protects his business from, among other things, hackers and viruses. The policy costs $14,000 a year, but Shipley says it is well worth the price to protect his company that now brings in more than $10 million in sales a year.[70]

A business may also purchase **surety insurance**, which protects against losses to customers that occur when a company fails to complete a contract on time or completes it incorrectly. Surety protection guarantees customers that they will get either the products or services they purchased or the money to cover losses from contractual failures.

Businesses also buy insurance to protect themselves from losses that occur when either finished goods or raw materials are lost or destroyed while being shipped. **Marine insurance** is designed to cover the risk associated with goods in transit. The name of this insurance goes back to the days when a ship's cargo was insured against high risks associated with ocean navigation.

Crime insurance does not deter crime, but it can reimburse the small business owner for losses from the "three Ds": dishonesty, disappearance, and destruction. Business owners should ask their insurance brokers or agents exactly what their crime insurance policies cover; after-the-fact insurance coverage surprises are seldom pleasant. Premiums for crime policies vary depending on the type of business, store location, number of employees, quality of the business's security system, and the business's history of losses. Coverage may include fidelity bonds, which are designed to reimburse business owners for losses from embezzlement and employee theft. Forgery bonds reimburse owners for losses sustained from the forgery of business checks.

LIFE AND DISABILITY INSURANCE. Unlike most forms of insurance, life insurance does not pertain to avoiding risk because death is a certainty for everyone. Rather, **life insurance** protects families and businesses against loss of income, security, or personal services that results from an individual's untimely death. Life insurance policies are usually issued with a face amount payable to a beneficiary upon the death of the insured. Life insurance for business protection, although not as common as life insurance for family protection, is becoming more popular. As you learned in the section on management succession, life insurance policies are an important part of many estate planning tools. In addition, many businesses insure the lives of key executives to offset the costs of having to make a hurried and often unplanned replacement of important managers.

When it comes to assets that are expensive to replace, few are more costly than the key people in a business, including the owner. What would it take to replace a company's top sales representative? Its production supervisor? Clearly, money alone cannot solve the problem, but it does allow a business to find and train their replacements and to cover the profits lost because of their untimely deaths or disabilities. That is the idea behind **key-person insurance**, which provides valuable working capital to keep a business on track while it reorganizes and searches for the right person to replace the loss of someone in a key position in the company.

Disability insurance protects an individual in the event of unexpected and often very expensive disabilities. Because a sudden disability limits a person's ability to earn a living, the insurance proceeds are designed to help make up the difference between what that person could have expected to earn if the accident had not occurred. Sometimes called income insurance, these policies usually guarantee a stated percentage of an individual's income—usually around 60 percent—while he or she is recovering and is unable to run a business. Short-term disability policies cover the 90-day gap between the time a person is injured and when workers' compensation payments begin. Long-term disability policies pay for lost income after 90 days or longer. In addition to the portion of income a policy will replace, another important factor to consider when purchasing disability insurance is the waiting period, the time gap between when the disability occurs and the disability payments begin. Although many business owners understand the importance of maintaining adequate life insurance coverage, fewer see the relevance of maintaining proper coverage for disabilities. For most people, the likelihood of a disability is three to five times greater than the risk of death; nearly 30 percent of workers between the ages of 35 and 65 will be unable to work for 90 days or longer due to a disability.[71]

Business owners can supplement traditional disability policies with **business overhead expense (BOE) insurance**. Designed primarily for companies with fewer than 15 employees, a BOE policy will replace 100 percent of a small company's monthly overhead expenses such as rent, utilities, insurance, taxes, and others if the owner is incapacitated. Payments typically begin 30 days after the owner is incapacitated and continue for up to 2 years.

HEALTH INSURANCE AND WORKERS' COMPENSATION. According to the National Federation of Independent Businesses (NFIB), small business owners' greatest concern for the last 25 years has been the skyrocketing cost of health insurance.[72] Currently, health care spending in the United States accounts for 17.3 percent of GDP, an amount that will increase to 20 percent by 2017.[73] The average small company spends on average $5,046 per year on health care insurance premiums for an employee. Because of the high cost of providing health care coverage for employees, only 68 percent of small businesses offer health insurance to their employees, compared to 99 percent of large companies (see Figure 7).[74] As health care costs steadily climb and the average age of the workforce continues to increase, small companies are having more difficulty providing coverage for their employees (see Figure 8). The primary reason cited by small business owners who do not offer health insurance is the high cost.[75] Small businesses actually pay 18 percent more than large companies for the same health insurance because of higher broker fees and costs of administering health care plans for a smaller number of employees.[76] "The corporate world really spoiled me," says Sandy Dixon, who left a large company to start Interior Arrangements, an interior redesign company in Evergreen, Colorado. "[When I started my business,] I was

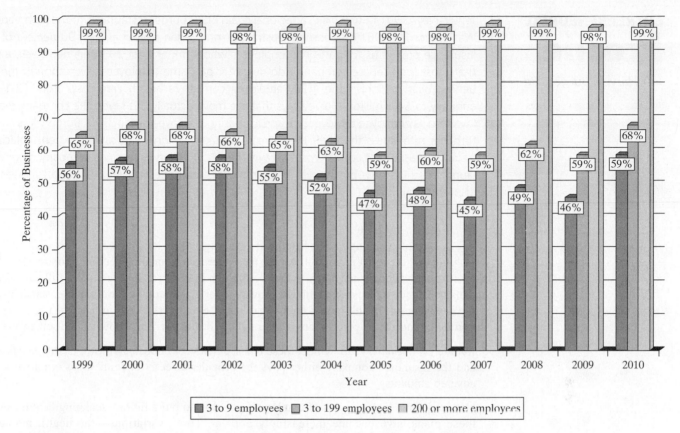

FIGURE 7
Percentage of Companies Offering Health Benefits by Company Size

Source: Employer Health Benefits: 2010 Summary of Findings, Kaiser Family Foundation and Health Research and Education Trust, p. 5.

really surprised by the high cost of health insurance and suddenly had a new appreciation for this corporate perk."[77]

Health insurance has become an extremely important benefit to most workers. Small companies that offer thorough health care coverage often find that it gives them an edge in attracting and retaining a quality workforce. In fact, 86 percent of business owners cite health care as the most important benefit to attracting and retaining quality workers.[78]

FIGURE 8
Average Annual Health Insurance Premiums for Family Coverage

Source: Employer Health Benefits: 2010 Summary of Findings, Kaiser Family Foundation and Health Research and Education Trust, p. 1.

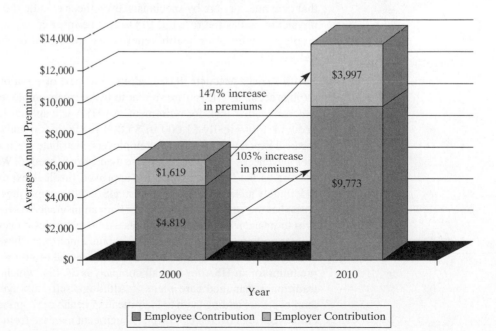

ENTREPRENEURIAL

Profile

Jeff Harvey: Burgerville

Jeff Harvey, CEO of Burgerville, a regional chain of 39 burger restaurants founded in Vancouver, Washington, in 1961 by George Propstra, recently began paying at least 90 percent of health insurance premiums for part-time employees who work at least 20 hours per week, a benefit that most food-service companies do not offer part-time employees. Even though the added benefit nearly doubled the 1,500-employee company's health care costs from $2.1 million annually to $4.1 million, Harvey says that the move actually has saved the company money by lowering its employee turnover rate and increasing employee productivity. Burgerville's employee turnover rate is less than half the industry average, a significant savings when replacing and training a restaurant worker costs on average $1,700. Harvey says the company is considering launching a wellness program to help employees lead healthier lifestyles and to lower health insurance claims.[79]

A key to providing proper health care coverage while keeping costs in check is to offer the benefits that are most important to your employees and to avoid spending money unnecessarily on coverage that does not apply to them. Although the Affordable Care Act, a bill passed in 2010 that is designed to provide health care coverage for a greater number of people, stands to change the mechanics of health care in the United States, employers face four basic health care options: traditional indemnity plans, managed care plans, health savings accounts, and self-insurance.

Traditional Indemnity Plans. Under these plans, employees choose their own health care providers, and the insurance company either pays the provider directly or reimburses employees for the covered amounts.

Managed Care Plans. As part of employers' attempts to put a lid on escalating health care costs, these plans have become increasingly popular. Three variations—the health maintenance organization (HMO), the preferred provider organization (PPO), and the point of service (POS)—are most common. An HMO is a prepaid health care arrangement under which employees must use health care providers who are employed by or are under contract with the HMO their company uses. Although they lower health care costs, employees have less freedom in selecting physicians under an HMO. Under a PPO, an insurance company negotiates discounts for health care with certain physicians and hospitals. If employees choose a health care provider from the approved list, they pay only a small fee for each office visit (often just $10 to $25). The insurance company pays the remainder. Employees may select a provider outside the PPO, but they pay more for the service. A POS is a hybrid of an HMO and a PPO that gives employees the freedom to select their health care providers (as with a PPO) and lowers costs (as with an HMO). As long as employees choose a primary care physician within the approved network, the POS will pay for that care and for care by specialists, even those outside the network, as long as the primary care physician makes the referral. PPOs are the most common managed care plans (53 percent of employers who offer health benefits use them), followed by POSs (25 percent) and HMOs (24 percent).[80]

Health Savings Accounts (HSAs). Created as part of a major Medicare overhaul in 2003, health savings accounts (HSAs) are similar to IRAs except employees' contributions are used for medical expenses rather than for retirement. An HSA is a special savings account coupled with a high-deductible (typically $1,000 to $5,000 for an individual) insurance policy that covers major medical expenses. Employees or employers contribute pre-tax dollars (up to a defined ceiling) from their paychecks into the fund and use them as they need to. Withdrawals from an HSA are not taxed as long as the money is used for approved medical expenses. Unused funds can accumulate indefinitely and earn tax-free interest. HSAs offer employees incentives to contain their health care costs, but the employer must choose both an insurance carrier to provide coverage and a custodial firm to manage employees' accounts. Although critics contend that consumer-driven plans push a greater portion of health care expenses onto employees, these plans continue to grow in popularity among small businesses because of their potential to rein in escalating costs. The average annual premium for an HSA for a small company is $4,454, which is 13.1 percent lower than the cost of traditional managed care plans.[81] Although self-employed individuals find HSAs attractive, employers are adding them to their menu of health care options for employees. More than 8 million employees are covered by HSAs, a significant increase from 1 million in 2005.[82]

ENTREPRENEURIAL
Profile

*Andrew Field and
PrintingforLess.com*

Andrew Field, owner of PrintingforLess.com, a Web-based printing company, had seen health care costs for his company's 130 employees increase by double-digit rates year after year and decided to switch from a traditional plan to an HSA plan. The change allowed him to provide his employees with better, more flexible coverage and the freedom to decide how to spend their health care dollars without any increase in cost. Although PrintingforLess.com did encounter a few problems in making the switch, Field and his employees are pleased with the HSA. "We were worried that it might have some bad side effects," he says. "but it's better than we thought."[83]

Self-Insurance. As you learned earlier in this chapter, some business owners choose to insure themselves for health coverage rather than to incur the costs of fully insured plans offered by outsiders. The benefits of self-insurance include greater control over the plan's design and the coverage it offers, fewer paperwork and reporting requirements, and, in some cases, lower costs. The primary disadvantage, of course, is the possibility of having to pay large amounts to cover treatments for several employees' major illnesses at the same time, which can strain a small company's cash flow. Many self-insured businesses limit their exposure to such losses by purchasing stop-loss insurance, under which the business owner pays for health care expenses up to a predetermined point; beyond that point, the stop-loss policy takes over the expenses.

Another type of health-related coverage is **workers' compensation**, which is designed to cover employees who are injured on the job or who become sick as a result of a work environment. Worker's compensation is a mandatory insurance program; companies that fail to offer workers' compensation must pay out-of-pocket for workers' claims and face penalties from the state. Before passage of workers' compensation legislation in 1911, an employee injured on the job had to bring a lawsuit to prove the employer was liable for the worker's injury. Because of the red tape and expenses involved in these lawsuits, many employees never received compensation for job-related accidents and injuries. Although the details of coverage vary from state to state, workers' compensation laws require employers to purchase insurance that provides benefits and medical and rehabilitation costs for employees injured on the job. The amount of compensation an injured employee receives depends on a fixed schedule of payment benefits based on three factors: the wages or salary that the employee was earning at the time of the accident or injury, the seriousness of the injury, and the extent of the disability to the employee.

Only two states, New Jersey and Texas, do not require companies to purchase workers' compensation coverage once they reach a certain size (usually three or more employees). Usually, the state sets the rates businesses pay for workers' compensation coverage, and business owners purchase their coverage from private insurance companies. Rapidly escalating workers' compensation rates, driven in large part by rising medical expenses, have become a major concern for small businesses across the nation. Companies in Alaska face the highest workers' compensation costs in the nation.[84] McGraw's Custom Construction in Sitka, Alaska, saw its workers' compensation costs go from $146,950 to $315,110 in just 2 years![85] Rates vary by industry, business size, and the number of claims a company's workers make. For instance, workers' compensation premiums are higher for a timber cutting business than for a retail gift store. Table 3 shows the 10 occupations with the greatest number of injuries and illnesses. Whatever industry they are in, business owners can reduce their workers' compensation costs by improving their employees' safety records.

ENTREPRENEURIAL
Profile

Core Systems

Core Systems, a plastic injection molding company based in Painesville, Ohio, was growing so fast that its accidents began to spiral out of control. Not only were employees being injured, but morale was down and workers' compensation costs were way up. In an effort to contain the rapidly rising costs, human resources director Maggine Fuentes, launched a safety system that combed through company records looking for accident and injury patterns and then focused on training and soliciting employee suggestions for improvement. The system made safety a priority at Core Systems and reduced both the number and the severity of accidents in the plant, which has lowered the company's workers' compensation cost by $277,000 so far.[86]

TABLE 3 Ten Most Dangerous Occupations

Rank	Occupation	Percentage of Total Injuries and Illnesses
1	Nonconstruction laborers	7.4%
2	Truck drivers (heavy)	5.4%
3	Nursing aides and orderlies	4.1%
4	Construction workers	2.9%
5	Retail salespeople	2.7%
6	Janitors and cleaners	2.6%
7	Truck drivers (light)	2.6%
8	Maintenance and repair workers	1.9%
9	Registered nurses	1.8%
10	Maids and housekeeping cleaners	1.7%

Source: "Workplace Safety/Workers Comp," Insurance Information Institute, *www.iii.org/facts_statistics/workplace-safety-workers-comp.html.*

▶ ENTREPRENEURSHIP IN ACTION ▶

What Can We Do to Help You Stay Healthy?

In 1997, when Jason Crawforth started Treetop Tech, a software development company in Boise, Idaho, he did not offer company-sponsored health insurance because he believed that his small company could not afford the cost. He soon realized, however, that he could not afford *not* to offer health insurance. "We started losing potential employees because of that," he says. In 2000, Crawforth added health insurance coverage to his employees' benefits package, just in time to watch premiums skyrocket over the next decade.

Crawforth, like many small business owners, is struggling to cope with health insurance premiums that have increased by 114 percent since 2000, compared to an increase of just 27 percent in the consumer price index over the same period. According to a survey by Aflac Inc. and Accelerant Research, 62 percent of small business owners say it is more difficult to offer a strong benefits package than 1 year before, and 52 percent say they have reduced their health insurance coverage. Donna Partin, who owns three Merry Maids franchises, two in Pennsylvania and one in Florida, that employ a total of 50 workers, says that her company's health insurance premiums have tripled since 2000. "I'm paying more for less and less [coverage] every year," she says. Partin pays $5,000 per month to insure her employees in Pennsylvania, where only one-third of her workforce has opted for coverage. The others cannot afford their portion of the health insurance premium. Partin says that she cannot afford coverage for her employees

in Florida, something that causes her concern because her business requires trustworthy workers to go into clients' homes to clean. As health care insurance costs continue to escalate, Partin, like many small business owners, worries that she will be at a disadvantage in attracting and retaining quality workers if she has to pare back or even eliminate coverage.

Thomas Johnson, owner of Thomas A. Johnson Furniture, a company that builds custom, handmade furniture in Lynchburg, Virginia, emigrated from Ghana, West Africa, to the United States with just $20, a willingness to work hard, and a desire to own a business. Today, the master craftsman has eight employee apprentices who work beside him, learning to make fine furniture. Unable to afford the premiums for a group health insurance plan, Johnson pays out-of-pocket for his employees' medical expenses. Skilled woodworkers are difficult to find, and Johnson cannot afford to lose any of his employees, in whom he has invested thousands of hours of training. "My workers are part of my business and part of my family," he says. To him, paying their medical expenses is a matter of honor—and practicality—but it also is risky. By paying for his workers' medical expenses, Johnson may have set a precedent that could obligate him to pay for all of his employees' expenses—even in the case of a catastrophic illness that might cost hundreds of thousands of dollars to treat.

About 70 percent of health care costs arise from *preventable* chronic diseases, a fact that has led many businesses to implement wellness programs that are designed to put the brakes on cost increases by giving employees incentives to get and stay healthy by quitting smoking, maintaining an ideal weight, reducing stress, and exercising regularly. Employers typically pay between $100 and $300 per person per year in incentives, a small price to pay compared to the additional $16,000 lifetime health care costs associated with an employee who smokes. The same holds true for overweight employees; health care costs are $1,400 more per year for obese workers than those who maintain a healthy weight. One-third of small companies offer wellness programs that include onsite fitness centers or memberships for offsite fitness centers, smoking cessation programs, online tracking tools, onsite health checks, and other features. Not only do wellness programs improve employees' health, but they also produce an impressive return on investment—up to $6 on average for every $1 invested. Mike Faith, founder of Headsets.com in San Francisco, California, stocks the break room with healthy snacks and fresh fruit for his 52 employees. He also offers them subsidized gym memberships and help with smoking cessation, including free nicotine patches.

"You don't need to spend a lot of money on these programs," says Dan Dauphinee, operations manager at Northeastern Log Homes, a small business in Kenduskeag, Maine. Northeastern Log Homes recently created a walking trail for its 100 employees, who are encouraged to exercise during their breaks. The company also offers fruits and vegetables in its snack room at subsidized prices. North-eastern Log Homes gives employees who engage in its wellness program discounts on their portion of health insurance premiums. Components of the wellness program range from nutrition lectures to walking challenges. "When you look at a culture that has healthy, happy employees and your health insurance costs are not going up, that's the justification," says Dauphinee.

1. Is it ethical for companies to reduce their health care costs by offering employees incentives to get and stay healthy? Explain.
2. How much control should companies have over employees' lifestyles away from the workplace?

Sources: Based on Patricia B. Gray, "HealthCure," *FSB*, February 2009, pp. 57–65; Robert Langreth, "Healthy Bribes," *Forbes*, August 24, 2009, p. 72; Mark Henricks, "An Apple a Day . . . " *Entrepreneur*, March 2008, pp. 19–20; E. B. Solomont, "Companies Find Inexpensive Ways to Promote Wellness," *Workforce Management*, March 2009, *www.workforce.com/section/benefits-compensation/feature/companies-find-inexpensive-ways-promote-wellness/index.html*; John Cummings, "Finding the ROI in Wellness Incentives," *Business Finance*, August 11, 2008, *http://businessfinancemag.com/article/finding-roi-wellness-incentives-0811;* Simone Richards, "Small Businesses Struggle to Offer Healthcare," *Black Enterprise*, July 15, 2009, *www.blackenterprise.com/business/business-news/2009/07/15/small-businesses-struggle-to-offer-healthcare/.*

LIABILITY INSURANCE. One of the most common types of insurance coverage is liability insurance, which protects a business against losses resulting from accidents or injuries people suffer on the company's property, from its products or services, and damage the company causes to others' property. Most BOPs include basic liability coverage; however, the limits on the typical policy are not high enough to cover the potential losses many small business owners face. For example, one "slip-and-fall" case involving a customer who is injured by slipping and falling on a wet floor could easily exceed the standard limits on a basic BOP. Claims from customers injured by a company's product or service also are covered by its liability policy. Although most product liability lawsuits are settled out of court, the median award for those that go to court is nearly $2 million.[87]

Even though courts have dismissed them, some small companies have been targets of frivolous lawsuits because they are seen as easy targets. Frivolous lawsuits can cost a small company thousands of dollars to defend, however. Jin and Soo Chung, owners of Custom Cleaners in Washington, D.C., recently were hit with a $54 million lawsuit by a customer after the dry cleaner lost a pair of the customer's pants! The trial court ruled for Custom Cleaners, but plaintiff Roy Pearson filed an appeal, extending the legal nightmare for the small business owners, who incurred $83,000 in legal fees to defend themselves.[88] With jury awards in product liability cases often reaching into the millions of dollars, entrepreneurs who fail to purchase sufficient liability coverage may end up losing their businesses. Most insurance experts recommend purchasing a commercial general liability policy that provides coverage of at least $2 million to $3 million for the typical small business. As a result, many business owners find it necessary to purchase additional liability coverage for their companies.

Another important type of liability insurance for many small businesses is **professional liability insurance**, or **"errors and omissions" coverage**. This insurance protects against damage a business causes to customers or clients as a result of an error an employee makes or an employees' failure to take proper care and precautions. For instance, a land surveyor may miscalculate the location of a customer's property line. If the landowner relies on that

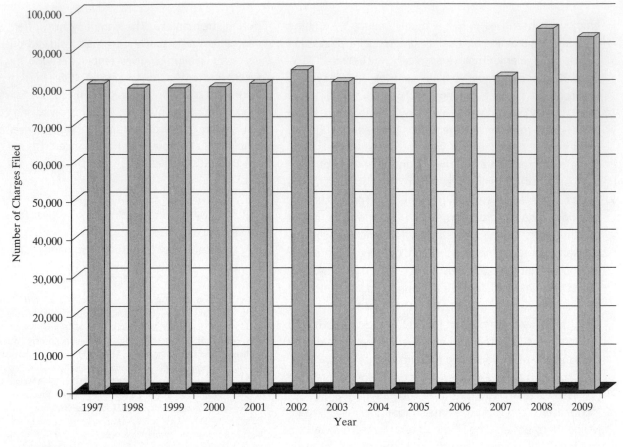

FIGURE 9
Number of Employment Charges Filed with EEOC

Source: Based on data from the Equal Employment Opportunity Commission, *www.eeoc.gov/eeoc/statistics/enforcement/all.cfm.*

property line to build a structure on what he thinks is his land and it turns out to be on his neighbor's land, the surveyor is liable for damages. Doctors, dentists, attorneys, and other professionals protect themselves through a similar kind of insurance, malpractice insurance, which protects them against the risk of lawsuits arising from errors in professional practice or judgment.

Employment practices liability (EPL) insurance provides protection against claims arising from charges of employment discrimination, improper discipline, wrongful termination, sexual harassment, and violations of the Americans with Disabilities Act, the Family and Medical Leave Act, and other employment legislation (see Figure 9). Although two-thirds of small business owners express concern that an employee will bring an EPL suit against them, only 1.2 percent carry EPL insurance.[89] Although most violations of these employment laws are not intentional but are the result of either carelessness or lack of knowledge, the company that violates them is still liable. Losing an employment practices liability case (employees win 58 percent of EPL cases) can be very expensive; the median jury award in EPL cases is $253,000.[90] Because they often lack full-time human resources professionals, small companies are especially vulnerable to charges of improper employment practices, making this type of insurance coverage all the more important to them. Seven employees at a franchised restaurant claimed that their supervisor had sexually harassed them by touching them inappropriately and making lewd comments and demands for sex. The young women complained about the harassment to the restaurant's general manager, who failed to investigate or act on their complaints. The restaurant owner negotiated an out-of-court settlement with the plaintiffs for $400,000, an amount that could force many small companies to close.[91]

Every business's insurance needs are somewhat unique, requiring owners to customize the insurance coverage they purchase. Entrepreneurs also must keep their insurance coverage updated as their companies grow; when companies expand, so do their insurance needs.

Controlling Insurance Costs

Small business owners face constantly rising insurance premiums. Entrepreneurs can take steps to lower insurance costs, however. To control the cost of insurance, owners should take the following steps:

1. *Pursue a loss-control program by making risk reduction a natural part of all employees' daily routine.* As discussed earlier in this chapter, risk reduction minimizes claims and eventually lowers premiums. Establishing a loss-control program means taking steps such as installing modern fire alarms, sprinkler systems, safety programs, and sophisticated security systems.

2. *Increase their policies' deductibles.* If a business can afford to handle minor losses, the owner can save money by raising the deductible to a level that protects the business against catastrophic events but, in effect, self-insures against minor losses. Business owners must determine the amount of financial exposure they can reasonably accept.

3. *Work with qualified professional insurance brokers or agents.* Business owners should do their homework before choosing insurance brokers or agents. This includes checking their reputation, credentials, and background by asking them to supply references.

4. *Work actively with brokers to make sure they understand business owners' particular needs.* Brokers need to know about entrepreneurs' businesses and objectives for insurance coverage. They can help only if they know their clients' needs and the degree of risk they are willing to take.

5. *Work with brokers to find competitive companies that want small companies' insurance business and have the resources to cover losses when they arise.* The price of the premium should never be an entrepreneur's sole criterion for selecting insurance. The rating of the insurance company should always be a primary consideration. What good is it to have paid low premiums if, after a loss, a business owner finds that the insurance company is unable to pay? Many small business owners learned costly lessons when their insurance companies, unable to meet their obligations, filed for bankruptcy protection.

6. *Utilize the resources of your insurance company.* Many insurers provide risk management inspections designed to help business owners assess the level of risk in their companies either for free or for a minimal fee. Smart entrepreneurs view their insurance companies as partners in their risk management efforts.

7. *Conduct a periodic insurance audit.* Reviewing your company's coverage annually can ensure that insurance coverage is adequate and can lead to big cost savings as well.

ENTREPRENEURIAL
Profile

Keith Alper: Creative Products Group

Keith Alper, owner of Creative Products Group (CPG), a business that produces videos for *Fortune* 500 companies, was surprised to discover that CPG was wasting thousands of dollars on policies it did not need. Many employees were classified incorrectly for workers' compensation coverage, several policies duplicated the coverage of others, and the company was paying for auto insurance on four cars when it had only three! In all, Alper was able to shave more than $10,000 off of the company's $75,000 annual insurance bill.[92]

8. *Compile discrimination, harassment, hiring, and other employment polices into an employee handbook and train employees to use them.* Companies that take an active approach to avoiding illegal employment practices have less exposure to lawsuits and, therefore, may be able to negotiate lower premiums.

Since World War II, businesses have been and continue to be the principal suppliers of health insurance in our society. To control the cost of health insurance, small business owners should consider the following steps:

1. *Increase the dollar amount of employee contributions and the amount of the employee deductibles.* Neither option is desirable, but rising medical costs have resulted in individuals becoming more responsible for their own health insurance and self-insuring to cover high deductibles.

2. *Switch to PPOs, POS plans, or HMOs.* Higher premium costs have encouraged some small business owners to reevaluate PPOs, POS plans, and HMOs as alternatives to traditional

health insurance policies. Although some employees resent limitations on their choice of providers, PPOs, HMOs, and POS plans have become the primary vehicles for companies to provide health care coverage to their employees.

3. *Consider joining an insurance pool.* Small businesses can lower their insurance premiums by banding together to purchase coverage. In many states, chambers of commerce, trade associations, and other groups form insurance pools that small businesses can join, spreading risk over a larger number of employees. In Cleveland, Ohio, for example, about 14,000 small companies purchase health insurance for their employees through the Council of Smaller Enterprises, a division of the chamber of commerce, at rates that are 8 percent below those that the owners could negotiate individually.[93]

4. *Keep employees informed.* By giving employees information about the costs and the benefits of various treatment alternatives and medications, employers empower their workers to make informed decisions that can lower health care costs.

5. *Conduct a yearly utilization review.* A review may reveal that your employees' use of their policies is statistically lower, which may provide you leverage to negotiate lower premiums or to switch to an insurer that wants a business with your track record and offers lower premiums.

6. *Make sure your company's health plan fits your employees' needs.* One of best ways to keep health care costs in check is to offer only those benefits that employees actually need. Getting employee input is essential to the process.

7. *Create a wellness program for all employees.* We have all heard the old adage that an ounce of prevention is worth a pound of cure, but when it comes to the high cost of medical expenses, this is especially true! Companies that have created wellness programs report cost savings of up to $6 for every $1 they invest. Employees involved in wellness programs not only incur lower health care expenses, but they also tend to be more productive as well. "Companies are reforming their own health care costs by recognizing that healthy workers cost less, are more productive, and are better for the company as a whole," says the president of a nonprofit health and productivity company.[94] Providing a wellness program does not mean building an expensive gym, however. Instead, it may be as simple as providing routine checkups from a nurse, incentives for quitting smoking, weight-loss counseling, or after-work athletic games that involve as many employees as possible. One recent study reports that 71 percent of companies offer their employees financial incentives to participate in wellness programs.[95]

Jon Wheeler, CEO of Wheeler Interests, a real estate management company based in Virginia Beach, Virginia, incorporated an employee wellness program into his business from the outset. He transformed empty office space into a small gym, brought in a personal trainer, and offered smoking cessation and other wellness programs for his employees. Wheeler also gives employees a mid-day kayaking break and allows them to set their own vacation times as long as they get their work done.[96]

8. *Conduct a safety audit.* Reviewing the workplace with a safety professional to look for ways to improve its safety has the potential for saving some businesses thousands of dollars a year in medical expenses and workers' compensation claims. The National Safety Council offers helpful information on creating a safe work environment.

9. *Create a safety manual and use it.* Incorporating the suggestions for improving safety into a policy manual and then using it will reduce the number of on-the-job accidents. Training employees, even experienced ones, in proper safety procedures is also effective.

10. *Create a safety team.* Assigning the responsibility for workplace safety to workers themselves can produce amazing results. When one small manufacturer turned its safety team over to employees, the plant's lost time due to accidents plummeted to zero for 3 years straight! The number of accidents is well below what it was when managers ran the safety team, and managers say that's because employees now "own" safety in the plant.

The key to controlling insurance costs is aggressive prevention. Entrepreneurs who actively manage the risks to which their companies are exposed find that they can provide the insurance coverage their businesses need at a reasonable cost. Finding the right insurance coverage to protect their businesses is no easy matter for business owners. The key is to identify the risks that represent the greatest threat to a company and then to develop a plan for minimizing their risk of occurrence and insuring against them if they do.

Chapter Review

1. Explain the factors necessary for a strong family business.
   - Nearly 90 percent of all companies in the United States are family owned. Family businesses generate 64 percent of the U.S. gross domestic product, account for 62 percent of employment, and pay 65 percent of all wages. Several factors are important to maintaining a strong family business, including shared values, shared power, tradition, a willingness to learn, behaving like families, and strong family ties.

2. Understand the exit strategy options available to an entrepreneur.
   - Family business owners wanting to step down from their companies can sell to outsiders, sell to insiders, or transfer ownership to the next generation of family members. Common tools for selling to insiders (employees or managers) include sale for cash plus a note, leveraged buyouts (LBOs), and employee stock ownership plans (ESOPs).
   - Transferring ownership to the next generation of family members requires a business owner to develop a sound management succession plan.

3. Discuss the stages of management succession.
   - Unfortunately, 70 percent of first-generation businesses fail to survive into the second generation, and, of those that do survive, only 12 percent make it to the third generation. One of the primary reasons for this lack of continuity is poor succession planning. Planning for management succession protects not only the founder's, successor's, and company's financial resources, but it also preserves what matters most in a successful business: its heritage and tradition. Management succession planning can ensure a smooth transition only if the founder begins the process early on.

4. Explain how to develop an effective management succession plan.
   - A succession plan is a crucial element in transferring a company to the next generation. Preparing a succession plan involves five steps: (1) Select the successor. (2) Create a survival kit for the successor. (3) Groom the successor. (4) Promote an environment of trust and respect. (5) Cope with the financial realities of estate taxes.
   - Entrepreneurs can rely on several tools in their estate planning, including buy-sell agreements, lifetime gifting, trusts, estate freezes, and family limited partnerships.

5. Understand the four risk management strategies.
   - Four risk strategies are available to the small business: avoiding, reducing, anticipating, and transferring risk.

6. Discuss the basics of insurance for small businesses.
   - Insurance is a risk transfer strategy. Not every potential loss can be insured. Insurability requires that it be possible to estimate the amount of actual loss being insured against and identify the specific risk and that there be enough policyholders to spread out the risk.
   - The four major types of insurance small businesses need are property and casualty insurance, life and disability insurance, health insurance and workers' compensation coverage, and liability insurance.
   - Property and casualty insurance covers a company's tangible assets, such as buildings, equipment, inventory, machinery, signs, and others that have been damaged, destroyed, or stolen. Specific types of property and casualty insurance include extra expense coverage, business interruption insurance, surety insurance, marine insurance, crime insurance, fidelity insurance, and forgery insurance.
   - Life and disability insurance also comes in various forms. Life insurance protects a family and a business against the loss of income and security in the event of the owner's death. Disability insurance, like life insurance, protects an individual in the event of unexpected and often very expensive disabilities.
   - Health insurance is designed to provide adequate health care for business owners and their employees. The most common managed health plans are preferred provider organizations (PPOs), point of service (POS) operations, and health maintenance

organizations (HMOs). Workers' compensation is designed to cover employees who are injured on the job or who become sick as a result of a work environment.

- Liability insurance protects a business against losses resulting from accidents or injuries people suffer on the company's property, from its products or services, and damage the company causes to others' property. Typical liability coverage includes professional liability insurance or "errors and omissions" coverage, which protects against damage a business causes to customers or clients as a result of an error an employee makes or an employee's failure to take proper care and precautions. Doctors, dentists, attorneys, and other professionals protect themselves through a similar kind of insurance, malpractice insurance, which protects them against the risk of lawsuits arising from errors in professional practice or judgment. Employment practices liability insurance provides protection against claims arising from charges of employment discrimination, sexual harassment, and violations of the Americans with Disabilities Act, the Family and Medical Leave Act, and other employment legislation.

Discussion Questions

1. What factors must be present for a strong family business?
2. Discuss the stages of management succession in a family business.
3. What steps are involved in building a successful management succession plan?
4. What exit strategies are available to entrepreneurs wanting to step down from their businesses?
5. What strategies can business owners employ to reduce estate and gift taxes?
6. Can insurance eliminate risk? Why or why not?
7. Outline the four basic risk management strategies and give an example of each.
8. What problems occur most frequently with a risk anticipation strategy?

9. What is insurance? How can insurance companies bear such a large risk burden and still be profitable?
10. Describe the requirements for insurability.
11. Briefly describe the various types of insurance coverage available to small business owners.
12. What kinds of insurance coverage would you recommend for the following businesses?
    a. A manufacturer of steel beams
    b. A retail gift shop
    c. A small accounting firm
    d. A limited liability partnership involving three dentists
13. What can business owners do to keep their insurance costs under control?

Family-owned businesses dominate the landscape of U.S. companies, but they face a dangerous threat from within: management succession. Most family businesses fail to survive into the second generation and beyond. The problem usually is the result of a lack of planning for a smooth transition from one generation of management to the next. The business plan can assist in this process.

On the Web

Under the tab on the Companion Web site at *www.pearsonhighered.com/scarborough* is a list of online resources that deal with succession planning and risk management. You will find resources that address issues related to managing a family business, planning for management succession, and managing business risk.

In the Software

If the business has issues regarding succession planning, capture those thoughts in your plan. This is also an opportunity to discuss risk management and exit strategies. What types of insurance coverage does your company require? Be sure to incorporate the cost of insurance coverage in your financial forecasts. Remember: You can add or modify outline topics within Business Plan Pro by right-clicking the outline in the left-hand navigation of the software.

Building Your Business Plan

One of the best ways to prevent a family-owned business from becoming just another management succession failure statistic is to develop a management succession plan early on in the life of the company. The business plan can be a vehicle to help with this discussion and document the plan to make this transition. The plan can also enable an entrepreneur to document ideas and plans regarding risk management and potential exit strategies.

Endnotes

1. "Facts About Family Business," S. Dale High Center for Family Business at Elizabethtown College, *www.centerforfamilybusiness.org/facts.asp;* MassMutual Family Business Network, *www.massmutual.com/fbn/index.htm;* "Family Business Facts," Family Business Institute, *www.ffi.org/looking/fbfacts_us.pdf.*

2. James Lea, "Five Ways Family Firms Can Thrive," Family Business Bizjournals.com, February 2, 2004, *www.bizjournals.com/extraedge/consultants/family_business/2004/02/02/column180.html.*

3. Thomas L. Kalaris, "Family Business: In Safe Hands?" *Barclays Wealth Insights,* 2009, p. 3.

4. "Country Comparison: GDP," *World Fact Book,* Central Intelligence Agency, *www.cia.gov/library/publications/the-world-factbook/rankorder/2001rank.html;* "A $238 Million Morning for the Walton Family," Wal-Mart Watch, March 5, 2009, *http://walmartwatch.com/blog/archives/a_238_million_dollar_morning_for_the_walton_family/;* "Wal-Mart Stores Inc," *CNNMoney,* November 10, 2010, *http://money.cnn.com/quote/quote.html?symb=WMT.*

5. Tony Taylor, "Small Businesses Show Relative Strength," *GSA Business,* September 4, 2006, p. 22; Jim Lee, "Family Firm Performance: Further Evidence," *Family Business Review,* June 2006, Vol. 19, No. 2, pp. 103–114.

6. "Research Reveals: Family Firms Perform Better," *Family Business Advisor,* March 2003, Vol. 12, No. 3, p. 1.

7. Nicholas Stein, "The Age of the Scion," *Fortune,* April 2, 2001, pp. 121–128.

8. Amol Sharma, "Reliance Rivals Vow to Play Nice," *Wall Street Journal,* May 24, 2010, *http://online.wsj.com/article/SB10001424052748704226004575262281639883648.html.*

9. "Facts and Perspectives on Family Business Around the World: United States," Family Business Institute, *www.ffi.org/looking/fbfacts_us.pdf.*

10. Ibid.

11. Ibid.

12. Peter Schworm, "End of a 378-Year Era," *Boston.com,* July 27, 2010, *www.boston.com/news/local/new_hampshire/articles/2010/07/27/nations_oldest_running_family_farm_put_on_market_in_nh/.*

13. *Kin in the Game,* PriceWaterhouseCoopers Family Business Survey, 2010–2011, p. 21.

14. Ibid.

15. "Facts and Perspectives on Family Business Around the World: United States," Family Business Institute, *www.ffi.org/looking/fbfacts_us.pdf.*

16. Sharon Nelton, "Ten Keys to Success in Family Business," *Nation's Business,* April 1991, pp. 44–45.

17. Toddi Gunter, "Moving Up to the Top of a Family Empire," *Wall Street Journal,* June 22, 2010, p. D4.

18. "Family Members Fight over Control of Texas Pete Hot Sauce Empire," *Greenville News,* May 17, 1997, p. 11D.

19. Stein, "The Age of the Scion," p. 124.

20. Eugenia Levenson, "Road Warrior," *Fortune,* November 27, 2006, p. 276; Hsiao-Ching Chao, "Maximilian Riedel Has the Stemware Industry in the Palm of His Hand," *Seattle Post-Intelligencer,* April 13, 2005, *http://seattlepi.nwsource.com/food/219827_riedel13.html;* Anthony Giglio, "Glass Menagerie," *Boston Magazine,* April 2006, *www.bostonmagazine.com/dining_food_wine/articles/boston_magazine_liquids_specialty_wineglasses/.*

21. Stein, "The Age of the Scion," p. 124.

22. Mike Armstrong, "PhillyInc: There's a Twist in the Pennsylvania Pretzel-Merger Saga," *Philly.com,* July 23, 2010, *www.philly.com/philly/business/homepage/20100723_PhillyInc__There_s_a_twist_in_the_Pennsylvania_pretzel-merger_saga.html.*

23. Bo Burlingham, "Why a CEO Needs to Have a Plan B," *Inc.,* May 2009, *www.inc.com/magazine/20090501/why-a-ceo-needs-to-have-a-plan-b.html.*

24. "Employee Ownership and Corporate Performance," National Center for Employee Ownership, *www.nceo.org/library/esop_perf.html.*

25. Paul J. Lim, "Putting Your House in Order," *U.S. News & World Report,* December 10, 2001, p. 38.

26. Lydia Dishman, "Keys to the Kingdom," *Black Box,* Quarter 1, 2010, pp. 67–71.

27. Claire Cain Miller, "Chapter Two," *Forbes,* December 25, 2006, p. 72.

28. Carol Tice, "Lost in Transition," *Entrepreneur,* November 2006, p. 102.

29. TCPN Quotations Center, *www.cyber-nation.com/victory/quotations/subject/quotes_subjects_f_to_h.html#f.*

30. Andy Bluestone, "Succession Planning Isn't Just About Money," *Nation's Business,* November 1996, p. 6.

31. Shelly Branch, "Mom Always Liked You Best," *Your Company,* April/May 1998, pp. 26–38.

32. Taylor, "Small Businesses Show Relative Strength," pp. 22, 24.

33. Patricia Schiff Estess, "Heir Raising," *Entrepreneur,* May 1996, pp. 80–82.

34. Tice, "Lost in Transition," pp. 101–103.

35. Jacquelyn Lynn, "What Price Successor?" *Entrepreneur,* November 1999, p. 146.

36. Craig E. Aronoff and John L. Ward, "Why Continue Your Family Business," *Nation's Business,* March 1998, pp. 72–74.

37. Jeremy Quittner, "Creating a Legacy," *BusinessWeek,* June 25, 2007, *www.businessweek.com/magazine/content/07_26/b4040443.htm?chan=search.*

38. Lee Smith, "The Next Generation," *Your Company,* October 1999, pp. 36–46.

39. "New Nationwide Survey Points to Bright Spot in American Economy—Family-Owned Businesses," MassMutual Financial Group, *www.massmutual.com/mmfg/about/pr_2003/01_22_03.html.*

40. Brett Pulley, "Murdoch Son Also Rises as Shareholders Study CEO Succession," *Bloomberg,* October 22, 2010, *www.bloomberg.com/news/2010-10-22/murdoch-son-also-rising-as-shareholders-focus-on-news-corp-ceo-succession.html.*

41. Annetta Miller, "You Can't Take It with You," *Your Company,* April 1999, pp. 28–34.

42. "Family Business Facts," Family Business Institute.

43. Frank Silverstein, "Daddy's Cowgirl Takes Over the Rodeo Business," MSNBC, August 30, 2009, *www.msnbc.msn.com/id/32573940/ns/business-small_business;* Courtney Elam, "Kirsten Vold," Harry Vold Rodeo Company, *www.harryvoldrodeo.com/staff.html.*

44. John Warrillow, "Leave the Business to the Kids? Maybe Not," *Wall Street Journal,* June 10, 2010, *http://online.wsj.com/article/SB10001424052748704575304575296523166009344.html.*

45. Karen E. Klein, "Succession Planning Without an Heir," *BusinessWeek,* June 20, 2007, *www.businessweek.com/smallbiz/content/jun2007/sb20070620_135303.htm?chan=search.*

46. Sharon Nelton, "Why Women Are Chosen to Lead," *Nation's Business,* April 1999, p. 51.

47. "New Nationwide Survey Points to Bright Spot in American Economy—Family-Owned Businesses," MassMutual Financial Group.

48. Dick Patten, "The Death Tax Is Killing Family Businesses," *Daily Caller,* October 8, 2010, *http://dailycaller.com/2010/10/08/the-death-tax-is-killing-family-businesses/;* Amanda Hill, "Estate Taxes Could Mean 'Death' of Family Farms and Ranches," *Texas Agriculture News,* September 27, 2010, *www.nodeathtax.org/news/estate-tax-could-mean-death-of-family-farms-and-ranches.*

49. Brad Hamilton and Jeane MacIntosh, "Death'$ Perfect Timing," *New York Post,* July 14, 2010, *www.nypost.com/p/news/local/death_perfect_timing_NusLyGlMu8cn8kyepprVJP?CMP=OTC-rss&FEEDNAME=.*

50. Patten, "The Death Tax Is Killing Family Businesses."

51. Quittner, "Creating a Legacy."

52. Joan Szabo, "Spreading the Wealth," *Entrepreneur,* July 1997, pp. 62–64.

53. Gay Jervey, "Family Ties," *FSB,* March 2006, p. 60.

54. Ibid.; Tom Herman, "Court Ruling Bolsters Estate Planning Tool," *Wall Street Journal,* May 27, 2004, p. D1.

55. Quittner, "Creating a Legacy."

56. William J. Dennis, "National Small Business Poll: Disasters," *National Federation of Independent Businesses,* 2004, Vol. 4, No. 5, pp. 5–6.

57. Joseph King, "Disasters Highlight Need for Business Continuity Planning," Institute for Business & Home Safety, September 7, 2010, *www.disastersafety.org/newsroom/view.asp?id=13291&Mode=List;* Emily Maltby, "Readying for the Worst," *Wall Street Journal,* September 9, 2009, *http://online.wsj.com/article/SB125250249415695553.html.*

58. Daniel Tynan, "In Case of Emergency," *Entrepreneur,* April 2003, p. 60.

59. Sarah E. Needleman, "Lights Out Means Lost Sales," *Wall Street Journal,* July 22, 2010, p. B6.

60. Elizabeth Hockerman, "When to Self-Insure?" *Small Business Times,* May 12, 2006, *www.biztimes.com/news/2006/5/12/when-to-self-insure.*

61. Jeanne Lee and Brandi Stewart, "Build Your Own Insurance Company," *FSB,* September 2007, pp. 28–31.

62. Tiana Velez, "A Home Business Needs Insurance," *Arizona Daily Star,* June 5, 2006, *www.azstarnet.com/allheadlines/132077.*

63. Kimberly Lankford, "Weird Insurance," *Kiplinger's Personal Finance Magazine*, October 1998, pp. 113–116.

64. "Costa Coffee Taster: One of the 10 Weirdest Insurance Policies," *The Telegraph*, March 9, 2009, *www.telegraph.co.uk/finance/personalfinance/insurance/specialrisks/4962817/Costa-Coffee-taster-Ten-of-the-weirdest-insurance-policies.html;* "Costa's Coffee Taster Has Tongue Insured for £10 Million," *The Telegraph*, March 9, 2009, *www.telegraph.co.uk/foodanddrink/foodanddrinknews/4957333/Costa-Coffees-taster-has-tongue-insured-for-10-million.html.*

65. John Fried, "Having Fun Yet?" *Inc.*, March 2006, pp. 75–77; "Incredible Adventures: Our Story," Incredible Adventures, *www.incredible-adventures.com/about_us.html;* Esther Dyson, "I Live and Die by Waivers," Esther Dyson's Flight School, May 11, 2007, *www.edventure.com/flightschool/blog/?p=4.*

66. Joyce M. Rosenberg, "Preparing a Disaster Plan Gets Serious," *Los Angeles Times*, August 16, 2007, *www.latimes.com/business/la-fi-smalldisaster16aug16,1,4272739.story?coll=la-headlines-business&ctrack=1&cset=true;* "Famed Restaurant Reopens Today," *Greenville News*, October 1, 2006, p. 4B.

67. Larry Kanter, "Smart Questions for Your Insurance Agent," *Inc.*, August 2006, p. 40; Michele Marchetti, "Thrown Off Track," *FSB*, February 2004, pp. 66–69.

68. Heidi Ernst, "The Best Line of Defense," Advertising Insert, *FSB*, July/August 2007, p. 80.

69. Jan Norman, "Business Disaster Can Strike at Any Time," *Greenville News*, April 4, 2004, p. E1.

70. Ilan Mochari, "A Security Blanket for Your Web Site," *Inc.*, December 2000, pp. 133–134.

71. Andrew Smyth, "Council for Disability Awareness Launches Consumer Website," *The Insurance Policy*, November 3, 2006, *www.theinsurancepolicy.com/new_insurance_agents/disability_insurance/.*

72. "Issues: Health Care Reform," National Federation of Independent Businesses, *www.nfib.com/issues-elections/healthcare.*

73. Kate Pickert, "The Unsustainable U.S. Healthcare System," *Time,* February 4, 2010, *http://swampland.blogs.time.com/2010/02/04/the-unsustainable-u-s-health-care-system/;* "Health Care Insurance Costs," National Coalition on Health Care, *www.nchc.org/facts/cost.shtml.*

74. *Employer Health Benefits 2010 Summary of Findings*, Kaiser Family Foundation and Health Research and Educational Trust, p. 5.

75. Ibid., p. 40.

76. Daniel Wityk, "Small Business Health Insurance," National Center for Policy Analysis, February 11, 2009, p. 1.

77. Eileen Figure Sandlin, "Finding Health Insurance as a Start-up," *Entrepreneur*, October 2006, *www.entrepreneur.com/management/insurance/typesofinsurance/article168504.html.*

78. *Intuit Payroll Survey 2009*, Intuit, *http://quickbooks.blogs.com/Intuit%20Payroll%20Survey%20-%20One%20Sheet.pdf*, p. 3.

79. Sarah E. Needleman, "Burger Chain's Health Care Recipe," *Wall Street Journal*, August 31, 2009, *http://online.wsj.com/article/SB125149100886467705.html.*

80. *Employer Health Benefits 2010 Survey*, Kaiser Family Foundation and Health Research and Educational Trust, p. 62.

81. Ibid., p. 15.

82. "Census Shows 8 Million People Covered by HSA/High-Deductible Health Plans," America's Health Insurance Plans, Center for Policy Research, January 2009, p. 4; *Behind the Numbers: Medical Cost Trends for 2010*, PriceWaterhouseCoopers, Health Research Institute, 2010, p. 7.

83. Colleen DeBaise, "Small Business Owners Try HSAs to Trim Health Costs," *Smart Money*, July 6, 2007, *www.smartmoney.com/smallbiz/index.cfm?story=20060511.*

84. "Workers' Compensation Insurance: The Role of State Funds, Market Trends, and Economic Influences," Insurance Information Institute, October 12, 2010, p. 16.

85. Greg O'Claray, "Alaska Needs Workers' Compensation Reform Now," National Federation of Independent Businesses, March 14, 2005, *www.nfib.com/object/IO_20952.html.*

86. Aaron Dalton, "Best Practices: Rapid Recovery," *IndustryWeek*, March 1, 2005, *www.industryweek.com/ReadArticle.aspx?ArticleId=10001.*

87. "Litigiousness," Insurance Information Institute, 2010, *www.iii.org/facts_statistics/litigiousness.html.*

88. Marc Fisher, "Judge Who Seeks Millions for Lost Pants Has His (Emotional) Day in Court," *Washington Post*, June 13, 2007, *www.washingtonpost.com/wp-dyn/content/article/2007/06/12/AR2007061201667.html;* "Dry Cleaner Raises Enough Cash to Pay Legal Fees," *WUSA9.com*, August 13, 2007, *www.wusa9.com/news/news_article.aspx?storyid=61690.*

89. "Employment Practices Liability Awareness Lacking for Some Small Business Owners," InsuranceNewsNet, February 3, 2010, *http://insurancenewsnet.com/article.aspx?id=157763.*

90. "Employment Law: Jury Awards, Trends, and Statistics," Thomas Fenner Woods Agency, November 2010, *www.tfwinsurance.com/news/11_2010/nl_employeem_9.php.*

91. "Employment Practices Liability Insurance for Restaurants," Restaurant Association of Maryland, October 2009, *www.marylandrestaurants.com/membership/foodserv_benefits/documents/09-199RAMEPLforRestaurants.pdf.*

92. Ilan Mochari, "Bug Your Broker," *Inc.*, August 2000, pp. 127–128.

93. Patricia B. Gray, "Health Care," *FSB*, February 2009, pp. 57–65.

94. Susan Caminiti, "Keeping America Fit," *Fortune*, May 3, 2010, p. S1.

95. Patricia F. Weisberg, "Wellness Programs: Legal Requirements and Risks," *Workforce Management*, March 2010, *www.workforce.com/section/legal/feature/wellness-programs-legal-requirements-risks/.*

96. Karene Spaeder, "Shape Up," *Entrepreneur*, September 2008, p. 26.

Ethics and Social Responsibility: Doing the Right Thing

Learning Objectives

Upon completion of this chapter, you will be able to:

1 Define business ethics and describe the three levels of ethical standards.

2 Determine who is responsible for ethical behavior and why ethical lapses occur.

3 Explain how to establish and maintain high ethical standards.

4 Define social responsibility.

5 Understand the nature of business's responsibility to the environment.

6 Describe business's responsibility to employees.

7 Explain business's responsibility to customers.

8 Discuss business's responsibility to investors.

9 Describe business's responsibility to the community.

Relativity applies to physics, not ethics.

—Albert Einstein

The high caliber organization is merely a reflection of its people.

—Price Pritchett

From Chapter 21 of *Effective Small Business Management: An Entrepreneurial Approach*, 10/e. Norman M. Scarborough.

Business ethics involves the moral values and behavioral standards that businesspeople draw on as they make decisions and solve problems. It originates in a commitment to do what is right. Ethical behavior—doing what is "right" as opposed to what is "wrong"—starts at the top of an organization with the entrepreneur. Entrepreneurs' personal values and beliefs influence the way they lead their companies and are apparent in every decision they make, every policy they write, and every action they take. Entrepreneurs who succeed in the long term have a solid base of personal values and beliefs that they articulate to their employees and put into practice in ways that others can observe. Values-based leaders do more than merely follow rules and regulations; their consciences dictate that they do what is right.

In some cases, ethical dilemmas are apparent. Entrepreneurs are keenly aware of the ethical entrapments awaiting them and know that society will hold them accountable for their actions. More often, however, ethical issues are less obvious, cloaked in the garb of mundane decisions and everyday routine. Because they can easily catch entrepreneurs off guard and unprepared, these ethical "sleepers" are most likely to ensnare business owners, soiling their reputations and those of their companies. To make proper ethical choices, entrepreneurs must first be aware that a situation with ethical implications exists.

Complicating the issue even more is that, in some ethical dilemmas, no clear-cut, right or wrong answers exist. There is no direct conflict between good and evil, right and wrong, or truth and falsehood. Instead, there is only the issue of conflicting interests among a company's **stakeholders**, the various groups and individuals who affect and are affected by a business. These conflicts force entrepreneurs to identify their stakeholders and to consider the ways in which they will deal with them (see Figure 1). For instance, when the founders of a small producer of frozen foods make business decisions, they must consider the impact of those decisions on many stakeholders, including the team of employees who own work there, the farmers and companies that supply the business with raw materials, the union that represents employees in collective bargaining, the government agencies that regulate a multitude of activities, the banks that provide the business with financing, the stockholders who own shares of the company's stock, the general public the business serves, the community in which the company operates, and the customers who buy the company's products. When making decisions, entrepreneurs often must balance the needs and demands of a company's stakeholders, knowing that whatever the final decision is, not every group will be satisfied. Figure 2 shows the results of a survey by McKinsey & Company of global CEOs about the stakeholders that will have the greatest effect on their businesses in the next 3 to 5 years.

Ethical leaders approach their organizational responsibilities with added dimensions of thought and action. They link ethical behaviors to organizational outcomes and incorporate social responsibility into daily decisions. They establish ethical behavior and concern for the environment as an integral part of organizational training and eventually as part of company culture. What does this mean from a practical standpoint? How does a commitment to "doing the right thing" apply to employees, customers, and other stakeholders, and how does it affect an

FIGURE 1
Key Stakeholders

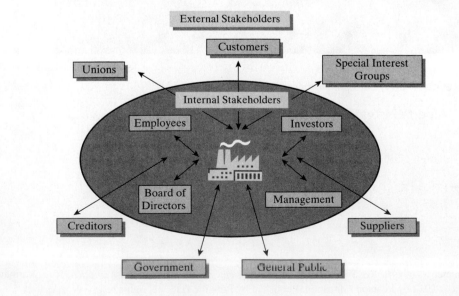

FIGURE 2
Which Stakeholders Will Have the Greatest Effect on Your Company's Economic Value in the Next 3 to 5 Years?

Source: McKinsey and Company, 2010.

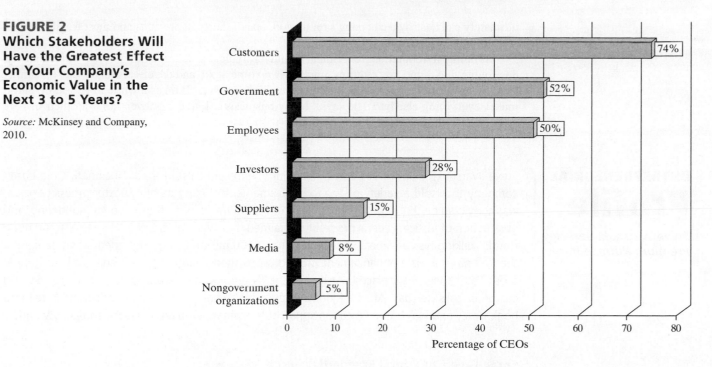

entrepreneur's daily decision making? For example, makers of PCs and laptops faced an ethical dilemma when China's Ministry of Industry and Information Technology issued a mandate that required every PC and laptop sold in China to be preloaded with Web filtering software that blocks access to particular Web sites. Government officials say that the software, Green Dam Youth Escort, prevents Chinese citizens from accessing pornographic Web sites. Critics contend that because the software also blocks access to Web sites with political content of which the Chinese government disapproves, it gives the government greater censorship power over Internet users inside China. If the managers of the computer makers decide not to sell their products in China (their largest market after the United States), they sacrifice hundreds of millions of dollars in sales and profits. If they fail to comply with the government mandate, they put at risk the investments that they have made in factories and research centers in China. Complying with the government's requirement, however, opens PC makers to a backlash from charges of supporting censorship and limits on basic human rights.[1] Balancing the demands of various stakeholders to make ethical decisions is no easy task.

Business operates as an institution in our often complex and ever-evolving society. As such, every entrepreneur is expected to behave in ways that are compatible with the value system of society. It is society that imposes the rules of conduct for all business owners in the form of ethical standards of behavior and responsibilities to act in ways that benefit the long-term interest of all. Society expects business owners to strive to earn a profit on their investments. Ethics and social responsibility simply set behavioral boundaries for decision makers. Ethics is a branch of philosophy that studies and creates theories about the basic nature of right and wrong, duty, obligation, and virtue. Social responsibility involves how an organization responds to the needs of the many elements in society, including shareholders, lenders, employees, consumers, governmental agencies, and the environment. Because business is allowed to operate in society, it has an obligation to behave in ways that benefit all of society.

An Ethical Perspective

1. Define business ethics and describe three levels of ethical standards.

Business ethics consist of the fundamental moral values and behavioral standards that form the foundation for the people of an organization as they make decisions and interact with stakeholders. Business ethics is a sensitive and highly complex issue, but it is not a new one. In 560 B.C., the Greek philosopher Chilon claimed that a merchant does better to take a loss than to make a dishonest profit.[2] Maintaining an ethical perspective is essential to creating and protecting a company's reputation, but it is no easy task. Ethical dilemmas lurk in the decisions—even the most mundane ones—that entrepreneurs make every day. Succumbing to unethical temptations ultimately can destroy a company's reputation, one of the most precious and most fragile possessions of any business.

Building a reputation for ethical behavior typically takes a long time; unfortunately, destroying that reputation requires practically no time at all, and the effects linger for some time. One top manager compares a bad reputation to a hangover. "It takes a while to get rid of, and it makes everything else hurt," he says.[3] Many businesses flounder or even fail after their owners or managers are caught acting unethically.

ENTREPRENEURIAL
Profile

Steve Warshak: Berkeley Premium Nutraceuticals

Steve Warshak, founder of Berkeley Premium Nutraceuticals (BPN), a Cincinnati, Ohio-based company that sold a variety of health supplements, including its blockbuster product Enzyte, was convicted on 93 counts of mail fraud, credit card fraud, bank fraud, money laundering, and obstruction of justice. Federal prosecutors claimed that Warshak created "a cycle of fraud upon fraud," bilking his customers out of more than $100 million by "giving" them a free sample of the "all natural male enhancement product" and then charging their credit cards for repeat orders that they never placed. At its peak, BPN employed 1,400 people and fielded 65,000 customer calls per day. After a judge sentenced Warshak to 25 years in prison, BPN fell into bankruptcy and was bought by a Cincinnati businessman, who renamed the company Vianda.[4]

Three Levels of Ethical Standards

There are three levels of ethical standards:

1. *The law*, which defines for society as a whole those actions that are permissible and those that are not. The law merely establishes the minimum standard of behavior. Actions that are legal, however, may not be ethical. Simply obeying the law is insufficient as a guide for ethical behavior; ethical behavior requires more. Few ethical issues are so simple and one dimensional that the law can serve as the acid test for making a decision.
2. *Organizational policies and procedures*, which serve as specific guidelines for people as they make daily decisions. Many colleges and universities have created honor codes, and companies rely on policies covering everything from sexual harassment and gift giving to hiring and whistle-blowing.
3. The *moral stance* that employees take when they encounter a situation that is not governed by levels one and two. The values people learn early in life at home, in the church or synagogue, in school, and at work are key ingredients at this level. Another determinant of ethical behavior is *training*. As Aristotle said thousands of years ago, you get a good adult by teaching a child to do the right thing. A company's culture can serve either to support or undermine its employees' concept of what constitutes ethical behavior.

Ethics is something that every businessperson faces daily; most decisions involve some degree of ethical judgment. Over the course of a career, entrepreneurs can be confident that they will face some tough ethical choices. But that is not necessarily bad! Situations such as these give entrepreneurs the opportunity to flex their ethical muscles and do what is right. Entrepreneurs set the ethical tone for their companies. The ethical stance employees take when faced with a difficult decision often reflects the entrepreneur's values.

Establishing an Ethical Framework

To cope successfully with the many ethical decisions they face, entrepreneurs must develop a workable ethical framework to guide themselves and the organization. Although many frameworks exist, the following four-step process works quite well.

Step 1. Recognize the ethical dimensions involved in the dilemma or decision. Before entrepreneurs can make informed ethical decisions, they must recognize that an ethical situation exists. Only then is it possible to define the specific ethical issues involved. Too often business owners fail to take into account the ethical impact of a particular course of action until it is too late. To avoid ethical quagmires, entrepreneurs must consider the ethical forces at work in a situation—honesty, fairness, respect for the community, concern for the environment, trust, and others—to have a complete view of the decision.

Step 2. Identify the key stakeholders involved and determine how the decision will affect them. Every business influences, and is influenced by, a multitude of stakeholders. Frequently, the demands of these stakeholders conflict with one another, putting a business in the position of having to choose which groups to satisfy and which to alienate. Before making a decision, managers must sort out the conflicting interests of the various stakeholders by determining which ones have important stakes in the situation. Although this analysis may not resolve the conflict, it will prevent the company from inadvertently causing harm to people it may have failed to consider. More companies are measuring their performance using a **triple bottom line (3BL)** that, in addition to the traditional measure of profitability, includes the commitment to ethics and social responsibility and the impact on the environment ("profit, people, and planet").

ENTREPRENEURIAL

Profile

King Arthur Flour Company

King Arthur Flour Company, founded in Boston, Massachusetts, in 1790, uses the 3BL to measure its performance. The company is profitable, with annual sales of more than $61 million, and it is now 100 percent owned by its 160 employees, each of whom receives up to 40 hours of paid time each year to work for a nonprofit organization of their choice. King Arthur Flour has a reputation as a good corporate citizen, donating 5 percent of its profits to charitable organizations and schools. The company also is an advocate of environmental sustainability, focusing on energy efficiency, recycling, preservation of natural resources, and other efforts.[5]

Step 3. Generate alternative choices and distinguish between ethical and unethical responses. When entrepreneurs are generating alternative courses of action and evaluating the consequences of each one, they can use the questions in Table 1 to guide them. Asking and answering questions such as these ensure that everyone involved is aware of the ethical dimensions of the issue.

Step 4. Choose the "best" ethical response and implement it. At this point, there likely will be several ethical choices from which managers can pick. Comparing these choices with the "ideal" ethical outcome may help managers make the final decision. The final choice must be consistent with the company's goals, culture, and value system as well as those of the individual decision makers.

TABLE 1 Questions to Help Identify the Ethical Dimension of a Situation

Principles and Codes of Conduct

- Does this decision or action meet my standards for how people should interact?
- Does this decision or action agree with my religious teachings or beliefs (or with my personal principles and sense of responsibility)?
- How will I feel about myself if I do this?
- Do we (or I) have a rule or policy for cases like this?
- Would I want everyone to make the same decision and take the same action if faced with these circumstances?
- What are my true motives for considering this action?

Moral Rights

- Would this action allow others freedom of choice in this matter?
- Would this action involve deceiving others in any way?

Justice

- Would I feel this action was just (right) if I were on the other side of the decision?
- How would I feel if this action were done to me or someone close to me?
- Would this action or decision distribute benefits justly?
- Would it distribute hardships or burdens justly?

Consequences and Outcomes

- What will be the short- and long-term consequences of this action?
- Who will benefit from this course of action?
- Who will be hurt?
- How will this action create good and prevent harm?

(continued)

TABLE 1 Continued

Public Justification

- How would I feel (or how will I feel) if (or when) this action becomes public knowledge?
- Will I be able to explain adequately to others why I have taken the action?
- Would others feel that my action or decision is ethical or moral?

Intuition and Insight

- Have I searched for all alternatives? Are there other ways I could look at this situation? Have I considered all points of view?
- Even if there is sound rationality for this decision or action, and even if I could defend it publicly, does my inner sense tell me it is right?
- What does my intuition tell me is the ethical thing to do in this situation? Have I listened to my inner voice?

Source: Sherry Baker, "Ethical Judgment," *Executive Excellence,* March 1992, pp. 7–8. Reprinted with permission by Leadership Excellence.

Who Is Responsible for Ethical Behavior?

2. Determine who is responsible for ethical behavior and why ethical lapses occur.

Although companies may set ethical standards and offer guidelines for employees, the ultimate decision on whether to abide by ethical principles rests with the *individual.* In other words, companies really are not ethical or unethical; individuals are. Managers, however, can greatly influence individual behavior within the company. That influence must start at the *top* of the organization. A founder or chief executive officer who practices ethical behavior establishes the moral tone for the entire organization. Table 2 summarizes the characteristics of the three ethical styles of management: immoral, amoral, and moral management:

- *Immoral management.* Immoral managers are motivated by selfish reasons such as their own gains or those of the company. The driving force behind immoral management is *greed*: achieving personal or organizational success at any cost. Immoral management is the polar opposite of ethical management; immoral managers do what they can to

TABLE 2 Approaches to Business Ethics

Organizational Characteristics	Immoral Management	Amoral Management	Moral Management
Ethical norms	Management decisions, actions, and behavior imply a positive and active opposition to what is moral (ethical). Decisions are discordant with accepted ethical principles. An active negation of what is moral is implicit.	Management is neither moral nor immoral; decisions are not based on moral judgments. Management activity is not related to any moral code. A lack of ethical perception and moral awareness may be implicit.	Management activity conforms to a standard of ethical, or right, behavior. Management activity conforms to accepted professional standards of conduct. Ethical leadership is commonplace.
Motives	Selfish. Management cares only about its or its company's gains.	Well intentioned but selfish in the sense that impact on others is not considered.	Good. Management wants to succeed but only within the confines of sound ethical precepts such as fairness, justice, and due process.
Goals	Profitability and organizational success at any price.	Profitability. Other goals are not considered.	Profitability within the confines of legal obedience and ethical standards.
Orientation toward law	Legal standards are barriers that management must overcome to accomplish what it wants.	Law is the ethical guide, preferably the letter of the law. The central question is, what can we do legally?	Obedience toward letter and spirit of the law. Law is a minimal ethical behavior. Prefer to operate well above what law mandates.
Strategy	Exploit opportunities for corporate gain. Cut corners when it appears useful.	Give managers free rein. Personal ethics may apply, but only if managers choose. Respond to legal mandates if caught and required to do so.	Live by sound ethical standards. Assume leadership position when ethical dilemmas arise. Enlightened self-interest.

Source: Archie B. Carroll, "In Search of the Moral Manager," *Business Horizons*, March–April, 1987, pp. 7–15.

circumvent laws and moral standards and are not concerned about the impact that their actions have on others.

■ *Amoral management.* The principal goal of amoral managers is to earn a profit, but their actions differ from those of immoral managers in one key way: They do not purposely violate laws or ethical standards. Instead, amoral managers neglect to consider the impact their decisions have on others; they use free-rein decision making without reference to ethical standards. Amoral management is not an option for socially responsible businesses.

■ *Moral management.* Moral managers also strive for success but only within the boundaries of legal and ethical standards. Moral managers are not willing to sacrifice their values and violate ethical standards just to make a profit. Managers who operate with this philosophy see the law as a minimum standard for ethical behavior.

The Benefits of Moral Management

One of the most common misconceptions about business is that there is a contradiction between earning a profit and maintaining high ethical standards. In reality, companies have learned that these two goals are consistent with one another. Tom Chappell, founder of Tom's of Maine and Rambler's Way Farm, companies known almost as well for their ethical and socially responsible behavior as for their natural personal care products and environmentally friendly clothing, says, "You can make money and do good at the same time. They are not separate acts."[6] Many entrepreneurs launch businesses with the idea of making a difference in society. They quickly learn that to "do good" their companies must first "do well." Fran Rathke, CFO of Vermont-based Green Mountain Coffee Roasters, a small company known for its commitment to social responsibility, says, "We are motivated to achieve success because the more profitable we are, the more good we can do in the world."[7] According to a survey by the public relations firm Edelman, 83 percent of U.S. consumers say that transparent and honest practices and operating as a business that one can trust are the most important factors in a company's reputation.[8]

ENTREPRENEURIAL **Profile** *Larry O'Toole: Gentle Giant Moving Company*	Larry O'Toole, who founded Gentle Giant Moving Company, a Boston, Massachusetts-based moving company, with $17 and a borrowed truck, understands the importance of moral management in building trust and a solid reputation for his business in the communities that it serves. "We want to give back," says O'Toole. "That's part of our culture." After a devastating earthquake struck Haiti, Gentle Giant used its moving trucks to collect medical supplies from local businesses and residents and donated them to the nonprofit group Partners in Health. The company also operates a charitable foundation that focuses on developing character in young people and preventing homelessness.[9]

Although behaving ethically has value in itself, there are many other benefits to companies that adhere to high ethical standards. First, companies avoid the damaging fallout from unethical behavior on their reputations. Unethical businesses usually gain only short-term advantages; over the long run, unethical decisions don't pay. It's simply not good business.

Second, a solid ethical framework guides managers as they cope with an increasingly complex network of influence from external stakeholders. Dealing with stakeholders is much easier if a company has a solid ethical foundation on which to build.

Third, businesses with solid reputations as ethical companies find it easier to attract and retain quality workers. Explaining why she came to work for Timberland, a socially responsible maker of shoes, Helen Kellogg, a senior manager, says, "I was looking for a company that had a conscience." Timberland gives every employee 40 hours of paid leave every year to work on volunteer projects. Bonnie Monahan, a Timberland vice president who organized a bike-a-thon that raised $50,000 for a local charity, says that she has turned down "several lucrative job offers" from larger companies to stay with Timberland, where "you don't have to leave your values at the door." Every year, Timberland sponsors Serv-a-palooza, a 1-day blitz of community service that involves 170 projects in 27 countries.[10]

Fourth, ethical behavior has a positive impact on a company's bottom line. Research by Dov Seidman, a management consultant, shows that companies that outperform their competitors ethically also outperform them financially.[11]

Finally, a company's ethical philosophy has an impact on its ability to provide value for its customers. The "ethics factor" is difficult to quantify, yet it is something that customers consider when deciding where to shop and which company's products to buy. "Do I want people buying Timberland boots as a result of the firm's volunteer efforts?" asks CEO Jeffrey Swartz. "You bet."[12] Timberland's commitment to "doing good" in addition to "doing well" is expressed in its slogan, "Boots, Brand, Belief." Like other social entrepreneurs, Swartz's goal is to manage the company successfully so that he can use its resources to combat social problems.

Entrepreneurs must recognize that ethical behavior is an investment in the company's future rather than merely a cost of doing business. Table 3 shows the results of a comprehensive study that was conducted by the American Management Association of global human resources directors, who were asked about the reasons for their companies' engaging in ethical behavior and the factors that drive business ethics today.

Why Ethical Lapses Occur

Even though most small business owners run their companies ethically, business scandals involving Enron, WorldCom, Tyco, and other high-profile companies have sullied the reputations of businesses of all sizes. The best way for business owners to combat these negative public perceptions is to run their business ethically. When faced with an ethical dilemma, however, not every entrepreneur or employee will make the right decision. According to KPMG's Integrity Survey, 74 percent of workers say that they have observed ethical lapses in their companies within the last year.[13] (Forty-six percent of employees say that misconduct they observed would cause "a significant loss of public trust if discovered.") Many unethical acts are committed by normally decent people who believe in moral values. Figure 3 shows the results of an integrity survey that identifies the primary causes of misconduct in businesses.

Let's explore some of these causes of ethical lapses in more detail.

AN UNETHICAL EMPLOYEE. Ethical decisions are individual decisions, and some people are corrupt. Try as they might to avoid them, small businesses occasionally find that they have hired a "bad apple." Eliminating unethical behavior requires eliminating these bad apples.

AN UNETHICAL ORGANIZATIONAL CULTURE. In some cases, a company's culture has been poisoned with an unethical overtone; in other words, the problem is not the "bad apple" but the "bad barrel." Pressure to prosper produces an environment that creates conditions that reward unethical behavior, and employees act accordingly. Studies show that companies with strong ethical cultures experience fewer ethical violations than those with weak ethical cultures.[14] To create an environment that encourages ethical behavior, entrepreneurs should:

■ *Set the tone.* "The character of the leader casts a long shadow over the organization and can determine the character of the organization itself," says one business executive.[15] What you do, how you do it, and what you say set the tone for your employees. The values you profess must be aligned with the behaviors you demonstrate.

TABLE 3 Reasons to Run a Business Ethically and the Factors That Drive Business Ethics

Top Five Reasons to Run a Business Ethically

1. Protect brand and company reputation
2. It is the right thing to do
3. Maintain customers' trust and loyalty
4. Maintain investors' confidence
5. Earn public acceptance and recognition

Top Five Factors That Drive Business Ethics

1. Corporate scandals
2. Marketplace competition
3. Demands by investors
4. Pressure from customers
5. Globalization

Source: The Ethical Enterprise: A Global Study of Business Ethics 2005-2015, American Management Association/Human Resource Institute, 2006, p. 2.

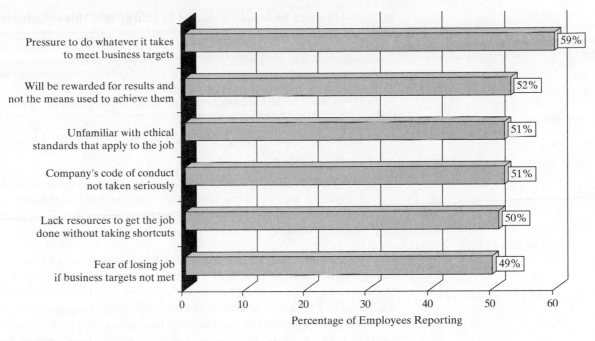

FIGURE 3
Causes of Ethical Lapses

Source: KPMG Integrity Survey, 2008–2009, KPMG LLC, 2009, p. 6.

- *Establish and enforce policies.* Set appropriate policies for your organization. Communicate them on a regular basis and adhere to them yourself so that others can see. Show zero tolerance for ethical violations and realize that the adage "Don't do as I do; do as I say" does *not* work. Without a demonstration of real consequences and personal accountability from the CEO, organizational policies are meaningless.
- *Educate and recruit.* Consider using a formal education program to enhance the understanding of and commitment to ethical behavior. Find colleges and universities that incorporate business ethics into courses and make them prime recruiting sources. Tina Byles Williams, owner of FIS Group, an investment advising and management firm, understands how important it is to hire honest employees with a strong sense of ethics. Although Williams knows that there is no foolproof hiring method, she has redesigned her company's selection process with an emphasis on screening for integrity.[16]
- *Separate related job duties.* This is a basic organizational concept. Not allowing the employee who writes checks to reconcile the company bank statement is one example.
- *Reward ethical conduct.* The reward system is a large window into the values of an organization. If you reward a behavior, people have a tendency to repeat the behavior.
- *Eliminate "undiscussables."* One of the most important things entrepreneurs can do to promote ethical behavior is to instill the belief that it is acceptable for employees to question what happens above them. Doing away with undiscussables makes issues transparent and promotes trust both inside and outside the company.[17]

MORAL BLINDNESS. Sometimes fundamentally ethical people commit unethical blunders because they are blind to the implications of their conduct. Moral blindness may be the result of failing to realize that an ethical dilemma exists, or it may arise from a variety of mental defense mechanisms. One of the most common mechanisms is rationalization:

"Everybody does it."

"If they were in my place, they'd do it too."

"Being ethical is a luxury I cannot afford right now."

"The impact of my decision/action on (whomever or whatever) is not my concern."

"I don't get paid to be ethical; I get paid to produce results."

TABLE 4 Ethics Research Reveals Features of Ethical Cultures

1. Leaders support and model ethical behavior.
2. Consistent communications come from all company leaders.
3. Ethics is integrated into the organization's goals, business processes, and strategies.
4. Ethics is part of the performance management system.
5. Ethics is part of the company's selection criteria and its selection process.

Source: The Ethical Enterprise: A Global Study of Business Ethics 2005–2015, American Management Association/Human Resource Institute, 2006, pp. 5, 6, 10.

Conducting ethics training and creating a culture that encourages employees to consider the ethical impact of their decisions reduces the likelihood of moral blindness. Instilling a sense of individual responsibility and encouraging people at all levels of an organization to speak up when they see questionable actions create a company-wide ethical conscience.

COMPETITIVE PRESSURES. If competition is so intense that a company's survival is threatened, managers may begin to view what were once unacceptable options as acceptable. Managers and employees are under such pressure to produce that they may sacrifice their ethical standards to reduce the fear of failure or the fear of losing their jobs. Without a positive organizational culture that stresses ethical behavior regardless of the consequences, employees respond to feelings of pressure and compromise their personal ethical standards to ensure that the job gets done.

OPPORTUNITY PRESSURES. When the opportunity to "get ahead" by taking some unethical action presents itself, some people cannot resist the temptation. The greater the reward or the smaller the penalty for unethical acts, the greater is the probability that such behavior will occur. If managers, for example, condone or even encourage unethical behavior, they can be sure it will occur. Those who succumb to opportunity pressures often make one of two mistakes: They overestimate the cost of doing the right thing, or they underestimate the cost of doing the wrong thing. Either error can lead to disaster.

GLOBALIZATION OF BUSINESS. The globalization of business has intertwined what once were distinct cultures. This cultural cross-pollination has brought about many positive aspects, but it has created problems as well. Companies have discovered that there is no single standard of ethical behavior that applies to all business decisions in the international arena. Practices that are illegal in one country may be perfectly acceptable, even expected, in another. Actions that would send a businessperson to jail in Western nations are common ways of working around the system in others.

Table 4 provides a summary of important ethics research concerning the characteristics that are most important to establishing an ethical culture.

Establishing Ethical Standards

3. Explain how to establish and maintain high ethical standards.

A study by the Southern Institute for Business and Professional Ethics found that small companies are less likely than large ones to have ethics programs.[18] Although they may not have formal ethics programs, entrepreneurs can encourage employees to become familiar with the following ethical tests for judging behavior:

- *The utilitarian principle.* Choose the option that offers the greatest good for the greatest number of people.
- *Kant's categorical imperative.* Act in such a way that the action taken under the circumstances could be a universal law or rule of behavior.
- *The professional ethic.* Take only those actions that a disinterested panel of professional colleagues would view as proper.
- *The Golden Rule.* Treat other people the way you would like them to treat you.
- *The television test.* Would you and your colleagues feel comfortable explaining your actions to a national television audience?
- *The family test.* Would you be comfortable explaining to your children, your spouse, and your parents why you took this action?[19]

Although these tests do not offer universal solutions to ethical dilemmas, they do help employees identify the moral implications of the decisions they face. People must be able to understand the ethical impact of their actions before they can make responsible decisions. Table 5 describes 10 ethical principles that differentiate between right and wrong, thereby offering a guideline for ethical behavior.

Maintaining Ethical Standards

Establishing ethical standards is only the first step in an ethics-enhancing program; implementing and maintaining those standards is the real challenge facing management. What can entrepreneurs do to integrate ethical principles into their companies?

CREATE A COMPANY CREDO. A **company credo** defines the values underlying the entire company and its ethical responsibilities to its stakeholders. It offers general guidance in ethical issues. The most effective credos capture the elusive essence of a company—what it stands for and why it's important—and they can be a key ingredient in a company's competitive edge. A company credo is especially important for a small company, where the entrepreneur's values become the values driving the business. A credo is an excellent way to transform those values into guidelines for employees' ethical behavior.

TABLE 5 Ten Ethical Principles to Guide Behavior

The study of history, philosophy, and religion reveals a strong consensus about certain universal and timeless values that are central to leading an ethical life.

1. *Honesty.* Be truthful, sincere, forthright, straightforward, frank, and candid; do not cheat, lie, steal, deceive, or act deviously.
2. *Integrity.* Be principled, honorable, upright, and courageous and act on convictions; do not be two-faced or unscrupulous or adopt an ends-justifies-the-means philosophy that ignores principle.
3. *Promise-keeping.* Be worthy of trust, keep promises, fulfill commitments, and abide by the spirit as well as the letter of an agreement; do not interpret agreements in a technical or legalistic manner in order to rationalize noncompliance or to create excuses for breaking commitments.
4. *Fidelity.* Be faithful and loyal to family, friends, employers, and country; do not use or disclose information earned in confidence; in a professional context, safeguard the ability to make independent professional judgments by scrupulously avoiding undue influences and conflicts of interest.
5. *Fairness.* Be fair and open-minded, be willing to admit error, and, when appropriate, change positions and beliefs and demonstrate a commitment to justice, the equal treatment of individuals, and tolerance for diversity; do not overreach or take undue advantage of another's mistakes or adversities.
6. *Caring for others.* Be caring, kind, and compassionate; share, be giving, serve others; help those in need and avoid harming others.
7. *Respect for others.* Demonstrate respect for human dignity, privacy, and the right to self-determination for all people; be courteous, prompt, and decent; provide others with the information they need to make informed decisions about their own lives; do not patronize, embarrass, or demean.
8. *Responsible citizenship.* Obey just laws [if a law is unjust, openly protest it]; exercise all democratic rights and privileges responsibly by participation [voting and expressing informed views], social consciousness, and public service; when in a position of leadership or authority, openly respect and honor democratic processes of decision making, avoid secrecy or concealment of information, and ensure others have the information needed to make intelligent choices and exercise their rights.
9. *Pursuit of excellence.* Pursue excellence in all matters; in meeting personal and professional responsibilities, be diligent, reliable, industrious, and committed; perform all tasks to the best of your ability, develop and maintain a high degree of competence, and be well informed and well prepared; do not be content with mediocrity, but do not seek to win "at any cost."
10. *Accountability.* Be accountable; accept responsibility for decisions, for the foreseeable consequences of actions and inactions, and for setting an example for others. Parents, teachers, employers, many professionals, and public officials have a special obligation to lead by example and to safeguard and advance the integrity and reputation of their families, companies, professions, and the government; avoid even the appearance of impropriety and take whatever actions are necessary to correct or prevent inappropriate conduct by others.

Source: Michael Josephson, "Teaching Ethical Decision Making and Principled Reasoning," *Ethics: Easier Said Than Done,* Winter 1988, pp. 28–29. *www.JosephsonInstitute.org.*

DEVELOP A CODE OF ETHICS. A **code of ethics** is a written statement of the standards of behavior and ethical principles a company expects from its employees. A code of ethics spells out what kind of behavior is expected (and what kind will not be tolerated) and offers everyone in the company concrete guidelines for dealing with ethics every day on the job. Although creating a code of ethics does not guarantee 100 percent compliance with ethical standards, it does tend to foster an ethical atmosphere in a company. Workers who will be directly affected by the code should have a hand in developing it.

ENFORCE THE CODE FAIRLY AND CONSISTENTLY. Managers must take action whenever they discover ethical violations. If employees learn that ethical breaches go unpunished, the code of ethics becomes meaningless. Enforcement of the code of ethics demonstrates to everyone that you believe that ethical behavior is mandatory.

CONDUCT ETHICS TRAINING. Instilling ethics in an organization's culture requires more than creating a code of ethics and enforcing it. Managers must show employees that the organization truly is committed to practicing ethical behavior. One of the most effective ways to display that commitment is through ethical training designed to raise employees' consciousness of potential ethical dilemmas. Ethics training programs not only raise employees' awareness of ethical issues, but they also communicate to employees the core of the company's value system.

HIRE AND PROMOTE THE RIGHT PEOPLE. Ultimately, the decision in any ethical situation belongs to the individual. Hiring people with strong moral principles and values is the best insurance against ethical violations. To make ethical decisions, people must have: (1) *ethical commitment*—the personal resolve to act ethically and do the right thing; (2) *ethical consciousness*—the ability to perceive the ethical implications of a situation; and (3) *ethical competency*—the ability to engage in sound moral reasoning and develop practical problem-solving strategies.[20]

PERFORM PERIODIC ETHICS AUDITS. One of the best ways to evaluate the effectiveness of an ethics system is to perform periodic audits. These reviews send a signal to employees that ethics is not just a passing fad.

ESTABLISH HIGH STANDARDS OF BEHAVIOR, NOT JUST RULES. No one can legislate ethics and morality, but managers can let people know the level of performance they expect. It is essential to emphasize to *everyone* in the organization the importance of ethics. All employees must understand that ethics is *not* negotiable. The role that an entrepreneur plays in establishing high ethical standards is critical; no one has more influence over the ethical character of a company than its founder. One experienced entrepreneur offers this advice to business owners: "Stick to your principles. Hire people who want to live by them, teach them thoroughly, and insist on total commitment."[21]

SET AN IMPECCABLE ETHICAL EXAMPLE AT ALL TIMES. Remember that ethics starts at the top. Far more important than credos and codes is the example the company's leaders set. If managers talk about the importance of ethics and then act in an unethical manner, they send mixed signals to employees. Workers believe managers' *actions* more than their words.

CREATE A CULTURE THAT EMPHASIZES TWO-WAY COMMUNICATION. A thriving ethical environment requires two-way communication. Employees must have the opportunity to report any ethical violations they observe. A reliable, confidential reporting system is essential to a whistle-blowing program, in which employees anonymously report breaches of ethical behavior through proper channels.

INVOLVE EMPLOYEES IN ESTABLISHING ETHICAL STANDARDS. Encourage employees to offer feedback on how to establish standards. Involving employees improves the quality of a company's ethical standards and increases the likelihood of employee compliance.

Social Responsibility and Social Entrepreneurship

4. Define social responsibility.

The concept of social responsibility has evolved from that of a nebulous "do-gooder" to one of "social steward," with the expectation that businesses will produce benefits not only for themselves but also for society as a whole. Society is constantly redefining its expectations of business and now holds companies of all sizes to high standards of ethics and social responsibility. Companies must

▶ E N T R E P R E N E U R S H I P   IN ACTION ▶

Is That Ethical?

Online Reviews

Buying online offers shoppers convenience, but making online purchases can be risky because of the potential for fraud. Another challenge that online retailers must overcome is shoppers' inability to examine merchandise firsthand, which explains the popularity of online reviews. A recent study by Nielsen reports that 70 percent of global online shoppers trust user reviews of products and services. Unfortunately, shoppers' trust in online reviews has led to some companies posting fake user reviews. Lifestyle Lift, a cosmetic surgery company that sells laser skin treatments that tighten and tone aging skin, was charged with posting fake user reviews of its procedures on several Web sites where customers rate and review products and services. The "patients" were not real patients after all; they turned out to be employees whom the company had paid to post positive reviews of its services. One critic says, "I know of other companies that do the same thing (post fake reviews), and they suffer from an underlying insecurity about the true value of their products and services and their business practices." Other companies, such as Overstock.com, post genuine customer reviews, even bad ones, so that customers can make more informed purchase decisions.

Advertising Buns

KFC, the world's most popular chicken fast-food chain, recently paid women on college campuses $500 to wear tight-fitting sweatpants with the words "Double Down" printed in large letters across the seat as they handed out discount coupons. The unusual advertising medium promoted the company's new line of bunless Double Down sandwiches. The campaign is aimed at the Double Down target market: young men between the ages of 18 and 25. KFC managers decided to take a different approach to reach its target customers after a survey of people aged 18 and 25 indicated that many young adults could not identify the company's signature character, Colonel Sanders, in its ads.

The ads caused some controversy on college campuses. "It's obnoxious to use women's bodies to sell fundamentally unhealthy products," says Terry O'Neill, president of the National Organization for Women. A marketing professor at one of the colleges included in the promotion says, "It'll get attention, but it probably will be a waste of money. I don't see how it helps." KFC's marketing vice president, however, believes the promotion is an effective way to reach target customers. "We've taken a page out of the book of some apparel companies and sororities that have promoted this way for years," he says.

1. Is it ethical for a company to post fake online reviews promoting its products and services? Does doing so cause harm? Explain.
2. Is KFC's advertising campaign ethical? Explain.

Sources: Based on Claire Cain Miller, "Company Settles Case of Reviews It Faked," *New York Times*, July 14, 2009, *www.nytimes.com/2009/07/15/technology/internet/15lift.html;* Bryan Stapp, "Fake User Reviews Are a No-No," *Loud Amplifier Marketing*, July 16, 2009, *www.loudamplifiermarketing.com/fake-user-reviews-are-a-no-no/;* Bruce Horovitz, "KFC Pays College Women for Ad Space on Buns," *USA Today*, September 22, 2010, *www.usatoday.com/money/industries/food/2010-09-22-kfc22_ST_N.htm;* Trang Do, "KFC Advertising Bun-less Sandwiches on Buns of College Students," WAFF 48 News, October 23, 2010, *www.waff.com/Global/story.asp?S=13208785.*

Source: © Scott Adams/Dist. by United Feature Syndicate, Inc.

go beyond "doing well"—simply earning a profit—to "doing good"—living up to their social responsibility. They also must recognize the interdependence of business and society. Each influences the other, and both must remain healthy to sustain each other over time.

Companies that are most successful in meeting their social responsibility select causes that are consistent with their core values and their employees' interests and skill sets. In fact, some entrepreneurs allow employees to provide input into the decision concerning which causes to support. A common strategy is to allow employees to provide pro bono work for the charitable organizations they support. Employees at Gumas Advertising, an advertising agency in San Francisco, founded by John Gumas, create marketing campaigns and perform other services for the San Francisco Giants Community Fund, a nonprofit organization that helps underprivileged youth to lead quality lives. Employees at the agency also benefit from their support of the cause. "It gives us a rallying point," says Gumas. [22]

A recent survey by SurePayroll reports that 55 percent of small business's mission statements include a reference to achieving some type of social goal. [23] Indeed, entrepreneurs are using their resources and sphere of influence not only to generate a profit but also to tackle challenging problems confronting the global economy, including pollution, habitat destruction, human rights, AIDS, hunger, poverty, and others. These **social entrepreneurs**, people who start businesses so that they can create innovative solutions to society's most vexing problems, see themselves as change agents for society. Social entrepreneurs use their creativity to develop solutions to social problems that range from cleaning up the environment to improving working conditions for workers around the world; their goal is to use their businesses to make money *and* to make the world a better place to live. The Global Entrepreneurship Monitor survey of entrepreneurial activity in 54 countries reports that 36 percent of entrepreneurs launch for-profit companies that also include a social responsibility focus. [24] Bill Drayton, founder of Ashoka, an organization that promotes social entrepreneurship, says, "Social entrepreneurs are not content just to give a fish or teach [someone] how to fish. They will not rest until they have revolutionized the fishing industry." [25]

ENTREPRENEURIAL
Profile

June Wilcox, Tim Mesaric, and John Hampson: TimesTwo

June Wilcox, Tim Mesaric, and John Hampson already were successful entrepreneurs when they decided to launch TimesTwo, a company based in Greenville, South Carolina, that donates a product to a charitable organization for every one that is sells. The three entrepreneurs operate Adec Group, a successful small company that manages Web content for large businesses, but were inspired by TOMS Shoes' business model to create a company with a focus on social responsibility. "Everyone in our company (Adec Group) has a servant heart," says Wilcox. "Each quarter we take turns choosing a service project we all do together. Those days, we're happiest and most satisfied. Then I saw an interview with TOMS Shoes founder Blake Mycoskie. He was sharing his story in hope that other businesses would copy his model of a business built to do good. I took the idea to my colleagues, and TimesTwo was born." TimesTwo's initial product offerings, all of which are adorned with the company's catchy "Buy. Give." logo, included a variety of baby products (e.g., blankets, towels, bibs, and snap shirts) but has expanded to include personal care items and school supplies. [26]

In a free enterprise system, companies that fail to respond to their customers' needs and demands soon go out of business. Today, customers are increasingly demanding the companies they buy goods and services from to be socially responsible. When customers shop for "value," they no longer consider only the price–performance relationship of the product or service; they also consider the company's stance on social responsibility. Whether a company supports a social or environmental cause has a significant effect on shoppers' behavior. A study by Cone LLC reports that 80 percent of U.S. consumers are likely to switch to a brand that they perceive is similar in price and quality if the company supports a cause. The study also concludes that 75 percent of consumers say that a company supporting a worthy cause affects where they shop and what they buy, and 76 percent say it affects the products and services they recommend to other people. [27] Other studies report that when price, service, and quality are equal among competitors customers buy from the company that has the best reputation for social responsibility.

Other studies show a connection between social responsibility and profitability. One team of researchers evaluated 52 studies on corporate social responsibility that were conducted over 30 years and concluded that a positive correlation existed between a company's profitability and its reputation for ethical, socially responsible behavior. The relationship also was self-reinforcing.

"It's a virtuous cycle," says Sara Rynes, one of the researchers. "As a company becomes more socially responsible, its reputation and financial performance go up, which causes them to become even more socially responsible."[28] The message is clear: Companies that incorporate social responsibility into their competitive strategies outperform those that fail to do so. Today's socially wired, transparent economy makes ethical and socially responsible behavior highly visible and, conversely, improper behavior more difficult to hide.

Putting Social Responsibility into Practice

One problem businesses face is defining just what socially responsible behavior is. Is it manufacturing environmentally friendly products? Is it donating a portion of profits to charitable organizations? Is it creating jobs in inner cities plagued by high unemployment levels? The nature of a company's social responsibility efforts depends on how its owners, employees, and other stakeholders define what it means to be socially responsible. Typically, businesses have responsibilities to several key stakeholders, including the environment, employees, customers, investors, and the community.

IN THE ENTREPRENEURIAL
SPOTLIGHT Making a Profit and Making a Difference

Entrepreneurs have learned that one of the most effective ways to connect with their customers is to support a cause about which their customers care. According to the Cone Cause Evolution Study, 85 percent of consumers say that they have a more positive image of a company when it supports a cause that is important to them. By forging partnerships with nonprofit and social causes, small businesses not only can make a difference in the world but also can improve their visibility in the marketplace and increase sales.

iContact

When Ryan Allis and Aaron Houghton met at the University of North Carolina at Chapel Hill, each of them owned companies that provided Web design and marketing services. The two joined forces to launch iContact Corporation, a business based in Morrisville, North Carolina, that provides a Web-based e-mail list management tool.

Just 2 years after launch, iContact became profitable, which allowed Allis and Houghton to do something that they had planned to do all along: implement the "4-1's Corporate Responsibility Program." Through the 4-1's, iContact would donate to charitable organizations 1 percent of its employees' time, 1 percent of its e-mail marketing products, 1 percent of its payroll (in addition to matching up to $300 of each employee's individual donations), and 1 percent of its equity to the iContact Foundation, which is designed to support a variety of worthy causes.

Houghton and Allis believe that the best way to make the world a better place to live is through social entrepreneurship. "My advice for college students who are considering starting a nonprofit is to consider doing it with a for-profit model," says Allis. The young entrepreneurs believe that for-profit companies produce better results by generating profits that they can funnel into important causes and charitable organizations than nonprofit entities whose leaders are distracted by having to chase donations constantly.

In just 5 years, iContact's revenue increased from $300,000 to $26.4 million, and the company now has more than 200 employees and an annual payroll of $11 million. In one recent year, iContact made $109,000 in cash donations, provided nearly 700 nonprofit organizations free use of its e-mail marketing management software, and gave its employees 500 paid days off to perform volunteer work for 63 different organizations. As their company grows, Allis and Houghton say that iContact's giving will grow in step. "Therein lies the power of social entrepreneurship," says Allis.

1. Do you agree with Ryan Allis' advice that the best way to support a cause is to create a for-profit business? Explain.
2. What benefits does iContact realize by dedicating a portion of their sales and business resources to charitable causes?
3. Select a local small business and work with a team of your classmates to brainstorm ideas for a social responsibility strategy that helps a charitable organization or social cause and produces benefits for the small company. What advice can you offer a small business that is considering supporting a nonprofit organization or social cause?

Sources: Based on 2010 Cone Cause Evolution Study, Cone LLC, p. 5; Joel Holland, "Save the World, Make a Million," *Entrepreneur*, April 2010, p. 76.

Business's Responsibility to the Environment

5. Understand the nature of business's responsibility to the environment.

Driven by their customers' interest in protecting the environment, companies have become more sensitive to the impact their products, processes, and packaging have on the planet. Environmentalism has become, and will continue to be, one of the dominant issues for companies worldwide because consumers have added another item to their list of buying criteria: environmental friendliness and safety. Companies have discovered that sound environmental practices make for good business. In addition to lowering their operating costs, environmentally safe products attract environmentally conscious customers and can give a company a competitive edge in the marketplace. Socially responsible business owners focus on the three Rs: reduce, reuse, and recycle:

- *Reduce* the amount of energy and materials used in your company, from the factory floor to the copier room.
- *Reuse* whatever you can.
- *Recycle* the materials that you must dispose of.

ENTREPRENEURIAL
Profile

Jonathan, Yair, and Helen Marcoschamer: Ecoist

Jonathan Marcoschamer and his mother, Helen Marcoschamer, displaying handbags that their company, Ecoist, makes from recycled candy wrappers, food packages, and soft drink labels.

Source: C.W. Griffin/Miami Herald/MCT/Newscom

After a family trip to Mexico, Jonathan, Yair, and Helen Marcoschamer were inspired by the handbags they saw in a street market that local artisans made from potato chip bags and candy wrappers. When they returned to their Miami, Florida, home, the three started Ecoist, a small company that makes a variety of stylish totes, bags, clutches, and bracelets from misprinted or discarded product packages. Ecoist has partnered with Coca-Cola, Disney, Frito-Lay, Mars, Cliff Bar, Aveda, and other companies to sponsor product lines using their products' packaging. To date, Ecoist has prevented more than 40 million wrappers from going into landfills and used them to create fashionable consumer products. "You can help save the planet and look good doing it," say the Marcoshamers. The company also partners with Trees for the Future to plant a tree for every bag it sells. Ecoist has planted more than 100,000 trees in Haiti, Uganda, India, and other countries.[29]

Many progressive small companies are taking their environmental policies a step further, creating redesigned, "clean" manufacturing systems that focus on *avoiding* waste and pollution and using resources efficiently. Such efforts require a different manufacturing philosophy. These companies design their products, packaging, and processes from the start with the environment in mind, working to eliminate hazardous materials and by-products and looking for ways to turn what had been scrap into salable products. This approach requires an ecological evaluation of every part of the process, from the raw materials that go into a product to the disposal or reuse of the packaging that contains it.

ENTREPRENEURIAL
Profile

Joshua Onysko and Pangea Organics

Joshua Onysko, founder of Pangea Organics, incorporates clean manufacturing principles into his business, which uses organic, all-natural ingredients such as beeswax, almond oil, and sweet basil to produce the company's line of soaps and body lotions. Pangea's packaging is made from 100 percent recycled paper using a "zero waste" process. The packages even include the seeds of herbs such as basil and amaranth. Once customers remove the product, they simply soak the package in water for 1 minute, plant it, and wait for the seeds to sprout! Pangea's 10,000-square-foot factory in Denver, Colorado, is powered completely by wind, and a 2,500-square-foot garden provides lunch for the company's 22 employees 7 months out of the year. Onysko says that Pangea is gearing up for an audit of its environmental impact so that the company can be even more environmentally sensitive.[30]

TABLE 6 Environmentally Responsible Questions

What can companies do to be more environmentally friendly? The following questions can help entrepreneurs evaluate their companies' impact on the environment.

- Are we trying to reduce the volume of our packaging?
- How do we deal with disposal?
- Are we recycling in the office?
- Can we get beyond the concept of volume sales to build products that last?
- Are we reducing waste and substituting toxic substances with nontoxic ones?
- Are we reformulating waste for resale?
- Do we have a formal environmental policy?
- Do we go beyond compliance?
- Are we uniformly stringent environmentally in operations outside, as well as inside, the United States?
- Do we educate employees about the hazards of working with toxic materials?
- Do we encourage employees to submit proposals on how to reduce waste?
- Do we conserve energy?
- Are we avoiding paying taxes, when those tax dollars might go to support environmental programs?
- How do our operations affect the communities they're in, including indigenous people in other countries?

Source: From Therese R. Welter, "A Farewell to Arms," *Industry Week*, August 20, 1990, p. 42. Reprinted with permission of Penton Media.

Table 6 offers a list of questions that environmentally responsible entrepreneurs should ask themselves.

Business's Responsibility to Employees

6. Describe business's responsibility to employees.

Few stakeholders are as important to a business as its employees. It is common for managers to *say* that their employees are their most valuable resource, but the truly excellent ones actually *treat* them that way. Employees are at the heart of increases in productivity, and they add the personal touch that puts passion in customer service. In short, employees produce the winning competitive advantage for an entrepreneur. Entrepreneurs who understand the value of their employees follow a few simple procedures by:

- Listening to employees and respecting their opinions.
- Asking for their input; involving them in the decision-making process.
- Providing regular feedback—positive and negative—to employees.
- Telling them the truth—always.
- Letting them know exactly what's expected of them.
- Rewarding employees for performing their jobs well.
- Trusting them; creating an environment of respect and teamwork.

ENTREPRENEURIAL
Profile

Tom, Kevin, and Larry Walter: Tasty Catering

Because of its employee-centered culture, Tasty Catering recently was named the Top Small Company Workplace in the United States.

Source: Tasty Catering

In 1984, brothers Tom, Kevin, and Larry Walter were operating Tasty Dawg, a hot dog stand in Elk Grove Village, Illinois, and received so many requests for catering jobs that they launched Tasty Catering. Today, the family-owned business, which caters an average of 30 events each day, has 58 full-time employees and annual sales of $6.1 million and was recently named Caterer of the Year and the Top Small Company Workplace in the United States. In 2007, Director of Communications Jamie Pritscher arranged for an outside provider to conduct a 65-question employee survey that included asking "What changes would you make if you owned Tasty Catering?" The survey led managers to launch a weekly bilingual employee newsletter that shows the company's financial status and includes articles featuring news and accomplishments in each department. Tasty Catering promotes from within, a strategy that increases employee loyalty; the average tenure of its employees is 7.5 years. "We have always tried to manage Tasty Catering on the philosophy that if we take care of our employees and our customers, we will be successful," says Kevin. The company also lives up to its social responsibility as a good corporate citizen, supporting programs at local schools and hosting an annual holiday party with food and gifts for families in need. Tasty Catering is working to make its operations more energy efficient and environmentally friendly. The plates it uses at picnics are made from recycled fiber, and the cups and cutlery are made from corn and potato starch. Tasty Catering recycles tons of material and has renovated its building to be as energy efficient as possible. Complimentary daily meals encourage employees to get together, learn from one another, and communicate more effectively.[31]

Entrepreneurs who are trying to meet their social responsibility to their employees face several important issues, including cultural diversity, drug testing, AIDs, sexual harassment, and privacy.

CULTURAL DIVERSITY IN THE WORKPLACE. The United States has always been a nation of astonishing cultural diversity (see Figure 4), a trait that has imbued it with an incredible richness of ideas and creativity. Indeed, this diversity is one of the driving forces behind the greatest entrepreneurial effort in the world, and it continues to grow. The United States, in short, is moving toward a "minority majority," and significant demographic shifts will affect virtually every aspect of business. Nowhere will this be more visible than in the makeup of the nation's workforce (see Figure 5). In 2020, members of five different generations will be working side-by-side in the United States.[32] By 2039, the *majority* of the workforce in the United States will be members of a minority.[33] The Hispanic population is the fastest growing sector in the United States, and Hispanics now comprise the largest minority population in the nation.

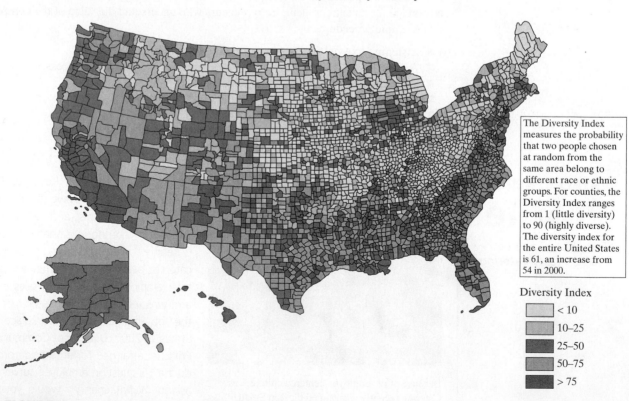

2010 Diversity Index by Country

The Diversity Index measures the probability that two people chosen at random from the same area belong to different race or ethnic groups. For counties, the Diversity Index ranges from 1 (little diversity) to 90 (highly diverse). The diversity index for the entire United States is 61, an increase from 54 in 2000.

Diversity Index
- < 10
- 10–25
- 25–50
- 50–75
- > 75

FIGURE 4
2010 Diversity Index by County

FIGURE 5
Composition of the
U.S. Workforce

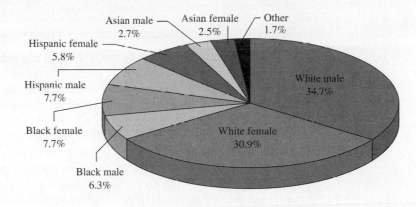

This rich mix of generations, cultures, and backgrounds within the workforce presents both opportunities and challenges to employers. One of the chief benefits of a diverse workforce is the unique blend of perspectives, skills, talents, and ideas employees have to offer. Also, the changing composition of the nation's population will change the customer base. What better way is there for an entrepreneur to deal with culturally diverse customers than to have a culturally diverse workforce? "No matter who you are, you're going to have to work with people who are different from you," says Ted Childs, vice president of global workforce diversity for IBM. "You're going to have to sell to people who are different from you, buy from people who are different from you, and manage people who are different from you."[34]

Managing a culturally diverse workforce presents a real challenge for employers, however. Molding workers with highly varied beliefs, backgrounds, and biases into a unified team takes time and commitment. Stereotypes, biases, and prejudices present barriers that workers and managers must constantly overcome. Communication may require more effort because of language differences. In many cases, dealing with diversity causes a degree of discomfort for entrepreneurs because of the natural tendency to associate with people who are similar to ourselves. These reasons and others cause some entrepreneurs to resist the move to a more diverse workforce, a move that threatens their ability to create a competitive edge.

How can entrepreneurs achieve unity through diversity? The only way is by *managing* diversity in the workforce. In *Best Practices of Private Sector Employers*, an Equal Employment Opportunity Commission task force suggests following a "SPLENDID" approach to diversity:

- *Study.* Business owners cannot solve problems they don't know exist. Entrepreneurs must familiarize themselves with issues related to diversity, including relevant laws.
- *Plan.* Recognizing the makeup of the local population, entrepreneurs must set targets for diversity hiring and develop a plan for achieving them.
- *Lead.* A diversity effort starts at the top of the organization with managers communicating their vision and goals to everyone in the company.
- *Encourage.* Company leaders must encourage employees at all levels of an organization to embrace the diversity plan.
- *Notice.* Entrepreneurs must monitor their companies' progress toward achieving diversity goals.
- *Discussion.* Managers must keep diversity on the company's radar screen by communicating the message that diversity is vital to business success.
- *Inclusion.* Involving employees in the push to achieve diversity helps break down barriers that may arise.
- *Dedication.* Achieving diversity in a business does not happen overnight, but entrepreneurs must be persistent in implementing their plans.[35]

The goal of diversity efforts is to create an environment in which all types of workers—men, women, Hispanic, African American, white, disabled, homosexual, elderly, and others—can flourish and can give top performances to their companies. In fact, researchers at Harvard University report that companies that embrace diversity are more productive than those that shun it. A distinguishing factor that companies supporting diversity share is the willingness of people to learn from their coworkers' different backgrounds and life experiences.[36]

Managing a culturally diverse workforce requires a different way of thinking, however, and that requires training. In essence, diversity training helps make everyone aware of the dangers of bias, prejudice, and discrimination, however subtle or unintentional they may be. Managing a culturally diverse workforce successfully requires a business owner to:

■ *Assess your company's diversity needs.* The starting point for an effective diversity management program is assessing a company's needs. Surveys, interviews, and informal conversations with employees can be valuable tools. Several organizations offer more formal assessment tools—cultural audits, questionnaires, and diagnostic forms—that also are useful.

■ *Learn to recognize and correct your own biases and stereotypes.* One of the best ways to identify your own cultural biases is to get exposure to people who are not like you. By spending time with those who are different from you, you will learn quickly that stereotypes simply don't hold up. Giving employees the opportunity to spend time with one another is an excellent way to eliminate stereotypes. The owner of one small company with a culturally diverse staff provides lunch for his workers every month with a seating arrangement that encourages employees to mix with one another.

■ *Avoid making invalid assumptions.* Decisions that are based on faulty assumptions are bound to be flawed. False assumptions built on inaccurate perceptions or personal bias have kept many qualified minority workers from getting jobs and promotions. Make sure that it does not happen in your company.

■ *Push for diversity in your management team.* To get maximum benefit from a culturally diverse workforce, a company must promote nontraditional workers into top management. A culturally diverse top management team that can serve as mentors and role models provides visible evidence that nontraditional workers can succeed.

■ *Concentrate on communication.* Any organization, especially a culturally diverse one, will stumble if lines of communication break down. Frequent training sessions and regular opportunities for employees to talk with one another in a nonthreatening environment can be extremely helpful.

■ *Make diversity a core value in the organization.* For a cultural diversity program to work, top managers must "champion" the program and take active steps to integrate diversity throughout the entire organization.

■ *Continue to adjust your company to your workers.* Rather than pressure workers to conform to the company, those entrepreneurs with the most successful cultural diversity programs are constantly looking for ways to adjust their businesses to their workers. Flexibility is the key.

As business leaders look to the future, an increasingly diverse workforce stares back. People with varying cultural, racial, gender, and lifestyle perspectives seek opportunity and acceptance from coworkers, managers, and business owners. Currently, women make up nearly 48 percent of the U.S. workforce, and minority workers comprise more than 34 percent of the labor force.[37] Businesses that value the diversity of their workers and the perspectives they bring to work enjoy the benefits of higher employee satisfaction, commitment, retention, creativity, and productivity than those companies that ignore the cultural diversity of their workers. In addition, they deepen the loyalty of their existing customers and expand their market share by attracting new customers. In short, diversity is a winning proposition from every angle!

DRUG TESTING. One of the realities of our society is substance abuse. The second reality, which entrepreneurs now must face head on, is that substance abuse has infiltrated the workplace. In addition to the lives it ruins, substance abuse takes a heavy toll on business and society. Drug and alcohol abuse by employees results in reduced productivity (an estimated $81 billion per year), increased medical costs, higher accident rates, and higher levels of absenteeism. Alarmingly, 77 percent of all substance abusers are employed.[38] Small companies bear a disproportionate share of the burden because they are less likely to have drug-testing programs than large companies, and thus are more likely to hire people with substance abuse problems. Abusers who know that they cannot pass a drug test simply apply for work at companies that do not use drug tests. In addition, because the practice of drug testing remains a controversial issue, its random use can lead to a variety of legal woes for employers, including invasion of privacy, discrimination, slander, or defamation of character.

An effective, proactive drug program should include the following five elements:

1. *A written substance abuse policy.* The first step is to create a written policy that spells out the company's position on drugs. The policy should state its purpose, prohibit the use of

drugs on the job (or off the job if it affects job performance), specify the consequences of violating the policy, explain the drug testing procedures the company will use, and describe the resources available to help troubled employees.

2. *Training for supervisors to detect substance-abusing workers.* Supervisors are in the best position to identify employees with alcohol or drug problems and to encourage them to get help. The supervisor's job, however, is not to play "cop" or "therapist." The supervisor should identify problem employees early and encourage them to seek help. The focal point of the supervisor's role is to track employees' performances against their objectives to identify employees with performance problems. Vigilant managers look for the following signs:

- Frequent tardiness or absences accompanied by questionable excuses
- Long lunch, coffee, or bathroom breaks
- Frequently missed deadlines
- Withdrawal from or frequent arguments with fellow employees
- Overly sensitive to criticism
- Declining or inconsistent productivity
- Inability to concentrate on work
- Disregard for personal safety or the safety of others
- Deterioration of personal appearance

3. *An employee education program.* Business owners should take time to explain the company's substance abuse policy, the reasons behind it, and the help that is available to employees who have substance abuse problems. Every employee should participate in training sessions, and managers should remind employees periodically of the policy, the problem, and the help that is available. Some companies have used inserts in pay envelopes, home mailings, lunch speakers, and short seminars as part of their ongoing educational efforts.

4. *A drug testing program, when necessary.* Experts recommend that business owners seek the advice of an experienced attorney before establishing a drug testing program. Pre-employment testing of job applicants generally is a safe strategy to follow, as long as it is followed consistently. Testing current employees is a more complex issue, but, again, consistency is the key.

5. *An employee assistance program (EAP).* No drug-battling program is complete without a way to help addicted employees. An **employee assistance program (EAP)** is a company-provided benefit designed to help reduce workplace problems such as alcoholism, drug addiction, a gambling habit, and other conflicts and to deal with them when they arise. Although some troubled employees may balk at enrolling in an EAP, the company controls the most powerful weapon in motivating them to seek and accept help: *their jobs.* The greatest fear that substance-abusing employees have is losing their jobs, and the company can use that fear to help workers recover. EAPs, which cost between $18 and $30 per employee each year to operate, are an effective weapon in the battle against workplace substance abuse. Research shows that EAPs can pay for themselves quickly by reducing absenteeism and tardiness by 25 percent and increasing productivity by 25 percent.[39]

ENTREPRENEURIAL
Profile

Eastern Industries

Eastern Industries, a Pennsylvania-based company that produces building supplies, concrete, asphalt, and stone, operates in an industry that traditionally has been plagued by substance abuse problems. (A recent study shows that 15.1 percent of workers in the construction industry had substance abuse problems, second only to the food service industry.) Initially, Eastern's substance abuse policy was simple: We test for drugs, and if you fail the test you are fired. The all-or-nothing policy affected the company's ability to keep and retain skilled workers, and company managers decided to change it to a policy that includes prevention, testing, and rehabilitation. Eastern includes educational sessions on substance abuse in its employee orientation program and ongoing programs for all workers. If an employee fails a drug test, he or she can enroll in an employee assistance program that includes rehabilitation that, once successfully completed, allows the worker to return to his or her job. Managers at Eastern say the program has been a tremendous success, allowing them to keep good workers they would have lost under the old policy and giving employees the opportunity to correct bad decisions and keep their jobs.[40]

HIV/AIDS. One of the most serious health problems to strike the world is HIV/AIDS (acquired immune deficiency syndrome). Health care experts estimate that more than 1.5 million people in the United States have HIV/AIDS, and 56,000 new cases are diagnosed each year. HIV/AIDS claims the lives of about 18,000 people annually.[41] This deadly disease, for which no cure yet exists, poses an array of ethical dilemmas for business, ranging from privacy to discrimination. AIDS has had an impact on our economy in the form of billions of dollars in lost productivity and increased health care costs. For most business owners, the issue is not one of *whether* one of their employees will contract AIDS but *when*.

Coping with AIDS in the workplace is not like managing normal health care issues because of the fear and misunderstanding the disease creates among coworkers. When confronted by the disease, many employers and employees operate out of misconceptions and fear, resulting in "knee-jerk" reactions that are illegal, including firing the worker and telling other employees. Too many entrepreneurs know very little about their legal obligation to employees with AIDS. In fact, AIDS is considered a disability and is covered by the Americans with Disabilities Act (ADA). This legislation prohibits discrimination against any person with a disability, including AIDS, in hiring, promoting, discharging, or compensation. In addition, employers are required to make "reasonable accommodations" that will allow an AIDS-stricken employee to continue working. Some examples of these accommodations include job sharing, flexible work schedules, job reassignment, sick leave, and part-time work.

Coping with AIDS in a socially responsible manner requires a written policy and an educational program, ideally implemented *before* the need arises. When dealing with AIDS, entrepreneurs must base their decisions on facts rather than on emotions, so they must be well informed. As with drug testing, it is important to ensure that a company's AIDS policies are legal. In general, a company's AIDS policy should include the following:

- *Employment.* Companies must allow employees with AIDS to continue working as long as they can perform the job.
- *Discrimination.* Because AIDS is a disability, employers cannot discriminate against qualified people with the disease who can meet job requirements.
- *Employee benefits.* Employees with AIDS have the right to the same benefits as those with any other life-threatening illness.
- *Confidentiality.* Employers must keep employees' medical records strictly confidential.
- *Education.* An AIDS education program should be a part of every company's AIDS policy. The time to create and implement one is before the problem arises. As part of its AIDS program, one small company conducted informational seminars, distributed brochures and booklets, established a print and video library, and even set up individual counseling for employees.
- *Reasonable accommodations.* Under the ADA, employers must make "reasonable accommodations" for employees with AIDS. These may include extended leaves of absence, flexible work schedules, restructuring a job to require less-strenuous duties, purchasing special equipment to assist affected workers, and other modifications.

SEXUAL HARASSMENT. Sexual harassment is a problem in the workplace, and thousands of workers file sexual harassment charges with the Equal Employment Opportunity Commission against their employers every year (see Figure 6). A survey by Reuters-Ipsos reports that 10 percent of workers in 24 countries say that they have been physically or sexually harassed. Employees in India were most likely to report sexual harassment (26 percent), and those in France and Sweden were least likely (3 percent). The incidence of sexual harassment in the United States is slightly below the global average at 9 percent.[42] Sexual harassment is a violation of Title VII of the Civil Rights Act of 1964 and is considered to be a form of sex discrimination. Studies show that sexual harassment occurs in businesses of all sizes, but small businesses are especially vulnerable because they typically lack the policies, procedures, and training to prevent it. Even cartoon strip characters are not immune to sexual harassment charges. In Mort Walker's long-running "Beetle Bailey" comic strip, Miss Buxley once filed charges against General Halftrack because of his leering stares and sexual and untoward comments.[43]

Sexual harassment is any unwelcome sexual advance, request for sexual favors, and other verbal or physical sexual conduct made explicitly or implicitly as a condition of employment. Women bring about 84 percent of all sexual harassment charges.[44] Jury verdicts reaching into the millions of dollars are not uncommon. Retaliation such as demotions and assignments to less attractive work against employees who file complaints of sexual harassment occurs too often. The

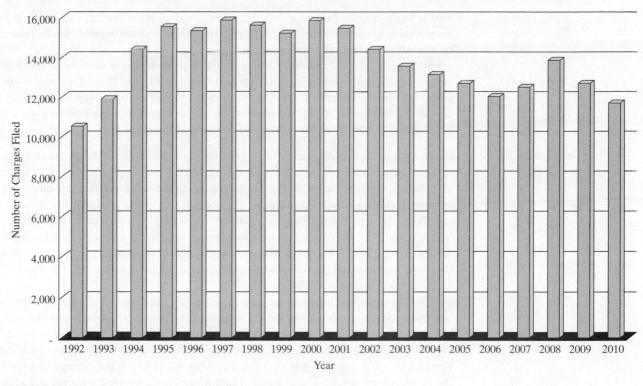

FIGURE 6
Number of Sexual Harassment Charges Filed

Source: Equal Employment Opportunity Commission, 2010.

most common form of employer retaliation is termination. Several types of behavior may result in sexual harassment charges.

Quid Pro Quo Harassment. The most blatant, and most potentially damaging, form of sexual harassment is *quid pro quo* ("something for something"), in which a superior conditions the granting of a benefit (promotion, raise, etc.) upon the receipt of sexual favors from a subordinate. Only managers and supervisors, not coworkers, can engage in *quid pro quo* harassment.

Only managers can engage in *quid pro quo* sexual harassment.

Source: RubberBall/SuperStock, Inc.

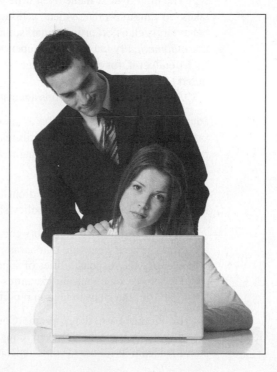

Hostile Environment. Behavior that creates an abusive, intimidating, offensive, or hostile work environment also constitutes sexual harassment. A hostile environment usually requires a *pattern* of offensive sexual behavior rather than a single, isolated remark or display. When judging whether a hostile environment exists, courts base their decisions on how a "reasonable woman" would perceive the situation. (The previous standard was that of a "reasonable person.") Although not easily defined, a hostile work environment is one in which continuing unwelcome sexual conduct in the workplace interferes with an employee's work performance. Most sexual harassment charges arise from claims of a hostile environment.

Harassment by Nonemployees. An employer can be held liable for third parties (customers, sales representatives, and others) who engage in sexual harassment if the employer has the ability to stop the improper behavior. For example, one company required a female employee to wear an extremely skimpy, revealing uniform. She complained to her boss that the uniform encouraged members of the public to direct offensive comments and physical contact toward her. The manager ignored her complaints, and later she refused to wear the uniform, which resulted in her dismissal. When she filed a sexual harassment claim, the court held the company accountable for the employee's sexual harassment by nonemployees because it required her to wear the uniform after she complained of the harassment.[45]

No business wants to incur the cost of defending itself against charges of sexual harassment, but those costs can be devastating for a small business. Multimillion-dollar jury awards in harassment cases are becoming increasingly common because the Civil Rights Act of 1991 allows victims to collect punitive damages and emotional distress awards. A jury awarded Shannen De La Cruz $2.16 million in damages after she won a lawsuit in which she claimed that her supervisor at the casino where she worked as a card dealer made inappropriate comments and sexual innuendo towards her. After De La Cruz reported the behavior to the company's human resource manager, a woman who also had filed (and settled) a sexual harassment suit against the company, the supervisor began disciplining her for minor and fabricated violations. Managers at the company did nothing to stop the supervisor's actions. The supervisor fired De La Cruz after he discovered that she was exploring legal action against the company over the harassment. On appeal, a judge affirmed the lower court's ruling but reduced the award to $1.26 million.[46]

The U.S. Supreme Court has expanded the nature of an employer's liability for sexual harassment, rejecting the previous standard that the employer had to be negligent to be liable for a supervisor's improper behavior toward employees. In *Burlington Industries v. Ellerth,* the Court ruled that an employer can be held liable *automatically* if a supervisor takes a "tangible employment action," such as failing to promote or firing an employee whom he has been sexually harassing. The employer is liable even if he was not aware of the supervisor's conduct. If a supervisor takes no tangible employment action against an employee but engages in sexually harassing behavior, such as offensive remarks, inappropriate touching, or sexual advances, the employer is not *automatically* liable for the supervisor's conduct. However, an employer would be liable for such conduct if, for example, he knew (or should have known) about the supervisor's behavior and failed to stop it.[47]

A company's best weapons against sexual harassment are education, policy, and procedures.

Education. Preventing sexual harassment is the best solution, and the key to prevention is educating employees about what constitutes sexual harassment. Training programs are designed to raise employees' awareness of what might be offensive to other workers and how to avoid sexual harassment altogether.

Policy. Another essential ingredient is a meaningful policy against sexual harassment that management can enforce. The policy should:

- Clearly define what behaviors constitute sexual harassment.
- State in clear language that harassment will not be tolerated in the workplace.
- Identify the responsibilities of supervisors and employees in preventing harassment.
- Define the sanctions and penalties for engaging in harassment.
- Spell out the steps to take in reporting an incident of sexual harassment.

In another case, the Supreme Court ruled that an employer was liable for a supervisor's sexually harassing behavior even though the employee never reported it. The company's liability stemmed from its failure to communicate its sexual harassment policy throughout the organization.

This ruling makes employers' policies and procedures on sexual harassment the focal point of their defense.

Procedure. Socially responsible companies provide a channel for all employees to express their complaints. Choosing a person inside the company (perhaps someone in the human resources area) and one outside the company (a close advisor or attorney) is a good strategy because it gives employees a choice about how to file a complaint. At least one of these people should be a woman. When a complaint arises, managers should:

- Listen to the complaint carefully without judging. Taking notes is a good idea. Tell the complainant what the process involves. Never treat the complaint as a joke.
- Investigate the complaint *promptly*, preferably within 24 hours. Failure to act quickly is irresponsible and illegal. Table 7 offers suggestions for conducting a sexual harassment investigation.
- Interview the accused party and any witnesses who may be aware of a pattern of harassing behavior *privately* and separately.
- Keep findings confidential.
- Decide what action to take, relying on company policy as a guideline.
- Inform both the complaining person and the alleged harasser of the action taken.
- Document the entire investigation.[48]

The accompanying "Lessons from the Street-Smart Entrepreneur" feature includes a quiz on sexual harassment for both employees and managers.

PRIVACY. Modern technology has given business owners the ability to monitor workers' performances as they never could before, but where is the line between monitoring productivity and invasion of privacy? With a few mouse clicks, it is possible for managers to view e-mail messages employees send to one another, listen to voice-mail or telephone conversations, and actually see what is on their monitors while they are sitting at their computer terminals. Managers use electronic monitoring to track customer service representatives, word processing clerks, data entry technicians, and other workers for speed, accuracy, and productivity. Even truck drivers, the lone rangers of the road, are not immune to electronic tracking. Most major trucking companies

TABLE 7 What to Do When an Employee Files a Sexual Harassment Complaint

When an employee files a sexual harassment complaint, the Equal Employment Opportunity Commission (EEOC) recommends that employers (1) question both parties in detail and (2) probe for corroborative evidence. Here is a checklist to help when following these EEOC recommendations:

- Analyze the victim's story for sufficient detail, internal consistency, and believability.
- Do not attach much significance to a general denial by the accused harasser.
- Search completely and thoroughly for evidence that corroborates either person's story.
- You can do this by:
  - interviewing coworkers, supervisors, and managers;
  - obtaining testimony from individuals who observed the accuser's demeanor immediately after the alleged incident of harassment; and
  - talking to people with whom the alleged victim discussed the incident (e.g., coworkers, a doctor, or a counselor).
- Ask other employees whether they noticed changes in the accusing individual's behavior at work or in the alleged harasser's treatment of him or her.
- Look for evidence of other complaints, either by the victim or other employees.
- Follow up on evidence that other employees were sexually harassed by the same person.

To make a fair and legal decision on a sexual harassment complaint, you must find out as much information as you can, not only on the incident itself, but also on the victim's and accuser's personalities, surroundings, and relationships. To accomplish this task, you need to ask many questions not only of the victim and the accuser but also of any witnesses to the incident.

Source: "Questions for Investigations," Women's Studies Database at the University of Maryland, *www.mith2.umd.edu/WomensStudies/GenderIssues/SexualHarassment/questions-for-investigations.*

LESSONS FROM THE STREET-SMART ➡ entrepreneur

How to Avoid Sexual Harassment Charges

The Equal Employment Opportunity Commission (EEOC) handles about 13,000 charges of sexual harassment each year from both women and men. Not surprisingly, women file 84 percent of the charges. Experts say that many other employees are sexually harassed but never file charges because of the stigma associated with doing so. What can you do to ensure you provide your employees a safe work environment that is free of sexual harassment? Consider the following case and then take the quizzes that follow on sexual harassment.

Theresa Waldo was the only woman working in the transmission lines department, a traditionally male-dominated job in which workers maintain and repair high-voltage power lines, sometimes at heights up to 250 feet, for Consumers Energy (CE). Her supervisor told her that the company did not "have women in this department," had never had them there, and that "they are not strong enough" to do the job. Despite resistance from her supervisor and her coworkers, Waldo, who started her career with CE as a meter reader, was participating in a 4-year Line Apprentice Training Program that would entitle her to a higher paying job. On several occasions, Waldo's supervisor told her that he would "wash her out" of the apprenticeship program.

During her time in the apprenticeship program, Waldo alleges that she faced an "abusive and dysfunctional environment" in which she was constantly "bombarded with sexually abusive and derogatory language and conduct." Male coworkers subjected her to magazines, calendars, playing cards, and other items that contained photographs of nude women. They also referred to Waldo using derogatory, sexually offensive names and on one 90-degree day intentionally locked her in a port-a-potty for 20 minutes. On another occasion, her supervisor ordered her to clean up the tobacco spit of the male workers; when she refused, her coworkers locked her in a trailer. Waldo complained to the company's management about the sexual harassment on several occasions, but managers failed to take any meaningful action to stop the behavior.

After Waldo had successfully completed 3 years of the apprenticeship program, CE removed her from it and transferred her to the Sub Metro Department, where her pay was $4 less per hour. She filed a sexual harassment charge, alleging that the company had created a hostile work environment, committed sexual harassment, and engaged in gender discrimination and retaliation.

Does Waldo have a legitimate sexual harassment complaint? Explain.

Yes. Although the jury in the trial ruled in favor of the *employer* on all claims, the judge granted Waldo's motion for a new trial, acknowledging that the jury's verdict on the hostile work environment and sexual harassment should be set aside because of the "clear evidence presented" in the case. The court ruled that the evidence "demonstrated egregious actions and sexually offensive and demeaning language" directed at Waldo. The court concluded that the harassment created "an intimidating, hostile, and offensive work environment" and that CE "knew of the harassment and failed to implement proper and appropriate corrective action." At the second trial, a jury ruled in Waldo's favor and granted her $400,000 in compensatory damages and $7.5 million in punitive damages.

One of the primary causes of sexual harassment in the workplace is the lack of education concerning what constitutes harassment. The following quizzes ask you to assume the roles of an employee and of a manager when answering the questions. Learning from these quizzes can help your company avoid problems with sexual harassment.

Test for Employees

Answer the following true/false questions:

1. If I just ignore unwanted sexual attention, it will usually stop.
2. If I don't mean to sexually harass another employee, he or she cannot perceive my behavior as sexually harassing.
3. Some employees don't complain about unwanted sexual attention from another worker because they don't want to get that person in trouble.
4. If I make sexual comments to someone and that person doesn't ask me to stop, I can assume that my behavior is welcome.
5. To avoid sexually harassing a woman who comes to work in a traditionally male workplace, men simply should not haze her.
6. A sexual harasser may be told by a court to pay part of a judgment to the employee he or she harassed.
7. A sexually harassed man does not have the same legal rights as a woman who is sexually harassed.
8. About 84 percent of all sexual harassment in today's workplace is done by males to females.
9. Sexually suggestive pictures or objects in a workplace don't create a liability unless someone complains.

10. Displaying nude pictures can constitute a hostile work environment even though most employees in the workplace think they are harmless.

11. Telling someone to stop his or her unwanted sexual behavior usually doesn't do any good.

Answers: (1) False, (2) False, (3) True, (4) False, (5) False, (6) True, (7) False, (8) True, (9) False, (10) True, (11) False.

Test for Managers

Answer the following true/false questions:

1. Men in male-dominated workplaces usually have to change their behavior when a woman begins working there.

2. Employers are not liable for the sexual harassment of one of their employees unless that employee loses specific job benefits or is fired.

3. Supervisors can be liable for sexual harassment committed by one of their employees against another.

4. Employers can be liable for the sexually harassing behavior of management personnel even if they are unaware of that behavior and have a policy forbidding it.

5. It is appropriate for a supervisor, when initially receiving a sexual harassment complaint, to determine whether the alleged recipient overreacted or misunderstood the alleged harasser.

6. When a supervisor tells an employee that an allegation of sexual harassment has been made against the employee, it is best to ease into the allegation instead of being direct.

7. Sexually suggestive visuals or objects in a workplace don't create a liability unless an employee complains about them and management allows them to remain.

8. The lack of sexual harassment complaints is a good indication that sexual harassment is not occurring.

9. It is appropriate for supervisors to tell an employee to handle unwelcome sexual behavior if they think that the employee is misunderstanding the behavior.

10. The *intent* behind employee A's sexual behavior is more important than the *impact* of that behavior on employee B when determining whether sexual harassment has occurred.

11. If a sexual harassment problem is common knowledge in a workplace, courts assume that the employer has knowledge of it.

Answers: (1) False, (2) False, (3) True, (4) True, (5) False, (6) False, (7) False, (8) False, (9) False, (10) False, (11) True.

Sources: Reprinted with permission from *IndustryWeek*, November 18, 1991, p. 40. Copyright Penton Publishing, Cleveland, Ohio; *Sexual Harassment Manual for Managers and Supervisors* (Chicago: Commerce Clearing House), 1992, p. 22; Andrea P. Brandon and David R. Eyler, *Working Together* (New York: McGraw-Hill), 1994; *Theresa Waldo v. Consumers Energy Company*, 2010 U.S. District Lexus 55068; 109 Fair Employment Practices Case (BNA) 11348, June 4, 2010; John Agar, "Consumers Energy Ordered to Pay $8 Million in Sexual Harassment Lawsuit Verdict," *Mlive*, October 8, 2010, *www.mlive.com/news/grand-rapids/index.ssf/2010/10/consumers_energy_ordered_to_pa.html*.

outfit their trucks with GPS devices that they use to monitor drivers' exact locations at all times, regulate their speed, make sure they stop only at approved fueling points, and ensure that they take the legally required hours of rest. Although many drivers support the use of these devices, others worry about their tendency to create George Orwell's "Big Brother" syndrome.

E-mail also poses an ethical problem for employers. Internet users send more than 247 billion e-mails each day.[49] Although most e-mails are unwanted spam, e-mail messages are a common way for employees to communicate with one another. Most workers do not realize that, in most states, employers legally can monitor their e-mail and voice-mail messages without notification. Only two states (Connecticut and Delaware) require companies to notify employees that they are monitoring e-mail. According to the Electronic Monitoring & Surveillance Survey, 43 percent of businesses monitor employees' e-mail and 28 percent have fired employees for misusing e-mail.[50] To avoid ethical (and legal) problems, business owners should follow these guidelines:

■ *Establish a clear policy for monitoring employees' communications.* Employees should know that the company is monitoring their e-mails and other forms of communication, and the best way to make sure they do is to create an unambiguous policy. Once you create a policy, be sure to follow it. Some managers ask employees to sign a consent form acknowledging that they have read and understand the company's monitoring policy.

■ *Create guidelines for the proper use of the company's communication technology and communicate them to everyone.* A company's policies and guidelines should be reasonable and should reflect employees' reasonable expectations of privacy.

■ *Monitor in moderation.* Employees resent monitoring that is unnecessarily invasive. In addition, excessively draconian monitoring may land a company in a legal battle.

▶ E N T R E P R E N E U R S H I P ▶ IN ACTION ▶

Think Before You Send That E-mail

Bonita Bourke and Rhonda Hall worked as customer service representatives for Nissan Motor Corporation, where they helped managers and employees at dealerships resolve problems with a new computer system that the company had implemented to help run dealerships more efficiently. During a training session on the system, one of Bonita Bourke's coworkers, Lori Eaton, was demonstrating how dealerships could use the system's e-mail feature as a management tool. As part of the demonstration, she randomly selected an e-mail that Bourke had sent to an employee at a Nissan dealership. Unfortunately, the e-mail was a personal one rather than one with a business purpose and contained sexual comments.

Eaton reported the incident to her supervisor, who reviewed the e-mails of all of the employees in Bourke's work group. He found a substantial number of e-mails from Bourke and Hall with similar content, much of it sexual and inappropriate in a business setting. The supervisor issued written warnings to both Bourke and Hall for violating the company's policy that prohibits the use of Nissan's e-mail system for personal purposes.

According to previous job evaluations, Bourke's job performance was substandard, and after the e-mail incident her performance declined. Eleven months after the e-mail incident, Bourke's job evaluation was rated "needs improvement," the second lowest category. Hall also received negative performance reviews during this time. Her supervisor wrote that she spent too much time on personal business and that she needed to demonstrate more initiative to learn the new computer system. She received the lowest performance rating, which was "unsatisfactory." Two months later, Bourke and Hall filed complaints with the human resources department, claiming that the company had invaded their privacy by reading their e-mail messages.

Two weeks later, Bourke's supervisor told her that if her performance did not improve over the next 3 months, she would be fired. She resigned the next day, the same day that Nissan fired Hall. Bourke and Hall filed a lawsuit against Nissan, alleging invasion of privacy, wrongful termination, and violation of the right to privacy under the U.S. Constitution. They argued that because the company gave them passwords to access the computer system and told them to safeguard their passwords, they believed that their e-mail messages would remain private. In its answer to the lawsuit, Nissan argued that employees had no reasonable expectation of privacy in their e-mail communications. The company pointed to a statement of company policy that the plaintiffs had signed: It is "company policy that employees restrict their use of company-owned computer hardware and software to company business." Furthermore, both employees knew that managers sometimes reviewed the e-mail messages that employees sent. Nissan argued that given these facts, employees could not reasonably expect that their e-mail communications were private.

Many e-mail privacy cases, including *Bourke v. Nissan Motor Corporation,* have landed in the courts in recent years. E-mail monitoring is a common practice among companies; 43 percent of companies say they monitor employees' e-mail. The best way for companies to avoid legal problems over e-mail privacy is to create a policy that states that employees have no expectation that their e-mails are private and that the company reserves the right to monitor e-mail activity. The policy also should address the appropriate use of the company's e-mail system. Employees should sign the policy as well.

Many workers are blissfully unaware that their e-mail activity is anything but private. "If your e-mails are being monitored and you send a message that violates your company's policy and you are terminated for that message, you will have a hard time making a claim of invasion of privacy stick," says one expert. However, courts in some states have upheld employees' right to e-mail privacy because they require "all party consent" for an employer to monitor e-mail communications. In other words, both the sender and the receiver of the e-mail message must be aware that the company is monitoring their communications.

1. If you were the judge in the *Bourke v. Nissan Motor Corporation* case, how would you rule? Explain your reasoning.
2. What steps can companies that monitor employees' e-mail take to protect themselves against invasion of privacy lawsuits?

Sources: Adapted from 2005 Electronic Monitoring & Surveillance Survey, "Many Companies Monitoring, Recording, Videotaping—and Firing—Employees," American Management Association, *www.amanet.org/press/amanews/ems05.htm*; Andrea Coombes, "Privacy at Work: Don't Count on It: Employers Are Tracking E-mail," *CareerJournal.com*, July 1, 2005, *www.careerjournal.com/myc/killers/20050701-coombes.html*; *Bourke v. Nissan Motor Corporation,* No. B068705 (Cal. Ct. App. July 26, 1993).

Business's Responsibility to Customers

7. Explain business's responsibility to customers.

One of the most important groups of stakeholders that a business must satisfy is its *customers.* Building and maintaining a base of loyal customers is no easy task; it requires more than just selling a product or a service. The key is to build relationships with customers. Socially responsible companies recognize their duty to abide by the Consumer Bill of Rights, first put forth by President John Kennedy. This document gives consumers the following rights.

RIGHT TO SAFETY. The right to safety is the most basic consumer right. Companies have the responsibility to provide their customers with safe, quality products and services. The greatest breach of trust occurs when businesses produce products that, when properly used, injure customers. Product liability cases can be controversial, such as the McDonald's coffee lawsuit, in which a jury found that the fast-food giant's coffee was too hot when served and caused a serious injury when a customer at a drive-through window spilled coffee in her lap. In other situations, the evidence is clear that a product suffers from fundamental flaws in either design or construction and caused an injury to its user when used properly.

Many companies have responded by placing detailed warning labels on their products that sometimes insult customers' intelligence. Consider the following actual examples from product warning labels:

- "Do not eat toner" on a toner cartridge for a laser printer
- "Never operate your speakerphone while driving," a warning attached to a "Drive 'N' Talk" speakerphone for use with cell phones
- "Do not use orally" on a toilet bowl cleaning brush
- "Do not try to dry your phone in a microwave oven" in the instructions for a cellular phone
- "Caution: Remove infant before folding for storage" on a baby stroller[51]

RIGHT TO KNOW. Consumers have the right to honest communication about the products and services they buy and the companies that sell them. In a free market economy, information is one of the most valuable commodities available. Customers often depend on companies for the information they need to make decisions about price, quality, features, and other factors. As a result, companies have a responsibility to customers to be truthful in their advertising.

Unfortunately, not every business recognizes its social responsibility to be truthful in advertising. The Federal Trade Commission (FTC) filed a false advertising lawsuit against a small company that was selling an exercise device that the company claimed would allow users "to lose from 4 to 14 inches guaranteed in just 7 days" by "supercharging their blood with fat-burning oxygen." The infomercial that promoted the $54.85 device (including shipping and handling) ran more than 2,000 times on cable channels across the nation. As a result of the FTC's action, the company agreed to refund to customers $2.6 million and to stop their false advertising campaign.[52] Businesses that rely on unscrupulous tactics may profit in the short-term, but they will not last in the long-run.

Right to Be Heard

The right to be heard suggests that the channels of communication between companies and their customers run in both directions. Socially responsible businesses provide customers with a mechanism for resolving complaints about products and services. Some companies have established a consumer ombudsman to address customer questions and complaints. Others have created customer hotlines, toll-free numbers designed to serve customers more effectively.

Another effective technique for encouraging two-way communication between customers and companies is the customer report card. The Granite Rock Company, a business that supplies a variety of building materials to construction companies, relies on an annual report card from its customers to learn how to serve them better. Although the knowledge a small business owner gets from customer feedback is immeasurable for making improvements, only 1 in 12 small companies regularly schedules customer satisfaction surveys like Granite Rock's.

RIGHT TO EDUCATION. Socially responsible companies give customers access to educational programs about their products and services and how to use them properly. The goal is to give customers enough information to make informed purchase decisions. A product that is the wrong solution to the customer's needs results in a disappointed customer who is likely to blame the manufacturer or retailer for the mistake. Consumer education is an inexpensive investment in customer satisfaction and the increased probability that a satisfied customer is a repeat buyer.

RIGHT TO CHOICE. Inherent in the free enterprise system is the consumer's right to choose among competing products and services. Socially responsible companies do not restrict competition, and they abide by the United States' antitrust policy, which promotes free trade and competition in the market. The foundation of this policy is the Sherman Antitrust Act of 1890, which forbids agreements among sellers that restrain trade or commerce and outlaws any attempts to monopolize a market.

Business's Responsibility to Investors

8. Discuss business's responsibility to investors.

Companies have the responsibility to provide investors with an attractive return on their investment. Although earning a profit may be a company's *first* responsibility, it is not its *only* responsibility; meeting its ethical and social responsibility goals is also a key to success. Investors today want to know that entrepreneurs are making ethical decisions and acting in a socially responsible manner. In a survey by Opinion Research Corporation, 76 percent of investors say that they would move their investments from companies that engage in unethical but legal behavior, even if the company's action produced a high return on their investment.[53] Another study shows that a company's financial returns are the *least* important factor that influences public perception of its reputation.[54] Maintaining high standards of ethics and social responsibility translates into a business culture that sets the stage for a profitable business operation.

Companies also have the responsibility to report their financial performances in an accurate and timely fashion to their investors. Businesses that misrepresent or falsify their financial and operating records are guilty of violating the fiduciary relationship with their investors.

ENTREPRENEURIAL
Profile

Richard Priddy and Charles Sample: TVI Corporation

Richard Priddy, CEO of TVI Corporation, and Charles Sample, the company's CFO, were sentenced to prison and ordered to pay $595,000 in restitution for defrauding the company of more than $1.4 million. Priddy and Sample learned that they could purchase from a company in Seattle at significantly lower prices the same parts that TVI had been buying from another vendor. Rather than allow TVI to switch to the lower cost supplier, they formed a separate company, Containment & Transfer Systems, LLC (CATS), to purchase the parts from the Seattle company and resell them to TVI. Over the next 5 years, Priddy and Sample hid the fact that they owned CATS from the TVI board and investors and defrauded TVI of more than $1.4 million before board members discovered the executives' illicit actions.[55]

Business's Responsibility to the Community

9. Discuss business's responsibility to the community.

As corporate citizens, businesses have a responsibility to the communities in which they operate. In addition to providing jobs and creating wealth, companies contribute to the local community in many different ways. Socially responsible businesses are aware of their duty to put back into the community some of what they take out as they generate profits; their goal is to become a neighbor of choice.

Experts estimate that 80 percent of companies worldwide engage in some type of socially responsible activity.[56] The following are just a few examples of ways small businesses have found to give back to their communities:

- Act as volunteers for community groups such as the American Red Cross, United Way, literacy programs, and a community food bank.
- Participate in projects that aid the elderly or economically disadvantaged.
- Adopt a highway near the business to promote a clean community.

In a recent survey, 75 percent of consumers say that companies living up to their social responsibility is important even during economic recessions.[57] Even small companies that may be short on funding can support causes by choosing them strategically and discovering creative ways to help them. The key to choosing the "right" cause is finding one that makes an impact and whose purpose resonates with customers, employees, and owners. Small companies can commit their employees' talent and know-how, not just dollars, to carefully chosen social causes and then tell the world about their cause and their dedication to serving it. By forging meaningful partnerships, both the businesses and the causes benefit in unique ways. Over the years, companies have helped social causes enjoy financial rewards and unprecedented support. In addition to doing good, companies have been able to enhance their reputations, deepen employee loyalty, strengthen ties with business partners, and sell more products or services.

ENTREPRENEURIAL
Profile

Ray Booska: Glacier Tek

Bomb-sniffing dogs in the Middle East wearing body-cooling vests donated by Glacier Tek, the small company that created the special vests.

Source: Glacier Tek

Ray Booska, founder of Glacier Tek, a West Melbourne, Florida-based company that makes body-cooling vests for a variety of applications, learned about the challenges that the intense heat in the Middle East creates for bomb-sniffing dogs stationed there on military duty and decided that his company could help. Booska and his team of designers tested several prototypes on Booska's retired police dog, Fritz, before finding one that worked to their satisfaction. The vest is made of a nontoxic coolant that works like gel ice packs and can be recharged in just 15 minutes. Glacier Tek added the canine vest to its product line but has donated more than 500 of them to dogs in military zones in the Middle East. "These dogs save the lives of our sons and daughters," says Booska, "and we're going to do everything we can to help them."[58]

Entrepreneurs such as Booska who demonstrate their sense of social responsibility not only make their communities better places to live and work but also stand out from their competitors. Their efforts to operate ethical, socially responsible businesses create a strong sense of loyalty among their customers and their employees.

Conclusion

Businesses must do more than merely earn profits; they must act ethically and in a socially responsible manner. Establishing and maintaining high ethical and socially responsible standards must be a top concern of every business owner. Managing in an ethical and socially responsible manner presents a tremendous challenge, however. There is no universal definition of ethical behavior, and what is considered ethical may change over time and may be different in other cultures.

Finally, business owners and managers must recognize the key role they play in influencing their employees' ethical and socially responsible behavior. What owners and managers *say* is important, but what they *do* is even more important! Employees in a small company look to the owner and managers as models; therefore, these owners and managers must commit themselves to following the highest ethical standards if they expect their employees to do so.

Chapter Review

1. Define business ethics and describe the three levels of ethical standards.
   - Business ethics involves the fundamental moral values and behavioral standards that form the foundation for the people of an organization as they make decisions and interact with the organization's stakeholders. Small business managers must consider the ethical and social as well as the economic implications of their decisions.
   - The three levels of ethical standards are (1) the law, (2) the policies and procedures of the company, and (3) the moral stance of the individual.

2. Determine who is responsible for ethical behavior and why ethical lapses occur.
   - Managers set the moral tone of the organization. There are three ethical styles of management: immoral, amoral, and moral. Although moral management has value in itself, companies that operate with this philosophy discover other benefits, including a positive reputation among customers and employees.
   - Ethical lapses occur for a variety of reasons:
     Some people are corrupt ("the bad apple").
     The company culture has been poisoned ("the bad barrel").
     Competitive pressures push managers to compromise.
     Managers are tempted by an opportunity to "get ahead."
     Managers in different cultures have different views of what is ethical.

3. Explain how to establish and maintain high ethical standards.
   - Philosophers throughout history have developed various tests of ethical behavior: the utilitarian principle, Kant's categorical imperative, the professional ethic, the Golden Rule, the television test, and the family test.
   - A small business manager can maintain high ethical standards in the following ways:
     Create a company credo.
     Develop a code of ethics.
     Enforce the code fairly and consistently.
     Hire the right people.
     Conduct ethical training.
     Perform periodic ethical audits.
     Establish high standards of behavior, not just rules.
     Set an impeccable ethical example at all times.
     Create a culture emphasizing two-way communication.
     Involve employees in establishing ethical standards.

4. Define social responsibility.
   - Social responsibility is the awareness of a company's managers of the social, environmental, political, human, and financial consequences of their actions.

5. Understand the nature of business's responsibility to the environment.
   - Environmentally responsible business owners focus on the three Rs: reduce, reuse, recycle: *reduce* the amount of materials used in the company from the factory floor to the copier room; *reuse* whatever you can; and *recycle* the materials that you must dispose of.

6. Describe business's responsibility to employees.
   - Companies have a duty to act responsibly toward one of their most important stakeholders: their employees. Businesses must recognize and manage the cultural diversity that exists in the workplace; establish a responsible strategy for combating substance abuse in the workplace (including drug testing) and dealing with AIDS; prevent sexual harassment; and respect employees' right to privacy.

7. Explain business's responsibility to customers.
   - Every company's customers have a right to safe products and services; to honest, accurate information; to be heard; to education about products and services; and to choices in the marketplace.

8. Discuss business's responsibility to investors.
   - Companies have the responsibility to provide investors with an attractive return on their investments and to report their financial performances in an accurate and timely fashion to their investors.

9. Describe business's responsibility to the community.
   - Increasingly, companies are seeing a need to go beyond "doing well" to "doing good"—being socially responsible community citizens. In addition to providing jobs and creating wealth, companies contribute to the local community in many different ways.

Discussion Questions

1. What is ethics? Discuss the three levels of ethical standards.
2. In any organization, who determines ethical behavior? Briefly describe the three ethical styles of management. What are the benefits of moral management?
3. Why do ethical lapses occur in businesses?
4. Describe the various methods for establishing ethical standards. Which is most meaningful to you? Explain.
5. What can business owners do to maintain high ethical standards in their companies?
6. What is social responsibility?
7. Describe business's social responsibility to each of the following areas:
   - The environment
   - Employees
   - Customers
   - Investors
   - The community
8. What can businesses do to improve the quality of our environment?
9. Should companies be allowed to test employees for drugs? Explain. How should a socially responsible drug testing program operate?
10. Many owners of trucking companies use electronic communications equipment to monitor their drivers on the road. They say that the devices allow them to remain competitive and to serve their customers better by delivering shipments of vital materials exactly when their customers need them. They also point out that the equipment can improve road safety by ensuring that drivers get the hours of rest the law requires. Opponents argue that the surveillance devices work against safety. "The drivers know they're being watched," says one trucker. "There's an obvious temptation to push." What do you think? What ethical issues does the use of such equipment create? How should a small trucking company considering the use of such equipment handle these issues?
11. What rights do customers have under the Consumer Bill of Rights? How can businesses ensure those rights?

Businesses have a responsibility to both "do well"—earn a profit, remain financially sound, and stay in business—and "do good"—operate ethically and meet their responsibility to society. It is critical for business owners to recognize their obligation to operate their businesses in an ethical and socially responsible manner. They must consider these issues as essential elements of a successful and sustainable business. They must create a culture that encourages employees to recognize ethical dilemmas and to do what is right when faced with ethical dilemmas. Values-based leaders integrate the ethical dimensions of their actions and decisions as well as those of their employees into the fabric of their companies' culture. They establish ethical guidelines, conduct training sessions in ethics, and, most important, set an example for ethical behavior in the organization. These leaders understand that ethical behavior does not simply happen in an organization; it is the result of a conscious effort that involves everyone. They also recognize that their companies have a responsibility to society that extends far beyond merely earning a profit. The business plan must capture this broader sense of ethical and social responsibility to all stakeholders.

On the Web

The Internet offers a wealth of information regarding business ethics and a company's responsibility to investors, employees, customers, the community, and the environment. You will find some of these resources on the Companion Web Site at *www.pearsonhighered.com/scarborough*. These links may help you to integrate ethical standards into the fabric of your business plan.

In the Software

Review all divisions of your plan. Attempt to take an objective look to determine whether your plan communicates a values-based leadership approach. Consider these questions:

- How does your plan describe the company's responsibility to its employees?
- How does the plan describe its responsibility to investors?
- How does your plan describe its responsibility to customers?
- What does the business plan communicate about the company's responsibility to the community?
- Does the plan explain how the business operates in an environmentally responsible manner?
- Does the plan describe a business that offers long-term sustainability?

Building Your Business Plan

The business plan will help you to identify the key stakeholders in your company, verbalize your philosophy of business ethics, identify the best way to establish high ethical standards, and explain the level of your company's commitment to socially responsible actions. Consider including the description of your philosophy of ethics and social responsibility in the plan's "Strategy and Implementation" section. Your analysis of these important issues also may lead you to modify your company's mission statement.

Endnotes

1. Michael Barkoviak, "PC Makers Still Not Pleased with Chinese Censorship Software," *Daily Tech*, June 30, 2009, *www.dailytech.com/ PC+Makers+Still+Not+Pleased+With+Chinese+Censorship+Software/ article15560.htm*; Rex Crum, "PC Makers Assess How to Deal with China's Green Dam," *Market Watch*, June 23, 2009, *www.marketwatch.com/ story/green-dam-issue-grows-between-pc-makers-and-china*; Loretta Chao, "China Squeezes PC Makers," *Wall Street Journal*, June 8, 2009, pp. A1, A10.

2. Vernon R. Loucks, Jr., "A CEO Looks at Ethics," *Business Horizons*, March–April 1987, p. 2.

3. Susan Caminiti, "The Payoff from a Good Reputation," *Fortune*, February 10, 1992, p. 74.

4. Amy Wallace, "The Rise and Fall of the Cincinnati Boner King," *GQ*, September 2009, *www.gq.com/news-politics/mens-lives/200909/ smilin-bob-enzyte-steve-warshak-male-enhancement*.

5. "Top Small Workplaces—2008 Winner: King Arthur Flour Company," *Winning Workplaces*, *www.winningworkplaces.org/topsmallbiz/ 2008winners/tsw2008_kingarthurflour.php*; "Good Works," King Arthur Flour Company, *www.kingarthurflour.com/about/ goodworks.html*.

6. Richard C. Morais, "A River Runs Through It," *Forbes*, March 16, 2009, p. 90.

7. Kate O'Sullivan, "Virtue Rewarded," *CFO*, October 2006, p. 51.

8. *2010 Edelman Trust Barometer*, Edelman Financial Services, 2010, p. 6.

9. Jim Witkin, "Despite Struggles, Entrepreneurs Find Ways to Give Back," *New York Times*, September 15, 2010, *www.nytimes.com/ 2010/09/16/business/smallbusiness/16sbiz.html*.

10. O'Sullivan, "Virtue Rewarded"; Jennifer Reingold, "Walking the Walk," *Fast Company*, November 2005, pp. 81–85; Joseph Pereira, "Doing Good and Doing Well at Timberland," *Wall Street Journal*, September 9, 2003, pp. B1–B10.

11. Richard McGill Murphy, "Why Doing Good Is Good for Business," *Fortune*, February 8, 2010, pp. 91–95.

12. Pereira, "Doing Good and Doing Well at Timberland."

13. *Integrity Survey 2008–2009*, KPMG LLC, 2009, p. iii.

14. *The Importance of Ethical Culture: Increasing Trust and Driving Down Risks*, Ethics Resource Center, Arlington, Virginia, 2010, p. 5.

15. Patricia Wallington, "Honestly?!" *CIO*, March 15, 2003, p. 42.

16. Mark Henricks, "Well, Honestly!" *Entrepreneur*, December 2006, p. 103.

17. Patricia Wallington, "Total Leadership—Ethical Behavior Is Essential," *CIO*, March 15, 2003, *www.cio.com/article/31779/Total_ Leadership_Ethical_Behaviour_Is_Essential*.

18. Joshua Kurlantzick, "Liar, Liar," *Entrepreneur*, October 2003, pp. 68–71.

19. Gene Laczniak, "Business Ethics: A Manager's Primer," *Business*, January–March 1983, pp. 23–29.

20. Michael Josephson, "Teaching Ethical Decision Making and Its Principled Reasoning," *Ethics: Easier Said Than Done*, Winter 1988, p. 28.

21. John Rutledge, "The Portrait on My Wall," *Forbes*, December 30, 1996, p. 78.

22. Jim Witkin, "Despite Struggles, Entrepreneurs Find Ways to Give Back," *New York Times*, September 15, 2010, *www.nytimes.com/ 2010/09/16/business/smallbusiness/16sbiz.html*.

23. SurePayroll Insights Survey: Economy Woes Squeeze Small Business Charity, SurePayroll, May 28, 2008, *www.surepayroll.com/spsite/press/ releases/2008/release052808.asp*.

24. Niels Bosma and Jonathan Levie, *Global Entrepreneurship Monitor 2009 Global Report*, 2009, *www.gemconsortium.org*, p. 49.

25. "What Is a Social Entrepreneur?" Ashoka, *www.ashoka.org/ social_entrepreneur*.

26. Katrina Daniel, "Customers Buy, Company Gives," *Womenetics*, November 23, 2010, *www.womenetics.com/philanthropy/733- customers-buy-company-gives*.

27. *2010 Cone Cause Evolution Study*, Cone LLC, Boston, Massachusetts: 2010, pp. 6, 8.

28. Edward Iwata, "Businesses Grow More Socially Conscious," *USA Today*, February 14, 2007, *www.usatoday.com/money/companies/ 2007 02 14 high-purpose-usat x.htm*.

29. "About Ecoist," Ecoist, *www.ecoist.com/pc/about/intro.asp*.

30. Chris Penttila, "Shades of Green," *Entrepreneur*, August 2007, pp. 19–20; "Nature Meet Nurture," Pangea Organics, *www.pangeaorganics.com/home.html*.

31. "Top Small Company Workplaces 2010 Winner," Winning Workplaces, *www.winningworkplaces.org/topsmallbiz/2010winners/tsw2010_ tastycatering.php*; Bruce Christian, "Caterer of the Year," *Catering Magazine*, May 2008, pp. 28–30.

32. Jennifer J. Salopek, "The 2020 Workplace," *Workforce Management*, June 2010, pp. 36–40.

33. Juan Rodriguez, "U.S. Workforce Will Be Smaller, More Diverse in 2050," *Diversity Jobs*, August 14, 2008, *http://diversityjobs.com/ news/us-workforce-will-be-smaller-more-diverse-in-2050/*.

34. Keith H. Hammonds, "Difference Is Power," *Fast Company*, July 2000, p. 58.

35. Best Practices of Private Sector Employers, Equal Employment Opportunity Commission (Washington, DC, 2003), *www.eeoc.gov/ abouteeoc/task_reports/prac2.html*.

36. Martha Lagace, "Racial Diversity Pays Off," Harvard Business School: *Working Knowledge*, June 21, 2004, *http://hbsworkingknowledge.hbs.edu/ item.jhtml?id=4207&t=organizations*.

37. Fay Hanson, "Diversity of a Different Color," *Workforce Management*, June 2010, pp. 23–26.

38. Amy Preiss, "Substance Abuse in the Workplace," University of Phoenix, June 29, 2009, *www.phoenix.edu/profiles/faculty/amy-preiss/ articles/abuse-in-the-workplace.html*.

39. Gina Ruiz, "Expanded EAPs Lend a Hand to Employer's Bottom Line," *Workforce Management*, January 16, 2006, pp. 46–47.

40. *The President's National Drug Control Strategy*, February 2007, *www.whitehousedrugpolicy.gov/publications/policy/ndcs07/*, pp. 14–15; "Nationwide Survey Shows Most Illicit Drug Users and Heavy Alcohol Users Are in the Workplace and May Pose Special Problems," Substance Abuse and Mental Health Services Administration, U.S. Department of Health and Human Services, July 17, 2007, *http://oas.samhsa.gov/work2k7/press.htm*.

41. *The National Survey on Drug Abuse and Health Report*, Substance Abuse and Mental Health Services Administration, U.S. Department of Health and Human Services, December 2010, p. 1.

42. Belinda Goldsmith, "Indians Most Likely to Report Sexual Harassment at Work—Poll," *Reuters*, August 12, 2010, *http://in.reuters.com/ article/idINIndia-50803120100812*.

43. Amy Wilson, "Inappropriate Behavior Lands Beetle Bailey's General in Hot Water," *Greenville News*, November 22, 1992, p. 20D.

44. "Sexual Harassment Charges," Equal Employment Opportunity Commission, 2010, *www.eeoc.gov/eeoc/statistics/enforcement/ sexual_harassment.cfm*.

45. *Sexual Harassment Manual for Managers and Supervisors* (Chicago: Commerce Clearing House, 1992), pp. 25–26.

46. Lori A. Carter, "$2 Million Harassment Verdict Against Petaluma Card Room," *Press Democrat*, August 5, 2010, *www.petaluma360.com/ article/20100805/COMMUNITY/100809800?p=3&tc=pg&tc=ar*; Lori A. Carter, "Judge Reduces Jury Award in Petaluma Card Room Sexual Harassment Case," *Press Democrat*, October 8, 2010, *www.pressdemocrat.com/ARTICLE/20101008/ARTICLES/101009447*.

47. *Burlington Industries v. Ellerth* (97-569) 123 F.3d 490; "Employer Liability for Harassment," Equal Employment Opportunity Commission, *www.eeoc.gov/types/harassment.html*.

48. Nicole P. Cantey, "High Court Rules Same Sex Harassment Is Against the Law," *South Carolina Business Journal*, August 1998, p. 3; Jack Corcoran, "Of Nice and Men," *Success*, June 1998, pp. 64–67.

49. "Internet 2009 in Numbers," Royal Pingdom, January 22, 2010, *http://royal.pingdom.com/2010/01/22/internet-2009-in-numbers/*.

50. *2007 Electronic Monitoring and Surveillance Survey*, American Management Association, February 28, 2008, *http://press.amanet.org/ press-releases/177/2007-electronic-monitoring-surveillance-survey/*.

51. "13th Annual Wacky Warning Labels Contest Winners Selected on National Television," Wacky Warning Labels, July 12, 2010, *www .wackywarninglabelstv.com/press-releases/2010/7/12/13th-annual- wacky-warning-labels-contest-winners-selected-on.html*; "M-Law's Tenth Annual Wacky Warning Label Contest," Wacky Warning Labels, January 4, 2007, *www.wackywarnings.com*; "Things People Said: Warning Labels," Rinkworks, *www.rinkworks.com/said/ warnings.shtml*.

52. "FTC Charges BodyFlex with False Advertising," ConsumerAffairs.com, November 10, 2003, *http://consumeraffairs.com/ news03/bodyflex.html*; "BodyFlex to Offer $2.6 Million in Refunds," ConsumerAffairs.com, September 1, 2004, *www.consumeraffairs.com/news04/bodyflex.html*.

53. Thomas Kostigen, "Ethics Trumps Returns," Market Watch, July 13, 2007, *www.marketwatch.com/news/story/story.aspx?guid= %7BC3CA306A-4BD5-4250-85C2-98D60F699CAB%7D&siteid=rss*.

54. *2010 Edelman Trust Barometer*, Edelman Financial Services, 2010, p. 6.

55. "Examples of Corporate Fraud Investigations 2010: Corporate CEO, Vice President and Accountant Sentenced for Defrauding Maryland Company of Over $1.4 Million," Internal Revenue Service, *www.irs.gov/compliance/enforcement/article/0,,id=213768,00.html*.

56. Ruben Hernandez-Murillo and Christopher J. Martinek, "Corporate Social Responsibility Can Be Profitable," *Regional Economist*, April 2009, pp. 4–5.

57. Corporate Social Responsibility Branding Survey, Penn, Schoen, Berland and Burson-Marseller, 2010, *www.psbresearch.com/ files/CSR%20 Branding%20Survey%202010%20EXTERNAL% 20FINAL.pdf*, p. 1.

58. Elise Reinemann, "Chilly Dogs," *FSB*, September 2008, pp. 18–19.

Global Marketing Strategies

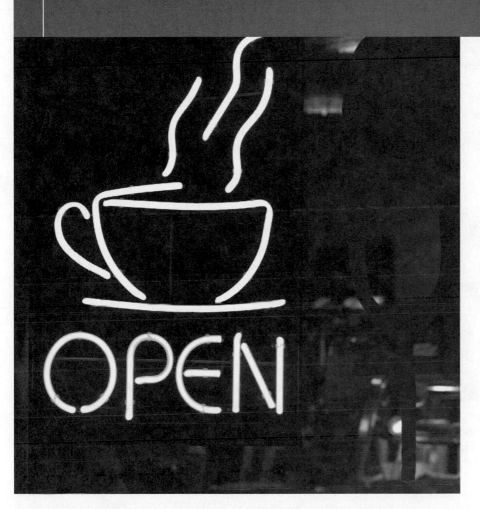

Learning Objectives

Upon completion of this chapter, you will be able to:

1 Explain why "going global" has become an integral part of many small companies' strategies.

2 Describe the nine principal strategies small businesses can use to go global.

3 Explain how to build a successful export program.

4 Discuss the major barriers to international trade and their impact on the global economy.

5 Describe the trade agreements that have the greatest influence on foreign trade.

You can't do business in the world today unless you are a global citizen. We live in a world that is so small now that the "community" is the people on the planet.

—Margaret Lee

It is easier to go to the moon than it is to enter the world of another civilization. Culture—not space—is the greatest distance between two people.

—Jamake Highwater

From Chapter 12 of *Effective Small Business Management: An Entrepreneurial Approach*, 10/e. Norman M. Scarborough.

Until recently, the world of international business was much like the world of astronomy before Copernicus, who revolutionized the study of the planets and the stars with his theory of planetary motion. In the sixteenth century, his Copernican system replaced the Ptolemaic system, which held that the earth was the center of the universe, with the sun and all the other planets revolving around it. The Copernican system, however, placed the sun at the center of the solar system with all of the planets, including the earth, revolving around it. Astronomy would never be the same.

In the same sense, business owners across the globe were guilty of having Ptolemaic tunnel vision when it came to viewing international business opportunities. Like their pre-Copernican counterparts, owners saw an economy that revolved around the nations that served as their home bases. Market opportunities stopped at their homeland's borders. Global trade was only for giant corporations that had the money and the management to tap foreign markets and enough resources to survive if the venture flopped. That scenario no longer holds true in the twenty-first century. Indeed, a survey by consulting firm Grant Thornton of medium-size businesses reports that 56 percent of CEOs view globalization as an opportunity for their companies; just 19 percent of CEOs see it as a threat.[1]

Fifteen years ago, if a company was considered to be multinational, everyone knew that it was a giant corporation; today, that is no longer the case. The global marketplace is as much the territory of small, upstart companies as it is that of giant multinational corporations. Powerful, affordable technology, the Internet, increased access to information on conducting global business, and the growing interdependence of the world's economies have made it easier for companies of all sizes, many of which had never before considered going global, to engage in international trade.

ENTREPRENEURIAL
Profile

Ethan Siegel: Orb Audio

Ethan Siegel, founder of Orb Audio, and his wife, Lelenya

Source: Alex Quesada/*New York Times*-Maps and Graphics

In 2003, Ethan Siegel and a friend launched Orb Audio, a New York City–based company that makes high-end, orb-shaped speakers for home theater and stereo systems. The business, which generates most of its sales online, grew slowly, but in 2008, when the value of the U.S. dollar dropped against foreign currencies, Siegel saw a dramatic increase in inquiries from customers from other countries. Spotting an opportunity, Siegel began targeting customers in Canada, Australia, Great Britain, and Finland with country-specific Web pages and Internet ads on sites that are popular with customers in those countries. International sales at Orb Audio now comprise 35 percent of total sales. The growth in international sales has more than offset the decline in domestic sales for the company, which generates more than $5 million in revenue per year. Orb Audio now has customers around the globe, including places as far away as Zimbabwe, Africa, and Easter Island, located 2,300 miles off the coast of Chile and home to the famous moai stone statues.[2]

Just a few years ago, military might governed world relationships; today, commercial trade and economic benefit have become the forces that drive global interaction. Since 1948, the value of world merchandise exports has risen from $58.0 billion to $12.5 *trillion*.[3] Countries at every stage of development are reaping the benefits of increased global trade. Forecasts show that the economies of emerging markets such as China and India will expand faster than those of mature markets such as the United States and Germany. Consulting firm Grant Thornton has created an emerging-markets opportunity index that reflects countries' population and economic growth, involvement in world trade, and other factors. The countries that top the list are China, India, Russia, Mexico, and Brazil.[4] The International Monetary Fund estimates that China, where economic growth has been among the fastest in the world, will boast the largest gross domestic product (GDP) in the world by 2030.[5] The message is clear: Global markets present a tremendous opportunity for small companies that are prepared to market to them.

Political, social, cultural, technological, and economic changes continue to sweep the world, creating a new world order—and a legion of both threats and opportunities for businesses of all sizes. Market economies are replacing centralized economies in countries where only decades ago private ownership of productive assets was unthinkable. Technology advances have cut the cost of long-distance communications and transactions so low that conducting business globally often costs no more than doing business locally. Even the smallest companies are using their Web sites to sell in foreign markets at minimal costs. Small businesses are buying raw materials and services from all over the globe, wherever the deals are best. Jack Stack, CEO of Springfield Remanufacturing Corporation, a Springfield, Missouri-based company that refurbishes automotive engines and parts, was surprised when he learned that the company was purchasing parts from suppliers in 56 different countries! "Here we were, minding our business in Springfield, Missouri," says Stack, "and suddenly we discover that we've gone global."[6] Entrepreneurs are seeing new markets emerge in countries around the world as the ranks of their middle classes surge. These business owners realize that the size of these fast-growing markets is small today compared to their potential in the near future. Changes such as these are creating instability for businesses of *any* size going global, but they also are creating tremendous opportunities for those small companies ready to capitalize on them. One writer explains why entrepreneurs, with their unique perspective on risk taking, stand ready to embrace going global:

> Globalizing is risky. The risks include potential spoilers such as an unfamiliar language, an alien business landscape, untested partners, and political volatility. Still, the chance to try new things in new places is like a jumper cable to the entrepreneurial engine. Like the Internet companies of a decade ago, company owners [who go global] are working out the rules as they go, drawing lessons from the failures and the successes alike. They see the scale of battle growing, and they are girding for it.[7]

Expanding a business beyond its domestic borders actually enhances a small company's overall performance. Several studies have concluded that small companies that export earn more money, grow faster, create higher paying jobs, and are more likely to survive than their purely domestic counterparts.

Why Go Global?

1. Explain why "going global" has become an integral part of many small companies' strategies.

Small companies can no longer consider themselves to be strictly domestic businesses in this hotly competitive global environment. "In the global economy, the competitor six time zones away is potentially as serious a threat as the competitor six blocks away," says one expert.[8] For companies across the world, going global is a matter of survival, not preference. No matter where a company's home base is, competitors are forcing it to think globally. "There are an awful lot of people in the rest of the world who think they are pretty good at doing your business," warns Lester Thurow.[9] Companies that fail to see the world as a global marketplace risk being blindsided in their markets both at home and abroad. "Just being part of the domestic market and depending on that source of revenue isn't cutting it anymore," says Maryann Stein, director of a development agency in Erie, Pennsylvania, that helps small companies break into global markets. "We haven't really had to explore other markets because U.S. companies have been OK just selling domestically. That's not the case anymore."[10]

Failure to cultivate global markets can be a lethal mistake for modern businesses—whatever their size. In short, to thrive in the twenty-first century, small businesses must take their place in the world market. Today, the potential for doing business globally for businesses of all sizes means that where a company's goods and services originate or where its headquarters is located is insignificant. To be successful, companies must consider themselves to be businesses without borders.

ENTREPRENEURIAL
Profile

Brad Oberwager:
Sundia Inc.

Dan Hoskins, general manager and founder of Sundia, a company that sells fruit and fruit juices to upscale grocery stores around the world. Sundia's founder, Brad Oberwager, established the company as a global business from the outset.

Source: ZUMA Press

Brad Oberwager, chairman and founder of Sundia, a company that sells cut fruit and fruit juices to upscale grocery stores around the world, operates the business from an office in the basement of his home in San Francisco, California, but employs workers across the United States, India, and the Philippines. From the outset, Oberwager set up Sundia to be a micro-multinational business, and he relies on Web-based business systems to coordinate the company's far-flung activities. For instance, suppose that a customer in Europe orders several cases of watermelon–pomegranate juice (which is processed in Washington from fruit grown in Mexico and California) by calling Sundia's San Francisco telephone number. The call is forwarded to a customer service center in the Philippines, where a representative takes the order and submits it to a warehouse that is closest to the customer, in this case, London. The warehouse ships the order to the customer and notifies the accounting department, which is housed in India. The accounting department generates a customer invoice, sends it to company headquarters in San Francisco, which forwards the invoice to the customer in Europe. In less than 2 years, Oberwager's global strategy has made Sundia the largest watermelon brand in the world and the fastest growing produce brand in the United States.[11]

Going global can put a tremendous strain on a small company, but entrepreneurs who take the plunge into global business can reap many benefits, including the ability to offset sales declines in the domestic market, increase sales and profits, improve the quality of their products to meet the stringent demands of foreign customers, lower the manufacturing cost of their products by spreading fixed costs over a larger number of units, and enhance their competitive positions to become stronger businesses. In a recent study conducted by CompTIA of small and medium-size businesses that export, 64 percent of owners say that doing business globally has made their companies significantly more competitive. In addition, 86 percent of these business owners say that their companies' export sales are growing faster than their domestic sales.[12]

Unfortunately, many entrepreneurs have not learned to view their companies from a global perspective. Indeed, learning to *think globally* may be the first—and most threatening—obstacle an entrepreneur must overcome on the way to creating a truly global business. One British manager explains:

> If you are operating in South America, you'd better know how to operate in conditions of hyperinflation. If you're operating in Africa, you'd better know a lot about government relations and the use of local partners. If you're operating in Germany, you'd better understand the mechanics of codetermination and some of the special tax systems that one finds in that country. If you're operating in China, it's quite useful in trademark matters to know how the People's Court of Shanghai works. . . . If you're operating in Japan, you'd better understand the different trade structure.[13]

Gaining a foothold in newly opened foreign markets or maintaining a position in an existing one is no easy task, however. Until an entrepreneur develops the attitude of operating a truly global company rather than a domestic company that happens to be doing business abroad, achieving success in international business is difficult. That attitude starts at the top in the executive's office. Success in the global economy also requires constant innovation; staying nimble enough to use speed as a competitive weapon; maintaining a high level of quality and constantly improving it; being sensitive to foreign customers' unique requirements; adopting a more respectful attitude toward foreign habits and customs; hiring motivated, multilingual employees; and retaining a desire to learn constantly about global markets. In short, the path to success requires businesses to become "insiders" who see the world as their market rather than just "exporters."

Before venturing into the global marketplace, an entrepreneur should consider six questions:

1. Is there a profitable market in which our company has the potential to be successful over the long run? Table 1 shows a country-screening matrix designed to help entrepreneurs decide which countries offer the best opportunities for their products.
2. Do we have and are we willing to commit adequate resources of time, people, and capital to a global campaign?
3. Are we considering going global for the right reasons? Are domestic pressures forcing our company to consider global opportunities?
4. Do we understand the cultural differences, history, economics, values, opportunities, and risks of conducting business in the countries we are considering?
5. Do we have a viable exit strategy for our company if conditions change or the new venture does not succeed?
6. Can we afford *not* to go global?

TABLE 1 A Country-Screening Matrix

For an entrepreneur considering launching a global business venture, getting started often is the hardest step. "The world is such a big place! Where do I start?" is a typical comment from entrepreneurs considering global business. The following matrix will help you narrow your options. Based on preliminary research, select three to five countries that you believe have the greatest market potential for your products. Then, use the following factors to guide you as you conduct more detailed research into these countries and their markets. Rate each factor on a scale of 1 (lowest) to 5 (highest). Based on your ratings, which country has the highest score?

Market factor	Country 1 Rating	Country 2 Rating	Country 3 Rating
Demographic/physical environment			
■ Population size, growth, density			
■ Urban and rural distribution			
■ Climate and weather variations			
■ Shipping distance			
■ Product-significant demographics			
■ Physical distribution and communication network			
■ Natural resources			
Political environment			
■ System of government			
■ Political stability and continuity			
■ Ideological orientation			
■ Government involvement in business			
■ Attitudes toward foreign business (trade restrictions, tariffs, nontariff barriers, bilateral trade agreements)			
■ National economic and developmental priorities			
Economic environment			
■ Overall level of development			
■ Economic growth: GNP, industrial sector			
■ Role of foreign trade in the economy			
■ Currency: inflation rate, availability, controls, stability of exchange rate			
■ Balance of payments			
■ Per capita income and distribution			
■ Disposable income and expenditure patterns			
Social/cultural environment			
■ Literacy rate, educational level			
■ Existence of middle class			
■ Similarities and differences in relation to home market			
■ Language and other cultural considerations			

(continued)

TABLE 1 Continued

Market access			
■ Limitations on trade: high tariff levels, quotas			
■ Documentation and import regulations			
■ Local standards, practices, and other nontariff barriers			
■ Patents and trademark protection			
■ Preferential treaties			
■ Legal considerations for investment, taxation, repatriation, employment, code of laws			
Product potential			
■ Customer needs and desires			
■ Local production, imports, consumption			
■ Exposure to and acceptance of product			
■ Availability of linking products			
■ Industry-specific key indicators of demand			
■ Attitudes toward products of foreign origin			
■ Competitive offerings			
Local distribution and production			
■ Availability of intermediaries			
■ Regional and local transportation facilities			
■ Availability of manpower			
■ Conditions for local manufacture			
Total Score			

Source: Adapted from "International Business Plan," *Breaking into the Trade Game: A Small Business Guide,* U.S. Small Business Administration Office of International Trade (Washington, DC: 2001), *www.sba.gov/oit/info/Guide-To-Exporting/trad6.html.*

► ENTREPRENEURSHIP **IN ACTION** ►

Stay at Home or Go Abroad?

Joan Denizot came up with the idea for her business when she realized that other people faced the same problem that she did. Denizot, 52, is one of the millions of Americans struggling to lose weight with the help of an exercise regimen. For Denizot, one of the most appealing forms of exercise is cycling. While recovering from gastric bypass surgery, Denizot tried cycling but quickly realized that every bicycle she tried out was too small for her full figure. "I'd get on bikes, and the tires would flatten," she says.

Denizot searched the Internet for plus-sized bikes but found very little. "They talked about how much the bike and all of its parts weighed but never about how much weight the bike would carry," she recalls. "Even bikes that were built for 'large riders' went up to only 225 pounds." She considered finding someone to build a custom bicycle that would be sturdy enough for her frame, but she wanted to help others like her to get outside, exercise, and become healthier. That's when she decide to launch Super Sized Cycles.

The company, which is based in Vermont, currently sells about 100 bicycles per year through its Web site

(*www.supersizedcycles.com*) and generates sales of $104,000. Sales have increased each of the 5 years that the company has been in business, but Denizot's business earns a modest profit and can afford to pay her only a very small salary. Super Sized Cycles offers six bicycle models that range in price from $669 for the entry-level model to $3,395 for a tricycle version with a small electric motor. Because of their strong steel frames and broad, sturdy tires, the bikes can accommodate riders up to 6 feet, 7 inches tall and who weigh up to 550 pounds. The company's best-selling models are A New Leaf and Time of Your Life, both of which Denizot designed herself. They sell for $2,070 each.

Depending on the specific model, Denizot pays $400 to $500 for bicycle frames, which are made in Iowa and shipped to Vermont, where the company's master assembler, Timothy Mathewson, builds each bike to the customer's specifications, which adds another $1,250 to her costs. Although Super Sized Cycles' gross profit margin is low, Denizot says that some potential customers balk at the company's prices. Taking the advice of a private investor who helped finance Super Sized Cycle's start up, Denizot outsourced production of 70 New Leaf bicycles to a manufacturer in Taiwan as a test.

She was pleased with the quality of the bicycles manufactured by the Taiwanese company and was even more pleased with the price she paid. Denizot says that, despite one-time costs associated with placing the order, she would be able to purchase fully assembled bicycles designed to her specifications for just $550, allowing her to offer customers lower prices and increase her company's profit margin. Denizot is caught in a quandary. She sees many advantages of keeping production in the United States: fast delivery times, the ability to oversee quality easily, and the ability to provide extraordinary customer service thanks to the technical skills of her "bike guru," Timothy Mathewson. She also likes the idea of keeping manufacturing jobs in the United States. "There's a lot to be said for helping a community and creating jobs here," she says, "but I need to be competitive, and I need to make a quality product."

1. Should Denizot keep production of her company's bicycles in the United States or outsource production to the manufacturer in Taiwan? Explain. What other recommendations can you offer her?

2. If Denizot were to outsource production to Taiwan, what steps do you suggest she take to maintain the quality of her products and protect her designs from piracy?

Sources: Based on John Grossman, "Make Bikes in the U.S., or Go Abroad to Cut Costs?" *New York Times,* June 2, 2010, *www.nytimes.com/2010/06/03/business/smallbusiness/03sbiz.html;* "About Us," Super Sized Cycles, *www.supersizedcycles.com/index.php?l=page_view&p=about_us.*

Going Global: Strategies for Small Businesses

2. Describe the nine principal strategies small businesses can use to go global.

The globalization of business actually *favors* small businesses because it creates an abundance of niche markets that are ideal for small companies to serve. "In this global economy, the competitive edge is swiftness to market and innovation," says John Naisbitt, trend-spotting author of *The Global Paradox,* and those characteristics are the hallmarks of entrepreneurs.[14] Their agility and adaptability gives small firms the edge in today's highly interactive, fast paced global economy. "The bigger the world economy, the more powerful its smallest players," concludes Naisbitt.[15]

Becoming a global business depends on instilling a global culture throughout the organization that permeates *everything* the company does. Entrepreneurs who conduct international business successfully have developed a global mind-set for themselves and their companies. As one business writer explains:

> The global [business] looks at the whole world as *one market*. It manufactures, conducts research, raises capital, and buys supplies wherever it can do the job best. It keeps in touch with technology and market trends around the world. National boundaries and regulations tend to be irrelevant, or a mere hindrance. [Company] headquarters might be anywhere.[16]

As cultures across the globe become increasingly interwoven, companies' ability to go global will determine their degree of success. Small companies pursuing a global presence have nine principal strategies available: creating a presence on the Web, relying on trade intermediaries, establishing joint ventures, engaging in foreign licensing arrangements, franchising, using countertrading and bartering, exporting products or services, establishing international locations, and importing and outsourcing (see Figure 1).

FIGURE 1
Nine Global Strategies

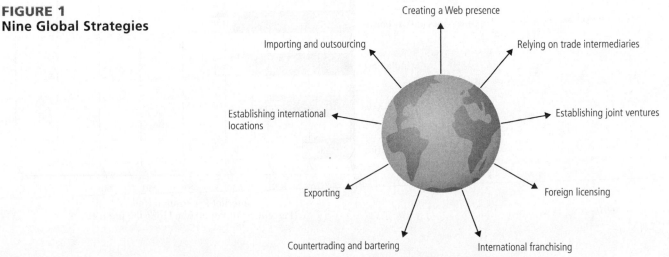

Creating a Web presence

Importing and outsourcing

Relying on trade intermediaries

Establishing international locations

Establishing joint ventures

Exporting

Foreign licensing

Countertrading and bartering

International franchising

Creating a Presence on the Web

Approximately 96 percent of the world's consumers live outside the United States, and the simplest and least expensive way for a small business to begin to reach them is to establish a Web site. The Web gives small businesses tremendous marketing potential all across the globe without having to incur the expense of opening international locations. With a well-designed Web site, a small company can extend its reach to customers anywhere in the world—without breaking the budget! A Web site is available to anyone, anywhere in the world and provides 24-hour-a-day exposure to a company's products or services, making global time differences meaningless.

Establishing a presence on the Web is an essential ingredient in the strategies of small companies trying to reach customers outside the borders of the United States. Although Internet usage varies greatly by region of the world (see Figure 2), the number of Internet users is growing extremely fast—nearly 400 percent worldwide since 2000. Another important factor for U.S. entrepreneurs to note is that 86 percent of the estimated 1.8 billion Internet users worldwide live *outside* of North America.[17]

FIGURE 2A
Internet Users Worldwide

Source: "Internet Usage Statistics: The Big Picture," Internet World Stats 2009, *www.internetworldstats.com/stats.htm.*

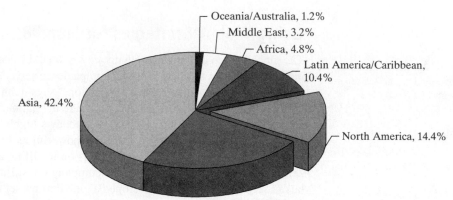

Oceania/Australia, 1.2%
Middle East, 3.2%
Africa, 4.8%
Latin America/Caribbean, 10.4%
Asia, 42.4%
North America, 14.4%
Europe, 23.6%

FIGURE 2B
Internet Penetration Rate by World Region

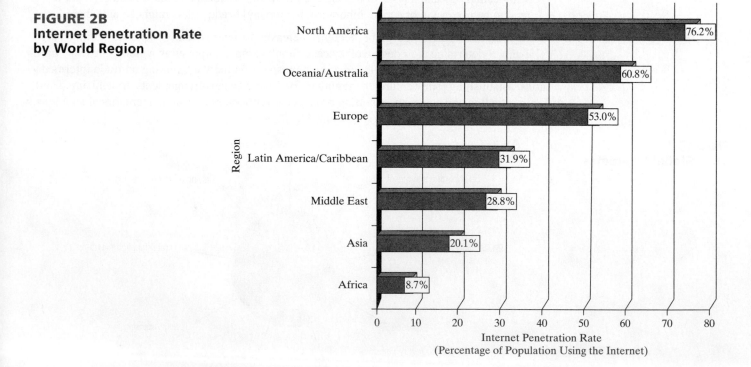

North America 76.2%
Oceania/Australia 60.8%
Europe 53.0%
Latin America/Caribbean 31.9%
Middle East 28.8%
Asia 20.1%
Africa 8.7%

Region

Internet Penetration Rate
(Percentage of Population Using the Internet)

Before the advent of the Internet, small businesses usually took incremental steps toward becoming global businesses. They began selling locally, and, then, after establishing a reputation, expanded regionally, and perhaps nationally. Only after establishing themselves domestically did small businesses begin to think about selling their products or services internationally. The Web makes that business model obsolete because it provides small companies with a low-cost global distribution channel that they can utilize from the day they are launched. Designed properly, a Web site can be an engaging marketing tool.

ENTREPRENEURIAL
Profile

Greg Jackson: Carolina Classic Boats

Shortly after starting his company, Greg Jackson created a Web site for his boat- and auto-brokering business, Carolina Classic Boats and Cars (*www.carolina-classic-boats.com*), which specializes in buying, selling, and trading antique wooden boats made from the 1920s to the 1950s by manufacturers such as Chris Craft, Gar Wood, Atlas, Hacker Craft, and Riva. Jackson recently added classic cars to his product line of "big-boy toys." Although Jackson operates his business in Clinton, South Carolina, a small town of fewer than 10,000 residents, his company operates globally with the help of the Web site, where customers can see photographs and read detailed descriptions of the boats and cars they are considering. Jackson has bought, sold, and shipped classic boats and cars all over the world, from Europe to Australia. "As long as I have a cell phone and a laptop, it doesn't matter where I am," he says.[18]

Entrepreneurs who do not want to take the time to set up their own Web sites can still sell to international customers through the Internet giant eBay, which has a wide global reach of 90 million active users. eBay handles an average of $2,000 worth of transactions every second, and 54 percent of all eBay transactions take place outside the United States.[19] eBay's international sales are growing twice as fast as its domestic sales.

ENTREPRENEURIAL
Profile

Lanny and Deena Morton: Sports Closeouts

In 2002, Lanny Morton spotted 20 baseball bats priced at just $40 each. His girlfriend and, now wife, Deena, encouraged him to buy them and resell them on eBay. Morton had to borrow $800 to make the purchase and quickly resold the bats for $1,300 on eBay. Recognizing a potential business, Deena invested $1,300 to purchase more discount sporting goods, which the pair sold for $2,600. Soon, Lanny and Deena had a successful eBay business selling quality sporting goods at discount prices. They used their 1,400 square-foot home in Glendale, Arizona, as their warehouse (with boxes of items often stacked to the ceiling in almost every room) until their business, Sports Closeouts, outgrew the space. "We started out on the living room floor," recalls Lanny, "writing labels and shipping out 10 or 15 items at a time. Eventually, the product just consumed the house." The Mortons have created their own Web site (*www.sportscloseouts.com*) but still sell items on eBay. Now operating out of a 7,200 square-foot warehouse, Sports Closeouts sells to customers across the globe and generates more than $4 million in annual revenue.[20]

Rather than merely counting on international customers to find their Web sites, small companies can take a proactive approach by translating their sites into other languages. Business owners can determine which countries to target by using Web analytics reports to identify the countries in which their existing online customers live. Hiring someone who understands the nuances of the language and the culture of the target countries to translate a site is the safest strategy and avoids embarrassing cultural blunders.

Relying on Trade Intermediaries

Another alternative for low-cost and low-risk entry into international markets is to use a trade intermediary. Trade intermediaries are domestic agencies that serve as distributors in foreign countries for domestic companies of all sizes. They rely on their networks of contacts, their

IN THE ENTREPRENEURIAL SPOTLIGHT

Building a Global Business in the Middle of a War Zone

During his regular evening reading time, Bill McNeely came across several articles about the iPhone's short battery life, and the inspiration for a business struck him. "I saw a big market and not that many players," he says. Although McNeely has no technical background, he had a simple idea that he was confident would work: a sleek, external battery that snaps onto the bottom of an iPhone, extending its battery life. All he needed was someone to design the battery and manufacture it for him. He went to Alibaba.com, a Web site that serves as a marketplace for importers, exporters, and suppliers from more than 240 countries, and within a few weeks found a reliable Chinese manufacturer that would transform his idea into a real product. He then went to Elance, a Web site that allows entrepreneurs to hire and manage freelance employees, and found a graphic designer to create the packaging for his iPhone battery, which he calls the 3GPower2. McNeely used the Web to find a consultant with a Harvard Business School degree to help him with his business plan, and an article in the *New York Times* led him to a Web designer, who helped him create his company's Web site, *www.3GPower2.com*.

With a total investment of $6,000, McNeely had 3GPower2 up and running as a global business in less than 3 months, something not all that unusual for modern entrepreneurs. However, one fact makes McNeely's accomplishments noteworthy: He built his company while managing the logistical operations of a police training base in one of the most dangerous places in the world: Kunduz, Afghanistan, a city mired in battle with the Taliban. The camp where McNeely works trains Afghan police and is under constant threat of attack from terrorists. Recently, a rocket launched by the Taliban landed only a few hundred feet from the base. "I've been through some pretty rough stuff," admits McNeely. He recalls the day when he was working for a defense contractor in southern Afghanistan when terrorists attacked his convoy, killing several drivers and destroying McNeely's SUV. Somehow McNeely survived the attack. His goal is to build his business to the point where he can retire from his job with the defense contractor and go back home to Texas to operate 3GPower2 full-time.

In the meantime, McNeely's wife, Suzy, handles the day-to-day operations of the business, including shipping, from the couple's home in Temple, Texas. Bill McNeely spends a great deal of time making Skype calls at night and on weekends to Suzy about 3GPower2. Currently, the McNeelys are focusing on search engine optimization techniques to boost the company's placement in search engines and on creating a coupon through Groupon (*www.groupon.com*).

1. How does the Internet enable entrepreneurs to create global businesses at start up? Has this always been the case?
2. What lessons can you draw from Bill McNeely's experience launching 3GPower2?

Source: Based on Jason Del Rey, "Report from the War Zone," *Inc.*, April 2010, pp. 25–26.

extensive knowledge of local customs and markets, and their experience in international trade to market products effectively and efficiently all across the globe. Trade intermediaries serve as export departments for small businesses. Although a broad array of trade intermediaries is available, the following are ideally suited for small businesses:

EXPORT MANAGEMENT COMPANIES (EMCS). **Export management companies (EMCs)** are an important channel of foreign distribution for small companies just getting started in international trade or for those lacking the resources to assign their own people to foreign markets. Most EMCs are merchant intermediaries, working on a buy-and-sell arrangement with small domestic companies. They provide small businesses with a low-cost, efficient, independent international marketing department, offering services ranging from market research on foreign countries and advice on patent protection to arranging financing and handling shipping. More than 1,000 EMCs operate across the United States, and many of them specialize in particular products or product lines. The chief advantage of using an EMC is that a small business's products get international exposure without having to tie up its own resources.

ENTREPRENEURIAL
Profile

*Steven Meier and
David Cisneros: Western
Export Services*

Western Export Services (WES), an export management company in Denver, Colorado, founded by Steven Meier and David Cisneros, specializes in selling food and beverage products from U.S.-based small and medium-size companies in markets across the globe. Recently named "Exporter of the Year," WES represents food and beverage suppliers from across the United States in the Pacific Rim, the Middle East, Latin America, and Europe.[21]

The greatest benefits that EMCs offer small companies are ready access to global markets and an extensive knowledge base on foreign trade, both of which are vital for entrepreneurs who are inexperienced in conducting global business. In return for their services, EMCs usually earn an extra discount on the goods they buy from their clients or, if they operate on a commission rate, a higher commission than domestic distributors earn on what they sell. EMCs charge commission rates of about 10 percent on consumer goods and 15 percent on industrial products. Although EMCs rarely advertise their services, finding one is not difficult. The Federation of International Trade Associations (FITA) provides useful information for small companies about global business and trade intermediaries on its Web site (*http://fita.org*), including a *Directory of Export Management Companies*. Industry trade associations and publications and the U.S. Department of Commerce's Export Assistance Centers* also can help entrepreneurs to locate EMCs and other trade intermediaries.

EXPORT TRADING COMPANIES (ETCs). Another tactic for getting into international markets with a minimum of cost and effort is through an export trading company (ETC). ETCs have been an important vehicle in international trade throughout history. The Hudson's Bay Company and the East India Company were dominant powers in world trade in the sixteenth, seventeenth, and eighteenth centuries.

Export trading companies are businesses that buy and sell products in a number of countries, and they typically offer a wide range of services, such as exporting, importing, shipping, storing, distributing, and others, to their clients. Unlike EMCs, which tend to focus on exporting, ETCs usually perform both import and export trades across many countries' borders. However, like EMCs, ETCs lower the risk of exporting for small businesses. Some of the largest trading companies in the world are based in the United States and Japan. In fact, many businesses that have navigated successfully Japan's complex system of distribution have done so with the help of ETCs.

In 1982, Congress passed the Export Trading Company Act to allow producers of similar products to form ETC cooperatives without the fear of violating antitrust laws. The goal was to encourage U.S. companies to export more goods by allowing businesses in the same industry to band together to form export trading companies.

MANUFACTURER'S EXPORT AGENTS (MEAs). **Manufacturer's export agents (MEAs)** act as international sales representatives in a limited number of markets for various noncompeting domestic companies. Unlike the close, partnering relationship formed with most EMCs, the relationship between an MEA and a small company is a short-term one, in which the MEA typically operates on a commission basis.

EXPORT MERCHANTS. **Export merchants** are domestic wholesalers who do business in foreign markets. They buy goods from many domestic manufacturers and then market them in foreign markets. Unlike MEAs, export merchants often carry competing lines, which means they have little loyalty to suppliers. Most export merchants specialize in particular industries— office equipment, computers, industrial supplies, and others.

RESIDENT BUYING OFFICES. Another approach to exporting is to sell to a **resident buying office**, a government-owned or privately-owned operation established in a country for the purpose of buying goods made there. Many foreign governments and businesses have set up

*A searchable list of the Export Assistance Centers is available at the Export.gov Web site
(*www.export.gov/eac/index.asp*).

buying offices in the United States. Selling to them is just like selling to domestic customers because the buying office handles all the details of exporting.

FOREIGN DISTRIBUTORS. Some small businesses work through foreign distributors to reach international markets. Small domestic companies export their products to these distributors who handle all of the marketing, distribution, and service functions in the foreign country.

ENTREPRENEURIAL
Profile

Peter Cole: Gamblin Artists Colors

In 2007, when Peter Cole took over Gamblin Artists Colors, a company that makes handcrafted oil paints, varnishes, and other artists' supplies, international sales accounted for less than 5 percent of the company's revenue. Cole realized that foreign markets represented a significant opportunity for the company's high-quality products and traveled to several countries that basic market research helped managers select as prime targets. Logging more than 80,000 miles in less than 1 year, Cole established relationships with foreign distributors in Israel, Australia, Mexico, Great Britain, and Spain. Gamblin Artists Colors now generates more than $5 million in annual sales, and international sales account for 10 percent (and growing) of the total.[22]

THE VALUE OF USING TRADE INTERMEDIARIES. Trade intermediaries such as these are becoming increasingly popular among businesses attempting to branch out into world markets because they make that transition much faster and easier. Most small business owners simply do not have the knowledge, resources, or confidence to go global alone. Intermediaries' global networks of buyers and sellers allow their small business customers to build their international sales much faster and with fewer hassles and mistakes. Entrepreneurs who are inexperienced in global sales and attempt to crack certain foreign markets quickly discover just how difficult the challenge can be. However, with their know-how, experience, and contacts, trade intermediaries can get small companies' products into foreign markets quickly and efficiently. The primary disadvantage of using trade intermediaries is that doing so requires entrepreneurs to surrender control over their foreign sales. Maintaining close contact with intermediaries and evaluating their performance regularly help to avoid major problems, however.

The key to establishing a successful relationship with a trade intermediary is conducting a thorough screening to determine which type of intermediary—and which one in particular—will best serve a small company's needs. The 50 World Trade Centers (most of which are affiliated with the U.S. government) and the Export Assistance Centers located in more than 100 cities across the United States and in 80 countries around the world offer valuable advice and assistance to small businesses wanting to get started in conducting global business. In addition, entrepreneurs can find reliable intermediaries by using their network of contacts in foreign countries and by attending international trade shows while keeping an eye out for potential candidates. Table 2 describes various resources that can help entrepreneurs locate trade intermediaries.

Joint Ventures

Joint ventures, both domestic and foreign, lower the risk of entering global markets for small businesses. They also give small companies more clout in foreign lands. In a **domestic joint venture**, two or more U.S. small businesses form an alliance for the purpose of exporting their goods and services abroad. For export ventures, participating companies get antitrust immunity, allowing them to cooperate freely. The businesses share the responsibility and the costs of getting export licenses and permits, and they split the venture's profits. Establishing a joint venture with the right partner has become an essential part of maintaining a competitive position in global markets for a growing number of industries.

In a **foreign joint venture**, a domestic small business forms an alliance with a company in the target nation. The host partner brings to the joint venture valuable knowledge of the local market and the customs and the tastes of local customers, making it much easier to conduct business in the foreign country. "For a small business, a far less risky approach to selling goods or services in a distant market is to work through local partners who understand the market and often have built-in distribution channels," says Edward Wes, a partner in a law firm that specializes in international business.[23] Forming a joint venture with a local company also is the best way for a business to negotiate the maze of government regulations in some countries. Some foreign countries

TABLE 2 Resources for Locating a Trade Intermediary

Trade intermediaries make doing business around the world much easier for small companies, but finding the right one can be a challenge. Fortunately, several government agencies offer a wealth of information to businesses interested in reaching into global markets with the help of trade intermediaries. Entrepreneurs looking for help in breaking into global markets should contact the International Trade Administration, the U.S. Commerce Department, and the Small Business Administration first to take advantage of the following services:

- *Agent/Distributor Service (ADS)*. Provides customized searches to locate interested and qualified foreign distributors for a product or service. (Search cost, $250 per country)
- *Commercial Service International Contacts (CSIC) List.* Provides contact and product information for more than 82,000 foreign agents, distributors, and importers interested in doing business with U.S. companies.
- *Country Directories of International Contacts (CDIC) List.* Provides the same kind of information as the CSIC List but is organized by country.
- *Industry Sector Analyses (ISAs).* Offer in-depth reports on industries in foreign countries, including information on distribution practices, end-users, and top sales prospects.
- *International Market Insights (IMIs).* Include reports on specific foreign market conditions, upcoming opportunities for U.S. companies, trade contacts, trade show schedules, and other information.
- *Trade Opportunity Program (TOP).* Provides up-to-the-minute, prescreened sales leads around the world for U.S. businesses, including joint venture and licensing partners, direct sales leads, and representation offers.
- *International Company Profiles (ICPs).* Commercial specialists will investigate potential partners, agents, distributors, or customers for U.S. companies and will issue profiles on them.
- *Commercial News USA.* A government-published magazine that promotes U.S. companies' products and services to 400,000 business readers in 176 countries at a fraction of the cost of commercial advertising. Small companies can use *Commercial News USA* to reach new customers around the world for as little as $499.
- *Gold Key Service.* For a small fee, business owners wanting to export to a specific country can use the Department of Commerce's Gold Key Service, in which experienced trade professionals arrange meetings with prescreened contacts whose interests match their own.
- *Platinum Key Service.* The U.S. Commercial Service's Platinum Key Service is more comprehensive than its Gold Key Service, offering business owners long-term consulting services on topics such as building a global marketing strategy, deciding which countries to target, and how to reach customers in foreign markets.
- *Matchmaker Trade Delegations Program.* This program helps small U.S. companies establish business relationships in major markets abroad by introducing them to the right contacts.
- *Multi-State/Catalog Exhibition Program.* The Department of Commerce presents companies' product and sales literature to hundreds of interested business prospects in foreign countries for as little as $450.
- *Trade Fair Certification Program.* This service promotes U.S. companies' participation in foreign trade shows that represent the best marketing opportunities for them.
- *Globus and National Trade Data Bank (NTDB).* With the NTDB (*http://www.wand.com/ntdb/*), small companies have access to leads on trading partners (both suppliers and customers) around the world.
- *International Trade Library.* At the Bureau of National Affairs Web site (*http://www.bna.com/ products/corplaw/itlw.htm*), entrepreneurs can access the International Trade Library, where they can learn about managing currency exchange risks, find country-specific market research, read Country Commercial Guides, and access a treasure trove of information on doing business globally. The Global Business Opportunity Leads section helps entrepreneurs locate leads and make business contacts for conducting international business.
- *Economic Bulletin Board (EBB).* Provides online trade leads and valuable market research on foreign countries compiled from a variety of federal agencies.
- *U.S. Export Assistance Centers.* The Department of Commerce has established 19 export assistance centers (USEACs) in major metropolitan cities around the country to serve as one-stop shops for entrepreneurs who need export help. Visit *www.sba.gov/aboutsba/sbaprograms/internationaltrade/ useac/index.htm*l for more information.
- *Trade Information Center.* The center helps locate federal export assistance, provides export assistance, and offers a 24-hour automated fax retrieval system that gives entrepreneurs free information on export promotion programs, regional market information, and international trade agreements. Call USA-TRADE.

(continued)

TABLE 2 Continued

■ *Office of International Trade.* Through the Office of International Trade, the Small Business Administration works with other government and private agencies to provide a variety of export development assistance, how-to publications, online courses, and information on foreign markets.

■ *Export-U.com.* This Web site (*www.export-u.com*) offers free export Webinars to business owners on topics that range from the basics, "Exporting 101," to more advanced topics, such as export financing arrangements. The site also provides links to many useful international trade Web sites.

■ *U.S. Commercial Service.* The U.S. Commercial service, a division of the International Trade Administration (*www.trade.gov*), provides many of the services listed in this table. Its Web site (*www.buyusa.gov/home/*) is an excellent starting point for entrepreneurs who are interested in exporting.

■ *Export.gov.* This Web site (*www.export.gov*) from the U.S. Commercial Service is an excellent gateway to a myriad of resources for entrepreneurs who are interested in learning more about exporting. The site includes market research, trade events, trade leads, and much more.

■ *Federation of International Trade Associations (FITA).* The FITA Global Trade Portal (*www.fita.org*) is an excellent source for international import and export trade leads and events and provides links to about 8,000 Web sites related to international trade.

place limitations on how joint ventures operate. Some nations, for example, require domestic (host) companies to own at least 51 percent of the venture. Sometimes, says one international manager, "the only way to be German in Germany, Canadian in Canada, and Japanese in Japan is through alliances."[24] When Subway, one of the leading franchises in the world, enters foreign markets with one of its sandwich shops, it often looks for a local company with which to form a joint venture. "Nobody knows an area like a local partner," says Don Fertman, a director of international development at Subway.[25]

The most important ingredient in the recipe for a successful joint venture is choosing the right partner. A productive joint venture is much like a marriage, requiring commitment, trust, and understanding. In addition to picking the right partner(s), a second key to creating a successful alliance is to establish common objectives. Defining *exactly* what each party in the joint venture hopes to accomplish at the outset minimizes the opportunity for misunderstandings and disagreements later on. One important objective should always be to use the joint venture as a learning experience, which requires a long-term view of the business relationship. Issues to address *before* entering into a joint venture include:

■ What contributions will each party make?
■ Who will be responsible for making which decisions?
■ How much control will each party have over the joint venture's direction?
■ How will the earnings from the joint venture be allocated?
■ How long will the joint venture last? Under what circumstances can the parties terminate the relationship?

ENTREPRENEURIAL
Profile

Bombardier Inc.: Joint Ventures with Sifang Locomotive, Rolling Stock, and Shenyang Aircraft Corporation

Bombardier Inc., a Quebec, Canada-based company that manufactures aircraft and trains, used a joint venture as part of its strategy to enter the Chinese market. Recognizing that China's decision to invest 3.2 trillion yuan in upgrading its infrastructure, including railways and airports (97 new airports by 2020), presented a tremendous business opportunity for both its aircraft and train divisions, Bombardier forged joint ventures with Chinese companies, one in the rail industry and the other in the aircraft industry. Bombardier will partner with Sifang Locomotive and Rolling Stock Ltd. to build its new ZEFIRO 380 trains that can go nearly 240 miles per hour. The company also has created a joint venture with China's Shenyang Aircraft Corporation to build its Q400 turboprop and C series regional aircraft. Thanks to these joint ventures, Bombardier forecasts call for China to become the company's third largest market behind North America and Europe.[26]

Unfortunately, most joint ventures fail. That makes it essential for the companies in an alliance to establish a contingency plan for getting out in case the joint venture doesn't work. Common problems leading to failure include improper selection of partners, incompatible management styles, failure to establish common goals, lack of flexibility, and failure to trust one another. What can entrepreneurs do to avoid these pitfalls in joint ventures?

- Understand their partner's reasons and objectives for joining the venture.
- Select a partner that shares their company's values and standards of conduct.
- Spell out in writing exactly how the venture will work, what each partner's responsibilities are, and where decision-making authority lies.
- Select a partner whose skills are different from but compatible with those of their own companies.
- Prepare a "prenuptial agreement" that spells out what happens in case of a "business divorce."

Foreign Licensing

Rather than sell their products or services directly to customers overseas, some small companies enter foreign markets by licensing businesses in other nations to use their patents, trademarks, copyrights, technology, processes, or products. In return for licensing its assets, a small company collects royalties from the sale of its foreign licenses. Licensing is a relatively simple way for even the most inexperienced business owners to extend their reach into global markets. Licensing is ideal for companies whose value lies in its intellectual property, unique products or services, recognized name, or proprietary technology. Although many businesses consider licensing only their products to foreign companies, the licensing potential for intangibles such as processes, technology, copyrights, and trademarks often is greater. Some entrepreneurs earn more money from licensing their know-how for product design, manufacturing, or quality control than they do from actually selling their finished goods in a highly competitive foreign market with which they are not familiar. Foreign licensing enables a small business to enter foreign markets quickly, easily, and with virtually no capital investment. Risks to the company include the potential loss of control over its manufacturing and marketing processes and creating a competitor if the licensee gains too much knowledge and control. Securing proper patent, trademark, and copyright protection beforehand can minimize those risks, however.

International Franchising

Franchising has become a major export industry for the United States. A survey by the International Franchise Association reports that 52 percent of U.S.-based franchisors have an international presence, and more domestic franchisors are looking to expand abroad.[27] Franchises are attracted to international markets, where they find it easier to increase sales and profits because the domestic market has become increasingly saturated with outlets and is much tougher to wring growth from than in the past. As a growth strategy, international franchising works best for experienced franchisors. Both the cost and the complexity of franchising increase as the distance between franchisor and franchisees increases. Before committing to global expansion, franchisors should meet the following criteria:

The International Franchise Association reports that 52 percent of U.S.-based franchisors have an international presence. Pictured here are McDonald's and KFC outlets in Dubai, United Arab Emirates.

Source: vario images GmbH & Co. KG/Almay Images

- Sufficient financial and managerial resources to devote to globalization
- A solid track record of success in the United States
- Adequate trademark protection for the franchise's brand
- Time-tested training, support, and reporting procedures that help franchisees succeed[28]

International franchisors sell virtually every kind of product or service imaginable—from fast food to child day care—in global markets. In some cases, the products and services sold in international markets are identical to those sold in the United States. However, most franchisors have learned that they must adapt their products and services to suit local tastes and customs. Fast-food chains operating in other countries often must make adjustments to their menus to please locals' palates.

<table>
<tr><td>

ENTREPRENEURIAL

Profile

McDonald's and Domino's Pizza

</td><td>

In Japan, McDonald's (known as "Makudonarudo") outlets sell koroke burgers (made of mashed potatoes and cabbage), rice burgers, and katsu burgers (cheese wrapped in a roast pork cutlet topped with katsu sauce and shredded cabbage) in addition to their traditional American fare. In the Philippines, the McDonald's menu includes a spicy Filipino-style burger, spaghetti, and chicken with rice. In Germany, McDonald's restaurants sell McBeer, and in Great Britain they offer British Cadbury chocolate sticks. Some McDonald's outlets in Canada sell poutine, French fries topped with cheese curds and gravy, and the McHomard, a sandwich made of chunks of lobster meat on a roll. Domino's Pizza operates more than 3,500 restaurants in 60 international markets, where local managers have developed pizza flavors such as shrimp, squid, broccoli, fried garlic, and cheese (Japan), lamb and pickled ginger (India), tuna and sweet corn (England), crab, shrimp, onions, and peapods, (Taiwan), and reindeer sausage (Iceland) to cater to customers' preferences.

</td></tr>
</table>

Although franchise outlets span the globe, Europe is the primary market for U.S. franchisors, with Pacific Rim countries and Canada following. Because they are the most populous nations on earth, China and India are becoming franchising "hot spots." These markets are most attractive to franchisors because they offer large middle-class populations, rising personal incomes, significant numbers of young consumers with purchasing power and a fascination with Western products, growing service economies, and spreading urbanization. Because the franchise industry is nascent in both China and India, the potential for growth is tremendous, and U.S. franchisors are taking note. Many franchisors are laying the groundwork to enter these markets, whose unique cultures pose challenges to foreign companies who do business there.

Growth potential is the primary attraction of international markets. Franchisors that decide to expand internationally should take these steps:

1. ***Identify the country or countries that are best suited to the franchisor's business concept.*** Factors to consider include a country's business climate, demographic profile, level of economic development, rate of economic growth, degree of legal protection, language and cultural barriers, and market potential. Franchisors making their first forays into global markets should consider focusing on a single nation where cultural barriers are minimal (such as Canada) or a small group of similar nations.

2. ***Generate leads for potential franchisees.*** Franchisors looking for prospective franchisees in foreign markets have many tools available to them, including international franchise trade shows, their own Web sites, trade missions, and brokers. Many franchisors have had success with trade missions, such as those sponsored by trade groups such as the International Franchise Association, the U.S. Department of Commerce's Gold Key Program, or various state programs. These trade missions are designed to introduce franchisors to qualified franchise candidates in target countries. Some franchisors rely on brokers who have extensive business contacts in specific countries.

3. ***Select quality candidates.*** Just as in any franchise relationship, the real key to success is choosing the right franchisee. Because of the complexity and cost of international franchising, selecting quality franchisees is essential to success.

4. *Structure the franchise deal.* Franchisors can structure international franchise arrangements in a variety of ways, but three techniques are most popular: direct franchising, area development, and master franchising.

- **Direct franchising**, which is common in domestic franchise deals, involves selling single-unit franchises to individual operators in foreign countries. Although dealing with individual franchisees makes it easier for the franchisor to maintain control, it also requires more of the franchisor's time and resources.
- **Area development** is similar to direct franchising except that the franchisor allows the franchisee to develop multiple units in a particular territory, perhaps a province, a county, or even an entire nation. A successful area development strategy depends on a franchisor selecting and then supporting quality franchisees.
- **Master franchising** is the most popular strategy for companies entering international markets. In a master franchising deal, a franchisor sells to a franchisee the right to develop subfranchises within a broad geographic area or, sometimes, an entire foreign country. In short, master franchising turbo charges a franchisor's growth. Many franchisors use this method to open outlets in international markets more quickly and efficiently because their master franchisees understand local laws and the nuances of selling in local markets. Although master franchising simplifies a franchisor's expansion into global markets, it gives franchisors the least amount of control over their international franchisees.

Countertrading and Bartering

As business becomes increasingly global, companies are discovering that attracting customers is just one part of the battle. Another problem global businesses face when selling to some countries is that their currencies are virtually worthless outside their borders, so getting paid in a valuable currency is a real challenge! Companies wanting to reach these markets must countertrade or barter. A **countertrade** is a transaction in which a company selling goods and services in a foreign country agrees to help promote investment and trade in that country. The goal of the transaction is to help offset the capital drain from the foreign country's purchases. As entrepreneurs enter more developing nations, they will discover the need to develop skill at implementing this global trading strategy.

Countertrading does suffer from numerous drawbacks. Countertrade transactions can be complicated, cumbersome, and time consuming. They also increase the chances that a company will get stuck with useless merchandise that it cannot move. They can lead to unpleasant surprises concerning the quantity and quality of products required in the countertrade. Still, countertrading offers one major advantage: Sometimes it's the only way to make a sale!

Entrepreneurs must weigh the advantages against the disadvantages for their companies before committing to a countertrade deal. Because of its complexity and the risks involved, countertrading is not the best choice for a novice entrepreneur looking to break into the global marketplace.

Bartering, the exchange of goods and services for other goods and services, is another way of trading with countries lacking convertible currency. In a barter exchange, a company that manufactures electronics components might trade its products for the coffee that a business in a foreign country processes, which it then sells to a third company for cash. Barter transactions require finding a business with complementary needs, but they are much simpler than countertrade transactions.

ENTREPRENEURIAL
Profile

Howard Dahl: Amity Technology

Howard Dahl, owner of Amity Technology, a North Dakota–based manufacturer of farm equipment, was part of the first wave of entrepreneurs to enter Russia after the communist regime in the former Soviet Union collapsed. Conducting business in those early years was challenging, and Dahl's company often relied on bartering. "[The Russians] would trade rapeseed, which you could use to make vegetable oil, for our machinery," he says. "We would then sell the seeds to a German agribusiness in a back-to-back transaction." Dahl is glad that he didn't give up the Russian export market; today, exports to Russia account for 40 percent of Amity Technology's total sales.[29]

Exporting

For years, small businesses in the United States could afford the luxury of conducting business at home in the world's largest market, never having to venture outside its borders. However, a growing number of small companies, realizing the incredible profit potential that exporting offers, are making globalization an ever-expanding part of their marketing plans. Approximately 95 percent of the world's population lives outside the United States, and more than 75 percent of the world's purchasing power lies outside the borders of the United States. Companies that export can tap into that purchasing power.[30] A recent study by CompTIA reports that small and medium-size companies that export generate, on average, 12 percent of their revenues from exports.[31]

Large companies continue to dominate export sales, however. Less than 1 percent of the nearly 30 million businesses in the United States export their goods and services.[32] Although small companies with fewer than 100 employees account for 90.7 percent of the 266,500 U.S. businesses that export goods and services, they generate only 21.0 percent of the nation's export sales.[33] Their impact is significant, however; small companies generate $1.1 billion each day in export sales.

Experts estimate that at least twice as many small companies are capable of exporting but are not doing so.[34] One of the biggest barriers facing companies that have never exported is not knowing where or how to start (see Figure 3). Paul Hsu, whose company sells ginseng across the globe, explains, "Exporting starts with a global mind-set, which unfortunately, is not all that common among owners of small- and medium-sized businesses in the United States. Most entrepreneurs in the United States envision markets only within domestic and sometimes even state borders, while foreign entrepreneurs look at export markets first."[35]

Breaking the psychological barrier to exporting is the first—and most difficult—step in setting up a successful program. The U.S. Chamber of Commerce's Trade Roots initiative, an international trade leadership program that networks more than 3,000 local U.S. chambers of commerce, is a useful resource for entrepreneurs looking to launch into global business. The program provides information on the benefits and methods for its members' who want to engage in international trade but aren't sure where to start. The U.S. Commercial Service's *Export Programs Guide* provides entrepreneurs with a comprehensive list of federal programs designed to help U.S. exporters. Another valuable source of information are the U.S. Export Assistance Centers (*www.sba.gov/oit/export/useac.html*), which serve as single contact points for information on the multitude of federal export programs that are designed to help entrepreneurs who want to start exporting. Entrepreneurs who want to learn more about exporting should investigate *A Basic Guide to Exporting* (*www.unzco.com/basicguide/*), which is published by the Department of Commerce and Unz and Company. The U.S. government export portal, *www.export.gov*, gives entrepreneurs access to valuable information about exporting in general (finance, shipping, documentation, and others), as well as details on individual nations (market research, trade

FIGURE 3
Small Business Exporting Survey, 2010

Source: NSBA/SBEA Small Business Exporting Survey, 2010.

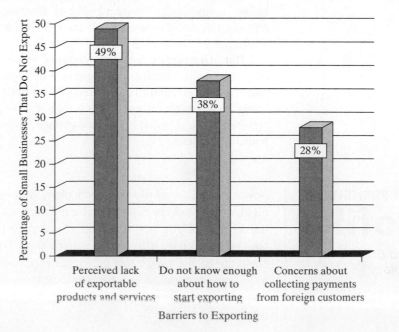

Barriers to Exporting

agreements, statistics, and more). Learning more about exporting and realizing that it is within the realm of possibility for small companies—even *very* small companies—is the first, and often most difficult, step in breaking the psychological barrier to exporting.

The next challenge is to create a sound export strategy. In fact, a study of 346 small exporting companies by Pierre-André Julien and Charles Ramangahahy found that small companies with well-defined export strategies outperformed those that merely dabbled in exporting.[36] What steps must entrepreneurs take to build a successful export strategy?

1. ***Recognize that even the tiniest companies and least experienced entrepreneurs have the potential to export; help is available.*** Size and experience are not prerequisites for a successful export program.

ENTREPRENEURIAL
Profile

John & Nancy Kleppe: J&N Enterprises

In 1985, when John and Nancy Kleppe launched J&N Enterprises, a company that sells the Gas Trac, a portable combustible gas detector, in the spare bedroom of their home in Union, Indiana, they had no intention of operating their tiny business globally. J&N Enterprises grew over time, and in 2003, the company moved into a new high-tech 14,000-square-foot building in nearby Valparaiso. With the help of state agencies, president Scott Kleppe, the couple's son, attended a trade show in China, which led to orders that increased the company's sales by 22 percent. Today, J&N Enterprises exports its expanded product line to 16 countries, including Australia, Korea, Mexico, and Turkey and recently was named the Indiana Exporter of the Year by the U.S. Small Business Administration.[37]

2. ***Analyze your product or service.*** Is it special? New? Unique? High quality? Priced favorably due to lower costs or exchange rates? Does it appeal to a particular niche? In which countries would there be sufficient demand for it? In many foreign countries, products from the United States are in demand because they have an air of mystery about them! Exporters quickly learn the value foreign customers place on quality. Ron Schutte, president of Creative Bakers of Brooklyn, a company that makes presliced cheesecakes for restaurants, saw an opportunity to sell in Japan. The only modification Schutte made to his high-quality cheesecakes was reducing the portion size from 4.5 ounces to 2.25 ounces to accommodate Japanese diners' smaller appetites.[38]

3. ***Analyze your commitment.*** Are you willing to devote the time and the energy to develop export markets? Does your company have the necessary resources to capitalize on market opportunities? In any international venture, patience is essential. One expert estimates that penetrating a foreign market requires at least 3 years.[39] Laying the groundwork for an export operation can take from 6 to 8 months (or longer), but entering foreign markets isn't as tough as most entrepreneurs think. "One of the biggest misconceptions people have is that they can't market overseas unless they have a big team of lawyers and specialists," says one export specialist. "That just isn't true."[40] Table 3 summarizes key issues managers must address in the export decision.

4. ***Research markets and pick your target.*** The average small or medium-size business exports to eight countries (see Figure 4).[41] Before investing in a costly sales trip abroad, however, entrepreneurs should make a trip to the local library or visit the Web sites of the Department of Commerce and the International Trade Administration. Exporters can choose from a multitude of guides, manuals, books, statistical reports, newsletters, videos, and other resources to help them research potential markets. Armed with research, small business owners can avoid wasting time and money on markets with limited potential for their products and can concentrate on those with the greatest promise. According to the Economist Intelligence Unit, the fastest growing economies outside the United States between 2006 and 2020 will be China, India, Brazil, and Russia. Asian economies in particular will be attractive markets for small exporters, increasing their share of global GDP from 35 percent today to 43 percent in 2020.[42] India alone has a rapidly expanding middle class the size of the entire U.S. population that is becoming increasingly well-educated, making it an attractive export target.[43]

Research also shows export entrepreneurs whether they need to modify their existing products and services to suit the tastes and preferences of their foreign target customers. Sometimes foreign customers' lifestyles, housing needs, body sizes, traditions, and cultures require exporters to make alterations to their product lines. When Peter Cole, CEO of Gamblin Artists Colors, the

TABLE 3 Management Issues in the Export Decision

I. Experience

1. With what countries has your company already conducted business (or from what countries have you received inquiries about your product or service)?
2. What product lines do foreign customers ask about most often? Prepare a list of sales inquiries for buyer by product and by country.
3. Is the trend of inquiries or sales increasing or decreasing?
4. Who are your primary domestic and foreign competitors?
5. What lessons has your company learned from past export experience?

II. Management and Personnel

1. Who will be responsible for the export entity's organization and staff? (Do you have an export "champion"?)
2. How much top management time
   a. Should you allocate to exporting?
   b. Can you afford to allocate to exporting?
3. What does management expect from its exporting efforts? What are your company's export goals and objectives?
4. What organizational structure will your company require to ensure that it can service export sales properly? (Note the political implications, if any.)
5. Who will implement the plan?

III. Production Capacity

1. To what extent is your company using its existing production capacity? Is there any excess? If so, how much?
2. Will filling export orders hurt your company's ability to make and service domestic sales?
3. What will additional production for export markets cost your company?
4. Are there seasonal or cyclical fluctuations in your company's workload? When? Why?
5. Is there a minimum quantity foreign customers must order for a sale to be profitable?
6. To what extent would your company need to modify its products, packaging, and design specifically for its export targets? Is your product quality adequate for foreign customers?
7. What pricing structure will your company use? Will the prices be competitive?
8. How will your company collect payment on its export sales?

IV. Financial Capacity

1. How much capital will your company need to begin exporting? Where will it come from?
2. How will you allocate the initial costs of your company's export effort?
3. Does your company have other expansion plans that would compete with an exporting effort?
4. By what date do you expect your company's export program to pay for itself?
5. How important is establishing a global presence to your company's future success?

Source: Adapted from *A Basic Guide to Exporting* (Washington, DC: U.S. Department of Commerce, 1986), p. 3.

**FIGURE 4
Number of Countries
to Which Small
Businesses Export**

Source: Elizabeth Clark, *Small and Medium-Sized Exporting Companies: A Statistical Handbook*, International Trade Administration, Office of Trade and Industry Information (Washington, DC: 2005), p. 19.

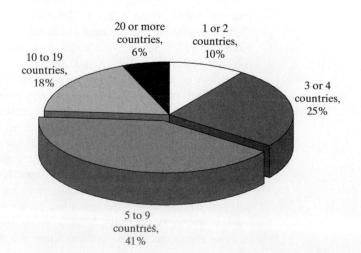

20 or more countries, 6%
1 or 2 countries, 10%
10 to 19 countries, 18%
3 or 4 countries, 25%
5 to 9 countries, 41%

TABLE 4 Questions to Guide International Market Research

- Is there an overseas market for your company's products or services?
- Are there specific target markets that look most promising?
- Which new markets abroad are most likely to open up or expand?
- How big is the market your company is targeting, and how fast is it growing?
- What are the major economic, political, legal, social, technological, and other environmental factors affecting this market?
- What are the demographic and cultural factors affecting this market: e.g., disposable income, occupation, age, gender, opinions, activities, interests, tastes, and values?
- Who are your company's present and potential customers abroad?
- What are their needs and desires? What factors influence their buying decisions: price, credit terms, delivery terms, quality, brand name, etc.?
- How would they use your company's product or service? What modifications, if any, would be necessary to sell to your target customers?
- Who are your primary competitors in the foreign market?
- How do competitors distribute, sell, and promote their products? What are their prices?
- What are the best channels of distribution for your product?
- What is the best way for your company to gain exposure in this market?
- Are there any barriers such as tariffs, quotas, duties, or regulations to selling your product in this market? Are there any incentives?
- Are there any potential licensing or joint venture partners already in this market?

Source: Adapted from *A Basic Guide to Exporting* (Washington, DC: Department of Commerce, 1986), p. 11.

company that makes handcrafted oil paints, varnishes, and other artists' supplies, began exporting to Australia, he quickly realized the importance of modifying the size of the products. "In Australia, they want larger sizes of paints—sizes we had not contemplated for the U.S. market," says Cole. "People tend to paint bigger and thicker."[44]

Japan is the second largest international market for coffee retailer Starbucks. Since entering Japan in 1996, Starbucks has customized its menu to appeal to local customers' tastes. For instance, menu additions include a Sakura Steamer (steamed milk infused with a flavored syrup), a Roasted Green Tea Latte, and a Sakura steamed bun filled with red bean paste.[45] Making modifications such as these often spells the difference between success and failure in the global market. In other cases, products destined for export need little or no modification. Experts estimate that one-half of exported products require little modification; one-third require moderate modification; only a few require major changes. Table 4 offers questions to guide entrepreneurs as they conduct export research.

5. *Develop a distribution strategy.* Should you use an export intermediary or sell directly to foreign customers? As you learned earlier in this chapter, many small companies just entering international markets prefer to rely on trade intermediaries or a joint venture partner to break new ground. Using intermediaries or joint ventures often makes sense until an entrepreneur has the chance to gain experience in exporting and to learn the ground rules of selling in foreign lands. Figure 5 illustrates the various distribution strategies that micro-size companies (those with less than $1 million in annual sales) and small companies (those with annual sales between $1 million and $20 million) use to export their products and services.

6. *Find your customer.* Small businesses can rely on a host of export specialists to help them track down foreign customers. (Refer to Table 2 for a list of some of the resources available from the government.) The U.S. Department of Commerce and the International Trade Administration should be the first stops on an entrepreneur's agenda for going global. These agencies have market research available through the U.S. Commercial Service Web site (*www.buyusa.gov*) that can help entrepreneurs locate the best target markets for its products or services and specific customers within those markets. Industry Sector Analysis (ISA), International Market Insights (IMIs), and Customized Market Analysis (CMA) are just some of the reports and services that global entrepreneurs find most useful. These agencies also have knowledgeable staff specialists experienced in the details of global trade and in the intricacies of foreign cultures. Through the Platinum Key Service, Commercial Service agents consult with companies as they build their global strategies, evaluate markets, and decide how to reach foreign markets.

One of the most efficient and least expensive ways for entrepreneurs to locate potential customers for their companies' products and services is to participate in a trade mission. These

FIGURE 5
Export Distribution Strategies

Source: Small and Medium-Size Business Export Insights and Opportunities, CompTIA, 2010, p. 8.

missions usually are sponsored by either a federal or a state economic development agency or an industry trade association for the purpose of cultivating international trade by connecting domestic companies with potential trading partners overseas. A trade mission may focus on a particular industry or may cover several industries but target a particular country. "We set up meetings for them with distributors, suppliers, manufacturers, customers, accountants, law firms, the whole gamut, to be able to provide them with the necessary resources to get into that market," says Christian Bartley, president of the World Trade Center Wisconsin, an organization that regularly sponsors trade missions to foreign countries for Wisconsin entrepreneurs who are interested in exploring export markets.[46] Fourteen small companies participated in a recent trade mission to China sponsored by Automation Alley, an organization that specializes in trade missions for high-tech companies. The trip resulted in 15 sales contracts from Chinese companies and added nearly $18.5 million in export sales to the participating companies' revenue streams. "As a direct result of the China Trade Mission, we signed up four highly qualified distributors," says Lee King, a top manager at Numatics Inc., one of the trade mission participants. "We have generated $500,000 in sales and, as a result of exporting, we have hired 15 more employees."[47]

7. *Find financing.* One of the biggest barriers to small business exports is lack of financing. The trouble is that bankers and other sources of capital don't always understand the intricacies of international sales and view financing them as highly risky ventures. In addition, among major industrialized nations, the U.S. government spends the least per capita to promote exports.

ENTREPRENEURIAL
Profile

Cindy Lowry: Blossom Bucket

Cindy Lowry started Blossom Bucket as a part-time business, making simple crafts for decorating homes and selling them at trade shows. Before long, sales accelerated, and Lowry became a full-time entrepreneur. At one trade show, Lowry landed $200,000 in orders, many of them from foreign customers, for a new line of holiday ornaments that one of her friends had designed. "I went to three banks for financing," she says, "and none of them would lend me any money. [They said] that orders are not money. You can cancel an order." Lowry turned to the only source of capital she could find: credit cards. "I got as many credit cards as I could and filled those orders," she says. "Now we are off and running."[48]

Access to adequate financing is a crucial ingredient in a successful export program because the cost of generating foreign sales often is higher and collection cycles are longer. Several federal, state, and private programs are operating to fill this export financing void, however. Loan programs from the Small Business Administration include its Export Working Capital program (90 percent loan guarantees up to $1,500,000), Export Express (a streamlined approach to obtaining SBA-guaranteed financing up to $250,000), and International Trade Loan program (75 percent loan guarantees up to $1,500,000). In addition, the Export-Import Bank (*www.exim.gov*), the Overseas Private Investment Corporation, and a variety of state-sponsored programs offer export-minded entrepreneurs both direct loans and loan guarantees. (Recall that the *Export Programs Guide* provides a list of the 20 government agencies that help companies to develop their export potential.) The Export-Import Bank, which has been financing the sale of U.S. exports for more than 70 years, provides small exporters with export credit insurance and loans through its working capital line of credit and a variety of pre-export loan programs. The Bankers Association for Foreign Trade (*www.baft.org/jsps/*) is an association of 150 banks around the world that matches exporters needing foreign trade financing with interested banks.

ENTREPRENEURIAL
Profile
Craig Matheson:
Web Press

Web Press, a maker of newspaper-printing equipment founded in 1968 and based in Kent, Washington, had generated orders from customers in Europe, Mexico, and Nigeria but needed financing because of the longer collection periods involved in export sales. When the company's bank balked at extending credit on export sales, CEO Craig Matheson worked with the Export Finance Assistance Center of Washington to secure a line of credit from another bank that carried a guarantee from the SBA's Export Working Capital Program. Web Press has since closed export deals with customers in Vietnam, Costa Rica, and Canada.[49]

8. *Ship your goods.* Export novices usually rely on international freight forwarders and customhouse agents—experienced specialists in overseas shipping—for help in navigating the bureaucratic morass of packaging requirements and paperwork demanded by customs. These specialists, also known as *transport architects,* are to exporters what travel agents are to passengers and normally charge relatively small fees for a valuable service. They move shipments of all sizes to destinations all over the world efficiently, saving entrepreneurs many headaches. Good freight forwarders understand U.S. export regulations, foreign import requirements, shipping procedures (such as packing, labeling, documenting, and insuring goods), customs processes, and maintaining proper records for paying tariffs. In addition, because they work for several companies, freight forwarders can aggregate payloads to negotiate favorable rates with shippers. "[A freight forwarder] is going to be sure that his client conforms with all the government regulations that apply to export cargo," explains the owner of an international freight forwarding business. "He acts as an agent of the exporter, and, in most circumstances, is like an extension of that exporter's traffic department." The Johnston Sweeper Company, a manufacturer of street sweepers, ships its 20,000-pound pieces of equipment worldwide with the help of an international freight forwarder.[50]

Exporters can find an online directory of more than 400 freight forwarders located in 120 countries at Freightbook (*www.freightbook.net*). Another useful resource is the National Customs Brokers and Forwarders Association of America (*www.ncbfaa.org*), which represents more than 800 freight forwarders and customs brokers. Table 5 features common international shipping terms and their meaning.

9. *Collect your money.* Collecting foreign accounts can be more complex than collecting domestic ones; however, by picking their customers carefully and checking their credit references closely, entrepreneurs can minimize bad-debt losses. Businesses engaging in international sales can use four primary payment methods (ranked from least risk to most risky): cash in advance, a letter of credit, a bank (or documentary) draft, and an open account. The safest method of selling to foreign customers is to collect cash in advance of the sale. This is the safest option for the seller because it eliminates the risk of collection problems and provides immediate cash flow. However, requiring cash payments up front may severely limit a small company's base of foreign customers.

One tool that small exporters can use to minimize the risk of bad-debt losses on foreign sales is export credit insurance, which protects a company against the nonpayment of its open accounts due to commercial and political problems. The cost of export credit insurance usually is a very

TABLE 5 Common International Shipping Terms and Their Meaning

Shipping Term	Seller's Responsibility	Buyer's Responsibility	Shipping Method(s) Used
FOB ("Free on Board") Seller	Deliver goods to carrier and provide export license and clean onboard receipt. Bear risk of loss until goods are delivered to carrier.	Pay shipping, freight, and insurance charges. Bear risk of loss while goods are in transit.	All
FOB ("Free on Board") Buyer	Deliver goods to the buyer's place of business and provide export license and clean onboard receipt. Pay shipping, freight, and insurance charges.	Accept delivery of goods after documents are tendered.	All
FAS ("Free Along Side") Vessel	Deliver goods alongside ship. Provides an "alongside" receipt.	Provide export license and proof of delivery of the goods to the carrier. Bear risk of loss once goods are delivered to the carrier.	Ship
CFR ("Cost and Freight")	Deliver goods to carrier, obtain export licenses, and pay export taxes. Provide buyer with clean bill of lading. Pay freight and shipping charges. Bear risk of loss until goods are delivered to buyer.	Pay insurance charges. Accept delivery of goods after documents are tendered.	Ship
CIF ("Cost, Insurance, and Freight")	Same as CFR plus pay insurance charges and provide buyer with insurance policy.	Accept delivery of goods after documents are tendered.	Ship
CPT ("Carriage Paid to . . .")	Deliver goods to carrier, obtain export licenses, and pay export taxes. Provide buyer with clean transportation documents. Pay shipping and freight charges.	Pay insurance charges. Accept delivery of goods after documents are tendered.	All
CIP ("Carriage and Insurance Paid to . . .")	Same as CPT plus pay insurance charges and provide buyer with insurance policy.	Accept delivery of goods after documents are tendered.	All
DDU ("Delivered Duty Unpaid")	Obtain export license, pay insurance charges, and provide buyer documents for taking delivery.	Take delivery of goods and pay import duties.	All
DDP ("Delivered Duty Paid")	Obtain export license and pay import duty, pay insurance charges, and provide buyer documents for taking delivery.	Take delivery of goods.	All

Source: Adapted from *Guide to the Finance of International Trade,* edited by Gordon Platt (HBSC Trade Services, Marine Midland Bank, and the Journal of Commerce), *http://infoserv2.ita.doc.gov/efm/efm.nsf/503d177e3c63f0b48525675900112e24/6218a8703573b32985256759004c41f3/$FILE/Finance_.pdf,* pp. 6–10. Reprinted with permission by the Journal of Commerce.

small percentage of the sale that the company is insuring. Private insurers and the Export-Import Bank offer export credit insurance. The Export-Import Bank provides nearly $3 billion in export credit insurance annually to small businesses. Applied Fabric Technologies (AFT), a company based in Orchard Park, New York, that specializes in products to contain oil spills, regularly uses export credit insurance to lower the risk associated with its foreign sales. A customer in Liberia placed an order with AFT and insisted on "net 30" credit terms from the receipt of the merchandise, risky terms on an international sale, especially for a small company. Rather than pass up the sale, AFT purchased an export credit insurance policy through the Export-Import Bank. The company has since used a similar strategy on sales to customers in Taiwan, South Africa, Australia, and Egypt.[51]

Financing foreign sales often involves special credit arrangements such as letters of credit and bank (or documentary) drafts. A **letter of credit** is an agreement between an exporter's bank and the foreign buyer's bank that guarantees payment to the exporter for a specific shipment of goods. In essence, a letter of credit reduces the financial risk for the exporter by substituting a bank's creditworthiness for that of the purchaser (see Figure 6). A **bank draft** is a document the seller draws on the buyer, requiring the buyer to pay the face amount (the purchase price of

FIGURE 6
A Letter of Credit

Seller   Buyer

Foreign buyer agrees to buy
products; seller agrees to ship
goods if buyer arranges a letter
of credit.

Seller ships goods to buyer
according to letter of credit's
terms and submits shipping
documents to bank issuing letter
of credit.

Seller's bank   Buyer's bank

Letter of credit

Buyer requests that his bank grant a letter of
credit, which assures exporter payment if she
presents documents proving goods were
actually shipped. Bank makes out letter of
credit to seller and sends it to seller's bank
(called the confirming bank).

Buyer's bank makes payment
to seller's (confirming) bank.
Confirming bank then pays
seller amount specified in
letter of credit.

the goods) either on sight (a sight draft) or on a specified date (a time draft) once the goods are shipped. Rather than use letters of credit or drafts, some exporters simply sell to foreign customers on open account. In other words, they ship the goods to a foreign customer without any guarantee of payment. This method is the riskiest because collecting a delinquent account from a foreign customer is even more difficult than collecting past-due payments from a domestic customer. The parties to an international deal should always come to an agreement in advance on an acceptable method of payment.

Establishing International Locations

Once established in international markets, some small businesses set up permanent locations there. Establishing an office or a factory in a foreign land can require a substantial investment that reaches beyond the budgets of many small companies. In addition, setting up an international office can be an incredibly frustrating experience. In some countries, business infrastructures are in disrepair or are nonexistent. Getting a telephone line installed can take months in some places, and finding reliable equipment to move goods to customers is nearly impossible. Securing necessary licenses and permits from bureaucrats often takes more than filing the necessary paperwork; in some nations, bureaucrats expect payments to "grease the wheels of justice." In fact, the Foreign Corrupt Practice Act, passed in 1977, considers bribing foreign officials to be a criminal act. One study by the World Bank of "grease payments" for the purpose of minimizing the red tape imposed by foreign regulations concludes that the payments do not work; in fact, companies that actually used them experienced greater government scrutiny and red tape in their international transactions.[52] In another study, risk management company Simmons & Simmons reports that 35.4 percent of companies said that they had refused to make investments in certain countries because of the nation's reputation for corruption.[53] Finally, finding the right person to manage an international office is crucial to success; it also is a major challenge, especially for small businesses. Small companies usually have lean management staffs and cannot afford to send key people abroad without running the risk of losing their focus.

Small companies that establish international locations can reap significant benefits. Start-up costs are lower in some foreign countries (but not all!), and lower labor costs can produce significant savings as well. In addition, by locating in a country a business learns firsthand how its culture influences business and how it can satisfy customers' demands most effectively. In essence, the business becomes a local corporate citizen.

Importing and Outsourcing

In addition to selling their goods in foreign markets, small companies also buy goods from distributors and manufacturers in foreign markets. In fact, the intensity of price competition in many industries—from textiles and handbags to industrial machinery and computers—means that more companies now shop the world market, looking for the lowest prices they can find. Because labor costs in countries such as China and India are far below those in other nations, businesses there offer goods and services at very low prices. Increasingly, these nations are home to well-educated, skilled workers that are paid far less than comparable workers in the United States or Western Europe. For instance, a computer programmer in the United States might earn $100,000 a year, but in India a computer programmer doing the same work earns $25,000 a year or less. As a result, many companies either import goods or outsource work directly to manufacturers in countries where costs are far lower than they would be domestically. According to TPI, a leading outsourcing consulting firm, global outsourcing is a $424 billion per year industry (up from $232 billion in 2000).[54]

ENTREPRENEURIAL
Profile

Valerie Johnson: Big Feet Pajama Company

Valerie Johnson, founder of Big Feet Pajamas.

Source: John Gurzinski/The New York Times/ Redux

Valerie Johnson left a corporate career to pursue her entrepreneurial dream and launched the Big Feet Pajama Company in 2005 in the basement of her Las Vegas, Nevada, home. Her company, which makes more than 50 styles of footed pajamas for men, women, and children and generates annual sales of more than $1 million, includes among its customers celebrities such as Taylor Swift and Niecy Nash. One of Johnson's first challenges was to locate a company to manufacture her pajama designs. She turned to Alibaba.com, a Web site that connects importers, exporters, and suppliers from more than 240 countries, to screen potential suppliers. Johnson narrowed her choices to three factories before boarding a plane to make onsite visits. The factory she chose "was not the least expensive," she says, "but I was confident in the quality and efficiency of its operation and how it treated employees."[55]

Entrepreneurs who are considering importing goods and service or outsourcing their service or manufacturing jobs to foreign countries should follow these steps:

■ *Make sure that importing or outsourcing is right for your business.* Even though foreign manufacturers often can provide items at significant cost savings, using them may not always be the best business decision. Entrepreneurs sometimes discover that achieving the lowest price may require a trade-off of other important factors, such as quality and speed of delivery. When Patrick Kruse, owner of Ruff Wear, a business that sells dog booties, began outsourcing many of his company's products to Chinese factories, he discovered that the quality of the goods was poor. "We actually had to refuse some shipments, which really hurt our business," he says.[56] In addition, some foreign manufacturers require sizeable minimum orders, perhaps $200,000 or more, before they will produce a product.

■ *Establish a target cost for your product.* Before setting off on a global shopping spree, entrepreneurs first should determine exactly what they can afford to spend on manufacturing a product and make a profit on it. Given the low labor costs of many foreign manufacturers, products that are the most labor intensive make good candidates for outsourcing.

■ *Do your research before you leave home.* Investing time in basic research about the industry and potential suppliers in foreign lands is essential before setting foot on foreign soil. Useful resources are plentiful, and entrepreneurs should use them. Refer to Table 2 for a list of some of the most popular sources of information on foreign countries and the companies that are based there.

■ *Be sensitive to cultural differences.* When making contacts, setting up business appointments, or calling on prospective manufacturers in foreign lands, make sure you understand what is acceptable business behavior and what is not. Once again, this is where your research pays off; be sure to study the cultural nuances of doing business in the countries you will visit.

■ *Do your groundwork.* Once you locate potential manufacturers, contact them to set up appointments, and go visit them. Preliminary research is essential to finding reliable sources of supply, but "face time" with representatives from various companies allows entrepreneurs to judge the intangible factors that can make or break a relationship. After months of online research, Cathy Raff, founder of My Stone Company, a business that markets religious jewelry and The Friendship Stone, flew to South Africa to evaluate several mines that were potential suppliers of the stones her company used. "I needed to go meet the people I would be working with," says Raff, who also flew to China to select the factory that produces the embroidered suede pouches that hold her company's products. "Outsourcing is the best way to go because you can get really high quality work from these countries at much lower rates," she says.[57]

■ *Protect your company's intellectual property.* A common problem that many entrepreneurs have encountered with outsourcing is "knockoffs." Some foreign manufacturers see nothing wrong with agreeing to manufacture a product for a company and then selling their own "knockoff" version of it. Securing a nondisclosure agreement and a contract that prohibits such behavior helps, but experts say that securing a patent for the item in the source country itself (not just the United States) is a good idea.

■ *Select a manufacturer.* Using quality, speed of delivery, level of trust, degree of legal protection, costs, and other factors as criteria, select the manufacturer that can do the best job for your company. Be aware that delivery times may be longer—sometimes much longer—for outsourced goods. Items that domestic suppliers can supply within a week or two may take months to arrive from some foreign countries.

■ *Provide an exact model of the product you want manufactured.* Providing a manufacturer with an actual model of the item to be manufactured will save lots of time, mistakes, and problems. One entrepreneur learned this lesson the hard way when he submitted a rough prototype of a product to a Chinese factory with which he had contracted for production. When the first shipment of the products arrived, he was shocked to see that they were exact duplicates—including imperfections and flaws—of the prototype that he had submitted!

■ *Stay in constant contact with the manufacturer and try to build a long-term relationship.* Communication is a key to building and maintaining a successful relationship with a foreign manufacturer. Weekly teleconferences, e-mails, and periodic visits are essential to making sure that your company gets the performance you expect from a foreign manufacturer.

Going global by employing one or more of these nine strategies can put tremendous strain on a small company, but the benefits of cracking international markets can be significant. Not only does going global offer attractive sales and profit possibilities, but it also strengthens the company's competitive skills and enhances its overall reputation. Pleasing tough foreign customers also keeps companies on their competitive toes.

Barriers to International Trade

4. Discuss the major barriers to international trade and their impact on the global economy.

Governments have always used a variety of barriers to block free trade among nations in an attempt to protect businesses within their own borders. The benefit of protecting their own companies, however, comes at the expense of foreign businesses, which face limited access to global markets. Ultimately, customers in nations that restrict free trade pay the price in the form of higher prices and smaller supplies of goods available. Numerous trade barriers—both domestic and international—restrict the freedom of businesses in global trading. Despite these barriers, international trade has grown to more than $14.2 trillion.[58]

Domestic Barriers

Sometimes the biggest barriers potential exporters face are right here at home. Three major domestic roadblocks are common: attitude, information, and financing. Perhaps the biggest barrier to small businesses exporting is the attitude that "I'm too small to export. That's just for big corporations." The first lesson of exporting is "Take nothing for granted about who can export and what you can and cannot export." The first step to building an export program is recognizing that the opportunity to export exists.

Another reason entrepreneurs neglect international markets is a lack of information about how to get started. The key to success in international markets is choosing the correct target market and designing the appropriate strategy to reach it. That requires access to information and research. Although a variety of government and private organizations make volumes of exporting and international marketing information available, many small business owners never use it. A successful global marketing strategy also recognizes that not all international markets are the same. Companies must be flexible and willing to make adjustments to their products and services, promotional campaigns, packaging, and sales techniques.

Another significant obstacle is the lack of export financing available. A common complaint among small exporters is that they lose export business simply because they cannot get the financing to support it. Financial institutions that serve small companies often do not have experience in conducting international business and simply deny loans for international transactions as being too risky.

International Barriers

Domestic barriers are not the only ones export-minded entrepreneurs must overcome. Trading nations also erect obstacles to free trade. Two types of international barriers are common: tariff and nontariff.

Source: (2009) Thaves. Reprinted by permission. Newspaper dist. by UF.

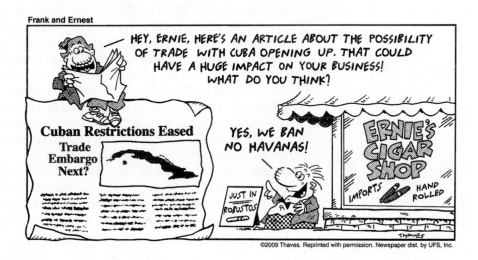

©2009 Thaves. Reprinted with permission. Newspaper dist. by UFS, Inc.

TARIFF BARRIERS. A **tariff** is a tax, or duty, that a government imposes on goods and services imported into that country. Imposing tariffs raises the price of the imported goods—making them less attractive to consumers—and protects the makers of comparable domestic products and services. Established in the United States in 1790 by Alexander Hamilton, the tariff system generated the majority of federal revenues for about 100 years. Today, the *Harmonized Tariff Schedule*, which sets tariffs for products imported into the United States, includes 37,000 categories of goods. The United States imposes tariffs on thousands of items, ranging from brooms and fish fillets to costume jewelry and fence posts. The average tariff on goods imported into the United States is just 1.3 percent, but the U.S. International Trade Commission estimates that eliminating tariffs would expand U.S. exports by $5.5 billion and increase imports by $13.1 billion.[59] After sales of tires exported to the United States from China tripled in just 4 years and several U.S. tire factories closed, the U.S. government imposed a 35 percent tariff on auto and light truck tires. The result was a significant decrease in the supply of low-end tires, those priced between $50 and $60 each, which caused prices to increase by 20 to 25 percent.[60]

Nations across the globe rely on tariffs to protect local manufacturers of certain products. For instance, Japan's tariffs average 5.4 percent, and those in China average 10 percent. If a small company's products are subject to those tariffs, exporting to that nation becomes much more difficult because remaining price competitive with products made by local manufacturers is virtually impossible.

NONTARIFF BARRIERS. Many nations have lowered the tariffs they impose on products and services brought into their borders, but they rely on other nontariff structures as protectionist trade barriers.

Quotas. Rather than impose a direct tariff on certain imported products, nations often use quotas to protect their industries. A **quota** is a limit on the amount of a product imported into a country. The United States imposes quotas on sugar imports from 40 countries, limiting the amount of sugar they can sell in the United States each year.[61] The result of these trade restrictions is that in the United States sugar sells for 56 cents per pound, but the international market price is just 23 cents per pound, 59 percent lower. Other countries impose quotas on everything from shoes to movies in an attempt to protect domestic industries. For instance, China allows only 20 foreign films to be released each year. In addition, foreigners can invest in Chinese cinemas, but they can own no more than 49 percent of the joint venture.[62]

Embargoes. An **embargo** is a total ban on imports of certain products or all products from a particular nation. The motivation for embargoes is not always economic but can involve political differences, environmental disputes, terrorism, and other issues. For instance, the United States imposes embargoes on products from nations it considers to be adversarial, including Cuba, Iran, Iraq, and North Korea, among others. An embargo on trade with Cuba, begun in 1962, still exists today. In other cases, embargoes originate from cultural differences or health reasons. Many countries, including the United States, imposed embargoes on live birds from nations where avian influenza outbreaks occurred.

Dumping. In an effort to grab market share quickly, some companies have been guilty of **dumping** products, selling large quantities of them in foreign countries below cost. The United States has been a dumping target for steel, televisions, shoes, and computer chips in the past. More than 60 nations now have antidumping laws. Under the U.S. Antidumping Act, a company must prove that the foreign company's prices are lower here than in the home country and that U.S. companies are directly harmed. In response to a complaint from U.S.-based companies, the U.S. International Trade Commission ruled that Chinese honey producers were dumping thousands of tons of honey illegally in the United States at unfairly low prices and, as a result, were damaging the ability of U.S. producers to compete. "It's been a struggle for many [beekeepers] to survive," says John Talbert, owner of Sabine Creek Honey Farm in Josephine, Texas. The ITC imposed tariffs of 200 percent and more on honey imported from China.[63]

Piracy. Another barrier to conducting business globally is the threat that counterfeit and pirated products pose to businesses and their customers. The OECD estimates that the proportion of counterfeit and pirated goods in world trade has increased from 1.85 percent in 2000 to 1.95 percent today. Counterfeit and pirated goods cost the U.S. economy $250 billion per year.[64] Pirates and counterfeiters ply their illegal, unethical trade to almost every kind of product, from designer handbags and smartphones to birth control pills and industrial equipment. Not only do counterfeit products erode the profitability of the companies that make the "genuine" articles, but they also can be dangerous or even deadly to consumers who purchase them.

Political Barriers

Entrepreneurs who go global quickly discover a labyrinth of political tangles. Although many American business owners complain of excessive government regulation in the United States, they are often astounded by the complex web of governmental and legal regulations and barriers they encounter in foreign countries.

Companies doing business in politically risky lands face the very real dangers of government takeovers of private property; attempts at coups to overthrow ruling parties; kidnappings, bombings, and other violent acts against businesses and their employees; and other threatening events. Companies' investments of millions of dollars may evaporate overnight in the wake of a government coup or the passage of a law nationalizing an industry (giving control of an entire industry to the government). In 2005, Jeff Ake, owner of Equipment Express, was kidnapped by militants in Iraq while installing bottling equipment that his La Porte, Indiana, company manufactured. His kidnappers called his wife to demand a ransom, and a video of Ake being held at gunpoint appeared on Arabic television network Al-Jazeera. His wife and four children still do not know what happened to Ake.[65]

Business Barriers

U.S. companies doing business internationally quickly learn that business practices and regulations in foreign lands can be quite different from those in the United States. Simply duplicating the practices they have adopted (and have used successfully) in the domestic market and using them in foreign markets is not always a good idea. Perhaps the biggest shock comes in the area of human resources management, where international managers discover that practices common in the United States, such as overtime, women workers, and employee benefits, are restricted, disfavored, or forbidden in other cultures. Business owners new to international business sometimes are shocked at the wide range of labor costs they encounter and the accompanying wide range of skilled labor available. In some countries, what appear to be "bargain" labor rates turn out to be excessively high after accounting for the quality of the labor force and the mandated benefits their governments impose—from company-sponsored housing, meals, and clothing to required profit sharing and extended vacations. For instance, in most European nations, workers are accustomed to 4 to 6 weeks of vacation compared to 2 weeks in the United States.

ENTREPRENEURIAL
Profile

*Harry Tsao and
Talmadge O'Neill:
Smarter.com*

In 2003, Harry Tsao and Talmadge O'Neill launched Smarter.com, a comparison-shopping Web site, in Monrovia, California. The entrepreneurs thought that by hiring software engineers in China they could keep their operating costs low. They opened a branch in Shanghai to handle the back office of their e-commerce operation and hired 10 engineers at bargain salaries. Then Tsao and O'Neill discovered that companies operating in China must pay exorbitant payroll taxes, an unforeseen technicality that cost their fledgling company an unexpected $26,000. "I had no choice," recalls Tsao. "I had to take on those costs."[66]

In many nations, labor unions represent workers in almost every company, yet they play a very different role from the unions in the United States. Although management–union relations are not as hostile as in the United States and strikes are not as common, unions can greatly complicate a company's ability to compete effectively.

Cultural Barriers

The **culture** of a nation includes the beliefs, values, views, and mores that its inhabitants share. Differences in cultures among nations create another barrier to international trade. The diversity of languages, business philosophies, practices, and traditions make international trade more complex than selling to the business down the street. Entrepreneurs wanting to do business in international markets must have a clear understanding and appreciation of the cultures in which they plan to do business. Consider the following examples:

- A U.S. entrepreneur, eager to expand into the European Community, arrives at his company's potential business partner's headquarters in France. Confidently, he strides into the meeting room, enthusiastically pumps his host's hand, slaps him on the back, and says "Tony, I've heard a great deal about you; please, call me Bill." Eager to explain the benefits of his product, he opens his briefcase and gets right down to business. The French executive politely excuses himself and leaves the room before negotiations ever begin, shocked by the American's rudeness and ill manners. Rudeness and ill manners? Yes—from the French executive's perspective.
- Another American business owner flies to Tokyo to close a deal with a Japanese executive. He is pleased when his host invites him to play a round of golf shortly after he arrives. He plays well and manages to win by a few strokes. The Japanese executive invites him to play again the next day, and again he wins by a few strokes. Invited to play another round the

following day, the American asks, "But when are we going to start doing business?" His host, surprised by the question, says, "But we *have* been doing business."

■ The CEO of a successful small company is in China negotiating with several customers on deals, any of which would be significant to the company. On the verge of closing one deal, the CEO sends in his place to the negotiation a young sales representative, thinking that the only thing that remained is to sign the contract. At the meeting, the manager of the Chinese company remarks, "Ah, you are about the same age as my son." Much to the U.S. entrepreneur's surprise, the deal falls through.[67]

When American businesspeople enter international markets for the first time, they often are amazed at the differences in foreign cultures' habits and customs. In the first scenario described, for instance, had the entrepreneur done his homework, he would have known that the French are very formal (back slapping is *definitely* taboo!) and do not typically use first names in business relationships (even among long-time colleagues). In the second scenario, a global manager would have known that the Japanese place a tremendous importance on developing personal relationships before committing to any business deals. Thus, he would have seen the golf games for what they really were: an integral part of building a business relationship. In the final scenario, the U.S. entrepreneur did not understand that status (*shehui dengji*) is extremely important to the Chinese. The Chinese executive would consider negotiating a deal with an executive whose rank in the organization did not at least equal his to be a great insult. That particular deal was doomed the minute the lower-level salesperson walked into the room.

Understanding and heeding these often subtle cultural differences is one of the most important keys to international business success. "There's more to business than just business," says one writer, "particularly when confronting the subtleties of deeply ingrained cultural customs, conventions, and protocols that abound in today's global marketplace."[68] Conducting a business meeting with a foreign executive in the same manner as one with an American businessperson could doom the deal from the outset. Business customs and behaviors that are acceptable—even expected—in this country may be taboo in others.

Entrepreneurs who fail to learn the differences in the habits and customs of the cultures in which they hope to do business are at a distinct disadvantage. When it comes to conducting international business, a lack of understanding of cultures and business practices can be as great a barrier to structuring and implementing a business transaction as an error in the basic assumptions of the deal. Consider, for instance, the American who was in the final stages of contract negotiations with an Indonesian company. Given the size of the contract and his distance from home, the American business executive was nervous. Sitting across from his Indonesian counterpart, the American propped his feet up. Obviously angered, the Indonesian business owner stormed out of the room, refused to sign the contract, and left the American executive totally bewildered. Only later did he discover that exposing the soles of one's shoes to an Indonesian is an insult. Profuse apologies and some delicate negotiations salvaged the deal.[69]

An American businesswoman in London was invited to a party hosted by an advertising agency. Unsure of her ability to navigate the streets and subways of London alone, she approached a British colleague who was driving to the party and asked him, "Could I get a ride with you?" After he turned bright red from embarrassment, he regained his composure and politely said, "Lucky for you I know what you meant." Unknowingly, the young woman had requested a sexual encounter with her colleague, not a lift to the party![70]

Inaccurate translations of documents into other languages often pose embarrassing problems for companies conducting international business.

ENTREPRENEURIAL
Profile

Interactive Magic

Interactive Magic, a North Carolina software company, had introduced several computer games in Germany that had been quite successful. Executives at the small company expected that their newest release, "Capitalism," would be the best selling game yet. After the game hit store shelves in Germany, however, managers discovered that the instructions told customers to use a nail file to get the game running on their computers. In the translation from English to German, the word *file* somehow lost its electronic meaning and became a beauty accessory![71]

Mistranslated ads have left foreign locals scratching their heads, wondering why a company's advertising message would say that. For example, when an ad for KFC that was supposed to say "Finger lickin' good" was translated into Chinese, it came out as "Eat your fingers off." An ad for the Parker Pen Company that was supposed to say "Avoid embarrassment" in Spanish actually said "Avoid pregnancy," leaving Parker Pen executives quite embarrassed themselves.[72]

The accompanying "Lessons from the Street-Smart Entrepreneur" feature shows the importance of learning about a nation's culture before conducting business there.

LESSONS FROM THE STREET-SMART → entrepreneur

The Secret Language of International Business

When U.S. businesspeople enter international markets for the first time, they often are amazed at the differences in foreign cultures' habits and customs. Understanding and heeding these often subtle cultural differences is one of the most important keys to international business success. The maze of cultural variables from one country to another can be confusing, but with proper preparation and a little common sense any manager can handle international transactions successfully. In short, before you pack your bags, do your homework. In most cases, conducting international business successfully requires managers to have unlimited patience, a long-term commitment, and a thorough knowledge of the local market, business practices, and culture. The key for entrepreneurs is learning to be sensitive to the business cultures in which they operate. Consider these pointers from the Street-Smart Entrepreneur:

- Patience is a must for doing business in Spain. Like the French, Spaniards want to get to know business associates before working with them. In the United States, business comes before pleasure, but in Spain business is conducted after dinner, when the drinks and cigars are served. "I've known American businessmen who have shocked their Spanish host by pulling out their portfolios and charts before dinner is even served," says one expert. In Spain, women should avoid crossing their legs; it is considered unladylike. Men usually cross their legs at the knees.

- In India, entrepreneurs who rush in to close a deal quickly often find that the deal never materializes. As in Spain, businesspeople in India prefer to get to know prospective business partners before doing business with them. Indian culture also is far less focused on time than American business is. Entrepreneurs should not be surprised or angered if meetings, dinners, and other events do not start promptly at the appointed hour. Dress codes in India tend to be conservative. Entrepreneurs should avoid

using a person's first name until they are invited to do so; in some parts of India, doing so is considered rude. In restaurants, do not order beef. Although some Indians eat beef, many are vegetarian.

- In Great Britain, businesspeople consider it extremely important to conduct business "properly" with formality and reserve. Boisterous behavior such as backslapping or overindulging in alcohol and ostentatious displays of wealth are considered ill-mannered. The British do not respond to hard-sell tactics but do appreciate well-mannered executives. Politeness and impeccable manners are useful tools for conducting business successfully in Great Britain.

- In Mexico, making business appointments through a well-connected Mexican national will go a long way to assuring successful business deals. "People in Mexico do business with somebody they know, they like, or they're related to," says one expert. Because family and tradition are top priorities for Mexicans, entrepreneurs who discuss their family heritages and can talk knowledgeably about Mexican history are a step ahead. In business meetings, making extended eye contact is considered impolite.

- In China, entrepreneurs will need an ample dose of the "three Ps": patience, patience, patience. Nothing in China—especially business—happens fast! In conversations and negotiations, periods of silence are common; they are a sign of politeness and contemplation. The Chinese view personal space much differently than Americans; in normal conversation, they will stand much closer to their partners. Before doing business with someone, especially foreigners, Chinese businesspeople look to build a personal relationship (*renji hexie*) that demonstrates trust and harmony. Doing so often involves invitations to sporting events, sight-seeing, long dinners that involve talking about everything but business, and home visits, all of which may take months. Be careful when selecting gifts for your Chinese hosts. Clocks, umbrellas, white flowers, and handkerchiefs are inappropriate gifts because of their association with separation and death. A traditional part of Chinese culture involves haggling over the terms of a deal, and Chinese negotiators are very good at it! Howard Schultz, CEO of Starbucks, the coffee retailer, says that China, where Starbucks has nearly 400 stores and plans for hundreds more, "is a complicated market that requires significant discipline and thoughtfulness."

■ American entrepreneurs doing business in the Pacific Rim should avoid hard-sell techniques, which are an immediate turnoff to Asian businesspeople. Harmony, patience, and consensus make good business companions in this region. It is also a good idea to minimize the importance of legal documents in negotiations. Although getting deals and trade agreements down in writing always is advisable, attempting to negotiate detailed contracts (as most U.S. businesspeople tend to do) would insult most Asians, who base their deals on mutual trust and benefits.

■ Japanese executives conduct business much like the British: with an emphasis on formality, thoughtfulness, and respect. Greeting a Japanese executive properly includes a bow and a handshake—showing respect for both cultures. In many traditional Japanese businesses, exchanging gifts at the first meeting is appropriate. Also, a love of golf (the Japanese are crazy about the game) and a willingness to participate in karaoke are real pluses for winning business in Japan. Don't expect to hear Japanese executives say "no," even during a negotiation; they don't want to offend or to appear confrontational. Instead of saying "no," a Japanese negotiator will say, "It is very difficult," "Let us think about that," or "Let us get back to you on that." Similarly, a "yes" from a Japanese executive doesn't necessarily mean that. It could mean, "I understand," "I hear you," or "I don't understand what you mean, but I don't want to embarrass you."

■ In Japan and South Korea, exchanging business cards, known in Japan as *meishi,* is an important business function (unlike Great Britain, where exchanging business cards is less popular). A Western executive who accepts a Japanese companion's card and then

slips it into his pocket or scribbles notes on it has committed a major blunder. Tradition there says that a business card must be treated just as its owner would be—with respect. Travelers should present their own cards using both hands with the card positioned so the recipient can read it. (The flip side should be printed in Japanese, an expected courtesy.)

1. What steps should an entrepreneur take to avoid committing cultural blunders when conducting global business?
2. Select a foreign country in which you are interested. Use the Internet to learn about other tips for conducting business there in a way that shows respect for the culture and its people. Prepare a one-page report on your findings.

Sources: Based on Mariko Sanchanta, "Starbucks Plans Big Expansion in China," *Wall Street Journal,* April 14, 2010, p. B10; John L. Graham and N. Mark Lam, "The Chinese Negotiation," *Harvard Business Review,* October 2003, pp. 82–91; Laura Fortunato, "Japan: Making It in the USA," *Region Focus,* Fall 1997, p. 15; David Stamps, "Welcome to America," *Training,* November 1996, p. 30; Barbara Pachter, "When in Japan, Don't Cross Your Legs," *Business Ethics,* March–April 1996, p. 50; Tom Dunkel, "A New Breed of People Gazers," *Insight,* January 13, 1992, pp. 10–14; M. Katherine Glover, "Do's and Taboos," *Business America,* August 13, 1990, pp. 2–6; Deidre Sullivan, "An American Businesswoman's Guide to Japan," *Overseas Business,* Winter 1990, pp. 50–55; Stephanie Barlow, "Let's Make a Deal," *Entrepreneur,* May 1991, p. 40; "Worldly Wise," *Entrepreneur,* March 1991, p. 40; David Altany, "Culture Clash," *IndustryWeek,* October 2, 1998, pp. 13–20; Edward T. Hall, "The Silent Language of Overseas Business," *Harvard Business Review,* May–June 1960, pp. 5–14; John S. McClenahen, Andrew Rosenbaum, and Michael Williams, "As Others See U.S.," *IndustryWeek,* January 8, 1990, pp. 80–82; James Bredin, "Japan Needs to be Understood," *IndustryWeek,* April 20, 1992, pp. 24–26; David L. James, "Don't Think About Winning," *Across the Board,* April 1992, pp. 49–51; "When in Japan," *Small Business Reports,* January 1992, p. 8; Bernie Ward, "Other Climates, Other Cultures," *Sky,* March 1992, pp. 72–86; Roger E. Axtell, *Gestures: The Do's and Taboos of Body Language Around the World,* New York: John Wiley & Sons, 1991; Suzanne Kreiter, "Customs Differ Widely from Those in the U.S.," *Greenville News,* September 26, 1993, p. 15D; Bradford W. Ketchum, "Going Global: East Asia-Pacific Rim," *Inc.* (Special Advertising Section), May 20, 1997; Valerie Frazee, "Getting Started in Mexico," *Global Workforce,* January 1997, pp. 16–17; Shawna McAlearny, "Business Mistakes: 11 Cultural Faux Pas You Should Never Make in China," *CIO,* April 21, 2009, *www.cio.com/article/490168/ Business_Mistakes_11_Cultural_Faux_Pas_You_Should_Never_Make_i n_China*; Shawna McAlearny, "Business Mistakes: 10 Cultural Faux Pas You Should Never Make in India," *CIO,* April 17, 2009, *www.cio.com/ article/489763/Business_Mistakes_10_Cultural_Faux_Pas_You_Should_ Never_Make_in_India.*

International Trade Agreements

5. Describe the trade agreements that have the greatest influence on foreign trade.

In an attempt to boost world trade, nations have created a variety of trade agreements over the years. Although hundreds of agreements are paving the way for free trade across the world, the following stand out with particular significance: the World Trade Organization (WTO), the North American Free Trade Agreement (NAFTA), and the Dominican Republic-Central American Free Trade Agreement (CAFTA-DR).

World Trade Organization

The World Trade Organization (WTO) was established in January 1995 and replaced the General Agreement on Tariffs and Trade (GATT), the first global tariff agreement, which was created in 1947 and designed to reduce tariffs among member nations. The WTO, currently with 153 member countries, is the only international organization that establishes rules for trade among nations. Its member countries represent more than 97 percent of all world trade. The rules and agreements of the WTO, called the **multilateral trading system**, are the result of negotiations among its members. The WTO actively implements the rules established by the Uruguay Round negotiations of General Agreement on Tariffs and Trade from 1986 to 1994 and continues to negotiate additional trade agreements.

Through the agreements of the WTO, members commit themselves to nondiscriminatory trade practices. These agreements spell out the rights and obligations of each member country. Each member country receives guarantees that its exports will be treated fairly and consistently in other member countries' markets. The WTO's General Agreement on Trade in Services (GATS) addresses specific industries, including banking, insurance, telecommunications, and tourism. In addition, the WTO's intellectual property agreement, which covers patents, copyrights, and trademarks, defines rules for protecting ideas and creativity across borders.

In addition to the development of agreements among members, the WTO is involved in the resolution of trade disputes among members. The WTO system is designed to encourage dispute resolutions through consultation. If this approach fails, the WTO has a multi-stage procedure that culminates in a ruling by a panel of experts.

The North American Free Trade Agreement

The North American Free Trade Agreement (NAFTA) created the world's largest free trade zone among Canada, Mexico, and the United States. A **free trade zone** is an association of countries that have agreed to eliminate trade barriers—both tariff and nontariff—among partner nations. Under the provisions of NAFTA, these barriers were eliminated for trade among the three countries, but each remained free to set its own tariffs on imports from nonmember nations.

NAFTA forged a unified U.S.–Canada–Mexico market of 456.5 million people with a total annual output of more than $17 trillion of goods and services. This important trade agreement binds together the three nations on the North American continent into a single trading unit stretching from the Yukon to the Yucatan. NAFTA has made trade less cumbersome and more profitable for companies of all sizes and has opened export opportunities for many businesses. Today, Canada and Mexico are the largest trading partners for companies in the United States.

The Dominican Republic-Central America Free Trade Agreement

The Dominican Republic-Central America Free Trade Agreement (CAFTA-DR) is to Central America what NAFTA is to North America. The agreement, which took effect on August 2, 2005, is designed to promote free trade among the United States and six Central American countries: Costa Rica, El Salvador, Guatemala, Honduras, Dominican Republic, and Nicaragua. U.S. exports to these seven nations are $20 billion a year.[73]

In addition to reducing tariffs among these nations, CAFTA-DR protects U.S. companies' investments and intellectual property in the region, simplifies the export process for U.S. companies, and provides easier access to Central American markets.

ENTREPRENEURIAL
Profile

Maureen Coughlin:
Clabber Girl

Lower tariffs and the elimination of other trade barriers through CAFTA-DR allowed Clabber Girl, a small company in Terre Haute, Indiana, to increase export sales of its line of baking powder, baking soda, corn starch, and gourmet cookie mixes to Central America. The company worked with a variety of trade agencies to develop customers in Central America and has since expanded its export program to include South America and Asia. "Because of reduced tariffs on our products, buyers in this region are more interested in importing our products," says Maureen Coughlin, the company's export sales manager. "We find that free trade agreement countries cultivate stronger import–export trade relations."[74]

Conclusion

For a rapidly growing number of small businesses, conducting business on a global basis will be the key to future success. A small company going global exposes itself to certain risks, but, if planned and executed properly, a global strategy can produce huge rewards. To remain competitive, businesses of all sizes must assume a global posture. Global effectiveness requires managers to be able to leverage workers' skills, company resources, and customer know-how across borders and throughout cultures across the world. Managers also must concentrate on maintaining competitive cost structures and a focus on the core of every business—the *customer*! Robert G. Shaw, CEO of International Jensen Inc., a global maker of home and automobile stereo speakers, explains the importance of retaining that customer focus as his company pursues its global strategy: "We want [our customers] to have the attitude of [our] being across the street. If we're going to have a global company, we have to behave in that mode—whether [the customer is] across the street—or 7 miles, 7 minutes, or 7,000 miles away."[75]

Few businesses can afford the luxury of limiting their target markets to the boundaries of their home country's borders. The manager of one global business, who discourages the use of the word *domestic* among his employees, says, "Where's 'domestic' when the world is your market?"[76] Although there are no sure-fire rules for going global, small businesses wanting to become successful international competitors should observe these guidelines:

- Make yourself at home in all three of the world's key markets—North America, Europe, and Asia. This triad of regions is forging a new world order in trade that will dominate global markets for years to come. Small companies that focus on business opportunities in the fast-growing economies of Brazil, Russia, India, and China are likely to benefit most because forecasts call for these four nations to account for 44 percent of global GDP by 2050.[77]
- Appeal to the similarities within the various regions in which you operate but recognize the differences in their specific cultures. Although the European Union is a single trading bloc composed of 27 countries with a combined population of 498 million people, smart entrepreneurs know that each country has its own cultural uniqueness and do not treat them as a unified market.
- Be willing to commit the necessary resources to make your global efforts successful. Going global requires an investment of time, talent, money, and patience.
- Develop new products for the world market. Make sure your products and services measure up to world-class quality standards.
- Use the many resources available, such as the U.S. Commercial Service and the International Trade Administration, to research potential markets and to determine the ideal target market for your products.
- Familiarize yourself with foreign customs and languages; constantly scan, clip, and build a file on the cultures of countries where you are likely to do business—their lifestyles, values, customs, and business practices.
- Learn to understand your customers from the perspective of *their* culture, not your own. Bridge cultural gaps by being willing to adapt your business practices to suit their preferences and customs.
- "Glocalize." Make global decisions about products, markets, and management, but allow local employees to make tactical decisions about packaging, advertising, and service. Building relationships with local companies that have solid reputations in a region or a country can help overcome resistance, lower risks, and encourage residents to think of them as local companies.
- Make positive and preferably visible contributions to the local community. A company's social responsibility does not stop at the borders of its home country. Seattle-based Starbucks enhances its reputation in the Chinese communities in which it does business by donating coffee and snacks for local celebrations such as the Autumn Moon Festival. Once, when a group of protesters approached the U.S. Embassy in Beijing, they stopped at a nearby Starbucks café to buy coffee. Rather than being the object of a protest, the branch actually saw sales climb![78]
- Train employees to think globally, send them on international trips, and equip them with state-of-the-art communications technology.

- Hire local managers to staff foreign offices and branches.
- Do whatever seems best wherever it seems best, even if people at home lose jobs or responsibilities.
- Consider using partners and joint ventures to break into foreign markets you cannot penetrate on your own.
- Be patient. International business often takes time to cultivate. "Selling to the world does not happen overnight," says Laurel Delaney, an international business expert and author. "It is a slow process that requires thought, discipline, and lots of hard work. However, go global today, and you could fulfill your own version of the American dream."[79]

By its very nature, going global can be a frightening experience for an entrepreneur considering the jump into international markets. Most of those who have already made the jump, however, have found that the benefits outweigh the risks and that their companies are much stronger because of it.

Chapter Review

1. Explain why "going global" has become an integral part of many entrepreneurs marketing strategies.
   - Companies that move into international business can reap many benefits, including offsetting sales declines in the domestic market; increasing sales and profits; extending their products' life cycles; lowering manufacturing costs; improving competitive position; raising quality levels; and becoming more customer-oriented.
2. Describe the nine principal strategies for going global.
   - Perhaps the simplest and least expensive way for a small business to begin conducting business globally is to establish a site on the World Wide Web. Companies wanting to sell goods on the Web should establish a secure order and payment system for online customers.
   - Trade intermediaries such as export management companies, export trading companies, manufacturer's export agents, export merchants, resident buying offices, and foreign distributors can serve as a small company's "export department."
   - In a domestic joint venture, two or more U.S. small companies form an alliance for the purpose of exporting their goods and services abroad. In a foreign joint venture, a domestic small business forms an alliance with a company in the target area.
   - Some small businesses enter foreign markets by licensing businesses in other nations to use their patents, trademarks, copyrights, technology, processes, or products.
   - Over the last decade, a growing number of franchises have been attracted to international markets to boost sales and profits as the domestic market has become increasingly saturated with outlets and much tougher to wring growth from. International franchisors sell virtually every kind of product or service imaginable in global markets. Most franchisors have learned that they must modify their products and services to suit local tastes and customs.
   - Some countries lack a hard currency that is convertible into other currencies, so companies doing business there must rely on countertrading or bartering. A countertrade is a transaction in which a business selling goods in a foreign country agrees to promote investment and trade in that country. Bartering involves trading goods and services for other goods and services.
   - Although small companies account for 91 percent of the companies involved in exporting, they generate only 21 percent of U.S. export sales. However, small companies, realizing the incredible profit potential it offers, are making exporting an ever-expanding part of their marketing plans.
   - Once established in international markets, some small businesses set up permanent locations there. Although they can be very expensive to establish and maintain, international locations give businesses the opportunity to stay in close contact with their international customers.

3. Explain how to build a thriving export program.
   - Building a successful export program takes patience and research. Steps include: realize that even the tiniest firms have the potential to export; analyze your product or service; analyze your commitment to exporting; research markets and pick your target; develop a distribution strategy; find your customer; find financing; ship your goods; and collect your money.
4. Discuss the major barriers to international trade and their impact on the global economy.
   - Three domestic barriers to international trade are common: the attitude that "we're too small to export," lack of information on how to get started in global trade, and a lack of available financing.
   - International barriers include tariffs, quotas, embargoes, dumping, and political business, and cultural barriers.
5. Describe the trade agreements that have the greatest influence on foreign trade.
   - Created in 1947, the General Agreement on Tariffs and Trade (GATT), the first global tariff agreement, was designed to reduce tariffs among member nations and to facilitate trade across the globe.
   - The World Trade Organization (WTO) was established in 1995 and replaced GATT. The WTO has 153 member nations and represents more than 97 percent of all global trade. The WTO is the governing body that resolves trade disputes among members.
   - The North American Free Trade Agreement (NAFTA) created a free trade area among Canada, Mexico, and the United States. The agreement created an association that knocked down trade barriers, both tariff and nontariff, among these partner nations.
   - The Dominican Republic-Central America Free Trade Agreement (CAFTA-DR) is designed to promote free trade among the United States and six Central American countries.

Discussion Questions

1. Why must entrepreneurs learn to think globally?
2. What forces are driving small businesses into international markets?
3. Outline the nine strategies that small businesses can use to go global.
4. Describe the various types of trade intermediaries small business owners can use. Explain the functions they perform.
5. What is a domestic joint venture? A foreign joint venture? What advantages does taking on an international partner through a joint venture offer? What are the disadvantages?
6. What mistakes are first-time exporters most likely to make? Outline the steps a small company should take to establish a successful export program.
7. What are the benefits of establishing international locations? What are the disadvantages?
8. Describe the barriers businesses face when trying to conduct business internationally. How can a small business owner overcome these obstacles?
9. What is a tariff? A quota? What impact do they have on international trade?

10. Thirty furniture makers in the United States recently asked the U.S. International Trade Commission (ITC) to impose high tariffs on Chinese makers of wooden bedroom furniture for dumping their products in the U.S. market at extremely low prices. The U.S. manufacturers claimed that the Chinese imports single-handedly sent their industry into a deep tailspin. The Chinese factory owners contend that their low-cost furniture is the result of taking a labor-intensive product and building it with low-priced workers in high-tech modern factories. Identify the stakeholders in this trade dispute. What are the consequences for each stakeholder likely to be if the ITC were to impose tariffs on Chinese furniture? What impact do tariffs have on international trade? If you served on the ITC, what factors would you consider in making your decision? How would you vote in this case? Explain.
11. What impact have the WTO and NAFTA had on small companies wanting to go global? What provisions are included in these trade agreements?
12. What advice would you offer an entrepreneur interested in launching a global business effort?

Are there global opportunities for your business? If so, include them as an "opportunity" in your SWOT analysis. Review

the other sections that will benefit from incorporating these global plans into your business plan strategy. For example, you may need to address your global strategy in the marketing strategy and the Web site sections of your business plan. You may need to include additional expenses in the financial section of your business plan relating to your global strategy.

On the Web

A number of Web resources are available that may assist you with developing global strategies. You will find several of those links at the Companion Web site at *www.pearsonhighered.com/scarborough*.

In the Software

If you plan to employ a global strategy, make certain that you have addressed that intent in your business plan. International activity of any kind will have implications to several sections of your business plan, including your products and services, market analysis, strategy, implementation, Web plans, management, and financial sections.

This is also an excellent time to review your entire plan, paying specific attention to the summary sections at the beginning of each major section. You may have used these areas for notes and now is a good time to review what you

have written in each of these sections. Make certain the summaries provide a brief overview of what each section contains. Those sections include:

- Company
- Product and Services
- Market Analysis
- Strategy and Implementation
- Web Plan
- Management Plan
- Financial Plan

These initial introductory statements will add flow to your plan. You may also want to review each section to avoid redundancy and optimize the efficiency of your overall plan.

Building Your Business Plan

As you near the final stages of creating your business plan, have others review your plan. Do they understand the "story" your business plan is telling? Do they follow your rationale? Do they have questions that the plan should address? Based on their comments, assess whether the plan is successful at communicating your message. If there are deficiencies, make the necessary changes to improve your plan.

Endnotes

1. "International Business Owners Survey 2006: Key Findings," Grant Thornton, June 2006, *www.internationalbusinessreport.com/main/index1.php?page=14&lang=en&id=120811&country_id=0*; "U.S. Business Embraces Global Growth," *Sales & Marketing Management's Performance Newsletter*, October 15, 2006, p. 1.
2. Ian Mount, "Tips for Increasing Sales in International Markets," *New York Times*, April 21, 2010, *www.nytimes.com/2010/04/22/business/smallbusiness/22sbiz.html*.
3. "International Trade Statistics 2009: World Merchandise Exports by Region and Selected Economy," World Trade Organization, *www.wto.org/english/res_e/statis_e/its2009_e/its09_toc_e.htm*.
4. "Emerging Markets: Leading the Way to Recovery," International Business Report, Grant Thornton, 2010, p. 5.
5. Ibid., p. 3.
6. Jack Stack with Bo Burlingham, "My Awakening," *Inc.*, April 2007, pp. 93–97.
7. Leigh Buchanan, "Going Global," *Inc.*, April 2007, p. 91.
8. Ted Miller, "Can America Compete in the Global Economy?" *Kiplinger's Personal Finance Magazine*, November 1991, p. 8.
9. Bernard Wysocki, Jr., "Going Global in the New World," *Wall Street Journal*, September 21, 1990, p. R3.
10. Matt Glynn, "Setting Sites on Small Business Exports," *Buffalo News*, April 21, 2010, *www.buffalonews.com/2010/04/20/1025651/setting-sights-on-small-business.html*.
11. Michael V. Copeland, "The Mighty Micro-Multinational," *Business 2.0*, July 2006, pp. 106–114.
12. "Small and Medium Size Businesses Export Insights and Opportunities: Executive Summary," CompTIA, January 2010, pp. 3, 4.
13. "Globesmanship," *Across the Board*, January–February 1990, p. 26.
14. Michael Barrier, "Why Small Looms Large in the Global Economy," *Nation's Business*, February 1994, p. 9; Vivian Pospisil, "Global Paradox: Small Is Powerful," *IndustryWeek*, July 18, 1994, p. 29.
15. Michael Barrier, "A Global Reach for Small Firms," *Nation's Business*, April 1994, p. 66.
16. Jeremy Main, "How to Go Global—And Why," *Fortune*, August 28, 1989, p. 70.
17. "Internet Usage Statistics: The Big Picture," Internet World Stats 2009, *www.internetworldstats.com/stats.htm*.
18. Joey Holleman, "Classic Wooden Boats Ready to Fulfill Dreams," *The State*, March 14, 2010, *www.thestate.com/2010/03/14/1198132/classic-wooden-boats-ready-to.html*.
19. "Who We Are," eBay, *www.ebayinc.com/who*; Rick Aristotle Munarriz, "Lights Out eBay," The Motley Fool, January 24, 2008, *www.fool.com/investing/general/2008/01/24/lights-out-ebay.aspx*.
20. "Sports Closeouts Equal Millions," *Rich Couples*, June 14, 2007, *www.richcouples.com/sport-closeouts-equal-millions/*; "eBay Success Story: From $800 to $3.3 Million in 3 Years," *Fox News*, March 28, 2007, *www.youtube.com/watch?v=eTnf2cJUxLQ*.
21. "Think Global," Kentucky World Trade Center, July 14, 2006, *www.kwtc.org/enews/071406/eleven.htm*; "About Us," IMPEX, *www.rgrana.com/about.htm*; "About Arch Environmental," Arch Environmental, *www.aeec.com/Help/About.aspx*.
22. Ian Mount, "Tips for Increasing Sales in International Markets," *New York Times*, April 21, 2010, *www.nytimes.com/2010/04/22/business/smallbusiness/22sbiz.html*.
23. Jennifer LeClaire, "How to Take Your Small Business Global," *E-Commerce Times*, June 20, 2006, *www.ecommercetimes.com/story/50910.html?wlc=1276800833*.
24. Joseph E. Pattison, "Global Joint Ventures," *Overseas Business*, Winter 1990, p. 25.
25. Polly Larson, "Opening Doors to Emerging Markets," International Franchise Association, *www.ifa.org/intl/News/Prjf6.asp*.
26. Scott Deveau, "Bombardier Joint Venture Wins Big in China," *Financial Post*, September 28, 2009, *www.financialpost.com/news-sectors/story.html?id=2042464*.
27. David J. Kaufman, "What a Ride!" *Entrepreneur*, May 2007, pp. 108–113.
28. William Edwards, "International Expansion: Do Opportunities Outweigh Challenges?" *Franchising World*, February 2008, *www.franchise.org/Franchise-News-Detail.aspx?id=37992*.
29. Howard Dahl, "How I Did It," *Inc.*, April 2007, pp. 102–105.
30. Rich Laden, "International Trade a Key for Local Businesses, Chamber Speaker Says," *Colorado Springs Gazette*, May, 18, 2010, *www.gazette.com/articles/international-99007-trade-local.html*.
31. *Small and Medium Size Business Export Insights and Opportunities*, CompTIA, January 2010, p. 3.
32. Ian Mount, "Tips for Increasing Sales in International Markets," *New York Times*, April 21, 2010, *www.nytimes.com/2010/04/22/business/smallbusiness/22sbiz.html*.
33. *A Profile of U.S. Exporting Companies, 2006–2007*, U.S. Census Bureau, U.S. Department of Commerce, Washington, DC: April 9, 2009, p. 6.
34. Geoff Williams, "It's a Small World After All," *Entrepreneur*, May 2004, pp. 39–43; Joshua Kurlantzick, "Stay Home?" *Entrepreneur*, February 2003, pp. 58–59; *Small and Medium-Sized Exporting*

Companies: A Statistical Handbook, International Trade Administration, Office of Trade and Industry Information (Washington, DC: 2005), p. 1.

35. Paul C. Hsu, "Profiting from a Global Mind-Set," *Nation's Business*, June 1994, p. 6.

36. David Newton, "Shipping News," *Entrepreneur*, February 2004, p. 22.

37. "Success Stories: J&N Enterprises," Indiana Small Business Development Center, *www.isbdc.org/default.aspx?action=SuccessStories&id=29.*

38. Jan Alexander, "To Sell Well Overseas, Customize," *Your Company*, Fall 1995, p. 15.

39. Joshua Kurlantzick, "Stay Home?" *Entrepreneur*, February 2003, pp. 58–59.

40. Frances Huffman, "Hello, World!" *Entrepreneur*, August 1990, p. 108.

41. *Small and Medium Size Business Export Insights and Opportunities*, CompTIA, January 2010, p. 6.

42. "Foresight 2020: Economic, Industry, and Corporate Trends," Economist Intelligence Unit, *The Economist*, 2006, p. 7.

43. Lee Smith, "Modern India," Special Advertising Section, *Fortune*, April 12, 2010, pp. S1–S12.

44. Ian Mount, "Tips for Increasing Sales in International Markets," *New York Times*, April 21, 2010, *www.nytimes.com/2010/04/22/business/smallbusiness/22sbiz.html.*

45. Mariko Sanchanta, "Starbucks Plans Big Expansion in China," *Wall Street Journal*, April 14, 2010, p. B10.

46. Eric Decker, "The Art of the Trade Mission," *Small Business Times*, June 8, 2007, *www.biztimes.com/news/2007/6/8/the-art-of-the-trade-mission.*

47. "Trade Missions Testimonials," Automation Alley, *www.automationalley.com/autoalley/International+Business+Center/Trade+Missions/Testimonials.htm*; "Past Missions," Automation Alley, *www.automationalley.com/autoalley/International+Business+Center/Trade+Missions/Past+Missions/China2002.htm.*

48. Marcia Pledger, "Woman Builds Craft Hobby into Multimillion Dollar Importing Business," *Everything Cleveland*, November 19, 2009, *www.cleveland.com/business/index.ssf/2009/11/post_19.html.*

49. "Success Stories," Export Finance Center of Washington, *www.efacw.org/success-stories/*; "News," Web Press, *www.webpresscorp.com/News2.html.*

50. Charlotte Mulhern, "Fast Forward," *Entrepreneur*, October 1997, p. 34.

51. Matt Glynn, "Setting Sites on Small Business Exports," *Buffalo News*, April 21, 2010, *www.buffalonews.com/2010/04/20/1025651/setting-sights-on-small-business.html.*

52. Daniel Kaufmann and Shang-Jin Wei, "Does 'Grease Money' Speed Up the Wheels of Commerce?" World Bank, *www.worldbank.org/wbi/governance/pdf/grease.pdf.*

53. *International Business Attitudes to Corruption*, Simmons & Simmons, 2006, p. 7.

54. Clemmie Newton-Taylor, "Trends in the Global Outsourcing Market," *Executive View*, June 9, 2010, *www.executiveview.com/knowledge_centre.php?id=11693.*

55. "The Growing Company: Big Feet Pajamas," Advertising Insert, *Fast Company*, June 2009, p. 18; "Company Overview," Alibaba.com, *http://news.alibaba.com/specials/aboutalibaba/index.html?tracelog=24581_foot_company_info.*

56. Mark Henricks, "The New China?" *Entrepreneur*, February 2006, pp. 17–18.

57. Michelle Wu, "How I . . . Hopscotched the Globe to Build My Business," *Wall Street Journal*, January 15, 2010, *http://online.wsj.com/article/SB10001424052748704281204575002943447096122.html.*

58. "International Trade Statistics 2009," World Trade Organization, *www.wto.org/english/res_e/statis_e/its2009_e/its09_toc_e.htm.*

59. *The Economic Effects of Significant U.S. Import Restraints, Sixth Update*, United States International Trade Commission (Washington, DC: February 2009), pp. ix–x.

60. Edmund L. Andrews, "U.S. Adds Tariffs on Chinese Tires," *New York Times*, September 11, 2009, *www.nytimes.com/2009/09/12/business/global/12tires.html*; Timothy Aeppel, "Tariff on Tires to Cost Consumers," *Wall Street Journal*, September 14, 2009, p. A3.

61. Bob Meyer, "Sugar Import Quota Increase Being Considered," *Brownfield Ag News for America*, April 14, 2010, *http://brownfieldagnews.com/2010/04/14/sugar-import-quota-increase-being-considered/*; Mattie Duppler, "Sickeningly Sweet—Sugar Quotas and Obama's Protectionism," *Americans for Tax Reform*, August 25, 2009, *www.atr.org/sickeningly-sweet-sugar-quotas-obamas-protectionism-a3758.*

62. Chi-Chi Zhang, "China: Theaters Must Meet Domestic Movie Quota," *ABC News*, January 27, 2010, *http://abcnews.go.com/Entertainment/wireStory?id=9672337.*

63. Eric Berger, "Honey from China Adds to U.S. Beekeepers' Woes," *Spartanburg Herald-Journal*, May 16, 2010, p. A4.

64. *Magnitude of Counterfeiting and Piracy of Tangible Products: An Update*, Organization for Economic Cooperation and Development, November 2009, pp. 1–2.

65. Jason Hanna, "Five Years After Iraq Abduction, Family Tries Making Own Closure," *CNN*, April 11, 2010, *www.cnn.com/2010/LIVING/04/11/missing.iraq.ake.altaie/index.html.*

66. Michelle Tsai, "Shanghai Surprises: The Perils of Opening an Office in China," *Inc.*, March 2007, pp. 47–49.

67. John L. Graham and N. Mark Lam, "The Chinese Negotiation," *Harvard Business Review*, October 2003, p. 87.

68. Stephen J. Simurda, "Trade Secrets," *Entrepreneur*, May 1994, p. 120.

69. Edward T. Hall, "The Silent Language of Overseas Business," *Harvard Business Review*, May–June 1960, pp. 5–14.

70. Lawrence Van Gelder, "It Pays to Watch Words, Gestures While Abroad," *Greenville News*, April 7, 1996, p. 8E.

71. Anton Piëch, "Speaking in Tongues," *Inc.*, June 2003, p. 50.

72. Anton Piëch, "Lost in the Translation," *Inc.*, June 2003, *www.inc.com/magazine/20030601/25511.html.*

73. "CAFTA-DR," Office of the United States Trade Representative, *www.ustr.gov/trade-agreements/free-trade-agreements/cafta-dr-dominican-republic-central-america-fta.*

74. "Indiana Food Supplier Doubles International Business Thanks to Food Export Midwest Programs and Services," Food Export USA, 2009, *www.foodexportusa.org/success/story19.htm*; "Free Trade Agreements Open Door to Foreign Markets," *Global Food Marketer*, May–June 2008, p. 1.

75. John S. McClenahen, "Sound Thinking," *IndustryWeek*, May 3, 1993, p. 28.

76. Jeremy Main, "How to Go Global—And Why," *Fortune*, August 28, 1989, p. 70.

77. "Businesses Capitalising on Opportunities in the World's Fastest Growing Economies," Grant Thornton, February 2007, *www.internationalbusinessreport.com/main/index1.php?page=131&lang=en&id=114557&country_id=0.*

78. Orit Gadiesh and Jean-Marie Pean, "Think Globally, Market Locally," *Wall Street Journal*, September 9, 2003, p. B2.

79. Jennifer LeClaire, "How to Take Your Small Business Global," *E-Commerce Times*, June 20, 2006, *www.ecommercetimes.com/story/50910.html?wlc=1276800833.*

Case
Dogswell

Will a small company's new product line put it in peril?

Within months of the failure of his first company, Clear Day, a natural beverage company, Marco Giannini was busy launching another business, Dogswell, a company that makes all-natural, healthy dog treats that contain supplements to help with conditions such as hip dysplasia and arthritis—problems that his childhood dog, Emily, suffered from. Giannini experimented with recipes before hitting on the right one and found a manufacturer to make the treats. In a tribute to guerrilla marketing, Giannini loaded his car with Dogswell treats and visited more than 200 independent pet stores, asking them to give his new product, Happy Hips, a chance. Many of them did, and in its first year Dogswell's revenue was $500,000. Four years later, Dogswell appeared on *Inc.* magazine's list of the fastest growing small companies in the United States, with 21 employees and sales of $17 million.

Giannini had bigger plans, however. He wanted to launch a line of pet foods to round out the company's successful pet treats, taking the company into the much larger market for natural pet food. "I wanted to become a household name, and I figured food was the way to get us there," he says. He worked with several food scientists to develop a recipe for a healthy grain-free dry dog food called Nutrisca and set up a series of canine focus groups. The results were even better than Giannini had expected: Dogs preferred Nutrisca 15 to 1 over the leading natural dog food brand. Giannini sent his sales force into the field to conduct focus groups with pet owners to determine the most effective packaging.

Giannini faced the same question he had years before when he first launched Dogswell: What is the best way to launch a product on a limited marketing budget? Making personal calls on retailers was impractical now that major chains such as Target and Whole Foods carried the company's products. Giannini hired 15 new people, most of them in sales, to roll out the new line of dog food. To entice customers to try Nutrisca, Dogswell offered coupons for a free bag of Nutrisca (normally priced at $10.99) with every purchase of a bag of Dogswell treats, which retail between $16 and $20.

As with many new products, sales were slow, and the coupons that retailers were submitting for rebates were straining the company's cash flow. However, Giannini and CFO Berenice Officer were distracted by ongoing meetings with TSG Consumer Partners, a San Francisco-based private investment company that Dogswell had been negotiating with for months in an effort to raise capital to fund the company's brand-building strategy. Giannini and Officer closed an equity investment deal with TSG on December 31, but when they returned to their Los Angeles headquarters they discovered that the coupon giveaway was costing the company $100,000 a month and devastating its profits and cash flow. In addition, the promotion was not generating repeat buyers fast enough. Giannini and Officer also realized that customers purchased dog food less often than they did treats and that the profit margins on dog food were less than those on dog treats. For the first time in its history, Dogswell had incurred a quarterly loss and was clearly heading for another one. "I felt like I was losing control of the company," says a frustrated Giannini.

Giannini and Officer had less than 3 months to create a plan to stop the damage that the pet food line was causing and put together a presentation for TSG explaining their strategy and why it would work. Giannini knew all too well the stories of other companies whose equity investors had ousted their founders at the first sign of trouble. Would he suffer the same fate?

Questions

1. What dangers do entrepreneurs face when they court equity investors to provide capital to finance their companies' growth? What steps can they take to minimize these risks?
2. Develop a strategy to return Dogswell to profitability.
3. Outline at least five components for a guerrilla marketing strategy for Nutrisca. How could Dogswell tap into the power of social marketing as part of its guerrilla marketing strategy?

Source: Based on Nitasha Tiku, "Case Study: Dogswell," *Inc.*, December 2009–January 2010, pp. 56–63.

From Case 1 of *Effective Small Business Management: An Entrepreneurial Approach*, 10/e. Norman M. Scarborough.

Case
Zatswho LLC

Can a mother–daughter team be successful entrepreneurs?

Trish Cooper, 52, spent the last 13 years of her career working as the chief financial officer for a small telecommunications company near her home in Hope, New Jersey. When the company merged with another business and moved out of state, Cooper lost her job. She sent out lots of resumes to other businesses but knew that her job prospects were slim because of her age and an ongoing recession. She began spending more time with her granddaughter, Gianna, using family photographs to teach the child about family members. There was only one problem: "She was destroying my photos," says Cooper, who began laminating the photographs.

That's when Cooper had a flash of inspiration. "Our 'photo recognition' game was such fun, and she was learning so much," says Cooper. "What if I make a 'real' game out of it, using individual photo flashcards that are soft and she can hold in her own little hands?" Cooper envisioned a learning tool for toddlers that consisted of soft, flexible protective frames into which parents could slip family photographs and create their own flashcards. She began researching the market. "I learned there were no products on the market like that," she says.

Cooper made a few prototypes herself from nontoxic foam and put them in a small tote-bag carrying case but realized that she would need help to launch her business. Cooper turned to the one person who had been advising her all along: her 26-year-old daughter Carrie Schwinoff. "She was a stay-at-home mom," says Cooper. "I said, 'Look, you are not going to have another opportunity like this to be a business owner.'" Schwinoff agreed because she wanted to supplement her family's income but retain flexibility in her schedule to care for Gianna. She also liked the idea of building a business with her mother. "She's my best friend, my partner in crime," laughs Schwinoff.

Cooper invested $30,000 in the startup, which they named Zatswho, and the two women assembled 500 sets of Zatswho cards and began selling them. One of their first decisions was dividing business responsibilities. Cooper has a strong financial background and serves as CEO and CFO. Schwinoff, who has a degree in marketing, is responsible for sales and marketing. "Tweeting wasn't something I could wrap my head around,"

says Cooper. As in any business, disagreements arise, but the mother–daughter entrepreneurs have managed them effectively. For instance, Schwinoff thought that her mother's use of the word "tactile" on the product's packaging missed the mark. "Why don't we say 'pliable' or 'sensory?'" asked Schwinoff. "People get that more easily." They changed the wording on the packaging to "soft" and "easy to hold." "Because I am the mother and she is my daughter, my natural feeling might be, 'I know better because I am more experienced.' But I have to listen to her point of view. We are both learning that it takes discipline and respect to make this work."

Cooper and Schwinoff are negotiating with a U.S.-based company that has a manufacturing operation in China to mass-produce Zatswho flashcards, which currently sell for $15.95 per set in stores in seven states.

Questions

1. What tips can you offer Cooper and Schwinoff about family members who start and run a business together? What pitfalls would you warn them to avoid?
2. Suppose that Cooper and Schwinoff had approached you when they were launching Zatswho concerning the form of ownership they should use. Which form of ownership do you recommend they use. Why?
3. Work with a team of your classmates to brainstorm potential groups of people who make up Zatswho's target market.
4. Help Cooper and Schwinoff develop a guerrilla marketing strategy for Zatswho. Write a two-page memo to Cooper and Schwinoff that highlights the key points of your strategy and the reasoning behind each one.
5. Visit the Zatswho Web site at *www.zatswho.com*. What recommendations can you make for improving the site?

Sources: Based on Colleen Debaise, Emily Maltby, and Sarah E. Needleman, "Parent & Child Inc.," *Wall Street Journal*, November 15, 2010, *http://online .wsj.com/article/SB10001424052748703794104575546553171806306.html? KEYWORDS=family+business+mother+daughter;* "About," Zatswho, *www.zatswho.com/pages/About-.html.*

Case
Penn Brewery

Should an entrepreneur buy back the brewery that he launched nearly a quarter-century before?

Tom Pastorius and his wife Mary Beth started Penn Brewery, an authentic German microbrewery in Pittsburgh, Pennsylvania, in 1986. They built the brewery into a successful business, producing more than 15,000 barrels a year and generating annual sales of $3.5 million. Along the way, their microbrewery won 14 medals at the Great American Beer Festival and built a base of devoted customers for its brands, which included Penn Pilsner, Penn Oktoberfest, and others. They also added a German-themed restaurant that Mary Beth managed. In 2003, Tom and Mary Beth, both approaching 60, decided to cash out and sold the brewery to Birchmere Capital, a local private equity firm. Tom retained 20 percent ownership and agreed to stay on as president of the company for 5 years. He had lived up to his contract but was miserable working for the new owners, who made many significant changes to the company's strategy. "I am not a good employee," says Tom. "I'm a solo act."

Not only did Birchmere Capital close the brewery's restaurant, but it also decided to outsource production of beer to the Lion Brewery in nearby Wilkes-Barre and close Penn's brewing operation. The moves proved to be disastrous; once-devoted customers departed, and sales tumbled. "It was so hard to sit back and watch this place sink," says Tom, who was becoming bored with retirement. Then Birchmere offered to sell the brewery back to Pastorius for a fraction of what they had paid him for it a few years before. Tom was ready to buy the brewery back and restore it to its former grandeur, but convincing Mary Beth would take some doing. She had been instrumental in its success but told Tom that she had no intention of going back to it. "It's too risky at our age (now 65)," she says. "We don't have the luxury of time." Besides, Mary Beth had launched a retirement business of her own, a company that restores historic buildings.

Tom, however, could not get rid of the idea of owning Penn Brewery again. He began working clandestinely on a business plan preparing a risk-benefit analysis. The principal risks he identified included the brewery's $1 million debt, the tarnished brand name, and the fact that he would be buying back his former business at age 65. However, he was still very energetic and had the experience necessary to turn around the foundering brewery. He was confident that he could restore the luster to the Penn Brewery name by returning beer production to the Victorian-style red brick building in which he had launched the company years before. After weeks of candid discussions, Mary Beth told Tom, "If you want to do it, you are crazy, but keep me out of it."

Questions

1. Should Tom Pastorius buy Penn Brewery? Explain.
2. Tom Pastorius says, "I'm not a good employee." What does he mean? Do you think the same is true of most entrepreneurs?
3. What challenges does selling the businesses they create pose for entrepreneurs?
4. If Pastorius decides to buy the brewery, what steps should he take before closing the deal?

Sources: Based on Cristina Rouvalis, "Case Study: Penn Brewery," *Inc.*, July–August 2010, pp. 71–74; "The Pennsylvania Brewing Company," *www.pennbrew.com/data/english/about.htm.*

From Case 5 of *Effective Small Business Management: An Entrepreneurial Approach*, 10/e. Norman M. Scarborough.
Copyright © 2012 by Pearson Education. Published by Prentice Hall. All rights reserved.

Case: James Confectioners

From Case 6 of *Effective Small Business Management: An Entrepreneurial Approach*, 10/e. Norman M. Scarborough.

Case
James Confectioners

How can a confectioner cope with rising costs?

Telford James and his wife Ivey are the second-generation owners of James Confectioners, a family-owned manufacturer of premium chocolates that was started by Telford's father, Frank, in 1964 in Eau Claire, Wisconsin. In its nearly 50 years, James Confectioners has grown from its roots in a converted hardware store into a large, modern factory with sophisticated production and quality control equipment. In the early days, all of Frank's customers were local shops and stores, but the company now supplies customers across the United States and a few in Canada. Telford and Ivey have built on the company's reputation as an honest, reliable supplier of chocolates. The prices they charge for their chocolates are above the industry average but are not anywhere near the highest prices in the industry even though the company is known for producing quality products.

Annual sales for the company have grown to $3.9 million, and its purchases of the base chocolate used as the raw materials for their products have increased from 25,000 pounds 20 years ago to 150,000 pounds today. The Jameses are concerned about the impact of the rapidly rising cost of the base chocolate, however. Bad weather in South America and Africa, where most of the world's cocoa is grown, and a workers' strike have disrupted the global supply of chocolate, sending prices upward. There appears to be no relief from high chocolate prices in the near future. The International Cocoa Organization, an industry trade association, forecasts that world production of cocoa, from which chocolate is made, will decline by 7.2 percent this year. Escalating milk and sugar prices are squeezing the company's profit margins as well. Much to James and Ivey's dismay, James Confectioners' long-term contracts with its chocolate suppliers have run out, and the company is purchasing its raw materials under short-term, variable-price contracts. They are concerned about the impact that these increases in cost will have on the company's financial statements and on its long-term health.

Ivey, who has the primary responsibility for managing James Confectioners' finances, has compiled the balance sheet and the income statement for the fiscal year that just ended. The two financial statements are as follows:

Balance Sheet, James Confectioners
December 31, 2xxx

Assets	
Current Assets	
Cash	$161,254
Accounts receivable	$507,951
Inventory	$568,421
Supplies	$84,658
Prepaid expenses	$32,251
Total current assets	$1,354,536
Fixed Assets	
Land	$104,815
Buildings, net	$203,583
Autos, net	$64,502
Equipment, net	$247,928
Furniture and fixtures, net	$40,314
Total fixed assets	$661,142
Total Assets	$2,015,678

Liabilities	
Current Liabilities	
Accounts payable	$241,881
Notes payable	$221,725
Line of credit payable	$141,097
Accrued wages/salaries payable	$40,314
Accrued interest payable	$20,157
Accrued taxes payable	$10,078
Total current liabilities	$675,252
Long-term Liabilities	
Mortgage	$346,697
Loan	$217,693
Total long-term liabilities	$564,390

Owner's Equity	
James, Capital	$776,036
Total liabilities and owner's equity	$2,015,678

**Income Statement,
James Confectioners**

Net sales revenue		$3,897,564
Cost of goods sold		
Beginning inventory, 1/1/xx	$627,853	
+ Purchases	$2,565,908	
Goods available for sale	$3,193,761	
– Ending inventory, 12/31/xx	$568,421	
Cost of goods sold		$2,625,340
Gross profit		$1,272,224
Operating expenses		
Utilities	$163,698	
Advertising	$155,903	
Insurance	$74,054	
Depreciation	$74,054	
Salaries and benefits	$381,961	
E-commerce	$38,976	
Repairs and maintenance	$58,463	
Travel	$23,385	
Supplies	$15,590	
Total operating expenses		$986,084
Other expenses		
Interest expense	$119,658	
Miscellaneous expenses	$1,248	
Total other expenses		$120,906
Total expenses		$1,106,990
Net income		$165,234

To see how the company's financial position changes over time, Ivey calculates 12 ratios. She also compares James Confectioners' ratios to those of the typical firm in the industry. The following table shows the value of each of the 12 ratios from last year.

	James Confectioners		Confectionery
Ratio	**Current Year**	**Last Year**	**Industry Median***
Liquidity Ratios			
Current ratio		1.86	1.7
Quick ratio		1.07	0.8
Leverage Ratios			
Debt ratio		0.64	0.7
Debt-to-net-worth ratio		1.71	1.0
Times interest earned ratio		2.49	2.3
Operating Ratios			
Average inventory turnover ratio		4.75	4.9
Average collection period (days)		34.6	23.0
Average payable period (days)		31.1	33.5
Net sales to total assets		2.17	2.1
Profitability Ratios			
Net profit on sales ratio		7.40%	7.1%
Net profit to assets ratio		9.20%	5.6%
Net profit to equity ratio		29.21%	16.5%

Annual Statement Studies: Financial Ratio Benchmarks, Risk Management Association.

"How does the financial analysis look for this year, Hon?" Telford asks.

"I'm about to crunch the numbers now," says Ivey. "I'm sure that rising chocolate prices have cut into our profit margins. The question is 'how much?'"

"I think we're going to have to consider raising prices, but I'm not sure how our customers will respond if we do," says Telford. "What other options do we have?"

Questions

1. Calculate the 12 ratios for James Confectioners for this year.
2. How do the ratios you calculated for this year compare to those Ivey calculated for the company last year? What factors most likely account for those changes?

3. How do the ratios you calculated for this year compare to those of the typical company in the industry? Do you spot any areas that could cause the company problems in the future? Explain.
4. Develop a set of recommendations for improving the financial performance of James Confectioners using the analyses you conducted in questions 1–3.
5. What pricing recommendations can you make to Telford and Ivey James?

Source: Cocoa forecast information obtained from "Cocoa Forecasts," International Cocoa Organization, May 27, 2009, *www.icco.org/about/press2.aspx?Id=0ji12056.*

Case
James Confectioners—Part 2

How can a small confectioner forecast cash flow?

Telford James and his wife Ivey, the second-generation owners of James Confectioners, a family-owned manufacturer of premium chocolates that was started by Telford's father, Frank, in 1964 in Eau Claire, Wisconsin, have become increasingly concerned that turmoil in the banking and financial industries could have a negative impact on their business. They have read the headlines about bank closures, heightened government scrutiny of the banking industry, and tight credit conditions, especially for small businesses. The company has a $150,000 line of credit with Maple Leaf Bank, but the Jameses want to increase it to $250,000 as a precautionary move. Last week, they contacted Claudia Fernandes, their personal banker at Maple Leaf, about increasing their line of credit. Fernandes said that in addition to

reviewing the James Confectioners' most recent balance sheet and income statement, she would need a cash flow forecast for the upcoming year.

Although Telford and Ivey have prepared budgets for James Confectioners and have analyzed their financial statements using ratio analysis, they have not created a cash flow forecast before. They expect sales to increase 6.2 percent next year to $4,139,213. Credit sales account for 96 percent of total sales, and the company's collection pattern for credit sales is 8 percent in the same month in which the sale is generated, 54 percent in the first month after the sale is generated, and 34 percent in the second month after the sale is generated. The Jameses have gathered the following estimates from their budget for the upcoming year:

	Jan	Feb	Mar	Apr	May	Jun	Jul	Aug	Sep	Oct	Nov	Dec
Other cash receipts	$105	$55	$60	$75	$85	$55	$65	$60	$65	$85	$95	$110
Purchases	365,280	174,400	294,300	190,750	193,745	125,350	209,825	185,300	152,600	220,725	269,774	321,549
Utilities	13,600	14,100	13,700	13,200	13,200	13,600	14,800	15,900	14,900	14,100	13,800	14,000
Advertising	18,000	11,000	10,000	7,000	9,000	10,000	12,000	12,000	15,000	20,000	22,000	24,000
Insurance	0	0	19,650	0	0	19,650	0	0	19,650	0	0	19,650
Salaries and benefits	33,583	33,583	33,583	33,583	33,583	33,583	33,583	33,583	33,583	33,583	33,583	33,583
E-commerce	2,700	4,500	2,900	3,000	1,900	2,400	3,200	3,300	3,400	3,900	5,000	6,000
Repairs and maintenance	5,000	5,000	5,000	5,000	5,000	5,000	5,000	5,000	5,000	5,000	5,000	5,000
Travel	4,100	2,700	2,700	2,000	3,000	2,600	2,200	3,100	3,800	4,500	5,500	6,500
Supplies	1,088	1,836	1,190	1,207	782	1,309	1,156	952	1,377	1,683	2,006	2,414
Loan payment	10,000	10,000	10,000	10,000	10,000	10,000	10,000	10,000	10,000	10,000	10,000	10,000
Other cash disbursements	125	125	125	125	125	125	125	125	125	125	125	125

The company's cash balance as of January 1 is $22,565. The interest rate on James Confectioners' current line of credit is 8.25 percent.

Questions

1. Develop a monthly cash budget for James Confectioners for the upcoming year.

2. What recommendations can you offer Telford and Ivey James to improve their company's cash flow?

3. If you were Claudia Fernandes, the James's banker, would you be willing to increase the company's line of credit? Explain.

From Case 7 of *Effective Small Business Management: An Entrepreneurial Approach*, 10/e. Norman M. Scarborough.

Case
eMusic

Should an online music company with a base of loyal fans sign on with a major music house and raise its prices?

Danny Stein is considering making some significant changes to his online music retail business, eMusic, the company that he had founded in 1998 and built into the nation's second largest music download site. eMusic has established itself as *the* place for music aficionados to discover the latest independent artists, but recently several independent labels, including Drag City and Tzadik, dropped eMusic as a distributor because they complained that the prices it charged were too low and left their artists with royalty payments as low as 15 cents per track. In fact, pricing has been an issue for eMusic for some time. Originally, customers could pay just $9.99 per month for unlimited downloads, but Stein switched to higher monthly rates with limits on the number of downloads. Songs at eMusic still are bargains—about 25 cents each—compared to iTunes and Amazon, where tracks sell for 69 cents to $1.29. Stein wants to avoid other labels dropping eMusic because of low prices and is considering a tiered pricing arrangement that ranges from $11.99 for up to 24 tracks to $35.99 for up to 73 tracks. Even if eMusic adopts the new pricing strategy, music downloads will average between 49 cents and 89 cents, still 20 to 50 percent lower than iTunes' pricing. Another issue is how to deal with the long-time customers whose "legacy" contracts allow them to pay far lower prices than new customers. These legacy customers now number in the tens of thousands, and their outdated pricing schedules are creating a drag on eMusic's revenue.

An even bigger change that Stein is considering is adding songs from one of the major music labels, Sony BMG. Under the deal, Sony BMG would make its back catalog of 1 million songs available to eMusic customers. The idea of partnering with the biggest of the major music houses would have been unthinkable in the early days of eMusic's history, but Stein believes that he has to offer customers something new if he raises prices. In addition, the landscape in the digital music business is changing fast, and online music aficionados are looking for a broader range of music content. A deal with Sony BMG would provide that breadth, but Stein knows that adding content from a major music house might alienate eMusic's core customers, who would see the move as a betrayal of the cool, alternative music niche that eMusic has carved out. eMusic's image always has been linked closely to its identity as the place to discover cool, up-and-coming, independent musical artists, and a deal with Sony BMG could mar that image. However, Stein believes that most ardent music fans care more about finding the music they like rather than the record label it is on. The question is whether they would be willing to pay more for access to a greater selection of music.

Stein has two very important and very difficult decisions to make. He has called in his executive team to seek their ideas and input.

Questions

1. What are the risks that eMusic faces if it raises prices? If it does *not* raise prices?
2. Should eMusic raise its prices using the new tiered pricing schedule? If so, how should the company communicate the price increase to its customers? Compose an e-mail to existing customers that explains the rationale behind a price increase.
3. What are the risks that eMusic faces if it signs the deal with Sony BMG to expand its online music catalog? If it does *not* sign the deal with Sony BMG?
4. Should eMusic sign the deal with Sony BMG? Explain.

Sources: Based on Adam Bluestein, "Case Study: eMusic," *Inc.*, March 2010, pp. 55–58; Bruce Houghton, "eMusic Relaunches with Variable Pricing," *Hypebot*, November 2011, *www.hypebot.com/hypebot/2010/11/emusic-relaunches-with-variable-pricing.html;* Chris Foresman, "eMusic Changes Pricing Structure to Nab Major Music Tracks," *ARS Technica*, November 2010, *http://arstechnica.com/media/news/2010/11/emusic-changes-pricing-structure-to-nab-major-label-tracks.ars.*

Case
Fikes Products

How can the CEO of a fast-growing company improve his poor track record at hiring stars?

In 1997, Mark Sims began working in sales and service for Fikes Products, a company in Kent, Washington, with 30 employees that sells janitorial supplies and services to restaurants, retailers, and other businesses. In 2003, Sims became the owner of the company when his parents, the founders of the company, retired. Sims used his sales talent to increase annual sales at Fikes to more than $4 million and opened a branch in Portland, Oregon. He is proud of the company's growth but realizes that it has created a problem: The day-to-day tasks of managing a fast-growing company are draining him professionally and personally. He wants to hire several employees, including an office administrator, two route drivers, and a warehouse worker. Dan Price, a fellow entrepreneur and mentor, suggests that Sims also hire an operations manager to handle the daily operations of the company and allow Sims to focus on leading the company. "There is no one to take work off of Mark's plate," says Price. Yet he understands Sims' hesitation. "A first senior hire is daunting for an entrepreneur," he says.

Sims also is a bit gun shy when it comes to making hiring decisions because his track record is not that good. Recently, he hired several employees who seemed "fine," but none of them lasted. A route driver that he found on Craigslist wrecked a new vehicle before he quit. A new office staffer spent 30 percent of her workday on personal social media, distracting coworkers and raising their ire. Sims also sees the time he spends sorting through resumes as unproductive because he could be out in the field landing new customers. The high unemployment rate means that the number of applicants, qualified or not, for each job has surged. "I get resumes for driver positions from applicants who don't even have a driver's license," he laments. "We aren't attracting the quality candidates we'd hoped for," he says, citing a "deteriorating work ethic" among many applicants. "I want to get people excited about working here—even if we do sell toilet paper and Dumpster deodorizers."

To find candidates for the operations manager's position and lower-level jobs, Sims is considering placing employment ads on state employment agency Web sites because they are free. He also has considered hiring a professional recruiting company but is hesitant because recruiters typically charge a fee that is the equivalent of 20 to 30 percent of the new hire's first year salary. Sims knows that his company has to attract quality workers if it is to continue to grow and prosper, but he is unsure of the best way to find them.

Questions

1. What steps should Mark Sims take to ensure that he hires the right employees for Fikes Products?
2. Write a two-page memo to Sims that outlines a selection process that will produce the results he wants.
3. Where should Sims look for quality employees? How should he structure the interviews for prospective employees?
4. What methods should Sims use to motivate his employees to achieve higher levels of performance?

Sources: Based on Adriana Gardella, "Hiring Employees, With Help or Without," *New York Times*, October 27, 2010, *www.nytimes.com/2010/10/28/business/smallbusiness/28sbiz.html?ref=casestudies;* "Meet the Owner," Fikes Products, *www.fikesproducts.com/company/meet-the-owner.*

From Case 9 of *Effective Small Business Management: An Entrepreneurial Approach*, 10/e. Norman M. Scarborough.

Index